THE
NAG HAMMADI
SCRIPTURES

EDITED BY

MARVIN MEYER

WITH CONTRIBUTIONS BY

Wolf-Peter Funk, Karen L. King, Jean-Pierre Mahé, Marvin Meyer,
Elaine H. Pagels, Birger A. Pearson, Paul-Hubert Poirier, Michel Roberge,
James M. Robinson, Madeleine Scopello, Einar Thomassen,
and John D. Turner

BASED ON THE WORK OF

the Berliner Arbeitskreis für koptisch-gnostische Schriften,
the Bibliothèque copte de Nag Hammadi, Université Laval, and
the Coptic Gnostic Library Project, Institute for Antiquity
and Christianity, Claremont Graduate University

ADVISORY BOARD

Wolf-Peter Funk
Paul-Hubert Poirier
James M. Robinson

THE
NAG HAMMADI
SCRIPTURES

THE INTERNATIONAL EDITION

HarperOne

An Imprint of HarperCollins*Publishers*

HarperOne

HarperCollins books may be purchased for educational, business, or sales promotional use. For information please write: Special Markets Department, HarperCollins Publishers, 10 East 53rd Street, New York, NY 10022.

HarperCollins Web site: http://www.harpercollins.com

HarperCollins®, 📖®, and HarperOne™ are trademarks of HarperCollins Publishers.

FIRST HARPERCOLLINS PAPEERBACK EDITION PUBLISHED IN 2008

Library of Congress Cataloging-in-Publication Data is available upon request.
ISBN 978–0–06–162600–5

13 14 15 RRD(H) 20 19 18 17 16 15 14 13 12

To

HANS-MARTIN SCHENKE

1929–2002

Esteemed colleague, dear friend,

Coptologist extraordinaire

CONTENTS

PREFACE

James M. Robinson

The Nag Hammadi Scriptures is a collection of thirteen papyrus codices—bound books, not scrolls—that were buried near the city of Nag Hammadi in Upper Egypt most likely in the second half of the fourth century CE. They had been brought together earlier in that century and then buried in a jar for safekeeping at the foot of the Jabal al-Tarif, a cliff close to the hamlet Hamra Dum. In all, there are some fifty-two tractates in the collection of Nag Hammadi codices, and since six are duplicates, there are forty-six different texts. Of these, forty-one are texts that were not previously extant, but ten are very fragmentary, so that one may say that the discovery has added about thirty-one new texts to our knowledge of religion and philosophy in antiquity. This is indeed a dramatic escalation of source material on early Christian, Neoplatonic, Hermetic, Sethian, and Valentinian thought. The precise dates of the composition of these texts are uncertain, but most are from the second and third centuries CE. All were originally written in Greek and translated into Coptic.

The people who wrote, copied, translated, recopied, read, collected, and finally buried these texts are unknown. Since most of the tractates are Gnostic, it is assumed that there must have been a sympathetic community in the region that collected, cherished, and then buried its library. The cartonnage—the discarded papyrus used to thicken the inside of the leather covers—contains references to the region near where they were discovered and dates on receipts just before and in the middle of the fourth century. Thus, the time and place of the production of the codices coincides with the emergence of the Pachomian monastic order, with which there may be some association. In fact, fragments of a Coptic letter from a Papnoute to a certain Pahome may be from Papnoutios, the "business manager" of the nearby monastery, to its founder, Pachomius. In 367, Athanasius, the orthodox patriarch of Alexandria, wrote an Easter letter to be read in all the monasteries of Egypt, calling upon them to eliminate from their libraries apocryphal writings; in the letter he listed those books that were to be included as acceptable—the oldest extant list of the twenty-seven books in the New Testament. It has been suggested that the Nag Hammadi codices were among the books that had to be excluded but were buried for safekeeping in a sealed jar by those who valued them.

Another codex, Papyrus Berolinensis 8502, which has been in Berlin for a century, contains duplicates of two tractates in the Nag Hammadi collection, the *Secret Book of John* and the *Wisdom of Jesus Christ*, as well as two other texts, the *Gospel of Mary* and the *Act of Peter*. They have been included in the present edition, as have the texts from Codex Tchacos, the *Gospel of Judas* and the *Book of Allogenes*.

The English translation of the Nag Hammadi scriptures published in the present volume is the result of the close collaboration of three teams of scholars who over the past generation have prepared English, French, and German translations. The English-language team has had its center in the Coptic Gnostic Library Project of the Institute for Antiquity and Christianity of Claremont Graduate University in Claremont, California. It was first to publish a preliminary translation of the whole discovery, *The Nag Hammadi Library in English*, in 1977, in order to make the tractates available promptly to a wider audience. The Claremont team published a critical edition of the Nag Hammadi texts, The Coptic Gnostic Library, as a subseries in the broader series Nag Hammadi Studies (now Nag Hammadi and Manichaean Studies), in twelve volumes in 1975–95, followed by a five-volume paperback reprint in 2000. The project was founded and directed by James M. Robinson.

The German-language team has been based in the Berliner Arbeitskreis für koptisch-gnostische Schriften of the Theological Faculty of the Humboldt University of Berlin. It published preliminary translations in the periodical *Theologische Literaturzeitung*, followed by a number of dissertations addressing individual tractates, and more recently, in 2001 and 2003, the Berlin team produced a complete two-volume German translation, *Nag Hammadi Deutsch*. The Arbeitskreis was founded by Hans-Martin Schenke and is currently directed by Hans-Gebhard Bethge.

The French-language team has been centered in the Institut d'études anciennes and the Faculté de théologie et de sciences religieuses of the Université Laval in Québec, Canada. Founded by Jacques-É. Ménard and Hervé Gagné, the team is currently directed by Louis Painchaud, Wolf-Peter Funk, and Paul-Hubert Poirier. It is publishing critical editions with commentaries of each of the Nag Hammadi tractates in its Bibliothèque copte de Nag Hammadi (1977–) as well as a one-volume French translation edited by Jean-Pierre Mahé and Paul-Hubert Poirier, *Écrits gnostiques*, to appear in Paris in the Bibliothèque de la Pléiade. The Laval team has enlisted Wolf-Peter Funk from the Berlin Arbeitskreis and John D. Turner from the Claremont Project, and it has been the congenial host of the meetings at which the present volume was prepared (August 2003, January 2004, August 2004, and August 2005). These work sessions were attended by Wolf-Peter Funk, Marvin Meyer, Birger A. Pearson, Paul-Hubert Poirier, James M. Robinson, John D. Turner, and others.

The Nag Hammadi Scriptures seeks to take advantage of the generation of scholarship that has taken place at each of the three centers and elsewhere. The advisory board for this volume consists of James M. Robinson, representing the American team, Wolf-Peter Funk, representing the German team, and Paul-Hubert Poirier, representing the French-Canadian team. The translation published here seeks to build on the contributions of these international teams as well as other scholars around the world, and the contributors to the present volume have attempted to incorporate the insights of the other scholars. The translators have also smoothed out the often verbose formulations of the Coptic texts into a more crisp, intelligible English rendition in order to produce a volume in which the texts are presented as accurately as possible in readable, contemporary English.

For many years our colleague Hans-Martin Schenke played a major role in the collaborative work on the Nag Hammadi library. He not only organized and directed the Berlin team, but also worked for two years in Québec and taught three semesters in Claremont, thus bringing his scholarly mastery of the texts and his congenial goodwill into play in all three centers. With gratitude we dedicate this volume to him.

THE
NAG HAMMADI
SCRIPTURES

INTRODUCTION

Marvin Meyer and Elaine H. Pagels

The Nag Hammadi Scriptures

The present volume, entitled *The Nag Hammadi Scriptures*,[1] offers a new edition of some of the most remarkable texts that have come to light in the last century. Since the discovery of the thirteen codices of the Nag Hammadi library in 1945, the Berlin Gnostic Codex 8502 a few decades before, and Codex Tchacos more recently, such texts as the *Gospel of Thomas* and the *Gospel of Mary* have become a significant part of cultural and religious life, and they have come to be known and read not only by students of early Christianity, but also by a wide variety of people interested in religion in general and the early Christian movement in particular. These and the other texts from the Nag Hammadi library, the Berlin Gnostic Codex, and Codex Tchacos invite us to reconsider the nature of our religious and philosophical heritage, the development of Christianity and the Judeo-Christian-Islamic tradition, and the enduring questions raised by religious and philosophical inquiry.

The Nag Hammadi Scriptures includes nearly fifty texts that were read as sacred literature and gathered in collections found near Nag Hammadi and elsewhere in Egypt—hence the title of this volume. The texts published here, however, do not constitute scripture in the narrow sense of a closed canonical collection, as is the case with the Jewish scriptures, the New Testament, or the Qur'an. Rather, the documents from the Nag Hammadi library, the Berlin Gnostic Codex, and Codex Tchacos are scriptural in the broader sense of texts composed, read, translated, and copied as books recognized as inspired—and inspiring—for those seeking God. The texts included here were translated into Coptic, a form of the Egyptian language used from the Roman period until more recent times, though they were likely composed in Greek. Portions of Greek editions of the texts, some

---

1. In this Introduction, Marvin Meyer is chiefly responsible for "The Nag Hammadi Scriptures" and "Reading the Nag Hammadi Scriptures," Elaine H. Pagels for "What Are the Nag Hammadi Scriptures?"

found in an ancient garbage heap at Oxyrhynchus and some from other sources, are also translated and presented in this volume.

The Coptic texts included here have come from discoveries that have occurred in southern and central Egypt. In 1896 a German scholar, Carl Reinhardt, bought the Berlin Gnostic Codex from a dealer from Akhmim, in central Egypt, who claimed that the codex had been discovered with feathers covering it in a recessed place in a wall; Carl Schmidt, the first editor of the codex, suspected that it may have come from a cemetery near Akhmim. Schmidt published the last text of the codex—the *Act of Peter*—in 1903, but it was not until 1955 that Walter C. Till was able to see the first three texts of the codex—the *Gospel of Mary*, the *Secret Book of John*, and the *Wisdom of Jesus Christ*—through the press. Hans-Martin Schenke published a second, revised edition of the Berlin Gnostic Codex in 1972: *Die gnostischen Schriften des koptischen Papyrus Berolinensis 8502*.[2]

Meanwhile, around the end of 1945, the texts known as the Nag Hammadi library were discovered, not at the city of Nag Hammadi itself, but near the base of a majestic cliff, the Jabal al-Tarif, which flanks the Nile River a few kilometers from Nag Hammadi. The villages closest to the Jabal al-Tarif bear the names Hamra Dum, al-Busa, al-Dabba (the site of the Monastery of the Angel, Deir al-Malak), al-Qasr (the site of the Pachomian monastery at Chenoboskion), and Faw Qibli (the site of the Pachomian monastery at Pbow). Five years after the discovery, the French scholar Jean Doresse explored the region and tried to find out the circumstances of the discovery of the Nag Hammadi library. He published his story in his book *The Secret Books of the Egyptian Gnostics*. According to Doresse, he spoke with some people from the area, and they directed him to the southern part of an ancient cemetery. They reported that peasants from Hamra Dum and al-Dabba, searching for natural fertilizer (manure), found somewhere near this locale a large jar filled with papyri bound in the form of books. Doresse writes:

> The vase was broken and nothing remains of it; the manuscripts were taken to Cairo and no one knows what then became of them. As to the exact location of the find, opinion differed by some few dozen yards; but everyone was sure that it was just about here. And from the ground itself we shall learn nothing more; it yields nothing but broken bones, fragments of cloth without interest and some potsherds.[3]

He concludes:

> We have never been able to discover exactly where the Coptic Manichaean manuscripts came from, nor the *Pistis-Sophia*, nor the

---

2. On the story of the discovery of the Berlin Gnostic Codex, see Karen L. King, *The Gospel of Mary of Magdala*, 7–12; Marvin Meyer, *The Gnostic Discoveries*, 19–20; Michael Waldstein and Frederik Wisse, *The Apocryphon of John*, 2–3.

3. Jean Doresse, *The Secret Books of the Egyptian Gnostics*, 133.

Bruce Codex. So it was well worth the trouble to find out, in a pagan cemetery a few miles from Chenoboskion, the exact site of one of the most voluminous finds of ancient literature; thus to be a little better able to place this library in the frame of history to which it belongs; and to support, with concordant details, the hypotheses that have been made about its antiquity.[4]

James M. Robinson has offered another version of the story of the discovery. For a number of years, Robinson conducted interviews with people from the towns and villages in the Nag Hammadi area, in particular Muhammad Ali of the al-Samman clan, a resident of al-Qasr, and from the interviews he pieced together a fascinating account of how the Nag Hammadi codices were uncovered. Where possible, Robinson attempted to confirm dates and events from official records. As Robinson has reconstructed the story, the discovery of the Nag Hammadi library took place in about December of 1945, when several Egyptian fellahin, including Muhammad Ali, his brothers Khalifah Ali and Abu al-Magd, and others, were riding their camels to the Jabal al-Tarif in order to gather *sabakh*, a natural fertilizer that typically accumulates around there. They hobbled their camels at the foot of the Jabal, the account continues, and began to dig around a large boulder on the talus, or slope of debris, that had formed against the cliff face. As they were digging, they unexpectedly came upon a large storage jar buried by the boulder, with a bowl sealed on the mouth of the jar as a lid. Apparently the youngest of the brothers, Abu al-Magd, initially uncovered the jar, but Muhammad Ali, as the oldest, took control of the operation. In his account of what transpired, Muhammad Ali has suggested to Robinson that he paused before removing the lid or breaking open the jar, out of fear that the jar might contain a *jinni*, or spirit, that could cause trouble if released from the jar. It seems that Muhammad Ali also recalled stories of hidden treasures buried in Egypt, and his love of gold overcame his fear of *jinn*. He smashed the jar with his mattock, and indeed something golden in color and glistening in the sunlight—fragments of papyrus, we might conclude—flew out of the jar and disappeared into the air. And when he looked into the broken jar to see what remained, he found only a collection of old books—the codices of the Nag Hammadi library.[5]

Robinson's version of the story is carefully documented, and it includes colorful anecdotes and detailed accounts of events. For instance, Robinson reminisces about how he persuaded Muhammad Ali to return to the site of the discovery, so close to Hamra Dum, where a family caught up in acts of vengeance with the family of Muhammad Ali lived. Robinson recalls:

I had to go to Hamra Dum myself, find the son of Ahmad Isma'il, the man Muhammad Ali had butchered, and get his assurance that, since he had

---

4. Doresse, *Secret Books of the Egyptian Gnostics*, 136.

5. On this story of the discovery of the Nag Hammadi codices, see Meyer, *The Gnostic Discoveries*, 15–19; James M. Robinson, "From the Cliff to Cairo"; "Nag Hammadi: The First Fifty Years."

long since shot up a funeral cortège of Muhammad Ali's family, wounding Muhammad Ali and killing a number of his clan, he considered the score settled. Hence, he would not feel honor-bound to attack Muhammad Ali if he returned to the foot of the cliff. I took this good news back to Muhammad Ali, who opened his shirt, showed me the scar on his chest, bragged that he had been shot but not killed, yet emphasized that if he ever laid eyes on the son of Ahmad Isma'il again, he would kill him on the spot. As a result of this display of a braggadocio's fearlessness, he could be persuaded to go to the cliff, camouflaged in my clothes, in a government jeep, with me sitting on the "bullets" side facing the village and him on the safer cliff side, at dusk in Ramadan, when all Muslims are at home eating their fill after fasting throughout the daylight hours.[6]

More recently, in the 1970s (perhaps in 1978), yet another collection of manuscripts was unearthed in Egypt. The details of the story of this discovery remain shrouded in uncertainty, and the names of the fellahin have not been disclosed. According to what the researcher and writer Herbert Krosney has been able to reconstruct of the discovery, the manuscripts were found in Middle Egypt near al-Minya, in a cave used for burial, at the Jabal Qarara. The cave contained, among other things, Roman glassware in baskets or papyrus or straw wrappings. Krosney writes:

> The burial cave was located across the river from Maghagha, not far from the village of Qarara in what is known as Middle Egypt. The fellahin stumbled upon the cave hidden down in the rocks. Climbing down to it, they found the skeleton of a wealthy man in a shroud. Other human remains, probably members of the dead man's family, were with him in the cave. His precious books were beside him, encased in a white limestone box.[7]

The ancient books contained in this collection of codices are reported to have included (1) a Greek mathematical text, (2) a Greek edition of the book of *Exodus* from the Jewish scriptures, (3) a Coptic set of New Testament letters of Paul — and (4) a book now referred to as Codex Tchacos, with Coptic versions of the *Letter of Peter to Philip*, *James* (also called the *First Revelation of James*), the *Gospel of Judas*, and a text entitled, tentatively, the *Book of Allogenes*. For our purposes, Codex Tchacos is of particular interest, since it is a Nag Hammadi type of codex with two texts known from the Nag Hammadi library (the *Letter of Peter to Philip* and *James*) and two texts that were previously unknown or unavailable (the *Gospel of Judas* and the *Book of Allogenes*). Unfortunately, Codex Tchacos later was moved from place to place and passed from hand to hand, and the papyrus

---

6. Robinson, "Nag Hammadi: The First Fifty Years," 80.
7. Herbert Krosney, *The Lost Gospel*, 10.

book suffered extensive damage due to the greed and ineptitude of people. It was stored away in a safe-deposit box in humid Hicksville, New York, for sixteen years and was placed in a freezer in the Midwest in a misguided effort to separate papyrus pages.

At last the codex was acquired by Frieda Tchacos Nussberger and the Maecenas Foundation; it was given the necessary support for its publication by the National Geographic Society; and it was restored and conserved by Rodolphe Kasser, Florence Darbre, and Gregor Wurst. What was a box of hundreds and hundreds of papyrus fragments has become a legible codex once again. In the spring of 2006 the *Gospel of Judas* was released to the world, and it has generated international enthusiasm and excitement.[8]

The circumstances of the discovery of the Nag Hammadi library and the other Coptic texts are debated among scholars, and the debate is likely to continue into the future. However these various codices may have been uncovered, and whatever may be the implications of the discoveries, the discoverers could not have imagined the impact these texts would have on our understanding of early Christianity and the world of antiquity and late antiquity.

What Are the Nag Hammadi Scriptures?

Currently, in discussions among scholars throughout the world, the discovery of the Nag Hammadi library is transforming what we know about Christianity—and its mysterious founder. For more than fifteen hundred years, most Christians had assumed that the only sources of tradition about Jesus and his disciples are those contained in the New Testament, especially in the familiar gospels of *Matthew, Mark, Luke,* and *John.* Suddenly, however, the unexpected discovery of over fifty ancient texts, most of them Christian, has demonstrated what the church fathers long had indicated: that these familiar gospels are only a small selection from among many more traditions—and gospels—that, from the early generations of the Christian movement, circulated among groups throughout the known world. Now, for the first time in more than fifteen hundred years, scholars could open and read other gospels—the *Gospel of Thomas,* the *Gospel of Truth,* the *Gospel of Philip,* and the *Gospel of Mary* (*Mary* had been discovered in 1896)—sources that enormously widen our understanding of the scope of the early Christian movement.

Those who first investigated these writings quickly recognized that some of them, at least, date back to the earliest centuries of the Christian movement, but they assumed that these must be *false* gospels. Certain "fathers of the church" had mentioned by name such writings as the *Gospel of Thomas* and the *Gospel of Truth,* but apart from the names, such writings had remained virtually unknown, since some of the same church leaders had attacked them as "heresy." Irenaeus of

---

8. See Rodolphe Kasser, Marvin Meyer, and Gregor Wurst, eds., *The Gospel of Judas.* On the full story of the discovery of Codex Tchacos, see Herbert Krosney, *The Lost Gospel;* James M. Robinson, *The Secrets of Judas.*

Lyon, for example, who wrote around 160 CE, had discussed—and denounced—passages from the *Secret Book of John*, discovered complete at Nag Hammadi;[9] and his famous contemporary Hippolytus, a Christian writer in Rome, quoted some of the opening lines from perhaps the most famous book of the discovery, the *Gospel of Thomas*.[10] This shows that both of these texts—and, no doubt, many others—had been written and widely circulated among Christian groups by the middle of the second century. Irenaeus also mentioned a *Gospel of Truth*, which he said was written "recently," perhaps around 130–60 CE, by the Egyptian Christian poet Valentinus or one his followers—perhaps the same *Gospel of Truth* now discovered at Nag Hammadi.[11] Irenaeus specifically mentioned the *Gospel of Judas*, which, he said, teaches that Judas alone "knew the truth as no one else did" and enacted the "mystery of the betrayal," obeying a command from Jesus to initiate his sacrifice.[12] The *Gospel of Judas*, actually discovered only in the 1970s, has now been translated from Coptic and published for the first time in nearly two thousand years.[13]

Yet since scholars who relied upon Irenaeus's account also noticed that the bishop had classified all such gospels—and many other writings he dismissed along with them—as both "illegitimate" and "apocryphal," they assumed that the recently discovered texts they were reading must be what Irenaeus called them—"heresy." Irenaeus had insisted that such writings were "wholly unlike what has been handed down to us from the apostles," and he called those who revered such writings "heretics." He concluded, indeed, that "the heretics say they have more gospels than there really are; but really, they really have no gospel which is not full of blasphemy."[14]

Thus those who first read and published these texts assumed that the Christian texts among them were not really Christian, but "heretical"—the work of heretics who accepted what Irenaeus called "falsely so-called gnosis." What apparently had happened to these texts only confirmed that impression. Although they were originally written in Greek, like the New Testament gospels, these texts discovered in Egypt had been translated into Coptic, perhaps by Christian monks who treasured them as holy books in the library of one of the oldest monasteries in Egypt. But the monks' reverence for such writings apparently upset Athanasius, the archbishop of Alexandria, who sent out an Easter letter all over Egypt in the spring of 367, ordering believers to reject what he called "illegitimate and secret books."[15] Athanasius, who admired his predecessor Irenaeus for his strong stand against "heretics," also included a list of twenty-seven books of which he

---

9. *Against Heresies* 1.29.

10. *Refutation of All Heresies* 5.7.20. The renowned Egyptian teacher Origen, writing about a generation later, also mentions the *Gospel of Thomas*, along with the *Gospel of Matthias* and "many others" (*Homilies on Luke* 1).

11. *Against Heresies* 3.11.9.

12. *Against Heresies* 1.31.1.

13. Kasser, Meyer, and Wurst, eds., *The Gospel of Judas.*

14. *Against Heresies* 3.11.9.

15. *Festal Letter* 39.

approved, calling them the "springs of salvation." Strikingly, the twenty-seven books he names in this letter are precisely those that came to constitute the collection we call the "New Testament"—for which his letter provides our earliest known list. But apparently some monks defied the archbishop's order to reject all the rest; instead, they saved and protected over fifty texts from their library by sealing them in a heavy jar and burying them away from the monastery walls, under the cliff where they were found sixteen hundred years later.

Yet as we have seen, many of these writings already had been circulating widely throughout the ancient world before the archbishop took action. Two hundred years earlier, as we noted, Bishop Irenaeus, after charging that the many Christians among his congregations in rural Gaul (present-day France) who treasured such writings were actually "heretics," went on to insist that of the dozens of gospels revered by various Christians only four are genuine. And these four, Irenaeus declares, are the gospels now included in the New Testament, called by the names of Jesus's followers—*Matthew, Mark, Luke,* and *John*. All the rest are illegitimate, because, he says, "there cannot be more than four gospels, nor fewer."[16] Why not? Irenaeus explains that just as there are four corners of the universe and four principal winds, so there can be only four gospels—which he seems to take as a kind of scientific explanation. To those who would ask, "Why *these* four?" Irenaeus declares that only these are written by eyewitnesses of the events they describe—Jesus's disciples Matthew and John, or disciples of these disciples like Luke and Mark. Few scholars today would agree with Irenaeus. In the first place, we cannot verify who actually wrote any of these accounts, and many scholars agree that, although certain traditions were associated with certain disciples, the disciples themselves may not be their authors; second, nearly all the other "gospels" that Irenaeus detests are also attributed to disciples—often disciples from the same group as these.

When an international group of scholars first read and published the *Gospel of Thomas* in 1959,[17] the primary question in their minds, not surprisingly, was this: what can the *Gospel of Thomas* tell us about "Gnosticism"—that is, about "heresy"? Since Irenaeus and others had denounced such gospels, they assumed that *Thomas* must not only be a false, "Gnostic" gospel, but also that, being a "false gospel," it must have been written later than the "real" gospels. And since most people agree that Mark's gospel was written earliest, some forty years after Jesus's death, around the year 70, *Matthew* and *Luke* about ten years later, and *John* about 90–100, they assumed that *Thomas* must be later than any of these, and so they guessed that it dated to about 140 CE.

Further, since they assumed that this gospel was "heretical," they knew what to expect in terms of content: after all, church fathers like Irenaeus basically had defined—or, some would say, invented—heresy. Irenaeus explains that heretics

---

16. *Against Heresies* 3.11.8.

17. Antoine Guillaumont, Henri-Charles Puech, Gilles Quispel, Walter Till, and Yassah 'Abd al-Masih, *The Gospel According to Thomas.*

are "Gnostics," by which he means dualists who believe that the world was created by an evil power, and so they have a dismally negative view of the world and
the God who created it. Furthermore, following Irenaeus's lead, many of these
scholars also assumed that heretics are "nihilistic" and that the works they revered
would be full of philosophical speculation and bizarre mythology.[18] When the
first editors of Thomas's gospel found in it virtually no evidence for dualism,
nihilism, philosophical speculation, or weird mythology, most assumed that this
just goes to show how devious heretics are: they do not say what they really mean.
Many scholars decided that even if they could not find these elements in *Thomas*
explicitly, they must be there implicitly; consequently, some decided just to read
them into their understanding of the *Gospel of Thomas*. Most of the first publications did this; some still do even now.

When the discovery became available to scholars throughout the world, many
of us shared the excitement of investigating these nearly unknown texts. Hearing
about the discovery astonished everyone who heard it. This certainly was not
what we had expected to find in graduate school—nor, in fact, what we had
hoped to find. Most of us who set out to find out about Jesus and the early history
of Christianity imagined that we could find in first- and second-century sources a
kind of "golden age" of early Christianity, a simpler, purer Christian teaching
that existed when Jesus wandered with his disciples around the hills of Galilee—
what Professor Krister Stendahl, then dean of Harvard Divinity School, ironically
called "play Bible land." And since we assumed that there must have been only
one original, pure form of Christianity back at its beginning, we never imagined
that we would be asking the question that this discovery now raises for us: what
different Christian groups—and thus what *kinds* of early Christianity—were
there at the beginning of the movement?[19]

Yet by the time many of us arrived in graduate school, certain scholars already
had begun to embark upon a second stage of research. Examining the *Gospel of
Thomas*, scholars first noticed that it is not a narrative, like the New Testament
gospels; instead, it consists simply of a list of sayings attributed to Jesus. Scholars
like Helmut Koester, James M. Robinson, and John Dominic Crossan observed
that many sayings in *Thomas* are strikingly similar to sayings long familiar from
the New Testament gospels attributed to Matthew and Luke—for example, such
well-known parables about the kingdom of God as the parable of the mustard
seed and the parable of the sower and such sayings as "Blessed are the poor, for
yours is heaven's kingdom."[20] The research of this generation of scholars opened
up new questions: could the *Gospel of Thomas*, for example, possibly be not a
late, "Gnostic" gospel, as many of us first assumed, but, on the contrary, an early
collection of Jesus's teaching—perhaps even one that Matthew and Luke used to

18. See the influential book by Hans Jonas, *The Gnostic Religion*, an abridged translation of his 1934 monograph
published in Germany under the title *Gnosis und spätantiker Geist*.

19. See, e.g., Karen L. King, "Which Early Christianity?"

20. John Dominic Crossan, *Four Other Gospels: Shadows on the Contours of the Canon*.

compose their own gospels? Could it be the so-called Q source, a hypothetical first-century list of Jesus's sayings? Is it possible that the *Gospel of Thomas* might tell us a great deal not about heresy, but about Jesus and his teachings? Could this be an early source—maybe even our earliest source—of Jesus's teachings, collected in an unedited, unvarnished form?

Questions like these inspired a movement among a group of scholars looking for the "real, historical" Jesus and what Jesus actually taught. Professor Helmut Koester came to conclude that the *Gospel of Thomas* perhaps could be dated as early as the mid–first century—about twenty years after Jesus's death[21]—which would make it the earliest gospel we know, and certainly one of the most important. John Dominic Crossan and others have written books that follow this view, and many people are still engaged in this research.

At present, however, many do not share the view that the *Gospel of Thomas* is a kind of rough quarry of early Jesus sayings strung together with minimal editorial point of view. Even though our evidence cannot tell us for sure what came from "the historical Jesus," it can tell us a great deal, more than we ever knew before, about the early Christian movement—how it emerged and the astonishing variety of forms it took.

Recognizing this, many scholars today throughout the world have accepted the challenge articulated by our colleagues Michael A. Williams in his book *Rethinking "Gnosticism": An Argument for Dismantling a Dubious Category* and Karen L. King in *What Is Gnosticism?* Instead of regarding the many texts found at Nag Hammadi as a corporate collection, scholars today more often analyze each one separately or in relationship with contemporaneous Jewish, Christian, and pagan sources. Instead of assuming that all these texts deviate from what is "normal, mainstream" early Christianity, we are finding that they have opened up to us a far wider range of what we now understand to be early Christian sources. Instead of discriminating simply between what we used to call "orthodox" and "Gnostic" (or "proto-orthodox" and "proto-Gnostic," which amounts to the same thing), many scholars working on the Coptic texts are now investigating the new evidence along with the old to ask different questions. Many of us are discussing questions like whether it is misleading to classify these texts as "Gnostic." Given how varied they are, we realize that it is more accurate to look at them simply as a wide range of early Christian traditions that are unfamiliar to us, because the bishops intended to downplay viewpoints that diverged from their own. Professor Karen King has suggested that we should ask what evidence these many texts offer for various kinds of "early Christianities"; simultaneously, scholars of Judaism are investigating a wide range of "early Judaisms."[22] Finally, such investigation raises the question of what our familiar terminology means—and what it

---

21. Cf. Helmut Koester, "The Gospel of Thomas," in James. M. Robinson, ed., *The Nag Hammadi Library in English*, 125: "In its most original form, it may well date from the first century (the middle of the first century is usually considered the best date for the composition of 'Q')."
22. See King, "Which Early Christianity?"

obscures. What do we mean when we speak of what is "orthodox" and what is "heretical"? What characteristics differentiate and define what we mean when we speak of "Judaism" or "Christianity"?

In many ways, investigation of the Nag Hammadi texts is just beginning. This volume invites readers to participate in exploring the early Christian movement—with far more evidence of its amazing range than we had known before.

Reading the Nag Hammadi Scriptures

In this volume the texts of the Nag Hammadi library, the Berlin Gnostic Codex, and Codex Tchacos are presented in an edition that is intended to build upon the international scholarship that has been directed toward the texts in these codices since they were discovered and made available for research and study. In particular, the work of the Coptic Gnostic Library Project of the Institute for Antiquity and Christianity of Claremont Graduate University, the Berliner Arbeitskreis für koptisch-gnostische Schriften at the Theological Faculty of Humboldt University, and the French-Canadian team at the Institut d'études anciennes and the Faculté de théologie et de sciences religieuses of the Université Laval in Québec has been consulted in order to take advantage of the interpretations and insights of the scholars involved in these research projects. The published work of these projects includes the volumes of the Coptic Gnostic Library and *The Nag Hammadi Library in English* (edited by James M. Robinson), *Nag Hammadi Deutsch* (edited by Hans-Martin Schenke, Hans-Gebhard Bethge, and Ursula Ulrike Kaiser), and the Bibliothéque copte de Nag Hammadi and *Écrits gnostiques* (edited by Jean-Pierre Mahé and Paul-Hubert Poirier), all of which we have used in our translations of the texts.[23] Individuals from these three research teams have also functioned as members of the advisory board for this volume, in order that the contributions of each of the teams might gain a fair hearing, and we all have met together several times at Université Laval to discuss the translations prepared for the present volume. The result has been a collegial effort to produce a volume fully informed by the latest research on the Nag Hammadi library, the Berlin Gnostic Codex, and Codex Tchacos.

The English translations included in *The Nag Hammadi Scriptures* thus represent a new generation of translations, after the initial translations that appeared in the first editions of these texts. We have made a conscientious attempt to produce English translations that adhere closely to the meaning of the Coptic texts (and, as noted in a few instances, also some Greek texts) while being as readable and felicitous as possible. The present English versions of the texts are translations, not lexical equivalencies, and as a result they communicate the meaning of the texts in modern English rather than reproducing every grammatical feature of the Coptic text. We have given special attention to issues of gender in our transla-

---

23. These volumes will be referred to numerous times in the notes to the translations published here. For full bibliographical information about these volumes, see the Bibliography to the present volume.

tions, and we employ inclusive language where the spirit of the Coptic text recommends it and where it does not compromise the accuracy of the translations. Thus, most often the translations use "child of humanity" (where the gender of the figure referred to is uncertain or general) or "son of humanity" (where the gender of the figure referred to is masculine, as in the case of Jesus) instead of the more traditional "son of man." In some texts, such as the *Secret Book of John* and the *Holy Book of the Great Invisible Spirit*, that use exalted terms to describe how the divine transcends all finite categories, including gender categories, the translations read "it" for "he" or "him" in the Coptic (and sometimes use "parent" along with "father" in the Coptic) until the texts themselves distinguish between the Father and the Mother in their presentations. Nonetheless, a certain amount of gender bias has been allowed to remain in the translations as a reflection of the preferences of the translators, the specific contents of the texts, and the nature of the Coptic language, which has no neuter gender but makes use of the masculine to refer to what is indefinite or neutral.

The expressions "child of humanity" and "son of humanity," along with others, are capitalized when they function as titles for a given figure, though such a determination of function remains somewhat arbitrary. In general, we have struggled with matters of capitalization in English, and we have tried to reach a happy balance in the capitalization of personified terms that have both a mythological and a psychological function in the texts (e.g., Epinoia, "Insight").[24]

Usually terms in the texts, even technical terms (e.g., *aeōn*, *arkhōn*, *gnōsis*, *hupostasis*, and *plērōma*), are translated (as "eternal realm," "ruler," "knowledge," "reality," and "fullness," respectively), but sometimes they are retained in transliterated form (aeon, archon, gnosis, hypostasis, and pleroma) in the translations in order to preserve the particular style of the texts. The Coptic word *ptērᵉf* (and related terms), which frequently means "everything" or "the universe," often takes on a special meaning in the texts translated here, and when the word refers to the entirety of the divine realm above, it is usually translated "the All."[25] Terms, including technical terms, appearing in the titles of texts are translated as well, so that the present volume refers to the *Secret Book of James* and the *Secret Book of John* (rather than the *Apocryphon of James* and the *Apocryphon of John*), the *Revelations of Adam, James, Paul,* and *Peter* (rather than the *Apocalypses of Adam, James, Paul,* and *Peter*), the *Nature of the Rulers* (rather than the *Hypostasis of the Archons*), *Three Forms of First Thought* (rather than *Trimorphic Protennoia*), and so forth. The fifth tractate of Nag Hammadi Codex VI is entitled *Excerpt from Plato's Republic* and the eighth tractate *Excerpt from the Perfect Discourse*. In some texts, especially the Platonizing Sethian texts, where the language seems to be technical and reflective of Middle Platonic and Neoplatonic philosophy, more of the technical terminology is retained, often simply transliterated, and explained in the notes.

---

24. The Greek term *epinoia* can be translated variously, e.g., "insight," "reflection," "imagination," "creativity," "afterthought." See the notes to the *Secret Book of John*.

25. Cf. the Greek expression *to pan*, which can have a similar range of meanings.

Standard sigla are used in the present volume, though we have tried to keep sigla to a minimum for the sake of ease of reading. Within the English translations, the following signs are employed:

[ ]   Square brackets indicate a textual lacuna that has been restored. When the restoration entails only "a," "an," "the," or "and," such a minor restoration is usually not placed within square brackets. Ordinarily words are placed either entirely inside or outside square brackets. Exceptions to this policy are made in more fragmentary texts, in which portions of words may be placed inside square brackets.

< >   Angle brackets indicate an emendation of a scribal omission or error.

{ }   Braces indicate superfluous letters that presumably were added by a scribe. Some such instances are indicated in the translation. Instances of dittography (the inadvertent copying of a passage twice) are usually indicated in a note.

. . .   Ellipsis dots indicate unrestored lacunae—portions of Coptic (or Greek) text missing in the manuscripts that cannot be restored with confidence. Three dots indicate a lacuna of a Coptic line or less, that is, a short break in the flow of thought in the text. Six dots indicate a lacuna of more than a single Coptic line, that is, a major break in the flow of thought in the text. Ordinarily the extent of the longer lacuna is indicated in a note accompanying the translation. Occasionally the number of dots within a proper name indicates the number of letters missing in the name.

Within the translations, Coptic manuscript page numbers are provided for the sake of reference. In the case of the *Gospel of Thomas*, traditional sayings numbers are given, along with numbers for subdivisions of sayings.[26] In the case of the *Sentences of Sextus*, the system of numeration follows the standard edition of this tractate, which was composed in Greek and is known in Latin, Syriac, Armenian, and Georgian versions.[27] As in *Nag Hammadi Deutsch*, here also only Coptic page numbers are given, and not line numbers from the manuscripts. *The Nag Hammadi Scriptures* is not presented as an edition of Coptic manuscripts but a publication of texts in English translation, and for this reason the continuation of the use of references based upon line numbers in Coptic manuscripts seems inappropriate. Thus, in the notes to the translations, the cross-references to texts in the Nag Hammadi library, the Berlin Gnostic Codex, and Codex Tchacos are given with the titles of the texts and Coptic page numbers (or the other systems of

---

26. The tradition of dividing the *Gospel of Thomas* into 114 sayings is flawed, but it has become a nearly universal convention. The use of numbers for subdivisions of the sayings reflects an increasingly common means of reference.

27. See Henry Chadwick, *The Sentences of Sextus*.

numeration); when a particular text is preserved in more than one copy (as is the case, e.g., with the *Secret Book of John*), the codex number is also provided. Within the introductions to the tractates, however, the textual references include, in addition to the Coptic page numbers, the manuscript lines numbers as well, in case readers wish to refer directly to the Coptic manuscripts and the location of Coptic lines in the manuscripts.

Accompanying the translations in the present volume are several aids to interpretation. In addition to the volume introduction, each text is prefaced with its own introduction, which includes bibliographical suggestions for further reading and study. In the translations there are subheadings that are not in the texts themselves but have been provided by the translators as a way of indicating sections of the texts. The subheadings include references to Coptic page and line numbers in order to allow for another way of moving from the English translations to the Coptic manuscripts. Notes explain difficult passages and refer to parallel passages. In some cases, as with the Platonizing Sethian texts, the notes are somewhat more substantial, to help in the understanding of texts that may benefit from a fuller presentation. An epilogue, "Schools of Thought in the Nag Hammadi Scriptures," discusses Thomas Christianity, the Sethian and Valentinian schools of Gnostic thought, and Hermetic religion within the context of the questions surrounding the term "Gnostic," and a table of tractates provides an overview of the contents of the Nag Hammadi library, the Berlin Gnostic Codex, and Codex Tchacos. A bibliography and an index of proper names conclude the volume.

In *The Nag Hammadi Scriptures* we present a series of English translations prepared and introduced by scholars with different backgrounds and different points of view. Although we have attempted to achieve a degree of stylistic uniformity throughout the volume, some variety inevitably remains, and several voices can be detected in the introductions and translations. We consider such variety to be appropriate in a collection of texts as diverse as the Nag Hammadi library, the Berlin Gnostic Codex, and Codex Tchacos. It is our hope that in reading and studying this diverse collection of religious tractates, readers may join us in a process of seeking and finding, and that for those who explore these texts, in all their diversity, new light may be shed on the world of antiquity—and modernity. As one text in the Nag Hammadi collection, the *Gospel of Thomas*, puts it, "Know what is in front of your face, and what is hidden from you will be disclosed to you. For there is nothing hidden that will not be revealed."

THE PRAYER OF
THE APOSTLE PAUL

NHC I,1

Introduced by Madeleine Scopello
Translated by Marvin Meyer

The *Prayer of the Apostle Paul,* which is written on the front flyleaf of Nag Hammadi Codex I, may have been added after the Coptic scribe finished copying the fifth tractate of Codex I, the *Tripartite Tractate.* Since the first lines of the text are missing, we do not know if there was a title at the beginning of the text. In any case, a title has been conserved at the end of the treatise, "Prayer of the Apostle Paul," followed by a short colophon ("In peace. Holy is Christ"). Both the title and the colophon are in Greek, and the whole prayer was most likely translated from Greek into Coptic.

The *Prayer of the Apostle Paul* begins with a series of invocations addressed to the Redeemer. The person uttering the prayer, identified with the apostle Paul in order to give authority to this text, affirms connections with the divine: "[I am] yours; I have come from [you]" (A,3–6). Technical Gnostic terms are employed to portray the Redeemer by means of invocations employing the formula "you are," repeated for four times: you are mind, treasury, fullness, rest. Except for the word "treasury," which is translated into Coptic (*aho*), the terms are retained in Greek (*nous, plērōma, anapausis*); these terms are frequent in Valentinian literature, though they are also found elsewhere. Reflections on the treasury are also found in *Authoritative Discourse* 28,24, where it is said that the original home of the soul is the treasury, to which she will return and find rest.[1]

According to Dieter Mueller, this prayer is reminiscent of prayers of the *Corpus Hermeticum* (e.g., I.31–32; V.10–11; XIII.16–20) and invocations preserved in Greek and Coptic magical literature, and the beginning of the prayer recalls *Three Steles of Seth* 118,30–119,1.[2]

---

1. See Madeleine Scopello, *Femme, gnose et manichéisme,* 89–90.
2. See Dieter Mueller, in Harold W. Attridge, ed., *Nag Hammadi Codex I,* 2.1–5.

The second part of the *Prayer of the Apostle Paul* invokes the divine as "you who exist and preexisted." These titles, with a philosophical flavor, appear quite often in Valentinian as well as Sethian Gnostic literature in reference to the highest God. The formula "the name exalted above every name" derives from *Philippians* 2:9; as Dieter Mueller notes,[3] the author of the *Prayer* shows a clear knowledge of the *Psalms* and the Pauline epistles. We concur with this line of interpretation, especially concerning the five titles given to Jesus Christ: Lord of lords, King of the eternal realms (or aeons, ages), Son of Humanity, Spirit, Advocate (or Paraclete) of truth. The title "Lord of lords" is also present in 1 *Timothy* 6:15 and *Revelation* 17:14; 19:16, each time in connection with the title "King of kings." "King of the ages" appears as a title in *Tobit* 13:6–10, 1 *Timothy* 1:17, and *Revelation* 15:3. Although "Son of Humanity" is very frequent in the New Testament and early Christian literature, "Advocate of truth" seems to come from *John* 15:26 (cf. also, for "Paraclete," *John* 14:26; 16:7; 1 *John* 2:1).

The suppliant of the *Prayer of the Apostle Paul* also asks for "authority" (A,19: *exousia*, "power"), which indicates apostolic prerogatives. This theme seems to be linked to line 15, where the suppliant asks for God's "gifts." Both healing for the body and redemption for the enlightened soul are requested; the theme of the enlightened soul (or light soul) is very much at home in a Gnostic context.

Lines that bring to mind 1 *Corinthians* 2:9 (where Paul quotes *Isaiah* 64:3 and *Jeremiah* 3:16) and 1 *Corinthians* 2:8 (where the term "rulers" or "archons" is also used) lead the author of the *Prayer of the Apostle Paul* to a Gnostic reinterpretation that transforms the meaning of the term "ruler" from a political to a supernatural one. The statement that the human heart has been formed by the psychical god (A,30) refers to the creation and realm of the demiurge, a widespread conception in Gnostic and Valentinian thought.

Because the present text is included in a codex containing several Valentinian texts, it has been suggested that the *Prayer of the Apostle Paul* is a Valentinian prayer.[4] The place of origin of the tractate is difficult to determine: is it a text coming from the Italian branch of Valentinianism?[5] Its date of composition must be before the final copying of Codex I, in the mid-fourth century, but its themes situate the date of composition more probably at the beginning of the third century.

BIBLIOGRAPHY

Harold W. Attridge, ed., *Nag Hammadi Codex I*, 1.5–11; 2.1–5 (Dieter Mueller); Craig A. Evans, Robert L. Webb, and Richard A. Wiebe, eds., *Nag Hammadi Texts and the Bible*; Rodolphe Kasser et alii, *Oratio Pauli Apostoli*, in *Tractatus Tripartitus Partes II et III*; Hans-Martin Schenke, Hans-Gebhard Bethge, and Ursula Ulrike Kaiser, eds., *Nag Hammadi Deutsch*, 1.7–10 (Hans-Gebhard Bethge and Uwe-Karsten Plisch); Madeleine Scopello, *Femme, gnose et manichéisme*.

---

3. Mueller, in *Nag Hammadi Codex I*, 1.7.

4. See Rodolphe Kasser, *Oratio Pauli Apostoli*; for a somewhat more reserved attitude, cf. Mueller, in *Nag Hammadi Codex I*, 1.6–7.

5. So Kasser, *Oratio Pauli Apostoli*.

The Prayer of the Apostle Paul[1]

. . . . . .[2]
Grant me your [mercy].
[My] Redeemer, redeem me,
for [I am] yours;
I have come from [you].

You are [my] mind:
bring me forth.
You are my treasury:
open for me.
You [are] my fullness:[3]
accept me.
You are <my> rest:[4]
give me incomprehensible perfection.

I call upon you,
you who exist and preexisted,
in the name exalted above every name,[5]
through Jesus Christ,
[Lord] of lords,
King of the eternal realms.[6]
Give me your gifts, with no regret,
through the Son of Humanity,[7]
the Spirit,
the Advocate[8] of [truth].
Give me authority, [I] ask of you,
give [healing][9] for my body, since I ask you

---

1. Coptic text: NHC I,1: A,1–B,10 (front flyleaf). Editions: *The Facsimile Edition of the Nag Hammadi
Codices: Codex I*, 3–4; Harold W. Attridge, ed., *Nag
Hammadi Codex I*, 1.5–11, 2.1–5 (Dieter Mueller);
Hans-Martin Schenke, Hans-Gebhard Bethge, and
Ursula Ulrike Kaiser, eds., *Nag Hammadi Deutsch*,
1.7–10 (Hans-Gebhard Bethge and Uwe-Karsten
Plisch). 2. About two lines are missing at the beginning of the text. The letters just before the beginning
of the translation, at the end of the previous clause,
may be restored to read "[your] light" (*[pekou]aein*).
3. Pleroma, here and below. 4. The text reads only
"rest" (*tanapausis*, here emended to read *t<a>ana-
pausis*, "<my> rest"). 5. Cf. *Philippians* 2:9. 6. Or
"aeons," "ages." 7. Or "Son of Man." 8. Or "Paraclete." 9. Here the Coptic is restored to read *[tal]co*. It
may also be possible to restore it to read *[ta]co* (a variant of *[ta]ko*), "corruption," in which case the prayer
may be understood as Paul's prayer before his death.

through the preacher of the gospel,[10]
and redeem my eternal enlightened soul and my spirit,
and disclose to my mind the firstborn of the fullness of grace.

Grant what eyes of angels have not [seen],
what ears of rulers have not heard,
and what has not arisen in the human heart,[11]
which became angelic,
made in the image of the animate God[12]
when it was formed in the beginning.
I have faith and hope.
And bestow upon me
your beloved, chosen, blessed majesty,
the firstborn, the first-begotten, [**B**]
the [wonderful] mystery of your house.
[For] yours is power and glory
and praise and greatness,
forever and ever.

[Amen].

Prayer of the Apostle Paul

In peace.
Holy is Christ.

---

10. Or "evangelist," probably referring to Jesus, possibly to Paul himself or to another evangelist. **11.** Cf. 1 *Corinthians* 2:9; *Gospel of Thomas* 17; *Gospel of Judas* 47. **12.** Or "the psychical god," i.e., the demiurge.

THE SECRET BOOK OF JAMES

NHC I,2

Introduced by Madeleine Scopello
Translated by Marvin Meyer

W ritten for a fortunate few, the text called the *Secret Book of James* is a letter that James is said to have sent to an addressee whose name is unfortunately in a lacuna (only the last three letters [in Coptic] have survived: [. . .]*thos*). The tractate is a Coptic translation from a Greek original, now lost, and it occupies the first sixteen pages of Nag Hammadi Codex I. In general the text is well preserved, although some lines are in bad condition at the top of the first three pages. The text is untitled in the manuscript; however, the ancient author, who employs the authoritative pseudonym of James, refers to his letter as an "apocryphon" (*apokruphon*), or "secret book" (1,10)—hence the modern title of the tractate.

The *Secret Book of James* follows the ancient epistolary style for the opening of a letter (name of the sender, name of the addressee, salutation, and greeting of peace) as well as its conclusion. The letter has been sent by James, it is said, at the request of his addressee, and it contains an account of a secret revelation the Savior gave to James and Peter. James recalls that he wrote the letter, which is esoteric in its content, in Hebrew letters, and he asks his addressee not to share this writing with many: even the Savior did not want to deliver his message to the twelve disciples, but only to two of them (1,15–25). Doubtless the addressee is worthy of receiving this secret teaching, as is shown by the title James gives him: "a minister of the salvation of the saints" (the saints can be the members of a Gnostic community or, more generally, the elect believers who are deserving of salvation). And faith given through this discourse (*logos*) will automatically confer salvation upon them.

In the literary fiction of the *Secret Book of James*, the events depicted happen 550 days after the Savior's resurrection, at a time when the twelve disciples, all sitting together, are writing down in books what they remember of the words Christ told to each of them during his earthly life (2,7–15). This constitutes an important piece of information about how the disciples shaped Christ's *logia*, a process also recorded elsewhere in early Christian literature (e.g., in *1 Clement* 13.1–2). The gap of 550 days between the resurrection and the second coming of the Savior can be compared with a tradition recorded in the *Ascension of Isaiah*, a Jewish apocryphal text with Christian interpolations, which speaks of a period of 18 months, or 540 days.[1]

The intention of the Savior is to draw James and Peter apart from the other disciples and help them to "be filled"—a technical phrase in Gnostic thought linked to Pleroma and "fullness"—through his revelation. James is receptive to the words of the Savior, but Peter shows no understanding. The two figures have been interpreted as opposing symbols of the Gnostic community and the emerging orthodox church: members of the Gnostic community have no need of an intermediary to obtain salvation, while the members of the great church are grounded in an ecclesial structure that they need if they are to be saved.[2] Such ideas are advanced in *Secret Book of James* 2,23–33. The Savior's teachings are expressed through a series of opposing Gnostic metaphors: drunkenness and sobriety, waking and sleeping, being healed and being sick, emptiness and fullness. These metaphors belong to the common heritage of late antiquity, yet, taken together, they express themes typical of Gnostic teaching. The Savior utters teachings consisting of sayings, parables, and prophecies organized into a dialogue in which James asks questions of the Savior. As for Peter, he plays a small role in this dialogue, and he limits himself to a polemical statement showing his lack of comprehension (13,26–36).

The literary genre of the *Secret Book of James* is heterogeneous: the tractate is a letter reporting on a revelation shaped into the form of a dialogue.[3] Although the classical rules of epistolary style are known by the author, the treatise is marked by themes belonging to the genre of esoteric teaching.[4] The letter may even be a frame added later to the original content by a redactor.[5] As for the body of the text, it is an example of a revelatory dialogue, in which an inquirer asks questions about hidden matters and a revealer provides answers. Well attested in Jewish and Christian tradition, the revelatory dialogue has evolved from a real to an imaginary dialogue.[6] There are good parallels in Gnostic literature (*Dialogue of the Savior, Pistis Sophia, Books of Jeu*).

Two capstone themes are present in the *Secret Book of James*: that of fullness and pain (2,39–6,21) and that of prophecy (6,21–34). This part of the tractate is guided by the polemical intention of the author against Peter and the official church, but the polemical character of the *Secret Book of James* is veiled, and the author maintains a prudent attitude when dealing with these matters.[7] The

1. Donald Rouleau, *L'Épître apocryphe de Jacques*, 99; W. C. van Unnik, "The Origin of the Recently Discovered 'Apocryphon Jacobi.'"

2. Rouleau, *L'Épître apocryphe de Jacques*, 25–27.

3. Rouleau, *L'Épître apocryphe de Jacques*, 10.

4. Rouleau, *L'Épître apocryphe de Jacques*, 10–11.

5. Francis E. Williams, in Harold W. Attridge, ed., *Nag Hammadi Codex I*, 1.17–18.

6. See Pheme Perkins, *The Gnostic Dialogue*; Kurt Rudolph, "Der gnostische 'Dialog' als literarisches Genus."

7. Rouleau, *L'Épître apocryphe de Jacques*, 17.

polemical features of the text may suggest that the *Secret Book of James* speaks to a situation in which authoritative structures are being established and the text is reacting against them. Other Nag Hammadi texts (*Second Discourse of Great Seth, Revelation of Peter,* and *Testimony of Truth*) show similar concerns.

Some of the sayings attributed to Jesus in the *Secret Book of James* can be compared with *logia* in the canonical gospels,[8] but others have no parallels in New Testament tradition (e.g., the saying about the palm shoot, 7,24–35).

Jewish apocalyptic and esoteric themes are combined in the treatise: the theme of the "chariot of spirit" that bears the Savior aloft (14,3–36) recalls Jewish Merkavah speculations on the divine chariot of God; the vision James and Peter experience is paralleled in the Jewish pseudepigrapha, for example, in Enoch literature. After seeing and hearing angelic trumpets and a great deal of turmoil (15,10–13), the two disciples ascend to a higher place, where they can hear angels praising and rejoicing as well as celestial majesties (the highest classes of angels) singing hymns (15,15–23). Going further up in spirit, James and Peter approach the Majesty—the highest God—but they are allowed to hear and see no more (15,23–28).

The research on the *Secret Book of James* is rich. According to both Henri-Charles Puech and Gilles Quispel, followed by Jan Zandee and S. Kent Brown, this letter is a Gnostic composition belonging most likely to a Valentinian school of thought.[9] This interpretation is strengthened by the fact that the *Secret Book of James* is part of a codex with Valentinian features. Some expressions referring to the Savior have a Gnostic flavor. For example, the Savior says, "I shall return to the place from which I came" (2,23–24) and, in a similar vein, "I shall ascend to the place from which I have come" (14,20–22). For W. C. van Unnik, however, the present tractate is not Gnostic, and its provenance could well be situated in a small Egyptian community some time after the Jewish rebellion of 135 CE.[10] The Christology of the treatise shows no docetic tendencies, which are common in Gnostic texts, and the passion and suffering of the Savior are understood as having been real. Nevertheless, the Savior is said to be a preexisting entity (2,23–24).

The place and date of composition for the *Secret Book of James* can be fixed at the end of second century or at the beginning of the third, in Egypt, probably in Alexandria, in a milieu moving toward a break with the official church.

BIBLIOGRAPHY

Harold W. Attridge, ed., *Nag Hammadi Codex I*, 1.13–53; 2.7–37 (Francis E. Williams); S. Kent Brown, *James: A Religio-Historical Study of the Relations Between Jewish, Gnostic, and Catholic Christianity in the*

---

8. See Ron Cameron, *Sayings Traditions in the Apocryphon of James*; Robert W. Funk, *New Gospel Parallels*; Charles W. Hedrick, "Kingdom Sayings and Parables of Jesus in the Apocryphon of James: Tradition and Redaction"; Jean-Marie Sevrin, "Paroles et paraboles de Jésus dans les écrits gnostiques coptes."

9. See Henri-Charles Puech, "The Apocryphon of James (Apocryphon Jacobi)"; Henri-Charles Puech and Gilles Quispel, "La lettre de Jacques"; Jan Zandee, "Gnostische trekken in een Brief van Jacobus"; S. Kent Brown, *James: A Religio-Historical Study of the Relations Between Jewish, Gnostic, and Catholic Christianity in the Early Period Through an Investigation of the Traditions About James the Lord's Brother.*

10. Van Unnik, "The Origin of the Recently Discovered 'Apocryphon Jacobi.'"

Early Period Through an Investigation of the Traditions About James the Lord's Brother; Ron Cameron, *Sayings Traditions in the Apocryphon of James*; Robert W. Funk, *New Gospel Parallels*; Charles W. Hedrick, "Kingdom Sayings and Parables of Jesus in the Apocryphon of James: Tradition and Redaction"; Andrew K. Helmbold, "The Apocryphon of James"; Michel Malinine, Henri-Charles Puech, Gilles Quispel, Walter C. Till, Rodolphe Kasser, R. McL. Wilson, Jan Zandee, eds., *Epistula Iacobi Apocrypha*; Pheme Perkins, *The Gnostic Dialogue*; Henri-Charles Puech, "The Apocryphon of James (Apocryphon Jacobi)"; Henri-Charles Puech and Gilles Quispel, "La lettre de Jacques"; Donald Rouleau, *L'Épître apocryphe de Jacques*; Kurt Rudolph, "Der gnostische 'Dialog' als literarisches Genus"; Hans-Martin Schenke, Hans-Gebhard Bethge, and Ursula Ulrike Kaiser, eds., *Nag Hammadi Deutsch*, 1.11–26 (Judith Hartenstein and Uwe-Karsten Plisch); Jean-Marie Sevrin, "Paroles et paraboles de Jésus dans les écrits gnostiques coptes"; Terence V. Smith, "The Peter-Figure in Gnostic Sources "; W. C. van Unnik, "The Origin of the Recently Discovered 'Apocryphon Jacobi' "; Jan Zandee, "Gnostische trekken in een Brief van Jacobus."

The Secret Book of James[1]

The Letter of James (1,1–8)

[James][2] writes to . . . .[3]
Peace be [with you from] peace,
[love] from love,
[grace] from grace,
[faith] from faith,
life from holy life.

Secret Books (1,8–2,7)

You have asked me to send you a secret book revealed to me and Peter by the master,[4] and I could not turn you down, nor could I speak to you, so [I have written] it in Hebrew[5] and have sent it to you, and to you alone. But since you are a minister of the salvation of the saints, do your best to be careful not to communicate to many people this book that the Savior did not want to communicate even to all of us, his twelve disciples. Nonetheless, blessed will they be who will be saved through the faith of this treatise.

---

1. Coptic text: NHC I,2: 1,1–16,30. Editions: *The Facsimile Edition of the Nag Hammadi Codices: Codex I*, 5–20; Harold W. Attridge, ed., *Nag Hammadi Codex I*, 1.13–53, 2.7–37 (Francis E. Williams); Dankwart Kirchner, *Epistula Jacobi Apocrypha*; Donald Rouleau, *L'Épître apocryphe de Jacques*; Hans-Martin Schenke, Hans-Gebhard Bethge, and Ursula Ulrike Kaiser, eds., *Nag Hammadi Deutsch*, 1.11–26 (Judith Hartenstein and Uwe-Karsten Plisch). The title is construed from the contents of the text; the text may also be entitled the *Apocryphon of James*, the *Letter of James*, or the *Apocryphal Letter of James*. 2. Probably thought to be James the Just, brother of Jesus and leader of the Jerusalem church (cf. *Gospel of Thomas* 12; *First* and *Second Revelations of James*). 3. The restoration of the name or description of the recipient or recipients of the letter remains uncertain. The best suggestion is probably "the [student (lit., "son" or "child") Cerin]thos" (Coptic *ᵉm[pšēre kērin]thos*). Cf. Hartenstein and Plisch, in *Nag Hammadi Deutsch*, 1.18. A person named Cerinthos was a well-known second-century Christian teacher who was considered one of the first Gnostics by the heresiologists. The existing Coptic letters –*thos* could also be from such words as *pathos*, *sumpathos*, or *agathos*, and the restoration could indicate that the letter was written "to [one who embraces suffering]," "to [his companion in suffering]," "to [one who is good]," or the like. 4. Or "Lord," here and below. 5. Coptic (from Greek, preserving the Greek dative plural ending) *hᵉn hensheei mmᵉnthebraiois*, lit., "in Hebrew letters." No such Hebrew text is known.

Ten months ago I sent you another secret book[6] that the Savior revealed to me. Think of that book as revealed to me, James. But as for this book, [2] I [have not yet fully understood it, and it was also] revealed [for you and] those who are yours, so [try] to comprehend [its meaning]. This is how [you can be] saved, and [then] you should [also make it known].[7]

Jesus Appears to Peter and James (2,7–3,38)

The twelve disciples were all sitting together, recalling what the Savior had said to each of them, whether in a hidden or an open manner, and organizing it in books.[8] I was writing what is in [my book]. Look, the Savior appeared, after he had left [us, while we] were watching for him.

Five hundred fifty days[9] after he rose from the dead, we said to him, "Did you depart and leave us?"

Jesus said, "No, but I shall return to the place from which I came. If you want to come with me, come."

They all answered and said, "If you order us, we'll come."

He said, "I tell you the truth, no one will ever enter heaven's kingdom because I ordered it, but rather because you yourselves are filled. Leave James and Peter to me that I may fill them."

When he called the two of them, he took them aside and commanded the rest to keep doing what they were doing.

The Savior said, "You have been favored [3] [through the Father to receive my sayings. The other disciples also] have written [my sayings in their] books as if [they have understood, but be careful. They have done their] work without [really understanding]. They have listened like [foolish people], and . . . they have not understood.[10]

"Do you not want to be filled?

"Your hearts are drunk.

"Do you not want to be sober?

"You ought to be ashamed.

"From now on, awake or asleep, remember that you have seen the Son of Humanity[11] and have spoken with him and have listened to him.

"Woe to those who have seen the Son of Humanity.

"Blessed will you be who have not seen the human, or associated with him, or spoken with him, or listened to anything from him. Yours is life.[12]

"Understand that he healed you when you were sick, that you might reign.

---

6. No additional secret book of James is known. 7. The restoration of these lines remains tentative. Cf. Hartenstein and Plisch, in Nag Hammadi Deutsch, 1.18. 8. Cf. Gospel of Thomas Prologue; Book of Thomas 138. 9. Other texts, including Gnostic texts, also suggest long periods of time for appearances of Jesus, e.g., 18 months (540 days), 545 days (18 months plus five intercalary days?), or even 12 years. On 18 days (or months), cf. Secret Book of James 8. 10. The restoration of these lines remains tentative. Cf. Hartenstein and Plisch, in Nag Hammadi Deutsch, 1.19. The remaining lacuna has been restored, with hesitation, to read "[like deaf people]" (Nag Hammadi Deutsch, 1.19, n. 36). 11. Or "Son of Man," here and below. 12. Cf. Secret Book of James 12–13; John 20:29.

"Woe to those who have found relief from their sickness, for they will relapse into sickness.

"Blessed are you who have not been sick, and have known relief before getting sick. God's kingdom is yours.

"So I tell you, be filled and leave no space within you empty, or he who is coming will mock you."

Being Filled and Lacking (3,38–4,22)

Then Peter answered, "Look, three times you have told us, [4] 'Be [filled],' but we are filled."

The [Savior answered] and said, "For [this reason I have told] you, '[Be filled],' that you may not [lack. Those who lack] will not [be saved]. To be filled is good and to lack is bad. Yet since it is also good for you to lack but bad for you to be filled, whoever is filled also lacks. One who lacks is not filled in the way another who lacks is filled, but whoever is filled is brought to an appropriate end. So you should lack when you can fill yourselves and be filled when you lack that you may be able to [fill] yourselves more. Be filled with spirit but lack in reason, for reason is of the soul. It is soul."[13]

Believe in My Cross (4,22–6,21)

I answered and said to him, "Master, we can obey you if you wish, for we have forsaken our fathers and our mothers and our villages and have followed you. Give us the means not to be tempted by the evil devil."

The master answered and said, "What good is it to you if you do the Father's will, but you are not given your part of his bounty when you are tempted by Satan? But if you are oppressed by Satan and persecuted and do the Father's [5] will, I [say] he will love you, make you my equal, and consider you beloved through his forethought,[14] and by your own choice. Won't you stop loving the flesh and fearing suffering? Don't you know that you have not yet been abused, unjustly accused, locked up in prison, unlawfully condemned, crucified <without> reason,[15] or buried in the sand[16] as I myself was by the evil one? Do you dare to spare the flesh, you for whom the spirit is a wall surrounding you? If you consider how long the world has existed before you and how long it will exist after you, you will see that your life is but a day and your sufferings but an hour. The good will not enter the world. Disdain death, then, and care about life. Remember my cross and my death, and you will live."

I answered and said to him, "Master, do not mention to us the cross and death, for they are far [6] from you."

---

13. This paragraph is difficult to translate, but a significant distinction is made here between spirit (*pneuma*) and soul (*psukhē*). 14. Coptic *pronoia*. 15. The text is emended here (*hᵉnn oumᵉnt<a>logos*). The manuscript reads "with reason." 16. Coptic *hᵉnn oušou*; burial in sand is characteristic of Egypt. It is also possible to emend to read *hᵉnn ouš<ōs>*, "in <shame>."

The master answered and said, "I tell you the truth, none will be saved unless they believe in my cross, for God's kingdom belongs to those who have believed in my cross. Be seekers of death, then, like the dead who seek life, for what they seek becomes apparent to them. And what is there to cause them concern? As for you, when you search out death, it will teach you about being chosen. I tell you the truth, no one afraid of death will be saved, for the kingdom of death[17] belongs to those who are put to death.[18] Become better than I. Be like the child of the holy Spirit."[19]

The Head of Prophecy (6,21–8,27)

Then I asked him, "Master, how can we prophesy to those who ask us to prophesy to them? There are many who bring a request to us and look to us to hear our pronouncement."

The master answered and said, "Don't you know that the head of prophecy was cut off with John?"[20]

I said, "Master, it is impossible to remove the head of prophecy, isn't it?"

The master said to me, "When you realize what 'head' means, and that prophecy comes from the head, then understand the meaning of 'its head was [7] removed.'

"First I spoke with you in parables, and you did not understand. Now I am speaking with you openly, and you do not grasp it. Nevertheless, you were for me a parable among parables and a disclosure among things revealed.

"Be eager to be saved without being urged. Rather, be fervent on your own and, if possible, outdo even me, for this is how the Father will love you.

"Come to hate hypocrisy and evil intention. Intention produces hypocrisy, and hypocrisy is far from truth.

"Do not let heaven's kingdom wither away. It is like a palm shoot whose dates dropped around it. It produced buds, and after they grew, its productivity dried up. This is also what happened with fruit that came from this single root. After it was harvested, fruit was obtained by many. It certainly would be good if you could produce new growth now. You would find it.[21]

"Since I was glorified like this once before, why do you hold me back when I am eager to go? [8] After my labor[22] you have made me stay with you another eighteen days[23] because of the parables. For some people it was enough to listen to the teaching and understand 'The Shepherds,' 'The Seed,' 'The Building,' 'The Lamps of the Young Women,' 'The Wage of the Workers,' and 'The Silver Coins and the Woman.'[24]

---

17. Coptic *tmᵉntᵉr[r]o . . . ᵉmpmou*. The text may well be emended to read *tmᵉntᵉr[r]o . . . ᵉmp<n>ou<te>*, "<God's> kingdom." 18. Or "who put themselves to death," as voluntary martyrs. 19. Here the holy Spirit may be understood to be God the Mother. Cf. *Gospel of Thomas* 101; *Gospel of Philip* 55. 20. John the Baptizer; cf. *Gospel of Thomas* 46. 21. This parable of the date-palm shoot remains difficult to translate, and the translation given here is somewhat tentative. The reference to "it" in the last sentence apparently indicates the kingdom. 22. Coptic *ph[is]e*, which may also be translated "my suffering." 23. Or perhaps emend to read "eighteen months" (cf. *Secret Book of James* 2). 24. These are titles of or references to parables.

"Be eager for the word. The first aspect of the word is faith, the second is love, the third is works, and from these comes life.

"The word is like a grain of wheat. When someone sowed it, he had faith in it, and when it sprouted, he loved it, because he saw many grains instead of just one. And after he worked, he was saved because he prepared it as food and he still kept some out to sow.

"This is also how you can acquire heaven's kingdom for yourselves. Unless you acquire it through knowledge,[25] you will not be able to find it."

Be Sober, Be Saved (8,27–9,23)

"So I say to you, be sober. Do not go astray. And often have I said to you all together, and also to you alone, James, be saved. I have commanded you to follow me, and I have taught you how to speak before the rulers.

"See that I have come down and have spoken and have exerted myself and have won my crown [9] when I saved you. I came down to live with you that you might also live with me. And when I found that your houses had no roofs, I lived in houses that could receive me when I came down.

"Trust in me, my brothers. Understand what the great light is. The Father does not need me. A father does not need a son, but it is the son who needs the father. To him I am going, for the Father of the Son is not in need of you.

"Listen to the word, understand knowledge,[26] love life, and no one will persecute you and no one will oppress you other than you yourselves."

Woe to You, Blessed Are You (9,24–11,6)

"You wretches! You poor devils! You pretenders to truth! You falsifiers of knowledge! You sinners against the spirit! Do you still dare to listen when from the beginning you should have been speaking? Do you still dare to sleep when from the beginning you should have been awake so that heaven's kingdom might receive you? [10] I tell you the truth, it is easier for a holy person to sink into defilement and for an enlightened person to sink into darkness than for you to reign—or not to reign.[27]

"I have remembered your tears, your mourning, and your grief. They are far from us. You who are outside the Father's inheritance, weep when you should, mourn, and preach what is good. The Son is ascending, as is proper.

"I tell you the truth, if I had been sent to those who would listen to me and had spoken with them, I would never have come down to earth.[28] Now be ashamed.

"Look, I shall be leaving you and go away, and I do not want to stay with you any longer, just as you yourselves have not wanted this. Follow me quickly. This is why I tell you, for you I came down. You are loved ones. You are the ones who will

---

25. Gnosis. 26. Gnosis, here and below. 27. Coptic *ē at^emeire*, lit., "or not to do so." 28. Or "I would never ascend from the earth."

bring life to many people. Invoke the Father, pray to God frequently, and he will be generous with you.

"Blessed is one who has seen you with him when he is proclaimed among the angels and glorified among the saints. Yours is life. Rejoice and be glad as [11] children of God. Observe his will that you may be saved. Accept correction from me and save yourselves. I am mediating for you with the Father, and he will forgive you many things."

Few Find Heaven's Kingdom (11,6–12,17)

When we heard this, we were delighted. We had become gloomy because of what we[29] said earlier. But when he saw us happy, he said:

"Woe to you who are in need of an advocate.

"Woe to you who stand in need of grace.

"Blessed will they be who have spoken out and acquired grace for themselves.

"Compare yourselves to foreigners. How are they viewed in your city? Why are you anxious to banish yourselves on your own and distance yourselves from your city? Why abandon your dwelling on your own and make it available for those who want to live in it? You exiles and runaways, woe to you, for you will be captured.

"Or maybe you think that the Father is a lover of humanity, or that he is won over by prayers, or that he is gracious to one because of another, or that he tolerates whoever is seeking?

"He[30] knows about desire and what the flesh needs. Doesn't it desire the soul? The body does not sin apart from the soul just as [12] the soul is not saved apart from the spirit. But if the soul is saved from evil and the spirit too is saved, the body becomes sinless. The spirit animates the soul but the body kills it. The soul kills itself.[31]

"I tell you the truth, he certainly will not forgive the sin of the soul or the guilt of the flesh, for none of those who have worn the flesh will be saved. Do you think that many have found heaven's kingdom?

"Blessed is one who has seen oneself as a fourth one in heaven."[32]

Know Yourselves (12,17–13,25)

When we heard this, we became sad. But when he saw that we were sad, he said, "I say this to you that you may know yourselves.[33]

"Heaven's kingdom is like a head of grain that sprouted in a field. And when it was ripe, it scattered its seed, and again it filled the field with heads of grain for

---

29. Perhaps emend to read "he." 30. I.e., "The Father." 31. Or "herself"; "soul," *psukhē*, is feminine in gender. Here it is assumed that a person is composed of a body of flesh, an animating soul, and a vivifying spirit, as in Valentinian thought. Cf. also 1 *Thessalonians* 5:23. 32. This seems to be a way of saying that few are saved, and it may indicate one who is alone as a fourth one with God the Father, Mother, and Son, and thus is as close as one can get to the divine. 33. "Know yourself" was a maxim from the oracular center at Delphi, Greece.

another year. So with you, be eager to harvest for yourselves a head of the grain of life that you may be filled with the kingdom.

"And as long as I am with you, pay attention to me and trust in me, but when I am far from you, remember me. And remember me because I was with you and you did not know me.

"Blessed will they be who have known me.

"Woe to those who have heard and have not believed.

"Blessed will they be who [13] have not seen but yet have [believed].[34]

"Once again I appeal to you. I am disclosed to you as I am building a house useful to you when you find shelter in it, and it will support[35] your neighbors' house when theirs threatens to collapse.

"I tell you the truth, woe to those for whom I was sent down here.

"Blessed will they be who are going up to the Father.

"Again I warn you, you who exist. Be like those who do not exist that you may dwell with those who do not exist.[36]

"Do not let heaven's kingdom become a desert within you. Do not be proud because of the light that enlightens. Rather, act toward yourselves as I myself have toward you. I have put myself under a curse for you that you might be saved."

The Last Word (13,26–15,5)

Peter responded to these comments and said, "Sometimes you urge us on toward heaven's kingdom, but at other times you turn us away, master. Sometimes you encourage us, draw us toward faith, and promise us life, but at other times you drive us away from heaven's kingdom."

The master answered and said to us, "I have offered you faith many times—and have revealed myself to you, [14] James—and you have not known me. Now I see you often rejoicing. And although you are delighted about the promise of life, you are sad and gloomy when you are taught about the kingdom.

"Nevertheless, you, through faith and knowledge, have received life. So disregard rejection when you hear it, but when you hear about the promise, be joyful all the more.

"I tell you the truth, whoever will receive life and believe in the kingdom will never leave it, not even if the Father wants to banish him.

"This is all I shall tell you at this time. Now I shall ascend to the place from which I have come. When I was eager to go, you have driven me off, and instead of accompanying me, you have chased me away.

"Be attentive to the glory that awaits me, and when you have opened your hearts, listen to the hymns that await me up in heaven. Today I must take my place at the right hand of my Father.

---

34. Cf. *Secret Book of James* 3; John 20:29. **35.** Or "will be able to stand alongside" (Coptic *naš ōhe aret^ef*). **36.** On existing and not existing, cf. *Secret* *Book of John* II, 2–4; *Three Steles of Seth* 121–24; *Allogenes the Stranger* 61–64.

"I have spoken my last word to you; I shall depart from you, for a chariot of spirit[37] has carried me up, and from now on I shall strip myself that I may clothe myself.[38]

"So pay attention: blessed are those who have proclaimed the Son before he came down, so that, when I did come, I might ascend.

"Blessed three times over [15] are those who were proclaimed by the Son before they came into being, so that you might share with them."

Apocalyptic Ascent (15,5–16,11)

When he said this, he left. Peter and I knelt down, gave thanks, and sent our hearts up to heaven. We heard with our ears and saw with our eyes the noise of wars, a trumpet blast, and great turmoil.[39]

When we passed beyond that place, we sent our minds up further. We saw with our eyes and heard with our ears hymns, angelic praises, and angelic rejoicing. Heavenly majesties were singing hymns, and we rejoiced too.

Again after this we wished to send our spirits up to the Majesty. When we ascended, we were not allowed to see or hear anything. For the other disciples called to us and asked us, "What did you hear from the teacher? What did he tell you? Where did he go?"

We answered them, "He ascended. He gave us his right hand, and promised all of us life. He showed us children coming after us and commanded [16] [us] to love them, since we are to be [saved] for their sakes."

When they heard this, they believed the revelation, but they were angry about those who would be born. Not wishing to give them reason to take offense, I sent each of them to a different location. I myself went up to Jerusalem, praying that I might acquire a share with the loved ones who are to appear.[40]

Final Advice (16,12–30)

I pray that the beginning may come from you. This is how I can be saved. They will be enlightened through me, by my faith, and through another's that is better than mine. I wish mine to be the lesser.

Do your best to be like them, and pray that you may acquire a share with them. Beyond what I have said, the Savior did not disclose any revelation to us on their behalf. We proclaim a share with those for whom the message was proclaimed, those whom the lord has made his children.

---

37. On Jesus riding a chariot into heaven, cf. accounts of Elijah and Enoch traveling into heaven (2 *Kings* 2; 1 *Enoch* 70) as well as figures ascending to heaven in chariots on Roman commemorative coins. 38. Stripping and clothing refers to shedding the flesh as a garment and sometimes, as here, putting on a new heavenly garment. 39. Apocalyptic images. 40. This paragraph describes the dispersal of the apostles to preach throughout the world; cf. *Letter of Peter to Philip* 140. James stays in Jerusalem to lead the church there. The "loved ones who are to appear" are future believers, like the readers of the *Secret Book of James*.

THE GOSPEL OF TRUTH

NHC I,3; XII,2

Introduced by Einar Thomassen
Translated by Marvin Meyer

In *Against Heresies* 3.11.9, Irenaeus mentions that the Valentinians possess a work called "The Gospel of Truth." The third tractate of Codex I happens to begin with precisely those words, and most scholars are therefore inclined to identify the tractate with the work mentioned by Irenaeus. The tractate is not furnished with a title in the manuscript, but it can hardly be a coincidence that its opening words are identical with the title mentioned by Irenaeus. It is more reasonable to assume that the work was habitually referred to by its opening words, and that Irenaeus therefore understood them as its title.

The *Gospel of Truth* is not itself a "gospel" in the sense of other works that bear that name, nor is it intended to be. Instead, it is a discourse on the gospel, understood as the good news about the appearance of the Savior on earth and the message he brought to humanity.[1] The *Gospel of Truth* gives an interpretation of that event and explains how everything has been changed as a consequence of it. A peculiar feature of the text, however, is that the story of salvation seems to unfold simultaneously on two distinct levels. On one level we hear about the appearance of the Savior in the world of human beings: he taught them the truth, but he was persecuted by his enemies and was crucified and killed. However, his death brought life to mortal humans, and his instruction woke them up from forgetfulness and made them return to the Father, the source of their being. Parallel with this account, however, another, more mythological story is told in the text as a kind of metanarrative. This story tells how the world came into existence as the result of ignorance. Initially, the All, the Entirety of aeons or eternal realms, existed inside the Father, who was so vast and unfathomable that they were unable to perceive him. Because of this, ignorance, anguish, and terror took hold of the aeons; Error was produced instead of truth, and on this illusive basis the world was created as a solidification of ignorance and fear, a "fog."

---

1. On the *Gospel of Truth* (and other Nag Hammadi texts) as gospel or good news, see Marvin Meyer, *The Gnostic Gospels of Jesus*, xiii–xxviii.

The work of the Savior was not only to bring knowledge to earthly humans, but also to rectify the cosmic error. He revealed the unknown Father to the aeons and gave them a proper, harmonious relationship to their originator. Although the Savior, as a historical person, is identical with Jesus, he is also, from a higher and more fundamental perspective, the Son, the Word, and the Name of the Father; he is the first emanation, who manifests the Father to the aeons and causes them to come into being as perfect beings. Thus, the redemption of humans effected by Jesus in this world is a part of, and reflects, a larger process of cosmic scale and ontological significance, a process by which the aeons are properly brought into being and given knowledge about the Father. The discourse in the *Gospel of Truth* moves back and forth between the two levels, between the historical and the mythical, and one gets the impression that blurring the distinctions between them is a deliberate strategy of the writer.

An additional characteristic of the *Gospel of Truth* is its highly inventive use of images. For example, a long section is devoted to the concept of "the book of the living" (19,34–23,17). The theme is introduced following the presentation of the Savior as a teacher: instructing "the little children," he revealed the book, whose contents were the Father's thoughts, hidden from before creation. Naturally, therefore, the contents of the book is knowledge. However, the book is also compared to a will that lay hidden but was made public after the testator's death. Moreover, in being crucified, Jesus posted the book on the cross—thus it is also compared to a public proclamation. Further, the book of the living is a roll of names where those who have been appointed for salvation are written down. Finally, opening the book means that the names are called out, and whoever is called listens, turns around, and hastens toward the one who is calling. Even this list of meanings does not exhaust the richness of the symbolism of the "book" in this section of the *Gospel of Truth*, but may serve to give an impression of the author's sophisticated use of imagery.

In its composition, the *Gospel of Truth* moves from one theme to the next, prompted more by the association of images than by a linear logic of exposition. Thus, the initial description of the origin of error and illusion leads to the presentation of the Savior as the teacher. This in turns leads to the theme of the book of the living, which the Savior revealed. Next, a description of the book as a unity composed of many letters evolves into a portrait of the Savior as the Word that goes forth from the Father and permeates the All (23,17–24,9). The Word, moreover, is the Son, who reveals the Father, replacing ignorance with knowledge and dispersion with unity—in short, deficiency with fullness.

Unity and fullness then become the theme of the following section, where another central image is unfolded: the house and the jars (25,25–26,27). One moves to a new house, but only the good jars will be taken along—that is, the ones that are unbroken and full. The others are discarded. In this section, a tone of eschatological judgment is also present, though it is not clear precisely what the sorting of the jars refers to. Is it the general separation of spiritual and nonspiritual people that resulted from the appearance of the Savior? Or does the passage allude to a specific historical event, perhaps the moment when the Valentinian church separated from the rest of the Christian movement? Of course, the one interpretation does not exclude the other.

Next, the division between those who received the revelation and those who did not is radicalized as a distinction between being and not being: receiving knowledge means truly to come into being, to be manifested, whereas those who remain in error do not really exist at all (27,34–28,32). This idea inspires another impressive image, that of cosmic existence as a nightmarish dream, whose unreal nature is understood only when the dreamer wakes up (28,32–30,23). Aroused, the dreamer then receives the spirit, which enables him to stand up. The spirit, moreover, makes some people perceive the nature of the Savior (while others do not understand). He now becomes the way (31,29),[2] a catchword that in turn serves to introduce the parable of the lost sheep and the good shepherd (31,35–32,37)—a favorite topic among the Valentinians.[3] The good shepherd labored on the Sabbath, which means the world, and he brought the sheep into the higher day, which is pure light.

A paraenetic section next prescribes the behavior appropriate for those who belong to the heavenly day (33,1–32); and those who do the Father's will in this way are described as his "fragrance" (34,1). The text then reverts to the theme of the deficiency that has been transformed into fullness and to the image of the jars, and this time the text introduces the topic of anointing: the full jars are those that have been sealed with ointment (34,34–36,35). This is the clearest reference to ritual practices in the *Gospel of Truth*.[4]

Somewhat abruptly, the discourse now turns, with a protological perspective, to a description of the Word, which has revealed the hidden Thought of the Father, followed by a famous section where the Son is portrayed as the Father's Name—an idea that serves to express the indissoluble relationship between Father and Son as well as the Son's role as the revealer of the unnamable Father of the All (38,6–41,3). Finally, by stating that the Son revealed the origins and the destiny of the Father's children, the text is able to arrive at its concluding, eschatological theme: the place of rest in the Fullness.

This impressive composition, which adroitly chains together and inventively elaborates a series of striking images in a discourse interwoven with subtle allusions to New Testament texts, is no doubt the work of an important figure. Who he is we do not know. What we do know is that the *Gospel of Truth* known to Irenaeus was used by the Valentinians. The *Gospel of Truth* that we have was used by the *Tripartite Tractate*, an indubitably Valentinian text. The general vocabulary and the creative use of images are suggestive of Valentinianism. The *Gospel of Truth*, the *Treatise on Resurrection*, and the *Interpretation of Knowledge*

---

2. Cf. *John* 14:6.

3. Cf. *Matthew* 18:12–14; *Luke* 15:4–7; *Gospel of Thomas* 107; *John* 5:17; 10:7–18.

4. Cf. the *Valentinian Liturgical Readings*, including a reading "On Anointing," in NHC XI.

have many similarities, and the latter two texts are considered by most to be Valentinian. Moreover, these three tractates belong to the genres of homilies and letters, genres known to have been used in particular by the Valentinians.

On the other hand, the *Gospel of Truth* lacks any clear references to the distinctive mythology of Valentinianism, such as the myth of the fall of Sophia or the cosmogony and the anthropogony found in many of the systematic treatises. Instead of the story of Sophia's passion, which gave rise to matter, her subsequent repentance and joy at the vision of the Savior, from which soul and spirit originated, and the shaping of the cosmos from these three substances, the *Gospel of Truth* tells the allegorical tale of Error, from which the material cosmos came into being. This cosmogony is not only different from the standard Valentinian myth, it also implies a distinctly more negative view of the cosmos and a more dualistic ontology than is the case with Valentinian cosmology in general. According to the normal Valentinian position, matter and passion are certainly evil, but the cosmos, as matter and soul substance that have been given form and order by the Savior and the redeemed Sophia, is relatively good, "useful" for the plan of salvation. However, it may be possible to explain this discrepancy by hypothesizing that the *Gospel of Truth* was written at a time before the Valentinian systems had been fully developed. It may also be observed that a homily is a different genre from the systematic treatise, which means, first, that its main purpose is not the exposition of doctrine, but the exhortation of the faithful, and, second, that its style of address and rhetorical imagery may be more dualistic than in a treatise, since it aims to change the outlook and the behavior of its audience.

Although questions remain, it is, on balance, most reasonable to assign the *Gospel of Truth* to the Valentinian tradition. This is also the judgment of the majority of scholars. Whether the homily was actually composed by Valentinus himself, as some believe, cannot be confidently known.[5] However, the quality of the composition and the authority of the voice that speaks in it do point in the direction of the heresiarch himself, rather than some minor and unknown figure. Moreover, we know that Valentinus wrote homilies (Clement of Alexandria quotes from some of them), whereas it is doubtful whether he ever composed a systematic treatise. The lack of allusions to themes from the Valentinian systems is also suggestive of an early phase in the history of the movement. If the identification of the tractate with the writing known to Irenaeus is accepted, a date before 180 must in any case be assumed. In conclusion, the attribution to Valentinus is an attractive hypothesis, though it must inevitably be accompanied by a question mark.

---

5. For an argument in favor of attributing the authorship of the *Gospel of Truth* to Valentinus, see Bentley Layton, *The Gnostic Scriptures*, 251.

In addition to the complete copy of the *Gospel of Truth* in Codex I, some fragments of a different Coptic translation of the writing are preserved in Codex XII. Unfortunately, the fragments are too small to contribute substantially to textual criticism and to the study of the history of the text.

BIBLIOGRAPHY

Sasagu Arai, *Die Christologie des Evangelium Veritatis: Eine religionsgeschichtliche Untersuchung*; Harold W. Attridge, ed., *Nag Hammadi Codex I*, 1.55–117; 2.39–135 (Harold W. Attridge and George W. MacRae); Kendrick Grobel, *The Gospel of Truth: A Valentinian Meditation on the Gospel*; Jan Helderman, "Das Evangelium Veritatis in der neueren Forschung"; Jacques-É. Ménard, *L'Évangile de Vérité*; Tito Orlandi, *Evangelium Veritatis*; Hans-Martin Schenke, Hans-Gebhard Bethge, and Ursula Ulrike Kaiser, eds., *Nag Hammadi Deutsch*, 1.27–44 (Hans-Martin Schenke); Eric Segelberg, "Evangelium Veritatis: A Confirmation Homily and Its Relation to the Odes of Solomon."

The Gospel of Truth[1]

The Gospel of Truth (16,31–17,4)

The gospel of truth is joy for people who have received grace from the Father of truth, that they might know him through the power of the Word.[2] The Word[3] has come from the fullness[4] in the Father's thought and mind. The Word is called "Savior," a term that refers to the work he is to do to redeem those who had not known [17] the Father. And the term "gospel" refers to the revelation of hope, since it is the means of discovery for those who seek him.

Ignorance Brings Error (17,4–18,11)

All have sought for the one from whom they have come forth. All have been within him, the illimitable, the inconceivable, who is beyond all thought. But ignorance of the Father brought terror and fear, and terror grew dense like a fog, so that no one could see. Thus Error grew powerful. She worked on her material substance in vain.[5] Since she did not know the truth, she assumed a fashioned figure and prepared, with power and in beauty, a substitute for truth.

This was not humiliating for the illimitable, inconceivable one. For this terror and forgetfulness and this deceptive figure were as nothing, whereas established truth is unchanging, unperturbed, and beyond beauty.

For this reason despise Error.

Error[6] had no root; she was in a fog regarding the Father. She was there preparing works and deeds of forgetfulness and fear in order, by them, to attract those of the middle[7] and take them captive.

---

1. Coptic text: NHC I,3: 16,31–43,24; XII,2: 57,1–60,30 (fragments). The present translation is based on the Coptic text in NHC I. Editions: *The Facsimile Edition of the Nag Hammadi Codices: Codex I*, 20–47; Harold W. Attridge, ed., *Nag Hammadi Codex I*, 1.55–122, 2.39–135 (Harold W. Attridge and George W. MacRae); Jacques-É. Menard, *L'Évangile de Vérité*; Hans-Martin Schenke, Hans-Gebhard Bethge, and Ursula Ulrike Kaiser, eds., *Nag Hammadi Deutsch*, 1.27–44 (Hans-Martin Schenke). The title of the text comes from the incipit. 2. Cf. *John* 1:1. 3. "The Word" is added here and below for clarification. 4. Pleroma, here and below. 5. Here Error is personified and feminine in gender. Cf. her role with that of wisdom (Sophia) and the demiurge elsewhere in Gnostic texts. 6. Lit., "She." 7. The middle is the region between the Fullness of the divine above and this world below.

The forgetfulness of Error was not apparent. It is not [18] . . . from the Father. Forgetfulness did not come into being from the Father, but if it did come into being, it is because of him.[8] What comes into being within him is knowledge, which appeared so that forgetfulness might be destroyed and the Father might be known. Forgetfulness came into being because the Father was not known, so as soon as the Father comes to be known, forgetfulness will cease to be.

Jesus as Fruit of Knowledge (18,11–19,17)

This is the gospel of him whom they seek, revealed to the perfect through the Father's mercy. Through the hidden mystery Jesus Christ enlightened those who were in darkness because of forgetfulness. He enlightened them and showed the way, and that way is the truth he taught them.[9]

For this reason Error was angry with him and persecuted him, but she was re-strained by him and made powerless. He was nailed to a tree, and he became fruit of the knowledge of the Father. This fruit of the tree, however, did not bring de-struction when it was eaten, but rather it caused those who ate of it to come into being. They were joyful in this discovery, and he found them within himself and they found him within themselves.[10]

And as for the illimitable, inconceivable perfect Father who made all, the All is within him and needs him. Although he kept within himself their perfection, which he had not given to all, the Father was not jealous. What jealousy could there be between himself and his own members? For even if [19] the members of the eternal realm[11] had [received] their [perfection], they could not have ap-proached . . . the Father. He kept their perfection within himself, giving it to them as a means to return to him with complete, single-minded knowledge. He is the one who set the All in order, and the All is within him. The All was in need of him, just as a person who is not known to other people wants them to know him and love him. For what did the All need if not the knowledge of the Father?

Jesus as Guide and Teacher (19,17–34)

He became a guide, a person of rest who was busy in places of instruction. He came forward and spoke the word as a teacher. Those wise in their own eyes came to test him, but he refuted them, for they were foolish, and they hated him be-cause they were not really wise.

After them came the little children, who have knowledge of the Father. When they gained strength and learned about the expressions of the Father, they knew, they were known, they were glorified, they gave glory.

---

8. Here Bentley Layton translates this clause "and surely then not because of him!" (continuing the neg-ative from the previous clause; see *The Gnostic Scrip-tures*, 254). 9. Cf. John 14:6. 10. This reference to the tree recalls both the tree on which Jesus was crucified and the tree of the knowledge of good and evil in the Garden of Eden (described in *Genesis* and Gnostic texts). 11. Aeon, here and below.

The Living Book Is Revealed (19,34–21,25)

In their hearts the living book of the living was revealed, the book that was written in the Father's thought and mind and was, [20] since the foundation of the All, in his incomprehensible nature. No one had been able to take up this book, since it was ordained that the one who would take it up would be slain. And nothing could appear among those who believed in salvation unless that book had come out.

For this reason the merciful, faithful Jesus was patient and accepted his sufferings to the point of taking up that book, since he knew that his death would be life for many.[12]

As in the case of a will that has not been opened, the fortune of the deceased owner of the house is hidden, so also in the case of all that had been hidden while the Father of the All was invisible but that issues from him from whom every realm comes.

> Jesus appeared,
> put on that book,
> was nailed to a tree,
> and published the Father's edict on the cross.
> Oh, what a great teaching!
> He humbled himself even unto death,
> though clothed in eternal life.
> He stripped off the perishable rags
> and clothed himself in incorruptibility,
> which no one can take from him.[13]

When he entered the empty ways of fear, he passed by those stripped by forgetfulness. For he encompasses knowledge and perfection, and he proclaims what is in the heart [21]. . . . [He] teaches those who will learn. And those who will learn are the living who are inscribed in the book of the living. They learn about themselves, receiving instruction from the Father, returning to him.

Since the perfection of the All is in the Father, all must go up to him. When all have received knowledge, they receive what is theirs and draw it to themselves. For those who are ignorant are in need, and their need is great, because they need what would make them perfect. Since the perfection of the All is in the Father, all must go up to him and receive what is theirs. He inscribed these things first, having prepared them to be given to those who came from him.

---

12. Cf. *Hebrews* 2:17; *Mark* 10:45; 1 *Timothy* 2:6. 13.
Cf. *Philippians* 2:5–11. The reference to the perishable
rags describes the physical body of Jesus.

The Father Utters the Names of People Who Know
(21,25–23,17)

Those whose names he knew at the beginning were called at the end, as it is with every person who has knowledge. Such names the Father has uttered. One whose name has not been spoken is ignorant, for how could a person hear if that person's name had not been pronounced? Whoever remains ignorant until the end is a creature of forgetfulness and will perish with it. Otherwise why do these wretches have no [**22**] name, why no voice?

So whoever has knowledge is from above. If called, that person hears, replies, turns to the one who is calling, and goes up to him. He knows how he is called. That person has knowledge and does the will of him who called. That person wishes to please him, finds rest, and has the appropriate name. Those who have knowledge in this way know where they come from and where they are going. They know as one who, having become intoxicated, has turned from his drunkenness and, having come to his senses, has gotten control of himself.

He[14] has brought many back from Error. He went before them to the places from which they had turned when they followed Error, because of the depth of him who surrounds every place, though nothing surrounds him. Indeed, it is amazing that they were in the Father without knowing him and that they could leave on their own, since they were not able to contemplate or know the one in whom they were.

For if his will had not come from him . . . he revealed it as knowledge that is in harmony with the expressions of his will—that is, knowledge of the living book, which he revealed to the eternal realms at the end [**23**] as his [letters]. He showed that they are not merely vowels or consonants, so that one may read them and think them devoid of meaning. Rather, they are letters of truth; they speak and know themselves. Each letter is a perfect truth[15] like a perfect book, for they are letters written in unity, written by the Father for the eternal realms, so that by means of his letters they might come to know the Father.

The Word of the Father Appears (23,17–25,25)

As for the Word,
his wisdom[16] meditates on it,
his teaching utters it,
his knowledge has revealed it,
his patience is a crown upon it,
his joy is in harmony with it,

---

14. Apparently the Savior. 15. Coptic *me.* Or "thought" (correct to read *me<eue>*). 16. Sophia.

his glory has exalted it,
his character has revealed it,
his rest has received it,
his love has incarnated it,
his faith has embraced it.

Thus the Father's Word goes out in the All as the fruition [24] of his heart and expression of his will. It supports all and chooses all. It also takes the expression of all and purifies it, bringing it back to the Father, to the Mother, Jesus of infinite sweetness.[17]

The Father opens his bosom, and his bosom is the Holy Spirit. He reveals his hidden self, and his hidden self is his Son, so that through the Father's mercy the eternal realms may know him, end their wearying search for the Father, and rest in him, knowing that he is rest. For he has filled what was deficient and has done away with its appearance. The mere appearance of what was deficient is the world, and mere appearance serves in the world.

For where there is envy and strife there is deficiency, but where there is unity there is completeness. Since deficiency came about because the Father was not known, from the moment when the Father is known, deficiency will cease to be. As one's ignorance about another vanishes when one gains knowledge, and as darkness departs when light comes, [25] so also deficiency disappears in completeness. From then on the world of appearance will no longer be evident, but rather it will disappear in the harmony of unity.

Now the works of all lie scattered. In time unity will make the heavenly places complete, and in unity all individually will come to themselves. By means of knowledge they will purify themselves from multiplicity into unity, devouring matter within themselves like fire, darkness by light, death by life.

Since these things have happened to each of us, it is right for us to see to it above all that this house be holy and silent for the sake of unity.

Parable of the Broken Jars (25,25–26,27)

This is like people who moved from one house to another. They had jars around that were not good, and they broke, but the owner suffered no loss. Rather, the owner[18] was glad because instead of these defective jars there were full jars that were perfect.

This is the judgment that has come [26] from above and has judged every person, a drawn two-edged sword cutting on this side and that, since the Word that is in the heart of those who speak the Word appeared.[19] It is not merely a sound but it was embodied.

---

17. Cf. 1 *Peter* 2:2–3. 18. Lit., "she" (or emend to "he"). 19. On the two-edged sword, cf. *Hebrews* 4:12; *Revelation* 2:12, 16; 19:15; Philo of Alexandria *Who Is the Heir of Divine Things?* 130–40.

A great disturbance occurred among the jars, for some were empty and others were filled, some were ample and others were depleted, some were purified and others were broken.

All the realms were shaken and disturbed, for they had no order or stability. Error was agitated, and she did not know what to do. She was troubled, she lamented, she attacked herself, because she knew nothing.[20] For knowledge, which leads to the destruction of Error[21] and all her expressions, approached. Error is empty; there is nothing within her.

The Appearance of Truth and the Emanations of the Father (26,27–28,32)

Truth appeared, and all its expressions recognized it. They greeted the Father in truth and power that is complete and joins them with the Father.

Whoever loves truth, whoever touches [27] truth, touches the Father's mouth, because truth is the Father's mouth. His tongue is the Holy Spirit, and from his tongue one will receive the Holy Spirit. This is the manifestation of the Father and his revelation to his eternal realms. He revealed his hidden self and explained it. For who has anything within if not[22] the Father alone?

All the realms are from him. They know that they have come from him as children who were within a mature person but who knew that they had not yet received form or been given a name. The Father brings forth each of them when they receive the essence of his knowledge. Otherwise, though they were in him, they could not know him. The Father is perfect, and he knows every realm within himself. If he wishes, what he wishes appears when he gives it form and a name—and he does give it a name. He brings into being those who before coming into being were ignorant of the one who made them.

I am not saying that those who have not yet come to be are nothing.[23] They are [28] within one who may wish that they come into being if at some future point he so wishes. On the one hand, he knows, before anything appears, what he will produce. On the other hand, the fruit that has not yet appeared knows nothing and does nothing. Thus each realm in the Father comes from what is, but what has set itself up is from what is not. For whatever has no root has no fruit, and although thinking, "I have come into being," it will perish by itself. So whatever does not exist will never exist.

What, then, does he want such a one to think? It is this: "I have come into being like shadows and phantoms of the night." When the light shines, the person knows the terror that had been experienced was nothing.

---

20. Or "and cried out that she understood nothing" (Layton, Gnostic Scriptures, 258). 21. "Error" is added here for clarification. 22. Coptic petšōp eimēti, or "who exists" (read petšōpe imēti). 23. The author, writing in the first-person singular, notes that they have potential if not actual existence.

Ignorance Is a Nightmare (28,32–30,23)

Thus they were ignorant of the Father, for they did not see him. [29] Since there had been terror and confusion and uncertainty and doubt and division, there were many illusions among them, and inane ignorance—as if they were fast asleep and found themselves a prey to nightmares.[24] In these dreams they are fleeing somewhere, or they cannot get away when chased, or they are in a fight, or they themselves are beaten, or they are falling from on high, or they fly through the air with no wings. Or it seems people are trying to kill them, though there is no one chasing them, or they are killing their neighbors and are covered with their blood. This continues until those experiencing all these dreams wake up. Those caught in the middle of all these confusing things see nothing because the dreams are nothing.

So it is with those who cast off ignorance from themselves like sleep. They do not consider it to be anything, nor do they regard its [30] features as real, but they put them aside like a dream in the night and understand the knowledge of the Father to be the dawn. This is how each person acts while in ignorance, as if asleep, and this is how a person comes to knowledge, as if awakened. Good for one who comes to himself and awakens. And blessed is one who has opened the eyes of the blind.[25]

The spirit came to this person in haste when the person awakened. Having given its hand to the one lying prone on the ground, the spirit placed him firmly on his feet, for he had not yet risen.

The Beloved Son Reveals What Is New (30,23–31,35)

Knowledge of the Father and the revelation of his Son gave them the means of knowing. For when they saw and heard him, he let them taste him and smell him and touch the beloved Son. He appeared, informing them of the Father, the illimitable, and he inspired them with what is in the thought,[26] doing his will. Many received the light and turned [31] to him. But material people were strangers to him and did not discern his appearance or recognize him. For he came in the likeness of flesh, and nothing blocked his way, for incorruptibility cannot be grasped. Moreover, while saying new things and speaking about what is in the Father's heart, he produced the faultless Word. Light spoke through his mouth and his voice brought forth life. He gave them thought and understanding and mercy and salvation and the spirit of strength from the Father's infinity and sweetness. He made punishments and afflictions cease, for they caused those in need of mercy to stray from him in error and bondage. He destroyed them with might and confounded them with knowledge.

---

24. Descriptions of the nightmares follow in the text.
25. Cf. *Matthew* 11:5; *Luke* 7:21–22; *John* 9:10–11; 11:37.
26. Probably the thought of the Father.

He became a way for those who strayed,
knowledge for those who were ignorant,
discovery for those who sought,
support for those who tremble,
purity for those who were defiled.[27]

Parables of Sheep (31,35–32,37)

He is the shepherd who left behind the ninety-nine [32] sheep that had not strayed and went in search of the one that was lost.[28] He rejoiced when he found it. For ninety-nine is a number expressed with the left hand, but when another one is found, the numerical sum is transferred to the right hand. In this way what needs one more—that is, the whole right hand—attracts what it needs, takes it from the left and brings it to the right, and so the number becomes one hundred.[29] This is the meaning of the pronunciation of these numbers.

The Father is like that. He labored even on the Sabbath for the sheep that he found fallen into the pit. He saved the life of the sheep and brought it up from the pit.[30]

Understand the inner meaning, for you are children of inner meaning. What is the Sabbath? It is a day on which salvation should not be idle. Speak of the heavenly day that has no night and of the light[31] that does not set because it is perfect. Speak from the heart, for you are the perfect day and within you dwells the light that does not fail. Speak of truth with those who seek it and of knowledge with those who have sinned in their error. [33]

Do the Father's Will (33,1–32)

Steady the feet of those who stumble and extend your hands to the sick. Feed the hungry and give rest to the weary. Awaken those who wish to arise and rouse those who sleep, for you embody vigorous understanding. If what is strong acts like this, it becomes even stronger.

Focus your attention upon yourselves. Do not focus your attention upon other things—that is, what you have cast away from yourselves. Do not return to eat what you have vomited. Do not be moth-eaten, do not be worm-eaten, for you have already gotten rid of that. Do not be a place for the devil, for you have already destroyed him. Do not strengthen what stands in your way, what is collapsing, to support it. One who is lawless is nothing. Treat the lawless one more harshly than the just one, for the lawless does what he does because he is lawless, but the just does what he does with people because he is righteous. Do the Father's will, then, for you are from him.

---

27. Cf. the portrayal of Jesus as Word (Logos) in the *Gospel of John*, especially chap. 1. 28. Cf. *Matthew* 18:12–14; *Luke* 15:4–7; *Gospel of Thomas* 107. 29. In the Roman system of counting on the fingers, numbers 1–99 were counted on the left hand, and number 100 switched to the right. 30. On Jesus and the Father both working, cf. *John* 5:17. 31. Or "sun."

The Sweetness of the Father (33,33–34,34)

For the Father is sweet, and goodness is in his will. He knows what is yours, in which you find rest. By the fruit one knows what is yours.[32] For the Father's children [34] are his fragrance; they are from the beauty of his face. The Father loves his fragrance and disperses it everywhere, and when it mixes with matter, it gives his fragrance to the light. Through his quietness he makes his fragrance superior in every way to every sound. For it is not ears that smell the fragrance, but it is the spirit[33] that possesses the sense of smell, draws the fragrance to itself, and immerses itself in the Father's fragrance. Thus it[34] cares for it and takes it to where it came from, the original fragrance, which has grown cold in psychical form.[35] It is like cold water that has sunk into soft soil, and those who see it think there is only soil. Later the water evaporates when the wind draws it up, and it becomes warm. So cold fragrances are from division.

For this reason faith came, did away with division, and brought the warm fullness of love, so that what is cold may not return, but the unity of perfect thought may prevail.

The Father Restores Fullness (34,34–36,35)

This <is> the Word[36] of the gospel about the discovery of fullness, for those who await [35] salvation coming from above. Their hope, for which they are waiting, is in waiting, and this is their image, the light in which there is no shadow. At this time the fullness is about to come. Deficiency of matter is not from the infinity of the Father, who came to give time to deficiency. In fact, it is not right to say that the incorruptible would actually come in this manner. The Father's depth is profound, and the thought of error is not with him. It is something that has fallen, and something that can readily be set upright through the discovery of the one who has come to what he would restore.

This restoration is called repentance. The reason that the incorruptible breathed out and followed after the one who sinned was so that the sinner might find rest. Forgiveness is what remains for the light in deficiency, the Word of fullness. For a doctor rushes to where there is sickness, since that is the doctor's wish. The person in need does not hide it, because the doctor has what the patient needs. Thus fullness, which has no deficiency but fills up deficiency, [36] is provided to fill a person's need, so that the person may receive grace. While deficient, the person had no grace, and because of this a diminishing took place where there was no grace. When the diminished part was restored, the person in need was revealed as fullness. This is what it means to discover the light of truth that has shone toward a person: it is unchangeable.

---

32. Cf. *Matthew* 7:16; 12:33; *Luke* 6:44. 33. Or "breath" (Coptic *pna*, for *pneuma*). 34. The spirit. 35. The author is employing a pun in Greek by comparing *psukhē* ("psychical form, soul") and *psukhos* ("cold"). 36. Logos.

Because of the coming of Christ[37] it was said openly, "Seek, and the troubled will be restored, and he will anoint them with ointment." The ointment is the mercy of the Father, who will have mercy on them, and those anointed are the perfect. For filled jars are usually sealed with wax. But when the seal of a jar is broken, it may leak, and the cause of its defect is the lack of a seal. For then a breath of wind and the power that it has can make it evaporate. But on the jar that is without defect the seal is not broken, nor does it leak, and the perfect Father fills again what it lacks.

The Father Knows His Plants in Paradise (36,35–38,6)

He is good. He knows his plants because he planted them in his paradise. And his paradise is his place of rest. Paradise [37] is the perfection within the Father's thought, and the plants are the words of his meditation. Each of his words is the product of his will and the revelation of his speech. Since they were the depth of his thought, the Word that came forth caused them to appear, along with mind that speaks the Word, and silent grace. It[38] was called thought, because they dwelled in silent grace[39] before being revealed. So it happened that the Word[40] came forth when it was pleasing to the will of him who willed it.

The Father is at rest in will. Nothing happens without his pleasure; nothing happens without the Father's will. And his will is incomprehensible. His will is his footprint, but none can understand him, nor does he exist so that they might study him[41] in order to grasp him. Rather, when he wills, what he wills is this, even if the view does not please people before God: it is the Father's will. For he knows the beginning and the end of all, and at their end he will greet them. The end is the recognition of him who is hidden, and he is the Father, [38] from whom the beginning has come and to whom all will return who have come from him. They have appeared for the glory and joy of his name.

The Father's Name Is Revealed (38,6–41,3)

The Name of the Father is the Son. In the beginning he gave a name to the one who came from him, while he remained the same, and he conceived him as a Son. He gave him his Name, which belonged to him. All that exists with the Father belongs to him. He has the Name; he has the Son. The Son[42] can be seen, but the Name is invisible, for it alone is the mystery of the invisible, which comes to ears completely filled with it through his agency. Yet the Father's Name is not pronounced; it is revealed through a Son, and the Name is great.

Who then can utter his Name, the great Name, except him alone to whom the Name belongs, and the children of the Name, on whom the Father's Name rests, and who themselves rest on his Name? Since the Father has no beginning, he

---

37. I.e., "anointed one." 38. Probably the Word. 39. Lit., "it." 40. Lit., "it." 41. Or "nor is it possible for them to study him." 42. "The Son" is added here for clarification.

alone conceived it for himself as a name before he created the eternal realms, that the Father's Name might be supreme over them. This is the [39] true Name, which is confirmed by his authority in perfect power. This Name does not derive from ordinary words or name giving, for it is invisible.

He alone gave him a name,[43] because he alone saw him and he alone could name him. One who does not exist has no name, for what name would someone give to one who does not exist? One who exists exists with his name. He alone knows it, and to him alone he has given a name.[44] This is the Father, and his Name is the Son. He did not hide it within, but it was in existence, and the Son himself disclosed the Name. The Name, then, belongs to the Father, just as the Father's Name is the beloved Son. Otherwise where would he find a name except from the Father?

But someone may say to an acquaintance, "Who could give a name to someone who existed before himself? Do not children receive their names [40] from their parents?" First, we should consider this point: what is a name? This is the true Name, the Name from the Father, and this is the proper Name. He[45] did not receive the Name on loan, as is the case with others, who receive names that are made up. This is the proper Name, and there is no one else who gave it to him. He is unnamable, indescribable, until the time when the perfect one[46] spoke of him, for the perfect one alone is able to pronounce his Name and see him.

When it was pleasing to him that his Son should be his pronounced Name, and when he who came from the depth[47] disclosed this Name, he divulged what was hidden, for he knew that the Father is free of evil. That is why he brought him forth, so that he might speak about the place from which he had come and his place of rest, [41] and that he might glorify the fullness, the majesty of his Name, and the Father's sweetness.

The Place of Rest (41,3–43,24)

All will speak individually about where they have come from and how they were established in the place of rest. They will hasten to return and receive from that place, the place where they stood once before, and they will taste of that place, be nourished, and grow.

Their own place of rest is their fullness. All the emanations from the Father are fullnesses, and all his emanations find their root in the one who caused them all to grow from himself. He assigned their destinies. They all appear so that through their own thought [they might be perfected].[48] For the place to which they extend their thought is their root, which lifts them up through all the heights to the Father.

---

43. I.e., the Father gave the Son a name. 44. The meaning of the Coptic is uncertain. Perhaps correct to read: "<and he> alone <is in the position> to give him a name" (Schenke, in *Nag Hammadi Deutsch*, 1.42–43). 45. The Father. 46. Probably the Son. 47. Again, probably the Son. 48. This restoration remains tentative; cf. Schenke, in *Nag Hammadi Deutsch*, 1.43.

They embrace his head, which is rest for them, and they hold him close so that, in a manner of speaking, they have caressed his face with kisses. But they do not make [42] this obvious. For they neither exalt themselves nor diminish the Father's glory. And they do not think of him as insignificant or bitter or angry, but as free of evil, unperturbed, sweet, knowing all the heavenly places before they came into being, and having no need of instruction.

Such are those who possess something of this immeasurable majesty from above, as they await that unique and perfect One who is a Mother to them.[49] And they do not go down to the underworld, nor do they have envy or groaning, nor is death with them. They rest in one who rests, and they are not weary or confused about truth.

They are truth. The Father is in them and they are in the Father, perfect, inseparable from him who is truly good. They lack nothing at all but are at rest, fresh in spirit. They will hearken to their root and be involved with concerns in which they may find their root and do no harm to their souls.

Such is the place of the blessed, such is their place. As for the others, let them know, in their own places, that I should not [43] say more, for I have been in the place of rest. There I shall dwell, to devote myself, constantly, to the Father of the All and the true brothers and sisters,[50] upon whom the Father's love is lavished, and in whose midst nothing of him is lacking. They appear in truth dwelling in true and eternal life, and they speak of the perfect light filled with the Father's seed, which is in his heart and in the fullness. His spirit rejoices in this and glorifies him in whom it was. For he is good, and his children are perfect and worthy of his Name. Children like this the Father loves.

---

49. Or "who exists there for them" (Coptic *petoei* *ᵉmmeu neu*). 50. Or "true siblings"; lit., "true brothers."

THE TREATISE ON RESURRECTION

NHC I,4

Introduced by Einar Thomassen
Translated by Marvin Meyer

The title "The Treatise on Resurrection" is given to this work at the end of the text in the codex, but it is clear from the text itself that its literary form is that of a letter, addressed to a certain Rheginus—hence the title "The Letter to Rheginus" often used for this tractate. It is possible, on the other hand, that the epistolary genre is simply a literary device and that Rheginus is a fictitious person. The form of discourse resembles the philosophical diatribe; the topic under discussion is the doctrine of the resurrection.

The doctrine of the resurrection taught in this text takes its point of departure from Christological and soteriological considerations. The Savior was divine and human at one and the same time. This duality in the Savior's nature was a function of his redemptive task: in order to save humanity from its fallen condition, the Savior himself had to assume human nature, but because of his divinity he was also able to overcome the human fate of death (44,21–33). In this way, the Savior "swallowed death" (45,14–15)—an expression taken over from Paul.[1] This Christology of two natures and the understanding of redemption as an act of substitution are clearly in line with mainstream Christian theology (even anticipating later orthodox dogma), though this Christology also agrees with basic tenets of Eastern Valentinian soteriology.

However, the soteriology of the *Treatise on Resurrection* differs notably from later orthodox doctrine with regard to its views about the condition from which the Savior saved humanity. The "death" that the Savior brought to naught is not primarily a state of sin, but the condition of physical existence in a corruptible material world. The Savior's death and his incarnation are basically one and the same redemptive act. The fact that he entered this world and assumed a human

---

1. Cf. 1 *Corinthians* 15:54; 2 *Corinthians* 5:4.

body means that he accepted death. When the Savior later rose from the dead, he also freed himself from the body he had put on when he descended into the world and became once more a purely spiritual being. During this process, he "swallowed" the entire visible world: it was revealed as nothing.

Because the Savior assumed the physical existence of humans, they on their part acquired access to his spiritual form of being. This is their spiritual resurrection. Access to the resurrection depends on faith (46,3–22). The author stresses that the resurrection cannot be proven by philosophical arguments. Faith is a truth and a wisdom that has been received, and it cannot be understood by everybody. One is chosen and predestined for this kind of knowledge (46,25–34). Faith in the Savior is not primarily an intellectual act; it is a substantive relationship with the divine. Those who recognize the truth can do so because they are of the same spiritual substance as the Savior himself. When they attain knowledge, they are revealed: they come forth as the spiritual beings they really are (45,10–11.29–30; 48,5–6).

This idea is related to another important theme in the text: spiritual existence is fundamentally the only real form of existence. The world is in fact an illusion (48,14–15.22–28). This implies that the resurrection is thought of not just as the return to and the restoration of an original spiritual existence, but also as an act of knowledge in which one realizes that spiritual essence is something that one already has, hidden within oneself as one's true self. From this perspective, the salvific act of the Savior takes on a new significance. On the one hand, it was an event in history, in which the Savior put an end to corruptible existence by himself assuming a human body and subsequently discarding it through his resurrection (44,13–33; 45,14–23). On the other hand, the event of salvation is also understood as an awakening, whereby the mission of the Savior was to make the elect realize that they possess their spiritual nature already. From this point of view, salvation is no longer primarily seen as the liberation from the body and the attainment of spiritual existence in the sense of a redemptive event taking place in time and space. Rather, resurrection in this case means the realization that spiritual existence is something one already possesses and that time and space as such are illusions (47,24–30; 48,10–28). Thus, a change of focus is discernible in the text as it moves from the representation of salvation as a narrative, with fall and return as its main themes, to a perspective in which everything that takes place in time and space is regarded as unreal. This change of focus is not arbitrary, but follows logically from the basic concept of salvation in the *Treatise on Resurrection*: if salvation means the elimination of the physical world, it also means the elimination of the categories of time and space within which salvation as a narrative is represented.

In accordance with the view that the world and the body are no more than illusions, a purely negative "deficiency," while only spiritual reality, "fullness," is real, in the true sense of the word, those who realize that they belong to that reality will already be "resurrected." This means that the resurrection is a quality the elect already possess rather than an event by which they are saved. Several passages suggest that this is the view of the author (47,24–30; 48,3–6.30–33; 49,15–16). At the same time, however, the text retains the salvation-historical perspective according to which the incarnation and the resurrection of the Savior are necessary preconditions for salvation, and the resurrection is imagined as a return, made possible by the self-humiliation of the Savior, to the original form of being in the aeon, or the Fullness (45,19–40; 46,12–17). In this perspective there exists both an "already" and a "not yet." On account of their faith the elect already now share in the resurrection of the Savior; they share in him substantially, just like the rays of sunlight are parts of the sun itself (45,28–34; 48,38–49,5; 49,13–16). But the text also states that there will take place a resurrection after death, when one leaves one's body (45,35–39; 46,7–8; 47,1–23; 47,31–48,3). Toward the end of the letter it is even suggested that it is possible for the believer to go astray once more. Effort (gumnazein) and exercise (askein) are necessary in order not to succumb to the temptations of the body with its fragmented ways of existence and to realize the spiritual life, which is a life governed by unity (49,9–36). Judging from these statements, effort is required in order to attain resurrection after death; the resurrection is not automatically given by virtue of one's innate spiritual nature.

It will be clear that the soteriology of the Treatise on Resurrection points in different directions and is hardly consistent in all respects. Tension between different soteriological theories can be observed in Valentinianism generally. Eastern Valentinianism conceived of salvation according to a model of mutual exchange, where the incarnation, passion, death, and resurrection of the Savior was a precondition for the liberation of spiritual people from their passion-ridden lives in a corruptible material body. Western Valentinians, on the other hand, tended toward a doctrine that spiritual people were "saved by nature," so that the presence of the Savior in this world was purely symbolic and for the purpose of instruction and did not involve real corporeality, death, and resurrection. The Treatise on Resurrection clearly exemplifies the Eastern view, the soteriology of mutual exchange, though there are, as we have seen, also elements in the text that have affinities with the Western perspective on salvation as the manifestation of a preestablished spiritual nature. On the other hand, the text shows none of the characteristic Western Valentinian concern with the category of the psychical and the salvation of psychical humans.

The time of composition for the Treatise on Resurrection is usually assumed to be the second half of the second century. The author is unknown, and the name of the addressee, Rheginus, is otherwise unattested. The end of the letter shows that the author was a leader in the Valentinian movement. The suggestion that Valentinus himself was the author of the Treatise on Resurrection has not found favor with the majority of scholars, though the idea is not entirely impossible.

BIBLIOGRAPHY

Harold W. Attridge, ed., Nag Hammadi Codex I, 1.123–57; 2.137–215 (Malcolm L. Peel); Bentley Layton, The Gnostic Treatise on Resurrection from Nag Hammadi; Luther H. Martin, "The Anti-Philosophical Polemic and Gnostic Soteriology in 'The Treatise on the Resurrection'"; Hans-Martin Schenke, Hans-Gebhard Bethge, and Ursula Ulrike Kaiser, eds., Nag Hammadi Deutsch, 1.45–52 (Hans-Martin Schenke).

The Treatise on Resurrection[1]

The Letter to Rheginus (43,25–44,3)

Rheginus my son,[2] some people want to become intellectuals. That is their goal when they try to explain unsolved problems, and if they are successful, they have an exalted opinion of themselves. I do not think they are established on the word of truth. Rather, they seek their own rest, which we have received from Christ[3] our Savior and Lord. [44] We received rest[4] when we came to know the truth and rested on it.

Since you ask about the main issues on resurrection in such a pleasant way, I am writing to you. Resurrection is essential. Many do not believe in it and few find it, so let us discuss it in our treatise.

Christ as Son of God and Son of Humanity (44,3–39)

How did the Lord live his life? While he was in flesh and after he revealed himself as Son of God, he went about in this world where you live and spoke about the law of nature, which I call death. Rheginus, the Son of God was a son of humanity. He embraced both aspects, humanity and divinity, so that by being a son of God he might conquer death, and by being a son of humanity fullness[5] might be restored. For originally he was from above, a seed of truth, before the structure of the world, with all its dominions and deities, came into being.

The Resurrection of Christ (44,39–45,23)

I know I am presenting [45] this explanation in difficult terms, but there is nothing in the word of truth that is difficult. Christ came to provide the explanation, to

1. Coptic text: NHC I,4: 43,25–50,18. Editions: *The Facsimile Edition of the Nag Hammadi Codices: Codex I*, 47–50; Harold W. Attridge, ed., *Nag Hammadi Codex I*, 1.123–57, 2.137–215 (Malcolm L. Peel); Bentley Layton, *The Gnostic Treatise on Resurrection from Nag Hammadi*; Jacques-É. Ménard, *Le Traité sur la resurrection*; Hans-Martin Schenke, Hans-Gebhard Bethge, and Ursula Ulrike Kaiser, eds., *Nag Hammadi Deutsch*, 1.45–52 (Hans-Martin Schenke). The text is sometimes referred to as the *Epistle to Rheginus*. 2. Rheginus, to whom this letter is addressed, is known only from this text. 3. The term *pekhrēstos* may be understood as "the kind one," here and below. 4. Lit., "it." 5. Pleroma, here and below.

leave nothing hidden, but to reveal everything clearly about coming into being, the destruction of evil, and the revelation of the chosen.[6] This means the emergence of truth and spirit, and grace belongs to truth.

The Savior swallowed death. You must know this. When he laid aside the perishable world, he exchanged it for an incorruptible eternal realm.[7] He arose and swallowed the visible through the invisible, and thus he granted us the way to our immortality.

The Resurrection of the Believer (45,23–46,2)

As the apostle[8] said of him, we suffered with him, we arose with him, we ascended with him.[9]

Since we are visibly present in this world, we wear the garment of the world. From the Savior we radiate like beams of light, and we are sustained by him until our sunset, our death in this life. We are drawn upward by him, like rays by the sun, and nothing holds us down. This is the resurrection of the spirit, [46] which swallows the resurrection of the soul and the resurrection of the flesh.

Philosophers and Believers (46,3–19)

If some do not believe, they cannot be persuaded. My son, the affirmation that the dead will arise belongs to the realm of faith, not of argument.

Among the world's philosophers is there one who believes? Certainly that philosopher will arise. But that philosopher should not trust anyone who turns to himself alone, even for our faith.[10]

We know the Son of Humanity, and we believe that he arose from the dead. We say of him, "He became death's destroyer."

Thought and Mind Will Not Perish
(46,19–47,1)

The object of belief is great and the believers are also great. The thought of believers will not perish and the mind of those who know[11] will not perish. We are chosen for salvation and redemption, since from the beginning it was determined that we would not fall into the folly of the ignorant, but we would enter into the understanding of those who know the truth.

The truth they guard cannot be lost. Nor will it be. The system of the Fullness is strong; what broke loose and became the world is insignificant. What is held fast is the All. It did not [47] come into being. It was.

---

6. Or "what is superior." 7. Aeon, here and below. 8. Paul. 9. Cf. *Romans* 8:17; *Ephesians* 2:4–6; *Colossians* 2:12; 3:1–3. 10. The translation of this sentence remains tentative, and the Coptic text may need emendation. 11. Lit., "know it" or "know him."

Flesh and Spirit (47,1–30)

So never doubt the resurrection, Rheginus my son. Although once you did not exist in flesh, you took on flesh when you entered this world. Why is it, then, that you will not take your flesh with you when you ascend into the eternal realm? What is better than flesh is what animates the flesh.[12] What came into being because of you,[13] isn't it yours? If it is yours, doesn't it exist with you?

But while you are in the world, what are you missing? Is that what you have attempted to learn about: the outflow[14] of the body, which is old age? Are you nothing but corruption?

Leaving this behind will profit you, for you will not give up the better part when you leave. The inferior part will suffer loss, but there is grace for it.[15] Nothing redeems us from this world, but we are of the All, and we are saved. We have been saved from start to finish. Let us think about it in this way; let us accept it in this way.

What Is the Resurrection? (47,30–48,19)

Some inquire further and want to know whether one will be saved immediately, if the body is left behind. Let there be no doubt about this. Surely the visible parts of the body are dead [48] and will not be saved.[16] Only the living parts that are within will arise.

What is the resurrection? It is always the disclosure of those who have arisen. If you remember reading in the gospel that Elijah and Moses appeared with Jesus,[17] do not think that the resurrection is an illusion. It is no illusion. It is truth. It is more appropriate to say that the world is illusion rather than the resurrection that came into being through our Lord and Savior Jesus Christ.

Reality and Illusion (48,19–49,9)

What am I telling you?
All at once the living die.
How do they live in illusion?
The rich become poor,
kings are overthrown,
everything changes.

---

12. The soul is what animates the flesh. 13. The flesh comes into being because of a person. 14. Or "the afterbirth" (*pkhorion*). 15. This difficult passage may mean that the inferior body finds grace, either because it embodies a soul in this world, because its suffering and its existence come to an end, or because aspects of its existence continue on as the sort of resurrected spiritual body that Paul discusses in 1 *Corinthians* 15. Conversely, the passage could conceivably refer to the better, spiritual self and suggest that the spiritual self finds grace by being liberated from the body. Cf. Ismo Dunderberg, "The School of Valentinus"; Layton, *The Gnostic Treatise on Resurrection from Nag Hammadi*; Peel, in *Nag Hammadi Codex I*, 2.137–215. 16. Or "How come the visible parts of the body are dead and will not be saved?" 17. This reference is to the accounts of the transfiguration in *Matthew* 17:1–8; *Mark* 9:2–8; *Luke* 9:28–36.

The world is illusion.
Let me not speak so negatively.
The resurrection is different.
It is real,
it stands firm.
It is revelation of what is,
a transformation of things,
a transition into newness.
Incorruptibility [49] [flows] over corruption,
light flows over darkness, swallowing it,
Fullness fills what it lacks.
These are symbols and images of resurrection.
This brings goodness.

Resurrection Is Already Here (49,9–37)

Rheginus, do not get lost in details, nor live according to the flesh for the sake of harmony. Flee from divisions and bonds, and then you already have resurrection.[18] If the mortal part knows itself,[19] knows that it will die even though it has lived many years in this life, why not look at yourself and see that you already have arisen and have been received in?

You have the resurrection but go on as if you are to die when it is that mortal part that knows it is dead. Why am I so patient? Only because of your lack of training. Everyone needs to practice ways to be released from this element so as not to wander in error, but rather to recover what one was at the beginning.

Conclusion (49,37–50,18)

What I received through the generosity of my [50] Lord Jesus Christ I have taught you and your brothers and sisters, who are my children, about them, and I have left out nothing that may strengthen you. If anything in the explanation of the treatise is too deep, ask and I shall clarify it.

Do not be worried about sharing this treatise with anyone among you, for it can be helpful. Many are awaiting what I have written to you. I say, peace and grace be with them.

I greet you and those who love you with the love of family.[20]

The Treatise on Resurrection

---

18. Cf. the position of Hymenaeus and Philetus according to 2 *Timothy* 2:16–18. 19. Cf. the Delphic maxim "Know yourself," and *Gospel of Thomas* 3 and other texts. 20. Lit., "brotherly love."

THE TRIPARTITE TRACTATE

NHC I,5

Introduced and Translated by Einar Thomassen

N o title is preserved in the manuscript for this massive treatise of Valentin-ian theology, though it cannot be totally excluded that a title was provided at the end, on the last, fragmentary page. The title by which the work is currently known is, at any rate, an invention by modern scholars: it refers to the fact that the scribe has divided the text into three parts by means of decorative lines on pages 104 and 108.[1] This partition roughly corresponds to a division of the contents. The first and longest part (51–104) deals with the Father, the Son, and the emanation of the Pleroma, or Fullness, the fall of the youngest aeon, and the creation of the cosmos. The second, quite short part narrates the creation of the first human and his transgression and expulsion from paradise. The last part (108–138) describes the many confused opinions among people about the nature of the cosmos, the advent of the Savior, the establishment of the church, and the fates of the various categories of humans.

The importance of this tractate is above all that it contains a version of the Valentinian system that is distinctly Valentinian at the same time that it differs on many points from the well-known systems reported by the church fathers. For this reason, it helps us understand better what are the constant and indispensable fea-tures of the Valentinian systems and what are individual and local variations. Thus, the system of *Tripartite Tractate* does not have a Pleroma of thirty aeons and does not list the names of the aeons; its aeons are numberless and nameless. Instead of presenting the Pleroma as being unfolded by means of arithmetical and geometrical derivations, the *Tripartite Tractate* describes the emanation process in embryological terms as a gradual formation of the Pleroma within the Father that ends in the birth of the aeons as autonomous beings. Further, there are not two Sophias, as in the systems reported by Irenaeus and Hippolytus, but only one. In fact, the fallen aeon is not called Sophia at all, but simply a logos, or word (logos being used as a generic name for the aeons). Finally, there is no

---

1. On these decorative lines, see *The Facsimile Edition of the Nag Hammadi Codices: Codex I*, 108, 112.

"psychical Christ" in the *Tripartite Tractate*—the figure that the Savior puts on when he descends into the world and who suffers and is crucified while the Savior himself remains passionless. Instead, the Savior is himself incarnated in a human body, suffers, dies, and is redeemed. These differences between the system of the *Tripartite Tractate* and those found in the church fathers demonstrate that the latter, far from representing "the" Valentinian system (as the church fathers claim), are merely local variants of it.

In its Christology and soteriology, the *Tripartite Tractate* in fact agrees with the Eastern Valentinian Theodotus, who says that the Savior himself was in need of redemption after having descended into the world of matter (*Excerpts from Theodotus* 22.7; cf. *Tripartite Tractate* 124,32–125,4). The idea that the Savior participated fully in the human condition in order for humans to share in his spiritual being (cf. *Tripartite Tractate* 115,3–11) is a distinctive Eastern Valentinian doctrinal feature. The *Tripartite Tractate* therefore seems to be the only preserved example of a complete Eastern Valentinian systematic treatise.

The outline of the treatise follows a pattern familiar from the heresiological presentations of the Valentinian system and whose main features can be found in certain other Gnostic treatises as well, such as the *Secret Book of John*. The main divisions are:

1. First principles: the Father, the Son, and the Church of aeons (51,1–59,38)

2. The projection of the aeons (60,1–75,17)

3. The passion of the youngest aeon and the origin of the material powers (75,17–80,11)

4. The conversion of the aeon-logos and the origin of the psychical powers (80,11–85,15)

5. The mission of the Savior and the origin of the spiritual kind (85,11–95,16)

6. The creation of the cosmos and the region of the Middle (95,17–104,3)

7. The creation of humanity and the expulsion from paradise (104,4–108,12)

8. The errors of humankind and the prophecies (108,13–113,5)

9. The advent and work of the Savior (113,5–118,14)

10. The destiny of the three kinds of humans (118,14–138,27)

In several respects, the system of the *Tripartite Tractate* is simpler than the parallel accounts in the church fathers. Instead of the complex hierarchies of aeons as found in Irenaeus and Hippolytus, the transcendent world is described here as the relationships among three factors: the Father, the Son, and the Church. The Son is eternally generated by the Father as his self-reflective and self-admiring Thought, and the Church is the multiplicity of divine qualities that inhere in this self-reflective activity, "in the same way as kisses, when two people abundantly embrace one another in a good and insatiable thought—it is a single embrace but consists of many kisses" (58,22–29).[2] It is clear that the multitudinous aeons generated in this way are aspects or attributes of the Father himself. However, they also evolve into a congregation of autonomous beings through a process that brings them forth from the Thought, like children from a womb. The successive phases of this divine gestation are the theme of *Tripartite Tractate* 60,1–75,17.

"Church" is not a common name for the Pleroma in the extant (Western) versions of the Valentinian system, but the idea it expresses is certainly presupposed there as well. In the *Tripartite Tractate* the term serves to highlight the correspondence between the Pleroma as a congregation of aeons and the "Church in the flesh" (125,4–5). The earthly church is an image of the Pleroma, and this relationship is an essential element in the system as a whole. The origin of the earthly church goes back to before the creation of the world. It is narrated as an episode in the story of the fallen aeon, a story that tells how everything in the lower world came into being. The fallen aeon—called the Logos, or Word, in the *Tripartite Tractate*—first experienced a passion, which came alive as a multitude of rebellious powers, the powers of materiality. The Logos's second emotion was repentance and prayer for help; this gave rise to a superior set of powers having a psychical nature. In response to the prayer for help, the aeons then collectively produced and sent out the Son-Savior, who manifested the totality of the Pleroma to the Logos. Seeing him, the Logos experienced a third emotion: joy. Expressing this emotion by jubilant thanksgiving, the Logos gave birth to the third kind of beings, the spiritual seed. These beings form the spiritual church, which is established as a special region below the Pleroma. This church was an image of the Pleroma because it originated from the Logos's vision of the Son and Savior.

The account of the origin of matter, soul, and spirit closely parallels the story of the lower Sophia in the Valentinian systems of Irenaeus and Hippolytus. It explains how the building blocks of the cosmos came into being, and it is followed, as in those systems, by a cosmogony and an anthropogony. The cosmogonic myth explains how the cosmos was made from the substances of matter and soul; the anthropogony narrates how the material and psychical powers each contributed to the composition of the first human. In addition to body and soul, however, the first human received an input of spiritual seed from the region of the Logos and the spiritual church, a region now situated in the middle between the cosmos and the Pleroma. In consequence, some humans carry the spiritual seed from above inside them, but it is hidden in body and soul and not fully conscious of itself. At best, it inspired prophecies about a Savior and revealer coming in the future.

---

2. On this image, cf. *Gospel of Truth* 41,28–42,11.

At a certain moment in time the Savior appeared on earth, assuming a human body and soul. Coming down, however, he also brought with him, as his spiritual body, the church of the spiritual seed from the intermediary region of the Logos. This idea of a preexistent church and body of the Savior, which was incarnated together with him, is an important and very characteristic Valentinian notion. The descended church participates in the Savior's work to redeem the spiritual seed hidden in humans; in addition, however, it needs instruction and redemption itself, since it still remains for it to be reunited with the Pleroma, its model. In this way, the cosmos serves as a training ground and an arena of redemption for the spiritual seed. To fulfill this purpose the church exists in the world, teaching, performing baptism, and doing similar sorts of things. Eventually the whole spiritual seed will have passed through the cosmos on its journey back to the Pleroma. The existence of the cosmos is thus a necessary element in the Father's plan of salvation—the *oikonomia*—and has been willed by him from the beginning.

The *Tripartite Tractate* also gives a great deal of attention to the category of psychical beings (humans and cosmic powers). Psychical humans were made by the demiurge-archon, the cosmic ruler. Thus, they do not possess the spiritual seed, but ultimately derive, like all psychical substance, from the emotion of repentance first experienced by the Logos. In consequence, psychical beings have the capacity for recognizing the Savior, submitting to him, and being of service to the church. Those who do so will be saved, the *Tripartite Tractate* asserts, but, in spite of lengthy discussions of the topic, it finally remains unclear what their salvation will consist in. Will they be admitted to the Pleroma as well, or is there a lower level of redemption in store for them, as the main Valentinian system of Irenaeus states? Other psychical people have, on the contrary, persisted in denying the Savior and will be lost, having chosen for themselves the ultimate fate of destruction, just like the material ones, the third category of beings. The *Tripartite Tractate*'s concern with the psychical people lacks parallels in other extant Eastern Valentinian sources and is a feature that seems, on the surface, more akin to the Western systems. On the other hand, the *Tripartite Tractate* clearly subscribes to the Eastern view of the Savior's body (the church) as embracing the spiritual category only.

The author of the *Tripartite Tractate* is unknown. Dating the treatise is difficult. On the one hand, the text shows some affinity with Origen (185–254) and his school: the argument from "Father" to "Son" (51,12–15); the argument from the oneness of the Father to the only-begotten nature of the Son (57,8–23); the notion of the eternal generation of the Son (56,30–35; 58,7–8); the idea that the end will be like the beginning, that is, a unity (127,23–25; 132,20–23); and the emphasis throughout the text on providence, education, and economy in the salvation process, a perspective that also provides justification for creation and the temporary cosmic existence of humanity. (However, the *Tripartite Tractate* explicitly

3. On the *Tripartite Tractate* and Origen, see Jean-Daniel Dubois, "Le *Traité Tripartite* (Nag Hammadi I, 5) est-il antérieure à Origène?"

rejects another idea often found in Origen and his followers, the concept of a "substance" of the Father [53,34–35].)[3] If these similarities are significant, a date in the second half of the third century must be assumed. On the other hand, the treatise also contains elements that point toward an early phase of Valentinian theology, like the theory that the aeons initially existed inside the Father as in a womb—a theory also attested for Valentinus himself (Tertullian *Against the Valentinians* 4.3) and found in the *Gospel of Truth*. It is not unlikely that the *Tripartite Tractate* incorporates materials and ideas from different Valentinian sources, some of which may be significantly older than the treatise itself.

BIBLIOGRAPHY

Harold W. Attridge, ed., *Nag Hammadi Codex I*, 1.159–337; 2.217–497 (Harold W. Attridge and Elaine H. Pagels); Jean-Daniel Dubois, "Le *Traité Tripartite* (Nag Hammadi I, 5) est-il antérieure à Origène?"; Rodolphe Kasser, et al., *Tractatus Tripartitus*; Einar Thomassen and Louis Painchaud, *Le Traité tripartite*; Hans-Martin Schenke, Hans-Gebhard Bethge, and Ursula Ulrike Kaiser, eds., *Nag Hammadi Deutsch*, 1.53–93 (Hans-Martin Schenke).

The Tripartite Tractate[1]

Part One (51,1–104,3)

Introduction (51,1–8)

In order to be able to speak about exalted things, it is necessary that we begin with the Father, who is the root of the All and from whom we have obtained grace to speak about him. For he existed before anything else had come into being except him alone.

The Father (51,8–54,35)

The Father is singular while being many.[2] For he is first and he is unique, though without being solitary. How else could he be a father? For from the word "father" it follows that there is a "son." That singular one who is the only Father is in fact like a tree that has a trunk, branches, and fruit.

Of him it may be said that he is a true father, incomparable and immutable, because he is truly singular and God. For no one is god for him and no one is father to him—he has not been born—and no other has brought him into being. For whoever is the father of somebody, or his maker, himself has a father and a maker in turn. It is certainly possible that he may become the father and the maker of whoever comes into being from him and is made by him; still, he is not a father in the true sense or a god, insofar as [52] someone has given [birth to him and] has brought him into being. The only Father and God in the true sense, therefore, <is> the one who has been born by no one, but who, on the contrary, has given birth to the All and has brought it into being.

He is without beginning and without end. For not only is he without end—being unborn makes him immortal as well—but he is also unchangeable in his

---

1. Coptic text: NHC I,5: 51,1–138,27. Editions: *The Facsimile Edition of the Nag Hammadi Codices: Codex I*, 55–142; Harold W. Attridge, ed., *Nag Hammadi Codex I*, 1.159–337, 2.217–497 (Harold W. Attridge and Elaine H. Pagels); Louis Painchaud and Einar Thomassen, *Le traité tripartite*; Hans-Martin Schenke, Hans-Gebhard Bethge, and Ursula Ulrike Kaiser, eds., *Nag Hammadi Deutsch*, 1.53–93 (Hans-Martin Schenke). The title is construed from the contents of the text. Within the translation a substantial number of terms are capitalized as personified concepts in the Valentinian cosmological account. 2. Or "like a number." Here the Coptic word is ambiguous and can mean either "numeral" or "multitude." Since "one" was not usually regarded as a numeral in antiquity and "number" was conceived as essentially implying plurality, the most likely interpretation here is that the Father is a "number" in the sense that he is many (as well as being singular). The context seems to support this interpretation.

eternal being, in that which he is, in that which makes him immutable and that which makes him great. He does not move himself away from what he is, nor can anyone else force him against his will to cease being what he is. For no one has made him what he is.

Therefore neither does he change himself, nor will another be able to move him from that in which he is, from what he is, from his way of being, or from his greatness—thus he cannot be moved, nor is it possible for another to change him into a different form, either by reducing him or changing him or making him less. For this is truly and veritably <how> he is unchangeable and immutable, being clothed in immutability. Thus he is called "without beginning" and "without end," not only because he is unborn and immortal, but also because, just as he is without beginning, he is also without end. In his manner of being he is incomprehensible [53] in his greatness, inscrutable in his wisdom, invincible in his might, and unfathomable in his sweetness.

In the true sense he alone, the good, unborn, and perfect Father who lacks nothing, is complete—filled with everything he possesses, excellent and precious qualities of every kind. Moreover, he has no envy, which means that all he owns he gives away, without being affected and suffering no loss by his gifts. For he is rich from the things he gives away and finds rest in what he graciously bestows.

Therefore, his manner, his form, and his greatness are such that nothing else exists beside him from the beginning—neither a place in which he dwells, from which he has gone forth, or to which he will return; nor an original form that he used as a model for his work; nor fatigue that came over him as a result of what he did; nor matter that lay before him and from which he made the things that he made; nor a substance inside him and from which he brought forth the things he brought forth; nor a collaborator with whom he collaborated on the things that he created. To speak in such a way is ignorant. Rather, he himself, being good, lacking nothing, perfect, [54] and complete, is everything.

There is no name that suits him among those that may be conceived, spoken, seen, or grasped, however brilliant, exalted, or glorious. It is, to be sure, possible to speak such names in order to glorify and praise him, to the extent of the capacity of whoever wants to give glory. But the way he is in himself, his own manner of being—that no mind can conceive, no word express, no eye see, and no body touch, so incomprehensible is his greatness, so unfathomable his depth, so immeasurable his exaltedness, and so boundless his <extension>.[3]

Such is the nature of the unborn one. He does not get to work starting from something other than himself, nor does he have a partner—this would imply a limitation. But he has such an existence that he has neither figure nor form that can be perceived by the senses. This means that he is incomprehensible as well; and if he is incomprehensible, it follows that he is unknowable.

---

3. The text reads *ouōśe*, "will," here emended to read *ouōś*<*s*>, "<extension>."

The Generation of the Son (54,35–57,23)

Being inconceivable for any thought, invisible for any thing,[4] unutterable for any word, and untouchable for any hand, only he himself knows himself the way he [55] is, with his form and his greatness and his magnitude, and only he is able to conceive himself, name himself, and grasp himself. For he, the inconceivable, ineffable, incomprehensible, and unchangeable one, is mind for himself, eye for himself, mouth for himself, and form for himself, and it is also himself that he conceives, sees, speaks, and grasps. That which he conceives, sees, and speaks is nourishment and delight, truth, joy, and rest, and that which he thinks surpasses every wisdom, excels every mind, excels every glory, excels every beauty and every sweetness, every greatness, every depth, and every exaltedness.

Now, although he is unknowable in his nature and possesses all those supreme qualities I have described, he is nevertheless able, if he so desires, to grant knowledge in order that he may be known, out of his abundant sweetness. He possesses power, which is his will. For the moment, however, he holds himself back in silence, he who is the greatest, being the cause of the generation of the members of the All into eternal existence. [56]

For it is truly his ineffable self that he engenders. It is self-generation, where he conceives of himself and knows himself as he is. He brings forth something worthy of the admiration, glory, praise, and honor that belong to himself, through his boundless greatness, his inscrutable wisdom, his immeasurable power, and his sweetness that is beyond tasting. It is he himself whom he puts forth in this manner of generation, and who receives glory and praise, admiration and love, and it is also he who gives himself glory, admiration, praise, and love. This he has as a Son dwelling in him, keeping silent about him, and this is the ineffable within the ineffable, the invisible, the ungraspable, the inconceivable within the inconceivable.

This is how he exists eternally within himself. As we have explained, by knowing himself in himself the Father bore him without generation, so that he exists by the Father having him as a thought—that is, his thought about himself, his sensation [57] of himself and . . . of his eternal being. This is what in truth is meant by "Silence"—or "Wisdom,"[5] or "Grace," as the latter is also rightly called.

Just as the Father truly is one before whom no [other existed] and after [whom] there is no other unborn one, in the [same] way [the Son] as well is truly one before whom no other son existed and after whom there is no other. For that reason he is a firstborn and an only son—firstborn because there was no one before him, and the only son because there is no one after him.

The Preexistent Church (57,23–59,38)

Moreover, he has his fruit, though it remained unknown because of his overwhelming greatness. And he wished to make it known, because of his abundant

---

4. One expects "eye" here. The text may be corrupt.
5. Or "Sophia."

sweetness. He revealed his inscrutable power, and he mixed it with the plentiful abundance of his generosity. For not only the Son but also the Church exists from the beginning.

If somebody now thinks that this statement is contradicted by the fact that the Son is an only son, that is not so, because of the mystery of the matter. For just as [58] the Father is singular, and was shown to be his own father, so also the Son may be found to be his own brother, without generation and without beginning. It is himself that the Father admires [as] Father and to [whom] he gives [glory], praise, and [love], and it is equally himself that he conceives of as Son, in accordance with the qualities "without beginning" and "without end." This is how the matter is, being firmly established.

His offspring, the ones who are, are without number and limit and at the same time indivisible. They have issued from him, the Son and the Father, in the same way as kisses, when two people abundantly embrace one another in a good and insatiable thought—it is a single embrace but consists of many kisses. This is the Church that consists of many people and exists before the aeons and is justly called "the aeons of the aeons." This is the nature of these holy imperishable spirits upon which the Son rests since it is his essence, just as the Father rests [59] upon the Son . . . the Church exists in the properties and qualities in which the Father and the Son exist and which I have described earlier. Thus it consists of innumerable births of aeons, and these in turn give birth in infinite number through the qualities and properties in which they [exist]. These [are a] community [formed] with one another and [with the ones] who have gone forth from [them and] with the Son, because of whom they exist as glory.

For this reason no mind can conceive of <them>—such is the perfection of that place—nor can words speak of them. For they are ineffable, unnamable, and inconceivable. Only they are able to name themselves in order to conceive of themselves. For they are not rooted here below. Those who belong to that place are ineffable and innumerable, in accordance with the special structure[6] that this is. And <this is the form> and the manner, and this is the kind, the joy, and the delight of the nameless, unnamable, inconceivable, invisible, and ungraspable unborn one. It is the Fullness[7] of his fatherhood whereby his abundance becomes procreation. [60]

The All Before It Was Brought Forth (60,1–61,1)

. . . of the aeons existed eternally in the Father's Thought, and he was like a thought and a place for them. And once it was decided that they should be born, he who possesses all power desired to take and bring what was incomplete out of . . . those who [were within] him. But he is [as] he is, [for he is] a spring that is not diminished by the water flowing from it.

---

6. The text has *sustasis*, a technical term in Valentinianism. 7. Pleroma, here and below.

As long as they remained in the Father's Thought—that is, while they were in the hidden depth—the Depth himself certainly knew them, but they on their part were incapable of knowing the depth in which they found themselves, nor could they know themselves or anything else. In other words, they existed with the Father but did not exist for themselves. Rather, the kind of existence they had was like that of a seed, or it may be compared with that of an embryo. He had made them in the manner of the word,[8] which exists in a seminal state before the things it will bring forth have yet come into being.[9] [61]

The Father's Plan (61,1–62,5)

For that reason the Father had also thought in advance that they should exist not only for himself, but should exist for themselves as well—that they should remain[10] in [his] thought as mental substance, but also exist for themselves. He sowed a thought as a seed of . . . in order that [they might] understand [what kind of father] they have. He showed grace and [provided the] first form, that they might [perceive] whom [they have] for a father. The Name of the Father he granted them, by means of a voice calling out to them that he who is, is by that Name, and possessing it, one comes into being. How exalted the Name was, however, they did not realize. For as long as the infant is in the state of an embryo, it has what it needs without ever having seen the one who sowed it. For that reason, they had this only as an object to be sought after: they understood that he existed and they desired to find out who the existing one might be.

But the Father is good and perfect, and just as he did not <close> himself to them[11] so that they should remain forever in his Thought, but granted that they should come into being for themselves also, in the same way he would gracefully allow them to understand who the One Who Is is—that is, the one who knows himself eternally. [62] . . . receive form in order [to know] who the One Who Is is, in the same way as when one is brought forth here below: when one is born, one finds oneself in the light and is able to see one's parents.

The All Is Not Made Perfect from the Beginning
(62,6–33)

For the Father produced the All like a little child, like a drop from a spring, like a blossom from a [vine], like a . . . , like a shoot . . . , so that they needed [nourishment], growth, and perfection. He withheld the perfection for a time. Having kept it in his mind from the beginning, he possesses it from the beginning and looks at it, but he <concealed> it for those who had come forth from him. This

---

8. Or "logos," here and below. 9. Cf. *Gospel of Truth* 27–28; 37. 10. A negation has perhaps dropped out: "that they should <not> remain." 11. The codex has "listen to (sōt⁽ᵉ⁾m) them," which seems meaningless. The translation adopted here corrects the Coptic verb to <š>ōt⁽ᵉ⁾m, "close," following a suggestion made by Peter Nagel.

was not out of jealousy, but it was in order that the aeons should not receive their perfection from the beginning and thereby exalt themselves in glory as equal to the Father and think that they had achieved this perfection out of themselves. But just as they came into existence because it pleased him, so also it was because it pleased him that he benevolently granted them a perfect thought that would make them faultless.

The Father Reveals Himself in the Son Through the Hymns of the Mind (62,33–63,28)

That which he now made to rise like a light for those who had gone forth from himself, that by which they are given a name, that is the Son, the full and fault- lessly perfect one. The Father brought him forth while he remained united with the one from whom he had gone forth, [63] . . . receiving glory together . . . the All, according [to the ability] of each one to receive [him]. This is not yet his greatness that[12] they have received; rather, he exists only partially in the manner, the form, and the greatness that he is. For they are able to see him and to speak with regard to [what they] know about him—since they carry him and he carries them—and they are able to reach [him] as well, though [he] remains the way he is, the inimitable one, in order that the Father may be glorified by each and every one and reveal himself. And being hidden and invisible in his ineffability, he is admired in the mind.

For this reason his great exaltedness can be revealed when they speak about him and see him, gratefully singing hymns to him about his abundant sweetness.

The Ability of the Aeons to Procreate (63,29–64,27)

<. . .> and just as the marvels of silence are eternal births—births of mind—so also the faculties of the word are spiritual emissions.[13] Since they both belong to the word, [64] they are . . . and thoughts that are given birth by it, eternally living roots that have been manifested. For they are births that have issued from them, minds and spiritual births for the glory of the Father.

And there is no need of a voice, since they [are] spirits of mind and word, nor is there any need to perform [an action] for what they desire to [do], but in the same manner that [the Father] exists, so do [those] who have issued from him also bring forth all that they wish. And that which they think, that which they say, that which they move toward, that which they are in, and that which they sing as hymns, giving glory, he has[14] as son<s>. For this is their power of giving birth, as with the ones from whom they have gone forth: by mutual help, for they have been helping one another in the same way as those unborn.

---

12. It is here assumed that "the greatness" is intended as the object, and that the Coptic text is confused. 13. Or "emanations," here and below. 14. Perhaps read "they have."

The Distinction Between the Father and the Son (64,28–66,5)

Now the Father, insofar as he is elevated above the members of the All, is unknowable and incomprehensible. His greatness is so immense that if he had revealed himself at once and suddenly, even the highest of the aeons that have
gone forth from him would have perished. For that reason he withheld his power
and his impassibility in that in which he [65] is, [remaining] ineffable and unnamable, transcending all mind and all speech.

He, on the other hand, extended himself and spread himself out. It is he who
gave firmness, location, and a dwelling place to the All—according to one of his
names he is in fact "Father of the All"[15]—through his constant suffering on their
behalf, having sown in their minds the idea that they should seek what exceeds
their . . . , by making them perceive that he is and thus making them seek what he
might be. He was given them as delight and nourishment, joy and abundant illumination, and this is his compassion, the knowledge he provides, and his union
with them. And this is he who is called, and who is, the Son. He is the sum of the
All, and they have understood who he is, and he is clothed.[16]

On the other hand, that is the one by reason of whom he is called "Son," the
one about whom they perceive that he exists and that they have been seeking
him. This is the one who exists as Father, and of whom one can neither speak nor
think: he is the one who exists first. For no one can conceive of him, or think of
him, or draw near to that place, toward the exalted, toward the truly preexistent.
But every name that is thought [66] or spoken about him is brought forth in glorification as a trace of him, according to the capacity of each one of those who give
him glory.

The Son as the Name and the Names of the Father
(66,5–67,34)

He, however, whose light dawned from him, stretching himself out to give birth
and knowledge to the members of the All, he is all these names without falsehood, and he truly is the Father's only first Man. This is the one I [call] the form
of the formless, the body of the incorporeal, the face of the invisible, the word of
the inexpressible, the mind of the inconceivable, the spring that flowed from
him, the root of those who have been rooted, the god of those who are ready, the
light of those he illuminates, the will of those he has willed, the providence of
those for whom he provides, the wisdom of those he has made wise, the strength
of those he has given strength, the assembly <of> those with whom he is present,
the revelation of that which is sought after, the eye of those who see, the spirit of
those who breathe, the life of those who live, the unity of those who are united.

---

15. Alternately, "one of his names is in fact 'the one
through whom,' since he is the Father of the All." 16.
The metaphor of clothing expresses the union of the
Son with the members of the All, or the aeons: they
are the Son's "clothes."

While all the members of the All exist in the single one, as he clothes himself completely, and in his single Name, he is never called by it. And in the same unitary way they are simultaneously this single one as well as all of them. He is not divided as a body, nor is he split apart by the names in which he exists in the sense that this is one thing and that is [67] something [else; nor] does he change by . . . , nor does he alter through the names in which he is, being now like this and now something different, so that he would be one person now and someone else at another time. Rather, he is entirely himself forever; [he is] each and every one of the members of the All eternally at the same time. He is what all of them are, as Father of the All, and the members of the All are the Father as well. For he is himself knowledge for himself, and he is each one of his qualities and powers, and <he is> himself the eye for all that he knows, seeing all of it in himself, having a Son and form.

Thus, his powers and qualities are innumerable and inaudible because of the way <in which> he gives birth to them. The births of his words, his commands, and his members of the All are innumerable and indivisible. He knows them, for they are himself. When they speak, they are all in the one single Name; and if he brings them forth, it is in order that they may be found to exist as individual qualities forming a unity.

The Aeons Procreate (67,34–68,36)

He did not, however, reveal his multiplicity at once to the members of the All, nor did he reveal his sameness to those who had issued forth from him. Now, all those who had gone forth from him—<that> is, the aeons of the aeons, [68] [being] emissions born of a procreative nature—also <procreate> through their own procreative nature, to the glory of the Father, just as he had been the cause of their existence. This is what we said earlier: he makes the aeons into roots and springs and fathers. For that which they glorified, they bore.[17] For it possesses[18] knowledge and wisdom, and they have understood that they have gone forth from the knowledge and the understanding of the All.

If the members of the All had risen to give glory according to the individual <powers> of each aeon, they would have brought forth a glory that was only a semblance of the Father, who himself is the All. For that reason they were drawn, through the singing of praise and through the power of the oneness of him from whom they had come forth, into mutual intermingling, union, and oneness. From their assembled fullness they offered a glorification worthy of the Father, an image that was one and at the same time many because it was brought forth for the glory of the One, and because they had come forward toward him who himself is the entirety of the All.

---

17. The Coptic sentence is hardly correct. The sense seems to be that the aeons' praise of the Father is a procreative act whereby the praise they produce becomes a new generation of aeonic "children." 18. Perhaps read "they possess."

The Three Fruits of Glorification (68,36–70,19)

This, then, [69] was a tribute from the [aeons] to the one who had brought forth the All, a firstfruit offering of those who are immortal and eternal; for when it issued from the living aeons, it left them perfect and full, caused by something [perfect] and full, since they were full and perfect, having given glory in a perfect manner in communion.

For inasmuch as the Father lacks nothing, he returns the glory they give to those who glorify [him, so as to] make them manifest by what he himself is. The cause that brought about for them the second glorification is in fact that which was returned unto them from the Father, when they understood the grace from the Father through which they had borne fruit with one another, so that just as they had been bringing forth by glorifying the Father, in the same way they might also themselves be made manifest in their act of giving glory, so as to be revealed as being perfect.

They became fathers of the third glorification, which was produced in accordance with the free will and the power they had been born with, enabling them to give glory in unison while at the same time independently of one another, according to the will of each. Thus both the first and the second glorifications are perfect and full, for they are manifestations of the perfect and full Father and of the perfect things that issued from the glorification of him who is perfect. The fruit of the third glorification, however, is produced by the will of each individual aeon and of each of the Father's qualities and powers. This fruit is [70] a perfect Fullness to [the extent] that what the aeons desire and are capable of in giving glory to the Father comes from their union as well as from each of them individually.

For this reason they exist as minds over minds, words over words, superiors over superiors, degrees over degrees, being ranked one above the other. Each of those who glorify has his own station, rank, dwelling place, and place of rest, which is the glorification he brings forth.

The Harmony of the Aeons (70,19–71,7)

For those who glorify the Father all have their eternal offspring. They give birth by way of mutual help, and their emissions are unlimited and immeasurable. And no jealousy exists on the part of the Father toward those who have come forth from him because they are producing something like himself and his image; for it is he himself who is in the members of the All, giving birth and revealing himself. Whomever he desires to make a father—he himself is their Father; or a god—he himself is their God. And he makes into members of the All the ones <for whom> he himself is the All. [71] In that place rightfully belong all those good names that the angels and rulers who have come into being in the world share as well, although the latter have nothing in common with the eternal ones.

The Aeons Search for the Father (71,7–35)

The whole structure of aeons, then, is yearning and seeking to find the Father perfectly and completely, and this is their irreproachable union. Although the Father does reveal himself, he did not want them to know him from eternity, but he presented himself as something to be reflected upon and sought after, while keeping for himself that by which he is inscrutably preexistent. For the Father gave the aeons a starting point and a root, so that they are stations on the calm road leading to him, as to a school of good conduct; for he spread out faith and prayer for what they do not see, a firm hope in what they do not comprehend, a fertile love longing for what they do not behold, an eternally receptive understanding of the mind, a blessing that is richness and freedom, and, for their thoughts, the wisdom of one whose desire is the glory of the Father.

The Spirit (71,35–73,18)

For the Father, the exalted one, they know [**72**] by his Will, which [is] the Spirit that breathes through the members of the All and gives them a thought to search for the unknown, just as somebody is moved by a fragrance to seek the source of that fragrance—and the fragrance of the Father surpasses such unworthy things.[19] For its sweetness lets the aeons sense an indescribable pleasure, and gives them the thought that they should be united with the one who desires that they should know him in oneness, and that they should assist one another through the spirit that is sown in them. They find themselves in a great and powerful inbreathing where they are renewed in a speechless manner and are formed, having no occasion to turn away through thoughtlessness from that in which they are placed. For they do not speak but are silent about the glory of the Father, about him who has the power to speak.

He manifested [himself], though he cannot be spoken. They have <him> hidden in their thoughts; for that reason the aeons keep silent about the way the Father exists in his form, his nature, and his greatness, [**73**] but they have become worthy of knowing this through his Spirit. For he is unnamable and inaccessible, but through his Spirit, which is the trace by which he may be sought, he gives himself to them to be thought and spoken. For each of the aeons is a name corresponding to each of the Father's qualities and powers. Since he exists in many names, it is by mingling and through mutual harmony that they are able to speak of him, by means of a richness of speech.[20] Thus, the Father is a single Name because he is One, but nevertheless innumerable in his qualities and names.

---

19. The source of the fragrance must be something other than the physical surroundings of the one perceiving the fragrance. 20. Logos (plural).

The Nature of the Emission (73,18–74,18)

The emission[21] of the members of the All that comes from the One Who Is has not taken place by way of a division, as if it were <a> separation from the one who gave birth to them; rather, their birth has the form of a spreading out, by which the Father spreads himself out into that which he wishes, in order that [those] who have gone forth from him may be as well. For just as the present aeon is single, yet divided into ages, ages into years, years into seasons, seasons into months, months into days, days into hours, and hours into moments, in the same way [74] the true aeon also is single yet multiple, being glorified by small as well as by great names according to what each is able to comprehend. Or, to use other similes, it is like a spring that remains what it is even if it flows into rivers, lakes, streams, and canals; or like a root that spreads out into trees with branches and fruits; or like a human body that is indivisibly divided into limbs and limbs—main limbs and extremities, large ones and small.

Free Will, Wisdom, and the Collaboration of the Aeons
(74,18–75,17)

The aeons were brought forth according to the third fruit,[22] by using the freedom of the will and the wisdom the Father had graciously given them for their thoughts. They do not desire to give glory [together with] that which the individual Fullnesses[23] may produce in unison as words of [glorification], nor do they desire to give glory together with the All as a whole, nor does one desire to do so together with another aeon who has already attained a higher level or station than himself, without obtaining <what> has been desired from the one who resides in that higher name and the higher station. [75] He receives him with himself at that higher level, and the one who desired to ascend to him engenders, as it were, himself, engendering himself through that other with what he is, renewing himself with what has come to him from his brother, seeing him and praying to him about this matter.

In order that this may happen, the one who has desired to give glory does not say anything to him about it, except this only. For a Boundary to speech is placed in the Fullness, making them keep silent about the Father's unreachability, but allowing them to speak about their desire to reach him.

The Presumption of the Youngest Aeon (75,17–76,23)

It came upon one of the aeons that he should undertake to reach the inconceivability of the Father and to give glory to it as well as to his ineffability. It was a

---

21. The text reads *probolē*. 22. Cf. *Tripartite Tractate* 69–70. 23. Pleroma (plural). "Fullness" is here simply another word for the more frequently used terms "the All" and "aeon."

Word[24] belonging to the unity, [although][25] it was not one that arose out of the union of the members of the All, nor from him who had brought them forth—for he who has brought forth the All <is> the Father. For this aeon was one of those who had been given wisdom, with ideas first existing independently in his mind[26] so as to be brought forth when he wanted it. Because of that, he had received a natural wisdom enabling him to inquire into the hidden order, being a fruit of wisdom. Thus, the free will with which the members of the All had been born caused this one to do [76] what he wanted, with no one holding him back.

Now, the intention of this Word was good, because he rushed forward <to> give glory to the Father, even though <he> undertook a task beyond his power, having desired to produce something perfect from a union in which he did not share and without having received orders. This aeon was the last to <have been> brought forth through mutual assistance, and he was the youngest in age. And before he had yet produced anything to the glory of the Will and in the union of the members of the All, he acted presumptuously, out of an overflowing love, and rushed forward toward that which surrounds the realm of perfect glory.

This Happened in Accordance with the Father's Will (76,23–77,11)

It was not without the Will of the Father that this Word had been brought forth, nor that he should rush forward; rather, the Father had brought him forth for the things that he knew must take place. For the Father and the realm of the All now withdrew from him in order that the Boundary should be firm that the Father had fixed—for it does not exist to prevent the unreachable from being reached, but because of the Will [77] of the Father—and also in order that the things that happened should be for the sake of an economy[27] that was to come about—and it was <not> possible that it should not come to pass—for the revelation of the Fullness.

For this reason, then, it is wrong to condemn the movement that is the Word. Rather, we should speak about the movement of the Word as the cause that made an ordained economy come to pass.

The Word Is Divided (77,11–36)

Now, on the one hand, the Word gave birth to himself as a perfect single one, to the glory of the Father who had desired him and was pleased with him. The things he had wished to grasp and reach, however, he produced as shadows, phantoms, and imitations, for he could not bear to look at the light but looked at the depths, and he faltered. Because of this, he suffered a division and a turning away. From the faltering and the division came oblivion and ignorance of oneself and <of that> which is.

---

24. Logos, here and below, presented as a personified figure. 25. Perhaps read "It was a singular word, [since] . . ." 26. The translation is conjectural. The text reads, lit., "in whose thought each one preexisted." 27. Or "organization" or "plan of salvation," here and below.

His movement upward and his design to reach the unreachable hardened for him and remained in him. The sicknesses, however, which ensued when he was beside himself, arose from his faltering—that is, <his failure to approach> the glories of the Father, whose exaltedness is without end. That he did not reach, because he could not grasp it.

The Perfect Part of the Logos Reenters the Fullness
(77,37–78,28)

That which he had brought forth from himself [78] as a unitary aeon hastened upward to that which was his, and to his kin in the Fullness. He abandoned that which had come into being from deficiency and what had issued from him in an illusion, since they did not belong to him. However, the one who had brought him forth, with superior perfection, from himself, became weak after bringing him forth, like a female nature deprived of masculinity. For what issued from his presumptuous thought and his arrogance had existence from something that itself was deficient; because of that, what was perfect in him left him and [went] upward to his own. He remained in the Fullness, and the fact that [he had been] saved from the . . . served for him as a reminder.

The one who hastened on high and the one who drew him to himself did not remain idle, but they brought forth a fruit in the Fullness with a view to overthrowing what had come into being because of the deficiency.[28]

The Offspring of the Presumptuous Thought
(78,28–80,11)

Those who came into being from the presumptuous thought resemble in fact the Fullnesses of whom they are imitations, though they are phantoms, shadows, and illusions, deprived of reason and light, belonging to this empty thought, being nobody's offspring. For this reason also [79] their end will be like their beginning: coming from that which was not, they will return to that which will not be. In their own eyes, however, they are great and powerful beings, more [beautiful] than the names [that adorn] them, though they are only [their] shadows, made beautiful by way of imitation. For the beauty [one sees] in an image derives from what the image represents.

They thought of themselves that only they existed and that they had no beginning, since they saw no one existing before them. For this reason they exhibited disobedience and rebellion, being unwilling to submit to the one who had brought them into existence. For they desired to command one another and to lord it over them [in] their vain love of glory, and the glory that they acquired became the cause [of] the structure that was to be. [Being] imitations, then, of those

---

28. This passage anticipates what will be related in full at *Tripartite Tractate* 86–87.

above, <they> exalted themselves in lust for dominion, each one of them according to the magnitude of the name of which he was a shadow, fantasizing that he would become greater than his fellows.

Thus, the thought of these others was not idle, but in accordance with the model <of those> whose shadows they are, where every thought becomes a son, [80] so do the things they think about also become their offspring. Because of this, it came to pass that many issued from them as offspring: fighters, warriors, troublemakers, [rebels], disobedient folks who love to dominate, and all the others of that sort who derive from these.

The Conversion (80,11–81,26)

The Word, then, was the cause of these things coming into being, and he became increasingly desperate. He was dumbfounded. Instead of perfection he saw deficiency; instead of unity he saw division; instead of stability [he saw] disturbance; instead of [rest], upheaval. He was [unable] to bring their [love] of disturbance to an end, nor could [he] destroy it; he had become [utterly] powerless when his wholeness and his [perfection] had abandoned him.

Those who had come into being did not know themselves, nor did they know the Fullness from which they had originated, nor did they know him who had become the cause of their existence. For since the Word was in such an unstable condition, he no longer attempted to bring forth offspring in the form of emissions, which are Fullnesses of glory originated for the glory of the Father. Instead, what he brought [81] forth were feeble and small creatures, infected with the same sicknesses with [which] he himself had been infected.

The imitation that had taken place solitarily in this state was what had been the cause of the things that do not exist on their own account from the beginning. In this defective state he continued to produce such deficient beings, until he began to condemn the irrational things he had produced. This condemnation became a judgment directed against them—that is, those opposing the judgment—aiming at their destruction, [while] wrath pursues them. It is, however, a <helper> and a savior from their disposition and their rebelliousness, for from it [comes] the conversion that is also called repentance and that takes place [when] the Word takes on [a different] disposition and a different mind, having turned away from evil and having turned toward the good.

Remembrance and Prayer (81,26–82,9)

After conversion followed the remembrance of those who exist and the prayer on behalf of the one who had returned to himself by means of what is good. First he remembered the one who was in the Fullness and entreated him, then his brothers one by one, though always together with their fellows, then all of them together—but before all of these, the Father. [82]

This prayer and supplication helped to make [him] turn <toward> himself and toward the All, for their remembrance of him caused him to remember the preexistent ones, and this is the remembrance that calls out from afar and brings him back.

A New Order of Powers (82,10–83,33)

Now, all his prayer and remembrance were numerous powers, also produced in accordance with the Boundary[29] mentioned. For there was nothing idle in his thought. These powers were much better and greater than those belonging to the imitation. For the latter have the substance of [darkness], having come into being from illusory imitation and a [vain] and presumptuous [thought]. These, on the other hand, are from [a thought] that had known them in advance. Those, then, are like <oblivion> and heavy sleep; they are like people who have troubled dreams, in which <someone> pursues them and they are surrounded. These others, however, are for him like beings of light who are waiting for the rising sun, as when the dreamers have been able to see dreams in their sleep that are truly sweet.[30]

They [83] <. . .> the emissions of the remembrance. They did not have more substance, nor did they have greater glory, [for] <they> are not equal to the preexistent ones. If, on the other hand, they were superior [to] the imitations, the only thing that made them elevated above them was that they were from a good disposition—for they had not come out of the sickness that arose—which is the good disposition of <him who> searched after the preexistent, having prayed and brought himself to what is good. He sowed in them an inclination to seek and pray to what is glorious and preexistent, and he also sowed in them an ability to think about [it], and a power of reflection to make them realize that something greater than themselves existed before them, but they had not understood what it was. Bringing forth harmony and mutual love by means of that thought, they acted in unity and unanimity, since to unity and unanimity they owed their existence.

War Between the Two Orders (83,34–85,15)

The others, moreover, they now attempted to overpower in a lust for domination, because they were nobler [84] than those previous ones, and they had risen up against them. They had not surrendered. They thought they were self-engendered and without beginning and, with their manner of giving birth, the first to bring forth others. The two orders fought against each other, struggling for command with such a result that that they were engulfed by forces and material substances in accordance with the law of mutual combat, and they too acquired lust for domination and all the other passions of this sort; and consequently, empty vainglory pulls them all toward the desire of lust for domination, and not one of them remembers [what is superior] or confesses it.

The powers of remembrance were adorned with the <names> of the pre-

---

29. The text has *horos*. It is possible that this is not a reference to the Boundary encircling the Fullness, but instead to the "definition" or principle that all mental activity produces offspring (cf. *Tripartite Tractate* 79–80). 30. Cf. *Gospel of Truth* 29.

existent, whose likenesses they were; the order of those of this kind was in harmony with itself and with each other. It fought, however, the order of those of the imitation, because that order waged war against the likenesses, and so it acted against itself on account of its rage. [85] Because of this, it [happened . . . their] own . . . [against] one another, many . . . necessity placed them . . . as well, that they might prevail . . . he did not desist . . . their envy, [their] malice, rage, violence, lust, and ignorance ruled, as they were producing various kinds of matter and all sorts of powers, mixed with one another and in great number, while the Word who had been the cause of their production waited in his mind for the revelation of the [hope] that would come to him from above.

The Word's Hope (85,15–32)

For the Word that had moved possessed hope and expectation about what is superior. He turned away from those who belonged to the shadow, in every way, since they opposed him and were very rebellious, but in those who belonged to the remembrance he found rest. In those who had come into being by way of remembrance the Word invisibly gave birth, in accordance with what existed in them, to the one who had hastened upward, and who was in the superior state, remembering the one who had become deficient. The Word did this until there would shine forth on him from above the life-giving light born from the thought of brotherly love of the preexistent Fullnesses.

Intercession in the Fullness (85,33–86,23)

For the Father's aeons, who had not suffered, took upon themselves the fall that had happened as if it were their own, with concern, goodness, and great kindness. [86] . . . the All, that they should be instructed about . . . by the one . . . all be confirmed through the . . . to end the deficiencies.

The [order that now came] into being for him originated from <the one> who had hastened upward, and from that which he brought forth for him from himself and from the Fullness as a whole. He who had hastened upward became, on behalf of him who had become deficient, an intercessor with the emitted aeons who had come into being in accordance with what really exists. And after he had entreated them, they, on their part, consented with joy, benevolence, and harmonious agreement to help the one who had become deficient. They united and prayed to the Father with a salutary mind that help might come from above, from the hand of the Father, for his glory. For the one who had become deficient could be made perfect in no other way except by the Fullness of the Father consenting, pulling him toward itself, revealing him, and giving <what> he lacked.

The Fullness Produces the Son (86,23–88,8)

Through this joyously willed agreement that arose, they brought forth the Fruit as an offspring of their concord. It was a single one, since it came from the members of the All and manifested the countenance of the Father, of whom the aeons had been thinking when they gave glory and prayed for help for their brother, and the Father had shared their sentiment, so that they produced this Fruit willingly and with joy. The manifestation of the consent in which he had united with them, which is the Son of his Will, revealed itself. [87] The Son of the good pleasure of the All placed himself on them as a garment, by means of which he could give perfection to the one who had become deficient, and confirmation to the perfect. He is the one who is rightfully called Savior and Redeemer, the Well-Pleasing and the Beloved, the Advocate,[31] Christ, and the Light of those who are appointed, in accordance with the ones from whom he had been brought forth, for he had come into being clothed in the names of those who are established. Or what other name is there to call him except "Son," which we have already used? For he is the knowledge of the Father, who wished to become known.

The aeons not only produced the countenance of the Father whom they had been glorifying, as has been written above, but they produced their own as well. For in giving glory, the aeons produced their own countenance and aspect. They were produced as an army for him, as for a king, in which those who belong to this thought[32] share the command and are united in agreement. They went forth in a form that consisted of many forms, so that the one whom they were going to help should see those to whom he had prayed for help as well as the one who brought it to him. For the Fruit we have spoken about, of their concord with him, is vested with the power of the All. In him the Father placed all things, what was before, what is, and what will be.[33] [88] He was well equipped. He revealed the things Father had placed in him. He had not given but had entrusted them to him. He took charge of the economy of the All, by means of the authority vested in him from the beginning and the power needed to execute it. In this way he proceeded to carry out his revelation.

The Son Reveals Himself (88,8–89,4)

He in whom the Father dwells, and in whom dwell the members of the All, revealed himself first to the one who had lost his faculty to see and showed himself to those who wanted to gain vision, by shining forth with that perfect light. He first filled him with inexpressible joy, made him whole and complete, and also gave him that which came from each of the aeons. For this is the nature of the first joy. <He> also sowed in him, invisibly, a word designed for understanding and gave him the power to detach and dispel from himself those who were disobedient to him.

This is how he showed himself to him. To the ones who had come into being because of him, however, he revealed himself in a form beyond their comprehension. <He> came to them as a flash, revealing himself suddenly and then

---

31. Or "Paraclete." 32. "This thought" refers to the mental act performed in harmony by the aeons when they intercede with the Father, as is described earlier in the text. 33. *Matthew* 11:27; 28:18; *Luke* 10:22; *Ephesians* 1:21.

withdrawing, like a flash of lightning. He put an end to their mutual entangle-
ment [89] through this sudden revelation, for which they were unprepared and
which they did not expect, since they had no knowledge of it.

The Reactions of the Powers (89,4–90,13)

Because of this, they became afraid and collapsed, for they could not bear the
shock of the light that came upon them. The revelation was a blow to both of the
two orders. Those who belonged to the remembrance, however, who <have
been> named "small" since they have a small idea that something higher existed
before them, had sown in them an anticipation that what was higher would reveal
itself. For that reason they greeted his revelation and bowed down before him.
They became convinced witnesses for <him> and acknowledged that the light
that had appeared was stronger than their opponents.

Those who belonged to the imitation, however, were exceedingly frightened,
for they had never before heard talk that such a sight could exist. Therefore they
fell down into that pit of ignorance called "the outer darkness,"[34] chaos, Hades,
and the abyss. He placed them below the order of those who belong to the remembrance, since it had been shown to be stronger than they. So those were
found worthy of becoming rulers over the unspeakable darkness as their own
property and the lot that fell to them. This is what he granted them, so that they
too might become useful for the economy that was to be, [90] and of which
<they> were oblivious.

Thus, there is a [great] difference between the revelation to the one who had
come into existence and then had become deficient, and the revelation to those
who came into being because of him. For to him he revealed himself inside him,
being together with him, sharing his suffering, relieving him little by little, making him grow, raising him up, and finally giving himself to him to be enjoyed in a
vision. To those who were on the outside, however, he revealed himself in a leap
and a blow, and then withdrew immediately without letting them see him.

The Word Gives Thanks and Brings Forth a
Third Order of Powers (90,14–92,22)

After the Word who had become deficient was illuminated, his fullness came to
be. He freed himself from those who previously had been revolting against him,
became disentangled from them, and stripped himself of his former presumptuous thought. He acquired the unification of rest, as those who had been disobedient to him once before bowed down and succumbed to him.

Moreover, <he> rejoiced in the visitation of his brothers who had come to
visit him. He gave glory and praise to those who had revealed themselves to him
to give help, giving thanks that he had become free from those who had rebelled

---

34. Cf. *Matthew* 8:12; 22:13; 25:30.

against him, and admiring and praising the Greatness and those who had resolved to reveal themselves to him. He brought forth living images of the living
figures. Being handsome and good, since they derived from those who exist, they
resemble these in beauty, though they are not truly equal with them since they
had not issued from a union between him who had brought them [91] forth and
the one who had revealed himself to him. Nevertheless, he worked with wisdom
and understanding, uniting himself completely with the word given to him.
Therefore, what issued from him was great, just as that which exists is truly great.

Having admired the beauty of those <who> had revealed themselves to him,
he acknowledged, then, his thanks for their visitation. The Word effected this
work by means of the ones from whom he had obtained help, in order that those
who had come into being from him should be set aright and might receive something good, as he decided to pray that the fixed economy might attain all those
who had gone forth from him.

As a result, those whom he brought forth in accordance with this intention occupy chariots, in the same way as the existing ones who had revealed themselves,
so that they may traverse all regions of activities lying below, and each one may
obtain his fixed place in accordance with what he is.

This was a defeat for those who belong to the imitation, but for those who belong to the remembrance it was an act of beneficence, and it was a revelation of
the things that arose from the unitary and compassionate decision of the aeons,
even if they are only seeds that have not yet come into being for themselves.

For that which was manifested was a countenance of the Father and of the
concord. It was a garment composed of every grace, and food, consisting of
the things the Word had brought forth when he prayed, and it received the glory
and the praise [92] he had performed with his eyes fixed on the ones to whom he
prayed so as to make perfect by means of them the images he brought forth.

For the Word greatly increased mutual cooperation and expectant hope, and
they experienced happiness, deep rest, and undefiled pleasures. The things that
he at first had only remembered, when they were not before him in their perfection, he now brought forth with an object of vision before him. It is revealed to
him, but remaining in the hope and the faith of the Father, the completely perfect one, he has not yet been united with it, for fear that the ones who have come
into being might perish from looking at the light, since they cannot sustain a
greatness of such supreme magnitude.

The Aeon of the Images (92,22–94,10)

Now, this thought of the Word, when he turned toward his consolidation and became master over those who had come into being because of him, was called
"aeon" and "place" for all those he brought into being in accordance with the decision of the aeons. Further, it is called "assembly[35] of salvation," for it healed

---

35. In Coptic, from Greek, *sunagogē*.

him from the dispersion, which is the multiform thought, and turned him toward the single thought. Similarly, it is called "storehouse," because of the rest he attained and gave himself. [93] Moreover, it is called "bride," because of his joy over what was given to him, in the hope of the fruit that would issue from the union revealed to him. It is also called "kingdom," because of the consolidation he obtained when he rejoiced in his power over those who opposed him. And it is called "the joy of the Lord," because of the delight with [which he] clothed himself when the light was before him, giving him recompense for the good that was in him and the thought of freedom.

This aeon we here have been talking about is above the two orders of those who were fighting against one another. It shares nothing with those who hold dominion, nor is it implicated in the sicknesses and the weaknesses belonging to the remembrance or to the imitation. For that in which the Word established himself, filled with joy, was an aeon: it had the form of one, but it also had the constitution of its cause, which is what had been revealed, since it was an image of those who exist in the Fullness and who had come into being out of the abundant delight of the One Who Is.

In his joy, however, at the countenance of the one who had revealed himself, in his <pleasure>, his expectation, and the promise he had received of the things he had begged for, he possessed the word of the Son, together with his essence, his power, and his form. He was the one he desired and delighted in, [94] he was the one who had been prayed for in love. This aeon was light and a desire to be set aright, an openness for instruction and an eye designed for vision—qualities that it had from those above. Moreover, it was wisdom for his thought against the ones who were placed lower in the economy, a word for speech, and other perfect things of this kind.

The Individual Members of This Aeon (94,10–95,16)

Those, moreover, who had been formed together with him after the image of the Fullness have as their parents the ones who had revealed themselves, each one of them being a small impress of one of the figures. Being male forms, since they have not originated from the sickness, which is femaleness,[36] but from one who has already left the sickness behind, <they> possess the name "church." For harmoniously they resemble the harmony that reigns in the assembly of those who manifested themselves. That, in fact, which came into being after the image of the light is perfect itself, since it is an image of the single light that is, and that is the members of the All. Even if it was smaller than that of which it was an image,

---

36. An allusion to *Genesis* 1:27. The spiritual offspring of the Word, produced by his acts of thanksgiving and glorification as images of the revealed Fullness, are produced after the image of the Father, since the Fullness itself, united in the Son, is the countenance of the Father. The offspring of the Word therefore is understood to constitute a heavenly first human, brought forth "after the image" (i.e., the Fullness-Son) of the Father. In deliberate contrast to *Genesis* 1:27, it is here emphasized that the images produced by the Word are exclusively male.

it nevertheless possesses its indivisibility because it is a countenance of the indivisible light.

Those, however, who had come into being after the image of each one of the aeons are in essence that which we have said, but in their operation they are not equal to the aeons because it occurs in each of them separately. When they are united with one another, they have equality, [95] but as individuals they have not discarded what is proper to each. For that reason they are passions, and passion is a form of sickness; for they are not offspring from the unity of the Fullness, but from one who has not yet attained the Father, or the unity with the members of the All and his Will.

Nevertheless, it was a good thing for the economy that was to be, because it had been decided concerning them that they should pass through the lower stations, and the stations would not be able to accept them coming quickly through them unless they came one by one. And their coming was necessary because everything was to be fulfilled through them.

The Mandate of the Word in the Economy (95,17–96,16)

In short, then, at once the Word received all things, preexistent, present, and future, having been entrusted with the economy of all that exists. Some were already realities, since their coming into being had been useful; seeds that would come into being in the future, however, he kept within himself—seeds deriving from the promise, by which he had conceived, because it was a promise consisting of seeds of the future. And he gave birth to his offspring, which was the manifestation of that which he conceived. The seeds of the promise, however, were withheld for some time from coming into being, because they were such as had been appointed to be sent out at the advent of the Savior and his companions—it is they who are "the first"—for the knowledge and the glory of the Father.

It is necessary, [96] because of the prayer he made and the conversion that took place as a result, that some shall perish, others benefit, and others still be set apart. He prepared the punishment for those who had been disobedient, making use of the power of the one who was revealed and from whom he had received the authority over all things. In this way he set himself apart from the things below, and also situated himself at a distance from what is superior, and so <he> prepared the economy of everything that is on the outside[37] and accorded to each his appropriate region.

The Spiritual Level (96,17–97,27)

Arranging all things, the Word first set himself up as origin, cause, and ruler of the things that had come into being, after the model of the Father, who was the cause of the preexistent establishment.

---

37. I.e., of the Fullness.

Thereafter he established the images that already existed and that he had brought forth in thanksgiving and glorification. Then he arranged the abode of those he had brought forth by way of glorification, which is called "paradise," "enjoyment," "delight full of nourishment," and "delight <of> the preexistent ones," reproducing the image of all the good things that exist in the Fullness.

Then he arranged the kingdom, which is like a city filled with everything that is agreeable—brotherly love and great generosity—and which was filled [97] with the holy spirits and the strong powers that govern those the Word had brought forth, and thereby was established with strength.

Then he arranged the station of the Church that is assembled in this place and possessed the form of the Church that exists among the aeons that give glory to the Father.

After that he arranged the station of the faith and the obedience that arise [from] hope, the very things [the Word] had received when the light was revealed; and then the disposition of prayer and supplication leading to forgiveness, and the word about him who will be revealed.

All these spiritual stations are set apart by a spiritual power from those who belong to the remembrance, a power that consists of an image of what separates the Word from the Fullness.[38] The power is active in making them prophesy about the things to come, and it lets those who have come into being belonging to the remembrance <. . .>[39] the preexistent ones, without allowing them to mingle with those who had come into being through a vision of the figures before him.

The Two Lower Orders (97,27–99,19)

Now, although those who belong to the remembrance, which is excluded from this, are subordinate, they still reproduce the likeness of what belongs to the Fullness, and in particular because of their sharing in the names with which they are adorned. Subordinate to those who belong to the remembrance is conversion, and also the law of judgment, which is condemnation and rage, is subordinate to them.

Subordinate to these again is the power separating those who are below them, which throws them far off and does not allow them [98] [to] spread upward to those who belong to the remembrance and conversion. This power is fear and despair, oblivion, confusion, and ignorance. Even these inferior ones, who have come into being as an imitation from an illusion, are called by the higher names, <although they have no> knowledge about the ones from whom they have issued through a presumptuous thought, lust for dominion, disobedience, and falsehood.

To each <of> the two orders, moreover, he gave a name. Those who belong to the remembrance and the likeness are called "those on the right," "psychical," "fires," and "the middle ones," while those who belong to the presumptuous

---

38. I.e., the Boundary (cf. *Tripartite Tractate* 75–76).
39. Some Coptic text seems to have been lost

here, e.g., "<have an idea about>" (cf. *Tripartite Tractate* 83).

thought and the imitation are called "those on the left," "material," "darknesses," and "the last ones."

After having established each one in his rank—the images, the likenesses, and the imitations—the Word kept the aeon of the images pure from all its adversaries as a place of joy. To those who belong to the remembrance, however, he revealed the thought of which he had stripped himself, with the intention that it should draw them into a communion with the material. This was in order to provide them with a structure and a dwelling place, but also in order that by being drawn toward evil they should acquire a weak basis for their existence, so that, instead of rejoicing unduly in the glory of their own environment and thereby remaining exiled, they might rather perceive the sickness they were suffering from, [99] and so acquire a consistent longing and seeking after the one who is able to heal them from this weakness.

Over those who belong to the imitation, on the other hand, he placed the ordering word to provide them with form. He also placed over them the law of judgment, and, further, he also placed over them the powers that had their roots [in] the lust for dominion. He [placed] them to rule over them, so that the order should be kept in check either by the firmness of the wise word, by the threat of the [law], or by the power of the lust for dominion, all of which diminished that order's evilness, until the Word was content with them as useful for the economy.

The Hierarchy of the Cosmic Powers (99,19–100,18)

The Word knows that the two orders share a common lust for dominion, and he granted the desire of both these and all the others. To each he gave an appropriate rank for the exercise of command, so that each would become the ruler of one station and activity and renounce the place of whoever is superior to himself in order to command by his activity the inferior stations, being in charge of the activity that it befell him to control on account of his mode of being. Thus, there came to be commanders and subordinates in positions of dominion and servitude, angels [100] and archangels, with a variety of different kinds of activities.

Each of the rulers, with the category and the grade that came to be his lot in accordance with the way they had appeared, took his position, having been given his charge in the economy. And so none of them is without a command, and none is without a king above him, from the ends of the heavens to the ends of the [earth], as far as to the inhabited regions of the [earth] and those who are below the earth. There are kings and there are masters, as well as those whom they command; some are there to punish, others to give judgment, some to give relief and healing, others to instruct, and still others to keep watch.

The Ruler and Demiurge (100,18–101,5)

Over all these rulers he placed one ruler who is commanded by no one, since he is the lord of them all. This is the representation that the Word brought forth from his thought as a likeness of the Father of the All. Because of that he is adorned with every <name>, being a likeness of him, possessing all the qualities and all the glories. For he too is called "father," "god," "creator," "king," "judge," "place," "dwelling," and "law." The Word made use of him like a hand to order and work on the things below, and he used him like a mouth to say the things that should be prophesied. When he saw that the things he said and worked on were great, good, and marvelous, he rejoiced and was happy,[40] as [101] if he was the one who had spoken and had done these things by his own thoughts; for he was ignorant that the movement within him came from the spirit that moved him in a predetermined way toward what it wanted.

The Psychical Realm (101,6–102,26)

The things that came into being from him he spoke, and they came to be after the likeness of the spiritual stations we have discussed earlier in the section about the images. For he not only worked on but he himself also produced, in his capacity of father, [his] own economy and seeds. This took place, however, [through the] superior spirit that descended [through him] to the lower stations. And [not] only did he speak spiritual words as if they were his own <. . .> invisibly through the spirit that called out and produced things that were greater than his own nature. For since he was by nature a god and a father—and all the rest of such honorable titles—he thought that they were sprung from his own nature.

He established rest for those who obeyed him, but the disobedient <he sentenced> to punishments. With him is also a paradise and a kingdom and everything else that exists in the aeon before him, although those things stand above these imprints because of the thought with which the latter are joined and which acts like [102] a shadow or a veil so that he does not see what the nature of the existing things really is.

He set up for himself laborers and servants to assist him in the things he would do or say. For in every place where he worked he left his handsome figure by means of his name, while he worked and spoke the things he was thinking. [He] set up in his stations images of the light that had been revealed, and of [the] spiritual [places], images deriving from his own nature. As a result, the stations were everywhere adorned by him, stamped with the figure of the one who had put them in place. And so they were established: paradises, kingdoms, rests, promises, and multitudes of servants to do his will. Though they are lords with dominion, they are all placed under the one who is lord and has appointed them.

The Organization of the Material Realm (102,26–104,3)

After thus having listened to it well, he placed the lights that <constitute> the starting point <of> the structure over the organization of the things below. The

---

40. Cf. "And God saw that it was good," e.g., *Genesis* 1:9.

invisible spirit moved him in such a way that he [103] too desired to administer an economy by means of a servant of his own,[41] one that he also could make use of like a hand and a <mouth>, and as if he had a face. What he brought forth <were> order, threats, and fear, so that those who had been acting without instruction . . . should hold the position [they had been assigned to] keep, being fettered to their places by [the chains of the] rulers who are over them.

The whole constitution of matter [is] divided into three parts. The [first] powers, which the spiritual Word brought forth by illusion and presumption, he placed in the first, spiritual rank. The ones that these brought forth, moreover, through lust for dominion, he placed in the middle region, since they, [then], <were> powers of lust for dominion, so that they might rule and command the establishment under them with compulsion and violence. Those, finally, who had come into being from envy and jealousy, and all the other progeny from this kind of disposition, he placed as a servant order controlling the last things and commanding all existing things and all procreation. From these derive the diseases that instantly destroy, and they are also impatient to procreate, although their existence is nothing in the place they have issued from and to which they will once more return. Because of that, he placed over them commanding powers that continuously work on matter to ensure that [104] the offspring that come into being may also have durability. For this is their glory.

Part Two (104,4–108,12)

Humanity (104,4–18)

What, then, is the form of fluid matter? A cause, which is the blindness that derives from the powers . . . in it all of them . . . as they procreate together with them, and [perish]. The thought placed between those on the [right and] those on the left is a power of [simulation], <so that> all the things that the . . . desire to do, with the result that they bring them forth in the same way that a shadow is projected by a body it follows; these <are> the roots of the visible creations.

The Creation of the Human (104,18–106,25)

Now, the whole establishment and organization of the images, likenesses, and imitations has come into being for the sake of those who need nourishment, instruction, and form, so that their smallness may gradually grow, as through the instruction provided by the image of a mirror.[42] That, in fact, is why he created the human last, after having prepared and provided for him the things that he created for his sake.[43]

---

41. Apparently the devil, who is the ruler of the material realm. **42.** Cf. 1 Corinthians 13:12. For the Valentinians, the cosmos is not evil, but serves as a means of instruction, being a weak reflection of the Fullness. **43.** Cf. Genesis 1:26ff.

The creation of the human happened in the same way as everything else. The spiritual Word set it invisibly going, accomplishing it by means of the demiurge [105] and his subservient angels, who were joined in their modeling by the presumptuous thought and its rulers. Thus, the human became like an earthly shadow,[44] so that he would be of the same kind as [those who are] cut off from the members of the All, and a creature made by them all, the ones on the right as well as the ones on the left, each of the orders forming [the human just as] it itself was. For the [form] that the Word brought forth [was] deficient in such a way that he was [afflicted] by sickness. It did not resemble him, for he brought him forth into [oblivion], ignorance, . . ., and all the other sicknesses, having given him only the first form.

Now, the Word <gave him something> through the demiurge, without his knowledge, to let him know that there exists something higher and realize that he needed [it]. This is what the prophet called "the breath of life,"[45] and . . . of the superior aeon, and this is the living soul that gave life to the substance that was dead at first. For that which is dead is ignorance.

We must, therefore, conclude that the soul of the first human derives from the spiritual Word, even if the creator thought that it was his, because that which was breathed went through him as through a mouth.

The creator himself also sent down souls out of his own substance, since [he] too has the ability to procreate, [106] <being> derived from the likeness of the Father. And those on the left as well produced a sort of human being of their own, since they possess the imitation <. . .>.

The spiritual substance is one and a single image; . . . its sickness is the condition . . . form. As for the substance of those who are psychical, its condition is double, because it has an understanding of what is superior, and confesses it, but it is <also> inclined toward evil on account of the inclination of the presumptuous thought. And as far as the material substance is concerned, its impulses are diverse and take many forms. It was a sickness that assumed many kinds of inclinations.

The first human, then, is a mixed molding and a mixed creation, and a depository of those on the left and those on the right, as well as of a spiritual Word, and his sentiments are divided between each of the two substances to which he owes his existence.

Paradise and the Transgression of the First Human (106,25–108,12)

Because of this, it is also said that a paradise was planted for him, that he might eat from the fruit of three kinds of trees; it was a garden of the threefold order, and one that provides pleasures.[46] The noble and distinctive substance in him was much superior to <the> creation, and <was> a blow to them. For that reason, they issued a commandment, threatening him, and they brought over him great

---

44. *Genesis* 2:7. 45. *Genesis* 2:7. 46. *Genesis* 2:8–9.

danger: [107] death. Only the food of the bad trees did he allow him to eat and enjoy, whereas from that tree which had the double character [he] was not allowed to eat—and much less from that of life—in order that [he] might not acquire an honor [equal to] themselves, and also so that [he] should not . . . them.

Through the evil power called "the serpent"—for he is more crafty than all the other evil powers—the human <was> deceived, by a decision of those who belong to the remembrance and the desires.[47] It made him transgress the commandment, so that he should die. And he was expelled from that place and all its pleasures.

This is the expulsion they made him suffer, when he was expelled from the pleasures of those who belong to the imitation and those who belong to the likeness. It is, however, a work of providence, in order that it may be realized that the enjoyment the human being may have for such pleasures is short compared with the eternal existence of the place of rest. It was a work the Spirit had ordained, because it had planned in advance that the human should experience that great evil which is death—that is, the complete ignorance of all things—and also experience all the evils that arise from that, so that he, after the cravings and anxieties that result from these, might partake of the greatest [108] good, namely, eternal life, which is the complete knowledge of the All and the partaking of all good things.

Because of the transgression of the first human, death reigned.[48] It accompanied all humans in order to kill them as long as its [rule] remained, which it possessed and was given [for a] kingdom because of <the> economy of the Father's Will, of which we have spoken before.

Part Three (108,13–138,27)

Confusion in the World, Errors of Greeks and Barbarians (108,13–110,22)

Whenever the two orders, [those] on the right and those on the left, are brought together by means of that thought which lies between them[49] and gives them a common economy, it comes to pass that both of them perform their works with the same zeal, those on the right copying those on the left and those on the left also copying those on the right. Sometimes the evil order begins, in a foolish fashion, to work some evil, and the <wise> order emulates it in the shape of a malefactor, it too doing evil as if it were a power of evil. At other times the wise order sets out to do good, and the <foolish> order emulates it so as to do the same.

This is how it is with the things that are constituted in this way by such [109] deeds: they have come into being resembling things that are dissimilar, so that it has become impossible for the uninstructed to understand the cause of the things

---

47. Some Coptic text may be missing here. The idea is probably that the deception of the first human took place through a joint decision of the psychical powers ("those who belong to the remembrance") and the material powers. 48. Cf. *Romans* 5:14. 49. Cf. *Tripartite Tractate* 98–99.

that exist. Because of that, they have put forward different explanations. Some say that the existing things exist by providence; these are the ones who observe the regularity of the movement of the creation and its reliability. Others say that it is something alien; these are the ones who observe the <diversity> and the lawlessness of the powers and its evil character. Others again say that the existing things are what are destined to be; these are the ones who have occupied themselves with this matter. Others yet again say that it is in accordance with nature; and still others say that is accidental.[50] The great majority, however, have only reached as far as the visible elements and know of nothing more than these.

Those who have become wise among the Greeks and the barbarians have reached as far as the powers that came into being from illusion and a vain thought, <as well as> those who issued from these in turn by way of strife and in the manner of rebellion, and those powers have worked in them. Thus, when they spoke about the things they held to be "wisdom," it was imitation, presumption, and illusory ideas, for the <imitation> had deceived them: they thought that they had reached the truth, [110] though it was error they had reached. This was not only because the names they were using were small, but the powers themselves prevented them by giving the impression that they were the All.

From this it happened that this order was entangled in a struggle against itself, because of the presumptuous quarrelsomeness of . . . of the ruler who is . . . who is before him. For this reason, nobody agreed with anybody else about anything, either in philosophy, medicine, rhetoric, music, or mechanics, but these are all opinions and theories. Consequently, <verbosity> ruled, and <they> were confused, since they were at a loss to explain <those> who ruled and gave them their ideas.

The Insights of the Hebrews (110,22–113,1)

With regard to the things that have arisen from the <people> of the Hebrews, the scriptures <. . .> from the material powers <whose> model the Greeks <reproduce>, everything they thought so as to speak it, the powers on the right <. . .>, who moved them all to think <by means of> words and a likeness of themselves.[51] So they set out to reach the truth, and used the mixed powers that were working in them.

After that, they reached the order of the unmixed powers, <before> they reached the single one who is set up after the likeness of the Father—he is not invisible [111] in his nature, but is veiled in wisdom so as to reproduce the type of

---

50. The first three theories listed are those of the Stoics, the Epicureans, and the astrologers. Of the last two theories, the second ("accidental" or "spontaneous") is an Epicurean position, whereas the first (*kata phusin*, "according to nature") is basically given simply to indicate the opposite view, though it corresponds to an opinion held by Platonists as well as Stoics. A similar doxography is found in *Eugnostos the* *Blessed* (III 70) and the *Wisdom of Jesus Christ* (III 92–93). 51. A badly corrupt sentence that can no longer be confidently restored. The general meaning seems to be that the Jewish scriptures have been inspired by the psychical powers, unlike the writings of the Greeks, which reproduce the activities of the material powers.

the truly invisible one. Because of that, many angels have not attained a vision of him, nor have the humans of the Hebrew people, of whom we have spoken—that is, the righteous and the prophets.[52] They thought nothing and said nothing that came from illusion or imitation or from an obscure thought, but from the power that was working in him, and being attentive to what he saw and heard, each one of them spoke faithfully, with mutual harmony and concord after the manner of the ones who were working in them, because they preserved their <unity> and mutual harmony. This happened especially because they confessed that which was superior to themselves, and that something greater than themselves existed and had been established because they needed it. The spiritual Word had produced this with them as something that was in need of that which is superior, as a hope and anticipation deriving from remembrance. This is the seed of salvation, and an illuminating word, which is the remembrance, and its offspring and its emissions are the righteous and the prophets we have been speaking about. They preserve the confession and the testimony of their fathers concerning that which is great—those who came into being [112] with an anticipation of hope, and with attentiveness, and in whom was sown <the> seed of prayer and seeking, which is sown in many who have sought after confirmation. It manifests itself, and leads them to love that which is higher, so as to proclaim these things as being about the one and the same.

A single influence was working in them when they spoke; what they saw and spoke varied, however, because there were many who gave them their visions and their speech. Therefore, those who have listened to what has been said do not discard any of it, but have received the scriptures differently in their interpretations. They have set up many sects that remain even until now among the Jews. Some say that the god who made a proclamation in the ancient scriptures is one; others say that they are many. Some say that God is simple and that he was of a single mind as to his nature; others say that his actions embrace the principles of both good and evil. Some again say that he is the maker of the things that have come into being, whereas others say that [113] he made them through [his] angels.

The Prophecies Concerning the Savior (113,1–114,30)

Now, as to the many speculations of this kind, it is the great variety and the multiple forms of the scriptures that have given them <. . .> teacher<s> of the law.[53] The prophets, however, spoke nothing from themselves, but each of them from what he saw and heard of the proclamation about the Savior. That which he proclaimed, and which was the main point of their proclamation, was what he spoke about the coming of the Savior, namely, the fact of his coming. Sometimes, however, the prophets speak about him as if he is to come into being, while at other times as if the Savior is speaking through their mouths, saying that the Savior will come and show grace toward those who have not known him. Thus, by no means

---

52. Cf. *Matthew* 13:17. 53. Corrupt sentence.

did they all agree with one another in their testimony; rather, each one of them thought, by virtue of the activity by which he was empowered to speak about him and the station that he had happened to see, that over there was the place where the Savior would be born, and that he would come from that place. Consequently, none of them understood where he would come from or by whom he would be born. Instead, they were granted to say only this: he would be born and would suffer. As for his preexistent being, however, and that which he is, eternally, as unborn and impassible <. . .> not of the Word that came to be in the flesh [114] — that did not enter their thoughts.

And this is the word they were empowered to speak concerning his flesh that would appear. They say that it is something born from all of them, but above all that it derives from the spiritual Word, which is the cause of the things that came into being. He, from whom the Savior received his flesh, had indeed conceived him, in a seminal form, at the revelation of the light, as a word giving promise of his revelation; it <is>, in fact, <a> seed of those who are, though it was produced last. The one, however, whom the Father appointed so as to reveal the salvation through him, and who is the fulfillment of the promise, having been, when descending into life,[54] provided with all the instruments needed for his descent — his father is one, and this is his only true father, who is invisible, unknowable, and unattainable in his nature, and who is also[55] the god who, by his will alone, and his grace, let himself be seen, known, and attained.

The Incarnation (114,30–115,23)

What our Savior became, out of willing compassion, is the same as that which the ones for whose sake he appeared had become because of an involuntary passion: they had become flesh and soul, and this holds them perpetually in its grip, and they perish and die. Those, however, who had [come into being [115] as] an invisible human being, and invisibly,[56] them he instructed about himself in an equally invisible manner. For not only did he assume their death for the ones he had in mind to save, but in addition he also assumed their smallness, to which they had descended when they were <born> with body and soul; for he let himself be conceived and he let himself be born as a child with body and soul. All the other conditions as well that they, even if they possessed the light, shared with the ones who had fallen,[57] he entered into, though he was exalted above them because he let himself be conceived without sin, pollution, or defilement. He was born into life,[58] and he was in life, because it had been ordained that the former no less than the latter should become body and soul as a consequence of the passion and the aberrant sentiment of the Word that had moved.

---

54. The word for "life" here is *bios*, physical life. 55. Here the Coptic word *mᵉn* may represent a misinterpreted Greek word, *kai*. 56. Cf. *Tripartite Tractate* 104–5. 57. The text is obscure and probably incorrectly translated from the Greek. The basic meaning must be that the humans with a spiritual element (*Tri-* partite Tractate 104–5), whom the Savior came down to save, shared the condition of having a body and a soul with the ones that lack that element; for their sake, the Savior had to be incarnated with body and soul as well. 58. The word for "life" here is *bios*, physical life.

The Incarnation of the Spiritual Seed Together
with the Savior (115,23–117,8)

He, however, assumed, for the sake of the economy, that which resulted from the events we told about earlier—that which came into being from the radiant vision and the stable thought of the Word after he had turned himself around, after his movement.[59] In this way those who came with him received body and soul together with stability, firmness, and discernment. It had been planned that they too should come when the coming of the Savior was planned; they came, however, only after he had decided it. So they came, they too being far superior in their carnal emission compared to the ones who had been brought forth from deficiency. [116] For in [this] way they too were emitted bodily together with the Savior by being manifested in union with him.

These are such as belong to the single substance, and that is the spiritual one. The economy,[60] however, is variable, this being one thing, that another. Some have issued from passion and division; they need healing. Others derive from a prayer that the sick be healed; they have been appointed to care for those who have fallen. These are the apostles and the bringers of good tidings. They are, in fact, the disciples of the Savior: they are teachers for those who need instruction.

Why, then, did they too partake of those sufferings that those who had been brought forth from passion shared in, if, in accordance with the economy, they were brought forth in one body together with <the> Savior, who did not partake of these sufferings? Now, the Savior in fact was a bodily image of something unitary, namely the All. Therefore he preserved the model of indivisibility, from which is derived impassibility. They, however, are images of each of those who were revealed; for that reason they receive the division from their model, having been given form for that planting which exists down below, and which also [117] partakes of the evil that exists in the regions to which they have arrived. For the Will kept the All under sin, in order that by Will he might show mercy on the All and they might be saved, because a single one has been appointed to give life, whereas all the rest need salvation.

The Proclamation of Salvation (117,8–118,14)

Because of this, he was the first one among them to whom it was granted to distribute those gifts that were then proclaimed by the ones he found worthy of making a proclamation to the others. Because <the> seed of the promise about Jesus

---

59. Cf. *Tripartite Tractate* 90–91. Once again the Coptic syntax is less than transparent. It is standard Valentinian doctrine, however, that the Savior at his descent also assumes a spiritual body, composed of the spiritual offspring produced by Sophia in response to her vision of the Savior. This spiritual seed, which forms the heavenly church-body of the Savior, consti-

tutes the angelic counterpart of earthly spiritual humans. 60. Whereas the "economy" basically refers to the Father's plan of salvation, the word is often used by the Valentinians simply as a name for the cosmos, obviously because the cosmos is an essential element in the execution of the plan.

Christ had been deposited, whose revelation and unification we have ministered to, this promise now enabled instruction and a return to that which they had been from the beginning—that of which they possessed a drop inciting them to return to it—which is what is called redemption.

And that means to be released from captivity and to obtain freedom. The captivity is of those who were slaves of ignorance, which reigned in its own territories. Freedom, however, is the knowledge of the truth, which existed before ignorance came into being and which reigns eternally without beginning and without end; it is goodness, the healing of all things, the release from the slave nature in which those suffered who had been brought forth in a lowly and vain thought, the nature that inclines toward evil [118] owing to that thought, which drags them down into the lust for power. They acquired that treasure which is freedom, from the abundant grace that looks to the children but overthrows passion and brings to naught the things that had been caused by the Word. He had already rejected them at the moment when he separated them from himself, but he had postponed their destruction until <the> end of the economy, allowing them to exist because they too were useful for the things that had been ordained.

The Three Kinds of Human Beings (118,14–119,27)

Now, humanity came to exist as three kinds with regard to essence—spiritual, psychical, and material—reproducing the pattern of the three kinds of disposition of the Word, from which sprung material, psychical, and spiritual beings. The essences of the three kinds can each be known from its fruit. They were nevertheless not known at first, but only when the Savior came to them, shedding light upon the saints and revealing what each one was.

The spiritual kind is like light from light and like spirit from spirit. When its head appeared, it immediately rushed to it. At once it became a body for its head. It received knowledge straightaway from the revelation.

The psychical kind, however, being light from fire, tarried before recognizing [119] the one who had appeared to it, and still more before rushing to him in faith. Though it was instructed, moreover, only by means of voice,[61] <it> was content that in this way it was not far from the hope given by the promise, having received, in the form, as it were, of a pledge, the assurance of things to come.

The material kind, however, is alien in every respect: it is like darkness that avoids the shining light because it is dissolved by its manifestation. For it did not accept his <coming>, and is even <. . .> and filled with hatred against the Lord because he revealed himself.

Now, the spiritual kind will receive complete salvation in every respect. The material kind will perish in every respect, as happens to an enemy. The psychical kind, however, since it is in the middle by virtue of the way it was brought forth as

---

61. I.e., probably, by words about the Savior, rather than by a direct vision of him.

well as by virtue of its constitution, is double, being disposed to good as well as to evil, and the issue that is reserved for it is uncertain <. . .> and to proceed wholly into the things that are good.

The Various Fates of Psychical People (119,28–122,12)

On the one hand, those that the Word brought forth in his mind after the model of what was preexistent, when he remembered that which is superior and prayed for salvation, have salvation without any uncertainty. They will be completely saved, [because] of this saving thought, in accordance with what was produced from it. This is also the case [with the ones] that these in turn brought forth, [120] whether they be angels or humans: because they acknowledge that there is something higher than themselves, and they pray and search for it, they will obtain the same salvation as the ones who brought them forth. For they are of a disposition that is good. They were assigned to the service of the proclamation of the coming of the Savior before it happened as well as of his revelation after he had come. Whether angel or human, these have, by the fact of being nominated for this service, acquired the essence of their being.

On the other hand, those that issued from the thought of lust for domination, who originated from the assault of the ones who opposed him, are the products of that thought. Being, for that reason, mixed, the end they will get is uncertain. Those who rid themselves of the lust for domination that was given them temporarily and for short periods, who give glory to the Lord of glory and who abandon their rage, will be recompensed for their humility by being allowed to endure indefinitely.

Those, however, who arrogantly pride themselves in their vainglorious lust, who love temporary glory, who are oblivious to the fact that the power they have has been entrusted to them only for a limited time and period, and for that reason have not acknowledged that the Son of God [121] is the Lord of the All and the Savior, and who have failed to rid themselves either of their fury or their way of imitating those who are evil—they will receive judgment for their ignorance and their senselessness, namely, suffering.

This applies to those who have gone astray, all those among them who turned away or, even worse, who persisted in such a way that they too committed such indignities against the Lord as the powers on the left committed against him, even to the extent of causing his death, thinking, "We shall become the rulers of the All if he who has been proclaimed king of the All is killed." And those humans and angels who do not originate from the good disposition of the ones on the right, but from the mixture, endeavored to do this. They have willingly chosen for themselves transient honor and lust.

For those on the right who will be saved, the road to eternal rest leads from humility to salvation. After having confessed the Lord, having given thought to what is good for the Church, and having sung together with it the hymn of the humble, they will, for all the good they have been able to do for it, sharing its afflictions and sufferings like people who have consideration for what is good for the Church, partake of the fellowship in hope. This applies [122] to humans as well as to angels.

Similarly, the road for those who are of the order of those on the left leads to perdition—not only because they denied the Lord and plotted evil against him, but also because their hatred, envy, and jealousy are directed against the Church as well. And this is the reason for the condemnation of those who were agitated and rose up to cause <trials> for the Church.

The Election and the Calling (122,12–32)

The Election is consubstantial with the Savior and of one body with him. Because of its oneness and union with him, it is like a bridal chamber. For more than anything else it was for its sake that the Savior came. The Calling, on the other hand, occupies the place of those who rejoice at the bridal chamber, who are glad and happy on account of the union of the bridegroom and the bride.[62] Thus, the station that the Calling will have is the aeon of the images in the place where the Word has not yet been united with the Fullness. And for this the human being of the Church is glad, rejoices in it, and hopes for it; it was composed of spirit, soul, and body on account of the economy of the Planner.[63]

The Salvation of the Savior and of His Limbs
(122,32–123,22)

Now, the human inside him was a single one,[64] for he was the All and he was all of them, and he possessed what was flowing from the Father to the extent that the various [123] stations were able to receive it. But he also possessed those limbs that we have described above. Once the redemption had been proclaimed, the perfect human immediately received knowledge so as to return swiftly to his unity, to the place from which he came. Joyfully he returned back to the place from which he had originated, the place from which he had flowed forth.

His limbs, however, needed a school, such as exists in the regions that have been so fashioned as to provide it with the likeness of the images and the archetypes in the manner of a mirror, until all the limbs of the body of the Church <would be united> in one place and would attain the restoration[65] together, by appearing as the sound body <. . .> the restoration to the Fullness.

---

62. Election and Calling are common Valentinian terms for those who are spiritual (the elect) and those who are psychical (the called). 63. A somewhat obscure sentence. Apparently the Church is conceived of as a single human being (the *ekklēsia* as an *anthrōpos*), representing the Savior in his incarnation. This "human being of the Church" may thus be thought to include the psychical "Calling" as well as the spiritual "Election." In the following, however, the emphasis is clearly on the spiritual people only as constituting the limbs of the Savior and the Church, whereas the psychical people are, at best, assistants of the Church and not actually members of it as the body of the Savior. 64. The Savior is seen as "the inner human" of the *ekklēsia-anthrōpos*. 65. The text reads *apokatastasis*.

The Final Restoration (123,23–125,24)

The Fullness possesses a first mutual concord and union, which is the concord that exists for the glory of the Father, and through which the members of the All acquire a representation of him. The final restoration, however, <will take place> after the All is manifested in him who is the Son—the one who is the redemption, who is the road toward the incomprehensible Father, who is the return to the preexistent—and after the members of the All have been manifested in him who is truly the inconceivable, ineffable, [124] invisible, and ungraspable one, so that the All obtains its redemption.

The redemption is not only a release from the domination <of> those on the left, and not just an escape from the authority of the ones on the right, to each of whom we thought we were slaves or children, and from whom nobody gets loose without quickly becoming theirs once more. Rather, the redemption is also an ascent and <. . .> those levels that exist in the Fullness and with all those who have been given names and who comprehend them according to the capacity of each individual aeon, and it is an entry into that which is silent, where there is no need of voice, nor of understanding, comprehension, or illumination, but all things are luminous and have no need of illumination.

For not only earthly humans need the redemption, but the angels need the redemption as well, and the image,[66] and even the Fullnesses of the aeons and those marvelous luminous powers needed it—so as to leave no doubt with regard to anyone. And even the Son, who constitutes the type of the redemption of the All, [needed] the redemption, [125] having become human and having submitted himself to all that was needed by us, who are his Church in the flesh. After he, then, had received the redemption first, by means of the word that came down upon him, all the rest who had received him could then receive the redemption through him. For those who have received the one who received have also received that which is in him.

For the redemption began [to be] given among the humans who were in the flesh, with his firstborn and his love, the Son,[67] coming in the flesh, and the angels who were in heaven having been found worthy of forming a community, a community in him upon the earth—for this reason it is called the Father's angelic redemption—and with him comforting those who had suffered on behalf of the All for the sake of his knowledge, for he was given grace before anyone else.[68]

---

66. "The image" makes no sense here. Read probably "the images," i.e., the spiritual offspring of the Word in the aeon of images. 67. The original Greek may have read "his beloved Son." 68. The syntax of this complicated sentence has been reconstructed on the assumption that the Coptic translator has misconstrued a series of Greek participles by translating them as relative clauses instead of subordinate clauses. Logic dictates that the final clause must be dependent on the statement made at the beginning of the long sentence. The idea is that the whole process of salvation began with the redemption of the Savior and of earthly humans, after which followed, by way of a chain reaction, as it were, the redemption of the higher levels, including the Fullness itself.

The Father's Plan (125,24–127,25)

Now, the Father knew him in advance, since he existed in his deliberations before anything had yet come into being, where he also had the ones for whom he revealed him. He lay the deficiency upon that which lasts for limited periods of time, for the glory of his Fullness. It is the fact that he was unknown that made it possible for him to show his benevolence [by making himself known], [126] and thus, receiving knowledge about him is a manifestation of his generosity and the revelation of his abundant sweetness—which is the second glory. Consequently, in this way he is, in fact, the cause of ignorance as well as the originator of knowledge.

In hidden and inscrutable wisdom he guarded the knowledge until the end, until the members of the All would have labored in their search for God the Father, whom no one has found by his own wisdom and power. And then he grants them to attain knowledge of this great gift of his by means of that superior thought and that method which he has given them and which consists in ceaseless thanksgiving to him. Out of his immovable counsel, he then reveals himself for eternity to the ones who have proved worthy of receiving, by his will, the knowledge about the Father, who is unknowable in his nature.

It was premeditated in the Father's wisdom that the ones for whom he had planned that they should attain knowledge, as well as all the good things that come with it, should, in addition, also experience ignorance and its pains. Thus, they would taste the things that are evil, and would be trained through them, as a temporary . . . obtain the [enjoyment of the things that are good] for eternity. [127] The fact that they mark themselves out and are continually rejected and accused by their adversaries is something they carry as an ornament and a marvelous sign of the superior things. This was to make it evident that the ignorance of whoever was ignorant of the Father was of his own making, whereas that which gave them knowledge about him was a power from him enabling them to attain <it>.

This knowledge is rightly described as "the knowledge of everything that can be thought" and "a treasure." And, to give more knowledge in addition to that, it is also the revelation of the ones who were known in advance, and the road toward the concord and the preexistent, which means that those acquire greatness who have renounced the greatness that was theirs in the economy of the Will, in order that the end may be just as the beginning was.

Baptism (127,25–129,34)

As for the true baptism, into which the members of the All descend and where they come into being, there is no other baptism except the one—and that is the redemption—which takes place in God the Father, the Son, and the Holy Spirit, after confession of faith has been made in those names—[which] are the single name of the good tidings [128]—and after one has believed that the things one has been told are real.

And on account of this, whoever believes in their reality will obtain salvation, and that means to attain, in an invisible way, the Father, the Son, and the Holy Spirit, but only after one has borne witness to them in unfaltering faith and if one grasps them in a firm hope. In this way, it may happen that the fulfillment of what one has believed becomes a return to them, and that the Father becomes one with him—the Father, God, whom he has confessed in faith, and who has granted him to be united with himself in knowledge.

The baptism we have spoken about is called "the garment" <that> is not taken off by the ones who put it on and that is worn by the ones who have received redemption. And it is called "the confirmation of truth," which never fails in its constancy and stability and holds fast those who have obtained <restoration> while they hold on to it. It is called "silence" because of its tranquility and unshakability. It is also called "the bridal chamber" because of the concord and the inseparability of the ones [whom] <he has> known <and who> have known him. It is also [called] [129] "the unsinking and fireless light," not because it sheds light, but rather because those who wear it, and who are worn by it as well, are made into light. It is also called "the eternal life," which means immortality.

Thus it is called after all the fair things it contains, including the names that have been <left out>, in a manner that is simple, authentic, indivisible, irreducible, complete, and unchangeable. For how else can it be named, except by referring to it as the All? That is, even if it is called by innumerable names, they are spoken only as a way of expressing it in certain ways, although it transcends all words, transcends all voice, transcends all mind, transcends all things, and transcends all silence. This is how it is <. . .> with the things that belong to what it is. This is what it in fact is, with an ineffable and inconceivable character in order to be in those who have knowledge by means of what they have attained, which is that to which they have given glory.

The Salvation of Those Who Are Called (129,34–136,24)

Even if there are many more things that could be said on the subject of the Election, [130] and which it would be fitting to mention, it is nevertheless necessary that we <speak> once more about those who belong to the Calling—for this is how those on the right are named—and it would not be profitable for us to forget them. We have spoken about them as if the limited description above was sufficient. How, then, is it that we have spoken only partially about them?

Well, I said that all those who have gone forth from the Word, either from the condemnation of the things that are evil, or from the rage that fought against them, or the turning away from them, which is the conversion toward the superior things, or the prayer and the remembrance of the preexistent things, together with the hope and the faith that the salvation of that which is good might be [obtained]—all these have become worthy, because they originate from those good dispositions and they have as the cause of their birth a sentiment that derives from that which is.

Moreover, I said that before the Word himself had occupied himself with them in an invisible manner, and willingly, that which was superior had also supplied them with that thought which I mentioned above, because they had been [obedient] to it, [131] and that thought was what became the cause of their existence. And they did not exalt themselves because <they> were healed, as if no one existed before them; rather, they acknowledge that they have an origin of their existence, and they desire to know what that is that exists before them.

In addition to that, I said that they greeted the light when it appeared in the form of lightning, and they bore witness that it had appeared for their salvation.

Now, not solely about those who came forth from the Word did we say that they will attain that which is good, but the ones to whom these gave birth in turn in accordance with those good dispositions will also partake of that repose, as a consequence of the abundance of grace. And even those who were brought forth from the desire of lust for domination, having inside them the seed that is lust for domination, will receive the recompense of good things, if they have worked together with those who are predisposed toward good things, and provided they decide to do so deliberately, and are willing to abandon their vain love of temporary glory so as to [do] the command of the Lord [132] of glory, and instead of that small temporary honor they will inherit the eternal kingdom.

It was necessary for us to return to what we had spoken about earlier; now, however, we must join the premises thus laid down to the reasons and the <evidence> as to whether all those on the right, whether unmixed or mixed, may receive the grace of salvation and repose, so as to make a consistent argument. This means that we shall establish, in a compelling discourse, a demonstration from the form of their faith.

If, in fact, we confess the kingdom in Christ, it is for the abolishment of all diversity, inequality, and difference. For the end will regain the form of existence of a single one, just as the beginning was a single one—the place where there is no male and female, nor slave and free man, nor circumcised and uncircumcised, nor angel and human, but all in all is Christ.[69] How can one who did not exist at first be found to come into being, unless <. . .> the nature of the one who is not a slave, since he will take a place together with a [133] free man? For they will even obtain direct vision, so that they will no longer have to believe on account only of a small word produced by a voice that this is how things are.

For the restoration back to that which was is a single one. Even if some are exalted because of the economy, having been set up as causes for the things that happened, unfolding numerous physical forces and taking pleasure in them, [they]—angels [as well as] humans—will obtain the kingdom, the confirmation, and the salvation.

And here are the reasons. Those who had been revealed in the flesh believed without hesitation that he was the son of the unknown God, the one that had not been spoken about before and whom no one had been able to see. And they

---

69. Cf. *Galatians* 3:28; *Colossians* 3:11.

abandoned the gods they had served before and the lords who are in heaven as well as the ones on earth. Even before <he> had been taken up to heaven and even when he was still a child, these bore witness that he had already begun to preach. And when he lay in the tomb [as a] dead man, the angels thought that he was alive, [and they received] life [134] at the hand of the one who had died.

The many acts of worship and wonders they used to perform in the temples these now gave over to another. The confession is what gave these the power to do it, on account of their hastening toward him. That institution was something they had gotten only so that they should renounce it for the sake of the one who was not <shown honor> here below; but instead [they got] Christ, and they understood that he came from the [superior] place, the place from [which] they had come together with him, from a place divine and sovereign. The names that the ones they had been worshiping, tending to, and serving had received on loan they now gave over to the one who is truly called by them.

Those, however, realized only after his assumption that he was their lord, who has no lord over him. They then gave him their kingdoms, they rose [from their] thrones, and they laid down their crowns. He, however, revealed himself to them for the reasons we have mentioned before: that they might be healed and [turn to] the good thought toward . . . [135] friend and the angels . . . and the many good things they have done for it. In this [way] they were entrusted with the services that benefited the elect, as they brought the iniquity they suffered up to heaven, to be eternally tried by the incontrovertible and infallible [judgment]. And they remain for their sake, until they have all entered into earthly life and have passed out of it. As long as their bodies [remain] on the earth, they minister to all their . . . , and make [themselves] partners in their afflictions, persecutions, and tribulations, which have been brought upon the saints more than anyone else.

As for the servants of evil, however, since evil deserves destruction <. . .> with firmness on account of that [communal life] which is above all the worlds, and which is their good thought and friendship.

And the Church will remember them as good friends and faithful servants once it has been redeemed, and [it will give them] the reward consisting of the joy that reigns in the bridal [chamber], and the . . . [which] is in its house . . . which is in the thought . . . and that which it owes . . . [136] Christ, who is with it [and the] expectation of the Father [of] the All, and it will provide them with guiding and serving angels.

For the aeons will remember their benevolent thought with which they served the Church, <and> will give them their reward [for] all their consideration. This is an emission from them, in order that just as Christ . . . will, which brought forth the great and exalted [things] for the Church and gave them to it, <so> this emission too will become a thought for these and will provide them with dwelling places where they will dwell eternally [after they have] renounced the downward attraction of deficiency, and the power of the Fullness has pulled them upward, on account of the great generosity and the sweetness of the preexistent aeon.

The End of Time (136,24–138,27)

This is the nature of everything that was produced as a result of what [Christ] had with him when he shone upon them [with] a [light] that revealed . . . as his . . . which will be . . . just as his . . . the only difference [that] exists among those who have been . . . .[70] **[137]**

. . . those who are . . . by means of . . . value, in the way [I have] already explained, while the material beings will be left behind until the end to perish, for they will not give their . . . . If they have returned once more to that which . . . in the way that they were . . . while they do not exist . . . , but they had been useful . . . [for the] time that they were among them, even if they are not . . . at first, then . . . to do something else by means of the power they had in the establishment [to] oppose them.

Even if I continue to make use [of] such words . . . his thoughts . . . greatness . . . .[71] **[138]**

. . . all . . . angel . . . words [through] the [sound of a] trumpet, which will announce the great and complete reconciliation from the resplendent East, in the bridal [chamber], which [is] the love of God, the . . . , in accordance with the power that . . . of the greatness . . . the sweetness of his . . . , as he reveals himself to the greatnesses . . . his goodness . . . the praise, the power, and the [glory], through Jesus Christ, the Lord, the Savior, the Redeemer of all those who are embraced by the mercy of love, and through [his] Holy Spirit, from now throughout all generations forever and ever. Amen.

---

70. Five lines missing or untranslatable. 71. About five lines missing or untranslatable.

THE SECRET BOOK OF JOHN

NHC II,1; III,1; IV,1; BG 8502,2

Introduced by John D. Turner
Translated by Marvin Meyer

Discovered in the Berlin Gnostic Codex 8502 in 1896 but not published until 1955, the *Secret Book* (*Apocryphon*) *of John* is probably the most widely known of all the Sethian treatises. The popularity and importance of the *Secret Book of John* in antiquity is clearly evident. It now survives in no fewer than four separate manuscripts, a huge number of copies compared with what we have for most Gnostic texts. Two manuscripts (Nag Hammadi Codices II and IV) contain a somewhat longer version of the *Secret Book of John*, while the other two (Nag Hammadi Codex III and the Berlin Gnostic Codex 8502) contain somewhat shorter versions. All four codices contain other writings, but in the three Nag Hammadi codices, the *Secret Book of John* is always the first tractate copied into the codex. In *Against Heresies* 1.29 the late second-century anti-Gnostic Christian bishop Irenaeus summarized a work very similar to the first part of the *Secret Book of John*. Although Irenaeus attributed this work to certain "Gnostics," a later version of Irenaeus's report by the same title (*Against Heresies* 2, falsely attributed to Tertullian), ascribed this work to certain "Sethians" (*Sethoitae*), and Theodoret of Cyrrhus (*Summary of Heretical Fables* 13) identified these Gnostics as "Barbeloites." In addition, in his next chapter (*Against Heresies* 1.30) Irenaeus summarizes a work that features a revision of *Genesis* 1–9 quite similar to the second part of the *Secret Book of John*, attributing it to certain "others" (*alii*) whom Pseudo-Tertullian in *Against all Heresies* 2 first identified as "Ophites," and Theodoret (*Summary of Heretical Fables* 1.14) later identified also as Sethians, although the heavenly Seth plays a role only in the *Secret Book of John*.

According to Frederik Wisse,[1] one of the editors of the standard synopsis of the *Secret Book of John*, all four manuscripts (Nag Hammadi Codices II, III, and IV, and the Berlin Gnostic Codex) of the *Secret Book* are copies of independent translations into Sahidic Coptic from earlier Greek exemplars, one a shorter and

---

1. Frederik Wisse, "The Apocryphon of John," 899.

the other a longer version (both now lost). The versions in Codices II and IV are independent Coptic recensions of a previous Coptic translation of the original longer Greek version, and the shorter versions contained in Codex III and the Berlin Codex are independent translations of a single Greek exemplar of the shorter version. Aside from the question of the relationship of these two or three recensions of the *Secret Book of John* to the "Barbeloite" theogony and cosmogony summarized by Irenaeus, there is also the question of the relative priority among all these versions of the underlying myth: not only Irenaeus's account, but also that of both the two longer (II and IV) and two shorter versions (III and BG) of the *Secret Book of John*. At present this issue has not been decided, although it is obvious that even the material common to both the longer and shorter versions represents a text that has undergone substantial redaction and incorporated a number of separate sources, such as the introductory negative theology (II 3,17–33) and a short dialogical treatise on the salvation of various sorts of souls (BG 64,14–71,2; II 25,16–27,30). The longer versions differ from the shorter ones principally in their inclusion of the long citation from the *Book of Zoroaster* (II 15,29–19,10) and a hymnic monologue spoken by Forethought (Pronoia) as a conclusion for the entire work (II 30,11–31,25).

Although much of the material found in the *Secret Book of John*—arguably the earliest complete version of the "Sethian myth"—is echoed in other Sethian treatises, the concluding Forethought/Pronoia monologue seems actually to have served as the inspiration for the composition of an entire Sethian treatise, namely, *Three Forms of First Thought* (or *Trimorphic Protennoia*). One may accordingly conjecture that the shorter recension of the *Secret Book of John* (BG and NHC III), including the short excursus on the destiny of various sorts of souls, came into existence around 150 CE in the form of a dialogue between the resurrected Christ and his disciple John son of Zebedee. The longer version in Codices II and IV was created basically by the addition of the extended angelic melothesia of the earthly Adam's material body (from the *Book of Zoroaster*, II 15,29–19,10) and the inclusion of the Forethought/Pronoia monologue (II 30,11–31,25) at the end of the work and may have been completed during the last quarter of the second century. One may also conjecture a still earlier, nondialogical version consisting of the theogonic and cosmological material common to the *Secret Book of John* (BG 29,18–44,19; II 6,10–14,18), Irenaeus's *Against Heresies* 1.29, and *Three Forms of First Thought* 38,16–40,22, which may represent the earliest recoverable form of the *Secret Book of John*.

The *Secret Book* contains what purport to be secret teachings revealed by Christ in a postresurrection appearance to the apostle John the son of Zebedee. It thus constitutes a continuation of the Fourth Gospel, whose farewell dialogues between the precrucifixion Jesus and his uncomprehending disciples Peter, Thomas, and Philip concerning Jesus's promised return to the Father are now supplemented by John's postascension encounter with the very Savior who had indeed returned to the Father just as he had predicted. The veiled references to the many rooms of his Father's house to which the earthly Savior had promised to take his followers are now described in detail, and the unity between the Father and the Son is now clarified: Jesus is the Father, Mother, and Son; indeed, in his primordial capacity as the blessed Mother-Father, Christ had already raised up the seed of Seth to the Father's many-roomed house, namely, the four eternal realms, or aeons, which he himself had previously prepared before this world had ever come to be. In contrast to a future parousia at the end of days envisioned by *John* 21 and the Johannine letters, the *Secret Book of John* portrays this parousia as occurring shortly after the events described in the gospel and in effect challenges the leadership role *John* 21 assigns to Peter by having the postascension Jesus appoint John as the teacher of his fellow disciples.

Christ's ensuing lengthy discourse, punctuated at certain points by John's requests for clarification, consists of two parts, the Savior's lengthy monologue on theogony and cosmogony and a subsequent dialogue between John and the Savior on anthropogony and soteriology. According to Michael Waldstein,[2] with respect to its rapprochement with Jewish *Genesis* traditions, the first part tells of pre-*Genesis* realities and events about which Moses provides no information, and the second offers a rereading of *Genesis* 1–7. With respect to its rapprochement with Platonic traditions, especially Plato's *Timaeus*, the Jewish creator god is split "into an upper God of pure goodness, who is personally identified as the transcendent God of Middle Platonic theology who retained some central features of the God of Israel, and an evil lower God who was personally identified as the God of Israel, but is portrayed as a parody of the Platonic demiurge."[3]

In the first part, Christ reveals to John the nature of the supreme deity (the primal divine triad, Father, Mother, and Child), the divine realm brought into being by him (the All or Pleroma of light organized into Four Luminaries, Harmozel, Oroiael, Daveithai, and Eleleth), and its relation to the created order—how the creation, with its flaws and shortcomings originated (through the fall of Sophia/Wisdom and the creation of a lower world at the hands of her ill-begotten son, Yaldabaoth, and his demonic underlings) and became dominated by the inferior powers that now control it. This part concludes with Yaldabaoth's boast, "I am a jealous god and there is no other god beside me" (II 13,8–9), which marks the point of transition to the second part of the revelation, a dialogue wherein Christ makes the first of many textual allusions to *Genesis*. What makes the work distinctively Sethian is the understanding of the Four Luminaries as the respective aeonic dwellings of the archetypal Adam, Seth, his primordial seed (the seven Sethite generations from Seth through Noah), and Seth's postdiluvian progeny.

The second part of the *Secret Book of John* contains Christ's explanation of the true meaning of *Genesis* 1–9, revealing how Yaldabaoth created Adam as an initially weak copy, not yet spiritual, of the image of the archetypal human projected below from the divine world. John then asks the first of ten questions, introducing an element of dialogue not found in the first part; and the subject matter shifts

---

2. Michael Waldstein, *The Apocryphon of John: A Curious Eddy in the Stream of Hellenistic Judaism*, 82.
3. Michael Waldstein, "The Primal Triad in the *Apocryphon of John*," 154.

from theogony and cosmogony to soteriology and anthropogony. This part goes on to reveal how Adam acquired his true spiritual nature and was enlightened by Insight (Epinoia) appearing in the form of the spiritual Eve and by eating of the tree of knowledge, was expelled from paradise, and begot Seth. After a short dialogue on the salvation of various types of souls from the incarnational cycle and on the origin of the wicked spirit, Christ's revelation concludes with the story of Yaldabaoth's further enslavement of the human race through the origination of fate, the coming of the flood, and (note the reverse of the biblical order) how intercourse between the angels and human women led to humanity's sexual enslavement. The Savior then departs to the aeonic world with a reminder that salvation is certain, since the divine Mother has already enlightened her seed.

In the long monologue concluding the longer versions of the *Secret Book of John* (Codices II and IV) Forethought/Pronoia/Barbelo narrates in the first person her three salvific descents into the world of darkness to awaken her "seed" from their heavy sleep induced by the archontic powers and to elevate them into the supernal light by sealing them with "Five Seals." Several Sethian treatises present this final act of deliverance as a baptismal rite (the *Holy Book of the Great Invisible Spirit*, *Three Forms of First Thought*, *Melchizedek*, the *Revelation of Adam*, *Zostrianos*, and perhaps *Marsanes*), usually called the Five Seals (*Three Forms of First Thought*; the longer versions of *the Secret Book of John*; the *Holy Book of the Great Invisible Spirit*; and the untitled text of the Bruce Codex). Thus the ultimate restoration of Seth's progeny, who continue to live on earth, will be accomplished in the last days; its advent is marked by Barbelo's final act of raising up her seed by appearing either in her own person or in that of her child (the Word or Autogenes the Self-Generated or Seth or Christ or other similar figures) to reveal to the Sethians of those days—that is, the contemporary readers of the *Secret Book*—the true account of their spiritual origins and nature.

BIBLIOGRAPHY

Karen L. King, *The Secret Revelation of John*; "Approaching the Variants of the *Apocryphon of John*"; Louis Painchaud and Bernard Barc, "Les réécritures de l'Apocryphon de Jean à la lumière de l'hymne final de la version longue"; Zlatko Plese, *Poetics of the Gnostic Universe: Narrative and Cosmology in the Apocryphon of John*; Hans-Martin Schenke, Hans-Gebhard Bethge, and Ursula Ulrike Kaiser, eds., *Nag Hammadi Deutsch*, 1.95–150 (Michael Waldstein); Michel Tardieu, *Écrits gnostiques: Codex de Berlin*; Walter C. Till and Hans-Martin Schenke, *Die gnostischen Schriften des koptischen Papyrus Berolinensis 8502*; Michael Waldstein, *The Apocryphon of John: A Curious Eddy in the Stream of Hellenistic Judaism*; "The Primal Triad in the *Apocryphon of John*"; Michael Waldstein and Frederik Wisse, *The Apocryphon of John: Synopsis of Nag Hammadi Codices II,1; III,1; and IV,1 with BG 8502,2*; Frederik Wisse, "After the *Synopsis*: Prospects and Problems in Establishing a Critical Text of the *Apocryphon of John* and Defining Its Historical Location"; "The Apocryphon of John."

The Secret Book of John[1]

The Teaching of the Savior (1,1–4)

The teaching of the Savior, and [the revelation] of the mysteries [and the things][2] hidden in silence, things he taught his disciple John.

The Revealer Appears to John (1,5–2,25)

One day when John the brother of James, who are the sons of Zebedee, went up to the temple, it happened that a Pharisee named Arimanios[3] came up to him and said to him, "Where is your teacher, whom you followed?"

I said to him, "He has returned to the place he came from."

The Pharisee said to me, "This Nazarene really has deceived you, filled your ears with lies, closed [your minds], and turned you from the traditions of your ancestors."

When I, John, heard this, I turned away from the temple and went to a mountainous and barren place. I was distressed within, and I asked how the Savior was chosen:

> Why was he sent into the world by his Father?
> Who is his Father who sent him?
> To what kind of eternal realm[4] shall we go?
> And why did he tell us, when he spoke,
> that this eternal realm [to which we shall go]
> is modeled after the incorruptible realm,
> but he did not teach us what kind of aeon that one is?

---

1. Coptic texts: NHC II,1: 1,1–32,10; III,1: 1,1–40,11; IV,1: 1,1–49,28; BG 8502,2: 19,6–77,7. Editions: *The Facsimile Edition of the Nag Hammadi Codices: Codex II, 11–42; The Facsimile Edition of the Nag Hammadi Codices: Codex III, 7–44; The Facsimile Edition of the Nag Hammadi Codices: Codex IV, 7–57*; Walter C. Till and Hans-Martin Schenke, *Die gnostischen Schriften des koptischen Papyrus Berolinensis 8502*; Hans-Martin Schenke, Hans-Gebhard Bethge, and Ursula Ulrike Kaiser, eds., *Nag Hammadi Deutsch*, 1.95–150 (Michael Waldstein); Michael Waldstein and Frederik Wisse, *The Apocryphon of John: Synopsis of Nag Hammadi Codices II,1; III,1; and IV,1 with BG 8502,2*. The text is commonly referred to as the *Apocryphon of John*. The present translation is based mainly on the Coptic text of NHC II (the longer version of the *Secret Book of John*), and unless otherwise indicated the page numbers refer to the Codex II text. Where lacunae in the Codex II version may be confidently restored on the basis of readings preserved in the other texts, they are not placed within brackets. A few lines omitted from the Codex II text are added from the Codex IV text, the other text representing the longer version of the *Secret Book of John*. References to the texts of BG 8502 and NHC III, which represent the shorter version, are also included. 2. Or restore to read "[that are]." 3. This name recalls the evil Zoroastrian deity Ahriman. 4. Aeon, here and below.

At the moment I was thinking about this, look, the heavens opened, all creation under heaven lit up, and the world shook. [2] I was afraid, and look, I saw within the light [someone[5] standing] by me. As I was looking, it seemed to be an elderly person. Again it changed its appearance to be a youth.[6] Not that there were several figures before me. Rather, there was a figure with several forms within the light. These forms were visible through each other, and the figure had three forms.

The figure said to me, "John, John, why are you doubting? Why are you afraid? Aren't you familiar with this figure? Then do not be fainthearted. I am with you always. I am [the Father], I am the Mother, I am the Child. I am the incorruptible and the undefiled one. [Now I have come] to teach you what is, what [was], and what is going to come, that you may [understand] what is invisible and what is visible; and to teach you about the [unshakable generation of] the perfect [human]. So now, lift up your [head] that you may [hear] the things I shall tell you today, and that you may relate them to your spiritual friends who are from the unshakable generation of the perfect human."

The One (2,25–4,19)

I asked if I might understand this, and it said to me, The One[7] is a sovereign that has nothing over it. It is God and Parent, Father[8] of the All, the invisible one that is over the All, that is incorruptible, that is pure light at which no eye can gaze.

The One is the Invisible Spirit. We should not think of it as a god or like a god. For it is greater than a god, because it has nothing over it and no [3] lord above it. It does not [exist] within anything inferior [to it, since everything] exists within it, [for it established] itself.[9] It is eternal, since it does not need anything. For it is absolutely complete. It has never lacked anything in order to be completed by it. Rather, it is always absolutely complete in light.

The One is

> illimitable, since there is nothing before it to limit it,
> unfathomable, since there is nothing before it to fathom it,
> immeasurable, since there was nothing before it to measure it,
> invisible, since nothing has seen it,

---

5. Perhaps from the Coptic [ourōme]; here the shorter version in BG 8502, 20 reads oualou, "a child." 6. Coptic hal, "servant," probably is a translation of the Greek pais, which can mean "youth" or "servant." In the present context "youth" is much more likely. On Jesus appearing as a youth or child, cf., e.g., Gospel of Judas 33. 7. The text reads monas, "monad." The following lines offer a classic statement of divine transcendence formulated in terms of negation. This statement in the Secret Book of John is very similar to that in Allogenes the Stranger and reminiscent also of the via negativa of the Hindu Upanishads, with the insistence that the ultimate is neti neti, "not this, not that." 8. The text reads "Father" (eiōt), here and below, for the transcendent Great Invisible Spirit. The translation "Parent" is incorporated here to emphasize that the divine parent transcends gender categories, and the translation of this section seeks to provide an accurate means of addressing issues of gender in the Secret Book of John. For a slightly different translation of a portion of this section, see the note to Allogenes the Stranger 62–64. 9. The last clause is restored from NHC IV,4.

eternal, since it exists eternally,
unutterable, since nothing could comprehend it to utter it,
unnamable, since there is nothing before it to give it a name.

The One is the immeasurable light, pure, holy, immaculate. It is unutterable, and is perfect in incorruptibility. Not that it is just perfection, or blessedness, or divinity: it is much greater.

The One is not corporeal and it is not incorporeal.
The One is not large and it is not small.
It is impossible to say,
How much is it?
What [kind is it]?[10]
For no one can understand it.

The One is not among the things that exist, but it is much greater. Not that it is greater. Rather, as it is in itself, it is not a part of the aeons or time. For whatever is part of a realm was once prepared by another. Time was not allotted to it, since it receives nothing from anyone: what would be received would be on loan. The one who is first does not need to receive anything from another. It beholds itself in [4] its light.
The One is majestic and has an immeasurable purity.

The One is a realm that gives a realm,
life that gives life,
a blessed one that gives blessedness,
knowledge that gives knowledge,[11]
a good one that gives goodness,
mercy that gives mercy and redemption,
grace that gives grace.

Not that the One possesses this. Rather, the One gives immeasurable and incomprehensible light.
What shall I tell you about it? Its eternal realm is incorruptible, at peace, dwelling in silence, at rest, before everything.
It is the head of all realms, and it is the one who sustains them through its goodness.
We would not know [what is ineffable], we would not understand what is immeasurable, were it not for the one who has come from the Father. This is the one who has told these things to us [alone].

---

10. The parallel passages in the shorter version of the *Secret Book of John* in BG 8502, 24 and NHC III,5 and in *Allogenes the Stranger* 63 read "he is not a creature." The differences here may be related to a confusion of the Greek terms *poion*, "what kind," and *poiēton*, "creature." 11. Gnosis.

Barbelo Appears (4,19–6,10)

This Father[12] is the one who beholds himself in the light surrounding him, which is the spring of living water and provides all the realms. He reflects on his image everywhere, sees it in the spring of the Spirit, and becomes enamored of his luminous water, [for his image is in] the spring of pure luminous water surrounding him.[13]

His thought became a reality, and she who appeared in his presence in shining light came forth. She is the first power who preceded everything and came forth from his mind as the Forethought[14] of the All. Her light shines like the Father's[15] light; she, the perfect power, is the image of the Perfect and Invisible Virgin Spirit.[16]

She, [the first] power, the glory of Barbelo,[17] the perfect [5] glory among the aeons, the glory of revelation, she glorified and praised the Virgin Spirit, for because of the Spirit[18] she had come forth.

She is the first Thought, the image of the Spirit. She became the universal womb, for she precedes everything,

> the Mother-Father,[19]
> the first Human,
> the holy Spirit,
> the triple male,[20]
> the triple power,
> the androgynous one with three names,
> the aeon among the invisible beings,
> the first to come forth.

Barbelo asked the Invisible Virgin Spirit to give her Foreknowledge, and the Spirit consented.[21] When the Spirit consented, Foreknowledge appeared and

---

12. Here and elsewhere the word "Father" is used for clarity of translation when the Coptic uses only a personal pronoun. **13.** The Father gazes into the water and falls in love with his own image in a manner that calls to mind Narcissus in Greek mythology (see Ovid *Metamorphoses* 3.402–510). **14.** Pronoia, here and below. **15.** Lit., "his." **16.** Through this love of the Father for his own image the Father's thought (*ennoia*) emanated, and the First Thought or Forethought (*pronoia*) comes from the mind of the Father: the divine Mother, Barbelo. The Father thus produces an entity independently, without the aid of a lover. Other gods who are credited with acts of independent procreation include the Greek god Zeus, who produces Athena, the daughter of Metis (Wisdom or Skill), from his head alongside the River (or Lake) Triton (see Hesiod *Theogony* 886–900, 924–29), and the Egyptian god Atum, who mates with his hand and spits—i.e., he produces the seed of life by means of

masturbation. On Sophia conceiving independently, cf. *Secret Book of John* II, 9–10. **17.** Barbelo is the divine mother and the first emanation of the Father of the All in Sethian texts. She is also described as the Forethought of the Invisible Spirit. The name Barbelo may derive from Hebrew, and a possible translation is "God (cf. *'el*) in (*b-*) four (*arb[a]*)," with reference to the tetragrammaton, the ineffable four-letter name of God. **18.** Lit., "him" or "it," here and below. **19.** The text has *mētropatōr*, probably a term for an androgynous parent. **20.** This is a term of praise, in which maleness symbolizes all that is heavenly, like the divine Father, and maleness is amplified by being so three times over. Similar themes occur in *Gospel of Thomas* 114, the *Holy Book of the Great Invisible Spirit*, the *Three Steles of Seth*, and other texts. **21.** Or, throughout this section, "looked on," "looked on in agreement," or "nodded in agreement." Cf. the *Holy Book of the Great Invisible Spirit*.

stood by Forethought. This is the one who came from the Thought of the Invisible Virgin Spirit.[22] Foreknowledge glorified the Spirit and the Spirit's perfect power, Barbelo, for because of her Foreknowledge had come into being.

She asked again to be given Incorruptibility, and the Spirit consented. When the Spirit consented, Incorruptibility appeared and stood by Thought and Foreknowledge. Incorruptibility glorified the invisible one and Barbelo. Because of her they had come into being.

Barbelo asked to be given Life Eternal, and the Invisible Spirit consented. When the Spirit consented, Life Eternal appeared, and they stood together and glorified the Invisible Spirit and Barbelo. Because of her they had come into being.

She asked again to be given Truth, and the Invisible Spirit consented. Truth appeared, and they stood together and glorified the good Invisible [6] Spirit and its Barbelo. Because of her they had come into being.

These are the five aeons of the Father. They are:

> the first human, the image of the Invisible Spirit, that is,
> Forethought, which is Barbelo, and Thought,[23]
> along with Foreknowledge,
> Incorruptibility,
> Life Eternal
> and Truth.

These are the five androgynous aeons, which are the ten aeons, which is the Father.[24]

Barbelo Conceives (6,10–7,30)

The Father[25] gazed into Barbelo, with the pure light surrounding the Invisible Spirit, and his radiance. Barbelo conceived from him, and he produced a spark of light similar to the blessed light but not as great. This was the only Child of the Mother-Father that had come forth, the only offspring, the only Child of the Father, the pure light.[26] The Invisible Virgin Spirit rejoiced over the light that was produced, that came forth from the first power of the Spirit's Forethought, who is Barbelo. The Spirit anointed it with his own goodness[27] until it was perfect, with no lack of goodness, since it was anointed with the goodness of the

---

22. The one who comes from the Spirit's thought is most likely Forethought, or possibly Foreknowledge. 23. Or "thinking," "mind." 24. The five are *pentas*, the "pentad" or "quintet." It consists of Barbelo and the four spiritual attributes Barbelo requested. Since they are androgynous, they can also be called the ten (*dekas*). The five or the ten are the same as the Father in emanation. 25. Lit., "He." 26. Spiritual intercourse between the Father and Barbelo produces a Child of light. In the longer version of the *Secret Book* of *John*, the Father is considered to be the active procreative force. In the shorter version found in BG 8502 and NHC III, Barbelo is the one who gazes into the Father or the pure light, and then she gives birth. 27. Lit., "He (or It) anointed it with his own goodness." The Coptic reads m^{e}ntkhrs, here and below, from the Greek *khrēstos* ("good") or *khristos* (*christos*, "anointed"). The text apparently maintains that the divine Child is both good and anointed.

Invisible Spirit. The Child stood in the presence of the Spirit as the Spirit anointed the Child.[28] As soon as the Child received this from the Spirit, it glorified the holy Spirit and perfect Forethought. Because of her it had come forth.

The Child asked to be given Mind[29] as a companion to work with, and the Spirit consented. When the Invisible Spirit consented, [7] Mind appeared and stood by the anointed,[30] and glorified the Spirit[31] and Barbelo.

All these beings came into existence in silence.

Mind wished to create something by means of the word of the Invisible Spirit.[32] Its Will became a reality and appeared, with Mind and the light, glorifying it. Word followed Will. For the anointed, the divine Self-Generated,[33] created everything by the Word. Life Eternal, Will, Mind, and Foreknowledge stood together and glorified the Invisible Spirit and Barbelo, for because of her they had come into being.

The holy Spirit brought the divine Self-Generated Child of himself and Barbelo to perfection, so that the Child[34] might stand before the great Invisible Virgin Spirit as the divine Self-Generated, the anointed, who honored the Spirit[35] with loud acclaim. The Child came forth through Forethought. The Invisible Virgin Spirit set the true, divine Self-Generated over everything and caused all authority and the truth within to be subject to it, so that the Child might understand everything, the one called by a name greater than every name, for that name will be told to those who are worthy of it.

The Four Luminaries (7,30–8,28)

Now from the light, which is the anointed, and from Incorruptibility, by the grace of the Spirit, the Four Luminaries that derive from the divine Self-Generated gazed out[36] in order to stand [8] before it. The three beings are:

> will,
>
> thought,
>
> life.

The four powers are:

> understanding,
>
> grace,
>
> perception,
>
> thoughtfulness.

---

28. Lit., "He stood in his presence as he anointed him." 29. Nous, from Greek, here and below (the Coptic meeue is also used). 30. Or "Christ," here and below (pekhrs). 31. Lit., "it" or "him"; possibly "the anointed." 32. Here begins creation by the word, as in Genesis 1 and John 1 as well as the Egyptian creation text, the Memphite cosmogony, in which Ptah is described creating by means of the spoken word. 33. Or "Self-Engendered," "Self-Conceived," "Autogenes," here and below. 34. Lit., "he" or "it," here and below. 35. Or "whom the Spirit honored." 36. Or "appeared" (in BG 8502, 33).

Grace dwells in the eternal realm of the luminary Harmozel, who is the first angel.[37] There are three other aeons with this eternal realm:

> grace,
>
> truth,
>
> form.

The second luminary is Oroiael, who has been appointed over the second eternal realm. There are three other aeons with it:

> Insight,[38]
>
> perception,
>
> memory.

The third luminary is Daveithai, who has been appointed over the third eternal realm. There are three other aeons with it:

> understanding,
>
> love,
>
> idea.

The fourth eternal realm has been set up for the fourth luminary, Eleleth. There are three other aeons with it:

> perfection,
>
> peace,
>
> Sophia.

These are the Four Luminaries that stand before the divine Self-Generated; these are the twelve aeons that stand before the Child of the Great One, the Self-Generated, the anointed, by the will and grace of the Invisible Spirit. The twelve aeons belong to the Child, the Self-Generated, and everything was established by the will of the holy Spirit through the Self-Generated.[39]

---

37. Or "and is the first angel." **38.** Or "Reflection," "Imagination," "Creativity," "Afterthought," "Epinoia." On *pronoia* and *epinoia*, cf., in Greek mythology, the Titans Prometheus ("forethought") and Epimetheus ("afterthought"), who create human beings, though Epimetheus does his job imperfectly. Prometheus makes the humans stand upright, after the manner of the gods, and he takes fire from the gods and brings it down to earth. For his actions he is punished by being chained to a pillar in the mountains, where a bird of prey eats his liver. Eventually Heracles frees him. **39.** Or "before the Child of the great Self-Generated . . . to the Child of the Self-Generated." This could possibly be a reference to Pigeradamas; cf. *Secret Book of John* II, 9.

Pigeradamas and Seth (8,28–9,24)

From the Foreknowledge of the perfect Mind, through the expressed will of the Invisible Spirit and the will of the Self-Generated, came the perfect human, the first revelation, the truth. The Virgin Spirit named the human Pigeradamas,[40] and appointed him to [9] the first eternal realm with the great Self-Generated, the anointed, by the first luminary, Harmozel. Its powers dwell with it. The invisible one gave him an invincible power of mind.

Pigeradamas[41] spoke and glorified and praised the Invisible Spirit by saying,

> Because of you everything has come into being,
> and to you everything will return.
> I shall praise and glorify you,
> the Self-Generated,
> the eternal realms,
> the three, Father, Mother, Child,
> perfect power.

He appointed his son Seth to the second eternal realm, before the second luminary, Oroiael.

In the third eternal realm were stationed the offspring of Seth, with the third luminary, Daveithai. The souls of the saints were stationed there.

In the fourth eternal realm were stationed the souls of those who were ignorant of the Fullness.[42] They did not repent immediately, but held out for a while and repented later. They came to be with the fourth luminary, Eleleth.

These are creatures that glorify the Invisible Spirit.

The Fall of Sophia (9,25–10,19)

Now, Sophia, who is the Wisdom of Insight and who constitutes an aeon,[43] conceived of a thought from herself, with the conception of the Invisible Spirit and Foreknowledge. She wanted to bring forth something like herself, without the consent of the Spirit, who had not given approval, without her partner and without his consideration.[44] The male did not give approval. She did not find her part-

---

40. Or "Geradamas," here and below. Here BG 8502, 35 reads "Adam" and NHC III,13 reads "Adamas." The name Pigeradamas or Geradamas may mean "Adam the stranger" (Hebrew *gēr 'adam*), "holy Adam" (Greek *hier-adamas*), or "old (Greek *gerōn*) Adam." **41.** Lit., "He." **42.** Pleroma, here and below. **43.** Lit., "Sophia of Insight, being an aeon." **44.** Sophia tries to imitate the original procreative act of the Father. This account of Sophia bringing forth by herself seems to reflect ancient gynecological theories about women's bodies and reproduction. In Greek mythology the goddess Hera also imitates Zeus and brings forth a child by herself. According to one version of the myth, the child is the monster Typhon (*Homeric Hymn to Pythian Apollo* 300–362). According to another, it is the lame deity Hephaistos, whom Hera evicts from Olympus and sends down to the world below (Hesiod *Theogony* 924–29). Hephaistos is the artisan among the gods and is represented in Egypt by his counterpart Khnum, a ram-headed creator who molds creatures on a potter's wheel. In the *Secret Book of John* all the evils and misfortunes of this world derive from Sophia's blunder.

ner, and she considered this without the Spirit's consent and without the knowledge of her partner. Nonetheless, she gave birth. [10] And because of the invincible power within her, her thought was not an idle thought. Something came out of her that was imperfect and different in appearance from her, for she had produced it without her partner. It did not resemble its mother and was misshapen.

When Sophia saw what her desire had produced, it changed into the figure of a snake with the face of a lion. Its eyes were like flashing bolts of lightning.[45] She cast it away from her, outside that realm so that none of the immortals would see it. She had produced it ignorantly.

She surrounded it with a bright cloud and put a throne in the middle of the cloud so that no one would see it except the holy Spirit, who is called the Mother of the living. She named her offspring Yaldabaoth.

Yaldabaoth's World Order (10,19–13,13)

This is the first ruler, the archon who took great power from his mother. Then he left her and moved away from the place where he was born. He took control and created for himself other aeons with luminous fire, which still exists. He mated with the mindlessness[46] in him and produced authorities for himself:

The name of the first is Athoth, whom generations call the [reaper].[47]

The second is Harmas, who is the jealous eye.[48]

The third is Kalila-Oumbri.

The fourth is Yabel.

The fifth is Adonaios, who is called Sabaoth.[49]

The sixth is Cain, whom generations of people call the sun.

The seventh is Abel.

The eighth is Abrisene.

The ninth is Yobel. [11]

The tenth is Armoupieel.

The eleventh is Melcheir-Adonein.

The twelfth is Belias, who is over the depth of the underworld.[50]

---

45. On the child of Sophia with his eyes flashing, cf. *Gospel of Judas* 51. **46.** Or "was amazed in the mindlessness." Yaldabaoth's mating with his mindlessness (*aponoia*) probably suggests that he masturbated. **47.** The reading (*p[jaio]h's*) remains tentative. **48.** I.e., the evil eye (*pbal 'mpkōh*). BG 8502, 40 and NHC III,16 read "the eye of fire" (*pbal 'mpkōht*). **49.** Adonaios is also mentioned in the *Holy Book of the Great Invisible Spirit*, the *Second Discourse of Great Seth*, and the *Gospel of Judas*. On the first part of this list of names, cf. *Gospel of Judas* 52. **50.** The twelve cosmic authorities probably correspond to the signs of the zodiac. On this list of names, cf. *Holy Book of the Great Invisible Spirit* III, 58.

Yaldabaoth[51] stationed seven kings, one for each sphere of heaven, to reign over the seven heavens, and five to reign over the depth of the abyss.[52] He shared his fire with them, but he did not give away any of the power of the light he had taken from his mother. For he is ignorant darkness.

When light mixed with darkness, it made the darkness shine. When darkness mixed with light, it dimmed the light, and it became neither light nor darkness, but rather gloom.

This gloomy archon has three names: the first name is Yaldabaoth, the second is Sakla, the third is Samael.[53]

He is wicked in the mindlessness within him. He said, "I am God and there is no other god beside me,"[54] since he did not know from where his own strength had come.

The rulers each created seven powers for themselves, and the powers each created six angels, until there were 365 angels.[55] These are the names and the corresponding physiques:

The first is Athoth, and has the face of a sheep.

The second is Eloaios, and has the face of a donkey.

The third is Astaphaios, and has the face of a hyena.

The fourth is Yao,[56] and has the face of a snake with seven heads.

The fifth is Sabaoth, and has the face of a snake.

The sixth is Adonin, and has the face of an ape.

The seventh is Sabbataios,[57] and has a face of flaming fire.

This is the sevenfold nature of the week.[58]

Yaldabaoth has many [12] faces, more than all of these, so that he could show whatever face he wanted when he was among the seraphim.[59] He shared his fire with them, and lorded it over them because of the glorious power he had from his mother's light. That is why he called himself God and defied the place from which he came.

In his thought he united the seven powers with the authorities that were with him. When he spoke, it was done. He named each of the powers, beginning with the highest:

---

51. Lit., "He." 52. The seven kings probably correspond to the seven planetary spheres (for the sun, the moon, Mercury, Venus, Mars, Jupiter, and Saturn) described by ancient astronomers. 53. In Aramaic Yaldabaoth probably means "child of chaos" or "child of (S)abaoth," Sakla means "fool," and Samael means "blind god." Here and elsewhere in the text the first two names are spelled "Yaltabaoth" and "Saklas." 54. Isaiah 45:5–6, 21; 46:9. 55. The number of angels corresponds to the days in the solar year. 56. Yao (Iaō) is a form of Yahweh, the name of God, especially in Greek. Yao is a power of this world in some Gnostic texts and a son of Yaldabaoth in On the Origin of the World. In this section several of the names derive from Hebrew words, especially words that designate God. 57. Here the name is spelled "Sabbede." Other versions give the name as Sabbataios or Sabbadaios. Throughout the text the spelling of the names varies in the manuscripts, but only a few of the variant spellings are given here. 58. The seven powers correspond to the days of the week. 59. The seraphim are a class of angels, here angels of Yaldabaoth.

First is goodness, with the first power, Athoth.

Second is forethought, with the second power, Eloaios.[60]

Third is divinity, with the third power, Astaphaios.[61]

Fourth is lordship, with the fourth power, Yao.

Fifth is kingdom, with the fifth power, Sabaoth.[62]

Sixth is jealousy, with the sixth power, Adonin.

Seventh is understanding, with the seventh power, Sabbataios.[63]

Each has a sphere in its own realm.

They were named after the glory above for the destruction of the powers. Although the names given them by their maker were powerful, the names given them after the glory above would bring about their destruction and loss of power. That is why they have two names.

Yaldabaoth[64] organized everything after the pattern of the first aeons that had come into being, so that he might [13] create everything in an incorruptible form. Not that he had seen the incorruptible ones. Rather, the power that is in him, that he had taken from his mother, produced in him the pattern for the world order.

When he saw creation surrounding him, and the throng of angels around him that had come forth from him, he said to them, "I am a jealous god and there is no other god beside me."[65]

But by announcing this, he suggested to the angels with him that there is another god. For if there were no other god, of whom would he be jealous?

Sophia Repents (13,13–14,13)

Then the Mother began to move around. She realized that she was lacking something when the brightness of her light diminished. She grew dim because her partner had not collaborated with her.

I[66] said, "Lord, what does it mean that she moved around?"

The Lord laughed[67] and said, Do not suppose that it is as Moses said, above the waters.[68] No, when she recognized the wickedness that had taken place and the robbery her son had committed, she repented. When she became forgetful in the darkness of ignorance, she began to be ashamed. She did not dare to return, but she was agitated.[69] This agitation is the moving around.

The arrogant one took power from his mother. He was ignorant, for he thought no one existed except his mother alone. When he saw the throng of angels he had created, he exalted himself over them.

---

60. Here the name is spelled "Eloaio." Another version gives the name as Eloaios. 61. Here the name is spelled "Astraphaio." Another version gives the name as Astaphaios. 62. Here the name is spelled "Sanboth." Other versions give the name as Sabaoth. 63. Here the name is spelled "Sabbateon." Another version gives the name as Sabbataios. 64. Lit., "He." 65. Isaiah 45:5–6, 21; 46:9. 66. John. 67. On the laughter of Jesus, cf., e.g., the *Gospel of Judas*. 68. Genesis 1:2. 69. This sentence is restored from NHC IV,21.

When the Mother realized that the trappings[70] of darkness had come into being imperfectly, she understood that her partner had not collaborated with her. She repented [14] with many tears. The whole realm of Fullness heard her prayer of repentance and offered praise on her behalf to the Invisible Virgin Spirit, and the Spirit consented. When the Invisible Spirit consented,[71] the holy Spirit poured upon her some of the fullness of all. For her partner did not come to her on his own, but he came to her through the realm of Fullness, so that he might restore what she lacked. She was taken up not to her own eternal realm, but instead to a position above her son. She was to remain in the ninth heaven until she restored what was lacking in herself.[72]

The Human Appears (14,13–34)

A voice called from the exalted heavenly realm,

> Humanity[73] exists
> and the Child of Humanity.[74]

The first ruler, Yaldabaoth, heard the voice and thought it had come from his mother. He did not realize its source.

> The holy perfect Mother-Father,
> the complete Forethought,
> the image of the invisible one,
> being the Father of the All,
> through whom everything came into being,
> the first human—

this is the one who showed them and appeared in human shape.[75]

The entire realm of the first ruler quaked, and the foundations of the abyss shook. The bottom side of the waters above the material world was lit up by this image that had appeared. When all the authorities and the first ruler stared at this appearance, they saw the whole bottom side as it was lit up. And through the light they saw the shape of the image in the water.[76] [15]

---

70. Coptic *thbsō ᵉmpkake*; BG 8502, 46 reads "aborted fetus of darkness" (*phouhe mpkake*), with reference to Yaldabaoth. 71. This clause is restored from NHC IV,22. 72. Sophia dwells in the ninth sphere, above Yaldabaoth, who occupies the eighth sphere (sometimes called the Ogdoad and identified as the sphere of the fixed stars). Yaldabaoth himself is thus positioned over the seven kings in their seven spheres (sometimes called the Hebdomad; see above). See also the *Discourse on the Eighth and Ninth* and other Gnostic texts. 73. Or "Man." 74. Or "Son of Man," here and below. 75. In the longer version of the *Secret Book of John*, the figure that appears seems to be that of Forethought; in the shorter version it is that of the Father or first human Pigeradamas. 76. Yaldabaoth and his authorities look at the waters above the earth, and from underneath they see the reflection of a human shape in the water.

The Creation of Adam (15,1–19,10)

Yaldabaoth[77] said to the authorities with him, "Come, let's create a human being after the image of God and with a likeness to ourselves, so that this human image may give us light."[78]

They created through their respective powers, according to the features that were given. Each of the authorities contributed a psychical feature corresponding to the figure of the image they had seen. They created a being like the perfect first human, and said, "Let's call it Adam, that its name may give us power of light."[79]

The powers began to create:

> The first one, goodness, created a soul of bone.
>
> The second, forethought, created a soul of sinew.
>
> The third, divinity, created a soul of flesh.
>
> The fourth, lordship, created a soul of marrow.
>
> The fifth, kingdom, created a soul of blood.
>
> The sixth, jealousy, created a soul of skin.
>
> The seventh, understanding, created a soul of hair.

The throng of angels stood by and received these seven psychical substances from the authorities,[80] in order to create a network of limbs and trunk, with all the parts properly arranged.

> The first one, who is Raphao, began by creating the head,
>
> Abron created the skull,[81]
>
> Meniggesstroeth created the brain,
>
> Asterechme the right eye,
>
> Thaspomocha the left eye,
>
> Yeronumos the right ear,
>
> Bissoum the left ear,
>
> Akioreim the nose, [16]
>
> Banen-Ephroum the lips,
>
> Amen the teeth,
>
> Ibikan the molars,

---

77. Lit., "He." 78. *Genesis* 1:26. In the *Secret Book of John* a distinction is made between the image of God and the likeness of the creators. 79. Yaldabaoth and his authorities create a psychical man with a psychical body, i.e., they create a soul-man, his body composed entirely of the animating soul. His physical body of flesh and blood will be constructed later. 80. Or "and these seven psychical substances were taken by the authorities." 81. Or "The first one began by creating the head, Eteraphaope-Abron created the skull."

Basiliademe the tonsils,

Achcha the uvula,

Adaban the neck,

Chaaman the vertebrae,

Dearcho the throat,

Tebar the right shoulder,

N. . . the left shoulder,

Mniarchon the right elbow,

. . .e the left elbow,[82]

Abitrion the right underarm,

Euanthen the left underarm,

Krus the right hand,

Beluai the left hand,

Treneu the fingers of the right hand,

Balbel the fingers of the left hand,

Krima the fingernails,

Astrops the right breast,

Barroph the left breast,

Baoum the right shoulder joint,

Ararim the left shoulder joint,

Areche the belly,

Phthaue the navel,

Senaphim the abdomen,

Arachethopi the right ribs,

Zabedo the left ribs,

Barias the right hip,

Phnouth the left hip,[83]

Abenlenarchei the marrow,

Chnoumeninorin the bones,

Gesole the stomach,

Agromauma the heart,

Bano the lungs,

Sostrapal the liver,

---

82. These words are restored from NHC IV,25.
83. These words are restored from NHC IV,25.

Anesimalar the spleen,

Thopithro the intestines,

Biblo the kidneys,

Roeror the sinews,

Taphreo the backbone,

Ipouspoboba the veins,

Bineborin the arteries,

Aatoimenpsephei the breaths in all the limbs,

Entholleia all the flesh,

Bedouk the right buttock,

Arabeei the left [buttock],[84]

   . . . the penis,

Eilo the testicles,

Sorma the genitals,

Gormakaiochlabar the right thigh,

Nebrith the left thigh,

Pserem the muscles of the right leg,

Asaklas the muscle of the left,

Ormaoth the right leg,

Emenun the left leg,

Knux the [17] right shin,

Tupelon the left shin,

Achiel the right ankle,

Phneme the left ankle,

Phiouthrom the right foot,

Boabel its toes,

Trachoun the left foot,

Phikna its toes,

Miamai the toenails,

Labernioum . . .

Those who are appointed over all these are seven in number:

Athoth,

Armas,

---

84. The translation is tentative.

Kalila,
Yabel,
Sabaoth,
Cain,
Abel.[85]

Those who activate the limbs are, part by part:

the head, Diolimodraza,
the neck, Yammeax,
the right shoulder, Yakouib,
the left shoulder, Ouerton,
the right hand, Oudidi,
the left one, Arbao,
the fingers of the right hand, Lampno,
the fingers of the left hand, Leekaphar,
the right breast, Barbar,
the left breast, Imae,
the chest, Pisandraptes,
the right shoulder joint, Koade,
the left shoulder joint, Odeor,
the right ribs, Asphixix,
the left ribs, Sunogchouta,
the abdomen, Arouph,
the womb, Sabalo,
the right thigh, Charcharb,
the left thigh, Chthaon,
all the genitals, Bathinoth,
the right leg, Choux,
the left leg, Charcha,
the right shin, Aroer,
the left shin, Toechtha,
the right ankle, Aol,
the left ankle, Charaner,

---

85. The last three names are restored from NHC
IV,26.

the right foot, Bastan,
its toes, Archentechtha,
the left foot, Marephnounth,
its toes, Abrana.

Seven have been empowered over all these:

Michael,
Uriel,
Asmenedas,
Saphasatoel,
Aarmouriam,
Richram,
Amiorps.

Those who are over the senses are Archendekta,
the one who is over perception is Deitharbathas,
the one who is over imagination is Oummaa,
the one who is over arrangement [18] is Aachiaram,
the one who is over all impulse to action is Riaramnacho.

The source of the demons that are in the entire body is divided into four:

heat,
cold,
wetness,
dryness,

and the mother of them all is matter.

The one who is lord over heat is Phloxopha,
the one who is lord over cold is Oroorrothos,
the one who is lord over what is dry is Erimacho,
the one who is lord over wetness is Athuro.

The mother of all these, Onorthochras, stands in the midst of them, for she
is unlimited and mingles with them all. She is matter, and by her they are
nourished.
The four principal demons are:

> Ephememphi, the demon of pleasure,
> Yoko, the demon of desire,
> Nenentophni, the demon of grief,
> Blaomen, the demon of fear.

The mother of them all is Esthesis-Ouch-Epi-Ptoe.[86]
  From the four demons have come passions:

> From grief come jealousy, envy, pain, trouble, distress, hardheartedness, anxiety, sorrow, and others.
>
> From pleasure comes an abundance of evil, vain conceit, and the like.
>
> From desire come anger, wrath, bitterness, intense lust, greed, and the like.
>
> From fear come terror, servility, anguish, and shame.

All these are like virtues and vices. The insight into their true nature is Anaro, who is head of the material soul, [19] and it dwells with Esthesis-Z-Ouch-Epi-Ptoe.[87]

This is the number of angels. In all they number 365.[88] They all worked together until, limb by limb, the psychical and material body was completed. Now, there are others over the remaining passions, and I have not told you about them. If you want to know about them, the information is recorded in the *Book of Zoroaster*.[89]

Adam Receives Spirit and Life (19,10–20,28)

All the angels and demons worked together until they fashioned the psychical body. But for a long time their creation did not stir or move at all.

When the Mother wanted to take back the power she had relinquished to the first ruler, she prayed to the most merciful Mother-Father of the All. With a sacred command the Mother-Father[90] sent five luminaries down upon the place of the angels of the first ruler. They advised him so that they might recover the mother's power.

They said to Yaldabaoth, "Breathe some of your spirit into the face of Adam, and the body will arise."

---

86. "Sense perception is not in an excited state" (from Greek, *aisthēsis ouch epi ptoē*), a philosophical saying (see Bentley Layton, *The Gnostic Scriptures*, 43). 87. "The seven senses are (or sense perception is) not in an excited state" (again from Greek), another version of the philosophical saying (Bentley Layton). 88. The angels assembling the psychical body parts correspond to the days in the solar year, as above. 89. The precise identification of the *Book of Zoroaster* remains uncertain, but the title calls to mind the text *Zostrianos* or else Porphyry's *Life of Plotinos* 16, where Porphyry refers to other texts written under the name of Zoroaster, including a *Book of Zoroaster*. 90. Lit., "he" or "it."

He breathed his spirit into Adam.[91] The spirit is the power of his mother, but he did not realize this, because he lives in ignorance. The Mother's power went out of Yaldabaoth and into the psychical body that had been made to be like the one who is from the beginning.

The body moved and became powerful. And it was enlightened.

At once the rest of [20] the powers became jealous. Although Adam came into being through all of them, and they gave their power to this human, Adam was more intelligent than the creators and the first ruler. When they realized that Adam was enlightened and could think more clearly than they and was stripped of evil,[92] they took and threw Adam into the lowest part of the whole material realm.

The blessed, benevolent, merciful Mother-Father had compassion for the Mother's power that had been removed from the first ruler. The archons might be able to overpower the psychical, perceptible body once again. So with its benevolent and most merciful Spirit, the Mother-Father sent a helper to Adam—enlightened Insight, who is from the Mother-Father and who was called Life.[93] She helped the whole creature, laboring with it, restoring it to its fullness, teaching it about the descent of the seed,[94] teaching it about the way of ascent, which is the way of descent.[95]

Enlightened Insight was hidden within Adam so that the archons might not recognize her, but that Insight might be able to restore what the Mother lacked.

The Imprisonment of Humanity (20,28–22,28)

The human being Adam was revealed through the bright shadow within. And Adam's ability to think was greater than that of all the creators. When they looked up, they saw that Adam's ability to think was greater, and they devised a plan with the whole throng of archons and angels. They took fire, earth, [21] and water, and combined them with the four fiery winds.[96] They wrought them together and made a great commotion.[97]

The rulers brought Adam into the shadow of death so that they might produce a figure again, from earth, water, fire, and the spirit that comes from matter[98]—that is, from the ignorance of darkness, and desire, and their own phony spirit. This figure is the cave for remodeling the body that these criminals put on the human, the fetter of forgetfulness.[99] Adam became a mortal person, the first to descend and the first to become estranged.

Enlightened Insight within Adam, however, was rejuvenating Adam's mind.

---

91. *Genesis* 2:7. Here and below the name Adam is given in the translation in place of the masculine pronouns, since the text maintains that Adam is androgynous. 92. Perhaps parallel to *Genesis* 2:25. 93. Zoe. Cf. *Genesis* 3:20: Eve is named Zoe in the Septuagint. 94. Or "offspring." 95. Cf. *Three Steles of Seth* 127. 96. Here fiery winds replace air as the fourth element.

97. The scene recalls a workshop in which a statue or a fetter is being forged. 98. Here material spirit replaces air as the fourth element. 99. The description of a human being and a shadow in a cave may derive from the allegory of the cave in Plato's *Republic*, Book 7. Further, the body as the prison or tomb of the soul is also a well-known Platonic and Orphic teaching.

The archons took Adam and put Adam in paradise. They said, "Eat," meaning, Do so in a leisurely manner.[100] But in fact their pleasure is bitter and their beauty is perverse. Their pleasure is a trap, their trees are a sacrilege, their fruit is deadly poison, and their promise is death.

They put their tree of life in the middle of paradise.[101]

I[102] shall teach you what the secret of their life is—the plan they devised together, the nature of their spirit. The root of their tree is bitter, its branches are death, its shadow is hatred, a trap is in its leaves, its blossom is bad ointment, its fruit is death, desire is its seed, and it blossoms in darkness. The dwelling place of those who taste [22] of it is the underworld, and darkness is their resting place.

But the archons lingered in front of what they call the tree of the knowledge of good and evil, which is enlightened Insight,[103] so that Adam might not behold its fullness[104] and recognize his shameful nakedness.

But I[105] was the one who induced them to eat.

I[106] said to the Savior, "Lord, was it not the serpent that instructed Adam to eat?"

The Savior laughed and said, The serpent instructed them to eat of the wickedness of sexual desire and destruction so that Adam might be of use to the serpent.

The first ruler[107] knew Adam was disobedient to him because of enlightened Insight within Adam, which made Adam stronger of mind than he. He wanted to recover the power that he himself had passed on to Adam. So he brought deep sleep upon Adam.

I said to the Savior, "What is this deep sleep?"

The Savior said, It is not as Moses wrote and you heard. He said in his first book,[108] "He put Adam to sleep."[109] Rather, this deep sleep was a loss of sense. Thus the first ruler said through the prophet, "I shall make their minds sluggish, that they may neither understand nor discern."[110]

The Creation of Eve (22,28–23,35)

Enlightened Insight hid herself within Adam. The first ruler wanted to take her from Adam's side, but enlightened Insight cannot be apprehended. Although darkness pursued her, it did not apprehend her. The first ruler removed part of Adam's power and created another figure in the form of a female, like the image of Insight that had appeared to him. He put [23] the part he had taken from the power of the human being into the female creature. It did not happen, however, the way Moses said: "Adam's rib."[111]

---

100. *Genesis* 2:16–17. 101. Lit., "the tree of their life" (in NHC II). 102. The Savior, here Jesus. 103. Insight assumes the form of a tree, just as in Greek mythology Daphne changes into a laurel tree (see Ovid *Metamorphoses* 1.452–562; *Nature of the Rulers* 89; *On the Origin of the World* 116–17). Like Daphne, Insight is not to be apprehended. 104. Or "his fullness." 105. The Savior, here Jesus. 106. John. 107. Lit., "He" or "It." This probably refers to the first ruler, possibly the serpent. 108. Moses's first book is thought to be *Genesis*. 109. *Genesis* 2:21. 110. *Isaiah* 6:10. 111. *Genesis* 2:21–22.

Adam saw the woman beside him. At once enlightened Insight appeared and removed the veil that covered his mind. He sobered up from the drunkenness of darkness. He recognized his counterpart and said, "This is now bone from my bones and flesh from my flesh."[112]

For this reason a man will leave his father and his mother and will join himself to his wife, and the two of them will become one flesh. For his partner will be sent to him, and he will leave his father and his mother.[113]

Our sister Sophia is the one who descended in an innocent manner to restore what she lacked. For this reason she was called Life[114]—that is, the Mother of the living—by the Forethought of the sovereignty of heaven and by [the Insight that appeared] to Adam.[115] Through her have the living tasted perfect knowledge.[116]

As for me, I appeared in the form of an eagle[117] upon the tree of knowledge, which is the Insight of the pure enlightened Forethought, that I might teach the human beings and awaken them from the depth of sleep. For the two of them were fallen and realized that they were naked.[118] Insight appeared to them as light and awakened their minds.

Yaldabaoth Defiles Eve (23,35–25,16)

When Yaldabaoth realized that the humans had withdrawn from him, he cursed his earth. He found the woman as she was [24] preparing herself for her husband. He was master over her. And he did not know the mystery that had come into being through the sacred plan. The two of them were afraid to denounce Yaldabaoth. He displayed to his angels the ignorance within him, and he threw the humans out of paradise and cloaked them in thick darkness.[119]

The first ruler saw the young woman standing next to Adam and noticed that enlightened Insight of Life had appeared in her. Yet Yaldabaoth was full of ignorance. So when the Forethought of the All realized this, she dispatched emissaries, and they stole Life[120] out of Eve.

The first ruler defiled Eve and produced in her two sons, a first and a second: Elohim and Yahweh.[121]

> Elohim has the face of a bear,
> Yahweh has the face of a cat.
> One is just, the other is unjust.
> He placed Yahweh over fire and wind,
> he placed Elohim over water and earth.

---

112. *Genesis* 2:23. 113. *Genesis* 2:24. The manuscript includes an instance of dittography here. 114. Zoe, *Genesis* 3:20. 115. This clause is restored from NHC IV,36. 116. Gnosis. 117. The Savior appears as a heavenly bird; the eagle is the bird of Zeus. Cf. the *Hymn of the Pearl*, in which the royal letter flies as an eagle and becomes a voice of revelation. 118. *Genesis* 3:7, 10–11. 119. *Genesis* 3:22–24. 120. Zoe. 121. *Eloim* and *Yawe*, two names of God in the Hebrew scriptures. Elohim is a word that means God (though plural in form and ending); Yahweh is the name of God (based on the tetragrammaton, the ineffable four-letter name).

He called them by the names Cain and Abel,
with a view to deceive.[122]

To this day sexual intercourse has persisted because of the first ruler. He planted sexual desire within the woman who belongs to Adam. Through intercourse the first ruler produced duplicate bodies, and he blew some of his false spirit into them.

He placed these two rulers[123] over the elements so that they might rule over the cave.[124]

When Adam came to know the counterpart of his own foreknowledge, he produced a son like [25] the child of humanity. He called him Seth, after the manner of the generation in the eternal realms.[125] Similarly, the mother sent down her spirit, which is like her and is a copy of what is in the realm of Fullness, for she was going to prepare a dwelling place for the eternal realms that would come down.

The human beings were made to drink water of forgetfulness[126] by the first ruler, so that they might not know where they had come from. For a time the seed remained and helped so that when the spirit descends from the holy realms, it may raise up the seed and heal what it lacks, that the entire realm of Fullness may be holy and lack nothing.

On Human Destiny (25,16–30,11)

I said to the Savior, "Lord, will all the souls then be led safely into pure light?"

He answered and said to me, These are great matters that have arisen in your mind, and it is difficult to explain them to anyone except those of the unshakable generation.

Those upon whom the spirit of life will descend and whom the spirit will empower will be saved, and will become perfect and worthy of greatness, and will be cleansed there of all evil and the anxieties of wickedness, since they are no longer anxious for anything except the incorruptible alone, and concerned with that from this moment on, without anger, jealousy, envy, desire, or greed for anything.

They are affected by nothing but being in the flesh alone, and they wear the flesh as they look forward to a time when they will be met [26] by those who receive them. Such people are worthy of the incorruptible, eternal life and calling. They endure everything and bear everything so as to finish the contest[127] and receive eternal life.

I said to him, "Lord, will the souls of people be [rejected][128] who have

122. Genesis 4:1–2. 123. I.e., Elohim and Yahweh. 124. Or "the tomb" (as above). 125. Genesis 4:25; 5:3. 126. The water of forgetfulness recalls the water of the River Lethe in the Greek conception of the underworld. If a thirsty soul drinks of the water of this river, it forgets about its previous lives and thus may be reincarnated in another body. 127. The text reads pathlon in all the manuscripts except Codex II, which reads, apparently erroneously, "what is good" (pagathon). 128. Here the text reads senašo[one], restored from NHC IV,40; BG 8502, 66 and NHC III,34 read "be saved" (senaoujai).

not done these things, but upon whom the power and the spirit of life have descended?"

He answered and said to me, If the spirit descends upon them,[129] by all means they will be saved and transformed. Power will descend upon every person, for without it no one could stand.[130] After birth, if the spirit of life grows and power comes and strengthens that soul, no one will be able to lead it astray with evil actions. But people upon whom the false spirit descends are misled by it and go astray.

I said, "Lord, where will their souls go when they leave their flesh?"

He laughed and said to me, The soul in which there is more power than the contemptible spirit is strong. She escapes from evil, and through the intervention of the incorruptible one, she is saved and is taken up to eternal rest.[131]

I said, "Lord, where will the souls go of people who have not known to whom they belong?"

He said to me, The contemptible spirit has [27] grown stronger in such people while they were going astray. This spirit lays a heavy burden on the soul, leads her into evil deeds, and hurls her down into forgetfulness. After the soul leaves the body, she is handed over to the authorities who have come into being through the archon. They bind her with chains and throw her into prison.[132] They go around with her until she awakens from forgetfulness and acquires knowledge. This is how she attains perfection and is saved.

I said, "Lord, how can the soul become younger and return into its mother's womb,[133] or into the human?"

He was glad when I asked him about this, and he said to me, You are truly blessed, for you have understood. This soul will be made to follow another soul in whom the spirit of life dwells, and she is saved through that one. Then she will not be thrust into flesh again.

I said, "Lord, where will the souls go of people who had knowledge but turned away?"

He said to me, They will be taken to the place where the angels of misery go, where there is no repentance. They will be kept there until the day when those who have blasphemed against the spirit will be tortured and punished eternally.

I said, "Lord, where did the contemptible spirit come from?"

He said to me, The Mother-Father is great in mercy, the holy Spirit, who in every way is compassionate, [28] who sympathizes with you, the Insight of enlightened Forethought. This one raised up the offspring of the perfect generation and their thought and the eternal light of the human. When the first ruler

---

129. These clauses are restored from NHC IV,40.
130. This description of every person is like that of Adam moving and standing after receiving spirit from Yaldabaoth in Secret Book of John II, 19. 131. Feminine pronouns are used for the soul in the translation of this part of the Secret Book of John, since the soul (*psukhē*) is commonly depicted as being female in Greek and Gnostic literature. 132. The soul is thrown into another body and thus is reincarnated. 133. Lit., "nature," Coptic *phusis*, from Greek. Returning to the mother's womb is also a theme encountered in John 3:4.

realized that these people were exalted above him and could think better than he, he wanted to grasp their thought. He did not know that they surpassed him in thought and that he would be unable to grasp them.

He devised a plan with his authorities, who are his powers. Together they fornicated with Sophia, and through them was produced bitter fate,[134] the final, fickle bondage. Fate is like this because the powers are fickle. To the present day fate is tougher and stronger than what gods, angels, demons, and all the generations have encountered. For from fate have come all iniquity and injustice and blasphemy, the bondage of forgetfulness, and ignorance, and all burdensome orders, weighty sins, and great fears.

Thus all of creation has been blinded so that none might know the God that is over them all. Because of the bondage of forgetfulness, their sins have been hidden. They have been bound with dimensions, times, and seasons, and fate is master of all.

The first ruler regretted everything that had happened through him. Once again he made a plan, to bring a flood [29] upon the human creation.[135] The enlightened majesty of Forethought, however, warned Noah. Noah announced this to all the offspring, the human children, but those who were strangers to him did not listen to him. It did not happen the way Moses said, "They hid in an ark."[136] Rather, they hid in a particular place, not only Noah, but also many other people from the unshakable generation. They entered that place and hid in a bright cloud. Noah knew about his supremacy. With him was the enlightened one who had enlightened them, since the first ruler had brought darkness upon the whole earth.

The first ruler plotted with his powers. He sent his angels to the human daughters so they might take some of them and raise offspring for their pleasure.[137] At first they were unsuccessful. When they had proven unsuccessful, they met again and devised another plan. They created a contemptible spirit similar to the spirit that had descended, in order to adulterate souls through this spirit. The angels changed their appearance to look like the partners of these women, and filled the women with the spirit of darkness that they had concocted, and with evil.

They brought gold, silver, gifts, copper, iron, metal, and all sorts of things. They brought great anxieties to the people who followed them, [30] leading them astray with many deceptions. These people grew old without experiencing pleasure and died without finding truth or knowing the God of truth. In this way all creation was forever enslaved, from the beginning of the world until the present day.

The angels took women, and from the darkness they produced children similar to their spirit. They closed their minds and became stubborn through the stubbornness of the contemptible spirit until the present day.

---

134. In the Greco-Roman world fate (in Greek, *heimarmenē*, as here, in Coptic, *šimarmenē*) was considered to be the overwhelming force that determines the destiny of all that is earthly and heavenly. 135. Cf. *Genesis* 6:5–8:22. 136. *Genesis* 7:7. 137. Cf. *Genesis* 6:1–4; 1 *Enoch* 6–11.

Hymn of the Savior (30,11–31,25)

Now I, the perfect Forethought of the All, transformed myself into my offspring. I existed first and went down every path.[138]

I am the abundance of light,
I am the remembrance of Fullness.

I traveled in the realm of great darkness, and continued until I entered the midst of the prison. The foundations of chaos shook, and I hid from them because of their evil, and they did not recognize me.

Again I returned, a second time, and went on. I had come from the inhabitants of light—I, the remembrance of Forethought.

I entered the midst of darkness and the bowels of the underworld, turning to my task. The foundations of chaos shook as though to fall upon those who dwell in chaos and destroy them. Again I hurried back to the root of my light so they might not be destroyed before their time.

Again, a third time, I went forth—

I am the light dwelling in light,
I am the remembrance of Forethought—

so that I might enter the midst of darkness and the bowels [31] of the underworld. I brightened my face with light from the consummation of their realm and entered the midst of their prison, which is the prison of the body.

I said, Let whoever hears arise from deep sleep.[139]

A person wept and shed tears. Bitter tears the person wiped away, and said, "Who is calling my name? From where has my hope come as I dwell in the bondage of prison?"

I said,

I am the Forethought of pure light,
I am the thought of the Virgin Spirit, who raises you to a place of honor.
Arise, remember that you have heard
and trace your root,
which is I, the compassionate.
Guard yourself against the angels of misery,
the demons of chaos, and all who entrap you,

---

138. The concluding hymn of the Savior is found only in the longer version of the *Secret Book of John* (NHC II and IV). It reflects a hymn of heavenly Forethought, the divine Mother, as Savior. In the present Christianized version of the *Secret Book of John* read-ers may understand the Savior to be Jesus. Three descents of the Savior are also described in *Three Forms of First Thought*. 139. The call to awaken addresses a prototypal sleeper—any person who may awaken to knowledge and salvation.

and beware of deep sleep
and the trap[140] in the bowels of the underworld.

I raised and sealed the person in luminous water with Five Seals, that death might not prevail over the person from that moment on.

Conclusion (31,25–32,10)

Look, now I shall ascend to the perfect realm. I have finished everything for you in your hearing. I have told you everything for you to record and communicate secretly to your spiritual friends. This is the mystery of the unshakable generation.

The Savior communicated this to John for him to record and safeguard. He said to him, "Cursed be anyone who will trade these things for a gift, for food, drink, clothes, or anything [32] like this."

These things were communicated to him in a mystery, and at once the Savior[141] disappeared. Then John[142] went to the other disciples and reported what the Savior had told him.

Jesus Christ
Amen[143]

The Secret Book According to John

---

140. Or "enclosure," even "garment." 141. Lit., "he."
142. Lit., "he." 143. The shorter versions of the Se-   cret Book of John in BG 8502 and NHC III do not include this overtly Christian concluding statement.

THE GOSPEL OF THOMAS
WITH THE GREEK
GOSPEL OF THOMAS

NHC II,2; P. Oxy. 1, 654, 655; Hippolytus,
Refutation of All Heresies

Introduced and Translated by Marvin Meyer

The *Gospel of Thomas* is a collection of sayings of Jesus, numbered by scholars at 114 sayings, that are said to communicate salvation and life. In contrast to the New Testament gospels, which focus upon the crucifixion and resurrection as they set forth a gospel of the cross, the *Gospel of Thomas* presents a figure of Jesus who does not die for anyone's sins on the cross and does not rise from the dead on the third day. Rather, in the tradition of Jewish teachers of wisdom, the Jesus of the *Gospel of Thomas* utters wise sayings, one after another, and through these sayings the *Gospel of Thomas* proclaims a gospel of wisdom. The wise sayings of the *Gospel of Thomas* may be considered "sayings of the sages" (*logoi sophōn*) on account of their wisdom orientation,[1] or they may be likened to the "useful sayings" (*chreiai*) attributed appropriately to a specific speaker in Greco-Roman rhetorical discussions.[2] Further, although the *Gospel of Thomas* has some features in common with Gnostic texts, it is not easily classified as a Gnostic work without considerable qualification. The *Gospel of Thomas* receives its title from the titular subscript, and according to its incipit or Prologue the text consists of "the hidden (or secret) sayings (Coptic *ᵉnšaje ethēp*, Greek *hoi logoi hoi [apokruphoi]*) that the living Jesus spoke and Judas Thomas the Twin recorded." Judas Thomas was thought in some circles, particularly within Syriac Christianity, to be the twin brother of Jesus and as such the perfect person to function as guarantor of sayings of Jesus. Hence, the *Gospel of Thomas* may most appropriately be considered a sayings gospel with an incipient Gnostic perspective.

---

1. Cf. James M. Robinson, "LOGOI SOPHON: On the Gattung of Q."

2. Cf. Marvin Meyer, *The Gospel of Thomas*, 4–5; Ronald F. Hock and Edward N. O'Neil, *The Chreia in Ancient Rhetoric*.

The sayings in the *Gospel of Thomas* include a variety of aphorisms, parables, stories, and other utterances ascribed to Jesus, the interpretation of which, saying 1 announces, can lead to salvation and life. Saying 1 states, "Whoever discovers the interpretation (*hermēneia*) of these sayings will not taste death." There is hardly any narrative in the *Gospel of Thomas*, and the gospel does not tell a story of the life of Jesus. Rather, *Thomas*'s Jesus is a teacher of wisdom, and the value of Jesus lies in what he has to say and how his sayings lead to wisdom and understanding. In saying 2 Jesus describes the epistemological process whereby one comes to insight and knowledge—and the kingdom or reign of God: "Let one who seeks not stop seeking until one finds. When one finds, one will be troubled. When one is troubled, one will marvel and will reign over all." The Greek *Gospel of Thomas* adds an additional stage to the interpretive process: "and [having reigned], one will [rest]." In other words, the quest for an understanding of the sayings of Jesus is a worthy enterprise to be undertaken with commitment, and although the way to knowledge may be difficult and even disturbing, those who persevere will discover God's reign and God's rest.

As in Q and the New Testament gospels, especially the synoptic Gospels, Matthew, Mark, and Luke, Jesus in the *Gospel of Thomas* asks his disciples to seek and find. In the *Gospel of Thomas*, the sayings of Jesus are open to interpretation, so that disciples and readers are encouraged to search for the meaning of the sayings of Jesus and complete his thoughts after him. The *Gospel of Thomas* is an interactive gospel, and wisdom and knowledge come when readers creatively encounter sayings of Jesus and respond to the sayings in an insightful manner. A number of the sayings in the *Gospel of Thomas* are especially cryptic and riddlelike, and the need for creative interpretation is obvious. Much is at stake. Those who find the meaning of Jesus's sayings find life, the *Gospel of Thomas* proclaims, and they come to realize that they are children of the living Father. Or, as Jesus puts it in saying 108, those who drink from his mouth will be like him and he will be one with them, and they will understand what is hidden.

The interactive nature of the *Gospel of Thomas* and the sayings in the *Gospel of Thomas* is underscored by Richard Valantasis in his book *The Gospel of Thomas*, when he calls the theology of the *Gospel of Thomas* "a performative theology." He says that "the theology emerges from the readers' and hearers' responses to the sayings and their sequence and their variety."[3] At the very end of his book Valantasis writes:

> Knowledge emerges from an act of interpreting. The collection of sayings under the authorship of Jesus and editorship of Didymos Judas Thomas demands a performance to unlock their individual and collected meaning. It requires work and toil to perform these and to discover (note it is not to learn) the interpretation. . . . Whereas a narrative defines carefully the actors and their actions, sayings simply float meaning without careful

---

3. Richard Valantasis, *The Gospel of Thomas*, 7.

definition or careful control. This Gospel proclaims the priority of living voice over narrative, of textualized presence over narrative definition. The Gospel remains performative.[4]

This emphasis upon the living voice of Jesus in the *Gospel of Thomas* may be corroborated not only by the identification of Jesus as "the living Jesus" but also by a grammatical feature of the sayings themselves. The sayings are introduced by quotation formulas, "Jesus said," "He said," and the like, in Coptic *peje i(ēsou)s*, *pejaf*, and similar forms. The Greek fragments, however, employ the present indicative, *legei i(ēsou)s* or simply *legei*, and although in this volume we translate these quotation formulas with the English past tense, we could very well employ the English present tense. The German translation in *Nag Hammadi Deutsch* and the German and English translations in *Synopsis Quattuor Evangeliorum* do in fact use the present tense.[5] The sayings, coming from the living voice of Jesus, are not what Jesus once said as much as they are what Jesus continues to say.

Jesus in the *Gospel of Thomas* thus confronts his disciples and readers of the gospel with powerful sayings, but he does not pull rank. In the *Gospel of Thomas* Jesus assumes very few Christological titles, and as Stephen Patterson notes, Jesus in this gospel is just Jesus.[6] Jesus in the *Gospel of Thomas* is not designated the Christ or the Messiah, he is not acclaimed master or lord, and when he refers to himself once in the gospel, in saying 86, as child of humanity or son of man, he does so in the generic sense of referring to any person or to himself as a human being. If Jesus in the *Gospel of Thomas* is a child of humanity, so are other people called children of humanity (sayings 28; 106). Jesus in the *Gospel of Thomas* is not presented as the unique or incarnate son of God, and nothing is said of a cross with saving significance or an empty tomb.[7] Jesus is named the living Jesus, but God is also said to be a living one, and followers of Jesus are called living ones as well. Referring to Jesus as the living one, then, is not a specific reference to the resurrection; rather, this phrase indicates all that is part of the realm of life. And if Jesus is a living one in the *Gospel of Thomas*, he lives through his words and sayings.

Some of what Jesus says in the *Gospel of Thomas* has a familiar ring, and other utterances are quite new and startling. In general, it would appear that the *Gospel of Thomas* is not fundamentally dependent upon the New Testament gospels, but is an independent gospel and a primary source on the Jesus tradition.[8] As elsewhere,

---

4. Valantasis, *Gospel of Thomas*, 196.

5. Cf. Jens Schröter and Hans-Gebhard Bethge, in Hans-Martin Schenke, Hans-Gebhard Bethge, and Ursula Ulrike Kaiser, eds., *Nag Hammadi Deutsch*, 1.151–81; Kurt Aland, ed., *Synopsis Quattuor Evangeliorum*, 517–46.

6. Cf. Stephen J. Patterson, in Stephen J. Patterson, James M. Robinson, and Hans-Gebhard Bethge, *The Fifth Gospel*, 43.

7. The only mention made of the cross in the *Gospel of Thomas* is in saying 55, where the image of bearing the cross seems to be used in a metaphorical sense.

8. On the question of the relationship between the *Gospel of Thomas* and the New Testament gospels and the issue of intertextuality, see Ron Cameron, "Thomas, Gospel of"; Marvin Meyer, *The Gospel of Thomas*, 9–10.

including the New Testament gospels, Jesus in the *Gospel of Thomas* proclaims the kingdom or reign of God, but here the kingdom is both inside and outside (3:3). As elsewhere, Jesus speaks in parables and stories, and although some of the parables are well known, others are new parables (97, the parable of the jar of meal; 98, the parable of the assassin). In the *Gospel of Thomas*, Jesus echoes the words of the Delphic maxim and declares, "When you know yourselves, then you will be known, and you will understand that you are children of the living Father. But if you do not know yourselves, then you dwell in poverty, and you are poverty" (2:4–5). Jesus announces that children will enter the kingdom, but not business-people and merchants. He says that the two will be one and male and female will become "a single one" (22), but the female must become male in order to enter the kingdom (114).[9] Jesus seems to reject outward forms of piety and conventional family values, and instead he recommends spiritual observance and a new order of family. He states, tersely, "Be passersby" (42).[10] When Thomas addresses Jesus as "teacher" and admits that he is unable to compare him to anything, Jesus denies that he is a teacher who is the source of truth and knowledge: "I am not your teacher. Because you have drunk, you have become intoxicated from the bubbling spring that I have tended" (13). Jesus serves the spiritual beverage, but those with him must drink for themselves in order to be spiritually intoxicated.

The *Gospel of Thomas* survives as the second tractate in Codex II of the Nag Hammadi library, where it is preserved in Coptic translation. Three Greek fragments of copies of the *Gospel of Thomas* also survive (Papyrus Oxyrhynchus 1, 654, and 655) as well as testimonia in early Christian literature, especially Hippolytus of Rome, *Refutation of All Heresies* 5.7.20; 5.8.32. The variations among the several texts make it clear that the *Gospel of Thomas* went through several copies, and changes could be made from one copy to another. The Coptic text of the *Gospel of Thomas*, like the other texts in the Nag Hammadi library, is conserved at the Coptic Museum in Old Cairo, Egypt, and Papyrus Oxyrhynchus 1, 654, and 655 are housed, respectively, in the Bodleian Library at Oxford, the British Library in London, and Houghton Library at Harvard University.[11] Most likely the *Gospel of Thomas* was composed in Greek, probably in Syria, perhaps at Edessa, where Thomas was revered and his bones venerated.

Although some scholars prefer a second-century date for the composition of the *Gospel of Thomas*, a reasonable case can be made for a first-century date for a first collection of the sayings. The Coptic *Gospel of Thomas* from the Nag Hammadi library was translated no later than the middle of the fourth century, but the Greek papyrus fragments have been dated much earlier, at least as early as the first half of the third century. On the basis of such suggested dates, Bernard P. Grenfell and Arthur S. Hunt, the first editors of the Oxyrhynchus papyri, estimated that the original documents must have been composed at least half a century

---

9. On the interpretation of these two sayings, see Marvin Meyer, *Secret Gospels*, 76–106.

10. On the interpretation of saying 42, see Meyer, *Secret Gospels*, 59–75.

11. For new readings of the Greek text of the Oxyrhynchus Papyri by April D. DeConick and James M. Robinson, see the notes to the Greek *Gospel of Thomas*.

earlier, around 140 at the latest. More recently, Søren Giversen has revised these dates, and he has stated on papyrological grounds that the Oxyrhynchus papyrus fragments of the *Gospel of Thomas* may be assigned even earlier dates.[12] The textual evidence for an early date for the *Gospel of Thomas* thus may rival that of any of the New Testament gospels. The *Gospel of Thomas* also illustrates concerns often judged to be those that come to expression particularly in the first century: disagreements about apostleship, uncertainty about the role of James the Just, interest in sayings of Jesus and sayings collections, and the like. Sayings in the *Gospel of Thomas* also seem to be transmitted in a form that is earlier than what we have in the canonical gospels. Such may be noted, for instance, in parables, where *Thomas* preserves parables of Jesus simply as stories, but the New Testament gospels may append allegorical interpretations to the parables in an effort to explain them and apply them to new situations. One saying in the *Gospel of Thomas*, saying 17, offers words of Jesus—"I shall give you what no eye has seen, what no ear has heard, what no hand has touched, what has not arisen in the human heart"—that sound very much like what Paul cites in his description of wisdom Christians in Corinth (1 *Corinthians* 2:9) in the middle of the first century.[13]

The *Gospel of Thomas* is a sayings gospel representative of Thomas Christianity, and as such it has a goodly amount in common with another text from Codex II of the Nag Hammadi library, the *Book of Thomas*, as well as a text not in the Nag Hammadi collection, the *Acts of Thomas*. Sayings and themes from the *Gospel of Thomas* appear in the *Dialogue of the Savior*, and Judas—perhaps Judas Thomas—is one of the main participants in the discussion. In literary genre and contents, the *Gospel of Thomas* resembles to a considerable extent the synoptic sayings gospel Q, and some scholars have attempted to identify a common source behind *Thomas* and Q.[14] Unlike Q, however, the *Gospel of Thomas* has less of an apocalyptic and more of a mystical emphasis, and Jesus in *Thomas* critiques approaches of those who show apocalyptic concern. Though there are hints of dialogue and narrative in the *Gospel of Thomas*, the development of those literary forms are much more evident in the *Book of Thomas* and the *Dialogue of the Savior*, with discussions between Jesus and Judas Thomas (also involving, in the *Dialogue of the Savior*, Mary of Magdala and Matthew), and the *Acts of Thomas*, with the pious story narrating the adventures of Thomas in India.

Finally, the use of the *Gospel of Thomas* may be traced in other religious contexts as well. In the third century Mani adopted the concept of the twin and applied it to the divine presence that was with him, and later Manichaean authors incorporated materials from the sayings of *Thomas*'s Jesus into their own holy books—for example, the *Manichaean Psalm Book* and Manichaean *Kephalaia*. Many years thereafter, the medieval Islamic scholar Abu Hamid Muhammad

---

12. Søren Giversen, "The Palaeography of Oxyrhynchus Papyri 1 and 654–655."

13. See also the discussion in Stephen J. Patterson, *The Gospel of Thomas and Jesus*, 113–20.

14. See John Dominic Crossan, *The Birth of Christianity*.

al-Ghazali cited dozens of sayings of prophet 'Isa in his book *The Revival of the Religious Sciences*, and among them are sayings reminiscent of what Jesus says in the *Gospel of Thomas*.[15] Since its publication a few decades ago, the *Gospel of Thomas* has proved to be the most celebrated of the Nag Hammadi texts, and it has been an influential and provocative source in discussions of the historical Jesus and early interpretations of Jesus.

BIBLIOGRAPHY

Kurt Aland, ed., *Synopsis Quattuor Evangeliorum*, 517–46; April D. DeConick, *The Original Gospel of Thomas; Recovering the Original Gospel of Thomas*; Søren Giversen, "The Palaeography of Oxyrhynchus Papyri 1 and 654–655"; Bentley Layton, ed., *Nag Hammadi Codex II,2–7*, 1.37–128 (Helmut Koester, Bentley Layton, Thomas O. Lambdin, and Harold W. Attridge); Marvin Meyer, *The Gnostic Discoveries; The Gnostic Gospels of Jesus; The Gospel of Thomas; Secret Gospels*; Elaine H. Pagels, *Beyond Belief*; Stephen J. Patterson, *The Gospel of Thomas and Jesus*; Stephen J. Patterson, James M. Robinson, and Hans-Gebhard Bethge, *The Fifth Gospel*; Gregory J. Riley, *Resurrection Reconsidered*; Hans-Martin Schenke, Hans-Gebhard Bethge, and Ursula Ulrike Kaiser, eds., *Nag Hammadi Deutsch*, 1.151–81 (Jens Schröter and Hans-Gebhard Bethge); Risto Uro, *Thomas at the Crossroads*; Richard Valantasis, *The Gospel of Thomas*.

---

15. See Tarif Khalidi, *The Muslim Jesus*; Marvin Meyer, *The Unknown Sayings of Jesus*.

The Gospel of Thomas[1]

NHC II,2

Prologue   These are the hidden sayings that the living Jesus spoke and Judas Thomas the Twin[2] recorded.[3]

1   And he[4] said, "Whoever discovers the interpretation of these sayings will not taste death."[5]

2   (1) Jesus said,[6] "Let one who seeks not stop seeking until one finds. (2) When one finds, one will be troubled. (3) When one is troubled, one will marvel (4) and will reign over all."[7]

3   (1) Jesus said, "If your leaders say to you, 'Look, the kingdom is in heaven,' then the birds of heaven will precede you. (2) If they say to you, 'It is in the sea,'[8] then the fish will precede you. (3) Rather, the kingdom is inside you and it is outside you.[9]

     (4) "When you know yourselves, then you will be known, [33] and you will understand that you are children of the living Father. (5) But if you do not know yourselves, then you dwell in poverty, and you are poverty."[10]

4   (1) Jesus said, "The person old in days will not hesitate to ask a little child seven days old[11] about the place of life, and that person will live.[12] (2) For many of the first will be last[13] (3) and will become a single one."

---

1. Coptic text: NHC II,2: 32,10–51,28. Editions: *The Facsimile Edition of the Nag Hammadi Codices: Codex II*, 42–63; Bentley Layton, ed., *Nag Hammadi Codex II,2–7*, 1.37–128 (Helmut Koester, Bentley Layton, Thomas O. Lambdin, and Harold W. Attridge); Marvin Meyer, *The Gospel of Thomas*; Hans-Martin Schenke, Hans-Gebhard Bethge, and Ursula Ulrike Kaiser, eds., *Nag Hammadi Deutsch*, 1.151–81 (Jens Schröter and Hans-Gebhard Bethge). The text is referred to as the "Hidden Sayings of Jesus" in the incipit. The present translation is based on an ultraviolet collation of the Coptic text, by Marvin Meyer, at the Coptic Museum in 1988. Included in the translation are the traditional numbers for 114 sayings along with numbers of subdivisions of sayings, in keeping with an increasingly common convention. **2.** Didymos. **3.** Cf. *Secret Book of James* 2; *Book of Thomas* 138. **4.** Probably Jesus, possibly Judas Thomas. **5.** Cf. *Sirach* 39:1–3; *John* 8:51–52. **6.** Or "Jesus says," for such a quotation formula here and elsewhere in the text. In the Greek *Gospel of Thomas* the quotation formulas are given in the present tense. **7.** Or "the All." P. Oxy. 654.8–9 adds "and [having reigned], one will rest." For the saying in general, cf. *Gospel of the Hebrews* 4a; 4b; *Book of Thomas* 140–41; 145; *Matthew* 7:7–8 (Q); *Luke* 11:9–10 (Q); *Dialogue of the Savior* 129; *Wisdom of Solomon* 6:12, 17–20. **8.** P. Oxy. 654.13 reads "under the earth." **9.** Cf. *Luke* 17:20–21; *Gospel of Thomas* 113; *Manichaean Psalm Book* 160. **10.** "Know yourself" was among the Greek inscriptions at Delphi. On knowing and being known, cf. *Galatians* 4:8–9; *1 Corinthians* 8:1–3; 13:12; *Gospel of Truth* 19. **11.** Probably an uncircumcised child (Jewish boys were circumcised on the eighth day). **12.** Cf. Hippolytus *Refutation of All Heresies* 5.7.20, a saying said to derive from the *Gospel of Thomas*: "One who seeks will find me in children from seven years, for there, hidden in the fourteenth age, I am revealed." **13.** Cf. *Matthew* 20:16 (Q); *Luke* 13:30 (Q); *Matthew* 19:30; *Mark* 10:31; *Barnabas* 6:13.

5   (1) Jesus said, "Know what is in front of your face, and what is hidden from you will be disclosed to you.[14] (2) For there is nothing hidden that will not be revealed."[15]

6   (1) His disciples asked him and said to him, "Do you want us to fast? How should we pray? Should we give to charity? What diet should we observe?"[16]

    (2) Jesus said, "Do not lie, (3) and do not do what you hate,[17] (4) because all things are disclosed before heaven.[18] (5) For there is nothing hidden that will not be revealed, (6) and there is nothing covered that will remain undisclosed."[19]

7   (1) Jesus said, "Blessed is the lion that the human will eat, so that the lion becomes human. (2) And cursed[20] is the human that the lion will eat, and the lion will become human."[21]

8   (1) And he said, "Humankind[22] is like a wise fisherman who cast his net into the sea and drew it up from the sea full of little fish. (2) Among them the wise fisherman discovered a fine large fish. (3) He threw all the little fish back [34] into the sea and with no difficulty chose the large fish. (4) Whoever has ears to hear should hear."[23]

9   (1) Jesus said, "Look, the sower went out, took a handful of seeds, and scattered them. (2) Some fell on the road, and the birds came and pecked them up. (3) Others fell on rock, and they did not take root in the soil and did not produce heads of grain. (4) Others fell on thorns, and they choked the seeds and worms devoured them. (5) And others fell on good soil, and it brought forth a good crop. It yielded sixty per measure and one hundred twenty per measure."[24]

10 Jesus said, "I have thrown fire upon the world, and look, I am watching it until it blazes."[25]

11 (1) Jesus said, "This heaven will pass away, and the one above it will pass away.[26]

    (2) "The dead are not alive, and the living will not die.

    (3) "During the days when you ate what is dead, you made it alive. When you are in the light, what will you do?[27]

---

14. Cf. Manichaean *Kephalaia* 65 163,26–29, where a nearly identical version of this saying of Jesus is cited. 15. Cf. *Mark* 4:22; *Luke* 8:17; *Matthew* 10:26 (Q); *Luke* 12:2 (Q). On the last portion of the saying, cf. *Gospel of Thomas* 6:5–6. P. Oxy. 654.31 adds "and nothing buried that [will not be raised]." 16. Cf. *Matthew* 6:1–18; *Didache* 8:1–3. Saying 14 provides a more direct answer to these questions. 17. This is the negative formulation of the golden rule. 18. P. Oxy. 654.38 reads "truth" (Greek *alētheia*, equivalent to Coptic *me*; here the Coptic for "heaven" is *pe*). 19. Cf. *Gospel of Thomas* 5:2. 20. Or "foul." 21. Here the lion seems to symbolize what is passionate and bestial in human experience. A person may consume the lion or be consumed by it. Cf. Plato *Republic* 588e–589b. 22. Or "The human," "The man." 23. Cf. *Matthew* 13:47–50;

Babrius *Fable* 4. 24. Cf. *Matthew* 13:3–9; *Mark* 4:2–9; *Luke* 8:4–8; *Gospel of Judas* 43–44. 25. Cf. *Luke* 12:49 (Q?); *Pistis Sophia* 141. 26. Cf. *Matthew* 24:35; *Mark* 13:31; *Luke* 21:33; *Matthew* 5:18 (Q); *Luke* 16:17 (Q). 27. Cf. Hippolytus *Refutation of All Heresies* 5.8.32: "So they say, 'If you ate dead things and made them living, what will you do if you eat living things?'" In the light of this citation from Hippolytus, it is possible to imagine (so Hans-Martin Schenke, in an unpublished note) that the original wording of the saying may have been as follows: "During the days when you ate what is dead, you made it alive. <When you eat what is alive, what will you do? During the days when you were in the darkness, you saw the light.> When you are in the light, what will you do?"

(4) "On the day when you were one, you became two. But when you become two, what will you do?"

12 (1) The disciples said to Jesus, "We know that you are going to leave us. Who will be our leader?"

(2) Jesus said to them, "No matter where you have come from, you are to go to James the Just, for whose sake heaven and earth came into being."[28]

13 (1) Jesus said to his disciples, "Compare me to something and tell me what I am like."

(2) Simon Peter said to him, "You are like a just messenger."[29]

(3) Matthew said to him, [35] "You are like a wise philosopher."

(4) Thomas said to him, "Teacher, my mouth is utterly unable to say what you are like."[30]

(5) Jesus said, "I am not your teacher. Because you have drunk, you have become intoxicated from the bubbling spring that I have tended."

(6) And he took him, and withdrew, and spoke three sayings[31] to him.

(7) When Thomas came back to his friends, they asked him, "What did Jesus say to you?"

(8) Thomas said to them, "If I tell you one of the sayings he spoke to me, you will pick up rocks and stone me, and fire will come from the rocks and consume you."[32]

14 (1) Jesus said to them, "If you fast, you will bring sin upon yourselves, (2) and if you pray, you will be condemned, (3) and if you give to charity, you will harm your spirits.[33]

(4) "When you go into any region and walk through the countryside,[34] when people receive you, eat what they serve you and heal the sick among them.[35] (5) For what goes into your mouth will not defile you; rather, it is what comes out of your mouth that will defile you."[36]

15 Jesus said, "When you see one who was not born of woman, fall on your faces and worship. That is your father."[37]

16 (1) Jesus said, "Perhaps people think that I have come to impose peace upon the world. (2) They do not know that I have come to impose conflicts upon the earth: fire, sword, war. (3) For there will be five [36] in a house: there will be three against two and two against three, father against son and son against father, (4) and they will stand alone."[38]

17 Jesus said, "I shall give you what no eye has seen, what no ear has heard, what no hand has touched, what has not arisen in the human heart."[39]

---

28. On James the Just, see the New Testament *Acts of the Apostles*; *Gospel of the Hebrews* 7; the *Secret Book of James*; the *First* and *Second Revelations of James*; Hegisippus, in Eusebius *Church History* 2.23.4–7; Josephus *Jewish Antiquities* 20.200. 29. Or "angel." 30. Cf. *Gospel of Judas* 35. 31. Or "three words." The three sayings or words are unknown, and they may be mentioned as a device for the reflection of the reader. For examples of three words, see Hippolytus *Refutation of All Heresies* 5.8.4 (Kaulakau, Saulasau, Zeesar, from the Hebrew of *Isaiah* 28:10, 13); *Pistis Sophia* 136 (Yao Yao Yao, the ineffable name of God). 32. Cf. *Gospel of Bartholomew* 2:5. 33. Cf. the questions in *Gospel of Thomas* 6. 34. Lit., "walk in the places." 35. Cf. *Matthew* 10:8 (Q); *Luke* 10:8–9 (Q); 1 *Corinthians* 10:27. 36. Cf. *Matthew* 15:11; *Mark* 7:15. 37. Cf. *John* 10:30. 38. Or "as solitaries" (Coptic *monakhos*). Cf. *Matthew* 10:34–36 (Q); *Luke* 12:49 (Q?), 50, 51–53 (Q). 39. Cf. 1 *Corinthians* 2:9; *Isaiah* 64:4; *Apocalypse of Elijah* or *Secrets (Apocrypha) of Elijah*; Plutarch *How the Young Person Should Study Poetry* 17e; *Prayer of the Apostle Paul* A; *Gospel of Judas* 47.

18 (1) The disciples said to Jesus, "Tell us how our end will be."[40]

(2) Jesus said, "Have you discovered the beginning, then, so that you are seeking the end? For where the beginning is the end will be. (3) Blessed is one who stands at the beginning: that one will know the end and will not taste death."[41]

19 (1) Jesus said, "Blessed is one who came into being before coming into being.[42]

(2) "If you become my disciples and listen to my sayings, these stones will serve you.[43]

(3) "For there are five trees in paradise for you; they do not change, summer or winter, and their leaves do not fall. (4) Whoever knows them will not taste death."[44]

20 (1) The disciples said to Jesus, "Tell us what heaven's kingdom is like."

(2) He said to them, "It is like a mustard seed. (3) <It>[45] is the smallest of all seeds, (4) but when it falls on prepared soil, it produces a large plant and becomes a shelter for birds of heaven."[46]

21 (1) Mary said to Jesus, "What are your disciples like?"

(2) He said, "They are like [37] children living in a field that is not theirs.[47] (3) When the owners of the field come, they will say, 'Give our field back to us.' (4) They take off their clothes in front of them in order to give it back to them, and they return their field to them.[48]

(5) "For this reason I say, if the owner of a house knows that a thief is coming, he will be on guard before the thief arrives and will not let the thief break into the house of his estate and steal his possessions.[49] (6) As for you, then, be on guard against the world. (7) Arm yourselves with great strength, or the robbers might find a way to get to you, (8) for the trouble you expect will come.[50] (9) Let there be among you a person who understands.

(10) "When the crop ripened, the person came quickly with sickle in hand and harvested it.[51] (11) Whoever has ears to hear should hear."

22 (1) Jesus saw some babies nursing. (2) He said to his disciples, "These nursing babies are like those who enter the kingdom."

(3) They said to him, "Then shall we enter the kingdom as babies?"

(4) Jesus said to them, "When you make the two into one, and when you make the inner like the outer and the outer like the inner, and the

40. Cf. *Matthew* 24:3; *Mark* 13:3–4; *Luke* 21:7. **41.** Cf. *Gospel of Thomas* 49. **42.** Cf. *Gospel of Philip* 64; Lactantius *Divine Institutes* 4.8; Irenaeus *Proof of the Apostolic Preaching* 43. **43.** Cf., e.g., *Gospel of Thomas* 77:3. **44.** Five trees in paradise are mentioned elsewhere in Gnostic and Manichaean literature. Cf. *Genesis* 2:9. **45.** The Coptic text reads *sobᵉk*, emended to read *<s>sobᵉk*. **46.** Cf. *Matthew* 13:31–32 (Q); *Luke* 13:18–19 (Q); *Mark* 4:30–32. **47.** Here the editors of the *Gospel of Thomas* in *Synopsis Quattuor Evangeliorum*, ed. Kurt Aland, 525, understand *šēre šēm* ("children") to be a plural translation of the Greek word *pais*, "child, servant," and they assume the latter meaning of *pais* and hence translate the passage as follows: "They are like servants entrusted with a field that is not theirs." **48.** Cf. *Gospel of Thomas* 37. **49.** Cf. *Gospel of Thomas* 103; *Matthew* 24:43 (Q); *Luke* 12:39 (Q). **50.** The editors of the *Gospel of Thomas* in *Synopsis Quattuor Evangeliorum*, ed. Aland, 525, translate this clause: "For the necessities for which you are waiting (with longing) will be found" (an additional possible translation is given in a note: "For the possession you are watching out for they will find"). **51.** Cf. *Mark* 4:29; *Joel* 3:13.

upper like the lower, (5) and when you make male and female into a single one, so that the male will not be male nor the female be female, (6) when you make eyes in place of an eye, a hand in place of a hand, a foot in place of a foot, an image in place of an image, (7) then you will enter [the kingdom]."[52] [38]

23   Jesus said, "I shall choose you, one from a thousand and two from ten thousand, and they will stand as a single one."[53]

24   (1) His disciples said, "Show us the place where you are, for we must seek it."

(2) He said to them, "Whoever has ears should hear. (3) There is light within a person of light, and it[54] shines on the whole world. If it does not shine, it is dark."[55]

25   (1) Jesus said, "Love your sibling like your soul;[56] (2) protect that person like the pupil of your eye."[57]

26   (1) Jesus said, "You see the speck that is in your sibling's eye, but you do not see the beam that is in your own eye. (2) When you take the beam out of your own eye, then you will see clearly to take the speck out of your sibling's eye.[58]

27   (1) "If you do not fast from the world, you will not find the kingdom. (2) If you do not observe the Sabbath as a Sabbath, you will not see the Father."[59]

28   (1) Jesus said, "I took my stand in the midst of the world, and in flesh I appeared to them.[60] (2) I found them all drunk, and I did not find any of them thirsty. (3) My soul ached for the children of humanity,[61] because they are blind in their hearts and do not see, for they came into the world empty, and they also seek to depart from the world empty. (4) But now they are drunk. When they shake off their wine, then they will repent."

29   (1) Jesus said, "If the flesh came into being because of spirit, it is a marvel, (2) but if spirit came into being because of the body, it is a marvel of marvels. (3) Yet I marvel [39] at how this great wealth has come to dwell in this poverty."[62]

30   (1) Jesus said, "Where there are three deities, they are divine. (2) Where there are two or one, I am with that one."[63]

31   (1) Jesus said, "A prophet is not acceptable in the prophet's own town; (2) a doctor does not heal those who know the doctor."[64]

---

52. Cf. *Galatians* 3:27–28; *Gospel of the Egyptians*; *2 Clement* 12:2–6; *Martyrdom of Peter* 9; *Acts of Philip* 140; *Gospel of Thomas* 114. 53. Cf. *Deuteronomy* 32:30; *Ecclesiastes* 7:28; *Pistis Sophia* 134. 54. Or "he," here and below. 55. In general, cf. *Matthew* 6:22–23 (Q); *Luke* 11:34–35 (Q), 36 (Q?); *Dialogue of the Savior* 125–26. 56. Or "your life," "yourself." 57. Cf. *Matthew* 22:39; *Mark* 12:31; *Luke* 10:27; *Leviticus* 19:18; *Gospel of the Hebrews* 5; *Didache* 2:7. 58. Cf. *Matthew* 7:3–5 (Q); *Luke* 6:41–42 (Q). 59. Cf. Clement of Alexandria *Miscellanies* 3.15.99.4; Tertullian *Against the Jewish People* 4. 60. Cf. *John* 1:14; *1 Timothy* 3:16; *Proverbs* 1:20–33; *Baruch* 3:37. 61. Or "sons of men." 62. Cf. *Gospel of Thomas* 7. 63. P. Oxy. 1.23–30 has been reconstructed to read as follows: "[Jesus says], 'Where there are [three, they are without] God, and where there is only [one], I say, I am with that one. Lift up the stone, and you will find me there. Split the piece of wood, and I am there.'" See the notes for Greek *Gospel of Thomas* 30. On the conclusion of this version of the saying, cf. *Gospel of Thomas* 77:2–3. On the saying in general, cf. *Matthew* 18:19–20; Ephraem Syrus *Exposition on the Harmony of the Gospel* 14. 64. Cf. *Matthew* 13:57; *Mark* 6:4; *Luke* 4:23–24; *John* 4:44.

32   Jesus said, "A city built upon a high hill and fortified cannot fall, nor can it be hidden."[65]

33   (1) Jesus said, "What you will hear in your ear, in the other ear[66] proclaim from your rooftops. (2) For no one lights a lamp and puts it under a basket, nor does one put it in a hidden place. (3) Rather, one puts it on a stand so that all who come and go will see its light."[67]

34   Jesus said, "If a blind person leads a blind person, both of them will fall into a hole."[68]

35   (1) Jesus said, "You cannot enter the house of the strong and take it by force without tying the person's hands. (2) Then you can loot the person's house."[69]

36   Jesus said, "Do not worry, from morning to evening and from evening to morning, about what you will wear."[70]

37   (1) His disciples said, "When will you appear to us and when shall we see you?"

     (2) Jesus said, "When you strip without being ashamed and you take your clothes and put them under your feet like little children and trample them, (3) then [you] will see [40] the child of the living one and you will not be afraid."[71]

38   (1) Jesus said, "Often you have desired to hear these sayings that I am speaking to you, and you have no one else from whom to hear them. (2) There will be days when you will seek me and you will not find me."[72]

39   (1) Jesus said, "The Pharisees and the scholars have taken[73] the keys of knowledge[74] and have hidden them. (2) They have not entered, nor have they allowed those who want to enter to do so.[75] (3) As for you, be as shrewd as snakes and as innocent as doves."[76]

40   (1) Jesus said, "A grapevine has been planted away from the Father. (2) Since it is not strong, it will be pulled up by its root and will perish."[77]

41   (1) Jesus said, "Whoever has something in hand will be given more, (2) and whoever has nothing will be deprived of even the little that person has."[78]

42   Jesus said, "Be passersby."[79]

43   (1) His disciples said to him, "Who are you to say these things to us?"

---

65. Cf. *Matthew* 5:14; 7:24–25 (Q); *Luke* 6:47–48 (Q). 66. The phrase "in the other ear" may be a case of dittography, or it may refer to someone else's ear or even one's own "inner" ear. 67. Cf. *Matthew* 5:15 (Q); *Luke* 11:33 (Q); *Mark* 4:21; *Luke* 8:16. 68. Cf. *Matthew* 15:14 (Q); *Luke* 6:39 (Q). 69. Cf. *Matthew* 12:29 (Q?); *Mark* 3:27; *Luke* 11:21–22 (Q?). 70. Cf. *Matthew* 6:25–33 (Q), 34; *Luke* 12:22–31 (Q), 32. P. Oxy. 655.1–17 presents the following expanded saying: "[Jesus says, 'Do not worry], from morning [to nightfall nor] from [evening to] morning, either [about] your [food], what [you will] eat, [or] about [your robe], what clothing you [will] wear. [You are much] better than the lilies, which do not card or [spin]. And since you have one article of clothing, what (or why) . . . you . . . ? Who might add to your stature? That is the one who

will give you your clothing.'" See the notes for Greek *Gospel of Thomas* 36. 71. Cf. *Gospel of the Egyptians*; *Gospel of Philip* 75; Hippolytus *Refutation of All Heresies* 5.8.44; *Manichaean Psalm Book* 99,26–30. 72. Cf. *Matthew* 13:17 (Q); *Luke* 10:24 (Q); 17:22; *John* 7:33–36; *Proverbs* 1:23–28. 73. Or "have received." 74. Gnosis. 75. Cf. *Matthew* 23:13 (Q); *Luke* 11:52 (Q); Pseudo-Clementine *Recognitions* 2.30.1; Abu Hamid Muhammad al-Ghazali *Revival of the Religious Sciences* 1.49. 76. Cf. *Matthew* 10:16. 77. Cf. *Matthew* 15:13; *John* 15:5–6; *Isaiah* 5:1–7; *Gospel of Thomas* 57; *Matthew* 13:24–30; *Book of Thomas* 144. 78. Cf. *Matthew* 13:12; *Mark* 4:24–25; *Luke* 8:18; *Matthew* 25:29 (Q); *Luke* 19:26 (Q). 79. Cf. an Arabic inscription at the site of a mosque at Fatehpur Sikri, India; Petrus Alphonsi, *Clerical Instruction*.

(2) "You do not know who I am from what I say to you.[80] (3) Rather, you have become like the Jewish people, for they love the tree but hate its fruit, or they love the fruit but hate the tree."[81]

44 (1) Jesus said, "Whoever blasphemes against the Father will be forgiven, (2) and whoever blasphemes against the Son will be forgiven, (3) but whoever blasphemes against the holy Spirit will not be forgiven, either on earth or in heaven."[82]

45 (1) Jesus said, "Grapes are not harvested from thornbushes, nor are figs gathered from thistles, for they yield no fruit. (2) A good person brings forth [41] good from the storehouse; (3) a bad person brings forth evil things from the corrupt storehouse in the heart and says evil things. (4) For from the abundance of the heart this person brings forth evil things."[83]

46 (1) Jesus said, "From Adam to John the Baptizer, among those born of women, there is no one greater than John the Baptizer, so that his eyes[84] should not be averted.[85] (2) But I have said that whoever among you becomes a child will know the kingdom and will become greater than John."[86]

47 (1) Jesus said, "A person cannot mount two horses or bend two bows. (2) And a servant cannot serve two masters, or that servant will honor the one and offend the other.[87] (3) No person drinks aged wine and immediately desires to drink new wine. (4) New wine is not poured into aged wineskins, or they might break, and aged wine is not poured into a new wineskin, or it might spoil.[88] (5) An old patch is not sewn onto a new garment, for there would be a tear."[89]

48 Jesus said, "If two make peace with each other in a single house, they will say to the mountain, 'Move from here,' and it will move."[90]

49 (1) Jesus said, "Blessed are those who are alone[91] and chosen, for you will find the kingdom. (2) For you have come from it, and you will return there again."[92]

50 (1) Jesus said, "If they say to you, 'Where have you come from?' say to them, 'We have come from the light, from the place where the light came into being by itself, established [itself], [42] and appeared in their image.' (2) If they say to you, 'Is it you?'[93] say, 'We are its children, and we are the chosen of the living Father.' (3) If they ask you, 'What is the evidence of your Father in you?' say to them, 'It is motion and rest.' "[94]

---

80. Cf. *John* 14:8–11. 81. Cf. *Luke* 6:43–44 (Q); *Matthew* 7:16a, 16b (Q), 19–20; 12:33a–b, 33c (Q). 82. Cf. *Matthew* 12:31–32 (Q); *Luke* 12:10 (Q); *Mark* 3:28–29. 83. Cf. *Luke* 6:43–45 (Q); *Matthew* 7:16a, 16b (Q), 17, 18 (Q), 19–29; 12:33a–b, 33c (Q), 34a, 34b–35 (Q); *James* 3:12. 84. Most likely the person's eyes, possibly John's. 85. Lit., "be broken." On eyes being averted in modesty, cf. *Gospel of Judas* 35. 86. Cf. *Matthew* 11:11 (Q); *Luke* 7:28 (Q). 87. Cf. *Matthew* 6:24 (Q); *Luke* 16:13 (Q). 88. Cf. *Matthew* 9:17; *Mark* 2:22; *Luke* 8:37–39. 89. Cf. *Matthew* 9:16; *Mark* 2:21; *Luke* 5:36. 90. Cf. *Gospel of Thomas* 106; *Matthew* 18:19; 17:20b (Q); *Luke* 17:6b (Q); *Matthew* 21:21; *Mark* 11:23; 1 *Corinthians* 13:2. 91. Or "solitary" (Coptic *monakhos*). 92. Cf. *Gospel of Thomas* 18. 93. This may possibly be emended to read "<Who> are you?" (*ntōtn* <*nim*>). 94. This saying recalls the accounts of the career of the soul or of the person in the *Secret Book of John*, the *Hymn of the Pearl*, and the *Exegesis on the Soul*.

51 (1) His disciples said to him, "When will the rest[95] for the dead take place, and when will the new world come?"

(2) He said to them, "What you look for has come, but you do not know it."[96]

52 (1) His disciples said to him, "Twenty-four prophets[97] have spoken in Israel, and they all spoke of you."

(2) He said to them, "You have disregarded the living one who is in your presence and have spoken of the dead."[98]

53 (1) His disciples said to him, "Is circumcision useful or not?"

(2) He said to them, "If it were useful, children's fathers would produce them already circumcised from their mothers. (3) Rather, the true circumcision in spirit has become valuable in every respect."[99]

54 Jesus said, "Blessed are the poor, for yours is heaven's kingdom."[100]

55 (1) Jesus said, "Whoever does not hate father and mother cannot be a disciple of me, (2) and whoever does not hate brothers and sisters and bear the cross as I do will not be worthy of me."[101]

56 (1) Jesus said, "Whoever has come to know the world has discovered a carcass, (2) and whoever has discovered a carcass, of that person the world is not worthy."[102]

57 (1) Jesus said, "The Father's kingdom is like a person who had [good] seed. (2) His enemy came at night [43] and sowed weeds among the good seed. (3) The person did not let them pull up the weeds, but said to them, 'No, or you might go to pull up the weeds and pull up the wheat along with them.' (4) For on the day of the harvest the weeds will be conspicuous and will be pulled up and burned."[103]

58 Jesus said, "Blessed is the person who has labored[104] and has found life."[105]

59 Jesus said, "Look to the living one as long as you live, or you might die and then try to see the living one, and you will be unable to see."[106]

60 (1) <He saw>[107] a Samaritan carrying a lamb as he[108] was going to Judea.

(2) He said to his disciples, "That person is carrying the lamb around."[109]

95. Instead of "rest" (anapausis), the editors of the Gospel of Thomas in Synopsis Quattuor Evangeliorum, ed. Aland, 532, emend to read "<resurrection>" (ana<sta>sis). 96. Cf. Luke 17:20–21; Gospel of Thomas 113:4; John 3:18–19; 5:25; 2 Timothy 2:17–18; Treatise on Resurrection 49. 97. 2 Esdras 14:45 gives twenty-four as the number of books in the Jewish scriptures. 98. Cf. Augustine Against the Adversary of the Law and the Prophets 2.4.14. 99. Cf. Romans 2:25–29. 100. Cf. Matthew 5:3 (Q); Luke 6:20 (Q). 101. Cf. Matthew 10:37–38 (Q); Luke 14:26–27 (Q); Matthew 16:24; Mark 8:34; Luke 9:23; Gospel of Thomas 101. 102. Cf. Gospel of Thomas 80. This saying reads "carcass" (ptōma); saying 80 reads "body" (sōma). 103. Cf. Matthew 13:24–30. 104. Or "who has suffered." 105. Cf. Proverbs 8:34–36; Sirach 51:26–27; Gospel of Thomas 68–69. 106. Cf. Luke 17:22; John 7:33–36; 8:21; 13:33; Gospel of Thomas 38. 107. The emendation assumes Coptic letters were omitted due to haplography—hence the opening of the saying is restored to read <afnau>, "<He saw>." Also possible is <aunau>, "<They saw>." 108. Probably Jesus, possibly the Samaritan. 109. The Coptic text may be translated, lit., "That person is around the lamb." Possibly emend to read, "<Why does> that person <carry> around the lamb?" or the like. The editors of the Gospel of Thomas in Synopsis Quattuor Evangeliorum, ed. Aland, 534, offer a different interpretation of the Coptic and translation of the saying: "<He saw> a Samaritan who was trying to take away a lamb while he was on his way to Judea. He said to his disciples, 'That (person) is pursuing the lamb.' They said to him, 'So that he may kill it (and) eat it.'"

(3) They said to him, "Then he may kill it and eat it."[110]

(4) He said to them, "He will not eat it while it is alive, but only after he has killed it and it has become a carcass."

(5) They said, "Otherwise he cannot do it."

(6) He said to them, "So also with you, seek for yourselves a place for rest, or you might become a carcass and be eaten."[111]

61 (1) Jesus said, "Two will rest on a couch; one will die, one will live."[112]

(2) Salome said, "Who are you, mister? You have climbed onto my couch[113] and eaten from my table as if you are from someone."[114]

(3) Jesus said to her, "I am the one who comes from what is whole. I was given from the things of my Father."[115]

(4) "I am your disciple."

(5) "For this reason I say, if one is <whole>,[116] one will be filled with light,[117] but if one is divided, one will be filled with darkness."

62 (1) Jesus said, "I disclose my mysteries to those [who are worthy] of [44] [my] mysteries.[118] (2) Do not let your left hand know what your right hand is doing."[119]

63 (1) Jesus said, "There was a rich person who had a great deal of money. (2) He said, 'I shall invest my money so that I may sow, reap, plant, and fill my storehouses with produce, that I may lack nothing.' (3) These were the things he was thinking in his heart, but that very night he died. (4) Whoever has ears should hear."[120]

64 (1) Jesus said, "A person was receiving guests. When he had prepared the dinner, he sent his servant to invite the guests.

(2) "The servant went to the first and said to that one, 'My master invites you.'

(3) "That person said, 'Some merchants owe me money; they are coming to me tonight. I must go and give them instructions. Please excuse me from dinner.'

(4) "The servant went to another and said to that one, 'My master has invited you.'

(5) "That person said to the servant, 'I have bought a house and I have been called away for a day. I shall have no time.'

(6) "The servant went to another and said to that one, 'My master invites you.'

---

110. Or, lit., "So that he may kill it and eat it." 111. Cf. Gospel of Thomas 7; 11:3. 112. Cf. Luke 17:34–35 (Q); Matthew 24:40–41 (Q). 113. Or "bed." 114. Lit., "as from one." Bentley Layton, in Nag Hammadi Codex II,2–7, 1.74, notes two other possibilities. The Greek for "as a stranger" (hōs xenos) may have been mistranslated "as from one" (hōs ex henos), or the Greek for "as from whom" (hōs ek tinos) may have been mistranslated "as from someone" (hōs ek tinos, with a different accent). The editors of the Gospel of Thomas in Synopsis Quattuor Evangeliorum, ed. Aland, 534, opt for the translation "as a <stranger>." 115. Cf. Matthew 11:27 (Q); Luke 10:22 (Q); John 3:35; 6:37–39; 13:3–4. 116. Here the Coptic text reads efšēf, "desolate." It is emended to read efšē<š>, "<whole>." 117. Cf. John 8:12. 118. Cf. Matthew 13:11; Mark 4:11; Luke 8:10. 119. Cf. Matthew 6:3. 120. Cf. Luke 12:16–21 (Q?); Sirach 11:18–19.

(7) "That person said to the servant, 'My friend is to be married and I am to arrange the banquet. I shall not be able to come. Please excuse me from dinner.'

(8) "The servant went to another and said to that one, 'My master invites you.'

(9) "That person said to the servant, 'I have bought an estate and I am going to collect the rent. I shall not be able to come. Please excuse me.'

(10) "The servant returned and said to his master, 'The people whom you invited to dinner have asked to be excused.'

(11) "The master said to his servant, 'Go out on the streets and bring back whomever you find to have dinner.'[121]

(12) "Buyers and merchants [will] not enter the places of my Father."[122]

[45]

65 (1) He said, "A [usurer][123] owned a vineyard and rented it to some farmers, so that they might work it and he might collect its produce from them. (2) He sent his servant so that the farmers might give the servant the produce of the vineyard.(3) They seized, beat, and almost killed his servant, and the servant returned and told his master. (4) His master said, 'Perhaps he did not know them.'[124] (5) He sent another servant, and the farmers beat that one as well. (6) Then the master sent his son and said, 'Perhaps they will show my son some respect.' (7) Since the farmers knew that he was the heir to the vineyard, they seized him and killed him. (8) Whoever has ears should hear."[125]

66 Jesus said, "Show me the stone that the builders rejected: that is the cornerstone."[126]

67 Jesus said, "One who knows everything but lacks in oneself lacks everything."[127]

68 (1) Jesus said, "Blessed are you when you are hated and persecuted, (2) and no place will be found, wherever you have been persecuted."[128]

69 (1) Jesus said, "Blessed are they who have been persecuted in their hearts: they are the ones who have truly come to know the Father.[129] (2) Blessed are they who are hungry, that the stomach of the person in want may be filled."[130]

70 (1) Jesus said, "If you bring forth what is within you, what you have will save you. (2) If you do not have that within you, what you do not have within you [will] kill you."[131]

---

121. Cf. *Matthew* 22:1–10 (Q); *Luke* 14:16–24 (Q); *Deuteronomy* 20:5–7; 24:5. 122. Cf. *Sirach* 26:29. 123. Or "A [creditor]." The text reads *khrē*[*st.*]*s* (with one letter to be restored), which may be restored to read either "A [usurer]" (*khrē*[*stē*]*s*), as here, or "A [good person]" (*khrē*[*sto*]*s*). 124. Possibly emend to read "Perhaps <they> did not know <him>." 125. Cf. *Matthew* 21:33–41; *Mark* 12:1–9; *Luke* 20:9–16. 126. Cf. *Psalm* 118:22; *Matthew* 21:42; *Mark* 12:10; *Luke* 20:17; *Acts* 4:11; 1 *Peter* 2:7. 127. Cf. *Book of Thomas* 138. The editors of the *Gospel of Thomas* in *Synopsis Quattuor Evangeliorum*, ed. Aland, 536, translate this saying as follows: "Whoever knows all, if he is lacking one thing, he is (already) lacking everything." 128. Cf. *Matthew* 5:10, 11 (Q); *Luke* 6:22 (Q); *Gospel of Thomas* 58; 69. 129. Cf. *Gospel of Thomas* 68. 130. Cf. *Matthew* 5:6 (Q); *Luke* 6:21 (Q). 131. Cf. *Gospel of Thomas* 41; 67.

71   Jesus said, "I shall destroy [this] house, and no one will be able to build it again]."[132] [46]

72   (1) A [person said] to him, "Tell my brothers to divide my father's possessions with me."

(2) He said to the person, "Mister, who made me a divider?"

(3) He turned to his disciples and said to them, "I am not a divider, am I?"[133]

73   Jesus said, "The harvest is large but the workers are few. So beg the master[134] to send out workers to the harvest."[135]

74   Someone said,[136] "Master,[137] there are many around the drinking trough, but there is nothing[138] in the <well>."[139]

75   Jesus said, "There are many standing at the door, but those who are alone[140] will enter the wedding chamber."[141]

76   (1) Jesus said, "The Father's kingdom is like a merchant who had a supply of merchandise and then found a pearl. (2) That merchant was prudent; he sold the merchandise and bought the single pearl for himself.[142] (3) So also with you, seek his treasure that is unfailing, that is enduring, where no moth comes to devour and no worm destroys."[143]

77   (1) Jesus said, "I am the light that is over all things.[144] I am all: from me all has come forth, and to me all has reached.[145] (2) Split a piece of wood; I am there. (3) Lift up the stone, and you will find me there."[146]

78   (1) Jesus said, "Why have you come out to the countryside? To see a reed shaken by the wind?(2) And to see a person dressed in soft clothes, [like your] rulers and your [47] powerful ones? (3) They are dressed in soft clothes, and they cannot understand truth."[147]

79   (1) A woman in the crowd said to him, "Blessed is the womb that bore you and the breasts that fed you."[148]

(2) He said to [her], "Blessed are they who have heard the word of the Father and have truly kept it.[149] (3) For there will be days when you will say, 'Blessed is the womb that has not conceived and the breasts that have not given milk.' "[150]

---

132. Cf. *Matthew* 26:61; *Mark* 14:58; *Matthew* 27:40; *Mark* 15:29; *Acts* 6:14; *John* 2:19. The restoration "[again]" is tentative (*ⁿn[kesop]*), and may require a small blank space at the end of the line. For this reason the editors of the *Gospel of Thomas* in *Synopsis Quattuor Evangeliorum*, ed. Aland, 537, prefer to restore to read "[except me]" (*ⁿn[sabⁿllai]*). 133. Cf. *Luke* 12:13–14 (Q?); 'Abd al-Jabbar *Book on the Signs of Muhammad's Prophecy*. 134. Or "lord." 135. Cf. *Matthew* 9:37–38 (Q); *Luke* 10:2 (Q); *Pirke Avot* 2.20. 136. Lit., "He said." 137. Or "Lord." 138. Or "no one." 139. The Coptic text has *šōne*, "illness," here emended to read *šō<t>e*, "<well>." 140. Or "solitary" (Coptic *monakhos*). 141. Sayings 73–75 most likely

constitute a small dialogue. Cf. the *Heavenly Dialogue*, in Origen *Against Celsus* 8.15. For saying 75, cf. *Matthew* 25:1–13. 142. Cf. *Matthew* 13:45–46. 143. Cf. *Matthew* 6:19–20 (Q); *Luke* 12:33 (Q); *Matthew* 13:44. 144. Cf. *John* 8:12; *Wisdom of Solomon* 7:24–30. 145. Cf. *Romans* 11:36; 1 *Corinthians* 8:6; *Martyrdom of Peter* 10. 146. Cf. *Ecclesiastes* 10:9; *Habakkuk* 2:18–20; Lucian of Samosata *Hermotimus* 81. Also cf. *Gospel of Thomas* 30 and the note. 147. Cf. *Matthew* 11:7–8 (Q); *Luke* 7:24–25 (Q). 148. Cf. *Luke* 11:27–28 (Q?); Petronius *Satyricon* 94. 149. Cf. *John* 13:17; *James* 1:25. 150. Cf. *Luke* 23:29; *Matthew* 24:19; *Mark* 13:17; *Luke* 21:23; *Gospel of the Egyptians*.

80 (1) Jesus said, "Whoever has come to know the world has discovered the body, (2) and whoever has discovered the body, of that person the world is not worthy."[151]

81 (1) Jesus said, "Let one who has become wealthy reign, (2) and let one who has power renounce it."[152]

82 (1) Jesus said, "Whoever is near me is near the fire, (2) and whoever is far from me is far from the kingdom."[153]

83 (1) Jesus said, "Images are visible to people, but the light within them is hidden in the image of the Father's light. (2) He will be disclosed, but his image is hidden by his light."

84 (1) Jesus said, "When you see your likeness, you are happy. (2) But when you see your images that came into being before you and that neither die nor become visible, how much you will bear!"[154]

85 (1) Jesus said, "Adam came from great power[155] and great wealth, but he was not worthy of you. (2) For had he been worthy, [he would] not [have tasted] death."

86 (1) Jesus said, "[Foxes [48] have] their dens and birds have their nests, (2) but the child of humanity[156] has no place to lay his head and rest."[157]

87 (1) Jesus said, "How miserable is the body that depends on a body, (2) and how miserable is the soul that depends on these two."[158]

88 (1) Jesus said, "The messengers[159] and the prophets will come to you and give you what is yours. (2) You, in turn, give them what you have, and say to yourselves, 'When will they come and take what is theirs?'"[160]

89 (1) Jesus said, "Why do you wash the outside of the cup? (2) Don't you understand that the one who made the inside is also the one who made the outside?"[161]

90 (1) Jesus said, "Come to me, for my yoke is easy and my mastery[162] is gentle, (2) and you will find rest for yourselves."[163]

91 (1) They said to him, "Tell us who you are so that we may believe in you."

(2) He said to them, "You examine the face of heaven and earth, but you have not come to know the one who is in your presence, and you do not know how to examine this moment."[164]

---

151. Cf. *Gospel of Thomas* 56 and the note. 152. Cf. 1 *Corinthians* 4:8; *Gospel of Thomas* 110; *Dialogue of the Savior* 129. 153. Cf. Ignatius *Smyrnaeans* 4:2; Greek proverbs. Versions of this saying are also known from Origen, Didymus the Blind, an Armenian text from the monastery of St. Lazzaro, and in the *Gospel of the Savior*: "If someone is near me, that person will [burn]. I am the fire that blazes. Whoever is [near me] is near the fire; whoever is far from me is far from life" (Berlin 22220 107,39–48). 154. For sayings 83–84, cf. *Genesis* 1:26–28 and discussions in Philo of Alexandria and Gnostic accounts of creation. 155. Simon Magus was called the great power of God. Cf. *Acts* 8:9–10; *Concept of Our Great Power*. 156. Or "son of man." 157. Cf. *Matthew* 8:20 (Q); *Luke* 9:58 (Q); Plutarch *Life of Tiberius Gracchus* 9.4–5; Abu Hamid Muhammad al-Ghazali *Revival of the Religious Sciences* 3.153. 158. Cf. *Gospel of Thomas* 29; 112. 159. Or "angels." 160. Cf. *Secret Book of John* II, 25; *Authoritative Discourse* 32. 161. Cf. *Matthew* 23:25–26 (Q); *Luke* 11:39–41 (Q); Babylonian Talmud, *Berakoth* 51a; *Kelim* 25.1–9. 162. Or "lordship." 163. Cf. *Matthew* 11:28–30; *Sirach* 51:26–27. 164. Cf. *Matthew* 16:1, 2–3 (Q); *Luke* 12:54–56 (Q).

92 (1) Jesus said, "Seek and you will find.[165] (2) In the past, however, I did not tell you the things about which you asked me then. Now I am willing to tell them, but you are not seeking them.[166]

93 (1) "Do not give what is holy to dogs, or they might throw them upon the manure pile. (2) Do not throw pearls [to] swine, or they might make [mud] of it."[167]

94 (1) Jesus [said], "One who seeks will find; (2) for [one who knocks] it will be opened."[168]

95 (1) [Jesus said], "If you have money, [49] do not lend it at interest. (2) Rather, give [it] to someone from whom you will not get it back."[169]

96 (1) Jesus [said], "The Father's kingdom is like a woman. (2) She took a little yeast, [hid] it in dough, and made it into large loaves of bread. (3) Whoever has ears should hear."[170]

97 (1) Jesus said, "The [Father's] kingdom is like a woman who was carrying a [jar] full of meal. (2) While she was walking along a distant road, the handle of the jar broke and the meal spilled behind her [along] the road. (3) She did not know it; she had not noticed a problem.[171] (4) When she reached her house, she put the jar down and discovered that it was empty."[172]

98 (1) Jesus said, "The Father's kingdom is like a person who wanted to put someone powerful to death. (2) While at home he drew his sword and thrust it into the wall to find out whether his hand would go in. (3) Then he killed the powerful one."[173]

99 (1) The disciples said to him, "Your brothers and your mother are standing outside."

(2) He said to them, "Those here who do the will of my Father are my brothers and my mother. (3) They are the ones who will enter my Father's kingdom."[174]

100 (1) They showed Jesus a gold coin and said to him, "Caesar's people demand taxes from us."

(2) He said to them, "Give Caesar the things that are Caesar's, (3) give God the things that are God's, (4) and give me what is mine.[175]

---

165. Cf. *Gospel of Thomas* 2; 94; *Matthew* 7:7–8 (Q); *Luke* 11:9–10 (Q). 166. Cf. *John* 16:4–5, 12–15, 22–28. 167. Cf. *Matthew* 7:6. The restoration at the end of the saying is tentative (*šina je nouaaf ^enla[jte]*), but it fits the context. Bentley Layton, in *Nag Hammadi Codex II,2–7*, 1.86–87, notes the following additional suggestions for restoration: "or they might bring it [to naught]"; "or they might grind it [to bits]." 168. Cf. *Gospel of Thomas* 2; 92; *Matthew* 7:7–8 (Q); *Luke* 11:9–10 (Q). 169. Cf. *Matthew* 5:42 (Q); *Luke* 6:30 (Q), 34–35b (Q?), 35c (Q); *Didache* 1:5. 170. Cf. *Matthew* 13:33 (Q); *Luke* 13:20–21 (Q). 171. The edi-

tors of the *Gospel of Thomas* in *Synopsis Quattuor Evangeliorum*, ed. Aland, 542, prefer to emend (with Peter Nagel) to read "she had not noticed (anything) while <she> toiled" (*e<s>hise*). 172. This parable is known only here in early Christian literature, though a somewhat similar story is found in "Macarius" of Syria. 173. This parable is known only here in early Christian literature. In general, cf. *Gospel of Thomas* 35; *Matthew* 11:12–13 (Q); *Luke* 16:16 (Q). 174. Cf. *Matthew* 12:46–50; *Mark* 3:31–35; *Luke* 8:19–21; *Gospel of the Ebionites* 5. 175. Cf. *Matthew* 22:15–22; *Mark* 12:13–17; *Luke* 20:20–26.

101   (1) "Whoever does not hate [father] and mother as I do cannot be a [disciple] of me, (2) and whoever does [not] love [father and] mother as I do cannot be a [disciple of] me. (3) For my mother [gave me [50] falsehood],[176] but my true [mother][177] gave me life."[178]

102   Jesus said, "Woe to the Pharisees, for they are like a dog sleeping in the cattle manger, for it does not eat or [let] the cattle eat."[179]

103   Jesus said, "Blessed is the person who knows at what point[180] the robbers are going to enter, so that [he] may arise, bring together his estate, and arm himself before they enter."[181]

104   (1) They said to Jesus, "Come, let's pray today and let's fast."

      (2) Jesus said, "What sin have I committed, or how have I been undone? (3) Rather, when the bridegroom leaves the wedding chamber, then let people fast and pray."[182]

105   Jesus said, "Whoever knows the father and the mother will be called the child of a whore."[183]

106   (1) Jesus said, "When you make the two into one, you will become children of humanity,[184] (2) and when you say, 'Mountain, move from here,' it will move."[185]

107   (1) Jesus said, "The kingdom is like a shepherd who had a hundred sheep. (2) One of them, the largest, went astray. He left the ninety-nine and sought the one until he found it. (3) After he had gone to this trouble, he said to the sheep, 'I love you more than the ninety-nine.' "[186]

108   (1) Jesus said, "Whoever drinks from my mouth will become like me; (2) I myself shall become that person, (3) and the hidden things will be revealed to that person."[187]

109   (1) Jesus said, "The kingdom is like a person who had a treasure hidden in his field but did not know it. (2) And [when] he died, he left it to his [son]. The son [did] not know about it. He took over [51] the field and sold it. (3) The buyer went plowing, [discovered] the treasure, and began to lend money at interest to whomever he wished."[188]

---

176. This restoration is tentative (*ntas[ti naei *mpc]ol). Another possibility: "For my mother, who has [given birth to me, has destroyed me]" (see the note in Aland, ed., *Synopsis Quattuor Evangeliorum*, 543). It may even be possible, though more difficult, to restore to read saying 101:3 as follows: "For my mother [gave birth to me], but my true [mother] gave life to me." 177. Perhaps the holy Spirit; cf. *Gospel of the Hebrews* 3; *Secret Book of James* 6; *Gospel of Philip* 55. 178. Cf. *Matthew* 10:37–38 (Q); *Luke* 12:26–27 (Q); *Gospel of Thomas* 55. 179. Cf. *Matthew* 23:13 (Q); *Luke* 11:52 (Q); *Gospel of Thomas* 39:1–2; Aesop *Fable* 702. 180. This may refer to either the time or the place of entry. 181. Cf. *Gospel of Thomas* 21:5–9; *Matthew* 24:43 (Q); *Luke* 12:39 (Q). 182. Cf. *Matthew* 9:14–15; *Mark* 2:18–20; *Luke* 5:33–35; *Gospel of the Nazoreans* 2. 183. On despising physical connections, cf. *Gospel of Thomas* 55; 101; *Book of Thomas* 144. On Simon Magus, Helena, and the soul's prostitution, cf. Irenaeus *Against Heresies* 1.23.2; *Exegesis on the Soul*. On the tradition of Jesus as the illegitimate child of Mary, cf. Origen *Against Celsus* 1.28, 32; perhaps *John* 8:41. 184. Or "sons of man." 185. Cf. *Gospel of Thomas* 48; *Matthew* 18:19; 17:20b (Q); *Luke* 17:6b (Q); *Matthew* 21:21; *Mark* 11:23; 1 *Corinthians* 13:2. 186. Cf. *Matthew* 18:12–13 (Q); *Luke* 15:4–7 (Q); *Ezekiel* 34:15–16. 187. Cf. *Gospel of Thomas* 13; *John* 4:13–14; 7:37–39; *Sirach* 24:21. 188. Cf. *Proverbs* 2:1–5; *Sirach* 20:30–31; *Matthew* 13:44; Midrash Rabbah, *Song of Songs* 4.12.1; Aesop *Fable* 42.

110 Jesus said, "Let someone who has found the world and has become wealthy renounce the world."[189]

111 (1) Jesus said, "The heavens and the earth will roll up in your presence, (2) and whoever is living from the living one will not see death."[190]

(3) Doesn't Jesus say, "Whoever has found oneself, of that person the world is not worthy"?[191]

112 (1) Jesus said, "Woe to the flesh that depends on the soul. (2) Woe to the soul that depends on the flesh."[192]

113 (1) His disciples said to him, "When will the kingdom come?"

(2) "It will not come by watching for it. (3) It will not be said,[193] 'Look, here it is,' or 'Look, there it is.' (4) Rather, the Father's kingdom is spread out upon the earth, and people do not see it."[194]

114 (1) Simon Peter said to them, "Mary should leave us, for females are not worthy of life."

(2) Jesus said, "Look, I shall guide her to make her male, so that she too may become a living spirit resembling you males. (3) For[195] every female who makes herself male will enter heaven's kingdom."[196]

The Gospel According to Thomas

---

189. Cf. *Gospel of Thomas* 27:1; 81. 190. Cf. *Isaiah* 34:4; *Psalm* 102:25–27 (some ancient texts); *Hebrews* 1:10–12; *Revelation* 6:13–14. 191. This may be a later comment incorporated into the saying. 192. Cf. *Gospel of Thomas* 29; 87. 193. Or "They will not say." 194. Cf. *Mark* 13:21–23; *Matthew* 24:23–25, 26–27 (Q); *Luke* 17:20–22, 23–24 (Q); *Gospel of Thomas* 3:1–3; *Gospel of Mary* 8. 195. The editors of the Gospel of Thomas in *Synopsis Quattuor Evangeliorum*, ed. Aland, 546, understand this ("For," Coptic *je*) as an introduction to direct speech, and they read "(But I say to you): Every woman . . ." 196. Although the language of this saying may be shocking to our sensitivities, the intent of the saying seems to be liberating. Here the female may symbolize what is earthly and perishable and the male what is heavenly and imperishable, so that the female becoming male means that all who are mortal and of this world, men and women alike, become immortal and divine. *Gospel of Thomas* 22 uses gender categories in a somewhat different way but for similar purposes. Cf. Hippolytus *Refutation of All Heresies* 5.8.44; Clement of Alexandria *Excerpts from Theodotus* 79; *First Revelation of James* 41; *Zostrianos* 131; also *Second Discourse of Great Seth* 65, and *Gospel of Philip* 58, on the Valentinian concept of the female images of all of us being joined to the male angels in final union.

The Greek Gospel of Thomas[1]

P. Oxy. 1, 654, 655; Hippolytus, *Refutation of All Heresies*

Prologue   [**P. Oxy. 654**] These are the [hidden] sayings [that] the living Jesus spoke [and Judas, who is] also called Thomas, [recorded].

1   And he said, "[Whoever finds the interpretation] of these sayings will not taste [death]."

2   (1) [Jesus says], "Let one who [seeks] not stop [seeking until] one finds. (2) When one finds, [one will be astonished, (3) and having been] astonished, one will reign, (4) and [having reigned], one will [rest]."

3   (1) Jesus says, "[If] your leaders [say to you, 'Look], the kingdom is in heaven,' the birds of [heaven will precede you. (2) If they say] that it is under the earth, the fish of the sea [will enter, and will precede] you. (3) And [God's kingdom][2] is inside you [and outside you. (4) Whoever] knows [oneself] will find this. [And when you] know yourselves, [you will understand that] you are [children] of the [living] Father. (5) [But if] you do [not] know yourselves, [you are] in [poverty], and you are [poverty]."

4   (1) [Jesus says], "A [person old in] days will not hesitate to ask a [little child seven] days old about the place of [life, and] that person will [live]. (2) For many of the [first] will be [last, and[3]] the last first, (3) and they [will become one]."

5   (1) Jesus says, "[Know what is before] your face, and [what is hidden] from you will be disclosed [to you. (2) For there is nothing] hidden that [will] not [become] apparent, (3) and nothing buried that [will not be raised]."

6   (1) [His disciples] ask him and say, "How [shall we] fast? [How shall] we [pray]? How [shall we give to charity]? What [diet] shall [we] observe?"

---

1. Edition: Bentley Layton, ed., *Nag Hammadi Codex II,2–7*, 1.95–128 (Harold W. Attridge). 2. Or "[heaven's kingdom]," a reading that is based on a new collation of the text by April D. DeConick and is discussed in her book *The Original Gospel of Thomas*. See also DeConick, "Corrections to the Critical Reading of the *Gospel of Thomas*." 3. Perhaps omit "[and]," a suggestion based on a new collation of the text by April D. DeConick in her book *The Original Gospel of Thomas*. See also DeConick, "Corrections to the Critical Reading of the *Gospel of Thomas*."

(2) Jesus says, "[Do not lie, (3) and] do not do [what] you [hate, (4) because all things are disclosed before] truth. (5) [For there is nothing] hidden [that will not be apparent]."

7　[possible restoration] (1) . . . "Blessed is [the lion that a human eats, and the] lion will be [human. (2) And cursed is the human] that [a lion eats . . .]."

24　[possible restoration] (3) ". . . There [is light within a person] of light, [and it shines on the whole] world. [If it does not shine, then] it is [dark]."

26　[P. Oxy. 1] (2) ". . . and then you will see clearly to take out the speck that is in your brother's⁴ eye."

27　(1) Jesus says, "If you do not fast from the world, you will not find God's kingdom. (2) And if you do not observe the Sabbath as a Sabbath, you will not see the Father."

28　(1) Jesus says, "I took my stand in the midst of the world, and in flesh I appeared to them. (2) I found them all drunk, and I found none of them thirsty. (3) My soul aches for the children of humanity, because they are blind in their hearts and [do not] see . . . ."

29　(3) "[. . . comes to dwell in this] poverty."

30　(1) [Jesus says], "Where there are [three, they are without] God,⁵ (2) and where there is only [one], I say, I am with that one.

77　(2) "Lift up the stone, and you will find me there. (3) Split the piece of wood, and I am there."

31　(1) Jesus says, "A prophet is not acceptable in the prophet's hometown, (2) nor does a doctor perform healings on those who know the doctor."

32　Jesus says, "A city built on top of a high hill and fortified can neither fall nor be hidden."

33　(1) Jesus says, "<What> you hear in one ear of yours, [proclaim . . .]."

36　[P. Oxy. 655] (1) [Jesus says, "Do not worry], from morning [to nightfall nor] from evening [to] morning, either [about] your [food], what [you will] eat, [or] about [your robe], what clothing you [will] wear. (2) [You are much] better than the lilies, which do not card or [spin]. (3) And since you have one article of clothing, what⁶ . . . you . . . ?⁷ (4) Who might add to your stature? That is the one who will give you your clothing.'"

37　(1) His disciples say to him, "When will you be revealed to us and when shall we see you?"

(2) He says, "When you strip off your clothing and are not ashamed, (3) [. . . and you will not be afraid]."

---

4. Or "sibling's." 5. Or "they are gods," a reading that is based on a new collation of the text by April D. DeConick and is discussed in her book *The Original Gospel of Thomas*. See DeConick, "Corrections to the Critical Reading of the *Gospel of Thomas*." See also the Coptic wording of the saying. 6. Or "why." 7. A previous reading of the Greek text of this saying allowed for the following translation: "As for you, when you have no garment, what [will you put] on?" (cf. Harold W. Attridge, in *Nag Hammadi Codex II,2–7*, 1.121; but now see James M. Robinson, "Essays on the Original Reading Behind Q 12:27."

38 (1) [Jesus says, "Often you have desired to hear these sayings of mine], and [you have no one else from whom to hear them]. (2) And [there will come days when you will seek me and you will not find me]."

39 (1) [Jesus says, "The Pharisees and the scholars] have [taken the keys] of [knowledge;8 they themselves] have [hidden them. (2) Neither] have [they] entered, [nor] have they allowed those who are in the process of] entering [to enter. (3) As for you, be as shrewd] as [snakes and as] innocent [as doves]."

4   [Hippolytus, *Refutation of All Heresies* 5.7.20] (1) "One who seeks will find me in children from seven years, for there, hidden in the fourteenth age,9 I am revealed."

11 [Hippolytus, *Refutation of All Heresies* 5.8.32] (3) "If you ate dead things and made them living, what will you do if you eat living things?"

---

8. Gnosis. 9. Aeon.

THE GOSPEL OF PHILIP

NHC II,3

Introduced by Madeleine Scopello
Translated by Marvin Meyer

The *Gospel of Philip* (51,29–86,19) belongs to one of the most interesting codices of the Nag Hammadi library, Codex II, which contains three mythological treatises (NHC II,1; II,4; II,5), three texts published under the authority of apostles (II,2; II,3; II,7), and one allegorical tale on the soul (II,6). The Coptic translation of the *Gospel of Philip*, thirty-two pages long, derives from a lost Greek original, but it illustrates a knowledge of technical Syriac terms that may give some indication of the place of composition of the treatise (63,21–23; 56,7–9).[1] The papyrus is in good condition, with minor lacunae. The title appears at the end of the treatise (*Peuaggelion pkata Philippos*) and could have been added by the Coptic translator.

A summary of the contents of the *Gospel of Philip* is difficult to provide: several themes are intertwined and rehearsed over and over by the author. One of the first scholars who worked on the treatise, Hans-Martin Schenke, divided the text into 127 units, and he interpreted it as something of an anthology. For Schenke, the sequence of these units is marked by the presence of catchwords. This division of the text, accomplished in imitation of the system of sayings in the *Gospel of Thomas*, appeared in the first translations of the *Gospel of Philip*, but it is rarely followed today. Other scholars have proposed different views. Eric Segelberg speaks about a collection of sentences without a defined plan, a disorganized collection of diverse materials. Jacques-É. Ménard, on the other hand, judges that the repetition of catchwords connects sentences and allows readers to follow the progress of the author's thought. The message of the *Gospel of Philip* develops in a curious "spiral" manner, proceeding by free association and leading the author of the gospel from one theme to another.[2] Wesley W. Isenberg

1. See Jacques-É. Ménard, *L'Évangile selon Philippe*; Wesley W. Isenberg, in Bentley Layton, ed., *Nag Hammadi Codex II, 2–7*. Martha Lee Turner, *The Gospel According to Philip: The Sources and Coherence of an Early Christian Collection*, 165, disagrees ("this evidence is weak").

2. Ménard, *L'Évangile selon Philippe*, 2–6.

understands the *Gospel of Philip* to be a collection of excerpts from a Christian Gnostic catechesis that had not been inserted into a narrative framework. Bentley Layton concludes that the *Gospel of Philip* is a Valentinian anthology, containing some sources of other provenance. Jorunn Jacobsen Buckley finds the coherence of the treatise in an underlying symbolic system.[3]

The title of the tractate, the *Gospel of Philip*, does not provide a precise idea of the literary genre of the treatise. The *Gospel of Philip* is not a gospel (*euaggelion* means "announcement," "good news") in the canonical sense, that is, a narration made by an apostle whose aim was to transmit the message of Christ and to relate events in his life. Rather, the *Gospel of Philip* is good news in a broader sense of the word.

The *Gospel of Philip* may be defined as a collection of sayings and meditations belonging to different genres—"parables, paraenesis, narrative dialogue, canonical sayings, aphorism and analogy"[4]—that have not been organized in a logical fashion. An interesting perspective is provided by Martha Lee Turner, who compares the tractate with other collections of sentences in late antiquity. According to Turner, the coherence of the *Gospel of Philip* is to be found in the compiler's distinctive interests and not in the uniformity of the materials. Turner shows that "the document's organizing principles correspond to excerpting and collection practices in late antiquity."[5] The *Gospel of Philip* is a something of a notebook that has been rearranged a bit[6] or even an aid to memory.[7] It can be compared with other treatises having the same features, especially the *Sentences of Sextus*, a composition preserved in several languages, one version of which has been transmitted in Coptic in Codex XII of the Nag Hammadi library.

The *Gospel of Philip* includes traces of several Gnostic traditions, but Valentinian features seem to be most prevalent. Parallels can also be drawn with Thomas traditions[8] as well as with the contents of mythological treatises (the *Secret Book of John* and the *Nature of the Rulers*). Turner proposes that these different materials could have been chosen in order to focus on a number of specific questions: the *Gospel of Philip* has features of a speculator's sourcebook, and it recalls the structure of the *Excerpts from Theodotus*, which also brings together different materials.[9]

The *Gospel of Philip* contains several sayings of Jesus. Some are quite different from those found in the canonical gospels: 55,37–56,3 (Take from Every House); 58,10–14 (Prayer of Thanksgiving); 59,18–27 (Holy Spirit and Evil Forces); 63,25–30 (The Dye Works of Levi); 63,30–64,9 (Wisdom and Mary of Magdala); 64,9–12

---

3. On the sources of these interpretations, see the bibliography for this introduction.

4. Isenberg, in *Nag Hammadi Codex II*, 2–7.

5. Turner, *The Gospel According to Philip*, 239–55.

6. Turner, *The Gospel According to Philip*, 254.

7. Turner, *The Gospel According to Philip*, 261.

8. Bentley Layton, *The Gnostic Scriptures*; Turner, *The Gospel According to Philip*, 206–34.

9. Turner, *The Gospel According to Philip*, 257.

(One Who Is); 67,30–68,17 (The Inner and the Outer); 74,24–75,2 (Laughing). Other sayings recall *Matthew* 3:15; 6:6; 15:13; 16:17; 27:46; and *John* 6:53; 8:32, 34. Quotations of *Matthew* 3:10; 1 *Corinthians* 8:1; 15:50; and 1 *Peter* 4:8 are inserted into the text. The vocabulary of the *Gospel of Philip* includes expressions drawn from both the New Testament and the Jewish scriptures.

Why was this tractate published under the authority of Philip? And who is this Philip? Is he the apostle Philip or Philip the deacon, one of the seven? The person of Philip in the *Gospel of Philip* seems to be a composite figure, as in the apocryphal *Acts of Philip*, where the hero is a combination of the two figures of Philip in the New Testament. A similar Philip also appears in the *Pistis Sophia* and in Manichaean literature. Philip is mentioned just once in the *Gospel of Philip* (73,8), in connection with a story about Joseph the carpenter.

One of the major themes of the *Gospel of Philip* is the reunification of soul and spirit in a heavenly union (or syzygy) that realizes the identification of the soul with its true self. The myth of Sophia and her eagerness to rejoin her spiritual companion, the Logos, was very likely present in the mind of the Gnostic author, even if there is no explicit reference to the myth. The author focuses upon the metaphor of marriage, which communicates several symbolic features and allows for allegorical interpretations. Marriage is a symbol of the Pleroma, or Fullness, of the divine; it is a symbol of knowledge and truth, in opposition to the ignorance and falseness of the world; it is a symbol of freedom. As such, marriage is meant for free men, not for slaves: "Animals do not have a wedding chamber, nor do slaves or defiled women. The wedding chamber is for free men and virgins" (69,1–4)—free, that is, from the archons' domination and the burden of sexuality. Freedom comes from truth: "If you know the truth, the truth will make you free" (*John* 8:32; *Gospel of Philip* 84,8–9). Heavenly marriage is also a symbol of chastity, since it is spiritual and not carnal, and it is placed in contrast with sexual intercourse. This marriage is a mystery, and it belongs entirely to another dimension: "If defiled marriage is hidden, how much more is undefiled marriage a true mystery! It is not fleshly but pure. It belongs not to desire but to will. It belongs not to darkness or night but to the day and the light" (82,2–10). The union of the bride with her bridegroom leads to the restoration of androgyny. Through spiritual union male and female will become one, and there will no longer be male and female but rather a unique being.

If the worldly metaphor of marriage produces the idea of heavenly, spiritual sexuality, this concept is completely modified in the mystical union of androgyny. Androgynous union repairs the damage of the separation of male and female, which occurred when the female element fell into matter, according to the myth of Sophia. This separation led to death. The *Gospel of Philip* amplifies upon this point with a biblical example. When Adam and Eve were joined to each other in paradise, they were in a condition of unity and knowledge. Once they separated into two different beings, however, they fell into ignorance and death: "When Eve was in Adam, there was no death. When she was separated from him, death came. If <she> enters into him again and he embraces <her>, death will cease to be" (68,23–27).[10] So it is also with humanity: "If the female had not separated from the male, the female and the male would not have died. The separation of male and female was the beginning of death" (70,9–12). It is Christ who eliminates the separation: "Christ came to heal the separation that was from the beginning and reunite the two, in order to give life to those who died through separation and unite them" (70,12–17).

Serious attention is given to sacramental theology in the *Gospel of Philip*. A summary of these rituals is provided in 67,27–30: "The master [did] everything in a mystery: baptism, chrism, eucharist, redemption, and bridal chamber." The sacrament of the bridal chamber has been the object of various interpretations (since the time of the church fathers): does it have only a symbolic and spiritual value, or was it actually acted out in Gnostic groups?

The date of composition of the *Gospel of Philip* can be designated somewhere in the second half of the second century or the first decades of the third. The place of composition may be Syria, but other locales are also possible.

BIBLIOGRAPHY

Jorunn Jacobsen Buckley, "Conceptual Models and Polemical Issues in the Gospel of Philip"; Carmino J. de Catanzaro, "The Gospel According to Philip"; Bentley Layton, *The Gnostic Scriptures*, 325–53; Bentley Layton, ed., *Nag Hammadi Codex II, 2–7*, 1.129–217 (Wesley W. Isenberg and Bentley Layton); Jacques-É. Ménard, *L'Évangile selon Philippe*; Louis Painchaud, "La composition de l'Évangile selon Philippe (NH II,3): une analyse rhétorique"; Hans-Martin Schenke, *Das Philippus-Evangelium*; Hans-Martin Schenke, Hans-Gebhard Bethge, and Ursula Ulrike Kaiser, eds., *Nag Hammadi Deutsch*, 1.183–213 (Hans-Martin Schenke); Eric Segelberg, "The Coptic Gnostic Gospel According to Philip and Its Sacramental System"; Jean-Marie Sevrin, "Les noces spirituelles dans l'Évangile selon Philippe"; Einar Thomassen, "How Valentinian Is *The Gospel of Philip*?"; Martha Lee Turner, *The Gospel According to Philip: The Sources and Coherence of an Early Christian Collection*; Bas van Os, "Dispositio: Towards a Rhetorical Analysis of the Gospel of Philip"; R. McL. Wilson, *The Gospel of Philip*.

---

10. On the emendation of the Coptic text and the possibility of reading the passage without emendation, see the translation and note.

The Gospel of Philip[1]

Converts (51,29–52,2)

A Hebrew makes a Hebrew, and such a person is called a convert.[2] A convert does not make a convert. [Some people] are as they [are] and make others [like them], while others [52] simply are.

Inheriting the Living and the Dead (52,2–15)

A slave seeks only to be free and does not seek the master's estate.

For a child it is not enough to be a child, but a child claims the father's inheritance.

Heirs to the dead are dead, and what they inherit is dead. Heirs to the living are alive, and they inherit both the living and the dead. The dead inherit nothing, for how could a dead person inherit? If a dead person inherits the living, the living will not die and the dead will come to life.[3]

Jesus, Gentiles, Christians (52,15–24)

A gentile does not die, never having been alive so as to die. One who has believed in truth is alive, but this person is at risk of dying just by being alive.

Since Christ came, the world has been created, cities have been beautified, and the dead have been buried.

When we were Hebrews we were orphans, with only a mother, but when we became Christians we had a father and a mother.[4]

---

1. Coptic Text: NHC II,3: 51,29–86,19. Editions: *The Facsimile Edition of the Nag Hammadi Codices: Codex II, 63–98*; Bentley Layton, ed., *Nag Hammadi Codex II,2–7*, 1.129–217 (Wesley W. Isenberg and Bentley Layton); Hans-Martin Schenke, *Das Philippus-Evangelium*; Hans-Martin Schenke, Hans-Gebhard Bethge, and Ursula Ulrike Kaiser, eds., *Nag Hammadi Deutsch*, 1.183–213 (Hans-Martin Schenke). A number of the textual restorations incorporated here derive from these editions, and particularly from the work of Hans-Martin Schenke, including not only the works cited in this note but also another of his translations, "The Gospel of Philip," in *New Testament Apocrypha*, ed. Wilhelm Schneemelcher, 1.179–208. 2. Or "proselyte," here and in the next sentence. 3. Or "the dead will not die and will live all the more." Cf. *Gospel of Thomas* 11:2–3. 4. Cf. *Gospel of Thomas* 99; 101; 105.

Sowing and Reaping (52,25–35)

Whoever sows in winter reaps in summer. Winter is the world, summer is the other aeon, the eternal realm. Let's sow in the world to reap in summer. And for this reason we should not pray in winter.[5]

From winter comes summer. If someone reaps in winter, the person will not really reap but will pull out the young plants, and such do not produce a crop. [That person's field] is barren not only [now] but also on the Sabbath.[6]

Christ Came (52,35–53,14)

Christ came [53] to purchase some, to save some, to redeem some. He purchased strangers and made them his own, and he brought back his own whom he had laid down of his own will as a deposit. Not only when he appeared did he lay the soul of his own will as a deposit, but from the beginning of the world he laid down the soul, for the proper moment, according to his will. Then he came forth to take it back, since it had been laid down as a deposit. It had fallen into the hands of robbers and had been stolen, but he saved it. And he redeemed the good in the world and the bad.

Light and Darkness (53,14–23)

Light and darkness, life and death, and right and left are siblings[7] of one another, and inseparable. For this reason the good are not good, the bad are not bad, life is not life, and death is not death. Each will dissolve into its original nature, but what is superior to the world cannot be dissolved, for it is eternal.

Words and Names (53,23–54,5)

The names of worldly things are utterly deceptive, for they turn the heart from what is real to what is unreal. Whoever hears the word "god" thinks not of what is real but rather of what is unreal. So also with the words "father," "son," "holy spirit," "life," "light," "resurrection," "church," and all the rest, people do not think of what is real but of what is unreal, [though] the words refer to what is real. The words [that are] heard belong to this world. [Do not be] [54] deceived. If words belonged to the eternal realm, they would never be pronounced in this world, nor would they designate worldly things. They would refer to what is in the eternal realm.

---

5. Cf. *Gospel of Thomas* 14:2. 6. Cf. *Gospel of Thomas* 57. 7. Lit., "brothers," or more generally, "are related to one another."

The Name of the Father (54,5–13)

Only one name is not pronounced in the world, the name the Father gave the Son. It is the name above all; it is the Father's name. For the Son would not have become Father if he had not put on the Father's name. Those who have this name understand it but do not speak it. Those who do not have it cannot even understand it.

Truth (54,13–18)

Truth brought forth names[8] in the world for us, and no one can refer to truth without names. Truth is one and many, for our sakes, to teach us about the one, in love, through the many.

The Archons (54,18–31)

The rulers wanted to fool people, since they saw that people have a kinship with what is truly good. They took the names of the good and assigned them to what is not good, to fool people with names and link the names to what is not good. So, as if they are doing people a favor, they take names from what is not good and transfer them to the good, in their own way of thinking. For they wished to take free people and enslave them forever.

The Forces (54,31–55,5)

There are forces[9] that do [favors] for people. They do not want people to come to [salvation], but they want their own existence to continue. For if people come to salvation, sacrifice will [stop] . . . and animals will not be offered up [55] to the forces. In fact, those to whom sacrifices were made were animals.[10] The animals were offered up alive, and after being offered they died. But a human being[11] was offered up to God dead, and the human being came alive.

Christ Brought Bread (55,6–14)

Before Christ came there was no bread in the world, just as paradise, where Adam lived, had many trees for animal food but no wheat for human food, and people ate like animals. But when Christ, the perfect human, came, he brought bread from heaven,[12] that humans might be fed with human food.

---

8. Or "words," here and below. 9. In Gnostic texts the forces are among the rulers of this world. Here they are identified with the ancient gods and goddesses, to whom sacrifices were made. 10. Ancient gods and goddesses were often depicted as animals. 11. Perhaps humankind in general, or perhaps Christ. 12. Cf. John 6:31, 50–51; Exodus 16:4; Psalm 78:23–24.

The Archons and the Holy Spirit (55,14–19)

The rulers thought they did all they did by their own power and will, but the Holy Spirit was secretly accomplishing all[13] through them by the Spirit's will.[14]

Sowing and Reaping Truth (55,19–22)

Truth, which has existed from the beginning, is sown everywhere, and many see it being sown, but few see it being reaped.

Mary Conceiving (55,23–33)

Some said Mary became pregnant by the Holy Spirit.[15] They are wrong and do not know what they are saying. When did a woman ever get pregnant by a woman?[16]

Mary is the virgin whom none of the powers defiled. This is greatly repugnant to the Hebrews, who are the apostles and apostolic persons. This virgin whom none of the powers defiled [wishes that][17] the powers would defile themselves.

My Father (55,33–36)

The master[18] [would] not have said, "My [Father who is] in heaven,"[19] if [he] did not also have another father. He would simply have said, "[My Father]."

Take from Every House (55,37–56,3)

The master said to the disciples, "[Take something] [56] from every house and bring it to the Father's house, but do not steal while in the Father's house and take something away."

Jesus Is a Hidden Name (56,3–13)

Jesus is a hidden name,[20] Christ is a revealed name.[21] The name Jesus does not exist in any other language, but he is called by the name Jesus. The word for Christ in Syriac is *messias* and in Greek is *christos*, and likewise all other people have a word for it in their own language. Nazarene is the revealed form of the hidden name.

---

13. Or "the realm of the All." 14. Cf. 1 Corinthians 2:8. 15. Cf. Matthew 1:18; 20; Luke 1:35. 16. In Hebrew and other Semitic traditions the word for "spirit" is feminine in gender, and the Spirit may be considered to be the divine Mother. Cf. Secret Book of James 6; Gospel of Thomas 101; especially Gospel of the Hebrews 3, in which Jesus refers to his mother the holy Spirit. 17. The restoration is tentative (cf. Schenke, "The Gospel of Philip," 190). 18. Or "Lord," here and below. 19. Matthew 16:17. Cf. also Matthew 6:9; Luke 11:2 (the Lord's Prayer). 20. Or "private name, personal name" (so Bentley Layton, The Gnostic Scriptures, 332). 21. Or "public name" (so Layton, Gnostic Scriptures, 332).

Christ Has Everything (56,13–15)

Christ has everything within himself, whether human or angel or mystery, and the Father.

Christ Arose, Then Died (56,15–20)

Those who say that the master first died and then arose are wrong, for he first arose and then died. If someone is not first resurrected, wouldn't that person die? As God lives, that one would <die>.[22]

The Precious in the Worthless (56,20–26)

No one would hide something valuable and precious in a valuable container, but countless sums are commonly kept in a container worth only a cent.[23] So it is with the soul. It is something precious, and it has come to be in a worthless body.

Naked and Not Naked (56,26–57,22)

Some people are afraid that they may arise from the dead naked, and so they want to arise in flesh. They do not know that it is those who wear the [flesh] who are naked. Those who are [able] to take it off are not naked.

"Flesh [and blood will] not inherit God's kingdom."[24] What is this flesh that will not [57] inherit? It is what we are wearing. And what is this flesh that will inherit? It is the flesh and blood of Jesus.

For this reason he said, "One who does not eat my flesh and drink my blood does not have life within."[25] What does this mean? His flesh is the word and his blood is the Holy Spirit. Whoever has received these has food, drink, and clothing.

And I also disagree with others who say that the flesh will not arise. Both views are wrong. You say that the flesh will not arise? Then tell me what will arise, so we may salute you. You say it is the spirit in the flesh, and also the light in the flesh? But what is in the flesh is the word, and what you are talking about is nothing other than flesh.[26] It is necessary to arise in this sort of flesh, since everything exists in it.

In this world those who wear clothes are superior to the clothes. In heaven's kingdom the clothes are superior to those who wear them.

---

22. The restored letters (nam<ou>) are suggested for a blank space on the papyrus. 23. Lit., an assarius, a Roman coin of little value. 24. 1 Corinthians 15:50. 25. John 6:53. 26. The text employs the term logos for "word," as above, where it is said that the flesh of Jesus in the eucharist is the word. Here the indefinite article is used with logos, and thus a more general translation of logos may be preferred.

Baptism and Anointing (57,22–28)

By water and fire this whole realm is purified, the visible by the visible, the hidden by the hidden. Some things are hidden by the visible. There is water within water,[27] there is fire within the oil of anointing.

Jesus Tricked Everyone (57,28–58,10)

Jesus tricked everyone, for he did not appear as he was, but he appeared so that he could be seen. He appeared to everyone. He [appeared] to the great as great, he [appeared] to the small as small, he [appeared [58] to the] angels as an angel and to humans as a human. For this reason his word was hidden from everyone. Some looked at him and thought they saw themselves. But when he appeared to his disciples in glory upon the mountain, he was not small. He became great. Or rather, he made the disciples great, so they could see him in his greatness.

Prayer of Thanksgiving (58,10–14)

He[28] said on that day in the prayer of thanksgiving,[29]

> You who have united perfect light with Holy Spirit,
> unite the angels also with us, as images.[30]

The Lamb (58,14–15)

Do not despise the lamb, for without it no one could see the <king>.[31]

Meeting the King (58,15–17)

No one can meet the king while naked.

Children of the Perfect Human (58,17–59,6)

The heavenly person has more children than the earthly person. If the children of Adam are numerous but die, how much more numerous are the children of the perfect human, who do not die but are continually being born.

A father produces children but a child cannot produce children. One who has just been born cannot be a parent. Rather, a child gets brothers and sisters,[32] not children.

---

27. Baptismal water. 28. Philip? Jesus? 29. Lit., "the eucharist." 30. In Valentinian thought, this language means uniting the female images of all of us with the male angels in final union, as a result of the sacrament of the bridal chamber. 31. Or "the door." Translating this passage as "the <king>" assumes a slight emendation of the text (from *ro* to <*r*>*ro*). 32. Lit., "brothers."

All who are born in the world are born of nature, and the others [are nourished] from where they are born. People [are] nourished from the promise of the heavenly place. [If they would be] . . . from the mouth, from which the word comes, [59] they would be nourished from the mouth and would be perfect.

The perfect conceive and give birth through a kiss. That is why we also kiss each other. We conceive from the grace within each other.

Three Women Named Mary (59,6–11)

Three women always walked with the master: Mary his mother, <his> sister,[33] and Mary of Magdala, who is called his companion. For "Mary" is the name of his sister, his mother, and his companion.

Father, Son, Holy Spirit (59,11–18)

"Father" and "son" are simple names, "holy spirit" is a double name. They[34] are everywhere, above and below, in the hidden and in the visible. The Holy Spirit is in the visible, and then it is below, and the Holy Spirit is in the hidden, and then it is above.

Holy Spirit and Evil Forces (59,18–27)

Evil forces serve the saints, for they have been blinded by the Holy Spirit into thinking they are helping their own people when they really are helping the saints.

So a disciple once asked the master for something from the world and he said, "Ask your mother, and she will give you something from another realm."

Wisdom and Salt (59,27–60,1)

The apostles said to the disciples, "May our entire offering be provided with salt." For they called [Wisdom[35]] salt. Without it an offering is unacceptable.[36] Wisdom is barren, [with no] children, and so she is called [the pillar] of salt.[37] Whenever . . . the Holy Spirit . . . , [60] and she has many children.

Father and Child (60,1–6)

A father's possessions belong to his child. As long as the child is young, the child will not have what belongs to it. When the child grows up, the father will turn over all the possessions.

---

33. The text reads "her sister" (Coptic *tessōne*) here, and the translation may reflect that reading (but see the reading "his sister" just below). 34. This may be a reference to the Father and the Son, in contrast to the Spirit, mentioned next, or it may be a reference to the Spirit, or even to Father, Son, and Spirit together.

35. Or "Sophia," here and below. 36. Cf. *Leviticus* 2:13; *Mark* 9:49 (with the variant reading); *Colossians* 4:6. 37. The suggested restoration is tentative, and includes a possible reference to Lot's wife (cf. Schenke, "The Gospel of Philip," 192, 207).

The Lost (60,6–9)

Those who have gone astray, who are offspring of the Spirit, go astray also because of the Spirit. Thus from one Spirit the fire blazes and the fire is extinguished.

Wisdom and Wisdom of Death (60,10–15)

There is Echamoth and there is Echmoth. Echamoth is simply Wisdom, but Echmoth is the Wisdom of death—that is, the Wisdom that knows death, that is called little Wisdom.[38]

Tame and Wild Animals (60,15–34)

Some animals are tame, such as the bull, the donkey, and the like, while others are wild and live off in the wild. People plow fields with tame animals, and as a result people are nourished, together with animals, whether tame or wild.

So also the perfect human plows with powers that are tame and prepares everything to come into being. Thus the whole place has stability, good and evil, right and left. The Holy Spirit tends everything and rules over [all] the powers, whether tame or wild and running loose. For the Spirit is [resolved] to corral them, so that they cannot escape even if [they] wish.

Adam and Cain (60,34–61,12)

[The one] created[39] was [noble, and you would] expect his children to be [61] noble. If he had not been created but rather had been conceived, you would expect his offspring to be noble. But in fact he was created, and then he produced offspring.

And what nobility this is! First came adultery, then murder. One[40] was born of adultery, for he was the son of the serpent.[41] He became a murderer, like his father, and he killed his brother.[42] Every act of sexual intercourse between those unlike each other is adultery.

God the Dyer (61,12–20)

God is a dyer. Just as the good dyes, said to be genuine dyes, dissolve into what is dyed in them, so also those whom God dyes become immortal through his colors, for his dyes are immortal. And God dips[43] those to be dipped[44] in water.[45]

---

38. This passage seems to reflect the Valentinian distinction between a higher Wisdom (often called Sophia) and a lower Wisdom (often called Achamoth). In Hebrew and Aramaic *'ekh-moth* means "like death." **39.** Adam. **40.** Cain. **41.** Such Gnostic texts as the *Secret Book of John* and the *Nature of the*

Rulers describe how the ruler of this world, sometimes with his powers, seduced or raped Eve and thus produced Cain. **42.** Abel. **43.** Or "baptizes." **44.** Or "baptized." **45.** For another meditation on dyeing, see *Gospel of Philip* 63.

Seeing (61,20–35)

People cannot see anything that really is without becoming like it. It is not so with people in the world, who see the sun without becoming the sun and see the sky and earth and everything else without becoming them.

> Rather, in the realm of truth,
> you have seen things there and have become those things,
> you have seen the Spirit and have become Spirit,
> you have seen Christ and have become Christ,
> you have seen the [Father] and will become Father.[46]

[Here] in the world you see everything but do not [see] yourself, but there in that realm you see yourself, and you will [become] what you see.

Faith and Love (61,36–62,6)

Faith receives, love gives. [No one can [62] receive] without faith, and no one can give without love. So to receive we have faith and to love we give. If someone gives without love, that person gets no benefit from what was given.[47]

Anyone who receives something but does not receive the Lord is still a Hebrew.

Jesus's Names (62,6–17)

The apostles who came before us used the names *Iēsous nazōraios messias*, which means "Jesus the Nazorean, the Christ."[48] The last name is "Christ," the first name is "Jesus," the middle name is "the Nazarene."[49] *Messias* has two meanings, "Christ"[50] and "measured."[51] In Hebrew "Jesus" means "redemption."[52] *Nazara* means "truth," and so "the Nazarene" means "truth."[53] "Christ" has been "measured," thus "the Nazarene" and "Jesus"[54] have been measured out.

A Pearl in Mud (62,17–26)

If a pearl is thrown into mud, it will not lose its value, and if it is anointed with balsam, it will not increase its value. It is always precious in its owner's eyes.

---

46. The text suggests an eschatological perspective with a present realization of spiritual union with Christ and an anticipation of the future union with the Father. Such an eschatological perspective is also found in the letters of Paul. 47. Cf. the discussion of faith and love in 1 *Corinthians* 13 and *Secret Book of James* 8. 48. The Greek word *nazōraios* can indicate someone from Nazareth or someone who is an observant Jewish Christian. 49. The Greek word *nazarēnos* indicates someone from Nazareth. 50. In Greek *khristos (christos)* means "anointed." 51. In Syriac *mšiha* can have both meanings. 52. "Jesus" comes from the Hebrew and Aramaic names Yeshua and Yehoshua (Joshua), which mean "The Lord (Yahweh) is salvation" (or the like). 53. Schenke, in *Nag Hammadi Deutsch*, 1.198, emends to read "<the man of> the truth." 54. I.e., "truth" and "redemption."

Likewise, the children of God are precious in the eyes of the Father, whatever their circumstances of life.

The Name Christian (62,26–35)

If you say, "I am a Jew," no one will be moved. If you say, "I am a Roman," no one will be disturbed. If you say, "I am a Greek, barbarian, slave, free," no one will be troubled. If you say, "I am a Christian," the [world] will be shaken. May I [receive the one] whose name the [world] cannot bear to hear.

God Is a Man-Eater (62,35–63,4)

God[55] is a man-eater, [63] and so humans are [sacrificed] to him. Before humans were sacrificed, animals were sacrificed, because those to whom they were sacrificed were not gods.

Glass and Ceramic Vessels (63,5–11)

Glass and ceramic vessels are both made with fire. If glass vessels break, they are redone, since they have been made through breath.[56] But if ceramic vessels break, they are destroyed, since they have been made without breath.

A Donkey Turning a Millstone (63,11–21)

A donkey turning a millstone walked a hundred miles. When it was set loose, it found itself in the same place. Some people travel long distances but get nowhere. By nightfall they have seen no cities or villages, nothing man-made or natural, no powers or angels. These miserable people have labored in vain.

The Eucharist and Jesus (63,21–24)

The eucharist is Jesus. In Syriac it is called *pharisatha*, which means "that which is spread out." For Jesus came to crucify[57] the world.

The Dye Works of Levi (63,25–30)

The master went into the dye works of Levi, took seventy-two colored cloths,[58] and threw them into a vat. He drew them out and they all were white. He said, "So the son of humanity[59] has come as a dyer."[60]

---

55. Here God is the ruler of this world. On this passage, cf. *Testimony of Truth* 32. 56. Or "spirit," here and below. 57. Jesus was "spread out" on the cross. 58. Seventy-two is a traditional number of nations in the world according to Jewish lore. 59. Or "son of man," here and below. 60. For another meditation on dyeing, see *Gospel of Philip* 61.

Wisdom and Mary of Magdala (63,30–64,9)

Wisdom,[61] who is called barren, is the Mother of the angels.

The companion of the [Savior] is Mary of Magdala. The [Savior loved] her[62] more than [all] the disciples, [and he] kissed her often on her [mouth].

The other [disciples] [64] . . . said to him, "Why do you love her more than all of us?"

The Savior answered and said to them, "Why don't I love you like her? If a blind person and one who can see are both in darkness, they are the same. When the light comes, one who can see will see the light, and the blind person will stay in darkness."[63]

One Who Is (64,9–12)

The master said, "Blessed is one who is before coming into being. For whoever is, was and will be."[64]

Human Beings and Animals (64,12–22)

The superiority of human beings is not apparent to the eye, but lies in what is hidden. Consequently, they are dominant over animals that are stronger than they are and greater in ways apparent and hidden. So animals survive. But when human beings leave them, animals kill and devour each other. Animals have eaten each other because they have found no other food. Now, however, they have food, because humans till the ground.

Going Down into the Water (64,22–31)

Anyone who goes down into the water[65] and comes up without receiving anything and says, "I am a Christian," has borrowed the name. But one who receives the Holy Spirit has the name as a gift. A gift does not have to be paid back, but what is borrowed must be paid. This is how it is with us, when one of us experiences a mystery.

Marriage (64,31–65,1)

The mystery of marriage is great. [Without] it, the world would [not] exist. The existence of [the world depends on] people, and the existence [of people depends on] marriage. Then think of the power of [pure] intercourse, though its image [65] is defiled.

---

61. Or "Sophia." 62. Or, dividing the sentences differently, "Wisdom, who is called barren, is the mother of the angels and the companion of the [Savior]. The [Savior loved] Mary of Magdala . . ." 63. On the blind person in darkness, cf. Gospel of Thomas 34. 64. Cf. Gospel of Thomas 19:1. 65. The reference is to baptism.

Unclean Spirits (65,1–26)

Unclean spirits are male and female in form. Males have sex with souls that are female in form, and females cavort promiscuously with souls that are male in form. Souls cannot escape them if the spirits seize them, unless they receive the male or female power of the bridegroom and the bride. These are received from the mirrored bridal chamber.

When foolish females see a man by himself, they jump on him, fondle him, and pollute him. Likewise, when foolish males see a beautiful woman by herself, they seduce and violate her in order to pollute her. But when they see a husband and wife together, the females cannot make advances on the man and the males cannot make advances on the woman. So also if the image and the angel are joined, none can dare to make advances on the male or the female.[66]

Whoever Leaves the World (65,27–66,6)

Whoever leaves the world can no longer be held back as if still in the world. Such a person clearly is beyond desire . . . and fear, is dominant . . . , and is above envy.

If . . . ,[67] that person is grasped and choked. How can that person escape the [great grasping powers]? How can that person [hide from them]?

Some [say], "We are faithful," in order that they [may escape [66] unclean] spirits and demons. For if they had the Holy Spirit, no unclean spirit could grab them.

Do not fear the flesh and do not love it. If you fear the flesh, it will dominate you. If you love the flesh, it will swallow you up and strangle you.

This World, the Resurrection, and the Middle (66,7–21)

A person is either in this world or in the resurrection—or in the middle place.[68] May I not be found there! In this world there is good and evil, but the good of the world is not really good and the evil of the world is not really evil. After this world there is evil that is really evil: this is called the middle. The middle is death. As long as we are in this world, we should acquire resurrection, so that when we take off the flesh[69] we may be found in rest and not wander in the middle. For many go astray on the way.

Will and Action (66,21–29)

It is good to leave the world before one sins. Some have neither the will nor the strength to act. Others, even if they have the will, do themselves no good, for they

---

66. This meditation suggests that the state of salvific androgyny (the union of female image and male angel) protects against unclean spirits. Cf. *Gospel of Philip* 58. 67. The person described in this paragraph seems to be one who has not left the world. 68. The middle is the region between the Fullness of the divine above and this world below. 69. I.e., when we die.

have not acted. And if they do not have the will . . . . Righteousness is beyond their grasp, in either case. It always comes down to the will, not the action.[70]

Vision of Hell (66,29–67,1)

In a vision an apostolic person saw people who were locked up in a house of fire, bound with [chains] of fire, and thrown [into] . . . fire [on account of . . . false] faith. It was said, "[They might have] saved [their souls], but they did not want to, so they got [this place of] punishment called [67] the [outer] darkness . . . ."[71]

Water and Fire (67,2–9)

Soul and spirit have come into being from water[72] and fire. The attendant of the bridal chamber has come into being from water, fire, and light. Fire is chrism. Light is fire. I do not mean ordinary fire, which has no form, but other fire, which is pure white in appearance, beautifully bright and imparting beauty.

Truth and Nakedness (67,9–27)

Truth did not come into the world naked, but in symbols and images. The world cannot receive truth in any other way. There is rebirth and an image of rebirth, and it is by means of this image that one must be reborn. What image is this? It is resurrection. Image must arise through image. By means of this image the bridal chamber and the image must approach the truth. This is restoration.

Those who receive the name of the Father, Son, and Holy Spirit and have accepted them must do this. If someone does not accept them, the name[73] will also be taken from that person. A person receives them in the chrism with the oil of the power of the cross. The apostles called this power the right and the left. This person is no longer a Christian but is Christ.

Sacraments (67,27–30)

The master [did] everything in a mystery: baptism, chrism, eucharist, redemption, and bridal chamber.

The Inner and the Outer (67,30–68,17))

[For this reason] he[74] said, "I have come to make [the lower] like the [upper and the] outer like the [inner, and to unite] them in that place."[75] [He spoke] here in symbols [and images].

---

70. The translation of this paragraph remains tentative. 71. For a similar apocalyptic vision of hell, cf. Book of Thomas 142–43. 72. The water of baptism. 73. Probably the name "Christian." 74. Jesus. 75. Cf. Gospel of Thomas 22:4.

Those who say [there is a heavenly person and] one that is higher are wrong,[76] for they call the visible heavenly person [68] "lower" and the one to whom the hidden realm belongs "higher." It would be better for them to speak of the inner, the outer, and the outermost.[77] For the master called corruption "the outermost darkness,"[78] and there is nothing outside it. He said, "My Father who is in secret." He said, "Go into your room, shut the door behind you, and pray to your Father who is in secret,"[79] that is, the one who is innermost. What is innermost is the Fullness,[80] and there is nothing further within. And this is what they call uppermost.

Fall and Return to Fullness (68,17–22)

Before Christ some came from a realm they could not reenter, and they went to a place they could not yet leave. Then Christ came. Those who went in he brought out, and those who went out he brought in.[81]

When Eve Was in Adam (68,22–26)

When Eve was in Adam, there was no death. When she was separated from him, death came. If <she> enters into him again and he embraces <her>, death will cease to be.[82]

Why Have You Forsaken Me? (68,26–29)

"My God, my God, why, Lord, have you forsaken me?"[83] He spoke these words on the cross, for he had left that place.

True Flesh (68,29–37)

[The master] was conceived from what [is imperishable], through God. The [master rose] from the dead, but [he did not come into being as he] was. Rather, his [body] was [completely] perfect. [It was] of flesh, and this [flesh] was true flesh. [Our flesh] is not true flesh, but only an image of the true. [69]

The Wedding Chamber (69,1–4)

Animals do not have a wedding chamber,[84] nor do slaves or defiled women. The wedding chamber is for free men and virgins.

---

76. Perhaps cf. *Gospel of Thomas* 11:1. 77. Lit., "what is outside the outer." 78. *Matthew* 8:12; 22:13; 25:30. 79. *Matthew* 6:6. 80. Pleroma, here and below. 81. Christ brings people from the material world back to the realm of Fullness. 82. Emended. The Coptic text may read, without emendation, "If he again becomes complete and attains his former self, death will cease to be." This meditation suggests that death will be undone in the oneness of androgyny. 83. *Matthew* 27:46 and *Mark* 15:34, citing *Psalm* 22:1. 84. Or "bridal chamber," here and below.

Baptism (69,4–14)

We are born again through the Holy Spirit, and we are conceived through Christ in baptism with two elements. We are anointed through the Spirit, and when we were conceived, we were united.

No one can see oneself in the water or in a mirror without light, nor can you see yourself in the light without water or a mirror. So it is necessary to baptize with two elements, light and water, and light is chrism.

The Temple in Jerusalem (69,14–70,4)

There were three structures for sacrifice in Jerusalem. One opened to the west and was called the holy place; a second opened to the south and was called the holy of the holy; the third opened to the east and was called the holy of holies, where only the high priest could enter. The holy place is baptism; the holy of the holy is redemption; the holy of holies is the bridal chamber. Baptism entails resurrection and redemption, and redemption is in the bridal chamber. The bridal chamber is within a realm superior to [what we belong to], and you cannot find anything [like it . . . . These] are the ones who worship [in spirit and in truth,[85] for they do not worship] in Jerusalem. There are people in Jerusalem who [do worship] in Jerusalem, and they await [the mysteries] called [the holy] of holies, the curtain [of which] was torn. [Our] bridal chamber is the image [of the bridal chamber] [70] above. That is why its curtain was torn from top to bottom, for some people from below had to go up.[86]

Wearing the Light (70,5–9)

The powers cannot see those who have put on the perfect light, and they cannot seize them. One puts on the light in the mystery of union.

Union in the Bridal Chamber (70,9–22)

If the female had not separated from the male, the female and the male would not have died. The separation of male and female was the beginning of death. Christ came to heal the separation that was from the beginning and reunite the two, in order to give life to those who died through separation and unite them.

A woman is united with her husband in the bridal chamber, and those united in the bridal chamber will not be separated again. That is why Eve became separated from Adam, because she had not united with him in the bridal chamber.

---

85. Cf. *John* 4:23. **86.** On the restorations here, cf. Schenke, in *Nag Hammadi Deutsch*, 1.203; "The Gospel of Philip," 197–98. On the curtain of the temple being torn, cf. *Matthew* 27:51; *Mark* 15:38; *Luke* 23:45; *Hebrews* 10:19–20; *Gospel of Philip* 85.

Adam's Soul (70,22–34)

Adam's soul came from a breath.[87] The soul's companion is spirit, and the spirit given to him is his mother. His soul was [taken] from him and replaced with [spirit]. When he was united with spirit, [he] uttered words superior to the powers, and the powers envied him.[88] They [separated him from his] spiritual companion . . . hidden . . . bridal chamber . . . .

Jesus at the Jordan (70,34–71,3)

Jesus revealed himself [at the] Jordan River as the fullness of heaven's kingdom. The one [conceived] before all[89] [71] was conceived again; the one anointed before was anointed again; the one redeemed redeemed others.

The Mystery of the Virgin Birth (71,3–15)

It is necessary to utter a mystery. The Father of the All united with the virgin who came down, and fire shone on him.

On that day that one revealed the great bridal chamber, and in this way his body came into being.

On that day he came forth from the bridal chamber as one born of a bridegroom and a bride.

So Jesus established all within it, and it is fitting for each of the disciples to enter into his rest.

The Births of Adam and Christ (71,16–21)

Adam came from two virgins, the Spirit and the virgin earth.[90] Christ was born of a virgin to correct the fall that occurred in the beginning.

Two Trees in Paradise (71,22–72,4)

There are two trees growing in paradise. One produces [animals] and the other produces people. Adam [ate] of the tree that produces animals, and [he] became an animal and brought forth animals. As a result Adam's children worship animals.[91] The tree [whose] fruit [he ate] is the [tree of knowledge, and because of this, sins] increased. [If he had] eaten the [fruit of the other tree], the fruit of [the tree of life, which] produces people, [gods would] worship people. As [in paradise] God created people [that people] [72] might create God,[92] so also in this

---

87. Cf. *Genesis* 2:7 and Gnostic accounts of creation.
88. Cf. *Secret Book of John* II, 19–20. 89. Or "the All."
90. In *Genesis* 2:7 the name of Adam is connected to the Hebrew word *'adamah,* "earth," from which Adam

is made. 91. I.e., people worship gods depicted in the form of animals, as in Egypt. Cf. *Gospel of Philip* 54–55. 92. Possibly correct to read "worship God."

world people make gods and worship what they have created. It would be more fitting for gods to worship people.

Accomplishments (72,4–17)

The truth is, a person's accomplishments depend on that person's abilities, and for this reason we refer to accomplishments as abilities. Among such accomplishments are a person's children, and they come into being from a time of rest.[93] Now, one's abilities come to expression in what one accomplishes, and rest is clearly found in children. You will find this also applies to the image. These are the people made after the image,[94] who accomplish things through their strength and bring forth children through rest.

Slaves and the Free (72,17–29)

In this world slaves serve the free. In heaven's kingdom the free will serve the slaves and the attendants of the bridal chamber will serve the wedding guests.

The attendants of the bridal chamber have only one name, and that is rest. When they are together, they need no other form, [for they are in] contemplation . . . perception. They are superior . . . among those in . . . the glories of glories . . . .

Jesus Going Down into the Water (72,29–73,1)

[It] was [necessary for Jesus] to go down into the water [in order to perfect] and purify it. [So also] those who are [baptized] in his name [are perfected]. For he said, "[Thus] shall we perfect [**73**] all righteousness."[95]

Resurrection and Baptism (73,1–8)

People who say they will first die and then arise are wrong. If they do not receive the resurrection first, while they are alive, they will receive nothing when they die. So it is said of baptism, "Great is baptism," for if people receive it, they will live.

Joseph the Carpenter (73,8–19)

Philip the apostle said, "Joseph the carpenter planted a garden,[96] for he needed wood for his trade. He is the one who made the cross from the trees he planted, and his own offspring hung on what he planted. His offspring was Jesus and what he planted was the cross."

---

93. "Rest" is the term commonly employed in Gnostic texts to describe the state of ultimate bliss. 94. Cf. *Genesis* 1:26–27. 95. *Matthew* 3:15. 96. Lit., "a paradise."

The tree of life, however, is in the middle of the garden.[97] It is an olive tree, and from it comes chrism, and from chrism comes resurrection.

This World Eats Corpses (73,19–27)

This world eats corpses, and everything eaten in this world also dies. Truth eats life, and no one nourished by [truth] will die.[98] Jesus came from that realm and brought food from there, and he gave [life] to all who wanted it, that they might not die.

God Plants Paradise (73,27–74,12)

[God planted] a garden,[99] and humans [lived in the] garden. There are some [who dwell] with . . . God . . . .

This garden [is where] it will be said to me, ". . . [eat] this and do not eat that, [as you] [74] wish." This is where I shall eat everything, where the tree of knowledge is.[100]

That tree killed Adam, but here the tree of knowledge has brought people back to life. That tree was the law. It can give knowledge of good and evil, but it neither freed Adam from evil nor made him good, and it brought death to those who ate of it. For when it was said, "Eat this and do not eat that," death began.

Chrism Is Superior to Baptism (74,12–24)

Chrism is superior to baptism. We are called Christians from the word "chrism," not from the word "baptism." Christ[101] also has his name from chrism, for the Father anointed the Son, the Son anointed the apostles, and the apostles anointed us. Whoever is anointed has everything: resurrection, light, cross, Holy Spirit. The Father gave all this to the person in the bridal chamber, and the person accepted it. The Father was in the Son and the Son was in the Father. This is heaven's kingdom.

Laughing (74,24–75,2)

The master put it very well: "Some have gone into heaven's kingdom laughing, and they have come out [laughing]."

Someone said, "[That is] a Christian."

The person said [again, "That is the one who went] down into the water and came [up as lord] of all. [Redemption is no] laughing matter, but [a person goes laughing into] heaven's kingdom out of contempt for these rags.[102] If the person

---

97. Or "paradise." 98. Cf. *Gospel of Thomas* 11:2–3. 99. Or "paradise," here and below. 100. Cf. *Genesis* 3:1–7. Here the speaker seems to be Adam. The word for "knowledge" is gnosis, here and below. 101. I.e., "The anointed one." 102. This is the body worn as a garment, here a garment of rags.

despises [the body] and considers it a laughing matter, [the person will come out] laughing."

So it is also [75] with bread, the cup, and oil,[103] though there are mysteries higher than these.

Creation Through a Mistake (75,2–14)

The world came into being through a mistake. The creator wanted to make it incorruptible and immortal, but he failed and did not get what he hoped for. For the world is not incorruptible and the creator of the world is not incorruptible. Things are not incorruptible, but offspring[104] are. Nothing can receive incorruptibility unless it is an offspring.[105] And whatever cannot receive certainly cannot give.

Eucharist and Baptism (75,14–25)

The cup of prayer[106] contains wine and water, for it represents the blood for which thanksgiving is offered. It is full of the Holy Spirit, and it belongs to the completely perfect human. When we drink it, we take to ourselves the perfect human.

The living water is a body, and we must put on the living human. Thus, when one is about to go down into the water, one strips in order to put on the living human.[107]

Like Bring Forth Like (75,25–76,6)

A horse brings forth a horse, a human brings forth humans, a deity brings forth deities. So also bridegrooms and brides come from the [bridegroom and bride].

No Jews . . . from Greeks . . . from Jews . . . to Christians. [There was another generation of people], and these [blessed people] were called the chosen spiritual ones, [76] true humanity, the child of humanity, and the offspring of the child of humanity. This true generation is renowned in the world, and this is where the attendants of the bridal chamber are.

Strength and Weakness (76,6–17)

In this world, where strength and weakness are to be found, there is union of male and female, but in the eternal realm there is a different kind of union.

Although we refer to these things with the same words, there are also other words that are superior to every word that is pronounced.

---

103. Bread, the cup, and oil are elements in the sacraments of the eucharist and chrism. 104. Or "children." 105. Or "a child." 106. I.e., the cup of the eucharist. 107. This is baptismal imagery. Living or running water was commonly used in baptism, and a person being baptized was thought to take off the old and put on the new, namely, Christ.

These are above strength. For there is strength and there are those superior to strength, and they are not different but the same. This is incomprehensible to hearts of flesh.

Know Yourself (76,17–22)

All those who have everything should know themselves,[108] shouldn't they? If some do not know themselves, they will not enjoy what they have, but those who know themselves will enjoy their possessions.

Putting on Light (76,22–77,1)

The perfect human can neither be grasped nor seen. What is seen can be grasped. No one can obtain this grace without putting on perfect light and becoming perfect light. Whoever puts on light will enter [the place of rest]. This is perfect [light, and] we [must] become [perfect humans] before we leave [the world]. Whoever obtains everything [but does not separate] from this world will [not] be able [to attain] that realm but will [go to the] middle place,[109] for that one is not perfect. [77] Only Jesus knows the fate of that person.[110]

The Priest (77,2–7)

The holy person[111] is completely holy, including the person's body. The holy person who takes up bread consecrates it, and does the same with the cup or anything else the person takes up and consecrates.[112] So how wouldn't the person consecrate the body also?

The Water of Baptism and Death (77,7–15)

As Jesus perfected[113] the water of baptism, he poured death out. For this reason we go down into the water but not into death, that we may not be poured out into the spirit[114] of the world. When it blows, winter comes. When the Holy Spirit blows, summer comes.

Knowledge and Love (77,15–35)

Whoever knows[115] the truth is free,[116] and a free person does not sin, for "one who sins is a slave of sin."[117] Truth is the Mother, knowledge is the Father. Those who do not allow themselves to sin the world calls free. They do not allow themselves

---

108. "Know yourself" is the well-known Greek maxim from Delphi. 109. The middle is the place between the Fullness above and this world below. 110. The restorations here remain tentative. 111. Or "priest." 112. The references are to the eucharist.

113. Or "filled." Schenke, "The Gospel of Philip," 201, understands this to mean "Jesus filled the water of baptism with spirit." 114. Or "wind." 115. Gnosis, here and below. 116. Cf. John 8:32. 117. John 8:34.

to sin, and knowledge of the truth lifts them up[118]—that is, it makes them free and superior to all. But "love builds up."[119] Whoever is free through knowledge is a slave because of love for those who do not yet have freedom of knowledge. Knowledge enables them to be free.

Love [never says] it owns something, [though] it owns [everything]. Love does not [say, "This is mine]" or "That is mine," but rather, "[All that is mine] is yours."

Spiritual Love (77,35–78,12)

Spiritual love is wine and perfume. [78] People who anoint themselves with it enjoy it, and while these people are present, others who are around also enjoy it. If the people who are anointed leave them and go away, the others who are not anointed but are only standing around are stuck with their own bad odor.

The Samaritan gave nothing to the wounded person except wine and oil—that is, only ointment.[120] The ointment healed the wound, for "love covers a multitude of sins."[121]

Children and Love (78,12–25)

The children a woman brings forth resemble the man she loves. If it is her husband, they resemble her husband. If it is a lover, they resemble the lover. Often, if a woman must sleep with her husband but her heart is with the lover with whom she usually has sex, the child she bears will resemble the lover.

So, you who live with the Son of God, do not love the world but love the master,[122] that what you bring forth may not resemble the world, but may resemble the master.

Sex and Spirit (78,25–79,13)

Humans have sex with humans, horses have sex with horses, donkeys have sex with donkeys. Members of a species have sex with members of the same species. So also spirit has intercourse with spirit, word[123] mingles with word, light mingles [with light].

If [you] become human,
[a human] will love you.
If you become [spirit],
spirit will unite with you.
If you become word,
word [79] will have intercourse with you.

---

118. Or "puffs them up." Cf. 1 Corinthians 8:1. 119. 1 Corinthians 8:1. 120. Cf. Luke 10:34. 121. 1 Peter 4:8. 122. Or "Lord," here and below. 123. Logos, here and below.

If you become light,
light will mingle with you.
If you become one of those above,
those above will rest on you.
If you become a horse or donkey or bull
or dog or sheep or some other animal,
wild or tame,
then neither human nor spirit
nor word nor light can love you.
Those above and those within cannot rest in you,
and you have no part in them.

Slave and Free (79,13–18)

People who are slaves against their will can be free. People who are freed by favor of their master and then sell themselves back into slavery cannot be free again.

Farming (79,18–32)

Farming in this world depends on four things, and a harvest is gathered and taken into the barn as a result of water, earth, air,[124] and light.

God's farming also depends on four things: faith, hope, love, and knowledge.[125] Faith is the earth in which we take root. Hope is the water with which we are nourished. Love is the air through which we grow. Knowledge is the light by which we [ripen].[126]

Grace exists [in four ways. It is] earthly; it is [heavenly] . . . the highest heaven
. . . .

Blessed Is One Who Never Grieves Anyone (79,32–80,23)

[Blessed] is one who has never grieved [80] a soul. This is Jesus Christ. He came to the whole earth and never laid a burden upon anyone. Blessed is one like this, for this is a perfect human.

The word[127] tells us how difficult it is to bring this about. How can we accomplish such a feat? How can we give help[128] to everyone?

To begin with, one must not cause grief to anyone, whether great or small, unbeliever or believer, and one must not give help to those who are well off. There are some who profit by helping the rich. The person who does good deeds will not help the rich, for this person will not take just anything that may be desirable. Nor can such a person cause them grief, since this person does not give them

---

124. Or "wind," "spirit," here and below. 125. Gnosis, here and below. 126. On faith, hope, love, and knowledge, cf. 1 Corinthians 13 and Secret Book of   James 8. 127. Lit., "The logos," perhaps "Reason." 128. Or "rest," here and below.

trouble. The new rich sometimes cause others grief, but the person who does good deeds does not do this. It is the wickedness of these people that causes their grief. The person with the nature of a perfect human gives joy to the good, but some people are deeply distressed by all this.

A Householder and Food (80,23–81,14)

There was a householder who had everything: children, slaves, cattle, dogs, pigs, wheat, barley, chaff, fodder, [oil], meat, and acorns. The householder was wise and knew the food of each. He fed the children [baked] bread [and meat]. He fed the slaves [oil and] grain. [He fed] the cattle barley, chaff, and fodder. He threw the dogs some bones. He fed the pigs acorns [81] and gruel.

So it is with the disciples of God. If they are wise, they understand discipleship. Bodily forms will not deceive them, but they will examine the condition of each person's soul and speak appropriately with the person. In the world many animals have human form. If the disciples of God identify them as pigs, they feed them acorns. If cattle, they feed them barley, chaff, and fodder. If dogs, they throw them some bones. If slaves, they feed them what is preliminary. If children, they feed them what is complete.[129]

Creating and Procreating (81,14–34)

There is the Child of Humanity, and there is the child of the Child of Humanity. The Child of Humanity is the Lord, and the child of the Child of Humanity is the one who creates through the Child of Humanity. The Child of Humanity received from God the ability to create. He can also procreate. One who has received the ability to create is a creature, and one who has received the ability to procreate is an offspring. One who creates cannot procreate, but one who procreates can create. One who creates is said to procreate, but the "offspring" are really creatures, because these "offspring" are not children of procreation but [works of creation].

One who creates works openly and is visible. One who procreates does so [secretly] and is hidden, for one who procreates [is beyond every] image. So, then, one who creates does so openly, and one who procreates [produces] offspring secretly.

Pure Marriage (81,34–82,26)

No [one can] know when [a husband] [82] and wife have sex except those two, for marriage in this world is a mystery for those married. If defiled marriage is hidden, how much more is undefiled marriage a true mystery! It is not fleshly but

---

129. Layton, *Gnostic Scriptures*, 350, translates as follows: "if slaves, a first course (i.e., a single dish); if children, a complete meal."

pure. It belongs not to desire but to will. It belongs not to darkness or night but to the day and the light.

If marriage is exposed, it has become prostitution, and the bride plays the harlot not only if she is impregnated by another man, but even if she slips out of her bedchamber and is seen. Let her show herself only to her father and her mother, the friend of the bridegroom, and the attendants of the bridegroom. They are allowed to enter the bridal chamber every day. But let the others yearn just to hear her voice and enjoy the fragrance of her ointment, and let them feed on the crumbs that fall from the table, like dogs.[130]

Bridegrooms and brides belong to the bridal chamber. No one can see a bridegroom or a bride except by becoming one.

Abraham's Circumcision (82,26–29)

When Abraham [was able][131] to see what he was to see, [he] circumcised the flesh of the foreskin, thus teaching us that it is necessary to destroy the flesh.

Hidden Parts (82,30–83,18)

As long as their [insides] are hidden, [most] beings in the world are alive and well. [If their insides] are exposed, they die, as is clear by the example of the visible part of a person. [As long as] a person's intestines are hidden, the person is alive. [83] If the intestines are exposed and come out, the person dies. Likewise, while its root is hidden, a tree sprouts and grows. If its root is exposed, the tree withers.

So it is with all things produced in the world, not only the visible but also the hidden. As long as the root of evil is hidden, it is strong. When it is recognized, it is undone, and if it is brought to light, it dies. For this reason the word[132] says, "Already the ax is laid at the root of the trees."[133] It will not merely cut them down, for what is cut down sprouts up again. Rather, the ax will dig down until it cuts out the root. Jesus pulled out the root of the whole place, but others did so only in part.

The Root of Evil (83,18–30)

Let each of us also dig down after the root of evil within us and pull it out of our hearts from the root. It will be uprooted if we recognize it. But if we are ignorant of it, it takes root in us and produces fruit in our hearts. It dominates us. We are its slaves, and it takes us captive so that we do what we do [not] want and do [not] do what we want. It is powerful because we do not recognize it. As long as [it] exists, it stays active.

---

130. Cf. *Matthew* 15:27; *Mark* 7:28. 131. Or "[rejoiced]"; cf. *John* 8:56. 132. Or "scripture." 133. *Matthew* 3:10; *Luke* 3:9.

Ignorance Is the Mother of Evil (83,30–84,14)

Ignorance is the mother of [all evil]. Ignorance leads to [death, because] those who come from [ignorance] neither were nor [are] nor will be. [But those in the truth] [84] will be perfect when all truth is revealed. For truth is like ignorance. While hidden, truth rests in itself, but when revealed and recognized, truth is praised in that it is stronger than ignorance and error. It gives freedom.

The word[134] says, "If you know the truth, the truth will make you free."[135] Ignorance is a slave, knowledge[136] is freedom. If we know the truth, we shall find the fruit of truth within us. If we join with it, it will bring us fulfillment.

Things Visible and Hidden (84,14–20)

At present we encounter the visible things of creation, and we say that they are mighty and worthy and the hidden things are weak and insignificant. It is <not>[137] so with the visible things of truth. They are weak and insignificant, but the hidden things are mighty and worthy.

Temple, Cross, Ark (84,20–85,21)

The mysteries of truth are made known in symbols and images. The bedchamber is hidden, and it is the holy of the holy. At first the curtain[138] concealed how God manages creation, but when the curtain is torn[139] and what is inside appears, this building will be left deserted, or rather will be destroyed. And the whole god-head[140] will flee from here but not into the holy of holies, for it cannot mingle with pure [light] and [perfect] fullness. Instead, it will remain under the wings of the cross [and under] its arms.[141] This ark will be salvation [for people] when floodwaters [85] surge over them.[142]

Whoever belongs to the priestly order can go inside the curtain along with the high priest. For this reason the curtain was not torn only at the top, for then only the upper realm would have been opened. It was not torn only at the bottom, for then it would have revealed only the lower realm. No, it was torn from top to bottom. The upper realm was opened for us in the lower realm,[143] that we might enter the hidden realm of truth. This is what is truly worthy and mighty, and we shall enter through symbols that are weak and insignificant. They are weak compared to perfect glory. There is glory that surpasses glory, there is power that

---

134. Or "scripture." 135. *John* 8:32. 136. Gnosis. 137. The word "<not>" (Coptic <an>) presumably was omitted in the text, and it is supplied here. 138. A curtain or veil separates the realm of Fullness from the world below in Valentinian thought, and a curtain separates the holy of holies from the holy place in the temple in Jerusalem. Cf. the Boundary in the *Tripartite Tractate*. 139. On the curtain being torn, cf. *Gospel of Philip* 69–70, with references. 140. I.e., the lesser godhead, the realm of demiurge and demigod. Here and elsewhere in Valentinian literature, the ruler of this world can be a somewhat kinder and gentler demiurge who is not entirely diabolical. 141. This refers to the cross of Christ as source of salvation. 142. This refers to Noah's ark as source of salvation. 143. Or, with a slight correction, "the upper realm was opened for us <along with> the lower realm."

surpasses power. Perfect things have opened to us, and hidden things of truth. The holy of holies was revealed, and the bedchamber invited us in.

Revelation of the Seed (85,21–32)

As long as the seed[144] of the Holy Spirit is hidden, wickedness is ineffective, though it is not yet removed from the midst of the seed, and they are still enslaved to evil. But when the seed is revealed, then perfect light will shine on everyone, and all who are in the light will [receive the] chrism.[145] Then slaves will be freed and captives ransomed. "Every plant that my Father in heaven has not planted [will be] pulled out."[146] What is separated will be united, [what is empty] will be filled.

Eternal Light (85,32–86,19)

Everyone who [enters] the bedchamber will kindle the [light. This is] like marriages that occur [in secret and] take place at night. The light of the fire [shines] [86] during the night and then goes out. The mysteries of that marriage, however, are performed in the day and the light, and neither that day nor its light ever sets.

If someone becomes an attendant of the bridal chamber, that person will receive the light. If one does not receive it while here in this place, one cannot receive it in the other place.

Those who receive the light cannot be seen or grasped. Nothing can trouble such people even while they are living in this world. And when they leave this world, they have already received truth through images, and the world has become the eternal realm. To these people the eternal realm is Fullness.

This is the way it is. It is revealed to such a person alone, hidden not in darkness and night but hidden in perfect day and holy light.

The Gospel According to Philip

---

144. Or "offspring," here and below. 145. Or "be anointed." 146. *Matthew* 15:13.

THE NATURE OF THE RULERS

NHC II,4

Introduced and Translated by Marvin Meyer

The *Nature of the Rulers* is a Gnostic treatise classified by scholars as representing Sethian thought, which the author claims is being sent to an undisclosed recipient in order to clarify who the archons, or world rulers, are and how the struggle with the archons is to be carried out. In its present form, the *Nature of the Rulers* is a Christian text,[1] but most of the material in the text is reflective of Jewish thought, with the typical Hellenistic flourish. The author of the text, whose identity, like that of the recipient, is unknown, says that he or she is sending the text in response to certain questions that have been raised: "I have sent you this writing because you have asked about the real nature of the authorities" (86,26–27). Preserved as the fourth tractate in Nag Hammadi Codex II (86,20–97,23), the *Nature of the Rulers* is copied just before *On the Origin of the World*, another Gnostic text to which the *Nature of the Rulers* stands in some relation.

The title of the present text, *tthupostasis ⁿnarkhōn*, provided at the end of the tractate (97,22–23) and paraphrased twice in the opening section, has been translated variously as "The Hypostasis of the Archons,"[2] "The Reality of the Rulers,"[3] and, as here, "The Nature of the Rulers," depending on the interpretation of the technical Greek term *hupostasis*. We choose to translate the title of the text as "The Nature of the Rulers" (by implication, "the real nature"; cf. the use of that phrase for *thuposta[sis]* at 86,26–27) as a way of encompassing as much as possible of the full meaning of this rich Greek term. To be sure, a major point of the text is that the malevolent demiurge and archons are real and do exist, but when they are opposed vigorously by the children of the light, they will be defeated. Like other Gnostic texts, the *Nature of the Rulers* assumes a distinctive position in its concern for theodicy, the issue of the problem of evil in the world and the

---

1. Cf. the reference to Paul "the great apostle" and the citations of *Colossians* 1:13 and *Ephesians* 6:12 at the opening of the text.

2. See, e.g., Bernard Barc, *L'Hypostase des archontes*; Ursula Ulrike Kaiser, in Hans-Martin Schenke, Hans-Gebhard Bethge, and Ursula Ulrike Kaiser, eds., *Nag Hammadi Deutsch* ("Die Hypostase der Archonten").

3. See, e.g., Bentley Layton, *The Gnostic Scriptures*.

vindication of the goodness of God. Gnostic texts like the *Nature of the Rulers* take evil seriously—too seriously, opponents sometimes say, as when the great Neoplatonist philosopher Plotinus faults the Gnostics for being too hard on the world and the demiurge. Nonetheless, Gnostics bring a sense of urgency to the discussion of what evil is and how it is to be confronted when they insist, in a text like the *Nature of the Rulers*, that the archons are indeed real.[4]

The *Nature of the Rulers* is composed of two narrative parts that complement each other and overlap only a little. The first part (86,20–93,13) provides an account by the author of the text, and in this part the author gives a Sethian interpretation of the opening chapters of *Genesis* (1–6). Many familiar characters are introduced into the story—the Father of the All, Incorruptibility, Pistis Sophia, Samael the blind demiurge, a host of archons, and of course the figures from *Genesis*. This version of the story of *Genesis* begins with the arrogant and blasphemous utterance of Samael ("I am God; there is no other [but me]"), and this sets the tone for a text that means to disclose the true character of the archons. The divine figure of Incorruptibility is well known from the *Secret Book of John*, where she is associated with Forethought (Pronoia) or Barbelo; here Forethought and Barbelo are not mentioned, but Incorruptibility seems to assume a role like that of Forethought. In the *Nature of the Rulers* it is Incorruptibility who gazes out of heaven and whose image appears in the waters of the cosmos. The archons as described in the text are androgynous, with animal faces. They are a crude, lusty lot, and when they try to rape spiritual Eve, she, like Daphne in Greek mythology, turns into a tree, so they defile the shadow she leaves behind, apparently physical Eve (89,17–31).[5] Through it all, the female spiritual presence (*pneumatikē*)—who recalls Epinoia, Insight or Reflection, in the *Secret Book of John*—remains the active force working with the beleaguered humans in paradise as the Mother of the living, spiritual Eve, and even through the serpent as instructor. That is why Adam says to her and of her:

> You have given me life. You will be called the Mother of the living.
> For she is my mother.
> She is physician,
> woman,
> one who has given birth. (89,14–17)

Here Bentley Layton notes that these terms used by Adam to describe spiritual Eve are based upon puns in Aramaic on the Semitic name of Eve, and since these puns are incomprehensible in Greek (or Coptic), they must give evidence of connections between an early stage of the text or tradition of the *Nature of the Rulers* and the Semitic world.[6]

---

4. See Marvin Meyer, *The Gnostic Discoveries*, 98–99.

5. *On the Origin of the World* 116,8–117,15 tells essentially the same story of rape and sexual defilement. Cf. also *Secret Book of John* II 22,3–8, with the notes.

6. Layton, *Gnostic Scriptures*, 70–71.

The story of this first part of the *Nature of the Rulers* ends with the birth of Norea, daughter of Eve, and a portrayal of the events that transpired thereafter in her action-packed life. At the time of the great flood, Norea (or Orea) burns Noah's (first) ark after he refuses to allow her aboard, so that he has to rebuild the ark. Then she is confronted by the world rulers, who are as rapacious as ever, and they try to have sex with her. She calls to God for help, and when the angel Eleleth comes to her aid, the archons run for their lives. Eleleth, later described as one of the Four Luminaries of heaven, identifies himself to Norea: "I am Eleleth, Understanding (*tm^entsabe*),[7] the great angel who stands before the holy Spirit. I have been sent to speak with you and rescue you from the hand of the lawless ones. And I shall teach you about your root" (93,8–13).

With this self-disclosure of Eleleth, the first part of the *Nature of the Rulers* comes to a close. And although the narrative account of this section is filled with tales of violence and oppression, the overarching perspective is one of hope for oppressed human beings. God has a plan, and the will of God is going to be realized. In the words of the text, "All these things came to be by the will of the Father of the All" (88,10–11).

The same hopeful perspective is to be found in the second part of the *Nature of the Rulers* (93,13–97,21), particularly in the conclusion. The second part opens with Norea speaking in the first-person singular about the glory of the angelic luminary Eleleth, and her pious comments lead into a dialogue[8] between Norea and Eleleth in which Norea asks a number of questions and Eleleth provides revelatory answers. Norea is a prominent figure in the Nag Hammadi library and beyond. The figure of Norea, spelled variously,[9] is often related to the woman named Na'amah in *Genesis* 4:22, who is said to be the daughter of the Cainite Lamech and the sister of Tubal Cain. In much of the literature Norea is described as the sister and sometimes the wife of Seth son of Adam and Eve. Nag Hammadi Codex IX includes a short tractate entitled the *Thought of Norea*, and *On the Origin of the World* refers to two sources apparently written in the name of Norea: "the First Book of Noraia" (102,10–11) and "the First Discourse of Oraia" (102,24–25).[10]

Here in the *Nature of the Rulers*, Norea opens the dialogue, after comforting words from Eleleth, with questions about the authorities of the world, and Eleleth responds by telling a story of creation. Eleleth's story repeats a bit of what was recounted in the first part of the text, but Eleleth's story says more about Sophia and her lapse; Yaldabaoth, the misshapen child of Sophia; Zoe, the daughter of Sophia; and Sabaoth, the son of Yaldabaoth. Here and in *On the*

---

7. Perhaps cf. Sophia, Wisdom. Eleleth is usually described as the Fourth Luminary, and in the *Secret Book of John* Sophia is one of the aeons associated with Eleleth.

8. Cf. also the form of the dialogue described as "questions and answers" (*erotapokriseis*). See Kurt Rudolph, "Der gnostische 'Dialog' als literarisches Genus."

9. Orea in the *Nature of the Rulers* could be taken as a form of the Greek *hōraia*, "beautiful."

10. For a fuller discussion of traditions surrounding Norea, see the introduction to the *Thought of Norea* by John D. Turner below.

Origin of the World, Sabaoth turns out to be a pretty fine archon, as archons go.[11] Sabaoth repents of his ways and denounces his father, Yaldabaoth, and his mother, matter, and he praises Sophia and Zoe. Yaldabaoth takes the rejection of Sabaoth poorly, and this, Eleleth indicates, is where envy came from: "Envy produced death, death produced children, and death put each in charge of a heaven. All the heavens of chaos were full of their masses." Eleleth quickly adds, echoing a similar statement earlier in the text, "But all these things came to be by the will of the Father of the All, after the pattern of all that is above, so that the sum total of chaos might be reached" (96,8–15).

The *Nature of the Rulers* concludes with a few last words of encouragement from Eleleth. "All who know this way of truth," Eleleth assures Norea, "are deathless among dying humanity" (96,25–27). In the end the final liberation will come, "when the true human in human form reveals [the spirit of] truth that the Father has sent" (96,33–97,1), and then all will be resolved and completed. Eleleth, in the *Nature of the Rulers*, resorts to poetry to communicate the resultant bliss of the children of light, who will say, with a single voice:

> The Father's truth is just,
> the child is over all
> and with everyone,
> forever and ever.
> Holy, holy, holy!
> Amen. (97,17–21)

The text of the *Nature of the Rulers* was probably written in Greek. Scholars date the text to the second or third century, and a number of them suggest Alexandria as the place of composition, although Helmut Koester opts for Syria. Although Birger A. Pearson agrees that it likely came from Alexandria and proposes an early third-century date, he concedes that some of its sources must be older and could derive from Syria.[12] Bentley Layton's observations on Aramaic puns would suggest earlier, Semitic roots for some of the materials in the text.

BIBLIOGRAPHY

Bernard Barc, *L'Hypostase des archontes*; Roger A. Bullard, *The Hypostasis of the Archons*; Francis T. Fallon, *The Enthronement of Sabaoth*; Bentley Layton, *The Gnostic Scriptures*, 65–76; "The Hypostasis of the Archons or *The Reality of the Rulers*"; Bentley Layton, ed., *Nag Hammadi Codex II,2–7*, 1.219–59 (Roger A. Bullard and Bentley Layton); Peter Nagel, *Das Wesen der Archonten*; Hans-Martin Schenke, Hans-Gebhard Bethge, and Ursula Ulrike Kaiser, eds., *Nag Hammadi Deutsch*, 1.215–33 (Ursula Ulrike Kaiser).

11. Cf. the role of Adonaios, sometimes identified with Sabaoth, in the *Second Discourse of Great Seth*.

12. See Birger A. Pearson, *Gnosticism and Christianity in Roman and Coptic Egypt*, 63.

The Nature of the Rulers[1]

The Real Nature of the Authorities (86,20–27)

Concerning the reality of the authorities,[2] the great apostle,[3] through the spirit of the Father of truth, referred to the authorities of darkness[4] and told us "our struggle is not against flesh and [blood] but against the authorities of the world and the spirits of wickedness."[5] I[6] have sent you this writing because you have asked about the real nature of the authorities.

The Blind Demiurge (86,27–87,23)

The leader of the authorities is blind. [Because of his] power, ignorance, and arrogance he said, with [power], "I am God; there is no other [but me]."[7]

When he said this, he sinned against [the realm of the All]. This boast rose up to Incorruptibility,[8] [87] and a voice answered from Incorruptibility and said, "You are wrong, Samael"—which means "blind god."[9]

His thoughts were blind. He expressed his power—that is, the blasphemy he had uttered—and pursued it down to chaos and his mother the abyss, at the instigation of Pistis Sophia.[10] She[11] established each of his offspring according to its power, after the pattern of the eternal realms[12] above. For the visible originated from the invisible.

Incorruptibility looked down into the region of the waters. Her image appeared as a reflection in the waters, and the authorities of darkness fell in love with her. But they could not grasp the image that appeared to them in the waters, for they were weak, and what is only of soul cannot grasp what is of spirit. For the authorities were from below, but the image of Incorruptibility was from above.

This is why Incorruptibility looked down into that region, so that, by the Father's will, she might bring all into union with the light.

---

1. Coptic text: NHC II,4: 86,20–97,23. Editions: The Facsimile Edition of the Nag Hammadi Codices: Codex II, 98–109; Bernard Barc, L'Hypostase des archontes; Bentley Layton, ed., Nag Hammadi Codex II,2–7, 1.219–59 (Roger A. Bullard and Bentley Layton); Hans-Martin Schenke, Hans-Gebhard Bethge, and Ursula Ulrike Kaiser, eds., Nag Hammadi Deutsch, 1.215–33 (Ursula Ulrike Kaiser). The title of the text is sometimes translated as the Hypostasis of the Archons or the Reality of the Rulers. 2. Apparently the authorities are the same as the rulers or archons. 3. Paul. 4. Colossians 1:13. 5. Ephesians 6:12. 6. The author of the text. 7. Isaiah 45:5–6, 21; 46:9. 8. Incorruptibility is a female aeon related to Barbelo, divine Forethought, in Sethian thought. 9. Or "god of the blind." 10. "Faith Wisdom," a form of Sophia. 11. Pistis Sophia. 12. Aeons, here and below.

The Creation of Adam and Eve (87,23–89,17)

The rulers made plans and said, "Come, let's create a human of soil from the earth." They formed their creature as a being entirely of the earth.[13]

These archons have bodies that are both female [and male], and faces that are the faces of beasts.[14] They took [soil] from the earth and formed [their human], after their own bodies and [after the image] of God that had appeared [to them] in the water.[15]

They said, "[Come], let's grasp the image by means of the form we have shaped, [so that] the image may see its male partner [and fall in love with it], [88] and we may seize it with the form we have shaped." They did not understand the power of God, because they are powerless.

Samael[16] blew into his face, and the human acquired a soul and stayed upon the ground for many days. The rulers could not make him arise, because they are powerless. Like storm winds they kept on blowing, that they might try to capture the image that appeared to them in the waters. And they did not know what its power was.[17]

All these things came to be by the will of the Father of the All.

Later the Spirit saw the person of soul upon the ground. The Spirit came forth from the adamantine land.[18] It descended and made its home within him, and that person became a living soul.[19] And the Spirit[20] called his name Adam, since he was found moving around upon the ground.[21]

A voice came from Incorruptibility to help Adam. The rulers gathered all the animals of the earth and all the birds of the sky and brought them to Adam to see what Adam would call them, that he might give a name to each of the birds and all the animals.[22]

The rulers[23] took Adam and put him in the garden, that he might cultivate it and watch over it. They commanded him and said, "You may eat from [every] tree in the garden, but do not eat from the tree of knowledge of good and evil. Do not [touch] it, for the day you eat from it, you will surely die."[24]

They [said this to him], but they did not understand what [they said] to him. Rather, by the Father's will, [89] they said this in such a way that Adam[25] might eat, and Adam might <not>[26] perceive them as would a completely material person.

The rulers plotted together and said, "Come, let's make a deep sleep fall upon Adam."[27] So Adam slept. The deep sleep they made to fall upon him, and he slept, is ignorance. They cut open his side . . . like a living woman.[28] Then they repaired his side with flesh in place of her, and Adam had only a soul.

---

13. Cf. Genesis 2:7. 14. As restored here, the text describes the rulers of the world as androgynous with animal faces (cf. Secret Book of John II, 11; On the Origin of the World 101–2). 15. The image of Incorruptibility, above. 16. Lit., "He." 17. Cf. Genesis 2:7, again. 18. The adamantine land is not only steel-like or diamondlike in its heavenly character; it also may derive from the realm of heavenly Adamas or Pigeradamas (cf. Secret Book of John II, 8–9). 19. Genesis 2:7, again. 20. Lit., "it." 21. Sometimes the name Adam is re-

lated to the Hebrew word 'adamah, "ground, earth." See Genesis 2:7. 22. Genesis 2:19. 23. Lit., "They." 24. Genesis 2:16–17. 25. Lit., "he," here and below. 26. The negative, mistakenly omitted in the Coptic text, is restored here (<tᵉm>nau). 27. Genesis 2:21. 28. The Coptic of this sentence may need emendation. The sentence seems to suggest that one side of androgynous Adam, a female side, is removed; this is the spiritual side of Adam, the female spiritual presence—spiritual Eve.

The woman of spirit[29] came to him and spoke with him, saying, "Arise, Adam." When he saw her, he said, "You have given me life. You will be called the Mother of the living.

For she is my mother.
She is physician,[30]
woman,
one who has given birth."

Adam and Eve in the Garden (89,17–90,12)

The authorities approached their Adam. When they saw his female partner speaking with him, they became aroused and lusted after her. They said to each other, "Come, let's ejaculate our semen[31] in her," and they chased her. But she laughed at them because of their foolishness and blindness. In their grasp she turned into a tree,[32] and when she left for them a shadow of herself that looked like her, they defiled it sexually. They defiled the seal of her voice, and so they convicted themselves through the form they had shaped in their own image.[33]

Then the female spiritual presence came in the shape of the serpent, the instructor. The serpent taught Adam and Eve and said, "What did Samael [say to] you? Did he say, 'You may eat from every tree in the garden, but do not eat from [the tree] of knowledge of good and evil'?" [90]

The woman of flesh[34] said, "Not only did he say 'Do not eat,' but also 'Do not touch it. For the day you eat from it, you will surely die.' "

The serpent, the instructor, said, "You will not surely die, for he said this to you out of jealousy. Rather, your eyes will open and you will be like gods, knowing good and evil." And the female instructor was taken away from the serpent, and she abandoned it as something of the earth.

They Eat from the Tree (90,13–91,11)

The woman of flesh took from the tree and ate, and she gave to her husband as well, and thus these beings, who had only a soul, ate. Their imperfection became apparent in their ignorance. They recognized that they were stripped of the spiritual, and they took fig leaves and tied them around their naked bodies.[35]

The leader of the archons came and said, "Where are you, Adam?" For he did not know what had happened.

---

29. Coptic *tshime ᶜmpneumatikē*. The "woman of spirit," or "spiritual woman," is the female spiritual presence—described like spiritual Eve—while Adam is merely psychical again. 30. Or "midwife." 31. Or "sow our seed." 32. Perhaps thought to be the tree of life or the tree of the knowledge of good and evil (the latter is assumed in *Secret Book of John* II, 22, where in a similar scene Insight is embodied in the tree of knowledge). 33. This passage closely resembles the Greek myth of Daphne changing into a laurel tree; cf. *Secret Book of John* II, 22; *On the Origin of the World* 116–17. The last sentence seems to indicate that the rulers raped a shadow, and perhaps an echo, of the woman of spirit, after whom they lusted. This shadow seems to be physical Eve. 34. Coptic *tshime ᶜnsarkikē*. This is Eve of flesh, without the female spiritual presence. 35. *Genesis* 3:7.

Adam said, "I heard your voice and was afraid because I was naked, and so I hid."[36]

The ruler said, "Why did you hide, unless it is because you ate from the only tree from which I commanded you not to eat? You did eat!"

Adam said, "The woman you gave me [offered] me the fruit, and I ate." And the arrogant [ruler] cursed the woman.

The woman said, "The serpent deceived me, and I ate." [The rulers turned] to the serpent and cursed its shadow, [so that it was] powerless, and they did not know it was a form they themselves had shaped.[37] From then on, the serpent was under the curse of the authorities. The curse was on the serpent [91] until the perfect human was to come.

The rulers turned to their Adam. They took him and cast him and his wife out of the garden. They[38] have no blessing, for they are also under the curse.

The rulers threw humanity into great confusion and a life of toil, so that their people might be preoccupied with things of the world and not have time to be occupied with the holy Spirit.[39]

Cain, Abel, Seth, Norea (91,11–92,4)

After this Eve gave birth to Cain, their[40] son, and Cain farmed the land. Then Adam had sex with his wife. She became pregnant again and gave birth to Abel, and Abel was a shepherd. Cain brought in produce from his field, and Abel brought in an offering from his lambs. God looked with favor upon the offering of Abel, but he did not accept the offerings of Cain. Cain, man of flesh, pursued Abel his brother.

God said to Cain, "Where is your brother Abel?"

Cain answered and said, "Am I my brother's keeper?"

God said to Cain, "Listen. The voice of your brother's blood is calling to me. You have sinned with your mouth, and it will come back to you. Whoever kills Cain will release seven vendettas, and you will live groaning and shaking upon the earth."[41]

Adam [had sex] with his partner Eve again. She became pregnant and bore [Seth] for Adam. She said, "I have given birth to [another] person through God, in place [of Abel]."[42]

Eve became pregnant again and gave birth to [Norea].[43] Eve said, "He has produced for me a virgin to help many human generations." [92] Norea is the virgin whom the forces did not defile.

And humanity began to multiply and develop.

---

36. *Genesis* 3:10. 37. The serpent no longer has the spiritual presence but is a mere shadow of its former self. 38. Apparently the rulers of this world, possibly Adam and Eve. 39. Cf. *Genesis* 3:14–19. 40. As seems to be the case here, Cain is sometimes considered to be the son of Eve and the rulers of this world; in *Secret Book of John* II, 24 Cain and Abel both are sons of Eve and Yaldabaoth. Cf. the sexual defilement of the shadow, physical Eve, by the rulers. 41. On Cain and Abel, cf. *Genesis* 4:1–16. 42. Seth is the hero for the Sethian Gnostics; cf. *Genesis* 4:25–5:5. 43. Norea is a familiar figure, especially in Sethian literature; see also, perhaps, *On the Origin of the World* 102, and the *Thought of Norea*.

Noah and the Flood (92,4–18)

The rulers plotted together and said, "Come, let's cause a flood with our own hands and destroy all flesh, animal and human."[44]

When the ruler of the forces[45] learned of their plan, he said to Noah, "Make an ark of wood that will not rot and hide in it, you and your children and the animals and the birds of the sky, large and small. Put it on Mount Sir."[46]

Orea[47] came to Noah and wanted to board the ark. When he would not let her, she blew on the ark and made it burn up. So he rebuilt the ark.

Norea Opposes the Rulers (92,18–93,13)

The rulers went to meet Norea, for they planned to seduce her. Their leader said to her, "Your mother Eve came to us."

But Norea turned to them and said, "You are the rulers of the darkness. Damn you! You did not have sex with my mother but with one of your own ilk. For I am not from you. I am from the world above."

The arrogant ruler turned, with his might, and his expression was like a blazing [fire].[48] He was bold toward her and [said], "You must serve us sexually, as your mother Eve did, for I[49] have been given . . . ."

But Norea turned with the power of [God][50] and called in a loud voice to the holy one, the God of the All, [93] "Help me with these unrighteous rulers and rescue me from their hands—now!"

An angel came down from heaven and said to her, "Why are you calling to God? Why are you so bold toward the holy Spirit?"

Norea said, "Who are you?"

The unrighteous rulers had left her. The angel said, "I am Eleleth, Understanding, the great angel who stands before the holy Spirit. I have been sent to speak with you and rescue you from the hand of the lawless ones. And I shall teach you about your root."[51]

The Dialogue of Norea and Eleleth (93,13–32)

I[52] cannot describe the power of that angel. Its appearance is like fine gold and its garment is like snow. My mouth simply cannot bear to speak of its power and the appearance of its face.

---

44. *Genesis* 6–9. 45. This is Sabaoth, discussed later in the text, who is god of the forces. Sabaoth plays a similar role in *On the Origin of the World* 103–6, where he is portrayed as rebelling against the rulers of this world and creating Jesus and the virgin of the holy Spirit. 46. Mount Sir is a legendary site of wisdom and knowledge. 47. Orea, perhaps "beautiful" (cf. Greek *hōraia*); elsewhere, Norea. 48. Other restora- tions are possible, e.g., "like black [lead]" (see Bullard and Layton, in *Nag Hammadi Codex II,2–7*, 1.248–49). 49. Or "these" (Coptic *autinaei*). 50. Coptic p[*noute*]; other possible restorations include "the [light]" (Coptic p[*ouoein*]) or "the [spirit]" (Coptic p[*pna*], abbreviated). 51. On the root and tracing the root, cf. *Secret Book of John* II, 31. 52. Apparently Norea.

The great angel Eleleth spoke to me and said, "I am Understanding; I am one of the Four Luminaries who stand before the great invisible Spirit.[53] Do you think these rulers have power over you? None of them can overpower the root of truth, for on behalf of the root of truth a figure[54] has appeared in the last days, and these authorities will be restrained. These authorities cannot defile you or that generation,[55] for your home is with Incorruptibility, where the virgin Spirit dwells, who is superior to the authorities of chaos and their world."

Eleleth's Story of Creation (93,32–95,13)

I[56] said, "My lord, teach me about the [power of] these authorities. [How] did they come into being? With what kind of nature?[57] Of what material? [94] Who created them and their power?"

The great angel Eleleth, who is understanding, said to me, "Incorruptibility dwells within infinite realms. Sophia, who is called Pistis,[58] wanted to create something by herself, without her partner, and what she produced was from above.

"There is a curtain between the realms above and the aeons below. A shadow formed beneath the curtain,[59] and the shadow became matter, and the shadow was cast into a region.

"What she produced came to be something material like an aborted fetus. It took shape from the shadow, and it became an arrogant beast resembling a lion. It was androgynous, as I already said, because it came from matter.[60]

"The beast opened his eyes and saw a vast amount of matter without limit, and he became arrogant and said, 'I am God, and there is none but me.'[61]

"When he said this, he sinned against the realm of the All. A voice came from above the tyrannical realm and said, 'You are wrong, Samael'—which means 'blind god.'[62]

"He said, 'If anything exists before me, let me see it.'

"At once Sophia pointed her finger and brought light into matter, and she pursued it down to the region of chaos. When she returned up to her light, darkness once again [came upon] matter.

"This ruler was androgynous and made himself a huge realm, an expanse without limit. [95] He considered creating for himself offspring, and he created for himself seven offspring, androgynous like their parent.

"He said to his children, 'I am God of all.'[63]

---

53. Eleleth is one of Four Luminaries, with Harmozel, Oroiael, and Daveithai. **54.** Perhaps the perfect human; see below. **55.** The offspring of Seth, the Gnostics. The same phrase (*tgenea et^emmau*) is used in the *Gospel of Judas*. **56.** Again, Norea. **57.** Hypostasis, "nature, reality." **58.** Pistis Sophia, "Faith Wisdom," as above. **59.** The curtain or veil between heaven and earth keeps the light of heaven from shin-

ing upon the earth and produces a shadow. Similar ideas are found in Jewish thought, e.g., in Philo of Alexandria. Also cf. the curtain or Boundary in Valentinian texts. In a more general sense, cf. *Psalm* 104:2; *Isaiah* 40:22. **60.** The arrogant demiurge is also lionlike in *Secret Book of John* II, 10 and *On the Origin of the World* 100. **61.** Isaiah 45:5–6, 21; 46:9. **62.** Or "god of the blind." **63.** On this arrogant claim, see above.

"Zoe[64] daughter of Pistis Sophia called out and said to him, 'You are wrong, Sakla,' whose name is understood as Yaldabaoth.[65] Zoe breathed into his face, and her breath became for her a fiery angel, and that angel bound Yaldabaoth and cast him down into Tartaros, at the bottom of the abyss.[66]

The Story of Sabaoth (95,13–96,17)

"When Sabaoth son of Yaldabaoth[67] saw the strength of that angel, he repented and condemned his father and his mother, matter.

"Sabaoth loathed his mother,[68] but he sent songs of praise up to Sophia and her daughter Zoe. Sophia and Zoe took him up and established him over the seventh heaven, below the curtain between what is above and what is below. He is called 'god of the powers, Sabaoth,' because he is above the powers of chaos, for Sophia established him.

"When these things happened, Sabaoth[69] made himself a huge four-faced chariot of cherubim, and an infinity of angels as ministers, and harps and lyres.[70]

"Sophia took her daughter Zoe and made her sit at his right to teach him about the things that are in the eighth heaven,[71] and she put the angel of wrath at his left. [Since] that day, [his right] had been called 'life,' [96] and the left has represented the unrighteousness of the tyrannical realm above. These things happened before your time.

"When Yaldabaoth saw Sabaoth exalted in such great glory on high, he envied him, and his envy became something androgynous. This was the beginning of envy. Envy produced death, death produced children, and death put each in charge of a heaven. All the heavens of chaos were full of their masses.

"But all these things came to be by the will of the Father of the All, after the pattern of all that is above, so that the sum total of chaos might be reached.[72]

"Look, I have taught you about the form of the rulers, the matter in which the form was produced, their parent, and their world."

Conclusion (96,17–97,23)

I[73] said, "My lord, am I also from their matter?"

"You[74] and your offspring are from the Father, who was from the beginning. The souls come from above, from incorruptible light.[75] So the authorities cannot

---

64. Life. Zoe is the name for Eve in the Septuagint of *Genesis*. 65. The Coptic text reads Yaltabaoth. 66. Tartaros is the underworld, often the lower part of Hades, hence hell. On the passage, cf. *Revelation* 20:1–3. 67. Lit., "his son." 68. Lit., "He loathed her." 69. Lit., "he," here and below. 70. This chariot recalls the throne or chariot of God, the Merkavah, in *Ezekiel* and *Revelation*. 71. On the seventh and eighth heavens, see also the *Secret Book of John* and the *Discourse on the Eighth and the Ninth*. 72. This may indicate that the sum total of all things is attained, from the top in heaven to the bottom in the realm of chaos, as here. Bentley Layton, in *The Gnostic Scriptures*, 75, suggests this idea may come from Neoplatonic doctrine. 73. Norea. 74. Eleleth is speaking to Norea again. 75. The wording here is similar to *Gospel of Thomas* 50 and other texts.

approach them because of the spirit of truth within them, and all who know this way of truth[76] are deathless among dying humanity.

"But that offspring[77] will not appear now. It will appear after three ages and free them from the bondage of the authorities' error."

I[78] said, "My lord, how long will it be?"

He said to me, "Until the time when the true human in human form reveals [the spirit of] truth that the Father has sent. [97]

"Then he will teach them about everything and anoint them with the oil of eternal life, given from the generation without a king.

"Then they will be freed of blind thought. They will trample death, which is of the authorities. And they will ascend into the infinite light where this offspring is.

"Then the authorities will surrender their years and ages. Their angels will weep over their destruction, and their demons will mourn over their death.

"Then all the children of the light will know the truth, and their root, and the Father of the All, and the holy Spirit. They will all say with one voice:

> The Father's truth is just,
> the child[79] is over all
> and with[80] everyone,
> forever and ever.
> Holy, holy, holy![81]
> Amen."

The Nature of the Rulers

---

76. The text reads *hodos*, "way." The reference is to the work of the spirit of truth, just mentioned—hence the present translation. 77. Or "seed." 78. Norea. 79. Or "son." 80. Or "from." 81. The trisagion, "Holy, holy, holy," is sung by those around the divine throne in *Isaiah* and *Revelation*.

ON THE ORIGIN OF
THE WORLD

NHC II,5; XIII,2; Brit. Lib. Or. 4926(1)

Introduced and Translated by Marvin Meyer

On the Origin of the World, the fifth tractate in Nag Hammadi Codex II, is a long and thoughtful essay (97,24–127,17) that addresses questions about the creation of the world, the formation of humankind, and the end of the age. In addition to the complete Codex II version, the text is also known from a short fragment from Nag Hammadi Codex XIII and several fragments from a Coptic version housed in the British Library. The text is untitled in the extant manuscripts, and it has been given its present title on the basis of its contents. Elsewhere in the literature on the text, it is sometimes referred to with the unfortunate title "Untitled Work," "Schrift ohne Titel," and "Écrit sans titre." The Codex II version of the text is translated here, though the other texts have also been consulted.

On the Origin of the World is a learned work, a smart Gnostic essay by an author who uses argumentation, narration, and colorful illustration in order to demonstrate the basic points of a Gnostic worldview. Although On the Origin of the World does not discuss in any detail the unfolding of the divine Fullness above, it does follow the saga of Yaldabaoth, the creator of this world, and the adventures and misadventures of Adam, Eve, and the rest of humanity. In particular the text discusses themes from *Genesis*, in terms that recall *Jubilees* and the books of *Enoch*, and to these materials are added Greco-Roman, Egyptian, and Christian reflections. On the Origin of the World provides an accessible way of learning about various aspects of gnosis, and Hans-Gebhard Bethge suggests that the essay is presented "in the form of an apologetic tract designed for public effectiveness in attracting adherents."[1] It may well have been a popular tract, since portions of three copies have survived in the Nag Hammadi library and elsewhere. On the

---

1. Hans-Gebhard Bethge, in James M. Robinson, ed., *The Nag Hammadi Library in English*, 170; cf. Hans-Gebhard Bethge, in Hans-Martin Schenke, Hans-Gebhard Bethge, and Ursula Ulrike Kaiser, eds., *Nag Hammadi Deutsch*, 1.238.

Origin of the World builds self-consciously on a variety of literary sources, and within the text there are passages that seem to be related to at least two or three other Nag Hammadi texts. From the many parallels between the present text and the one immediately preceding it in Codex II, the *Nature of the Rulers*, it is obvious that there is a relationship between these two texts, though the precise nature of that relationship remains unknown. Louis Painchaud also sees similarities between *On the Origin of the World* and *Eugnostos the Blessed*. Further, the song of Eve, rehearsed in *On the Origin of the World* 114,2–24, is introduced in such a way as to recall the comments of Adam in *Nature of the Rulers* 89,14–17, but the song itself closely follows lines from the poetry of *Thunder* 13,19–14,9:

> I am the wife and the virgin.
> I am <the mother> and the daughter.
> I am the limbs of my mother.
> I am a barren woman
> who has many children.
> I have had many weddings
> and have taken no husband.
> I am a midwife
> and a woman who does not give birth.
> I am the solace of my own birth pains.
> I am bride and groom,
> and my husband produced me.
> I am the mother of my father
> and the sister of my husband,
> and he is my offspring.
> I am the servant of him who fashioned me,
> I am the ruler of my offspring.
> He [produced me] with a premature birth,
> and he is my offspring born on time,
> and my strength is from him.
> I am the staff of his power in his youth,
> and he is the rod of my old age,
> and whatever he wishes happens to me.

In addition to these parallels, the text of *On the Origin of the World* includes other features that help it inform and entertain. Within the text are numerous references to additional literature that, according to the author, may be consulted for further reading, and these references function as virtual notes to the essay. Among these notes are references to two texts of Norea, the *First Book of Noraia* and the *First Treatise of Oraia*, and others attributed to Moses and Solomon. The connection, if any, between these texts of Norea and the second part of the *Nature of the Rulers* (93,13–97,21), which features Norea, the *Thought of Norea* from Nag Hammadi Codex IX, and the works of Norea mentioned by Epiphanius (*Panarion* 26.1.3) is unclear. Another text noted in *On the Origin of the World*, the

Archangelic Book of Moses the Prophet, is cited in the Greek magical papyri.[2] The author of *On the Origin of the World* also incorporates etymological and other explanatory passages that seem intended to clarify the meaning of Gnostic points being addressed. Thus, the name Yaldabaoth, which ordinarily is thought by scholars to derive from the Aramaic for "child of chaos" or, less likely, "child of (S)abaoth," is said, in *On the Origin of the World* 100,12–14, to mean "Young man, move over here."[3] In a more lighthearted vein, it is claimed (100,29–101,23) that the names of the sons of Yaldabaoth—Yao, Eloai, and Astaphaios—come from the baby talk going on in Yaldabaoth's nursery. In one of the more exotic sections of the text, on phoenixes, water serpents, and bulls of Egypt (121,27–123,2), the author discusses these fantastic creatures as metaphors for Gnostic truths and then concludes, "These great images have [appeared] only in Egypt, not in other lands, indicating that Egypt is like God's paradise."

In his important study of the text *On the Origin of the World*, Louis Painchaud has determined that the overall structure of the tractate is informed by the Greco-Roman rhetorical handbooks of the day, and that the text itself employs the terminology of rhetoric at key points.[4] As a result, Painchaud proposes, the text is arranged in four major parts, and the flow of the discussion is determined by these rhetorical sections. Part 1, the *exordium* or *prooimion* (97,24–98,11), is the prologue, in which the author introduces a philosophical demonstration for the thesis that something existed before chaos. Part 2, the *narratio* or *diēgēsis* (98,11–123,2), constitutes the major portion of the text, and it provides a narrative account of the origin of the world and people in it. According to Painchaud, the elements in this section are organized in concentric and chiastic patterns. Part 3, the *probatio* or *pistis* (123,2–31), offers proof for how error and ignorance have grown strong in the world. Part 4, the *peroratio* or *epilogos* (123,31–127,17), brings matters to a conclusion through a discussion of immortal humanity, Jesus and the church, and the end of the age.

In what Painchaud identifies as the epilogue of the text, the author of *On the Origin of the World* promises that the end of things will be happiness and joy for all people of knowledge. With an eschatological flourish, the text states: "These people—the kingless, perfect generation—will enter the holy place of their Father, and they will reside in rest, and eternal, ineffable glory, and ceaseless joy. They already are kings. They are the immortal within the mortal, and they will condemn the gods of chaos and their powers" (125,7–14). After Jesus the Word comes and speaks of disclosing what is hidden[5] and the end times approach, all that is dark and deficient in the universe will be undone, and the cosmic structure of the creator and his powers will collapse. As the text concludes, "The light will [overcome the] darkness and banish it. The darkness will be like something that

---

2. Cf. Hans-Dieter Betz, ed., *The Greek Magical Papyri in Translation*, 172–95, especially 172, note 2.
3. On the Aramaic that may lie behind such a suggested etymology, see Louis Painchaud, *L'Écrit sans titre*, 264–66.
4. See Painchaud, *L'Écrit sans titre*.
5. Cf. *Matthew* 10:26; *Mark* 4:22; *Luke* 8:17; 12:2; *Gospel of Thomas* 5:2; 6:5–6.

never was, and the source of darkness will be dissolved. Deficiency will be pulled out by its root and cast down into the darkness, and the light will withdraw up to its root" (126,35–127,5).

On the Origin of the World is a Gnostic text, but it is difficult to classify the text more precisely than that. The tractate shows Christian features, especially in the last part but also earlier in the text (105,20–106,19), yet most of the text does not seem to be fundamentally shaped by Christian concerns. There are Sethian, Valentinian, and Manichaean motifs in the text, but the text itself cannot with confidence be identified specifically with any of those traditions. On account of the problems of language and comprehension, Bentley Layton has called the Coptic text an *opus imperfectum*, and Hans-Gebhard Bethge concurs.[6] *On the Origin of the World* was composed in Greek and, considering the Egyptian themes, the place of composition almost certainly was Egypt, perhaps the cosmopolitan city of Alexandria. Birger A. Pearson and other scholars tend to assign a fairly late date of composition to the text as we now have it (late third or early fourth century), but Pearson agrees with Painchaud that it may be based on earlier, second-century material.[7]

BIBLIOGRAPHY

Francis T. Fallon, *The Enthronement of Sabaoth*; Bentley Layton, *Nag Hammadi Codex II,2–7*, 2.11–134 (Hans-Gebhard Bethge, Bentley Layton, and Societas Coptica Hierosolymitana); Christian Oeyen, "Fragmente einer subschmimischen Version der gnostischen Schrift ohne Titel"; Louis Painchaud, *L'Écrit sans titre*; "The Literary Contacts Between the Writings Without Title 'On the Origin of the World' (CG II,5 and XIII,2) and 'Eugnostos the Blessed' (CG III,3 and V,1)"; "Something Is Rotten in the Kingdom of Sabaoth"; "The Writing Without Title of Nag Hammadi Codex II"; James M. Robinson, ed., *The Nag Hammadi Library in English*, 170–78 (Hans-Gebhard Bethge, Bentley Layton, and Societas Coptica Hierosolymitana); Hans-Martin Schenke, Hans-Gebhard Bethge, and Ursula Ulrike Kaiser, eds., *Nag Hammadi Deutsch*, 1.235–62 (Hans-Gebhard Bethge); Michel Tardieu, *Trois mythes gnostiques*.

6. Bethge, in *Nag Hammadi Deutsch*, 1.237.

7. Birger A. Pearson, *Gnosticism and Christianity in Roman and Coptic Egypt*, 69.

On the Origin of the World[1]

Prologue: In the Beginning (97,24–98,11)

Since everyone, both the gods of the world and people, says that nothing existed before chaos, I shall prove they all are wrong, because they do not know the [origin] of chaos or its root. Here [is the] proof.

Although certainly [98] people in general are [inclined] to say that chaos is darkness, in actuality chaos comes from a shadow, and it is the shadow that has been called darkness. The shadow comes from something that has existed from the beginning, and so it is obvious that something in the beginning existed before chaos came into being, and chaos came after what was in the beginning.[2]

Let us consider the facts of the matter, and particularly what was in the beginning, from which chaos came. In this way will the truth be clearly demonstrated.

Narration: Origin of Sophia and the Powers of the World (98,11–99,22)

After the world of the immortals was brought to completion out of the infinite, a being with this likeness, called Sophia, flowed from Pistis.[3] This being expressed its wish that it come to resemble the first light, and at once its wish appeared as a heavenly likeness with an incomprehensible greatness. This being came to be between the immortals and what came after them, like what is above, and Sophia served as a veil separating humanity from the things above.

The aeon of truth has no shadow <within> it[4] because infinite light shines everywhere within it. There is a shadow, however, outside it, and the shadow has been called darkness. From the shadow appeared a power set over the darkness, and the powers that came afterward called the shadow limitless chaos. From it

---

1. Coptic texts: NHC II,5: 97,24–127,17; XIII,2: 50,25–34 (fragment); British Library Oriental Manuscript 4926(1) (fragments). The present translation is based on the Coptic text in Nag Hammadi Codex II. Editions: *The Facsimile Edition of the Nag Hammadi Codices: Codex II*, 109–39. Bentley Layton, ed., *Nag Hammadi Codex II,2–7*, 2.11–134 (Hans-Gebhard Bethge, Bentley Layton, and Societas Coptica Hierosolymitana); Louis Painchaud, *L'Écrit sans titre*; Hans-Martin Schenke, Hans-Gebhard Bethge, and Ursula Ulrike Kaiser, eds., *Nag Hammadi Deutsch*, 1.235–62 (Hans-Gebhard Bethge). The title is construed from the contents of the text; the text has also been "entitled" by scholars the *Treatise Without a Title*. **2.** Cf. *Genesis* 1:1–2. **3.** Wisdom and Faith. **4.** The text is emended (*mpef<houn>*); the Coptic reads "outside it" (*mpefbol*).

[every] sort of deity emerged, [one after] another, along with the whole world. So [the shadow] came after [99] something that existed in the beginning, and then it became visible. The abyss also came from Pistis,[5] whom we have mentioned.

The shadow sensed that there was one stronger than it. It was jealous, and when it became pregnant by itself, all of a sudden it gave birth to envy. Since then the principle of envy has appeared in all the aeons and their worlds. But envy turned out to be an aborted fetus, without any spirit in it, and it came into being as a shadow in an expanse of watery substance. Bitter wrath came into being from the shadow and was cast into a region of chaos.

Since that day watery substance has been visible. What lurked[6] in the shadow flowed out and appeared in chaos. Just as all the afterbirth of a woman who gives birth to a baby flows out, so also the matter that came into being from the shadow was cast out. Matter did not come out of chaos; it was in chaos, in a region of chaos.

The Appearance of Yaldabaoth (99,23–100,29)

After these things happened, Pistis came and appeared over chaotic matter, which had been expelled like an aborted fetus, without any spirit in it. For chaos is all limitless darkness and unfathomable water. When Pistis saw what came into being from her deficiency, she was disturbed. And her disturbance appeared as something frightful, and it fled to her in the chaos. She turned to it and [blew] into its face in the abyss, [100] below all of the heavens.

When Pistis Sophia wanted to cause this thing with no spirit to be made into a likeness of the divine[7] and rule over matter and all its powers,[8] for the first time an archon appeared, out of the waters, lionlike in appearance, androgynous, with great authority in himself but ignorant of where he came from.

When Pistis Sophia saw him moving in the depth of the waters, she said to him, "Young man, move over here," which is the meaning of Yaldabaoth.

Since then the faculty of speech has come to expression, and the faculty of speech pertains to the gods, angels, and people. The gods, angels, and people have brought to completion what has come into being by means of the word.

The ruler Yaldabaoth[9] is ignorant of the power of Pistis. He did not see her face, but in the water he saw the likeness that spoke to him, and from that voice he called himself Yaldabaoth. Those who are perfect call him Ariael, because he is like a lion.[10]

After Yaldabaoth assumed authority over matter, Pistis Sophia withdrew up to her light.

---

5. Faith, here and below. 6. The meaning of this clause is uncertain. 7. Lit., "a likeness." Cf. *Genesis* 1:26. 8. Or "her powers." 9. The text reads "Yaltabaoth." 10. In Hebrew the name Ariel is commonly understood to mean "lion of God." The demiurge is also lionlike in *Secret Book of John* II, 10 and *Nature of the Rulers* 94.

Yaldabaoth Creates Heaven and Earth and Produces Sons
(100,29–101,23)

When the ruler saw his greatness, he saw only himself and nothing else except water and darkness. He thought that only he existed. His [thought] was completed by means of the word, and it [101] appeared as a Spirit moving to and fro over the waters.[11] When the Spirit appeared, the ruler separated the watery substance to one region and the dry substance to another region. From matter the ruler created for himself a dwelling place and called it heaven, and from matter he created a footstool and called it earth.

After this the ruler had a thought in accordance with his nature, and he created an androgynous being by means of the word. He opened his mouth and cooed to him. The child opened his eyes and saw his father, and he said to him, "EE," so his father called him Yao.[12]

The ruler created a second son and cooed to him. The child opened his eyes and said to his father, "EH," so his father called him Eloai.[13]

The ruler created a third son and cooed to him. The child opened his eyes and said to his father, "AS," so his father called him Astaphaios.

These are the three sons of their father.

The Seven Heavens of Chaos (101,24–103,2)

Seven androgynous beings appeared in chaos, and they have masculine names and feminine names.

> Yaldabaoth's feminine name is forethought[14] Sambathas,[15] which designates the week.
>
> His son is called Yao, and his feminine name is mastery.
>
> Sabaoth's[16] feminine name is divinity.
>
> Adonaios's feminine name is kingship.
>
> Eloaios's feminine name is envy.
>
> Oraios's feminine name is wealth.
>
> Astaphaios's feminine name [102] is Sophia.

These are the [seven] powers of the seven heavens of [chaos].

The powers were androgynous in accordance with the immortal pattern that existed before them and the will of Pistis, so that the likeness of what was from the beginning might have power to the end.

---

11. Cf. *Genesis* 1:2. 12. A form of the ineffable divine name Yahweh. In Greek Yao is spelled *Iaō* and the first letter (*iota*) is pronounced like a long *e* (or *y*), hence the baby talk "EE." 13. A name that resembles the Hebrew for God, El or Elohim. 14. Pronoia. 15. The name Sambathas resembles the Hebrew Shabbat, or Sabbath. 16. Sabaoth resembles the Hebrew for "hosts," as in "lord of hosts." The figure of Sabaoth is discussed extensively below.

You will find the function of the masculine names and powers in the *Archangelic Book of Moses the Prophet*.[17] The feminine names are in the *First Book of Noraia*.[18]

Since the chief creator[19] Yaldabaoth had great authorities at his disposal, he created beautiful heavens, by means of the word, as dwelling places for each of his sons, and in each heaven he created great glories, seven times glorious. Each son has within his heaven thrones, mansions, temples, chariots, virgin spirits, and their glories, extending up to an invisible realm,[20] as well as armies of divine, lordly, angelic, and archangelic powers, myriads without number, so they might serve.

You will find a precise account of this in the *First Discourse of Oraia*.[21]

Everything was completed in this <way>[22] up to the sixth heaven, the heaven of Sophia.

This heaven and earth were disrupted by the troublemaker who was beneath them all. The six heavens shook, for the powers of chaos did not know[23] who had disturbed the heaven beneath them. When Pistis found out about the harm caused by the troublemaker, she blew her breath, and she [bound him] and cast him down to Tartaros.

[Since then] heaven and [103] earth have established themselves through Sophia, who is the daughter of Yaldabaoth and is beneath them all.

Yaldabaoth Boasts That He Is God (103,2–32)

After the heavens, their powers, and their entire government were established, the chief creator exalted himself, and he was glorified by the whole army of angels. All the gods and their angels praised and glorified him.

He was delighted. He boasted over and over again and said to them, "I don't need anything."

He said, "I am God, and there is no other but me."[24]

When he said this, he sinned against all the immortals who speak forth,[25] and they watched him carefully.

When Pistis saw the impiety of the supreme ruler, she became angry. Without being seen, she said, "You are wrong, Samael"—which means "blind god." "An enlightened, immortal human exists before you and will appear within the forms you have shaped. The human will trample upon you as potter's clay is trampled, and you will descend with those who are yours to your mother the abyss. And when your work comes to an end,[26] all the deficiency that appeared from truth will be dissolved. It will cease to be, and it will be like what never was."

---

17. A text with this name is known from the Greek magical papyri. 18. Cf. the *Thought of Norea*. See also the reference to the *First Treatise of Oraia*, below. 19. The text reads *arkhigenetōr*, here and throughout. 20. The meaning of this phrase is uncertain, and the words may have been copied in error. 21. Perhaps emend to read Noraia, as above. 22. The Coptic is emended to read *hᵉn ti<h>e*. The text may also be read, as it stands, "from this heaven" (*hᵉn tipe*). 23. As noted by Wolf-Peter Funk, there are grammatical indications that the original text included the negative. 24. *Isaiah* 45:5–6, 21; 46:9. 25. The meaning of this clause is uncertain. 26. Or "after the consummation of your work."

After Pistis said this, she revealed the likeness of her greatness in the waters, and then she withdrew up to her light.

Sabaoth Praises Pistis (103,32–105,20)

When Sabaoth son of Yaldabaoth heard the voice of Pistis, he sang songs of praise to her, but he condemned his father [and mother] [104] on account of the word of Pistis. He glorified her because she told them about the immortal human and the light of the human. Pistis Sophia pointed her finger and poured over him light from her light, as condemnation of his father. When Sabaoth was enlightened, he received great authority over all of the powers of chaos, and since then he has been called "lord of the powers."[27]

He hated his father, who is darkness, and his mother, who is the abyss. He loathed his sister, who is the thought of the chief creator and who moves to and fro over the waters.

All of the authorities of chaos were jealous of Sabaoth[28] because of his light. They were upset, and they waged a great war in the seven heavens.

When Pistis Sophia saw the war, she sent seven archangels to Sabaoth from her light. The archangels carried him up to the seventh heaven and stood in his presence as his attendants. Then she sent three more archangels to him and established his kingdom above everyone, so that he might dwell above the twelve gods of chaos.

When Sabaoth occupied the place of rest because of his repentance, Pistis also gave him her daughter Zoe,[29] with great authority, so that she might tell him about everything in the eighth heaven. And since he had authority, he first made himself a mansion. It is immense, magnificent, seven times as great as all the mansions in the seven heavens.

In front of [105] his mansion he created a large throne on a chariot with four faces, called cherubim. The cherubim throne has eight figures on each side of the four corners, figures of lions, bulls, humans, and eagles, and there are a total of sixty-four figures. Seven archangels stand before the throne. Sabaoth[30] is the eighth, and he has authority, and so there are seventy-two figures in all. From this chariot the seventy-two gods took shape, so that they might rule over the languages of the seventy-two nations.[31] Beside that throne he created other, serpentlike angels called seraphim, who glorify him unceasingly.

Sabaoth Creates a Congregation of Angels, Israel, and Jesus (105,20–106,19)

Then he created a congregation of angels, thousands, myriads without number, which was like the congregation in the eighth heaven. He also created a firstborn

---

27. Or "lord of hosts," Yahweh Sabaoth. 28. Lit., "him." 29. Life, exalted Eve. Zoe is the name for Eve in the Septuagint of *Genesis*. 30. Lit., "He." 31. Seventy-two is a traditional number of nations in the world.

called Israel—that is, "the person who sees God"—and he created another being called Jesus Christ, who is like the Savior above in the eighth heaven and who sits at the right of Sabaoth[32] on a remarkable throne. At his left the virgin of the holy Spirit sits upon a throne and glorifies him. Seven virgins stand before her, with thirty harps and lyres and [106] trumpets in their hands, and they glorify him.[33] All the armies of angels glorify and praise him.

Sabaoth[34] sits on a throne covered by a great light cloud. No one was with him in the cloud except Sophia daughter of Pistis, and she taught him about all the things in the eighth heaven, so that what resembles these things might be created and his reign might last until the end[35] of the heavens of chaos and their powers.

Pistis Sophia moved him away from the darkness and summoned him to her right, and she put the chief creator at her left. Since then right has been called justice and left has been called injustice. They all received a realm in the congregation of justice, and injustice is set over all their creations.[36]

Yaldabaoth Produces Death (106,19–107,17)

When the chief creator of chaos saw his son Sabaoth and the glory in which he dwells, and recognized that he was the greatest of all the authorities of chaos, he was jealous of him. He was angry, and he engendered death from his own death. Death was established over the sixth heaven, for Sabaoth had been carried away from there. So the complete number of the six authorities of chaos was realized.

Since death was androgynous, he had sex with himself and produced seven androgynous children. These are the names of the males: envy, wrath, tears, sighs, grief, lament, tearful groans. These are the names of the females: anger, pain, lust, sighs, curses, bitterness, strife. They had sex with each other, and each one conceived seven children, so that the children total [107] forty-nine androgynous demons.

You will find their names and functions in the *Book of Solomon*.[37]

In the presence of these, Zoe, who dwells with Sabaoth, created seven good androgynous powers. These are the names of the males: the one not jealous, the blessed, the joyful, the true, the one not envious, the beloved, the faithful. These are the names of the females: peace, gladness, joyfulness, blessedness, truth, love, faith. Many good and pure spirits come from these powers.

You will find their accomplishments and functions in the *Configurations of the Fate of Heaven Beneath the Twelve*.[38]

---

32. Lit., "his right." 33. Possibly emend to read "while thirty others, with lyres and harps and trumpets in their hands, glorify him." On the virgins, cf. *Gospel of Judas* 50. 34. Lit., "He." 35. Or "consummation" (*sunteleia*), here and throughout 36. The meaning of this sentence is unclear, and the Coptic may need emendation. Possibly read the last clause as "where they all stand upon their foundations" (cf. Bethge, Layton, and Societas Coptica Hierosolymitana, in *Nag Hammadi Codex II,2–7*, 2.47). 37. The precise identity of this source is unknown. Several known texts are attributed to Solomon, such as the *Testament of Solomon*. 38. This source is unknown.

Yaldabaoth Is Distressed About His Mistake
(107,17–108,5)

When the chief creator saw the reflection of Pistis in the waters, he was deeply distressed, especially when he heard her voice, which was like the first voice that called to him out of the waters. When he knew that she was the one who gave him his name, he groaned. He was ashamed because of his transgression. And when he knew for certain that an enlightened, immortal human existed before him, he was greatly disturbed, because earlier he had said to all the gods and their angels, "I am God; there is no other but me."[39] For he feared that they might know another existed before him and condemn him.

But the chief creator was a fool. He had contempt for condemnation and acted rashly, and he said, "If [108] anything existed before me, let it appear so that we may see its light."

And at once, look, light shone out of the eighth heaven above and passed through all the heavens of the earth.

Adam of Light Shines Forth (108,5–109,1)

When the chief creator saw that the light was beautiful as it shone forth, he was amazed and very much ashamed. The light appeared and a human likeness was visible within it, and it was marvelous. No one saw it except the chief creator and Forethought,[40] who was with him. But its light was visible to all the powers of the heavens, and so they all were disturbed by it.

When Forethought saw this messenger of light,[41] she fell in love with him, but he hated her because she was in darkness. She desired to mate with him, but she was not able. When she was unable to satisfy her desire, she poured out her light upon the earth.

Since then this messenger has been called Adam of light, which means "the enlightened person of blood."[42] The earth upon <which the light of Forethought>[43] spread was called holy Adamas, which means "the holy adamantine earth."

From that time on all the authorities have honored the blood of the virgin, and the earth was purified because of the blood of the virgin.

Further, the water was purified by the reflection of Pistis Sophia, who had appeared to the chief creator in the waters. Rightly has it been said, "through the waters."[44] Since the holy water gives life to all, [109] it purifies all.

---

39. Isaiah 45:5–6, 21; 46:9. **40.** Pronoia. **41.** Lit., "messenger," "angel." **42.** This etymology may relate the name Adam to the Hebrew word *dam*, "blood." **43.** The text is emended to read <*ntaf>pōrš ebol ejōf.*

44. This reference to the waters recalls *Genesis* 1:26 and Gnostic interpretations of the appearance of the divine through the waters.

Eros (109,1–110,1)

Out of this first blood Eros[45] appeared. Eros is androgynous. His masculine side is Himeros,[46] because he is fire from the light, and his feminine side is a soul of blood from the substance of Forethought. He is extremely handsome in appearance, and more attractive than all the creatures of chaos.

When all the gods and their angels saw Eros, they fell in love with him. He appeared within them all and made them burn with desire. Just as many lamps are lit from a single lamp and all the light is the same but the light of the single lamp is not diminished, so also Eros was dispersed in all the creatures of chaos but was not diminished. Just as Eros appeared in the middle of light and darkness, and the sexual intercourse of Eros was accomplished in the middle of angels and people, so too the first sexual desire sprouted on the earth.

> Woman followed the earth,
> marriage followed woman,
> birth followed marriage,
> decay followed birth.

After Eros, a grapevine sprouted up from the blood that was shed upon the earth, and so those who drink of the fruit of the vine are filled with sexual desire.

After the grapevine, a fig tree and a pomegranate tree sprouted up from the earth, along with the rest of the trees, of every kind, and the seed of the trees came from the [110] semen of the authorities and their angels.

The Creation of Paradise (110,2–111,8)

Then justice created paradise. Paradise is beautiful, and is outside the circuit of the moon and the circuit of the sun in the land of pleasure, which is in the east in the rocky region. Desire dwells in the middle of the beautiful, stately trees. The tree of life eternal, as it appeared by the will of God, is in the north of paradise to give immortality to the souls of holy people,[47] who will leave their poor modeled bodies at the end of the age. The tree of life looks like the sun, and its branches are lovely. Its leaves are like the leaves of the cypress, its fruit is like a cluster of white grapes, and its height reaches the sky.

Next to it is the tree of knowledge,[48] which is endowed with the power of God. It is glorious as the moon shining brightly, and its branches are lovely. Its leaves are like fig leaves and its fruit is like a bunch of good, delicious dates. The tree of knowledge is in the north of paradise to arouse the souls from demonic stupor, so that they might come to the tree of life, eat its fruit, and condemn the authorities and their angels.

---

45. Eros is the Greek god of love and lover of Psyche in Greek mythology. 46. The text reads "Himireris." Himeros is the god of desire linked to Eros in Greek mythology. 47. Or "saints." 48. Gnosis, here and below.

The impact of this tree is described in the *Holy Book:*

You are the tree of knowledge,
which is in paradise,
from which the first man ate.
You opened his mind,
and he loved his female partner
and condemned [111] other strange figures,
and he loathed them.[49]

After this the olive tree sprouted, and it was to purify kings and high priests of justice who were to come in the last days. The olive tree appeared through the light of the first Adam for the sake of the oil of anointing that kings and high priests would receive.

The Creation of Plants, Animals, and Heavenly Bodies (111,8–112,25)

The first soul, Psyche, loved Eros,[50] who was with her, and she poured her blood upon him and upon the earth. From that blood the first rose sprouted upon the earth, out of a thorn bush, to give joy to the light that would appear in the bramble.

Next beautiful, fragrant flowers of every kind sprouted upon the earth from the blood of each of the virgin daughters of Forethought. They fell in love with Eros and poured their blood upon him and upon the earth.

Next, plants of every kind sprouted upon the earth, and they had the seed[51] of the authorities and their angels within them.

Then the authorities created animals, reptiles, and birds of every kind from the waters, and they had the seed[52] of the authorities and their angels within them.

But before all this, when Adam of light[53] appeared on the first day, he remained upon the earth about two days. He left the lower Forethought in heaven and ascended toward his light, and at once darkness covered the whole world. [112]

When she wished, Sophia, who is in the lower heaven, received authority from Pistis and created great heavenly lights and all the stars, and she placed them in the sky to shine upon the earth and designate chronological signs, seasons, years, months, days, nights, moments, and so on. Thus the whole region of the sky was organized.

When Adam of light wished to enter his light, which is the eighth heaven, he could not do so because of the poverty mingled with his light. So he created a

---

49. The source of this quotation is unknown. 50. Lit., "The first soul (or Psyche) loved Eros." 51. Or "semen." 52. Or "semen." 53. Lit., "he."

great aeon for himself, and in that eternal realm he created six more realms and their worlds, which are six in number and seven times better than the heavens of chaos and their worlds.

All these realms and their worlds are within the boundless region between the eighth heaven and chaos below it, and they are considered part of the world of poverty.

If you want to understand the organization of all these, you will find it described in the *Seventh Cosmos of Hieralias the Prophet.*[54]

The Creation of Humankind (112,25–114,4)

Before Adam of light made his return, the authorities saw him in chaos. They laughed at the chief creator because he lied when he said, "I am God; no one exists before me."

When they came to the chief creator, they said, "Is this being[55] not the God who ruined our work?"

He answered and said, "Yes. If you do not want him to be able to ruin our work, come, let's create a human being out of earth in the image of our body and with a likeness [113] to this being, to serve us, so that when this being sees his likeness, he may fall in love with it. Then he will no longer ruin our work, and we shall make the children of the light our slaves for this entire age."

All this happened in accordance with Pistis's forethought, so that humanity might appear in this likeness and condemn the authorities because of their modeled bodies. For their modeled bodies contained the light.

The authorities received knowledge[56] they needed to create humanity. Sophia Zoe, who is with Sabaoth, anticipated them. She laughed at their decision, because they are blind, and they created humanity in ignorance and against their own interests. They did not know what they were doing.

So she anticipated them. She created her own human being first, so that he might tell the modeled bodies of the authorities how to despise them and how to escape them.

The birth of the instructor happened like this. When Sophia let a drop of light fall, it landed on the water, and at once there appeared an androgynous human being. Sophia first made the drop into the form of a female body, and then she took the body and gave it a shape like the Mother who had appeared. She finished it in twelve months.

An androgynous human being was born, whom the Greeks call Hermaphrodite. The Hebrews call the child's mother Eve of life,[57] which means the female instructor of life, and the child born to her is lord. Later the authorities [114] called the child the beast so that it might lead their modeled bodies astray. The meaning of the beast is the instructor, for it turned out to be the wisest of all creatures.[58]

---

54. Another unknown source. 55. Adam of light. 56.
Gnosis. 57. Or "Eve of Zoe." 58. Cf. *Genesis* 3:1, on
the character of the serpent in paradise.

Song of Eve (114,4–24)

Eve is the first virgin, and she gave birth to her first child without a man. She was her own physician. For this reason she is said to have declared:

> I am part of my mother, and I am the mother.
> I am the wife, I am the virgin.
> I am pregnant, I am the physician,
> I am the comforter of birth pains.
> My husband produced me, and I am his mother,
> and he is my father and lord.
> He is my strength,
> he speaks of what he wants reasonably.
> I am becoming,
> but I have given birth to a lordly person.[59]

This was revealed by the will of Sabaoth and his Christ to the souls who were going to enter the modeled bodies of the authorities,[60] about whom the holy voice said, "Flourish and multiply, rule over all creatures."[61] These souls were taken captive, in accordance with their destinies, by the chief creator, and they were locked up in the prisons of the modeled bodies[62] <. . . until>[63] the end of the age.

The Rulers of the World Mold Adam (114,24–115,30)

Then the chief creator voiced his opinion about humankind to those who were with him. Then each of them ejaculated his semen into the middle of the navel of the earth.

Since then the seven archons have formed humanity with a body resembling their own body, but the likeness of humankind reflects the human being who appeared to them. The modeled body came into being, part by part, from each of the rulers, and the leader of the rulers created the brain and marrow.

Afterward the person appeared like the one before him. He became [115] a person with soul, and he was called Adam, which means father, after the name of the one who was before him.

After Adam was made, the chief creator abandoned him as a lifeless vessel, since Adam[64] was formed like an aborted fetus, with no spirit. When the chief ruler recalled the word of Pistis, he was afraid that the true human might enter his modeled body and rule over it. So he left his modeled body forty days without soul, and he withdrew and left him.

On the fortieth day Sophia Zoe blew her breath into Adam, in whom there was no soul. He began to crawl on the ground, but he could not stand up.

---

59. Cf. *Thunder* 13–14; *Genesis* 4:1. 60. This sentence is rearranged and restored. 61. *Genesis* 1:28. 62. The text reads "or" here, and this and what follows seem to be in error. 63. The text reads "at." 64. Lit., "he."

When the seven rulers came and saw him, they were greatly troubled. They approached him and grabbed him, and the chief ruler said to the breath within him, "Who are you? Where have you come from?"

He answered and said, "I have come through the power of the human to destroy your work . . . ."[65]

When they heard this, they glorified him, because he gave them rest from their fear and concern. They called that day the Day of Rest,[66] because they rested themselves from their troubles.

When they saw that Adam could not stand up, they were glad. They took him and put him in paradise, and withdrew up to their heavens.

Eve Gives Adam Life (115,30–116,8)

After the day of rest, Sophia sent her daughter Zoe, called Eve, as an instructor to raise Adam, in whom there was no soul, so that the children he would engender might be vessels of light.

[When] [116] Eve saw her male partner on the ground, she felt sorry for him and said, "Adam, live! Get up from the ground!"

At once her word became an accomplished deed. When Adam got up, at once he opened his eyes, and he saw her and said, "You will be called the Mother of the living, because you have given me life."[67]

The Powers Rape Earthly Eve (116,8–117,15)

The authorities were told that their modeled body was alive and had gotten up, and they were greatly troubled. They sent seven archangels to see what had happened.

They came to Adam, and when they saw Eve speaking with him, they said to each other, "Who is this enlightened woman? She looks like what appeared to us in the light. Come, let's seize her and ejaculate our semen into her, so that she may be unclean and unable to ascend to her light, and her children will serve us. But let's not tell Adam, because he is not one of us. Instead, let's put him to sleep and suggest to him in his sleep that Eve came from his rib, so that the woman may serve and he may rule over her."[68]

Since Eve was a heavenly power, she laughed at what they had in mind. She blinded their eyes and secretly left something that resembled her with Adam.

She entered the tree of knowledge and stayed there. The rulers chased her, and she revealed to them that she had entered the tree and had become a tree. The blind powers fell into great fear and ran away.

Later, when they recovered their sight, they came to [Adam]. They saw a female like that woman [117] with him, and they were troubled and thought this

---

65. There seems to be an awkward transition in thought here in the text, and a portion of the text may be missing. 66. The Sabbath Day. 67. Genesis 3:20. 68. Genesis 2:21–22.

was the true Eve. They acted rashly. They came to her, seized her, and ejaculated their semen upon her.

The powers acted wickedly. They defiled her in ways natural and obscene. First they defiled the seal of her voice, which had said to them, "What exists before you?" In this way they meant also to defile those who say that they were born at the end of the age through the word, through the true human.

The authorities and their angels erred. They did not know they defiled their own body and likeness in all these ways.

Eve Bears the Children of the Powers (117,15–118,6)

She first became pregnant with Abel from the first ruler, and then she gave birth to her other children from the seven authorities and their angels.

All this happened in accordance with the chief creator's forethought, so that the first mother might bear within herself every seed, every one mixed and joined with the fate of the world and its configurations, and justice.

A plan for Eve emerged, that the modeled bodies of the authorities might contain the light. Then the light would condemn the authorities through their own modeled bodies.

The first Adam of light is spiritual and appeared on the first day. The second Adam is psychical and appeared on the sixth day, called Aphrodite. The third Adam is earthly, a person of law, who appeared on the eighth day, called Sunday, [after] [118] the poor Day of Rest.[69]

The offspring of earthly Adam multiplied and filled the earth, and they acquired all the technical skills psychical Adam had. But they all were in ignorance.

The Trees of Paradise and the Beast (118,6–119,19)

Let me continue.

When the rulers saw him and the woman with him in error and ignorance, like animals, they were very pleased.

Then they found out that the immortal human was not going to pass them by and they would even have to fear the woman who turned into a tree. They were troubled and said, "Could this be the one who blinded us and taught us about the defiled woman who resembles the true human, in order to overpower us?"

The seven hatched a plot. They approached Adam and Eve carefully and said to him, "You may eat the fruit of every tree created for you in paradise, but be careful not to eat from the tree of knowledge. If you eat, you will die."[70] They gave them a great fright and withdrew up to their authorities.

The beast, the wisest of all creatures, came by. When it saw the likeness of their mother, Eve, it said to her, "What did God say to you? 'Do not eat from the tree of knowledge'?"

---

69. The Sabbath Day. 70. *Genesis* 2:16–17.

She said, "He not only said, 'Do not eat from it,' but 'Do not touch it, or you will die.'"

The beast said to her, "Don't be afraid. You certainly will [not die. He knows] that when you eat [119] from it your minds will become sober and you will be like gods, knowing the difference between evil and good people. He said this to you because he is jealous, so that you would not eat from it."[71]

Eve believed the words of the instructor. She looked at the tree and saw it was beautiful and appealing, and she liked it. She took some of its fruit and ate, and she gave it to her husband too, and he also ate. Their minds opened.

> When they had eaten,
> the light of knowledge[72] shone on them.
> When they clothed themselves with shame,
> they knew they were stripped of knowledge.
> When they became sober,
> they saw they were naked
> and they fell in love.
> When they saw their makers looked like beasts,
> they loathed them.

They understood a great deal.

The Rulers Confront Adam and Eve
(119,19–121,27)

When the rulers realized that Adam and Eve[73] had broken their commandment, they entered paradise and came to Adam and Eve with an earthquake and a great threat, in order to see what happened as a result of the help that was given. Adam and Eve were very much disturbed, and they hid in the trees in paradise. The rulers did not know where they were, and they said, "Adam, where are you?"

He said, "I'm here. I was ashamed and hid because I was afraid of you."

They said to him, ignorantly, "Who told you about the shame with which you clothed yourselves? Unless you ate from the tree!"

He said, "The woman you gave me gave it to me, and I ate."

They [said] to the woman, [120] "What have you done?"

She answered and said, "The instructor urged me to eat, and I ate."

The rulers approached the instructor. Their eyes were blinded by it, and they could not do anything to it. They were powerless, and they cursed it. Then they came to the woman, and they cursed her and her children. After the woman they cursed Adam and the earth and the fruit because of him. Everything they created they cursed. There is no blessing from them. Good cannot come from evil.

---

71. *Genesis* 3:1–5. 72. Gnosis. 73. Lit., "they."

Since then the authorities have known for certain that there is something stronger than they. They simply recognized that their commandment was broken. Great envy came into the world just because of the immortal human.[74]

When the rulers saw that their Adam had acquired different knowledge, they wanted to test him. They gathered all the domestic animals, wild beasts of the earth, and the birds of the sky, and brought them to Adam to see what he would call them. When he saw them, he gave names to the creatures of the rulers.

The rulers were troubled that Adam had recovered from all his anguish.[75] They gathered together and made a plan, and said, "Look, Adam has become like one of us, and he knows the difference between light and darkness. Now perhaps he will go astray as he did with the tree of knowledge and will come to the tree of life, eat from it, and become immortal and [rule] and despise us and consider [us] and all our glory to be foolish. And he will denounce [us and our] world. Come, let's throw him [121] out of paradise down to the earth, where he came from, so that he no longer can know anything better than we can."

So they threw Adam and his wife out of paradise.

What they had done did not satisfy them. They were still afraid. So they went to the tree of life and set great dreadful things around it, fiery living creatures called cherubim, and among them they put a flaming sword, constantly turning in a terrifying way, so that no one from the earth might ever enter that place.[76]

After this, since the rulers were jealous of Adam, they wanted to shorten the human life span, but they could not do so because of fate, which was established from the beginning. To each human being there was assigned a life span of one thousand years according to the circuit of the heavenly luminaries. Though the rulers were not able to do this, each one of the evildoers subtracted ten years, so the remaining time comes to nine hundred thirty years, and these are spent in grief and weakness and evil distractions. This is how life has gone, from that day until the end of the age.

Phoenixes, Water Serpents, and Bulls of Egypt (121,27–123,2)

When Sophia Zoe saw that the archons of darkness cursed her friends who were like her, she was angry. She came from the first heaven with all her power and chased the rulers from [their] heavens, and she cast them down into the sinful world so that they might dwell there as evil demons upon the earth.

[She sent a bird] [122] that was in paradise so that, until the end of the age, it might spend a thousand years in the rulers' world. The bird, a living creature endowed with soul, is called the phoenix, and it kills itself and revives itself as an image of the judgment against the rulers, because they dealt unjustly with Adam and his generation, until the end of the age.

---

74. Cf. Genesis 3:6–19. 75. The text reads *agōnia*; possibly correct to read *agnōsia*, "ignorance." 76. Cf. Genesis 3:21–24.

There are three human beings and their descendants in the world until the end of the age: the spiritual, the psychical, and the earthly. This circumstance is like the three kinds of phoenixes of paradise:[77] the first is immortal, the second lives a thousand years, and the third is consumed, according to what is written in the *Holy Book*. Likewise, there are three baptisms: the first is spiritual, the second is by fire, the third is by water.

As the image of the phoenix appears with reference to the angels, so the water serpents[78] in Egypt indicate those who go down for the baptism of a true human being.[79]

The two bulls in Egypt[80] indicate a mystery, the sun and the moon, which represent Sabaoth, because Sophia of the world has been exalted[81] above the sun and the moon from the time when she created them and sealed her heaven until the end of the age.

The worm that is born from the phoenix also represents[82] humanity. It is written of it, "The just will sprout like a phoenix."[83] The phoenix first appears alive, then dies, and then rises again, as an image of what appears at the end of the age.

These great images have [appeared] only in Egypt, not in other lands, indicating [123] that Egypt is like God's paradise.

Proof: The World Is in Error and Ignorance (123,2–31)

Let us return to the rulers of whom we spoke, so that we may offer an explanation of them.

When the seven rulers were cast from their heavens down to the earth, they created for themselves angels, numerous and demonic, to serve them. These angels taught people much about error, magic, potions, idolatry, bloodshed, altars, temples, sacrifices, and libations to all the demons of the earth. The angels work with fate,[84] which came into being by agreement of the gods of injustice and justice.

So when the world came into being, it went about in error and confusion all the time. All people on earth served the demons from the creation until the end of the age—both the angels of justice and the people of injustice. Thus the world was in confusion, ignorance, and stupor. All erred, until the appearance of the true human.

Enough on this. Next we shall consider our world so that we may present an accurate description of its structure and administration.

---

77. Perhaps the trees of paradise; see below. 78. Water *hudria*, perhaps water serpents, crocodiles, or otters. See Bethge, Layton, and Societas Coptica Hierosolymitana, in *Nag Hammadi Codex II,2–7*, 2.81. 79. The phoenixes may also be interpreted as palm trees, as in *Psalm* 91:13 in the Septuagint (see below), and the *hudria* as water pots like those in which Solomon confined the demons according to the *Testa-* ment of Solomon. Cf. Painchaud, *L'Écrit sans titre*, 473–75. 80. The two bulls in Egypt are most likely Apis and Mnevis. 81. Or "because Sophia has occupied the world." On "Sophia of the world," or "the wisdom of the world," cf. 1 *Corinthians* 1:20. 82. Or conceivably "does not (Coptic *an*) represent." 83. Or "like a palm tree"; *Psalm* 91:13 (in the Septuagint). 84. Coptic *šimarmenē*.

Then it will be clear how the proof of hidden things, which have been apparent from the foundation of the world to the end of the age, came about.[85]

Epilogue: The Blessed Little Innocent Spirits and the Church
(123,31–125,14)

Now I come to the main points [about] immortal humanity. I shall discuss all the beings belonging to immortal humanity and explain how they got here.

When a multitude of people had come into being through [Adam, who] [124] was formed from matter, and the world was filled, the rulers reigned over it—that is, they kept it in ignorance.

What is the reason? It is this. The immortal Father knows that deficiency of truth came to be among the aeons and their world. So when he wanted to bring down the rulers of perdition by means of their modeled creatures, he sent the blessed little innocent spirits, who are like you, down to the world of perdition. They are not strangers to knowledge.[86]

All knowledge is in one angel who appears to them. This angel stands before the Father and is not incapable of giving them knowledge.[87]

Whenever they appear in the world of perdition, the blessed spirits immediately reveal the pattern of incorruptibility so as to condemn the rulers and their powers.

When the blessed spirits appeared in the modeled bodies of the authorities, the authorities were jealous of them. Out of envy the authorities mixed their semen[88] with them in order to defile them, but they were not able.

When the blessed spirits appeared in an enlightened form, they appeared in different ways. They came from different realms and revealed their knowledge to the church[89] that appeared in the modeled bodies of perdition. The church was found to have all kinds of seed because of the seed of the authorities mixed [with it].

Then the Savior made all of them [one]. The spirits of these people [proved to be] superior, being blessed [125] but varying in election. There are many others who are kingless and superior to everyone before them.

So there are four generations. Three generations belong to the kings of the eighth heaven, and the fourth generation, which is the most exalted, is kingless and perfect.

These people will enter the holy place of their Father, and they will reside in rest, and eternal, ineffable glory, and ceaseless joy. They already are kings. They are the immortal within the mortal, and they will condemn the gods of chaos and their powers.

---

85. Or "Then it will be clear how the proof of hidden things is given <in> what has been apparent from the foundation of the world to the end of the age." 86. Gnosis. 87. Here in the manuscript occurs a case of dittography. 88. Or "seed." 89. Or "congregation" (*ekklēsia*), here and below.

Jesus the Word (125,14–32)

The Word[90] who is above all was sent for one reason only, to announce what is unknown. He[91] said, "There is nothing hidden that is not apparent, and what has not been known will be known."[92]

These people were sent to reveal what is hidden and expose the seven authorities of chaos and their godlessness, and so they[93] were condemned to death.

When all those who are perfect appeared in the modeled bodies of the rulers and revealed matchless truth, they put to shame all the wisdom of the gods.

> Their fate was condemnation,
> their power was dried up,
> their dominion was dissolved,
> their forethought was [empty],
> as was their glory.

The End of the Age (125,32–126,35)

Before the end [of the age], this whole region will shake with loud thunder. The archons will lament because of their [fear of] [126] death, the angels will grieve for their human beings, the demons will weep over their times and seasons, and their people will mourn and cry on account of their death.

Then the age will come, and they will be disturbed. Their kings will be drunk from the flaming sword and will wage war against each other, so that the earth will be drunk from the blood that is poured out. The seas will be troubled by war. The sun will darken and the moon will lose its light. The stars of the sky will abandon their circuits, and loud thunder will roar from a great power, above all the powers of chaos, where the firmament of the female[94] is located. She had produced the first creation, and now she will put away her wise fire of afterthought and put on irrational wrath.

Pistis Sophia will drive out the gods of chaos, whom she had created along with the chief creator, and she will cast them down to the abyss. They will be wiped out through their own injustice. They will be like mountains blazing with fire,[95] and they will consume one another until they are destroyed by their chief creator. When he destroys them, he will turn on himself and attack himself until he is no more.

The heavens of the gods of chaos will collapse upon one another and their powers will be consumed. Their realms will also be overthrown. The chief creator's heaven will fall and split in half. His [stars in their sphere][96] will fall

---

90. Logos. 91. Or "It," i.e., the Word. 92. *Matthew* 10:26; *Mark* 4:22; *Luke* 8:17; 12:2; *Gospel of Thomas* 5:2; 6:5–6. 93. This clause is ambiguous. Those con-demned are probably the authorities, possibly the holy people. 94. Apparently the heavenly female, Pistis Sophia. 95. Volcanoes. 96. The restoration is tentative.

down to the earth, [and the earth will not] be able to endure them. They will fall [down] to the abyss, and the abyss will be overthrown.

Light Overcomes Darkness (126,35–127,17)

The light will [overcome the] darkness and banish it. The darkness will be like [127] something that never was, and the source of darkness will be dissolved. Deficiency will be pulled out by its root and cast down into the darkness, and the light will withdraw up to its root.

The glory of the unbegotten will appear and fill all the eternal realms when the prophets and the writings of rulers[97] are revealed and fulfilled by those who are called perfect. Those who have not become perfect in the unbegotten Father will receive glory in their realms and the kingdoms of immortals, but they will never enter the kingless realm.

All must return to the place where they came from. By what they do and what they know all of them will reveal their natures.[98]

---

97. The prophets and writings designate scriptural books, specifically the Jewish scriptures. 98. Here the Coptic employs the singular ("Everyone . . ."), which is translated with the English plural for the sake of style.

EXEGESIS ON THE SOUL

NHC II,6

Introduced by Madeleine Scopello
Translated by Marvin Meyer

The tractate *Exegesis on the Soul*, extant only in the Coptic version preserved in Nag Hammadi Codex II, is a translation from an original Greek treatise, as is indicated by the Gnostic technical terminology preserved most often in Greek. The ten pages of the manuscript are in a good condition apart from a few lacunae. The title, which is given both at the beginning and the end of the text, reflects perfectly the purpose of its anonymous author: to offer an interpretation ("exegesis") of the story of the soul, built on the Gnostic myth of Psyche, from the account of her heavenly origin and her fall into the world to the description of her return to heaven. The author has chosen to tell this myth as a symbolic tale, whose heroine, the soul, is portrayed with female features.

The soul, the *Exegesis on the Soul* recounts, has a feminine name and a female nature (she even has a womb). She is virginal and androgynous in form when she is alone with her Father, but when she falls into a body and comes to life, she pollutes herself with many lovers. The soul's deceptions are many, and her lovers—brigands and bandits—treat her as a whore. She suffers when she understands that they are taking undue advantage of her, and she seeks other lovers. But even these compel her to live with them and make her their slave, for their sexual satisfaction. Though ashamed, the soul remains enslaved and submissive; her dwelling places are brothels, her steps lead her from one marketplace to another. The only gift she receives from her lovers is their polluted semen, by means of which she bears sick and feebleminded children (127,19–128,26).

The sexual and psychical captivity of the soul continues, the text maintains, until the day she becomes conscious of her unhappy situation and repents (128,26–30). She asks for help from her Father, and reminds him of the time when she was still a virgin in her maiden's quarters and stood by him (128,34–129,2). Seeing the soul so forlorn, the Father counts her worthy of his mercy: he makes her womb turn inward (131,19–24) so that the soul will regain her proper feminine character. In fact, the life of prostitution had changed the natural shape of her sexual organs: "The womb of the soul is turned to the outside like male sex organs, which are external" (131,25–27). This turning inward protects her from further sexual contamination. But this action is not sufficient to lead her to reproduce an unblemished offspring, so the Father sends her a bridegroom from heaven, who is her brother, the firstborn of the house of the Father (132,6–9).

As the bridegroom comes down to the soul, she cleanses herself of the pollution of the adulterers. She adorns herself in a bridal chamber, after having filled it with perfume, and sits there, waiting for her true lover. Her anxiety for his arrival combines with fear: she no longer remembers anything about him, just as she had forgotten everything about her Father's house. Nevertheless, a dream will restore the memory of the lover to her. The moment when bride and bridegroom meet again is sensually described, and the passionate love joining them, even if spiritual, is told in terms more proper to carnal intercourse (132,9–35). Good and beautiful children (meaning, in allegorical interpretation, virtuous ideas) are the fruit of this marriage (133,35–134,3). Finally, the soul regenerates herself and returns to her former state, coming back in the end to where she was in the beginning (134,6–11).

The special feature of the *Exegesis on the Soul* is the way in which it narrates the Gnostic myth of the soul as a romance, leaving aside the complex philosophical and theological language that is otherwise typical of this kind of literature. This tale seeks to explain the doctrine of gnosis in a rather simple and attractive manner, so that the metaphors and images that are used may be understood not only by philosophers and intellectuals but also by ordinary readers (see *Exegesis on the Soul* 131,31–34; 132,2–5).

Furthermore, the female heroine in the *Exegesis on the Soul* is dressed in the garb of Sophia, whose myth, as related in a general way by Irenaeus of Lyon (*Against Heresies* 1.1.1–9.5, about the doctrine of Ptolemy, a teacher of the school of Valentinus), is found here presented in a literary adaptation. The itinerary of the soul closely recalls Sophia's own journey: having left the perfection of the Pleroma, searching for new experiences, Sophia goes from wantonness to repentance, and finally she is accepted once again into her Father's dwelling. This myth, one of the key building blocks of Gnostic speculation, has often been interpreted in elaborate ways within Nag Hammadi literature and in the accounts of the church fathers. The myth finds in the *Exegesis on the Soul* a fresh and attractive presentation.

Two forms of literary tradition have certainly influenced the author in the composition of this treatise. These are Hellenistic and Jewish romance literature. Love and adventure are the chief ingredients of Hellenistic novels, and love produces action. These novels are governed by a single motif: the tragic separation of two lovers and their final reunion after many misadventures, with various tricks, storms, or brigands tempting the chastity of the heroine. Comparisons can be made between the *Exegesis on the Soul* and *Chereas and Callirhoe* by Chariton of Aphrodisia, *Leucippe and Clitophon* by Achilles Tatius, *Theagenes and Chariclea* (*The Ethiopics*) by Heliodorus, *Anthea and Abrocomes* by Xenophon of Ephesus, and *Daphnis and Chloe* by Longos.[1]

---

1. Madeleine Scopello, "Jewish and Greek Heroines in the Nag Hammadi Library," 78–82.

Nevertheless, two features can be observed in the *Exegesis on the Soul* that do not correspond to aspects of the Greek texts. First of all, the heroine of the Gnostic text is uniquely singular, and all of the meaning converges on the female heroine, while the male partner (the Spirit) plays a secondary role. In Greek novels the primary role is always given to a couple, a man and woman or a bridegroom and bride. Second, in Greek novels, the heroines wish to preserve their virginity at any cost: they are wise, virtuous girls. The heroine of the *Exegesis on the Soul*, however, has led, for a time, a life of prostitution.

Jewish influence is present as well in the *Exegesis on the Soul*. Jewish literature has preserved several stories and tales about women who symbolize, beyond their historical meaning, the search of the soul for God. Some such stories about women, who are said to have a questionable past but who return to God in repentance, are recounted in the Jewish scriptures and are picked up with great interest in the apocrypha and the pseudepigrapha: we may recall the stories of Tamar, Rahab, Ruth, and the wife of Uriah (all of whom are mentioned in the genealogy of Jesus according to *Matthew* 1:1–6).[2]

The influence of themes typical of trends in Jewish literature is even deeper. The intense focus on physical and spiritual pollution in the *Exegesis on the Soul* recalls Essene psychology (cf. the *Testaments of the Twelve Patriarchs* and Qumran literature). In the present Gnostic text as well as in Essene spirituality, purification and repentance are the only remedies for impurity. The turning inward of the womb of the female soul in the *Exegesis on the Soul* (131,19–31) can be compared with spiritual circumcision (cf. the Qumran *Community Rule* 5.5; this theme is also present in *Gospel of Philip* 82,26–83,2). Both of these images express a will to abandon what is on the outside, a symbol of worldly temptation.[3]

In the *Exegesis on the Soul*, the narrative is supported by another sort of narration, worked into the first one and built upon references to the Hebrew prophets and the poet Homer. This "parallel story" takes up the three key moments of the soul's life: the virginity in the beginning, prostitution on earth, and the return to the primal existence. Each moment is described in a series of quotations that were not collected by the author but were probably drawn from an anthology of quotations, traces of which have been preserved by Christian authors of Alexandria: Clement, Origen, and Didymos.[4] This helps to establish the milieu of the author of the *Exegesis on the Soul*. The author is dependent on an academic culture in which anthologies form an important part of an intellectual education. The use of biblical and Homeric references shows that Greek wisdom and Jewish wisdom have the same prophetic value for the Gnostic author. This standpoint is quite original, since Gnostic teachers generally employ a very critical approach toward the Jewish scriptures, which were written, according to the Gnostic teachers, under the inspiration of the demiurge. All these literary references in

---

2. Scopello, "Jewish and Greek Heroines in the Nag Hammadi Library," 82–85.

3. Madeleine Scopello, *L'exégèse de l'âme*, 57–93.

4. Madeleine Scopello, "Les 'Testimonia' dans le traité de l'*"Exégèse de l'âme.'"

the *Exegesis on the Soul* were meant to attract the attention of contemporary readers having a certain knowledge of biblical tradition as well as Greek culture. If the quotations drawn from the Hebrew prophets, which are rich in powerful imagery, provide a perfect completion to the Gnostic myth of the soul, the two references from Homer, which depict Helen and Odysseus far from their homeland, paint the despair of Gnostic humanity exiled on earth.[5]

The author of the *Exegesis on the Soul* also turns to allegory, a typical method of interpretation within the Platonic tradition of his time, in order to signify, through the career of the soul, the existential itinerary of every Gnostic seeking for his or her true origin. This allegory is easy to interpret, and its structure reveals the purposes of the writer, who wishes to communicate the message to a wider public and not only to the members of a Gnostic group. Exotericism, not esotericism (a frequent feature in Nag Hammadi literature), permeates this treatise on the soul.[6]

The attention given to the theme of marriage and the nuptial chamber in the *Exegesis on the Soul*, in which the soul and the Spirit ultimately come together in an androgynous union, leads us to situate the writer of the tractate in a Valentinian Gnostic context.[7] The text also gives some attention to the sacraments, though not to the extent of other Valentinian texts within the Nag Hammadi scriptures. All these elements suggest that the *Exegesis on the Soul* was composed in Alexandria, at the beginning of the third century, by a writer with a cultivated, syncretistic background.

BIBLIOGRAPHY

Hedda Bethge, "Die Exegese über die Seele"; Martin Krause and Pahor Labib, *Gnostische und hermetische Schriften aus Codex II und Codex VI*, 68–87; Bentley Layton, ed., *Nag Hammadi Codex II, 2–7*, 2.135–69 (Bentley Layton and William C. Robinson); Bernard Pouderon, "Hélène et Ulysse comme deux âmes en peine"; Hans-Martin Schenke, Hans-Gebhard Bethge, and Ursula Ulrike Kaiser, eds., *Nag Hammadi Deutsch*, 1.263–78 (Christina-Maria Franke); Madeleine Scopello, *Femme, gnose et manichéisme*; "Jewish and Greek Heroines in the Nag Hammadi Library"; "Les citations d'Homère dans le traité de *L'Exégèse de l'âme*"; *L'Exégèse de l'âme*; "Les 'Testimonia' dans le traité de l'*Exégèse de l'âme*'"; Jean-Marie Sevrin, *L'Exégèse de l'âme*; "La rédaction de *l'Exégèse de l'âme*."

---

5. Bernard Pouderon, "Hélène et Ulysse comme deux âmes en peine"; William C. Robinson, in Bentley Layton, ed., *Nag Hammadi Codex II,2–7*; Scopello, "Les 'Testimonia' dans le traité de *l'Exégèse de l'âme*'"; "Les citations d'Homère dans le traité de *L'Exégèse de l'âme*."

6. Madeleine Scopello, *Femme, gnose et manichéisme*, 179–200.

7. Jean-Marie Sevrin, *L'Exégèse de l'âme*.

Exegesis on the Soul[1]

Exegesis on the Soul

The Female Soul (127,18–22)

The sages who came before us gave the soul a feminine name. She is also feminine in nature, and she even has a womb.

Fall of the Soul (127,22–129,5)

While the soul was alone with the Father, she was a virgin and androgynous in form. When she fell down into a body and entered this life, she fell into the hands of many robbers. These shameless men passed her from one to the other and [violated] her. Some raped her, others seduced her with gifts. They defiled her, and she [lost her] [128] virginity.

In her body she became a whore and gave herself to everyone, and she considered each sexual partner to be her husband. After she gave herself to shameless, faithless adulterers for them to abuse her, she sighed deeply and repented.

But when she turned her face from those adulterers, she ran after others, and they made her live with them and serve them in their beds as if they were her masters. She was ashamed, and then she did not dare to leave them. For a long time they fooled her into thinking they respected her like faithful, true husbands. But finally they left and abandoned her.

She became a poor lost widow. She was helpless, and no one even gave ear to her in her pain. She got nothing from the adulterers except the filth they left when they had sex with her. The children she had from the adulterers are mute, blind, and sickly. They are disturbed.

Her Father on high noticed her. He looked down on her and saw her sighing in pain and disgrace and repenting of her prostitution. She began to call on him for help, and [she sighed] with all her heart and said, "My Father, save me. Look,

1. Coptic Text: NHC II,6: 127,18–137,27. Editions: *The Facsimile Edition of the Nag Hammadi Codices: Codex II*, 139–49; Bentley Layton, ed., *Nag Hammadi Codex II,2–7*, 2.144–69 (Bentley Layton and William C. Robinson); Hans-Martin Schenke, Hans-Gebhard Bethge, and Ursula Ulrike Kaiser, eds., *Nag Hammadi Deutsch*, 1.263–78 (Christina-Maria Franke); Madeleine Scopello, *L'Exégèse de l'âme*; Jean-Marie Sevrin, *L'Exégèse de l'âme*. The title of the text is also sometimes translated as the *Expository Treatise on the Soul*.

I shall tell [you how I] left home and [129] fled from my maiden's quarters. Restore me to yourself."

When he sees her in this condition, he will consider her worthy of his mercy. For many afflictions have come upon her because she left home.

On the Prostitution of the Soul (129,5–131,13)

The holy Spirit prophesies in many places about the prostitution of the soul. The Spirit said in the prophet Jeremiah:

> If a husband divorces his wife and she goes and takes another man, can she ever go back to him again? Has not such a woman utterly defiled herself? "You played the whore with many shepherds and you returned to me," said the Lord. "Lift up your eyes and see clearly where you went whoring. Were you not sitting in the streets defiling the land with your whoring and your vices? And you took many shepherds as a way of stumbling for you. You were shameless with everyone. You did not call on me as companion or father or guardian of your virginity."[2]

It is also written in the prophet Hosea:

> Come, accuse your mother, for she is not to be my wife nor I her husband. I shall remove her whoring from my presence and her adultery from between her breasts. I shall make her naked as on the day she was born and desolate as a waterless land. I shall make her childless with a [longing for children.[3] I] shall show her children no pity, for they are children of prostitution. Their mother played the whore and [shamed her children]. [130] She said, "I shall be a whore to my lovers. They gave me bread, water, garments, robes, wine, oil—everything I needed." Look, I shall block them so that she will not be able to run after her adulterers. When she seeks them but does not find them, she will say, "I shall go back to my former husband, for I was better off then than now."[4]

Again, it is said in Ezekiel:

> It happened that after much wickedness, the Lord said, you built yourself a brothel and made yourself a beautiful place in the streets. You built brothels in every alley and you wasted your beauty, you spread your legs in every alley and multiplied your acts of prostitution. You were a whore for the sons of Egypt, your neighbors, well-endowed men.[5]

---

2. *Jeremiah* 3:1–4. 3. Lit., "with a [thirst]." 4. *Hosea*
2:2–7. 5. *Ezekiel* 16:23–26.

What does "the sons of Egypt, well-endowed men" mean if not the realm of the flesh and the senses and the things of the earth by which the soul is defiled in this world? She receives from them bread, wine, oil, clothing, and the other external stuff surrounding the body, the things she thinks she needs.

But as to this prostitution, the apostles of the Savior commanded,

> Guard yourselves against it, purify yourself from it.[6]

They were speaking not just of the prostitution of the body but especially that of the soul. That is why the apostles write [to the churches] of God so that such [things] might not go on among us.

The greatest [struggle] is the prostitution [131] of the soul. From it comes the prostitution of the body. Thus Paul wrote to the Corinthians and said:

> I wrote to you in my letter, "Do not associate with whores," not meaning the whores of this world or the greedy or thieves or idol worshipers, since then you would have to leave the world.[7]

Here he is speaking spiritually:

> For our struggle is not against flesh and blood—as he said—but against the world rulers of this darkness and the spirits of evil.[8]

Restoration of the Soul *(131,13–132,27)*

As long as the soul keeps running here and there having sex with whomever she meets and defiling herself, she will suffer what she deserves. But when she perceives the trouble she is in and weeps before the Father and repents, the Father will pity her. He will make her womb turn from the outside back to the inside, so that the soul will recover her proper character. It is not so with a woman. The womb of the body is inside the body like the other internal organs, but the womb of the soul is turned to the outside like male sex organs, which are external.

When the womb of the soul, by the Father's will, turns to the inside, she is baptized, and at once she is free of the external pollution forced upon her, just as dirty [clothes] are soaked in [water and] are moved about until the dirt is removed and they are clean. The soul is cleansed so that she may regain what she had at first, [132] her former nature, and she may be restored. That is her baptism.

Then she will begin to rage like a woman in labor, who writhes and rages at the time of delivery. But since she is female and cannot conceive a child by herself, her Father sent her from heaven her man, her brother, the firstborn. The

---

6. Cf. *Acts* 15:20, 29; 21:25; 1 *Thessalonians* 4:3; 1 *Corinthians* 6:18; 2 *Corinthians* 7:1. 7. 1 *Corinthians* 5:9. 8. *Ephesians* 6:12.

bridegroom came down to the bride. She gave up her former whoring and cleansed herself of the pollution of adulterers, and she was restored to be a bride. She cleansed herself in the bridal chamber. She filled it with perfume and sat there awaiting the true bridegroom. She no longer went around the marketplace having sex with whomever she desired, but she stayed and waited for him, saying, "When will he come?" And she feared him. For she did not know what he looked like. She no longer remembered from the time she fell from her Father's house. Yet, by the Father's will, she dreamed of him like a woman who loves a man.

Marriage of the Soul to Her Beloved (132,27–133,31)

Then, by the Father's will, the bridegroom came down to her in the bridal chamber that had been prepared. And he decorated the chamber.

This marriage of the soul is not like a marriage of the flesh. In a marriage of the flesh, those who have sex with each other become satiated with sex, and so they leave behind them the annoying burden of physical desire and [turn their faces] from each other. This marriage of the soul [is different]. When the partners join [with each other], they become a single life. [133]

Thus the prophet said about the first man and woman,

They will become a single flesh.[9]

These partners were originally joined to each other when they were with the Father, before the woman led astray[10] the man, her brother. This marriage has brought them together again, and the soul has joined her true love and real master, as it is written:

The master of the woman is her husband.[11]

Gradually she recognized him. She was happy again, and she wept in his arms when she remembered the disgrace of her former widowhood. She adorned herself even more, so that he might be pleased to stay with her.

The prophet said in the Psalms:

Hear, my daughter, see and give ear,
    and forget your people and your father's house,
for the king has desired your beauty,
    and he is your master.[12]

Her master has her turn her face from her people and the many adulterers with whom she once was, to devote herself to her king, her real master, and to

---

9. *Genesis* 2:24. 10. Or "left." The translation "led astray" may reflect the story of Adam and Eve in *Gene-* *sis* 3. 11. Cf. *Genesis* 3:16; 1 *Corinthians* 11:1; *Ephesians* 5:23. 12. *Psalm* 44 (45):10–11 (Septuagint).

forget the house of the earthly father, with whom things went badly for her, but to remember her Father in heaven.

So also it was said to Abraham:

Leave your country and your relatives and your father's house.[13]

Rebirth of the Soul (133,31–135,4)

When the soul [adorned] herself again in her beauty, she [was eager] to enjoy her beloved. [He also] loved her. When she made love with him, she received [**134**] from him the seed,[14] which is the life-giving spirit. She bears good children by him and brings them up. This is the great, perfect, wonderful birth.

This marriage is consummated by the Father's will.

The soul needs to regenerate herself and become as she formerly was. So the soul stirred, and she received the divine from the Father, that she might be restored and returned to where she was before.

> This is resurrection[15] from the dead.
> This is freedom from captivity.
> This is ascent to heaven.
> This is the way up to the Father.

Therefore the prophet said:

> My soul, praise the Lord,
> all within me, praise his holy name.
> My soul, praise God,
> who forgave all your sins,
> who healed all your sicknesses,
> who freed your life from death,
> who crowned you with mercy,
> who satisfies your longing with good things.
> Your youth will be renewed like an eagle's.[16]

When the soul is renewed, she will arise and praise the Father and her brother, by whom she was rescued. In this way, through rebirth, the soul will be saved. This is not because of practical lessons or technical skills or learned books. Rather, it is the grace of the [Spirit],[17] it is the gift of the merciful [God], for it is from above.

Thus the Savior calls out: [**135**]

---

13. *Genesis* 12:1. **14.** Or "semen." **15.** Perhaps "the real resurrection," or "the resurrection that is . . ." (Coptic *tanastasis etšoop*). **16.** *Psalm* 102 (103):1–5 (Septuagint). **17.** The Coptic is restored to read *p[pna]* (abbreviated). It is also possible to restore the lacuna to read "Father" (*p[eiōt]*), "God" (*p[noute]*), or the like.

No one can come to me unless my Father draws and brings that one to me. I myself will raise that one on the last day.[18]

Praying with All Our Soul (135,4–136,16)

So we need to pray to the Father and call on him with all our soul, not outwardly with our lips but with the spirit, which is within and has come from the depth,

> sighing,
> repenting for the lives we led,
> confessing our sins,
> recognizing the vain deception
> and vain zeal we were in,
> weeping over our lives
> in darkness, as billows roll,
> mourning for ourselves
> that he might pity us,
> hating ourselves
> for what we are now.

Again, the Savior said:

> Blessed are they who mourn, for they will be pitied.
> Blessed are the hungry, for they will be filled.[19]

Again he said:

> One who does not hate one's own soul cannot follow me.[20]

The beginning of salvation is repentance. Thus:

> Before Jesus appeared John came and preached the baptism of repentance.[21]

Repentance takes place in sorrow and grief. The Father is good and loves people, and hears the soul that calls to him and sends her the light of salvation. Thus he said through the spirit to the prophet:

> Say to the children of my people,
> "[If] your sins reach [from earth to] heaven,

---

18. John 6:44. 19. Matthew 5:4, 6; Luke 6:21. 20. Luke 14:26. 21. Acts 13:24.

if they become [red] as scarlet and blacker than sackcloth,
[and if] [**136**] you return to me with all your soul
and say to me, 'My Father,'
I will listen to you as a holy people."22

Again, elsewhere:

> Thus says the Lord, the holy one of Israel,
> "If you return and sigh,
> you will be saved
> and know where you were
> when you trusted what is vain."23

And again he said:

> Jerusalem wept and wept, saying, "Pity me." He will have pity on the voice
> of your lamentation. When he noticed, he listened to you. And the Lord
> will give you bread of affliction and water of oppression. From now on
> those who deceive will never approach you again. Your eye will see those
> who would deceive you.24

Repentance of Odysseus and Helen (136,16–137,11)

We need to pray to God night and day and lift our hands to him as people do who
sail in the middle of the sea. They pray to God with all their heart without
hypocrisy. Those who pray with hypocrisy deceive only themselves. For God examines what is within and searches the depths of the heart to find out who is
worthy of salvation. And no one is worthy of salvation who still loves the place of
deception.

Thus it is written in the poet:

> Odysseus sat weeping and grieving on the island. He turned his face from
> the words of Calypso and from her tricks, and longed to see his village and
> smoke coming from it. If he had not [received] help from heaven, [he
> would not have been able to return] to his village.25

Again, [Helen also] says:

> My heart turned away from me. [**137**] I want to return to my own house.26

---

22. Here the text quotes an unknown prophet, perhaps an apocryphon of Ezekiel, also cited in 1 *Clement*
8:3. 23. *Isaiah* 30:15. 24. *Isaiah* 30:19–20. 25. Homer
Odyssey 1.48–59. 26. *Odyssey* 4.260–61.

She sighed and said:

> Aphrodite deceived me and brought me out of my village. I left my only
> daughter behind, and my good, understanding, handsome husband.[27]

When the soul leaves her perfect husband because of the deception of
Aphrodite, which happens in the act of conception in this world, the soul suffers
harm. But if she sighs and repents, she will be restored to her house.

Our Repentance (137,11–27)

Israel would not have once been visited by God and brought out of the land of
Egypt and the house of bondage if it had not sighed to God and wept about its op-
pressive labors.

Again, it is written in the Psalms:

> I have been deeply troubled
> in my groaning.
> I shall drench my bed and cover each night
> with my tears.
> I have become old among all my enemies.
> Depart from me, all you who do lawless things,
> for look, the Lord has heard the cry of my weeping,
> and the Lord has heard my prayer.[28]

If we truly repent, God, who is patient and abundant in mercy, will hear us. To
God be the glory forever and ever.

Amen.

Exegesis on the Soul

---

27. *Odyssey* 4.261–64. 28. *Psalm* 6:6–9.

THE BOOK OF THOMAS

NHC II,7

Introduced by John D. Turner
Translated by Marvin Meyer

The *Book of Thomas*, which occupies the final eight pages of Nag Hammadi Codex II, is virtually complete except for a few, often restorable lines at the bottom of each page. The tractate is a postresurrection dialogue between the risen Jesus and his twin brother Jude (Judas)[1] surnamed Thomas (from Aramaic *taumā*, Greek *didumos*, "twin"), ostensibly recorded by Mathaias[2] as he walked with them and recorded their conversation at a time shortly before Jesus's ascension into heaven. As the Savior's "true companion," Judas Thomas, with his already unparalleled earthly knowledge of his twin brother, is the ideal recipient of the Savior's truest and deepest teaching, which is now supplemented by a direct revelation of the Savior's postresurrection luminosity. This characterization of Thomas is part of the general theme of a favored confidant or "beloved disciple" singled out by Jesus as guarantor of his most secret and innermost teaching, as in the case of many Christian compositions, such as saying 13 of the *Gospel of Thomas*, the *Gospel of John*, and postresurrection dialogues such as the *Gospel of Mary* and the *Secret Book of John*. Other implied characters include the author's audience, which seems to reflect not only a debate between the members of an ideal ascetic community and the impure and lost masses beyond its borders

---

1. According to *Mark* 6:3, Jesus had four brothers, two of whom become prominent: James, who later replaced Peter as the leader of the Jerusalem Christians, and Judas, surnamed "Thomas" in the *Gospel of John* and perhaps to be identified with the reputed author of the New Testament *Letter of Jude* and the disciple/apostle Thomas in the synoptic gospels and *Acts*.

2. Whether this "Matthew" is meant to be identical with (1) the tax-collecting disciple of Jesus, (2) the author of the corresponding canonical gospel, (3) the chosen replacement for Judas Iscariot, or (4) a Matthaios elsewhere linked to certain secret teachings of Jesus (Hippolytus *Refutation of All Heresies* 7.20.1, 5; Clement of Alexandria *Miscellanies* 3.4.26.3) is hard to say. If an esoteric and ascetic connection is intended, then Mathaias along with Thomas is invoked as a prominent authority for Jesus's special teaching. According *Pistis Sophia* 1.43, Mariam exclaims to Jesus, "Concerning the word that you spoke to Philip, 'You and Thomas and Matthew are the three to whom it has been given, through the First Mystery, to write every word of the Kingdom of the Light, and to bear witness to them,' hear me and give the interpretation of the words that your light-power once prophesied through Moses: 'Through two and three witnesses everything will be established.' The three witnesses are Philip and Thomas and Matthew."

who refuse to listen to their preaching, but also an intracommunity debate between those who have achieved ascetic perfection and a less committed group
who know the truth, but whose preoccupation with the concerns of daily life lead
them astray from behaving in accord with it.

Like the *Gospel of Thomas* and the *Acts of Thomas*, so also the *Book of Thomas*
likely derives from the ascetic, pre-Manichaean Christianity of the Osrhoëne
(eastern Syria, between Edessa [modern Urfu] and Messene). The *Book of
Thomas* seems to seems to be a product of the late second century, occupying a
median position between the *Gospel of Thomas*—a sayings collection probably
originating in the first century—and the *Acts of Thomas*—a third-century Greek
romance about Thomas's exploits as a missionary in India—in three respects:
(1) date of composition, (2) relative predominance of the role played by Thomas
in these works, and (3) increasing predominance of narrative features as one
moves from sayings collection to dialogue to romance.

The basic and original theme of the text is an unbending asceticism that condemns anything to do with the flesh and sexuality, supplemented by the Platonic-
Gnostic-Hermetic theme of salvation by self-knowledge, familiar from the *Gospel
of Thomas*. The basic catchword is "fire": the fiery lustful and sexual passions of
the bestial body that infect the soul and condemn one to an eternal fiery punishment in hell, implementing a Dantean *contrapasso*—one is punished by that by
which one sins. The treatise evinces a metaphysical and ethical dualism of a radically ascetic stripe, but one that is more properly apocalyptic—much like infernal punishments of the last judgment in the Greek *Apocalypse of Peter*—than
mythological. The myth of the creation of the world by divine error or by an evil
power is neither mentioned nor apparently presupposed; indeed, the dualism of
the treatise is much more anthropological (the bestial body versus the divine soul,
the fire of sexual passion versus the tranquility of wisdom and self-control) than
cosmic (the transcendent ideal realm versus the earthly realm as its deficient
copy).

The genre of the *Book of Thomas* is composite. The subscript title designates
the complete work as the "book" of Thomas, identified as "the *athlētēs* (i.e., 'one
who struggles' against the fiery passions of the body) writing to the perfect"; the
opening lines designate the work as "hidden sayings" or "secret sayings" spoken
by Jesus to Judas Thomas and recorded by Mathaias as he heard them speaking.
The designation "sayings" does not really correspond to the apparent genre of the
work, which is a revelation dialogue. This type of dialogue is unlike the Platonic
dialogue, in which a conversational process of statement, counterstatement, and
clarification leads step by step to the birth of knowledge, but more related to the
literature sometimes called *erotapokriseis* ("questions and answers"), in which an
initiate elicits revealed truth from a spiritual authority or revealer figure in the
form of catechetical answers to topical questions.[3] The Christian dialogues of this

---

3. See Kurt Rudolph, "Der gnostische 'Dialog' als literarisches Genus."

sort are set at a time between the resurrection and ascension, when the risen Savior appeared on earth in his true divine form. In such a setting, both he and the true significance of his teaching became uniquely available to select apostles in a form unclouded by the materiality that was believed to account for the rather obscure and parabolic teaching of his earthly, preresurrection days.

The actual dialogue between Thomas and Jesus occupies only the first three-fifths of the treatise (138,4–142,21), while the remaining two-fifths (142,21–end) constitutes a long monologue of the Savior in which Thomas no longer plays a role. This and the detection of a transitional editorial seam at 142,21 suggest that the *Book of Thomas* may have resulted from a synthesis of two previously separate works, an introductory dialogue between Thomas and Jesus, perhaps entitled "The Book of Thomas, the Contender Writing to the Perfect," and a concluding monologue of the Savior's collected sayings, perhaps entitled "The Hidden Sayings That the Savior Spoke."[4] In its original form, the monologue occupying the last two-fifths seems to represent a late and decadent reflection of the literary genre of the sayings of Jesus, in which vestigial sayings formulas of Jesus ("Blessed are you . . . ," "Woe to you . . . ," "Watch and pray . . .")[5] have been supplemented with ascetic teaching whose content is quite alien to the synoptic tradition.

The dialogue portion of the *Book of Thomas* seems to have been created by the dissection of a preexisting epitome of Plato's teaching on the soul drawn principally from the *Phaedo, Phaedrus, Republic,* and *Timaeus* into expository units[6] placed on the lips of Jesus to serve as his answers to fictitious questions asked by his interlocutor Thomas to elicit the Savior's teaching as responses.[7] A later redactor then supplemented this dialogue with what amounts to a sayings collection reminiscent of the cluster of woes and macarisms (*Luke* 6:20–26 [Q]) to serve as Jesus's final testamentary speech prior to his ascension, and designated the whole as a collection of hidden sayings heard by Thomas and recorded by Mathaias. On this construction, the *Book of Thomas* is an interesting example of the Christianizing of Platonic teaching, or better yet, of the Platonizing of Jesus, as Platonic wisdom passes from the Socratic dialogue through popular Greco-Roman digests of Plato's thought onward to Christian revelation.

---

4. In Thomas's final words in 142,21–24, which immediately preface the Savior's concluding monologue, Thomas in effect designates Jesus's teaching as sayings: "But these sayings that you tell us are laughable and ridiculous to the world, since they are not understood."

5. Johannine traditions are also present; in the initial dialogue there is the formula "I tell you the truth" (142,27–29) and adaptations of *John* 3 in 138,21–36 and 140,5–18 as well as in the second and third macarisms of the concluding monologue (145,5–8). There is also a version of the synoptic parable of the weeds and tares (*Matthew* 13:24–30) adapted to the Johannine simile of the vine and branches (*John* 15:1–7) to form a parable of the grapevine (the soul) and the weeds (the body) in 144,21–36.

6. The Platonic teaching on the soul and its transmigration and incarnation into the body drawn from *Phaedo* (78e–80d; 81a–83e; 109d–e; 113a–114b), *Phaedrus* (246c–249c; 250e), *Republic* (VI 508c–509b, 514a–515d; X 571d–572a, 615e), and *Timaeus* (86b–e; 90e–91d) has been attributed to Jesus in the expository units of the initial dialogue, especially in 138,39–139,31; 140,1–5, 18–37; 141,5–8, 10, 14–18, 33–38; and 142,11–18. See especially John D. Turner, "The Book of Thomas and the Platonic Jesus."

7. A similar relationship exists between the *Wisdom of Jesus Christ* and *Eugnostos the Blessed.*

BIBLIOGRAPHY

Dankwart Kirchner, "Das Buch des Thomas"; Raymond Kuntzmann, *Le livre de Thomas*; Bentley Layton, ed., *Nag Hammadi Codex II,2–7*, 171–205 (John D. Turner); Pheme Perkins, *The Gnostic Dialogue*; Kurt Rudolph, "Der gnostische 'Dialogue' als literarisches Genus"; Hans-Martin Schenke, "The Book of Thomas (NHC II.7): A Revision of a Pseudepigraphical Epistle of Jacob the Contender"; *Das Thomas-Buch*; Hans-Martin Schenke, Hans-Gebhard Bethge, and Ursula Ulrike Kaiser, eds., *Nag Hammadi Deutsch*, 1.279–91 (Hans-Martin Schenke); Jesse W. Sell, *The Knowledge of the Truth—Two Doctrines: The Book of Thomas the Contender (CG II,7) and the False Teachers of the Pastoral Epistles*; John D. Turner, "The Book of Thomas and the Platonic Jesus"; *The Book of Thomas the Contender*; "A New Link in the Syrian Judas Thomas Tradition."

The Book of Thomas[1]

Hidden Sayings (138,1–4)

The hidden sayings that the Savior spoke to Judas Thomas, which I, Mathaias, in turn recorded.[2] I was walking, listening to them speak with each other.

Jesus Speaks with Brother Thomas (138,4–21)

The Savior said, "Brother Thomas, while you are still in the world, listen to me and I shall reveal to you what you have thought about in your heart.

"Since it is said that you are my twin and true friend, examine yourself and understand who you are, how you exist, and how you will come to be. Since you are to be called my brother, it is not fitting for you to be ignorant of yourself. And I know that you have understood, for already you have understood that I am the knowledge of truth. So while you are walking with me, though you do lack understanding, already you have obtained knowledge and you will be called one who knows himself.[3] For those who have not known themselves have known nothing, but those who have known themselves already have acquired knowledge about the depth of the All. So then, my brother Thomas, you have seen what is hidden from people, what they stumble against in their ignorance."

The Hidden and the Visible (138,21–139,31)

Thomas said to the master,[4] "That is why I beg you to tell me what I ask before your ascension. When I hear from you about what is hidden, I can speak of it. And it is clear to me that the truth is difficult to accomplish before people."

The Savior answered and said, "If what is visible to you is obscure to you, how can you comprehend what is invisible? If deeds of truth visible in the world are

---

1. Coptic text: NHC II,7: 138,1–145,19; 145,20–23 (scribal note). Editions: The Facsimile Edition of the Nag Hammadi Codices: Codex II, 150–57; Raymond Kuntzmann, Le Livre de Thomas; Bentley Layton, ed., Nag Hammadi Codex II,2–7, 2.171–205 (John D. Turner and Bentley Layton); Hans-Martin Schenke, Hans-Gebhard Bethge, and Ursula Ulrike Kaiser, eds., Nag Hammadi Deutsch, 1.279–91 (Hans-Martin Schenke). The text includes a secondary title in the manuscript: "The Contender Writing to the Perfect." 2. Here Judas Thomas is thought to be the twin brother of Jesus; cf. Gospel of Thomas Prologue. The name Mathaias resembles that of the original disciple Matthew and the replacement apostle Matthias, but his identity is unclear. 3. Cf. the Delphic maxim "Know yourself," and Gospel of Thomas 3:4–5. 4. Or "Lord," here and below.

difficult for you to accomplish, how will you accomplish things of the exalted majesty and fullness,[5] which are invisible?[6] How will you be called workers? You are beginners and have not attained the greatness of perfection."

Thomas answered and said to the Savior, "Tell us about these things that you say are invisible and hidden from us."

The Savior said, "[All] bodies [have come into being in the same irrational way] that animals are produced, and so they are visible, as [creatures lusting after creatures]. Those that are above, however, [do not exist like] those that are visible.[7] Rather, [they] live[8] [139] from their own root, and their crops nourish them. But the visible bodies feed on creatures that are like them, and so the bodies are subject to change. Whatever is subject to change will perish and be lost, and henceforth has no hope of life, because this body is an animal body. Just as an animal body perishes, these modeled forms also will perish. Are they not from sexual intercourse like that of the animals? If the body too is from intercourse, how will it give birth to anything different from them? So, then, you are children until you become perfect."

Thomas answered, "This is why I say to you, master, those who speak about what is invisible and difficult to explain are like people who shoot their arrows at a target during the night. Of course, they shoot their arrows as any people do, since they are shooting at the target, but it is not visible. When light comes, however, and banishes darkness, then the accomplishment of each person will be clear. And you, our light, bring enlightenment, master."

Jesus said, "It is through light that light exists."

Thomas spoke and said, "Master, why does this visible light that shines for people rise and set?"[9]

The Savior said, "Blessed Thomas, surely this visible light has shone for you not to keep you here, but that you might leave. And when all the chosen ones lay down their animal nature, this light will withdraw up to its being, and its being will welcome it to itself, because the light is a good helper."

Wisdom and Foolishness (139,31–141,2)

The Savior continued and said, "Oh, unsearchable love of light! Oh, bitterness of the fire! You blaze in the bodies of people and in the marrow of their bones, blazing in them night and day, burning their limbs and [making] their minds drunk and their souls deranged. [You dominate] males and females day and night; you move [and arouse] them secretly and visibly. When the males are [aroused, they are attracted to the] females and the females to the males.[10] That is why it is said

---

5. Pleroma. 6. This contrast between the visible and the invisible is a contrast between the lower world of body, change, perishability, and animal nature and the higher world of soul, constancy, immortality, and spiritual nature. Cf. the discussion of the soul in Plato's *Phaedo*. 7. The restoration of these lines re- mains somewhat tentative. Cf. Schenke, in *Nag Hammadi Deutsch*, 1.285. 8. Coptic e[u]onh. Or restore as "they are visible" (Coptic e[uou]onh). 9. I.e., the sun. 10. The restoration of these lines remains somewhat tentative. Cf. Schenke, in *Nag Hammadi Deutsch*, 1.286.

[140] that everyone who seeks truth from true wisdom[11] will fashion wings to fly, fleeing from the passion that burns human spirits. And one will fashion wings to flee from every visible spirit."

Thomas answered and said, "Master, this is precisely what I ask you, since I understand that you are beneficial to us through what you say."

Again the Savior answered and said, "This is why we must speak to you, because this is the teaching for the perfect. If you wish to become perfect, keep these sayings. If not, the name for you is 'ignorant,' since an intelligent person cannot associate with a fool. The intelligent person is perfect in all wisdom, but to the fool good and evil are the same. The wise person will be nourished by truth, and will be like a tree growing by the stream of water.[12] Some people have wings but rush toward visible things that are far from truth. The fire that guides them gives them an illusion of truth. It will shine on them with a perishable beauty, and it will imprison them in dark delight and capture them in sweet-smelling pleasure. And it will make them blind with insatiable desire, inflame their souls, and be like a stake that is jammed into their heart and can never be removed. Like a bit in the mouth, it leads them according to its own wish.[13]

"It has bound them with its chains, and tied all their limbs with the bitterness of the bondage of desire for those visible things that perish and change and fluctuate impulsively. They have always been drawn downward. When they are slain, they are drawn to all the animals of corruption."

Thomas answered and said, "It is clear and has been said that [many are] . . . those who do not know . . . soul."

[The Savior] answered and said, "[Blessed] is the wise person who has [sought truth, and] when it has been found, has rested [141] upon it forever, and has not been afraid of those who wish to trouble him."[14]

Our Own and the Others (141,2–142,26)

Thomas answered and said, "Master, is it beneficial for us to rest among our own?"

The Savior said, "Yes, it is useful, and it is good for you, since the things visible among people will pass away. For the vessel of their flesh will pass away, and when it disintegrates, it will come to be among visible things, among things that can be seen. The visible fire gives them pain, because of the love of faith they once had. They will be gathered back to the visible realm.[15] Moreover, among the invisible things, those who can see will perish, without the first love, in their concern for this life and the burning of the fire. There is only a little time before what is visible will pass away. Then shapeless phantoms will come and dwell forever in the midst of the tombs on corpses, in pain and destruction of soul."[16]

---

11. Sophia. 12. Cf. *Psalm* 1:3. 13. On the imprisonment of these people, see the discussion in Plato's *Phaedo*, especially 81c–82a; 83de. 14. Cf. *Gospel of Thomas* 2. 15. This passage refers to the death and decay of the body and the punishment and reincarnation of ignorant people. 16. On phantoms, cf. Plato's *Phaedo* 81c–e.

Thomas answered and said, "What can we say in the face of these things?[17] What shall we say to those who are blind? What teaching shall we give those miserable mortals who say, 'We have come to [do] good and not to curse,' and will [say] further, 'If we had not been born in the flesh, we would not have known iniquity'?"

The Savior said, "To tell the truth, do not think of these as human beings, but regard them [as] animals. As animals devour each other, so people like this devour each other. They are deprived of the kingdom,[18] since they love the delight of fire and are slaves of death and rush to deeds of corruption. They fulfill the desire of their parents. They will be cast down into the abyss and be afflicted by the compulsion of the bitterness of their evil nature. They will be whipped to drive them down to a place they do not know, and they will leave their limbs behind, not with fortitude but with despair. And they rejoice in [the fire, they love] madness and derangement, because they are [fools]. They pursue derangement, not realizing their madness but thinking they are wise. They . . . the love of their body . . . ,[19] [142] their hearts turning to themselves and their thoughts being on their affairs. But fire will consume them."

Thomas answered and said, "Master, what can one cast down to them do? I am very concerned about them, for many oppose them."

The Savior answered and said, "What is evident to you?"

Judas, called Thomas, said, "Master, you should speak and I should listen."

The Savior answered, "Listen to what I tell you and believe the truth. What sows and what is sown will pass away in their fire, in fire and water, and will be hidden in tombs of darkness. And after a long time the fruit of evil trees will appear and be punished and slain in the mouths of animals and people through the agency of the rains, the winds, the air, and the light shining above."[20]

Thomas answered, "You certainly have convinced us, master. We realize in our hearts it is clearly so, and your word is not meager. But these sayings that you tell us are laughable and ridiculous to the world, since they are not understood. How can we go forth and preach them when we are [not] respected in the world?"

Jesus Preaches About Judgment (142,26–143,7)

The Savior answered and said, "I tell you the truth, whoever listens to [your] word and turns away or sneers at it or smirks at these things, I tell you the truth, that person will be handed over to the ruler who is on high, who rules as king over all the powers, and the ruler will turn him away and cast him down from on high into the abyss, and he will be imprisoned in a cramped, dark place. So he cannot turn or move because of the great depth of Tartaros[21] and the [burdensome bitterness]

---

17. Or, "these people." 18. The Coptic is partially restored: tmᵉntᵉr[ro]. 19. The restoration of these lines is partial and somewhat tentative. Cf. Schenke, in Nag Hammadi Deutsch, 1.288. 20. On what sows and is sown, cf. Plato's Phaedo 83de and other descriptions comparing the life cycles of plants and humans. 21. The underworld, or hell. This description includes features typical of other descriptions in Hesiod, Plato, Christian apocalypses, and Dante.

of Hades. Whoever relies on what [is brought] to him . . . will not be forgiven [his] madness, but will [be judged. Whoever has] persecuted you will be handed over to the angel Tartarouchos,[22] [who has flaming] fire that pursues them,[23] [143] and fiery whips that spew forth sparks into the face of one pursued. If he flees to the west, he finds fire. If he turns south, he finds it there as well. If he turns north, the threat of erupting fire meets him again. Nor can he find the way to the east, to flee there and be saved, for he did not find it while embodied so as to find it on the day of judgment."

Woes upon the Godless (143,8–145,1)

Then the Savior continued and said, "Woe to you, godless people, who have no hope, who are secure in things that do not last.

"Woe to you who hope in the flesh and in the prison that will perish.[24] How long will you sleep and think that what is imperishable will also perish? Your hope is based upon the world, and your god is this present life. You are destroying your souls.

"Woe to you with the fire that burns within you. It is insatiable.

"Woe to you because of the wheel that turns in your minds.

"Woe to you because of the smoldering within you. It will devour your flesh visibly, tear your souls secretly, and prepare you for each other.

"Woe to you, prisoners, for you are bound in caves. You laugh, you rejoice in mad laughter. You do not perceive your destruction. Neither do you perceive your plight, nor have you understood that you dwell in darkness and death. Rather, you are drunk with fire and [full] of bitterness. Your hearts are deranged because of the smoldering within you, and the poison and blows of your enemies are a delight to you. Darkness has risen in you like the light, for you have surrendered your freedom to slavery. You have darkened your hearts and surrendered your minds to foolishness. You have filled your minds with the smoke of the fire within you, and your light has been hidden in the [dark] cloud. You [love] the garment[25] you wear, [although it is filthy], and you have been gripped [by] non-existent hope. [You have] believed in what you do [not] know. You all live in [bondage] but pride yourselves [in your freedom].[26] [144] You have baptized your souls in the water of darkness. You have pursued your own wishes.

"Woe to you who dwell in error, not seeing that the light of the sun, which judges the universe and looks down on the universe, will encircle everything to

---

22. Tartarouchos is the angel or power who controls Tartaros. 23. The restoration of these lines is somewhat tentative. Cf. Schenke, in Nag Hammadi Deutsch, 1.289. 24. The body is the perishable prison of the soul in Platonic and Orphic thought. Cf. also the prisoners bound in caves in Book of Thomas 143 and the allegory of the cave in Plato's Republic. 25. The garment is the body, which can be put on or taken off like an article of clothing. 26. The restoration of these lines is somewhat tentative. Cf. Schenke, in Nag Hammadi Deutsch, 1.290.

make slaves of the enemies. Nor do you perceive how the moon looks down night and day, seeing the bodies of your slaughters.

"Woe to you who love intercourse and filthy association with the female.

"And woe to you because of the powers of your bodies, for they will mistreat you.

"Woe to you because of the actions of the evil demons.

"Woe to you who entice your limbs with fire. Who will sprinkle a restful dew on you, to extinguish the many fires within you, and your burning? Who will make the sun shine on you, to dispel the darkness within you and hide the darkness and filthy water?

"The sun and the moon will give a fragrant aroma to you, as will the air, the spirit, the earth, and the water.[27] If the sun does not shine on these bodies, they will rot and perish just like weeds or grass. If the sun shines on them, they grow strong and choke the grapevine. But if the grapevine becomes strong and casts its shadow over the weeds and all the rest of the brush growing with it, and [spreads] and fills out, it alone inherits the land where it grows, and dominates wherever it has cast its shadow. So when it grows, it dominates the whole land, and it is productive for its master and pleases him greatly. He would have gone to great pains because of the weeds before pulling them out, but the grapevine by itself disposed of them and choked them, and they died and became like earth."

Then Jesus continued and said to them, "Woe to you, for you have not accepted the teaching, and those who [wish to accept it] will suffer when they preach. [You will persecute them], but you will rush into [your own traps]. You will cast them down [to the lions][28] and put them to death, daily,[29] [145] and they will rise from death.[30]

Blessed Are You (145,1–19)

"Blessed are you who understand beforehand the temptations and flee from things that are alien.

"Blessed are you who are mocked and are not respected because of the love your master has for you.

"Blessed are you who weep and are oppressed by those who have no hope, for you will be released from all bondage.

"Watch and pray that you may not remain in the flesh, but that you may leave the bondage of the bitterness of this life. And when you pray, you will find rest, for you have left pain and reproach behind. When you leave the pains and the

---

27. The four elements, with spirit replacing fire, since here fire is characteristic of passion, lust, and destruction. For "spirit" perhaps read "wind." 28. Cf. Daniel 6:16–18; Bel and the Dragon 31–32; Second Discourse of Great Seth 55. 29. The restoration of these lines is somewhat tentative. Cf. Schenke, in Nag Hammadi Deutsch, 1.291. 30. Lit., "that they may rise from death."

passions of the body, you will receive rest from the Good One. You will reign with the King, you united with him and he with you, from now on and forever. Amen."[31]

The Book of Thomas

The Contender Writing
to the Perfect

Scribal Note (145,20–23)

Remember me also, my brothers, in your prayers. Peace be with the holy[32] and the spiritual.[33]

---

31. Cf. *Gospel of Thomas* 2. 32. Or "saints." 33. The scribal note probably applies to the entire codex.

THE HOLY BOOK OF THE GREAT INVISIBLE SPIRIT

NHC III,2; IV,2

Introduced by John D. Turner
Translated by Marvin Meyer

The two Coptic versions of the *Holy Book of the Great Invisible Spirit* (III,2; IV,2) are copies of independent translations of basically the same Greek text; both copies are heavily damaged, the one in Codex IV more than the one in Codex III, but enough survives in them to be able to reconstruct about 90 percent of the text. The actual title of the text is preserved as "The Holy Book of the Great Invisible Spirit" in the subtitle and colophon of Codex III and in the initial lines of each copy, although since the late 1940s it has become customary to refer to it inappropriately as the "Gospel of the Egyptians," a title based on the name given to it at the beginning of the colophon in III 69,16–17.

As suggested by Hans-Martin Schenke,[1] the emphasis of the *Holy Book* seems to lie upon the well-defined ritual of baptism and the invocatory prayers that conclude the work (III 63,4–68,1; cf. IV 74,17–80,15), while the preceding sections seem to provide a mythological justification for them in the form of an elaborate theogony. In the second part, the three advents (*parousiai*) of Seth are summarized, namely, his descents at the flood, at the conflagration (of Sodom and Gomorrah), and at the judgment of the archons, to save his seed ("saints") who have gone astray in the world, a scheme of three descents similar to those of the illuminator in the *Revelation of Adam*. It is on his third descent that Seth is said to descend in a body begotten by the Word (Logos) and prepared for him by the "virgin" (probably Barbelo), put on Jesus, and defeat the powers of the thirteen aeons.

Like the *Revelation of Adam*, the *Secret Book of John*, and *Three Forms of First Thought*, the *Holy Book of the Great Invisible Spirit* portrays salvation as the culmination of a series of three descents of a heavenly being to earth. Both the *Holy*

---

1. Hans-Martin Schenke, "The Phenomenon and Significance of Sethian Gnosticism," 600–601.

Book and *Three Forms of First Thought* ascribe the final act of salvation to the third descent of the savior: in the former work, Seth as the Logos puts on Jesus, and in the latter, Protennoia (First Thought) as the Logos rescues Jesus from the cross (50,12–16; cf. the Ophite version of this theme in Irenaeus *Against Heresies* 1.30.12–13). In both cases this descent is associated with the bestowal of a ritual of baptismal ascent known as the Five Seals, in which the bodily and psychical garment of the spirit is replaced with light and immortal incorruptibility. The eschatological role of Jesus in these two texts clearly reflects Christian influence, positive in the *Holy Book*, but of a more polemical sort in *Three Forms of First Thought*, since there, rather than being the savior, Jesus becomes the one saved.

The first part of the *Holy Book of the Great Invisible Spirit* (III 40,12–62,24) consists of a lengthy theogony similar to but more complex than that of the *Secret Book of John*, featuring a series of at least six interlocking Father, Mother, and Child triads accounting for the generation of the supreme Five (Pentad) as well as of the self-begotten Son, Adamas, Seth, and his seed. Of these, the beings of the fourth, fifth, and sixth triads also form objects of praise in *Zostrianos* during each of his five baptisms in the name of the divine Self-Generated (Autogenes).

FATHER	MOTHER	CHILD
1. Invisible Spirit	Silence-Pronoia-Barbelo	Thrice Male Child–Great Christ
2. Triple-Male Child	Youel	Esephech, Child of the Child
3. Great Christ	Pronoia	Self-Generated Logos
4. Self-Generated Logos	Mirothoe	Adamas
5. Adamas, Self-Generated Logos	Prophania	Seth and the Four Luminaries
6. Seth	Plesithea	Seed of Seth

A possible seventh triad consists of the couple Self-Generated Logos and Edokla, who produce the race of morally good human beings, who, though not descendants of Seth, are guided by truth and justice, unlike the corrupt seed of Cain. The Self-Generated, who is the Child figure of the supreme Father-Mother-Child trinity of the *Secret Book of John*, is now demoted from the supreme trinity, becoming the child of a yet higher (triple-male) child, the great Christ, and redefined as Christ's (Self-Generated) Logos. Nevertheless, this Self-Generated Logos is still credited with establishing the Four Luminaries, and in the ritual conclusion to the treatise, he provides the body for Seth's final descent in the form of Jesus and serves as the name in which one is baptized.

Beginning with the emanation of Self-Generated and his successors Adamas, Seth with the Four Luminaries, Seth's seed, and their guardian angels, each emanation seems to be punctuated by five sixfold doxologies (IV 59,13–29; III 49,22–50,9; 53,12–54,6; 55,16–56,3; 61,23–62,1) directed to a series of principal transcendent beings whose origins were narrated in the preceding episodes of the theogony.[2] Apparently these five doxologies serve to celebrate the emergence of beings subsequent to the primal Five: the emergence of (1) the Self-Generated Logos, (2) Adamas, (3) Seth and the Four Luminaries, (4) Seth's seed, and (5) Aerosiel, Selmechel, and the four hundred ethereal angels who guard the seed of Seth until his final return. They seem to constitute traditional responses in a theogony articulated as a litany of versicle and community response: the responses would be the doxologies directed to the higher primal Five—perhaps thought of as the Five Seals—while the versicle portions would be spoken narratives of the emergence of beings subsequent to the primal Five. One may therefore suggest that this second portion of the theogony may have been recited aloud by an officiant, to which the candidates preparing for baptism responded with these doxologies.

Finally, the concluding parts of the theogony also include an account of the making of the lower world and the first creatures by its makers and rulers Sakla, Nebruel, and their twelve angels at the instigation of the fourth luminary Eleleth through the instrumentality of Sophia. It seems that the *Holy Book* knows the myth of Sophia from a version like that found in *Three Forms of First Thought*, wherein a voice from the fourth luminary Eleleth initiates the production of a ruler for chaos, in effect holding Sophia blameless for the creation of the lower world. In the *Holy Book*, this initiates the descent of the hylic Sophia cloud, who produces, not the chief archon Yaldabaoth as in other Sethian treatises, but first, apparently, the matter of the lower world, and second—upon the command of Gamaliel, minister of the first luminary Harmozel—two figures: the chief angel Sakla, the god of the thirteen aeons, and his demonic partner Nebruel,[3] who together create twelve aeons and angels and finally human beings. After Sakla's boast in his sole deity and the traditional voice from above announcing the prior existence of humanity and child of humanity, a double of Sophia named Metanoia ("Repentance") is introduced to make up for the deficiency in the aeon of Eleleth due to Sophia's descent. Metanoia then descends to the world called the "image of the night"[4] and prays for the repentance of created humans,

---

2. These principal beings constitute the divine Five, consisting of the Invisible Spirit as Father, the male virginal Barbelo as Mother, their offspring the triple-male Child, a secondary male virgin Youel as consort of the Child, and their offspring, Esephech Child of the Child as well as the great Doxomedon aeon that contains them (cf. *Zostrianos* 61,15–21 and *Holy Book* III 43,15–16, on the great aeon where the triple-male Child is).

3. In Manichaean tradition, Nebruel and her husband Ashaqlun (cf. Sakla) are parents of Adam and Eve; see Theodore bar Konai, *Liber Scholiorum* (ed. Scher), 317–18. Cf. The similar generation of Sakla and Nebro in *Gospel of Judas* 51,3–17.

4. Perhaps an etymology of Eleleth's name from Hebrew (*ēl*), "God," plus *laylāh*, "night," or "Lilith" of *Isaiah* 34:14 and later Jewish speculation, or perhaps *hēylēl*, "daystar," for *heōsphoros*, i.e., Lucifer; cf. *Isaiah* 14:12. The expression "the world resembles the night" or "the world that is the image of the night" occurs in III 51,4–5 (the earthly advent of Seth and his seed), 59,19–20 (the earthly advent of Metanoia, "Repentance," Sophia's lower double), and *Testimony of Truth* 44,27–29.

including the seed of Seth, suggesting that Eleleth rather than Sophia is ultimately responsible for the created order. Once the seed of Seth is sown into this world, these cosmic powers bring the flood and conflagration against which Seth and the guardian angels must protect the seed.

The second part of the *Holy Book* (III 62,24–68,1) begins by mentioning the three advents through which Seth passes at the times of the flood, the conflagration, and the (final) judgment, similar to the three descents of the illuminator mentioned in the *Revelation of Adam* (76,8–17). The *Holy Book* sets the tradition of Seth's advents in a baptismal context, since on his third descent he establishes a salvific baptism through a logos-begotten body that is prepared by the virgin (probably Barbelo). Both *Three Forms of First Thought* and the *Holy Book of the Great Invisible Spirit* equate the descent of the Logos upon the earthly figure of Jesus with the bestowal of the baptismal rite of the Five Seals.

The account of this bestowal is followed by a lengthy list of the various figures that are invoked in the course of the baptismal rite (III 64,9–65,26), which includes a multitude of new names, most of which show up in the baptismal sections of *Zostrianos*, alongside the more traditional ones, such as Micheus, Michar, Mnesinous, Gamaliel, and Samblo (in both the *Revelation of Adam* and *Three Forms of First Thought*), and Abrasax and Yesseus Mazareus Yessedekeus (in the *Revelation of Adam*), not to mention the Self-Generated and his companion Adamas, Seth and his companion Jesus, the seed of Seth, and "the souls of the children," who reside in the Four Luminaries Harmozel, Oroiael, Daveithe, and Eleleth, respectively (as in the *Secret Book of John* or *Three Forms of First Thought*). Thereafter follows the renunciation (of the world and the hostile powers of the thirteen aeons) and the receipt of those who receive them into the divine world (probably the ministers of the Four Luminaries). The concluding baptismal prayer (III 66,8–22) and postbaptismal profession (66,22–68,1) consist of two separate hymns of five strophes each, perhaps reflecting the Sethian baptismal tradition of the Five Seals known from the *Secret Book of John* and *Three Forms of First Thought*, which enumeration may also figure in the fivefold repetition of the doxologies demarcating the stages of the theogony in the first part of the *Holy Book* as well as the Pentad of beings comprising the Doxomedon aeon.[5]

It appears that the baptism may have involved a fivefold immersion during which the baptizand uttered a fivefold prayer to Yesseus Mazareus Yessedekeus, the living water (as "child of the child"). On completion of the baptism, the baptizand, having now become light, acknowledges that the name of the divine Self-Generated is now upon him. The whole proceeding concludes with the ritual acts of recognizing the Mother's grace by stretching out folded hands while the

5. The Doxomedon aeon contains the supreme Five of the Invisible Spirit, Barbelo, the triple-male Child, Youel, and Esephech (IV 56,23–57,1); cf. the Pentads of *Secret Book of John* II 6,2–10 (the Invisible Spirit, Barbelo, Foreknowledge, Incorruptibility, and Life Eternal), of *Eugnostos the Blessed* (Forefather [Propator], Father by Himself [Autopator], Immortal Human, Son of Humanity, and Savior/Son of Son of Humanity), of Irenaeus's (*Against Heresies* 1.30.1) Ophites (First Man, Ennoia, Second Man, Third Man, First Woman), and of Philo's "Ark" in *Questions and Answers on Exodus* 2.68 (the Logos plus the creative, ruling, merciful, and legislative "powers").

receipt of the purifying name of the Son is acknowledged by the statement that the incense or ointment of life has been mixed with the water of the archons.

Thus the *Holy Book*, in concert with *Three Forms of First Thought* and ritual materials in other Sethian treatises, gives evidence of a series of gestures and verbal performances capable of ritual enactment: renunciation, stripping, invocation and naming of holy powers, a doxological prayer to the living water, anointing, enthronement, investiture, baptismal immersion, and certain other manual gestures, such as extending the arms in a circle. Whether any of these acts, and if so, which ones, comprise the Five Seals is difficult to tell; certainly all these were frequently part of the baptismal rite in the wider Christian church as well.

BIBLIOGRAPHY

Alexander Böhlig and Frederik Wisse, eds., *Nag Hammadi Codices III, 2 and IV,2*; Régine Charron, *Concordance des texts de Nag Hammadi. Le Codex III*; Jean Doresse, "'Le Livre sacré du grand Esprit invisible' ou 'L'Évangile des Égyptiens'"; Hans-Martin Schenke, "Das sethianische System nach Nag-Hammadi-Handschriften"; "The Phenomenon and Significance of Sethian Gnosticism"; Hans-Martin Schenke, Hans-Gebhard Bethge, and Ursula Ulrike Kaiser, eds., *Nag Hammadi Deutsch*, 1.293–321 (Uwe-Karsten Plisch); Jean-Marie Sevrin, *Le dossier baptismal séthien*; John D. Turner, "The Sethian Baptismal Rite."

The Holy Book of the
Great Invisible Spirit[1]

The Holy Book (40,12–41,7)

The holy book of the . . . Great Invisible [Spirit],[2]

the Parent, the Father[3] whose name cannot be named,
who came from the heights of Fullness,
light of light of the realms of Light,
light of the silence[4] of Forethought
and the Father of silence,
light of word and truth,
light of the [41] incorruptions,
infinite light,
radiance from the realms of light
of the unrevealed, undisclosed,
unaging, unannounced Father,
aeon of aeons,
self-generated,[5] self-generating,
self-producing, foreign,
truly true eternal realm.

---

1. Coptic text: NHC III,2: 40,12–69,20; IV,2: 50,1–81,2 (the conclusion is lost). Editions: *The Facsimile Edition of the Nag Hammadi Codices: Codex III*, 44–69; *The Facsimile Edition of the Nag Hammadi Codices: Codex IV*, 58–89; Alexander Böhlig and Frederik Wisse, *Nag Hammadi Codices III,2 and IV,2*; Hans-Martin Schenke, Hans-Gebhard Bethge, and Ursula Ulrike Kaiser, eds., *Nag Hammadi Deutsch*, 1.293–321 (Uwe-Karsten Plisch). The text includes a secondary title in the copyist's note: "The Egyptian Gospel"; the text sometimes is referred to, erroneously, as the "Gospel of the Egyptians." The present translation is based primarily on the Codex III version; when the Codex IV version is used, this is indicated in the trans-

lation and notes. Where lacunae in one version may be confidently restored on the basis of readings preserved in the other version, they are not placed within brackets. 2. This is the reading of the Codex IV version. The Codex III version reads, "The book of the holy . . . of the Great Invisible [Spirit]." Possibilities for restoring the lacuna in the Codex IV version: "[prayers]," perhaps "[prayers of the] Great Invisible [Spirit]." 3. The text reads "Father" (*eiōt*), here and below, for the transcendent great invisible Spirit as well as the lower manifestations of the divine. 4. Cf. the role of silence in the *Secret Book of John*. 5. Autogenes.

Three Heavenly Powers Come from the Great Invisible Spirit
(41,7–42,4)

Three powers came forth from the Great Invisible Spirit:[6] the Father, the Mother, and the Child.[7] They came from the living silence of the incorruptible Father, from the silence of the unknown Father.

The aeon of Domedon Doxomedon[8] came from it, the eternal realm of eternal realms and the light of each of their powers.

The Child appeared fourth, the Mother [fifth], the Father sixth.[9] The Great Invisible Spirit was . . . unrecognized, undisclosed among all the powers, glories, and incorruptions.

So from the Great Invisible Spirit came three powers, [42] three realms of Eight that the Father brings forth from within,[10] in silence, with forethought: the Father, the Mother, and the Child.

The Father (42,5–11)

The first realm of Eight,[11] for whose sake the Child that is three times male came forth:

thought,

word,

incorruptibility,

[life] eternal,

will,

mind,

foreknowledge,

the androgynous Father.

The Mother (42,11–21)

The second power or realm of Eight:

the Mother,

the virgin Barbelo,[12]

Epititioch . . . ai,

---

6. Lit., "him" or "it," here and below. **7.** Or "Son," here and below. **8.** Domedon may mean "lord of the house," Doxomedon "lord of glory." Cf. Böhlig and Wisse, eds., *Nag Hammadi Codices III,2 and IV,2, 41.* **9.** This constitutes a second trinity. **10.** Lit., "from the bosom," here and below. **11.** Or "Ogdoad," here and below. **12.** On Barbelo, cf. the *Secret Book of John.*

> Memeneaimen . . . , who is over heaven,
> Karb . . . ,[13]
> Adonai,[14]
> . . . , the inexplicable power,
> the ineffable Mother.[15]

She shone and appeared, and she took pleasure in the Father of the silent silence.

The Child (42,21–43,8)

The third power or realm of Eight:

> the Child
> of the silent silence,
> the crown
> of the silent silence,
> the glory
> of the Father,
> the virtue
> of the [43] Mother.

From within, the Child[16] produces seven powers of great light, which are the seven vowels,[17] and the word completes them.

These are the three powers or three realms of Eight that the Father brought forth from within through forethought. He produced them there.

The Realm of Doxomedon (43,8–44,13)

Domedon Doxomedon appeared, the eternal realm of eternal realms, with thrones in it, powers around it, and glories and incorruptions. The Father of the great light [who came] forth in silence is [the great] realm of Doxomedon, in which [the triple-] male[18] Child rests. The throne of its glory was established in it, and the undisclosed name [is inscribed] on it, on the tablet, . . . the word, the Father of the light of the All, who came from silence and rests in silence, whose [44] name is in an invisible symbol. A hidden, [invisible] mystery came forth:

---

13. The Codex IV version reads ". . . *kaba*." 14. "Adone," inserted from the Codex IV version. 15. The Codex IV version includes ". . . *akroboriaor*. . . ." 16. Lit., "he" or "it." 17. Lit., "voices." 18. On this epithet, here and below, cf. the *Secret Book of John*.

IIIIIIIIIIIIIIIIIIIIII
ĒĒĒĒĒĒĒĒĒĒĒĒĒĒĒĒĒĒĒĒĒĒ
OOOOOOOOOOOOOOOOOOOOOO
UUUUUUUUUUUUUUUUUUUUUU
EEEEEEEEEEEEEEEEEEEEEE
AAAAAAAAAAAAAAAAAAAAAA
ŌŌŌŌŌŌŌŌŌŌŌŌŌŌŌŌŌŌŌŌŌŌ.[19]

And so the three powers offered praise to the Great Invisible Unnamable Ineffable Virgin Spirit, and the male virgin.

Yoel, Christ, Esephech (III 44,13–IV 58,22)

They asked for power.[20] A silence of living silence appeared, glories and incorruptions in the eternal realms, . . . aeons, myriads in addition, . . . triple-male beings, [triple]-male offspring, [male] generations, [glories of the Father], glories of the great [Christ and the] male offspring. The [generations][21] filled the great realm of Doxomedon with the power of the word of all the [Fullness].

The triple-male [Child, the great] Christ, whom the [Great] Invisible Spirit had anointed and whose power [is called] Ainon,[22] offered praise to the Great Invisible Spirit and the male virgin Yoel, and the silence of silent silence, and the majesty [55][23] . . . , ineffable . . . , unspeakable . . . , unanswered, uninterpreted, the first to [appear], unannounced . . . , [56] wonderful . . . , unspeakable . . . , who has all the majesties of majesty of the silence of silence there. The triple-[male Child] offered praise and asked for power from the [Great Invisible Virgin] Spirit.

There appeared in that place . . . [who] beholds [glories] . . . treasures . . . [invisible] mysteries . . . of silence . . . [the male] virgin [Youel].

[The child of the] child Esephech [appeared].

[So] it was completed:

the [Father],

the Mother,

the Child,

---

19. The mystery seems to be in the sequence of the vowels: IĒOU, E, A, Ō. Iēou, or Ieou, or Yeu, is the true name of God (cf. Yao) according to the Gnostic *Book of Jeu*; E, epsilon, may have the numerical value of five and is used later in the text, or conceivably it may represent the Greek word *estin*, "is"; A and Ō are alpha and omega, the first and last letters of the Greek alphabet. If E means "is," then the vowel series may read "Ieou is alpha and omega." Here each of the vowels is written twenty-two times; there are twenty-two letters in the Hebrew alphabet. Cf. Bentley Layton, *The Gnostic Scriptures*, 107. 20. The Codex IV version reads, "She (that is, Barbelo) asked for power." 21. These lines are added from Codex IV, 55. 22. On Ainon, perhaps cf. the site named Ainon in *John* 3:23 and on the Madaba mosaic map; or Ainon may be Greek for "praise" (accusative case) or "fearful, dreadful." 23. Pp. 45–48 are missing in the Codex III version. The following pages are added from Codex IV, 55–60.

the Five Seals,[24]
the invincible power,

who is the great [Christ] of all those who are incorruptible . . . [57] holy . . . the
end . . . incorruptible . . . are powers, [glories], and incorruptions . . . came forth
. . . . This one offered [praise] to the undisclosed hidden [mystery] . . . hidden . . .
in . . . the eternal realms . . . thrones, . . . and each one . . . myriads of [powers]
without number around [them, [58] glories] and incorruptions . . . and they . . .
the Father, the Mother, and the Child, and all [the Fullness], already [men-
tioned, and the] Five Seals, [and the mystery] of [mysteries]. They [appeared . . .
who] is [over] . . . and the eternal realms, in truth, truly, . . . eternal . . . and the
[eternal] realms, forever in truth, truly.

Divine Emanation (IV 58,23–59,29)

[An emanation[25] appeared in silence], with the [living] silence of the Spirit, the
Father's word, and light. [She . . . the Five] [59] Seals, which the [Father brought]
forth from within, and she passed [through] all the eternal realms, already mentioned. She established glorious thrones [and myriads] of angels [without] number around them, [powers and incorruptible] glories, and they all [sang songs],
gave glory, and offered praise with [one voice], with one accord, [with a sound]
that is never silent . . . to

the Father,
the [Mother],
the Child . . . ,
[all the] fullnesses, [already] mentioned,
that is, [the great] Christ,
who came from [silence],
who is the [incorruptible] Child,
Telmael Telmachael [Eli Eli] Machar Machar [Seth],
the power that truly lives,
[and the] male [virgin] with [him], Youel,
and Esephech, master of glory and [child] of the child,
and the [crown of] its glory,
. . . of the Five Seals,
the Fullness, [already mentioned].

---

24. On Five Seals, here and below, cf. the baptismal
reference in Secret Book of John II, 31. 25. The text
may be restored to read "[An emanation]" ([apohr]oia)
or "[Forethought]" ([pron]oia) or "[A thought]"
([enn]oia). On Forethought (often personified), cf. the
Secret Book of John.

The Word (IV 59,29–60,30)

The [60] great living Self-Generated [Word appeared, the] true [God], the un-born nature, whose name I utter by saying,

...AIA...THAŌTHŌSTH...,
Child of the [great] Christ,
Child of ineffable silence,
[who] came from the Great [Invisible] Incorruptible [Spirit].

The [Child] of silence appeared with [silence...invisible...hidden...and the] treasures of its glory. It appeared in the visible...and [established] four [eternal realms]. Through the Word it established them.

The Word offered [praise] to the Great Invisible Virgin Spirit, [the silence] of the [Father], in silence of the living silence of [silence], where humanity rests....

Mirothea and Adamas (IV 60,30–III 50,17)

Then there came forth from [49][26] that place the cloud of great light, living power, the Mother of the holy incorruptible ones, the great power Mirothea.[27] She gave birth to the being whose name I utter by saying,

[You are one],
you are one,
you are one,
EA EA EA.[28]

This is Adamas, light that has radiated [from light], the eye of the [light], the first human being,[29] through whom and to whom is everything, without whom is nothing.[30] The unknowable, incomprehensible Father came forth and descended from above to undo the deficiency.

The great divine Self-Generated Word and the incorruptible human Adamas joined with each other, and a human power of the word was produced. So humanity came into being through the word.

---

26. The Codex III version resumes with p. 49. 27. The text reads "Mirothoe." Mirothea is a Sethian name or epithet for the divine in several texts. The meaning is uncertain, but it may mean "divine destiny" (from Greek *moiro-theos*—cf. Moira, "destiny" in Greek mythology) or "divine anointed one" (from Greek *myro-theos*). Mirotheos is masculine in form, Mirotheos is masculine. Here Mirothea denotes the mother of Adamas (cf. Pigeradamas in the *Secret Book of John*). See John D. Turner, *Sethian Gnosticism and* the Platonic Tradition, 211. 28. The utterance is from the Codex IV version. "EA EA EA" may represent the Greek *ei a, ei a, ei a*, "you are one, you are one, you are one." The Codex III version reads "IEN IEN EA EA EA" three times. "IEN IEN" may be Greek, *ei hen, ei hen*, "you are one, you are one." E (epsilon) and A (alpha) may also be taken as numbers: "O five, one, five, one, five, one." The following lines are from Codex IV, 61. 29. Here the Codex III version resumes. 30. Cf. John 1:3.

This human power of the word offered praise to

the Great Invisible Incomprehensible Virgin Spirit,
the male virgin [Barbelo],[31]
the triple-male Child, [50]
the male [virgin] Youel,
Esephech, master of glory and Child of the Child,
the crown of its glory,
the great realm of Doxomedon,
the thrones in it,
the powers around it,
glories, incorruptions, and all their fullness, already mentioned,
the ethereal earth, receiving God,
where holy people of the great light take shape,
people of the Father of the silent living silence,
the Father and all their fullness, already mentioned.

Four Eternal Realms, Seth, Four Luminaries (50,17–52,3)

The great divine Self-Generated Word and the incorruptible human Adamas offered praise. They requested power and eternal strength for the Self-Generated,
so that four eternal realms may be fully completed and through them there may
appear [51] the glory and power of the invisible Father of the holy people of the
great light coming into the world. The world resembles the night.

Then the incorruptible human Adamas requested that a child come from
himself, so that the child may be father of the immovable incorruptible generation, and through this generation silence and speech may appear and through it
the dead realm may rise and then fade away.

So the power of the great light came from above. She was revelation,[32] and she
gave birth to Four Great Luminaries,[33]

Harmozel,
Oroiael,
Daveithe,
Eleleth,

along with great incorruptible Seth, son of the incorruptible human Adamas.

And so was completed the perfect realm of Seven, which exists in hidden mysteries. [52] When it receives [glory], it becomes eleven realms of Eight.

---

31. "[Barbelo]" is restored in the Codex IV version.
32. Or "Prophania." 33. On the Four Luminaries, cf.
the Secret Book of John.

Partners and Attendants for the Luminaries (52,3–54,11)

The Father nodded approval, and the entire Fullness of the Luminaries agreed. Partners for the Luminaries appeared to complete the realm of Eight of the divine Self-Generated:

> grace, for the first luminary Harmozel,
>
> perception, for the second luminary Oroiael,
>
> intelligence, for the third luminary Daveithe,
>
> understanding, for the fourth luminary Eleleth.

This is the first realm of Eight of the divine Self-Generated.

The Father nodded approval, and the entire Fullness of the Luminaries agreed. The attendants appeared:

> first, great Gamaliel, for the first great luminary Harmozel,
>
> great Gabriel, for the second great luminary Oroiael,
>
> great Samblo,[34] for the great luminary Daveithe,
>
> great Abrasax,[35] for [53] [the great luminary] Eleleth.

Partners for the attendants appeared by the will and good pleasure of the Father:

> memory, for the first, great Gamaliel,
>
> love, for the second, great Gabriel,
>
> peace, for the third, great Samblo,
>
> life eternal, for the fourth, great Abrasax.

Thus were the five realms of Eight completed, forty in all, as inexplicable power.

The great Self-Generated Word and the expression of the fullness of the Four Luminaries offered praise to

> the Great Invisible Unnamable Virgin Spirit
> the male virgin,
> the great realm of Doxomedon,
> the thrones in them,

---

34. Here the Codex IV version reads "Samblo" and the Codex III version reads "Samlo." **35.** Abrasax, here and below, is the name of a cosmic power in several traditions, including Gnostic traditions. The numerical value of the name Abrasax in Greek is 365, and thus it corresponds to the number of days in the solar year. The name Abrasax may come from the Hebrew *Arba* ("four," for the tetragrammaton or four-letter name of God, YHWH) *Sabaoth* ("hosts," "armies," shortened in the name), and thus Abrasax may reflect the meaning "Lord of hosts."

the powers around them,
glories, authorities, and powers,
the triple-male Child,
the male virgin Youel,
Esephech, [54] master of glory and [child] of the child,
the crown of its glory,
all the Fullness,
all the glories that are there,
the infinite fullnesses and the unnamable realms,

that they may call upon the Father as the fourth,[36] along with the incorruptible generation, and call the seed[37] of the Father the seed of great Seth.

The Luminaries Are Enthroned
(54,11–55,16)

Then everything shook, and the incorruptible ones trembled. The triple-male Child[38] came down from above to those unborn and self-generated, and to those conceived in the realm of birth. The Majesty appeared, all the Majesty of the great Christ, and established thrones of glory, myriads without number, in the four realms around them, myriads without number, powers, glories, [55] and incorruptions. They came forth in this way.

The incorruptible spiritual assembly[39] expanded within the Four Luminaries of the great living Self-Generated God of truth. They praised, sang, and gave glory with one voice, with one accord, with a mouth that is not silent, to

the Father,
the Mother,
the Child,
and all their fullness, already mentioned.
The Five Seals of the myriads,
the rulers over the realms,
and the couriers of the glory of the governors
were ordered to appear to those who are worthy.
Amen.

---

36. The meaning of "the fourth" is uncertain; the Codex III version originally read "the seventy-fourth," and this reading was corrected to the present reading. Perhaps cf. the trinities or divine triads in the *Holy Book of the Great Invisible Spirit* with the present Father as the fourth after a trinity; also note Heracleon *Commentary on John* 16 (on the Valentinian concept of forty and four, and the realm of Four, or tetrad); *Secret Book of James* 12 (on "a fourth one in heaven"). 37. Or "offspring," here and below. 38. This reading follows the Codex IV version; the Codex III version reads "The triple-male children." 39. Or "church" (*ekklēsia*).

The Seed of Great Seth (55,16–56,22)

Great Seth, son of the incorruptible human Adamas, offered praise to

the Great Invisible Unnamable Unspeakable Virgin Spirit,
the male virgin,
the triple-male Child,
the male[40] virgin Youel,
Esephech, master of glory,
the crown of its glory and Child of the Child, [56]
the great realms of Doxomedon,
and the Fullness, already mentioned.

Seth asked for his seed.
   Then Plesithea[41] came from that place,

the great power of great light,
mother of the angels,
mother of the Luminaries,
glorious mother,
virgin with four breasts,
bearing fruit from the wellspring of Gomorrah and Sodom,
fruit of the wellspring of Gomorrah within her.[42]

Plesithea came forth through great Seth.
   Great Seth rejoiced over the gift given him by the incorruptible child. He took his seed from the virgin with the four breasts and established it with him[43] in the four realms,[44] in the third great luminary Daveithe.

Sophia of Matter, Sakla, Nebruel, and Angels (56,22–58,22)

Five thousand years later the great luminary Eleleth said, "Let someone reign over chaos and Hades."
   A cloud [57] [named] Sophia of matter appeared . . . . [She] surveyed the regions [of chaos], and her face looked like . . . in her appearance . . . blood.[45]

---

40. Several phrases are inserted from the Codex IV version, p. 67. 41. The name Plesithea may mean "full goddess" or "nearby goddess." Cf. Böhlig and Wisse, eds., *Nag Hammadi Codices III,2 and IV,2*, 182; Bentley Layton, *The Gnostic Scriptures*, 113. 42. On the stories of Sodom and Gomorrah, cf. *Holy Book of the Great Invisible Spirit* III, 60–61; *Genesis* 18–19. Here and in other Gnostic texts—e.g., the *Paraphrase*

of *Shem*—Sodom and Gomorrah can be considered to be locales inhabited by Gnostics who are persecuted by the ruler of this world. 43. Or correct "with him" (*ᶜnmmaf*) to read "with <her>" (*ᶜnmma<s>*). 44. This reading follows the Codex IV version; the Codex III version reads "in the fourth realm." 45. On being defiled with blood, cf. *Gospel of Judas* 51.

[The great] angel Gamaliel spoke [to great Gabriel], the attendant of [the great luminary] Oroiael, and [said, "Let an] angel appear to reign over chaos [and Hades]."

The cloud[46] [agreed and produced] two individuals[47] . . . a little light . . . [the angel] she had established in the cloud [above].

Sakla[48] the great [angel observed] Nebruel the great demon[49] who is with him. [Together] they brought a spirit of reproduction to the earth, and [they produced] angelic assistants.

Sakla [said] to Nebruel the great [demon], "Let twelve realms come into being in the . . . realm, worlds . . . ."

Through the will of the Self-Generated One, [Sakla] the great angel said, [58] "There shall be . . . seven in number . . . ."

He said to the [great angels], "Go, [each] of you reign over your own [world]." And each [of these] twelve [angels] left.

[The first] angel is Athoth, whom [the great] generations of people call . . . ,

the second is Harmas, [the eye of fire],

the third [is Galila],

the fourth is Yobel,

[the fifth is] Adonaios, who is [called] Sabaoth,[50]

the sixth [is Cain, whom] the [great generations of] people call the sun,

the [seventh is Abel],

the eighth, Akiressina,

the [ninth, Youbel],

the tenth is Harmoupiael,

the eleventh is Archir-Adonin,

the twelfth [is Belias].[51]

These are set over Hades [and chaos].

---

46. I.e., the cloud of Wisdom, Sophia of matter. 47. Or "monads." 48. Sakla, whose name means "fool" in Aramaic, is the creator of this world, especially in Sethian texts. 49. In Manichaean thought the female Nebroel and the male Sakla are demons who create the creatures of the material world through sexuality. Cf. Nebro in Gospel of Judas 51. 50. Adonaios is also mentioned in the Secret Book of John, the Second Dis-

course of Great Seth, and the Gospel of Judas. On the first part of this list of names of angels, cf. Gospel of Judas 52. 51. Several of these names are restored from the similar list in Secret Book of John II, 10–11. For a possible restoration of the lacuna for the first angel Athoth, see the tentative restoration in the Secret Book of John.

The Arrogance of Sakla, the Coming of Repentance
(58,23–60,2)

After [the world] was founded, Sakla said to his [angels], "I am a [jealous] god, and nothing has [come into being] apart from me."[52] He] [59] felt certain of his nature.

A voice called from on high and said, "Humanity[53] exists, and the Child of Humanity."[54]

The first modeled creature was formed from the descent of the image above. The image resembles its voice on high, the voice of the image. The image gazed out, and from the gaze of the image above the first creature was formed. And for the sake of this creature repentance[55] came to be.

Repentance[56] was completed and empowered through the will and good pleasure of the Father. The Father approved of the great incorruptible immovable generation of great mighty people of great Seth, so that he might sow repentance in the aeons that had been produced, and through repentance the deficiency might become full. For Repentance came down from above to the world, which resembles the night. When she came, she prayed for the seed of the ruler of this aeon and the authorities derived from him, which is the defiled seed from the god who produces demons and who is destined to be destroyed, and she prayed for the seed [60] of Adam and great Seth, which is like the sun.

Hormos and the Seed of Seth (60,2–61,1)

Then the great angel Hormos[57] came to prepare the seed of great Seth, through the holy Spirit, in a holy body[58] begotten by the word, by means of virgins of the defiled sowing of seed in this aeon.[59]

Great Seth came with his seed, and he sowed it in the realms brought into being here below, whose number is the number of Sodom. Some say Sodom is the pastureland of great Seth—that is, Gomorrah. But others say great Seth took his crop from Gomorrah and planted it in a second location, which he named Sodom.

This is the generation that appeared through Edokla. For by the word she gave birth to truth and justice. This is the source of the seed of life eternal, which belongs to those who endure through knowledge[60] of where they came from. This is the great incorruptible generation that has come through three [61] worlds into this world.

---

52. *Exodus* 20:5; *Deuteronomy* 5:9; *Isaiah* 46:9. 53. Or "Man." Here this is Adamas. 54. Or "Son of Man." Here this is great Seth. 55. Metanoia. 56. Lit., "She," here and below. 57. The name Hormos means "refuge," "shelter," "haven." 58. Lit., "vessel." 59. A reference to the seed of Seth coming into this world, within bodied formed through sexual intercourse. 60. Here the Codex III version has *sooun*, the Codex IV version *gnōsis*.

Flood, Fire, Plagues, Famines, Temptations (61,1–62,12)

The flood has come to indicate the end of the age, and it will be sent into the world. Because of this generation a conflagration will come upon the earth, but to those who belong to this generation grace will be granted through prophets and guardians who protect the life of this generation. Because of this generation there will be famines and plagues, which will take place because of this great incorruptible generation. Because of this generation there will be temptations, and deception by false prophets.

Great Seth saw what the devil[61] was doing, his many guises, his schemes against the incorruptible immovable generation, the persecutions by his powers and angels, their deception. They acted rashly against themselves.

Great Seth offered praise to

> the Great Unnamable Virginal Spirit,
> the male [62] virgin Barbelo,[62]
> the triple-male Child Telmael Telmael Heli Heli Machar Machar Seth,
> the power that truly lives in truth,
> the male virgin Youel,
> Esephech, master of glory,
> the crown of its glory,
> the great realm of Doxomedon,
> the thrones in it,
> the powers around them,
> all the Fullness, already mentioned.

Guardian Angels and Incarnations of Seth (62,12–63,23)

Seth requested guardians for his seed. Four hundred ethereal angels came from the great realms, accompanied by great Aerosiel and great Selmechel,[63] to protect the great incorruptible generation, its fruitfulness, and the great people of great Seth, from the time and era of truth and justice until the end of the age and its rulers, whom the great judges condemned to death.

Great Seth was sent by the Four Luminaries, according to the will of the Self-Generated One [63] and all the Fullness, through the gift and good pleasure of the Great Invisible Spirit, the Five Seals, and all the Fullness.

Seth went through three advents, already mentioned: flood, conflagration, and judgment of the rulers, powers, and authorities. He did this to save the generation that went astray,

---

61. Sakla. 62. The text of the Codex III version reads
"Barbelon," here and below. 63. The Codex IV version reads "Selmelchel."

by means of the destruction[64] of the world,
and baptism through a body begotten by the word,
which great Seth prepared for himself,
mystically, through the virgin,
that the holy people may be conceived by the holy Spirit,
through invisible secret symbols,
through the destruction of world against world,[65]
through the destruction of the world
and the god of the thirteen realms,[66]
and the appeals of the holy ineffable incorruptible ones,
in the heart and great light of the Father,
which preexists in his forethought.

Seth Establishes Baptism Through Jesus (63,23–66,8)

Through forethought Seth has instituted the holy baptism that surpasses heaven, by means of the incorruptible one, [64] begotten by the Word, the living Jesus,[67] with whom great Seth has been clothed. He has nailed down the powers of the thirteen realms.[68] Through this means[69] he has established those who are brought in and go out,[70] and he has equipped them with armor of the knowledge of truth, with incorruptible, invincible power.

There appeared to them

the great attendant Yesseus Mazareus Yessedekeus,[71] the living water,

the great commanders, Jacob the great, Theopemptos, Isaouel,

one stationed over grace, Mep. .el,[72]

those stationed over the wellspring of truth, Micheus, Michar, Mnesinous,

one stationed over the baptism of the living, and the purifiers, Sesengenbarpharanges,[73]

---

64. In Coptic, *hōtb*; or read *hōtp*, "reconciliation." **65.** Or "the reconciliation of world with world." **66.** Cf. the thirteen kingdoms in *Revelation of Adam* 77–82. **67.** Cf. *Gospel of Thomas* Prologue. **68.** Cf. *Colossians* 2:8–15; *Revelation of Adam* 77–82. **69.** Lit., "Through it (or him)," with reference to baptism, or else to Seth, Jesus, or the act of nailing. **70.** This may refer to actions undertaken in the rite of baptism. **71.** The name Yesseus Mazareus Yessedekeus, here and below, may be related to the name of Jesus (cf. Jesus of Nazareth or Jesus the Nazarene [*nazōraios*] and Jesus the righteous [*ho dikaios*]). **72.** This line is added from the Codex IV version. **73.** The traditional spelling of a word or name of power, found in the Codex IV version (the Codex III version omits "bar"). Known from magical texts, Sesengenbarpharanges probably derives from Aramaic (S. son of [bar-] Ph.?). John G. Gager, *Curse Tablets and Binding Spells*, 269, refers to a drug from a fig tree in "the Baaras ravine" (Greek *pharangos* [genitive case]). More recently, at the international conference "Edicion de textos magicos de la Antigüedad y la Edad Media" held in Madrid and Toledo in 2005, Pablo Torijano presented a paper in which he attempts to trace the origin and transmission of the magical names Sesen, Sasm, Sesengen, and Sisinios in the multicultural world of late antiquity, in which there could be multiple linguistic transferences among Semitic and Greek texts.

those stationed over the gates of the waters, Micheus and Michar,

those stationed over the height, Seldao and Elainos,

those receiving the great generation,

the incorruptible mighty people of great Seth,

the attendants of the Four Luminaries,

great Gamaliel, great Gabriel, great Samblo, great [65] Abrasax,

those stationed over sunrise, Olses, Hupneus,[74] Heurumaious,

those stationed over the entrance into the state of rest of life eternal,

the governors[75] Mixanther and Michanor,

the guardians of chosen souls,[76] Akramas and Strempouchos,

the great power Heli Heli Machar Machar Seth,[77]

the Great Invisible Unnamable Unspeakable Virgin Spirit, and silence,

the great luminary Harmozel, where the living Self-Generated God of truth is,

with whom is the incorruptible human Adamas,

the second luminary Oroiael, where great Seth and Jesus are,

Jesus who has life

and who has come and crucified what is under the law,[78]

the third luminary Daveithe, where the children of great Seth are,

the fourth luminary Eleleth, where the souls of the children are at rest,

fifth, Yoel, stationed over the name of the one who will be ordained to baptize

with the holy incorruptible baptism that surpasses heaven.

From now on, [66] through the incorruptible human Poimael,[79] with regard to those worthy of the invocation and words of renunciation of the Five Seals in the baptism of running water,[80] they will know those who receive them, as they are instructed, and they will be known by them, and they shall not taste death.[81]

---

74. The Codex IV version reads "Umneos" or "Hum-neos." 75. Coptic, from Greek, *prutanis*; the Codex IV version reads "Phritanis." 76. The Codex IV version reads "slain souls." 77. The Codex IV version reads "Telmachael Telmachael Eli Eli Machar Machar Seth." 78. Cf. *Galatians* 4:4–5. 79. This name resembles the name Poimandres in Hermetic literature, and Poimandres probably derives from the Greek for "shepherd of men." The name Poimael may suggest Hermetic themes in the *Holy Book of the Great Invisible Spirit*; see the work of Régine Charron, Université Laval. 80. Or "the baptism of living water"; lit., "spring baptism." 81. Cf. *Gospel of Thomas* 1; 3.

Baptismal Hymn (66,8–68,1)

Yesseus[82]
ĒŌ OU ĒŌ ŌUA
in truth truly
Yesseus Mazareus Yessedekeus
living water
child of the child
glorious name
in truth truly
eternal being
I I I I
ĒĒĒĒ
EEEE
OOOO
UUUU
ŌŌŌŌ
AAAA
in truth truly
ĒI AAAA OOOO[83]
being who sees the eternal realms
in truth truly
A
EE
ĒĒĒ
I I I I
UUUUUU
ŌŌŌŌŌŌŌŌ[84]
being who exists forever
in truth truly
IĒA AIŌ[85]
in the heart
being who exists
U[86]
forever and ever

---

82. The translation of the baptismal hymn includes materials drawn from the Codex IV version. **83.** Possibly cf. Greek: *ei aaaa, ōōōō,* "You are alpha (four times), omega (four times)." Alpha and omega, as the first and last letters of the Greek alphabet, can symbolize the first and last, the beginning and the end; cf., e.g., *Revelation* 1:8; 21:6; 22:13. **84.** The Greek vowels in sequence; five omicrons are expected after four iotas, to maintain the sequence. In texts of ritual power such vowels may be arranged for visual effect—in this case, perhaps to form a pyramid. **85.** Greek *aiōn,* for "aeon, eternal realm"? **86.** Greek *huie,* for "son, child"?

you are what you are
you are who you are.[87]

This great name of yours is upon me,
you who lack nothing,
you Self-Generated One,
who are close to me.
I see you,
you who are invisible to all.
Who can comprehend you?

In another voice:[88] [67]

Having known you,
I have now mingled with your constancy.
I have armed myself with the armor of light.
I have become bright.
The Mother was there for the lovely beauty of grace.
So I have stretched out my two hands.
I have been formed in the circle of the riches of light
in my breast,
giving form to the many beings
produced in light beyond reproach.
In truth I shall declare your glory,
I have comprehended you:
yours,[89] Jesus;
look,
forever Ō
forever E[90]
O Jesus
O aeon, aeon,
God of silence,
I honor you completely.
You are my place of rest,
Child,
ĒS ĒS[91]
the E
formless one existing among formless ones,

---

87. These three lines are Greek: *aei eis aei, ei ho ei, ei hos ei*. 88. "In another voice" seems to be a liturgical rubric to indicate that the following portion of the baptismal hymn is to be chanted in a different voice. 89. If this is Greek *sou*, it may be translated "yours" or "it is yours." Otherwise it may be left as glossolalia, "SOU." The following lines also are Greek: *IĒS. Ide aei ō, aei e, ō IS*. 90. The numerical value of the letter epsilon is five, a number that plays a prominent role in Sethian texts. Cf. also Plutarch *On the E at Delphi*. 91. Greek for "Be. Be"? A reference to Esephech, twice?

raising the person by whom you will purify me into your life,
according to your imperishable name.
So the sweet smell of life is within me.
I have mixed it with water as a model for all the rulers,
that I may live with you in the peace of the saints,
you who exist forever,
in truth truly. [68]

Conclusion (68,1–69,5)

This is the book great Seth composed and placed high in mountains on which the sun has not risen and cannot rise. Since the days of the prophets, apostles, and preachers, the name has never risen in their hearts and cannot rise in their hearts, and their ears have not heard it.

Great Seth wrote this book letter by letter in a period of 130 years. He placed it on the mountain called Charaxio,[92] so that, at the end of the times and ages, according to the wish of the divine Self-Generated and the entire Fullness, through the gift of the unsearchable inconceivable fatherly will, he[93] may come forth and appear to this holy incorruptible generation of the great Savior and those dwelling with them in love, and the great invisible eternal Spirit and its only Child, and eternal light, [69] and its great incorruptible partner, and incorruptible Sophia, and Barbelo, and all the Fullness, in eternity. Amen.

Copyist's Note (69,6–20)

The Egyptian Gospel, a holy secret book, written by God. Grace, intelligence, perception, and understanding be with the copyist, Eugnostos the beloved in the Spirit—my worldly name is Gongessos[94]—and my fellow luminaries in incorruptibility. Jesus Christ, Son of God, Savior, ICHTHYS![95] The Holy Book of the Great Invisible Spirit is written by God. Amen.

The Holy Book of the Great Invisible Spirit

Amen.

---

92. Turner has suggested (*Sethian Gnosticism and the Platonic Tradition,* 88) that Charaxio may mean "mountain (Hebrew *har*) of the worthy (Greek *axiōn*)," or the like, where the worthy are the people of Seth. In this connection he also mentions that Ovid, in his *Metamorphoses,* refers to a certain Charaxus as a Lapith or a brother of Sappho. 93. Possibly read "it"—i.e., the book. 94. Lit., "in the flesh my name is Gongessos." The Latin form of this name is Concessus. 95. IKHTHUS, "fish," a common early Christian Greek acrostic, I(*ēsous*) KH(*ristos*) TH(*eou*) (H)U(*ios*) S(*ōtēr*). Cf. also *Teachings of Silvanus* 118.

EUGNOSTOS THE BLESSED

NHC III,3; V,1

Introduced by Madeleine Scopello
Translated by Marvin Meyer

T he tractate *Eugnostos the Blessed* is preserved in two codices in the Nag
   Hammadi library, Codex III and Codex V, and the two versions show some
differences. As the third treatise of Codex III, *Eugnostos* occupies pages
70,1–90,11. The first two lines of the text read, "Eugnostos the blessed, to those
who are his," and the title at the end of the tractate is given as "Eugnostos
the Blessed." For that reason the tractate is generally referred to as *Eugnostos the
Blessed*. Still, the opening of the version of the text in Codex V (1,1–17,17), even if
it is largely in a lacuna, cannot be reconstructed in the same way, and the title at
the conclusion of the document is merely "Eugnostos."

The two versions of *Eugnostos the Blessed* (or *Eugnostos*) provide translations
of a lost Greek document, as is underscored by the technical philosophical and
theological terminology communicated with Greek features in the text. It should
be noted that Codex III, where one version of *Eugnostos* is found, contains three
other treatises (*Secret Book of John, Holy Book of the Great Invisible Spirit, Wisdom of Jesus Christ*) that have also been copied either in another Nag Hammadi
codex or in the Berlin Gnostic Codex 8502. This point illustrates the wide diffusion of these texts, which were read by different Gnostic groups in Egypt, in Coptic translation, during the fourth century, even if they were composed in Greek,
as is the case with the great majority of texts in the Nag Hammadi library, in the
second and third centuries.

In style of writing and linguistic character, Codex III is quite different from
other Nag Hammadi codices.[1] *Eugnostos the Blessed* is well preserved in this
codex, though two pages are completely lacking (79 and 80). The version in
Codex V is more fragmentary. Codex V itself is of poorer quality than other
codices in the Nag Hammadi library; this may suggest that it was assembled for a
person or group with less financial means. Several lacunae are found in the
Codex V version of the tractate, and on some pages the ink has lost its color.

---

1. See Anne Pasquier, *Eugnoste*, 5.

But who is Eugnostos, and what is the meaning of this name? In Greek, *eugnōstos* is an adjective composed of *eu*, "good" or "well," and *gnōstos*, "known," and so Eugnostos means "well known," "familiar" (cf. Plato *Lysias*, frag. 17.3) or even "easy to understand" (cf. Plato *Sophist* 218e). The opposite of this term is *agnōstos*, "unknown," a term commonly used in philosophy to indicate the supreme God (cf. Epicurus *On the Nature of Things* 28.5). This adjective also has an active meaning, "the one who can know," "the one capable of knowing" (cf. Philo of Alexandria *On the Creation of the World* 154),[2] so that it may be a synonym of the term *gnōstēs* ("the one who knows," Acts 26:3). The link between *gnōstos* and *gnōstēs* makes the name Eugnostos highly symbolic. Here in the title of our text, this adjective is treated as a proper name, indicating the name of the author of the tractate.[3] The name Eugnostos also appears in another Nag Hammadi document, the *Holy Book of the Great Invisible Spirit* (NHC III,2; IV,2). In the final portion of this text (the colophon or copyist's note), the author introduces himself with his two names: Eugnostos, his spiritual name, and Gongessos, his ordinary, everyday name.

It may also be noted that in *Eugnostos the Blessed* the name Eugnostos is accompanied by the adjective "the blessed," an allusion to someone who finds in his condition of blessedness an intimate, peaceful feeling. This link between knowledge, *gnōsis*, and blessedness is, as Anne Pasquier observes, one of the themes of the tractate, which is entirely devoted to knowledge—knowledge that produces joy: "Rejoice in this, that you know" (III 70,2). Even if the name Eugnostos does not appear elsewhere in the tractate (apart from the opening line and the final title of the text), its meaning in relation to knowledge is in harmony with the tractate's emphasis on true knowledge.

Eugnostos the Blessed is a philosophical treatise presented in the form of a letter written by Eugnostos. We do not know if this letter, which contains the name of the sender, greetings for the recipients, and a formal conclusion, was real or fictitious. This is not simply a letter, but a letter meant to transmit an authoritative teaching on God and his heavenly realm. *Eugnostos* follows a well-articulated plan that shows clarity in its doctrine and is inspired by techniques employed in the philosophical schools of the time.[4] Anne Pasquier suggests that the tractate follows the rules of ancient rhetoric; it adopts the model of the *dispositio*, with a division of the text into four parts. Douglas M. Parrott, one of the first scholars to study *Eugnostos*, disagrees with this analysis. He believes that the tractate went through a number of stages of writing and rewriting, and that consequently it contains a wide variety of materials. The author of *Eugnostos* opens with a criticism of philosophical theories (an allusion to Stoics, Epicureans, and Babylonian scholars) and proceeds to focus on truth as a divine revelation, not a human construction. The author describes the divine realm inhabited by five be-

---

2. See Madeleine Scopello, *Femme, gnose et manichéisme*, 136–38.

3. See Michel Tardieu, *Écrits gnostiques*, 349–50; Pasquier, *Eugnoste*, 13.

4. Tardieu, *Écrits gnostiques*.

ings, each having his own aeon and heavenly followers, angels, and deities. These five beings are the unbegotten or unconceived Father, the Human Father by himself, the immortal Human, the Son of Humanity, and the Savior.

The perspective of the author of *Eugnostos* is not emanational; rather, the author posits a continuous chain of beings. The highest God, the unbegotten Father, is described by means of both negative theology (he is ineffable, without name, infinite, incomprehensible, unchanging, imperishable, untraceable, and so on) and positive theology (he surpasses everything, and he is blessed, perfect, and the like; III 71,13–72,23). This way of approaching the notion of God, common in Middle Platonic schools, is also taken up in several other Nag Hammadi philosophical texts, for example, the *Secret Book of John* and *Allogenes the Stranger*, with which *Eugnostos* can be usefully compared. Fed by Greek philosophical speculation, *Eugnostos* focuses as well on mystical Jewish elements. A deep interest in theoretical angelology appears in the tractate. Nevertheless, this angelology does not show any particular preoccupation with angelic names and their pronunciation, as generally may be seen in Jewish pseudepigrapha or other Nag Hammadi treatises. Michel Tardieu concludes that *Eugnostos* "is a text which represents, for the history of thought, the first (in a temporal sense) expository treatise of revelation where metaphysics serves angelology and where angelology changes constantly into metaphysics."[5]

Eugnostos the Blessed exerted an influence on or shared common traditions with other Nag Hammadi texts. Louis Painchaud sees a parallel between the tractate *On the Origin of the World* (NHC II,5) and our tractate. A comparison may also be drawn between the present treatise and an excerpt of a Valentinian letter cited by the heresiologist Epiphanius in *Panarion* 31.5.1–8.3, where quotations of *Eugnostos* have been found.[6] Valentinian tendencies can be detected,[7] especially concerning the theology of the name.[8] The theme of the five intellectual members of the primordial Human, which appears in the mythological doctrine of Mani (216–76 CE), may derive from *Eugnostos*.[9]

Eugnostos has been taken up and reused in another Nag Hammadi text appearing twice in two different codices: the *Wisdom of Jesus Christ* (NHC III,4; BG 8502,3). This technique of adapting and revising a text for new purposes is not unique in antiquity. In the case of *Eugnostos*, the author of the *Wisdom of Jesus Christ* transformed it in order to adapt it to a different public—a Christian Gnostic audience. In so doing, the author framed the philosophical treatise with a revelatory dialogue between Christ and his disciples. The dialogue provides the

---

5. Tardieu, *Écrits gnostiques*, 48.

6. Pasquier, *Eugnoste*; Tardieu, *Écrits gnostiques*.

7. A. H. B. Logan, "The Epistle of Eugnostos and Valentinianism."

8. Anne Pasquier, "Étude de la théologie du nom dans le traité gnostique d'Eugnoste à partir d'un fragment de Valentin."

9. Tardieu, *Écrits gnostiques*.

structure of the *Wisdom of Jesus Christ,* and the few sections deleted from the text of *Eugnostos* in the adaptation were apparently removed for doctrinal reasons.[10]

The original Greek text of *Eugnostos the Blessed* was probably composed in Egypt as early as the end of the first century.[11] From Egypt this tractate circulated in Syria, and it was known in the school of Bardaisan in the beginning of the third century.[12]

BIBLIOGRAPHY

Catherine Barry, ed., *La Sagesse de Jésus-Christ;* Paulinus Bellet, "The Colophon of the Gospel of the Egyptians: Concessus and Macarius of Nag Hammadi"; Werner Foerster, ed., *Gnosis,* 2.24–39 (Martin Krause); A. H. B. Logan, "The Epistle of Eugnostos and Valentinianism"; Deirdre J. Good, "Divine Noetic Faculties in Eugnostos the Blessed and Related Documents"; "Sophia in Eugnostos the Blessed and the Sophia of Jesus Christ"; Louis Painchaud, "The Literary Contacts Between the Writing Without Title 'On The Origin of the World' (CG II,5 and XIII,2) and 'Eugnostos the Blessed' (CG III,3 and V,1)"; Douglas M. Parrott, "The Significance of the Letter of Eugnostos and the Sophia of Jesus Christ for the Understanding of the Relation between Gnosticism and Christianity"; Douglas M. Parrott, ed., *Nag Hammadi Codices III,3–4 and V,1 with Papyrus Berolinensis 8502,3 and Oxyrhynchus Papyrus 1081;* Anne Pasquier, "Étude de la théologie du nom dans le traité gnostique d'Eugnoste à partir d'un fragment de Valentin"; ed., *Eugnoste;* Hans-Martin Schenke, Hans-Gebhard Bethge, and Ursula Ulrike Kaiser, eds., *Nag Hammadi Deutsch,* 1.323–79 (Judith Hartenstein); Madeleine Scopello, *Femme, gnose et manichéisme;* Michel Tardieu, *Écrits gnostiques.*

---

10. See Tardieu, *Écrits gnostiques.*

11. See Douglas M. Parrott, ed., *Nag Hammadi Codices III,3–4 and V,1 with Papyrus Berolinensis 8502,3 and Oxyrhynchus Papyrus 1081.*

12. See Tardieu, *Écrits gnostiques,* 60.

Eugnostos the Blessed[1]

Eugnostos Writing to Those Who Are His (70,1–71,13)

Eugnostos the blessed,[2] to those who are his.

Greetings. I want you to know[3] that all people born from the foundation of the world until now are of dust. They have inquired about God, who he is and what he is like, but they have not found him. The wisest of people have speculated about truth on the basis of the order of the universe, but their speculation has missed truth. Philosophers voice three different opinions about the order of the universe, and they disagree with each other. Some of them say that the universe has governed itself, others say that divine forethought has governed it, and still others that fate has been in charge. All these opinions are wrong. Of the three opinions I have mentioned, none of them is true. [71] Any life that comes from itself is empty, made by itself. Forethought is foolish. Fate is senseless.[4]

Whoever can avoid these three options I have mentioned, and come with another option to confess the God of truth and agree about everything concerning him, is immortal while living among mortal people.[5]

The One Who Is (71,13–73,3)

The One Who Is[6] is ineffable. From the foundation of the world, no power, no authority, no creature, no nature has known the One Who Is. Only the One Who Is knows itself.

---

1. Coptic Text: NHC III,3: 70,1–90,12; V,1: 1,1–17,18. Editions: *The Facsimile Edition of the Nag Hammadi Codices: Codex III,* 70–88; *The Facsimile Edition of the Nag Hammadi Codices: Codex V,* 9–25; Douglas M. Parrott, ed., *Nag Hammadi Codices III,3–4 and V,1*; Hans-Martin Schenke, Hans-Gebhard Bethge, and Ursula Ulrike Kaiser, eds., *Nag Hammadi Deutsch,* 1.323–79 (Judith Hartenstein). The present translation is based primarily on the Codex III version; when the Codex V version is used, this is indicated in the translation and notes. 2. The name Eugnostos, which means "well-versed in knowledge" (or the like; see the introduction), is also given as the spiritual name of the copyist of the *Holy Book of the Great Invisible Spirit* (III, 69). 3. The translation here follows the Codex V version. The greeting (Coptic, from Greek, *khaire*) is clear in the Codex V version. The text of the Codex III version reads "Rejoice in this (Coptic *raše hᵉn neei*), that you know . . ." Most likely the Coptic translator of the Codex III version has written *raše* for *khaire* and *hᵉn neei* for *hnai* ("It is pleasing to me . . ."). Here the Codex V version reads *tiouōš [etet]ᵉnᵉm[me]*. See Paulinus Bellet, "The Colophon of the Gospel of the Egyptians." 4. The text *On the Origin of the World* also opens with a consideration of various opinions about the origin and nature of the universe. 5. On this expression, cf. *Nature of the Rulers* 96. 6. Cf. the description of the divine in the Septuagint of *Exodus* 3:14 as *ho ōn,* "the One Who Is," for *'Ehyeh 'asher 'ehyeh,* "I am that I am" (or the like) in Hebrew. On account of these parallels with the Jewish scriptures, masculine personal pronouns may be preferred in the following lines. We employ gender neutral pronouns, however, because of the insistence in the text that the divine is infinite and transcends finite categories.

The One Who Is is immortal, eternal, without birth,
for whoever is born will die;
unconceived,[7] without a beginning,
for whoever has a beginning has an end;
undominated, [72] without a name,
for whoever has a name has been fashioned by another;
unnamable, with no human form,
for whoever has a human form has been fashioned by another.
The One Who Is has its own appearance,
not like what we have received and seen,
but an alien appearance that surpasses everything
and is superior to everything in the universe.
It looks everywhere and beholds itself in itself.

The One is infinite,
incomprehensible,
and constantly imperishable.
The One is unequalled,
immutably good,
without fault,
everlasting,
blessed,
unknowable,
yet it knows itself.
The One is immeasurable,
untraceable,
perfect,
without defect. [73]
The One is blessed,
imperishably,
and is called the Father of all.[8]

The Beginning of the Manifestation of the One Who Is
(73,3–74,7)

Before anything becomes visible among visible things—the majesty and the authorities that are in him—he grasps everything and nothing grasps him. He is all mind, thought, reflection, consideration, reason, and power, and all are equally

---

7. Or "unbegotten, unengendered, ungenerated" (*agennētos*), here and below. The language of conception is used more frequently in this translation because the text emphasizes creativity in both sexual and psy- chological terms. 8. Cf. *Secret Book of John* II, 2–4. The phrase "Father of all" may also be translated "Father of the All," here and below, perhaps referring to the divine realm of Fullness.

powerful.[9] These are the sources of all that is, and the entire generation, <from first> to last, was in the foreknowledge of the unconceived, for nothing had yet become visible.

There are differences among the imperishable realms. Let us consider it like this. Everything from the perishable will perish, since it is from the perishable. Everything [74] from the imperishable will not perish but will become imperishable, since it is from the imperishable. Many people have gone astray because they did not know about this distinction. They have died.

The Father, the Forefather, and the Kingless Generation (74,7–76,12)

This is enough. No one can argue with what I have said about the blessed, imperishable, true God. If anyone wishes to believe the words written here, that person will move from what is invisible to the end of what is visible, and this thought will teach how faith in what is invisible can be found in what is visible.

This is a principle of knowledge.[10]

The Lord of all is properly addressed not as Father but as Forefather. The Father is the beginning [75] of what is visible, and the Lord[11] is the Forefather without a beginning. The Forefather sees himself within himself as in a mirror, and his image appears as Father by himself,[12] Parent by himself, and reflection, because he reflects unconceived first existence.[13] He is as old as the one before him but not as powerful. Afterward he revealed many other beings, just as old and powerful as he, who are self-conceived and reflective. Glorious and without number, they are designated the generation over whom there is no kingdom among the kingdoms that exist. And all the beings of the realm with no kingdom over it, a multitude in number, are designated the children of the unconceived Father.[14] The unknowable one [76] is full of every imperishable glory[15] and ineffable joy, and all these beings are at rest in him, constantly rejoicing in ineffable joy over the unfading glory and unending praise never heard or known among the aeons and their worlds.

Enough of this, or we may go on endlessly.

The Immortal Human and Sophia Appear (76,12–78,15)

There is another principle of knowledge, from the perspective of what is conceived.[16]

---

9. These characteristics of mind are presented as mental powers in Manichaean texts. See also below, *Eugnostos the Blessed* 78; 83. 10. Coptic *sooun;* the Codex V version reads *gnōsis.* 11. Lit., "he," here and below. 12. Or "self-fathering Father" (*autopatōr*). 13. Cf. *Secret Book of John* II, 4, on the Father gazing at his reflection in the luminous water. 14. In Sethian texts, the people of Seth are often referred to as the generation without a king or the kingless generation. Cf., e.g., the *Nature of the Rulers,* the *Revelation of Adam,* and the *Gospel of Judas.* 15. This is the reading of the Codex V version; the Codex III version reads "is ever [full] of imperishability." 16. Here the Codex V version reads "from [his] only conceived, completely unique [word]."

The first to appear before the universe in infinity is the one who grows by himself, the self-made Father. He is full of bright, ineffable light. In the beginning he decided to turn his likeness into a great power, and at once the strength of that light appeared as an immortal androgynous Human. The male name of this human being [77] is [conceived] perfect [Mind], and the female name is all-wise mother Sophia. It is also said that she resembles her brother and companion. She is unchallenged truth. Here below, error lives with truth and challenges it.[17]

Through the immortal Human there first appeared a set of expressions, divinity and kingdom. The Father, called the Human Father by himself,[18] revealed this. He created an exalted aeon for his own majesty, and he gave him great authority. He ruled over all the created realms, and he created gods and archangels and angels, myriads without number, to serve him.

Through this Human there came divinity [78] [and kingdom]. For that reason the human being was called God of gods and King of kings. The first Human is Faith, Pistis,[19] for those who will come later. He has within himself a mind of his own, and thought, appropriate to him, and reflection, consideration, reason, and power.

All these attributes are perfect and immortal. They are equally imperishable but not equally powerful. There is a difference among them like the difference between father and son, and son and thought, and thought and what remains.

The Pattern Among the Immortals (III 78,15–V 8,27)

As I said before, about what was produced, the One is first, then the Two, then the Three, up to the tens. The tens dominate the hundreds, the hundreds dominate the thousands, the thousands dominate the ten thousands. This is the pattern among the immortals. [7]

The one and thought belong to the [immortal] Human. Insights are for the tens, the hundreds are [teachings, the thousands] are counsels, and the ten thousands are powers. Those [who] come [from] . . . exist with their . . . [in] every realm . . . . [8] [In the beginning, thought] and insights [came from] mind, [and then] teachings from insights, counsels [from teachings], and power [from counsels]. After all [the attributes], all that [was revealed] came from [his powers. From] what [was] created came what was [fashioned]. From what was [fashioned] came what was formed. From what was formed came what was named. The differences among what was conceived came from what was [named], from beginning to end, by the power of all the eternal beings.[20]

The immortal Human is full of all unfading glory and ineffable joy. His whole kingdom, and those never heard of or known in any of the aeons that [came] after them and their [worlds], rejoice in everlasting joy.

---

17. On the nature of error, sometimes personified, cf. the *Gospel of Truth*. 18. Or, again, "self-fathering Father" (*autopatōr*). 19. The text simply has Pistis, here and below. 20. This passage and later comments describe in detail the development of mental powers of thought in the universe.

The Child of God and Sophia, Love, Appear (V 8,27–III 81,21)

After that [another power] came from the immortal [Human], the self-perfected one who [conceives. When] his [companion great Sophia came together with him, he] disclosed [the first begotten androgyne, [9] called] the first begotten [Child of God].[21] The female name of the Child of God [is first] begotten Sophia, [Mother of the universe], whom some [name] love. The first begotten, with authority from his [father], created an exalted [eternal being] for his own majesty, as well as angels, myriads without number, to serve him. [81] The whole multitude of angels is designated the assembly of the holy, luminaries with no shadow. When they greet one another, their embraces become angels like themselves.

The first conceiving father is called Adam of light. The kingdom of the Child of Humanity[22] is full of ineffable joy and eternal praise. Those in the kingdom constantly rejoice in ineffable joy over their imperishable glory, which has never been heard and never been revealed to all the aeons that have come to be, and their worlds.

The Savior, Pistis Sophia, and Six Spiritual Beings Appear (81,21–83,10)

Then the Child, the Son of Humanity, came together with his companion Sophia and produced a bright androgynous light. [82] The masculine name of the light is Savior, the one who conceives all, and the feminine name is Sophia, the one conceiving all. Some call her Pistis, Faith.

The Savior came together with his companion Pistis Sophia[23] and disclosed six androgynous spiritual beings who are similar to those who preceded them. These are their male names:

first, unconceived,

second, self-conceived,

third, one who conceives,

fourth, first to conceive,

fifth, all-conceiving,

sixth, chief creator.[24]

These are the female names:

first, all-wise Sophia,

second, all-mother Sophia,

---

21. Or "[Son of God]," here and below. 22. Or "Son of Man," here and below. 23. On Pistis Sophia, cf. the *Nature of the Rulers, On the Origin of the World,* and the text entitled *Pistis Sophia.* 24. The text reads *arkhigenetōr.*

third, all-conceiving Sophia,

fourth, first-conceiving Sophia,

fifth, love Sophia, [83]

[sixth], Pistis Sophia.

[From the] union of those I have mentioned, thoughts appeared in the existing eternal realms,

and from thoughts, reflections,

from reflections, considerations,

from considerations, reasoned statements,

from reasoned statements, wills,

from wills, words.

More Spiritual Powers Appear, as Symbols of Time (83,10–84,11)

The twelve powers I have discussed came together with each other, and each disclosed <six> males and <six> females, for a total of seventy-two powers. Each of the seventy-two in turn disclosed five spiritual powers, bringing the number to three hundred sixty powers. They are united in will.[25]

In this way immortal Humanity came to symbolize our realm. The first one to conceive, [84] the Son of Immortal Humanity, functions as a symbol of time. The [Savior] symbolizes [the year]. The twelve powers are symbols of the twelve months. The three hundred sixty powers who derive from the Savior stand for the three hundred sixty days of the year. And the angels who came from them and who are without number stand for the hours and moments.[26]

Eternal Realms Appear (84,12–87,8)

As soon as those whom I have discussed appeared, the all-conceiving one, their father, moved to create twelve eternal realms to serve the twelve angels. In each realm there were six heavens, and thus there are seventy-two heavens with the seventy-two powers who came from him. In each of the heavens there were five firmaments, for a total of three hundred sixty [85] [firmaments] of the three hundred sixty powers who came from them.

When the firmaments were completed, they were referred to as the three hundred sixty heavens, after the name of the heavens that existed before them. All of them are perfect and good.[27]

---

25. Coptic *ouōš*. It is also possible to translate this sentence, with a different meaning for *ouōš*, "They are united in space." 26. On this section, cf. *Gospel of* *Judas* 49–50. 27. Cf. a very similar description of the creation of powers, aeons, heavens, and firmaments in *Gospel of Judas* 49–50.

This is how the defect of femaleness became apparent.[28]

The first eternal realm is that of immortal Humanity. The second eternal realm is that of the Child of Humanity, called the first one to conceive. The third is that of the offspring of the Child of Humanity, called the Savior.[29] What holds these is the realm over which there is no kingdom, the realm of the eternal infinite God, the aeon of aeons of the immortals in it, the aeon above the eighth realm that appeared in chaos.[30]

The immortal Human revealed realms, powers, and kingdoms, and gave authority to everyone [86] who [came from] him to make [whatever they wanted] until the days above chaos. They came together with each other and disclosed every majesty, even from spirit, and a multitude of lights, glorious and without number. The first, second, and third eternal realms were given names in the beginning, the first, the middle, and the perfect names. The first was called unity and rest. Each has its own name; the third realm was called assembly, after the great multitude that appeared in the One who is many. So, when the many gather and experience unity, they are called the assembly, from the assembly that surpasses heaven. The assembly of [87] the [eighth realm was] shown to be [androgynous] and was given male and female names. The male part was called the assembly and the female life, to indicate that from a female came life in all the realms.

The Names of the Eternal Realms All Come from Above
(87,8–88,17)

All the names came from the original source. That is the one who came together with thought, and powers called gods appeared. From their considerations the gods revealed gods of gods, and from their considerations the gods <of gods> revealed lords <of lords>, and from their words the lords of lords revealed lords, and from their powers the lords revealed archangels, and the archangels revealed angels, and from them came the ideas, [88] with structure [and form], for naming [all] the aeons and their worlds.

All the immortals I have described, all of them, have authority from the power of the immortal Human and his companion Sophia, who was called silence. She was named silence because she perfected her own majesty by reflecting without speaking. The imperishable beings had authority, and each established great kingdoms in all the immortal heavens and their firmaments, and thrones and temples, for their own majesty.[31]

---

28. The defect of femaleness refers to the fallen state of the world below, often described as being due to Sophia's mistake. Cf. *Wisdom of Jesus Christ* (BG 8502), 118–21. **29.** This sentence is added from the Codex V version. **30.** The eighth realm, or Ogdoad, is often understood to be the sphere of the fixed stars, and even the abode of the creator of this world. The exalted God, then, dwells beyond that. **31.** On divine silence, cf. *Secret Book of John* II, 4–7.

The Eternal Realms Are Completed (88,17–90,12)

Some of these, in dwellings and chariots, were in ineffable glory and could not be sent into any creature, and they produced for themselves hosts of angels, myriads without number, to serve [89] and glorify them, as well as virgin spirits and ineffable lights. They are free of sickness and weakness. There is only will, and it comes to expression at once.[32]

Thus the eternal realms were completed, with their heavens and firmaments, for the glory of the immortal Human and his companion Sophia. This is where <the ideas were for> all the realms and their worlds and those that were to follow, to provide patterns for those who would resemble them in the heavens and worlds of chaos. All natures, from the immortal one, from the unconceived one to the revelation in chaos, are in the light that shines with no shadow but with ineffable joy and unspeakable praise. They continue to rejoice over their glory that never fades and the state of rest that cannot be measured, which can neither be described [90] nor conceived among all the realms that have come to be, and their powers.

This is enough. I have told you all this so that you might accept it, until one who does not need to be taught appears among you. That one will tell you all these things in joy and pure knowledge.[33]

Eugnostos the Blessed

---

32. Cf. *Gospel of Judas* 49–50. 33. The final paragraph of the text, with its statement about one who is to come, may have prompted a Christian editor to rework *Eugnostos the Blessed* into a Christian text, with an identification of Jesus as the savior who reveals all these things and more, in the *Wisdom of Jesus Christ*. Here the Codex V version reads, "This is enough for you. I have told you all this so that you might keep it,

until the word (*šaje*) that does not need to be taught comes forth among you. It will interpret these things for you in unified and pure knowledge (gnosis). For whoever has will be given more." On a teacher who is untaught, cf. Paul's claim in *Galatians* 1:11–12. On the spirit as the advocate or paraclete to reveal truth, cf. *John* 14:16, 26; 15:26; 16:7–8.

THE WISDOM OF JESUS CHRIST

NHC III,4; BG 8502,3; P. Oxy. 1081

Introduced by Madeleine Scopello
Translated by Marvin Meyer

T he *Wisdom of Jesus Christ* (or the *Sophia of Jesus Christ*) is the fourth tractate of Nag Hammadi Codex III, where it occupies pages 90,14–119,18. Another version of the *Wisdom of Jesus Christ* has been preserved as the third text in
Berlin Gnostic Codex 8502 (pages 77,8–127,12), a Coptic codex discovered in
Upper Egypt at the end of the nineteenth century. The Berlin Gnostic Codex
contains a total of four tractates: the *Gospel of Mary*, the *Secret Book of John*, also
present in two versions within the Nag Hammadi library, the *Wisdom of Jesus
Christ*, and the *Act of Peter*. Furthermore, a fragment of the *Wisdom of
Jesus Christ* was found in a Greek papyrus (P. Oxy. 1081) from the beginning
of the fourth century. This fragment was identified by Henri-Charles Puech as a
part of the present text.[1] As with most Nag Hammadi documents, the *Wisdom of
Jesus Christ* was originally composed in Greek (the discovery of the Greek fragment strengthens this hypothesis) and then translated into Coptic.

The text of the *Wisdom of Jesus Christ* in Codex III is not complete. Pages 109,
110, 115, and 116 are missing, and various lacunae are to be noted on other pages as
well. On the other hand, the text in the Berlin Gnostic Codex is very well preserved, and only a few small lacunae appear here and there. The Oxyrhynchus
fragment of the *Wisdom of Jesus Christ* consists of fifty lines corresponding to
pages 96,21–99,13 in Codex III and pages 87,15–91,17 in the Berlin Gnostic
Codex. The two Coptic versions of the text along with the Greek fragment have
been published by Douglas M. Parrott.[2] These different versions show that the
treatise had a wide diffusion and was read during the fourth century by people
speaking Greek and Coptic in Egypt.

The Codex III version of the present tractate has the title ("The Wisdom of
Jesus Christ") inserted at the opening of the text; the final line of the tractate

---

1. Henri-Charles Puech, "Les nouveaux écrits gnostiques découverts en Haute-Égypte."
2. Douglas M. Parrott, ed., *Nag Hammadi Codices III,3–4 and V,1 with Papyrus Berolinensis 8502,3 and
Oxyrhynchus Papyrus 1081.*

reads simply "The Wisdom of Jesus." The first line of the Berlin Gnostic Codex version reads "The Wisdom of Jesus Christ," as does the concluding title. This title imitates such wisdom texts as the *Wisdom of Solomon* and the *Wisdom of Jesus, Son of Sirach*.[3] The *Wisdom of Jesus Christ* is closely connected with the tractate *Eugnostos the Blessed*, which precedes it in Nag Hammadi Codex III (see the introduction to *Eugnostos*).

The content of the *Wisdom of Jesus Christ* can be summarized as follows. After the resurrection, the twelve disciples and the seven women who faithfully followed Jesus's teaching go up on a mountain, in Galilee, called "Prophecy and Joy." They are puzzled about cosmological and soteriological matters, and the Savior appears to them in a spiritual form, resembling "a great angel of light." (This may be intended as a polemic against the concept of the resurrection of the body.) He greets them and laughs at their reaction of fear and surprise, and then he asks them why they are perplexed. Here begins a dialogue between the apostles and Christ that extends to the end of the tractate. The questions in the dialogue are short but the answers long. Most of what the author attributes to the Savior comes from the teachings found in *Eugnostos the Blessed*. The teachings are now presented in the form of a dialogue, after the manner of revelatory dialogues well known from Gnostic and apocryphal traditions in the first centuries of Christianity.[4]

The first question raised by the Savior addresses the reasons for the perplexity of the disciples (III 92,1–3). Philip answers for them all, explaining that they are puzzled "about the nature of the universe and the plan of salvation" (III 92,3–5). To this comment the Savior gives a long response (III 92,6–93,24). Matthew asks the Savior to reveal truth to them (III 93,24–94,4; the Savior's answer is given in III 94,4–95,18); Philip intervenes and asks how the One Who Is appears to the perfect ones (III 95,19–20; the Savior's answer is given in III 95,21–96,13), and Thomas wants an explanation about the coming into being of the imperishable ones (III 96,14–16; the Savior's answer is given in III 96,18–98,9). Then Mary also asks about what is perishable and imperishable (III 98,9–11; the Savior's answer is given in III 98,12–100,16). Matthew asks a question concerning the manifestation of Humanity (III 100,17–19; the Savior's answer is given in III 100,19–103,21). Bartholomew inquires about the name of Humanity and the Son of Humanity in the gospel (III 103,22–104,4; the Savior's answer is given in III 104,4–105,2). The disciples as a whole interrogate Christ a first time about the Human (III 105, 3–8; the Savior's answer is given in III 105,8–106,8), then a second time about the coming into the mortal world of the entities of the immortal realm (III 106, 9–14; the Savior's answer is given in III 106,14–108,16). Thomas wants to know the number of aeons (III 108,16–19; the Savior's answer is given in III 108,19 and following).

The next two pages (109 and 110) are missing in Codex III but may be supplied from the Berlin Gnostic Codex (106,14–107,13). The disciples ask again about the

---

3. See Michel Tardieu, *Écrits gnostiques*, 47.
4. See Pheme Perkins, *The Gnostic Dialogue*.

aeons of the immortal entities (BG 107,14–16; the Savior's answer is given in BG 107,16–114,11; only a portion of this answer is preserved in III 111,1–112,19). The holy apostles (previously called the disciples) question the Savior again about the inhabitants of the aeons, the angels (III 112,19–24; the Savior's answer is given in III 112,25–114,8). Mary asks a question that recalls *Excerpts from Theodotos* 78: "Holy master, where did your disciples come from, where are they going, and what should they do here?" (III 114,8–12; the Savior's answer is given in III 114,12 and following). The next two pages (115 and 116) are missing in Codex III (only a part of the Savior's answer is given, in III 117,1–119,9; the remainder may be read in the Berlin Gnostic Codex 117,18–126,16). The *Wisdom of Jesus Christ* concludes with the joy of the disciples, who receive this instruction and go to preach the "gospel of God" (III 119,13–15).

Having composed the text as a revelatory dialogue, the author of the *Wisdom of Jesus Christ* has made substantial use of *Eugnostos the Blessed*. This dependence is variously understood by scholars. As Michel Tardieu suggests, the author of the tractate has utilized his source, *Eugnostos*, within an artificial framework borrowed from the New Testament and apocryphal literature emphasizing the revelation of Christ to his disciples after the resurrection.[5] In so doing, the author has disrupted the literary and theological unity of *Eugnostos*, rewriting it and occasionally inserting other sources.[6] The highly philosophical character of *Eugnostos* and its description of the heavenly realm are distorted. The questions of the disciples are not really answered in the responses of the Savior. Further, the doctrine of *Eugnostos the Blessed* is profoundly transformed in the *Wisdom of Jesus Christ*. For example, the understanding of the Child or Son of Humanity (the Son of Man) changes from an angelological interpretation in *Eugnostos* to a Christological interpretation in the *Wisdom of Jesus Christ*. The angelology of *Eugnostos* describes the entities of the highest God; in the *Wisdom of Jesus Christ*, the attention is focused upon the entities of the demiurge, described as beings of poverty.[7]

According to Douglas M. Parrott, the non-Christian *Eugnostos* has undergone a process of transformation into a Christian Gnostic text, as is shown by (1) the integration of the person of Christ, identified with the heavenly revealer; (2) the addition of the myth of Sophia; (3) the focus placed on the god of the world and his sidekicks who enslave those who come from the heavenly realm; (4) the power of sexuality as the best weapon of the wicked powers to trap humankind; and (5) Christ as the one who breaks the bonds of the powers.[8] The approach of Catherine Barry is quite different from that of either Tardieu or Parrott. She considers the *Wisdom of Jesus Christ* a work to be evaluated on its own merits, not just as a Christian rewriting of *Eugnostos the Blessed*. The link between the two texts, to be sure, is strong, because the *Wisdom of Jesus Christ* develops points of the

---

5. Tardieu, *Écrits gnostiques*, 56.

6. See Anne Pasquier, *Eugnoste*, 1–2.

7. See Tardieu, *Écrits gnostiques*, 58–59.

8. Parrott, ed., *Nag Hammadi Codices III,3–4 and V,1*.

doctrine contained only implicitly in *Eugnostos*, especially in the version found in Nag Hammadi Codex III. Barry proposes that the *Wisdom of Jesus Christ* seeks to retrace the history of humankind from its preexistence in the unconceived or unbegotten One Who Is to the realization of salvation.[9] The author of the text tries to establish a theology of history, and this new historical perspective leads him to modify here and there the doctrine he found in *Eugnostos*. If Michel Tardieu underlines the incoherence between the questions of the disciples and the answers given by Jesus Christ, Catherine Barry judges that there actually is no discrepancy. For Barry, the questions of the *Wisdom of Jesus Christ* have a didactic aim, because they allow the author to present the topics he is going to discuss.[10] Other sources were also used in the composition of the text, including apocryphal gospels, the *Gospel of John*, and the Gnostic *Secret Book of John*; and Barry cites 1 *Corinthians* 15:45–47 as the point of departure of the anthropogonic myth on the creation and restoration of humanity given at the end of the tractate.[11]

What are the circumstances of the composition of this text? Douglas Parrott sees the presence of Sethian and Ophites traditions, as described by Irenaeus of Lyon in his work *Against Heresies*. Catherine Barry believes that Valentinian sources and Thomas traditions should also be acknowledged, even if "a Sethian hand has composed the original materials of the *Wisdom of Jesus Christ*."[12] Michel Tardieu considers this treatise "a catch-all and an all-purpose text"; its author "belongs to the milieu of plagiarists, not to the milieu of inventors, a milieu where there is not intellectual creation but copying and collecting."[13] Thus, the *Wisdom of Jesus Christ* can be dated in the middle of the third century, in Egypt. Parrott proposes, on the contrary, a date of composition in the second half of the first century, shortly after Egypt was Christianized.

BIBLIOGRAPHY

Harold W. Attridge, "P. Oxy. 1081 and the Sophia Jesu Christi"; Catherine Barry, ed., *La Sagesse de Jésus-Christ*; Werner Foerster, ed., *Gnosis*, 2.24–39 (Martin Krause); Helmut Koester, "Gnostic Writings as Witnesses for the Development of the Sayings Tradition"; Elaine H. Pagels, "The Mystery of the Resurrection: A Gnostic Reading of 1 Corinthians 15"; *The Gnostic Paul*; Douglas M. Parrott, "The Significance of the Letter of Eugnostos and the Sophia of Jesus Christ for the Understanding of the Relation Between Gnosticism and Christianity"; Douglas M. Parrott, ed., *Nag Hammadi Codices III,3–4 and V,1 with Papyrus Berolinensis 8502,3 and Oxyrhynchus Papyrus 1081*; Anne Pasquier, ed., *Eugnoste*; Pheme Perkins, *The Gnostic Dialogue*; Henri-Charles Puech, "Les nouveaux écrits gnostiques découverts en Haute-Égypte"; Hans-Martin Schenke, Hans-Gebhard Bethge, and Ursula Ulrike Kaiser, eds., *Nag Hammadi Deutsch*, 1.323–79 (Judith Hartenstein); Madeleine Scopello, *Femme, gnose et manichéisme*; Michel Tardieu, *Écrits gnostiques*; Walter C. Till and Hans-Martin Schenke, *Die gnostischen Schriften des koptischen Papyrus Berolinensis 8502*.

---

9. Catherine Barry, *La Sagesse de Jésus-Christ*, 20.

10. Barry, *La Sagesse de Jésus-Christ*, 32–33.

11. See also Elaine H. Pagels, "The Mystery of the Resurrection: A Gnostic Reading of I Corinthians 15"; *The Gnostic Paul*.

12. Barry, *La Sagesse de Jésus-Christ*, 34–35.

13. Tardieu, *Écrits gnostiques*, 60.

The Wisdom of Jesus Christ[1]

The Wisdom of Jesus Christ

The Savior Appears to His Followers After the Resurrection (90,14–93,24)

After he[2] rose from the dead, his twelve disciples and seven women continued to be his followers. They went to Galilee, up on the mountain [91] called "Prophecy and Joy."[3] As they gathered together, they were confused about the true nature of the universe, and the plan of salvation, and divine forethought, and the strength of the authorities, and everything the Savior was doing with them in the secret plan of salvation. Then the Savior appeared, not in his previous form but in invisible spirit. He looked like a great angel of light, but I must not describe his appearance. Mortal flesh could not bear it, but only pure and perfect flesh, like what he taught us about, in Galilee, on the mountain called Olivet.[4]

He said, "Peace be with you. My peace I give to you." They all marveled, and they were afraid.

The Savior [92] laughed and said to them, "What are you thinking about? Are you confused? What do you want to find out about?"

Philip said, "About the nature of the universe and the plan of salvation."

The Savior said to them, "I want you to know that all people born on earth from the foundation of the world until now are of dust, and though they have inquired about God, who he is and what he is like, they have not found him. The wisest of people have speculated on the basis of the order and movement of the universe, yet their speculation has missed the truth. It is said that philosophers

---

1. Coptic text: NHC III,4: 90,14–119,18; BG 8502,3: 77,8–127,12. Greek fragment: P. Oxy. 1081. Editions: *The Facsimile Edition of the Nag Hammadi Codices: Codex III*, 88–113; Michel Tardieu, ed., *Écrits gnostiques*; Walter C. Till and Hans-Martin Schenke, eds., *Die gnostischen Schriften des koptischen Papyrus Berolinensis 8502*; Catherine Barry, ed., *La Sagesse de Jésus-Christ*; Douglas M. Parrott, ed., *Nag Hammadi Codices III,3–4 and V,1*; Hans-Martin Schenke, Hans-Gebhard Bethge, and Ursula Ulrike Kaiser, eds., *Nag Hammadi Deutsch*, 1.323–79 (Judith Hartenstein). The title of the text is sometimes given as the *Sophia* *of Jesus Christ*. The present translation is based primarily on the Codex III version; when the BG 8502 version is used (mainly for pages missing in the Codex III version), this is indicated in the translation and notes. **2.** The Savior. **3.** Here the Coptic reads *mantē hi raše*, and *mantē* may be read as a form of Greek *manteia*, "prophecy, divination." *Mantē* could also be read as *ma n tē*, "Place of Harvest," which would suggest "Place of Harvest and Joy" for the name of the mountain. Perhaps cf. *John* 4:34–38. **4.** The geography is somewhat confused here, since Olivet—the Mount of Olives—is in Judea near Jerusalem.

voice three distinct opinions about the order of the universe, and they disagree with each other. Some of them say that the world governs itself, [93] others say that divine forethought governs it, still others that fate is in charge. All these opinions are wrong. Of the three opinions I have just mentioned, none of them comes close to the truth. They are mere human opinions.

"I have come from infinite light; I am here, and I can tell you exactly what the truth is. For any life that comes from itself is defiled, made by itself. Forethought lacks wisdom. Fate remains senseless.[5]

"It is given to you, however, to know the truth. Whoever deserves knowledge will receive it, whoever has not been conceived by the semen of unclean sexual rubbing[6] but by the first one who was sent, for that person is immortal among mortal people."[7]

The One Who Is (93,24–95,18)

Matthew said [94] to him, "Master,[8] no one can find truth except through you. Teach us the truth."

The Savior said, "The One Who Is[9] is ineffable. From the foundation of the world until now, no power, no authority, no creature, no nature has known the One Who Is. Only the One Who Is, and anyone to whom this One wishes to give revelation through the emissary from the first light, knows the One Who Is. Henceforth, I am the great Savior.

The One Who Is is
immortal and eternal, and being eternal, is without birth,
for whoever is born will die;
unconceived,[10] without a beginning,
for whoever has a beginning has an end;
undominated, without a name,
for whoever has a name has been made by another; [84][11]
unnamable, with no human form,
for whoever has a human form has been made by another.
The One Who Is has an appearance of its own, [95][12]
not like anything you have seen and received,
but an alien appearance that surpasses everything

---

5. The text *On the Origin of the World* also opens with a consideration of various opinions about the origin and nature of the universe. 6. A similar image of sexual rubbing, here and below, is found throughout the *Paraphrase of Shem*. 7. On this expression, cf. *Nature of the Rulers* 96. 8. Or "Lord," here and below. 9. Cf. the description of the divine in the Septuagint of Exodus 3:14 as *ho ōn*, "the One Who Is," for *'Ehyeh 'asher 'ehyeh*, "I am that I am" (or the like) in Hebrew. On account of these parallels with the Jewish scriptures, masculine personal pronouns may be preferred in the following lines. We employ gender neutral pronouns, however, because of the insistence in the text that the divine is infinite and transcends finite categories. 10. Or "unbegotten," "unengendered," "ungenerated" (*agennētos*), here and below. The language of conception is used more frequently in this translation because the text emphasizes creativity in both sexual and psychological terms. 11. The following section is added from BG 8502, 84. 12. Here the Codex III version resumes.

and is superior to the universe.
It looks everywhere and beholds itself in itself.

The One is infinite,
incomprehensible,
and constantly imperishable.
The One is unequalled,
immutably good,
without fault,
eternal,
blessed,
unknown,
yet it knows itself.
The One is immeasurable,
untraceable,
perfect,
without defect.
The One is blessed,
imperishably,
and is called the Father of all."[13]

The Beginning of the Manifestation of the One Who Is
(95,19–98,9)

Philip said, "Master, then how did the One Who Is appear to those who are perfect?"

The perfect Savior said, "Before anything becomes visible of visible things, the majesty and the authority are [96] in him, since he grasps everything while nothing grasps him. He is all mind; he is thought, consideration, reflection, reason, and power, and all are equally powerful.[14] These are the sources of all that is, and the entire generation, from first to last, was in the foreknowledge of the infinite unconceived Father."

Thomas said to him, "Master, Savior, why did these come to be, and why were they revealed?"

The perfect Savior said to him, "I have come from the infinite to tell you everything. The Spirit who is was the one who conceives, the one who has the power of conception [97] and can [give] form, so that the abundant wealth within might be revealed. In mercy and love the Spirit[15] wished to produce fruit independently, that the Spirit might not enjoy[16] goodness alone but that other spirits

13. Cf. *Secret Book of John* II, 2–4. The phrase "Father of all" (and similar phrases) may also be translated "Father of the All," here and below, perhaps referring to the divine realm of Fullness. 14. These characteristics of mind are presented as mental powers in Manichaean texts. See also below, *Wisdom of Jesus Christ* 102–3. 15. Lit., "he" or "it," here and below. 16. The word "enjoy" is emended in the Codex III version on the basis of the reading in the BG 8502 version.

of the unshakable generation[17] might produce bodies and fruit, glory and honor, in imperishability and the infinite grace of the Spirit. In this way the goodness of the Spirit could be revealed by the self-conceived God, the Father of all imperishability and those who were to come later. But nothing had become visible yet.

"There are many differences among the imperishable beings."

He spoke out and said, "Whoever has ears to hear about infinite things should hear.[18] It is to those who are awake that I speak."

He went on [98] and said, "Everything from the perishable will perish, since it is from the perishable. But everything from the imperishable does not perish but becomes imperishable, since it is from the imperishable.[19] Many people have gone astray because they did not know about this distinction, and they have died."

The Father and the Kingless Generation (98,9–100,16)

Mary said to him, "Master, then how can we know this?"

The perfect Savior said, "Bring yourselves from what is invisible to the end of those who are visible, and the emanation of thought itself will reveal to you how faith in what is invisible can be found in those who are visible, who belong to the unconceived Father. Whoever has ears to hear should hear.

"The Lord of the universe is addressed not as Father but as Forefather. <The Father is> the beginning of those who will appear, but the Lord[20] [99] is the Forefather without a beginning. When the Forefather saw himself within himself in a mirror, his resemblance appeared there, but his image appeared as the divine Father by himself and the reflection above reflections and the first-existing unconceived Father.[21] He is as old as the light before him but not as powerful. Afterward there was revealed a multitude of beings, just as old and powerful, who are self-conceived and reflective. Glorious and without number, their generation is designated the generation over whom there is no kingdom. You yourselves have appeared from the people of this generation. And the whole multitude of beings with no kingdom over them is designated [100] the children of the unconceived Father, God, Savior, Son of God, whose likeness is among you.[22] This is the unknowable one, who is full of imperishable glory and ineffable joy, and all these beings are at rest in him, constantly rejoicing in ineffable joy in the Father's unfading glory and unending praise that was never heard or known among the aeons and their worlds until now."

---

17. In Sethian texts, the people of Seth are commonly referred to as the unshakable generation. Cf., e.g., the *Secret Book of John*. 18. This injunction (with variations) to pay attention to the meaning of what is being said also occurs elsewhere in this text and throughout early Christian literature. 19. This clause is added from the BG 8502 version. 20. Lit., "he," here and below. 21. Cf. *Secret Book of John* II, 4, on the Father gazing at his reflection in the luminous water. 22. In Sethian texts, the people of Seth are often referred to as the generation without a king, or the kingless generation. Cf., e.g., the *Nature of the Rulers*, the *Revelation of Adam*, and the *Gospel of Judas*.

Immortal Humanity and Sophia Appear (100,16–103,21)

Matthew said to him, "Master, Savior, how was Humanity revealed?"

The perfect Savior said, "I want you to know that the being who appeared before the universe in infinity is the one who grows by himself, [101] the self-made Father. He is full of bright light and ineffable. In the beginning, when he decided to turn his likeness into a great power, at once the strength of that light appeared as an immortal androgynous Human, so that through that immortal Human, people might come to salvation and wake up from forgetfulness, through the interpreter who was sent, who is with you until the end of the time of poverty[23] of those who are robbers.[24]

"The companion of the immortal Human is great Sophia, who from the beginning was destined to be united with him, by the self-conceived Father, through the immortal Human who appeared as the first one and as divinity and kingdom. The Father, [102] called the Human, Father by himself,[25] revealed this. He created an exalted aeon, named the Eight,[26] for his own majesty, and he was given great authority. He rules over the impoverished creation, and he created gods and angels and archangels, myriads without number, to serve him, through that light, and the triple-male Spirit, which is of his companion Sophia.

"Through this God came divinity and kingdom. For that reason this God was called God of gods and King of kings. The first Human has a mind of his own within, and thought, appropriate to him, and consideration, reflection, reason, [103] and power.

"All these attributes are perfect and immortal. They are equally imperishable but not equally powerful. They are different, like the difference between father and son, <and son> and thought, and thought and the rest.

"As I said before, about what was produced, the One is first. After everything, all that was revealed came from his power. From what was created came what was fashioned. From what was fashioned came what was formed. From what was formed came what was named. This is how differences came to be among what was unconceived, from beginning to end."

The Child of God and Sophia, Love, Appear (103,22–106,9)

Then Bartholomew said to him, "How is it that this being was called [104] a human being and the Son of Humanity[27] in the gospel? To which of these figures is the Son related?"

The Holy One said to him, "I want you to know that the first Human is referred to as the one who conceives, the self-perfected mind. He reflected with his

---

23. On the present world as poverty, cf. *Gospel of Thomas* 3:5. 24. On the interpreter, cf. *Eugnostos the Blessed* 90. 25. Or "self-fathering Father" (*autopatōr*). 26. Or "the Ogdoad." The eighth realm, or Ogdoad, is often understood to be the sphere of the fixed stars, and even the abode of the creator of this world. 27. Or "Son of Man," here and below.

companion great Sophia and disclosed his first-begotten androgynous child. Its male name is first-begetting Son of God, its female name first-begetting Sophia, Mother of the universe. Some call her love, and the first-begotten is called Christ. With authority from his Father, he created a host of angels [105] without number to serve him, from spirit and light."

His disciples said to him, "Master, tell us about the one called the Human, so that we also might have a precise understanding of his glory."

The perfect Savior said, "Whoever has ears to hear should hear. The first-conceiving father is called Adam, eye of light, because he came from shining light, and his holy angels, ineffable and with no shadow, constantly rejoice in their reflections, received from their father. The entire kingdom of the Child of Humanity, who is called the Son of God, is full of ineffable joy, with no shadow, and eternal praise. They rejoice over his imperishable [106] glory, which until now has never been heard and never been revealed in the aeons that came later and their worlds.

"I have come from the self-conceived one and the first infinite light, to reveal everything to you."

The Savior, Pistis Sophia, and Other Powers Appear
(106,9–108,16)

His disciples said again, "Tell us exactly how they have come down from what is invisible, from the immortal realm to the world of mortality."

The perfect Savior said, "The Child, the Son of Humanity, came together with his companion Sophia and disclosed a bright androgynous light. The male name of the light is Savior, the one who conceives all, and the female name is all-conceiving Sophia. Some call her Pistis, Faith.[28]

"All who come into the world, like [107] a droplet from the light, are sent by him into the world of the ruler of the universe,[29] to be guarded by him. The fetter of his forgetfulness[30] has kept the light bound, by the will of Sophia, so that the reality of the circumstance might be <revealed> through the light to the whole impoverished world, on account of the arrogance and blindness of the ruler of the universe and the name of ignorance he was given.

"I have come from the places above by the will of the bright light, and I have escaped from that fetter. I have smashed the work of those who are robbers. I have awakened the droplet sent from Sophia, that it might produce an abundance of fruit through me, and be made perfect and never again be defective. Then the droplet from the light may be <made whole>[31] through me, the great Savior, and its glory may be revealed, and Sophia also may be vindicated of what

---

28. On Pistis Sophia, cf. the Nature of the Rulers, On the Origin of the World, and the text entitled Pistis Sophia. 29. The text reads pantokratōr, here and below. 30. On this phrase, cf. Gospel of Mary 17. 31. Here the text of the Codex III is emended to read eunanoh<b>f, on the basis of the BG 8502 version. This Coptic word may also be translated, more literally, "joined" or "integrated," or, by extension, "liberated."

was defective, and her [108] children may never again be defective, but may attain glory and honor and go up to their Father and know the words of the light of maleness.

"You in turn were sent by the Son, who was sent that you might receive light and escape the forgetfulness of the authorities. In this way the unclean sexual rubbing from the ferocious fire of the flesh of the authorities may never again come to expression through you. Trample on their evil intentions."

Eternal Realms and Aeons Appear (108,16–111,11)

Then Thomas said to [him], "Master, Savior, how many realms are there of those who surpass the heavens?"

The perfect Savior said, "I congratulate you for asking about the exalted realms, for your roots are in infinite places. [107][32] When those whom I have already discussed were revealed, the self-conceiving Father moved to create twelve eternal realms to serve twelve angels. They all are perfect and good. This is the way in which the defect of femaleness became apparent."[33]

They said to him, "How many realms are there for the immortals, starting with those that are infinite?"

The perfect Savior said, "Whoever has ears to hear should [108] hear. The first eternal realm is that of the Child of Humanity, who is called the first to conceive, and the Savior, who has appeared. The second eternal realm is that of the Human called Adam, eye of light. What holds these is the realm over which there is no kingdom, the realm of the eternal infinite God, the self-conceived aeon of the aeons in it, the eternal aeon of the immortals, whom I have already described. [109] This is the aeon above the seventh realm that appeared from Sophia, which is the first realm.

"The immortal Human has revealed realms, powers, and kingdoms, and has given authority to all who come through him, that they might do what they want until the last things above chaos. They came together with each other and disclosed every majesty, even from spirit, and a multitude of lights, glorious and without number. The first, the second, and the third eternal realms [110] were named in the beginning. The first is called unity and rest. Each has its own name, and the third realm was called assembly, after the great multitude that appeared.[34] A multitude of beings revealed themselves in One. Because the many [111] gather and experience unity, <they> are called the assembly, from the assembly that surpasses heaven. [111][35] We call them the assembly of the eighth realm. It appeared in an androgynous form and was given male and female names. The male part was called the assembly and the female part life, to indicate that from a female came life for all the realms.

---

32. Pp. 109–10 are missing from the Codex III version. The following pages are added from BG 8502, 107–11. **33.** The defect of femaleness refers to the fallen state of the world below, often described as being due to Sophia's mistake. The story of Sophia is recounted in

Wisdom of Jesus Christ (BG 8502), 118–21. **34.** Several minor emendations of numbers and other features of the preceding sentences have been made on the basis of the text of *Eugnostos the Blessed.* **35.** Here the Codex III version resumes.

The Names of the Eternal Realms All Come from Above
(111,11–112,19)

"All the names came from the original source. That is the one who united with thought, and at once powers appeared, called gods. From their wisdom the gods of gods revealed gods, and from their wisdom <the gods> revealed lords, and from their thoughts the lords of lords revealed lords, and from their power the lords revealed archangels, and from their words the archangels revealed angels, [112] and from them came ideas, with structure and form and names for all the aeons and their worlds.

"The immortals whom I have described, all of them, have authority from the immortal Human, who is called silence, because by reflecting without speaking the entire majesty of silence[36] was perfected. For the imperishable beings had authority, and each created a great kingdom in the eighth realm, and thrones and temples and firmaments for their own majesties. All these came to be by the will of the Mother of all."

The Eternal Realms Are Completed
(112,19–114,8)

Then the holy apostles said to him, "Master, Savior, tell us about those who are in the eternal realms, for we must ask about them."

The perfect [113] Savior said, "Whatever you ask about I shall tell you. These beings created hosts of angels, myriads without number, to serve and glorify them. They created virgin spirits, ineffable and unchangeable lights, and they are free of sickness and weakness. There is will, and they come to be at once.[37]

"Thus the eternal realms were completed, quickly, with the heavens and firmaments, in the glory of the immortal Human and his companion Sophia. This is where every realm and the world and those that were to follow got their ideas for their creation of patterns in the heavens of chaos and their worlds. All natures, beginning with the revelation of chaos, are in the light that shines with no shadow but with indescribable joy and unspeakable praise. They continue to rejoice over their unfading glory [114] and immeasurable rest, which cannot be described among all the realms that came to be later and all their powers. I have said all this to you so that you might shine in light even more brightly than these."

---

36. Here the Codex III version reads "her" (Sophia or silence) and the BG 8502 version "him" (the Human). In the *Wisdom of Jesus Christ* silence is an epithet of the immortal Human; in *Eugnostos the Blessed* silence is an epithet of the companion of the immortal Human, Sophia, who has disappeared from this section in the *Wisdom of Jesus Christ*. Hence the problem—which the BG 8502 version resolves with masculine pronouns. 37. This clause is added from the BG 8502 version. On the whole paragraph, cf. *Gospel of Judas* 49–50.

The Story of Sophia and Yaldabaoth
(III 114,8–BG 8502 119,16)

Mary said to him, "Holy master, where did your disciples come from, where are they going, and what should they do here?"[38]

The perfect Savior said to them, "I want you to know that Sophia, the Mother of all and the companion, desired all by herself to bring these creatures into being without her male companion. By the will of the Father of all, that his unimaginable goodness might be released, he created a curtain between the immortals and those who were to come later, so that this might follow [118][39] every realm and chaos, that what is defective from the female might appear, and error might contend with her.[40] These constituted [119] the curtain of the spirit.[41]

"From the eternal realms above the emanations of light, as I said before, a droplet from light and spirit came down to the lower regions of the ruler of the universe, in chaos, so that the forms they shaped might appear from that droplet. This is judgment against the chief creator,[42] called Yaldabaoth.[43]

The Story of Earthly Adam (BG 8502 119,17–121,13)

"That droplet revealed the forms they shaped, through breath, as a [120] living soul. This was withered and asleep in the ignorance of the soul. When this being was warmed by the breath of the bright light of the male, he formulated a thought, and names were given to everything in the world of chaos, through the immortal one, when breath blew into him.[44] This happened by the will of Mother Sophia, so that the immortal Human might reassemble [121] the garments there as judgment against those who are robbers. Then <he> welcomed the breath that was blown, but he was like soul and could not assume that power until the number of chaos and the time set by the great angel could be complete.[45]

The Restoration and Unification of Humanity
(BG 8502 121,13–III 119,8)

"I have taught you about the immortal Human, and I have freed him from the fetters of the robbers. I have broken the gates of [122] those without pity, right in

---

38. The story of Sophia, Yaldabaoth, Adam, and the restoration of humanity in the *Wisdom of Jesus Christ* expands upon the account in *Eugnostos the Blessed*. 39. Pp. 115–16 are missing in the Codex III version. The following pages are added from BG 8502, 118–22. 40. On the nature of error, sometimes personified, cf. the *Gospel of Truth*. 41. A curtain or veil also separates the realm of the divine from the world below in other Gnostic texts, e.g., Valentinian texts. 42. The text reads *arkhigenetōr*, here and below. 43. On the story of Sophia and Yaldabaoth, cf. *Secret Book of John* II, 9–14. 44. Cf. *Genesis* 2:7. 45. On the story of earthly Adam, cf. *Secret Book of John* II, 14–25.

front of them. I have humiliated their evil intentions, and they all have been put to shame and have emerged from their ignorance.[46]

"For this reason I have come here, that these may be united with spirit and breath, [117][47] and two may become one, as in the beginning.[48] Then you may produce an abundance of fruit and go up to the one who is from the beginning, in ineffable joy and glory and [honor and] grace of [the Father of all].

"Whoever knows [the Father in pure] knowledge [will depart] to the Father [and be at rest in] the unconceived [Father. Whoever knows him in a defective way] will depart [to what is defective] and experience the rest [that the eighth realm provides]. Let whoever knows the immortal [spirit] of light in silence, through reflection and agreement in truth, bring me signs of the invisible one, and such a person will become a light in the spirit of silence. Let whoever knows the Child of Humanity in knowledge and love bring me a sign [118] of the Child of Humanity, so that such a person may depart to the dwelling places with those in the eighth realm.

"Look, I have revealed to you the name of the perfect one, all the will of the mother of the holy angels, in order that the male [multitude] may be made complete here.[49] Then there [may appear, in the realms, the infinite beings and] those who [have come to be in the] untraceable [wealth of the great] invisible [Spirit,[50] and] all may receive from his goodness, even the wealth [of their rest] with no [kingdom over it].

"I have come [from the first] who was sent to reveal to you the one who is from the beginning, because of the arrogance of the chief creator and his angels, for they claim to be gods. I have come to eradicate their blindness, that I might tell everyone about the God who is above all. [119]

"So trample on their graves, humiliate their wicked intentions, break their yoke, and raise up those who are mine. I have given you authority over everything as children of light, to trample on their power with your feet."

The Savior Departs from His Followers (119,8–18)

This is what the blessed Savior [said, and then he disappeared] from them. [All the disciples] remained in [great, ineffable joy] in [the spirit from] that day on. [And his disciples] began to preach the gospel of God, the eternal, imperishable Spirit. Amen.

The Wisdom of Jesus[51]

---

46. On the claims of the Savior, in first-person statements, cf. the hymn of the Savior in *Secret Book of John* II, 30–31. 47. Here the Codex III version resumes. 48. Cf., e.g., *Gospel of Thomas* 22; 106; *Gospel of Philip* 70. 49. On the defect of femaleness and the salvation of maleness in the *Wisdom of Jesus Christ*, cf. *Gospel of Thomas* 114 and the notes. 50. Such Sethian texts as the *Secret Book of John* refer to the transcendent deity as the Great Invisible Spirit. 51. The Codex IV version concludes with the title "The Wisdom of Jesus Christ."

THE DIALOGUE OF
THE SAVIOR

NHC III,5

Introduced by Madeleine Scopello
Translated by Marvin Meyer

The *Dialogue of the Savior*, the fifth tractate of Nag Hammadi Codex III (120,1–147,23), is the only extant version of this text, which was originally composed in Greek. A number of lines on pages 127–32, 137–38, and 145–47 are poorly preserved, although the work of Stephen Emmel has allowed for a more substantial set of readings on pages 145–46.[1] The title appears at both the beginning and the end of the tractate. The Coptic manuscript includes several corrections made by the scribe, who added letters above the lines of text.

In its present form, the *Dialogue of the Savior* is a compilation of different sources that are intertwined and that thus contribute to the complexity of the document. Even if the tractate as a whole is called a "dialogue," the first part of the text (120,3–124,22) does not belong to this literary genre. The first section is a monologue the Savior delivers to his disciples, probably before leaving the world. The apparent timing of this monologue is of some interest, since many revelations of the Savior in Gnostic scriptures are said to have taken place after his resurrection.

The insertion of a prayer (121,3–122,1), which belongs to a later revision of this portion of the *Dialogue of the Savior*, divides the monologue into two parts. In the first part the Savior instructs his disciples about the theme of rest and the time of salvation. The Savior tells them, "Now the time has come, brothers and sisters, for us to leave our labor behind and stand at rest." He adds, "For whoever stands at rest will rest forever." These words imply that salvation has already come and a form of eschatology has been realized in the present life, a point of view common to several Gnostic currents of thought. The Savior also notes that he too has already come and opened the path for those who are chosen and alone (120,25–26;

---

1. Stephen Emmel, "A Fragment of Nag Hammadi Codex III in the Beinecke Library: Yale Inv. 784"; Stephen Emmel, ed., *Nag Hammadi Codex III,5*.

cf. *Gospel of Thomas* 49). Conversely, the second part of the monologue (122,1–124,22) refers to salvation yet to come at a future time, and the soul must still go through the archon's dreadful places after dissolution so as to attain the realm of truth.[2] We find here the well-known Gnostic theme of the archons, guardians of the spheres, trying to detain the soul in its ascent. The attitude the Savior recommends to the souls is that they neither fear the cosmic powers nor hesitate as they pass by. The prayer inserted between the two parts of the Savior's discourse is in tension with the monologue in that it indicates that the Son has already returned to the Father and the chosen have already been liberated from their bodies. Its terminology also shows that this part of the text was added by a redactor.

The actual dialogue of the *Dialogue of the Savior* begins at 124,23. The Savior addresses his disciples, but only three of them are individually named: Matthew, Judas (probably to be identified with Judas Thomas, the "twin" of the Lord, whose popularity was great in some Gnostic circles, especially in Syria, although Judas Iscariot is also a possibility), and Mary (Mary Magdalene), the two last disciples being among the most praised in Gnostic literature. Sometimes Matthew, Judas, or Mary raises questions, at other times the disciples as a whole do so. The questions and answers are generally short, especially at the beginning of the dialogue, but some answers are more fully developed by means of the insertion of additional materials: a fragment of a cosmogonic myth (129,20–131,16); a sapiential cosmological list (133,23–134 24); accounts of various actions (131,16–18; 132,23–24); and a description of an apocalyptic vision (135,4–136,5; 136,17–137,1).[3]

The *Dialogue of the Savior* is the only Nag Hammadi treatise to refer to the genre of dialogue in its title, even if this description does not apply to the entire text. Nevertheless, other dialogues are present in the Nag Hammadi library as well as in other Gnostic literature: they are typically revelatory dialogues in which the Savior communicates secret teachings to certain disciples through questions and answers. Among them are the *Secret Book of James*, the *Secret Book of John*, the *Gospel of Thomas*, the *Book of Thomas*, and, among Gnostic texts beyond the Nag Hammadi library, *Pistis Sophia*.[4] A difference can be noticed, however, between these works and the *Dialogue of the Savior*: in the *Dialogue of the Savior*, no reference is made to either the time when the dialogue occurred (whether before or after the Savior's resurrection) or where it took place.

Several traditional sayings of Jesus are included in the *Dialogue of the Savior*, and some of them recall sayings in the *Gospel of Thomas* and the *Gospel of John*.[5] One of the most noteworthy is a saying in the *Dialogue of the Savior* about seeking and finding (128,23–129,16), which brings to mind saying 2 of the *Gospel of Thomas*; another saying in the present text (143,3–5) recalls saying 1 of the same gospel.

---

2. Cf. Helmut Koester and Elaine H. Pagels, in Stephen Emmel, ed., *Nag Hammadi Codex III,5*; Pierre Létourneau, *Le Dialogue du Sauveur*.

3. Koester and Pagels, in *Nag Hammadi Codex III,5*; Létourneau, *Le Dialogue du Sauveur*.

4. See Pheme Perkins, *The Gnostic Dialogue*.

5. Koester and Pagels, in *Nag Hammadi Codex III,5*.

Several sources have contributed to the *Dialogue of the Savior* in its current form in the Nag Hammadi library. These sources do not belong to the same period of time, but "to various generations of Christianity."[6] The most ancient source is the dialogue itself, which may have been written before the end of the first century (as it is suggested by the simple theological interpretation of some sayings in comparison with the exegesis in the *Gospel of John*).[7] Eventually the tractate was revised by its final redactor, and it is in this form that we now know it. The original Greek text, which was later translated into Coptic, could have been composed during the second century, according to Helmut Koester and Elaine H. Pagels,[8] or between 250 and 275, according to Pierre Létourneau.[9]

Is the *Dialogue of the Savior* a Gnostic text? The question remains open, because on the one hand the treatise is characterized by typical Gnostic themes, but on the other hand it offers points of view that are shared with orthodox theology and doctrine. A balanced perspective of the tractate is given by Pierre Létourneau, who concludes that the *Dialogue of the Savior* belongs to a world of thought between what is Gnostic and what is orthodox.[10]

Some typical Gnostic ideas are lacking in the *Dialogue of the Savior*. Its author does not share, for instance, a pessimistic Gnostic opinion about the world based on the presence of a second, inferior deity. On the contrary, the world is presented as the creation of the Father through the word, or Logos (129,20–130,23). It is maintained that in creation the Father gathered together the water (cf. *Genesis* 1:9–10), and the word came forth and was told to fertilize the earth (a Stoic interpretation of *Genesis*, which may be compared with *Poimandres* 5–14).[11] Nevertheless, the world shows features of deficiency (139,13–20). It may also be observed that the myth of Sophia, a common feature of the Gnostic history of creation, does not appear in the tractate.

Some themes with Gnostic overtones do appear in the *Dialogue of the Savior*. One such theme is that of the bridal chamber (138,14–20), which is intertwined with another Gnostic motif, known from Valentinian traditions, namely, the garments of life (138,21–139,6) offered to the children of truth (143,12–144,21), who in turn are contrasted with the children of oblivion. A related Gnostic theme is the connection between the chosen or elect on earth and their partners (*syzygoi*) in heaven (125,10–16). It is not their destiny to perish but to recover their original androgynous oneness. To this set of Gnostic concepts we may add the theme of the archons placing obstacles in the way of the elect.

Another interesting point in the *Dialogue of the Savior* is the focus on the figure of Mary Magdalene, who is depicted by the Savior as "a woman who understood

---

6. Helmut Koester, in James M. Robinson, ed., *The Nag Hammadi Library in English*, 244.

7. Cf. Koester and Pagels, in James M. Robinson, ed., *The Nag Hammadi Library in English*, 244.

8. Koester and Pagels, in *Nag Hammadi Codex III,5*, 15–16.

9. Létourneau, *Le Dialogue du Sauveur*, 83.

10. Létourneau, *Le Dialogue du Sauveur*, 6.

11. Cf. Létourneau, *Le Dialogue du Sauveur*, 195–97.

everything" (139,11–13). Although this opinion is typical of Gnostic interpretation about the beloved disciple of Christ, the author does not make Mary Magdalene a symbol of secret knowledge, and in the tractate she does not come into conflict with the other disciples. Rather, she, along with the other disciples, learns to understand the teachings of the Savior by entering into a dialogue with him.

BIBLIOGRAPHY

April D. DeConick, "The *Dialogue of the Savior* and the Mystical Sayings of Jesus"; Stephen Emmel, "A Fragment of Nag Hammadi Codex III in the Beinecke Library: Yale Inv. 1784"; Stephen Emmel, ed., *Nag Hammadi Codex III,5*; Julian V. Hills, "The Three 'Matthean' Aphorisms in the *Dialogue of the Savior* 53"; Helmut Koester, *Ancient Christian Gospels*; Helmut Koester and Elaine H. Pagels, "Introduction," in Stephen Emmel, ed., *Nag Hammadi Codex III,5*, 1–17; "Report on the *Dialogue of the Savior* (CG III,5)"; Pierre Létourneau, *Le Dialogue du Sauveur*; Robert J. Miller, ed., *The Complete Gospels*, 343–56 (Julian V. Hills); Pheme Perkins, *The Gnostic Dialogue*; James M. Robinson, ed., *The Nag Hammadi Library in English*, 244–55 (Stephen Emmel, Helmut Koester, and Elaine H. Pagels); Hans-Martin Schenke, Hans-Gebhard Bethge, and Ursula Ulrike Kaiser, eds., *Nag Hammadi Deutsch*, 1.381–97 (Silke Petersen and Hans-Gebhard Bethge).

The Dialogue of the Savior[1]

The Dialogue of the Savior

The Savior Teaches About Rest (120,1–121,3)

The Savior said to his disciples, "Now the time has come, brothers and sisters,[2] for us to leave our labor[3] behind and stand at rest,[4] for whoever stands at rest will rest forever. I say to you, always rise above . . . time . . . . [I say] to you, . . . [do not] be afraid of [those] . . . you. I [say to you], anger is frightening, [and whoever] stirs up anger is a [frightening person]. But since you have [been able to endure], it may come from [you] . . . .

"People received these words about anger[5] with fear and trembling. Anger established rulers over them, for no one escapes anger. But when I came, I opened a path and taught people about the way of passage for those who are chosen and alone,[6] **[121]** who have known the Father and have believed the truth. And you offered praise.

Giving Praise to the Father (121,3–122,1)

"Now, when you offer praise, do so in this way:

Hear us, Father,
as you have heard your only Son
and have received him to yourself.[7]

---

1. Coptic text: NHC III,5: 120,1–147,23; Yale inv. 1784. Editions: *The Facsimile Edition of the Nag Hammadi Codices: Codex III*, 114–41; Stephen Emmel, ed., *Nag Hammadi Codex III,5*; Pierre Létourneau, *Le Dialogue du Sauveur*; Hans-Martin Schenke, Hans-Gebhard Bethge, and Ursula Ulrike Kaiser, eds., *Nag Hammadi Deutsch*, 1.381–97 (Silke Petersen and Hans-Gebhard Bethge). A substantial number of textual restorations have been incorporated here, and many of them have come from these editions, particularly from *Nag Hammadi Deutsch* and also from *Le Dialogue du Sauveur*. More speculative restorations are given in the notes. 2. Lit., "brothers." Here in the *Dialogue of the Savior* the circle of disciples includes Judas (probably Judas Thomas, or possibly Judas Iscariot—cf. the *Gospel of Judas*), Matthew (cf. the disciple Matthew, or Matthias the replacement apostle according to Acts 1:23–26, or Mathaias the scribe of the *Book of Thomas*), and Mary (probably Mary of Magdala). 3. Or "suffering." Cf. *Gospel of Thomas* 58. 4. Cf. *Gospel of Thomas* 50; 90. 5. Here and below the text reads "it" and the translation follows *Nag Hammadi Deutsch* and reads "anger" for the sake of clarity. 6. Or "solitary." Here and below, cf. *Gospel of Thomas* 16:4; 49:1; 75. 7. Cf. *John* 16:23; *Letter of Peter to Philip* 133–34.

[You have] given him rest from many [labors].
Your power is [invincible],
[because] your armaments are [invincible],
. . . light . . . alive . . . inaccessible . . . [alive].
The [true] word[8] [has brought] repentance for life,
[and this has come] from you.
You are the thought and supreme serenity
of those who are alone.[9]
Again, hear us
as you have heard your chosen.
Through your sacrifice the chosen will enter.
Through their good works they have freed their souls
from blind bodily limbs,
so that they may come to be [122] forever.
Amen.

Overcoming the Power of Darkness (122,1–124,22)

"I shall teach you. At the time of destruction the first power of darkness will come
upon you. Do not be afraid and say, 'Look, the time has come.' But when you see
a single staff . . . understand that . . . from some such thing . . . and the rulers . . .
come upon you . . . . In truth, fear is the power [of darkness]. So if you are afraid of
what is about to come upon you, it will overwhelm you, and not one among them
will spare you or show you mercy. Rather, look at [what is] within, since you have
mastered every word on earth. This [123] [will] take you up to a [place] where
there is no dominion [and no] tyrant. When you . . . you will see those . . . and you
will also [hear them. I] tell you, reflection . . . . Reflection is . . . [where] truth [is]
. . . but they . . . and you . . . truth. This [is . . . in] living [mind]. Therefore . . . and
your joy . . . in order that . . . your souls . . . lest the word . . . which they raised . . .
and they could not [understand] it . . . . Make what is [inside] you and what is
[outside you a single one].[10] To be sure, the place [124] of crossing is frightening
in [your] sight, but without hesitation pass by.[11] Its depth is great, [its] height [is]
staggering. [Be of a single mind] . . . and the fire . . . dew drops . . . all powers . . .
you. They will . . . and [all] powers . . . they . . . in front. I tell [you], . . . the soul . . .
becomes . . . in each one . . . you are . . . and that . . . sleep not . . . the children . . .
and you . . . you . . . ."

---

8. Logos. 9. Or "solitary." 10. Cf. *Gospel of Thomas*
3:1–3; 22:4–7; 89. 11. On the phrase "pass by," cf.
Gospel of Thomas 42.

The Savior and His Disciples Discuss the Inner Life
(124,23–126,5)

Matthew[12] said, "How . . . ?" [125]

The Savior said, "[If you do not keep] what is within you [in order, your work] will remain, but you [will not]."

Judas[13] [said], "Master,[14] [I want to understand all] the works of the souls [that are in] these little ones. When . . . , where will they be? . . . the spirit . . . ?"

The master [said, ". . . receive] them. They do not die and are not destroyed, because they have known [their] companions and the one who will receive them. For truth seeks the wise and the righteous."

The Savior [said], "The lamp [of the] body is the mind. As long as [what is within] you is kept in order—that is, [the soul][15]—your bodies are [enlightened]. As long as your hearts are dark, your light, which you [126] expect, [is far from you].[16] I have called [you to myself], since I am about to depart, so that [you may receive] my word among [yourselves. Look], I am sending it to [you]."[17]

Who Seeks, Who Reveals? (126,5–127,19)

His disciples [said, "Master], who seeks and [who] reveals?"

[The master] said [to them], "One who seeks [also] reveals."

Matthew [said to him again, "Master], when I [listen to you] and I speak, who is it who [speaks and] who listens?"

The [master] said, "One who speaks also [listens], and one who can see also reveals."

Mary[18] said, "Master, look, [while I] wear a body, where do my tears come from, where does my laughter come from?"

The master said, "[The body] weeps because of its works [and what] remains to be done. The mind laughs [because of [127] the fruits[19] of] the spirit. Whoever does not [stand] in darkness will [not] be able to see [the light].[20] I tell you, [what has no] light is darkness, [and whoever does not] stand in [darkness will] not [be able] to see the light. [The children of] falsehood, however, were taken out . . . . You will put on light, and [so you will live] forever . . . . [If] . . . ,[21] then [all] the powers above and below will treat you harshly. In that place [there will] be weeping and [gnashing] of teeth over the end of all."

---

12. Cf. the disciple Matthew, or Matthias the replacement apostle according to Acts 1:23–26, or Mathaias the scribe of the *Book of Thomas*. 13. Judas Thomas or Judas Iscariot. Cf. the *Gospel of Thomas* and the *Gospel of Judas*. 14. Or "Lord," here and below. 15. Or "[your nature]," "[your belief]." 16. Cf. *Gospel of Thomas* 24. 17. Cf. *John* 16:5–7. 18. Probably Mary of Magdala. 19. Or restore to read "[the strength]." On the fruits of the spirit, cf. *Galatians* 5:22–23. 20. It is also possible to restore this sentence without the negative, but cf. a few lines below, and *Dialogue of the Savior* 133. 21. Here Petersen and Bethge, in *Nag Hammadi Deutsch*, 1.389, restore to read, "[If you resemble] one [who never existed]."

The Creation of the World (127,19–128,23)

Judas said, "Tell [us], master, what [existed] before [heaven and] earth came into being?"[22]

The master said, "There was darkness and water, and [128] spirit upon [water].[23] And I tell you [the truth], look, what you seek and inquire about [is] within you, and it [has] the power and mystery [of the] spirit, for [it is] from [the spirit].[24] Wickedness entered [in order to destroy] the mind, [forever]. Look . . . ."[25]

[Matthew] said,[26] "Master, tell us, where is [the soul] established and where does the true [mind] dwell?"

The master [said], "The fire of the spirit came into existence [between] the two, and so there came to be [spirit][27] and the true mind within them. [If] someone establishes the soul on high, then [the person will] be exalted."

Seek, Find, Rejoice (128,23–129,19)

Matthew asked him [129], "[Isn't . . .[28] necessary], when it is understood [in the true sense]?"[29]

The master [said, ". . . is] more useful than your [work. Remove] from yourselves [what can] pursue you and everything [in] your hearts. For as your hearts . . . ,[30] so [will you find] a way to overcome the powers above and below. And I say to you, let one [who has] power renounce [it and] repent,[31] and let one who [knows] seek and find and rejoice."[32]

Judas said, "Look, [I] see that all things are [just] like signs over [the earth], and that is why they have come to be in this way."

The Emergence of the Word (129,20–131,18)

The master [said], "When the Father established the world, he [collected] some of its water, and the word[33] came from it. [130] It[34] experienced many [troubles, but] it was more exalted than the path [of the stars] around the entire earth."[35]

[He continued],[36] "The water collected [above] is beyond the stars, and [beyond] the water <is> a great fire encircling them like a wall. Periods of time

---

22. Cf. Genesis 1:1. 23. Cf. Genesis 1:2. 24. Lit., "from [it]." 25. Here Petersen and Bethge, in Nag Hammadi Deutsch, 1.390, restore to read "[wickedness thus has no existence]." 26. Or "[Judas] said [to him]." 27. Or "[movement]," "[mind]." 28. Here and below Petersen and Bethge, in Nag Hammadi Deutsch, 1.390, restore to read "circumcision." 29. Here and below the restoration is tentative. If the saying discusses physical circumcision and spiritual circumcision, then cf. Gospel of Thomas 53; Romans 2:25–29. 30. Perhaps read "[are circumcised]." 31. Cf. Gospel of Thomas 81:2. 32. Cf.

Gospel of Thomas 2. 33. Logos, here and below. The text reflects upon the primal water of creation and the place of the word in the creative process, according to Genesis 1. Apparently the water is both below and above, as in much of ancient cosmological thought. 34. Or "He"—i.e., the word—here and below. 35. These are the constellations and stars that rule over what happens on the earth, according to astronomical and astrological theory. 36. The restoration is tentative. This may simply be a continuation of the discussion in the previous section.

[began to be measured] once many of the beings [that] were within had separated from the rest.

"When the [word] was established, he looked [down]. The Father said to him, 'Go, [send[37] something] from yourself, so that [the earth] may not be in want from generation to [generation and] from age to age.'

"So [he] sent[38] from himself fountains of milk, fountains of honey, oil, wine, and fine fruit and delicious flavors and sound roots, [so that] the earth might not be deficient from generation [to] generation and from age to age.

"The word is above . . . [131] stood [and showed] his beauty . . . . And outside [was a great light], brighter [than] the one like it,[39] for that one rules over [all] the realms above and below. [Light was] taken from the fire and dispersed in the [firmament][40] above and below. Those over the heaven above and the earth below depend upon them. Everything is dependent upon them."

When Judas heard this, he bowed down, fell on his knees,[41] and praised the master.

The Savior and His Disciples Discuss the Place of Life
(131,19–132,19)

Mary asked her brothers, "Where are you going to store [these] questions you ask of the Son of [Humanity]?"[42]

The master [said] to her, "Sister, [no one] can ask about these things [except] someone who has a place [132] to store them in the heart. And such a person can leave [the world] and enter the place [of life], and will not be held back in this world of poverty."[43]

Matthew said, "Master, I want [to see] that place of life, [where] there is no wickedness but only pure light."

The master replied, "Brother Matthew, you will not be able to see it as [long as you] wear flesh."

Matthew said, "Master, [if I] cannot see it, at least let me understand it."

The master said, "Everyone who has known oneself[44] has seen oneself. Everything that person is given to do that person does. So such a person has come to [resemble] that place[45] in goodness."[46]

How Does an Earthquake Shake? (132,19–133,21)

Judas answered and said, "Tell me, master, how does an [earthquake] shake when it shakes the earth?"

---

37. Or "cast," "emit." 38. Or "cast," "emitted." 39. Probably the sun. 40. I.e., the dome of the sky around the earth, on which the sun, moon, and stars are set. Cf. *Genesis* 1:6–8. 41. Or "worshiped." 42. Or "Son of Man," here and below. 43. Cf. *Gospel of Thomas* 3:5.

44. Cf. the Delphic maxim "Know yourself"; *Gospel of Thomas* 3:4–5. 45. Lit., "it." This refers to the place of life under discussion in the context. 46. Lit., "his goodness" or "its goodness"—the goodness of that person or the goodness of that place.

The master picked up a stone and held it in his hand. [He [133] said to him, "What] am I holding in my hand?"

He answered, "[It is] a stone."

He said to them, "What supports the [earth] is also what supports heaven. When a word comes from the Majesty, it will go to what supports heaven and earth. The earth does not move. If it moved, it would collapse. But it does not, so that the first word might not fail. The word established the world and dwelled in it and smelled the fragrance from it.[47] I make known to you, all you children of humanity, all [the things] that do not move, for you are from that place. You live in the hearts of those who speak out in joy and truth. If the word comes from the Father's body, among people, and they do not receive it, it will return back to its place."

Coming to Understanding (133,21–134,24)

"Whoever does [not] know the work of perfection does not know anything.

"One who does not stand in the darkness cannot see the [134] light.

"One who does not [understand] how fire came to be will burn in it, not knowing its origin.[48]

"One who does not first understand water knows nothing. For what use is there for such a person to be baptized in it?

"One who does not understand how the wind that blows came to be will blow away with it.[49]

"One who does not understand how the body that a person wears came to be will perish with it.

"How will someone who does not know the Son know the [Father]?

"All things are hidden from one who does not know the root of all things.

"Whoever does not know the root of wickedness is no stranger to it.

"Those who do not understand how they came will not understand how they will go, and they are no strangers to this world, which will [exalt itself] and be humbled."

Judas, Matthew, and Mary Have an Apocalyptic Vision (134,24–137,3)

He [took] Judas, Matthew, and Mary [135] [to show them the final] consummation of heaven and earth, and when he placed his [hand] on them, they hoped they might [see] it. Judas gazed up and saw a region of great height, and he saw the region of the abyss below.

---

47. It is also possible to translate this sentence as follows: "The word established the world, and the world came to be through the word, and the world received fragrance from the word." The Coptic text employs ambiguous pronouns throughout the sentence. 48. Lit., "root." 49. On the wind blowing, cf. spirit. On the entire passage, cf. Genesis 1:2.

Judas said to Matthew, "Brother, who can ascend to such a height or descend to the abyss below? For there is great fire there, and great terror."

At that moment a word[50] issued from the height. As Judas was standing there, he saw how the word came [down].

He asked the word, "Why have you come down?"

The Son of Humanity greeted them and said to them, "A seed from a power was deficient, and it descended to the earth's abyss. The Majesty remembered [it] and sent the [word to] it. The word brought the seed up into [the presence] of the Majesty, so that [136] the first word might not be lost."[51]

[His] disciples marveled at everything he told them, and they accepted all of it in faith. And they understood that it was no longer necessary to keep an eye on evil.

Then he said to his disciples, "Didn't I tell you that, like a visible flash of thunder and lightning, what is good will be taken up to the light?"

All his disciples praised him and said, "Master, before you appeared here, who was there to praise you, for all praises are because of you? Or who was there to bless [you], for all blessing comes from you?"

As they were standing there, he saw two spirits bringing a single soul with them, and there was a great flash of lightning. A word came from the Son of Humanity, saying, "Give them their garments," and the small became like the great. They were [like] those who were received up; [137] [there was no distinction] among them.[52]

The [words] he [spoke convinced the] disciples.

Mary Asks About the Vision (137,3–138,2)

Mary [said to him, "Look, I] see the evil [that affects] people from the start, when they dwell with each other."

The master said [to her], "When you see them, [you understand] a great deal; they will [not stay there]. But when you see the one who exists eternally, that is the great vision."

They all said to him, "Explain it to us."

He said to them, "How do you wish to see it, [in] a passing vision or in an eternal vision?"

He went on to say, "Do your best to save what can come after [me], and seek it and speak through it, so that whatever you seek may be in harmony with you. For I [say] to you, truly the living God [is] in you, [138] [as you also are] in God."[53]

---

50. Logos. On the role of the word or logos, and Jesus as the incarnate word, cf. *John* 1, earlier passages in the *Dialogue of the Savior*, and other Gnostic texts. In the *Gospel of John*, as here, the word descends from the realm above, comes to this world below, and acts in a revelatory manner. 51. These references to seed, power, and deficiency are typical in Gnostic texts. 52. On garments clothing the soul, and on putting on perfect humanity as a garment, cf. *Gospel of Mary* 15; 18. On garments of light and life given to those who enter the bridal chamber, cf. *Dialogue of the Savior* 138–39. 53. For similarly mystical statements, cf. *Gospel of Thomas* 77; 108.

Judas Asks About the Rulers of the World and the Garments (138,2–139,7)

Judas [said], "I really want [to learn everything]."

The [master] said to him, "The living [God does not] dwell [in this] entire [region] of deficiency."[54]

Judas [asked], "Who [will rule over us]?"

The master replied, "[Look, here are] all the things that exist [among] what remains. You [rule] over them."

Judas said, "But look, the rulers[55] are over us, so they will rule over us."

The master answered, "You will rule over them. When you remove jealousy from yourselves, you will clothe yourselves in light and enter the bridal chamber."[56]

Judas asked, "How will [our] garments be brought to us?"

The master answered, "There are some who will provide them for you and others who will receive [them], [139] and they [will give] you your garments. For who can reach that place? It is very [frightening]. But the garments of life were given to these people because they know the way they will go.[57] Indeed, it is even difficult for me to reach it."[58]

Mary Utters Words of Wisdom (139,8–13)

Mary said, "So,

> The wickedness of each day <is sufficient>.[59]
> Workers deserve their food.[60]
> Disciples resemble their teachers."[61]

She spoke this utterance as a woman who understood everything.[62]

The Disciples Ask About Fullness and Deficiency, Life and Death (139,13–141,12)

The disciples asked him, "What is fullness and what is deficiency?"

He answered them, "You are from fullness, and you are in a place of deficiency. And look, his light has poured down on me."

---

54. The region of deficiency is this world below, where the light is obscured in darkness. 55. Or "archons," here and below. 56. On the rulers, or archons, who govern this world, cf. 1 Corinthians 6:3. On the bridal chamber, cf. the *Gospel of Philip*; *Gospel of Thomas* 75. 57. On the garments of the soul and the garments of light and life, cf. *Dialogue of the Savior* 136–137; *Gospel of Mary* 15; 18. 58. Cf. *Dialogue of the Savior* 145. 59. Cf. *Matthew* 6:34. 60. Cf. *Matthew* 10:10 (Q); *Luke* 10:7 (Q); 1 *Timothy* 5:18. 61. Cf. *Matthew* 10:25. If this third saying is emended by adding a negation ("Disciples do <not> resemble their teachers"; cf. Petersen and Bethge, in *Nag Hammadi Deutsch*, 1.394), then cf. *John* 13:16. Here in the *Dialogue of the Savior* it is Mary who utters these three sayings of wisdom. 62. Or "who understood completely."

Matthew asked, "Tell me, master, how the dead die and how the living live." [140] The master said, "[You have] asked me about a [true] saying that eye has not seen, nor have I heard it, except from you.[63] But I say to you, when what moves a person slips away, that person will be called dead, and when what is living leaves what is dead, it will be called alive."

Judas asked, "So why, really, do some <die> and some live?"

The master said, "Whatever is from truth does not die. Whatever is from woman dies."[64]

Mary asked, "Tell me, master, why have I come to this place, to gain or to lose?"[65]

The master replied, "You show the abundance of the one who reveals."

Mary asked him, "Master, then is there a place that is abandoned or without truth?"

The master said, "The place where I am not."

Mary said, "Master, you are awesome and marvelous, [141] and [like a devouring fire] to those who do not know [you]."

Matthew asked, "Why don't we go to our rest at once?"[66]

The master said, "When you leave these burdens behind."

Matthew asked, "How does the small unite with the great?"

The master said, "When you leave behind what cannot accompany you, then you will rest."[67]

Mary and the Other Disciples Discuss True Life with the Master (141,12–144,5)

Mary said, "I want to understand all things, [just as] they are."

The master said, "Whoever seeks life, this is their wealth. For the world's [rest] is false, and its gold and silver are deceptive."[68]

His disciples asked him, "What should we do for our work to be perfect?"

The master [said] to them, "Be ready in every circumstance. Blessed are they who have found [142] the [strife and have seen] the struggle with their eyes. They have not killed nor have [they] been killed, but they have emerged victorious."

Judas asked, "Tell me, master, what is the beginning of the way?"[69]

He said, "Love and goodness. If one of these had existed among the rulers, wickedness would never have come to be."

Matthew said, "Master, you have spoken of the end of the universe with no difficulty."

---

63. Cf. *Gospel of Thomas* 17; 1 *Corinthians* 2:9. 64. Cf. *Dialogue of the Savior* 144–45; *Gospel of the Egyptians*. 65. This place is the present world of deficiency and mortality. 66. Going to one's rest at once means dying now, so that this may be a question about why we do not experience the transformation from death to life now, or even why we do not commit suicide now. 67. Leaving the burden of the body behind and ascending to the fullness of the divine means attaining final rest. 68. Cf. *James* 5:3. 69. Cf. *John* 14:5.

The master said, "You have understood all the things I said to you and you have accepted them in faith. If you know them, they are yours. If not, they are not yours."

They asked him, "To what place are we going?"

The master said, "Stand in the place you can reach."

Mary asked, "Is everything established in this way visible?"

The master said, "I have told you, the one who can see reveals."

His twelve disciples asked him, "Teacher, [with] [143] serenity . . . teach us . . . ."

The master said, "[If you have understood] everything I have [told you], you will [become immortal, for] you . . . everything."[70]

Mary said, "There is only one saying I shall [speak] to the master, about the mystery of truth. In this we stand and in this we appear to those who are worldly."

Judas said to Matthew, "We want to understand what sort of garments we are to be clothed with when we leave the corruption of the [flesh]."

The master said, "The rulers and the administrators[71] have garments that are given only for a while and do not last. But you, as children of truth, are not to clothe yourselves with these garments that last only for a while. Rather, I say to you, you will be blessed when you strip off your clothing. For it is no great thing [144] [to lay aside what is] external."[72]

. . .[73] said, "Do I speak and do I receive . . . ?"

The master said, "Yes, [one who receives] your Father in [a reflective way]."[74]

Mary Questions the Master About the Mustard Seed
(144,5–146,20)

Mary asked, "[Of what] kind is the mustard seed?[75] Is it from heaven or from earth?"

The master said, "When the Father established the world for himself, he left many things with the Mother of all.[76] That is why he sows and works."[77]

Judas said, "You have told us this from the mind of truth. When we pray, how should we pray?"

The master said, "Pray in the place where there is no woman."

Matthew says, "He tells us, 'Pray in the place where there is no woman,' which means, destroy the works of the female,[78] not because there is another form of birth[79] but because they should stop [giving birth]."

---

70. Here Petersen and Bethge, in *Nag Hammadi Deutsch*, 1.395, restore to read "you [will sustain] everything." 71. The archons and other powers of the cosmos. 72. On putting on the garment of the body and taking it off, cf. *Dialogue of the Savior* 136–39; *Gospel of Mary* 15; *Gospel of Thomas* 21:2–4; 37:2–3. 73. Possibly restore to read "Judas" (Petersen and Bethge, in *Nag Hammadi Deutsch*, 1.395). 74. The restoration is tentative; cf. Petersen and Bethge, in *Nag Hammadi Deutsch*, 1.395. 75. Cf. the parable of the mustard seed in *Gospel of Thomas* 20; *Matthew* 13:31–32 (Q); Luke 13:18–19 (Q); Mark 4:30–32. 76. Or "Mother of the All"—i.e. the Mother of the divine realm above. 77. Or "speaks and acts." Here the Father is God the Father, and the Mother may be Sophia (Wisdom) or another female manifestation of the divine. 78. Or "womanhood," here and below. 79. This statement seems to deny the possibility of being born again.

Mary said, "Will they never be destroyed?"

The master said, "[You] know they will perish [once again], [145] and [the works] of [the female here] will be [destroyed as well]."[80]

Judas said [to Matthew], "The works of the [female] will perish. [Then] the rulers will [call upon their realms], and we shall be ready for them."

The master said, "Will they see [you and will they] see those who receive you? Look, a true word[81] is coming from the Father to the abyss, silently, with a flash of lightning, and it is productive.[82] Do they see it or overcome it? No, you know more fully [the way] that [neither angel] nor authority [knows]. It is the way of the Father and the Son, for the two are one. And you will travel the [way] you have come to know. Even if the rulers become great, they will not be able to reach it. I tell you the [truth], it is even difficult for me to reach it."[83] [146]

[Mary] asked [the master], "If the works [are destroyed, what actually] destroys a work?"

[The master said], "You know that [when] I destroy [it, people] will go to their own places."

Judas said, "How is the spirit disclosed?"

The master said, "How [is] the sword [disclosed]?"

Judas said, "How is the light disclosed?"

The master said, "[It is disclosed] through itself eternally."

Judas asked, "Who forgives whose works? Do the works [forgive] the world or does the world forgive the works?"

The master [answered], "Who [knows]? For it is the responsibility of whoever has come to know the works to do the [will] of the Father.

Conclusion (146,20–147,23)

"As for you, work hard to rid yourselves of [anger] and jealousy, and strip yourselves of your [works], and do not [147] . . . . . .[84] reproach . . . . For I say to [you], . . . you receive . . . many . . . one who has sought, having [found true life]. This person will [attain rest and] live forever. I say to [you, watch yourselves], so that you may not lead [your] spirits and your souls into error."[85]

[The Dialogue] of the Savior

---

80. Cf. *Dialogue of the Savior* 140; *Gospel of the Egyptians; Gospel of Thomas* 114. 81. Coptic *šaje;* cf. logos. 82. Cf. *Dialogue of the Savior* 135. 83. Cf. *Dialogue of* the Savior 139. 84. About twelve lines missing or untranslatable. 85. The concluding restorations are tentative.

THE REVELATION OF PAUL

NHC V,2

Introduced by Madeleine Scopello
Translated by Marvin Meyer

A short tractate of seven pages, the *Revelation of Paul* is found in a codex largely made up of apocalyptic treatises (*First Revelation of James*, V,3; *Second Revelation of James*, V,4; *Revelation of Adam*, V,5). The title is preserved both at the beginning (partially in a lacuna) and at the end of the tractate. Originally written in Greek, the Coptic text is the only extant copy of the *Revelation of Paul*. The text is in a good condition, except for pages 17 and 18, where several lines are lacking.

Written in a style that might attract the attention of readers or hearers, the *Revelation of Paul* makes use of the literary framework of the ascension to heaven of a privileged person—here, the apostle Paul—and through the ascension, it is said, divine revelation (the first meaning of the term *apokalupsis*) is unveiled. This framework, a prevalent one in Jewish pseudepigrapha (e.g., *Ascension of Isaiah*, 1 and 2 *Enoch*, *Testament of Abraham*, *Apocalypse of Abraham*), was often adopted by Gnostic writers to illustrate a central theme in Gnostic thought: the return of the soul to God after a dangerous ascent through the heavenly spheres. The person being initiated into Gnostic thought, identified as the elect soul, is taken up during a dream or in ecstasy and ascends to heaven, guided by a divine being or an angel who helps and instructs him. The favorite places of origin for this mysterious trip are savage and remote—a desert or a mountain, for example. One of the Nag Hammadi texts that best illustrates the theme of the heavenly journey is the *Revelation of Paul*.

The *Revelation of Paul* opens with a meeting of Paul and a little child on a mountain of Jericho (an imaginary place: no mountain exists in Jericho).[1] The child (an epiphany of the resurrected Christ[2] or an allusion to the angelic figure

---

1. Jean-Marc Rosenstiehl and Michael Kaler, *L'Apocalypse de Paul*, 26–34.
2. William R. Murdock and George W. MacRae, in Douglas M. Parrott, ed., *Nag Hammadi Codices V, 2–5 and VI*.

of Enoch-Metatron, the "young one"?[3]) invites Paul to accompany him during a journey to the heavenly Jerusalem (18,1–20). Since Paul is the one blessed from his mother's womb (18,16–17; cf. 23,1–4),[4] he will be able to endure this ascension, which has already been planned by divine will. The child knows who Paul is, even if he asks him to pronounce his name (the name is the essence of a person), and he reveals to the apostle his true nature: he is the Spirit (18,7–22). He also discloses to Paul that the goal of the journey is to obtain knowledge: "Awaken your mind, Paul, and notice that this mountain where you are standing is the mountain of Jericho, so that you may come to know the things hidden in what is visible" (19,10–14). Looking up at the apostles (the chosen or elect spirits), whom only his eyes can distinguish (19,18–20), Paul is brought by the child up to the third heaven, and he passes beyond to the fourth, where he can contemplate his likeness upon the earth (19, 26–29). This suggests that only Paul's spirit has undertaken the heavenly trip; his body, his likeness, has been left in the world.

Paul's journey takes on, here and there, the character of a visit to the infernal realms: he assists in the judgment and punishment of a soul, led by angels at the gate of the fourth heaven and whipped by them (20,6–12). Once the soul is face-to-face with the gatekeeper or toll collector who guards this sphere, she complains and asks that witnesses be called (20,13–25). Three of them come forward and accuse the soul of misdeeds she committed during her life. At last, the soul is cast down in a body prepared in advance for her (20,25–21,22) — an allusion to the soul's transmigration from one body to another (cf. 19,5–7). Encouraged by his guiding Spirit, Paul ascends to the fifth heaven, where he meets his fellow apostles and has a vision of a great angel holding an iron staff (21,26–22,10). He also catches a glimpse of three angels competing with each other with whips in their hands and leading other souls to judgment. Having ascended to the next heavenly sphere, Paul contemplates a light shining down on the sixth heaven and orders the gatekeeper to open the gate for him and the guiding Spirit (22,17–24).

At the seventh heaven Paul beholds a magnificent scene: an old man, bathed in shining light and covered with a white garment, sits on a throne seven times brighter than the sun (22,25–30). This man asks three questions of Paul, and Paul is summoned by the Spirit to answer (23,1–7). In his first question, the old man asks where Paul is going, and Paul answers: "I am going to the place I came from" (23,8–10). In his second question, the old man asks, "Where are you from?" (23,11) and Paul replies in such a way as to show that he is going down to the realm of death (23,12–17). Under the counsel of the Spirit, Paul does not answer the third question ("How will you be able to escape me?"), but instead Paul gives a sign, so that the old man opens for him the doors of the eighth heavenly realm (23,19–28). Here Paul sees the twelve apostles and ascends with them to the ninth heaven, and then to the tenth, where he greets those who have become his fellow spirits (23,29–24, 8).

---

3. Rosenstiehl and Kaler, *L'Apocalypse de Paul*, 77.

4. This formula recalls *Galatians* 1:15.

The *Revelation of Paul* offers an allegorical interpretation of a tradition related in *Galatians* 1:11–17 about the revelation Paul received directly from Christ and additional trips to Jerusalem. In *Galatians* 1:17, Paul maintains that initially he did not go to Jerusalem to visit the apostles. Paul then states, in *Galatians* 1:18, that he "ascended" to Jerusalem three years later, looking for Cephas. Fourteen years later, Paul writes in *Galatians* 2:1–2, he "ascends" to Jerusalem again, with Barnabas and Titus, obeying a revelation, and there he meets the apostles. The geographical meaning of ascending to Jerusalem is changed into a symbolic one in the *Revelation of Paul*, strengthened by what is related in *2 Corinthians* 12:2–4. In *2 Corinthians* Paul makes mention of revelations and visions from the Lord and his ascent to the third heaven—whether in his body or outside his body, he cannot tell.

Traditions about Paul's journey to heaven were widespread in early Christianity, and they were described in a well-known text, the *Vision of Paul*.[5] Translated from Greek into several languages (a long version exists in Latin; a Coptic version is also extant), this document exerted a great influence on authors during the Middle Ages, and it was one of the sources of Dante's *Divine Comedy*. Nevertheless, there is no evidence of specific literary parallels between the *Vision of Paul* and the Coptic *Revelation of Paul*.

When mentioning a Gnostic tradition about Paul's privileged role and his ascension to heaven, the Christian heresiologists Irenaeus of Lyon (*Against Heresies* 2.30.7), Tertullian (*Prescription Against Heretics* 24.5–6), Hippolytus of Rome (*Refutation of All Heresies* 5.8), and Epiphanius of Salamis (*Panarion* 38.2.5) refer to a particular text, but whether this corresponds to what we know as the Coptic *Revelation of Paul* cannot be proved, since there are no quotations from a Gnostic text about Paul and his apocalyptic experience.

It is clear that the *Revelation of Paul* is heavily dependent on Jewish apocalyptic literature.[6] Nevertheless, the author reworks the traditional apocalyptic traditions by offering a Gnostic interpretation marked by a pessimistic way of looking at life and creation. For example, the person of the old man whom Paul encounters at the gate of the seventh heaven is drawn from *Daniel* 7:13 and is also recognized in *1 Enoch* 46–47, but this heavenly figure becomes, in the Gnostic treatise, the symbol of the demiurge, the lord of destiny, who tries to prevent the soul from returning to the place of her origin (cf. *Excerpt from the Perfect Discourse* 76,22). The scene of the punishment of the soul (cf. *Testament of Abraham* 10, long recension)[7] is portrayed with Gnostic literary motifs, and gatekeepers, toll collectors, and angels punish the soul. The depiction of the gatekeeper who guards this heavenly sphere brings to mind passages in the *First Revelation of James* (33,2–27) and Origen's *Against Celsus* (7.31.40) as well as Mandaean literature (*Left Ginza*

5. Theodore Silverstein, *Visio Sancti Pauli: The History of the Apocalypse in Latin Together with Nine Texts*; Silverstein and Hilhorst, *Apocalypse of Paul*.

6. Murdock and MacRae, in *Nag Hammadi Codices V, 2–5 and VI*; Rosenstiehl and Kaler, *L'Apocalypse de Paul*; Madeleine Scopello, "Contes apocalyptiques et apocalypses philosophiques dans la bibliothèque de Nag Hammadi."

7. Murdock and MacRae, in *Nag Hammadi Codices V, 2–5 and VI*.

3.70).[8] Angels torturing the soul are also described in the *Excerpt from the Perfect Discourse* (78,24–32), the *Book of Thomas* (141,36–39), and *Pistis Sophia*. The competing angels could come from Greek mythology.[9] The three questions of the old man recall the three questions about Gnostic destiny in *Excerpts from Theodotus* 78, transmitted by Clement of Alexandria: "Where have I come from? Where am I? Where shall I go?" Such questions are typical of the Gnostic quest for the true nature of the human self.

The *Revelation of Paul* was probably composed in the second century in Egypt by an author familiar with Jewish traditions[10] or reacting strongly against them.[11] It is conceivable that the author was connected to a Valentinian school of thought in which Paul was highly praised.[12]

BIBLIOGRAPHY

Alexander Böhlig and Pahor Labib, eds., *Koptisch-gnostische Apokalypsen aus Codex V von Nag Hammadi im Koptischen Museum zu Alt-Kairo*, 15–26; William R. Murdock, "The Apocalypse of Paul from Nag Hammadi"; Louis Painchaud, Marie-Pierre Bussières, and Michael Kaler, "The Coptic *Apocalypse of Paul*, Irenaeus' *Adv. Haer.* II.30.7, and the Second-Century Battle of Paul's Legacy"; Douglas M. Parrott, ed., *Nag Hammadi Codices V, 2–5 and VI*, 47–63 (William R. Murdock and George W. MacRae); Jean-Marc Rosenstiehl and Michael Kaler, *L'Apocalypse de Paul*; Hans-Martin Schenke, Hans-Gebhard Bethge, and Ursula Ulrike Kaiser, eds., *Nag Hammadi Deutsch*, 2.399–405 (Uwe-Karsten Plisch); Wilhelm Schneemelcher, ed., *New Testament Apocrypha*, 2.695–700 (Wolf-Peter Funk); Madeleine Scopello, "Contes apocalyptiques et apocalypses philosophiques dans la bibliothèque de Nag Hammadi"; Theodore Silverstein, *Visio Sancti Pauli: The History of the Apocalypse in Latin Together with Nine Texts*; Theodore Silverstein and Anthony Hilhorst, *Apocalypse of Paul*.

8. Scopello, "Contes apocalyptiques et apocalypses philosophiques."

9. Murdock and MacRae, in *Nag Hammadi Codices V, 2–5 and VI*.

10. Rosenstiehl and Kaler, *L'Apocalypse de Paul*; Scopello, "Contes apocalyptiques et apocalypses philosophiques."

11. Murdock and MacRae, in *Nag Hammadi Codices V, 2–5 and VI*.

12. Rosenstiehl and Kaler, *L'Apocalypse de Paul*.

The Revelation of Paul[1]

[The Revelation[2] of] Paul

A Little Child Gives a Revelation to Paul (17,19–19,20)

. . . . . .[3] [18] the road. [He[4] asked him, "Which] road [shall I take to go] up to [Jerusalem]?"[5]

The little child [answered and said], "First tell me your name, so that [then I may show] you the way."

[The little child] knew [very well who Paul was]. He only wished to engage him in conversation with these words, [that] he might find an excuse to speak with him.

The little child[6] continued and said, "I know who you are, Paul, for you have been blessed from your mother's womb.[7] Since I have [seen] that you were [going up to Jerusalem] to your fellow [apostles],[8] that is why [I] was [sent to you]. I am the [Spirit who is with] you. [Awaken your mind, Paul] . . . .[9] [19] For . . . all . . . among the [dominions and] these authorities and archangels and powers and the whole generation of demons. [Recognize][10] the one who fashions bodies for a seed of soul."[11]

After he finished saying these things, he went on and said to me, "Awaken your mind, Paul, and notice that this mountain where you are standing is the mountain of Jericho, so that you may come to know the things hidden in what is visible. You will meet the twelve apostles, for they are chosen[12] spirits, and they will welcome[13] you." He lifted up his eyes and saw them as they were welcoming him.

---

1. Coptic text: NHC V,2: 17,19–24,9. Editions: *The Facsimile Edition of the Nag Hammadi Codices: Codex V, 25–32*; Douglas M. Parrott, ed., *Nag Hammadi Codices V,2–5 and VI, 47–63* (William R. Murdock and George W. MacRae); Jean-Marc Rosenstiehl and Michael Kaler, *L'Apocalypse de Paul*; Hans-Martin Schenke, Hans-Gebhard Bethge, and Ursula Ulrike Kaiser, eds., *Nag Hammadi Deutsch*, 2.399–405 (Uwe-Karsten Plisch); 2. Or "Apocalypse," here and below. 3. About eight lines are mostly missing or untranslatable at the beginning of the text, with only a few letters that are legible. 4. Paul. 5. Either the earthly or the heavenly Jerusalem; here probably heavenly Jerusalem. 6. The little child is probably to be understood as Christ the revealer (cf. *Secret Book of John* II, 2; *Gospel of Judas* 33; *Acts of John* 88). In the text the child is identified as the Spirit. See the discussion in the introduction. 7. Cf. *Galatians* 1:15. 8. On Paul going up to Jerusalem, cf. *Galatians* 1:11–2:10; *Acts* 9; 15; 21. 9. About six lines missing. 10. The restoration is tentative; cf. Plisch, in *Nag Hammadi Deutsch*, 2.403. 11. Or restore to read "<prepared> for souls" (*euc<ar>c ⁱmpsukhē*). 12. Or "elect." 13. Or "greet," here and below.

Paul Ascends to the Fourth Heaven (19,20–21,22)

Then the holy [Spirit] who was speaking with [him] snatched him up on high to the third heaven,[14] and he went on further to the fourth [heaven].[15] The [holy] Spirit addressed him and said, "Look there and see what is like you on the earth." And he [looked] down and saw those [on] the earth. He stared[16] [and saw] those . . . . [Then [20] he] looked [down again and] saw the twelve apostles on his right and left in the created world, and the Spirit was walking ahead of them.

In the fourth heaven I[17] saw angels resembling gods in their rank, and they were bringing a soul from the land of the dead. The angels put the soul at the gate of the fourth heaven, and they were flogging her.[18]

The soul asked, "What sin did I commit in the world?"

The gatekeeper[19] in the fourth heaven answered and said, "It was wrong for you to commit all those lawless actions that are typical of the world of the dead."

The soul replied, "Bring witnesses and let them [tell] you in what body I committed lawless actions. [Do you want] to bring a book and [read from it]?"

Three witnesses came. The first said, "Wasn't I [in] the body? Around the second hour[20] I [came and] rose up against you, [21] until [you fell] into anger, rage, and envy."

The second said, "Wasn't I also in the world? Around the fifth hour[21] I entered, and I saw you and desired you. Look, now I accuse you of murders you committed."

The third said, "Didn't I come to you around the twelfth hour of the day, near sunset?[22] I brought you darkness, until you completed your sins."

When the soul heard these things, she looked down in dejection. Then she looked up again, but she was cast down. The soul that was cast down [entered] a body prepared [for her].[23] And look, the witnesses [against her] finished testifying.

The Fifth Heaven (21,22–22,12)

I [looked] up and [saw the] Spirit saying [to me], "Paul, step over here and come [by] me." As I [went], the gate opened, and I ascended to the fifth [heaven]. I saw my fellow apostles coming [with me] [22] and the Spirit accompanying us. And I saw a great angel in the fifth heaven, holding an iron staff in his hand, and three other angels were with him. I stared into their faces. They were competing with each other, their whips in their hands, driving souls to judgment.[24] But I went along with the Spirit, and the gate opened for me.

---

14. Cf. 2 *Corinthians* 12:2–4, where Paul describes his ascent to the third heaven. 15. On the ascent of the soul and the interrogation by the gatekeepers, cf. *Gospel of Thomas* 50; *First Revelation of James* 32–36; *Gospel of Mary* 15–17. 16. Perhaps Paul looks up at this point. 17. Paul now speaks in the first person. 18. The soul is often personified as a female in ancient lit-

erature. 19. Or lit., "toll collector" (*telōnēs*), here and below. 20. 8:00 a.m. 21. 11:00 a.m. 22. 6:00 p.m. 23. The soul is reincarnated in another body. 24. On the judgment and punishment of souls in the fourth and fifth heavens, cf. *Book of Thomas* 142–43; *Testament of Abraham* 10. On three angels whipping souls, cf. the furies in Greek mythology.

The Sixth Heaven (22,13–23)

Then we ascended to the sixth heaven. I saw my fellow apostles coming with me, and the holy Spirit was leading me before them. And I gazed up on high and saw a great light shining down on the sixth heaven.

I spoke to the gatekeeper in the sixth heaven and said, "[Open] for me and the [holy] Spirit [who goes] before [me]." The gatekeeper opened for [me].

The Seventh Heaven (22,23–23,28)

[Then we] ascended to the seventh [heaven. In the middle] of the light [I saw] an old man [in] white [clothing. His throne], which is in the seventh heaven, was [seven] times brighter than the sun.[25] **[23]** The old man spoke to [me] and said, "Where are you going, Paul, you blessed one, set apart from your mother's womb?"[26]

I looked at the Spirit, and he was nodding his head and saying to me, "Speak with him."

I replied to the old man, "I am going to the place I came from."

The old man responded to me, "Where are you from?"

I answered and said, "I am going down to the world of the dead in order to take captive the captivity that was taken in the Babylonian captivity."[27]

The old man said to me, "How will you be able to escape me? Look and see the dominions and authorities."

The Spirit said, "Give him the sign[28] you have, and [he will] open for you."

I gave [him] the sign, and he turned his face down toward his creation and his own authorities.

The Eighth, Ninth, and Tenth Heavens (23,29–24,9)

Then the <seventh>[29] heaven opened, and we ascended to the **[24]** eighth realm.[30] I saw the twelve apostles, and they welcomed me. We ascended to the ninth heaven, and I greeted all those in the ninth heaven.[31] We ascended to the tenth heaven, and I greeted my fellow spirits.

The Revelation of Paul

---

25. On the old man on his throne, cf. *Daniel* 7:13; 1 *Enoch* 46–47. Here the old man is a hostile figure, reminiscent of the demiurge or one of his lackeys, who attempts to hinder the ascent of Paul (and the Spirit) to the eighth realm. **26.** Cf. *Galatians* 1:15, again. **27.** Cf. *Ephesians* 4:8–10; *Psalm* 68:18. **28.** The sign is the soul's passport, the indication of the true identity of the person (here Paul) ascending to the heavens. **29.** Here the manuscript mistakenly reads "sixth" (*so*) and is corrected to read "<seventh>" (*<saŝfe>*). **30.** Or "the Eight," "the Ogdoad." **31.** On the eighth and ninth heavens, cf. the *Discourse on the Eighth and Ninth*. In the tenth heaven Paul meets his fellow spirits.

THE FIRST REVELATION
OF JAMES

NHC V,3; Codex Tchacos 2

Introduced and Translated by Wolf-Peter Funk

N ag Hammadi Codex V contains two works entitled simply "The Revelation of James." According to the order in which these two texts were
copied in this particular manuscript, modern scholarship has named them the
"first" and the "second" to distinguish them. These attributes do not suggest any
inherent order or sequence of events.

The James of these two texts is the brother of Jesus, traditionally nicknamed
"James the Just" (or "the Righteous," for his extensive practice of prayer, which
also plays a certain role in these two revelations), who after Peter's departure was
the sole leader of the early Christian community in Jerusalem. Both texts presuppose his being known as Jesus's brother, but while the second uses this relationship as a point of departure for far-reaching theological developments, the first
only mentions it in passing, even taking issue with its reality (James is the brother
of Jesus, but "not physically," 24,26).

The *First Revelation of James* takes the form of a series of dialogues between
Jesus and James, with only a few narrative passages intervening, notably one to
mark the point in time of Jesus's passion (30,11–15) and another, at the end of the
text, to relate the deliberations leading up to James's own condemnation and martyrdom (43,7–44,8). The topics covered by these conversations are fairly diverse,
and many of them are considered only briefly. Thus, for instance, at the beginning and the end of the work mention is made of the issue of maleness and
femaleness in relation to salvation; the first part also touches upon various questions of Gnostic theology and worldview, mostly in terse statements the understanding of which clearly presupposes prior knowledge of more elaborate
accounts of Gnostic thought.[1]

---

1. On maleness and femaleness in Nag Hammadi texts, cf. *Gospel of Thomas* 22; 114; and numerous other
tractates.

The center of the revelation in the *First Revelation of James* is doubtless found in the long speech that the risen Christ makes after explaining the meaning of his apparent suffering, to prepare James for his own destiny. The scene of his martyrdom and the suffering he has to face from the hands of the lynching people here in this world will immediately be transformed—with no mention being made of his "death"—into a kind of hearing or examination presumably situated in the lower heavens, where he is confronted by three "toll collectors" (later they are called "detainers"), who will try to stop him from continuing his rise into the higher regions. His deliverance from earthly sufferings is thus virtually indistinguishable from his deliverance from the hands of these powers. Successful performance in this latter case, however, can only be assured by his knowledge of the right answers to their questions, answers that will prove him to be of superior origin. Those questions and answers—presumably meant to be of crucial importance not only in James's ascent but also in any other Gnostic believer's ascent—are specified in detail in Jesus's discourse. The statements found in the answers are more or less identical with liturgical formulas recorded by Irenaeus of Lyon (*Against Heresies* 1.21.5) for the group of Valentinians that he calls Marcosians and later on by Epiphanius of Salamis (*Panarion* 36.3.1–6) for a group he calls Heracleonites. The hearing that Jesus in the *First Revelation of James* predicts will happen during James's ascension through the heavens therefore appears to be a dramatization of traditional liturgical formulas.

Apart from the information about the correct responses to be given in such a hearing, this discourse, in its narrative and dialogic context, also serves the purpose of comforting and strengthening a visibly shaken and fearful James. His faintheartedness is countered by Jesus on several occasions in the course of these dialogues, and both the explanation of Jesus's sufferings and the means he provides to James for overcoming his own sufferings are obviously meant to be an encouragement for martyrdom in general (a feature found only rarely in Gnostic writings).

Another equally peculiar and intriguing topic of the conversations between Jesus and James has to do with the chain of transmission that Jesus stipulates for his revelation. Obviously bypassing the twelve apostles, Jesus asks James to keep all these things to himself until he has a chance to communicate them to Addai, the person known as the legendary founder of Syrian Christianity.[2] With the ensuing further instructions for Addai, which involve a number of persons named explicitly, we are unfortunately more and more left hanging because of the increasing deterioration of the papyrus toward the center of the codex. It follows from indirect data provided by the passage just mentioned that, although the precise individual who authored this work is unknown, we can be reasonably sure that the work was composed in Syria, in some part of the Jewish Christian community exiled from Jerusalem. Taking into account the use of a Valentinian litur-

---

2. On Addai and Syrian Christianity, cf. the legend of Abgar of Edessa as discussed in Eusebius of Caesarea *Church History* 1.13.1–5.

gical formula, the composition of this text can hardly have taken place earlier than the second half of the second century, possibly somewhat later.

Another version of the *First Revelation of James* is preserved, under the title *James*, as the second tractate of Codex Tchacos. In the translation that follows, the conclusion of the Codex Tchacos version, which provides valuable new readings, and considerably more text is included in the notes.

The study of this other version has far-reaching consequences for the establishment of a more reliable and readable text of the *First Revelation of James*, but most of this work remains to be done. Since the new text has become accessible only recently, it is not possible to take the newly available information fully into account here. Updating is possible in a limited number of cases, where a more reliable reading becomes immediately evident through an examination of the parallel text.[3]

BIBLIOGRAPHY

Wolf-Peter Funk, "The First Apocalypse of James"; "Notizen zur weiteren Textkonstitution der zweiten Apokalypse des Jakobus"; Douglas M. Parrott, ed., *Nag Hammadi Codices V,2–5 and VI, 65–103* (William R. Schoedel); Wilhelm Pratscher, *Der Herrenbruder Jakobus und die Jakobustradition*; Hans-Martin Schenke, Hans-Gebhard Bethge, and Ursula Ulrike Kaiser, eds., *Nag Hammadi Deutsch*, 2.407–18 (Imke Schletterer and Uwe-Karsten Plisch); Armand Veilleux, eds., *La première apocalypse de Jacques; La seconde apocalypse de Jacques*.

---

3. Those cases are NHC 25,24–25; 26,17–18; 30,23–26; 32,26; 36,3; 40,25; 41,15; 43,11–12; 44,5–8.

The First Revelation of James[1]

The Revelation of James

Jesus Speaks with His Brother James About the One Who Is and the Coming Suffering (24,10–25,9)

It happened that the master[2] spoke to me: "See now the completion of my deliverance. I have already given you a sign of these things, my brother James. For not without reason have I called you my brother, though you are not physically my brother. I know you well. So when I give you a sign, pay attention and listen.

"Once nothing existed except the One Who Is.[3] That one is unnamable and ineffable. I also am unnamable, from the One Who Is, although I have been [given] many names. <We> both <come> from the One Who Is, but I am before you.

"Since you have inquired about femaleness, I tell you, femaleness did exist, but femaleness was not first. [It] prepared divine powers for itself, but [it] did not yet exist [when] I came to be, [25] for I am an image of the One Who Is. I brought forth the image [of the One Who Is], that the children of the One Who Is might know what is theirs and what is alien to them.[4] Look, I shall reveal to you every aspect of this mystery. They will arrest me the day after tomorrow, but my deliverance will be near."

---

1. Coptic text: NHC V,3: 24,10–44,10. Editions: *The Facsimile Edition of the Nag Hammadi Codices: Codex V*, 32–52; Douglas M. Parrott, ed., *Nag Hammadi Codices V,2–5 and VI*, 65–103 (William R. Schoedel); Hans-Martin Schenke, Hans-Gebhard Bethge, and Ursula Ulrike Kaiser, eds., *Nag Hammadi Deutsch*, 2.407–18 (Imke Schletterer and Uwe-Karsten Plisch); Wilhelm Schneemelcher, ed., *New Testament Apocrypha*, 1.313–26 (Wolf-Peter Funk); Armand Veilleux, ed., *La première apocalypse de Jacques; La seconde apocalypse de Jacques*. The text is commonly referred to as the *First Revelation* (or *Apocalypse*) of *James* in order to distinguish it from the text that follows it in Nag Hammadi Codex V, also entitled "The Revelation of James." Another version of the *First Revelation of James* has been discovered in Codex Tchacos; there the title is simply *James*. 2. Or "Lord," here and throughout. 3. Cf. the description of the divine in the Septuagint of *Exodus* 3:14 as *ho ōn*, "the One Who Is," for *'Ehyeh 'asher 'ehyeh* in Hebrew. 4. On femaleness, cf. also *First Revelation of James* 34–35; 41.

Jesus and James Discuss the Hostility of the Rulers of This World (25,10–28,4)

James said, "Rabbi, you said, 'They will arrest me.' What can I do?"

He said to me, "Don't be afraid, James. You too will be arrested. [Leave] Jerusalem, for this city always gives the cup of bitterness[5] to the children of light. This is the dwelling place of many archons, but your deliverance will deliver you from them. In order that you may know who they are and what they are like, you should [flee]. Listen: it is not [everything] but only [firstfruits]. The twelve . . . . . .[6] [every one of them] [26] on his own realm of Seven."

James said, "Rabbi, then are there twelve realms of Seven and not seven, as in the scriptures?"

The master said, "James, the one who spoke through this scripture had limited understanding. I shall reveal to you what has come from the one who is innumerable; I shall give you a sign concerning their number. And as for what has come from the immeasurable, I shall give you a sign concerning their measure."

James said, "Rabbi, how is that? Look, I have received their number: they are seventy-two vessels."[7]

The master said, "These are the seventy-two inferior heavens that belong to them. These are the powers of all their might. They have been established by them, and they have been assigned to every place under the [authority] of the twelve rulers. The power in them, insignificant as it is, [brought forth] for itself angels and hosts without number. But [the One Who Is] was given . . . because of . . . the One Who Is . . . without number. [27] If you wish to number them now, you will not be able to do so until you throw off blind thought, this bond of flesh surrounding you. Only then will you attain to the One Who Is, and then you will no longer be James, but you are that One Who Is. And all those without number will have names given to them."

"Rabbi, how shall I attain to the One Who Is, since all these powers and hosts are armed against me?"

He said to me, "These powers are armed not against you alone but also against others. These powers are armed against me, and they are armed with other [powers]. They are armed against me [with] judgment. I have not been given . . . in it . . . through them . . . here . . . suffering. I shall . . . . . .[8] [28] and I shall not reprove them. But within me will be silence and a hidden mystery. I am faint of heart before their anger."[9]

---

5. Cf. *Mark* 10:38; 14:34, 36; *John* 18:11. 6. Four lines missing or untranslatable. 7. On seventy-two powers or heavens, cf. *Eugnostos the Blessed* III, 83–84. Seventy or seventy-two is the traditional number of nations in the world according to Jewish lore. 8. One line missing or untranslatable. 9. Cf. *Mark* 14:34, 61; 15:4–5.

James Professes That Jesus Came with Knowledge, and Jesus Goes to His Passion (28,5–30,15)

James said, "Rabbi, if they arm themselves against you, still there is no reason to blame you.

> You have come with knowledge[10]
> to reprove their forgetfulness.
> You have come with remembrance
> to reprove their ignorance.
> I was worried about you.
>
> For you have come down into profound ignorance,
> but you were not defiled by any of it.
> You have come down into thoughtlessness,
> but your memory stayed with you.
> You walked in mud,
> and your garments did not get dirty.
> You were not inundated with their filth,
> and they did not apprehend you.
> I was not like them,
> but I have clothed myself in all that is theirs.
> There is in me forgetfulness,
> but I remember what is not theirs.
> There is in me . . . ,
> and I am in their . . . .
> I have found knowledge,
> and . . . not for their sufferings . . . .

Yet I am afraid of them, since they have power. Tell me, what [29] will they do? What can I say? What word can I utter to escape them?".

The master said, "James, I praise your understanding and your fear. If you continue in your commitment, do not be concerned about anything other than your deliverance. For look, I shall complete what is destined here on earth, as I once said from the heavens. And I shall reveal to you your deliverance."

James said, "Rabbi, how is that? After this will you appear to us again? After they have arrested you and you complete what is destined, you will go up to the One Who Is."

The master said, "James, after this I shall make everything clear to you, not only for your sake but also because of the unbelief of people, that [faith] may come to be among them. For many will [attain] to faith, and they will grow in . . .

---

10. Gnosis, here and below.

until they . . . . [**30**] And after this I shall appear to rebuke the rulers, and I shall show them that there is one who is invincible. If that one is seized, he will seize all of them. But now I shall go. Remember the things I have told you, and let them enter your heart."

James said, "Master, I shall hurry to do as you have said."

The master said good-bye to him, and he fulfilled what was fitting.[11]

When James heard of the master's sufferings, he was deeply distressed.

The Risen Master Appears and Explains to James the Real Meaning of His Passion (30,16–32,28)

They were waiting for the sign of his coming, and it came after some days. James was walking on the mountain called Gaugela,[12] along with his disciples, who still listened to him with desire. They had a comforter,[13] and they said, "This is the second [teacher]." The crowd dispersed, but James remained [behind and] prayed . . . , as [**31**] was his custom.

The master appeared to him. He stopped praying, embraced him, and kissed him, saying, "Rabbi, I've found you. I heard of the sufferings you endured, and I was greatly troubled. You know my compassion. Because of this I wished, as I reflected upon it, that I would never see these people again. They must be judged for what they have done, for what they have done is not right."

The master said, "James, do not be concerned for me or these people. I am the one who was within me. Never did I suffer at all, and I was not distressed. These people did not harm me. Rather, all this was inflicted upon a figure of the rulers, and it was fitting that this figure should be [destroyed] by them. Also . . . the rulers . . . . The just [God became] angry with [you, since you had been] [**32**] a servant to him. Because of this you have the name James the Just. You see how you will become sober once you have seen me. You stopped praying because you are a just man of God, and you embraced and kissed me. I tell you the truth, you have set in motion great anger and wrath against yourself. But this has happened so that these other things might occur."

James was fearful, and he wept. He was greatly troubled. They sat down together on a rock, and the master said to him, "James, this is how you will face these sufferings. Do not be sad. The flesh is weak,[14] and it will get what is ordained for it. But as for you, do not be timid or afraid."

The master [paused].

When James heard this, he wiped away the tears that were in [his eyes], and he was greatly relieved [from the sadness he had felt].

---

11. I.e., Jesus goes off to his passion and crucifixion.
12. Perhaps Golgotha (in Syriac, Gagultha), or a certain mountain named Gaugal that is mentioned in Syriac texts. 13. Cf. the Comforter, Advocate, or Paraclete in *John* 14:16, 26; 15:26; 16:7–8; *Prayer of the Apostle Paul* A. 14. Cf. *Mark* 14:38.

Jesus Reveals to James How He Also Will Be
Delivered from Suffering (32,28–38,11)

The master said to him, "James, look, I shall [33] reveal to you your deliverance. When you are arrested and you face these sufferings, a multitude of people will arm themselves against you in order to seize you. Three in particular will lay hold of you—those who sit as toll collectors. Not only do they demand toll, they also take away souls by theft.

"If you fall into their hands, the one who is their guard will say to you, 'Who are you, and where are you from?' You are to say to him, 'I am a son, and I am from the Father.' He will say to you, 'What kind of son are you, and to what father do you belong?' You are to say to him, 'I am from the preexistent Father, and I am a son in the preexistent one.' [He will say] to you, '[With what mandate have you come]?' You are [to say to him, 'I have come] at the behest of the [preexistent one], that I [may see those who are ours, those] who [have become aliens].'[15] He will say to you, 'Of what kind [34] are these aliens?' You are to say to him, 'They are not entirely alien, but they are from Achamoth,[16] who is female. She produced them when she brought this generation down from the preexistent one. So they are not aliens; they are ours. They are ours, because she who rules over them comes from the preexistent one. Yet they are aliens, because the preexistent one did not have intercourse with her when she was about to produce them.' When he says to you again, 'Where will you go?' you are to say to him, 'I shall return to the place I came from.'[17] If you say these things, you will avoid their attacks.

"If you fall into the hands of the three detainers, who carry off souls by theft in that place, [in order to . . . them], you are to [say to them, 'I am] a vessel [that is] more [precious] than [the female who] . . . [35] who is your [mother. As long] as she is [ignorant] of her root, you [also] will not become sober [again]. But I shall call upon imperishable knowledge, who is Sophia,[18] who is in the Father and is the Mother of Achamoth. Achamoth had no father or male companion, but she is a female from a female. She created you by herself without a male, since she was ignorant of those who [attain] to her mother, and she thought that she alone existed. I shall cry up to her mother.'[19]

"Then they will be troubled, and they will blame their root and the generation of their mother. But you will go up to [what is] yours, after [you have thrown off] their fetters . . . . . .[20] [36] the preexistent one. [They are] prototypes of the twelve disciples and the [seventy]-two companions . . . Achamoth, which is translated Sophia.

"You are to hide within yourself who I am, and who imperishable Sophia is, through whom you will be delivered, and who all the children are of the One

---

15. Or "strangers," here and below. 16. Achamoth, who is a lower form of Wisdom (cf. Hebrew *Hokhmah*) and is the daughter of Sophia, higher Wisdom, is known in particular in Valentinian traditions; cf. *Gospel of Philip* 60. 17. On this paragraph, cf. Irenaeus of Lyon *Against Heresies* 1.21.5. On the ascent of the soul and the interrogation by the toll collectors or gatekeepers, cf. *Gospel of Thomas* 50; *Revelation of Paul* 19–24; *Gospel of Mary* 15–17. 18. Wisdom. 19. On Wisdom producing a child without a male partner, cf. *Secret Book of John* II, 9–10. 20. Three lines missing or untranslatable.

Who Is, these matters that they have known and have hidden within themselves. Be quiet about these things, but reveal them to Addai.[21] As soon as you leave, there will be war waged against this land, so weep for anyone who dwells in Jerusalem.[22] Let Addai take these things to heart. In the tenth year Addai is to sit down and write them out. When he has written them out, . . . and they are to give them [to] . . . . He has the . . . . . .[23] [37] the [first], who is called by the [name] Levi.[24] Then he is to bring forth . . . without words. On the basis [of what was] prophesied earlier, I say, [he is to take] a wife [outside] Jerusalem in her . . . , and he <is to> produce [two] sons from her. [They are] to inherit these things, and the understanding of the one who will rise [even higher]. They are to receive from him a portion of his mind.

"The smaller is the greater among them. Let these things be shared with him and hidden within him until [he] is seventeen years old . . . . . .[25] [38] from [them]. He will be severely persecuted at the hands of his fellow . . . . He will be proclaimed [through] them, and [he will] proclaim this word. Then [it will become] a seed of [salvation."

Jesus and James Conclude Their Conversation, and James Faces His Martyrdom (38,12–44,10)

James said, "[I am] encouraged . . . and they are . . . [for] my soul. Yet I ask you [something else]: who are the seven women who have [become] your disciples? Look, all the women bless you. But I wonder how it can be that [powerless] vessels have become strong through the perception within them?"

The master [said], "You . . . well . . . . . .[26] [39] a spirit of . . . , a spirit of thought, [a spirit] of counsel and . . . , a spirit of . . . , a spirit of knowledge, [a spirit] of fear.[27]

"When we passed through the region of [this archon, called] Adonaios,[28] [we] . . . him, and . . . he was ignorant. When I passed by him, [he] thought I was a son of his. He treated [me] graciously at that time, as though I were his son. Then, before <I> appeared in this place, they were cast among [this] people. But from that . . . the prophets did not . . . . . .[29] [40] upon you."

James [said], "Rabbi, . . . them [all] together. Who [are those] . . . among them more [than] . . . ?"

The master said, "[James], I praise you [for the] accuracy [of your] . . . word which is . . . . For [you have] cast away from [yourself] the cup, which is

---

21. Addai is the legendary founder of Syrian Christianity, and he is reputed to have particular ties with Edessa. Sometimes he is identified with Thaddaeus (*Mark* 3:18) or with one of the seventy (or seventy-two) disciples (*Luke* 10:1). See Eusebius of Caesarea *Church History* 1.13., on Addai/Thaddaeus and Abgar of Edessa as well as the *Doctrine of Addai* and the *Chronicle of Arbela*. 22. Cf. *Matthew* 23:37–39; *Luke* 13:34–35; 23:28. The war alluded to in these texts is the Jewish revolt against the Romans in 66–70. 23. Seven lines missing or untranslatable. 24. On figures named Levi in early Christian literature, cf. the New Testament gospels; *Gospel of Philip* 63; *Gospel of Mary* 18; Wilhelm Schneemelcher, ed., *New Testament Apocrypha*. 25. Seven lines missing or untranslatable. 26. Seven lines missing or untranslatable. 27. Cf. *Isaiah* 11:2. 28. Adonaios, whose name derives from Adonai (Hebrew for "my Lord"), is often described as the son of the creator of this world, and the Jewish people are sometimes said to be linked to him. 29. Nine lines missing or untranslatable.

bitterness.[30] None of [the rulers will be able] to stand against you, for you [have begun] to understand [their] roots from beginning to end. Cast away from yourself all lawlessness, and beware lest they touch you. When you speak these words of such great perception, exhort this . . . . Salome, Mary . . . , Arsinoe[31] . . . .[32] [41] These he [offers up as] burnt offerings and sacrifices. But I [will] not [do] so. Rather, [I will bring] firstfruits of the [imperishable] . . . , that the power [of truth] may be clear. The perishable has gone [up to] the imperishable, and the work of femaleness has attained to the work of this maleness."[33]

James said, "Rabbi, into these three, then, has their . . . been cast. For they have been despised and persecuted by . . . ."[34] [42]

[The master said, "James], ...[35] Look, [I] have [imparted] everything [to you. I] have . . . in no way . . . . For you have received [the firstfruits] of knowledge,[36] and [you know] now the [place] in [which you will] walk. You will [find] . . . . But I shall go [forth] and [reveal] . . . , because they have trusted you, that they may be convinced, for their blessing and salvation, and that this revelation may come to pass."

Then he went at once and admonished the twelve, and he instilled in them contentment [about] the way of knowledge . . . .[37] [43]

Most of [the judges], when they saw [that] there was no case [against him, left] him alone. [But] the other ones [and the people resisted. Rising up, they] said, "Let [us take] this person away from the earth, for he is not worthy of life." The first ones were afraid, and they rose up and said, "We have no part in this man's blood, for a just man will perish unjustly." James left, in order to . . . . . . ,[38] [44] "[My] Father [in the heavens, forgive] them, for [they do] not [know] what [they are doing]."[39]

The Revelation of James

---

30. Cf. *First Revelation of James* 25. 31. This passage has been understood and translated in various ways. Attempts have been made to restore a number descriptive of the women: "[four]" or "[seven]." Cf. four women in the present passage and seven women in *First Revelation of James* 38. Schletterer and Plisch (in *Nag Hammadi Deutsch*, 2.417) understand this passage quite differently and translate as follows: "Be content with this [word]. Salome, Mary [of Magdala], Arsinoe . . . ." On the names (partially restored) of these four women, cf. *Manichaean Psalm Book* 192,21–24; 194,19–22. Some of these women are well known from early Christian traditions. On Salome, cf. also *Gospel of Thomas* 61. On Mary (probably Mary of Magdala, possibly Mary sister of Martha and Lazarus), cf. especially the *Gospel of Mary*. 32. Nine lines missing or untranslatable. 33. Cf. *Gospel of Thomas* 114 and the notes. The *Wisdom of Jesus Christ* also discusses femaleness, maleness, and salvation. 34. Six lines missing or untranslatable. 35. Four lines missing or untranslatable. 36. Gnosis, here and below. 37. Thirteen lines missing or untranslatable. 38. Thirteen

lines missing or untranslatable. 39. The end of the version of the text in Codex Tchacos (*James* 29–30) reads as follows: "It happened [a while] later that they arrested Jam[es] instead of another man, against whom they had brought charges, for he had fled from . . . . And . . . prison, but it was another man named Jam[es] who got out of the prison. They arrested this person [instead] of him, and they brought him before the judges. Most of the judges saw that he was innocent, and they let [him go]. But the others and all the people resisted and [said], 'Take him away from the earth; he is not [worthy of] life!' But those were afraid, [rose up], and said, 'We have no [part in] . . . .' (about three lines missing) . . . he remembered . . . he became . . . , for the men . . . him, but the . . . . And when they were stoning [him], he said, 'My Father [in] heaven, forgive them, for they do <not> know what they are doing'" (Rodolphe Kasser, François Gaudard, Marvin Meyer, and Gregor Wurst, eds., *Codex Tchacos*).

THE SECOND REVELATION
OF JAMES

NHC V,4

Introduced and Translated by Wolf–Peter Funk

T he *Second Revelation of James*[1] has a rather complicated literary structure. Although it contains little real dialogue, it presents itself as a lengthy report that an anonymous priest gives to a certain Theudas, who is said to be the father of James the Just, apparently in an attempt to muster help in the dangerous situation in which James finds himself as he is facing the death penalty for his activities; and the work ends with a short narrative describing the stoning of James while he is uttering a prayer. The main part of the priest's report consists of a discourse that James is said to have recently given to the assembled crowd of people (and that has provoked the accusation of blasphemy against him). Within this discourse, James legitimizes himself as a proclaimer of true knowledge and reports about the special revelation Jesus imparted to him after his resurrection. These discourses of Jesus, stylized as doubly reported, are the central part of the writing and represent its "revelation" in a narrower sense.

A striking feature of the literary makeup of Gnostic enlightenment as found in Jesus's address to James is the unique use made of the brotherly relationship between Jesus and James. Although their physical relationship as seen in this text is not quite clear (mostly because of lacunae in the manuscript), the discussion of this issue is soon elevated to a metaphysical level, following the programmatic words, "Your father is not my Father, but my Father has become a father to you" (51,19–22). In other words, the revelation of transcendent knowledge (*gnōsis*) is here expressed in terms of a new father-son relationship that James is entitled to, a wakening call (52,13–18) with regard to the true God of eternal life instead of the one he has worshiped so far, the God of the Old Testament whose promises only extend to the visible land as an inheritance. This focus on the opposition between two gods—one with terrestrial and the other with celestial promises, one acting as

---

1. For the epithet "second" in the title of the text, see the introduction to the *First Revelation of James*.

a judge and the other with compassion—bears a strong resemblance to Marcion's *Antitheses*.

Thus the fragmentary pieces found in the *Second Revelation of James* of some sort of Gnostic myth (especially pp. 53–54) are placed under the general topic of a change of orientation in terms of a switch from one father to another. Since the creator god has set out to capture and assimilate "those who are from the Father," Jesus has come down to set into motion a process of liberation, and he has chosen James as his principal tool in this process. The ensuing hymnic description of James's multifold responsibility as liberator (55,15–56,14), apparently based upon his historical role as Jesus's vicar in Jerusalem and expanding this role into transcendent dimensions, is comparable only to the unique status that James is given in *Gospel of Thomas* 12, somehow focusing the entire salvation process on his person.

James's death prayer, which concludes the *Second Revelation of James*, fits the literary context in which it is presented here—that is, his approaching death as a result of being stoned—only to a limited extent. It is in fact a prayer for death and, as such, one of the finest examples of a barely investigated type of prayer found in several corpora of Gnostic affiliation.[2] In agreement with other examples of this kind of prayer, the prayer of James features the request that this life of earthly existence come to an end by maintaining that "the hour has come," and it includes a request for help in surmounting the hostile powers that will oppose the departing person during ascension. Whether or not such prayers were part of a ritual in certain Christian Gnostic communities (a "mass for the dead" or for those about to die), we do not know.

Although there is nothing in the *Second Revelation of James* to indicate the precise time and place of its composition, the claim it lays to the James tradition makes it likely that the writing originated in a portion of the exiled Jerusalem community, most likely in some part of Syria, and its closeness to Marcionite theology may suggest a time during the second century.

BIBLIOGRAPHY

Wolf-Peter Funk, "Notizen zur weiteren Textkonstitution der zweiten Apokalypse des Jakobus"; "The Second Apocalypse of James"; *Die zweite Apokalypse des Jakobus aus Nag-Hammadi-Codex V*; Douglas M. Parrott, ed., *Nag Hammadi Codices V,2–5 and VI*, 105–49 (Charles W. Hedrick); Wilhelm Pratscher, *Der Herrenbruder Jakobus und die Jakobustradition*; Hans-Martin Schenke, Hans-Gebhard Bethge, and Ursula Ulrike Kaiser, eds., *Nag Hammadi Deutsch*, 2.419–32 (Ursula Ulrike Kaiser and Uwe-Karsten Plisch); Armand Veilleux, ed., *La première apocalypse de Jacques; La seconde apocalypse de Jacques*.

---

2. Cf., e.g., the *Acts of Thomas*, *Pistis Sophia*, and Mandaean and Manichaean sources (for more details, see Wolf-Peter Funk, "The Second Apocalypse of James").

The Second Revelation of James[1]

The Revelation of [James]

The Discourse of James (44,11–16)

This is the discourse that James the Just delivered in Jerusalem and Mareim[2] wrote down.

The Beginning of the Priest's Report (44,16–45,25)

One of the priests told it to Theudas,[3] the father of this just man, since he was a relative of his.

He said, [Hurry] and come with [Mary] your wife and your relatives . . . .[4] [45] So hurry. Perhaps, [if] you yourself lead us to him, [he will] come to his senses. For look, there are many who are disturbed at his [slander]. They are extremely angry [with him, for he has said], "They [do not] pray . . . ." [He has said] these things often, and other things too.

He used to say these things while the multitude of the people was seated. But on this occasion he entered and sat down <not> in his customary place but on the fifth flight of steps, [which] is the favored place.[5]

---

1. Coptic text: NHC V,4: 44,11–63,32. Editions: *The Facsimile Edition of the Nag Hammadi Codices: Codex V*, 52–73; Wolf-Peter Funk, ed., *Die zweite Apokalypse des Jakobus aus Nag-Hammadi-Codex V*; Douglas M. Parrott, ed., *Nag Hammadi Codices V,2–5 and VI*, 105–49 (Charles W. Hedrick); Hans-Martin Schenke, Hans-Gebhard Bethge, and Ursula Ulrike Kaiser, eds., *Nag Hammadi Deutsch*, 2.419–32 (Ursula Ulrike Kaiser and Uwe-Karsten Plisch); Wilhelm Schneemelcher, ed., *New Testament Apocrypha*, 1.327–41 (Wolf-Peter Funk); Armand Veilleux, ed., *La première apocalypse de Jacques; La seconde apocalypse de Jacques*. The text is commonly referred to as the *Second Revelation* (or *Apocalypse*) *of James* in order to distinguish it from the text that precedes it in NHC V,

also entitled "The Revelation of James." 2. Mareim is named as the scribe who copied down the discourse of James. 3. Here Theudas is said to be the husband of Mary and the father of James. It is conceivable that Theudas is envisioned as the second husband of Mary, after Joseph. According to the *Protevangelium of James*, Joseph was already an old man at the time of the birth of Jesus, and it may be imagined that he died shortly thereafter. That, however, is only a guess. Cf. Kaiser and Plisch, in *Nag Hammadi Deutsch*, 2.426. 4. About twelve lines missing or untranslatable. 5. James is described as speaking at the temple, perhaps at the Nicanor gate (cf. the "beautiful gate" mentioned in Acts 3:2). See also the scene in Pseudo-Clementine *Recognitions* 1.66–73.

The Discourse of James: James Speaks of Jesus and of Himself (45,25–47,20)

While all our [people[6] . . . . . . ,[7] James spoke]:

"... [46]
[Blessed] is the person [who] . . . out of . . . ,
[and will come] to . . . ,
[of whom it is said] that he is . . . .
I am the one who received revelation from the fullness[8] of imperishability,
who was summoned by the one who is great,
who obeyed the [master].[9]
It is he who passed through the [worlds without being recognized],
who [came down after] stripping off his clothing,
and walked about naked,
who was found in perishability
though destined to be brought up to imperishability.[10]

"This same master [came] down as a son who can see, and as a brother. He was [rejected] when he was on his way to [the one whom] the [Father] produced, in order that [he might . . . him] and induce him to free himself [from the fetters of] death . . . . . .[11] [47] [who] came to [me in faithfulness] . . . .[12] Now again am I rich in knowledge.[13] I have a unique deliverer—one who alone was conceived from above and was the first [to] come from . . . . I am . . . [to the Father] whom I have come to know. What was revealed to me was hidden from everyone, yet that will be revealed through him. I < . . . > the two who see.[14]

James Recalls the Life and Words of Jesus (47,21–49,end)

"It was once proclaimed, 'He will be judged with the unrighteous.'[15]

He who lived [without] blasphemy
died through [blasphemy].
He who was cast out
[has been exalted].
He who [was] . . .
is . . . .[16] [48]

"[It was the master who] said,

---

6. "Our [people]" may be the Jewish people. 7. Four lines missing or untranslatable. 8. Pleroma. 9. Or "Lord," here and below. 10. Cf. 1 Corinthians 15:42–54. 11. Three lines missing or untranslatable.

12. Four lines missing or untranslatable. 13. Gnosis, here and below. 14. Perhaps cf. the two blind men in Matthew 9:27–31; 20:29–34. 15. Cf. Isaiah 53:12; Luke 22:37. 16. Three lines missing or untranslatable.

'. . . . . . .[17]
I . . . flesh,
[and yet] I shall come forth from the flesh in [fulfillment].
I shall surely die,
but I shall be found in life.
I came to the world to be judged,
[and I shall] come forth [victorious].

"'I do not judge, [and I do] not [confuse] the servants of his [will], whom I hurry to set free. And if [I] help them, I wish to take them above the one who wants to rule over them. In a secret [way] I am the brother who scorned this [pitiless] one . . . .[18] [49]

I [am the] . . . of imperishability
[and the] first among [those who shall rise].[19]
I [am the] first [son] who was conceived
and who will destroy the dominion of [them] all.
I [am] the beloved.
I am the just one.
I am the son of the Father.

I speak as [I] have heard.
I command as [I] have received the command.
I teach you as I have [found].

Look, I speak, that I may come forth.
Pay attention to me, that you may see me.
If I have come into being, who am I?
For I have come as I am [not],
and I shall not appear as I am.[20]

"'I lived on the earth for only a short time. [I] did [not] have . . . .'[21] [50]

James Describes an Appearance of the Risen Christ
(50,4–51,13)

"One time when I was sitting and meditating, the one whom you hated and persecuted opened the door and came in to me, and he said to me,

Hello, my brother; brother, hello.

---

17. Three lines missing or untranslatable. 18. Seven lines missing or untranslatable. 19. Cf. 1 *Corinthians* 15:20–28. 20. Cf. *Gospel of Philip* 57–58; *Wisdom of* *Jesus Christ* 91. 21. Nine lines missing or untranslatable.

"As I raised my [head] to look at him, mother said to me, 'Don't be afraid, my son, because he said to you, "My brother." You were both nourished with the same milk. That is why he says to me, "My mother." He is not a stranger to us; he is your stepbrother. [I am] not . . . .'[22]

"[After] she [had spoken these words . . . .[23] He said] [**51**] to me, 'My [brother], . . . these words . . . . [Those] whom I shall [find will] come forth. [But] I am the stranger, and none of them knows me in [their] thoughts, because they know me only in [this body]. But it would be fitting that others would come to knowledge through you.

James Tells What Jesus Said Regarding Two Fathers
(51,14–54,15)

"'I tell you, listen and understand.

> For many, when they hear, will be fainthearted,
> but you, understand in the way I can tell you.

> Your father is not my Father,
> but my Father has become a father to you.[24]

Like this virgin, about whom you hear, you [have chosen] rest [for yourself, in that you escaped].'

"When I [did not understand, he said], 'Listen . . . virgin . . . .'

"[I said], '. . . . . .[25] [**52**] this virgin. [I] have [understood] how [she returned].'

"He said to me, '[Pay attention. Anyone who] unsettles what I [promise] does not [act] as I wish. For to this you are to turn [your] face, and this [also] is to your advantage.

> Your father, whom you consider rich,
> will grant that you inherit
> all that you see.[26]
> But I proclaim to you
> that I shall give you
> what I shall say,
> if you listen.
> So open your ears,

---

22. On the relationship between Jesus, James, and the other members of the family, cf., e.g., the *Protevangelium of James*. Here the view of the relationship is unclear. It may be thought that Jesus is James's stepbrother, foster brother, or cousin. The text may be read as "he is the brother [of] your father" (Coptic *pson* [*em*]*pekeiōt pe*) or "he is the brother [by way of] your father" (Coptic *pson* [*ha*] *pekeiōt pe*). 23. About four lines missing or untranslatable. 24. Cf. *John* 20:17; perhaps also *Gospel of Thomas* 55; 101. 25. About two lines missing or untranslatable. 26. This father is the father below—i.e., the God of the Jewish scriptures.

and understand,
and walk accordingly.

"'When they come for you, being dispatched by one considered glorious and intending to bring confusion and violence, [pay no attention to them], but . . . . And . . . . . .[27] [53] he set his hand [to something he] did not [understand], nor did [those] sent by him to prepare this present [creation]. Later, when [he] is put to shame, he will [be troubled] that his work, which is far removed [from] the eternal realms,[28] comes to nothing. His inheritance, which he boasted about, claiming it was great, will prove to be insignificant. His gifts are not blessings and his promises are evil intrigues. You are not of <the children> of his compassion, but he does violence against you. He wants to do injustice against us. And he will have dominion for a period of time appointed for him.[29]

"'But understand and know the Father who has compassion, who was not given an inheritance, whose inheritance is unlimited, with an unlimited number of days.[30] Rather, it is an eternal [day], and it is [light]. It exists [in places the creator [54] himself cannot] perceive and he merely uses, for he is not from those places. Because of this he [utters curses], and because of this he boasts, that he may not be rebuked. For this reason he is superior to those who are below, who were looked down upon, in order to be perfected in them. After he captured those who are from the Father, he seized them and shaped them to resemble himself, and so they are with him.

James Recalls What Jesus Said About Salvation and the Mediator of Salvation (54,15–56,14)

"'I saw from on high those who came into being, and I have explained how they came into being. They were visited while they were in another form. While I was watching, [I] recognized that those I know are like me. In the presence of those who came into being, they will [depart], for I know that everyone who [was] forced down to this place [55] will come [to me like] little children. [I] want to give [them] a revelation through you and the [Spirit of] power, and the Spirit will give revelation [to those] who are yours, and through you those who wish to enter may go through a good door. They turn around, that from now on they may walk on the path that leads before this door. They follow you and enter, [and you] accompany them inside and give each of them a share of the reward.[31]

For you are not the deliverer
nor a helper of strangers.

---

27. About three lines missing or untranslatable. 28. Aeons. 29. Cf. *First Revelation of James* 31–34. 30. This father is the Father above—i.e., the exalted God and Father of Jesus. 31. On the role of James the Just as a leader in the early church, cf. also, among other texts, the *First Revelation of James*; *Gospel of Thomas* 12; *Galatians* 1–2; *Gospel of the Hebrews*; *Protevangelium of James*; Hegesippus *Memoirs* (*Hypomnēmata*); *Ascents of James* (*Anabathmoi Iakōbou*).

You are an illuminator and deliverer
of those who are mine,
and now those who are yours.
You shall give revelation,
and you shall bring good among them all.

You [they shall] admire
because of all your miracles.
You the heavens bless.
You he shall envy,
[who] called himself the [jealous one].[32]
You . . . .[33]
[Those who live] in forgetfulness [56]
are instructed in these things with [you].

Because of you
[they] will be taught about [these things]
and come to rest.
Because of you
they will come to reign
and become kings.[34]
Because of [you]
pity will be taken
on those to be pitied.

As you are the first
who clothed yourself,
so also are you the first
who will strip off your clothes.
And you will become as you were
before you took off your clothes.'

James Recounts the End of the Revelation (56,14–57,19)

"He kissed me on the mouth and embraced me, saying, 'My beloved! Look, I shall reveal to you what the heavens have not known, nor their rulers. Look, I shall reveal to you what that one did not know—the one who boasted [and said, "I am God, and there is no other] [57] except me. I am alive, because I am a father. Don't I have [power] over everything?"[35] Look, I shall reveal [to you] all things. My beloved, understand and know these things, [that] you may come

---

32. Cf. *Exodus* 20:5. 33. Three lines missing or untranslatable. 34. Cf. 1 *Corinthians* 4:8; *Gospel of Thomas* 2. 35. Cf., e.g., *Isaiah* 44:6; 45:5–6, 21; 46:9;

Second Discourse of Great Seth 53; 64; the *Secret Book of John*.

forth from this womb[36] and be as I am. Look, I shall reveal to you what [is hidden]. Reach out your [hand] and embrace me.'

"At once I reached out my [hands], but I did not find him as I thought he would be. After this I heard him say, 'Understand, and embrace me.' Then I understood, and I was afraid, yet I rejoiced with great joy.

James Professes the Divinity of Jesus (57,20–58,end)

"Therefore I say to you, you who judge have been judged. You did not spare, but you have been spared. Be sober and [recognize him. For the one] you [judged is actually not the one you] thought . . . . . .[37] [58] you did not know.

> He was [the one]
> whom he who created heaven and earth and dwelled in it
> [could] not [see].[38]
> He was the one [who] is life.
> He was the light.

> He was the one who will be
> and will provide an ending for [what] has begun
> and a beginning for what will come to an end.
> He was the holy Spirit
> and the invisible one
> who did not come down on the earth.
> He was the virgin,
> and what he wishes happens to him.
> I saw he was naked,
> and there was no garment clothing him.
> What he wills happens to him . . . .[39] [59]

James Urges the Members of the Audience to
Walk with the Lord (59,1–60,23)

"Abandon this difficult path, which is so irregular, and walk in accordance with the one who wants you to become free people [with] me, after you have overcome every dominion. He will not [judge] you for what you have done, but he will have mercy on you, [for] it was not you who did these things but [your] Lord. He was [not] someone wrathful, but he was a kind father.

> You have judged yourselves,
> and so you will remain in their fetters.
> You have burdened yourselves,

---

36. Or "from the body." 37. One line missing or untranslatable. 38. In his blindness the creator of this world could not see the exalted divine being of Christ. 39. Three lines missing or untranslatable.

and you will repent,
but you will not profit at all.
Look upon the one who speaks,
and seek the one who is silent.
Know who came to this place,
and understand who went away.
I am the just one,
yet I do <not> judge.
I am not a master,
but I am a helper.

"He, the master, was rejected before he stretched out his hand. [But] as for me, [he has] opened [my ears] . . . .[40] [60] He makes me hear the <silencing> of your trumpets, your flutes, and your harps [for this] house. It is the Lord who has taken you captive, closing your ears that they may not hear the sound of my speech, yet you [will be able to pay] attention in your hearts, and you will call me 'the Just.' Thus I say to you <in the name of the Lord>,[41] look, I have given you your house, which you say God has made, through which the one who dwells in it has promised to give you an inheritance. I shall tear down this house, to the ruin and derision of those who live in ignorance."[42]

The Conclusion of the Priest's Report
(60,23–61,15)

Look, those who hold the office of judge are deliberating, to pass [judgment on all he said . . . . . .[43] [61] on] that day. All the [people] and the crowd were confused, and it was clear that they were not convinced. He got up and left after saying these things.

Another day he came in again and spoke for a few hours. I was with the priests, and I said nothing of our relationship, because they were all saying with one voice, "Come, let us stone 'the Just.'"

The Martyrdom of James: The Execution
(61,15–62,12)

They arose and said, "Yes, let us kill this man, that he may be removed from our midst. For he will be of no use to us at all."

---

40. Three lines missing or untranslatable. **41.** This phrase has apparently been mistakenly copied in line 7 of the manuscript. We read it here in line 14. **42.** On threats against the temple, cf. accounts of Jesus and charges against Jesus in the New Testament gospels, the story of the martyrdom of Stephen in the *Acts of the Apostles*, and James traditions in Hegesippus's *Memoirs*. **43.** Two lines missing or untranslatable.

They were there, and they found him standing by the pinnacle of the temple, next to the mighty cornerstone. They determined to throw him down from the height, and they did just that.

[When] they [looked at him], they saw [he was alive. So] they arose [and went down], [62] and they seized him and [abused] him, dragging him on the ground. They stretched out his body and rolled a stone on his abdomen, and they trampled him with their feet and said, "O you who have gone astray!"

Since he was still alive, they raised him up again, made him dig a hole, and forced him to stand in it. They covered him up to his abdomen and stoned him in this manner.[44]

The Death Prayer of James (62,12–63,29)

But he reached out his hands and uttered this prayer—not the prayer he was accustomed to speak:

> My God and Father,
> who saved me from this dead hope,
> who made me alive through the mystery of your good pleasure,
> do not let these days in the world be prolonged for me,
> but let the day of your light, in which [no night] remains,
> [shine upon me].
> [Bring me to where my] [63] salvation is,
> and deliver me from this [place of] sojourn.
> Let not your grace be squandered on me,
> but let your grace be pure.
> Save me from an evil death.
> Bring me from the tomb alive,
> for your grace is alive in me,
> the desire to accomplish a work of fullness.[45]
> Save me from sinful flesh,
> because I have trusted in you with all my strength,
> for you are the life of life.
> Save me from an enemy that would humiliate me,
> and do not let me fall into the hands of a harsh judge.
> <Save me> from sin,
> and forgive me all the debts of my days.
> For I am alive in you,

---

44. On the martyrdom of James, cf. also *First Revelation of James* 43–44; Josephus *Antiquities of the Jews* 20.200; Eusebius of Caesarea *Church History* 2.1; *Manichaean Psalm Book* 142.25–26; 192.8–9. On the Jewish regulations for stoning established in the Mishnah, see *Sanhedrin* 6.6. The account here in the *Second Revelation of James* reflects rather accurately the Mishnaic regulations. **45.** Pleroma.

your grace is alive in me.
I have renounced everything,
but you I have confessed.
Save me from evil affliction.
Now is the [time] and the hour.
Holy [Spirit], send me salvation.
Light [from] light, crown [me] with [imperishable] . . . power.

The Death of James and the Conclusion to the Account
(63,30–32)

When he finished speaking, [he] fell silent.[46] After this his word [was written down. This is] the account[47] . . . .

---

46. I.e., he died. 47. Logos.

THE REVELATION OF ADAM

NHC V,5

Introduced by Madeleine Scopello
Translated by Marvin Meyer

The *Revelation of Adam* is the last tractate of Nag Hammadi Codex V, which contains three other texts belonging to the same literary genre: the *Revelation of Paul* (V,1), the *First Revelation of James* (V,3), and the *Second Revelation of James* (V,4). A translation from a Greek original, the *Revelation of Adam* fills twenty-one pages; the writing is quite irregular, probably because of the cheap quality of the papyrus (the hand that copied this text is unique in the Nag Hammadi library). Several mistakes present in the Coptic text were partially corrected by the scribe. Here and there words are added in the margin either because the Coptic scribe considered a particular reading to be difficult[1] or because the scribe had two different versions of the tractate in front of him.[2] The last lines of pages 65–72 are missing; pages 73–79, 81, 83–84 offer minor lacunae on the bottom of the pages. Other lacunae are scattered throughout the text.

A title opens the tractate, and the theme of the title is picked up in the first lines of the text: "The revelation (or apocalypse) that Adam taught his son Seth in the seven hundredth year" (64,2–4). The tractate closes with the same title, preceded by a few lines recalling the contents of the text: "These are the revelations (*niapokalupsis*) Adam disclosed to his son Seth, and his son taught them to his offspring" (85,19–22).

The *Revelation of Adam* is appropriately titled, since the tractate provides a revelation transmitted by Adam to his beloved son Seth, the only child of Adam to have inherited the divine spark of knowledge and thus to have the possibility of returning to his heavenly home above. In contrast, a negative judgment is pronounced on the lineage of Shem and, to a somewhat lesser extent, on Ham's and Japheth's descendants. The seed of Seth represents the chosen ones, who seek

---

1. See Alexander Böhlig and Pahor Labib, *Koptisch-gnostische Apokalypsen aus Codex V von Nag Hammadi im Koptischen Museum zu Alt-Kairo.*
2. See George W. MacRae, in Douglas M. Parrott, ed., *Nag Hammadi Codices V,2–5 and VI.*

true knowledge through all their generations. This point of view is shared by other Nag Hammadi tractates and confirmed by church fathers who describe what we now commonly refer to as a Sethian Gnostic group. The analysis of these texts has led scholars of Gnostic religion to consider Sethians as a Gnostic school of thought with its own traditions and holy scriptures.

As the *Revelation of Adam* begins, Adam recalls the time when he and Eve became conscious of their resemblance to the great angels. They also came to know that they were superior to the god who created their bodies. Adam recalls the wrath of this god, the archon of the present aeon, who put restrictions on Eve and himself, to keep them in slavery. But the knowledge they had lost did not disappear: it entered into another great aeon and another great generation. We may note that the adjective "great" is frequent in the *Revelation of Adam*, and it defines beings and situations in the heavenly world. Adam explains to his son Seth that he was named by Adam himself after the name of the celestial human who is "the seed of the great generation" (65,5–9), and this functions as a promise of eternal knowledge given to Seth and his descendants.

After this introductory speech, Adam recounts to Seth the revelation he received in his sleep. Three persons, who could not be identified because they were from the world above, appeared to him (65,24–32) and invited him to arise from the sleep of death and hear about "the eternal realm and the seed of that human to whom life has come" (66,1–6). This revelation, which begins at the *Revelation of Adam* 67,14, relates the stages of the struggle between the divine figures descending periodically into this world and the inferior creator of this world, called Sakla. At each coming of these great ones, the creator, identified with the Old Testament god, reacts by provoking a natural catastrophe, and he intends thereby to destroy those people who come from the seed of life and gnosis. But through each event, first the flood (69,1–16) and then destruction by fire, sulfur, and asphalt (75,9–16), the elect will be saved by the intervention of celestial angels appearing on clouds of light. A third time, in the future, an illuminator of knowledge will manifest himself and perform signs and wonders (77,1–3). His mission is to deliver the souls of the elect, and the creator will unleash his anger on him until he suffers in his flesh (77,16–18), but the cosmic powers will be unable to see him. During the eschatological struggle between the opposing forces, the glory will withdraw to a holy dwelling place.

The origin of the heavenly figure of the illuminator is discussed at length in the *Revelation of Adam* (77,27–82,19), and thirteen false stories of explanation are enumerated. Each one is attributed to a "kingdom" and rooted either in biblical traditions or in pagan mythology. The fourteenth explanation (82,19–28) is set in contrast with the preceding stories and attributed not to a "kingdom" but to "the generation without a king." This entire section is structured rather like a hymn, and it is probably an interpolation added to the original apocalyptic treatise.[3]

---

3. Charles W. Hedrick, *The Apocalypse of Adam*, 130–54.

The *Revelation of Adam* belongs to the literary genre of the apocalypse, as the title itself shows,[4] and this is a well-known genre in apocryphal and pseudepigraphical Jewish literature. By attributing the writing to Adam, the author of the treatise endows it with significant authority. This sort of attribution to important figures of the past is hardly unique in Jewish literature or in the Nag Hammadi scriptures, and several texts recounting the exceptional career of Adam circulated in Jewish and Christian circles. Among them are the *Struggle of Adam*, the *Testament of Adam*, and the *Life of Adam and Eve*. In addition to the Nag Hammadi text, there is also a reference to revelations or apocalypses of Adam in the heresiologist Epiphanius of Salamis, who states in *Panarion* 26.8 that some Gnostics read apocalypses of Adam.[5]

Among the motifs in the *Revelation of Adam* that are typical of apocalyptic writing, we may recall the instruction received in a dream from an angelic entity, the transmission of the revelation to a son or a disciple, the further communication of the revelation from the disciple to chosen followers, and the command to hide books containing the revelation in a safe place—in the present case, on a mountain.

The *Revelation of Adam* has striking parallels with other Nag Hammadi texts that focus attention on the person of Seth: the *Holy Book of the Great Invisible Spirit*, the *Second Discourse of Great Seth*, and the *Three Steles of Seth*. With the *Holy Book* it shares, for example, a common angelology and Jewish esoteric motifs.[6] Connections can also be drawn with the untitled text of the Bruce Codex.

The *Revelation of Adam* has probably been the object of redactional attention. Charles W. Hedrick sees two distinct redactional sources in the composition of the treatise; Françoise Morard, on the other hand, underscores the coherence of the text. There is no agreement among scholars about the background of this apocalypse. Is it a Jewish text that offers a polemic against mainstream Judaism? Is it a pre-Christian Gnostic text that has been influenced by Jewish apocalypticism and has adapted traditional apocalyptic themes to Gnostic thought? Is it possible to distinguish in it any Christian references, especially in the description of the third illuminator?[7] The date of the text can be ascribed to the end of the first century or the beginning of the second; interpolations, particularly the hymnic section of stories of the origin of the illuminator, can be dated somewhat later.

BIBLIOGRAPHY

Alexander Böhlig and Pahor Labib, eds., *Koptisch-gnostische Apokalypsen aus Codex V von Nag Hammadi im Koptischen Museum zu Alt-Kairo*; James H. Charlesworth, ed., *The Old Testament Pseudepigrapha*, 1.707–19 (George W. MacRae); Charles W. Hedrick, *The Apocalypse of Adam*; "The Apocalypse of Adam: A Literary and Source Analysis"; Rodolphe Kasser, "Bibliothèque gnostique V: Apocalypse d'Adam";

---

4. See Pheme Perkins, "Apocalypse of Adam: The Genre and Function of a Gnostic Apocalypse."

5. Françoise Morard, *L'Apocalypse d'Adam*, 8.

6. See George W. MacRae, in James M. Robinson, ed., *The Nag Hammadi Library in English*; Morard, *L'Apocalypse d'Adam*.

7. See Morard, *L'Apocalypse d'Adam*, 100–102.

Bentley Layton, *The Gnostic Scriptures*, 52–64; George W. MacRae, "The Apocalypse of Adam Reconsidered"; Françoise Morard, ed., *L'Apocalypse d'Adam*; "*L'Apocalypse d'Adam* de Nag Hammadi: Un essai d'interprétation"; "Thématique de l'*Apocalypse d'Adam* du Codex V de Nag Hammadi"; Douglas M. Parrott, ed., *Nag Hammadi Codices V,2–5 and VI*, 151–95 (George W. MacRae); Pheme Perkins, "Apocalypse of Adam: The Genre and Function of a Gnostic Apocalypse"; James M. Robinson, ed., *The Nag Hammadi Library in English*, 277–86 (George W. MacRae and Douglas M. Parrott); Hans-Martin Schenke, Hans-Gebhard Bethge, and Ursula Ulrike Kaiser, eds., *Nag Hammadi Deutsch*, 2.433–41 (Walter Beltz); Gedaliahu A. G. Stroumsa, *Another Seed: Studies in Gnostic Mythology*.

The Revelation of Adam[1]

The Revelation of Adam

The Revelation of Adam to Seth (64,1–6)

The revelation that Adam taught his son Seth in the seven hundredth year.[2] And he said, Listen to my words, my son Seth.

Adam and Eve Are Created (64,6–65,23)

After God created me out of earth, along with your mother Eve, I went about with her in a glory that she had beheld in the eternal realm[3] we had come from. She instructed me in the knowledge[4] of the eternal God.[5] We resembled the great eternal angels, for we were superior to the god who had created us and the powers with him, whom we did not know.

God, the ruler[6] of the realms and the powers, angrily divided us. Then we became two beings,[7] and the glory in our hearts departed from your mother Eve and me, as did the previous knowledge that breathed in us. The glory fled from us and entered another great [aeon] and another great [generation]. [65] It was not from this present aeon, from which your mother Eve and I derive, that knowledge [came]. Rather, knowledge entered the seed of great eternal beings. For this reason I myself have called you by the name of that human who is the seed of the great generation, or from whom it comes.[8] After those days, the eternal knowledge of the God of truth left your mother Eve and me, and from then on we learned about mortal things, like human beings.

---

1. Coptic text: NHC V,5: 64,1–85,32. Editions: *The Facsimile Edition of the Nag Hammadi Codices: Codex V*, 74–95; Douglas M. Parrott, ed., *Nag Hammadi Codices V,2–5 and VI*, 151–95 (George W. MacRae); Françoise Morard, *L'Apocalypse d'Adam*; Hans-Martin Schenke, Hans-Gebhard Bethge, and Ursula Ulrike Kaiser, eds., *Nag Hammadi Deutsch*, 2.433–41 (Walter Beltz). The text is also referred to as the *Apocalypse of Adam*. 2. In the Septuagint of *Genesis* 5:3–5, it is said that Adam was 230 years old when Seth was born, and Adam lived 700 years after that. The *Revelation of Adam* is thus Adam's testament just before his death. 3. Aeon, here and below. 4. Gnosis, here and below. 5. Or "I went about with her in glory (or innocently). When she beheld him (i.e., the creator) from the eternal realm we had come from, she instructed me in the knowledge of the eternal God." 6. Archon, here and below. 7. Lit., "aeons." Originally androgynous, the human being is divided by the creator into male and female. 8. The translation is tentative. The text reads, lit., "or from it (or him)"; the text may be corrupt, or this may be a scribal note added for explanation. "The name of that human" is the name of heavenly Seth.

Then we came to recognize the god who had created us, for his powers were not foreign to us. We served him in fear and subservience. And after that we grew dim in our minds.

Adam Has a Revelation in His Sleep (65,24–67,14)

I was asleep in the thought of my mind, and I saw in front of me three persons whose appearance I could not recognize, since they were not from the powers of the god who had [created us].[9] They surpassed . . . glory . . . , [66] saying to me, "Adam, arise from the sleep of death, and hear about the eternal realm and the seed of that human to whom life has come, who came from your partner Eve and you."

When I had heard these words from the great persons standing before me, Eve and I sighed in our hearts. The Lord, the God who had created us, stood before us and said to us, "Adam, why were you both sighing in your hearts? Don't you know that I am the god who created you? And that I breathed into you a spirit of life, so you might be a living soul?"[10]

Our eyes became dim. Then the god who created us created a son[11] from himself and [your] mother Eve . . . . . .[12] in . . . [67] the thought [of procreation].[13] I felt a sweet desire for your mother. The power of our eternal knowledge was gone and weakness overtook us, and the days of our life became few. I realized I had come under the authority of death.

Adam Communicates the Revelation to His Son Seth (67,14–69,1)

So now, my son Seth, I shall reveal to you what those people[14] whom I once saw before me revealed to me. After I have completed the times of this present generation and the years of [the generation] have come to an end, then [Noah will come, a] servant [of the Lord God who created us].[15] [69]

Noah and the Flood (69,2–71,8)

In order that [God], the ruler of the universe,[16] might destroy [all] flesh from the earth because of what they seek, his rainstorms will pour down on those who are from the offspring of people to whom has passed the life of knowledge, which came from your mother Eve and me.[17] For those people were strangers to him. After that great angels will come on high clouds, and they will bring those people

---

9. On the three persons, cf. *Secret Book of John* II, 2; *Genesis* 18:2; *Testament of Abraham* 6. 10. Cf. *Genesis* 2:7. 11. Cain. Cf. *Secret Book of John* II, 24; *Nature of the Rulers* 91. 12. About two lines missing or untranslatable. 13. The restoration is tentative. 14. Throughout the text, the references to "those people" (*nirōme et'mmau*) indicate the offspring of Seth. Cf. the de- scriptions of "that generation" (*tgenea et'mmau*) in the *Gospel of Judas*. 15. The restoration, though tentative, is suggested by Martin Krause, in Werner Foerster, ed., *Gnosis*, 2.17. Coptic p. 68 is blank. 16. Or "almighty" (*pantokratōr*), here and below. 17. Cf. *Genesis* 6–9.

into the place where the spirit of life dwells . . . . . .[18] [70] come from heaven to [earth]. The whole population of fleshly beings will be lost in the [waters].

Then God will rest from his wrath. He will cast his power on the waters and endow his sons[19] and [their wives] with power, by means of the ark, along with the animals that pleased him and the birds of heaven that he called and released on the earth.

God will say to Noah, whom generations will call Deucalion,[20] "Look, I have protected <you> in the ark, along with your wife, your sons, their wives, their animals, and the birds [of heaven] that you called [and released on the earth] . . . . . .[21] [71] Therefore I shall give you and your sons the [earth]. You and your sons will rule over it as kings, and you will refrain from producing offspring of people who will stand in some other glory instead of in my presence."

Noah and Another Generation (71,8–72,15)

Then people will come to be like a cloud of great light.

Those people who have been expelled[22] from the knowledge of the great eternal realms and the angels will come forward and stand before Noah and the realms.

God will say to Noah, "Why have you ignored what I told you? You have created another generation so that you might bring contempt upon my power."

Noah will say, "I testify before the might of your arm that the generation of these people did not come from me or [my] sons . . . ."[23] [72]

. . . knowledge . . . . Those people will be brought into the land they deserve, and a holy dwelling place will be built for them. And they will be called by that name and live there six hundred years in knowledge of incorruptibility, and angels of the great light will be with them. They will have no improper thought in their hearts, but only the knowledge of God.

Noah Divides the Earth Among His Sons (72,15–73,12)

Then Noah will divide the entire earth among his sons, Ham, Japheth, and Shem. He will say to them, "My sons, listen to my words. Look, I have divided the earth among you.[24] But serve God in fear and subservience all the days of your life, and do not let your offspring turn away from the face of God, the ruler of the universe, . . . your . . . and I . . . ."[25] [73]

[Then Shem][26] the son of Noah [will say, "My] offspring will be pleasing before you and your power. Seal it with your strong hand by fear and commandment. None of the offspring that have come from me will turn away from you and

---

18. About seven lines missing or untranslatable. 19. Apparently the sons of Noah. 20. Deucalion is the hero of the Greek story of the great flood. 21. About four lines missing. 22. Or "sent out." Those people, the seed or offspring of Seth, may be understood to have been "expelled" from paradise (with its tree of knowledge) or "sent out" from the realms of knowledge. 23. About five lines missing or untranslatable. 24. Cf. Genesis 9:18–10:32. 25. About five lines missing or untranslatable. 26. The restoration is tentative but reasonable; cf. Ham and Japheth, just below.

God, the ruler of the universe, but they will serve in humility and fear within the limits of their perception."[27]

The Four Hundred Thousand (73,13–74,26)

Then others from the offspring of Ham and Japheth, four hundred thousand in number, will go out and enter another land and sojourn there with those people who came from the great eternal knowledge. The shadow of their power will protect those who sojourn with them from all evil and all unclean desires.

Then the offspring of Ham and Japheth will form twelve kingdoms,[28] and their other offspring will enter the kingdom of another group of people.[29]

[Then] . . . will take counsel . . . aeons . . . [74] mortal . . . the great realms of incorruptibility. They will approach their god Sakla,[30] and they will go in to the powers and accuse the great people who are in their glory.

They will say to Sakla, "What is the power of these people who have stood in your presence, who have separated from the offspring of Ham and Japheth and are <four hundred thousand>[31] in number? They have been received into another realm, one from which they have come, and they have overturned all the glory of your power and the dominion of your hand. The offspring of Noah through his son has fully accomplished your will and the will of all the powers in the realms where your mighty power reigns supreme. But those people and the people who sojourn in their glory have not done your will, and they have turned aside your entire throng."

The Creator Sends Fire, but the Generation of Those People Is Rescued (74,26–76,7)

Then the god of the aeons will hand over to them some who serve [him] . . . . They will come to that land [75] where the great people will be, who have not been defiled and will not be defiled by any desire. For their souls came not from a defiled hand, but from a great commandment of an eternal angel.

Then fire, sulfur, and asphalt will be cast upon those people, and fire and smoke will cover those realms.[32] The eyes of the powers of the heavenly luminaries[33] will be darkened, and the inhabitants of the realms will not be able to see in those days.

But great clouds of light will descend, and more clouds of light will come down on them from the great eternal realms. Abrasax, Sablo, and Gamaliel[34] will

---

27. Coptic *peueime*. 28. In the Septuagint of *Genesis* 10:2, 6, Ham and Japheth are said to have twelve sons. 29. The thirteenth kingdom of the four hundred thousand. 30. Sakla, "fool" in Aramaic, is a name commonly given to the creator of the world. 31. The text mistakenly reads "four hundred" and is emended here. 32. Cf. the description of the destruction of Sodom and Gomorrah in *Genesis* 19 and apocalyptic accounts of the destruction of the world. In *Holy Book of the Great Invisible Spirit* III, 56, the seed of Seth is associated with Sodom and Gomorrah. 33. The sun and moon are the eyes of the sky. 34. On these rescuers, cf. *Holy Book of the Great Invisible Spirit* III, 52–53; 64–65; *Three Forms of First Thought* 48. Perhaps emend "Sablo" to read "Sa<m>blo," as in the other texts.

descend and rescue those people from the fire and wrath, and take them above the realms and domains of the powers, and [take] them away . . . living . . . and take them [away] . . . the realms . . . [76] dwelling place of the great . . . there with the holy angels and the eternal realms. The people will become like those angels, for they are not foreign to them. Rather, they labor with the incorruptible seed.

The Illuminator of Knowledge Comes (76,8–77,18)

Once again, for a third time, the illuminator[35] of knowledge will pass by in great glory,[36] in order to leave behind some of the offspring of Noah and the sons of Ham and Japheth, to leave behind for himself trees that bear fruit.[37] The illuminator will redeem their souls from the day of death. For all creation that came from mortal earth will be under the authority of death, but those who reflect in their hearts on the knowledge of the eternal God will not perish. They have received spirit not from this kingdom, but from something eternal, angelic . . . illuminator . . . will come . . . mortal . . . [77] Seth. And he will perform signs and wonders in order to bring contempt upon the powers and their ruler.

The god of the powers will be troubled and say, "What is the power of this human who is superior to us?"

He will arouse great wrath against that human, and the glory will depart and dwell in holy houses it has chosen for itself. The powers will not see it with their own eyes, and they will not see the illuminator either.

Then they will punish the flesh of the human on whom the holy Spirit has come.[38]

The Origin of the Illuminator (77,18–83,4)

The angels and all the generations of the powers will use the name erroneously and ask,[39] "Where did this[40] come from?" Or again, "Where did the words of falsehood, which all the powers have failed to understand, come from?"[41]

> Now the first kingdom [says of him],
> He came [from] . . . .[42] [78]
> A spirit . . . up.

---

35. Or "luminary," here and below. 36. The illuminator comes for a third time, after the flood and the fire. On three descents of the Savior, cf. the concluding hymn of the Savior in the longer version of the *Secret Book of John, Holy Book of the Great Invisible Spirit* III, 63, and *Three Forms of First Thought*. 37. The reference to trees bearing fruit is a metaphor for productive, fruitful people. Cf. *Revelation of Adam* 85. Conversely, on trees that do not bear fruit, cf. *Gospel of Judas* 39. 38. The illuminator of knowledge will be persecuted. It is possible, though probably unlikely, that this description of persecution recalls the crucifix- ion of Jesus as a manifestation of Seth (as in Christian Sethian texts). 39. Or "The angels and all the generations of the powers will use the name. In their error they will ask . . ." 40. The word "this" refers either generally to "all this" or more specifically to "error" (cf. "erroneously"—i.e., "in error"). 41. There follow legends about the origin of the illuminator from the twelve kingdoms and the thirteenth kingdom. The true account is that of the generation without a king—i.e., the Sethians. 42. Two lines missing or untranslatable.

He was nourished in the heavens.
He received its glory and power.
He came to the bosom of his mother,
and in this way he came to the water.[43]

The second kingdom says of him,
He came from a great prophet.
A bird came, took the child who was born,
and brought him onto a high mountain.
He was nourished by the bird of heaven.
An angel came from there and said to him,
"Arise, God has given you glory."
He received glory and strength,
and in this way he came to the water.

The third kingdom says of him,
He came from a virgin womb.
He was banished from his city, with his mother,
and was brought to a desert place.
He nourished himself there.
He came and received glory and power,
and in this way he came to the water.

The fourth kingdom says of him,
He came [from a virgin] . . . .
[Solomon] [79] sought her,
along with Phersalo and Sauel
and his armies that had been sent out.
Solomon himself sent his army of demons[44]
to search for the virgin.
They did not find the one they sought,
but rather the virgin who was given to them.
They brought her, Solomon took her,
and the virgin became pregnant
and gave birth to the child there.
She nourished him on a border of the desert.
When he was nourished,
he received glory and power
from the seed from which he had been conceived,
and in this way he came to the water.

---

43. Or "he came on the water," here and below. This refrain most likely refers to the illuminator coming to the world; it could also refer to coming to baptism. Cf. *Second Discourse of Great Seth* 50. **44.** In the *Testament of Solomon* and other texts, King Solomon is said to have harnessed the power of the demons.

The fifth kingdom says of him,
He came from a heavenly droplet
and was cast into the sea.
The abyss received him, gave birth to him,
and bore him up.
He received glory and power,
and in this way he came to the water.

The sixth kingdom [says],
A . . . [went] down to the realm [80] below
to gather flowers.
She became pregnant from desire for the flowers,
and gave birth to him in that place.
The angels of the flower garden nourished him.
He received glory and power there,
and in this way he came to the water.[45]

The seventh kingdom says of him,
He is a droplet and came from heaven to earth.
Dragons brought him down to their caves,
and he became a child.
A spirit came over him
and brought him on high
to where the droplet had come from.
He received glory and power there,
and in this way he came to the water.

The eighth kingdom says of him,
A cloud came over the earth
and enveloped a rock, and he came from it.[46]
The angels over the cloud nourished him.
He [received] glory and power there,
and [in this way he] came to [the water]. [81]

The ninth kingdom says of him,
One of the nine muses went away by herself.
She came to a high mountain and relaxed there,
so that she desired herself alone
to become androgynous.
She fulfilled her desire

---

45. Cf. the legend, in Philostratus, about Apollonius of Tyana being born in a meadow after his mother went out to pick flowers. **46.** In traditions about the Mithraic mysteries, Mithras is depicted as being born from a rock.

and became pregnant from it.
He was born.
The angels over desire nourished him.
He received glory and power there,
and in this way he came to the water.

The tenth kingdom says of him,
His god loved a cloud of desire.
He produced him by his hand
and ejaculated some of the droplet
upon the cloud near him,
and he was born.[47]
He received glory and power there,
and in this way he came to the water.

The eleventh kingdom says of him,
The father desired his [own] daughter,
and she became pregnant from her father.
She cast . . . tomb out in the desert. [82]
The angel nourished him there,
and in this way he came to the water.

The twelfth kingdom says of him,
He came from two luminaries.[48]
They nourished him there.
He received glory and power,
and in this way he came to the water.

And the thirteenth kingdom says of him,
Every offspring of their ruler[49] is a word,[50]
and this word received a mandate there.[51]
He received glory and power,
and in this way he came to the water,
so that the desire of those powers might be satisfied.

But the generation without a king[52] says,
God chose him from all the eternal realms.
He made knowledge of the undefiled one of truth
to come to be [in] him.

---

47. In other words, God masturbated, and from the divine semen the illuminator was born. 48. The sun and moon. 49. Archon. 50. Logos. 51. The account of the thirteenth kingdom suggests that the illuminator is the divine word or logos who receives an authoritative mandate. Cf. the law received by the Hebrew people—i.e., the people of Shem. Less convincing are parallels with the logos hymn in *John* 1:1–18. 52. Or "the kingless generation," "the generation with no ruler over it"—i.e., the seed or offspring of Seth.

He said, "The [great] illuminator has come
[from] foreign air, [from a] great eternal realm."
And [he] [83] illumined the generation of those people,
whom he had chosen for himself,
so that they might illumine the whole eternal realm.

Final Vindication of the Seed of Seth (83,4–85,3)

Then the offspring, who will receive his name in the water, and that of them all,[53] will oppose the power, and a dark cloud will overshadow them.

The people will cry out with a loud voice and say, "Blessed are the souls of those people, because they have known God with knowledge of truth. They will live for ever and ever, because they have not been corrupted by their desires, as the angels have, and they have not accomplished the deeds of the powers. Rather, they have stood before him in knowledge of God, like light that has come from fire and blood.

"But we have done everything through the foolishness of the powers. We have boasted about the transgression of [all] our deeds. We have cried out against [the God] of [truth], because all of his work . . . [84] is eternal. Take pity on our spirits. For now we know our souls will surely die."

Then a voice came to them <from> Micheus, Michar, and Mnesinous,[54] who are over holy baptism and living water, saying, "Why were you crying out against the living God with lawless voices and unlawful tongues and souls full of blood and foulness? You are filled with deeds far from truth, yet your ways are full of fun and laughter. You have defiled the water of life and have drawn it to the will of the powers, into whose hands you have been given, to serve them.[55]

"Your thought is not like that of those people whom you persecute . . . desire . . . . [85] Their fruit does not wither.[56] Rather, they will be known up to the great eternal realms."

The Revelation Is Preserved on a Mountain (85,3–18)

The preserved words of the God of the eternal realms were not copied in a book or put in writing. Angelic beings, whom none of the human generations know, will convey them, and they will be placed on a high mountain, on a rock of truth.[57] They will be called words of incorruptibility and truth for those who

---

53. The reading is uncertain here. Perhaps ". . . in the water—even from them all—will oppose the power"?
54. Micheus, Michar, and Mnesinous are connected to baptism in Sethian tradition. Cf. *Holy Book of the Great Invisible Spirit* III, 64; *Zostrianos* 6; *Three Forms of First Thought* 48. Here in the *Revelation of Adam* the text remains difficult, and it may also be translated: "Then a voice came to them, saying, 'Micheus, Michar, and Mnesinous, you who are over holy bap-

tism and living water! Why were you crying out . . .'"
55. Defiling the water of baptism probably means practicing an inappropriate sort of baptism, the baptism of the creator god and the powers of the world.
56. Cf. *Revelation of Adam* 76. 57. On divine revelation preserved on monuments or steles and sometimes on a mountain, cf. *Holy Book of the Great Invisible Spirit* III, 68; *Discourse on the Eighth and Ninth* 61–62; *Three Steles of Seth* 118; *Allogenes the Stranger* 68.

know the eternal God, through wisdom of knowledge and teaching of the eternal angels, because the eternal God knows all things.

Conclusion (85,19–32)

These are the revelations Adam disclosed to his son Seth, and his son taught them to his offspring. This is the hidden knowledge of Adam that he gave to Seth, and this is holy baptism for people who have eternal knowledge, through those born of the word and the incorruptible illuminators,[58] who have come from the holy seed,

Yesseus Mazareus Yessedekeus,[59]
the living water.

The Revelation of Adam

---

58. Or "luminaries"—perhaps the Four Luminaries, Harmozel, Oroiael, Daveithai, and Eleleth). 59. Also connected to baptism in Sethian tradition. Cf. *Holy Book of the Great Invisible Spirit* III, 64; 66; *Zostrianos* 47.

THE ACTS OF PETER AND
THE TWELVE APOSTLES

NHC VI,1

Introduced by Madeleine Scopello
Translated by Marvin Meyer

N ag Hammadi Codex VI contains a wide range of tractates; eight treatises are of different orientations, three of which belong to Hermetic gnosis, and the opening tractate in the codex is the *Acts of Peter and the Twelve Apostles*. This tractate is well preserved, and it occupies pages 1,1–12,22 of the codex. A Coptic translation of a lost Greek original, the tractate has a title at the end of the text; the title could be a later addition after the final lines describing the apostles worshiping Christ.[1]

This highly allegorical treatise opens with an account uttered by the apostle Peter, who relates how, some time after the crucifixion, he and his companions wish to accomplish the ministry Christ entrusted to them and embark on a ship. After having sailed a day and a night, they encounter what is probably a providential sign: the wind brings them to a small city in the middle of the sea. Once on the dock, Peter is told that the name of the town is "Abide-in-endurance." As he inquires for a place where he may lodge with his companions, he encounters a fine-looking man holding a book and a box made of precious wood. This man, whose body is only partly visible to Peter, cries out "Pearls! Pearls!" (2,10–32). The apostle addresses him, thinking he is an inhabitant of the city, and asks him about a place to lodge, since he and his friends are strangers in the city. But the man is a stranger himself (2,34–3,11). The announcement about pearls catches the attention of rich people only for a very short time, but poor people, on the contrary, surround the man, eager to see a shining pearl, even if they cannot afford to buy it. This foreign merchant tells them that they will be able to see the pearl if they agree to come to his city, and they may even be able to own it, if they wish: he will graciously offer the pearl to them (3,14–5,1). At this point in the story, Peter asks

---

1. See R. McL. Wilson and Douglas M. Parrott, in Douglas M. Parrott, ed., *Nag Hammadi Codices V,2–5 and VI*.

the man to disclose his name. Peter also wants to find out about the hardships of the trip to the merchant's city, because he and his companions are entrusted with spreading the word of God everywhere (5,8–14). The merchant reveals his name, Lithargoel, as well as its meaning, "light bright stone"—an appropriate name for someone who sells luxury items.

Lithargoel goes on to describe the way to his city, which is named after its nine gates. Only those who have left everything behind (an allusion to the well-known theme of renunciation) are able to reach it (5,19–25). The way is extremely dangerous, and people may be attacked by robbers and wild beasts. After seeing a dramatic vision of a city surrounded by waves and walls, Peter sets off with his companions, and they avoid the hazards of the road, thanks to the advice of the merchant. When they arrive at the gates of the city, Lithargoel comes to meet them. He does not look like a merchant but rather like a physician, holding an unguent box and followed by a young disciple carrying a pouch full of medicine (8,14–19). At first the apostles do not recognize Lithargoel, and Peter asks the man to show him Lithargoel's house, but shortly thereafter the mysterious physician reveals himself as Christ (9,2–19). He exhorts the disciples to go and heal the sick people of the city who believe in his name, and he offers his pouch of medicine to them. John points out that he and his companions have not been taught how to heal. He says, "How, then, shall we know how to heal bodies, as you have told us?" (11,10–14). Christ answers him by stating that "the doctors of this world heal what is of the world, but the doctors of souls heal the heart" (11,16–19). He counsels them to heal bodies first, without worldly medicine, so that people will believe in their power to heal illnesses of the heart. After a final warning about rich people who are even within the churches—a polemical aside directed toward orthodox Christianity—the treatise ends with the apostles prostrating themselves in front of Christ and worshiping him.

In the lively style of the novel, the *Acts of Peter and the Twelve Apostles* addresses the theme of the missionary journeys of the apostles, a motif developed especially in the apocryphal acts of the apostles. An interesting parallel can be drawn between the *Acts of Peter and the Twelve Apostles* and the *Acts of Philip*. In the latter text, Philip arrives at the city of Azotus, on the coast of Palestine (3.15), after a dangerous voyage from Candace, in Ethiopia, and when he reaches the city gates, he asks for a place to lodge. As in several apocryphal acts, the author of the *Acts of Peter and the Twelve Apostles* focuses on the need for the renunciation of worldly possessions in order to be saved.[2] Wild beasts and brigands are commonly found in apocryphal, Gnostic, and monastic texts describing the temptations inflicted on those who seek after truth.

The symbol of the pearl is central to the present text. Also known from the famous *Hymn of the Pearl* in the apocryphal *Acts of Thomas*, the pearl in the *Acts of Peter and the Twelve Apostles* symbolizes spiritual salvation.[3] The name

---

2. See Yves Haas, "L'exigence du renoncement au monde dans les Actes de Pierre et des douze apôtres, les Apophtegmes des pères du désert et la Pistis Sophia."

3. Antoine Guillaumont, "De nouveaux actes apocryphes: Les actes de Pierre et des douze apôtres."

Lithargoel, said to be the name of Christ, is composed of two Greek words: *lithos,* "stone," and *argos,* "shining," followed by the Semitic honorific suffix *el,* which refers to God and appears often in angelic names. Andrea Lorenzo Molinari remarks that the figure of the pearl merchant Lithargoel could thus be understood as "the pearl of God," a possible reference to the parable of the pearl in *Matthew* 15:46. Lithargoel is an angel name in the *Book of the Installation of the Angel Gabriel*[4] and is also known, in a similar form, in Nubian traditions.[5] In the *Acts of Peter and the Twelve Apostles,* Lithargoel is a key figure, portrayed with multiple forms, and he appears as Christ and a holy physician.

The theme of the physician of foreign origin healing bodies and souls is another key element in the *Acts of Peter and the Twelve Apostles.* This same theme is found in the *Doctrine of the Apostle Addai,* a fifth-century Syriac text that is dependent on earlier traditions, as well as *Acts of Philip* 5, a text also written later than the Greek original of the *Acts of Peter and the Twelve Apostles,* and this fact may suggest that the *Acts of Peter and the Twelve Apostles* could have influenced other early Christian texts and particularly the fifth *Act of Philip,* which was composed in Asia Minor at the end of the fourth century.[6] The emphasis placed on poverty and renunciation of the world in the *Acts of Peter and the Twelve Apostles* may also recall the *Acts of Philip* and apocryphal literature in general. This leads us to ask whether the *Acts of Peter and the Twelve Apostles* is a Gnostic text[7] or simply a treatise used by Gnostics because of the presence of themes familiar to them.[8]

The tractate has been understood by Martin Krause, Douglas M. Parrott, and R. McL. Wilson as being composite, perhaps consisting of four major sections (or two major sections, according to Andrea Lorenzo Molinari): (1) an introduction; (2) the story of the meeting of Peter with the pearl merchant and the reaction of the rich and poor people; (3) the account of the trip of Peter and his companions to the city of Lithargoel, along with Peter's vision; and (4) the revelation of Lithargoel as physician and Christ. There are some contradictions among these four accounts, and it is possible that they were assembled by an editor who used parables that were already available in order to communicate an episode of the apostolic mission.[9] The date of composition of the tractate can be assigned to the end of second century or the beginning of the third, a date that a number of parallels with the *Shepherd of Hermas* would seem to support.[10]

---

4. See the note to the translation as well as Stephen J. Patterson, "Sources, Redaction and *Tendenz* in the *Acts of Peter and the Twelve Apostles.*"

5. See J. Kubińska, "L'ange Litakskuel en Nubie."

6. See Madeleine Scopello, *Femme, gnose et manichéisme,* 342–46.

7. See Pheme Perkins, *The Gnostic Dialogue,* 125–28.

8. See Wilson and Parrott, in *Nag Hammadi Codices V,2–5 and VI.*

9. See Mitzi Jane Smith, "Understand Ye a Parable! *The Acts of Peter and the Twelve Apostles* as Parable Narrative."

10. See Douglas M. Parrott and R. McL. Wilson, in James M. Robinson, ed., *The Nag Hammadi Library in English.*

BIBLIOGRAPHY

Victor C. Ghica, *Les actes de Pierre et des douze apôtres*; Antoine Guillaumont, "De nouveaux actes apocryphes: Les actes de Pierre et des douze apôtres"; Yves Haas, "L'exigence du renoncement au monde dans les Actes de Pierre et des douze apôtres, les Apophtegmes des pères du désert et la Pistis Sophia"; Martin Krause, "Die Petrusakten in Codex VI von Nag Hammadi"; Martin Krause and Pahor Labib, *Gnostische und hermetische Schriften aus Codex II und Codex VI*; J. Kubińska, "L'ange Litakskuel en Nubie"; Andrea Lorenzo Molinari, *The Acts of Peter and the Twelve Apostles*; "The Acts of Peter and the Twelve Apostles: A Reconsideration of the Source Question"; Douglas M. Parrott, ed., *Nag Hammadi Codices V,2–5 and VI*, 197–229 (R. McL. Wilson and Douglas M. Parrott); Stephen J. Patterson, "Sources, Redaction and *Tendenz* in the Acts of Peter and the Twelve Apostles"; Pheme Perkins, *The Gnostic Dialogue*, 125–28; James M. Robinson, ed., *The Nag Hammadi Library in English*, 287–94 (Douglas M. Parrott and R. McL. Wilson); Hans-Martin Schenke, Hans-Gebhard Bethge, and Ursula Ulrike Kaiser, eds., *Nag Hammadi Deutsch*, 2.443–53 (Hans-Martin Schenke); Wilhelm Schneemelcher, ed., *New Testament Apocrypha*, 2.412–25 (Hans-Martin Schenke); Madeleine Scopello, *Femme, gnose et manichéisme*; Jesse Sell, "Jesus the 'Fellow-Stranger'"; Mitzi Jane Smith, "Understand Ye a Parable! *The Acts of Peter and the Twelve Apostles* as Parable Narrative."

The Acts of Peter
and the Twelve Apostles[1]

The Apostles Set Sail (1,1–2,6)

. . . [words] that . . . occasion . . . as follows: it happened when we [were sent] out to [preach] . . . we, the apostles, . . . that we sailed, while we . . . of the body, with others who were anxious of [heart].

Still, we were one of [mind], and we decided to complete the ministry to which the lord appointed us. We came to an agreement with each other, and we went down to the sea at the right time, which we learned from the master. We discovered a ship moored at the shore, ready to sail, and we spoke with the sailors of the ship about whether we could come aboard with them. They were very friendly to us, as was arranged by the master.

It happened that after we put out to sea, we sailed for a day and a night. Then a wind blew the ship and brought us to a small city in the middle of the sea.

I, Peter, asked residents standing on the dock about the name of this city. [One] of [them] [2] answered [and said, "The name] of this [city is 'Abide' —that] is to say, establish yourself—'[in]-endurance.' So your[2] leader within [you will] . . . a palm branch at the edge . . . ."[3]

The Apostles Meet a Man Giving Out Pearls (2,7–3,31)

Now, when we went ashore [with the] baggage, I entered the city to inquire . . . about lodging. A man came out wearing a linen cloth bound around his waist with a gold belt,[4] and a shawl was tied on his chest, going over his shoulders and covering his head and hands.

I was staring at the man, because he was good-looking in appearance and demeanor. I saw four parts of his body: the soles of his feet, a portion of his chest, the palms of his hands, and his face. That was all I could see.

---

1. Coptic text: NHC VI,1: 1,1–12,22. Editions: *The Facsimile Edition of the Nag Hammadi Codices: Codex VI,* 5–16; Douglas M. Parrott, ed., *Nag Hammadi Codices V,2–5 and VI,* 197–229 (R. McL. Wilson and Douglas M. Parrott); Hans-Martin Schenke, Hans-Gebhard Bethge, and Ursula Ulrike Kaiser, eds., *Nag Hammadi Deutsch,* 2.443–53 (Hans-Martin Schenke).

2. The gender of the pronoun indicates that the city itself is being addressed. 3. Wilson and Parrott, in *Nag Hammadi Codices V,2–5 and VI,* 206–7, restore to read "at the edge of [the dock]." 4. According to *Daniel* 10:5, *Revelation* 15:6, and other texts, heavenly beings may be dressed in linen clothing with gold belts.

There was a bound book like that of an official[5] in his left hand and a staff of styrax wood in his right hand. He spoke slowly, with a resonating voice, and called out in the city, "Pearls! Pearls!"[6]

I was assuming he was a resident of that city, and I said to him, "My brother and my friend." [3]

[He answered] me [and said, "You] are [right] to say, '[My brother and] my friend.' What do you [want] from me?"

I said to him, "[I want to ask] you [about] lodging for me and my brothers, since we are strangers here."

He said [to] me, "That is why I said, 'My brother and my friend,' for I too am a stranger along with you."

When he said this, he called out again, "Pearls! Pearls!"

The wealthy people of that city heard his voice and came out of their hidden chambers. Some were peering out of the rooms of their houses; others looked from their upper windows. They saw nothing in him, for there was no bag over his shoulder and no bundle within his linen cloth or shawl.[7] In their arrogance they did not even ask who he was, and he in turn did not make himself known to them. They went back to their rooms and said, "Is this man mocking us?"[8]

The Poor Approach the Man Offering Pearls (3,32–5,1)

The poor [4] [of that city] also heard [his voice, and they approached] the man [who offered to sell this pearl and said to him], "Please [show us the] pearl so that [at least we can see] it. We are [poor] and don't have the money to buy it. But [show it to us], and then we can tell our friends that [we saw] a pearl with our own eyes."

He answered and said to them, "If you can, come to my city, so that I may not only show it to you but may give it to you free of charge."[9]

When the poor of that city heard this, they said, "We are beggars, and we know that nobody gives a pearl to a beggar. Beggars usually get bread and money. So we ask you this favor, that you show us the pearl, and then we can brag to our friends that we saw a pearl with our own eyes. For this does not happen among poor people, especially beggars like us."

He answered and said to them, "If you can, you should come to my city, that I may not only show it to you but may give it to you free of charge."

The poor and the beggars rejoiced because of [5] the man [who gives] free of charge.

---

5. Apparently a book, or codex, and not a scroll. 6. Cf. Wisdom calling out to people in *Proverbs* 8 and other texts. On the pearl, sometimes used as a symbol of the soul or the knowledge of the soul, see *Matthew* 13:45–46, and especially the *Hymn of the Pearl* in the *Acts of Thomas*. 7. Cf. *Matthew* 10:9–10; *Mark* 6:8–9; *Luke* 9:3. 8. Cf. the wealthy as portrayed in such texts as *Matthew* 19:16–30; *Mark* 10:17–31; *Luke* 18:18–30. 9. In 2 *Corinthians* 11:7 Paul declares that in his preaching he offers the gospel free of charge.

The Man Named Lithargoel Discusses Hardships (5,1–6,28)

Some people [asked] . . .[10] about hardships. Peter replied and told [them] what he heard on the way, for they had endured hardships in their ministry.

He said to the man who offered to sell the pearl, "I would like to know your name and what hardships there are on the way to your city. We are strangers and servants of God, and we must be obedient and spread God's word in every city."

The man[11] answered and said, "Since you ask, my name is Lithargoel, which means 'light bright stone.'[12] And concerning the way to this city, which you also have asked about, I shall tell you. None can travel that road unless they renounce all their possessions and fast daily from one night's stay to the next. There are many robbers and wild beasts on that road. If people[13] take bread on the road, black dogs kill them because of the bread. If they carry expensive garments of this world, robbers kill them [6] [because of the] garments. [If they carry] water, [wolves kill them because of the water], for the wolves are thirsty. [If they] are concerned about [meat] and vegetables, lions eat them because of the meat, and [if] they get away from the lions, bulls devour them because of the vegetables."

When he said this to me, I groaned within and said, "What great hardships are on the way! May Jesus give us the strength to walk this path."

He saw that my face was downcast and that I was groaning, and he said to me, "Why are you groaning if you know the name of Jesus and believe in him? He is a power great enough to give you strength. For I also believe in the Father who has sent him."[14]

I asked him again, "What is the name of the city you are going to?"

He said to me, "This is the name of my city: In nine gates let us praise God, and consider that the tenth gate is the main gate."[15]

After this I left him in peace and went to call my friends.

Peter Learns About Abiding in Endurance (6,28–7,19)

I saw waves and huge walls of water around the shores of the city, and I was amazed at the marvelous things I saw. Then I saw an old man sitting there, and I

---

10. Perhaps restore to read "[Peter]." 11. Lit., "He." 12. Lithargoel is an angel of healing known from a text entitled the *Book of the Installation of the Angel Gabriel*, in which the angel (said to be the fifth angel of a group of five) states, "I am Litharkuel, in whose hand is the medicine chest, filled with the medicine of life; I heal every soul"; see Hans-Martin Schenke, in Wilhelm Schneemelcher, ed., *New Testament Apocrypha*, 2.418–19. Schenke also mentions the base of a statue, now in Warsaw, of a figure identified as Litarkuel (or Litaxkuel). Schenke likens Lithargoel to "a Jewish Asclepius." Wolf-Peter Funk also notes that *litharguros* ("silver stone") is the Greek name of a stone that is light in color and is sometimes used in medicine to help in cauterization. 13. In the following sentences the Coptic text has singular pronouns ("he," "him"); for stylistic reasons the translation employs the plural ("they," them"). 14. The expression "the Father who has sent him" recalls similar expressions in the *Gospel of John*. 15. The gates of the city bring to mind the gates of Jerusalem—and of heavenly Jerusalem—and the ten heavenly realms (cf. the *Revelation of Paul*). Cf. also, with Schenke (in Schneemelcher, ed., *New Testament Apocrypha*, 2. 417), the *Book of the Installation of the Archangel Michael*, in which the angels and gates of the heavenly city are mentioned.

asked him if the name of the city was really [7] [the one] he had [given when he said, "Abide-in-endurance]."

He said to me, "[You speak] the truth. We abide here because [we] endure."

I answered and said, "Rightly . . . have people called endurance the first virtue. Cities are populated with people [who] endure their temptations, and a noble kingdom comes from them, because they endure through the deceptions and difficulties of the storms. This goes to show how the city of everyone who bears the burden of the yoke of faith will be populated,[16] and these sorts of people will be included in the kingdom of heaven."

Peter and the Others Go to the City of Lithargoel (7,19–8,13)

I rushed off and called my friends, that we might go to the city to which Lithargoel directed us. In a pact of faith we renounced everything, as he had told us. We avoided the robbers because they did not find the garments they were looking for with us. We avoided the wolves because they did not find the water they were thirsty for with us. We avoided the lions because they did not find the meat they wanted with us. [8] [We avoided the bulls because . . . they did not find any] vegetables.[17] We [were filled with] great joy and freedom from care, in peace, [in] our master. We [rested] in front of the gate and talked together. This was not a casual conversation about this world. Rather, we lingered in a deep discussion of the faith, and we recalled the robbers we avoided on the way.

Lithargoel Appears and Reveals That He Is Christ (8,13–9,17)

Lithargoel appeared, and he looked different from before. Now he took the form of a doctor with a medicine case under his arm, and there was a young student following him with a bag full of medicine. We did not recognize him.

Peter spoke up and said, "We wish you to do us a favor, since we are strangers. Take us to the house of Lithargoel before evening comes."

He said, "With an upright heart I shall show it to you. But I wonder how you know this fine man. He does not reveal himself to everyone, because he is the son of a great king. Rest a little while, and I shall go and treat this patient and then return."

He hurried off, and he returned [9] soon.

He said to Peter, "Peter!"

Peter was startled that he knew his name was Peter. Peter responded to the Savior, "How do you know me, for you called me by my name?"

Lithargoel answered, "I want to ask you, who gave you the name Peter?"

He said to him, "It was Jesus Christ, the son of the living God. He gave me this name."[18]

---

16. Cf. the concept of the yoke of the Torah, or law, within Judaism. 17. Cf. *Acts of Peter and the Twelve Apostles* 5–6. 18. Cf. *Matthew* 16:16–18.

He answered and said, "It is I. Recognize me, Peter."

He loosened the garment be was wearing, the one he had put on so that we did not recognize him.

Lithargoel Sends the Apostles Out (9,17–10,30)

When he revealed to us that this really was he, we fell down and worshiped him. We were eleven disciples.[19] He reached out his hand and made us stand up. We spoke with him in a humble manner, and with our heads bowed down in modesty we said, "We shall do whatever you wish. Just give us the strength always to do what you wish."

He gave them the medicine case and the bag that was in the student's hand, and he offered these instructions [10] and said, "Return to the city you came from, called Abide-and-remain-in-endurance, and teach all who have believed in my name that I too have endured adversities of faith. I shall grant you your reward. To the poor of that city give what they need to live, until I present to them what is better, about which I told <them>, 'I shall give it to you free of charge.' "[20]

Peter answered and said to him, "Master, you have taught us to renounce the world and everything in it. We have forsaken these things for your sake. Now we are concerned only about food for a single day. Where can we find what the poor need, which you ask us to give to them?"

The master answered and said, "Peter, it was necessary for you to understand the parable I told you. Don't you know that my name, which you teach, is worth more than all riches, and the wisdom of God is worth more than silver and gold and precious stones?"[21]

The Apostles Are to Heal Bodies and Souls (10,31–12,22)

He gave them the bag of medicine and said, "Heal all the people of the city who are sick and believe [11] [in] my name."

Peter was afraid to take issue with the master a second time, so he motioned to John, who was next to him: "You say something this time."[22]

John answered and said, "We are afraid to say too much in your presence, but you have asked us to practice this art. We have not been taught to be doctors. How, then, shall we know how to heal bodies, as you have told us?"

He answered him, "You have said it well, John: 'I know that the doctors of this world heal what is of the world, but the doctors of souls heal the heart.' So, first heal bodies, that through the real powers[23] of healing their bodies, with no medicine of this world, they may come to believe in you, that you also have the power to heal sicknesses of the heart.

---

19. The twelve become the eleven disciples after the betrayal of Judas Iscariot; cf. *Matthew* 28:16; *Mark* 16:14; *Luke* 24: 9, 33; *Acts* 1:26; the *Gospel of Judas*. 20. Cf. *Acts of Peter and the Twelve Apostles* 4–5. 21. Cf. *Proverbs* 8:10; *Acts* 3:6; 1 *Corinthians* 3:9–15. 22. Perhaps cf. *John* 13:23–24. 23. Or "miracles."

"As for the wealthy people of this city, who did not even bother to ask who I was but reveled in their wealth and arrogance, [12] do not dine with them in their houses and do not have fellowship with them, or their partiality[24] may influence you. For many people in the churches have shown partiality to the rich, and thus they sin and also lead others to sin. Judge them in uprightness, that your ministry may be glorified and my name also may be glorified in the churches."[25]

The disciples answered and said, "Yes, in truth, this is what we should do."

They fell down and worshiped him. He made them stand up, and he departed from them, in peace.

Amen.

The Acts of Peter
and the Twelve Apostles

---

24. Or "snobbishness." 25. Cf. *James* 2:1–13.

THUNDER

NHC VI,2

Introduced by Paul-Hubert Poirier
Translated by Marvin Meyer

The tractate entitled *Thunder*, or *Thunder, Perfect Mind*, is a kind of anomaly in the Nag Hammadi library. It belongs to none of the literary genres attested in the collection; it features no known Gnostic entity; and it has neither a narrative nor a didactic frame. The Nag Hammadi texts it resembles most closely are *Three Forms of First Thought* (XIII,1) and the hymn of the Savior (Forethought or Pronoia) at the end of the longer version of the *Secret Book of John* (II,30–31).

Thunder takes the form of a discourse, composed for the most part of self-predications in the first-person singular (Coptic *anok pe/te*, Greek *egō eimi*) interspersed with exhortations and reproaches addressed to an unidentified audience. The speaker remains unnamed, but many features in the text show that the person or entity speaking is a feminine being. This characteristic explains why the tractate was at first compared with the Isis aretalogies—the self-proclamations in which the goddess Isis presents herself and lists her feats—or with the public addresses of female Wisdom in the Jewish scriptures (*Proverbs* 8:4–36; *Sirach* 24:3–22), but these parallels remain only partial.

The genre of *Thunder* is rather to be defined according to the opening statement of the speaker: "I was sent from the power and have come to those who contemplate me and am found among those who seek me" (13,2–5). These lines evoke the kind of discourse by which, in ancient societies, an envoy or ambassador would introduce himself, name his sender, and state his qualifications and status. The *Gospel of John* provides good example of such declarations (see *John* 7:28–29; 8:14–18; 8:42).

Despite the absence of a clear literary structure, the text does show some kind of organization. It opens with a prologue (13,2–15) in which the speaker identifies herself and invites her listeners (or readers) to be attentive to her message, and it closes with a final exhortation to hear and learn her words in order to live and not die again (20,26–21,32). In between, the text is made up of sections more or less organized, of which the most striking feature is the constant use of contradictory statements.

The feminine entity who speaks throughout *Thunder* presents herself as "the first and the last" (13,15–16), the only one who exists and has no one to judge her (21,18–20). She transcends and abolishes all kinds of relationships and dependencies, whether familial, spousal, or domestic. She declares, "I am <the mother> and the daughter. I am the limbs of my mother. . . . I am the mother of my father and the sister of my husband, and he is my offspring" (13,20–32). Furthermore, the speaker claims two modes of existence characterized by paradox and contradiction: she is simultaneously "honored" and "scorned" (13,17), "whore" and "holy" (13,18), "despised" and "professed" (16,29–31), "foolish" and "wise" (15,29–30).

Even if the female speaker of *Thunder* calls for universal acceptance, being "the wisdom [of the] Greeks and the knowledge of the barbarians," "the judgment of Greeks and barbarians" (16,3–6), she has nevertheless a precise ethnic identity: she is "a barbarian among barbarians" (16, 2–3). The opposition of Greek and barbarian was well known and used in antiquity (cf. *Romans* 1:14), usually in a polemical way. Here the claim by the speaker to be a barbarian is given a rather positive value. Though she is "the one whose image is great in Egypt and who has no image among the barbarians" (16,6–9), called "death" and "lawless," "godless" and "uneducated" (16,12–15.24) — that is, deprived of the Greek *paideia* — she is in reality life and law, and people learn from her and the many gods of the Greeks manifest her presence. All those contradictory statements are best explained if we hypothesize that the reference to the "barbarians" is a cryptic designation of the Jews, and the female speaker of the tractate is a metamorphosis of the Jewish Wisdom or Sophia.

Like Wisdom, the speaker of *Thunder* is a feminine figure who delivers a first-person speech composed of self-predications and powerful statements, and these must be received and heard. Just like Sophia, the speaker resembles a divine entity, second only to the first principle, to which she alone provides access (cf. *Proverbs* 8:22). But, at the same time, she exhibits features that the biblical wisdom tradition attributes to the opposite of Sophia, Folly, the "foolish woman" of *Proverbs* 9:13–18, depicted as a courtesan and a prostitute (*Proverbs* 7:10). Although biblical Wisdom gives intelligence and knowledge to the simple, the heroine of our tractate, though providing learning, declares herself "uneducated" (16,27–29). Such a contradictory statement — and there are many others in the tractate — is best explained if the speaker is seen as a drastic reinterpretation of Jewish Wisdom. But there are in the biblical sapiential tradition elements that anticipate the paradoxical portrait of the speaker: Wisdom knows how to walk "on tortuous paths" and to torment her listeners by her discipline in order to test them (*Sirach* 4:17). She dwells in the highest heavens and, at the same time, walks with the human race (*Proverbs* 8:30–31; *Sirach* 24:3–7). Therefore, the speaker of *Thunder* is a universalistic radicalization of biblical Wisdom, of which the best illustration is perhaps the Simonian Wisdom of the Pseudo-Clementines: an "all-bearing being, for whose sake the Greeks and barbarians fought, having before their eyes but an image of truth," while she was with the Supreme God (*Homily* 2.25.2; trans. T. Smith). The universalism of the tractate evokes also Plutarch's ideal, who declares that the gods are not to be regarded "as different among different peoples nor as barbarian and Greek and as southern and northern" (*Isis and Osiris* 67; trans. J. Gwyn Griffiths).

Even though *Thunder* is indebted to the Jewish wisdom tradition, there are indications in the text that suggest other backgrounds, either Gnostic, Isiac, or philosophical. First, there is a section of the tractate (13,19–14,9: "I am the wife and the virgin . . . and whatever he wishes happens to me") that has clear parallels in two Nag Hammadi tractates, *On the Origin of the World* (114,7–15) and the *Nature of the Rulers* (89,16–17). Those parallels are so close that we are compelled to suppose that one tractate is dependent upon the others or that the three of them draw from a common source. In *On the Origin of the World* and the *Nature of the Rulers*, the parallel passages are introduced as a quotation. In *Thunder*, there is no formal indication of a citation, but the vocabulary of these lines indicates that they were borrowed from somewhere else and introduced into the tractate, probably because of their stylistic similarity to the rest of the writing. Consequently, it cannot be argued, on the basis of this common stock, that *Thunder* maintains the same Gnostic perspective as the other two tractates. Nevertheless, our tractate shows obvious parallels with Gnostic texts or doctrines that suggest it could have been composed in a milieu familiar with Gnostic ideas.

It has also been suggested that *Thunder* could be read in the light of the Isis aretalogies. In fact, *Thunder* shares many features with the aretalogies: a feminine persona, the self-predications themselves, and an identical claim to universal recognition. *Thunder*'s speaker is not far from Isis, who in her many forms and names encompasses in herself all gods and goddesses. But there are irreducible differences between *Thunder* and the Isiac aretalogies. The aretalogies convey only the positive part of *Thunder*'s oppositions: whereas the speaker introduces herself as "the honored and the scorned, . . . the whore and the holy" (13,16–18), the Hellenistic Isis is univocally sacred and blameless. Once again, we have a common atmosphere rather than a case of literary dependency.

Finally, many elements in *Thunder* point toward a philosophical model[1] widely used in the second and third centuries to describe the metaphysical first principles, and especially the second principle, seen as a self-generating Mind, like the present tractate's "Perfect Mind," which is both the mother and the daughter, and the mother of her own father (13,20–21.30–31). Of course, *Thunder* is not a philosophical tractate, and its author wishes not only to teach the readers, but also to exhort and convert them. Nevertheless, and despite its "prophetic" style, the tractate reflects the brand of Platonism known to us from Porphyry and Iamblichus.

The tractate *Thunder, Perfect Mind,* is a Sahidic Coptic translation of an otherwise lost Greek original. This translation could have been done at any time in the

---

1. See John Whittaker, "Self-Generating Principles in Second-Century Gnostic Systems."

first half of the fourth century, since Codex VI of the Nag Hammadi library, the only witness to the text, was very likely copied and bound in the mid-fourth century.

Thunder most likely comes from a milieu characterized by proselytizing and marked by apocalypticism and an eschatological orientation. The epilogue of the tractate announces the fulfillment of the "words" and "texts" (21,12–13) and promises to the listeners a "place of rest" where they will find life after their death. The style of the tractate is to be compared with what the pagan philosopher Celsus terms "the most perfect type of prophecy among people of Phoenicia and Palestine":

> They are many, he says, who are nameless, who prophesy at the slightest excuse for some trivial cause both inside and outside temples; and there are some who wander about begging and roaming around cities and military camps; and they pretend to be moved as if giving some oracular utterance. It is an ordinary and common custom for each one to say, "I am God (or a son of God, or a divine Spirit). And I have come. Already the world is being destroyed. And you, O men, are to perish because of your iniquities. But I wish to save you. And you shall see me returning again with heavenly power. Blessed is he who has worshipped me now!" (Cited in Origen *Against Celsus* 7.9; trans. Chadwick)

In both *Celsus* and *Thunder*, we have a divine envoy who calls to conversion and claims to bring about salvation.

This prophetic milieu of *Thunder* must have been Jewish or at least akin to Judaism. The peculiarity of the form and contents of *Thunder* suggests, however, that this Jewish or Judaizing milieu must have been marginal—in sum, a milieu opened to the literary and doctrinal diversity exemplified by Codex VI, one of the most disparate of the Nag Hammadi collection, with its Hermetic, apocryphal, and Gnostic writings.[2] It would not be too daring an assumption to suppose that the Gnostics who gathered the Nag Hammadi tractates included *Thunder* because they saw in its feminine speaker an evocation of Barbelo as she appears in *Three Forms of First Thought* or the *Three Steles of Seth*. The Gnostic Barbelo could easily be reinterpreted in sapiential or philosophical as well as mythological terms.

As to the place and date of composition, we are left with no positive indications. The mention of Egypt in *Thunder* 16,7 points toward an Egyptian milieu, perhaps Alexandria, but this remains hypothetical. The comparison with the excerpt from *Celsus* cited above suggests that the Greek original of *Thunder* might have been composed around the end of the second century or the beginning of the third. The philosophical background we have evoked hints in the same direction.

---

2. See Michael A. Williams, "Interpreting the Nag Hammadi Library as 'Collection(s)' in the History of 'Gnosticism(s)'"; Michael A. Williams and Lance Jenott, "Inside the Covers of Codex VI."

BIBLIOGRAPHY

Bentley Layton, *The Gnostic Scriptures*, 77–85; Douglas M. Parrott, ed., *Nag Hammadi Codices V, 2–5 and VI*, 231–55 (George W. MacRae); Paul-Hubert Poirier, ed., *Le Tonnerre, intellect parfait*; Hans-Martin Schenke, Hans-Gebhard Bethge, and Ursula Ulrike Kaiser, eds., *Nag Hammadi Deutsch*, 2.455–66 (Uwe Karsten Plisch); John Whittaker, "Self-Generating Principles in Second-Century Gnostic Systems"; "The Historical Background of Proclus' Doctrine of the *authupostata*"; Michael A. Williams, "Interpreting the Nag Hammadi Library as 'Collection(s)' in the History of 'Gnosticism(s)' "; Michael A. Williams and Lance Jenott, "Inside the Covers of Codex VI."

Thunder[1]

Thunder
Perfect Mind

I was sent from the power
and have come to those who contemplate me
and am found among those who seek me.

Look at me, you who contemplate me,
and you who hear, listen to me.
You awaiting me, take me to yourselves.
Do not banish me from before your eyes.
Do not let your voice be hateful toward me,
nor your hearing.
Do not be ignorant of me,
in any place, at any time.
Be alert; do not be ignorant of me.[2]

For I am the first and the last.[3]
I am the honored and the scorned.
I am the whore and the holy.
I am the wife and the virgin.
I am \<the mother\> and the daughter.
I am the limbs of my mother.
I am a barren woman
who has many children.
I have had many weddings
and have taken no husband.

---

1. Coptic text: NHC VI,2: 13,1–21,32. Editions: *The Facsimile Edition of the Nag Hammadi Codices: Codex VI*, 17–25. Douglas M. Parrott, ed., *Nag Hammadi Codices V,2–5 and VI*, 231–55 (George W. MacRae); Paul-Hubert Poirier, ed., *Le Tonnerre, intellect parfait*; Hans-Martin Schenke, Hans-Gebhard Bethge, and Ursula Ulrike Kaiser, eds., *Nag Hammadi Deutsch*, 2.455–66 (Uwe-Karsten Plisch). 2. These statements recall the role of Wisdom in Jewish wisdom literature. 3. Or "For it is I who am the first and the last." This grammatical construction with the Coptic cleft sentence is employed throughout the text, and Wolf-Peter Funk refers to such extensive use of the cleft sentence as "hyperclefting."

I am a midwife
and a woman who does not give birth.
I am the solace of my own birth pains.
I am bride and groom,
and my husband produced me.
I am the mother of my father
and the sister of my husband,
and he is my offspring.
I am the servant of him who fashioned me,
I am the ruler [14] of my offspring.
He [produced me] with a premature birth,
and he is my offspring born on time,
and my strength is from him.
I am the staff of his power in his youth,
and he is the rod of my old age,
and whatever he wishes happens to me.[4]
I am silence that is incomprehensible
and insight[5] whose memory is great.
I am the voice whose sounds are many
and the word whose appearances are many.
I am the utterance of my own name.

You who hate me, why do you love me
and hate those who love me?
You who deny me, confess me,
and you who confess me, deny me.
You who tell the truth about me,
tell lies about me,
and you who have lied about me,
tell the truth about me.
You who know me, be ignorant of me,
and as for those who have not known me,
let them know me.

For I am knowledge and ignorance.
I am shy and bold.
I am shameless; I am ashamed.
I am tough and I am terror.
I am war and peace.

Be attentive to me.
I am disgraced and great.

---

4. Cf. *On the Origin of the World* 114. **5.** "Insight," Epinoia, is an emanation of the divine and a heavenly aeon in the *Secret Book of John* and other Sethian texts.

Be attentive to my [15] poverty and my wealth.
Do not be arrogant toward me
when I am thrown down on the ground,
and you will find me
in those [who] are to come.
If you see me on the dung heap,
don't go and leave me thrown there.
You will find me in the kingdoms.
If you see me when I am thrown out
with the disgraced in the most sordid places,
don't mock me.
Don't throw me down violently
with those in need.
I, I am compassionate and I am cruel.
Take care not to hate my obedience,
but love my self-control.
In my weakness do not disregard me,
and do not fear my power.

For why do you despise my terror
and denounce my pride?
I am present in all fears,
and I am strength in agitation.
I am a weak woman,
and I am well in a pleasant locale.
I am foolish and I am wise.
Why have you hated me in your counsels?
Because I shall be silent among the silent
and I shall appear and speak? [16]
Why have you hated me, you Greeks?
Because I am a barbarian among barbarians?

For I am the wisdom[6] [of the] Greeks
and the knowledge[7] of the barbarians.
I am the judgment of Greeks and barbarians.
I am the one whose image is great in Egypt
and who has no image among the barbarians.
I have been hated everywhere and loved everywhere.
I am the one called life,[8]
and you have called me death.
I am the one called law,

---

6. Sophia. 7. Gnosis. 8. Coptic *pōnᵉh*. Cf. Zoe, Greek
for "life," the name of Eve in the Septuagint.

and you have called me lawless.
I am one you pursued,
and I am one you seized.[9]
I am one you have scattered,
and you have gathered me together.
I am one before whom you have been ashamed,
and you have been shameless to me.
I am a woman who does not celebrate festivals,
and I am she whose festivals are many.
I, I am godless,
and I have many gods.
I am one you have professed,[10]
and you have scorned me.
I am uneducated,
and people learn from me.
I am one you have despised,
and you profess me.
I am one from whom you have hidden,
and you appear to me.
Whenever you hide, I shall appear. [**17**]
For [whenever] you [appear], I [shall hide] from you.

As for those who have . . . foolishly . . . ,
take me away [from] their [understanding], from grief,
and receive me, from understanding and grief.
Receive me, from low places in creation,
and take from the good, even if in a lowly way.
From shame, take me to yourselves shamelessly.
From shamelessness, and shame,
put my members to shame within you.

Draw near to me,
you who know me and you who know my members,
and establish the great among the insignificant first creatures.
Draw near to childhood,
and do not despise it because it is small and insignificant.
Do not make what is great turn away,
part by part, from what is small,
for what is small is known from what is great.

---

9. Eve is described as being seized or raped in the *Secret Book of John* and other texts. **10.** Cf. Poirier, ed., *Le Tonnerre, intellect parfait*, 267.

Why do you curse me and honor me?
You have smitten and you have shown mercy.
Do not separate me from the first ones, [18]
whom you have [known].
Do not cast anyone [out]
[nor] turn anyone away . . . .
Turn yourselves . . .
. . . do not [know] . . . what is mine . . . .
I know the first ones,
and those after them know me.

I am [perfect] mind,[11]
and rest . . . .[12]
I am the knowledge of my search,
the discovery of those who seek me,
the command of those who ask of me,
the power of powers, through my knowledge,[13]
of angelic ambassadors, through my word,
of gods among gods, through my counsel,
of spirits of all people dwelling with me,
of women dwelling within me.

I am honored and praised,
and scornfully despised.
I am peace, and war has come because of me.
I am alien[14] and citizen.
I am substance and a woman without substance.
Those from union with me are ignorant of me,
and those sharing in my being know me.[15]
Those near me have been ignorant of me,
and those far from me have known me.
On the day I am near [19] [you],
[you] are far [from me],
and on the day I [am far] from you,
[I am near] you.

I [am] . . . a lamp of the heart.
[I am] . . . of natures.
I am . . . of the creation of spirits,
[and the] request of souls.

---

11. Cf. the title of the present text. 12. Plisch, in *Nag Hammadi Deutsch*, 2.463, restores to read "of the [thunder]." 13. Gnosis. 14. Or "stranger." The theme of the alien or stranger is well known in Gnostic texts.

15. Plisch, in *Nag Hammadi Deutsch*, 2.463, emends to read "those <not> (<an>) from <union> with me (*ta<sun>ousia*) know me."

I am restraint and lack of restraint.
I am unity and dissolution.
I abide and dissolve.
I am descent, and people ascend to me.
I am judgment and pardon.
I, I am sinless,
and the root of sin comes from me.
I am desire outwardly,
and within me is self-control.
I am hearing adequate for everyone
and speaking that cannot be repressed.[16]
I cannot talk or speak,
and plentiful are my words.

Hear me in gentleness,
and learn from me in roughness.

I am the woman crying out,
and I am cast upon the face of the earth.
I prepare bread, and my mind within.[17]
I am the knowledge[18] of my name.
I cry out and I listen. [20]
I appear . . . walk . . .
. . . seal[19] . . . sign of refutation . . . .
I am [the judge, I] am the defense . . . .
I am the one called justice,
but violence [is my name].

You honor me,
[you who overcome],
and you whisper against [me],
you who are overcome.
Judge before you are judged,
because in you are judge and partiality.
If you are condemned by it,
who will pardon you?
Or if you are pardoned by it,
who can detain you?
For what is within you is outside you,
and the one who fashions you on the outside

---

16. Or "grasped." 17. On this difficult line, possibly in need of emendation, cf. Plisch, in *Nag Hammadi Deutsch*, 2.464; Poirier, ed., *Le Tonnerre, intellect par-* fait, 195. 18. Gnosis. 19. The text reads *phragis*; possibly read *phrasis*, "utterance" (cf. Poirier, ed., *Le Tonnerre, intellect parfait*, 194).

has formed you within.[20]
What you see outside you, you see within you.[21]
It is visible, and it is your garment.[22]

Hear me, you listeners,
and learn my words, you who know me.

I am hearing adequate for everything.
I am speaking that cannot be repressed.[23]
I am the name of the voice and the voice of the name.
I am the sign of the letter and the indication of division.
I [21] . . . light . . . and [shadow].
[Hear me], you listeners,
. . . [take me] to yourselves.
As [the Lord], the great power, lives,
the one who [stands] will not change the name.
It is [the one who] stands who created me.
I shall utter his name.[24]

Look at the words of this one,
and all the texts that have been written.
Pay attention, you listeners,
and you also, you angels,
and you who have been sent,
and you spirits who have risen from the dead.
I alone exist,
and I have no one to judge me.
For there are many sorts of seductive sins
and deeds without restraint
and disgraceful desires
and fleeting pleasures that people embrace,[25]
until they become sober
and rise up to their place of rest.
They will find me there,
and they will live and not die again.

---

20. Cf. *Gospel of Thomas* 22; 89. 21. Cf. *Gospel of Thomas* 3:3; *Gospel of Mary* 8. 22. The garment is the body that clothes the inner person. 23. Or "grasped." 24. On these lines, note the description of the teachings of Simon Magus and his companion Helena in the New Testament *Acts* and other early Christian literature, where Simon's concept of the divine can be referred to as the great power and Simon himself can be described as one who stands. Cf. also the *Concept of Our Great Power* (also NHC VI). 25. Or read with Poirier, ed., *Le Tonnerre, intellect parfait*, 198: "For there are many sorts of pleasant people with numerous sins and deeds without restraint and disgraceful desires and fleeting pleasures that hold them back, . . ."

AUTHORITATIVE DISCOURSE

NHC VI,3

Introduced by Madeleine Scopello
Translated by Marvin Meyer

*A*uthoritative Discourse, a Coptic tractate based on an original Greek text, occupies thirteen pages in Nag Hammadi Codex VI. It is quite well preserved, but there are extensive lacunae in the first four or five lines of pages 22–28. The title is found at the end of the text (*Authentikos Logos*); we cannot know if the title was also mentioned at the beginning because of the lacuna on page 22,1–3. This title features two significant terms: *logos* probably refers to a speech or a teaching, given here in written form; *authentikos* can be understood either as a speech of authority containing true statements (probably in opposition to other non-Gnostic teachings) or as an authentic presentation of the Gnostic tradition. The title can also refer to the literary genre of *logoi*, well known in Hermetic circles.[1] The present *logos* tells the story of the soul from her heavenly origin to her fall into the world and her return back to the realm of perfection, a place of rest where the light shining on her never sets (35,16–18).

Authoritative Discourse opens with a scene in which a fiancé (the Spirit) secretly nourishes his bride (the soul, Psyche), who has fallen into the world, and he heals her wounded eyes with an ointment so that she can see with her mind and perceive her true origin (22,23–25). The food and the medicine are constituted by the logos. The healing accomplished by the Spirit on the eyes of Psyche shows that she is literally blind. Through the metaphorical language of the text, we can distinguish the ignorance and forgetfulness that characterize the worldly sojourn of the soul. This major theme is resumed in *Authoritative Discourse* 27,25–29, where blindness is connected to ignorance and leads to darkness.

The most intense passages of *Authoritative Discourse* concern the soul's prostitution, a theme common in other Nag Hammadi tractates and especially the *Exegesis on the Soul* of Codex II. Here prostitution seems to be the result of the free

---

1. George W. MacRae, "A Nag Hammadi Tractate on the Soul."

choice of the soul, since death and life are set before everyone (24,6–13). The period of time the soul spends in the world is described in a metaphorical way: "When the spiritual soul was cast into a body, it became a sibling to lust, hatred, and envy, that is, to material souls" (23,12–17). The soul has fallen into bestiality and left knowledge behind (24,20–22). Veiled in metaphor, the mythical story of the text reflects the grim reality of life in the world: "If a lustful thought arises in a person who is a virgin, that person [already] has become contaminated" (25,6–9).

The author of *Authoritative Discourse* also characterizes the soul as a strong heroine. By virtue of the medicine she is to put on her eyes and in her mouth, she will be able to reject matter. She is now a triumphant woman, represented by the symbols of royalty and capable of overcoming the hostile forces that fight against her, and she can even blind them with her light (28,10–22). Since her adversaries are supernatural powers (the rulers, or archons, of Gnostic mythology), the refuge of the soul will be spiritual: a treasure-house, a storehouse, where she is secure and no stranger can enter (28,22–30).

But evil tempts the soul with seductive offers in order to entice her into ignorance and lead her to conceive material offspring. The themes of deceptive gifts and polluted offspring recall similar motifs in the *Exegesis on the Soul*. The author of *Authoritative Discourse* pays particular attention to the semantic field of poisons, hooks, and nets capable of capturing the soul and drawing her into ignorance (29,3–30,28; 31,8–24).

According to the author of *Authoritative Discourse*, the soul is not a naive creature: she has tasted human temptations and realizes that sweet passions are transitory. She is conscious about evil and despises this life because, like human passions, this life is transitory. The soul is able to distinguish between healthy food, which will give her life, and unhealthy food, which will poison her and lead her to death (31,24–32,1). The soul also becomes conscious of her power, her original light, when she is endowed with her true spiritual clothing as a beautiful bride, having left behind the pride of flesh for the beauty of the mind (32,2–8). If she once was a slave, she now is a queen. As the author writes, "The soul returned the body to those who had given it to her. They were ashamed, and those who deal in bodies sat down and wept because they could not do their business with that body, and that was the only commodity they had. They had gone to great pains to shape the body for this soul, and they had intended to bring down the invisible soul" (32,16–27). The soul fools the dealers in bodies, keeping her superior nature, her spiritual body, secret from them (32,30–33,3). Their fault is their ignorance, because they do not seek after God (33,4–5). The soul, on the other hand, possesses gnosis because of her intellectual curiosity about God and her constant labor in seeking the inscrutable one (34,32–35,7).

The conclusion of the soul's existential trip is marked by love and rest. In the bridal chamber she will eat of the banquet she has hungered for and partake of immortal food, and she will find what she has been looking for (35,8–15).

Authoritative Discourse recalls, in its literary genre, homilies with a didactic goal, as it proclaims to its readers how to deal with the soul's adversaries in order to obtain freedom and recover her true origin.[2] The tractate also recalls the genre of the novel as it tells the story of a soul, portrayed with feminine features, going from her heavenly homeland to a body and prostitution, and returning back to the country of knowledge.[3] This Gnostic tale shares themes and terminology with other Nag Hammadi texts, most notably the *Exegesis on the Soul*, and a similar tension between prostitution and virginity can be found in both treatises. This factor may allow us to conclude that the authors of these two treatises may have come from a similar cultural milieu.

Authoritative Discourse is built upon a series of motifs typical of Gnostic speculation (bride and bridegroom; the bridal chamber; union in love; the opposition of the malicious archons; a material way of life of the soul culminating in prostitution). The themes of forgetfulness and drunkenness are emphasized as well, and although they recall similar statements in Gnostic texts, these themes are also present in Philo of Alexandria.

The descriptions of the soul in *Authoritative Discourse*, first as a whore and then as a bride, are often interspersed with quotations of proverbs or sayings typical of a well-schooled writer of the Greco-Roman world. Among the wise sayings are those that make use of the metaphors of wheat and chaff and of the good shepherd. The insertion of elements that do not belong to the narrative creates some awkwardness in the Gnostic account of the soul, and stylistic breaks (25,26) and changes in person (26,20: plural "we") suggest that the text is a collection of separate accounts.[4]

The struggle of the soul against the archons is described with metaphors that are somewhat unusual in comparison with Christian or Greco-Roman sources. The image of those who fish for people may be based on *Habakkuk* 1:13–17, and other similar occurrences may be found in Qumran and Manichaean literature.[5] The image of the dealers in bodies, who are deceived by the soul, may be an allusion to slave traders.[6]

One of the main themes of *Authoritative Discourse* is the sickness of the soul. This sickness is blindness, which wounds the soul's eyes. Blindness is the symbol of ignorance in Gnostic speculation, while the ability to see is the image of true knowledge.[7] The sickness of the soul is provoked by the forces of matter, and the remedy is provided when the bridegroom anoints the eyes of the soul with medicine (22, 22–34); later it is said that the soul applies the medicine herself (27,25–33). This seems to be both a medical and a ritual act, and it is reminiscent of the account in the book of *Tobit*.[8]

2. MacRae, "A Nag Hammadi Tractate on the Soul"; Jacques-É. Ménard, *L'Authentikos Logos*.

3. Madeleine Scopello, *Femme, gnose et manichéisme*; "Jewish and Greek Heroines in the Nag Hammadi Library."

4. George W. MacRae, in Douglas M. Parrott, ed., *Nag Hammadi Codices V,2–5 and VI*.

5. MacRae, "A Nag Hammadi Tractate on the Soul."

6. Scopello, *Femme, gnose et manichéisme*.

7. Ménard, *L'Authentikos Logos*; Scopello, *Femme, gnose et manichéisme*.

8. Scopello, *Femme, gnose et manichéisme*.

The themes of the illness of the soul, her feeble state, and her poverty bring to mind Valentinian concepts, as do descriptions of the bridal chamber.[9] The story of the soul also recounts in a simplified way the myth of Sophia—her fall from her Father's place, her sojourn into the world, and her return to glory.[10]

This story of the soul in *Authoritative Discourse* applies to everybody. The soul is the image of every Gnostic, whether a man or a woman, who, while reading this literature, sees his or her own personal story retraced in a mythical mode. The journey of the soul from prostitution to virginity is, at the same time, the journey made by every Gnostic from ignorance to knowledge, from the material world to the realm of spirit.

Authoritative Discourse, a tractate written with the goal of simplifying and proclaiming the Gnostic myth of the soul, may have been composed in Alexandria at the end of the second century or the beginning of the third. Some scholars deny any philosophical background to this text, while others maintain that it finds its rightful place in the Platonic tradition.[11]

BIBLIOGRAPHY

Wolf-Peter Funk, "Authentikos Logos: Die dritte Schrift aus Nag-Hammadi-Codex VI"; Wolf-Peter Funk, "Der verlorene Anfang des Authentikos Logos"; Martin Krause and Pahor Labib, *Gnostische und hermetische Schriften aus Codex II und Codex VI*, 133–49; George W. MacRae, "A Nag Hammadi Tractate on the Soul"; Jacques-É. Ménard, ed., *L'Authentikos Logos*; Douglas M. Parrott, ed., *Nag Hammadi Codices V,2–5 and VI*, 257–89 (George W. MacRae); Hans-Martin Schenke, Hans-Gebhard Bethge, and Ursula Ulrike Kaiser, eds., *Nag Hammadi Deutsch*, 2.467–81 (Katharina Heyden and Cornelia Kulawik); Madeleine Scopello, *Femme, gnose et manichéisme*; "Jewish and Greek Heroines in the Nag Hammadi Library"; Roelof van den Broek, "The Authentikos Logos: A New Document of Christian Platonism."

---

9. Ménard, *L'Authentikos Logos*.

10. Ménard, *L'Authentikos Logos*; Scopello, "Jewish and Greek Heroines in the Nag Hammadi Library."

11. Roelof van den Broek, "The Authentikos Logos: A New Document of Christian Platonism."

Authoritative Discourse[1]

The Origin of the Soul Is from Above (22,1–22)

......[2] in heaven ... in him ... anyone appears ... the hidden heavens ... appear, and [before] the invisible, ineffable worlds became visible.[3]

From these came the invisible soul of righteousness, one member with them, one body with them, one spirit with them. Whether she is coming down or is in the realm of Fullness,[4] she is not apart from them, but they see her and she looks at them, through the invisible word.[5]

The Word Is Like Food and Medicine for the Soul (22,22–23,4)

Secretly her bridegroom obtained the word. He held it to her mouth to make her eat it like food. He applied it to her eyes like medicine to make her see with her mind, and perceive those who are kin to her,[6] and learn about her root, that she may be able to hold on to the branch from which she has come, receive what is hers, and renounce matter[7] [23] ......[8]

The Soul Is Like a Child Among Stepchildren (23,4–25,12)

[When a man marries a woman] who already has children, the natural children [of the man], conceived from his semen, call the children of the woman "our siblings." Similarly, when the spiritual soul was cast into a body, it became a sibling to lust, hatred, and envy, that is, to material souls. So the body came from lust, and lust came from material substance. That is why the soul became a sibling to

1. Coptic text: NHC VI,3: 22,1–35,24. Editions: *The Facsimile Edition of the Nag Hammadi Codices, Codex VI*, 26–39; Jacques-É. Ménard, *L'Authentikos Logos*; Douglas M. Parrott, ed., *Nag Hammadi Codices V,2–5 and VI*, 257–89 (George W. MacRae); Hans-Martin Schenke, Hans-Gebhard Bethge, and Ursula Ulrike Kaiser, eds., *Nag Hammadi Deutsch*, 2.467–81 (Katharina Heyden and Cornelia Kulawik). The text is also referred to as *Authentikos Logos* (the Greek title preserved in the Coptic text). 2. Five and a half lines missing or untranslatable. 3. Approximately three lines are missing from the tops of pp. 22–28.

Here, at the beginning of the text, Wolf-Peter Funk, in "Der verlorene Anfang des Authentikos Logos," suggests that p. 22, lines 1–8 could conceivably be restored as follows: "[Authoritative Discourse. Before anything came into being, it is the Father of the All who alone existed, the invisible and hidden one] resting [in his incorruptible] heavenly [glory that was] in him [before] anything was manifest." 4. Pleroma. 5. Logos, here and below. 6. On the word as food and medicine, cf. Philo of Alexandria *Allegorical Interpretation* 3.174–78; *Who Is the Heir?* 79. 7. Cf. *Romans* 11:16–21. 8. About four lines missing.

them. Yet they are stepchildren, unable to inherit from the male, but they will inherit from their mother alone.[9]

When the soul wishes to inherit along with the stepchildren—for the possessions of the stepchildren are exalted passions, life's pleasures, hateful jealousies, boastful expressions, foolish experiences, reproachful words [24] . . . .[10]

. . . [If a soul who is ignorant chooses a spirit of prostitution], he casts [her] out [and throws] her into a brothel. He [has left] her to [corruption, because] she [has abandoned] modesty.

Death and life are placed before everyone, and people choose for themselves which of these two they want.[11]

That soul will fall into drinking too much wine in a corrupt manner. Wine corrupts.[12] The soul forgets her siblings and her father, and sensual pleasures and sweet things deceive her. She has abandoned knowledge and has fallen into the life of an animal. A person devoid of sense lives like a beast, not knowing what one should say or should not say.

The gentle child inherits with joy from the father, and the father rejoices over his child, because everyone praises the father on account of the child, and the child also looks for a way to duplicate what was received.

The stepchildren [25] . . . .[13] [Their lust cannot] mix with [sobriety].

If a lustful thought arises in a person who is a virgin, that person [already] has become contaminated. This sort of appetite cannot mix with moderation.

This Is Like Wheat Mixed with Chaff (25,12–27)

For if chaff is mixed with wheat, it is not the chaff that is contaminated but the wheat. Since they are mixed together, no one will buy the contaminated wheat. They will coax the dealer and say, "Give us this chaff," for they see the wheat mixed with it. Then they will take the chaff and throw it out with the rest of the chaff, and that chaff will become mixed with all other material stuff.[14]

Pure seed is kept in storehouses that are secure.

We now have discussed all these things.

The Father Establishes a Contest in the World
(25,27–26,end or 27,beginning)

Before anything was, the Father alone existed, before the worlds in the heavens appeared, or the world on earth, or principalities or authorities or powers[15] [26] . . . . . .[16] appeared . . . and [they produced others].

Nothing came to be without the Father's will.[17]

---

9. On children inheriting, cf. *Gospel of Philip* 52. 10. About four lines missing. 11. On choosing between death and life, cf. *Deuteronomy* 30:15, 19; *Jeremiah* 21:8; *John* 5:24. 12. On wine corrupting, cf. *Ephesians* 5:18. 13. About four lines missing. 14. On wheat and chaff, cf. *Matthew* 3:12; *Luke* 3:17. 15. Cf. 1 *Corinthians* 15:24. 16. About three and a half lines missing. 17. Cf. *John* 1:3.

The Father wished to reveal his [wealth] and his glory, and so he established a great contest in this world. He wanted to make the contestants come up and leave behind what is of the created world, and despise these things with exalted, incomprehensible knowledge, and run to the one who is. We are to be triumphant over the ignorance of those who contend with us, the adversaries who contend against us, through our knowledge, for we already have known the inscrutable one from whom we have come.[18] We have nothing in this world, or else the world's authority that came to be might hold us back in the worlds of the heavens, where death is universal,[19] surrounded by individual [27] . . . .[20]

We Withdraw from the World (27,beginning–25)

. . . [the powers] of the world, [who oppose us].

We now have been put to shame [in the] worlds, but we are not interested in them when they speak ill of us. We ignore them when they curse us. We stare at them in silence when they treat us shamefully, directly to our face.

They go about their business, and we go about in hunger and thirst, looking to our dwelling place, which we perceive through our lifestyle and our conscience. We do not hang on to created things, but we withdraw from them. Our hearts are set on what truly is, and although we are sick, weak, and in pain, there is great strength hidden within us.

The Word Heals the Soul's Blindness (27,25–28,22)

Our soul is sick because she lives in a house of poverty, and matter strikes her eyes in order to blind her. For this reason the soul pursues the word and applies it to her eyes as medicine, and she <opens> her eyes and casts off [28] [blindness] . . . . . .[21] thought of . . . blindness . . . after that, if such a one is in ignorance once again, that one is in complete darkness and is a material being. That is why the soul always [takes] a word and applies it to her eyes as medicine, so that she may be able to see.[22] Then her light may overwhelm the foes that oppose her, and she may blind them with her light, capture them in her presence, make them collapse in exhaustion, and act boldly with her strength and her scepter.

The Soul Finds Shelter in Her Treasure-House (28,22–29,3)

While her enemies look at her in shame, she flees up to her treasure-house, where her mind is, and to her storehouse, which is secure. No one in creation has been able to grasp her, and she has taken no stranger into her house. Many of

---

18. On athletic imagery, cf., e.g., *Philippians* 1:30; *Hebrews* 12:1. 19. On not belonging to this world, cf. the *Gospel of John*, e.g., 15:19. 20. About three and a half lines missing. 21. About three and a half lines missing. 22. Cf. *Authoritative Discourse* 22.

those born in her house oppose her day and night, and they do not rest [29] day or night, for their lust oppresses them.[23]

We Are Like Fish That May Be Caught in Nets (29,3–17)

This is why we do not fall asleep and forget about the nets, hidden from view, that are lying in place to catch us. For if we are caught in a single net, it will swallow us down within it, and water will wash over us and splash into our faces, and we shall be pulled down into the dragnet. We shall not be able to come up from the deep, because the water is high above us, flowing down from above, making our hearts sink down in filthy mud. We shall not be able to get away from them.[24]

We Shall Be Consumed by Man-Eaters (29,17–30,4)

Man-eaters[25] will grab us and consume us, and they will enjoy themselves like a fisherman who is casting a hook and line into the water. For a fisherman casts different kinds of bait into the water, because each kind of fish has its own food. The fish smells the food and swims after the fragrance of the food, but when it bites into the bait, the hook hidden within snares it and draws it up by force from the deep water. Nobody can catch that fish down in the deep water [30] unless a fisherman finds a way to trap it. By tricking the fish with food, the fisherman has caught the fish on the hook.[26]

The Adversary Tries to Poison Us with the Food of This World (30,4–25)

We live like this in the world, like fish. The adversary is on the lookout for us and is lying in wait for us, like a fisherman, to catch us. The adversary is delighted to consume us. [He dangles] many kinds of food before our eyes, the stuff of this world, because he hopes to make us desire just one kind of food and to taste only a little of it, that he then may catch us with his hidden poison and take us from freedom into slavery.[27] For when he catches us with a single kind of food, we cannot help but desire the rest of the food. In the end, such things become the food of death.[28]

The Devil Lies in Wait with Food (30,26–31,24)

These are the kinds of food with which the devil lies in wait for us. First he plants pain in your heart so that you feel heartache over something trivial in this life,

---

23. On treasures and the treasure-house, cf. *Matthew* 6:19–21; *Luke* 12:33–34. 24. On people being caught like fish in nets, cf. *Habakkuk* 1:14–17. 25. On the creator god as a man-eater, cf. *Gospel of Philip* 62. 26. Here and below, the text continues to employ the vivid image of being caught like fish in nets. 27. On freedom and slavery, cf. *Romans* 8:21; *Galatians* 5:1. 28. On tasting death, cf. *Gospel of Thomas* 1 and many other texts.

and he catches us with his poisons. After that he introduces the desire for an article of clothing, so that you will be proud [**31**] of it, and then love of money, pride, vanity, envy rivaling envy, beauty of body, and covetousness. The worst of all these are ignorance and laziness.

All such kinds of food the adversary prepares in an attractive way and spreads it out before the body. The adversary wants to make the thought of the soul turn the soul to some kind of food, and thus he hopes to overwhelm her.[29] As with a hook he draws the soul by force, in ignorance, and deceives her, until she conceives evil and bears fruit of matter and behaves badly, pursuing many desires and cravings, seduced in ignorance by the pleasure of the flesh.

The Soul Finally Eats the Food of Life
(31,24–32,16)

The soul who has tasted these things has come to realize that sweet passions are fleeting. She has learned about evil, has forsaken these passions, and has adopted a new lifestyle.[30]

After her experiences, the soul disdains this life, because it lasts only for a time. She seeks the kinds of food that will bring her life, [**32**] and she leaves behind the food of falsehood. She learns about the light, and she goes about and strips off this world. Her true garment clothes her within, and her bridal gown reveals beauty of mind rather than pride of flesh. She learns about the depth of her being. She runs into her sheepfold as her shepherd stands at the door.[31] In return for all the shame and scorn she experienced in this world, she receives ten thousand times as much grace and glory.

The Soul Has a True Shepherd (32,16–33,3)

The soul returned the body to those who had given it to her. They were ashamed, and those who deal in bodies sat down and wept because they could not do their business with that body, and that was the only commodity they had.

They had gone to great pains to shape the body for this soul, and they had intended to bring down the invisible soul.

Now they were ashamed of what they had done, for they lost what they had worked hard to accomplish. They did not realize that the soul has an invisible spiritual body,[32] but they thought, "We are her shepherd and we feed her." They did not realize that she knows [**33**] another way, hidden from them. This is what her true shepherd taught her, in knowledge.[33]

---

29. On the food of people and souls, cf. *Gospel of Philip* 80–81. 30. On sweet fleeting passions, cf. *Thunder* 21. 31. On the sheepfold and the shepherd at the door, cf. *John* 10:1–6; *Revelation* 3:20. 32. On the spiritual body, cf. 1 *Corinthians* 15:44. 33. On the true shepherd, cf. *John* 10:7–18.

The Ignorant Are More Wicked Than Pagans (33,4–34,32)

Those, however, who are ignorant do not seek God, and they do not look for their dwelling place, which is a place of rest, but instead they live like animals. They are more wicked than pagans. To begin with, they do not inquire about God. Their hardheartedness drags them down so that they act in a cruel manner. Then, if they find someone asking about salvation, in their hardness of heart they work on that person. If the person keeps on asking, they kill him with their cruelty, and they think they have done something good for themselves. Without a doubt, they are children of the devil.[34] Even pagans give to charity, and they know that God who is in the heavens exists, the Father of the universe, exalted over the idols they worship, [34] although they have not heard the word, so as to inquire about the ways of God.[35]

The mindless person hears the call, but is ignorant of the place to which he or she has been called. He has not asked during the preaching, "Where is the temple into which I should go and worship my hope?" Such a person is mindless and worse than a pagan, for pagans know the way to their temples of stone, which will perish, and they worship their idol, with their hearts set upon it, because this is their hope. The word has been preached to this mindless person, and it has taught him, "Seek and inquire about the ways you should go, for there is nothing as important as this." So the substance of the hardness of heart strikes the person's mind, with the force of ignorance and the demon of error, and these things prevent the person's mind from recovering and being capable of working at seeking and understanding hope.

The Rational Soul Learns About God and Comes to Rest
(34,32–35,24)

The rational soul, on the other hand, [35] has worked at seeking, and she has learned about God. She has struggled to inquire, enduring bodily distress, wearing out her feet after the preachers,[36] and learning about the inscrutable one.

> She has found her rising.
> She has come to rest in the one who is at rest.
> She has reclined in the bridal chamber.
> She has eaten of the banquet
> for which she has hungered.
> She has partaken of immortal food.
> She has found what she has sought.

---

34. On children of the devil, cf. *John* 8:44. **35.** Cf. *Acts* 17:22–31; *Romans* 1:18–23; 10:14–17. **36.** Or "evangelists,"—i.e., preachers of the good news (*neuaggelistēs*).

She has received rest from her labors,
and the light shining on her does not set.
To the light belongs the glory
and the power and the revelation,
forever and ever.
Amen.

Authoritative Discourse

THE CONCEPT OF
OUR GREAT POWER

NHC VI,4

Introduced by Madeleine Scopello
Translated by Marvin Meyer

The *Concept of Our Great Power* is a tractate that exists only in the Coptic version of Nag Hammadi Codex VI. Translated from an original Greek text, it is twelve pages in length (36,1–48,15), and it has a few short lacunae. The Coptic employed by the translator is Sahidic, with a few dialectical characteristics in portions of the treatise,[1] and this distinguishes it from the other texts of the same codex. The title at the beginning of the tractate ("Intellectual Perception of Understanding; The Concept of the Great Power") is different from the title at its end ("The Concept of Our Great Power"). The first title may be a later insertion of an editor who is trying to suggest an interpretation that helps to capture the meaning of the shorter title at the end. The terms "perception" (*aisthēsis*) and "intellectual" and "understanding" (*dianoia*) belong to philosophical language and shed some light on the "concept" (*noēma*) of "our great power." The Coptic term "power" (*com*) is the equivalent of the Greek word *dunamis*, a technical term in Gnostic texts. The "perception" is to be understood not as sensory perception but as a mental perception.[2]

The *Concept of Our Great Power* opens with a discourse uttered by the great Power himself. The name of the great Power designates the highest God; this name is unique in the Nag Hammadi library, but similar formulations occur in the Coptic magical papyri.[3] In his discourse the great Power promises invisibility and safety to those who know him and offers salvation to everyone, "from seven days old to one hundred twenty years old," in whom his form (Greek *morphē*) will

---

1. See Pierre Chérix, *Le concept de notre grande puissance*; Francis E. Williams, *Mental Perception: A Commentary on NHC VI,4, The Concept of Our Great Power*, 249–53.

2. See Williams, *Mental Perception*.

3. See Marvin Meyer and Richard Smith, *Ancient Christian Magic: Coptic Texts of Ritual Power*.

appear. These people will be able to see the great Power and prepare their future dwelling places in him. The supreme deity offers the hearers a profound teaching about past and present: "Come to know how what has gone has come to be, that you may know <how> what is alive <will> come to be" (36,27–31). The deity also encourages his hearers to ask the most essential questions about their present condition in the world and their aim for the future life — "what that aeon looks like, what its nature is, and how it came into being. [Why] don't you ask what your [nature] will be, or how you have come into being?" (36,32–37,5). These questions are typical of Gnostic self-examination, and the way the questions are formulated recalls the well-known words of the Valentinian *Excerpts from Theodotus* 78.2: "Who are we? What have we become? Where are we? Where have we been cast? Where shall we go?"

In the present text the great Power recounts what resembles salvation history, built on biblical facts and divided into two main periods: the age of flesh and the age of the soul. If the first age is the equivalent of the antediluvian period, the second age depicts postdiluvian time.

The account of these two periods of history is preceded by a sketch of creation in which materials from the first chapters of *Genesis* are intermingled with features of Stoic physics (37,6–12). Creation consists of water, earth, and air, but it also has another constitutive element, fire, which is present especially in darkness and the underworld. Even if the great Power is not the maker of the universe, he still intervenes in it by providing the Spirit to people, "so that they may receive life from the Spirit day by day" (37,25–27). During the period of the age of flesh, giants come to existence ("giant bodies," 38,14). They bring about the experience of lust and corruption and enter into flesh, and they provoke the vengeance of the father of the flesh — a metaphor for the Old Testament god. The father of the flesh, who is also identified in the text with the water, sends the flood to humanity but constructs a wooden ark to save pious Noah.

Whereas the age of flesh is characterized by huge dimensions, the age of the soul is trivial and small. This age is a period of mixing and mingling during which souls are polluted by their association with bodies. It is during this period that "there will come the human who knows the great Power" (40,26–27). This human, who will speak in parables and proclaim the aeon that is to come, is Christ, even if he is never called by name in the tractate. His descent to Hades to destroy the power of its ruler is recorded in the text, and the wrath of the archons is painted with strong colors (41,15–33). The Savior, whose nature cannot be grasped (42,1–3 — a typical Gnostic doctrine, influenced by docetism), abolishes the law of the aeon by his word (42,5–6). An impressive number of signs and events announcing that the power of the archons is coming to a close is included in the text, and these sorts of descriptions are deeply rooted in Jewish apocalypticism. A "ruler of the west" arises in these troubled times. Is he a mythical figure or a veiled allusion to a real or political personage? According to Francis E. Williams, this could be an allusion to Emperor Julian, seen as a forerunner of the Antichrist because of his restoration of pagan religion (this passage is understood to be an interpolation of the last redactor of the *Concept of Our Great Power*).[4] From page 44,31 to page 45,24, the coming of the Antichrist is described, and his coming is accompanied by signs and wonders. As new manifestations of the approaching end also appear in nature, the great Power withdraws with those who know him, and all enter into the light. Protected by holy garments, they cannot be harmed by darkness or fire. When the domination of the archons, which lasts for 1,468 years, is finished, all the children of matter will perish. Then will come the "aeon of beauty," and the followers of the great Power will taste knowledge, light, and rest. The souls, which have come from simple copies (*tupoi*, 38,8–9), will become images of the great Power and reflections of his light.

The *Concept of Our Great Power* belongs to the literary genre of the apocalypse, a revelation by a divine entity with concern for the events of the end and the signs of the eschaton. In expressing these themes, the treatise has drawn its inspiration from Jewish, Christian, and Gnostic materials. Francis E. Williams points to Samaritan Jewish themes (especially in liturgical materials) and Gnostic parallels with the doctrine of Simon Magus and his followers in the *Concept of Our Great Power*.[5] These Simonian parallels deal with the doctrine of the great Power (cf. Hippolytus *Refutation of All Heresies* 6.9–18), the supreme deity. But the rich and syncretistic approach of the *Concept of Our Great Power* cannot be ascribed to only one author. The *Concept of Our Great Power* is a text that has been reworked by several hands at different times and has gone through more than one redaction. The treatise can be understood as the combination of two main documents, one that is Christian and another that is not. This appears clear from the rough transitions in some parts of the text, and from abrupt changes of personal pronouns (first and third person) in the course of the narration. Furthermore, some sentences are practically meaningless, and this can be attributed either to clumsy work on the Greek text by the last editor or to a misunderstanding by the Coptic translator.

The place of composition of the *Concept of Our Great Power* could be Asia Minor, if we take into account the reference to the east as "the place where the word (*logos*) first appeared" (44,3). As to the date, if the "ruler of the west" is to be identified with Emperor Julian, as Williams has suggested, the last version of the tractate could have been written shortly after 360. If we understand the term *nianhomoion* at 40,7 to refer to the Anomoean heresy of the fourth century (see the note to the translation), that would confirm this fourth-century date. In any case, some portions of the document have certainly been composed earlier, probably during the second century.

---

4. See Williams, *Mental Perception*.

5. Williams, *Mental Perception*, 203–31.

BIBLIOGRAPHY

Pierre Chérix, *Le concept de notre grande puissance*; Douglas M. Parrott, ed., *Nag Hammadi Codices V, 2–5 and VI, 291–323* (Frederik Wisse and Francis E. Williams); James M. Robinson, ed., *The Nag Hammadi Library in English*, 311–17 (Francis E. Williams and Frederik Wisse); Hans-Martin Schenke, Hans-Gebhard Bethge, and Ursula Ulrike Kaiser, eds., *Nag Hammadi Deutsch*, 2.483–93 (Hans-Martin Schenke); Francis E. Williams, *Mental Perception: A Commentary on NHC VI,4, The Concept of Our Great Power.*

The Concept of Our Great Power[1]

Intellectual Perception
The Concept of the[2] Great Power

Whoever Knows the Great Power Will Be Saved (36,1–37,5)

Whoever knows our great Power[3] will become invisible. Fire will be unable to consume such a person, but it will purify. And it will destroy all that you possess.

For all those in whom my[4] form appears, from seven days old to one hundred twenty years old,[5] will be saved.[6] Upon them are placed these obligations, to gather together all that is lost and the letters[7] of our great Power, that the great Power may write your name in our bright light and bring the thoughts and deeds of others to an end. Then these may be purified, scattered, destroyed, and brought together in the place no one can see.

You will see me and prepare your dwelling places in our great Power.

Come to know how what has gone has come to be, that you may know <how> what is alive <will> come to be. And know how to recognize this, and what that aeon looks like, [37] what its nature is, and how it came into being.

[Why] don't you ask what your [nature] will be, or how you have come into being?

In the Beginning Are Water and Spirit (37,6–34)

Think about how immense this water is, that it is incomprehensibly immeasurable. It has no beginning; it has no end. It supports the earth and blows into the air

---

1. Coptic text: NHC VI,4: 36,1–48,15. Editions: *The Facsimile Edition of the Nag Hammadi Codices: Codex VI*, 40–52; Pierre Chérix, *Le Concept de Notre Grande Puissance*; Douglas M. Parrott, ed., *Nag Hammadi Codices V,2–5 and VI*, 291–323 (Frederik Wisse and Francis E. Williams); Hans-Martin Schenke, Hans-Gebhard Bethge, and Ursula Ulrike Kaiser, eds., *Nag Hammadi Deutsch*, 2.483–93 (Hans-Martin Schenke); Francis E. Williams, *Mental Perception: A Commentary on NHC VI,4, The Concept of Our Great Power*. The text is also provided with the titles "Intellectual Perception" and "The Concept of the Great Power" (which may be emended; see the note) at the opening of the text. 2. Perhaps emend to read "<Our>," as in the version of the title at the end of the text and the opening line of the text itself. 3. Great Power designates the divine in a number of traditions, including that of Simon Magus. Cf. *Acts* 8:10; *Thunder* 21. 4. When the first-person singular pronoun ("I") is used, the speaker often seems to be the great Power. 5. On one hundred twenty years, cf. *Genesis* 6:3. 6. Cf. *Gospel of Thomas* 4. 7. Or "writings." On the letters of God written in the living book, cf. *Gospel of Truth* 22–23.

where the gods and angels are. There is fear and light in the one exalted over all this, and my letters are visible in that one.[8]

I have provided them as a service for the creation of the flesh. For no one can stand without that one, and the aeon cannot live without that one.

That one has what is within, and thinks in a pure way.

Look at the Spirit and understand where it[9] is from.

The Spirit was given to people so that they may receive life from it day by day. It has life within and gives to all.

Then darkness and the underworld received the fire.

It[10] will release from itself what is mine.

Its eyes could not endure my light.

The First Age of Flesh Begins (37,34–39,15)

The winds and waters moved. [38] The rest also came into being, along with the entire aeon of creation.

From the depths came the fire.

Power came to be in the midst of the powers.

The powers desired to see my image.

The soul became a copy of it.

This is what came into being. Notice what it is like, that before coming into being it could not be seen.[11]

Since the aeon of the flesh came to be in giant bodies, long periods of time in creation were assigned to them.[12]

When they became corrupt after entering the flesh, the father of the flesh,[13] the water, acted in judgment.

When the father of the flesh, who holds the angels in subjection, found Noah, who was pious and worthy, Noah proclaimed a message of piety for one hundred twenty years, but no one listened to him. So he made a wooden ark, and whoever he found went in. Then the flood came, [39] and Noah and his sons were saved.[14]

If there had been no ark for a person to enter, the flood water would not have come.

Thus that one had a thought and planned to save the gods, the angels, the powers, and the majesty of all of them, and the luxurious way of life, by moving them out of that aeon and providing a life for them in places that endure.

The judgment of the flesh[15] came to an end. Only the work of Power remained steadfast.

8. Cf. *Genesis* 1:1–7. 9. Or "he," here and below. 10. Darkness. 11. On creation in the image of God, cf. *Genesis* 1:26; *Secret Book of John* II, 14–15. 12. On the giants and long periods of time, cf. *Genesis* 5:1–6:8. 13. The father of the flesh is the god of this world. 14. Cf. *Genesis* 6:9–9:29. 15. I.e., the flood.

The Second Age of the Soul Follows (39,16–40,23)

Next is the aeon of the soul. It is trivial, entangled with bodies and the conception of souls and defilements. The first defilement of creation gained strength.

It produced all sorts of things—many works of wrath, anger, envy, jealousy, hatred, slander, contempt, and warfare, lies and evil advice, sorrows and pleasures, disgraces and defilements, deceits and diseases, and unjust judgments given arbitrarily.

Still you sleep [40] and dream dreams. Wake up, come back, taste and eat the food of truth.

Make the word and the water of life available.[16]

Avoid evil lusts and desires and whatever deviates from who you are.[17] These are evil dispositions that are unsound.

The mother of the fire did not have Power. She sent fire upon the soul and the land, and she burned all the dwellings in it, until her consuming rage[18] ceased. When she can find nothing else to burn, she will consume herself.

The fire will become incorporeal, with no body, and it will burn matter until it has purified everything, including all that is wicked. When it can find nothing else to burn, it will turn on itself until it consumes itself.[19]

The Revealer Comes into the World and Is Persecuted (40,24–41,32)

Then in this aeon of the soul there will come the human who knows the great Power.[20] He will receive it and know me. He will drink from the milk of the mother of the work that was done. He will speak in parables and proclaim the aeon that is to come, [41] just as he spoke in the first aeon of the flesh to[21] Noah. When he uttered his words, he spoke in seventy-two languages.[22] He opened the gates of the heavens with his words. He put the ruler of the underworld[23] to shame, he raised the dead, and he destroyed the dominion of the ruler of the underworld.[24]

Then there was a great disturbance. The rulers rose up in wrath against him, and they wanted to give him over to the ruler of the underworld.

---

16. The food and water may designate eucharist and baptism. 17. The text reads *nianhomoion* (in Greek *anomoios* means "unlike"). Here some scholars prefer to read "the Anomoeans," and they refer to the mid-fourth-century Anomoean heresy, an extreme form of Arian thought that maintained God the Father and Christ were essentially unlike each other. See Wisse and Williams, in *Nag Hammadi Codices V,2–5 and VI*, 304. 18. Coptic *mane*; cf. Greek *mania*. The meaning of the Coptic word is unclear; it could mean "shepherd," but that seems inappropriate in the current context, and *mania* seems more likely. On fire that destroys dwellings and more, cf. apocalyptic fire, and perhaps even the fire that destroyed Sodom and Gomorrah. 19. Cf. Irenaeus of Lyon *Against Heresies* 1.7.1, where Irenaeus reports that in the system of the Valentinian teacher Ptolemy it is said that at the end, when the fire in the world has consumed matter, it will pass into nonexistence. 20. This human is the Gnostic revealer, who comes to expression in the figure of Jesus. 21. Or "in" (Coptic *'n*). 22. Seventy or seventy-two is the traditional number of nations in the world according to Jewish lore. Hence the revealer here is said to speak all the languages of the world. 23. Hades. 24. Cf. *Hebrews* 2:14.

They knew one of his followers,[25] and a fire burned in that person's soul. He handed him over, since no one knew who he was.

They did it, they seized him, but they brought judgment upon themselves. They delivered him up to the ruler of the underworld.[26] They gave him over to Sasabek and Berotth.[27]

He prepared himself to go down and prove them wrong.

The Revealer Triumphs over the Archons and Ascends
(41,32–42,31)

Then the ruler of the underworld took him, [42] but he discovered that his flesh was such that it could not be seized and shown to the archons. He kept saying, "Who is this? What is this?"[28]

His word[29] has abolished the law of the aeon.[30]

He is from the word of the Power of life. He was stronger than the command of the rulers, and they could not dominate him by their action.

The rulers searched to find out what had happened. They did not know that this was the sign of their demise and the moment of change of the aeon.

The sun went under during the day, and the day became dark.[31] The demons were shaken.

After this he will appear as he is ascending.

The sign of the aeon that is to come will become visible, and the aeons will be dissolved.

Blessed will they be who understand what is discussed with them and will be revealed to them. Blessed will they be, for they will come to understand truth: you have found rest in the heavens.

Many Follow the Revealer and Record His Words
(42,31–43,29)

Then many will follow him, and they will labor in the regions where they were born. [43]

They will go about and write down his words as they wish.[32]

Observe that these aeons are gone. How large is the water of the aeon that has dissolved? What are the dimensions of aeons? How will people prepare themselves, how will they be established, how will they become indestructible aeons?

At first, after his preaching, he proclaims the second aeon, along with the first.

The first aeon must perish with the passing of time.

---

25. Judas Iscariot. **26.** This refers to the crucifixion of Jesus. **27.** Coptic *berōtth*. Some scholars have translated this as "nine bronze coins" (*berōtth*); cf. the payment made to Judas Iscariot according to *Matthew* 26:15; 27:3; Wisse and Williams, in *Nag Hammadi Codices V,2–5 and VI*, 308–9. **28.** Cf. *Three Forms of First Thought* 43. **29.** Logos, here and below. **30.** Cf. *Romans* 10:4; *Ephesians* 2:15. **31.** Cf. *Matthew* 27:45; *Mark* 15:33; *Luke* 23:44–45. **32.** These comments describe the expansion of the emerging orthodox church and the proclamation of words of Jesus or the composition of texts about Jesus.

He spent time in the first aeon, as he went about in it until it perished, and he preached for one hundred twenty years.[33] This is the perfect number, which is held in high regard.[34]

He made the border of the west desolate, and he destroyed the east.

Your seed and those who wish to follow our great word[35] and his proclamation <...>.

The Archons Attack the Place Where the Word First Appeared (43,29–44,31)

Then the wrath of the rulers burned. They were ashamed of their dissolution.

They fumed and grew angry at life. Cities were overthrown; mountains dissolved.

The ruler came, with the [44] rulers of the west, to the east, to the place where the word first appeared.[36]

Then the earth trembled and the cities were shaken.[37]

The birds ate and had their fill of their dead.[38]

The earth mourned, along with the inhabited world. They were desolate.

When the times were completed, wickedness increased greatly, until the final end of the word.

Then the ruler of the west arose.[39] He will act from the east and will teach people his wickedness. He wishes to eradicate all teaching of words of true wisdom,[40] for he loves false wisdom.[41]

He raised his hand against what is old, with the intent of bringing wickedness in and dressing in the clothing of dignity. He could not do it, because his garments are exceptionally filthy.

Then he got angry and made an appearance. He wished to go up and pass over to that place.

The moment came, and he approached. He changes the ordinances.

The Imitator Reigns over the Earth and Leads People Astray (44,31–45,24)

Then the time came when the child grew up. When he reached maturity, [45] the rulers sent the imitator[42] to that person,[43] so that they might come to know our

---

33. On one hundred twenty years, cf. *Concept of Our Great Power* 38. 34. Wisse and Williams note, in *Nag Hammadi Codices V,2–5 and VI*, 312, that Philo of Alexandria considers one hundred twenty to be the "perfect number" because it is an "image and imitation of the circle of the zodiac" (*On Rewards and Punishments* 65). 35. Logos. 36. The east, where the Logos first appeared, is probably Palestine. 37. These images and those that follow are typical of apocalyptic literature. 38. On birds eating the dead, cf. *Ezekiel* 39:17–20; *Revelation* 19:21. 39. The paragraphs that follow seem to reflect statements about the activity of the Antichrist as that is described in such texts as Hippolytus of Rome *On the Antichrist*. Apparently it is thought that the Antichrist will come from the west, imitate the person of Jesus, and attempt to establish Jewish customs. On the possible identity of this figure, see the introduction. 40. Or "true Sophia." 41. Or "false Sophia." 42. Or "imposter" (*pantimeimon*). Cf. *Revelation of Peter* 71; 78–79. 43. Apparently Jesus the revealer.

great Power. They expected that he would work a sign for them, and he performed great signs.[44]

He[45] reigned over the whole earth and all who are under heaven. He set his throne over the end of the earth.

It is said, "I shall make you God of the world."

He will perform signs and wonders.

The people will turn from me and go astray.

Those people who follow the imitator will introduce circumcision. He will pronounce judgment upon those who are from the uncircumcision, who are the real people.

For he has sent many preachers beforehand, and they have preached on his behalf.

Souls Are Purified as Apocalyptic Signs Appear
(45,24–47,2)

When he has completed the time set for the kingdom of the earth, the purification of souls will occur, for wickedness has become stronger than you.

The powers will tremble. All the seas will dry up. The firmament will not send down dew.

The springs will stop giving water. The rivers will no longer flow [46] back to their springs. The waters of the springs of the earth will stop flowing.[46]

The depths will be laid bare and will lie open.

The stars will expand and the sun will stop shining.[47]

I shall withdraw with all those who know me.

They will enter into immeasurable light, where there is no being of flesh or seduction of fire to seize them. They will be free and holy, and no one will be able to drag them down. I am protecting them with my hand, and they have holy garments that fire cannot touch.

Next are darkness, wind, and a moment as short as the blink of an eye.

Then he will come to destroy everything.

They will be chastised until they are pure.

The period of time allotted for them to have power is 1,468 years.[48]

When the fire has consumed everything and can find nothing else to burn, it will extinguish itself.[49]

Then the [47] [judgment of fire], which is the [second] power, will be completed.

---

44. On this statement and what follows, cf. *Revelation* 13, on the two beasts, those who worship the beasts, and signs and wonders. 45. Apparently the Antichrist. 46. I.e., the cycle of the origin, flow, and replenishment of water in the world will no longer work. 47. Cf. *Excerpt from the Perfect Discourse* 73. 48. In Manichaean sources 1,468 years is the period of time of the final conflagration in which the cosmos will burn and the last light particles will be freed from matter and return to paradise. See Schenke, in *Nag Hammadi Deutsch*, 2.492. 49. Cf. Irenaeus of Lyon *Against Heresies* 1.7.1.

The Third Age of the Spirit Is an Aeon of Beauty
(47,2–48,15)

Then mercy will come . . . through Sophia . . . .

The firmaments [will collapse] down to the abyss.

The children of matter will perish. From that moment they will not exist.

Then will appear the souls who are holy through the light of the Power that is exalted above all powers, the immeasurable, the universal. That is I, and all who know me.

They will be in the aeon of beauty, of the aeon of marriage,[50] and they will be adorned through Sophia.

After praising the one who is in incomprehensible oneness, they behold him[51] on account of his[52] will that is within them.

They all have come to be as reflections in his light. They all have shone, and they have found rest in his rest.

The one who is in oneness will free the souls being chastised, and they come to live in purity.

They will see the holy ones and call out to them, "Have mercy on us, Power above all powers."[53] For [48] . . . in the iniquity that exists . . . to him their eyes.

[They] do not seek him because they do not seek us, nor do they believe us. They have acted in accordance with the creation of the rulers and the other rulers of creation. We also have behaved according to our fleshly origin, in the creation of the rulers, which establishes law.

Yet we are the ones who have come to live in the unchangeable aeon.[54]

The Concept of Our Great Power

---

50. Coptic *hap*, which could also be translated "judgment." 51. Or "it." 52. Or "its," here and below. 53. Cf. *Secret Book of John* II, 26–27; *Paraphrase of* *Shem* 48; *Luke* 16:22–24. 54. The final state of those who follow the great Power will be rest in the eternal realm.

EXCERPT FROM PLATO'S REPUBLIC

NHC VI,5

Introduced and Translated by Marvin Meyer

The *Excerpt from Plato's Republic* is the fifth tractate of Nag Hammadi Codex VI, and it provides a Coptic version of a portion of the parable of Socrates in Plato's *Republic*, Book 9, 588a–589b, on the human soul. In the parable Socrates compares the soul to a creature of three forms: a many-headed beast, a lion, and a human. The many-headed beast, Socrates suggests, stands for the lower passions, the lion for the higher passion of courage, and the human for reason, and the point of the parable is that the human—that is, reason—should watch over and cultivate the various aspects of the soul.

This passage from the *Republic* reads as follows in the English translation of the Greek by Benjamin Jowett:

> "Well," I said, "and now having arrived at this stage of the argument, we may revert to the words which brought us hither: was not someone saying that injustice was a gain to the perfectly unjust who was reputed to be just?"
>
> "Yes, that was said."
>
> "Now then, having determined the power and quality of justice and injustice, let us have a little conversation with him."
>
> "What shall we say to him?"
>
> "Let us make an image of the soul, that he may have his own words presented before his eyes."
>
> "Of what sort?"
>
> "An ideal image of the soul, like the composite creations of ancient mythology, such as the Chimera or Scylla or Cerberus, and there are many others in which two or more different natures are said to grow into one."
>
> "There are said to have been such unions."

"Then do you now model the form of a multitudinous, many-headed monster, having a ring of heads of all manner of beasts, tame and wild, which he is able to generate and metamorphose at will."

"You suppose marvelous powers in the artist; but, as language is more pliable than wax or any similar substance, let there be such a model as you propose."

"Suppose now that you make a second form as of a lion, and a third of a man, the second smaller than the first, and the third smaller than the second."

"That," he said, "is an easier task; and I have made them as you say."

"And now join them, and let the three grow into one."

"That has been accomplished."

"Next fashion the outside of them into a single image, as of a man, so that he who is not able to look within, and sees only the outer hull, may believe the beast to be a single human creature."

"I have done so," he said.

"And now, to him who maintains that it is profitable for the human creature to be unjust, and unprofitable to be just, let us reply that, if he be right, it is profitable for this creature to feast the multitudinous monster and strengthen the lion and the lionlike qualities, but to starve and weaken the man, who is consequently liable to be dragged about at the mercy of either of the other two; and he is not to attempt to familiarize or harmonize them with one another—he ought rather to suffer them to fight and bite and devour one another."

"Certainly," he said, "that is what the approver of injustice says."

"To him the supporter of justice makes answer that he should ever so speak and act as to give the man within him in some way or other the most complete mastery over the entire human creature. He should watch over the many-headed monster like a good husbandman, fostering and cultivating the gentle qualities, and preventing the wild ones from growing."[1]

The Coptic version of the *Excerpt from Plato's Republic* has presented interesting challenges to interpreters of the Nag Hammadi texts since it was first identified by Hans-Martin Schenke.[2] This section of the *Republic* was popular during the early centuries of the common era, and it is cited by Eusebius of Caesarea in *Preparation for the Gospel* 12.46.2–6 and alluded to by the Neoplatonist authors Plotinus and Proclus. It may well have been included in a handbook of quotations for students of philosophy in the world of late antiquity.[3] Schenke proposes that practitioners of Hermetic religion may have found Plato particularly attrac-

---

1. Benjamin Jowett, *The Republic and Other Works.*

2. See Hans-Martin Schenke, "Zur Faksimile-Ausgabe der Nag-Hammadi-Schriften."

3. See Hans-Martin Schenke, in Hans-Martin Schenke, Hans-Gebhard Bethge, and Ursula Ulrike Kaiser, eds., *Nag Hammadi Deutsch*, 2.495–96; James Brashler, in Douglas M. Parrott, ed., *Nag Hammadi Codices V,2–5 and VI*, 325–26.

tive and may have thought of him as a student of Hermes, so that they could have associated this section from Plato's *Republic* with other Hermetic texts—and three such Hermetic texts follow the *Excerpt from Plato's Republic* in Nag Hammadi Codex VI.

The Coptic *Excerpt from Plato's Republic* differs from the Greek text in significant respects, and scholars have offered several explanations to account for the differences. Some have maintained that the Coptic translator misunderstood the Greek text;[4] others have judged that the differences reflect deliberate gnosticizing tendencies on the part of the translator.[5] Howard M. Jackson also refers to "the incapability of the Coptic language to render the complexities and niceties of Plato's style."[6] It is most likely that all these considerations contributed to the state of the Coptic translation that has been transmitted in Codex VI of the Nag Hammadi library. It is apparent that upon occasion the Coptic translator has misunderstood the Greek.[7] At the same time, the text from Plato, with its emphasis upon images, the evil beast, the lion, the weakness of the human, and the need for the human being to act with justice and strength, would have been very appealing to people with ascetical or gnosticizing proclivities, and the Coptic translation of the *Excerpt from Plato's Republic* may have emphasized these very points even more. As a result, the *Excerpt from Plato's Republic* may be read, profitably, along with a text like the *Secret Book of John*, with its understanding of creation in the image of the divine, life in the cosmos of the lionlike demiurge, and salvation for humanity, above and below, through insight and knowledge.

BIBLIOGRAPHY

Benjamin Jowett, *The Republic and Other Works*; Tito Orlandi, "La traduzione copta di Platone"; Louis Painchaud, ed., *Fragment de la République de Platon*; Douglas M. Parrott, ed., *Nag Hammadi Codices V,2–5 and VI*, 325–39 (James Brashler); James M. Robinson ed., *The Nag Hammadi Library in English*, 318–20 (James Brashler, Howard M. Jackson, and Douglas M. Parrott); Hans-Martin Schenke, "Zur Faksimile-Ausgabe der Nag-Hammadi-Schriften"; Hans-Martin Schenke, Hans-Gebhard Bethge, and Ursula Ulrike Kaiser, eds., *Nag Hammadi Deutsch*, 2.495–97 (Hans-Martin Schenke).

4. See Schenke, "Zur Faksimile-Ausgabe der Nag-Hammadi-Schriften"; Brashler, in *Nag Hammadi Codices V,2–5 and VI*.

5. See Tito Orlandi, "La traduzione copta di Platone."

6. Howard M. Jackson, in James M. Robinson, ed., *The Nag Hammadi Library in English*, 318.

7. Examples of such apparent mistakes in translation may be found in the notes to the translation below.

Excerpt from Plato's Republic[1]

"Since we have reached this point in the discussion, let's return to the first things said to us. We shall find that someone[2] says, 'Good for one who has been treated in a completely unjust way,[3] for that one is justly glorified.' Wasn't that one refuted in this way?"

"Yes, in exactly that way."

I[4] said, "Now then, we have spoken of this because someone has said[5] that the unjust and the just both have power."

"How is that?"

"That person said, 'The reasoning faculty[6] of the soul is an image with nothing like it,' and the one who said this will [49] understand."

"The person [said, 'Is] it really [like this] or not? We [say it] is for me.' But all these [mythical figures][7] that the rulers have revealed now turn out to be natural creatures, including Chimera[8] and Cerberus[9] and all the rest that are mentioned. They all have come down and have cast off forms and images and have become a single image. It was said, 'Do it now.' The single image has become the image of a complex, many-headed beast, often[10] like the image of a wild beast, and then it can cast off the first image. All these rough and rugged forms come from that image with some effort, for they are formed arrogantly. And all that resemble them are formed through the word, and this now is a single image. Further, the image of a lion is one thing and the image of a human is another.[11] [50] The

---

1. Coptic text: NHC VI,5: 48,16–51,23. Editions: *The Facsimile Edition of the Nag Hammadi Codices: Codex VI*, 52–55; Louis Painchaud, *Fragment de la République de Platon*; Douglas M. Parrott, ed., *Nag Hammadi Codices V,2–5 and VI*, 325–39 (James Brashler); Hans-Martin Schenke, Hans-Gebhard Bethge, and Ursula Ulrike Kaiser, eds., *Nag Hammadi Deutsch*, 2.495–97 (Hans-Martin Schenke). The *Excerpt from Plato's Republic* presents *Republic* 588a–589b. 2. Lit., "he." In the Coptic this may be assumed to be a previous speaker. 3. Here the Greek of the *Republic* employs the active form of the verb and hence communicates a different meaning. 4. In the Greek Socrates is speaking in the first person. 5. Lit., "he." Here the Greek of the *Republic* reads "we have agreed (or determined)." The Coptic reading may assume another speaker. 6. Logos. 7. The restorations are tentative. 8. In Greek mythology Chimera is a female monster with features of the lion, goat, and dragon or serpent. 9. In Greek mythology Cerberus is the three-headed dog that guards the entrance to Hades. 10. Lit., "some days" (*henhoou*). Here the Greek of the *Republic* reads *hēmerōn*, "tame," which the Coptic translator may have understood as *hēmerōn* (with a different accent), "days." 11. Here and throughout this passage, cf. *Gospel of Thomas* 7. In the *Secret Book of John* II, 10, the demiurge has the figure of a snake with the face of a lion.

[image of what] is joined is a single [image], and this [is] much more complex [than the] first image.[12] And the second image[13] [is] small."

"It has been formed."

"Now then, join them together and make the three into a single one,[14] so that they grow together and all are in a single image, the outward image of a human who cannot see what is inside but only what is outside. And it is apparent what creature the image is in, and that it[15] was formed in a human image.

"I spoke with one who said that it is profitable for a person to act unjustly. But one who acts unjustly really does not profit or find any good. What is profitable for a person is this: to cast down every image of the evil beast and trample them along with the images of the lion.[16] But the human being is weak in this respect, and everything he does is weak. So he is drawn to the place where he first[17] spends time with them.[18] [51] He does [not reconcile them to each other or take them] to himself, but they put up a [fight] against anyone hostile among [them]. They devour each other in animosity.[19] Yes, he said all this to everyone who praises unjust actions."

"And isn't it profitable to speak justly?"

"If a person does these things and speaks about them, these things take firm hold within a person. For this reason in particular a person tries to care for them and nourishes them as a farmer nourishes the produce day by day[20] and the wild beasts keep it from growing."

---

12. The restoration is tentative. The first image is the image of the lion. 13. The second image is the image of the human. 14. The phrase "single one" is also used in the *Gospel of Thomas*, and in *Gospel of Thomas* 22; 106 it is said that the two become one. Here the three become a single one. 15. Or "he." 16. Here the Coptic text differs considerably from the Greek text of the *Republic*. 17. Here the Greek of the *Republic* reads *hopoteron*, "wherever" (or the like— the English is a little different in the Jowett translation, above), which the Coptic translator may have under-stood as *proteron*, "former" or "first." 18. The images. 19. On the restoration, cf. Brashler, in *Nag Hammadi Codices V,2–5 and VI*, 339. Here the Greek of Plato's *Republic* reads: "But he lets them fight and bite and devour one another" (589a—the English is only slightly different in the Jowett translation). 20. Here the Greek of the *Republic* reads *hēmera*, "tame" (Jowett: "gentle"), which the Coptic translator may have understood as *hēmera* (with a different accent), "day."

THE DISCOURSE ON THE EIGHTH AND NINTH

NHC VI,6

Introduced by Jean-Pierre Mahé
Translated by Marvin Meyer

The title of the sixth tractate of Nag Hammadi Codex VI has been accidentally torn off. On the basis of 53,23–26, it can be approximately reconstructed as the *Discourse on the Eighth and Ninth*. The text is a dialogue between a "father," sometimes called "Hermes" (58,28; 59,11; 63,24) or "Trismegistus" (59,15.24), and a "son," addressed as "my child" without any proper name.[1]

This disciple in the *Discourse on the Eighth and Ninth* is far from being a novice. Hermes has already explained to him all of his "general lectures" and his "detailed lectures" (63,1–2). There is only one thing left to be done: the disciple needs to pass through the last stage of spiritual perfection, which does not consist merely of learning but demands full personal involvement. In fact, he has to undergo an initiation into the divine mysteries of the Eighth and the Ninth, so that he may be born again and become a new person, directly inspired by God's mind.

This goal cannot be reached by ordinary teaching. The dialogue is composed mainly of prayers and praises to God mingled with ecstatic visions. From the very beginning (52,27), the father's guidance takes the form of instruction about prayer. Moreover, the spiritual power that brings about new birth is conveyed through a kiss (57,26), a symbol and instrument of divine love.

In both form and content, the *Discourse on the Eighth and Ninth* is most similar to the *Secret Dialogue of Hermes Trismegistus on the Mountain: On Being Born Again and on the Promise to Be Silent* (*Corpus Hermeticum* XIII). The latter text, however, is formally less perfect. The author constantly wavers between visionary enthusiasm and scholastic discussion. In our dialogue, on the other hand, when the heavenly forces come down (57,28–29), the theoretical discussion has

---

1. Throughout this introduction the translation used (with minor modifications) for Hermetic writings beyond the Nag Hammadi library is that of Brian P. Copenhaver.

been over for some time, giving way to praise and gratitude, which alone can lift one up to the supreme vision.

Supposedly the dialogue of the *Discourse on the Eighth and Ninth* takes place in Egypt, a point that is strongly emphasized in the epilogue. After giving thanks to God for his favor, the disciple is told to carve the book of his vision on turquoise steles—a color typical of Alexandrian glazed ceramics—which shall be put on the esplanade of Hermes' shrine in Diospolis. This place name is likely to be identified with Diospolis Magna, ancient Thebes, where Thoth's temple can still be found in Kasr al-Agouz.

But to what extent does the subject matter of the dialogue—the revelation of the Eighth and the Ninth—derive from ancient Egyptian beliefs? Along with the Coptic numbers "eighth" and "ninth," our text also uses the Greek forms "Ogdoad" and "Ennead," which to Egyptologists indicate groups of primordial deities that were worshiped mainly in Hermopolis and Heliopolis. Thoth, the Egyptian ancestor of Hermes Trismegistus, was closely associated with these deities for many centuries. Thus he could be called "the lord of the city of the Eight"—that is, Hermopolis-Ashmouneïn (from Coptic *šmoun*, "eight")—or "the lord of the Ennead." Our text explicitly names the "nine of the sun" (62,4–5) and mentions frog- and cat-faced keepers (62,8.10), which may be zoomorphic emblems of the Ogdoad and the Ennead.

Nevertheless, in the second century CE, when the Greek original of the *Discourse on the Eighth and Ninth* was written, these terms would have evoked astrological ideas, namely, the eighth and the ninth heavenly spheres, rather than the primeval deities of Egypt. Of course, even the reinterpretation of the Ogdoad in astrological terms might have been furthered by ancient Egyptian speculation. For instance, the theologians of Heliopolis tried to work the Ogdoad into their system by assimilating it to the so-called eight Hehous, the pillars that hold up the heavens. Yet the movement of our text depends almost completely on the Hellenistic belief in astral fatalism.

Soaring up to the eighth sphere, the Ogdoad, means first of all getting rid of the influence of the seven planets and gaining access to the superior world, the abode of the highest God. In the oath that concludes our dialogue (63,16–32), Hermes sketches a vertical section of the universe. Above the ground floor, where the material elements (air, earth, fire, and water) are, dwell the seven Ousiarchs, who in this context must be identified with the seven planetary governors of *Poimandres* (*Corpus Hermeticum* I, 14.16). They constitute the Harmonia, the cosmic framework moved by fate (I, 19) or the demiurgic spirit (I, 11). Then comes the Begotten One, the rational soul of the cosmos, on the same level as the Eighth, the abode of individual souls and angels (58,17–20; 59,29–30). One step higher we meet the Self-Begotten One, divine Mind and its powers, on the same level as the Ninth. Over the heights of heavens reigns the Unbegotten God.

Why does rising again to the eighth and the ninth spheres necessarily mean being born again, or being granted regeneration? Because humanity's coming down here below is, by contrast, a degeneration. In the first nineteen paragraphs of *Poimandres* (*Corpus Hermeticum* I), which can be read as a rewriting of *Gene-*

sis 1:1–10:1, God the Almighty, the maker of everything, to whom are addressed the eighteen blessings of the Kedusha, consists of a triad of Sovereignty (*Authentia*), Mind, and Holy Word, the latter most likely being identical with the spirit of God, who according to *Genesis* 1:2 was moving upon the face of the water. The first two entities can be regarded as unbegotten and self-begotten, whereas the Holy Word is begotten, since it is "the son of God coming from his mind" (*Corpus Hermeticum* I, 6).

As to the origin of humankind, according to *Poimandres*, first the Mind gives birth, after its image, to an androgynous Human within the superior world (*Corpus Hermeticum* I, 12). By being mirrored in the watery nature of the inferior world, this first Human produces a form after his own likeness (I, 14). Thus is the begotten second androgynous human, who is twofold—mortal in his body and immortal in his essential being (I, 15). The latter in turn begets seven androgynous human beings made out of material nature (I, 16). Then the two sexes are separated, time starts its course, along with the revolutions of the heavenly spheres, and human generations like ours are brought into being (I, 19).

Poimandres teaches that salvation consists in "recognizing oneself as immortal, in knowing that love is the cause of death, and in becoming acquainted with all that exists" (*Corpus Hermeticum* I, 18). This goal can be reached by living piously (I, 22). Then, at the moment of death, when the soul is freed from the material body, "the human being rushes up through the cosmic framework" (I, 25) and "enters the eighth sphere" (I, 26). Then he "hears certain powers that exist above the eighth sphere and sing hymns to God with sweet voices." God himself dwells on a higher level. All those who have received knowledge are bound to enter into him (I, 26).

The Discourse on the Eighth and Ninth obviously takes up the same ten levels of beings. But instead of waiting for a posthumous ascent to the superior world, our Hermetic author aims at anticipating the process here below by strengthening within himself the mental faculties—soul and mind—that humanity has received from the eighth and the ninth spheres.

In order to advance in "the way of immortality" (*Discourse on the Eighth and Ninth* 63,10–11) under the guidance of Trismegistus, the disciple must pass through an initiatory mystery, a rite of regeneration. The central experience of this mystery seems to be a vision of oneself: "I see myself" (58,8; 61,1; cf. *Corpus Hermeticum* XIII, 13). Not only does this vision bring about the regeneration of the initiate—"for this is rebirth, my child" (XIII, 13)—but it also enables him to recognize in the one initiating him—the father—the figure of Trismegistus himself. The name Trismegistus occurs only twice in our text, and it does so precisely between the two visions of the self.

How can we live through such an experience? We need spiritual exercise and grace. The main exercise is prayer. Prayer aims at beseeching God's free assistance (55,14–15) and complements the meditative contemplation of the beauty of the soul that was begun during the previous days. Those who pray become "a reflection of the Fullness," the superior world surrounding God (57,8–10). By praising the divinity, the disciple first joins his brothers who live in this world, the congregation of Hermes' spiritual sons (53,27–30). Eventually he also meets the souls and the angels of the eighth sphere as well as the power of the ninth one. True prayer is a spiritual sacrifice offered to God (57,19). It can be compared with some kind of seraphic trisagion uniting in one and the same hymn all of the souls and the spirits here below as well as in the highest of heavens. The kiss that follows the first prayer and brings about ecstatic vision is by itself an angelic liturgy.

By miming the contents of the most blessed vision—that is, the choir of angels and powers praising God with their silent mind—we become able to conceive ourselves as pure minds, released from our bodies and able to receive from above "the power that is light" (57,29–30). Thus will we change our abstract meditation and our persistent effort to concentrate on the superior world into "a clear and joyful vision" (*Corpus Hermeticum* I, 4) that is "sharper than the ray of the sun and is full of immortality" (X, 4).

No doubt, for the Hermetic writer, this luminous power is nothing but divine Mind itself. It consists in divine self-contemplation and manifestation of oneself to oneself. Whoever sees himself by the power of this Mind tends to recover his "essential" self and become assimilated to the Self-Begotten Human. Then he can also see the source of the Unbegotten One (*Discourse on the Eighth and Ninth* 52,19; 55,22; 58,13).

There are three main reasons scholars have had a particular interest in the *Discourse on the Eighth and Ninth*. Unlike the other two Hermetic writings from the Nag Hammadi library (the *Prayer of Thanksgiving* and the *Excerpt from the Perfect Discourse*), this tractate was previously unknown. In addition, by describing an initiation mystery, the *Discourse on the Eighth and Ninth* shows us the religious and existential dimensions of Hermetic thought. The concern of Trismegistus is to open a path, to guide his disciples up to spiritual rest and illumination. This goal could hardly be met without the organization of communities and mystery ceremonies. Finally, the mythological basis of our tractate clearly alludes to Egyptian religion and to the same tradition as the Nag Hammadi tractate *Eugnostos the Blessed* (NHC III,3; V,1). *Eugnostos the Blessed* offers a Jewish interpretation of *Genesis*; but from a Hermetic point of view, there is not the slightest discontinuity between Egyptian and Jewish inspiration, since Moses supposedly was a disciple of Hermes Trismegistus.

BIBLIOGRAPHY

Brian P. Copenhaver, *Hermetica*; Jean-Pierre Mahé, ed., *Hermès en Haute Égypte*; Douglas M. Parrott, ed., *Nag Hammadi Codices V,2–5 and VI*, 341–73 (James Brashler, Peter A. Dirkse, and Douglas M. Parrott); Hans-Martin Schenke, Hans-Gebhard Bethge, and Ursula Ulrike Kaiser, eds., *Nag Hammadi Deutsch*, 2.499–518 (Karl-Wolfgang Tröger).

The Discourse on the Eighth and Ninth[1]

Introduction to the Ceremony (52,1–55,22)

"[My father],[2] yesterday you promised [me you would take] my mind to the eighth stage[3] and after that you would take me to the ninth. You said this is the sequence of the tradition."

"Yes, my child,[4] this is the sequence, but the promise was made about human nature. I told you this when I initiated the promise, and I said it on the condition that you will remember each of the stages. After I received the spirit through the power, I established the action for you. Clearly understanding resides in you. In me it is as if the power were pregnant, for when I conceived from the spring that flows to me, I gave birth."

"Father, you have spoken every word rightly to me, but I am amazed at what you say. You said, 'The power in me.'"

He said, "I gave birth to the power, as children are born."

"Then, father, I have many siblings[5] if I am to be counted among the generations."

"Right, my child. This good thing is counted [53] ......[6] always. So, my child, you must know your siblings and honor them rightly and well, since they have come from the same father. I have addressed each of the generations. I have named them, since they are offspring like these children."

"Then, father, do they also have mothers?"[7]

---

1. Coptic text: NHC VI,6: 52,1–63,32. Editions: *The Facsimile Edition of the Nag Hammadi Codices: Codex VI*, 57–67; Jean-Pierre Mahé, *Hermès en Haute Égypte*; Douglas M. Parrott, ed., *Nag Hammadi Codices V,2–5 and VI*, 341–73 (James Brashler, Peter A. Dirkse, and Douglas M. Parrott); Hans-Martin Schenke, Hans-Gebhard Bethge, and Ursula Ulrike Kaiser, eds., *Nag Hammadi Deutsch*, 2.499–518 (Karl-Wolfgang Tröger). The title is construed from the contents of the text. 2. A line missing at the very opening of the text must have contained the title ("[The Eighth and Ninth]"? "[On the Eighth and Ninth]"? "[The Eighth Reveals the Ninth]"?). 3. Here the text reads simply "the eighth," referring to the eighth stage of as-

cent to the divine. Cf. also the levels of the spheres of heaven, where beyond the seven planetary spheres are realms for the fixed stars and sometimes the demiurge, Sophia, and the divine. 4. Lit., "my son," translated throughout the text as "my child." 5. Lit., "brothers," throughout the text. 6. About four lines missing or untranslatable. 7. Coptic *ouⁿtau hōou ⁿmmau*. Cf. Mahé, ed., *Hermès en Haute Égypte*, 1.66–67; Tröger, in *Nag Hammadi Deutsch*, 2.509. Brashler, Dirkse, and Parrott, in *Nag Hammadi Codices V,2–5 and VI*, 348–49, prefer to read "do they have a day?" and refer to a birthday. It may also be possible to translate "do they themselves possess something?"

"My child, they are spiritual, for they exist as forces nurturing other souls. That is why I say they are immortal."

"Your word is true, and from now on it cannot be refuted. Father, begin the discourse on the eighth and ninth, and count me also with my siblings."

"Let us pray, my child, to the Father of the All, with your siblings, who are my children, that he may grant the spirit and I may speak."

"How do they pray, father, when they are united with the generations? Father, I want to obey." [54]

". . . . . . [8] [This is not from necessity] or law. Rather, one rests [in] her [and she loves] him, and loving makes you remember[9] the progress you have experienced as wisdom from the books.[10] My child, think of your early years of life. Like a little child you have raised senseless and foolish questions."

"Father, I have experienced progress and foreknowledge from the books, and they are greater than what is lacking. These matters are my first concern."

"My child, when you understand the truth of your statement, you will find your siblings, who are my children, praying with you."

"Father, I understand nothing else than the beauty I have experienced in the books."

"This is what you call the beauty of the soul—the edification you have experienced in stages. May understanding come to you, and you will become wise."

"Father, I have understood each of the books, and especially [55] . . . that is in . . . ."[11]

"My child, . . .[12] in praises from those who raise [them]."

"Father, I shall receive from you the power of the discourse [you will] utter. As it was spoken to the two of us, father, let us pray."

"My child, it is fitting for us to pray to God with all our mind and all our heart and our soul, and to ask him that the gift of the eighth reach us, and that each receive from him what belongs to him. Your job is to understand, mine is to be able to utter the discourse from the spring that flows to me."

Prayer for the Ascent to the Eighth and Ninth (55,23–57,25)

"Let us pray, father:

> I call upon you,
> who rules over the kingdom of power,
> whose word is an offspring of light,
> whose words are immortal,

---

8. About two lines missing or untranslatable. 9. On these restorations, cf. Máhe, *Hermès en Haute Égypte*, 1.68–69. The feminine singular pronoun may refer to the soul. 10. Or "generations," here and below (*jōme*). It may well be suggested here that instruction with books constitutes the lower stages of spiritual enlightenment. "Generations," however, are also mentioned in the same context. 11. The text cannot be restored with confidence. One possibility: "the [hymn] that is in [silence]." The first part of the lacuna could also be restored as "[matter]." 12. Again, the text cannot be restored with confidence. It may read something like "[it is offered]" (Tröger, in *Nag Hammadi Deutsch*, 2.511).

eternal, immutable,
whose will produces life for forms everywhere,
whose nature gives form to substance,
by whom [56] souls, [powers], and angels are moved,
[whose] word [reaches all] who exist,
whose forethought[13] reaches everyone [in] that [place],
[who] produces everyone,
who has [divided] the eternal realm[14] among spirits,[15]
who has created everything,
who, being self within self, supports everything,
being perfect,
the invisible God to whom one speaks in silence,
whose image is moved when it is managed,
and it is so managed,
mighty one in power,
who is exalted above majesty,
who is superior to those honored,
ZŌXATHAZŌ
A
ŌŌ EE
ŌŌŌ ĒĒĒ
ŌŌŌŌ ĒĒ
ŌŌŌŌŌŌ OOOOO
ŌŌŌŌŌŌ UUUUUU
ŌŌŌŌŌŌŌŌŌŌŌŌŌŌŌ
ZŌZAZŌTH.[16]
Lord, grant us wisdom from your power that reaches us,
that we may relate to ourselves the vision of the eighth and ninth.
Already we have advanced to the seventh,
since we are faithful
and abide in your law.
Your will we fulfill always.
We have walked in [57] [your way]
[and have] renounced [evil],[17]
so the vision[18] may come.
Lord, grant us truth in the image.
Grant that through spirit we may see
the form of the image that lacks nothing,
and accept the reflection of the Fullness[19]

---

13. Or "providence" (*pronoia*). 14. Aeon. 15. The restorations here and in the preceding lines are proposed by Máhe, *Hermès en Haute Égypte*, 1.72–73. 16. Glossolalia. 17. On the restoration, cf. Máhe, *Hermès en Haute Égypte*, 1.74–75. Here Tröger, in *Nag Hammadi Deutsch*, 2.512, restores to read "[our childhood]," with reference to *Discourse on the Eighth and Ninth* 54. 18. Or "your vision." 19. Pleroma.

from us through our praise.
Recognize the spirit within us.
From you the universe received soul.
From you, one unbegotten,
the begotten one came to be.
The birth of the self-begotten is through you,
the birth of all begotten things that exist.
Accept these spiritual offerings from us,
which we direct to you
with all our heart, soul, and strength.
Save what is within us,
and grant us immortal wisdom."

Vision of the Eighth and Ninth (57,26–61,17)

"My child, let us embrace in love.[20] Be happy about this. Already from this, the power that is light is coming to us. I see, I see ineffable depths. How shall I tell you, [58] my child? [We now have begun to see] . . . the places.[21] How [shall I tell you about] the All?[22] I am [mind[23] and] I see another mind, one that [moves] the soul. I see the one that moves me from pure forgetfulness. You give me power. I see myself. I wish to speak. Fear seizes me. I have found the beginning of the power above all powers, without beginning. I see a spring bubbling with life. I have said, my child, that I am mind. I have seen. Language cannot reveal this. For all of the eighth, my child, and the souls in it, and the angels,[24] sing a hymn in silence. I, mind, understand."

"How does one sing a hymn through silence?"

"Can no one communicate with you?"

"I am silent, father. I want to sing a hymn to you while I am silent."

"Then sing it. I am mind."

"I understand mind—'Hermes,' which cannot be explained[25] because it stays in itself. I am happy, father, to see you smiling. The universe [59] [is happy]. No creature will lack your life, for you are lord of the inhabitants everywhere. Your forethought keeps watch. I call you father, aeon of aeons, spirit, divine being,[26] who through spirit sends moisture on everyone.[27] What do you tell me, father Hermes?"

---

20. Or "in truth" (*hᵉn oume*). **21.** So it is restored, in part, by Máhe, *Hermès en Haute Égypte*, 1.76–77. Here Tröger, in *Nag Hammadi Deutsch*, 2.513, reads: "How should I tell you, my child, [if you] already [have begun to see the seven] places? How [do you see] the All?" **22.** Or "the universe." **23.** Nous, here and below. **24.** The souls and the angels are thought to dwell in the eighth. **25.** This is a pun on the name Hermes: it cannot be explained (*hermēneue*) because the *hermēneia* stays in *Hermes*. **26.** Coptic, from Greek, *ppna on theion*. It is also possible to divide the letters as *ppna o ntheion* and translate "great divine spirit." **27.** Or "sends rain on everyone." The text also refers to "a spring bubbling with life," and other Gnostic texts likewise mention water, including living water.

"My child, I say nothing about this. It is right before God for us to remain silent about what is hidden."

"Trismegistus, do not let my soul be deprived of the vision. O divine being,[28] everything is possible for you as master of the universe."

"Sing <praise> again, my child, and sing while you are silent. Ask what you want in silence."

When he finished praising, he called out, "Father Trismegistus, what shall I say? We have received this light, and I myself see this same vision in you. I see the eighth, and the souls in it, and the angels singing a hymn to the ninth[29] and its powers. I see the one with the power of them all, creating [60] <those> in the spirit."[30]

"From [now on] it is good for us to remain silent, with head bowed.[31] From now on do not speak about the vision. It is fitting to sing [a hymn] to the Father until the day we leave the body."

"What you sing, father, I also want to sing."

"I am singing a hymn in myself. While you rest, sing praise. You have found what you seek."

"But is it right, father, for me to sing praise when my heart is filled?"

"What is right is for you to sing praise to God so it may be written in this imperishable book."

"I shall offer up the praise in my heart as I invoke the end of the universe, and the beginning of the beginning, the goal of the human quest, the immortal discovery, the producer of light and truth, the sower of reason, the love of immortal life. No hidden word can speak of you, lord. My mind wants to sing a hymn to you every day. I am the instrument of your spirit, mind is your plectrum, and your guidance makes music with me. I see [61] myself. I have received power from you, for your love has reached us."

"Right, my child."

"O grace! After this, I thank you by singing a hymn to you. You gave me life when you made me wise. I praise you. I invoke your name hidden in me,

A
Ō EE
Ō ĒĒĒ
ŌŌŌ III
ŌŌŌŌ OOOOO
ŌŌŌŌŌ UUUUUU

---

28. Coptic *ttheōreia on theion*. It is also possible to divide the letters as *ttheōreia o ntheion* and translate "great divine vision." 29. Mind dwells in the ninth. 30. Without emendation the text reads "creating spirits"; with a slight emendation, "creating in the spirit." 31. Lit., "leaning forward" (*hᶜn oumᶜnt[pro]petēs*).

The translators in *Nag Hammadi Codices V,2–5 and VI*, 363, suggest "in a reverent posture," while Mahé and Tröger understand the phrase to mean "from this moment"—which fits well with what follows in the text.

ŌŌŌŌŌŌ ŌŌŌŌŌ
ŌŌŌŌŌŌŌ ŌŌŌŌ[32]
You exist with spirit.
I sing to you with godliness."

Instructions for the Preservation of the Text (61,18–63,32)

"My child, copy this book for the temple at Diospolis,[33] in hieroglyphic characters, and call it the Eighth Reveals the Ninth."

"I shall do it, <father>,[34] as you command."

"<My child>,[35] copy the contents of the book on turquoise steles.[36] My child, it is fitting to copy this book on turquoise steles in hieroglyphic characters, for mind itself has become the supervisor [62] of these things. So I command that this discourse be carved in stone and that you put it in my sanctuary.[37] Eight guards watch over it with nine[38] of the sun:[39] the males on the right have faces of frogs, the females on the left have faces of cats.[40] Put a square milk-stone at the base of the turquoise tablets and copy the name on the azure stone tablet in hieroglyphic characters. My child, you must do this when I[41] am in Virgo, and the sun is in the first half of the day, and fifteen degrees have passed by me."

"Father, all you say I shall gladly do."

"Copy an oath in the book, so that those who read the book may not use the wording for evil purposes or try to subvert fate. Rather, they should submit to the law of God, and not transgress at all, but in purity ask God for wisdom and knowledge.[42] And whoever [63] is not begotten beforehand by God develops through the general and instructional discourses. Such a person will not be able to read what is written in this book, even though the person's conscience is pure within and the person does nothing shameful and does not go along with it. Such a person progresses by stages and advances in the way of immortality, and so advances in the understanding of the eighth that reveals the ninth."

"I shall do it, father."

"This is the oath: I adjure you who will read this holy book, by heaven and earth and fire and water, and seven rulers of substance and the creative spirit in them, and the <un>begotten[43] God and the self-begotten and the begotten, that you guard what Hermes has communicated. God will be at one with those who keep the oath and everyone we have named, but the wrath of each of them will come upon those who violate the oath. This is the perfect one who is, my child."

---

32. More glossolalia. The sequence of vowels seems to be imperfect. 33. Diospolis Magna is Thebes (Luxor); Diospolis Parva is Heou (near Nag Hammadi). 34. Emended; the Coptic text reads "my child." 35. Emended; the Coptic text reads "My father." Here Máhe, *Hermès en Haute Égypte*, 1.82–83, takes "My father" as a vocative with a question from the student to the teacher: "My father, should I copy the contents of the book on turquoise steles?" 36. The *Three Steles of Seth* also assumes such monuments. 37. The

meaning of this Coptic word is uncertain (*ouōpe*). Cf. Tröger, in *Nag Hammadi Deutsch*, 2.516 (with reference to a suggestion by Hans-Martin Schenke). 38. Here Tröger, in *Nag Hammadi Deutsch*, 2.516, reads "attendants." 39. Helios—the Sun. 40. Egyptian deities often are depicted with faces of animals. 41. I.e., Hermes, the planet Mercury. 42. Gnosis. 43. Here the Coptic is emended to read <a>*gennētos* (*ge* may have been crossed out in the manuscript by a scribe).

THE PRAYER OF THANKSGIVING

NHC VI,7

Introduced by Jean-Pierre Mahé
Translated by Marvin Meyer

The *Prayer of Thanksgiving*, which appears in Codex VI of the Nag Hammadi library as an epilogue to the *Discourse on the Eighth and Ninth*, was originally an independent writing destined to be recycled in different contexts. It also serves as the conclusion to both a Greek magical collection of texts (in the so-called Papyrus Mimaut) and *Asclepius*, a Latin adaptation of the Greek *Perfect Discourse* of Hermes Trismegistus. In the latter dialogue (*Asclepius* 41), the prayer is flanked by two liturgical rubrics containing instructions for the use of the prayer. Thus, before the text of the prayer, we read, "When someone wants to entreat God at sunset, he should direct his gaze to that quarter, and likewise at sunrise toward the direction they call east." A similar instruction (*Corpus Hermeticum* XIII, 16) is also given in the *Secret Hymn* (XIII, 17–20) contained in another Hermetic writing. Similarly, the following words of recommendation bring the prayer to a conclusion: "with such hope we turn to a pure meal that includes no living thing." Although the second rubric for the use of the prayer has been preserved in Nag Hammadi Codex VI (65,2–7), the first has been replaced with a narrative introduction, "This is the prayer they offered" (63,33), which obviously echoes a previous sentence in the *Discourse on the Eighth and Ninth*: "When he finished praising, he called out" (59,23–24).[1]

The *Prayer of Thanksgiving* is particularly appropriate to conclude a dialogue describing the final stage of Hermetic initiation. Its contents may be summarized as follows:

Narrative introduction
Invocation of the divine name

---

1. Throughout this introduction the translation used (with minor modifications) for Hermetic writings beyond the Nag Hammadi library is that of Brian P. Copenhaver.

Enumeration of divine gifts
Gift of mind, word, and knowledge
Divinizing effects of knowledge
Revelation of the divine essence: light and life, Father and Mother
Final request: to be preserved in knowledge
Liturgical rubric: ritual kiss and sacred meal

In the central part of the *Prayer of Thanksgiving*, the three gifts of mind, word, and knowledge seem to be granted simultaneously. We know, however, from other Hermetic writings, that these three fulfill successive functions on the "way of immortality" (*Discourse on the Eighth and Ninth* 63,11). For example, word or discourse and mind share the task among themselves as follows: "Discourse does not get to the truth, but mind is powerful, and when it has been guided by the discourse up to a certain point of the road, it has the means to get as far as the truth. After mind has included everything in an all-embracing glance and has discovered that all of it is in harmony with the interpretation of the discourse, it comes to believe, and in this beautiful belief it finds his rest" (*Corpus Hermeticum* IX, 10). Thus we learn that word or discourse and mind cover two different stages of the Hermetic way. In fact, they are rather two successive steps or stages (*Discourse on the Eighth and Ninth* 52,13; 54,28; 63,9), since the way is ascending to the uppermost regions.

Knowledge, as "the goal of learning" (*Corpus Hermeticum* X, 9), cannot possibly be a once-for-all fixed science. Rather, knowledge consists in gradually becoming aware of transcendent truth (IX, 4) by crossing, in some way, the sill of a "portal" (VII, 2). Knowledge is a fervent search for the absolute, kindled with "piety" (I, 27; VI, 5; IX, 4)—a radical shift from ignorant lack of concern for religion to the firm conviction that God exists and "wishes to be known" (I, 31). "Thus, knowledge is not a beginning of the good, but it provides us with means of beginning to know it" (IV, 9). Significantly enough in the Coptic version of the prayer, the Coptic verb *sooun* appears as a translation not of the Greek *gignōskein*, "to know," with an absolute meaning, but of *epigignōskein* (64,14), "to find out, to discover," or *gnōrizein* (64,22.24.25.27), "to gain knowledge, gradually to become acquainted with."

Knowledge divinizes human beings not by itself alone, but jointly with word and mind, which both remain indispensable to cover the "way of immortality" up to its end. For "this is the final good for those who have received knowledge: to be made gods" (*Corpus Hermeticum* I, 26). Such a knowledge produces an ecstatic joy, which our text expresses by repeating thrice "we are happy" or "we rejoice" (64,15.16.17) and four times "we have known you" (64,22.24.25.27).

Prayer is instrumental in acquiring the knowledge of God. Indeed, a reverent soul that mind leads to the light of knowledge "never has its fill of hymning and praising" (*Corpus Hermeticum* X, 21). As a result, such a soul still fans the flame of its own fervor, and it comes to know God more and more, so that it may truly affirm, according to our text, "The thanksgiving of one approaching you is this alone: that we know you" (64,20–22).

We should not be surprised by the realism of the sexual metaphors depicting the divine Father as endowed with male and female genitals, so that he never stops impregnating his own womb in order to fill up the universe with new creatures. In a manner reflective of traditional Egyptian sources, the Hermetic author regards sexual intercourse as a "marvelous image" (*Excerpt from the Perfect Discourse* 65,16–17), apt to arouse spiritual contemplation of the divine essence.

In fact, carnal generation is but a symbol of the ineffable. The "male and female" Hermetic God (*Corpus Hermeticum* I, 9) is not only a phallus and a womb, but also "light of mind" (64,23) and "life of life" (64,24)—that is, in Greek, *phōs*, a male principle, and *zōē*, a female principle, both of which God conveys to his most perfect creature, the primordial Human who is in his image (*Corpus Hermeticum* I, 12), male and female, like his Father (I, 15). Eventually when man and woman were separated from each other (I, 18), the first earthly man was Phos (either "Light" or "Mortal," depending on the accent), and the first woman was Zoe ("Life," or Eve, according to the Septuagint version of *Genesis* 4:20). Conceiving God as the source of Phos and Zoe means having an intuition or even a mystical vision of the first human couple, just released from God's hand, endowed with divine likeness and perfect knowledge of their creator.

Contemplating divine sexuality is a pledge of spiritual rebirth. The *Secret Dialogue on Being Born Again* opens with these words: "I do not know what sort of womb humanity was born from, O Trismegistus, nor what kind of seed—My child, the womb is the wisdom of understanding in silence, and the seed is the true good—Who sows the seed, Father ? . . .—The will of God, my child" (*Corpus Hermeticum* XIII, 1–2).

Since the *Prayer of Thanksgiving* sums up in a vividly lyrical form the whole experience of mental progress and the successive steps of the Hermetic ascent to heavenly immortality, it could rightly be thought to provide an excellent conclusion to the last stage of initiation described in the *Discourse on the Eighth and Ninth*. In addition, immediately after the liturgical rebirth, it would allow the newly born again child of Trismegistus to be immersed in the community ritual of a fraternal banquet.

BIBLIOGRAPHY

Brian P. Copenhaver, *Hermetica*; Jean-Pierre Mahé, ed., *Hermès en Haute Égypte*; Douglas M. Parrott, ed., *Nag Hammadi Codices V,2–5 and VI*, 375–93 (Peter A. Dirkse, James Brashler, and Douglas M. Parrott); Hans-Martin Schenke, Hans-Gebhard Bethge, and Ursula Ulrike Kaiser, eds., *Nag Hammadi Deutsch*, 2.519–25 (Karl-Wolfgang Tröger).

The Prayer of Thanksgiving[1]

This is the prayer they[2] offered:

We thank you;
every soul and heart reaches out to you,
O name free of trouble, [64]
honored with the designation God,
praised with the designation Father.
To all and all things
come fatherly kindness and affection and love.
And if there is sweet and simple instruction,[3]
it grants us mind, word, and knowledge:[4]
mind, that we may understand you,
word, that we may interpret you,
knowledge, that we may know you.
We are happy,
enlightened by your knowledge.
We are happy.
You have taught us about yourself.
We are happy.
While we were in the body,
you have made us divine through your knowledge.

The thanksgiving of one approaching you
is this alone:
that we know you.
We have known you,
light of mind.

---

1. Coptic text: NHC VI,7: 63,33–65,7; 65,8–14 (scribal note). Editions: *The Facsimile Edition of the Nag Hammadi Codices: Codex VI*, 67–89; Jean-Pierre Mahé, *Hermès en Haute Égypte*; Douglas M. Parrott, ed., *Nag Hammadi Codices V,2–5 and VI*, 375–93 (Peter A. Dirkse, James Brashler, and Douglas M. Parrott); Hans-Martin Schenke, Hans-Gebhard Bethge, and Ursula Ulrike Kaiser, eds., *Nag Hammadi Deutsch*, 2.519–25 (Karl-Wolfgang Tröger). The title is con- strued from the contents of the text. The text is also preserved as a part of the *Perfect Discourse* (or *Asclepius*); cf. Papyrus Mimaut 591–611; Latin *Asclepius* 41. 2. In the present context, those offering the prayer must be the teacher and the student of the *Discourse on the Eighth and Ninth*. 3. Here the Greek reads, "To all and all things you have shown fatherly kind- ness, affection, love, and even sweeter action." 4. Gnosis, here and below.

Life of life,
we have known you.
Womb of every creature,
we have known you.
Womb pregnant with the Father's nature,
we have known you.
Eternal constancy of the Father who conceives,
so have we worshiped your goodness.
One favor we [65] ask:
we wish to be sustained in knowledge.[5]
One protection we desire:
that we not stumble in this life.

When they prayed and said these things, they embraced[6] and went to eat their sacred bloodless[7] food.

Copyist's Note (65,8–14)

I have copied this one of his discourses.[8] A great many have come into my hands, but I have not copied them because I thought they were already in your possession. I even hesitate to copy these things for you, since perhaps you may already have received them and the matter may annoy you, for that person's discourses that have come into my hands are many.

---

5. Or, reading with the Greek and Latin versions, "your knowledge" (*tē sē gnōs[ei], cognitionis tuae*).   6. Perhaps they kissed each other in a ritual embrace.   7. Vegetarian food.   8. Apparently Hermes' discourses.

EXCERPT FROM THE
PERFECT DISCOURSE

NHC VI,8

Introduced by Jean-Pierre Mahé
Translated by Marvin Meyer

The eighth tractate of Nag Hammadi Codex VI derives from a teaching of Hermes Trismegistus to his main disciples Asclepius, Tat, and Ammon (72,30). Only small fragments of the Greek original, whose title was *Perfect Discourse*, have been preserved. The Latin *Asclepius*, sometimes attributed to Apuleius, provides us with a complete version of the work. However, a comparison of all the extant evidence proves that the Coptic is a fairly accurate translation from the Greek, whereas the Latin is a rather free adaptation.[1]

The Coptic *Excerpt from the Perfect Discourse* contains the central elements of the dialogue (*Asclepius* 21–29), with a vibrant eulogy to Egypt. More than any other Hermetic writing, this text raises the question of the links between Alexandrian culture and old Egyptian literature and civilization. We cannot fully explain the prediction of Trismegistus concerning Egypt and its gods by simply looking for hints in the historical events of the third century CE. In fact, the text revives a literary genre that appeared as early as the first intermediate period (2190–2070 BCE). The *Lamentations of Ipou-our*, from that period, is not exactly a prediction. It deplores the present misfortune of Egypt and recalls the happiness of the old days. It concludes by describing an appeasement, which is less a prophecy than a wish. Nevertheless, its evocation of foreign invasions, slaughters, inversion of moral values, and exaltation of traditional piety are rather close to our Hermetic oracle.

Later on, about 2000 BCE, *Neferty's Prediction* pretends to foretell to Snefru, the father of Kheops, the disturbances of the first intermediate period and the successful reign of Amenemhat I. As in the *Perfect Discourse*, the text has two

---

1. Throughout this introduction the translation used (with minor modifications) for Hermetic writings beyond the Nag Hammadi library is that of Brian P. Copenhaver.

parts: it anticipates a catastrophe and the gradual restoration of order. Through foreign invasions, human disorder brings about cosmic disasters. The *Demotic Chronicle* of the third century BCE comments upon several oracles concerning the last Egyptian pharaohs as well as Persian and Macedonian invaders. Just like the Hermetic writer of the *Perfect Discourse* (74,7–11), the chronicler refers to astral necessity to account for the rebirth of Egypt after foreign domination.

Shortly after the victorious campaigns of Ptolemy III (246–231 BCE), who had brought back to Egypt the statues of the gods captured by the Persians, the *Oracle of the Lamb* offers what is intended as a prediction of these events to King Bocchoris (722–716 BCE). Likewise, in the *Perfect Discourse*, Hermes foretells to his disciples (75,27–33) the retreat of the gods and the foundation of the Alexandrian shrines.

About 130 BCE, the Greek *Oracle of the Potter*—a cryptic name of Khnum, the ancestral god of the Hermetic Good Genius—deals with the same themes as Trismegistus: withdrawal of the gods, foreign wars, omnipresence of death, return of Egypt to the desert, horrible crimes, perversion of values, cosmic perturbations, and final restoration of order. Just as in the *Oracle of the Potter*, the prediction of Trismegistus in the *Perfect Discourse* contains an invocation to Egypt (70,36) and an allusion to "a city that is in a corner of Egypt" (75,28–29), which is sure to be Alexandria.

However, when the Hermetic dialogue was written in the late third century, Egypt had been open to foreign cultural influences for several centuries. Thus, although our text is quite different from Jewish apocalyptic, the mention of "wicked angels" leading men into evil deeds (73,5–12) may well be an echo of the book of *Enoch*. Moreover, the Hermetic author of the *Perfect Discourse* revisits the Egyptian myth of successive births of the cosmos in the light of Greek physics and philosophy. The harmonious functioning of the universe demands a balanced sharing of the four elements. Whenever some disorder brings about the overabundance of fire or water, human beings become victims either of drought or flood. In spite of the Nile's protection, Egypt undergoes such calamities (73,32) until the demiurge restores his previous creation (74,1).

Furthermore, the judgment of the soul and its journey in the underworld are well known in pharaonic literature. But Trismegistus portrays aerial hells that are nothing like the Egyptian underworld. He adapts Plato's myths of the great beyond (*Gorgias* 524d; *Phaedo* 107d; *Republic* X, 614a) to cosmological ideas of his time concerning the heavenly spheres and the various obstacles that may thwart the ascent of the soul toward the uppermost dwellings of blessedness. Thus, despite authentic and quite distinctive Egyptian colors, the *Perfect Discourse* also displays cultural features of the Hellenistic and Roman period.

In comparison with the other Hermetic writings preserved in Nag Hammadi Codex VI, the *Perfect Discourse* seems at first glance confused, down-to-earth, and polytheistic. We feel far removed from the unfathomable heights of the *Discourse on the Eighth and Ninth*, and we nearly forget spiritual devotion to the Most High. In the *Perfect Discourse* the ceiling is usually low. No sooner have we raised our mind above the summit of heavens, up to an immaterial place (75,9), than we go back to Kore and the anonymous forces of the inferior world. Scarcely have we contemplated the sidereal kinship of human beings to astral gods (68,7) than we praise earthly divinities, crafted with mortal hands and just as corporal as their manufacturers (69,19).

Such a contrast is understandable if we keep in mind that Hermetism is not a philosophical system but a spiritual way. We cannot possibly progress toward God unless we ascend and pass through all of the strata of the universe, one after the other. Whoever gazes into heaven (72,19), at the beginning of the road, will feel the same admiration as Hermes in the face of "the beautiful world of God, an incomparable work, virtue in action, a vision of many forms, an abundance that does not hold back, full of every vision" (72,9–16). But as soon as we seek God more deeply, if we try to penetrate heavenly mysteries, the splendid ornaments of the cosmos turn into a screen and an obstacle: "Can you see, my child, how many bodies we must pass through, how many troops of demons, cosmic connections, and stellar circuits, in order to hasten towards the One and Only?" (*Corpus Hermeticum* IV, 8).

We cannot resist such cosmic weariness unless we have received appropriate training. Before starting, we have to gain an overall survey of the route and learn how to increase our steps gradually. No doubt the *Perfect Discourse* marks out only the first two stages of the journey—knowledge and rational speech. Since Hermetic knowledge is closely connected to reverent piety (*Corpus Hermeticum* I, 27; VI, 5; IX, 4), we might ask what the difference is between common and well thought out piety filled with divine knowledge. In this respect, we should be wary of imitating most of the philosophers who sharply criticize popular devotion, for such a method would yield exactly the reverse of what we are searching for: instead of progressing toward holiness, we would only swell the ranks of the unbelievers, the blasphemers, the atheists, and the impious people (66,1–2). No form of piety should be rejected; every one of them should be observed in its proper place and at its appropriate level.

The highest level of being is merely immaterial. It applies to the invisible Unbegotten God (75,9–14). The second level is the abode of the star gods, who are made of a pure, imperishable matter and are bound to eternal and inflexible trajectories (67,18). The lowest level belongs to the earthly gods who dwell in temples (69,26). There is an analogy between the invisible God, creator of the heavenly images of the stars, and humanity, that privileged creature endowed with science and knowledge, modeling material images after the likeness of astral gods (68,20–69,16).

For each of these levels, there is an appropriate form of worship. Since our text describes the beginning of spiritual progress, it mainly aims at justifying traditional Egyptian religion. The gods who are worshiped by common people have been crafted by humankind. Consequently, they consist, unlike star gods, not only of heads, but also of all the others members of the body (69,19–21). As a result, they are subject to wrath and other passions (*Asclepius* 37). By presenting them with offerings, people can obtain from them oracles and healings for themselves and sicknesses and calamities for their foes (69,36–37). Nevertheless,

Asclepius does not seem fully convinced of the might of these earthly gods, and so Trismegistus delivers his prediction in order to show the necessity of their cults.

All rites should be performed advisedly, as we learn from the Armenian *Hermetic Definitions* (VIII, 3): "Those who worship idols worship plain pictures. For if they worshiped with knowledge, they would not have gone astray, but since they do not know how they should worship, they have gone astray, far from piety." "To worship with knowledge" means to understand that the statues of the gods are more than inert images (69,29). They are divine souls, "portioned out, as it were—having come from the one soul of the All" (*Corpus Hermeticum* X, 7), but not discontinuous from the divine Mind. Indeed, through all these idols and their various names, the Hermetist has to look for the hidden name (*Discourse on the Eighth and Ninth* 61,9) of the Most High.

As corporal beings, humans have two kinds of duties here below: "wondering at heavenly beings and worshiping them, tending earthly beings and covering them" (*Asclepius* 8). In his prediction concerning Egypt in the *Perfect Discourse*, Trismegistus reveals what happens when these duties are neglected. As soon as people suppress temple worship, they begin despising the world (72,9), so that eventually nobody cares about either soul or heaven (72,20.27). By contrast, restoration of order after the cataclysm makes the world worthy again of admiration, and its creator receives new praises (74,3–4).

Starting from the earthly gods, whose energies liven up all existing beings (75,25), we gradually ascend to mightier deities, such as Kore, "who produces crops," Plutonian Zeus, who is "lord over earth and sea," and Zeus, called life, the demiurge who reigns "between heaven and earth" (75,13–25). Above them stretches the realm of heavenly gods, those radiant stars created by the supreme God.

"Who might come to know heaven without heavenly favor, or find God without being part of his court?" (Manilius II, 115–16). By calculating the trajectories of stars and planets, by detecting their influence on individual or collective destiny, humanity becomes "related to the gods" (68,7). Contemplation of them means a vocation, a challenge, and a limit. It is a vocation because the stars are only "heads" and abide by immutable and merely logical laws. Their example invites people to rid themselves of passions in order to behave only on the basis of science and knowledge (67,24–28). But the immortality of the stars depends only on the imperishable matter out of which they are made. On the contrary, human beings, with a "twofold nature" (67,32), must take up the challenge of making effective the virtual immortality latent within themselves thanks to the divine gifts of science and knowledge. Finally, the star gods mark, for human beings, the limit between the visible and the invisible. As radiant as they are, these star gods remain visible and material, whereas God's abode is located above the sky, in a mysterious place that has no stars or material things (75,11–19).

Except for this reference, the supreme God is not explicitly described in our text. Yet the words of Hermes are permeated with his omnipresence. How could God not be the source of divine Providence, who grants science and knowledge to people in order to protect them from evil? Regardless of whether God acts directly by himself or through a demiurge, the divine will makes human beings different from other creatures (67,22) and even superior to heavenly gods (67,35), and it opposes disorder and evil (73,27) and is eternally identical to the good (74,12).

Should one ask for further investigation of the mystery, Hermes' advice would be to meditate on the wonderful image of sexual intercourse (65,15–38). More than merely a symbol of divine fecundity, this image appeals to the innermost intuition of everyone; carnal union can either feed the jokes of the scornful and the impious or sustain the contemplation of the reverent person who regards it as a sacred mystery revealing the effect of God's activity.

Thus we may observe that there is some distance between the *Excerpt from the Perfect Discourse* and such initiatory texts as *Poimandres* and the *Discourse on the Eighth and Ninth*. In the present text Hermes neither directly reveals the supreme God nor shows us the way to reach him in the superior world. He does not even indicate the specific kind of worship the Most High deserves—spiritual offerings and silent praises. The dialogue limits itself to the preliminary stage: deepening traditional piety, opening higher levels, and meditating on the visible image of the invisible.

BIBLIOGRAPHY

Brian P. Copenhaver, *Hermetica*; Jean-Pierre Mahé, ed., *Hermès en Haute Égypte*; Douglas M. Parrott, ed., *Nag Hammadi Codices V,2–5 and VI*, 395–451 (Peter A. Dirkse and Douglas M. Parrott); Hans-Martin Schenke, Hans-Gebhard Bethge, and Ursula Ulrike Kaiser, eds., *Nag Hammadi Deutsch*, ed. 2.527–41 (Jens Holzhausen).

Excerpt from the Perfect Discourse[1]

The Nature of the Mystery (65,15–38)

"If you wish to see the nature of this mystery,[2] consider the marvelous image of sexual intercourse between male and female. For when the male reaches his climax, the semen is ejaculated. At that moment the female receives the strength of the male and the male receives the strength of the female, as the semen does this.

"Therefore the mystery of intercourse is performed in secret, so that the two genders may not be embarrassed in front of many who have not tried it. Each of them contributes to procreation. But if intercourse takes place in the presence of those who do not understand it, it is laughable and unbelievable. Moreover, these are holy mysteries of both words and deeds,[3] because they are neither heard nor seen.

Knowledge Leads to Learning (65,38–66,26)

"For this reason [66] such ignorant people are blasphemers. They are godless, impious. There are not many people who are different from this, and godly people are few in number. That is why there is wickedness among the masses, since learning about what is right is nowhere to be found among them. Knowledge[4] of what is right is truly healing for the passions of material existence, and learning comes from knowledge.

"But if there is ignorance, and no learning in the soul of a person, then incurable passions persist in that soul. And more evil comes with the passions in the form of an incurable sore, and the sore gnaws at the soul, so that the soul produces worms from the evil sore and it stinks. God does not cause these things, since God has sent knowledge and learning to people."

---

1. Coptic text: NHC VI,8: 65,15–78,43. Editions: *The Facsimile Edition of the Nag Hammadi Codices: Codex VI*, 69–82; Jean-Pierre Mahé, *Hermès en Haute Égypte*; Douglas M. Parrott, ed., *Nag Hammadi Codices V,2–5 and VI*, 395–451 (Peter A. Dirkse and Douglas M. Parrott); Hans-Martin Schenke, Hans-Gebhard Bethge, and Ursula Ulrike Kaiser, eds., *Nag Hammadi Deutsch*, ed. 2.527–41 (Jens Holzhausen).

The Perfect Discourse (Ho Logos teleios) is the original Greek title; the text is also known as *Asclepius* or the *Apocalypse of Asclepius*. The portion included in the *Excerpt from the Perfect Discourse* is *Asclepius* 21–29. 2. I.e., the mystery that the divine is both male and female. 3. In the mystery religions it is said that there were *legomena* ("things said") and *drōmena* ("things done, acted out"). 4. Gnosis, here and below.

Knowledge and Learning Among Gods and People
(66,26–67,34)

"Trismegistus, has God sent knowledge and learning to people alone?"

"Yes, Asclepius, God has sent these things to people alone. We should tell you why God has granted knowledge and learning to people alone as a share of his goodness.

"Listen! God, the Father and Lord, created humanity after the gods, and he took humanity from [67] the material realm. [Since God has given] matter [a place equal to spirit] in creation, there are passions in it, and they flow over a person's body.[5] Such a living thing can only exist if it eats this food, for it is mortal. It is also inevitable that inappropriate desires, which cause harm, come to be within such a person. Now, the gods have come into being out of pure matter and do not need learning and knowledge, for the immortality of the gods is learning and knowledge, since they have come out of pure matter. Immortality serves as their knowledge and learning. Of necessity God has determined a place for humanity and established humanity in learning and knowledge.

"God[6] has perfected learning and knowledge,[7] as we have been discussing, so that by means of learning and knowledge he might restrain passions and vices, by his will. God has brought human mortality into immortality, and humanity[8] has become good and immortal, as I have said. So God has created a twofold nature in humanity, immortal and mortal.

People Surpass Gods (67,34–69,6)

"It turned out this way because of the will [68] of [God] that people should be better than the gods, since the gods are immortal but only people are both immortal and mortal. People are related to the gods, and they know about each other with certainty. The gods know the concerns of people and people know the concerns of the gods. Asclepius, I am talking about people who have attained learning and knowledge. About people who lack these things we should not say anything bad, since we are divine and are going into sacred subjects.

"Since we have begun the discussion of the communion between gods and people, Asclepius, understand what people can do. For just as the Father, the Lord of the universe, creates gods, so too people—mortal, earthly, living things, who are not[9] like God—create gods. People give and receive power. People become divine and create gods. Are you surprised, Asclepius? Are you too an unbeliever, like so many?" [69]

---

5. On the restoration of this sentence, cf. Mahé, *Hermès en Haute Égypte*, 2.159. 6. Lit., "He," here and below. 7. Lit., "these things," here and below. 8. Lit., "he" or "it," here and below. 9. Coptic *an*; cf. Mahé, *Hermès en Haute Égypte*, 2.223. It is possible to translate this Coptic word as "also," thus "who are also like God."

"Trismegistus, [I agree with] what has been said to me, and I believe you when you speak, but I am astonished by this discourse. I conclude that people are blessed, because they have enjoyed this great power."

Images and Their Capabilities (69,7–70,2)

"Asclepius, what is greater than all this is worthy of wonder. It is obvious to us, and we agree with everyone, that the generation of the gods has come into being out of pure matter, and they are endowed only with heads. But what people fashion is only an image of the gods. They[10] are from the lowest part of matter, and what they fashion[11] is from the external part of the image[12] of people. People fashion not only heads for the gods but also all the other body parts, in their own image. As God has wished that the inner person be created to be like God,[13] so also earthly people create gods in their own image."

"Trismegistus, you are not talking about idols, are you?"

"Asclepius, you are the one talking about idols. You see, Asclepius, that again you do not believe this discourse. You talk about things that have soul and breath and great accomplishments, and you call them idols. You talk about things that foretell the future and make [70] people sick and cure them and [send] plagues as well, and you call them idols.[14]

The Apocalypse: Egypt Will Be Despised (70,3–71,9)

"Asclepius, don't you know that Egypt is the image of heaven, moreover, that it is the dwelling place of heaven and all the forces in heaven? To tell the truth, our land is the temple of the world. But you should know that a time will come when it will seem that Egyptians have served the divine in vain, and all their holy worship will be despised. All that is divine will depart from Egypt and fly up to heaven. Egypt will be widowed, abandoned by the gods. Foreigners will come into Egypt and rule it. Egypt, or Egyptians, will be prohibited from worshiping God, and whoever among them is found worshiping and serving God will face the most severe punishment.

"In that day the country that was more godly than any other country will become impious. It will not be full of temples but of tombs, not of gods but of corpses. You, O Egypt, Egypt, will be the stuff of fables, and no one [71] will believe your divine practices, [neither] the marvelous deeds nor the holy words, not even if your wondrous words are written on stones.[15] Barbarians will surpass you, O Egyptian, in godliness, whether they are Scythians or Hindus or others like them.

---

10. The antecedent of this pronoun is uncertain. Here the pronoun "They" is understood to refer to human beings; the pronoun may also refer to the gods. 11. Lit., "it." 12. Coptic *einai*, which may be read as the Greek infinitive "to be, being" or the Coptic noun *eine*, "image" (an instance of itacism). Cf. Holzhausen, in *Nag Hammadi Deutsch*, 2.535. 13. Lit., "like him." 14. On the restoration of this sentence, cf. Mahé, *Hermès en Haute Égypte*, 2.169. In this passage images of the gods are understood to be animated and powerful. 15. On the restoration of this sentence, cf. Holzhausen, in *Nag Hammadi Deutsch*, 2.536.

The Egyptians Will Perish (71,9–35)

"What do I have to say about the Egyptians? They will not[16] leave Egypt, but when the gods have left the land of Egypt and have flown up to heaven, all the Egyptians will die, and Egypt will be deserted by the gods and the Egyptians. For you, O river,[17] the day will come when you will flow more with blood than with water. Dead bodies will be piled higher than the dams, and the dead will be not be mourned as much as the living. Once again the living will be recognized as Egyptians by their language. Asclepius, why are you weeping? They will seem like foreigners in terms of their customs. And divine Egypt will suffer even worse evils than these. Egypt, lover of God, dwelling place of the gods, school of religion, will become the picture of impiety.

The World Will Be Desolate (71,35–73,22)

"On that day the world will no longer be admired, [72] [because of its wickedness] and godlessness, nor will it be revered. About it we cannot say that it is either good or beautiful as something that exists now or as something that is envisioned, but it runs the risk of becoming a burden to all people.[18] So the world will be despised, the beautiful world of God, an incomparable work, virtue in action, a vision of many forms, an abundance that does not hold back, full of every vision. People will prefer darkness to light and death to life. No one will gaze up to heaven. The godly will be considered mad, and the impious will be honored as wise. The coward will be considered strong, and the good person will be punished as a criminal.

"Concerning the soul, and the things of the soul, and whatever has to do with immortality, along with the rest of what I have explained to you, Tat, Asclepius, and Ammon,[19] these things will not only be considered ridiculous, they will also be regarded as being nothing. Believe me, people like this will expose themselves to the ultimate danger to their souls. A new law will be established [73] . . . . . .[20] and the good [spirits] will [depart],[21] but the wicked angels will remain among people and be with them, and lead them recklessly into what is evil and into godlessness, war, and pillage, by teaching them things contrary to nature.

"In those days the earth will be unstable, and people will not sail the sea or discern the stars in heaven. Every sacred voice of the word of God will become silent, and the air will be unhealthy. This is the senility of the world: godlessness, dishonor, contempt for noble words.

---

16. Coptic *an*, which Mahé, *Hermès en Haute Égypte*, 2.175, translates "also." 17. The Nile River. 18. On the restoration of these sentences, cf. Holzhausen, in *Nag Hammadi Deutsch*, 2.537. 19. These participants in the Hermetic discussion have names of Egyptian deities. Tat's name comes from Thoth, god of wisdom and the divine scribe. Asclepius is often identified with the deified Egyptian sage Imhotep, vizier of Djoser and architect of the stepped pyramid at Sakkara. Ammon is named for Amun, leading god of the New Kingdom and the wind god promoted to sun god as Amun-Re. 20. About two and a half lines missing or untranslatable. 21. On the restoration of this sentence, cf. Mahé, *Hermès en Haute Égypte*, 2.183.

End of the Apocalypse: God Restores the Universe
(73,23–74,17)

"Asclepius, when all this has happened, and the Lord, the Father and God and creator from[22] the first and only deity, has seen what has happened, he formulates his plan, a good plan, against the chaos. He eradicates error and eliminates evil, sometimes drowning it in a flood, at other times burning it in a conflagration, and at still other times subduing it in wars and plagues, until he brings [74] . . . . . .[23] of this work.[24]

"This is the birth of the world. The restoration of the nature of the pious and the good will take place in a period of time without a beginning. For the will of God has no beginning, even as his nature, which is his will, has no beginning. God's nature is will, and his will is the good."

The World Is Good (74,17–75,13)

"Trismegistus, does intention[25] correspond to will?"

"Yes, Asclepius, since will is included in deliberation. <God>[26] does not will what he has from some deficiency. Rather, since God is filled everywhere, he wills what he fully has. God has everything good, and what he wills he wills, and he has the good he wills. God has everything, and God wills what he wills. And the good world is an image of the good."

"Trismegistus, is the world good?"

"Yes, Asclepius, it is good, as I shall teach you. For just as [75] [God bestows . . . . . .[27] spirit, soul, and] life, [the world produces what is good from] matter:[28] the changes in climate, the growth and ripening of fruit, and the like. So God rules over the heights of heaven; he is everywhere and sees everywhere. Where he is, there is not heaven or stars or anything corporeal.

The Masters of the Earth Rule in an Egyptian City to the West
(75,13–76,19)

"The creator rules in the place between heaven and earth. He is called Zeus, which means life.[29] Plutonian Zeus[30] is lord over earth and sea, but he does not

---

22. Or "of." 23. About four and a half lines missing or untranslatable. 24. On the basis of the Latin *Asclepius* and the Greek parallel in Lactantius *Divine Institutions*, it is possible to conclude that the content of these lines must have been similar to the following: "until he brings the world back to its previous state. Thus God will be honored as creator and restorer of this great work." Throughout this paragraph the Coptic text employs the perfect tense and Lactantius the aorist. The English translation opts for the present tense; cf. the grammatical discussion in Holzhausen, in *Nag Hammadi Deutsch*, 2.538. 25. Or "deliberation" (*boulēsis*). 26. Lit., "He," here and below. 27. About two lines missing or untranslatable. 28. On the restoration of these sentences, cf. Holzhausen, in *Nag Hammadi Deutsch*, 2.539. 29. The name of Zeus is here related to the Greek word for "life" (*zōē*). 30. I.e., Zeus of the underworld, Zeus of the afterlife. Plutonian Zeus is probably Sarapis, "Osiris-Apis," a prominent deity in Alexandria during the Hellenistic period and after.

possess the sustenance for all mortal living creatures, for Kore[31] is the one who produces crops. These forces are always powerful around the earth, but other forces are always from the One Who Is.[32]

"The masters of the earth will withdraw and establish themselves in a city that is in a corner of Egypt and that will be built toward the setting of the sun.[33] Everybody will enter the city, whether they come by sea or by land."

"Trismegistus, where will they settle then?"

"Asclepius, they will be in the great city that is on the [Libyan] mountain. [76] . . . . . .[34] [death frightens . . . as a] great [evil because of] ignorance of the topic.[35] Death is the dissolution of the labors of the body and the number of the body, when death completes the number of the body. For the number is what joins the body together.[36] The body dies when it cannot support a person. And this is death: the dissolution of the body and the loss of bodily sensation. There is no need to be afraid of this or because of this. People are afraid because of what they do not know and do not believe."

The Great Demon Judges Human Souls
(76,19–77,12)

"What is it they do not know or believe?"

"Listen, Asclepius. There is a great demon[37] that the supreme God has appointed as overseer or judge of human souls. God has placed him in the middle of the air between earth and heaven. When a soul comes from a body, it must meet this demon. At once the demon will turn this person around and examine him with regard to the character he developed during his lifetime. If the demon finds that the person accomplished all his deeds in a godly manner, deeds for which he came into the world, the demon will let him [77] . . . turn him . . . .[38] But [if the demon observes and becomes angry] at a person [who] spent his life doing [evil] deeds, he grabs him on his way up and throws him back down so that he is suspended between heaven and earth and punished severely.[39] There will be no hope for such a soul, and it will be in great pain.

---

31. Kore, "girl" in Greek (*korē*), is a grain goddess and the daughter of Demeter in the Eleusinian mysteries. 32. Cf. the description of the divine in the Septuagint of *Exodus* 3:14 as *ho ōn*, "the One Who Is," for *'Ehyeh 'asher 'ehyeh*, "I am that I am" (or the like) in Hebrew. The reading of the end of this sentence is uncertain. Cf. Holzhausen, in *Nag Hammadi Deutsch*, 2.539; Mahé, *Hermès en Haute Égypte*, 2.193. 33. I.e., toward the west. The city is most likely Alexandria, and the masters of the earth are probably the Ptolemaic rulers. 34. About two lines missing or untranslatable. 35. On the basis of the Latin *Asclepius* and the Greek text of Stobaeus, it is possible to suggest the following general reading of the missing lines: "But now we must speak about death, for death frightens many people as a great evil because of ignorance of the topic." 36. In this passage the text reads *arithmos*, "number" (from Greek), and in the parallel passage in Stobaeus the Greek text reads *harmōn* (nominative, *harmoi*), "joints." The translator has apparently confused *arithmos* with *arthrōn* (nominative, *arthra*), another Greek word for "joints," and this confusion has led to confusion in the Coptic text. 37. The text reads *daimōn*, here and below. 38. Here the Latin *Asclepius* reads, "the demon lets him dwell in the regions under his authority." 39. On the restoration of these sentences, cf. Holzhausen, in *Nag Hammadi Deutsch*, 2.540.

The Wicked Will Be Punished (77,12–78,31)

"That soul does not have a place on earth or in heaven, but it has come to be in the open air[40] of the universe, where there is blazing fire, freezing water, streams of fire, and massive turbulence. The bodies are tormented in various ways. Sometimes they are cast into raging water; at other times they are thrown down into fire in order that the fire may destroy them. I am not saying that this is the death of the soul, for the soul has been delivered from evil. Nonetheless, it is a death sentence.

"Asclepius, we must believe these things and fear them so that they may not happen to us. Unbelievers are impious and commit sin. Later they will be made to believe, but they will not simply listen to words. They will experience the reality of these things, for they were convinced they would not have to go through them."

"Not only [78] . . . ."[41]

"First of all, [Asclepius], all those who are earthly are [subject to death] and [those who are] corporeal [to loss] . . . evil . . . with such as these. For those here are not like those there. As the demons[42] . . . people, they despise . . . there. So it is not the same. But in truth, the gods in that place will always punish more severely whoever has concealed something here."

"Trismegistus, of what sort is the wickedness in them?"

"Asclepius, you think that when someone steals from a temple, the person is impious, for that kind of person is a thief and a robber. This is a matter between gods and people. But do not compare what happens here with what happens in the other place. I would like to speak this discourse to you confidentially; people will believe none of it. The souls that are full of much that is evil will not come and go in the air, but they will be situated in the places of demons, places full of pain and forever full of blood and slaughter, and their food is weeping, mourning, and groaning."

Who Are the Demons? (78,31–43)

"Trismegistus, who are these demons?"

"Asclepius, some are called stranglers, some roll souls downhill, some whip them, some throw them into the water, some throw them into the fire, some bring about the pains and afflictions of people. For those who are like this[43] are not from a divine soul, nor from a rational human soul, but they are from terrible evil."

---

40. Lit., "the open sea of the air." 41. Here the Latin *Asclepius* reads, "Then, Trismegistus, are the crimes of people not punished by human law alone?" 42. The text reads *daimōn*, here and below. 43. This may refer either to people or to demons.

THE PARAPHRASE OF SHEM

NHC VII,1

Introduced and Translated by Michel Roberge

The *Paraphrase of Shem* is an apocalypse, a revelation given by Derdekeas, the son of infinite Light, to Shem, the son of Noah. The fictional narrative framework describes Shem's ecstatic ascent to the summit of creation (1,5–16) and his awakening and transformation (41,21–42,11). The actual revelation consists of a cosmogony (1,16–23,8) and an anthropogony (23,9–24,29), followed by an interpretation of history that focuses on an account of the flood (a past event in the narrative fiction, 24,30–28,8), the destruction of Sodom (28,8–29,33), the baptism of the Savior (29,33–38,27), and his ascent by means of his crucifixion (38,28–40,31). This revelation concludes with an address to Shem concerning his mission on earth (40,31–41,20). To this apocalypse were added, probably later, a first eschatological discourse of Derdekeas (42,11–45,31), Shem's own description of his ascent to the planetary spheres at the end of his life (45,31–47,31), a second eschatological discourse of Derdekeas (47,32–48,30) and, as a conclusion to the whole writing, a final address to Shem (48,30–49,9).

The key to understanding the *Paraphrase of Shem* must be sought in its anthropology, and its most original feature lies in the devaluation of mind (*nous*) and the central place given to thought. According to this treatise, human beings consist of (1) a body originating from Darkness and Fire; (2) a soul (*psukhē*) brought forth through the defilement of the winds and the demons; (3) a particle of Mind, which was first Darkness's possession but was rescued by the Spirit and to whom the Savior granted a light called Faith (Pistis); and (4) a thought produced by the astonishment of the Spirit (*pneuma*). The combination of these four constituents defines three classes of people: (1) psychics (material people), who are ruled by the soul and belong to Darkness (they have a body and soul); (2) noetics (mental people), who are ruled by the mind and belong to Faith (they have a body, soul, and mind); and (3) pneumatics (spiritual people), who are ruled by thought and belong to the Spirit (they have a body, soul, mind, and thought).

The creation myth of the *Paraphrase of Shem* was written to account for this conception of humanity and to explain the function of the pneumatic race toward the noetics in the history of salvation. It is divided into three parts: the primeval harmony; the fall of the Spirit; and the gathering of the fallen light of the Spirit and the salvation of Mind.

The first part of the story of creation (1,16–2,19) opens with the description of the three great powers, or roots, that existed in the beginning: Light, Darkness, and the Spirit. At the top reigns the infinite Light, whose name is Majesty and who is characterized as thought filled with hearing and word. What should be noted in particular is that the *Paraphrase of Shem* avoids defining the supreme principle as Mind (*nous*) thinking himself or as Thought generating a Mind that would contain the ideas of created beings. Absolutely transcendent, Light has no female consort, is not the object of beatitude, and never enters into direct contact with creation. The link with the created world is reserved for the Spirit and Mind. But though the supreme principle never intervenes directly in the production of beings, in the last analysis everything that comes to pass always depends on his will.

The middle principle, the Spirit, is characterized as a quiet, humble light. Like the biblical Spirit (cf. *Genesis* 1:2), the Spirit in the *Paraphrase of Shem* possesses a certain transcendence and acts independently. When the Spirit falls into chaos while revealing himself to Darkness, he will act as an active principle and will initiate the process that culminates in the separation of Mind from Darkness. At the time of the formation of the universe, it will be astonishment (*thauma*), a power emitted by the Spirit, who will play the role of an immanent active principle.

In the precosmic chaos of the *Paraphrase of Shem*, Darkness, the evil principle, reigns with his Mind and his members, the primordial elements: fire, water, and wind. The author imagines the elements associated with Darkness as superimposed regions: at the top, water; in the water, wind; under the water, the chaotic fire enveloping Mind; and at the bottom, Darkness. These cosmic entities are endowed with intelligence and emotions and, as in Stoic philosophy, the treatise uses cosmobiological analogy to describe the formation of the universe. Darkness plays the role of the masculine principle and water the role of the feminine principle. Winds are also considered feminine entities, and they will be given a womb in order to receive the semen of the demons at the time of the formation of humankind. Fire concentrates in itself the power (*dunamis*) of Father Darkness, his generating force. It makes up the fiery forms that the Spirit will place at his own service when he reveals himself to Darkness.

But how to account for Mind's presence in the precosmic chaos? Indeed, the text alludes to no previous act of aggression on the part of Darkness with the purpose of snatching Mind, and does not mention that Mind is in chaos because it fell there. The hypothesis can therefore be made that the author intended to maintain the demiurgic function of Mind in the organization of the universe. But since the author assumed the existence of a first principle that was absolutely transcendent and never involved in creation and the existence of a middle principle, the Spirit, acting as a Stoic active principle, he had no other place to locate Mind than in chaos. In fact, the author uses a Middle Platonist model, that of Numenius of Apamaea or of the *Chaldean Oracles*; these two systems postulate the existence of two Minds. The first Mind or first god, an indivisible monad containing the ideas, is father of a second god, who is the demiurgic Mind. This second Mind presents a dyadic character in that it is turned either toward the world of ideas in order to contemplate them or toward matter in order to introduce the ideas or forms into it and to organize the sensible world. By uniting with matter to bring it to order, the second Mind constitutes the world's good Soul. The author of the *Paraphrase of Shem* adopts this model, but reverses it, so that the organization of the universe proceeds from below.

Moreover, as in the *Chaldaean Oracles*, the author places a feminine entity, the cosmic womb (the goddess Hecate in the *Chaldaean* system), between the first and the second Mind, and describes their succession according to the biological generative mode. The formation of the universe, therefore, is no longer understood as arising from the transcendent world of ideas, but as an embryological process in which the Spirit plays the role of an active principle and the forms or ideas are assimilated to rational seeds, which Nature uses to construct the material world (cf. *Paraphrase of Shem* 10,37–11,6).

However, if the *Paraphrase of Shem* shares with the *Oracles* the doctrine of the two Minds, the paternal and the demiurgic, it does not keep its notion of the demiurge's dyadic character: the absence of transcendent intelligible forms renders the contemplative function of the demiurge useless. Rather, the text affirms the existence of a third Mind proceeding from the seed of Nature's forms, entirely distinct from the second Mind and called to reign over the universe (cf. 22,9–23,8).

The state of harmony that ruled at the beginning between the roots occurred because each root governed in its own kingdom with no mixing with the others. However, the text insists on the inequality of the principles. Light possesses a great power and knows the lowliness of Darkness, while Darkness is completely unaware of the existence of a root higher than himself. So long as Darkness checks his malice and stays covered by water, harmony is preserved.

The second part of the creation myth in the *Paraphrase of Shem* (2,19–3,29) narrates the fall of the Spirit, which is permitted for the purpose of the salvation of Mind. Through a sudden stirring of Darkness, the Spirit discovers the existence of the evil root and realizes at the same time that this root ignores the existence of the infinite Light. By the will of Majesty, water separates and Darkness emerges with his eye, his Mind. The Spirit reveals himself to Darkness, who tries through his Mind to attain equality with the Spirit. By revealing himself to Darkness, however, the Spirit has forfeited a part of his light and has rendered Mind active. Mind raises himself up and illumines chaos with a fiery light, his forms.

The third part of the creation myth (3,30–24,29) relates how the Savior, Derdekeas, the son of the infinite Light, through different interventions, rescues Mind and gathers the fallen light of the Spirit. With the goal of making Mind exit Hades, Derdekeas manifests himself first under the aspect of the Spirit. His coming from above immediately starts the process of forming the universe. To render Darkness inert or inoperative (*argos*) by depriving him of his power—that is, the generative power of the fiery forms—Mind, who is already partially similar to the Spirit, first has fire go up from between Darkness and water. This provokes water's transformation into mist, then into the womb. The chaotic fire, which is error, goes into the womb and tricks Darkness. At the sight of the womb, Darkness becomes impure: he unites with her and ejaculates his mind as seed that, mixing with the power of Darkness (the fiery forms), makes all the forms appear in the womb (3,30–5,6).

For his part, Mind, the paternal seed, has generated in the womb an image of himself, a second Mind, fiery in nature, but one that takes on the likeness of the Spirit, thereby clashing with him. Now Mind must ascend and attach himself to the womb. Yet the womb, having no principle of motion, is incapable of pushing Mind to the bottom of herself in order to retain him. To understand this episode, we must take account of the physiological process of conception as described by Soranos of Ephesus. According to this early second-century BCE physician, conception involves two main steps: (1) *analēpsis*, or "ascent" of the seed toward the bottom of the womb, and (2) *sullēpsis*, or "retention" of the seed by the womb, which is, properly speaking, the actual conception. Animation of the embryo follows this second step.[1] That is why the Savior provokes the division of Nature into four clouds that will constitute the different spheres of the universe. From the top down they are called hymen, placenta (also called silence), power (also called middle), and water. The first three, which are fiery clouds, then draw the embryonic Mind out of the harmful waters (*analēpsis*), so he may turn toward the center of his power (the fiery forms), in the middle of Nature, where he will cling (*sullēpsis*) (5,6–6,14).

However, heavy from the weight of the embryonic Mind, the Spirit—that is, the light of the Spirit in water—has produced the power of astonishment, and this power turns Mind toward his heat. Mind puts on the Spirit's light and through this active principle sets Nature in motion. Astonishment continues to rise and fastens onto the cloud of hymen, whereas Mind settles in the middle of Nature (6,14–30).

The Spirit beseeches the infinite Light to have mercy on his light. The Savior appears as a whirlwind and blows from the cloud of hymen: the clouds separate so that the light of the Spirit might return, and Mind takes shape like an embryo (6,30–7,30).

Then Derdekeas, having put on his universal garment of light, comes with the appearance of the Spirit and prompts the ascent of the light out of Darkness and the cloud of water. Following this rescue, astonishment in the cloud of hymen conceives a great power, a Thought, the primal Human. The Savior reveals to Shem that he himself is this great power, the principle of the pneumatic race. Therefore the *Paraphrase of Shem* will say about the race of Shem that it is issued from the cloud of light (cf. 26,17–20) and that its members possess a thought from the light of the power of astonishment (cf. 24,5–9). At the consummation they will rest at the place of their root, the unbegotten Spirit (7,30–12,15).

---

1. See Soranos of Ephesus *Gynecology* 1.43.

In order to bring to perfection the light of the Spirit in the cloud of hymen, the Savior discards his universal garment and puts on a trimorphic (three-formed) one. But as he appears in the hymen, the cloud cannot endure both the light of the garment and the light of astonishment. It sheds this power and a part of the light falls onto the middle, carrying with it also the light that was in the cloud of silence—this light had remained in the cloud of silence during the ascent of astonishment. This second fall of a luminous entity has a salvific goal: the part of light separated from astonishment illumines the womb and produces spiritual seeds, which are to be sown later in the elect people by the winds, the stars, and the demons to constitute the pneumatic race, whose function will be to live among the noetics and to teach them (12,15–13,23).

Through a second coming into the cloud of hymen, the Savior grants astonishment the fullness of universal thought and word, whereas the light of silence, for its part, returns to its place. As for the light separated from astonishment, it is troubled and casts off the weight of the cloud. But the dark fire (cf. *Paraphrase of Shem* 9,13–15), no longer restrained by the light of the cloud of silence, mixes with the waters in order to make them noxious. And Nature, which had been repelled (cf. 13,13–15), immediately climbs out of the waters and conceives the fiery power, which is the archon of creation (cf. 27,1–21). His likeness appears in the water in the shape of a frightful beast with many faces, the serpent (13,23–15,16).

The next saving action is accomplished by the Spirit's gaze from out of the clouds toward the depths of Nature in order to neutralize the power of the womb and fire. This gaze is an illumination, a ray of light that crosses the middle and rejoins the light imprisoned in the depths of Nature (cf. 6,16–22). Through the Savior's will and by means of this gaze, light reascends with the womb. The light in the middle then illumines the womb, who sees those she had not seen, that is, the spiritual seeds (cf. 13,13–15). Thinking she possesses the light's strength, she rejoices, but she has been rendered inert by the luminous ray that came down to her. Further, the pneumatics, who possess in themselves a seed sprung from astonishment, are assured of being beyond the grasp of Nature's power (15,17–16,23).

The light diverted into the middle lifts its eyes toward the higher Light and begs him to take pity on it and straighten it. In response to this prayer, Derdekeas takes off his trimorphic garment within the hymen and comes into the cloud of silence. There he clothes himself in the light, whose two parts are immediately revealed under a unique form. Likewise, he takes off his garment in the cloud of silence, penetrates into the middle, and there clothes himself with the light separated from astonishment. This light receives the knowledge about the immortal realities and prays that his light will also be removed from harmful Nature (16,24–18,1).

The Savior lays aside his light-garment and puts on one that is fiery and formless. He penetrates into Nature and settles upon her eye, a light that has come forth from the Spirit, which the Spirit has prepared for him as a garment and place of rest. In view of the creation of heaven and earth (cf. 20,2–10), this light gives its voice to Nature for a while. Through his fiery garment, the Savior prostitutes himself with Nature. As a consequence of the orgasm provoked by the garment's caress, the womb dries up Mind and expels him from herself in the form of a fish. Troubled, the womb is seized with sorrow and, in tears, also casts out the Spirit's power, the light with which Mind had clothed himself. The Savior clothes himself in the Spirit's light and then rests (18,27–19,13). As the fruit of the Savior's fornication, numerous animal forms, the zodiacal signs, proceed from the womb and come into existence in Hades (18,1–19,26).

After this Derdekeas puts on the beast (cf. 15,14–16) as a garment and prompts Nature to produce heaven and earth and all kinds of seeds. Derdekeas's garment arises in the midst of Nature and shines upon the whole world until Nature becomes dry. Darkness, which had been Nature's garment, is cast into the harmful water, and the middle of Nature is purified (19,26–21,1).

The Savior asks Nature to bring into existence a seed and a power upon the earth. Immediately, Nature's forms, which are male and female, couple and produce winds and demons. However, one of the womb's forms has been left by itself and has not coupled with the others. It masturbates and brings forth a wind possessing a power from fire, Darkness, and the Spirit. The winds and demons are then outfitted with genital organs: the winds receive a womb and the demons a penis (22,4–9). From then on, these demiurgic forces are able to engage in sexual activity similar to that indulged in at the beginning by Darkness and the womb, thus liberating the power of fire and light they received during the copulation between Nature's forms (21,2–22,9).

But then the forms of Nature that had united to produce the winds and demons turn away from one another and expel the power, that is, Mind. With this coitus interruptus the program announced in *Paraphrase of Shem* 21,2–12 has been carried out: part of the power has passed into the winds and demons, the remainder being expelled and appearing in Nature as Mind. Then the Savior grants Mind the right to reign over the winds and demons, and he gives him "a likeness of fire, light, and hearing, with a share of the guileless word." By virtue of this part of the Spirit's light that he received from the Savior, Mind is perfected in his own power. That is why at the consummation he will rest "in the honored place," the hymen (cf. 35,24–31), since he will be found faithful (*pistos*) because of his disgust at the defilement of Nature and Darkness (22,9–23, 8).

The creation myth of the *Paraphrase of Shem* ends with the formation of prediluvian humankind. First, the copulation of the winds and demons, described in very crude fashion, ends in the conception and birth of "all sorts of filthy things." This concerns the production of beings with a body and a material soul. Indeed, the soul and the body are referred to in the treatise by the same scornful expressions: the soul is a "work of uncleanness" (24,25–26) and a "burden of Darkness" (24,21); likewise, the body is an "unclean work" (32,24–25) and a "burden" (47,8–13). However, it should be noted that for the *Paraphrase of Shem*'s author, what is transmitted by the demons' sperm is not the soul, since in the following episode sterile men and women are generated through the sexual activity of the wind on its own. What the demons transmit is referred to here simply as "power." It can therefore be specified that this concerns the noetic element, for the term "power" is used in the narrative about humankind after the flood as a parallel to the expression "power of Mind" (27,31; 27,35–28,1). But for the moment the author seems uninterested in categorizing individuals; the account's entire interest is concentrated on the final affirmation that the product of this sexual union is impure (23,9–30).

Then through the masturbation of one of the winds, barren women and sterile men are begotten. These are the psychics, who possess a body and a material soul and are bound to dissolve in Darkness (23,31–24,2).

Finally, the author describes the appearance of the pneumatic class of people. This episode must be read as the extension of the first, to which it explicitly refers in its mention of what Shem's race has received through the joint action of the winds and demons. What came from the winds are the body and the material soul, the unclean part of their being, of which they must rid themselves. The noetic element is what the demons transmit to them as coming from themselves. But what characterizes Shem's race is the presence in its members of a "thought from the light of the power of astonishment" (24,2–15).

The historical survey of the *Paraphrase of Shem* is divided into three periods. As in many other Gnostic works,[2] the *Paraphrase of Shem* narrates three major crises: the flood, the destruction of Sodom, and the crucifixion of the Savior, which is linked to the end of time (cf. 43,28–33; 45,8–11). In accordance with the apocalyptic genre, the narrator underlines the fact that in each crisis the wickedness of Nature reaches its paroxysm (cf. 24,30–31; 29,27–31; 39,26–28) and, in a typically Gnostic way, he reverses the meaning of the flood and of the destruction of Sodom by interpreting these events as attempts of Nature to annihilate the pneumatic race.

The flood is the result of a plot of Nature's sin with water and Darkness so as "to seize the light and to take it away from Faith." Nature therefore decides to annihilate the race of the pneumatics, in order to keep for herself the light particles and establish her ascendancy over a human race from which the thought of astonishment's light would be excluded—that is, a human race furnished only with the particle of Mind and at the beck and call of Nature. But Nature's intention has backfired, because the Savior has decreed the construction of a tower. Whereas through the Savior's teaching the members of his race have been able to return to their root, the unbegotten Spirit, Shem has escaped the cataclysm by entering the tower with Noah. The Savior explains to him that he has "remained in a body outside the cloud of light" so that he "might abide patiently with Faith." In fact, by accepting an alliance with the evil demiurge (cf. *Genesis* 8:20–22; 9:8–17), Noah has tied himself to Nature's observances and has thus inaugurated the rule by the economy of faith (cf. *Hebrews* 11:7).

From then on, from the flood to baptism, through the agency of the archon of creation, Nature will exert herself to keep the race of the noetics under her power

---

2. Cf. the *Secret Book of John*, the *Revelation of Adam*, *Three Forms of First Thought*, and the *Holy Book of the Great Invisible Spirit*.

by imposing on it her teaching and commands—that is, "her faith" (40,2–3), in the form of circumcision, law, and finally baptism. Shem and his followers therefore have the mission of living in the company of the noetics, whose particle of Mind is subject to the obligations Nature has imposed. That is why the Savior adds, for Shem's benefit, that Faith's thought "will be taken and given to you in bright consciousness." This means that he possesses within himself the light of true Faith, a particle of Mind formed by the word of the Spirit, with an eye to teaching the noetics. Until the consummation (or, in apocalyptic terms, during the whole time from the "appointed time of Faith," 43,15), the pneumatics will have to coexist patiently with the noetics. To gain salvation, the latter, after the example of their root, the luminous Mind, will have to loathe "the defilement of Nature" and so receive "a share of the guileless word" (24,30–26,36).

After the flood, the womb expels from her genitals the fiery power she possessed from the beginning through her intercourse with Darkness. This fiery power is the demon, the deceiver, the pantocrator "who aroused the womb toward every form." Fire therefore rises and shines upon creation as the material sun "instead of the righteous one"—that is, the Savior and his invincible garment. Until the return of the righteous one, the archon of creation, who is "the light that was corrupted," reigns over the world with his members, the stars, and he, along with Nature, will plan the destruction of Sodom (27,1–21).

In order to control the generation and the fate of living beings, Nature grants the demons and the winds a star each. Then beasts are brought forth and a new humanity repopulates the earth. The narrator lists three principles, (1) Darkness and fire, (2) the power of Mind, and (3) the Light, at the beginning of two classes of human, the pneumatics and the noetics. Both classes possess a body and a material soul, alluded to by mentioning Darkness and fire. In addition, the pneumatics have received something that has come forth from the power of Mind and Light. The existence of a class of human beings provided with a particle of Mind but not with a thought of the Light is confirmed by a restrictive clause: "Since the thought of the Light, my eye, is from the Spirit, it does not exist in every person." The reason for this seems to be given in the following lines, which refer to the corruption of humanity before the flood (cf. *Genesis* 6:3, 5): "For before the flood came about through the winds and the demons, <evil> came to people." The passage gives no mention of the race of psychics, but the eschatological texts take their existence for granted (27,22–28,8).

When Nature undertakes the unjust burning of Sodom, Shem, for his part, will have to proclaim to the Sodomites his "universal teaching." The Sodomites will then accomplish the universal testimony and will rest, with a pure conscience, in the place of their repose, the unbegotten Spirit (28,8–30,4).

Finally, when the archon of creation tries to impose the faith of Nature in its "last likeness"—that is, when he appears in the person of John the Baptizer in order to keep the noetics under his rule by binding them up with the impure rite of baptism—then the Savior will manifest himself to rescue "the members of the thought of Faith" by descending into the water. In order to make the light of Faith pass into his garments of light, he will use his terrestrial body, the demon Soldas.

On this occasion the Savior will reveal for the pneumatics and the noetics the passwords, that is, the list of the names of the celestial and cosmic entities who played a part in the creation myth and that is called the "testimony." The knowledge of these names will allow them to pass without hindrance through the planetary spheres as they return to their root. The noetics will bear the "testimony of Faith" and ascend to the cloud of hymen, the place of Faith (30,4–38,27). Thanks to the "universal testimony" (the memorial of Derdekeas and the testimony of Faith), the pneumatics will ascend to the place of the Spirit.

After this the Savior foretells his ascent through his crucifixion in terms that recall the Johannine presentation of the crucifixion as a lifting up of the Savior. In her anger Nature will try to seize him, but will only manage to nail Soldas, the terrestrial Jesus. The following allegory, which narrates the beheading of Rebouel, explains for the noetics the meaning of the crucifixion of the Savior: it does not have the effect of purifying the water of baptism,[3] but rather it brings about a division between light and darkness. Just as Rebouel is declared blessed in her beheading, so the noetics should not hesitate to separate from the great church (early orthodoxy), which practices baptism, and enter the community of those who possess gnosis. To ascend to their root, they must follow Mind's example and loathe the impurity of Nature in order to be found faithful. They will not be saved by the observance of the law or by a rite bound to water, but through conversion and the possession of the testimony of Faith (38,28–40,31).

It seems that the *Paraphrase of Shem* knew the gospel tradition about the Savior's baptism and the Johannine interpretation of his crucifixion. And if we take into account the meaning of Shem's mission, the anti-Pauline interpretation of the function of Faith in the salvation history (cf. *Hebrews* 11), the allusions to the universal (catholic) character of Shem's doctrine (cf. *Paraphrase of Shem* 29,14), the total rejection of any baptismal rite, and the meaning of the allegory of the beheading of Rebouel (cf. 40,4–31), we may conclude that the writing is best explained as the product of a group living on the fringe of Christianity and urging the members of the great church to separate and join the community of those who possess gnosis. It is not impossible, however, that the polemic may also be directed at the Elchasaites, whose practices were centered on multiple water baptisms and especially on therapeutic baths (cf. 36, 29–31).

Notwithstanding some traits related to the so-called Sethian gnosis—for instance, the awareness of forming a chosen race out of a common ancestor and the division of history according to a tripartite plan—it cannot be said that the *Paraphrase of Shem* discloses Sethian gnosis. A fundamental element is lacking: the originating triad of Father, Mother, and the Self-Generated One. The Sethian metaphysics is triadic, while that of our tractate is dyadic, with Spirit constituting an intermediate being, inferior in nature to the Father and his Son. The *Paraphrase of Shem*'s absolute dualism does not fit the Sethian system any more than does its absolute rejection of all forms of baptism.

---

3. Cf. Ignatius of Antioch *Ephesians* 18:1–2.

The *Paraphrase of Shem* was largely inspired by the Valentinian system in the tripartite structure of its anthropology, and in its eschatology, which visualizes salvation on two levels. Again, it is in the sense of Valentinian teaching that the text explains the process of individuation and recounts the cohabitation of pneumatics and psychics in the history of salvation. But here again the author of the *Paraphrase of Shem* parts from his model by conferring a lower status on Mind, who draws his origin from the evil principle and gains transcendence only after a dual generation. Still, Mind occupies a lower echelon than the Spirit, because the place of its repose is the hymen, beneath Spirit's sphere. In the *Paraphrase of Shem*, the highest God is not Mind, nor is the noblest part of the human being a particle of Mind, but a thought from the astonishment of the Spirit. Besides, it is on this fundamental point of Mind's status that, despite similarities in detail, our tractate is also distinguished from Hermetic texts, notably the *Poimandres*.

To sum up, while dipping liberally into the springs of the major Sethian and Valentinian systems, the author of the *Paraphrase of Shem* turns his back on them and follows his own way, in many respects anticipating Manichaeism. In this regard, we note especially the preexistence of the evil principle, the representation of chaos in stages, the hierarchy of principles, the jealousy of the evil principle and the fall of the Light-being (interpreted as a ruse by the higher principle for conquering the evil one), the notion of Light's homogeneity, the various scenarios that employ sexual analogy to describe the origin of the beings of creation, the encratism of the text, the antibaptismal polemic, and the image of the "dark lump" (*bōlos*) used to describe the end of material creation. This gives us a set of traits pointing unequivocally toward Manichaeism. But fundamental differences remain, the principal ones being the *Paraphrase of Shem*'s much greater emphasis on the lower status accorded to Mind and on the transcendent character of the supreme deity.

As for the relationship between *The Paraphrase of Shem* and the tractate entitled the *Paraphrase of Seth*, which is referred to by the heresiologist Hippolytus in his report on the Sethians,[4] although there are similarities in the description of chaos and some common themes and terminology, the differences between the two doctrines, especially with regard to anthropology and baptism, are too great to warrant the assumption of any direct link between the two works. We could contend, at the very most, that both writings use traditions stemming from the same school or circle of thought. In any case, we cannot regard the *Paraphrase of Seth* as a Christianized version of the *Paraphrase of Shem*.

The *Paraphrase of Shem* is written in the Sahidic dialect of Coptic, with considerable influence from other dialects.[5] The present text contains traces that point to the original composition in Greek. The forty-nine pages of the text are in an excellent state of preservation except for the top and the bottom of a few pages. Among the inscribed fragments of papyri found in the cartonnage of the cover of

---

4. Hippolytus of Rome *Refutation of All Heresies* 5.19–22.

5. Lycopolitan dialects (especially L5).

Codex VII, there is a deed of surety addressed to the chairman of a city council and dated October 348 CE. This provides us with a *terminus a quo* for the manufacture of the codex.

The *Paraphrase of Shem* presents a very sophisticated cosmological and anthropological system, and its Gnostic terminology, which recalls Valentinianism, is quite expansive. It could have been written at a time when the main Gnostic systems were already constituted and the polemic against the great church was at its peak, perhaps in the first half of the third century. At this time, also, the Elchasaite movement underwent a revival through the preaching of Alcibiades of Apamea (ca. 220).

The author of the *Paraphrase of Shem* is unknown, but the text was probably written in Syria. The relationship between its creation myth and passages in the Aramaic philosopher Bardaisan (154–222 CE), its underlying encratism, and its polemical attitude against baptism all point to a common area of interacting traditions. The region that best meets this description appears to be eastern Syria, with Edessa as its center.

BIBLIOGRAPHY

Jean-Daniel Dubois, "Contribution à l'interprétation de la *Paraphrase de Sem*"; Henriette Havelaar, "Wie spricht Gott in der Schöpfungsgeschichte von Codex VII,1?"; Birger A. Pearson, ed., *Nag Hammadi Codex VII*, 15–127 (Frederik Wisse); Michel Roberge, ed., *La Paraphrase de Sem*; "Le rôle du *Noûs* dans la *Paraphrase de Sem*"; "Anthropogonie et anthropologie dans la *Paraphrase de Sem*"; "Chute et remontée du Pneuma dans la *Paraphrase de Sem*"; "La crucifixion du Sauveur dans la *Paraphrase de Sem*"; "*La Paraphrase de Sem* (NH VII,1) et le problème des trois natures"; "The *Paraphrase of Sem* (NH VII,1) as an Ascent Apocalypse"; James M. Robinson, ed., *The Nag Hammadi Library in English*, 339–61 (Michel Roberge and Frederik Wisse); Hans-Martin Schenke, Hans-Gebhard Bethge, and Ursula Ulrike Kaiser, eds., *Nag Hammadi Deutsch*, 2.543–68 (Hans-Martin Schenke).

The Paraphrase of Shem[1]

The Paraphrase of Shem

Incipit and Introduction: Shem's Ecstatic Experience (1,1–16)

The paraphrase about the unbegotten Spirit—what Derdekeas[2] revealed to me, Shem.

In accordance with the will of the Majesty, my thought in my body snatched me away from my race[3] and carried me up to the summit of creation,[4] close to the light that shone on the whole inhabited world.[5] I saw no earthly likeness there, but only light, and my thought left my body of darkness as though in sleep.

Derdekeas Utters a Revelation to Shem About the Harmony of the Primeval World (1,16–2,19)

I heard a voice speaking to me:

Shem, since you are from pure power and you are the first being on earth, listen and understand what I am about to tell you concerning the great powers who existed in the beginning, before I appeared. In the beginning there was Light and Darkness and Spirit between them. Your root, the unbegotten Spirit, fell into forgetfulness, and so I am revealing to you the precise nature of the powers.

---

1. Coptic text: NHC VII,1: 1,1–49,9. Editions: *The Facsimile Edition of the Nag Hammadi Codices: Codex VII, 7–55*; Michel Roberge, *La Paraphrase de Sem*; Birger A. Pearson, ed., *Nag Hammadi Codex VII*, 15–127 (Frederik Wisse); Hans-Martin Schenke, Hans-Gebhard Bethge, and Ursula Ulrike Kaiser, eds., *Nag Hammadi Deutsch*, 2.543–68 (Hans-Martin Schenke). In the manuscript the title is given as "The Paraphrase of Sēem." Another text with a similar title, the *Paraphrase of Seth*, is known from the writings of Hippolytus of Rome, but it seems to have been a different work; see the introduction. 2. The name Derdekeas probably derives from the Aramaic *drdq'*, "male child." If so, the name may bring to mind the savior-child who frequently appears in the literature of antiquity and is commonly attested in the Nag Hammadi texts (cf. *Secret Book of John, Holy Book of the Great Invisible Spirit, Revelation of Paul, Zostrianos*). 3. Or "genera-

tion," here and throughout. 4. In the conclusion of the apocalypse (*Paraphrase of Shem* 42), the author uses the expression "the top of the earth." This expression recalls the summit of a mountain, at the edge of heaven, according to the apocalyptic imagination (cf. *1 Enoch, Testament of Levi,* and the Cologne Mani Codex). 5. The light Shem mentions is the light produced by the Savior's fiery garment, which he put on to reveal himself in chaos (*Paraphrase of Shem* 18). After the creation of heaven and earth, this fiery garment lifted up in the middle of the cloud of Nature and, like a sun, shone upon all creation. This divine light was supplanted by the physical sun, the fiery power, which the cosmic womb expelled from herself after the flood in order that it might shine on the whole of creation (*Paraphrase of Shem* 26–27). For this reason the past tense is used here.

Light was thought full of hearing and word[6] united in one form.

Darkness was [2] wind in the waters, and Darkness had a Mind wrapped in restless fire.

Between them was Spirit, a quiet, humble light.

These are the three roots.

These three each reigned alone, each by its own power, and they were hidden from one another. But the power of the Light was great, and the Light knew how deep Darkness was and what was wrong with Darkness: his root was not pure. The problem with Darkness was that he was ignorant, and he told himself that there was no one above him.[7] As long as he was able to deal with his evil, he remained covered with water.[8]

The Spirit Discovers the Evil Root, and His Light Becomes Entangled with the Mind of Darkness: The First Mind (2,19–3,29)

Darkness stirred, and the Spirit was frightened by the noise. He raised himself up as high as he could, and when he saw a huge expanse of dark water, he was disgusted. Meanwhile, the thought of the Spirit looked down and saw his infinite light. The evil root did not notice this.[9]

By the will of the great Light, the dark water separated, and Darkness emerged, covered with vile ignorance.

After Darkness stirred, the light of the Spirit appeared to him, so that his Mind might leave him, because he prided himself in his Mind. [3] When Darkness saw the light of the Spirit, he was astonished, for he did not know that there was another power above him. And when he saw that his appearance was dark compared with the Spirit, he was overcome with grief. In his grief he lifted up his Mind as high as he could. Among the members of Darkness, the Mind of Darkness was the eye of the bitterness of evil. Darkness made his Mind take shape partly from the members of the Spirit, thinking that by staring at his evil he would be able to equal the Spirit. He could not do it; he wanted to do something impossible, and it did not happen. But in order that the Mind of Darkness, which is the eye of the bitterness of evil, might not remain inactive, since he had been made in part like the Spirit, he arose and shone with a fiery light upon all of Hades, and in this way the purity of the faultless Light was revealed. For the Spirit made use of every form of Darkness, because he had appeared in his greatness.[10]

---

6. Logos, here and throughout. 7. Cf. the statements of God in Isaiah 45:5–6, 21; 46:9, interpreted in the *Secret Book of John* and many other Gnostic texts. 8. Cf. Genesis 1:1–2. 9. From the highest part of his place, the Spirit looks below; the light he then sees cannot be the superior Light but must be his own light, since the Spirit is also said to be infinite. This is the same process of self-knowing as what is said about the superior Light (*Paraphrase of Shem* 1), but in the case of the Spirit, this process is dramatized and transferred into spatial categories. 10. Thanks to the light of the Spirit that he partially received, Mind is able to shine upon Hades with his fiery forms. But Mind's light, because it is mixed with fire, is a defiled light compared to the pure and homogeneous light of the Majesty or the light of the Spirit (*Paraphrase of Shem* 1).

The Savior Appears in the Likeness of the Spirit, a Cosmic Womb Is Formed, and a Second Mind Is Conceived (3,30–5,19)

The exalted, infinite Light appeared, and he was exceedingly joyful. He wished to reveal himself to the Spirit, so the likeness of the exalted Light appeared to the unbegotten Spirit. [4]

I appeared. [I] am the Son of incorruptible, infinite Light. I appeared in the likeness of the Spirit, for I am the ray of universal Light and the appearance of Light. This took place in order that the Mind of Darkness might not remain in Hades, for Darkness had made himself like his Mind among some of the members.

<I> appeared in the likeness of the Spirit, O Shem, so that Darkness might cast a shadow on himself alone. In accordance with the will of the Majesty, in order that Darkness might lose every form of his power,[11] Mind drew the fire of chaos, which was covered by water, from the midst of Darkness and water. Out of Darkness the water became a mist, and from the mist the womb took shape. The fire of chaos, which is deceitfulness, came to the womb.[12]

When Darkness saw the womb, he became defiled. And stirring up the water, Darkness rubbed the womb. The Mind of Darkness was ejaculated down to the depths of Nature, and it mingled with the power of the bitterness of Darkness. The eye of power was torn from wickedness, so that she would not bring forth Mind again. For this was [5] the seed of Nature from the dark root.

When Nature had conceived[13] Mind by means of the dark power, every form took shape in her.

When Darkness had produced the likeness of Mind, it resembled the Spirit. Actually, Nature tried to hold it in, but she could not do so, since she did not receive any form from Darkness. So she brought it forth in the cloud, and the cloud shone. Mind appeared in it like a frightful, harmful fire, and Mind collided with the unbegotten Spirit, since it had a likeness from the Spirit.[14]

---

11. Power here indicates the whole assemblage of the fiery forms or ideas, which Darkness possesses through his Mind and the Spirit has rendered active (*Paraphrase of Shem* 3). 12. The appearance of the Savior initiates the process of the formation of the universe. Through the division of water, Darkness and his Mind could ascend to the top of his multilayered realm (*Paraphrase of Shem* 2–3). From this upper place, Mind, who has already received some light from the Spirit, draws fire from the midst of Darkness and water. This provokes the transformation of water into a cloud, and out of the cloud the womb takes shape. 13. Lit., "When Nature had taken to herself." The underlying Greek verb means in this context "to conceive, to become pregnant" (the same verb is used in *Paraphrase of Shem* 15). Being ejaculated like sperm into the depth of Nature, Mind mixes himself with power and thus transfers the fiery forms into the cosmic womb, where he also generates an image of himself. Nature is then provided with the fiery forms, which she will use as *logoi spermatikoi* (rational seeds) to construct the material world (*Paraphrase of Shem* 10–11). The program stated in *Paraphrase of Shem* 4 is thus realized: Darkness has become inert, being deprived of every form of his power. 14. Since Nature received no form or configuration from Darkness— i.e., what makes up her constituent parts as a womb— she cannot help the seed go up. She then conceives the image of the paternal intellect in the cloud of water. There this second Mind collapses with the image of the Spirit (*Paraphrase of Shem* 9).

Nature Is Divided into Four Clouds, and the Spirit Produces the Power of Astonishment (5,19–6,30)

In order that Nature might become free of raging fire, Nature was quickly divided into four parts. These parts became clouds that varied in their appearance, and they were called hymen, placenta, power, and water. Hymen, placenta, and power were raging fires. They draw Mind from the midst of Darkness and water, since Mind was in the midst of Nature and dark power, in order that the harmful waters might not cling to it. [6]

So Nature was divided, in accordance with my will, in order that Mind might return to his power, which the dark root received from him and which was mixed with him and had appeared in the womb. Thus, by the division of Nature, the power of Mind separated from the dark power, since the power had something from Mind. Mind entered into the midst of his power, that is, into the middle of Nature.

The Spirit of light, when Mind weighed him down, was astonished. The power of his astonishment cast off this burden, and it turned toward the heat of astonishment and put on the light of the Spirit. When Nature had been set in motion by the power of the light of the Spirit, the burden returned. Thus the astonishment of the light of the <Spirit> cast off the burden and stuck to the cloud of hymen. All the clouds of Darkness, who had separated from Hades, cried out because of the alien power: it was the Spirit of light who had come among them.[15]

The Savior Appears as a Ray of Light and a Gust of Wind (6,30–7,11)

By the will of the Majesty, the Spirit gazed up at the infinite Light, in order that his light might be pitied and his likeness might be brought up from Hades.

When the Spirit looked out, I, the Son of Majesty, flowed [7] out like a ray of bright light and a gust of the immortal Spirit. I blew from the cloud of hymen upon the astonishment of the unbegotten Spirit, and the cloud separated and shed light on the other clouds. They separated so that the Spirit might return. Because of this, Mind took form; his repose was over.[16]

---

15. This episode refers back to *Paraphrase of Shem* 5. By producing the power of astonishment, the Spirit allows this power to ascend with the second Mind when Mind is drawn out from the cloud of water by the three fiery clouds. During this ascent, astonishment turns Mind toward the cloud of power, where the fiery forms are, in order that he may cling to it, whereas he himself continues to ascend to the cloud of hymen. Here the author of the text seems to employ the Stoic distinction of three fires—*augē*, *aithēr*, and *anthrax*—that determine three regions of the cosmos: empyrean, ethereal, and material. 16. Through the Savior's blowing, the clouds divide, opening the way for the ascent of the light of the Spirit, and Mind takes shape. This is the end of the conception—the formation of the embryo. The conclusion of this episode ("its repose was over") is best explained by means of a text from Philo of Alexandria: "Now seed is the original starting point of living creatures. That this is a substance of a very low order, resembling foam, is evident to the eye. But when it has been deposited in the womb and becomes solid, it acquires movement, and at once enters upon natural growth. But growth is better than seed, since in created things movement is better than quiescence."

Comment on the Four Clouds (7,11–30)

The hymen of Nature was a cloud that cannot be grasped: it was a great fire. Likewise, the placenta of Nature was the cloud of silence: it was a majestic fire. The power, which was mixed with Mind, also was a cloud of Nature mingled with Darkness, who had aroused Nature to unclean behavior. And the dark water was a frightful cloud. The root of Nature below was twisted, since it is burdensome and noxious. The root was blind before the bound light, which was imperceptible, since it had many appearances.

The Savior Appears Wearing a Universal Garment, to Free the Light of the Spirit (7,31–9,3)

I had pity on the light <of> the Spirit that Mind had taken.[17] I returned to my place in order to pray to the exalted, infinite Light, [8] that the power <of the light> of the Spirit might increase on his place and become full, not with dark defilement but with what is pure.

I said, "You are the root of the Light. Your hidden form has appeared, and it is exalted, infinite. May all the power of the Spirit become pure, and may it be filled with its light. The infinite Light will not be able to join with the unbegotten Spirit, and the power of astonishment will not be able to mingle with Nature."

In accordance with the will of the Majesty, my prayer was accepted. The voice of the word was heard saying from the Majesty <to> the unbegotten Spirit, "Look, the power has attained its fullness. The one who was revealed by me appeared in the Spirit."

I shall appear again. I am Derdekeas, the Son of undefiled, infinite Light. The light of the infinite Spirit came down into feeble Nature for a short time until all the defilement of Nature was withdrawn.[18]

So that the darkness of Nature might be put to shame, I put on my garment, the garment of the light of Majesty. That is what I am. I took on the appearance of [9] the Spirit in order to consider all the light in the depths of Darkness.

The Light of the Spirit Arises out of the Depths of Darkness and Gives Praise (9,3–10,15)

In accordance with the will of the Majesty, that by means of the word the Spirit might be filled with his light apart from the power of the infinite Light, and in accordance with my own will, the Spirit arose through his own power. His greatness was granted to him, that he might be filled with all his light and emerge from the

---

17. This refers to the light that revealed itself to the first Mind in the depths of chaos (cf. *Paraphrase of Shem* 3; 9). **18.** In receiving Mind like semen through her sexual intercourse with Darkness, Nature received the forms of the material beings. Thus those beings are the product of impurity. At the end of time, when Nature will have given birth to all material beings, she will become empty of all impurity and will return to chaos (*Paraphrase of Shem* 45).

entire burden of Darkness. For what was behind was a dark fire, blowing and pressing on the Spirit. The Spirit rejoiced because he had been protected from the frightful water. His light was not as bright as the Majesty, but <whatever> was granted him by the infinite Light was given so that in all his members he might appear in pure light. And when the Spirit arose above the water, the dark image of the water became apparent.[19]

The Spirit paid homage to the exalted Light: "Surely you alone are the infinite one, for you are above everything unbegotten and you have protected me from Darkness. At your wish I arose above the dark power."

In order that nothing may be hidden from you, Shem, the thought that the Spirit had begotten through his greatness came into being, [10] since Darkness was not able to restrain his evil. Once it appeared, the three roots became known as they were from the beginning. If Darkness had been able to check his evil, Mind would not have separated from him, and another power would not have appeared. But from the time it appeared, I, the Son of Majesty, have been seen, so that the light of the Spirit might not become deaf[20] and that Nature might not reign over him, because he gazed at me.

Derdekeas Reveals to Shem His True Nature (10,16–12,15)

Then, by the will of the Majesty, my purity was revealed, in order that what comes from power might appear. You are the great power that came into being, and I am the perfect Light above the Spirit and Darkness, the one who puts Darkness to shame in the intercourse of risqué rubbing. For it is through the division of Nature that the greatness of the Spirit wishes to protect itself with honor up to the height of the thought of the Spirit. The Spirit was receiving rest in his power. For the image of Light is inseparable from the unbegotten Spirit.[21] The lawgivers did not give it a name from all the clouds of Nature, nor is it possible to name it. For every form [11] into which Nature has divided is a power of restless fire; this is the seed of matter. The fire that receives the power of Darkness has enclosed it in the midst of the members of Nature.

By the will of the Majesty, in order that Mind and all the light of the Spirit might be protected from every burden and labor of Nature, a voice came from the Spirit to the cloud of hymen. The light of astonishment began to praise with the voice granted to him. The great luminous Spirit was in the cloud of hymen. He honored the infinite Light and the universal likeness—and that is what I am: "Son of Majesty, you who are called rising and setting,[22] you are the infinite Light

---

19. The Spirit expresses his joy for having been preserved from the frightful water, the cloud of water. And although the light of the Spirit is not equal in dignity to that of the Majesty, the light he is granted is pure and unmixed. But when the light of the Spirit rises above the water, the water loses its luminous particles and becomes again what it was when the Spirit saw it for the first time—a huge expanse of dark water (*Paraphrase of Shem* 2). **20.** This refers to the call of

the word or logos—i.e., the garment of the Savior said to be "the voice of immeasurable thought" (*Paraphrase of Shem* 12). **21.** This is the portion of light that has fallen into chaos (*Paraphrase of Shem* 6). **22.** Or "Anasses Duses." These titles are given to the Savior because, as a spiritual light—the sun of justice— Derdekeas is the rising (*anastasis*) and the setting (*dusis*).

given by the will of the Majesty to establish every light of the Spirit upon the place and to separate Mind from Darkness. For it was unsuitable for the light of the Spirit to remain in Hades. At your wish the Spirit arose to gaze at your greatness."

Shem, I have told you these things so that you might understand [12] that my likeness, the Son of Majesty, is from my infinite thought, since I am for the Majesty a universal likeness that does not lie, and I am over every truth and the principle of the word. His appearance is in my beautiful garment of light, which is the voice of immeasurable thought. We are the unique Light that came into being alone. This Light appeared in another root in order that the power of the Spirit might be raised from feeble Nature.

The Savior Appears in the Cloud of Hymen with His Threefold Garment, and a Part of Astonishment Falls (12,15–13,23)

By the will of the great Light, I came from the exalted Spirit down to the cloud of hymen without my universal garment. Then the word received me from the Spirit in the first cloud of the hymen of Nature, and I put on that word, of which the Majesty and the unbegotten Spirit had made me worthy.[23]

The threefold unity of my garment appeared in the cloud, by the will of the Majesty, in a single form, and my likeness was covered with the light of my garment. The cloud was disturbed, unable to support my likeness. It shed the first power, which it had taken from the Spirit and which had shone on him from the beginning, before <I> appeared in the word of the Spirit. The cloud [13] could not support both of them. Then the light that came from the cloud passed through the silence, until it came into the middle.[24]

By the will of the Majesty, the light <of> the Spirit that is in the silence, that had been separated from the luminous Spirit, mingled with it. It had been separated by the cloud of silence. The cloud of the middle was disturbed. It was the light of silence that gave rest to the flame of fire. It pressed down the dark womb, in order not to reveal other seed. Out of Darkness, it held them back, in the middle of Nature, to their position in the cloud. The seeds were troubled since they did not know where they were, for they did not yet possess the universal knowledge of the Spirit.[25]

---

23. The garment the Savior puts on is a word or logos that calls, since it is also a voice. This is a threefold garment, since it must be heard through the three spheres of the cosmos, from hymen through silence to the middle. **24.** The first fall of a spiritual entity was caused by looking down at chaos; this time, the fall is caused by looking at something above. **25.** The portion of light broken off from astonishment produces luminous seeds in the womb. These seeds will pass through the forms of Nature at the same time with the noetic powers—the powers of the Mind—and then through the winds and the demons (*Paraphrase of Shem* 21; 34). These will sow them with the particles of Mind at the time of birth. Later, in *Paraphrase of Shem* 24, it is mentioned that the power of astonishment gives birth to a pneumatic race—a spiritual race—from the womb; this makes explicit what is said elsewhere about the other race. This also explains why the text asserts that the spiritual person possesses in himself "a thought from the light of the power of astonishment."

The Savior Appears, to Bring to Perfection the Light in the Cloud of Hymen, and Nature Conceives the Archon of Creation (13,23–15,16)

I prayed to the Majesty, toward the infinite Light, that the troubled power of the Spirit might go to and fro and the dark womb might become inactive, and that my likeness might appear in the cloud of hymen, as if I were wrapped in the light of the Spirit that had gone before me. Then, by the will of the Majesty and through the prayer, I was in the cloud, in order that through my garment, which was from the power [14] of the Spirit, the fullness[26] of the word might bring power to the members in Darkness.

Because of them, I appeared in this insignificant place. I am a helper to everyone who has been given a name. For when I appeared in the cloud, the light of the Spirit began to save itself from the frightful water and from the clouds of fire that had been separated from dark Nature. And I gave them eternal honor, that they might not again mingle with unclean sexuality.[27]

The light in the hymen was troubled by my power, and it passed through the very middle of me. It was filled with universal thought and the word of the light of the Spirit. It turned to its repose and took form in its root. It shone, since it was without deficiency.

But the light that had come with it from the silence departed from the middle and returned to its place. Then the cloud shone, and from it came unquenchable fire.

The part that had separated from astonishment had put on forgetfulness; it had been tricked by the fire of Darkness. The trouble of its restlessness cast off the burden of the [15] cloud. It was evil, for it was unclean.

The fire mixed with water in order that the waters might become noxious. Nature, which had been driven back, immediately climbed out of the still waters, for her descent had been shameful. Nature conceived the power of fire, and that one became strong because of the light of the Spirit in Nature. His likeness appeared in the water in the shape of a frightful beast that had many faces and was twisted below.

The Savior Appears, to Give Revelation About the Light Within the Womb (15,16–16,23)

A light descended into chaos, filled with mist and dust, in order to harm Nature. The light of astonishment, which was in the middle, cast off the burden of Darkness

---

26. Pleroma. 27. The Savior's prayer first concerns the fallen light of the Spirit, that it "might go to and fro" through all the spheres of the cosmos and might be filled with the wholeness of the word. This purpose begins to be fulfilled as soon as the Savior comes down in the cloud of hymen. The prayer also concerns the womb, which should become inert or inoperative—i.e., she should release every power of the light of the Spirit she possesses. This purpose will be fulfilled at the time of the intervention of the Savior along with a special light going down into chaos (*Paraphrase of Shem* 15–16).

and came toward it. It rejoiced when the Spirit arose, for the Spirit looked down from the clouds toward the dark waters at the light in the depths of Nature.

For this reason I appeared, that I might find occasion to go down to Tartaros,[28] to the light of the Spirit that was weighed down, so that I might protect it from the evil of the burden. Thanks to the downward gaze of the Spirit at the dark region, the light [16] came up once more, in order that the womb might again rise from the water.

The womb rose by my will. Guilefully, the eye opened, and the light that had appeared in the middle and had separated from astonishment rested. It shone upon the womb, and the womb saw those she had not seen before. She rejoiced, jubilant in the light, in her wickedness, although what had appeared in the middle was not hers. When the light had shone on her, the womb thus saw those she had not seen before.

The womb was brought back down to the water. She thought she had obtained the power of light, but she did not know that her root had been made inactive through the likeness of the light, and that she was the one toward whom the light had run.

The Savior Appears, to Save the Light in the Clouds of Silence and the Middle (16,23–18,1)

The light that was in the middle, that was beginning and end, looked amazed. At once its thought gazed up at the exalted Light, and it cried out and said, "Lord, have mercy on me, for my light and my effort have gone astray. If your goodness does not establish me, I really do not know where I am."

The Majesty heard it and had mercy on it. I appeared from the cloud of hymen in the silence [17] without my holy garment. By my will I honored my garment of three forms in the cloud of hymen. The light that is in the silence, that emanated from the exulting power, received me into itself, and I put it on. Its two parts appeared in a single form. Its parts had not appeared on account of the fire, and I had been unable to speak in the cloud of hymen, for its fire was frightful, flaring up without weakening.[29]

In order that my greatness and the word might appear, in the same way I likewise laid down my garment in the cloud of silence. I went into the middle and put on the light that was in it, that was lost in forgetfulness and separated from the Spirit of astonishment, for it had cast the burden from him. At my wish, nothing mortal appeared to it, but only immortal realities that the Spirit granted to it. Then the light of the middle said in the thought of the light, "AI EIS AI OU PHAR DOU IA EI OU,"[30] which means, "I was in great rest," in order that the

---

28. The underworld, or hell. 29. The garments are voices (cf. *Paraphrase of Shem* 12; 20). The Savior could not let his voice be heard from the cloud of hymen to the clouds of silence and the middle.

30. These letters are explained in the following lines. They could be an example of glossolalia or they could have a symbolic or magical meaning.

Spirit might give rest to my light in its root and may bring it out of [18] noxious Nature.

The Savior Appears in a Garment of Fire to Separate Mind from Womb (18,1–19,26)

Then, by the will of the Majesty, I discarded my bright garment and put on another garment that was of fire and without form, from the Mind of power, which had been separated and prepared for me, in accordance with my will, in the middle. The middle covered it with dark power. In order to go and put it on, I descended into chaos, that I might rescue all the light from it. For without dark power I could not oppose Nature.

Once I penetrated into Nature, she could not withstand my power. I rested on her staring eye: it was a light that emanated from the Spirit, and it had been prepared for me as a garment and repose by the Spirit. Through me it opened its eyes down to Hades, and he granted Nature his voice for a while.[31]

My garment of fire, in accordance with the will of the Majesty, went down to the strong one, to the unclean part of Nature the dark power was covering. My garment rubbed Nature with its material, and her unclean femaleness grew strong. The passionate womb came up and [19] dried Mind up, in the form of a fish with a spark of fire and the power of fire. But when Nature expelled Mind from herself, she was troubled, and she wept. When she felt hurt and was in tears, she expelled from herself the power of the Spirit. She remained as quiet as I. I put on the light of the Spirit, and I rested with my garment at the sight of the fish.[32]

In order that the deeds of Nature might be condemned, since she is blind, many animal shapes came from her[33] in accordance with the number of winds that blow. They all came into existence in Hades, in search of the light of Mind that gives shape, but they could not rise up against it. I rejoiced over their ignorance. They found me, the Son of Majesty, in front of the manifold womb.

The Savior Appears, Puts on the Beast, and Requests That Heaven and Earth Be Formed (19,26–21,1)

I clothed myself in the beast, and I made a great request of Nature: that heaven and earth come into existence, in order that all the light might rise up. For the only way that the power of the Spirit could be liberated from bondage was for me to appear to her in the shape of a beast. So she agreed, [20] as though I were her son.

---

31. Once in Nature, the Savior rests on Nature's eye, "a light that emanated from the Spirit" (*Paraphrase of Shem* 15) and that had been prepared for him as a garment and repose. This light grants his voice to Nature for a while (cf. *Genesis* 1:3–29, on the creative voice of the word). This luminous garment will be called upon in the testimony as "unquenchable spark, who is an eye of heaven and a voice of light" (*Paraphrase of Shem* 46). 32. On the fish, cf. the role of the fish in the worship of the Syrian goddess, who sometimes takes the form of a mermaid, or of Aphrodite, who is connected to the sea. 33. These animal shapes are the signs of the zodiac.

On account of my request, Nature arose, since she had some of the power of the Spirit and Darkness and fire. She had taken off her forms. Once she had turned, she blew on the water. Heaven was created, and from the foam of heaven the earth came into existence.

At my wish the earth brought forth all kinds of food in accordance with the number of the beasts. It produced dew from the winds for your sake and for those who will be begotten a second time upon the earth.[34] The earth possessed the power of restless fire, and so it brought forth every seed.[35]

After heaven and earth had been created, my garment of fire arose in the midst of the cloud of Nature. It shone upon the whole creation until Nature dried up. Darkness, which was earth's garment, was cast into the noxious waters, and the middle was cleansed of Darkness.

The womb grieved about what had come into existence. She saw among her parts water that looked like a mirror. When she saw this, she wondered how it had come to be. Thus she remained a widow, and as for Darkness, he was [21] astonished, because he no longer was in her.

The Savior Appears, to Bring the Power in Nature to Perfection: The Third Mind (21,2–23,8)

Yet the forms still possessed power of fire and light. This power remained in Nature until all the powers were taken away from her. For just as the light of the Spirit has been perfected in three clouds, so also it is necessary that the power in Hades be brought to perfection at the appointed time.

Because of the kindness of the Majesty, I appeared to Nature in water a second time. My face pleased her, and her face also was relaxed. I said to her, "May seed and power come from you on the earth."

She obeyed the will of the Spirit, that she might become inactive. Her forms held each other and rubbed their tongues together, and they had sex and produced winds and demons with the power from fire, Darkness, and the Spirit.

A form that stayed alone cast off the beast from herself. She did not have intercourse, but rather she masturbated. She produced a wind possessing power from fire, Darkness, and the Spirit.

In order that the [22] demons also might become devoid of the power they possessed through defiled intercourse, a womb came into existence with the winds in a watery form. Then an unclean penis came into being with the demons in accordance with the example of Darkness and in the way he had rubbed the womb in the beginning.

Yet, when the forms of Nature had come together, they pulled away from one another and ejaculated the power; they were astonished about the deceit they had experienced. They grieved with eternal grief and covered themselves with their

---

34. These lines are written from the point of view of the narrator and are addressed to the race of Shem and those who will be born after the flood. 35. Cf. *Genesis* 1:6–13.

power. When I had put them to shame, I arose with my garment in the power—that is, with my garment that is higher than the beast, since it is bright—in order that I might leave Nature desolate.

At my wish, the Mind that appeared in dark Nature, that was the eye of the heart of Darkness, reigned over the winds and the demons. I gave him a likeness of fire, light, and hearing, with a share of the guileless word. In this way he was given some of the greatness, so that he might find strength in his own power, yet without the power, without the light of the Spirit, and without the intercourse of Darkness, in order that, at the end of time, [23] when Nature will be destroyed, he may rest in the honored place. For he will be found faithful, having loathed the defilement of Nature and Darkness. The strong power of Mind has come from Mind and from the unbegotten Spirit.

Humankind Is Formed Before the Great Flood (23,9–24,29)

The winds, which are demons from water, fire, darkness, and light, had intercourse unto perdition. Through their intercourse the winds received in their womb foam from the penis of the demons, and they conceived a power in their vulva through inhalation. The wombs of the winds huddled together until the times of birth came. The winds went down to the water. But it is through inhalation, in the midst of the sexuality that leads to pregnancy, that the power was conceived. Every form of conception took shape through inhalation. When the times of birth drew near, all the winds gathered out of the water near the earth, and they gave birth to all sorts of filthy things.

At the place where the wind came by itself, it acted in a defiled manner. Barren women and sterile men came into existence from this, [24] for as one is begotten, so one begets.

For your sakes the image of the Spirit appeared on the earth and in the water. For you are like the light, and you possess a share of the winds and the demons and a thought from the light of the power of astonishment. It was not good for the womb that each one brought forth by the light from the womb upon the earth came into existence. Her groan and her pain occurred because of the image that had appeared in you from the Spirit. You are exalted in your hearts.

It is a blessing, Shem, if a share is given to someone and that person leaves the soul for the thought of the light. The soul is a burden of Darkness, and those who know where the root of the soul comes from will be able to apprehend Nature as well. For the soul is a work of uncleanness and an object of scorn for bright thought. And I am the one who revealed the return of all that is unbegotten.

Nature Plots with Water to Destroy the Offspring of Shem (24,29–26,36)

In order that the sin of Nature might be filled, I saw to it that the womb, which had been disturbed, found blind wisdom pleasant, so that I might make her inactive. At my wish, [25] sin and dark water as well as Darkness plotted to wound

every form of your heart, since, by the will of the light of the Spirit, they surrounded you and bound you with Faith.[36] And the light sent a demon to cause the
plan of Darkness to fail, so that the plan of the wickedness of the womb might be
proclaimed—a plan to bring about a flood and destroy your race, and thereby to
seize the light and take it away from Faith.

But I hurried to proclaim by the mouth of the demon that a tower be built for
the particle of light left in the demons and their race, which was in them,[37] in
order that the demon might be protected from restless chaos. The womb planned
these things, in accordance with my will, so that she might pour everything out.
So a tower was constructed by the demons.[38]

Darkness was disturbed in his deficiency, and he relaxed the muscles of the
womb. Then the demon who was going to enter the tower was protected, that the
generations might continue and expand through him, for he possesses power
from every form.

Return, from this moment on, [26] O Shem, and rejoice [greatly] in your race
and Faith, for without body and necessity it is protected from every body of Darkness, since it bears witness to the holy things of greatness—that which was revealed to them in their thought by my will. They will rest in the unbegotten Spirit
without grief.

As for you, Shem, you remained in a body outside the cloud of light so that
you might abide patiently with Faith and Faith might come to you. The thought
of Faith will be taken and given to you in bright consciousness. I told you these
things for the benefit of your race from the cloud of light. Likewise, I shall reveal
to you all that I say, until the end, so that you may reveal these things to all who
will come to be upon the earth a second time.

O Shem, the disturbance that occurred at my wish happened in order that
Nature might become empty. The wrath of Darkness subsided. O Shem, Darkness was silenced. The light that shone for creation no longer appears in it, in accordance with my will. And after Nature said that her wish had been fulfilled,
every form was swallowed up in the bottom of the waters. [27]

Nature Casts Off Fire and Establishes Fate (27,1–28,8)

In prideful ignorance, Nature turned over her dark womb and expelled the power
of fire that was in her from the beginning through the sexuality of Darkness. The
fire raised itself up and shone upon the whole creation instead of the righteous
one. All the forms of the womb sent their powers like flames of fire up to heaven
to help the light that was corrupted, that had raised itself up. They were the

---

36. Pistis, here and throughout. 37. Or "<in> water."
38. The tower of Babel; cf. *Genesis* 11:1–9. This passage, which provides a reinterpretation of the *Genesis*
account, recalls the *Secret Book of John* (II, 29), where
the ark is replaced by a luminous cloud. The *Chronicle of Edessa* relates how on the occasion of a cata-
strophic flood of the city in 201, King Abgar VIII

(177–212) sought refuge in the great tower called "(the
tower) of the Persians"; see J. B. Segal, *Edessa*, 24–25.
It may also be recalled that in the *Shepherd of Hermas*,
Vision 3.3.5, the tower symbolizes the church. Shem's
presence in the tower could thus symbolize the situation of the pneumatics within the great church.

members of the restless fire. She did not realize she had harmed herself alone. When she cast out the power that is powerful, she expelled it from her genitals. It was the demon, a deceiver, who aroused the womb toward every form.[39]

In her ignorance, as though she were doing a great work, Nature granted the demons and the winds a star each. Without wind and star nothing happens on the earth. It is through every power that the earth is filled, since they are released from Darkness and fire, from power and light. For in the place where their darkness and their fire mingled with each other, beasts were brought forth.

It was in the place of Darkness and fire, of the power [28] of Mind and Light, that human beings came into existence. Since the thought of the Light, my eye, is from the Spirit, it does not exist in every person. For before the flood came about through the winds and the demons, <evil> came to people.

Nature Plans to Destroy Sodom (28,8–30,4)

In order that the power that was in the tower might still be brought forth and might rest on the earth, Nature, which had been disturbed, wanted to harm the seed that would come into being on the earth after the flood. Demons were sent to them, as well as the deceit of the winds, the burden of the angels, the fear of the prophet, and verbal condemnation, that I may teach you, O Shem, from what blindness your race is protected.[40]

When I have revealed to you all that has been said, then the righteous one will shine upon creation with my garment. Night and day will separate from one another. I shall hurry down to creation to bring the light to that place Faith possesses, and I shall appear to those who will have acquired the thought of the light of the Spirit. Because of them my greatness appeared. When he will appear, O Shem, on the earth, [in] the place that will be [29] called Sodom, safeguard the insight I shall give you. For those whose heart is pure will gather close to you because of the word you will reveal.[41]

When you appear in creation, dark Nature will shake against you, as well as the winds and their demons, so that they may destroy insight. But you, proclaim quickly to the Sodomites your universal teaching, for they are your members. The demon in human form will depart from that place since, by my will, he is ignorant. He will guard this teaching.

---

39. After the flood, the womb expels from her genitals the fiery power she possessed from the beginning through her intercourse with Darkness. This fire rises and shines upon creation as the physical sun "instead of the righteous one"—i.e., instead of the Savior and his invincible garment. Until the return of the righteous one (cf. *Paraphrase of Shem* 37; 47), the evil demiurge—the archon of creation, the corrupted light—reigns over the world with his members, the stars. **40.** In order to keep the postdiluvian generations for herself and under her dominion, Nature plans to destroy the race of Shem, the spiritual seed. She first establishes her faith, the Jewish religion, through Abraham and the law of circumcision (cf. *Genesis* 17:1–15; 19:13). **41.** Derdekeas reveals to Shem the appearance of the righteous one at the time of the destruction of Sodom. The righteous one is the Savior who appears in creation with his garment of fire. He is the luminous cloud that, as the sun of justice, separates day and night—i.e., good and evil. He is both light and darkness (cf. *Exodus* 14:20): salvation for the spiritual people and judgment for the others. Shem is urged to teach those who will gather around him. From this point on, the narrator uses the future tense.

The Sodomites, however, in accordance with the will of the Majesty, will bear witness to the universal testimony. They will rest with a pure conscience in the place of their repose, which is the unbegotten Spirit. As these things happen, Sodom will be burned unjustly by perverse Nature. Evil will not cease, so that your greatness may appear there.[42]

Then [30] the demon will depart with Faith, and he will appear in the four regions of creation.[43]

The Faith of Nature Appears, and the Savior Is Baptized (30,4–31,4)

When Faith appears in the last likeness, her appearance will be exposed. For the firstborn is the demon who appeared in the celestial framework of Nature with many faces in order that Faith might be manifested in him. When he appears in creation, evil wrath will break out, and earthquakes, wars, famines, and blasphemies. Because of him, the whole world will be disturbed. He will seek the power of Faith and Light, but he will not find it.

At that time the demon will also appear on the river to baptize with an imperfect baptism and to disturb the world with bondage of water. It is necessary for me, then, to appear among the members of the thought of Faith, in order to reveal the great works of my power. I shall separate thought out of the demon who is Soldas, and I shall mix the light, which has something from the Spirit, with my invincible garment as well as with the one whom I shall reveal [31] in the darkness for your sake and for the sake of your race, which will be protected from evil Darkness.[44]

The Memorial and Testimony of Derdekeas (31,4–32,5)

Know, O Shem, that without Elorchaios, Amoia, Strophaia,
Chelkeak, Chelkea, <Chelke>, and Aileos,
no one will be able to pass by this wicked station.
This is my memorial,

---

42. It is through Shem that the righteous one will reveal himself (*Paraphrase of Shem* 41; 42). Through Shem, the luminous cloud will illumine the spiritual people, the members of Shem, and gather them at the place of their salvation, when Nature will burn Sodom unjustly. Abraham will go forth from Sodom and accept the teaching of the angels sent by Nature, but the Sodomites will bear witness to the universal testimony and rest in the unbegotten Spirit. 43. Abraham will depart from Sodom and bring the Faith of Nature to the four regions of creation (cf. *Genesis* 12:3; 13:14; 18:18; 25:6; *Hebrews* 11:13). 44. The archon of creation, the demon, will manifest himself upon the river through John the Baptizer to bind people with the im-

pure rite of water, but the Savior will appear through the demon Soldas, who is the terrestrial Jesus. In order to make the light of Faith pass onto his garment of light, the Savior avails himself of an earthly garment (*Paraphrase of Shem* 30), his demonic body of fire he has put on to trick the archon. The "members of the thought of Faith" with whom the Savior clothes himself can be identified with the righteous of the old covenant, who observed the law in good faith and who await the Savior, as Valentinian Gnostic thought teaches. See *Excerpts from Theodotus* 18 and 37–38. For the *Paraphrase of Shem*, the *descensus ad inferos* takes place at baptism, not after the crucifixion.

because through it I have triumphed
over the wicked station
and I have rescued the light of the Spirit
from the frightful water.
For when the appointed days set for the demon,
the one who will baptize in error,
draw near, I shall appear
in the baptism of the demon
to reveal with the mouth of Faith
a testimony for those who are hers.
I testify to you, unquenchable spark,
Osei,[45] the elect of the Light, the eye of heaven,
and to you, Faith,[46] the first and the last,
and to you, Sophia,[47]
and to you, Saphaia,
and to you, Saphaina,
and to you, righteous spark,
and to you, impure light,
and to you, east and west and north and south,
upper air and lower air,
and to all the powers and authorities, [32]
you are in [creation];
and to you, Moluchtha, as well as Soch,
who are from every work and every impure effort of Nature.

The Savior Descends to the Water (32,5–27)

Then, through the demon, I shall descend into the water. Whirlpools of water and flames of fire will rise up against me, and I shall put on the light of Faith and the unquenchable fire and ascend from the water, so that through my help the power of the Spirit may get across, the power sown in creation by the winds and demons and stars. Through them every defilement will be filled.

Henceforth, O Shem, count on yourself alone to become better through the thought of the light. Do not let your thought get involved with the fire and the dark body, which was an unclean work. What I teach you is right.

The Paraphrase of the Memorial and Testimony (32,27–34,16)

This is the paraphrase, for you did not remember that it is from the firmament that your race has been protected. Elorchaios is the name of the great Light, the

---

45. The name Osei is probably a transcription of the Greek *hos ei* ("who is," "who (you) are") here wrongly interpreted as a name, but rightly translated in *Para-* *phrase of Shem* 46: "who is (*peto*) an eye of heaven." **46.** Pistis. **47.** Or "Wisdom."

place from which I have come, the word without equal. The likeness is my glorious garment. Derdekeas is the name [of] his word [33] in the voice of the Light. Strophaia is the blessed gaze, which is the Spirit. Chelkeach is my garment, who has come from astonishment; this is the one who was in the cloud of hymen, which appeared as a cloud with three forms. Chelkea is my garment with two forms; this is the one who was in the cloud of silence. Chelke is my garment given to him from every region; it was given to him in a single form from the greatness, who was in the cloud of the middle. The star of the Light that was mentioned is my invincible garment I wore in Hades; this is the mercy located above the thought and the testimony of those who bear witness.

This is the testimony that was mentioned: the first and the last, Faith, the Mind of the wind of Darkness. <Sophia> and S<a>phaia and Saphaina are in the cloud of those who have been separated from the restless fire. The righteous spark is the cloud of light, which has shone in your midst. In it my garment will go down to chaos. The defiled [34] light exists as power; it appeared in Darkness and belongs to dark Nature. The upper air as well as the lower air, the powers and the authorities, the demons and the stars, all possessed a particle of fire and light from the Spirit. Moluchtha is a wind, and without it nothing is brought forth upon the earth. He resembles a serpent and a unicorn, and he has manifold wings that he unfolds. What is left is the womb that has been overthrown.

Derdekeas Teaches Shem About the Last Things (34,16–36,24)

You are blessed, Shem, for your race has been protected from the dark wind with many faces. They will bear witness to the universal testimony and the unclean sexuality of <Nature>, and they will be uplifted through the memorial of Light. O Shem, none of those who wear the body will be able to complete these things, but by remembering they will be able to grasp them, so that when their thought separates from the body, then these things may be revealed to them. They have been revealed to your race.

O Shem, it is difficult for someone wearing a body to complete [these things about which] I have spoken to you. [35] Only a few people will complete them, people who possess the particle of Mind as well as the thought of the light of the Spirit, and they will protect their thought from risqué rubbing. Many in the generation of Nature will seek the security of power, but they will not find it, nor will they be able to fulfill the will of Faith. For they are the seed of universal Darkness. And the winds and the demons will hate those who will be found to have put forth great efforts. Bodily bondage is great indeed.

For where the winds, the stars, and the demons sow seeds from the power of the Spirit, there repentance and testimony will appear among them, and mercy will lead them to the unbegotten Spirit. As for those who are repentant, they will find rest in the consummation of the age with Faith in the place of hymen. This is the Faith that will fill the place left empty. As for those who have nothing from the luminous Spirit or Faith, they will be dissolved in Darkness, [36] where repentance has not come.

I opened the eternal gates closed from the beginning. To those who long for nobility of life and who are worthy of the repose, he revealed them. I granted perception to the perceptive; I disclosed to them all the concepts and teaching of the righteous. In no way did I become their enemy, but when I endured the wrath of the world, I was triumphant. Not one of them knew me. The gates of fire and endless smoke opened against me, and all the winds rose up against me. For a time thunder and lightning will rise up against me, and they will bring their wrath upon me. Because of me, as far as flesh is concerned, they will rule over them tribe by tribe.[48]

Derdekeas Denounces Defiled Baptism (36,25–38,28)

Then many who wear flesh that leads them astray will descend into the harmful waters by means of the winds and the demons, and they are bound with the water. But water will provide an ineffective treatment. It will mislead and bind the world. And those who do the will of Nature, their part . . . [37] two times in the day of the water and the forms of Nature. Nothing will be granted to them, when Faith confounds them in order to greet the righteous one.

O Shem, it is necessary that thought be called by the word, so that, in bondage, the power of the Spirit may be saved from the frightful water. It is indeed a blessing if it is granted to someone to understand what is exalted and to know the ultimate time and bondage. Water is an insignificant body, and people are not released, since they are bound in water, just as from the beginning the light of the Spirit was bound.

O Shem, people are deceived by the many forms of demons, and they think that through the baptism of unclean water this substance that is dark, feeble, ineffective, and disturbing will take away sins. They do not know that coming from the water and going to the water are bondage, error, defilement, envy, murder, adultery, false witness, heresies, robberies, lusts, babbling, wrath, bitterness, [insults] . . . . [38] For this reason an abundance of water burdens their thoughts.

I proclaim to those who have a mind that they must abandon defiled baptism, and those who possess thought from the light of the Spirit will not get involved with sexual rubbing. Their heart will not vacillate, nor will they be cursed, nor will they show honor to the water. Where the curse is, there is deficiency, and where honor is, there is blindness. When they mix with the evil ones, they become

---

48. The Savior completes the teaching he already has given to Shem (cf. *Paraphrase of Shem* 32) about the meaning of his future baptism by presenting his descent into the water as a descent into the underworld. The vocabulary and images are those traditionally used in reports of the descent into the underworld — e.g., the mention of gates. In ancient thought, the three regions of the universe (heaven, earth, and underworld) were connected by gates (cf. *Matthew* 16:18; *Revelation* 4:1). In traditional Christian teaching, the descent of the Savior into the underworld after his crucifixion was intended to express in a dramatic and mythic way how people already dead could benefit from his death. For the *Paraphrase of Shem*, however, the main saving event is not the crucifixion, but baptism. The descent to the underworld is therefore transferred to baptism, thus establishing a link between the descent into the river and the descent of the Savior into the cloud of water in order to rescue the light of the Spirit (cf. *Paraphrase of Shem* 18–19).

empty in dark water. For where water has been invoked, there is Nature with a ritual formula, a lie, and injury. Only in the unbegotten Spirit, where the exalted Light has rested, has water not been invoked, nor can it be invoked.[49]

The Savior Ascends Through His Crucifixion
(38,28–40,31)

This is my revelation. When I have completed the days assigned to me upon the earth, I shall cast from me . . . and [39] my incomparable garment will shine on me, as well as all my other garments that I put on in all the clouds and that were from the astonishment of the Spirit. The air will divide my garment. My garment will shine and divide in all the clouds to the root of the Light. Mind is repose with my garment. My other garments are on the left and the right, and they will shine behind me so that the image of the Light may appear. The garments I put on in the three clouds will, in the last day, rest in their root, in the unbegotten Spirit, since they will have no more deficiency from the division of the clouds.

That is why I have appeared, without deficiency, because the clouds are not of uniform character, and in order that the wickedness of Nature might be brought to completion. For at that time Nature wished to seize me. She will nail Soldas, who is a dark flame, who will stand on the [height] . . . of error, [40] that he might seize me. She took care of her faith, being vain.

At that time the Light was about to separate from Darkness and a voice was about to be heard in creation, saying, "Blessed is the eye that has seen you and the Mind that has supported your greatness, by my will." And it will be said from above, "Blessed is Rebouel among all generations of people, for you alone have seen and will listen." They will behead the woman who has the perception you will reveal upon the earth.

In accordance with my will, the woman will bear witness and will rest from every vain effort of Nature and chaos. For the woman they will behead at that time is the arrangement of the power of the demon, who will baptize the seed of Darkness with harshness in order to mix it with uncleanness. He engendered a woman, and she was named Rebouel.[50]

---

49. This passage develops a harsh polemic against baptism. Baptism is the last means used by Nature to enslave people, and those who do the will of Nature will not be saved with Faith, when she will receive the Savior, the righteous one. The reason for rejecting baptism is the fact that in the beginning water kept the light of the Spirit bound (*Paraphrase of Shem* 37). Baptism cannot be given for the forgiveness of sins, because water is itself a source of sin. Since water was associated in the beginning with the sexual intercourse between Darkness and the cosmic womb, baptism is assimilated to sexual rubbing. Therefore, those who want to rest with the exalted Light in the unbegotten Spirit cannot call upon the dark water. 50. Since the Savior has delivered the "members of the thought of Faith," Nature will try to regain her light by seizing him, but she will only succeed in crucifying Soldas, "who is the dark flame"—i.e., the terrestrial body of the Savior. The use of the Greek verb *pessein* appears to be a clear allusion to the crucifixion; it means "to stick or fix in," "stick or fix on," "fix upon an object." On Rebouel, see the introduction.

Derdekeas Tells Shem About His Mission on Earth
(40,31–41,21)

Look, O Shem, all the things I have told you have been fulfilled . . . and the things you [41] lack, in accordance with my will, will be revealed to you at that place upon the earth where you may reveal them as they are. Do not let your thought get involved with the body. For I have told you these things with the voice of fire. I entered through the midst of the clouds, and I spoke in the language of each one. This is my language that I have spoken to you and that will be received from you. You will speak with the voice of the world upon the earth, and it will appear to you with this face and this voice.

This is all that I have said to you. From now on, proceed with the Faith that shone in the depths of creation.

Shem Returns to His Senses and Receives the Power of Light
(41,21–42,11)

I, Shem, awoke as from deep sleep.[51] I was astonished when I received the power of Light and all his thought. I went with Faith, which shone with me. The righteous one followed us with my invincible garment, and all that he told me would happen upon the earth did happen.[52]

Nature was handed over to Faith, so that Faith might overturn her and establish her in Darkness. Nature developed a circular motion by [42] turning night and day, without rest, with the souls. This brought her deeds to completion.[53]

Then I rejoiced in the thought of Light. I departed from Darkness and proceeded in Faith where the forms of Nature are, up to the top of the earth, to the things that are prepared.

Derdekeas Delivers His First Discourse on Eschatology
(42,11–45,31)

Your Faith rules over the earth the entire day. For all night and all day Faith keeps Nature turning so that she may receive the righteous one. Nature is burdened

---

51. This narrative conclusion closes the revelation of Derdekeas (cf. *Paraphrase of Shem* 1). In the first part of the conclusion, Shem tells of his transformation and his association with Faith and the righteous one. The second part is an explanation of the interactions between Faith and Nature. In the third part, Shem describes his cosmic ascent with Faith up to the forms of Nature in a way that recalls the first part. The last lines of the conclusion mention the ascent of Shem to the top of the earth in terms that recall the ascent of Enoch in *Genesis* 5:24 and his investiture in *1 Enoch* 71:13–17. **52.** To carry out his mission as an illuminator, Shem receives the fullness of the thought of the Spirit. He is also assimilated to the righteous one by re- ceiving his invincible garment (cf. *Holy Book of the Great Invisible Spirit* III, 64, where it is said that great Seth has put on Jesus). Since the function of the righteous one was to illumine creation with his invincible garment, he now accomplishes this in the figure of Shem, as promised (cf. *Paraphrase of Shem* 28). **53.** Previously the text has explained how the Mind, with his light, was established as king over the forms of Nature, the winds and the demons (*Paraphrase of Shem* 22–23). Now, after the flood, Nature is once again put under the rule of Faith, who is the light of Mind; Nature then sets in motion the rotation of the spheres, which leads to the incarnation of souls.

and troubled. None will be able to open the forms of the womb except Mind alone, who was entrusted with their configuration. The configuration of the two forms of Nature—the one that is blind—is frightful.[54]

Those who have a free conscience will remove themselves from the babbling of Nature and will bear witness to the universal testimony. They will strip off the burden of Darkness; they will put on the word of Light, and they will not be kept back [43] in an insignificant place. Moreover, what they possess from the power of Mind they will give back to Faith. They will be accepted without suffering. Finally, they will abandon the chaotic fire they possess in the middle of Nature, and they will be received by my garments, which are in the clouds. They guide their members, and they will rest in the Spirit without suffering.

Because of this the appointed time of Faith was manifested on the earth for a little while, until Darkness is taken away from her and her testimony is revealed—the testimony revealed by me. Those who will be found from her root will strip off Darkness and chaotic fire. They will put on the light of Mind and will bear witness. For all that I have said will come to pass.

After I cease to be on the earth and I withdraw above to my repose, a great, harmful deceit will come upon the world as well as many evils, in accordance with the number of forms of [44] Nature. Evil days will come, and when the time of Nature approaches destruction, darkness will come upon the earth. The number of the elect will be limited.[55]

A demon will rise up from the power, with a likeness of fire. He will tear the sky and rest in the depth of the east. The whole creation will be shaken, and the deceived world will be disturbed. Many places will be flooded because of the envy of the winds and the demons, whose names are meaningless: Phorbea, Chloerga. They govern the world with their teaching and lead many hearts astray because of their disorder and defilement. Many places will be sprinkled with blood, and there will be five generations that eat their own children. But the regions of the south will accept the word of Light. Those outside the error of the world < . . . >.

From the east, then, a demon will come from the belly of the serpent. He was [45] hidden in a deserted place, and he will perform many wonders. Many will

---

54. Without any transition, Derdekeas begins a new revelation by addressing Shem directly: "Your Faith . . ." The first lines of his discourse resume the teaching already given about the cosmic functions of Faith and Mind. From the flood to the last coming of the righteous one, Faith and Mind are at work in order that Nature may be emptied of her forms through the production of material beings and the incarnation of souls and thereby rendered inactive. The forms of nature are the signs of the zodiac that the cosmic womb produced after she cast out the demiurgic Mind. Cf. *Paraphrase of Shem* 19. The blind configuration refers to ancient astrological ideas. The zodiacal signs, considered to be living beings, were associated with one another through various geometrical combinations known as configurations. One of them was the association of the signs with parallel lines having the same latitude—i.e., located on lines parallel to the equator. These signs were said to be looking at each other. But in this configuration, the Crab (Cancer) and the Ram (Aries), situated on the lines of the summer and winter solstices, could not see each other and were said to be blind. According to Numenius, the Crab and the Ram are the doors through which souls come down to the earth and go up after their terrestrial life (Numenius, fragments 31–35). 55. The third part of Derdekeas's discourse deals with cosmic eschatology. The final crisis that is described here and that leads to the destruction of Nature seems to be linked to the crucifixion of the Savior (cf. *Paraphrase of Shem* 38).

loathe him. Wind will come forth from his mouth, with a female likeness, and her name will be called Abalphe. He will reign over the world, from the east to the west.[56]

Then Nature will have one last moment. The stars will disappear from the sky, and the mouth of error will be opened so that evil Darkness may become ineffective and silent. In the last day the forms of Nature will be eliminated with the winds and all their demons. They will turn into a dark lump, just as they were in the beginning. And the sweet waters, burdened by the demons, will dry up. For where the power of the Spirit has gone, there are my sweet waters. No further works of Nature will appear; they will mingle with the waters of Darkness, which are limitless, and all her forms will recede from the middle.

Shem Recites the Memorial and Testimony and Ascends to the Planetary Spheres (45,31–47,32)

I, Shem, have completed these things. My heart began to separate from the body of Darkness, and my [46] time was up. Then my heart put on the immortal memorial, and I said,

> I agree with your memorial
> that you have revealed to me:
> Elorchaios,
> and you, Amoiaias,
> and you, Sederkeas,
> and your guilelessness,
> and then, Strophaias,
> and you, Chelkeak,
> and you, Chelkea,
> as well as Chelke and Elaios,
> you are the immortal memorial.
> I testify to you, unquenchable spark,
> who is an eye of heaven and a voice of light,
> and to you, Soph{a}ia,
> and to you, Saphaia,
> and to you, Saphaina,
> and to you, righteous spark,
> and to you, Faith, the first and the last,
> and to you, upper air,
> and to you, lower air,[57]

---

56. This passage makes use of Jewish and Christian traditions about the coming of the Antichrist at the end of time (see *Assumption of Moses*; *4 Ezra*; *3 Sibylline Oracles*; Mark 13; Revelation 12–13). He "will come from the belly of the serpent"—i.e., he will be sent by the evil demiurge. He will bring with him all kinds of plagues and false prophets, and he will act as a wonder-worker. His coming will give rise to a world empire, symbolized here by a woman (cf. 3 *Sibylline Oracles* 75–90). **57.** The preceding lines are inadvertently copied twice—a case of dittography.

and to you, all the powers and authorities in creation,
and to you, impure light,
and to you also, east,
and to you, west,
and to you, south,
and to you, north,
you are the four cardinal points [47] of the inhabited world;
and to you also, Moluchtha,
and to you, Essoch,
you are the root of evil
and every work and defiled effort of Nature.

These are the things I completed while bearing witness.[58]

I am Shem. On the day when I was to come forth from the body, when my thought had completed its time in the body, I arose as if from deep sleep. When I arose as though out of the burden of my body, I said, "Just as Nature has grown old, so is it also today with humanity. Blessed are they who have known, as they have fallen asleep, in what power their thought has rested."

When the Pleiades separated, I saw clouds, which I shall pass through. The cloud of Spirit is like pure beryl, the cloud of hymen is like shining emeralds, the cloud of silence is like flourishing amaranths, and the cloud of the middle is like pure jacinth.[59]

Derdekeas Delivers His Second Discourse on Eschatology (47,32–48,30)

When the righteous one appeared in Nature, then Nature, once in a state of excitement, felt hurt. She granted [48] to Morphaia to explore heaven. If the righteous one explores during twelve periods, it is in order that he may explore them during a single period, that his time may be completed quickly and Nature may become ineffective.

Blessed are they who guard themselves against the deposit of death, against the burdensome water of Darkness. It is only for a few moments that they will be dominated, since they will hasten to come forth from the error of the world. As long as they are dominated, they will be kept back. They will be tormented in darkness until the time of the consummation. When the consummation comes

---

58. This discourse, uttered by Shem, does not fit the narrative fiction of the revelation of Derdekeas, which presupposes that the seer records the teaching he received from Derdekeas during his celestial journey. Here Shem narrates how he ascended to the celestial sphere at the end of his life, wearing the memorial as a garment and delivering the testimony of Faith. 59. Shem narrates his departure from terrestrial life, stressing the opposition between thought and body.

The theme of the aging of humanity (cf. 4 Ezra 14:10–12) is resumed in the last discourse of Derdekeas. Shem's discourse ends abruptly with the description of the celestial spheres. These are compared to precious stones (cf. Revelation 21:11, 18–21), except for the sphere of silence. The order of presentation starts from the highest sphere, although Shem is supposed to be ascending.

and Nature is destroyed, their thoughts will separate from Darkness. Nature has burdened them for a short time. They will be in the ineffable light of the unbegotten Spirit, without a form. So also it is with Mind, as I have said from the start.[60]

Conclusion (48,30–49,9)

From now on, O Shem, proceed in grace and remain in Faith upon the earth. For all the powers of light and fire will be completed by me [49] for your sake. Without you they will not be revealed until you speak of them openly. When you leave the earth, they will be communicated to the worthy. And apart from this revelation, let them speak about you upon the earth, since they will inherit the land, free of care and in harmony.

---

60. The context for the first part of this new eschatological teaching given by Derdekeas is to be found in the conclusion of the revelation (*Paraphrase of Shem* 41–42). The presence of the righteous one in creation initiates the new order of the universe after the flood (cf. *Genesis* 8:22). The archon of creation, Morphaia, revolves through heaven and settles the course of the stars in order to control the fate of humankind. But this new order is also "the appointed time of Faith." During this time, the righteous one, the sun of justice, carries out his cosmic acts of salvation, particularly as the illuminator. In the apocalyptic tradition, the history of salvation is divided into predetermined periods of time (cf. 1 *Enoch* 91–104), twelve according to 4 *Ezra* 14:10–17, and the twelfth period of the visit of the Savior is the last one (cf. 2 *Enoch* 65:4–5; 3 *Sibylline Oracles* 92). According to the *Paraphrase of Shem*, Nature will then become inactive. The second part of the revealer's teaching seems to suppose or foresee a situation of persecution, and the faithful are urged to persevere. At the end of time the pneumatics will rest in the light of the unbegotten Spirit and the noetics in the light of the Mind.

THE SECOND DISCOURSE
OF GREAT SETH

NHC VII,2

Introduced and Translated by Marvin Meyer

The *Second Discourse of Great Seth*, traditionally entitled the "Second Treatise (or Logos) of the Great Seth," is a speech or message of Jesus about
salvific knowledge and the true meaning of the crucifixion in the face of the theology of the emerging orthodox church. The title of the text, given entirely in
Greek at the end of the document (*deuteros logos tou megalou sēth*), calls the text
the second *logos*, apparently in contrast to the first discourse, which may be referred to near the opening of the text: "I have uttered a discourse for the glory of
the Father . . ." (49,20–22). Apart from this inference, we know nothing more
about a "First Discourse of Great Seth." In both instances the discourse may be a
spoken word—here a spoken word that has been written down. If that interpretation is correct, this text consists of a second speech or message of great Seth. The
title may also refer to the personified *logos*, the divine word, as in *John* 1 and many
Gnostic texts. Great Seth, mentioned only in the title of the text, is a leading character in other Gnostic texts, especially Sethian texts, such as the *Holy Book of the
Great Invisible Spirit*. In Christian Sethian traditions the heavenly figure of Seth
can come to expression in the person of Christ, who may conceivably be the incarnation of Seth. Thus, the *Second Discourse of Great Seth* may be understood
to be the second speech or message delivered by Jesus, the manifestation of
heavenly Seth.

In his analysis of the *Second Discourse of Great Seth*, Gregory Riley suggests
that the text most resembles a homily delivered to encourage and rouse faithful
Gnostic Christians in the face of the theological and political opposition of the
emerging orthodox church.[1] The organization of the homily is hardly systematic.
Rather, it seems to presuppose knowledge of the basic mythological, theological,
and philosophical tenets of the religious tradition, and it offers its homiletical

---

1. Gregory Riley, in Birger A. Pearson, ed., *Nag Hammadi Codex VII*, 129.

insights with thematic progression. The basic message of the text is that the Savior has come down from the divine Majesty above into the cosmos of Yaldabaoth and his archons, and here in this world he has requisitioned a human body, thrown out the previous tenant, and made it his place of residence. That is how the Savior has become Christ the anointed. As a stranger here below, Jesus proclaims a message of gnosis and unity among all those who are kin to him, and after undergoing a passion that was, put bluntly, simply a joke, the Savior returns to heaven to enjoy a wedding celebration with "a wedding of truth" (67,5–6) and "a feast of love" (67,17). The good news for the readers of the text is that they too can experience the same joy, truth, and love when they realize their oneness with the Savior and the One Who Is, the Father of the All.

The speaker throughout the *Second Discourse of Great Seth* is Jesus himself. Jesus proclaims the good news of salvation in the first-person singular, so that the text presents itself as the good news according to Jesus. Jesus explains that when he came down from the Majesty of the Spirit, the rulers of the world were confused and upset at the divine stranger in their midst, although at least one of the powers, whose name is Adonaios and who is known from other Gnostic texts, including Sethian texts, did not join the other archons in their opposition to Jesus. Adonaios's name is taken from Adonai, Hebrew for "my Lord." Adonaios appears to be Lord of the Jewish people in the *Second Discourse of Great Seth*, and he is a fairly good archon.[2]

The rest of the world rulers tried to kill Jesus, but in their ignorance they were unable to do so. Jesus says:

> The death they think I suffered they suffered in their error and blindness. They nailed their man to their death. Their thoughts did not perceive me, since they were deaf and blind. By doing these things they pronounce judgment against themselves. As for me, they saw me and punished me, but someone else, their father, drank the gall and the vinegar; it was not I. They were striking me with a scourge, but someone else, Simon, bore the cross on his shoulder. Someone else wore the crown of thorns. And I was on high, poking fun at all the excesses of the rulers and the fruit of their error and conceit. I was laughing at their ignorance. (55,30–56,20)

The understanding of the crucifixion in the *Second Discourse of Great Seth* is one of the most fascinating aspects of the text. There is a significant amount of laughter in the *Second Discourse of Great Seth*, as in the text that follows it in Codex VII, the *Revelation of Peter*, where the real Jesus—the living Jesus—is also portrayed laughing at the crucifixion.[3] In the *Revelation of Peter* Jesus tells Peter:

---

2. Cf. the role of Sabaoth, sometimes associated with Adonaios, in the *Nature of the Rulers* and *On the Origin of the World.*

3. For another Gnostic text that resounds with the laughter of Jesus, cf. the *Gospel of Judas.*

The one you see smiling and laughing above the cross is the living Jesus. The one into whose hands and feet they are driving nails is his fleshly part, the substitute for him. They are putting to shame the one who came into being in the likeness of the living Jesus. Look at him and look at me. (81,15–24)

What makes the crucifixion laughable is the ignorance of the powers who think they can execute the real, living Jesus. The mention made of Simon in the text is reminiscent of the role of Simon of Cyrene in the New Testament (*Matthew* 27:32; *Mark* 15:21; *Luke* 23:26), where it is said that he carries the cross for Jesus, or it may call to mind the observations of Irenaeus (*Against Heresies* 1.24.4) and Epiphanius (*Panarion* 24.3), who claim that according to the Gnostic teacher Basilides, Simon of Cyrene was crucified in place of Jesus. Yet in the *Second Discourse of Great Seth* Simon is never actually crucified, and Jesus says that it is "their man" that the world rulers put to death—the physical body that the heavenly Savior borrowed. Further, the comment by Jesus in the *Second Discourse*, "Though they punished me, I did not die in actuality (*h^{e}n outajro*) but only in appearance (*h^{e}m petouon^{e}h*)" (55,16–19), may recall classic formulations of docetic views of the crucifixion and even the position of the Qur'an, which states in Sura 4 that the opponents of 'Isa—Jesus—did not kill him for sure, but "he was made to resemble another for them" or "they thought they did."[4]

The leaders and members of the emerging orthodox church, Jesus goes on to say, mistakenly focus upon the story of the crucifixion, which they misunderstand, and they establish their theology on it. Like Paul, they claim that baptism is dying with Christ,[5] but Christ himself says, in the present text, that true baptism means people come to be in Christ and Christ in them: "The scripture regarding the ineffable water in use among us is this word: I am in you and you are in me, just as the Father is in me <and in> you, with no guile at all" (49,29–50,1). In the emerging orthodox church, people preach "the doctrine of a dead man" (60,22), and they behave in a legalistic fashion, so that they are in bondage, though some of them use the name of Christ and claim to be proponents of Christ. Actually, they serve two masters, Christ and Yaldabaoth, the world ruler, and even more, probably Yaldabaoth's fellow cosmic bureaucrats. Further, Jesus says, Yaldabaoth is a laughingstock, as are all those folks, from Adam to John the Baptizer, who are Yaldabaoth's lackeys. The so-called Christians are the very people who, along with the ignorant, oppose the members of the perfect assembly or church. In this way the *Second Discourse of Great Seth*, like Valentinian texts, may suggest a threefold division of people into the ignorant (people of flesh), ordinary Christians (people of soul), and the members of the perfect assembly—Gnostics (people of spirit).

According to the *Second Discourse of Great Seth*, Jesus teaches that he has come to his own and has united with them. He says, "Our thought was one with

---

4. Cf. F. E. Peters, "Jesus in Islam," 267–68.
5. Cf. Paul's presentation of baptism as dying with Christ in *Romans* 6:1–14.

their thought, so they understood what I was saying" (59,12–15). In word and peace they have united in the knowledge of Jesus, and Jesus concludes:

> They have come to know fully and completely that the One Who Is is one, and all are one. They have been taught about the One and the assembly and the members of the assembly. For the Father of the All is immeasurable and immutable, mind, word, division, jealousy, fire, yet he is simply one, all in all in a single principle, because all are from a single spirit. (68,10–25)

The *Second Discourse of Great Seth* is to be found in Nag Hammadi Codex VII, tractate 2, immediately after the long *Paraphrase of Shem*.[6] The *Second Discourse of Great Seth* has been translated into Coptic but originally was composed in Greek. The Coptic is difficult to understand and translate, with more than a few beguiling passages, and peculiarities, obscurities, and ambiguities in the content of the document present more challenges for translation and interpretation. Whether the text may be read as a unified whole has been debated among scholars. Nonetheless, it is probably best to assume the essential integrity of the text and to read it as a single literary piece. In spite of the problems that linger in the text, the *Second Discourse of Great Seth* is a document with poetry and power. The text is also difficult to classify, and although the title refers to great Seth and may imply that Christ is the manifestation of Seth, as in Sethian literature, the title may be the most Sethian part of the text. Gregory Riley posits that the *Second Discourse of Great Seth* may have been written in the latter half of the second century, perhaps in Alexandria, and that suggestion may be as good as any.

BIBLIOGRAPHY

Hans-Gebhard Bethge, "Zweiter Logos des grossen Seth"; Louis Painchard, ed., *Le Deuxième Traité du Grand Seth*; Birger A. Pearson, ed., *Nag Hammadi Codex VII*, 129–99 (Gregory Riley); Hans-Martin Schenke, Hans-Gebhard Bethge, and Ursula Ulrike Kaiser, eds., *Nag Hammadi Deutsch*, 2.569–90 (Silvia Pellegrini).

---

6. On the theory that the *Paraphrase of Shem* may function as the "First Discourse of Great Seth," cf. the positions of Jean Doresse and Henri-Charles Puech addressed by Silvia Pellegrini in Hans-Martin Schenke, Hans-Gebhard Bethge, and Ursula Ulrike Kaiser, eds., *Nag Hammadi Deutsch*, 2.571–72. It is interesting to observe that the *Paraphrase of Shem* has its title only at the opening of the text and the *Second Discourse of Great Seth* only at the end. In this regard Pellegrini also mentions the "Paraphrase of Seth" discussed by Hippolytus, in *Refutation of All Heresies* 5.19.1–22.1, and multiple books written under the name of Seth according to Epiphanius, in *Panarion* 39.5.1.

The Second Discourse of
Great Seth[1]

Perfect Majesty, the Mother, and the Savior
(49,10–20)

Perfect[2] Majesty is at rest in ineffable light, in truth, the Mother of all things. Since I[3] alone am perfect, all of you attain to me on account of the word. For I dwell with all the Majesty of the Spirit, who is a friend equally to us and to our kin.

The Word and Baptism (49,20–50,1)

I have uttered a discourse[4] for the glory of our Father, through his goodness and imperishable thought, and this word comes from him. It is a matter fit for slavery to say, We shall die with Christ,[5] which means with imperishable and undefiled thought. What an incomprehensible wonder! The scripture regarding the ineffable water in use among us is this word: I am in you and you are in me, just as the Father is in me <and in> you, [50] with no guile at all.[6]

---

1. Coptic text: NHC VII,2: 49,10–70,12. Editions: *The Facsimile Edition of the Nag Hammadi Codices: Codex VII*, 55–76; Louis Painchaud, *Le Deuxième Traité du Grand Seth*; Birger A. Pearson, ed., *Nag Hammadi Codex VII*, 129–99 (Gregory J. Riley); Hans-Martin Schenke, Hans-Gebhard Bethge, and Ursula Ulrike Kaiser, eds., *Nag Hammadi Deutsch*, 2.569–90 (Silvia Pellegrini). The text is sometimes referred to as the *Second Treatise of the Great Seth* or the *Second Logos of the Great Seth*. Matyas Havrda and Steven Johnson have provided valuable assistance in the completion of the present translation. 2. The presence of the Greek connective particle *de* ("and," "but") after the first word of the text may indicate that this sentence follows additional material that is now lost. 3. Throughout the *Second Discourse of Great Seth* speaker uses the first-person singular ("I"), and the speaker identifies himself as Christ. Thus the text presents itself as the discourse of Christ himself. 4. Or "word," "speech," "message," here, above, and below, including in the title. It is also possible to translate the title "The Second Treatise of the Great Seth." This reference to a discourse previously uttered, however, suggests a spoken discourse, and this reference may indicate the first discourse or speech or message of great Seth, given prior to the present second discourse of great Seth. 5. This is a reference to Paul's understanding of baptism as dying with Christ (cf. *Romans* 6:1–14), an interpretation the present text vigorously rejects in favor of an understanding of baptism as union with Christ who is "imperishable and undefiled thought." See also *Second Discourse of Great Seth* 60. 6. Cf. *John* 17:21–23. The emendation is proposed by Painchaud, *Le Deuxième Traité du Grand Seth*, 24.

The Call for the Salvation of Divine Thoughts (50,1–51,20)

Let's call together an assembly.[7] Let's examine this creation of his[8] and send someone, just as he also examined thoughts[9] in the regions below.[10]

I said this to all the members of the whole vast assembly of the Majesty, so that they rejoiced, and the entire household of the Father of truth rejoiced. Since I am of them, I reminded them of the thoughts that had come from the undefiled Spirit and had descended to the water—that is, to the regions below. A single thought was in all of them, since it came from a single source. They expressed their decision to me, and I concurred and went forth to reveal glory to my kin, my friends in spirit.

Those in the world had been prepared by the will of our sister Sophia,[11] whose indiscretion[12] was without guile. She was not sent out, nor did she request anything from the realm of the All, the Majesty of the assembly, and the Fullness[13] when she first came [51] to prepare homes and habitations for the child of light. From the elements below she derived collaborators to construct bodily dwellings for them, but in their vainglory they fell into ruin. Yet it was in these dwellings that those in the world came to live.[14] And since they were prepared by Sophia, they are ready to receive the saving word of the ineffable One[15] and the Majesty of the assembly of all those who still are in waiting and those who already are in me.

Coming to This World (51,20–52,10)

I approached a bodily dwelling and evicted the previous occupant, and I went in.[16] The whole multitude of archons was upset, and all the material stuff of the rulers and the powers born of earth began to tremble at the sight of the figure with a composite image.[17] I was in it, and I did not look like the previous occupant. He was a [52] worldly person, but I, I am from above the heavens. I did not defy them, and I became an anointed one,[18] but neither did I reveal myself to them in the love coming from me. Rather, I revealed that I am a stranger to the regions below.

Unrest and Confusion in the World (52,10–53,27)

There was a great disturbance, with confusion and restlessness, in the whole world and in the council of the archons.

---

7. The text reads *ekklēsia*, which may also be translated "church," here and below. 8. Probably the creation or realm of the heavenly Father, possibly the creation, here below, of the world ruler. 9. Ennoia, here and below. 10. Or "send someone from him to examine thoughts in the regions below." This is a declaration of the heavenly decision to send someone from the realms above to seek out and save spiritual people ("thoughts") in the world below. 11. Personified Wisdom, here and elsewhere in the text. 12. Coptic, from Greek, *pronikos* (for *prounikos*), a term that can refer to a whore, a disreputable person, or a hired porter. 13. Pleroma. 14. The antecedents of pronouns in this section are vague, and the translation suggests a probable interpretation. 15. Monad. God is called the One several times in the *Second Discourse of Great Seth*. Cf. the divine One in the *Secret Book of John* and other texts. 16. A reference to the incarnation of Christ. 17. The human figure now has a different and alien appearance because of the entry of the heavenly Christ into the earthly body. 18. I.e., a Christ.

Some were convinced when they saw the mighty deeds I accomplished. They are of the generation of Adonaios[19] and are descended from the one who fled from the throne to Sophia of hope, since she had previously given indication about us and all those with me.[20] They all were moving about.

Others hurried to inflict every sort of punishment on me from the world ruler and his accomplices. They were restless of mind about what they would plot against me. They thought their majesty was everything, and they also told lies about the human being[21] and all the Majesty [53] of the assembly. They were incapable of knowing the Father of truth, the human being of Majesty. They usurped the name through corruption and ignorance, <through>[22] a flame of fire and a vessel created for the destruction of Adam, made to conceal all those who likewise are theirs.

The rulers from the realm of Yaldabaoth disclosed the circuit of the angels.[23] This is what humanity was seeking, that they might not know the true human, for Adam the modeled creature appeared to them. So throughout their dwelling place there was agitation and fear that the angels surrounding them might take a stand against them.

For those offering praise I died, though not really, that their archangel might be useless.

The Arrogance of the World Ruler (53,27–55,9)

Then the voice of the world ruler announced to the angels, "I am God, and there is no other beside me."[24] I laughed heartily when I reflected upon how conceited he was. He kept saying, over and over, "Who [54] is the human being?"[25] The whole host of his angels, who had seen Adam and his dwelling place, laughed at its insignificance. Thus their thought turned away from the heavenly Majesty, who is the true human, whose name they perceived in the insignificance of a dwelling place. They are inferior, senseless in their empty thought, in their laughter, and so they were corrupted.

The entire Majesty of the Fatherhood of the Spirit was at rest in his realms, and I was with him, since I have a thought of a single emanation from the eternal and unknowable ones, undefiled and immeasurable. I disturbed and frightened the whole multitude of the angels and their ruler, and I placed a small thought in the world. I examined all with flame and fire through my thought, and all they did they did through me.

---

19. In some texts Adonaios, whose name derives from Adonai (Hebrew for "my Lord") and who is also called Sabaoth, is the son of Yaldabaoth who turns against his father and gives his loyalty to Sophia (cf. *On the Origin of the World* 101–7). Here those of the generation of Adonaios (the people of Adonai) seem to be the Jewish people. Adonaios is also mentioned in the *Holy Book of the Great Invisible Spirit* III, 58; *Secret Book of John* II, 10; and *Book of Baruch* 26.4. **20.** Those through whom Sophia offers insights into the future seem to be Hebrew prophets. **21.** The heavenly human, here and below, is equated with the Father of truth. **22.** The text is emended here to read *et<b>e*, "<through>," rather than *ete*, "which" (for "which (is)"?). Cf. Pellegrini, in *Nag Hammadi Deutsch*, 2.582. **23.** This is the heavenly circuit of the planets in astronomy and astrology. **24.** Cf. *Isaiah* 45:5–6, 21; 46:9. In the *Secret Book of John* and other texts Yaldabaoth makes the same arrogant claim. **25.** Cf. *Psalm* 8:4; *Secret Book of John* II, 14.

There was trouble and strife around the seraphim and the cherubim, whose glory will perish, [55] and commotion around Adonaios, on every side, and around their dwelling place, all the way to the world ruler, who said, "Let us seize him." Others said, "This plan will never work out." For Adonaios knows me, through hope.[26]

In the Mouths of Lions (55,9–56,20)

I was in the mouths of lions.[27] They hatched a plot against me, to counter the destruction of their error and foolishness, but I did not give in to them as they had planned. I was not hurt at all. Though they punished me, I did not die in actuality but only in appearance, that I might not be put to shame by them, as if they are part of me. I freed myself of shame, and I did not become fainthearted because of what they did to me. I would have become bound by fear, but I suffered only in their eyes and their thought, that nothing may ever be claimed about them. The death they think I suffered they suffered in their error and blindness. They nailed their man to their death. Their thoughts did not perceive [56] me, since they were deaf and blind. By doing these things they pronounce judgment against themselves. As for me, they saw me and punished me, but someone else, their father, drank the gall and the vinegar; it was not I. They were striking me with a scourge, but someone else, Simon,[28] bore the cross on his shoulder. Someone else wore the crown of thorns. And I was on high, poking fun at all the excesses of the rulers and the fruit of their error and conceit. I was laughing at their ignorance.[29]

Coming Down Past the Rulers (56,20–57,7)

I brought all their powers into subjection. When I came down, no one saw me, for I kept changing my forms on high, transforming from shape to shape, so when I was at their gates, I assumed their likeness.[30] I passed by them quietly. I saw their realms, but I was not afraid or ashamed, because I was pure. I was speaking with them and mingling with them, through those who are mine. Jealously I trampled on those who [57] are harsh toward them, and I put out the fire. I was doing all this by my will, to complete what I willed in the will of the Father above.

Bringing Up the Child of the Majesty from the Region Below (57,7–58,13)

We brought the child of the Majesty, hidden in the region below, to the height. There I am, in the aeons that no one has seen or understood, where the wedding

---

26. Cf. Sophia of hope, above. 27. Cf. *Psalm* 22:13. Yaldabaoth is often said to resemble a lion in appearance; cf. *Secret Book of John* II, 10. 28. Cf. Simon of Cyrene in *Matthew* 27:32; *Mark* 15:21; *Luke* 23:26. In the present text the body Christ adopted seems to be what is crucified, not Simon of Cyrene. 29. Cf. *Reve-* lation of Peter 81–83; *Round Dance of the Cross* 96; Irenaeus *Against Heresies* 1.24.4 (on Basilides); Qur'an, sura 4. 30. Christ passes through the heavenly gates, guarded by cosmic powers, on his way from the realms above to the world below.

of the wedding robe is. It is the new wedding, not the old, and it does not perish, for the new bridal chamber is of the heavens, and it is perfect.[31]

As I have revealed, there are three ways, and this is an undefiled mystery in the spirit of the eternal realm that is not destroyed or divided or even discussed, for it is indivisible, universal, and permanent.

The soul from on high will not discuss error here or carry herself[32] away from these realms that are here. She will be carried forth when she is liberated and treated nobly in the world, and she stands [58] before the Father with no difficulty or fear, forever communing with the mind of ideal power. These will see me from every side with no animosity, for they see me, and they are seen, mingling with them. They did not put me to shame, and they were not ashamed. They were not afraid in my presence, and they will pass by every gate without fear and be perfected in the third glory.[33]

The Crucifixion Interpreted (58,13–59,19)

The world was not receptive to my visible exaltation, my third immersion in an image that was perceptible.[34] The flame of the seven authorities was extinguished, the sun of the powers of the rulers set, darkness overcame them, and the world became impoverished. They bound this one with many bonds and nailed him to the cross, and they secured him with four bronze nails. He ripped the temple veil with his own hands. An earthquake shook earth's chaos, for the souls of the dead were released and resurrected, and they walked out in the open. They laid aside [59] ignorant jealousy and lack of insight by the dead tombs, and they put on the new person. They had come to know the blessed, perfect one of the eternal, incomprehensible Father and the infinite light. That's what I am.[35]

When I came to my own and united them with me, there was no need for many words. Our thought was one with their thought, so they understood what I was saying. We made plans for the destruction of the rulers, and in this I did the will of the Father. That's what I am.

Opposed and Persecuted in the World (59,19–60,12)

When we left our home and came down to this world and became embodied in the world, we were hated and persecuted both by those who are ignorant[36] and by

---

31. The bridal chamber is referred to in *Gospel of Thomas* 75 and *Dialogue of the Savior* 138, and it is discussed extensively in the *Gospel of Philip*. 32. In Greek the word *psukhē*, "soul," is feminine in gender, and the soul is typically personified as the young female Psyche. 33. The souls of those who are liberated pass through the heavenly gates in their ascent to the realms above. Cf. *Gospel of Mary* 15–17. 34. The three immersions are probably birth, water baptism, and baptism in blood, and the crucifixion is the "third im-

mersion." Cf. Riley, in *Nag Hammadi Codex VII*, 171. 35. This passage provides a Gnostic interpretation of the account of the crucifixion of Jesus in *Matthew* 27. 36. These people are unbelievers, people who are not Christians. They may recall the material people, people of body and flesh, in Valentinian texts, and this description in general resembles the Valentinian threefold designation of people as hylics, psychics, and pneumatics (people of fleshly body, soul, and spirit).

those who claim to be enriched with the name of Christ,[37] though they are vain and ignorant. Like irrational animals they do not know who they are. They hate and persecute those whom I have liberated.[38] If these people would only shut their mouths for once, they would start weeping and groaning in futility, because [60] they have not really known me. Rather, they have served two masters[39]—and even more.[40]

You, however, will be winners in everything, in combat, fights, and schism with jealousy and anger. In the uprightness of our love, we are innocent, pure, and good, and we have the mind of the Father in an ineffable mystery.

The Opponents Are Insignificant and Ignorant
(60,13–62,1)

It was a joke, I tell you, it was a joke. The rulers do not know that all this is an ineffable unity of undefiled truth like what is among the children of light. They have imitated it, and they proclaim the doctrine of a dead man,[41] along with false teachings that mock the freedom and purity of the perfect assembly. In their doctrine they bind themselves to fear and slavery and worldly concerns and improper forms of worship, for they are ignorant and of no significance. They do not accept the nobility of truth. They hate the one to whom they belong, and they love the one to whom they do not belong.

They do not have the [61] knowledge[42] of the Majesty, that it is from above, from the fountain of truth and not from slavery, jealousy, fear, and love of the material world. Boldly and freely they make use of what is not theirs and what is theirs. They do not covet because of their authority and their law that addresses what they desire.[43] And those who are without the law are in dire straits: they do not have it and they still desire. These people mislead folks who through them resemble those who have the truth of their freedom, so as to place us under a yoke and coerce us with anxiety and fear.[44] One person is subjected to bondage; another is controlled by God through threats and violent force.

Noble people of the fatherhood, however, are not controlled, since they control themselves by themselves, without command or force. They belong to the thought of the fatherhood, and they are one with their will, that the fatherhood may be perfect and inexpressible through [62] the living water.

---

37. These people are ordinary believers, who claim to be Christians, in the emerging orthodox church. They may recall the people of soul, or psychics, in Valentinian texts. 38. These people are the Gnostics of the *Second Discourse of Great Seth*, who are opposed and persecuted by people in the emerging orthodox church. They may recall the people of spirit, or pneumatics, in Valentinian texts. 39. Cf. *Matthew* 6:24. Here Christ seems to suggest that ordinary believers actually serve both Christ and Yaldabaoth, the ruler of the world. 40. Probably all the powers of Yaldabaoth. 41. This is the proclamation of Christ crucified, the gospel of the cross, in the emerging orthodox church. See *Second Discourse of Great Seth* 49. 42. Gnosis. 43. The opponents make use of the law, including the Ten Commandments, one of which states, "You shall not covet." On the food laws, cf. *Second Discourse of Great Seth* 64. 44. The law, or Torah, is sometimes referred to as a yoke, comparable to the yoke placed upon an animal to guide it; hence being under the law is said to resemble being under a yoke.

The Perfect People Who Live in Harmony and Friendship
(62,1–27)

Be[45] wise among yourselves, not only in words that are heard but also in deeds, in words that are fulfilled. In this way those who are perfect are worthy to be established and united with me, and they will have no enmity. With good friendship I do everything through the one who is good, for this is the unity of truth, that people should have no adversary. If some cause division, they do not learn wisdom, because they cause division and are not friends. They are enemies. But those who live in the harmony and friendship of love of brother and sister, naturally and not only of necessity, completely and not merely in part, those truly reflect the will of the Father. This is universal and perfect love.

Adam and His Descendants Were a Joke (62,27–64,17)

Adam was a joke.[46] He was created by the ruler of the seventh realm[47] in a phony way, in the shape of a human, as though he had become stronger than I and my siblings.[48] We are blameless toward him, and we have not sinned.

Abraham was a joke, as were Isaac and Jacob, since they were called patriarchs in a phony way by the ruler of the seventh realm, as though [63] he had become stronger than I and my siblings. We are blameless toward him, and we have not sinned.

David was a joke, since his son was named Son of Humanity[49] and was put in power by the ruler of the seventh realm, as though he had become stronger than I and my kin. We are blameless toward him; we have not sinned.

Solomon was a joke, since he became arrogant through the ruler of the seventh realm and thought he was the anointed,[50] as though he had become stronger than I and my siblings. We are blameless toward him; I have not sinned.

The twelve prophets were a joke, since they appeared as imitations of the true prophets. They came in a phony way through the ruler of the seventh realm, as though he had become stronger than I and my siblings. We are blameless toward him, and we have not sinned.

Moses was a joke, called a faithful servant[51] and friend.[52] The testimony about him was wrong, since he never knew me. He did not know me, and none of those before him, from Adam to Moses and John the Baptizer, knew me or [64] my siblings. They had instruction from angels to observe food laws and submit to bitter slavery. They never knew truth and they never will, because their souls are enslaved and they can never find a mind with freedom to know, until they come to

---

45. Here we read *šōpe*; the manuscript has *ešōpe*. Cf. also Pellegrini, in *Nag Hammadi Deutsch*, 2.586. **46.** Adam and the rest of the prominent characters in the Jewish scriptures, along with John the Baptizer, are said to be laughingstocks, because they are understood to be mere servants of the world ruler. **47.** The ruler of the seventh realm, or Hebdomad, is Yaldabaoth the world ruler. **48.** Lit., "my brothers," here and below. **49.** Or "Son of Man," here and below. **50.** Christ. **51.** Cf. *Numbers* 12:7; *Hebrews* 3:5. **52.** Cf. *Isaiah* 41:8; *James* 2:23.

know the Son of Humanity. On account of my Father, I was the one the world did not know, and for this reason it rose up against me and my siblings. But we are blameless toward it; we have not sinned.

The Ruler of the World Is a Joke (64,17–65,2)

The ruler was a joke, for he said, "I am God, and no one is greater than I. I alone am Father and Lord, and there is no other beside me. I am a jealous god, and I bring the sins of the fathers upon the children for three and four generations"[53]—as though he had become stronger than I and my siblings. We are blameless toward him, and we have not sinned. In this way we mastered his doctrine, but he is conceited and does not agree with our Father. So through our friendship we overcame his doctrine, since he is arrogant and conceited and does not agree with our Father. He was a joke, with his [65] judgment and false prophecy.

I Am Christ (65,2–67,27)

O you who cannot see! You do not perceive that on account of your blindness this is[54] one unknown. Neither did those people ever know or understand him. They would not listen to an accurate account of him, and so they practiced their lawless justice and raised their filthy, murderous hands against him as if they were beating the air. Those who are mindless and blind are always mindless, always slaves of law and worldly fear.

I am Christ, Son of Humanity, one from you who is within you. For you I am despised, that you may dismiss what is impermanent. Don't become female, lest you give birth to evil and what is related, jealousy, dissension, anger, wrath, dishonesty, and greed.[55]

To you I am an ineffable mystery. Once, before the foundation of the world, when the whole multitude of the assembly in the realm of the Eight[56] came together [66] and made plans, they united in spiritual marriage.[57] The marriage was consummated in these ineffable places by means of a living word, through the mediator Jesus, who dwells in all of them and rules over them with pure profound love.[58] He transformed himself and appeared as a single manifestation of all of them, as Thought, Father, One. He stands apart from them, for he came forth all by himself.

He is life,
he from the Father of truth,[59]

---

53. Cf. *Isaiah* 44:6; 45:5–6, 21; 46:9; *Exodus* 20:5. Similar claims are made by Yaldabaoth in the *Secret Book of John* and other texts. 54. Here Pellegrini, in *Nag Hammadi Deutsch*, 2.587, emends the text to read "<I> am," so that the pronouns in the succeeding sentences refer to "me" instead of "him." 55. Cf. *Gospel* of *Thomas* 114. 56. The realm of the Eight, or Ogdoad, is the heavenly region of the fixed stars. In the *Second Discourse of Great Seth* the heavenly assembly lives there. 57. On the bridal chamber and spiritual marriage, cf. *Second Discourse of Great Seth* 57. 58. Or "will." 59. Cf. *John* 14:6.

ineffable, perfect,
the Father of those there,
the unity of peace,
friend of the good,
eternal life and spotless joy,
in complete harmony of life and faith,
through eternal life
of fatherhood, motherhood, sisterhood,
and rational wisdom.

These were one with mind
that extends itself,
that will extend itself,
in joyful union.
He is honored [67]
and listens faithfully
to the One.

This is
in fatherhood, motherhood, brotherhood
of the word,
and wisdom.
This is a wedding of truth,
incorruptible rest,
in a spirit of truth,
in every mind,
perfect light
in unnamed mystery.

This does not happen and will not happen among us in any regions and locales where there is dissension and disruption of peace. Rather, this is union, a
feast of love,[60] and all are fulfilled in the One Who Is. This love also is to be found
in the regions under heaven that are joined to the realms above. Those who have
come to know me through salvation and unity, and those who have lived for the
glory of the Father and truth, once were separate, but they have been united with
the One through the living word.

I Am with Those Who Are Friends (67,28–68,25)

I am in the spirit and truth of motherhood, where unity is, and I am with
those who are always friends to each other. They know nothing of enmity and

---

60. Cf. the *agapē* meal, or love feast or eucharist, in
Christian tradition.

wickedness, but they are united [68] by my knowledge[61] in word and peace, which dwells completely with everyone and in everyone. Those who have taken on the likeness of my form will take on the likeness of my word, and they will emerge in the light forever, in mutual friendship and the spirit. They have come to know fully and completely that the One Who Is is one, and all are one. They have been taught about the One and the assembly and the members of the assembly. For the Father of the All is immeasurable and immutable, mind, word, division, jealousy, fire, yet he is simply one, all in all in a single principle, because all are from a single spirit.

Why Did You Not Know the Mystery? (68,25–69,20)

O you who cannot see, why really didn't you know the mystery? The archons around Yaldabaoth were disobedient because of the thought that came down to him from Sophia the sister of thought, and they got together with those who were with them in a conflagration of [69] fiery cloud, which was their jealousy, along with all the others produced by their own creatures. They acted as though they had brought together the noble pleasure of the assembly. Instead they showed their own collective ignorance through a phony image of fire and earth and murderer.[62] They are few, they are uneducated, and they are ignorant. They were bold to do these things, but they did not understand that light associates with light and darkness with darkness, and what is impure associates with what is perishable and what is imperishable with what is pure.

This Is What I Have Given You (69,20–70,12)

This is what I have presented to you. I am Jesus the Christ, Son of Humanity, exalted above the heavens. You who are perfect and undefiled, I have presented this to you on account of the mystery that is undefiled and perfect and ineffable, that you understand that we ordained these things before the foundation of the world, so that when we appear throughout the world, we may present the symbols of incorruption from the spiritual union with [70] knowledge. You do not know this because of the cloud of flesh that overshadows you.

It is I who am the friend of Sophia.[63] From the beginning I have been close to the Father, where the children of truth are, and the Majesty.[64] Rest in me, my friends in spirit, my brothers and sisters, forever.

Second Discourse of Great Seth[65]

---

61. Gnosis. 62. The murderer may be Yaldabaoth or Cain. Cf. Gospel of Philip 61. 63. Or "wisdom." 64. Cf. John 1:18. 65. The concluding title is given entirely in Greek in the manuscript. Great Seth is also referred to by that name in the Holy Book of the Great Invisible Spirit.

THE REVELATION OF PETER

NHC VII,3

Introduced and Translated by Marvin Meyer

The *Revelation of Peter* from Codex VII of the Nag Hammadi library is a Christian Gnostic apocalypse in which the Savior reveals to the apostle Peter the meaning of the crucifixion and the nature of genuine Christianity. The text occupies the majority of fifteen manuscript pages of the codex (70,13–84,14), and a title is copied down in Greek for the text at both the beginning and the end: *apokalupsis petrou,* "Revelation of Peter." The Nag Hammadi *Revelation* (or *Apocalypse*) *of Peter* should not be confused with the *Apocalypse of Peter* that was composed in Greek and is now preserved mainly in Ethiopic translation, nor with later Ethiopic and Arabic versions of the *Apocalypse of Peter*.[1] The earlier Ethiopic *Apocalypse of Peter* contains fiendishly brilliant descriptions of the punishments due to the wicked, in anticipation of Dante's *Inferno*, and it bears no apparent relationship to the present text from the Nag Hammadi library. The Nag Hammadi *Revelation of Peter* follows the text *Second Discourse of Great Seth,* the second tractate of Codex VII, and it shares with the *Second Discourse* similar interests in a laughing Jesus who offers a creative interpretation of his crucifixion and disputes the positions of other Christians in the early church.

The *Revelation of Peter* opens with a scene in the temple at Jerusalem on the night before the crucifixion, only a short time before Peter's denial (72,2–4), and the Savior is said to be seated in the temple and speaking with Peter.[2] Peter is the apostolic protagonist in the text, and the text is ostensibly dictated or written by Peter, since first-person singular pronouns are used to refer to Peter throughout much of the text. Although Peter is portrayed as wrathful and misogynist in the *Gospel of Thomas,* the *Gospel of Mary,* and *Pistis Sophia,*[3] here the role of Peter is essentially very positive, and he is described as a friend of gnosis. In the present

---

1. Cf. Wilhelm Schneemelcher, ed., *New Testament Apocrypha,* 2.620–38 (C. Detlef G. Müller).
2. On the textual difficulties in the opening lines, see the translation and notes. On the question of whether the temple is understood to be the earthly temple or the heavenly temple, see Michel Desjardins, in Birger A. Pearson, ed., *Nag Hammadi Codex VII,* 203.
3. See Marvin Meyer, *The Gospels of Mary.*

text Peter is the sole recipient of the revelation of the Savior, and although he sometimes appears timid and fearful, he comes to an awareness of the insight and knowledge conveyed by the Savior. The Savior announces to Peter, "Through you I have begun a work for the remnant whom I called to knowledge" (71,19–21). Other texts within the Nag Hammadi library and the Berlin Gnostic Codex (*Secret Book of James, Acts of Peter and the Twelve Apostles, Letter of Peter to Philip, Act of Peter*) and a host of documents written from many different early Christian perspectives also try to lay claim to Peter and his apostolic authority. As the *Revelation of Peter* helps to clarify, the tradition of Peter, as with the other apostles, was discussed, interpreted, and fought over by a wide variety of people in the early church — including Christian Gnostics — in the interests of establishing apostolic authority for one group or another. Peter is professed as the rock in the *Gospel of Matthew*, and this profession finds its way onto the dome of St. Peter's Basilica in Rome, yet he is also the apostolic hero of Gnostic tradition in the *Revelation of Peter*.

The teachings of the Savior in the *Revelation of Peter* address the crucifixion of Jesus and disagreements among Christians. Peter receives the revelation in a vision, and only at the very end of the text does he return "to his senses."[4] Peter envisions the threats of priests and people, and after revelatory words from the Savior, Peter sees him seemingly being arrested and crucified. Peter asks, "What do I see, master? Is it really you they are seizing, and are you holding on to me? And who is the one smiling and laughing above the cross? Is it someone else whose feet and hands they are hammering?" (81,7–14). The Savior explains that the one who is above (or beside) the cross, who is smiling and laughing, is "the living Jesus,"[5] and the one actually being crucified is the man of flesh — later called "the man of Elohim, the man of the cross, who is under the law" (82,24–26). The fleshly body of Jesus was crucified, but the living Jesus is an immortal being who does not suffer and die. All in all, this account of the Savior in the *Revelation of Peter* resembles what the Savior also says, a few pages earlier in the codex, in *Second Discourse of Great Seth* 55,30–56,20: during the crucifixion, Christ stands apart, laughing at the ignorance of the world rulers, who are trying in vain to kill the divine Christ but end up crucifying "their man" of flesh.

The Christological perspective of the *Revelation of Peter* leads to a careful set of distinctions between the living Jesus and the fleshly body of Jesus, and only the body of flesh is susceptible to suffering and death. Yet the Christology of the text may be more subtle and nuanced. According to *Revelation of Peter* 82,1–3, the Savior reflects upon the visionary crucifixion scene and the hostile powers who are present, and he observes that "they have put to shame the son of their own glory instead of the one who serves me" — and the one who serves the Savior, who is distinguished from the Savior, is the living Jesus. This statement would suggest that there may well be another more exalted aspect of the Gnostic redeemer be-

---

4. On techniques for seeing and hearing in the vision, cf. *Revelation of Peter* 72,4–73,23.

5. On "the living Jesus," cf. *Gospel of Thomas* Prologue.

yond the living Jesus, namely, the Savior as a transcendent spiritual being. Peter seems to glimpse this aspect of the Savior, and he describes what he sees:

> Then I saw someone about to approach us who looked like the one laughing above the cross, but this one was intertwined with holy spirit, and he was the Savior. And there was an unspeakably bright light surrounding them and a multitude of ineffable and invisible angels praising them. When the one who glorifies was revealed, I myself saw the Savior. (82,3–9)

The Savior confirms for Peter the true identity of his glorious being with an aretalogical self-predication: "I am the spirit of thought filled with radiant light. The one you saw approaching me is our fullness of thought, which unites the perfect light with my holy spirit" (83,8–15). Ultimately, the *Revelation of Peter* proclaims, the Savior is the transcendent spiritual presence manifesting the thought and fullness of the divine.

In the *Revelation of Peter*, as in the *Second Discourse of Great Seth*, the Savior has strong words about some in the Christian church who claim to follow Christ but fall into error. In contrast to "the little ones,"[6] who are the true believers and the authentic Christians, the misguided folks "hold on to the name of a dead man" (74,13–14)—that is, the crucified Christ—just as the opponents in the *Second Discourse of Great Seth* "proclaim the doctrine of a dead man" (60,21–22). They follow "an evil deceiver with complicated doctrines" (74,18–20), conceivably the apostle Paul himself, the champion of the gospel of the cross,[7] and they are led astray into "heresy." That term of derision for the opponents—heresy—is used here in a Christian Gnostic text to characterize the error of other Christians, including,[8] it would seem, those who are in the emerging orthodox church. These other Christians have bishops and deacons, and they appeal to the divine authority that resides in their leaders, but they are all "dry canals" (79,31).[9] These people are dubbed the "sisterhood," as opposed to the "brotherhood" of the little ones, who are a part, though an oppressed part, of the same Christian community. "For a specified time proportionate to their error," the Savior declares, "they will rule over the little ones" (80,8–11). Eventually, however, truth will triumph over error and the little ones will be vindicated. They will rule, and in the end their immortal souls will receive their reward. Hence, the Savior says to Peter:

> You are to present what you have seen to those who are strangers, who are not of this age. For there will be no grace among those who are not

---

6. The phrase "little ones" refers to true believers, and it is particular familiar from another Petrine text, though with a very different message, the *Gospel of Matthew* (e.g., 18:1–14).

7. See Desjardins, in *Nag Hammadi Codex VII*, 212, and the notes to the translation, below.

8. Cf. also the references in the text (with the notes) to those who follow a man and a naked suffering woman, and Hermas.

9. Cf. 2 *Peter* 2:17.

immortal, but only among those chosen because of their immortal nature, which has shown it can receive the one who gives in abundance. (83,15–26)

The *Revelation of Peter* was almost certainly composed in Greek and translated into Coptic. Andreas Werner suggests that the text may have been written around the end of the second century or the beginning of the third, perhaps in Syria or Palestine.[10] The reference within the text to "dry canals," revised from the "dry springs" of 2 *Peter*, seems to suggest an Egyptian setting for the text at some stage of composition, translation, or transmission, and on the basis of this sort of evidence Birger A. Pearson prefers to assign the text to "third-century Egypt, probably Alexandria."[11]

BIBLIOGRAPHY

James Brashler, "The Coptic *Apocalypse of Peter*"; Henriette Havelaar, *The Coptic Apocalypse of Peter*; Birger A. Pearson, "The Apocalypse of Peter and Canonical 2 Peter"; Birger A. Pearson, ed., *Nag Hammadi Codex VII*, 201–47 (Michel Desjardins and James Brashler); Pheme Perkins, *The Gnostic Dialogue*; Hans-Martin Schenke, Hans-Gebhard Bethge, and Ursula Ulrike Kaiser, eds., *Nag Hammadi Deutsch*, 2.591–600 (Henriette Havelaar); Wilhelm Schneemelcher, ed., *New Testament Apocrypha*, 2.700–12 (Andreas Werner); Ulrich Schoenborn, *Diverbium Salutis: Studien zur Interdependenz von literarische Struktur und theologische Intention des gnostischen Dialogs am Beispiel der koptischen 'Apokalypse des Petrus'*; Terence V. Smith, *Petrine Controversies in Early Christianity*.

---

10. Andreas Werner, in Wilhelm Schneemelcher, ed., *New Testament Apocrypha*, 2.702.

11. Birger A. Pearson, *Gnosticism and Christianity in Roman and Coptic Egypt*, 73. Cf. also Henriette Havelaar, in Hans-Martin Schenke, Hans-Gebhard Bethge, and Ursula Ulrike Kaiser, eds., *Nag Hammadi Deutsch*, 2.593.

The Revelation of Peter[1]

Revelation of Peter[2]

The Savior Speaks with Peter in the Temple
(70,13–72,4)

The Savior was sitting in the temple, in the three hundredth <year> since its foundation, <in the month of> the completion of the tenth pillar, and he was at rest in the plentitude of the living, incorruptible Majesty. He said to me,[3] "Peter, blessed are those who belong to the Father, for they are above the heavens. It is he[4] who through me revealed life to people from life. I reminded those built on what is strong[5] that they should listen to my teaching and learn to tell the difference between words of unrighteousness or lawlessness and words of righteousness, which [71] come from the height of every word of the fullness of truth. These people have been enlightened in good pleasure by him whom the principalities sought but did not find, nor was he proclaimed among any of the generations of the prophets; now I[6] have appeared among these people as the Son of Humanity,[7] exalted above the heavens, among a <huge number> of people of the same nature.[8]

"Peter, you are to become perfect in keeping with your name,[9] along with me, the one who has chosen you, for through you I have begun a work for the

---

1. Coptic text: NHC VII,3: 70,13–84,14. Editions: *The Facsimile Edition of the Nag Hammadi Codices: Codex VII*, 76–90; Henriette Havelaar, *The Coptic Apocalypse of Peter*; Birger A. Pearson, ed., *Nag Hammadi Codex VII*, 201–47 (James Brashler and Michel Desjardins); Hans-Martin Schenke, Hans-Gebhard Bethge, and Ursula Ulrike Kaiser, eds., *Nag Hammadi Deutsch*, 2.591–600 (Henriette Havelaar). Also referred to as the *Apocalypse of Peter*, the present text is not to be confused with the Ethiopic or Arabic *Revelations* or *Apocalypses of Peter*. 2. The title is written in Greek both at the beginning and at the end of the text. 3. The opening of the text is difficult to understand, and the numbers are obscure. The sentences may be translated as follows, lit.: "The Savior was sitting in the temple, in the three hundred (or hundredth) of the foundation (or covenant), in the completion (or agreement, convergence) of the tenth pillar, and he was resting on the number of the living, incorruptible Majesty. He said to me . . ." The translation given here follows the interpretation of Andreas Werner, in Wilhelm Schneemelcher, ed., *New Testament Apocrypha*, 2.705. In *Nag Hammadi Codex VII*, 219, Brashler offers a different translation and interpretation: "As the Savior was sitting in the temple, in the inner part of the building at the convergence of the tenth pillar, and as he was at rest above the congregation of the living, incorruptible Majesty, he said to me . . ." 4. The Father. 5. Cf. 1 Peter 2:5. 6. Lit., "he"; the antecedent of the pronoun indicates that this is Jesus speaking about himself. 7. Or "Son of Man." 8. The text has *šbēr ᵉnousia*; cf. *homoousios*, as well as *John* 1:11. 9. Peter means "rock."

remnant whom I called to knowledge.[10] So be strong until the imitator[11] of righteousness < . . . > of the one who first called you.[12] He called you so that you might understand him properly with regard to the distinction between the sinews of his hands and feet and the crowning by those of the middle region over against his radiant body.[13] He will be brought in hope of [72] providing a reward of honor, and tonight he will reprove you three times."[14]

The Priests and the People Threaten Jesus and Peter
(72,4–73,23)

When he said this, I saw the priests and the people running toward us with stones as if they would kill us, and I was afraid we would die.

He said to me, "Peter, I have told you many times that they are blind and have no leader.[15] If you want to know their blindness, put your hands on the eyes of your garment[16] and tell me what you see."

When I did this, I saw nothing, and I said, "No one sees in this way."

Then he told me, "Do it again."

Fear and joy arose in me, for I saw a new light brighter than the light of day,[17] and it came down on the Savior. I told him what I saw.

He said to me again, "Put your hands to your ears and listen to what [73] the priests and the people are saying."

I listened to the priests as they were sitting with the scholars, and the multitude was shouting with a loud voice.

When he heard what I said about this, he said to me, "Use your ears and listen to what they are saying."

I listened again. "They are praising you as you are sitting here."

When I said this, the Savior replied, "I have told you that these people are blind and deaf. Now listen to the things I am telling you in secret and keep them. Do not tell them to the children of this age. For they will denounce you during these ages, since they are ignorant of you, but they will praise you when there is knowledge.[18]

Some First Follow the True Savior, but Then
Turn Away to Worship a Dead Man (73,23–75,7)

"At first many will accept our words, but they will turn away again according to the will of the father of their error, because they have done his will, and the father of error will disclose them in his judgment as servants of the word. Those who

---

10. Cf. *Matthew* 16:17–19. 11. Or "imposter" (*pi-antimimon*, here and below). Cf. *Concept of Our Great Power* 45. 12. On imitators of the true Savior, cf. *Matthew* 24; *Mark* 13; *Luke* 21; *Concept of Our Great Power* 44–45. 13. Or "He called you so that you might understand him properly with regard to the rejection he underwent, and the sinews of his hands and feet, and the crowning by those of the middle region, and his radiant body." 14. A reference to the three times Peter denied Jesus at the time of the arrest of Jesus. 15. Cf. *Matthew* 9:36; 15:14; 23:16–19. 16. This is probably the body as the garment of the soul. 17. The sun. 18. Gnosis.

have [74] associated with people of error will become their prisoners, since they are without perception. But the good person, who is pure and upright, will be handed over to the dealer in death,[19] in the kingdom of those who praise a Christ of a future restored world.[20] And they also praise people who preach this falsehood, people who will come after you.[21] They will hold on to the name of a dead man,[22] thinking that in this way they will become pure, but instead they will become more and more defiled. They will fall into a name of error and into the hand of an evil deceiver with complicated doctrines, and they will be dominated by heresy.[23]

"Some of them will blaspheme the truth and proclaim evil teachings, and they will speak evil against each other. Some of them will give themselves a name, for they stand in the power of the rulers: the name of a man and a naked woman of many forms and many sufferings.[24] And [75] those who say all this will inquire into dreams, and if they claim that a dream came from a demon, which is appropriate for their error, they shall be granted perdition instead of incorruption.

Mortal Souls Are Different from Immortal Souls (75,7–76,23)

"Evil cannot produce good fruit.[25] Everything, wherever it comes from, produces what is like it. Not every soul is of the truth or of immortality. In our opinion, every soul of these present times[26] is assigned to death and is always enslaved, since this soul is created to serve its own desires. These souls are destined for eternal destruction, in which they are and from which they are, for they love the creatures of matter that came into being with them.

"But immortal souls are not like these, Peter. Still, as long as the hour[27] has not yet come, an immortal soul resembles mortal souls. It[28] will not reveal its true nature: it alone is [76] immortal and contemplates immortality, and has faith, and desires to renounce these mortal souls.

"People do not gather figs from thistles or thorns, if they are wise, nor grapes from thornbushes.[29] Something always stays in that state in which it exists. If

---

19. Or "executioner." **20.** The text reads *ᵉnhrai hᵉn ouapokatastasis.* On salvation as the future restoration of all things, cf. *Acts* 3:21 and the eschatology of later authors, e.g., Origen. According to the Gnostic teacher Basilides, all things will be restored at the time of Jesus's return. **21.** Church leaders who come after Peter. **22.** The crucified Christ. On this critique of Christians who proclaim the crucified Christ, cf. the *Second Discourse of Great Seth.* **23.** In Coptic, *hᵉn oumᵉntheresis.* This may be a polemical reference to Paul and his teaching, comparable to what is in the Pseudo-Clementine literature. The teaching of Christ crucified and raised from the dead, as opposed here, is central to Paul. **24.** This may be a reference to Simon Magus and his companion Helena. Simon apparently called himself the great power of God, and he was described as the one who stands. Helena was a prostitute in Tyre who was identified by Simon as the first thought of the divine. She was said to have incarnated and reincarnated as thought or soul in one human body after another— e.g., Helen of Troy—and to have suffered through these various incarnations. Desjardins, in *Nag Hammadi Codex VII,* 212, also suggests that the man and naked suffering woman could be Paul and Thecla. **25.** Cf. *Matthew* 7:18; 12:35; *Luke* 6:43; *Gospel of Thomas* 45; *James* 3:12. **26.** Or "ages," "aeons." **27.** I.e., the final hour in which all is to be resolved. **28.** Or "She," here and below, since the soul commonly is personified as a female in ancient texts. **29.** Cf. *Matthew* 7:16; *Luke* 6:44; *Gospel of Thomas* 45.

something is in a bad state, that becomes destruction and death for the soul. But the soul[30] abides in the eternal one,[31] the source of life and immortality of life[32] that these[33] resemble.[34]

"All that does not really exist will dissolve into nothingness, and those who are deaf and blind associate only with people like them.

Some Church Leaders Lack Knowledge and Lead People Astray (76,23–78,31)

"Others will wander from evil words and mysteries that lead people astray. Some who do not understand the mysteries and speak of what they do not understand will boast that the mystery of truth is theirs alone. In arrogance [77] they will embrace pride and will envy the immortal soul that has been used as down payment. For every authority, principality, and power of the ages[35] wants to be with the immortal souls in the created world, in order that these powers, who do not come from what exists and have forgotten who they are, may be glorified by the immortal souls that do exist. The powers have not been saved or shown the way by them, though they always have wished to become imperishable. For if an immortal soul is empowered by a spirit of thought, at once it is joined[36] by one of those who were led astray.

"Many others, who oppose truth and are messengers of error, will ordain[37] their error and their law against my pure thoughts. Since they see from one perspective only, they think that good and evil come from the same source. They do business in [78] my word.[38] And they will establish harsh fate in which the generation of immortal souls will run in vain, until my return.[39] For the immortal souls will surely remain among them. And I have forgiven the transgressions into which they have fallen through their adversaries, and I have redeemed them from their slavery, to give them freedom.

"Some will create a mere imitation of the remnant in the name of a dead man, who is Hermas,[40] the firstborn of unrighteousness, in order that the little ones[41] may not believe in the light that is. These are the workers who will be cast into the outer darkness,[42] away from the children of light. For they will not enter, nor do they allow those who are going to their destination, for their deliverance, to enter.[43]

---

30. Here the text simply reads "she." 31. Or "For what is produced always comes from its root. If something comes from what is bad, that becomes destruction and death for the soul. But the soul comes from the eternal source . . ." 32. Cf. the tree of life in paradise. 33. Souls, as produce or fruit. 34. Or "that resemble him" (i.e., the eternal one). 35. Or "realms." 36. Or "they are joined." Probably either the immortal soul or the soul and spirit together are in mind. On the other hand, Werner (in Schneemelcher, ed., *New Testa-* *ment Apocrypha*, 2.707) emends the text to read "<the demons>" as the subject of the clause: "then immediately <the demons> of those (already) led astray rush upon them." 37. Or "will lie in ambush with." 38. Cf. *2 Corinthians* 2:17. 39. Parousia. 40. Cf. the writings of Hermas in the *Shepherd of Hermas*. 41. This phrase used to refer to true believers, here and below, is familiar from *Matthew* 10:42; 18:6, 10, 14. 42. Cf. *Matthew* 8:12. 43. Cf. *Matthew* 23:13; *Luke* 11:52; *Gospel of Thomas* 39; 102.

Others, Who Are Martyrs, Bishops, and Deacons, Are Dry Canals (78,31–79,31)

"Still others among them endure suffering and think they will perfect [79] the wisdom of the brotherhood that really exists, the spiritual fellowship with those united in communion, through which the wedding of incorruptibility will be revealed. Instead, what will appear is a mere imitation, the kindred generation of the sisterhood. These people oppress their brothers and say to them, 'Through this fellowship our God has mercy, since salvation comes to us alone through this.'[44] They do not know the punishment of those who rejoice at what was done to the little ones, those who watched when the little ones were taken captive.

"And there are others among those outside our number who call themselves bishops and deacons, as if they have received authority from God, but they bow before the judgment of the leaders.[45] These people are dry canals."[46]

The Little Ones Eventually Will Reign (79,31–81,3)

I[47] said, "I am afraid because of what you have told me. Although [80] there are only a few phonies among us,[48] there are many others who lead astray and subdue multitudes of living ones. And when they speak your name, people will believe them."

The Savior replied, "For a specified time proportionate to their error, they will rule over the little ones. And after the completion of error, the being of immortal understanding, who does not grow old, will become new, and the little ones will rule over their rulers. That being will pull out their error by its root, and put it to shame and expose it for all the liberties it has taken. Peter, such people will never change.

"Come, let's proceed to the fulfillment of the good pleasure of the incorruptible Father. For look, those who will bring judgment on themselves are approaching and will put themselves to shame. They cannot touch me. Peter, you will stand in their midst, but don't be afraid, though you are fainthearted. [81] Their understanding will be gone, for the invisible one has taken a stand against them."

Peter Sees the Crucifixion and the Savior Explains It (81,3–82,3)

When he said this, I saw him apparently being arrested by them. I said, "What do I see, Lord? Is it really you they are seizing, and are you holding on to me? And

---

44. This seems to be the profession that salvation comes only through the church—i.e., the emerging orthodox church. 45. Lit., "the first places" (cf. Matthew 23:6). 46. Cf. 2 Peter 2:17. The modification of the image from dry springs (in 2 Peter) to dry canals (in the Revelation of Peter) may be an accommodation to the Egyptian context. 47. Peter is speaking once again. 48. On this image of the phonies, cf. Second Discourse of Great Seth 62–63; 69.

who is the one smiling and laughing above[49] the cross? Is it someone else whose feet and hands they are hammering?"

The Savior said to me, "The one you see smiling and laughing above the cross is the living Jesus. The one into whose hands and feet they are driving nails is his fleshly part, the substitute for him. They are putting to shame the one who came into being in the likeness of the living Jesus. Look at him and look at me."

When I looked, I said, "Lord, no one sees you. Let's get out of here."

He answered me, "I told you they are blind. Forget about them. Look at how they do not know what they are saying. [82] For they have put to shame the son of their own glory instead of the one who serves me."

The Savior Appears to Peter in a Bright Light (82,3–83,15)

Then I saw someone about to approach us who looked like the one laughing above the cross,[50] but this one was intertwined[51] with holy spirit, and he was the Savior. And there was an unspeakably bright light surrounding them and a multitude of ineffable and invisible angels praising them. When the one who glorifies[52] was revealed, I myself saw him.

He said to me, "Be strong, for these mysteries have been given to you so that you might know clearly[53] that the one they crucified is the firstborn, the abode of demons, the stone vessel in which they live,[54] the man of Elohim, the man of the cross, who is under the law.[55] But the one who is standing near him is the living Savior, who was in him at first and was arrested but was set free. He is standing and observing with pleasure that those who did evil to him are divided among themselves. [83] And he is laughing at their lack of perception, knowing that they were born blind. The one capable of suffering must remain, since the body is the substitute, but what was set free was my bodiless body. I am the spirit of thought filled with radiant light. The one you saw approaching me is our fullness of thought, which unites the perfect light with my holy spirit."

The Savior Tells Peter to Proclaim What Has Been Revealed (83,15–84,14)

"You are to present what you have seen to those who are strangers,[56] who are not of this age.[57] For there will be no grace among those who are not immortal, but

---

49. Or "beside," here and below. 50. Lit., "like him, even (or and [m^e n]) the one laughing above the cross." If m^e n is taken as the conjunction "and," then two beings are mentioned in the comparison with the spiritual Savior, most likely the crucified one and the laughing Jesus. 51. Or "interwoven," as with a garment (Coptic sēh). Brashler, in Nag Hammadi Codex VII, 242–43, prefers to emend the text and read <m>ēh, "filled." 52. Or, with an emendation of the text, "the one who <is> glorified." 53. Or "through revelation." 54. According to the Testament of Solomon, Solomon confined the demons in such vessels. Cf. Testimony of Truth 70; perhaps On the Origin of the World 122. Here these vessels refer to physical bodies, particularly the physical body that was crucified on the cross. 55. Cf. Paul's statements about the cross and the law, e.g., in Galatians. 56. Or "aliens, foreigners" (niallogenēs). Cf. the use of this term elsewhere, particularly in the title Allogenes the Stranger, from NHC XI and in the Book of Allogenes from Codex Tchacos. 57. Or "realm," "aeon."

only among those chosen because of their immortal nature, which has shown it can receive the one who gives in abundance.[58]

"For this reason I have said, Whoever has will be given more, and this person will have in abundance. But whoever does not have—that is, the person of this world,[59] who is completely dead,[60] who derives[61] from the planting of creation and procreation, [84] who thinks he can lay hold of someone else of immortal nature when such a person appears—this will be taken away from that person and added to whatever exists.[62]

"So be courageous and fear nothing. For I shall be with you that none of your enemies may prevail over you. Peace be with you. Be strong."

When the Savior said these things, Peter came to his senses.[63]

Revelation of Peter

---

58. I.e., the spirit. 59. Lit., "this place." 60. Or "who exists entirely as a dead person." 61. Or "is taken." 62. Cf. *Matthew* 13:12; 25:29; *Mark* 4:24–25; *Luke* 8:18; 19:26; *Gospel of Thomas* 41. 63. Lit., "When he said these things, he came to his senses."

THE TEACHINGS OF SILVANUS

NHC VII,4

Introduced and Translated by Birger A. Pearson

The *Teachings of Silvanus* is extant only in the Coptic version found in Nag Hammadi Codex VII, a translation from the original Greek. There is a short Coptic text attributed to St. Antony that corresponds to a section of our tractate (97,9–98,22). That text, preserved on a parchment folio now in the British Museum,[1] is part of a collection of maxims attributed to the great hero of Egyptian monasticism. It is either from a source also used by the author of the *Teachings of Silvanus* (so Wolf-Peter Funk)[2] or an excerpt from the *Teachings of Silvanus*.[3]

The *Teachings of Silvanus* is the only non-Gnostic tractate in Nag Hammadi Codex VII and one of the few non-Gnostic tractates in the corpus as a whole. In form, it is a wisdom writing similar to classical Jewish wisdom compendia such as the biblical book of *Proverbs* or the deuterocanonical *Ecclesiasticus* (*Sirach*). In such literature a teacher offers instructions and admonitions to a pupil whom he refers to as his "son." The tractate also utilizes two other literary genres common in early Hellenistic Judaism, the "diatribe" form, derived from popular Stoic and Cynic philosophy, and the "Hellenistic hymn," in which praises are offered up to God or to personified Wisdom.[4] Pagan examples of the latter are the hymns or aretalogies associated with the cult of the Greco-Egyptian goddess Isis.

Although attempts have been made to understand the tractate as a "unified whole,"[5] it is clearly an agglutinative text that has grown over a considerable period of time. The basic and oldest stratum of material stems from Hellenistic Jewish wisdom and philosophy such as was characteristic of first-century Alexandrian Judaism. The most important exemplars of this variety of Judaism are the *Wisdom*

---

1. British Museum 979; see Wolf-Peter Funk, "Ein doppelt überliefertes Stück spätägyptischer Weisheit."
2. Funk, "Ein doppelt überliefertes Stück spätägyptischer Weisheit,"18–20.
3. Roelof van den Broek, "The Theology of the Teachings of Silvanus," 257.
4. William R. Schoedel, "Jewish Wisdom and the Formation of the Christian Ascetic"; Malcolm L. Peel, in Birger A. Pearson, ed., *Nag Hammadi Codex VII*, 250–54.
5. Jan Zandee, *The Teachings of Sylvanus*, 1.

of Solomon and the writings of Philo Judaeus. Of course, the *Teachings of Sil-vanus* as we now know it is clearly a Christian writing, parts of which may be as early as the first century and other parts as late as the early fourth century.

The tractate consists of two main parts. The first part (84,16–98,20) is devoted largely to moral philosophy and can be regarded as a Jewish compendium of moral teaching influenced by Stoicism and Platonism, to which Christian features have been added. The Christian additions consist largely of crediting Jesus Christ as the source of the teacher's wisdom. The second part (98,20–118,7) is more explicitly theological and reflects the theological and Christological teachings of the Alexandrian teachers Clement and Origen.

The first part of the tractate begins with the teacher exhorting his "son" to rely on his divinely given mind (*nous*) and his reason (*logos*) in the struggle for moral rectitude (84,16–87,4). The pupil is encouraged to attend to his moral education and to pay attention to the teacher's instruction, for it is ultimately Christ who supplies the power for self-mastery (87,4–88,34). The pupil must heed the summons of Wisdom (*sophia*) and reject foolishness (88,35–90,28), so as not to bring trouble to the divine element (*nous*) within him (90,29–92,10).

The next section is an interesting example of Alexandrian Jewish anthropology,[6] teaching that the human being is made up of three essential parts: body, soul, and mind (92,10–93,3). "Know yourself," the teacher says. "Understand that you have come into being from three races (*genos*): from the earth, from the formed (*plasma*), and from the created." The body (*sōma*) is of the earth, the soul (*psukhē*) and body are "formed," and the immaterial mind (*nous*) is that which is created according to the image of God. This teaching is based on Philo of Alexandria's interpretation of the key texts in the Greek version of *Genesis* (the Septuagint) dealing with the creation of Adam: "God formed (*eplasen*) the man from dust of the earth, and breathed into his face the breath of life, and the man became a living soul" (*Genesis* 2:7); "and God created man according to the image of God" (*Genesis* 1:27). The teacher goes on to make the point that his pupil should "live in accordance with the mind" and turn away from "the earth-engendered nature" (93,3–94,19). In what can be taken as a Christian addition, the teacher reminds his pupil of his baptism, when he was "illuminated in mind" (94,19–29).

In what follows, the pupil is warned to beware of the adversary (the devil), whose wiles include "strange kinds of knowledge," "spurious knowledge . . . disguised as mysterious sayings." One should rely on Christ alone (94,29–97,3). In material that is also attributed to St. Antony, it is asserted that a wise person watches his speech (97,3–17) and does not put his trust in human friendship, but trusts in God alone (97,18–98,20). This section has been labeled "the most Egyptian" of all the material in the *Teachings of Silvanus*.[7]

The second main part of the tractate begins with a discussion of Christ as the

---

6. Birger A. Pearson, "Philo, Gnosis, and the New Testament," 179–80.

7. Funk, "Ein doppelt überliefertes Stück spätägyptischer Weisheit," 21.

"true light and the sun of life." God in his own incorporeal being is impossible to know. He can only be known through Christ, "who bears the image of the Father" (98,20–101,13). As for Christ, "even if he was begotten, he is unbegotten," comprehensible in his human nature but "incomprehensible in terms of his actual being (*hupostasis*)"—that is, his divine nature (101,13–102,7). God is ineffable, and speculation as to his being is dangerous (102,7–22). Examine yourself to make sure that you have your mind turned "toward the light of heaven," and walk in the way of Christ (102,23–103,33).

The teacher then goes on to refer to the descent of Christ to "the underworld" (103,34–104,14), here taken as a reference to Christ's incarnation.[8] One should choose "the gift of Christ" and guard oneself from every kind of evil (104,15–106,22). In a hymnic passage Christ is praised as "Wisdom," "Word," "life," "power," "door," "light," "angel," and "good shepherd." One should entrust oneself entirely to him (106,22–107,25) and gladly drink of "the true vine of Christ" (107,26–108,3). One can avoid sin by fearing and pleasing God, for where Christ is, sin is idle (108,3–109,11). One should let Christ into the temple of the soul and thus become truly blessed (109,11–110,14).

In another hymnic passage, Christ is again praised for his descent to the underworld, that is, his incarnation on behalf of humanity, that "humanity might become like God" (110,14–111, 20). The teacher then alludes to the apostle Paul as the epitome of piety and wisdom (111,20–112,8). Christ is praised as the one who, victorious as the first contender, will give the crown to every contender (112,8–29). In another hymnic passage, the teacher praises God, who has glorified his Word (112,27–37). He then launches into a hymn of praise to Christ as "light from the power of God" and "a pure emanation of the glory of the Almighty" (112,37–113,23), a hymn whose first part is a rephrasing of the hymn to Wisdom in the *Wisdom of Solomon* 7:25–26.

Christ is praised for his efforts on behalf of everyone, helping the contender to "fight the great fight" against the powers of the adversary (113,24–114,30). He is praised as the "hand" of God the Father, who "fashions all things," for he exists "always as Son of the Father," the eternal "image of the Father" (114,30–115,35). It is impossible to know God as he is, and one lacking in self-knowledge will not even be able to know Christ or the angels or other incorporeal beings (115,36–117,5). The author concludes his teachings with exhortations to his pupil to open the door to the knowledge of God by "knocking" on himself. He should guard the wisdom of Christ in the knowledge that "God's way is always profitable" (117,5–118,7).

The colophon at the end of the tractate (118,8–9) is written entirely in Greek: "Jesus Christ, Son of God, Savior. Indescribable Wonder!" It is marked off with decorations and indecipherable symbols. It is probably not to be taken as part of the tractate.[9] The exemplar that the scribe of Codex VII used in copying the

---

8. Malcolm L. Peel, "The 'Descensus ad Inferos' in the 'Teachings of Silvanus.'"

9. In spite of the position of Peel, in *Nag Hammadi Codex VII*, 250.

Teachings of Silvanus was probably the last tractate in a codex, followed by the colophon.[10] (Codex VII has its own colophon following the last tractate.)

The *Teachings of Silvanus* reflects considerable influence from Greek philosophy, especially Stoicism and Middle Platonism,[11] and the Bible, both testaments.[12] The author was familiar with the writings of the Jewish philosopher Philo[13] and with those of the Alexandrian Christian writers Clement[14] and Origen.[15] Although one scholar has argued that the tractate is a Gnostic work,[16] it can be shown, on the contrary, that it contains a number of anti-Gnostic polemics. In addition to the texts cited above warning against "strange kinds of knowledge" (*gnōsis*, 94,31–33) and "spurious knowledge" (96,3), the author attacks those who regard the Creator as ignorant (116,5–9), clearly a reference to a Gnostic theology such as one might find in the *Secret Book of John*. Nevertheless, there are certain affinities in the *Teachings of Silvanus* with Gnostic teachings, especially with Valentinian Gnostic thought.[17] So it is not out of the question that our author was familiar with Gnostic writings, such as those of the Alexandrian teacher Valentinus. The ascetic strain that comes through in the tractate from beginning to end can be found in many Gnostic writings and certainly must have appealed to the fourth-century Egyptian monks who treasured this and other tractates in the Nag Hammadi corpus.[18]

Although it has been argued that the title of the tractate could refer to a fourth-century Egyptian teacher named Silvanus,[19] it is more likely that the Silvanus referred to in the title is meant to refer to the co-worker of the apostle Paul (2 *Corinthians* 1:19; 1 *Thessalonians* 1:1; 2 *Thessalonians* 1:1) and Peter (1 *Peter* 5:12). Of course, attribution to the historical Silvanus is impossible, as can be seen from the tractate's content. The title is probably secondary, meant to attribute the tractate to the co-worker of the apostle Paul, who is explicitly named in it (108,30). But who the real author (or final editor) was, no one knows.

There can be no question where this author was active, namely, Alexandria. Although the original Greek version of the *Teachings of Silvanus* as we know it in translation has been dated to the fourth century, after the Council of Nicea in

---

10. Hans-Martin Schenke and Wolf-Peter Funk, in Hans-Martin Schenke, Hans-Gebhard Bethge, and Ursula Ulrike Kaiser, eds., *Nag Hammadi Deutsch*, 2.604.

11. Jan Zandee, "Die Lehren des Silvanus: Stoischer Rationalismus und Christentum im Zeitalter der frühkatholischen Kirche"; "Origène et 'les enseignements de Silvain'"; *Teachings of Sylvanus*, 523–38.

12. Zandee, *Teachings of Sylvanus*, 485–515.

13. Jan Zandee, "'Les Enseignements de Silvanos' et Philon d'Alexandrie"; *Teachings of Sylvanus*, 516–22.

14. Jan Zandee, *"The Teachings of Silvanus" and Clement of Alexandria.*

15. Zandee, "Origène et 'les enseignements de Silvain'"; Malcolm L. Peel, *The Teachings of Silvanus*, 265–67; Van den Broek, "The Theology of the Teachings of Silvanus."

16. Jerry L. Sumney, "The 'Teachings of Silvanus' as a Gnostic Work."

17. Zandee, *Teachings of Sylvanus*, 539–51; Peel, *Teachings of Silvanus*, 267–70.

18. Cf. Peel, *Teachings of Silvanus*, 271.

19. Van den Broek, "The Theology of the Teachings of Silvanus," 257–58.

325,[20] it more likely comes from a time before Nicea.[21] Since the tractate reflects knowledge of the teachings of Origen, it should probably be dated to sometime after his death in 254, sometime in the late third century. What is important to remember, however, is that the tractate contains very early material, including traditions that could even go back to first-century Alexandrian Christianity.[22]

BIBLIOGRAPHY

Régine Charron, *Concordance des textes de Nag Hammadi: Le Codex VII*; Wolf-Peter Funk, "Ein doppelt überliefertes Stück spätägyptischer Weisheit"; Yvonne Janssens, *Les Leçons de Silvanos*; "Les Leçons de Silvanos et le monachisme"; Birger A. Pearson, "Christians and Jews in First-Century Alexandria"; "Philo, Gnosis, and the New Testament"; Birger A. Pearson, ed., *Nag Hammadi Codex VII, 249–369* (Malcolm L. Peel and Jan Zandee); Malcolm L. Peel, "The 'Descensus ad Inferos' in the 'Teachings of Silvanus'"; Hans-Martin Schenke, Hans-Gebhard Bethge, and Ursula Ulrike Kaiser, eds., *Nag Hammadi Deutsch*, 2.601–32 (Hans-Martin Schenke and Wolf-Peter Funk); William R. Schoedel, "Jewish Wisdom and the Formation of the Christian Ascetic"; "'Topological' Theology and Some Monistic Tendencies in Gnosticism"; Jerry L. Sumney, "The 'Teachings of Silvanus' as a Gnostic Work"; Roelof van den Broek, "Juden und Christen in Alexandrien im 2. und 3. Jahrhundert"; "The Teachings of Silvanus and the Greek Gnomic Tradition"; "The Theology of the Teachings of Silvanus"; Jan Zandee, "'Les Enseignements de Silvain' et le Platonisme"; "'Les Enseignements de Silvanos' et Philon d'Alexandrie"; "'Die Lehren des Silvanus' als Teil der Schriften von Nag Hammadi und der Gnostizismus"; "Die Lehren des Silvanus: Stoischer Rationalismus und Christentum im Zeitalter der frühkatholischen Kirche"; "Origène et 'les enseignements de Silvain'"; *The Teachings of Silvanus*; "The Teachings of Silvanus" and Clement of Alexandria.*

---

20. Van den Broek, "The Theology of the Teachings of Silvanus."
21. Peel, *Teachings of Silvanus*, 272–74.
22. Birger A. Pearson, "Christians and Jews in First-Century Alexandria," 95–99.

The Teachings of Silvanus[1]

The Teachings of Silvanus[2]

Let Your Mind Be Your Guide (84,15–85,29)

Put an end to every kind of immature conduct. Acquire for yourself[3] strength of mind and soul, and strengthen your struggle against every kind of foolishness consisting of the passions of erotic love,[4] base wickedness, love of praise, fondness for strife, tiresome jealousy, wrath, anger, and avaricious desire.

> Guard your[5] encampment with weapons and spears. Arm yourself
> with all the soldiers, which are words,
> with the commanders, which are counsels,
> and with your [85] mind as a guiding principle.[6]

My child, throw every robber out of your gates. Guard all your gates with torches, which are the words,[7] and by these means you will acquire a tranquil life.

But the person who will not guard these things will become like a captured city, desolate and trampled by wild animals. For thoughts that are not good are evil beasts. Your city will be filled with robbers, and you will not obtain peace, only all kinds of savage beasts. The evil one,[8] who is a tyrant, is lord over them.[9]

---

1. Coptic text: NHC VII,4: 84,15–118,7; 118,8–9 (colophon). Editions: *The Facsimile Edition of the Nag Hammadi Codices: Codex VII*, 90–124; Régine Charron, *Concordance des textes de Nag Hammadi: Le Codex VII*; Yvonne Janssens, *Les Leçons de Silvanos*; Birger A. Pearson, ed., *Nag Hammadi Codex VII*, 249–369 (Malcolm Peel and Jan Zandee); Hans-Martin Schenke, Hans-Gebhard Bethge, and Ursula Ulrike Kaiser, eds., *Nag Hammadi Deutsch*, 2.601–24 (Hans-Martin Schenke and Wolf-Peter Funk); Jan Zandee, *The Teachings of Sylvanus*. The present translation has also, at some points, adopted suggestions made by Roelof van den Broek. 2. The superscript title is set off by decorations. The fictitious author is presumably meant to be the co-worker of Paul (2 *Corinthians* 1:19; 1 *Thessalonians* 1:1; 2 *Thessaloni-*

ans 1:1) and Peter (1 *Peter* 5:12). 3. The fictitious recipient of Silvanus's teaching, here addressed in the second-person singular, is often addressed as "my son," as is typical of classical Jewish wisdom literature; cf., e.g., *Proverbs* 1:8; *Sirach* 2:1. "My son" is here translated throughout as "my child." 4. Greek *erōs*. 5. The plural is used here. The only other use of the second-person plural in the text is at *Teachings of Silvanus* 89. 6. Greek *hēgemonikon*, a term derived from Stoic philosophy. 7. Presumably Silvanus's words of instruction. 8. Greek *phaulos*, here a reference to the devil; cf. *Teachings of Silvanus* 88. The term *phaulos* is used by Philo of the wicked person who builds a city for a tyrant (*Confusion of Tongues* 83). Cf. Zandee, *Teachings of Silvanus*, 95. 9. The beasts, understood as evil thoughts and impulses.

While he is directing this he dwells beneath the great mud.[10] The whole city, which is your soul, will suffer destruction.

Remove yourself from all these things, O wretched soul. Bring in your guide and your teacher. The mind is the guide, and reason is the teacher. They will bring you out of the dangers of destruction.[11]

Be a Human Being, Not an Animal (85,29–86,13)

Listen, my child, to my advice. Don't show your back [to] your enemies and run away. Instead, go after them as a [strong person]. [86] Don't be an animal, with men pursuing you; instead, be a human being, with you pursuing the evil beasts, lest somehow they prevail over you and trample you like a corpse and you perish through their wickedness. O you poor man, what will you do if you fall into their hands? Watch yourself, that you not be given over to your enemies.

Your Mind and Reason Will Protect You (86,13–87,4)

Entrust yourself to this pair of friends, reason and mind, and no one will prevail over you. May God dwell in your camp, may his Spirit protect your gates, and may the divine Mind[12] protect the walls. Let holy reason become a torch in your mind, burning the wood which is all sin.

If you do these things, O my child, you will prevail over all your enemies, and they will not be able to wage war against you. They will neither be able to stand firm, nor be able to get in your way. For if you encounter these, you will despise them as mere gnats.[13] They will speak to you with [cajolery] and entreaties, not because they are [afraid] [87] of you, but because they are afraid of those who dwell within you, the guardians of the divine teaching.[14]

Attend to Your Education (87,4–88,34)

My child, accept for yourself the education and the teaching. Do not flee from the education and the teaching, but when you are taught accept it joyfully. And when you are educated in any subject, do what is good. You will weave a crown of education by your guiding principle.[15] Put on the holy teaching like a robe. Make yourself noble by your good conduct. Gain for yourself the austerity of good discipline. Judge yourself like a wise judge. Do not stray from my teaching and develop ignorance, lest you lead your people astray. Do not flee from the divine and

---

10. Or "mire" (*borboros*), a term drawn from Greek religion depicting a region of the underworld. 11. Lit., "the destruction and the dangers." The pronouns in this paragraph are feminine, referring to the soul (*psukhē*). 12. The "divine Mind" (*nous*) here is probably a reference to Christ. Cf. *Teachings of Silvanus* 112 and the note. 13. Here following Janssens, taking *calme* as a new form of *šalmes*, "gnat." Peel takes the word as a new construct form of *cal + me*, and translates "deniers of truth." 14. Lit., "of the divinity and the teaching." The "guardians" are reason (*logos*) and mind (*nous*). 15. Cf. *Teachings of Silvanus* 85 and the note.

the teaching within you, for your teacher loves you very much and will leave you a worthy austerity.

Throw out the animal nature that is within you, and don't give access to bad thought. For it is a beautiful thing for you to attain maturity by knowing the way I am teaching you. If it is good to rule over the [few],[16] as you see it, [how] much better it is for you to [88] rule over everyone, since you are exalted above every congregation and every people and prominent in every respect with divine reason. You have become master over every power that kills the soul.

My child, does anyone want to be a slave? Why, then, do you trouble yourself for the wrong reason?[17] My child, do not fear anyone except God alone, the exalted one. Cast away from you the deceitfulness of the devil. Accept the light for your eyes, and cast the darkness from you. Live in Christ, and you will obtain treasure in heaven. Don't become a bag stuffed with many useless things, and don't become a guide for your blind ignorance.

My child, listen to my good and useful teaching, and bring an end to the sleep that weighs heavily upon you. Come away from the forgetfulness that fills you with darkness. For if you were powerless to do anything, I would not have said these things to you.

But Christ came to give you this gift. Why do you pursue the darkness when the light is at your disposal? Why do you drink brackish water when sweet water is available to you?

Wisdom Summons You (88,35–89,26)

Wisdom[18] summons [you], [89] yet you desire folly. It is not by your own wish that you do these things, but it is the animal nature within you that does them. Wisdom summons you in her goodness, saying, "Come to me, all of you foolish ones, that you may receive as a gift the understanding that is good and excellent. I am giving you a high-priestly vestment that is woven from every kind of wisdom."

What else is evil darkness except familiarity with forgetfulness? Cast your anxiety upon God alone.[19] Do not become a lover of gold and silver, which have no profit in them. But clothe yourself with wisdom like a robe, put knowledge on yourself like a crown, and be seated upon a throne of perception. These are yours, and you will receive them again on high at another time.

The Foolish Person's Folly (89,26–90,28)

For a foolish person puts on folly like a robe, and like a garment of sorrow he puts on shame. He crowns himself with ignorance, and seats himself on a throne of

---

16. The text reads *nho[lig]on*. Janssens, and Schenke and Funk read *nho[rat]on*, "the visible things." 17. Lit., "evilly" (*kakōs*) or "wrongly." 18. Here Wisdom (Sophia) is personified and contrasted with folly.

Cf. *Proverbs* 14. 19. *Psalm* 54 (55):23; cf. 1 *Peter* 5:7. Here and below, references to *Psalms* are given according to the chapter numbers of the Septuagint, with the chapter numbers of the Hebrew Bible in parentheses.

[incomprehension]. Since he is [irrational], [90] he leads only himself astray, for he is guided by ignorance, and he follows the ways of every passionate desire.[20]

He swims in life's desires—and has already sunk to the depths—thinking that he finds profit in doing things that are of no profit. The poor wretch who goes through all these things will die because he does not have the mind as a helmsman. But he is like a ship tossed to and fro by the wind, and like a loose horse that has no rider.[21] For this person needed the rider, which is reason. The poor wretch went astray because he didn't want advice. He was tossed to and fro by three evils: he got for himself death as a father, ignorance as a mother, and evil counsels he got as friends and brothers. O fool, you ought to weep for yourself.

Return to Your Divine Nature (90,29–92,10)

From now on, then, my child, return to your divine nature. Cast from [yourself] these evil, deceiving friends. [Take for] yourself Christ, the true friend, [91] as a good teacher. Cast death from yourself, which had become a father to you. For death did not exist at first, nor will it exist in the end. But since you cast from yourself God, the holy Father, the true life, the spring of life, you have consequently inherited death as your father, and ignorance you have gotten as your mother. They have robbed you of the true knowledge.

My child, return to your first father, God, and Wisdom, your mother, from whom[22] you came into being from the beginning. Return, that you might fight against all of your enemies, the powers of the adversary.[23]

My child, listen to my advice. Do not be arrogant, opposing every good opinion, but take for your <teacher>[24] of divinity the Word.[25] Keep the holy commandments of Jesus Christ, and you will reign over every place on earth, and be honored by the angels and archangels. Then you will acquire them as friends and fellow servants, and you will get for yourself places in [heaven above]. [92]

Do not bring grief and trouble to the divine[26] [which is] within you. But when you foster it, request of it that you remain pure, and become self-controlled in your soul and body. Then you will become a throne of wisdom and a member of God's household. He will give you a great light through it.[27]

Know Yourself (92,10–94,29)

But before everything else, know yourself,[28] that is, from what substance you are, or from what race,[29] or from what species. Understand that you have come into

---

20. Lit., "the desire of every passion." 21. These traditional images derive from Plato *Phaedrus* 246b; 247c. 22. Wisdom (Sophia), as is clear in the Coptic text. 23. The devil or Satan. The word translated "adversary" (*antikeimenos*) is used for Satan in other early Christian texts; see, e.g., 1 Timothy 5:14–15; 1 Clement 51:1. 24. Accepting Funk's emendation, *sa<h>*, "teacher." The text reads *sa*, "side." 25. Or "reason," as Peel renders it (*logos*). Here the Word is taken to refer to Christ, reflecting the "Logos Christology" of the Gospel of John (1:1–18). Cf. *Teachings of Silvanus* 106. 26. The mind (*nous*). 27. Wisdom. 28. The ancient Delphic maxim, here interpreted in terms of a traditional Hellenistic-Jewish anthropology probably going back to Philo of Alexandria. 29. Or "class," "genus" (*genos*).

being from three races: from the earth, from the formed,[30] and from the created.[31] The body came into being from the earth with an earthly substance, but the formed, for the sake of the soul, came into being from the thought of the divine. The created, however, is the mind that came into being according to the image of God. The divine mind has substance from the divine, but the soul is that which he formed within them. For I think it exists as wife of what came into being according to the image.[32] But as for the body that came into being from the earth, its substance is matter.[33] [If] you mix yourself, you will get for [yourself] the [93] three parts as you fall from heavenly virtue into earthly inferiority.

Live in accordance with the mind. Don't think about the things of the flesh. Get strength for yourself, because the mind is strong. If you fall from this other,[34] you have become a female male. And if you cast out of yourself the substance of the mind, which is thought,[35] you have cut off the male part and turned yourself to the female part alone. You have become psychical,[36] since you have received the substance of the formed. When you cast out this last part, so as not to get a human part—you have thus taken for yourself the animal thought and likeness—you have become fleshly by taking on an animal nature.

It is difficult to find a psychical person; how much more so to find the Lord! I say that God is the spiritual one.[37] Human beings have[38] taken shape from the substance of God. The divine soul shares partly in him. Moreover the soul shares partly in the flesh. The base soul tends to turn from one side to the other.

How would it seem to truth? [It is good] for you, O man, [94] to turn yourself toward the human rather than the animal nature, I mean the fleshly nature. You will take on the likeness of the part toward which you turn yourself.

I'll tell you something else: Once again, in what will you take pleasure?

Did you[39] wish to become animal when you came into this kind of nature?[40] Wouldn't you rather take part in a true nature of life? Animality will guide you[41] into the earthly race, but the intellectual[42] nature will guide you to intelligible forms. Turn toward the intellectual nature, and cast from yourself the earth-engendered nature.

O obstinate soul, be sober and shake off your drunkenness, which is the work of ignorance. If you are obstinate and live in the body, you dwell in a boorish condition. When you entered into a bodily birth, you were begotten. <When you were born again,>[43] you came to be inside the bridal chamber,[44] and you were illuminated in mind.

---

30. *Plasma*, reflecting the verb *eplasen* in *Genesis* 2:7. 31. Cf. *Genesis* 1:27. 32. The soul (*psukhē*, feminine) is "wife" of the mind (*nous*, masculine). 33. Greek *hulē*, a common term in Middle Platonic philosophy. 34. Heavenly virtue (*aretē*). 35. I.e., "thought" (*noēsis*) is the "substance" (*ousia*) of the mind (*nous*). 36. *Psukhikos*, from *psukhē*, "soul," here taken to be the "substance" of "the formed" (*plasma*). An exegesis of *Genesis* 2:7 is in the background here. 37. *Pneumatikos*. Cf. the contrast Paul makes between the "spiritual" and the "psychical" or "unspiritual" in 1 Co-

rinthians 2:14–16. The "spiritual," for Paul, are those who have the Spirit of God. 38. Lit., "man has." 39. Feminine. Here the soul is being addressed. Cf. *Teachings of Silvanus* 94. 40. A reference to the soul's descent into corporeality. 41. Masculine. Here Silvanus's "son" is being addressed. 42. The text has *noeros*, related to Greek *nous*, "mind," "intellect." Its next occurrence here is translated as "intelligible." 43. Here following Schenke and Funk. The reference is to Christian baptism. 44. The text reads *nymphōn*; cf. *Exegesis on the Soul* 132. The bridegroom is Christ.

Beware of the Adversary (94,29–97,3)

My child, do not swim in just any kind of water, and do not allow yourself to be defiled by strange kinds of knowledge.[45] Don't you know that [95] the schemes of the adversary[46] are not few, and that he has a variety of tricks? They have especially robbed the <foolish> person[47] of the proverbial snake's shrewdness.[48] For it is right for you to be in agreement with these two,[49] with the snake's shrewdness and the dove's innocence. Otherwise, he[50] will come to you in the guise of a flatterer and true friend, saying, "I advise good things for you." But if you received him as a true friend, you did not recognize this one's deceitfulness.

For he casts into our heart evil thoughts disguised as good ones, hypocrisy as secure shrewdness, avarice as conservative frugality, love of glory as what is beautiful, boastfulness and pride as great austerity, and godlessness as [great] godliness. [96] For the one who says, "I have many gods," is godless.[51] And he[52] casts spurious knowledge[53] into your heart disguised as mysterious sayings.

Who will be able to comprehend his thoughts and various devices? For those who wish to accept him as king he is a "great mind." My child, how will you be able to comprehend this one's schemes or his soul-killing counsel? For his devices and the schemes of his wickedness are many. And how will you be able to perceive his ways of entry, that is, how he will enter your soul? And how will you be able to perceive in what garment he will enter you?

Accept Christ, who is able to set you free. He has taken on that one's devices, so that through these he might destroy him with guile! For this is the king you have, who is forever invincible. Against him no one will be able to fight or speak a word. This is your king and your father. There is none like him. The divine teacher is with [you at] [97] all times as a helper. He meets you because of the good you have within you.[54]

Watch Your Speech (97,3–17)

Do not put a malicious word in your disposition. For every malicious person harms only himself. Only a foolish person walks toward his own destruction,[55] but a wise person knows his way. A foolish person does not keep from telling a secret. A wise person, on the other hand, does not blurt out every word, but scrutinizes those who hear. Don't utter every word in the presence of those you don't know.

---

45. Gnosis. This is a warning against Gnostic heresies. Cf. 1 Timothy 6:20. 46. Cf. Teachings of Silvanus 91 and the note. 47. Adopting the emendation offered by Schenke and Funk: p<a>noētos. The text reads pnoētos, "the intelligent person." 48. Matthew 10:16. 49. Text: {h^en tm^entr^em^enhēt} ^empesnau, "{with the shrewdness} of these two," correcting a scribal error, as suggested by Schenke and Funk. 50. The adversary.

51. Cf. Sentences of Sextus 599: "A person with many gods is godless." Cf. also the Gospel of Thomas 30 (Greek version). 52. The adversary. 53. Cf. Teachings of Silvanus 94 and the note. 54. Probably a reference to the divine mind within. 55. What follows here is a passage that has a parallel in teachings attributed to St. Antony.

Do Not Trust Anyone as a Friend
(97,18–98,8)

Have a good number of friends, but not many counselors. First, examine your counselor, and don't honor[56] anyone who flatters. Their[57] speech is sweet as honey, but their hearts are full of poison.[58] For whenever they think they have become a reliable friend, then they will deceitfully turn against you and throw you down into the mud.

Do not trust anyone as a friend. For the whole world has become deceitful, and every [person] is troubled [in vain].[59] All things [of] [98] the world are without profit; they happen in vain.[60] There is no real <friend>,[61] not even a brother, since each person seeks his own advantage. My child, do not have anyone as a friend. If you acquire one, do not entrust yourself to him.

Entrust Yourself to God Alone (98,8–20)

Entrust yourself to God alone, both as father and as friend. For everyone goes about in deceit. The whole earth is full of suffering and pain, things in which there is no profit. If you wish to lead your life in tranquility, do not keep company with anyone. Even if you do keep company with them, be as if you do not. Be pleasing to God, and you will not need anyone.

Christ Is the True Light (98,20–99,15)

Live with Christ, and he will save you.[62] For he is the true light and the sun of life. Just as the visible sun shines on physical eyes,[63] so Christ illuminates every mind and heart. For if one who is wicked during his lifetime[64] has an evil death, how much more so does one who has a blind mind. For every blind person [remains incapable] of seeing it.[65] [So it is] [99] with people who do not have a sound mind. They[66] do not delight in acquiring the light of Christ, which is reason.[67]

For everything visible is a copy of what is invisible. As a fire burns in a place without being confined to it, so it is with the sun in the sky: all of its rays extend to places on earth. It is a single being[68] that Christ has, and he gives light to every place.

---

56. The text from "don't honor" to "into the mud" (lines 21–30) is missing from the Antony parallel. 57. The flatterers'. 58. Lit., "helebore" (*helleboron*), a poisonous herb, a variety of which was given to the insane in antiquity. 59. Cf. *Ecclesiastes* 1:12ff. 60. This sentence is lacking in the Antony parallel. 61. The Coptic manuscript lacks "friend" (here given as "real friend"), but it is found in the Antony parallel.

62. The Antony parallel ends here. 63. Lit., "the eyes of the flesh." 64. Lit., "a wicked man in the body." 65. The sun. Restorations of lacunae in this passage are those suggested by Wolf-Peter Funk and incorporated in the work of Schenke and Funk. 66. Lit., "the one (masculine) who does not . . . he." 67. The reason (*logos*) in the human mind (*nous*) is the connecting link to Christ the Logos. 68. Or "hypostasis."

Is the Mind in a Place? (99,15–28)

This is also the way he speaks about our mind, using the image of a lamp burning and lighting up the whole place.[69] <Existing> only in a part of the soul, it still gives light to all the parts of the body.

In addition, I will say something more important. The mind, in terms of its actual being, is in a place, which means it is in the body. But in terms of the thought process, the mind is not in a place. For how can it be in a place when it contemplates every place?

God Is Incorporeal and in No Place (99,29–100,13)

But we are able to say something still more important than this. Do not think in yourself that God is [in a] place. If you localize the [Lord of] all [100] in a place, then you could say that the place is more exalted than the one who dwells in it. For what contains is superior to what is contained.

For there is no place that can be called incorporeal. It is not right for us to say that God is corporeal. The consequence would be that we attribute both <increase> and decrease to the body, and also that one who is subject to these will not remain imperishable.

Knowledge of God Comes Through Knowledge of Christ (100,13–31)

Now, the creator of all creatures is not difficult to know, but it is impossible to comprehend what he is like. For it is not only difficult for human beings to comprehend God, but it is also difficult for every divine nature, the angels and the archangels. For it is necessary to know God in the way he is.[70] You cannot know God through any means except through Christ, who bears the image of the Father. For this image reveals the true likeness of God in a visible way. A king is usually not known apart from an image.[71]

God Is Everywhere and Nowhere (100,31–101,13)

Consider these things about God: He is in every place; on the other hand, he is in [no] place. [In terms of power], [101] he is in every place, but in terms of divinity, he is in no place. So, then, it is possible to know God a little. In terms of his power, he fills every place, but in his exalted divinity nothing contains him.

---

69. Cf. *Matthew* 6:22, where Jesus speaks of the eye as "the lamp of the body." Here the eye is interpreted as the mind; in Platonic thought the mind is the "eye of the soul" (cf. *Republic* 7.533b). **70.** I.e., in the way he is knowable. Later on the author makes it clear that no one can know God "as he is." See *Teachings of Silvanus* 116 and the note. **71.** I.e., a sculpture or painted portrait, such as those of a Roman emperor.

Everything is in God, but God is not in anything. What is it to know God? Everything that partakes of the truth is God.

Christ Is the Light of the Father (101,13–102,7)

But it is as impossible to look at Christ as it is to look at the sun.[72] God sees everyone; no one looks at him. Christ receives and gives ungrudgingly. He is the light of the Father. Thus, he sheds light on every place. Christ is All, who has inherited everything from the One Who Is.[73] For the All is Christ, apart from his incorruptibility.

When you consider sin, it is not anything real.[74]

The apprehension of imperishability is the apprehension of Christ. He is the light shining undefiled. For the sun shines on every impure place, yet it is not defiled.

So it is with Christ. Even if he is in deficiency, yet he is without deficiency. Even if [he was begotten] [102] he is unbegotten. So it is with Christ: if, on the one hand, he is comprehensible, on the other, he is incomprehensible in terms of his actual being.[75] Christ is the All. Whoever does not possess the All cannot know Christ.

God Is Ineffable (102,7–22)

My child, do not dare to speak a word about this One, and do not confine the God of all to mental images. For will the one who condemns not be judged by the One who condemns?[76] It is good to ask and to know who God is. "Reason" and "mind"[77] are masculine nouns. Let the person who wishes to know about this One ask quietly and reverently. For there is no small danger in speaking about these things, since you know that you will be judged on the basis of everything you say.

The Light Comes from Above (102,23–103,11)

Understand by this that the one who is in darkness will not be able to see anything without receiving the light, by which means he can see. Examine yourself, to see whether you really have the light, so that if you ask about these things, you may understand how you will escape. For many are seeking in darkness, and they grope about wishing to understand, since there is no light for them.

---

72. Christ has already been compared to the sun; see *Teachings of Silvanus* 98. 73. Cf. *Exodus* 3:14 (Septuagint). 74. Lit., "being" (*ousia*). This sentence seems out of place, for the premise is left undeveloped. 75. Or "hypostasis." Cf. *Teachings of Silvanus* 99 and the note. 76. *Matthew* 7:12. The translation here reflects a suggestion made by Roelof van den Broek (*Studies in Gnosticism and Alexandrian Christianity*, 264–65). 77. *Logos* and *nous*, in contrast to sense perception (*aisthēsis*, a feminine noun). Cf. the warning above (*Teachings of Silvanus* 93) against casting out the "substance of the mind" and turning oneself only to the female part. It is only through reason and mind that one can know who God is.

My [103] child, do not let your mind stare downward, but rather let it look with the light at things above. For light always comes from above. Even if it[78] is located on earth, let it seek to pursue the things above. Illuminate your mind with heavenly light, so that you may turn toward the light of heaven.

Walk in the Way of Christ (103,11–33)

Do not tire of knocking on the door of the Word, and do not cease walking in the way of Christ. Walk in it that you may receive rest from your labors. If you walk in another way, the way you take is of no profit. For those who walk in the broad way[79] will in the end go down to muddy perdition.[80] For the underworld[81] is wide open to the soul, and the place of perdition is broad. Accept Christ, the narrow way. For he is oppressed and bears affliction for your sin.

O obstinate soul,[82] in what ignorance you exist! For who is your guide into the darkness? How many likenesses did Christ take on because of you!

Christ's Saving Work (103,34–104,14)

Although he was divine, he [was found] [104] among humans as a human.[83]

He descended to the underworld.[84] He released the children of death. They were suffering birth pangs, as the scripture of God has said,[85] and he sealed the heart within it.[86] He completely broke its[87] strong bows.[88] And when all the powers had seen him they fled, so that he might bring you, poor wretch, up from the abyss and die for you as a ransom for your sin.[89] He saved you from the strong hand of the underworld.

Choose the Gift of Christ (104,15–24)

But as for you, give him utterly and completely your assent by taking decisive action,[90] that he may take you up with joy. That assent is the gift of Christ, which is humility of heart. The acceptable sacrifice is a contrite heart.[91] If you humble yourself, you will be greatly exalted; and if you exalt yourself, you will be exceedingly humbled.[92]

---

78. The mind. 79. *Matthew* 7:13–14. 80. Lit., "the perdition of the mud." Cf. *Teachings of Silvanus* 85 and the note. 81. Coptic em^ente. Amente is the underworld of Egyptian religion. 82. Cf. *Teachings of Silvanus* 94. Here, as in the earlier passage, the soul is addressed, and the second-person pronouns are feminine. 83. Cf. *Philippians* 2:6–7. 84. Cf. 1 *Peter* 3:19; 4:6. The traditional Egyptian term is used here, as above. The "underworld" here refers to this world, as pointed out by Malcolm Peel, "The 'Descensus ad Infernos' in the 'Teachings of Silvanus.'" 85. The reference may be to *Psalm* 17 (18):5. 86. This obscure sentence may imply, with its reference to "sealing" (*sphragizein*), that Christ administered baptism to the denizens of the underworld. 87. The underworld's. Or perhaps "his"—i.e., Death's. 88. Cf. *Psalm* 45 (46):9. 89. Cf. *Mark* 10:45. 90. Lit., "by means of a footstep." 91. *Psalm* 50 (51):17. 92. Cf. *Matthew* 23:12.

Guard Yourself Against Evil (104,24–106,22)

My child, guard yourself against evil, and do not let the spirit of evil[93] throw you down into the abyss. For he is mad and bitter. He is terrifying, and throws everyone he can into a pit of mud.[94]

It is a very good thing not to love fornication, and not even to think of that wretched subject at all, [105] for to think of it is death. It is not a good thing for any person to fall into death. For a soul that is dead[95] will be without reason. It is better not to live at all than to acquire an animal's life. Watch yourself, so that you are not burned by the fires of fornication.[96] Many shooters of the arrow[97] are slaves to it.[98] These whom you don't know are your enemies.

O my child, strip off the old garment of fornication, and put on the clean and shining garment. In it you are beautiful. When you have this garment, protect it well. Release yourself from every bond, that you may acquire freedom for yourself. If you cast away from yourself desire, with its many devices, and release yourself from sins of pleasure, < . . . >.[99]

Listen, O soul,[100] to my advice. Do not become a nest of foxes and snakes, or a hole for lizards[101] and asps, or a lair for lions, or a shelter for vipers. When these things happen to you, O soul, what will you do? For these are the powers [106] of the adversary.[102] Through them everything dead will gain entrance to you. For their food is everything dead and everything impure. When these are within you, what living thing will come into you? The living angels will detest you. You were a temple, but you made yourself a tomb. Stop being a tomb, and become a temple again, that uprightness and divinity may remain in you. Light the light within you, and don't put it out. For no one lights a lamp for wild animals or their young.

Raise your dead who have died. For they were once living, and they died on your[103] account. Give them life, and they will live again. For the tree of life[104] is Christ.

Christ Is the Wisdom of God (106,22–107,25)

He is Wisdom.[105]
He is Wisdom and also the Word.[106]
He is the life,[107] the power,[108] and the door.[109]
He is the light,[110] the angel,[111] and the good shepherd.[112]

Entrust yourself to this one who became all for your sake. Knock on your inner self as upon a door, and walk within yourself as on a straight road. For if you walk

---

93. The devil. 94. Cf. *Teachings of Silvanus* 85 and the note. 95. Lit., "that has been found in death." Spiritual death is meant here. 96. Cf. *1 Corinthians* 7:9. 97. Taking *refjalᵉk sote* as a combination of agential *ref* + *jōlᵉk*, "bend (a bow)" and *sote*, "arrow," with Janssens, and Schenke and Funk. Peel sees here a combination of *jōlᵉk*, "be submerged," and *sate*, "fire," and translates "who are submerged in fire." 98. Fornication. 99. The conclusion to the sentence is missing. One would expect, "you will . . ." 100. The second-person pronouns in this paragraph are feminine. 101. "Dragons" (*drakōn*). 102. Cf. *Teachings of Silvanus* 91 and the note. 103. The pronoun is masculine, indicating that this paragraph is no longer addressing the soul. 104. *Genesis* 2:9. 105. *1 Corinthians* 1:1–18. 106. *John* 1:1–18. 107. *John* 14:6. 108. *1 Corinthians* 1:24. 109. *John* 10:7, 9. 110. *John* 3:19–21. 111. Justin *1 Apology* 63.4–5. 112. *John* 10:11.

on the road, you won't be able to go astray. [107] And if you knock on this one,[113] you knock on hidden treasures.

Since he[114] is Wisdom, he makes the foolish person wise. She[115] is a holy kingdom and a shining robe. Having much gold, she gives you great honor.

The Wisdom of God became for your sake a foolish form, that she[116] might pick you up, O foolish one, and make you wise.

And the life died for you when he was powerless, so that through his death he might give life to you who once were dead.

Entrust yourself to the Word, and remove yourself from animality. It is clear what an animal is: one who lacks reason. For many think they have reason, but if you take a good look at them, their speech is animality.

Drink of the True Vine (107,26–108,3)

Give yourself gladness from the true vine of Christ.[117] Satisfy yourself with the true wine in which there is neither drunkenness nor dregs. The true wine entails the end of drinking, since it can give joy to the soul and mind through the Spirit of God. [108] But first, before you drink of it, nurture your reasoning powers.

Avoid Sin (108,3–17)

Do not stab yourself with the sword of sin.[118] Do not burn yourself, O wretched one, with the fire of pleasure. Do not surrender yourself to barbarians like a prisoner, or to savage beasts that want to trample you. For they are like lions roaring very loudly. Don't be a corpse, or they will trample you. Since you are human, it is possible for you through reasoning to conquer them.

The Rational Person Fears God (108,17–109,4)

The person who does nothing worthy <of God is> not the rational person.[119] The rational person is the one who fears God. The one who fears God does nothing insolent. The one who keeps himself from doing anything insolent is someone who keeps his guiding principle.[120] This person, though existing on earth as a human being, makes himself like God.[121] The one who makes himself like God is someone who does nothing <un>worthy of God. According to the statement of Paul this person is one who has become like Christ.[122]

Who can worship God without wanting to do things that are pleasing to God? For worship of God is something that comes [109] from the heart, and worship of God from the heart characterizes every soul that is near to God.

---

113. Feminine, referring to Wisdom. 114. Christ. 115. Wisdom. 116. The reference is to Christ as Wisdom (feminine). 117. John 15:1. 118. Sirach 21:3. 119. Following the emendation offered by Van den Broek (*Studies in Gnosticism and Alexandrian Christianity*, 271). The uncorrected text reads, "the person who does nothing is not worthy . . ." 120. Cf. *Teachings of Silvanus* 85 and the note. 121. Assimilation to the divine is a traditional goal in Platonism; see Plato *Theaetetus* 176ab. 122. Or, with Peel, "according to the statement of Paul who has become like Christ." Cf. 1 *Corinthians* 11:1.

Where Christ Is, Sin Is Idle (109,4–11)

The soul that is a member of God's household is one that is kept pure, and the soul that has put on Christ[123] is one that is pure, and it is impossible for it to sin.[124] Where Christ is, sin is idle.

Let Christ Enter Your World (109,11–110,14)

Let Christ alone enter your world, and let him bring to nothing all powers that have come upon you. Let him enter the temple that is within you, that he might throw out all the merchants.[125] Let him dwell in your inner temple, and you become for him a priest and a Levite entering in purity.

Blessed are you, O soul, if you find this one[126] in your temple. Blessed are you still more if you perform his service.

But whoever defiles God's temple God will destroy.[127] For you are revealed for what you are, O man, if you throw this one[128] out of your temple. For whenever the enemies do not see Christ in you, then they will come into you armed in order to crush you.

O my child, I have given you orders about these things many times, [110] so that you would always guard your soul. It is not you who will throw him out, but he will throw you out. For if you flee from him, you will fall into great sin. Again, if you flee from him, you will become food for your enemies. All who are worthless run away from their masters, and the person who is worthless in terms of virtue and wisdom runs away from Christ. Everyone who is separated from him falls into the paws of the wild beasts.

Know Who Christ Is (110,14–111,20)

Know who Christ is, and acquire him as a friend, for he is the true friend. He is also God and teacher. He, being divine, became human for your sake.

He is the one who broke the underworld's[129] iron bars and bronze bolts.
He is the one who attacked and threw down every arrogant tyrant,
the one who loosened the bonds with <which he> was being held,[130]
and brought up the poor from the abyss and the mourners from the underworld,
the one who humbled the arrogant powers,
the one who, through humility, put arrogance to shame,
the one who, through weakness, threw down the strong and the boaster,[131]

---

123. *Romans* 13:14. 124. 1 *John* 3:3, 6. 125. Cf. *Matthew* 21:12. 126. Christ. 127. 1 *Corinthians* 3:17. 128. Christ. 129. Coptic *am^ente*. Amente is the underworld of Egyptian religion. 130. Accepting the emendation offered by Schenke and Funk, *ene<u>amahte ^emmo<f>*. The text reads *enefamahte ^emmoou*, "of which he had taken hold." 131. Cf. *Luke* 1:51–52.

the one who, through his shame, scorned what [111] is thought to be
  honorable,
that humility for God's sake might be highly exalted,
the one who put on humanity and is God, the divine Word,
the one who always bears patiently with humanity,
and wished to instill humility in the exalted one.

The one who has exalted humanity became like <humanity>,[132] not that he might bring God down to humanity but that humanity might become like God.[133] O this great goodness of God!

O Christ, king who have revealed to humans the great divinity,
  king of every virtue and king of life,
  king of the ages and Great One of the heavens,
  Hear my words and forgive me!

Where Is Wisdom? (111,20–112,8)

Furthermore, he[134] manifested a great zeal for piety: "Where is a wise person or one powerful in intelligence, or a person whose wanderings are many because he knows wisdom? Let him speak wisdom; let him utter great boasting! For everyone has become foolish."[135]

He[136] spoke of his own knowledge when he said, "He[137] confounded the counsels of guileful people, and caught those wise in their own understanding. Who will be able to discover the counsel of the Almighty, or describe divinity, or express it correctly?"[138] [112]

If we have not been able to understand the counsel of our companions, who will be able to comprehend divinity or the heavenly divinities? If we scarcely find things on earth, who will search for heavenly things?

Everything Has Been Made New (112,8–27)

A great power and a great glory[139] has been revealed to the world. And the life of heaven wishes to make everything new, that he may cast out what is weak and every black garment,[140] and everyone shine with great brilliance in heavenly garments, to make manifest the command of the Father. And, that he might crown

---

132. Accepting the emendation offered by Van den Broek (*Studies in Gnosticism and Alexandrian Christianity*, 254). The text reads "God." 133. Cf. *Teachings of Silvanus* 108 and the note. 134. A reference to Paul, as noted by Schenke and Funk. Paul has already been cited by name (*Teachings of Silvanus* 108). Several paraphrases of and allusions to 1 Corinthians follow. The abrupt change of subject suggests that there is something missing here. 135. 1 *Corinthians* 1:20–25. 136. Paul. 137. Christ. 138. 1 *Corinthians* 3:19; 2:16. 139. Christ. 140. Lit., "form" or "shape" (*skhēma*). The word came to be used of ecclesiastical or monastic clothing ("habit") in the church, and such usage may be reflected here. On the association of "black garments" with vices, cf. *Shepherd of Hermas, Similitudes* 9.15.3.

those wishing to contend well,[141] Christ is the judge of the contest and the one who has given each one the crown. He teaches everyone to contend—he who, as the first contender, received the crown, gained the victory, and appeared, giving light to everyone. Everything has been made new through the Holy Spirit and the Mind.[142]

Who Can Glorify God Adequately? (112,27–37)

O Lord Almighty, how much praise shall I give you?
No one has been able to glorify God adequately.
It is you who have glorified your Word[143] in order to save everyone,
    O merciful God!
It is he who has come forth from your mouth,
the firstborn,[144] Wisdom,[145]
the prototype, the first light.

Hymn to Christ[146] (112,37–113,23)

For he is light from [113] the power of God,
and he is a <pure> emanation of the glory of the Almighty.[147]
He is the spotless mirror of the activity of God,
and he is the image of his goodness.

For he is also the light of light forever.
He is the eye that looks at the invisible Father.
He is always serving and creating by the Father's will,
he who alone was begotten by the Father's good pleasure.

For he is an incomprehensible Word,
and he is Wisdom and life.
All living things and powers he vivifies and nourishes;
just as the soul gives life to all the members of the body.
He rules over all with power, and gives life to them.
For he is the beginning and the end of everyone.[148]
He watches over all and encompasses them.

---

141. Cf. 1 Corinthians 9:14–15. 142. A title of Christ (nous); cf. Epistle to Diognetus 9.6. 143. Cf. John 8:54. 144. Colossians 1:15; Hebrews 1:6. This is an attribute of personified Wisdom; cf. Sirach 1:4. 145. Cf. Teachings of Silvanus 106 and the note. 146. The first part of this hymn is a reworking of a hymn to personi-fied Wisdom (Sophia); cf. Wisdom of Solomon 7:25–26. 147. The text reads, "an emanation of the pure glory of the Almighty." The emended placement of "pure" is based on Wisdom of Solomon 7:25 (so Schenke and Funk). 148. Revelation 22:13.

Christ Takes Pains on Behalf of Everyone (113,24–31)

He takes pains on behalf of everyone, and he rejoices and also mourns. He mourns for those who have gotten the place of punishment as their lot. On the other hand, he takes pains on behalf of everyone whom he arduously brings to instruction. And he rejoices over everyone who lives in purity.

Fight the Good Fight (113,31–114,30)

So take care that you not fall into the hands of the robbers. Do not give sleep to your eyes or slumber to your eyelids, that you may be saved like a gazelle from snares, and like a [114] bird from a trap.[149]

Fight the great fight as long as the contest lasts, while all the powers are staring at you, not only the holy ones, but also all the powers of the adversary. Woe to you if you are vanquished in the presence of everyone watching you! If you fight the fight and gain the victory over the powers that fight against you, you will bring great joy to everyone who is holy, and you will bring great grief to your enemies. The judge of your contest[150] is entirely helpful, since he wants you to prevail.

Listen, my child, and do not be slow of hearing.[151] Soar aloft like an eagle, when you have left your old self[152] behind. Fear God in all your acts, and glorify him through good work. You know that every person who is not pleasing to God is the child of perdition, and will go down to the abyss of the underworld.

O this patience of God, which bears with everyone, which desires that everyone who has become subject to sin be saved!

God's Hand in Creation (114,30–115,10)

But no one prevents him[153] from doing what he wants. For who is stronger than he, that he might prevent him? To be sure, it is he who touches the earth, causing it to quake, and causing the mountains to give off smoke.[154]

He it is who gathered the waters of such a great sea [115] as in a wineskin,[155] and weighed all the water in the palm of his hand.[156]

Only the hand of the Lord has created all these things.[157]

This hand of the Father is Christ, and it fashions all things. Through it,[158] everything has come into being, since it became the mother of everything. It is he alone,[159] existing always as Son of the Father.

---

149. *Proverbs* 6:4–5. 150. Christ; cf. *Teachings of Silvanus* 112. 151. Lit., "delay with your ears." 152. Lit., "old man"; cf. *Romans* 6:6. 153. God. 154. *Psalm* 103 (104):32. 155. *Psalm* 32 (33):7. 156. Cf. *Isaiah* 40:12. 157. Cf. *Isaiah* 48:13. 158. The hand (feminine)—i.e., Christ. 159. Christ.

Christ the Divine Son (115,10–23)

Consider these things about God: the Almighty who always exists was not always reigning as king without also needing the divine Son.[160] Everything subsists in God, that is, the things that came into being through the Word,[161] who is the Son as the image of the Father. For God is near at hand, and not far off.[162] Where is his limit? Divine entities[163] are all related to God.

God's Gift to the Human Race (115,23–35)

Therefore, if this divine[164] agrees with you in anything, even partially, know that the entire divine agrees with you. But this divine is not content with anything evil. For it is this which teaches everyone about what is good. This is what God has given to the human race, so that for this reason every human might be superior to all the angels and the archangels.

God Is Both Hidden and Revealed (115,36–117,5)

God does not need to test anyone. [116] He knows all things even before they happen, and he knows the hidden things of the heart. They are all revealed and found wanting in his presence. Let no one ever say that God is ignorant, for it is not right to attribute ignorance to the creator[165] of every creature. For even things that are in darkness are before him like light.

So there is nothing hidden except God alone. But he is revealed to everyone, yet very hidden. He is revealed because God knows everything. Even if people do not wish to say it, they will be corrected by their hearts. He is hidden because no one perceives the things of God. For he is incomprehensible and unfathomable when it comes to knowing God's counsel.

Further, it is difficult to search him out,[166] difficult even to find Christ.[167] For he[168] it is who dwells in every place and in no place. For no one who wants to can know God as he is,[169] not even Christ or the Spirit, or the chorus of angels, or the

---

160. This sentence is not completely clear, but it gives expression to the coeternality of the Son with the Father, a doctrine first taught by Origen (*On First Principles* 1.2.2, 4). **161.** *John* 1:1–3. **162.** Cf. *Acts* 17:27–28. **163.** "Divine" (*theios*) here presumably refers to human minds. Cf. especially the "divine mind" (*nous theios*) that is part of the human constitution (*Teachings of Silvanus* 92). **164.** The mind; cf. the previous note. **165.** Or "demiurge" (*dēmiourgos*), a term used by some Gnostics for the ignorant creator. For other examples of anti-Gnostic sentiment, see *Teachings of Silvanus* 94; 96 and the notes. The term *dēmiourgos* is used positively of God here, probably reflecting the influence of Philo of Alexandria (e.g., *On the Creation* 36); it is derived from Plato (*Timaeus* 29a). **166.** Or "find his traces," Coptic *ᵉnᵉnratᵉf*, which is here taken to be equivalent to Greek *exikhniasai* (from *exikhniazein*). Cf. *Romans* 11:33: God's ways are "inscrutable" (*anexikhniastoi*). **167.** This clause may be a secondary gloss. **168.** God. **169.** Cf. Philo's distinction between knowing God "as he is," which is impossible, and knowing "that he is" (see, e.g., *On Rewards and Punishments* 44). The former knowledge is denied here even to Christ (so Van den Broek, *Studies in Gnosticism and Alexandrian Christianity*, 195–96). Cf. *Teachings of Silvanus* 100. Alternatively, one can take Christ, the Spirit, and the others as object of the knowing (so Peel, Janssens, and Schenke and Funk).

archangels [117], together with the thrones of the spirits, and exalted lordships, and the "great mind."[170] If you do not know yourself,[171] you will not be able to know any of these.

Concluding Exhortations (117,5–118,7)

Open the door for yourself, that you may know the One Who Is. Knock on yourself, that the Word may open to you. For he is the door[172] of faith and the sharp sword. He became all for everyone, because he wishes to have mercy on everyone.

My child, prepare yourself to escape from the world rulers of darkness and the air of the sort that is full of powers.[173] If you have Christ, you will prevail over this whole world.[174] What you open for yourself, you will open. What you knock upon for yourself, you will knock upon, with benefit to yourself. Help yourself, my child, by not proceeding with things in which there is no profit.

My child, first purify yourself for the outward life, that you may be able to purify the inward.

Don't be a merchant of the word of God.[175]

Put all words to the test before you utter them.

Don't wish to acquire honors that are insecure or [118] the boastfulness that brings you to ruin.

Accept for yourself the wisdom of Christ, who is patient and mild, and guard this, O my child, knowing that God's way is always profitable.

Colophon (118,8–9)[176]

Jesus Christ, Son of God, Savior.[177]
Indescribable Wonder!

---

170. Possibly a reference to the adversary (Satan), who was earlier referred to as "a great mind." See *Teachings of Silvanus* 96. 171. Cf. *Teachings of Silvanus* 92 and note 27. 172. Coptic *p^erro*, "the ruler," as translated by Peel. Following Schenke and Funk, the word is here taken as a variant of *pro*, "the door." 173. *Ephesians* 6:12. 174. 1 *John* 5:4–5. 175. 2 *Corinthians* 2:17. 176. The colophon, entirely in Greek, is accompanied by decorations and indecipherable symbols. It may have occurred at the end of the codex with which the scribe was working when he was copying the *Teachings of Silvanus*, which then would have been the last tractate in that codex. Codex VII has its own colophon at the end (127,28–32). 177. IKHTHUS, "fish," a common early Christian Greek acrostic, I(*ēsous*) KH(*ristos*) TH(*eou*) (H)U(*ios*) S(*ōtēr*). Cf. also *Holy Book of the Great Invisible Spirit* III, 69.

THE THREE STELES OF SETH

NHC VII,5

Introduced and Translated by John D. Turner

I n the *Three Steles of Seth*, which shows no traces of Christian influence, the
traditional two steles, or tablets of stone and brick, on which Seth was said to
have preserved from destruction by flood or fire the vast sum of astrological lore
revealed to him (cf. Josephus *Jewish Antiquities* 1.67.1–71.5) have now become
three steles recording three doxological hymns. The hymns are addressed by Seth
to, in ascending order, his own father, Pigeradamas (the heavenly Adam), and the
three members of the Sethian trinity, the Self-Generated Son, the divine mother
Barbelo, and the preexistent Father. These hymns of praise, anciently preserved
for the elect "living and unshakable generation" and supposedly discovered by
Dositheos, the reputed founder of Samaritan Gnostic religion, constitute a virtual Sethian hymnal. After Seth's initial praise of his father Pigeradamas (as in the
Secret Book of John, Zostrianos, and *Melchizedek,* the "senior [heavenly, arche-
typal] Adam," *ho geraios Adamas,* Hebrew *Adam qadmōn*) and the divine Self-
Generated One (regarded as Pigeradamas's parent) in the first-person singular,
the doxologies directed to Barbelo and the supreme preexistent One are cast in
the first-person plural, as if to be used during a communal ritual of celestial ascent practiced by a community considering themselves to be Seth's descendants.
The hymns of the first stele, addressed to Pigeradamas, the Self-Generated One,
and the male virginal Barbelo (addressed as masculine), are used as a prelude to
the ascent through the Aeon of Barbelo in the second stele, where she is addressed in the feminine—except in 122,6–13—as a threefold divine Intellect. The
hymn of the third stele is used in the salvific ascent to the preexistent paternal
nonbeing, addressed in the masculine. Once this spiritual acme is achieved, the
worshipers enter into a silent act of praise tantamount to cognitive assimilation to
the supreme Father, after which they descend through the three levels in reverse
order. One is led to suppose that a mystagogue may have spoken these prayers in
the presence of a group of contemplative practitioners, as a way of articulating
the stages of mental abstraction and contemplation they undergo.

After an initial revelation and various macarisms rendered by Seth (118,5–
120,28), who praises the bisexual Pigeradamas as a "Mirotheid" (i.e., begotten of

his mother Mirothea as in the *Holy Book of the Great Invisible Spirit* and *Zostrianos*) and as Mirotheos (perhaps "divine anointed one"), the rest of the treatise uses the first-person plural for ascribing praise to (1) the Self-Generated (also called Mirotheos), originator of "another race," (2) the Triple-Male Barbelo (addressed also as Kalyptos and Protophanes), emanated from the Triple-Powered One and characterized by being, living, and knowing, and (3) the supreme preexistent One, who is characterized as a triad of existence, life, and mind, which in *Zostrianos* comprise the three powers of the Invisible Spirit, and in *Allogenes the Stranger* and *Marsanes* comprise the three powers of an independent being called the Triple-Powered One. The whole concludes with a rubric (126,32–127,22) that explains the use of the steles in the practice of descent from the third to the second to the first; likewise, the way of ascent is the way of descent.

The *Three Steles of Seth* represents a somewhat simplified version of the same ontological doctrine and ascensional technique found in *Zostrianos* and *Allogenes the Stranger*. It specifically exhibits two main transcendent levels in addition to the sensible cosmos: that of the supreme and absolutely singular preexistent One or truly living Spirit (clearly the same as the supreme Invisible Spirit in most Sethian treatises), altogether beyond determinate being, and that of its product, which has become "numerable" in a threefold way, the Aeon of Barbelo as generator of subsequent multiplicity. Although there is no mention of a distinct being such as the Triple-Powered One, Barbelo is clearly said to have originated in "triple-powered" fashion (120,19–22) and is explicitly called a "triple power . . . from an undivided Triple-[Powered] One" (121,29–33; 123,23–24), implying that in the *Three Steles of Seth*, the Triple-Powered One does not appear as a distinct entity, but is in fact Barbelo's prefigurative self before, during, and after her emergence from her source, the supreme preexistent Spirit.

The *Three Steles of Seth* (122,1–14) reflects a doctrine of the emanation of the Aeon of Barbelo similar to that in *Zostrianos* and *Allogenes the Stranger*. Barbelo is addressed as the "first shadow of the holy Father, light from light," originating as a shadow of him: "You are Kalyptos." Like *Zostrianos*, *Melchizedek*, and the *Secret Book of John* (but unlike *Allogenes* and *Marsanes*), *Three Steles* preserves the name of Seth's father, the heavenly Adam, Pigeradamas. At the point where the *Three Steles of Seth* shifts from Seth as the speaker to the "we" of the Sethian community, the "Triple-Male" Barbelo is blessed as the unifier and completer of the All and Savior of the perfect individuals (120,34–121,16; cf. *Allogenes* 58,13–15). He is the giver of crowns, which in *Zostrianos* (57,12–58,16) are given by Gamaliel and Gabriel and described by Youel as bearing seals that are the three kinds belonging to Kalyptos, Protophanes, and the Self-Generated. This suggests that the author of the *Three Steles of Seth* may have used the term "Triple-Male," originally an epithet of Barbelo, to designate that phase of Barbelo that has gone forth into (or from) the middle, namely, the Self-Generated.

As one might expect in a set of doxological hymns to be employed in a communal praxis of visionary ascent, the process of the Barbelo Aeon's emanation from the One is not specifically narrated, although it is clearly called a monadic "shadow" (a projected image) from the One that has become triple (122,1–12) and that supplies all subsequent reality with Substantiality, Vitality, and Mentality as well as Being, Life, and Mind (122,19–34; 123,18–26). Although the names Kalyptos, Protophanes, and the Self-Generated One occur in this treatise, the Self-Generated One is not specifically treated as a member of the Aeon of Barbelo, who forms the central object of praise in the second of the three steles, but is a distinct object of praise near the end of the first stele in his capacity as the Mirotheos, immediate parent of Seth's Mirotheid father Pigeradamas. On the other hand, Protophanes and Kalyptos are specifically mentioned as contained in the Aeon of Barbelo: you (Barbelo) "have become Protophanes, a great first-appearing male mind" (123,4–5); "You are Kalyptos, a Hidden One; you are a world of knowledge" (122,14–15). Ontological realms below that of the Aeon of Barbelo are not specifically denominated, although it appears that both Seth and his parent Pigeradamas are considered to be heavenly beings, while his descendants or seed, for whom Dositheos recites the three steles inscribed by Seth, presumably still inhabit the sensible cosmos.

The position of the *Three Steles of Seth* relative to the other three Platonizing Sethian treatises is more indeterminate, since the title does not seem to be echoed in any ancient testimonia, perhaps because it was an in-house liturgical text. If anything, it is closer in terminology and spirit to *Allogenes the Stranger*, yet, like *Zostrianos*, it seems to preserve more of the basic Sethian dramatis personae than does *Allogenes*, such as Pigeradamas and Emmacha Seth. Like *Allogenes*, the complete absence of baptismal motifs seems to represent a phase of Sethianism in which the ascensional rite has become detached from the older baptismal mystery in favor of a practice of contemplative ascent. It contains little of the profusion of aeonic beings evident in *Zostrianos*; it lacks the Triple-Male Child, Youel, and Ephesech triad that tends to disrupt the otherwise strictly triadic structure (Kalyptos, Protophanes, the Self-Generated One) of the Barbelo Aeon. Many of the beings produced in the course of the theogony of the *Holy Book of the Great Invisible Spirit* (upon which *Zostrianos* builds its aeonic structure) are never mentioned in the *Three Steles of Seth*, which reflects the ascensional praxis of *Zostrianos* and *Allogenes*, but without the transcendental baptismal schemata that one finds in *Zostrianos*. Of all four treatises, its portrayal of the emergence of Barbelo from the Invisible Spirit is extremely close to Moderatus's account of the emergence of Quantity within his second "One" (late first century; cf. Simplicius *Commentary on Aristotle's Physics* 230.34–231.26). On the whole, the *Three Steles of Seth* is probably contemporary with *Zostrianos* and *Allogenes* but earlier than *Marsanes* and the Bruce Codex, even though it seems to preserve a simpler and perhaps earlier version of the basic structure and function of the Barbelo Aeon than do the other Platonizing Sethian treatises.

BIBLIOGRAPHY

Paul Claude, "Approche de la structure des Trois Stèles de Seth"; *Les Trois Stèles de Seth*; Bentley Layton, *The Gnostic Scriptures*, 152–58; Birger A. Pearson, ed., *Nag Hammadi Codex VII*, 386–421 (James E. Goehring and James M. Robinson); James M. Robinson, "The Three Steles of Seth and the Gnostics of Plotinus"; Hans-Martin Schenke, Hans-Gebhard Bethge, and Ursula Ulrike Kaiser, eds., *Nag Hammadi Deutsch*, 2.625–632 (Hans-Martin Schenke); John D. Turner, *Sethian Gnosticism and the Platonic Tradition*.

The Three Steles of Seth[1]

Dositheos's Witness to the Three Steles of Seth (118,10–24)

Dositheos's revelation of the three steles[2] of Seth, father of the living and unshakable generation. Dositheos[3] remembered what he saw, understood, and read, and gave it to the chosen, just as it was written there.

Often I have joined with the powers in giving glory, and I became worthy of immeasurably majestic things.

The steles read as follows:

The First Stele of Seth

Seth's Hymn to Pigeradamas, the Divine Adam (118,25–119,15)

I praise you, father Pigeradamas,[4]
I, your son Emmacha Seth,
whom you have engendered without procreation
for the praise of our God.
I am your son
and you [119] are my mind, O my father.
I have sown and procreated,

---

1. Coptic text: NHC VII,5: 118,10–127,32. Editions: *The Facsimile Edition of the Nag Hammadi Codices: Codex VII*, 124–33; Paul Claude, *Les Trois Stèles de Seth*; Birger A. Pearson, ed., *Nag Hammadi Codex VII*, 371–421 (James E. Goehring and James M. Robinson); Hans-Martin Schenke, Hans-Gebhard Bethge, and Ursula Ulrike Kaiser, eds., *Nag Hammadi Deutsch*, 2.625–32 (Hans-Martin Schenke). **2.** See the tradition of the two steles or tablets of ancient lore preserved by Seth for his progeny, one of stone (to resist the flood) and the other of brick (to resist the conflagration) in Josephus *Jewish Antiquities* 1.67.1–71.5; *Life of Adam and Eve* 49.1–51.3; Pseudo-Malalas *Chronologica* 6.7–20; and Georgias Monachus *Chronicon* 10.12–24. At the conclusion of his ascent and descent, Zostrianos says that he "wrote three wooden tablets, and left them as knowledge for those who come after me, the living elect" (*Zostrianos* 130; cf. *Holy Book of the Great Invisible Spirit* III, 68, and the turquoise steles at the temple of Diospolis in *Discourse on the Eighth and Ninth* 61). **3.** Samaritan tradition (*Asatir* II.3) knows of certain Dositheans, followers of a Samaritan prophet Dusis, who considered themselves sons of Seth; they constituted a baptizing sect of the first and second centuries CE (Abul Fath *Annals* 151–59 [Vilmar]; Origen *Against Celsus* 1.57; 6.11; Eusebius *Church History* 4.22; cf. James A. Montgomery, *The Samaritans*, 255–63). The Pseudo-Clementine *Homilies* 2.15–24 and *Recognitions* 1.54–63; 2.8, though of questionable historical value, link Dositheos with John the Baptizer and Simon Magus, suggesting an original association of Gnostic religion and baptizing sectarianism with first-century Samaria. **4.** As in the *Secret Book of John* and other Sethian texts, Pigeradamas is the perfect exalted human being, Adamas or the heavenly Adam, the father of Seth.

but you have seen majestic things
and have endlessly stood at rest.
I praise you, father.
Praise me, father.
Because of you I exist,
because of God you exist,
because of you I exist in the presence of that one.
You are light and see light.
You have revealed light.
You are a Mirotheid,
you are my Mirotheos.[5]
I praise you as god,
I praise your divinity.

Seth's Hymn to Autogenes, the Self-Generated (119,15–120,17)

Great is the good Self-Generated One who stood,
the God who was first to stand at rest.[6]
You came in goodness,
you appeared,
and you revealed goodness.
I shall utter your name,
for you are a primary name.[7]
You are unborn,
you have appeared to reveal eternal things.
You are the One Who Is,
so you have revealed those who really are.[8]
You are uttered by a voice,
but by mind you are glorified.
You are powerful everywhere,
so the sensible world also knows you,

---

5. Mirotheos, perhaps "divine anointed one" (*muro-theos*) or "divine destiny" (*meiro-theos*) or divine "part" (*meros*, derived from *meiromai*). In *Three Forms of First Thought* 38 and 45, Mirothea is a feminine cognomen for Barbelo; in *Holy Book of the Great Invisible Spirit* III, 49 and *Zostrianos* 6 and 30, Mirothea is the mother of the heavenly Adam Pigeradamas; and in *Melchizedek* 6 and 18, one finds Meirocheirothetos (perhaps "one anointed with myrrh"). In the *Three Steles of Seth* this name (spelled variously as *mirōtheas, mirōtheos, mirotheos*) is an attribute applied to Seth's father, Pigeradamas (119), the "Mirotheid" child of his mother Mirothea and his father Autogenes, the Self-Generated, who, as Mirothea's masculine consort, can also be considered a Mirotheos (120). **6.** Autogenes, the Self-Generated, is the lowest of the three levels of the Barbelo Aeon and contains the "perfect individuals," souls that are no longer subject to reincarnation but have not yet achieved perfect union with their ideal counterparts. In later Platonic thought, standing at rest is the condition of transcendental being not subject to change, the end result of a product's emanation from its higher source, here probably the emanation of Autogenes from Barbelo's three powers. **7.** In the *Holy Book of the Great Invisible Spirit* and *Zostrianos*, one is spiritually baptized in the name of Autogenes, the Self-Generated. **8.** Autogenes, as "One Who Is," contains the stable and determinate "things that are" (Greek *ta onta*) as well as reveals their divine archetypes, the "things that really are" (Greek *ta ontōs onta*), contained in the Protophanes level just above him.

because of you and your seed.[9]
You are merciful, [120]
you are from another race,[10]
and it presides over another race.
Now you are from another race,
and it is placed over another race.[11]
You are from another race,
you are different.
You are merciful,
you are eternal.
You are placed over a race,[12]
you made them all to increase
because of my seed,
and you know it experiences procreation.
But they are from other races,
they are different.
They are placed over other races,
they are placed in life.
You are a Mirotheos.[13]
I praise its power given to me.

Communal Hymn to Barbelo (120,17–121,16)

You who made the masculinities
that really are to be triple male,[14]
you who were divided into five,[15]
who were given to us in triple power,
who were generated without birth,
who came from the superior
and for the inferior entered the midst,[16]

---

9. Or "offspring" (of Seth); see the previous note.
10. Coptic *kegenos*, "another kind, race, class, genera-tion" (a term very similar to *allogenēs*, "foreigner, stranger") is a play on the designation of Seth as "an-other seed (*sperma heteron*) in place of Abel who killed Cain" in *Genesis* 4:25 (Septuagint). Cf. *Book of Allogenes* 60. "The Stranger (Allogenes) answered and said, 'Get away from me, Satan, for I do not seek you but my Father, who is superior to all the great realms. For I have been called the Stranger because I am from another race. I am not from your race.'" 11. This sen-tence is a possible instance of dittography, although the liturgical nature of the text may easily allow for such repetition. 12. In Sethian texts, the Greek (and Coptic) word *genos* normally refers to a special "genus," "class," "kind," "race," "generation," or "stock"

of morally earnest human beings descended from Seth son of Adam and thus distinct from other ordi-nary humans descended from Cain and Abel. 13. See n. 5. 14. Cf. triple-male, in the *Secret Book of John* and elsewhere, as a term of praise in which maleness symbolizes transcendence. See also n. 15. 15. The text reads *pentas*. Cf. the description of the divine realm as a quintet or pentad of divine beings emanated by the Invisible Spirit in *Secret Book of John* II, 6. Here five may signify Barbelo plus her three levels (Kalyptos, Protophanes, Autogenes) plus her triple-male child, or, in Platonic/Neopythagorean terms, the union of her original form as a feminine indeterminate dyad (group of 2) and her subsequent defined reality as a male triadic aeon (see *Marsanes* 9). 16. I.e., the realm of generation and change.

you are a father[17] through a father,
a word from a command.
We praise you, Triple-Male,[18]
you have unified the All through them all,
you have empowered us.
You have come into being from Unity,[19]
you have gone forth from Unity,
you have come to Unity.
You saved,
you saved,
you saved us,
you who are crowned
and who crown.[20] **[121]**
We praise you eternally,
we praise you,
we who are saved,
who are perfect individuals,
who are perfect because of you,
who have become perfect with you.
You who are perfect,
who perfect,
who are perfect through all these,
who are everywhere similar,
Triple-Male,
you came to stand,
you were first to come to stand.
You have been divided everywhere,
and you have remained one.
Whomever you wished
you have saved,
and you wish
that all who are worthy be saved.
You are perfect,
you are perfect,
you are perfect.

The First Stele of Seth

---

17. Or "parent," in the sense that Barbelo and the supreme One transcend gender categories. **18.** In the *Three Steles of Seth*, the *Secret Book of John*, and *Three Forms of First Thought*, "triple-male" is a Sethian epithet of Barbelo. In the *Holy Book of the Great Invisible Spirit*, the Triple-Male Child is the offspring of Barbelo, while in *Zostrianos* and *Allogenes the Stranger the Stranger* the

Triple-Male (Child) is a denizen of the Barbelo Aeon without obvious parentage. **19.** Coptic *oua* (masculine), here and below. **20.** In *Zostrianos* 57 and 129, one who approaches the Protophanes level of the Barbelo Aeon receives a luminous crown with three seals representing the vision of the Barbelo Aeon's three levels.

The Second Stele of Seth

Communal Hymn to the Barbelo Aeon, Unified Author of Multiplicity (121,20–123,13)

Great is the first aeon,
male virgin Barbelo,[21]
the first glory of the invisible Father.
You who are called perfect
first saw
that the one who really preexists
is nonbeing.[22]
From and through that one
you have eternally proceeded,
the nonbeing one from an undivided Triple-[Powered] One.
You are a triple power,
you are a great oneness[23] from a pure oneness. [122]
You are a superior oneness,
first shadow[24] of the holy Father,
light from light.
[We] praise you,
producer of perfection,
supplier of aeons.
You saw that those who are eternal
derive from a shadow.
You have given rise to multiplicity,
yet you turned out to remain one,[25]
while still conferring multiplicity through division.
You are a threefold replication;
truly you are replicated threefold.
You are One,[26] of the One,[27]
and you are from its shadow.
You are Kalyptos, a Hidden One;[28]
you are a world of knowledge;

---

21. "Male virgin" is a traditional Sethian epithet designating Barbelo's androgyny. 22. Nonbeing in the sense of "beyond being," even preexisting the origin of pure, determinate being. 23. Monad, *monas* (feminine), often regarded as a metaphysically distinct entity from the "one," Coptic *oua* (masculine/neuter) or *ouei* (feminine, as in the immediately following lines). 24. Coptic *haibes*, lit., "shadow," here and on pp. 122 and 124, in the sense of something cast or projected from a light source (the supreme One). 25. Coptic *ouei* (feminine) for Greek *mia*. 26. Coptic *ouei* (feminine). 27. Coptic *oua* (masculine) for Greek *heis* (masculine) or *hen* (neuter). 28. Kalyptos, the Hidden One, is the uppermost level of the Barbelo Aeon, containing the universal forms, "the things that really exist."

you know that those of the One[29] are from a shadow.
And these are yours in thought.
Because of these you have empowered the eternal ones by Substantiality;
you have empowered divinity by Vitality;
you have empowered Mentality by goodness;[30]
by blessedness you empowered the shadows
flowing from the One.
You empowered one in knowledge,
you empowered another in <quality>.[31]
You made the equal and the unequal,
the same and the different.[32]
With generation and forms
you have empowered others in the realm of Being
[to flourish] with generation.
To these [you have given] power. [**123**]
As a hidden one, you have empowered these by thought.
You have emanated into these and out of these.
You are divided among them
and have become
Protophanes, a great first-appearing male mind.[33]
Fatherly God,
divine child,
producer of multiplicity,
in a division of all who really are,
you appeared to them all as a rational principle.[34]
You possess them all without generation,
eternally, imperishably.

Communal Petition to the Barbelo Aeon to Enable the Ascent (123,14–124,13)

Because of you salvation has come to us,
from you is salvation.
You are wisdom,[35]
you are knowledge,[36]

---

29. Coptic *oua* (masculine), here and below. **30.** As in *Zostrianos*, *Allogenes*, the anonymous *Parmenides Commentary* 14,10–26, and Proclus *Elements of Theology* 103, the triad Substantiality (Greek *ousiotēs*) or Existence (Greek *huparxis*), Vitality (Greek *zōotēs*), and Mentality (Greek *noētēs*) are the three components of the triple power by which a higher entity, often regarded as pure "substantiality" beyond determinate being emits an indeterminate power of life (vitality) that achieves substantial determination as the divine Intellect by intellectually (as "mentality") turning back upon and contemplating its source. "Blessed-ness" is an equivalent to mentality that signifies the attribute of self-knowledge. **31.** The manuscript has Coptic *tamio*, translating Greek *poiēton* ("creature"), probably erroneously for Greek *poion*, "quality." **32.** For the categories of equality, inequality, sameness, and difference, see Plato *Parmenides* 139b–140d, 146ad–151e, 160d–165a, *Timaeus* 35a–36d, and the "greatest kinds" (being, sameness, otherness, rest, and change) of *Sophist* 254b–258e. **33.** Protophanes is the median level of the Barbelo Aeon, containing ideal forms in union with the intellectual entities that contemplate them. **34.** Logos. **35.** Sophia. **36.** Gnosis.

you are truth.
Because of you is life,
from you is life.
Because of you is mind,
from you is mind.
You are mind,
you are a world of truth.
You are a triple power,
you are a threefold replication,
truly you are threefold,
the aeon of eternal aeons.
You alone see purely
the eternal and unengendered primal principles,
and to the extent that you have been divided,
also the primal divisions.
Unify us as you have been unified.
Teach us what you see.
Empower us
so we may [124] be saved to eternal life.
We are a shadow[37] of you
even as you are already a shadow of the preexistent one.
Hear us first.
We are eternal.
Hear us as perfect individuals.
You are the aeon of aeons,
the all-perfect one, who is unified.
You have heard,
you have heard.
You have saved,
you have saved.
We give thanks,
we praise you always,
we shall glorify you.

The Second Stele of Seth

---

37. See n. 24.

The Third Stele

Communal Doxology and Petition to the Supreme One
(124,17–127,6)

Opening Communal Doxology (124,17–126,5)

We rejoice,
we rejoice,
we rejoice.
We have seen,
we have seen,
we have seen what really preexists,
that it really exists
and is the first eternal one.
You unengendered one,
from you are the eternal ones
and the aeons,
the all-perfect ones, who are unified,
and the perfect individuals.[38]
We praise you, insubstantial one,
Existence prior to existences,
prime Substance before substances,
father of divinity and Vitality,
creator of Mind,
supplier of goodness,
supplier of blessedness.[39]
We all praise you,
you who know,
with [glorifying] praise,
you, [125] [because of] whom all [these] are,
[you who know those that truly exist],[40]

---

38. The all-perfect ones who are in unity with their objects of contemplation inhabit the median (Protophanes) level of the Barbelo Aeon, while the perfect individuals who have not achieved this unity inhabit its lowest level, Autogenes, the Self-Generated. 39. Cf. this hexad of attributes (Existence-Divinity-Vitality-Mind-Goodness-Blessedness) to the similar hexad (Substantiality-Divinity-Vitality-Mentality-Goodness-Blessedness) on p. 122, and to the triplets of similar attributes (Perfection, Blessedness, and Divinity) in Secret Book of John II, 3, and to the triplets Divinity, Blessedness, and Perfection in Allogenes the Stranger 62–63 (cf. 55; Zostrianos 15; Victorinus Against

Arius 1.50.16–21; 52,3–5). The triad of Perfection, Divinity, and Blessedness may be a precursor of the Existence-Vitality-Mentality (or Blessedness) triad to be found in the anonymous Parmenides Commentary 14,10–26 and in Three Steles of Seth 122 (see note 30) and often in Zostrianos and Allogenes the Stranger. Proclus (Commentary on Timaeus 1.357,9–11) uses a similar triad of attributes to distinguish between the paradigm, the demiurge, and the copy in Plato's Timaeus: "the divinity of the paradigm, the goodness of the maker, and the perfection of the product." 40. Restoring [ᵉntok etei]m[e eniont]ōs et[šoop].

who know yourself through yourself alone.
For there is nothing active prior to you.
You are spirit,[41] alone and living.
You know the One:[42]
we cannot speak of this unity,
which belongs to you everywhere.
Your light enlightens us.
Command us to see you
that we may be saved.
Knowledge[43] of you is the salvation of us all.
Command!
If you command,
we have been saved.
Truly we are saved.
We have seen you through mind.
You are all these
and save them all,
you who will not be saved
nor have been saved by them.
You have commanded us.
You are One,
you are One.
Just as one would say of you that you are one,
you are a single, living spirit.
How shall we give you a name?
We have none.
You are the Existence of all these,
you are their Life,
you are their Mind.[44]
In you they all rejoice. [126]
You commanded them all to be saved
through your word
[to the extent that] they [are able].

Traditional Doxology to the Supreme
Preexistent One (126,5–17)

O [single] preeminent glory,[45]
O hidden one,

---

41. The Sethian supreme deity is normally the Invisible Spirit. 42. Coptic *oua*, here and below. 43. Gnosis. 44. Existence, Life, and Mind, a triad found in *Zostrianos*, *Allogenes the Stranger*, and often in Neoplatonic texts; see n. 30. 45. This ecstatic prayer, directed by the ascending visionary to the supreme preexistent One, is very similar to those found in *Allogenes the Stranger* 54 and *Zostrianos* 51–53, 86, 88. The names Sunaōn, Mell[e]phaou, El[l]emm[aōni], Smoun, and Eptaōn occur as part of the colophon of a papyrus published by William Brashear, "Seth-Gebet."

blessed Senaon,
who generated himself,
Asineus
Mephneus
Optaon
Elemaon, the great power
Emouniar
Nibareus
Kandephoros
Aphredon
Deiphaneus
you who are Armedon for me,[46]
you generator of powers,
Thalanatheus
Antitheus.[47]
You are in yourself,
you are before yourself,
and none became active after you.

Final Doxology to the Supreme One (126,18–127,6)

How shall we praise you?
We cannot,
but we give thanks to you,
we who are inferior.
For you commanded us,
you who are superior,
to glorify you
as we can.
We praise you because we are saved
and we always glorify you.
Now we glorify you
that we might be saved to eternal salvation.
We have praised you
for we can.
We have been saved.
You always wished
us all to do this.
We all have done this . . . [127]
. . . we together with those who [have been saved].

---

46. Possibly correct to read "for these." **47.** For other instances of the ecstatic invocation of these divine names, see *Zostrianos* 51, 86, and 88, and *Allogenes the Stranger* 54.

Using the Steles for the Mystical Ascent and Descent (127,6–26)

Whoever remembers these things[48] and always glorifies will be perfect among the perfect and free of suffering beyond all things. They all praise these, individually and collectively, and afterward they will be silent.

As it has been ordained for them, they ascend. After silence, they descend from the third. They praise the second, and afterward the first. The way of ascent is the way of descent.[49]

So understand as those who are alive that you have succeeded. You have taught yourselves about things infinite. Marvel at the truth within them, and at the revelation.

The Three Steles of Seth

Colophon: Scribal Note and Benediction (127,28–32)

This is the father's[50] book,[51] and the son wrote it. Bless me, father. I bless you, father, in peace. Amen.

---

48. Or perhaps "these steles." 49. Cf. Heraclitus, frag. B60 [Diels]: "The way up and the way down are one and the same." This paragraph gives instructions for the use of the hymns, with intervening silence, in the liturgy of ascent and descent. 50. Lit., "the father-hood's." 51. Whether this refers specifically to the *Three Steles of Seth* or to the entire codex is unclear.

ZOSTRIANOS

NHC VIII,1

Introduced and Translated by John D. Turner

Zostrianos contains a pseudonymous account of the otherworldly journey of Zostrianos, legendary son of Yolaos and father of Armenios, said by Plato (*Republic* X 614b) to be the father of Er the Pamphylian, who was later assimilated with Zoroaster (cf. Clement of Alexandria *Miscellanies* 5.14.103.2). Probably originally composed in Greek in late second- or early third-century Alexandria, it reflects a non-Christian form of Gnostic Sethianism that had thoroughly reinterpreted its ritual and mythological traditions by means of a massive fund of second-century Neopythagorean and Middle Platonic metaphysical speculation whose originality had commended *Zostrianos* and its sister treatise *Allogenes the Stranger* to the critical attention of Plotinus and his circle in third-century Rome. Those two treatises and the *Three Steles of Seth* and *Marsanes* are all sufficiently heavily indebted to Platonism as to merit the designation "Platonizing Sethian treatises."

The basic scheme of *Zostrianos* is built around the reception of a graded series of revelations and visions of the transcendental beings encountered by the Sethian visionary during his or her supracelestial ascent. At each level of the ascent, Zostrianos is instructed about its character and spiritual inhabitants, whereupon he contemplates them and is assimilated to their nature. Each successive stage of the ascent is delineated by particular transcendental baptisms and sealings modeled on the Sethian baptismal rite of the "Five Seals." In *Zostrianos*, this rite, originally entailing immersion in ordinary water, has become entirely transcendentalized beyond the earthly plane, implemented by a heavenly ascent in which one is directly assimilated to the higher spiritual beings. This interpretation of baptism owes to the influence upon *Zostrianos* of a tradition of visionary ecstatic ascent achieved as a self-performable technique typical of religious Platonism.

Two interwoven structural units dominate *Zostrianos*: the narrative of Zostrianos's successful quest for enlightenment, and a sequence of four main revelation discourses that delimit the stages of Zostrianos's quest and form the main content of *Zostrianos*. This narrative depicts Zostrianos's gradual progress toward enlightenment. His initial rejection of the materialistic life in favor of a quest for the truth about ultimate reality, his dissatisfaction with traditional religious answers, and his eventual suicidal despair of finding enlightenment by his own unaided efforts culminate in the sudden appearance of divine aid in the form of a sequence of revealers who enable his escape from the earthly realm and step-by-step visionary ascent through the transcendent realms of true being. After 125 pages of visions and revelations, the narrative concludes with his descent to earth, where he now is able to master the physical aspect of his existence. He records the revelations he has received on three wooden tablets and launches a mission to awaken ordinary mortals to the dangers of lustful materiality, exhorting them to enter into the authentic being offered by the unfailingly trustworthy Father. As Zostrianos moves from materiality to authenticity, from the despair of self-effort to reliance upon revealed truth, from psychological instability to stable confidence, and from ignorance to knowledge, the text progressively guides its reader toward his or her own enlightenment and salvation.

The major characters within *Zostrianos* are the following:

1. Zostrianos, the central character and narrator of the treatise's content.

2. The angel of light, who rescues Zostrianos from suicidal despair and escorts him on a cloud of light through the sublunary and superlunary realms, the Aeonic Copies, Sojourn, and Repentance up to the Self-Generated Aeons.

3. The "great preeminence" Authrounios, a "helper" Glory in the Self-Generated Aeons, who reveals the origin of the physical cosmos from the acts of Sophia and the archon of creation and the nature of the Aeonic Copies.

4. The Child of the Child Ephesech, who, just prior to Zostrianos's final baptism in the name of the divine Autogenes, reveals to Zostrianos the three powers of the Invisible Spirit, the origin and nature of the Barbelo Aeon, the nature of baptism, and the nature of the various kinds of souls in Sojourn, Repentance, and the Self-Generated Aeons. In the *Holy Book of the Great Invisible Spirit* he appears as Esephech, the offspring of the Triple-Male Child and the virgin Youel.

5. The all-glorious virgin Youel/Yoel, the mother of the Glories residing in the Aeon of Kalyptos. As in *Allogenes the Stranger*, she reveals the nature and ontological characteristics of the Aeons of Autogenes and Protophanes, as well as the nature of certain crowns and seals Zostrianos sees there, and administers Zostrianos's final baptism in which he receives a holy spirit and becomes "truly existing."

6. The Luminaries of the Barbelo Aeon, a triad of revealers, Salamex, Semen, and the all-perfect Arme. As in *Allogenes the Stranger*, they convey the highest teaching concerning the supreme Triple-Powered Invisi-

ble Spirit and how he gave rise to the Aeon of Barbelo and its principal subaeons, Kalyptos ("hidden"), Protophanes ("first-appearing"), and Autogenes ("self-generated").

The divine hierarchy of *Zostrianos* is complex, but it illustrates many of the familiar entities of Sethian lore:

1. The Triple-Powered Invisible Spirit, the supreme Sethian deity, utterly beyond being and comprehension. His three powers, Existence, Vitality or Life, and Blessedness or Mentality, give rise to the Aeon Barbelo, a transcendental divine intellect to whose three sublevels (Kalyptos, Protophanes, and Autogenes) and their peculiar baptismal waters they are intimately related.

2. The Barbelo Aeon, the First Thought of the Invisible Spirit and his only direct product. As the universal Intellect containing the archetypes of all things, it comprises the highest realm of pure, determinate being. As One-in-Many, it is completely unified, yet also contains three distinguishable ontological levels usually referred to as Kalyptos, Protophanes, and Autogenes, whose names represent three phases in the unfolding of the Barbelo Aeon: its initial latency or potential existence, its initial manifestation, and its self-generated actualization.

3. The Aeon of Kalyptos ("Hidden One"), the first and highest subaeon within the Aeon of Barbelo. This is the domain of intelligible reality defined by the authentic existents ("those that truly exist"), the universal ideas or paradigms of Platonic metaphysics. Zostrianos receives a vision of this realm, but apparently does not enter it.

4. The Aeon of Protophanes ("First Appearing One"), the second highest subaeon within the Barbelo Aeon. Called a great perfect male Mind, this is the domain of the "all-perfect ones who are unified (that is, they exist together)." These beings seem to be potentially distinct intelligences and souls unified with their objects of contemplation, the ideal forms in Kalyptos. This realm seems to be the highest level achieved by Zostrianos during his visionary ascent.

5. The Aeon of Autogenes ("Self-Generated"), the lowest of the three ontological levels within the Barbelo Aeon. He presides over the domain of the "perfect individuals" who are differentiated, individual forms and souls. His activity is directed to the ordering of his Self-Generated Aeons, and perhaps even the ordering of realms extending to the moon or to the earth itself. In other Sethian treatises, he forms the third member of the supreme divine triad of Father (the Invisible Spirit), Mother (Barbelo), and Son (Autogenes).

6. The Triple-Male Child, a prominent figure in the Barbelo Aeon closely related to the "individual" forms and souls that reside in the Autogenes aeon as well as to "those who exist together" in Protophanes. He seems to be a savior or mediator who brings undifferentiated beings in the Aeon of Protophanes into differentiated existence in the Aeon of Autogenes and, conversely, helps the differentiated beings in the Aeon of Autogenes to ascend to the Aeon of Protophanes.

7. The Self-Generated Aeons, the aeons presided over by Autogenes, where Zostrianos is baptized five times in the name of Autogenes (which may reflect the Sethian baptismal rite of the Five Seals). They contain the vast majority of the divine beings traditionally associated with the Sethian baptismal rite: the Living Water (Yesseus Mazareus Yessedekeus), the baptizers Micheus and Michar (and Mnesinous), the purifier Barpharanges, and Seldao, Elenos, and Zogenethlos. In addition to these, the Self-Generated Aeons also contain the Four Luminaries; Sophia; Mirothea, the consort of Autogenes and mother of the archetypal Adam, Pigeradamas; Prophania, the mother of the heavenly Seth and of the Four Luminaries; and Plesithea, mother of the seed of Seth, called "the angels." Souls that reside in the Self-Generated Aeons are "perfect individuals" who possess "an intelligent, ineffable rational expression (Logos) of the truth" as well as self-generated power and eternal life.

8. The Four Luminaries, Armozel (or Harmozel), Oroiael, Daveithe, and Eleleth, established by the divine Autogenes as the celestial dwelling places of the primordial line of Seth (*Genesis* 5:1–32). As in the *Secret Book of John* and the *Holy Book of the Great Invisible Spirit*, Adamas dwells in Armozel (or Harmozel), (Emmacha) Seth dwells in Oroiael, the seed of Seth dwells in Daveithe, while Sophia and the repentant souls of later generations dwell in Eleleth (or in the level of Metanoia immediately below the Self-Generated Aeons).

9. Sophia, divine Wisdom, who according to Sethian tradition resides in Eleleth, the lowest of the Four Luminaries, and inaugurates the coming into being of the perceptible cosmos by attempting to emulate the creative power of the supreme Invisible Spirit by giving rise to the world creator. In *Zostrianos*, Sophia does not produce the world creator, but merely shows forth the model for earthly things, of which the already existing creator sees only a dim reflection, which he uses, together with his own imagination, to shape the created order (i.e., below the moon). Having thus illumined the darkness below her, as in other Sethian treatises, Sophia repents and receives a place of rest, perhaps in the Luminary Eleleth, while the world creator is condemned to perishability. Nevertheless, Sophia becomes the cause of the descent and reincarnation of souls.

10. Repentance, a lower aeon whose name seems to derive from the Sethian tradition concerning Sophia's repentance. It contains immortal souls that are satisfied with knowledge, renounce dead and worldly things, and zealously embrace their immortal mind and soul. Although they are repentant, they can and do commit sins, probably unintentionally. Repentance is said to contain six subaeons arranged according to the types of sins committed.

11. Sojourn, an aeon whose name may also mean something like "exile" or even "transmigration," perhaps inspired by the Sethian tradition of Sophia's brief descent below the divine world. This is the traditional realm of disembodied souls after death. Souls that inhabit it can avoid reincarnation if they discover the truth and stand apart from the wicked; nevertheless, lacking self-generated power, they tend to "follow practices of others."

12. The Aeonic Copies, probably the realm of the seven planetary orbits from the moon to Saturn, where Zostrianos is baptized seven times. They are essentially a temporary holding place for the inferior souls of mortals who are still in the world, a place where they can be trained and enlightened for immortality, perhaps by certain eternal glories that also reside there. This realm may also include the fixed stars that function as the images of the ideal divine realities that the archon of creation sees reflected in lower matter and uses to shape the created order.

13. The archon of creation, who plays a role similar to the demiurge of Plato's *Timaeus*. But instead of fixing his gaze on a transcendent paradigm, he looks downward and perceives merely the reflection of the model for worldly things projected below by Sophia; from these and his imagination he simulates a perceptible world over which he rules.

14. The atmospheric realm, "the airy earth," probably the realm extending from the moon down to the level of the clouds, or even to the earth itself.

15. The thirteen aeons, probably the realm between the earth and the clouds, or even the atmospheric realm itself, consisting of thirteen zones containing the angelic host presided over by the archon. It is the realm of embodiment, which the soul must transcend.

Zostrianos is the sole copy of a heavily damaged (pp. 89–112 are almost completely obliterated and almost all the others have suffered damage) fourth-century Coptic translation of an essentially pagan Greek apocalypse (Porphyry *Life of Plotinus* 16: "There were in his time and circle many Christians and others, and sectarians who ... used to adduce apocalypses by Zoroaster and Zostrianos and Nikotheos and Allogenes and Messos and other people of the kind") produced in the late second or early third century. In the period 244–269 CE, a Greek version of *Zostrianos*, perhaps originally composed around 225 CE, circulated in

Plotinus's Roman seminar, where various of its doctrines were attacked by Plotinus in *Ennead* II, 9 [33][1] and refuted at greater length by Amelius and Porphyry himself. Along with the *Three Steles of Seth* and *Allogenes the Stranger*, the text displays evidence of having been originally translated into a northern Coptic dialect, whose syntactic features still remain largely intact, and later into a southern dialect by a scribe concerned to employ Sahidic orthography, suggesting that these Coptic translations, possibly originating in Alexandria, circulated down the Nile valley, moving gradually south, among various collectors and readers.

Zostrianos was composed mainly on the basis of mythologumena drawn from the theogonical and baptismal doctrine most evident in the *Holy Book of the Great Invisible Spirit*, and from Middle Platonic theological interpretations of Plato's dialogues, especially the *Phaedo, Phaedrus, Timaeus, Republic,* and *Parmenides*, available in popular Platonic tracts, epitomes, or commentaries. It thereby effected a rapprochement between traditions at home in Gnostic Sethianism and a Middle Platonism of a strongly Neopythagorean bent. The hymns, doxologies, prayers, and invocations directed to various celestial powers during Zostrianos's ascent clearly reflect the baptismal liturgies of earlier Sethian treatises like the *Holy Book, Three Forms of First Thought, Melchizedek,* and the *Revelation of Adam*. In particular, *Zostrianos* (51,24–52,8; 88,9–25) shares a traditional doxological prayer with *Allogenes the Stranger* (54,11–37), *Three Steles of Seth* (125,24–126,17), and the final lines of a fragmentary "prayer of Seth" in Papyrus Berolinensis 17207.

The author of *Zostrianos* used Middle Platonic metaphysics and epistemology to account for the nature of the Sethian divine and cosmic hierarchy and for the manner in which the baptismal rite of the Five Seals mentioned in earlier Sethian literature could afford a saving enlightenment and direct experience of the divine without any recourse to earthly ritual practices. By attributing its doctrine to an ancient revelation granted to Zostrianos, great-grandfather of Zoroaster, the author of *Zostrianos* implicitly claimed an authority more ancient than Plato himself for his version of Platonic metaphysics and approach to the knowledge of transcendent reality. According to Plotinus, the entire metaphysics of the Platonizing Sethian texts, especially *Zostrianos*, probably the main target of his critique in *Ennead* II, 9 [33] 6, was a grand misrepresentation of Plato's philosophy and a violation of philosophical method; rather than flatly asserting the authority of revealed truth as the basis of their novel interpretations, the authors and users of such texts ought to present their own opinions with courtesy and philosophical method.

Of special interest is the source shared in common between *Zostrianos* (66,14–68,13; 74,17–75,21) and the later, fourth-century Christian theologian Marius Victorinus's *Against Arius* (I, 50,1–21), which seems to be an epitome or commentary on Plato's *Parmenides*, especially its first hypothesis, 137c–142a. On

---

1. In fact, it appears that in his treatise *Against the Gnostics* (*Ennead* II, 9 [33] 10,19–33), Plotinus actually cites *Zostrianos* 10,1–20.

the grounds that *Zostrianos* was circulated and read in Plotinus's Roman seminar (Porphyry *Life of Plotinus* 16), Michel Tardieu[2] has argued that "the totality of *Zostrianos*—whose content we know through the Coptic version in the Nag Hammadi codices—was already written in 263, at the time of the arrival of the Gnostics in the School of Plotinus." He furthermore notes that the anonymous *Parmenides Commentary*, which Pierre Hadot has attributed to Porphyry, contains a statement (fragment IX 1–4: "Others, although they affirm that he has robbed himself of all that which is his, nevertheless concede that his power and intellect are co-unified in his simplicity") that depends upon both the *Chaldaean Oracles* (frag. 3: "the Father snatched himself away and did not enclose his own fire in his intellectual Power"; and 4: "For power is with him, but intellect is from him") and the theological source common to Marius Victorinus's *Against Arius* (I, 50,10: "Since he is one in his simplicity, containing three powers: all Existence, all Life, and Blessedness") and *Zostrianos* (66,14–20: "For they are [triple] powers of his [unity, complete] Existence, Life and Blessedness. In Existence he exists [as] a simple unity"). This suggests that this common source not only predates Plotinus, but also the anonymous *Commentary* itself, and that we may have to do with several theological expositions of the *Parmenides* in pre-Plotinian times. Thus *Zostrianos* becomes a signally important witness to the history of the development of later Platonic metaphysics.

    Zostrianos initiated a creative attempt to integrate older Sethian traditions into a new conceptual framework. This author sought to explain the inner meaning of the Sethian baptismal rite by means of the Middle Platonic metaphysics of the divine Intellect and its generation from the supreme deity. According to 24,28–25,22, various baptisms mark the stripping away of the influence of worldly concerns and a resultant vision of transcendent reality and a "knowledge of everything," an almost exact paraphrase of the doctrine of the baptism of the Five Seals most fully expounded in *Three Forms of First Thought* and elaborated in liturgical terms in the *Holy Book of the Great Invisible Spirit* (III 62,24–68,1). Although these earlier treatises reflect the baptismal rite of the Five Seals as an earthly communal ritual by which immersion in ordinary water affords immersion in the transcendental "living water" of enlightenment and ultimate salvation, *Zostrianos* sets the practice of baptismal enlightenment not in the context of an earthly, communal ritual, but in the context of philosophical inquiry focused on a set of questions concerning the origin of multiplicity from unity; since the answers to these questions cannot be achieved in this world, they are revealed to Zostrianos during his ascent to the Self-Generated Aeons, which in effect become a new, transcendent setting for the erstwhile earthly baptismal rite.

    Earlier Sethian treatises, such as the *Secret Book of John, Three Forms of First Thought,* and the *Holy Book of the Great Invisible Spirit,* present the Mother Barbelo as the principal initiator and agent of enlightenment and salvation,

---

2. Michel Tardieu, *Recherches sur la formation de l'Apocalypse de Zostrien et les sources de Marius Victorinus,* 100–101, 112.

which she conveys through a series of temporally successive descents into this world, culminating in her gift of the baptismal rite of the Five Seals. On the other hand, starting with *Zostrianos*, the Platonizing Sethian treatises exhibit a more vertical, nontemporal, suprahistorical scheme in which salvation is achieved not through earthly visitations of the Mother, but through a graded series of visionary ascents beyond the earthly realm enacted by the eventual recipient of salvation. During a contemplative ascent through a vertical hierarchy of levels of intelligible being, the visionary becomes assimilated to their nature. The upward progression from Autogenes to Protophanes to Kalyptos is the progression from sequential discursive thought, to a simultaneous union of knowing subject and known object, to the total awareness or direct intuition of pure being. Beyond this, there is introduced yet another, higher triad of powers within the supreme Invisible Spirit itself, namely, its Triple Power, contemplation of which is possible only by transcending intellect altogether by a sudden flash of insight or revelation, which *Allogenes the Stranger* characterizes as a nonknowing knowledge. Although in *Zostrianos* the ascent culminates at the intellectual level of the Barbelo Aeon, in *Allogenes* and perhaps the *Three Steles of Seth* the ascent continues through the levels of the Invisible Spirit's Triple Power, culminating in a nonknowing, mentally vacant revelatory encounter with the Unknowable One at the summit of all.

The inevitable result is increased reliance upon self-performable techniques of enlightenment and decreased reliance upon the salvific initiatives of the Mother Barbelo. In effect, the Aeon of Barbelo has now become only a stage on the path of ascent, no longer its goal or even its author. This shift is evidently the product of a deeper degree of involvement with a contemplative Platonism that takes its start in Plato's *Symposium* and leads directly to Plotinus. In *Zostrianos* and the other Platonizing Sethian treatises, the earlier Father, Mother, Child nomenclature for the supreme theogonical triad becomes obsolete and is replaced by the "the Triple-Powered One," a derivational triad of powers (Existence, Life, Blessedness) latent within the Invisible Spirit. On a lower level, the older triad of Barbelo's attributes—Foreknowledge (Prognosis), Incorruptibility (Aphtharsia), and Life Eternal (Aionia Zoe), as in the *Secret Book of John*—is replaced by a triad of ontological levels, Kalyptos, Protophanes, and Autogenes. As the Knowledge or Intellect of the Invisible Spirit, Barbelo's traditionally maternal identity as merciful Mother and Womb of the All becomes replaced by a masculine identity as a Platonic universal Intellect called the Aeon of Barbelo.

BIBLIOGRAPHY

Catherine Barry, Wolf-Peter Funk, Paul-Hubert Poirier, and John D. Turner, eds., *Zostrien*; William Brashear, "Seth-Gebet"; Pierre Hadot, *Porphyre et Victorinus*; "'Porphyre et Victorinus': Questions et hypothèses"; Hans-Martin Schenke, "The Phenomenon and Significance of Gnostic Sethianism"; Hans-Martin Schenke, Hans-Gebhard Bethge, and Ursula Ulrike Kaiser, eds., *Nag Hammadi Deutsch*, 2.633–62 (Hans-Martin Schenke); Madeleine Scopello, "Youel et Barbélo dans le traité de l'Allogène"; John H. Sieber, ed., *Nag Hammadi Codex VIII*, 7–225 (John H. Sieber and Bentley Layton); Michel Tardieu, "Recherches sur la formation de l'Apocalypse de Zostrien et les sources de Marius Victorinus"; John D. Turner, *Sethian Gnosticism and the Platonic Tradition*; Michael A. Williams, "Stability as a Soteriological Theme in Gnosticism"; *The Immovable Race*.

Zostrianos[1]

Authorial Ascription (1,1–7)

[The book] of the [glory] of the eternally living words [that] I, Zos[trianos,[2] wrote]
. . . and Yolaos when I came into the world for the sake of those of my generation
and [those] after me, the living elect.

Kerygmatic Pronouncement (1,8–10)

The God [of] truth lives in very truth and knowledge and eternal light!

Zostrianos's Autobiographical Prologue
(1,10–29)

After I mentally abandoned my inner corporeal darkness, psychical chaos, and
dark, lustful femininity with which I was unconcerned, and after I had discovered
the boundlessness of my materialism and reproved the dead creation within me
as well as the perceptible divine world ruler, I powerfully proclaimed wholeness
to those with unrelated parts.[3] Although I had tried their ways for a little while insofar as the necessity of birth brought me visibility, I was never satisfied with
them. Instead, I always used to separate myself from them because I had come
into being through a holy—although procreative—[birth].

---

1. Coptic text: NHC VIII,1: 1,1–132,9. Editions: *The Facsimile Edition of the Nag Hammadi Codices: Codex VIII*, 11–138; Catherine Barry, Wolf-Peter Funk, Paul-Hubert Poirier, and John D. Turner, *Zostrien*; Hans-Martin Schenke, Hans-Gebhard Bethge, and Ursula Ulrike Kaiser, eds., *Nag Hammadi Deutsch*, 2.633–62 (Hans-Martin Schenke); John H. Sieber, ed., *Nag Hammadi Codex VIII*, 7–225 (Bentley Layton and John H. Sieber). 2. According to later tradition, Zostrianos was the grandfather of Zoroaster (whose name occurs only in the colophon, on p. 132, probably added secondarily), who, according to Arnobius (*Against the Pagans* 1.52; cf. Clement of Alexandria *Miscellanies* 5.14.103.2 and other late sources), was the father of the Armenius, said by Plato (*Republic* 10.614b) to be the grandfather of Er the Pamphylian, who was at some point assimilated with Zoroaster. The *Secret Book of John* (II, 14–19) quotes from an (otherwise unknown) *Book of Zoroaster*. The figure of Yolaos, Zostrianos's putative father (cf. 4), is attested in Hesiod's *Theogony* (102; 323; 340; 467) as a great warrior. Diodorus Siculus (*Library of History* 5.15.2) identifies him as the son of Herakles' brother Iphikles; in a fit of madness Herakles betrothed his own first wife, Megara, to his nephew Yolaos. 3. Lit., "I powerfully uttered a cry of the All (i.e., the universe) to those who have strange/alien parts."

Initial This-Worldly Vision of the Perfect Child
(1,30–2,24)

When I had improved my sinless soul, then I strengthened [2] the intellectual
[spirit within me] and I [was able to awaken from] the [dark sleep and find] my
[paternal] God . . . . Although I had [worked on this in every way],[4] I was strengthened by a holy spirit higher than God. [It settled] upon me alone as I was improv-
ing myself, and I saw the perfect Child,[5] [who he is] as well as what [he possesses].
He often and [variously] appeared to me like a consenting [unity] while I was
seeking the [male] father of all things,[6]

> things [that are] conceptual and sensible,
> specific and generic,
> [partial]and whole,
> containing and contained,
> corporeal and incorporeal,
> essential and material,

and [matters] pertaining to all these, and the Existence that is combined with
them and with the god of this <perfect Child>,[7] the unengendered Kalyptos, the
power [in] them all.

Initial Puzzles Concerning the Relationship of the Ideal and
Phenomenal Worlds (2,24–3,13)

Now as for existence: how can beings—since they are from the aeon of those who
derive from an invisible and undivided self-generated spirit as triform unengendered images—both have an origin superior to existence and preexist all [these]
and yet have come to be in the [world]? How do those in its presence with all
these [3][originate from the] good [that is above]? What sort [of power] and
[cause does it have, and] what is [its] place? What is its principle? How does its
product belong both to it and all these? How, [being a] simple [unity], does it differ [from] itself, given that it exists as existence, form, and blessedness and, being
vitally alive, grants power? How has existence that has no being appeared in a
power that has being?

---

4. Perhaps restore "although I had [worked (ᶜrh[ōb])
on this in every way]" as "although I had [feared
(ᶜrh[ote]) him (Zostrianos's paternal god) in every
way]." 5. The "perfect Child" is probably the "perfect
Triple-Male Child," the principal savior figure of the
treatise, who resides in the Barbelo Aeon. 6. This
father could be the Aeon of Barbelo, the Self-
Generated One, or, less likely, the Invisible Spirit. 7.
The "perfect Child" is probably the "perfect Triple-
Male Child," the principal savior figure of the treatise,
who resides in the Barbelo Aeon.

Diligent but Fruitless Attempts to Find Answers (3,14–28)

Seeking to understand these things, after the custom of my kind I would offer them up daily to the god of my fathers. I would praise them all, since my forefathers and ancestors who sought found.

As for me, I did not stop seeking a place of rest worthy of my spirit, where I would not be bound in the perceptible world. Then, as I was deeply troubled and gloomy because of the feeblemindedness that surrounded me, I dared to act and to deliver myself to the wild beasts of the desert for a violent death.[8]

This-Worldly Appearance of the Angel of Knowledge (3,28–4,19)

There stood before me the angel of the knowledge[9] of eternal light, and he said to me, "Zostrianos, why have you gone mad as though you were ignorant of the great eternal beings [4] who are above? [Don't you know that you are a chosen person] and therefore you were informed about [what you are to do] so that you might now be saved? Never ever [become] destructive, nor [pay attention] to those you are familiar with in order to save others [whom] the father on high will choose. [Do you suppose] that you are the father of [your kind]? Or that Yolaos is your father? [You have] a divine angel [that has shown] you [the way] through holy persons. Come and transcend these [realms]! You will return to them another [time] to proclaim a living [race], to save those who are worthy and to empower the chosen. For great is the struggle of this age, but the time [in] this world is short."

Zostrianos's Spiritual Ascent Through the Aeons (4,20–129,16)

The Luminous Cloud (4,20–5,17)

When he had said this [to me], I very eagerly and gladly embarked with him upon a great luminous cloud, and [left] my molded bodily form upon the earth, guarded by glories.[10] [We] eluded the entire world and the thirteen aeons in it, as well as their angelic host.[11] We were not seen, but their chief was disturbed at [our passage,] since [our] luminous cloud, [5] [a substance] superior [to everything in the cosmos], was ineffable. Its beauty shone brightly. It has an ability to [guide]

---

8. Contrast Zostrianos's suicidal perplexity with Allogenes' confidence (*Allogenes the Stranger* 57). **9.** Gnosis, here and throughout. **10.** Cf. Jesus's ascension on a cloud (*Acts* 1:9) or Nephele's rescue of Phrixus from Ino's plot to sacrifice him (Pseudo-Apollodorus *Library* 1.9.1). Certain "glories" (spiritual helpers, 46) will protect Zostrianos's physical body from tampering until he descends and reassumes it as the vehicle for his mission of proclaiming what he has learned to the rest of the elect. **11.** The world and its thirteen aeons designate the earth and its sublunar atmosphere governed by the archon of creation (8–10) and his angelic host; cf. "the god of the thirteen realms" in the *Holy Book of the Great Invisible Spirit* III, 63 and the "thirteen kingdoms" of the *Revelation of Adam* (77–82).

pure spirits, since it is a vitalizing spirit and an intelligent reason, [not] like those things in the world [that are made] of pliable matter and persuasive reason.[12]

Then I knew that my inner power had overcome the darkness, because it contained total light. I was baptized there, and I received the image of the glories there and became like one of them.

The Atmospheric Realm and the Aeonic Copies (5,17–23)

I traversed the atmospheric [realm][13] and passed by the Aeonic Copies after immersing myself [there] seven times [in] living [water], once for each [of the] aeons without pausing until [I had traversed] them all at once.

The Sojourn, Repentance, and Arrival at the Self-Generated Aeons (5,24–56,23)

The Ascent Beyond the World (5,24–6,7)

I ascended to the [truly] existent Sojourn. [I] was baptized, and [I abandoned the world]. I ascended to the truly existent Repentance [and was] baptized there [six] times.[14] I passed through the [6] sixth[15] [and was empowered from this very one]. I ascended to the [Self-Generated] Aeons, and stood there after having seen a really existing and true light; it was truly existing from its self-generated root, [along with] great angels and glories [beyond] measure.

The First of Five Baptisms in the Name of Autogenes, the Self-Generated (6,7–7,1)

I was baptized[16] in the [name of] the divine Self-Generated One [by]
those powers that preside [over the] living water, Michar and Mi[cheus].
I was purified by the great Barpharanges.
I was [glorified] and inscribed in glory.
I was sealed by those who preside over these powers,
[Michar], Micheus, Seldao, Ele[nos], and Zogenethlos.

---

12. "Pliable matter and persuasive reason": see *Timaeus* 48a, where Plato attributes the origin of the universe to reason persuading the recalcitrant necessity of disordered matter. 13. The atmospheric realm (lit., "the airy earth") is probably the region that included the seven planets (moon, sun, Mercury, Venus, Mars, Jupiter, Saturn) in each of whose orbits Zostrianos is baptized in "living water," a Sethian metaphor for enlightenment through receipt of saving knowledge. 14. This terminology for the upper realms inhabited by disincarnate souls, the Sojourn (*paroikēsis*), Repentance (*metanoia*), and the Aeonic Copies (*antitupoi*), was known to Plotinus (*Ennead* II,

9 [33] 6.1–10). 15. Perhaps Zostrianos's sixth baptism at the level of the Repentance. 16. Upon each of the first four baptisms, Zostrianos becomes a different sort of angel, coming to "stand" upon each of four aeons, probably the Four Luminaries (7). The account of his fifth baptism in the name of the Self-Generated One, where he becomes "divine" and stands upon the "fifth" aeon, is narrated forty-six pages later, after the lengthy revelations of Authrounios and Ephesech the Child of the Child. The fivefoldness of Zostrianos's baptisms in the name of the divine Self-Generated One probably stems from the well-attested traditional Sethian baptismal rite of the "Five Seals."

I [became] a [contemplative] angel and stood upon the first—that is, the fourth—aeon together with the souls. I blessed

> the divine Self-Generated One
> and the forefather Pigeradamas,
> [an eye of] the Self-Generated One, the first perfect [human being];
> and Seth Emm[acha Seth],
> the son of [A]damas, the [father of] the [immovable race];
> and the [Four] Luminaries, [Armozel and Oroiael, Daveithe and Eleleth];
> and Mirothea the mother [of Adamas],
> and Prophania [the mother] of the luminaries,
> and Ple[sithea] the [mother of the angels].[17] [7]

The Second of Five Baptisms in the Name of the Self-Generated One (7,1–9)

I was [baptized for the] second time in the name of the divine Self-Generated One by these same powers. I became an angel of masculine gender. I stood upon the second—that is, the third—aeon along with the children of Seth, and I blessed these same ones.

The Third of Five Baptisms in the Name of the Self-Generated One (7,9–16)

And I was baptized for the third time in the name of the divine Self-Generated One by these same powers. [I] became a holy angel and stood upon the third—that is, the second—[aeon], and [blessed] these same ones.

The Fourth of Five Baptisms in the Name of the Self-Generated One (7,16–22)

And I was baptized for the fourth time by these [same] powers. I became a perfect [angel and stood upon] the fourth—[that is, the first]—aeon, and [blessed these same ones].

Zostrianos Seeks the Single Reality Underlying the Self-Generated Aeons (7,22–8,7)

Then I sought [a single power belonging to them]. I spoke [these words, saying], "I . . . of . . . ." And I [was asking] him [about how they should be understood]: "Why [are there differences] in the ability [to hear] them, given the differences in human hearing? [8] [Are these very things] their powers? Or are they the same things, but with names that differ from one another? Does soul differ from soul? Why are human beings different from one another? How and to what extent are they human?"

---

17. See the similar list of beings praised at Zostrianos's fifth baptism in the name of the Self-Generated One in 51. In the *Holy Book of the Great Invisible Spirit*, many of these beings are also invoked in its concluding baptismal ritual (III, 64–65), and in III, 49–56 one finds an account of their origin.

The Revelation of Authrounios (8,7–13,6)

THE REALMS BELOW THE SELF-GENERATED AEONS (8,7–28)

The great preeminence, Authrounios, said to me:

"Are you asking about those things through which you have passed?[18] Or why this atmospheric realm has this worldly pattern? Or how many Aeonic Copies there are? Or why they are [un]disturbed? Or about the Sojourn and Repentance and about the [aeonic] creation and the world that [does not truly exist?[19] I will openly teach] you about [all these things you ask] of me. [No revelation] or [mandate can appear] to you, [even from the] Invisible [Spirit, until you know these things] and the [doctrine that . . . . . . Eleleth . . . that] will appear to you."

[And the two of us joined with the aeons] that I had [traversed].

THE ORIGIN OF THE PHYSICAL COSMOS AND SOPHIA'S ROLE (8,30–10,28)

And [9] the [great] preeminence Authrounios said [to me], "The atmospheric realm came into being by a rational principle, and it incorruptibly manifests generated and perishable things for the sake of the advent of the great judges,[20] lest they experience perception and be enclosed in the creation. But when they came upon it and thereby perceived the works of the world, they condemned its ruler to a perishability characteristic of the world, since it is a [substance] and principle of matter, that dark, corrupt [product].

"When Sophia looked [down],[21] she saw the darkness, [illumining it] while maintaining [her own station], being a model for [worldly] things, [a principle] for the [insubstantial] substance [and the form]less form . . . a [shapeless] shape. [It makes room] for [every cosmic thing] . . . the All . . . [the corrupt product, since it is a rational principle that persuades] the darkness. [He sows from his] reason, since it [is im]possible [for the ruler] of [creation] to see any of the eternal entities. [10] He saw a reflection, and with reference to the reflection that he [saw] in it, he created the world. With a reflection of a reflection he worked upon the world, and then even the reflection of what appeared was taken from him.

"But Sophia was given a place of rest in exchange for her repentance. As a result, since there was within her no pure, original image—either preexisting in him or that had already come to be through him—he used his imagination and fashioned the remainder, for the image belonging to Sophia is always corrupt and deceptive. But the archon—[since he simulates] and embodies by [pursuing the image] on account of the superabundance [that inclined downward]—looked down."

---

18. I.e., the thirteen aeons of the archon, the sublunar atmospheric realm, the planetary realm of the Aeonic Copies, the Sojourn, and Repentance. 19. "That which truly does not exist" is a technical term derived from later Platonic systematization of the modes of being mentioned in Plato's *Sophist* 240b, 254d. 20. Probably the stars. 21. From her position just above the fixed stars (the "judges"), Sophia illumines preexisting matter and serves the archon of creation as his model for creating the world. While Plato's demiurge looks above to the ideal forms contained in the "truly living being" (*Timaeus* 39e), the archon of creation can only look downward to their faint reflection in the matter illumined by Sophia. Plotinus's critique of Gnostic views of creation in *Ennead* II, 9 (33) 10.19–33 (cf. 11.14–30) may actually be citing *Zostrianos* 10.

When [I heard these things and when] I saw [them, I was able to understand] the mind of [these who set their mind] upon the things they do not [know]. Since he has set [his mind upon . . . the] aeons . . . greater than . . . .

THE RESTORATION OF SOPHIA (10,28–11,2)

And [again he said, "Sophia became] perfect[22] through [the will of the commander] through whom [the atmospheric realm persists], having [11] [immutably averted] the destruction of the world.

THE AEONIC COPIES AND THE ILLUMINATION OF SOULS (11,2–13,6)

"Now the Aeonic Copies[23] exist as follows: they have not attained an equipotent form, [but] they possess eternal glories, and they exist as judgment seats for each of the powers. But when souls are illumined by the light within these copies and by the pattern that often arises [effortlessly] in them, then the soul thinks that she sees [the truth] and the eternal [cause in] the blessed [idea that exists] as the single unity . . . each of . . . light that . . . all, and she . . . whole, and she and a . . . and she . . . she who . . . she . . . of [the Sojourn. And the evidence] for the Repentance [is with the souls] [12] according to the power [within them that] they might stand.

"And inferior [souls] are trained by the Aeonic Copies, which receive a replica of their souls while they are still in the world. After the individual emergence of the aeons, they come into being and are individually transferred from the copy of the Sojourn to the truly existent Sojourn, from the copy of the Repentance to the truly existent Repentance, [and from the] copy of the Self-Generated Aeons [to the] truly existent [Self-Generated Aeons], and so on . . . . The souls . . . exist in a [light] . . . them all [through the] Aeonic [Copies].

"[On the one hand, they] see, [but when] . . . and certain . . . forth . . . the . . . outside . . . light . . . of . . . [all] those [who] are . . . [as they [13] bless]

[the god] above the [great] aeons,
and the [unengendered] Kalyptos,
the great male Protophanes,
the perfect [Child] who is higher than god,
and his eye, Pigeradamas."

Zostrianos Invokes Ephesech, Child of the Child (13,7–26)

I called upon the Child of the Child Ephesech.[24] He stood before me and said, "O messenger of god, child of the father, [you are] the perfect human.

---

22. Remaining traces suggest this passage may have related the restoration of Sophia, a common theme in Sethian literature, known also to Plotinus (*Ennead* II, 9 [33] 4,15–19). It is unclear whether the subject of 10–11 "[reveals]" (*eaf[ou]ōn[ᵉh]*) or "[averts]" (*eaf[pō]ōn[e]*) the destruction of the world; in *Genesis* 6:11–13 the creator elects to destroy his creation. **23.** The Aeonic Copies serve as a pattern by which incarnate souls are enabled to "think" that they see the ideal reality that

truly exists, thus giving them an initial orientation toward intelligible reality, enabling them to be transferred from the mere visible copies of heavenly realities to their archetypal "patterns" contained in the truly existent Sojourn, Repentance, and Self-Generated Aeons. **24.** Ephesech is known also from the *Holy Book of the Great Invisible Spirit*, where he is named Esephech, Child of the Child, son of the Triple-Male Child and the male virgin Youel (IV, 56).

[Why] are you calling on me and asking about the things you know, as though you were [ignorant] of them?"

[But I said], "I am inquiring about the water: [so how does] it make perfect and give [its power]? What are [its] powers? [The names] in which we receive baptism? [Why are] these names [different from those]? And why [are the waters different] from one [another? And are they complete] in the . . . [from] others . . . humans . . . ? [Why are they different in this way from one another]?"

The Revelation of Ephesech: Part I, Baptism and Assimilation to the Barbelo Aeon (13,27–44,22)

THE THREE POWERS OF THE INVISIBLE SPIRIT AND THE ORIGIN OF THE BARBELO AEON (13,27–14,28)

[The Child of the Child Ephesech, the Savior, answered], [14] saying:

"[Zost]trianos, hear about [all] these things! Now the pre[existent] principles are three in number, although they have appeared from a single principle [of] the Barbelo Aeon,[25] not as an indefinite number of principles and powers, nor as derivatives of just any origin and power. On the contrary,

> they have manifested every principle
> and empowered every power,
> and have appeared in that which is far superior to them,
> these ones who are Existence, Blessedness, and Life.

"[These have appeared] with one [another and have appeared] from a [single unity], and therefore . . . they were named [for their] greater [glory . . . single] . . . and [certain] . . . a perfect . . . from [a single principle, and it is] a [simple unity] . . . always . . . . [15]

THREE BAPTISMAL WATERS OF THE BARBELO AEON, THREE POWERS OF THE INVISIBLE SPIRIT (15,1–16,2)

"And [there exists] a water for [each] of them. Therefore they are [three] perfect waters:[26]

> It is the water of Life
> that belongs to Vitality
> in which you now have been baptized in the Self-Generated One.

---

25. The "single origin of the Barbelo aeon" is the supreme Invisible Spirit, who contains three preexistent principles, Existence, Blessedness, and Life, the three powers or phases by which the Barbelo Aeon originates as the First Thought of the "triple-powered" Invisible Spirit. Preexisting within the Invisible Spirit as a prefigurative, indeterminate Existence (*huparxis*), it proceeds forth as a purely indeterminate Vitality (*zōotēs*), finally achieving the fully determinate being as the Aeon of Barbelo by an act of contemplative reflection (known as Mentality, *noētēs*, or Blessedness, *makariotēs*) upon its original prefiguration still latent within its source, the Invisible Spirit. In *Zostrianos*, the *Three Steles of Seth*, and Victorinus *Against Arius* (1.48–64 and 3.1–10), "Blessedness" is a technical term for being turned toward oneself in an act of self-determining insight or self-knowledge. 26. Baptism into these waters signifies a mental assimilation to the three preexistent principles Existence, Blessedness, and Life (named here in the standard Neoplatonic order rather than in the order Existence, Life, and Blessedness as used in the *Three Steles of Seth* (124; 125), *Allogenes the Stranger* (59–60; 61), and in the negative theology of *Zostrianos* (64–75, 80).

It is the [water] of Blessedness
that [belongs] to Knowledge
in which you will be [baptized] in the Protophanes.

It is the water of Existence
[that] belongs to Divinity,
that is, to Kalyptos.

And the water of Life [exists with respect to] power,
that of [Blessedness] with respect to essence,
and that of [Divinity] with respect to [Existence].

"But all [these are likenesses and forms of the] Triple-Powered One. It is [they] that [flow from the] pure water . . . [it] is also [the pattern . . . water] according to . . . [when they] depart . . . [male . . . there] . . . [16] Existence [as he] is.

The Generation of Determinate Being: The Barbelo Aeon (16,2–17,5)

"Not only [did they dwell] in thought, but he [made room for] them, since he is [Becoming] in the following way: he imposed a [limit] upon Being, lest it become endless and formless; instead, Becoming was truly delimited[27] while it was a new entity in order that [it] might become an entity having its proper [place], Existence together with [Being], standing with it, existing with it, surrounding it, [and being like it] on every side.[28] [It withdrew] from the [living water that it might] receive the [pre]existent [stability] of . . . activity . . . visible . . . his word also . . . these after . . . they became . . . [making room] for a . . . . [17] And the power exists together with the Essence and the Existence of Being, while this water exists. And the name in which one is baptized is a verbal expression of this water.

The Receipt of Enlightenment and Stable Being Through Baptism (17,5–18,10)

"Therefore the first perfect water of the Triple-Powered One, <that of> the Self-Generated One, [is] Life for the perfect souls,[29] since it is a rational expression of the coming into being of both the perfect [mind and of] that [one].[30] For the source of all [those] is the Invisible Spirit, while the others derive [from knowledge], since they are likenesses of him. [But] he who simultaneously knows

---

27. Note the Platonic contrast between unstable, indeterminate Becoming and determinate, stable Being. Perhaps the Coptic translator confused an original *diaperainein* ("delimit," "bring to an end") with *diaperan*, ("traverse," normally rendered by Coptic *jioor*). 28. Prefigurative being proceeds forth as an indeterminate, formless Vitality, which, if unchecked, would proceed to infinity. By placing a limit on it, it becomes defined (comes to "stand") as true, stable Being with its own "dwelling place"; cf. *Allogenes the Stranger* 49. 29. Perfect souls, having partaken of the living water

and having entered into the indeterminate limitlessness of Vitality, achieve stable existence by an act of knowledge, just as Barbelo did in the course of her own emanation from the Invisible Spirit. Although it appears that Zostrianos is never baptized in the waters of Protophanes (the "water of Blessedness"), he nevertheless sees them, and since he apparently never enters the Kalyptos Aeon, he never sees the waters ("of Existence") there, although he does "hear" about them. 30. I.e., the Self-Generated One.

[how he exists] and what [the living water is—such a one] lives by [knowledge. That which belongs to knowledge] is the [water of Vitality]. And in [becoming, Life] becomes [limitless, so that it may receive] its [own Being . . . and] the name . . . . . .[31] [18] he truly exists; this is so since he limits himself. They [approach] this water according to this equivalence in power and rank.

"Protophanes, the great male invisible perfect mind, has his own water, as you [will see] when you arrive at his place. So also does the unengendered Kalyptos.

THE STRUCTURE OF THE BARBELO AEON (18,11–26,19)

The Barbelo Aeon (18,11–19,3). "In relation to each one there exists a partial and [initial] form, so that they might thus become complete. Now the Self-Generated Aeons are four complete instances of the all-perfect ones [that exist before] the [perfect individuals]. And the [fifth] aeon [contains] the [divine] Self-Generated One, for [they] all [derive from the perfect, divine Triple]-Male [Child].[32] For [they are] wholes . . . perfect [divine . . . the Triple-Male . . . the perfect] individuals . . . in the . . . . . .[33] [19] perfect,[34] those who exist by species, genus, whole, and partial difference.

The Self-Generated One, the Triple-Male Child, Protophanes, and Kalyptos (19,4–21,1). "The path of ascent that is higher than perfect <is> likewise with Kalyptos.

"The divine Self-Generated One is chief ruler of his own aeons and angels as parts of him, since those that individually comprise the four simultaneously comprise the fifth aeon, and the fifth exists in unity. Taken individually, the four [comprise] the fifth. But all these are individually complete [because they] have a [single principle].

"So also [the Triple-Male] is a [perfect individual], for he is a [power] of the divine [Self-Generated One]. And [Protophanes], the invisible [perfect] male mind, [is the dwelling place] of those who [are unified within the aeons]. A . . . . . .[35] [like] [20] living and perfect parts.

"Now as for the All, both the all-perfect kind and that which is higher than perfect and blessed:

"The self-generated Kalyptos is a preexistent principle of the Self-Generated One, a deity and forefather, a cause of Protophanes, a father of his own parts. A paternal deity, he is apprehended, but not comprehended. As he is a self-derived power, he is his own father, therefore he is [fatherless].

"The invisible Triple-Powered One, the forethought [of them] all, the Invisible Spirit, is [the source of them all] and [an insubstantial Existence prior to Essence] and Existence [and Being. Existences are prior to] Life, [for it is] the [cause of] Blessed[ness. And] . . . the [magnitude] . . . all [these] . . . the . . . . . .[36] [21] [exist] in them.

---

31. Four lines missing. **32.** Souls must progress from the "perfect individuals" in the Self-Generated Aeons to the "all-perfect ones" in the Aeons of Protophanes and Kalyptos. The Self-Generated Aeons are four in number, defined by the Four Luminaries that preside over each; as a group of four they are presided over by the divine Self-Generated One as a sort of "fifth aeon." **33.** Five lines missing. **34.** Probably "perfect individuals." **35.** Four lines missing. **36.** Three lines missing.

Baptism and the Ascent and Unification of Souls Within the Barbelo Aeon (21,1–24,17). "[They descended] among others, but they [are all] intermingled in many places, whatever place is desirable and pleasing. They are everywhere and they are nowhere. They contain spirit—for they are incorporeal—yet they transcend incorporeal things. They are undivided, with living thoughts and a power of truth, together with those purer than they, since in this respect they are spiritually purer and unlike bodies that are in a single location. Above all, they are without compulsion, whether in whole or part. So their path of ascent is pure [because it is imperishable]. Each [of their powers has] set [aside for itself] its own [root]. And . . . them . . . . . . its [22] particular aeons. Then [he knows] how he can receive an eternal pattern.

"And the universal intelligence joins in when the water of the Self-Generated One is complete. When one knows it and all these, one has to do with the water of Protophanes; when one unites with him and all these, one has to do with Kalyptos. Similarly among the aeons: as regards knowing these individually along with their parts, they are [perfect]. Those of the All, where knowledge is, and that which they know have [become distinct], yet they have something in common with one another. The All and all [these have the] immersion in the [baptism of the Self-Generated One].[37]

"If the . . . perfect . . . .[38] The [23] one who shows that he has come to know how he belongs to him and experiences mutual fellowship has washed in the baptism of Protophanes.

"And if one understands their origin, how they are all manifest in a single principle, and how all who are joined become divided, and how those who were divided join together again, and how the parts [join with] the wholes and the species with the [genera]—when one understands these things, one has washed in the baptism of Kalyptos.

"For each locale one has a portion of the eternal ones and ascends [to them. As] one [becomes pure and] simple, just so one continually [approaches] unity. Being [always] pure and [simple], one is filled [with Mentality,] with Existence, [and spirit], even a holy Spirit. There is [24] nothing of him outside of him.

On the one hand, with perfect soul he [sees] those of the Autogenic ones;
with Intellect, those of the Triple-Male;
with holy Spirit, those of the Protophanic ones.

On the other hand, he hears about Kalyptos
through the powers of the Spirit from whom they have come forth
in a far superior revelation of the Invisible Spirit.

---

37. Baptism in the water of the Self-Generated One brings knowledge of souls and ideas as distinct entities; baptism in the waters of Protophanes unifies the individuated souls and ideas in the Self-Generated One according to the universal ideas in Kalyptos. Baptism in the water of Kalyptos (apparently not achieved by Zostrianos) entails a thorough understanding of incorporeal reality by both an analytic and a synthetic knowledge of the relation of parts to the whole, and of species to their genus, and vice versa. 38. Five lines missing.

And by means of the thought that now exists in silence,
even within the First Thought,
he hears about the Triple-Powered Invisible Spirit;

it is, moreover, an audition and a silent power
purified with life-giving Spirit,
the perfect, [first] perfect, and all-perfect one.[39]

Preservation of Those Who Are Worthy by the Glories (24,17–30). "Therefore there are glories[40] appointed as [nourishers] over them. Those who have been truly baptized in knowledge and those who are worthy are guarded, but those who [are] not from this kind [are mere things] and they [return] to [their own root. One deriving from] the fifth is [satisfied with those of the Aeonic] Copies. [For each] of the aeons [there is] a baptism [of this sort].

Various Baptisms and Degrees of Knowledge (24,30–26,19). "Now if [one] strips off the world [**25**] and lays aside [nature], whether one is a sojourner without dwelling place or power, following the practices of others, or whether one repents, having committed no sin, being satisfied with knowledge and without concern for anything worldly, baptisms are appointed respectively for these:

"There is first the path into the Self-Generated ones, the one in which you have now been baptized each time, which is appropriate for seeing the [perfect] individuals. It is a knowledge of everything, having originated from the powers of the Self-Generated ones.

"Next there is the baptism you will perform when you transfer to the all-perfect aeons.

"When you wash in the third baptism, [then] you will hear about those [that] truly [exist] in [that] place.

"Now concerning [these] names,[41] they are like this: there is a unity, [and it is a single genus] like [things that are perfect] by virtue of [coming into being among] things that are, and [they have come into being because] there is a rational expression of them [and because] [**26**] it is a name that truly exists [as] they do.

"Now on the one hand, existing things exist in a concept similar to them, and its generic similarity is its innate property; on the other hand, an individual sees, understands, enters, and becomes like his genus by audible speech and hearing. But by mere hearing they are powerless, because they are sensible and corporeal, and so they merely take things as they are able to receive them; it's a [faint] image of the sort that comes from sensation or reasoning, superior to material nature but inferior to the intellectual essence.

---

39. The contemplative ascent from Protophanes to Kalyptos to the supreme Invisible Spirit corresponds to an epistemological progression from active and discursive seeing to the passive hearing of revelation (given by the luminaries of *Zostrianos* 64–96) to pure silent intuition. **40.** The glories, "conceptual patterns of salvation available as helpers to anyone who wishes to transcend this world" (63), inhabit all ontological levels, from the top level of the Barbelo Aeon to the earth itself. Most of the named glories, including Authrounios, Ephesech Child of the Child, and Youel Mother of the Glories, exist in the Barbelo Aeon. **41.** Baptismal names are apparently rational expressions (*logoi*) of stable and changeless things, namely, archetypal ideas and forms. In Platonic metaphysics, *logos* is a transcendent entity that can act upon and give shape to physical, sensible things.

VARIOUS KINDS OF SOULS AND THEIR LEVEL OF AEONIC ATTAINMENT
(26,19–28,30)

Types of Incarnate Souls (26,19–27,14). "Do not be amazed about the differences among souls. When one thinks that they are different, then they are [not] similar, although they are [parts] of things that [endure].

> [Now] one[42] [appears] in a [soul] and has [completely] perished;
> their [souls are disem]bodied.
> Another [who is within] his time [appears] for a while; [**27**]
> their soul is [em]bodied.

> Now those who have completely [perished] are four,
> while those [within] time are nine.
> Each of them has its character and habit.
> Although similar, they are different;
> although individually distinct, they are at least stable.

"And other immortal souls associate with all these souls because of Wisdom who looked down. For there are three species of immortal souls:

Types of Disincarnate Souls in the Sojourn (27,14–21). "The ones who have taken root upon the Sojourn do not have self-generated power; they follow the ways of others. Now this is a single species, [self-contained].

Types of Disincarnate Souls in the Repentance (27,21–28,10). "Second, those that stand [upon the] Repentance, who [were not ambivalent about] sin, since knowledge is sufficient [for] them: since they are neophytes, [they still sin]. Yet this kind also has distinctions: there are [those] who have sinned; others [also who] [**28**] have repented; and still others [who only intend to repent]. For there are [three] classes of these last ones: those who have committed all the sins and have repented; those who have sinned partially; or those who only intended to sin. Therefore, their aeons also are six according to the place attained by each of their souls.

Types of Disincarnate Souls in the Self-Generated Aeons (28,10–30). "The third kind is that of the souls of the Self-Generated ones; they have an ineffable and knowledgeable, rational account of the truth, as well as self-generated [power] and eternal [life. And] they have four distinctions in the same manner: the forms of angels, those who love the truth, those who hope, and those who believe. [Indeed], they [also] have [mates] and exist [within them]. They exist [as four places of] the Self-Generated ones: [the first] is the one of [perfect Life]; the

---

42. The fourfoldness of completely perished souls may be related to the succession of births experienced by the soul: e.g., the four grades of souls in *Phaedo* 113d–114e. Likewise, the ninefoldness of souls still in their time may be related to the nine births of *Phaedrus* 248c–e. Those of the Sojourn, Repentance, and the Self-Generated Aeons are apparently souls that are disembodied during the period in which they must make a choice of the kind of life and body they will have in their next incarnation. Sojourners merely follow the "practices" or "ways" of others (27). Repenters have entered upon a morally scrupulous life, no longer ambivalent about sin, but aware of the sins they do commit. Inhabitants of the Self-Generated Aeons, baptized like Zostrianos in living water, have "eternal life"; their virtues (angelic form, and love, hope, and faith) resemble the triad of "abiding" virtues in Paul's encomium on love in 1 *Corinthians* 13:13.

[second] is [the one of Mentality]; the [third is the one of eternal] knowledge; the fourth is the one [belonging to the] immortal [souls]. [29]

THE RELATION OF THE FOUR LUMINARIES AND THEIR
DENIZENS TO THE SOUL'S ASCENT (29,1–32,10)

"The Four Luminaries exist [there] in the same way:

> [Arm]ozel [is set] over the first aeon,
> a desire for god and truth, a uniter of souls;
> Oroiael, a seer of truth, is set over the second;
> Daveithe, a vision of knowledge, is set over the third;
> Eleleth, an eager appetite and readiness for truth, is set over the fourth.

"The four exist as rational expressions of truth and knowledge. They exist, although they belong not to Protophanes but to the Mother.

"It is a thought of the perfect mind of light that causes immortal souls to acquire knowledge. [He who suffices] for them is the [divine] Self-Generated One, Arse[n]oas,[43] a revelation [of the power] of them all, [since] he is an [intelligent], ineffable rational expression [of the] truth who [speaks openly] about the [perfect Mind], namely, that it is a higher [principle that is indivisibly [30] joined] in a partnership between itself and an [intellectual] light and thought within its own aeon.

"And Adam is the [perfect] human, being an eye of the Self-Generated One. It is his knowledge that <knows> that the divine Self-Generated One is a rational expression of the perfect Mind of truth.

"The son of Adam, Seth, comes to each of the souls as knowledge sufficient for them. Therefore, the living [seed] originated from him.

"Mirothea is [the one in whom] the divine Self-Generated One [appeared] together with [Adamas]; she is a thought of the perfect Mind concerning her own Existence, what she is, [how] she used to exist, and how she now exists.

"Therefore the divine Self-Generated One is a rational principle and knowledge, knowledge [that derives from a rational power]. Accordingly, [the soul of] Adamas [is simple. It is the power] of the [simple ones to whom] it appeared; [it is a] transformation of souls; it is also [a power of the] perfect [Mind]. On behalf of [the perfect ones and] the angelic host [31] [it has often appeared].

"[If] therefore [there exists the cosmic] soul [that produces them and preexists the perceptible world as well], the Aeonic Copies [that] truly [exist and the Sojourn] that [truly exists and] the Repentance [are the ascent] to this place, up [to the Self-Generated] Aeons that [truly] exist.[44]

"If [the soul finds] and loves [the truth], it will stand upon [the fourth] aeon, [possessing] the luminary Eleleth; [it will] become a contemplative [thought].

---

43. Perhaps "male mind"; possibly read "[S]orso[r]oas."
44. The restoration of this paragraph is extremely conjectural.

"[And if] it hopes and perceives, it is an [angel] of the [masculine] gender that has come to stand upon [the third, possessing the luminary Daveithe]. [32]

"[If] it is joined [with the truth, then it will] stand [upon the] first [aeon, possessing the luminary] Ar[mozel].

"[If you become] an [angel of the intelligible world, and if you ascend] to [that power], you [will] stand upon [the first aeon], the light that [is over them all].

NEGATIVE AND POSITIVE PROSPECTS FOR SOULS IN THE
SELF-GENERATED AEONS (32,11–35,10)

"Immeasurable [and great is] that aeon! [Now if you attain] only those, [you will fall away] from the perfect [aeons and] that power, [whether] or [not it is] possible for one [to consolidate] every [form] of his [immortal] soul, not [only] the perceptible and [measurable, but] also the in[expressibly] individually [perfect] one.

". . . . . .[45] [33] Adamas, and . . . [the divine] Autoge[nes]. And he ascends [to the great perfect] Mind [Protophanes]. The divine [unengendered] Kalyptos [who fore]knows . . . . . .[46] [35] [she stands. And if] a soul . . . [it again becomes an angel], and [if the angels and the other divine beings become] worldly, the holy [soul is] superior.

AEONIC LEVELS AND WATERS BELOW THE SELF-GENERATED AEONS (35,10–17)

"Now as for the aeons that are [below the Self-Generated] ones, [they too] have [other] waters, the [water of the holy soul and also those of] the archons. [But these waters] have [still other distinctions] about which it is not [fitting for] the soul to speak.

THE TRIPLE-MALE CHILD AND THE THREE SUBAEONS OF THE
BARBELO AEON (35,17–42,6)

"[The invisible] male [stands before] it and [before] the divine [Autogen]es . . . which exists . . . hear . . . Self-Generated One . . . of . . . [any [36] pattern at all. He] has [a rational expression] of Existence [in order that he might become] Life [for all those that] exist on account of [an intelligent] rational expression [of the truth].

"The [perfect Triple]-Male Child [is] a form [of the] divine [Self-Generated One, a power of the Invisible] Spirit [and a thought within] the perfect [Mind, and an] agreement of [a prime principle] with a principle [and of a prime] source with [a source. He is a power] of Barbel[o. And he is a revelation] and a [thought within] the perfect Mind.[47]

"[Now the] secondary principles are those of [the knowledge of the] thought [that originated] from the [light that exists] in Barbel[o] . . . . And Kalyptos . . . [37] in that one. [Either she derives from] the power [of] that one, [or else she] derives

---

45. The bottom seven lines of p. 32, the first seventeen and last six lines of p. 33, and all of p. 34 are nearly obliterated and unreconstructable. 46. Three lines missing. 47. I.e., Barbelo.

from [its aeon]. But she derives from the power of that one, [the one who truly exists], since she [exists] as his [image. He is the preexistent one]; although they are pre[existent, they are derivatives] of that preexistence [which is his alone]. And he is the [the immutable one]; it is he alone [that can] suffice for himself, [for he has no] deficiency . . . . [48] [38]

"[The Triple-Male Child is] a [thought] of the perfect [Mind, since he is knowledge] and he [is a] perfect [triple-powered] spirit. [He is a] perfect [male], living forever, [since he is an invisible god]. And [he exists because] this one exists [before him. He is the rational expression] of the [perfect Mind, since] he is [a rational expression] from . . . which is in . . . [they have] all these eternally . . . [exist in] the Triple-[Powered] . . . is in the . . . [they resemble] those that [are unified, being] perfect . . . the Protopha[nes perfect] Mind, but . . . . [49] [39]

". . . [him] as if he [alone] exists and as if [he is] other [than existing things], that is, [that which has] privation . . . . [50] [40] [The Triple-Male Child's] knowledge [is Protophanes, the invisible perfect male mind. And] he has [his own Existence] within the unengendered [Kalyptos. He possesses the] third [of those aeons, since he] possesses [Mentality]. And he [contains those who] dwell together [in order that they become] all-perfect [and blessed], since there is no . . . . . . [51] [41] [Pr]oto[phanes, the male perfect] Mind, [possesses all] the powers [that dwell] entirely [unified] within [him] and he [dwells among them].

"And his knowledge [is a great deity], the Self-Generated [One]. And [the divine Self-Generated One is a principle] of the [perfect] Triple-Male Child. And this male [is a pattern and species of the] perfect [Mind]—although it does not contain [these] within a [single] knowledge like that one—[and he is] a measure of the individuals and a single knowledge of the individuals, [both] the wholly [and individually] perfect.

"And the [perfect] male Mind [is] a [knowledge of] the Kalyptos, and the divine [unengendered] Kalyptos [is a principle and cause] and a power [and an existence] of them all . . . truly . . . . . . [Pro]to[phanes . . . Pro]-[42]to[phanes] . . . one another . . . mind . . . they [exist together . . . wholly . . . the] unengendered [Kalyptos]. . . .

FIVE KINDS OF PERSONS AND THEIR PROSPECTS FOR SALVATION (42,6–44,22)

Mortality Necessitates Salvation (42,6–19). ". . . human . . . since they [belong to all those who will be saved] and to the one who [will save them].[52]

"Now the [one who repents and] the sojourner [and the one inhabiting] the perceptible [world] live with what is dead. [They] all [resemble a single thing.

---

48. Lines 13–29 unreconstructable. 49. 38,19–39,8 unreconstructable. 50. 39,13–40,5 unreconstructable. 51. 40, 18–41,2 unreconstructable. 52. Of these five categories, worst off are persons that not only inhabit a dead body, but everything else about them is dead. Slightly better off are those merely materialistic persons who fail to seek the higher realities and practice a utilitarian ethic as if there were no soul or eternal god.

Even better are the sojourners who at least seek the truth and the repentant who zealously seek immortal things. The "self-generated power" of those in the Self-Generated Aeons leads them not only to earnestly seek the truth, but in fact to live the life of the philosopher, "finding itself and its intellect" (cf. *Phaedo* 114b–c).

They] attain salvation [apart from] the dead. Now [none] of them needed salvation initially, but salvation is needed more now that they are degraded.

Materialistic Persons with Dead Souls (42,20–43,1). "As for the type of person that is dead: its soul, [its mind], and its body [are] all [dead]. Sufferings [of the subtle], fathers of [material men, they are demons that] the fire [consumes. They are worldly] . . . [43] that is transformed.

Materialistic Persons with Living Souls (43,1–12). "The second type of person is the immortal soul that inhabits dead things, concerning itself with them; [for] it then [undertakes] a search for particular benefits [and it] experiences bodily suffering. The soul [is treated corporeally], and it [forgets that it has] an eternal god; it associates with demons.

Those Who Sojourn (43,13–19). "Now the humanity in the Sojourn: if it inwardly possesses a discovery of the truth, it is far from the deeds of others who live [wickedly] and [stumble].

Those Who Repent (43,19–30). "As for the type of person that repents: if it renounces dead things and desires real things—immortal mind and immortal soul—[it is going to] be zealous about them by first undertaking for itself an inquiry, not just about action but of the results. From this he [receives another way of thinking. The entire place] and [every] attainment [will be his]. [44]

Those Who Are Saved (44,1–22). "Now the type of person that can be saved is the one that seeks itself and its intellect and finds each of them. And how much power this type has!

"The person that has been saved is one who has not known about these things [merely] as they seem to exist, but one who is personally involved with the rational faculty as it exists [in him]. He has grasped their [image that changes] in every situation as though they had become simple and one. For then this type is saved who can pass through [them] all; [he becomes] them all. Whenever he [wishes], he again parts from all these matters and withdraws into himself; for he becomes divine, having withdrawn into god."

Zostrianos's Response to Ephesech's First Revelation (44,22–45,9)

[Now] this is what [I] heard, and I offered up praise[53] to

the living and unengendered God [who is] in truth,
and the unengendered [Kalyptos],
Protophanes the invisible male perfect Mind,
the invisible Triple-Male Child,
and the divine Self-Generated One. [45]

I said to the Child of the Child Ephesech who was with me, "Can your wisdom instruct me about the dissipation of the type of person that is saved? What

---

53. Cf. this doxology with *Allogenes the Stranger* 58.

are the things mixed with it, and what are those that divide it, so that the living elect might know?"

The Revelation of Ephesech: Part II (45,9–47,27)

SOULS THAT CAN BE SAVED NEED ASSISTANCE TO
ESCAPE REINCARNATION (45,9–46,15)

Then the Child of the Child Ephesech, [speaking] openly, told me:

"When this type[54] repeatedly withdraws into itself alone and is occupied with the knowledge of other things, since the intellect and immortal [soul] do [not] intelligize, it thereupon experiences deficiency, since even it turns aside, has nothing, and separates from the intellect, stands [apart] and experiences an alien [appetite] instead of becoming a unity. So that type of person resembles many forms. And when it turns aside, it comes into being seeking things that don't exist. When it descends to them in thought, it cannot understand them in any other way unless [46] it be enlightened, and so it becomes a mere physical object. Accordingly, this type of person descends into generation and becomes speechless because of the difficulties and indefiniteness of matter. Although possessing eternal, immortal power, this type is bound in the clutches of the body, [removed], and [continually] bound within strong bonds, is lacerated by every evil spirit, until it once more [reconstitutes itself] and begins again to inhabit it.

THE GLORIES ENABLE SALVATION (46,15–47,27)

"Therefore, for their salvation, there have been appointed specific powers, and these same ones inhabit this world.[55] And among the Self-Generated ones there stand at each [aeon] certain glories, so that one who is in the [world] might be saved alongside [them]. The glories are perfect living concepts; it is [im]possible that they perish, because [they are] patterns of salvation—that is to say, anyone receiving them will be rescued to them. Being patterned, one will be empowered by it. And, having that glory as a helper, one thus passes through the world [and every aeon].

"And there [47] are the guardians of the immortal soul:[56]

Gamaliel and Strempsouchos;
Akramas and Loel, and Mnesinous [are] immortal spirits;
Yesseus [M]azareu[s] Ye[s]sedekeus is [the commander]
[who] belongs to the Child, [the Savior],
the Child of the Child, even [the one who knows you];

---

54. In spite of their self-generated power to escape the body and assimilate themselves to the divine realm, the souls of the saved can become occupied with the affairs of the body, whose clutches force them to undergo another cycle of reincarnation. 55. The glories assist one's ascent through the world and the aeons above. Their chief is Youel/Yoel, "the all-glorious one" ("she-of-all-the-glories"), the masculine Mother of all the glories that provide the noetic "patterns of salvation" to anyone seeking enlightenment (see 54). 56. Cf. the similar list of beings involved in the Sethian baptismal ritual portrayed in *Holy Book of the Great Invisible Spirit* III, 64–65.

and Ormos is [delimiter] over the living seed,
and Kam[ali]el is the spirit-giver;
The attendants are Isauel and Audael and [A]brasax;
the myriads, Phaleris, Phalses, and Eurios;
the guardians of glory, Stetheus, Theo[pe]mptos, Eurumeneus, and
    Olsen.
The helpers [in] every matter are Ba[thor]mos, [I]son, Eir[o]n,
    Lalameus, Eidomeneus, and Authrou[n]ios;
the judges are Sumphthar, Eukrebos, and Keilar;
the rapturer, Samblo;
the angels who guide the misty clouds are Sappho and Thouro."

Zostrianos's Vision and Praise of Self-Generated Aeons and the Triple-Male Child (47,27–53,14)

THE VISION OF ZOSTRIANOS (47,27–56,1)

When he had said these things, he told me about all those in the Self-Generated Aeons. They were all [48] eternal lights and perfect, being individually complete. At each of the aeons I saw a living earth, a living water, luminous [air], and an [unconsuming] fire.[57] All [these], being simple, are also immutable and simple [eternal living creatures], possessing a variety [of] beauty, trees of many kinds that do not perish, as well as plants of the same sort as all these, imperishable fruit, human beings alive with every species, immortal souls, every shape and species of intellect, gods of truth, angels dwelling in great glory with an indissoluble body and unengendered offspring and unchanging perception. There was also that which impassively experiences passion, for it was a power of a power . . . . [58] [51]

ZOSTRIANOS PREPARES FOR HIS FIFTH BAPTISM (51,6–53,14)

. . . we were blessing[59]

[the Self-Generated One]
and Pigeradamas
[and Mirothea the] mother of [the one glorified by] her who glorifies
    [him who begets divinity],
[and Prophania] the mother [of the luminaries],
and Plesithea [the mother] of the angels,
and [the son] of Adam, Se[th Emma]cha Seth, father of the immovable
    [race],

---

57. Cf. similar descriptions of the contents of the ideal aeonic world in 55 (the Self-Generated Aeons) and 116–17 (the aeon of Kalyptos). **58.** Pp. 49–50 and the top five lines of p. 51 are nearly obliterated. **59.** Cf. n. 17 and the beings praised during Zostrianos's first four baptisms in the name of the Self-Generated One in *Zostrianos* 6–7.

and [those who belong to the] Four Luminaries, Arm[ozel, Oroia]el,
Daveithe, Eleleth.

[These] we blessed by name: [the self]-seer, the ruler of glory, the triple-[powered
and] Triple-Male Child. [With] majesty we said,[60]

> You are one, you are [one], you are one, O Child [**52**] of ...,
> Yato[menos] ... exist ... you ....

> You are one, you [are one] ..., Semelel ... Telmachae[l] ...
> Omothem ...,
> male ... the engenderer [of glory, the] ruler of [glory, the] lovable one,
> he [of] all the absolutely all-perfect ones, Akron ...,
> O Triple-Male: AA[AAA] ŌŌŌŌŌ BI TREIS E[IS]!

> You are spirit from spirit;
> you are light from light;
> you are [silence] from silence;
> [you are] thought from thought,
> O [perfect] Child of the god ....

> Let us say ... [**53**]
> ... [let us say]
> ... [let us say]
> ... [let us say]
> ... word ... the great ... and the [great ... God] ....

[All together] we [blessed ... the] invisible [aeon of B]arbelo ... the un-... the
[Triple]-Male Prones,[61] and the all-glorious one, Youel.

The Fifth of Five Baptisms in the Name of the Self-Generated One (53,14–24)

[When I was] baptized the fifth [time] in the name of the Self-Generated One
by these same powers, I became divine.[62] [I] stood upon the [fifth] aeon, a habita-
tion for all [of them]; I saw all those belonging to the Self-Generated One, [those]
who truly exist.

---

60. This ecstatic prayer (directed to the Barbelo
Aeon) and the ones in 86 and 88 (directed by the
Kalyptos Aeon to the Barbelo Aeon) are very similar to
those found in *Three Steles of Seth* 126 (directed by the
ascending visionary to the supreme preexistent One)
and in *Allogenes the Stranger* 54 (directed by Youel to
the Barbelo Aeon). The names Sunaon, Mell[e]phaou,
El[l]emm[aoni], Smoun, and Eptaon as well as the
word *hupsiphronē*, the feminine being featured in the

Nag Hammadi tractate by that name, *Hypsiphrone*
(NHC XI,4), also occur as part of the colophon
of a papyrus published by William Brashear, "Seth-
Gebet." **61.** "The Triple-Male Prones" is an otherwise
unattested name of the Triple-Male Child. Here (and
throughout the *Holy Book of the Great Invisible Spirit*)
his consort is the all-glorious Youel. **62.** Zostrianos's
fifth baptism in the name of the Self-Generated One;
for the first four, see 6–8.

Zostrianos Sees all the Self-Generated Aeons (53,25–56,23)

Indeed, I was immersed five [**54**] times [by Audael] and I[saouel, the guardians] of the [great Yesseus Ma]zareu[s Yessedekeus, the one] from . . . that one and . . . perfect . . . and the great [virginal] glory, [the all-glorious one, she of the great divine male gender], the [mother who] revealed [all] the doubly perfect [aeons, even] the one belonging to all the male species, the [ruler] of the glory, the mother of the glories Youel, and the [Four] Luminaries of [the male] Mind Protophanes: Selmen [and the one] with him, the god-[revealers] Zachth[os] and Yachthos, Sethe[us] and Antiphan[te]s, [Sel]dao and Ele[n]os [**55**] . . . .[63]

There are in [each] of the aeons a living [earth] and a [living] water, air made of light and a blazing fire that does not [consume],[64] and living animals and [trees]; souls and minds and human beings and all those who dwell [with them], gods [or] powers or even angels, for all these [**56**] . . . . . .[65] and those [who come forth through] the Self-Generated [One. And I] was shaped by them.

And the aeons [of the] Self-Generated One opened; a [great light] came forth upon [me] from the [perfect] male aeons, and they [were glorified]. The four aeons were spread [out] within a [single] aeon in the form of a single [aeon] existing [alone].

Zostrianos Approaches the Aeon of Protophanes (56,24–63,20)

Ephesech Departs, and Zostrianos Sees the Light-Crown and Seals (56,24–57,12)

Then E[phesech], the Child of the Child, [brought me][66] . . . . [**57**] . . . . . .[67] [there stood Yesseus] Maza[reus Yessede]keus [together with those who give the crown] of [light with seals] upon it, [namely, Gamaliel] and Gabrie[l, who are under the great luminaries.[68] And] there were seals of four kinds.

The Revelation of Youel (57,13–60,23)

YOUEL APPEARS (57,13–21)

There came before me the glorious male and [virginal] Yoel. [I] wondered about the crowns, and she [said] to me:

---

63. Twelve lines unreconstructable. **64.** For the unconsuming fire, see *Zostrianos* 116; cf. Plato *Timaeus* 58c5–7 for the kind of (celestial) fire that "issues from flame, but which does not burn, but supplies light to the eyes." **65.** Ten lines unreconstructable. **66.** Although he apparently never actually enters into the Aeons of Protophanes and Kalyptos or receives baptism in their respective waters, Zostrianos does come to stand immediately before the Protophanes Aeon, where Youel baptizes him twice more with living water after she has instructed him about certain "crowns." Thereupon he becomes all-perfect, receives a crown, and descends back to earth. **67.** Three lines missing. **68.** In several Sethian treatises, the servants of the Four Luminaries.

The Crowns and Their Seals (57,21–59,7)

"Why [does] your spirit wonder [about] the crowns and the [seals] on them? [They] are the crowns that empower every [spirit] and every soul; and the seals that are [upon] them are of three kinds,[69] and [belong to] the Invisible Spirit. [58] . . . .[70] And the seals [of these] kinds are those belonging to [the Self-Generated One] and Protophanes and Kalyptos.

"The [Invisible] Spirit [is] a psychic and intellectual power, a knower and a foreknower. Therefore he is mediated by [Ga]briel the spirit-giver, [so that] when he gives a holy spirit, he might seal one with the crown and crown him, as though [he has] gods and [59] . . . .[71]

The Perfect Individuals (59,8–18)

"[The individuals are] spirits [that exist and know him in order that they may] become [perfect. They exist by themselves] and they are not [intermingled] in order that they may [become] simple and [might not] be replicated [in] any respect. [These] are the simple, perfect individuals.

The All-Perfect Who Are Unified (59,19–60,23)

"[The All] and all these, [the aeons] of aeons, [complete] him, [as well as] all those who are collectively all-perfect. It takes great [effort] to see them, for [the invisible] [60] Protophanes, the great male mind . . . perfect . . . in the [Existence] . . . every [power . . . truly] exist, [for] it [was a great thing for all those who] hear him [openly]. And [they were existing] in thought and Forethought, [since] it is powerful and perfect.

"[But] it is fitting for you to [preach] about everything here and [about] the things you will hear through a thought of those higher than perfect, the things you will [recognize] with a soul [of] the perfect ones."

Youel Baptizes Zostrianos in Living Water (60,23–61,15)

[When] she had said these things, she [baptized me[72] [61] in living water] . . . of [the great male invisible perfect Mind Protophanes-Armedon] . . . the first . . . . I received power [from her] and [she appeared to me and I] received form [and semblance]. I received [a light] that was beyond my [calculation, and I] received a holy spirit. [I] became [truly] existing.

Zostrianos Sees the Triple-Male Child (61,15–22)

Then she brought me into the great [aeon] where the perfect Triple-Male is. I saw the invisible Child within an invisible light.

---

69. The untitled text of the Bruce Codex 240 mentions crowns containing every "triple-powered genus" and goes on to say that they are worn by the baptismal "receivers" (paralēmptōres). 70. Twelve lines unreconstructable. 71. Seven lines unreconstructable. 72. Youel (spelled Yoel in 57 and 62) administers the last two of Zostrianos's twenty-two baptisms, where-

upon he sees the Triple-Male Child and is instructed by Ephesech to call upon the luminaries of the Barbelo Aeon, Salamex, Semen, and Arme, who (as in Allogenes the Stranger 59–68) deliver to Zostrianos his final and highest revelation (called a "primary revelation" in Allogenes).

Youel Administers Zostrianos's Last Baptism (61,22–63,8)

Then [she] baptized me again[73] in [62] [living water] . . . . . .[74] I was able to [see in the presence of] the great and perfect [Self-Generated ones].

And Yoel the all-[glorious] one said to me, "You have [received] all the [baptisms] in which it is fitting to [be] baptized, and you have become [perfect for] the hearing of all [these matters]. Therefore [call] now upon Salamex and S[emen] and the all-perfect Ar[me],[75] the luminaries of the Barbelo [Aeon], the immeasurable knowledge. [They] will reveal [to you [63] those of the] invisible, [great perfect male Protophanes, and the unengendered Kalyptos and then they will teach you about the virginal Barbelo Aeon and] the Invisible [Triple]-Powered Spirit."

Zostrianos Invokes the Luminaries of the Barbelo Aeon (63,8–20)

[When] the all-[glorious] Youel [had said this] to me, she [set me down] and went and stood before Proto[phan]es. Then I [stood at rest] upon my spirit, praying fervently to the great luminaries by thought. I was calling upon Salamex and Se[m]en and the all-perfect [Ar]me.

Zostrianos Is Anointed, Enters the Aeon of Protophanes, and Is Crowned (63,20–129,16)

The Revelation of the Luminaries of the Barbelo Aeon: Part I (63,20–96,3)

Zostrianos Is Anointed and Sees a Vision (63,20–64,13)

And I saw [glories] greater than powers, and they anointed me. I was capable [64] and I . . . in [this one] . . . and [then] the all-[perfect male virginal Youel departed, having] covered [them] all.

[And I saw] Salamex [and Semen, those] who revealed everything [to me], saying,

Negative and Positive Predications of the One (64,13–66,14; cf. Victorinus, *Against Arius* 49,9–40)

"Zostrianos, [hear] about the things you sought:[76]

---

73. According to the extant text, Zostrianos's twenty-second baptism. **74.** Six lines unreconstructable. **75.** The name of the third luminary (Armē) is restored with the help of 63; cf. also *Allogenes the Stranger* 56. **76.** At the beginning of the luminaries' revelation, the author incorporates a portion of a Middle Platonic theological commentary on the second half of Plato's *Parmenides* concerning the nature of the supreme One, which he identifies with the Invisible Spirit. Citations from this treatise, originally in Greek, are to be found both in the Coptic of *Zostrianos* 64–75 and in the Latin of Marius Victorinus *Against Arius* 49,9–40; 50,5–16, which serves as the basis for the restoration of missing text. Here and in the following passages, the

text restored from Marius Victorinus is italicized in the translation. An exhaustive analysis of this common source is provided by its joint discoverers, Pierre Hadot, "Porphyre et Victorinus": *Questions et hypotheses*, and Michel Tardieu, *Recherches sur la formation de l'Apocalypse de Zostrien et les sources de Marius Victorinus*. As the supreme deity, the One is characterized by means of a negative (the *via negativa*) and superlative (the *via eminentiae*) theology, supplemented by a long series of positive affirmations about the One's identity as a threefold Spirit (*Zostrianos* 66–68; 74–75; *Against Arius* 1.50,1–21). Most of the negative attributes of the Spirit—such as immeasurable, invisible, indiscernible, and partless—derive from the first hypothesis

[He] was a [unity] and a single one,
existing prior to [all those] that truly exist,
an immeasurable Spirit, completely indiscernible by anything else
that [exists] in him and [outside] him and [remains] after him.

It is he alone who delimits himself, [65]
[part]less, [shape]less, [quality]less,
[color]less, [specie]less, [form]less to them [all].
[He precedes] them all:
[he is pre-principle of every principle],
fore[thought of] every thought,
[strength] of every power.

[He is faster] <than> [his motion],
he is more stable <than> [stability],
he [surpasses] compaction
[as well as] rarefaction.

And he is farther than any unfathomableness,
and he is more [definite] than any corporeal entity,
he is purer than any incorporeal entity,
he is more penetrating <than> any thought and any body.

[Being] more powerful than them all,
any genus or species,
He is their totality: [66]
the whole of [true] existence
and [those who truly exist];

---

of the *Parmenides* (137c–142a), while others are transferred from the *Phaedrus* or derive from the description of matter in the *Timaeus*. Cf. *Against Arius* 1.49,9–40: "*Before all the authentic existents was the One or the Monad or One in itself, One before being was present to it. For one must call 'One' and conceive as One whatever has in itself no appearance of otherness. It is the One alone, the simple One, the One so-called by concession. It is the One before all existence, before all existentiality and absolutely before all inferiors, before Being, for this One is prior to Being; he is thus before every entity, substance, hypostasis, and before all realities with even more potency. It is the One without existence, without substance, <life>, or intellect*—for it is beyond all that—*immeasurable*, invisible, *absolutely indiscernible by anything else, by the realities that are in it, by those that come after it, even those that come from it; for itself alone, it is distinct and defined by its own existence, not by act, of such a sort that its own constitution and knowledge it has of itself is not something other than itself; absolutely indivisible, without shape, without quality* or lack of quality, nor qualified by absence of quality; *without color, without species, without form,* privated of all the forms, without being the form in itself by which all things are formed. It is the *first cause of all* the existents whether they are universals or particulars, the *principle prior to every principle, intelligence prior to every intelligence, the vigor of every power, more mobile than movement itself, more stable than rest itself*—for it is rest by an inexpressible movement and it is a superlative movement by an ineffable rest; *more condensed than every continuity, more exalted than every distance; more definite than every body* and greater than every magnitude, *purer than every incorporeal entity, more penetrating than every intelligence and every body; of all realities it has the most potency,* it is the potency of all potencies; *more universal than everything, every genus, every species,* it is in an absolutely universal way the truly Existent, *being itself the totality of the authentic existents, greater than every totality whether corporeal or incorporeal, more particular than every part, by a <pure> ineffable potency being <preeminently> all the authentic existents.*"

[he is] all [these];
[*for he is greater than the whole*],
[*corporeal and incorporeal alike*],
[*he is more*] *particular* [*than all the*] *parts.*

Existing by a [*pure un*]*knowable* [*power*],
[*he*] *from whom* [*derive*] *all those that truly exist,*
that derive from the [truly] existent Spirit, the sole One.

THE THREE POWERS OF THE SPIRIT (66,14–68,13; CF. VICTORINUS, *Against Arius* 50,10–16; 50,1–8)

For they are [*triple*] *powers of his* [*unity*],[77]
[*complete*] *Existence, Life, and Blessedness.*
In Existence *he exists* [*as*] *a simple unity,*
his own [*rational expression*] *and idea.*
Whomever he will find he brings into being.
[And in] Vitality, he is alive and [**67**] [becomes];
[in *Blessedness* he comes to have Mentality].

[And he] knows [that]
all these [become] uniquely him,
for a divinity [*is unconcerned with anything*]
except [*what is his*] *alone,*
and he [is a unity]
within himself [and by himself],
the single, [*perfect Spirit*].

---

77. Here the source common to Zostrianos and Victorinus apparently shifted to a consideration of the three powers preexisting in the supreme One that will come forth to make a "second One." These three powers are Existence, Vitality, and Blessedness (in the sense of self-knowledge) or sometimes Mentality, by which a higher entity, often regarded as an infinitival Existence beyond determinate being, emits or projects an indeterminate power of life (Vitality) that achieves substantial determination (e.g., as a divine Intellect, the Aeon of Barbelo) by intellectually contemplating its source. The second One (the Aeon of Barbelo) is the "One Who Is" of the second hypothesis of the *Parmenides* (142b–144e), identified by Marius Victorinus with the Son of God and by *Zostrianos* with the Aeon of Barbelo. It appears that Victorinus continued to copy the common source, while the author of *Zostrianos* only excerpted from it. Cf. *Against Arius* 1.50,1–21: "This (One) is God, this is the Father, preintelligence preexisting and preexistence preserving itself in its own *Blessedness* and a motionless motion and, because of this, *having no need of other beings*; perfect beyond perfect things, triple powered in ac-

cord with the *unicity of the Spirit, perfect* and beyond Spirit; for he does not breathe; rather, the *Spirit is only in that which is his being*, Spirit breathing into itself so that it may be Spirit, since the Spirit is *not separate* from itself. He is at the same time *residence and resident*, existing at the same time *everywhere and nowhere* remaining in himself, alone in himself alone. Since he is one in its simplicity, he nevertheless interiorly unites in himself these three powers: *universal existence, universal life, and Blessedness; but all these are one, even a simple one,* and it is predominantly in the power of being—i.e., Existence—that the powers of Life and Blessedness exist, for that by which it is and exists is the power of Existence, and this is also the power of Life and Blessedness. He is himself and by himself *the idea and rational expression (logos) of himself. He has his living and acting in his own nonexistent Existence;* union *without distinction of the Spirit* with itself, *divinity, substantiality, blessedness, mentality, vitality, goodness,* being *absolutely all things* in a universal mode, *purely unengendered, preexisting, unity of union* which is not itself union."

For *he dwells [within] that which is his,*
which [exists as] an idea of an idea,
a unity of the [Henad].[78]

He exists as [the Spirit],
inhabiting it by intellect,
and it inhabits him.
He is not about to come forth to any place,
because he [is] a single perfect, simple Spirit.
He is his own place,
and he is its inhabitant.
Indeed <he is> everything.

And on the other hand [there] is
the one who [68] [comes to be in Mentality] and [Life],
even [his] inhabitant.
And the Life is an activity of the insubstantial [Existence].
That which exists in [them]
[exists] in him;
and because of [him]
[they exist as] Blessed[ness] and perfect[ion].
And [Life is the power]
that exists in [all those] that truly exist.

IMPLICATIONS FOR SALVATION (68,14–74,16)

Blessed[79] is the [Idea] of the activity that exists! By receiving Existence it receives potential [for] perfection. Since it never divides, it is then perfect. Therefore, it is perfect because it is not divisible with itself. For nothing exists before it except [the perfect] unity [73][80] [that is its] Existence, [since] it is salvation [for the wholes].

And he [of whom] it is [not] even possible or [fitting to speak], if one [affirms] him for himself, all such things [will come to pass], for he [who abides] in the Existence [of] this one [exists] in every way in Life; by Blessedness he knows; and if he participates in the [wholes], he is perfect. But if he participates in [two] or one, he is of the sort that he has merely participated:

For [this] reason there are those with soul and those without soul;
for this reason those who will be saved;
for this reason those who will [perish] if they had no [share] in him;
for [this] reason there is matter and bodies;

---

78. Or "One," here and below. 79. It appears that pp. 69–72 (71 and 72 are lost) were blank, although counted in the scribes' pagination, so that the text is continuous from the bottom of p. 68 to the top of p. 73.

Since this material does not appear in Victorinus, here the author of *Zostrianos* has probably inserted his own commentary on the material in the common source. 80. Pp. 69–72 are blank.

for this reason [**74**] [there is a desirable] in[corporeality];
Therefore [they are derivatives of a whole].

For all [these reasons]
it is he who [pre]exists and [is pure], since
he is a [simple] Unity, a single, unnamable Spirit,
even his own [Existence], Idea, and [Being], both
[in accord with the] activity that is [his] Life, and
in accord with the perfection that [is] luminous intellectual power.
And the three stand together, moving together.

THE ATTRIBUTES OF THE SPIRIT (74,17–76,1; CF. VICTORINUS,
Against Arius 50,9–10; 50,16–21)

> *It is everywhere and nowhere* that
> he [empowers] and activates them all.
> The ineffable, unnamable one—
> it is from himself that he [truly] exists,
> resting himself [in] in his perfection—
> has [not] shared in [any] form; [**75**]
> therefore [he is invisible to] them [all].
> [He has taken no pattern for himself],
> [nor is he anything at all of] those [that exist]
> [among the perfect ones]
> and [those that are unified].

> The one [belonging to the All] *exists in Existence*
> [and he] dwells in the [Vitality] of *Life*;
> *and* in Perfection and [Mentality] <and> *Blessedness*.
> All [these] were existing [in the] indivisibility of the Spirit.
> *And it is Mentality on account of* [*which*] *is*
> [*divinity*] *and insubstan*[*tiality*][81]
> *and Blessedness and Life*
> *and Mentality and goodness.*

> *And he is a Henad with Unity,*
> *and absolutely all things,*
> *the unengendered purity,*
> thanks to whom they preexist,
> all these as well as the . . . . [**76**]

---

81. Perhaps for "insubstantiality" read "substantiality."

THE EMERGENCE OF THE BARBELO AEON FROM THE TRIPLE-POWERED SPIRIT (76,2–88,22FF.)

The Barbelo Aeon Appears (76,2–81,21). . . .[82] his . . . within the . . . . . . [like a fragrance it reaches the] light [anterior to their] aeon. It is a [power that] inhabits a [part of the] unengenderedness, for it always exists. It [sought] after him, seeing him [there] and existing as a simple [unity]. Since he is Blessedness in perfection, he [was] a perfect and [blessed] unity. She lacks his unity because she lacked him, since he would supplement her with knowledge. And his knowledge dwells outside of him with that which contemplates him inwardly. A reflection and an [image [77] that] lacks . . . . . . and . . . it would [have fallen down]. Therefore she [came to exist outside his] fullness. It was not for herself that she desired this aspect of her that she [established] outside the [perfection]; she became distinct because she is an all-perfect instance [of] perfection existing as contemplation.

With respect to that one, [she] is an offspring that supplements him, even that which derives from his ineffable power. She has a pre-potency, even the primal unengenderedness succeeding that one, because with respect to all the rest [she is] a first aeon. [78] . . . . . .[83][all who are pure because of the insubstantial Existence. It is she who] grants [rest. It is she who knows] and [who foreknows] herself, [truly existing] as a [single] aeon in act and potency and [Existence]. It is not [in] time that she originated, but [she appeared] eternally, having eternally stood in his presence. She was overshadowed by the majesty of his [goodness]. She stood looking at him and rejoicing. Being filled with kindness [she did not become separate]. But when she was [filled [79] . . . . . .[84] of the glories. And she is an insubstantial Existence and a power] that [truly exists. She is the] first [insubstantial] Existence [after] that one.

[And from] the undivided One toward Existence in act move the [intellectual] perfection and intellectual Life that were Blessedness and divinity. The [entire] Spirit, perfect, simple and invisible, [has] become a unity in existence and act, even a simple Triple-[Powered] One, an Invisible Spirit, an image of the one that truly exists, the one [80] . . . .[85] [It is impossible to comprehend] true [existence] since it is her [source], while she is an image.

[She began to] strive, since it was [im]possible to unite with his [image]. She saw its [privation] while it was [next to] his all-perfection, since he preexists and is situated over all these, preexisting, being known as three-powered. The Invisible Spirit has never [been] incognizant: [he did not merely] make an act of knowing, but was instead [abiding in] perfection and Blessedness. [Now] when [she] [81] became incognizant . . . and she . . . body after . . . [in] another way . . . [en]lighten . . . she [was] existing [individually as cause] of [the declination]. Lest she come forth anymore or get further away from perfection, she knew herself and him, and

---

82. Both Victorinus and *Zostrianos* immediately move beyond their common expositions of the supreme One to expound the process by which the indeterminate preexistence within the One Spirit gives rise to a subsequent hypostasis: for Victorinus the Son of God (*Against Arius* 1.50,22–51,43), and for *Zostri-* *anos* the Aeon of Barbelo (76–84). Similarities in these accounts suggests they may have been influenced by a common source, perhaps an exposition of hypothesis II of the *Parmenides* as a "second One" that was generated from the First One. **83.** Three lines missing. **84.** Three lines missing. **85.** Five lines missing.

she stood at rest and spread forth on his [behalf]—since she was [from] true existence, she was from what truly exists in common with all things—to know herself and the one that preexists.

The Emergence of Kalyptos (81,21–86,10). Having supplemented him, they came into existence. {They came into existence.} And they are manifest through those [82] [who pre]exist. And . . . through the . . . since they had appeared [as a] second [Mentality]. And they appeared [through the one][86] who foreknows him, being an eternal space, having become a secondary form of his knowledge, even the duplication of his knowledge, the unengendered Kalyptos. And the truly existent ones also stood at rest upon Kalyptos, for she accordingly knew him in order that those following her might come into being having a place, and that those that come forth might not precede her but might become holy and simple.

She is the introspection of the god [83] who pre[exists. She] spread [forth] . . . to the simple . . . salvation . . . salvation . . . . And he . . . the light that is fore[known]. She was called Barbelo by virtue of thought, the perfect virginal male of three kinds. And it is her own knowledge through which she originated lest [she be drawn] down and come forth further by the things that exist in her and that follow her. Rather, she is simple in order that she might be able to know the god who preexists, since she became better than those when she [revealed her product [84] without] engenderment.

[And she became a] third [aeon. There are] two [differences in form] among [aeons, and they differ] in this way:

On the one hand [she is a first aeon] with the [second] unengendered [nature], a second [image]. She stood at rest [as the] first instance of that [which] truly exists.

In [another way she is] truly the Blessedness of the Invisible [Spirit], the knowledge of the primal Existence within the simplicity of the Invisible Spirit—"within the Henad" resembles "within the Unity"—that which is pure and shape[less] . . . . [87] [85]

. . . and the [Mentality] and the [perfection] acted upon it and [it came to rest], the first [divine] Kalyptos, all of them: existence and activity, divinity, kind, and species. And the powers are a unity.

Now how is he a unity, that is, not as a particular thing, but as a whole? What is the unity that is the Henad? . . . . . . [88] [86] [Existence].

Kalyptos Praises Her Source (86,10–88,8). A perception [of the] truth of [that] all-perfect one said [by way of praise],[89]

"You are great, Aphr[edon]. You are perfect, Neph[redon]."

To his Existence she says,

---

86. I.e., Barbelo. 87. 84,22–85,7 unreconstructable. 88. 85,21–86,9 unreconstructable. 89. Here the text apparently makes an abrupt shift from the emanation of Barbelo to the product of her self-determination: she becomes a tripartite Intellect in analogy with the three powers of the Invisible Spirit, which she herself is. She is compared to the receptacle (or "space," *khōra*) of *Timaeus* 48e–52d as an "eternal space" (*khōrēma*) who has become a secondary form or duplication of the Invisible Spirit's Knowledge.

"You are great, Deipha[neus]"—she [is] his activity and life and divinity—
"You are great, Harmedo[n], the [all]-glorious one, Epiph[aneus]"—his
Blessedness and the perfection [of] the unity.

All [of that which belongs to a single one] is unified [87] . . . . . .[90] eternal . . . intellectual . . . [perfect the virginal Barbelo] through the simplicity of the Blessedness of the Triple-Powered Invisible Spirit.

She who has known that one has known herself. And that one, being everywhere one, being undivided, [brought her to] himself [so that] she might know
[herself as] his activity. [He] who does not know [himself is one] who is known
[while existing] within another [88] [one] . . . .[91]

Ecstatic Doxology to Barbelo (88,8–22ff.)

. . . , "[I] bless [you] . . . ,[92]
O Be[ritheus, Erigenaor], Or[imeni]os, Ar[amen], Alphl[eges],
    Elilio[upheus], Lalameus, Noetheus!
Your name is great and strong.
He who knows [you] knows everything.
You are one, you are one, Sious, Ei[ron], Aphredon!
You are the [aeon] of the aeons of the perfect great one,
the first Kalyptos of the [third] activity!"

The Revelation of the Luminaries of the Barbelo Aeon: Part II (96,20–128,18)[93]

THE CONTENTS OF THE KALYPTOS AEON (113,1–123,25)

The Kalyptos Aeon (113,1–116,24). ". . .[94] [113] and angels, daimons, minds,
souls, living creatures, trees and bodies and those prior to them,

those of the simple elements of simple principles,
and those that are in [mixture]
and those that are unmixed:

air and water,
earth and number,
pairing and motion,
[limitation] and order,
and breath, and all the rest.

---

90. Six lines missing. 91. Seven lines missing. 92. For this fragment of the traditional ecstatic doxology in the Platonizing Sethian treatises, see n. 60. 93. Surviving traces suggest that the second part of the luminaries' revelation probably began somewhere on p. 96. The remainder of pp 88 and pp. 89–108, which contained the second part of the revelation from the luminaries of the Barbelo Aeon, are nearly obliterated, while pp. 109–112 are entirely missing. Remaining traces suggest pp. 88–96 contained the implications of the first part of the luminaries' revelation for Zostrianos, and his response to it. 94. When legible text returns, the topic of the luminaries' revelation has shifted to the contents of the Kalyptos Aeon, the highest level of the Barbelo Aeon, whose four subaeons contain the ideal forms or paradigms of ideal eternal entities like powers, wholes, kinds, souls, archetypal trees and bodies, and the primal elements.

There are fourth powers that are [in] the fourth aeon,
those [that] are in the [totalities] and perfections of all these,
the powers [of] powers,
[wholes] of [the wholes],
[genera] of [the genera],
[angels of the] angels,
souls [of the] souls,
living animals [of the] living animals,
trees [of the trees],
bodies [of the bodies].

And . . . . . .[95] [114] his own.

There are [those] that are as if generated,
and those that are in an unengendered generation;
and there are those that are holy and eternal,
those that are changeless within change
and in corruption within incorruptibility.
And there are those that exist as wholes;
there are those [that are generic]
and those that inhabit an order and a rank;
there are those in [incorruptibility],
and there are the primary ones [that stand] at rest
with the secondary ones [among] them all,
[all] those [that derive] from them
and [those that] exist [among] them
and [from] these that [follow] them
[and from them] . . .
these . . . .

"And [they] stood at rest [upon the] fourth aeon . . . they dwell . . . they dwell . . . the whole . . . [115] in them, since it is scattered abroad. They do not conflict with one another, but they too are alive; among themselves they exist and agree with one another as those who derive from a single principle. They dwell united because they all inhabit a single aeon of Kalyptos, [although] they become distinct in capability. For aeon by aeon they abide, standing at rest as they ought.

"[But] Kalyptos is a single aeon; [it] contains four different aeons. Each of the aeons has capabilities, not like firsts and seconds, for they [are] all eternal, and they differ merely [in] rank and glory. [And the others] that are [within the] fourth aeon and [in the aeons] that preexist it [are] divine . . . they are . . . . [116]

All of them exist in unity,
unified and individually,

---

95. Two lines missing.

perfected in fellowship
and filled with the aeon that truly exists.

"There are those among them that have come to stand as if they exist essentially. And there are those that are actively or [passively] quasi-[essential]; they
exist secondarily, for it is the unengenderedness of the truly existent unengendered entities that indwells them. When the unengendered ones have come into
being, their power stands at rest.

There is there an incorporeal essence
with an imperishable [body];
in [that place] there is the [truly] existent [immutable one],
[even] that which changes [with] change;
[with all of them] stands
[the unconsuming and in]destructible fire.

The Ideal Cosmos of the Kalyptos Aeon and the Modes of Nonbeing (116,24–118,8;
cf. *Victorinus*, To Candidus the Arian 8,8–21; 11,1–12)

"And . . . [117] he stands.[96]
It is there that all living creatures are,
existing individually,
although unified.
The knowledge of the knowledge is there
as well as a basis for ignorance.
Chaos is there
as well as a [place] for all of them,

---

96. In the Kalyptos Aeon, all living creatures (cf.
55–56; 47–48) exist "individually although unified." It
is possible that the phrase "living creatures," although
in the plural, was inspired by the "Living Creature,"
the formal paradigm of everything in the cosmos, in
Timaeus 39e: "According then as intellect contemplates the forms (ideas) in the really existing Living
Creature (*ho esti zōion*), such and so many as exist
therein did he reason (*dienoēthē*) that this world
should also contain." The existence in the Kalyptos
Aeon of "the knowledge of the knowledge" is reminiscent of Plotinus's critique (*Ennead* II, 9 [33] 1,33–57)
of those who hold that there is one intellect that knows
and another that knows that it knows. The Kalyptos
Aeon contains pairs of contraries. The "true light" in
the Kalyptos Aeon may be the same as the unconsuming and imperishable fire mentioned in *Zostrianos* 116;
its contrary is darkness, although of an "enlightened"
sort, which suggests something like Plotinus's "intelligible matter" (cf. *Ennead* II, 4 [12] 5.15–23). The pair of
contraries "that [which] is not truly existent" (*pē[et]e*

<n>ſšoop an ontōs = to ouk ontōs on) and "the nonexistent ones that are not at all" (*ouk ontōs ouk on*)
are intermediate metaphysical entities, in this case, souls
and sensible or physical reality like bodies, derived
from the categories of being and nonbeing developed
by Plato in *Sophist* 240b7.12; 254d1 and *Parmenides*
162a3. In *On the Heavens* 282a4–b7 (reflected also in
the *Categories*), Aristotle makes the same distinctions,
using *aei* instead of *ontōs*. Cf. *Allogenes the Stranger*
55 and the untitled text of the Bruce Codex 237. According to R. Tournaire, "La classification des exis-
tants selon Victorin l'Africain," the predicate *on*
means innately organized (intelligible or psychical),
ouk on means innately unorganized (sensible, material), while the qualifier *ontōs* signifies what is stable
or stabilized (intelligible or material), and *ouk ontōs*
signifies perceptible or intelligible reality subject to
change. See the lengthy discussion in Pierre Hadot,
Porphyre et Victorinus and *Marius Victorinus, Traités
théologiques sur la Trinité, II: Commentaire*, 712.

it being [complete]
while they are incomplete.
True light is there,
as well as enlightened darkness
together with *that which truly is nonexistent,*
that [which] is not truly existent,
[as well as] *the nonexistent ones that are not at all.*[97]

But he <is> the [Good]
from which derives what is good and pleasant,
even the god from [whom] derives the divine
as well as that which [is beyond divine], that which is great.[98]

"For [there is nothing] partial; [there is no] form together with the god [of that one] and that [which is superior to] god . . . all these . . . guilessness . . . [118] and genus.

He has not commingled with anything,
but he remains alone in himself
and rests himself within his limitless limit.
He is the god of those that truly exist,
a self-[seer] and god-revealer.

Barbelo Praises Herself and the Invisible Spirit (118,9–119,3). "Having empowered him who [knows], Barbelo—the Aeon, the Knowledge of the Invisible Triple-Powered Perfect Spirit—[glorified] herself as she said,

He [is alive with] life.
I am alive in [unity].
You, O Unity, are alive.
He is alive, [he] who is three.
You are the [triad] who [is] thrice [replicated: AAA] EEE.

"[They are] the first seven [vowels]. The third [seven and] the second [seven are EEE]EEEE AAAAAAA . . . . And this [has four] . . . knowledge . . . [119] part.

What mind!
What wisdom!

---

97. Enlightened darkness is probably something like Plotinus's "intelligible matter"; "that which truly is nonexistent" is probably gross matter; "that which is not truly existent" is probably the soul; and "the nonexistent ones that are not at all" are probably sensibles. Cf. Proclus *Commentary on Plato's Parmenides* 1.233,1–4: "Accordingly certain of the ancients call the noetic realm 'truly existent,' the psychic 'not truly exis-tent,' the perceptible 'not truly nonexistent,' and the material 'truly nonexistent.'" 98. The attributes of Kalyptos are akin to those Numenius assigns to his first and second Gods respectively (fragment 16.8–10 [des Places]): "If indeed the demiurge of becoming is good, doubtless the demiurge of being would be the Good-in-itself, innate to being."

What knowledge!
What doctrine![99]

The Four Luminaries of the Kalyptos Aeon (119,3–122,5). "His luminaries are given names:[100]

the first [is Aphre]don and his consort is [Arme];
the second is Diphane[us and] his consort is Deiph[anea];
the third is [Marsed]on and his consort is . . . ;
the fourth is [Solmi]s and his consort is Olmis.

"And there is Kalyptos, having [joined] with his Idea. And [he is] invisible to all these so that they all might be empowered by him, since [<he is> a god] dwelling in the all-perfect [aeon].

"There are fourths that dwell [beside Kalyptos] and the First. [And the fourths] are in a [union proper] to him alone [and B]arbelo; [he is next after her since she is their totality].

"[The first] luminary . . . [he who] [120] knows him and the one who is placed second. Now the first of the aeons is Harmedon, the paternal glory.

"The second luminary <is> one that [does know] him, but all the [individuals] <are> a wisdom [of him who] resides in the fourth [aeon], which has revealed [him] and all the glories.

"[The third] luminary <is> one [who] does not [see] him, being the rational expression of all [the forms] as well as the [glory. He is] the understanding [that is] in the third [aeon]. Four inhabit him: Malsedon and M. .nios.[101]

"The fourth luminary is the one who sees [him, he] of all the forms [that are] unified, dwelling [in] an instruction and glory and truth of the [four aeons] O[l]mis, . . . and the . . . the [121] fifth.

"The first—that is, the second—is the all-perfect Kalyptos, for there are the Four Luminaries. It is Kalyptos who has divided again. They are unified, and these knowers are all those that are glories; all of them are perfect. It is he [that] knows everything about them all, since he is all-perfect.

From him is every power, and every one is with its entire aeon.
It is to him and from him that they all come,
the power of them all, the principle of them all.

When he knows [himself],
he becomes a [second] aeon and
a [second] unengenderedness.

---

99. For similar instances of praise celebrating acts of generation, see *Holy Book of the Great Invisible Spirit* IV, 59; III, 49–50; 53–54; 55–56; 61–62; and *Secret Book of John* II, 5–7. 100. Like the Aeon of the Self- Generated One, the Kalyptos Aeon also has Four Luminaries; the restoration of their names here is rather conjectural. 101. Only two of the four are named.

"[They have] other aeons [within] them . . . . [If he] [**122**] becomes a Barbelo, he becomes a first aeon because of the eternity of the Invisible Spirit; since Kalyptos is the second unengenderedness.

The Glories of the Kalyptos Aeon (122,5–123,25). "These are all the glories:

> the limitless Aphredons,
> the ineffables,
> the revealers,
> the immutables,
> all the . . . ,
> the glory-revealers;
> the pairwise manifested Marsedons,
> the limitless Solmises,
> the self-revealers,
> those who are [full] of glory,
> those who [attend the] glories,
> the blessers,
> the M[alse]dons,
> the hidden ones that [are manifest],
> the limits [that] exceed the limits,
> [and the thoughts] that are [above the thoughts].

"[And he establishes them upon . . . . . .[102] having] [**123**] ten thousand glories in them. Therefore, it is a complete glory so that whenever it can harness and control, it may become complete. Thus, even if it enters a body and a material transformation, they do not receive greater honor for their all-perfection, which is from him; all these and their associates are perfect.

"So too each aeon has ten thousand aeons in itself, so that it may collectively become a complete aeon, and each dwells in the [Blessedness] of the perfect Invisible Triple-Powered [Spirit in the presence of] the silence [of the God] who is fore[known], even the knowledge . . . .[103] [**124**]

THE PROTOPHANES AEON AS THE IMAGE OF KALYPTOS (123, BOTTOM–126,1)

". . . . . .[104] a silence of the second knowledge, the first thought within an agreement of the Triple-Powered One, since he commanded her to know him so that he might become all-perfect. And he is inherently perfect. It is by simplicity and Blessedness that he is recognized. [He received] goodness through that successor of the Barbelo Aeon who grants him being. It was not the power of the former,

---

102. Five lines missing. **103.** Five lines missing. **104.** Somewhere in the broken text at the bottom of p. 123 there must have been a transition from the treatment of the Kalyptos Aeon to a portrayal of the Protophanes Aeon, since it appears that the Protophanes Aeon is being described at the top of

p. 124. Like Kalyptos (and the Self-Generated One), Protophanes also contains an ideal living world consisting of undifferentiated but potentially distinct intelligences and souls ("those that exist together") that contemplate the universal forms ("those that truly exist") in Kalyptos.

but of the latter. The aeons that truly exist abide silently. Existence was inactivity, and the knowledge of the self-established Kalyptos was ineffable.

"Having come [from the] fourth, the [thought of his] thought, the Proto[phanes], the great perfect male [mind, . . . Arme]do[n] . . . .[105] [125] He is his image, equal to him in glory and power, superior to him in rank, though not in aeonic level. Like him he possesses them all, alive, dwelling together in unity with the aeon within the aeons. He shares a fourfold difference with all the rest that are there.

"And Kalyptos truly exists, and with him is located the all-glorious one, Youel, the male virginal glory, through whom are seen all the all-perfect ones.

"Those that stand before him are the three:

[the divine] Child,
the Triple-[Male],
and the [divine] Self-Generated One.

"He possesses [three] within one, which [makes four. The one who] also dom-inates the . . . dwelling upon . . . [126] ten thousand–fold.

THE FOUR AEONS OF THE PROTOPHANES AEON (126,1–127,11)

"The first aeon inhabiting him[106] <is . . .>, from whom comes
the first luminary Solmis and the god-revealer,
infinite according to the pattern in the Kalyptos and Doxomedon
aeons.
The second aeon is Akremon the ineffable, containing
the second luminary Zachthos and Yachthos.
The third aeon is Ambrosios the virgin, containing
the third luminary Setheus and Antiphantes.
The fourth aeon is the [triple]-gendered blesser containing
the fourth luminary [Seldao] and Elenos.

He is [dominated] by [the perfect Mind Protophanes] Arm[edon] . . . . . . :[107] [127]

PHOĒ ZOĒ ZĒOĒ ZĒ[OĒ] ZŌSI ZŌSI ZAŌ ZĒOOO ZĒSEN ZĒSEN!
The individuals and the four who are eightfold are alive!

---

105. Four lines missing. 106. The Protophanes Aeon is apparently conceived as consisting of four aeons each containing two luminaries. The Doxomedon aeons on p. 126 are mentioned nowhere else in *Zostrianos*; the author may have added this phrase under the influence of the authority of the *Holy Book of the Invisible Spirit*, where the Doxomedon Aeon, mentioned in the five doxologies that punctuate the various phases of its theogony, seems to define the primal pentad (the Invisible Spirit, Barbelo, the Triple-Male Child, Youel, and Ephesech Child of the Child). Probably the Doxomedon Aeon of the *Holy Book* is the conceptual precursor of the Barbelo Aeon in *Zostrianos* and the other Platonizing Sethian treatises. It is perhaps this very concept that encouraged the re-formulation of the Mother Barbelo into the masculine Aeon of Barbelo. 107. Four lines missing.

ĒOOOO ĒA ĒŌ![108]

It is you who are before them, you who are in them all!

They are within the perfect male Armedon-Protophanes, the actuality of all these dwelling together.

The Aeon of the Self-Generated One and Its Four Subaeons (127,11–128,7)

"Since all the individuals[109] were existing as perfect ones, the activity of all the individuals appeared again. As for the divine Self-Generated One, he stands within an aeon containing four different Self-Generated Aeons.

> The first aeon in him of the first luminary is
> [Harmozel], Orneos, Euthrounios, also called . . . .
> The second [aeon of the second luminary is]
> [Oroiael, Yo]udas[i]os, Ap. . , [128] Arros[iel].
> The third aeon of the third luminary is
> Daveithe, Laraneus, Epiphanios, Eideos.
> The fourth aeon of the fourth luminary is
> Eleleth, Kodere, Epiphanios, Allogenios.

Conclusion: Those That Reside in Matter (128,7–18)

"Now all the others that reside in matter were all persistent.[110] It was because of their knowledge of majesty, their audacity and power, that they came into existence and adorned themselves. Because they did not know God, they shall pass away.

"Behold, Zostrianos, you have heard all these things of which the gods are ignorant and that are undefined for angels."

Zostrianos's Response to the Luminaries' Revelation (128,19–129,16)

As for me, I became bold and said, "I am [still] wondering about the Triple-Powered Invisible perfect Spirit—how it exists for itself, [even the cause] for them all [and of] those that truly exist . . . what is the [place of that one] and [of what

---

108. The ecstatic exclamation on p. 127 seems to play on various forms, mostly defective, of *zōē*, "life," and *zaō*, "to live," while that on p. 127 may mean something like "may he be (*ē*) four O's, may he be first (A), may he be last (Ō)," in which the four O's may represent the Greek masculine definite article or the numeral for seventy or simply four entities that are not further specified. 109. "Perfect individuals" is the generic name for the contents of the Aeon of the Self-Generated One (18; 59; 129). The four aeons of the Self-Generated One are named in the order of the Four Luminaries Armozel (or Harmozel), Oroiael,

Daveithe, and Eleleth, each of which is accompanied by three other beings who do not correspond to the members of similar lists found in the *Secret Book of John* and the *Holy Book of the Great Invisible Spirit*; in particular, one notes the absence of Sophia, the last of twelve aeons distributed among the Four Luminaries. 110. The luminaries' revelation concludes by informing Zostrianos that his knowledge of ultimate reality transcends the knowledge of gods and is undefined ("limitless") for angels. In *Allogenes the Stranger* 50, Youel prefaces her revelation of the Barbelo Aeon to Allogenes in much the same language.

sort is it?" And after I] said [these things, I was] [**129**] greatly [glorified], and they set [me] down and departed.

Apophantes and Aphropais the Virgin-light came before me and brought me to Protophanes, the great male perfect Mind.

> There I saw all of them as they dwell in unity.
> I united with them all and blessed
> the Kalyptos Aeon,
> the virginal Barbelo,
> and the Invisible Spirit.
> I became all-perfect and was empowered.
> I was inscribed in glory and sealed.
> There I received a perfect crown.[111]

Zostrianos's Descent from the Aeons and Recording of the Revelation (129,16–130,14)

I came forth to the perfect individuals.[112] All of them were questioning me, listening to the majesty of the knowledge, rejoicing and receiving power.

When I again came down to the Self-Generated Aeons, I received a true image, pure, worthy of perception.

I came down to the Aeonic Copies and came down thence [**130**] to the atmospheric [realm].

I wrote three wooden tablets and left them as knowledge for those who would come after me, the living elect. Then I came down to the perceptible world and put on my image. Because it was uninstructed, I empowered it and went about preaching the truth to everyone. Neither the angelic beings of the world nor the archons saw me, for I nullified a multitude of [disgraces] that brought me near death.

Zostrianos Issues the Call to Awakening (130,14–132,5)

But an errant multitude I awakened, saying: "Understand, you who are alive, the holy seed of Seth! Do not [be] disobedient to me. [Awaken] your divine part as

---

111. Cf. the crowns whose nature and seals are explained by Youel in *Zostrianos* 56–59. 112. Zostrianos now makes his descent, first to the Aeon of the Self-Generated One, where the "perfect individuals" eagerly hear his newly acquired knowledge. Here Zostrianos receives a perceptible image, perhaps some kind of psychic envelope or subtle body. Descending through the planetary world of the Aeonic Copies and the sublunar atmospheric realm, Zostrianos records for the elect his revelation, which will live after his own time on three wooden tablets (cf. the three tablets of Seth read by Dositheos and delivered to the elect in *Three Steles of Seth* 118). The making of heavenly books is frequent in apocalyptic literature; see *4 Ezra* 14:42–15:2; *1 Enoch* 81:1–82:3. Oddly, there is no explicit connection between these three heavenly wooden tablets and the text of *Zostrianos* itself, called

"[the book] of the [glory] of the eternally living words" (1) that Zostrianos claims he has written. That he leaves the tablets in the heavenly world for the living elect who come after him suggests that they would be read only by those who, like Zostrianos, were able to ascend to the atmospheric realm and read them there, presumably after having read *Zostrianos* itself. After inscribing the tablets, Zostrianos reenters the perceptible world and dons his "image," the physical body he had left on earth guarded by glories during his ascent (4), to supplement the psychic envelope he had just received in the Self-Generated Aeons; he then instructs this body to serve as his vehicle for preaching the truth, yet it still remains invisible to the angels and archons, just as was the luminous cloud on which Zostrianos originally ascended to the Self-Generated Aeons (cf. 4–5).

divine, and empower your sinless elect soul. Mark the passing of this world and seek immutable unengenderedness. The [Father] of all these invites you as he awaits you. And even when you are ill-treated, [**131**] he will not abandon you.

"Do not baptize yourselves with death nor entrust yourselves to things inferior to you as if to superior things. Flee the madness and the bondage of femininity, and choose for yourselves the salvation of masculinity.[113]

"You have not come to suffer; rather, you have come to escape your bondage. Release yourselves, and that which has bound you will be nullified. Save yourselves, so that one[114] may be saved.

"The kind Father has sent you the Savior[115] and empowered you! Why do you hesitate? Seek when you are sought; when you are invited, listen. For the time is short. Do not be led astray.

"Great is the aeon of the aeons of the living ones, and the [punishment] of those who are unconvinced. Many bonds and chastisers surround you. [**132**] Flee quickly before destruction reaches you. Behold the light! Flee the darkness. May you not be led astray to destruction."

Title and Colophon (132,6–9)

Zostrianos

Words of Truth of
Zostrianos. God of Truth.
Words of Zoroaster[116]

---

113. Zostrianos explicitly warns the seed of Seth not to be baptized with death or entrust themselves to inferiors, which sounds like some kind of polemic against other baptizing groups, perhaps Christians or even other Sethians who continue to practice the earthly ritual of the Five Seals rather than the transcendental baptisms into knowledge characteristic of Zostrianos's visionary ascent (cf. the Archontics' rejection of baptism in Epiphanius *Panarion* 39–40 and the similar rejection in *Revelation of Adam* 84). The admonition to flee the bondage of femininity and embrace the salvation of masculinity matches Zostrianos's own rejection of "psychical chaos and lustful femininity" prior to his ascent on the luminous cloud (1; cf. Plotinus *Ennead* III, 5 [50] 1.31–38, 55–63; Porphyry *On Abstinence* 4.20.18–21). In the context of Gnostic and ascetic discourse, "becoming male" signifies the development of a higher spirituality as well as a return to a primordial unity prior to the division of *Genesis* 2:18–25; Gnostic salvation can therefore be conceived as a kind of "masculinization." In *Galatians* 3:28 and in the *Gospel of Thomas* 22; 37 (cf. 114), baptism symbolizes the reunification of the sexes and the return to a primordial unity; indeed at Zostrianos's second baptism in the name of the Self-Generated One, he becomes "an

angel of masculine gender" and "stands with the children of Seth" (7). The self-actualized nature of salvation is clear from Zostrianos's exhortation: although the Father through Zostrianos has issued the invitation and sent the Savior, the individual is alone responsible for choosing and working out the salvation of masculinity: awaken your divine part, empower your soul, release yourself, save yourself. 114. I.e., your soul. 115. Perhaps the Triple-Male Child or even Zostrianos himself. 116. The colophon (*logia alētheias Zostrianou theou alētheias logoi Zōroastrou*) is a Greek cryptogram consisting of a substitutionary permutation of the twenty-four letters of the Greek alphabet plus the Coptic letter *fai* and a form of the Greek *sampi*. It designates *Zostrianos* as a collection of oracles, sayings, or discourses communicated by Zostrianos, although the work is technically an apocalypse, and provides no warrant for conceiving Zostrianos as a "god," even though he becomes "divine" at his fifth baptism in the name of the divine Self-Generated One (53). The subtitle provides no warrant for ascribing any of *Zostrianos's* content to Zoroaster, whose teachings in the *Gathas* and later Persian literature are completely different.

THE LETTER OF PETER TO PHILIP

NHC VIII,2; Codex Tchacos 1

Introduced and Translated by Marvin Meyer

The *Letter of Peter to Philip* is the second and concluding tractate of Nag Hammadi Codex VIII, after the long and sprawling Sethian text *Zostrianos*, and it occupies most of the last pages of the codex (132,10–140,27). The present text opens with a superscribed title that is written as a title (with appropriate scribal decorations) but is more periphrastic and descriptive of the opening of the text: *tepistolē ᵉmpetros etafjoous ᵉmphilippos*, "The Letter of Peter Which He Sent to Philip" (132,10–11). In the literature, this title is ordinarily shortened and simplified to read "The Letter of Peter to Philip." Another version of the text has come to light, as the opening tractate of Codex Tchacos, and it includes the titular subscript [t]epistolē ᵉmpetros ša philippos, "The Letter of Peter to Philip."[1]

The *Letter of Peter to Philip* is a Christian Gnostic text that is described as a letter but also incorporates other traditional materials characteristic of Gnostic literature and acts of apostles. The *Letter of Peter to Philip* opens as a letter of Peter, and to that extent the tractate may be included, along with several other letters (e.g., the New Testament 1 and 2 *Peter* and the *Epistula Petri* at the opening of the Pseudo-Clementines), within the Petrine corpus of letters. The letter within the tractate makes use of epistolary conventions, but the letter itself fills only a few lines of the tractate (132,10–133,8), and thereafter the text presents no formal conclusion and no further reference to the letter. The letter simply provides the occasion for Philip and the other apostles to come together in order to hear what the risen Christ has to say and discuss matters of mission with each other.

The balance of the *Letter of Peter to Philip* (133,8–140,27) depicts meetings of the apostles, often in the form of a dialogue of the risen Savior with the apostles or even the form called "questions and answers" (*erotapokriseis*),[2] and the themes

---

1. Cf. Marvin Meyer, in John Sieber, ed., *Nag Hammadi Codex VIII*, 232; Rodolphe Kasser, Marvin Meyer, and Gregor Wurst, eds., *The Gospel of Judas*.
2. Kurt Rudolph, "Der gnostische 'Dialog' als literarisches Genus."

and terms that are employed call to mind passages in the *Gospel of John* and early Christian acts of apostles, particularly the first, Petrine section of the New Testament *Acts* (chaps. 1–12). These features of the *Letter of Peter to Philip* may cause the text to be more at home in the world of the acts of apostles, and it may be tempting to classify the text as an "Act of Philip"—comparable to the *Act of Peter* in Berlin Gnostic Codex 8502—perhaps even the "First Act of Philip."[3] The *Letter of Peter to Philip* provides an alternative understanding of "Pentecost" stories as they are told in the New Testament (*Acts* 1–2; *John* 20). In the *Letter of Peter to Philip*, the apostles assemble, hear revelatory teachings from the risen Christ and a spirit-filled sermon from Peter, receive the Holy Spirit, and go forth to preach the gospel. In the *Letter of Peter to Philip*, as in *Acts* 2:14–42, Peter preaches a sermon on Jesus and his passion; and as in *John* 20:19–23, the apostles see the risen Christ, who greets them with a greeting of peace and promises his power and presence, and then they depart on their missionary journeys.[4]

The contents of the teachings of the resurrected Christ in the *Letter of Peter to Philip* reflect Christian Gnostic concerns, including some that are somewhat reminiscent of Sethian formulations. After the apostles receive the letter of Peter and gather together, they offer one prayer to the Father of the light and another to the Son of life and immortality, and Jesus Christ appears as a light and voice. The apostles raise several questions for the risen Christ to answer, and these questions function as a virtual table of contents for much of the tractate. The apostles ask about the deficiency of the aeons, the fullness or pleroma, detainment in this world, and the battle against the powers of this world (134,20–135,2).

Jesus addresses these concerns—"again," he says, reminding the apostles that he had spoken of these matters before—in fairly brief sketches providing Gnostic explanations of deficiency, fullness, and the other points. In his revelatory answer on the deficiency of the aeons (135,8–136,15), Jesus delivers an abbreviated version of the myth of the Mother in terms that may recall both the fall of mother Eve in *Genesis* 3 and the fall of Sophia (divine Wisdom) as portrayed in Gnostic texts. There are no overtly Christian elements whatsoever in the story of the Mother in the *Letter of Peter to Philip*. In overall presentation and terminology, the story of the Mother resembles aspects of the story of Sophia in the Sethian *Secret Book of John* and in the account of the Gnostics or Barbelognostics in Irenaeus *Against Heresies* 1.29.1–4. All these sources focus upon the action of the Mother (*maau, mater*) and caricature the demiurge as the arrogant one (*authadēs, authadia*). Nonetheless, the similarities with Sethian texts are not overwhelming, and it is most appropriate to conclude that the *Letter of Peter to Philip* may simply reflect some of the themes and terms often thought to be typical of Sethian Gnostic thought.

---

3. Cf. Hans-Gebhard Bethge, in Wilhelm Schneemelcher, ed., *New Testament Apocrypha*, 1.342–45; Hans-Martin Schenke, in Hans-Martin Schenke, Hans-Gebhard Bethge, and Ursula Ulrike Kaiser, eds., *Nag Hammadi Deutsch*, 2.848.
4. See Klaus Koschorke, "Eine gnostische Pfingstpredigt."

In his next revelatory answer in the *Letter of Peter to Philip*, Jesus answers the query about the fullness or pleroma (136,16–137,13). Jesus declares that he himself is the fullness, and in a way like that of the hymn to the word in *John* 1:1–18, he describes how he was sent down from above and went unrecognized by people in this world, but when he spoke with his own, his own responded to him. Jesus announces, "I gave him authority to enter into the inheritance of his fatherhood. And I took [him] . . . filled . . . through his salvation. Since he was deficiency, he became fullness" (136,26–137,4). The implication here, in spite of the intrusion of lacunae, seems to be that those who hearken to the word of Christ and are his own will also attain the joy and fullness of the divine. Like Christ, they will become fullness.[5]

Jesus goes on to address other problems raised by the apostles concerning the struggle with the archons of this world. The apostles are fretting about the rulers who dominate and oppress humankind, and Jesus replies by acknowledging that a war is going on, but he indicates that it is a spiritual war and the world rulers are fighting against "the inner person" (137,22). If the struggle in this world is a spiritual struggle, then the weapons taken up in the struggle must also be spiritual.[6] Jesus advises the apostles, and all who would follow him, to equip themselves with the power of the Father, gather in worship and prayer, and teach and preach salvation in the world. Jesus assures the apostles, "Surely the Father will help you, as he helped you by sending me. Don't [be afraid. I am with you forever], as I already said to you when I was in the body" (137,28–138,3).

A little later in the *Letter of Peter to Philip*, Peter himself preaches a sermon on the suffering and death of Jesus and those who follow Jesus. The apostles, it is said, gather yet again, this time for Peter's "Pentecost" sermon (139,9–140,1). Peter, filled with holy spirit, recites a traditional credo on the suffering, death, and resurrection of Christ, and then he offers an interpretation of the credo. "Jesus," Peter proclaims, "is a stranger to this suffering." People die because of the transgression of the Mother—Eve or Sophia—but Jesus is the "Son of the Father's immeasurable glory," and if he suffers, he does so, Peter maintains just prior to his sermon, "for us" (*etbēētᵉ[n]*). "He suffered for us," Peter says, "and we must also suffer for our smallness" (138,18–20), where "smallness" means the insignificance of mortal existence. As for the suffering of Jesus, Peter continues in his sermon, "Jesus is a stranger to this suffering," and all that he accomplishes he does "symbolically among us," or "in a likeness to us," or "like us" (*kata oueine hrai nhētn*, 139,25). According to the *Letter of Peter to Philip*, Jesus suffers, though not to atone for human sins. Jesus suffers as a divine being in this world who illustrates what it means to enter into and overcome mortal existence. A Christological tension remains in the sermon of Peter in the *Letter of Peter to Philip* as Peter affirms the passion and death of Christ and still professes the glorious divinity of the Savior, for whom suffering and death are strange and foreign, and who is also

---

5. See Klaus Koschorke, "Eine gnostische Paraphrase des johanneischen Prologs."
6. Cf. *Ephesians* 6:10–20.

able to transcend death and embrace life and thereby show the way for mortal people to do the same. As Peter states near the end of his sermon, the Lord Jesus is "the author—*piarkhēgos*, the originator, the pioneer—of our life" (139,27–28).[7]

The *Letter of Peter to Philip* was composed in Greek, probably in the late second or early third century, though the date of composition remains tentative. Where the text was composed and by whom are unknown; Syria or Alexandria are reasonable conjectures for where such a text may have been written. Within the translation that follows, the most significant variant readings from the version of the text in Codex Tchacos are given in the notes.

BIBLIOGRAPHY

Hans-Gebhard Bethge, "Der Brief des Petrus an Philippus"; Rodolphe Kasser, François Gaudard, Marvin Meyer, and Gregor Wurst, eds., *Codex Tchacos*; Rodolphe Kasser, Marvin Meyer, and Gregor Wurst, eds., *The Gospel of Judas*; Klaus Koschorke, "Eine gnostische Paraphrase des johanneischen Prologs"; "Eine gnostische Pfingstpredigt"; Antti Marjanen, "The Suffering of One Who Is a Stranger to Suffering"; Jacques-É. Ménard, *La Lettre de Pierre à Philippe*; Marvin Meyer, *The Letter of Peter to Philip*; Kurt Rudolph, "Der gnostische 'Dialog' als literarisches Genus"; Hans-Martin Schenke, Hans-Gebhard Bethge, and Ursula Ulrike Kaiser, eds., *Nag Hammadi Deutsch*, 2.663–76 (Hans-Gebhard Bethge); Wilhelm Schneemelcher, ed., *New Testament Apocrypha*, 1.342–53 (Hans-Gebhard Bethge); John H. Sieber, ed., *Nag Hammadi Codex VIII*, 227–51 (Marvin Meyer and Frederik Wisse).

---

7. Cf. also *Letter of Peter to Philip* 140,4: the Lord Jesus Christ is the "author (*parkhēgos*) of our rest."

The Letter of Peter to Philip[1]

The Letter of Peter
Which He Sent to Philip

Peter Writing to Philip (132,10–133,8)

Peter, apostle of Jesus Christ,[2] to Philip, our beloved brother and our fellow apostle,[3] and the brothers who are with you: greetings.

I want you to understand, our brother, that we received orders from our Lord, the Savior of the whole world, that we should come together to teach and preach concerning the salvation that was promised us by [133] our Lord Jesus Christ.[4] But you were separated from us, and you did not wish us to come together and learn how to organize ourselves that we might tell the good news. So would it be agreeable to you, our brother, to come according to the orders of our God Jesus?

The Apostles Gather and Jesus Christ Appears (133,8–135,8)

When Philip received and read this, he went to Peter, rejoicing with gladness.

Then Peter gathered the others. They went to the mountain called Olivet, where they used to gather with the blessed Christ when he was in the body.

When the apostles came together and fell on their knees, they prayed in this way and said:

> Father, Father, Father of the light,
> you who possess the incorruptions,
> hear us,

---

1. Coptic text: NHC VIII,2: 132,10–140,27; Codex Tchacos 1: 1,1–9,15. Editions: *The Facsimile Edition of the Nag Hammadi Codices: Codex VIII*, 138–46; Rodolphe Kasser, François Gaudard, Marvin Meyer, and Gregor Wurst, eds., *Codex Tchacos*; Hans-Gebhard Bethge, *Der Brief des Petrus an Phillipus*; Jacques-É. Ménard, *La Lettre de Pierre à Philippe*; Marvin Meyer, *The Letter of Peter to Philip*; Hans-Martin Schenke, Hans-Gebhard Bethge, and Ursula Ulrike Kaiser, eds., *Nag Hammadi Deutsch*, 2.663–76 (Hans-Gebhard Bethge); John Sieber, ed., *Nag Hammadi Codex VIII*, 227–51 (Marvin Meyer and Frederik Wisse). The title is derived from the expanded title in the manuscript. In the copy of the *Letter of Peter to Philip* discovered in Codex Tchacos, the title is given as "The Letter of Peter to Philip" rather than "The Letter of Peter Which He Sent to Philip." 2. As in the *Acts of the Apostles*, Peter is the leader of the apostles in the *Letter of Peter to Philip*. 3. Cf. Philip the disciple in the New Testament gospels and Philip the evangelist in the *Acts of the Apostles*. 4. Cf. *Luke* 24:44–49; *Acts* 1:1–8.

just as [you] have taken pleasure
in your holy child Jesus Christ.
For he has become for us a luminary [134]
in the darkness.
Yea, hear us.

And they prayed again and said,

Son of life, Son of immortality,
you who are in the light,
Son, Christ of immortality,
our Redeemer,
give us strength,
because they are searching for us
to kill us.

Then a great light appeared, and the mountain shone from the vision of the one who appeared. And a voice called out to them and said, "Listen to my words that I may speak to you. Why are you looking for me? I am Jesus Christ, who is with you forever."

The apostles answered and said, "Lord, we would like to understand the deficiency of the aeons and their fullness. And how are we detained in this dwelling place?[5] How have we come to this place? In what way shall we leave? How do we possess [135] the authority of boldness? Why do the powers fight against us?"[6]

Then a voice called to them from the light and said, "It is you who bear witness that I have said all these things to you. But because of your unbelief I shall speak again.

The Deficiency of the Aeons (135,8–136,15)

"To begin with, concerning [the deficiency] of the aeons, this is the deficiency.[7] When the disobedience and foolishness of the Mother[8] appeared,[9] without the command of the majesty of the Father, she wanted to set up aeons.[10] When she spoke, the arrogant one[11] followed. But when she left behind a portion,[12] the arrogant one grabbed it, and it became a deficiency. This is the deficiency of the aeons.

---

5. Here Codex Tchacos reads, "Lord, [how] do the deficiency (*cōĵ°b*; NHC, *šōōt*) of the aeons and their fullnesses (*neumouh*; NHC, *peuplērōma*) detain us [in our] dwelling [place]?" (*Letter of Peter to Philip* 3). 6. On the prayers and questions of the apostles, cf. *Book of Allogenes* 59. 7. A fuller version of this abbreviated story of the origin of the world is given in the *Secret Book of John* and other Gnostic texts. 8. Cf. Mother Sophia and Mother Eve in the *Secret Book of* *John, Genesis,* and other texts. 9. Here Codex Tchacos reads, "And the Mother, showing poor judgment" (*Letter of Peter to Philip* 3). 10. Here Codex Tchacos reads, "He (i.e., the Great One) is the one who wished, from the beginning, to set up aeons" (*Letter of Peter to Philip* 3). 11. Here and below, NHC uses the word *authadēs* and Codex Tchacos the word *jasihēt*. 12. Here Codex Tchacos reads "body part" (Coptic *melos*) where NHC has "portion" (*meros*).

"When the arrogant one took a portion,[13] he sowed it. He placed powers and authorities over it, and he confined it within the mortal realms.[14] All the powers of the world rejoiced that they had been brought forth. [136] But they do not know the preexistent [Father], since they are strangers to him. Rather, the arrogant one[15] was given power, and they served him and praised him.

"The arrogant one grew proud because of the praise of the powers. He was jealous and wanted to make an image in place [of an image] and a form in place of a form.[16] He assigned the powers within his authority to mold mortal bodies.[17] And they came into being from a misrepresentation of the appearance that had come forth.[18]

The Fullness (136,16–137,13)

"Concerning the fullness,[19] it is I.[20] I was sent down in the body for the seed[21] that had fallen away. And I came down to their mortal model.[22] But they did not recognize me, thinking I was a mortal. I spoke with the one who is mine, and he listened to me[23] just as you also who have listened today. I gave him authority to enter into the inheritance of his fatherhood. And I took [him] [137] . . . filled . . . through his salvation.[24] Since he was deficiency, he became fullness.

"Concerning the fact that you are being detained, it is because you are mine. When you strip yourselves of what is corruptible, you will become luminaries in the midst of mortal people.

"Concerning the fact that you are to fight against the powers, it is because they do not have rest like you, since they do not want you to be saved."

Fighting the Archons (137,13–138,7)

The apostles worshiped again and said, "Lord, tell us, how shall we fight against the rulers,[25] since the rulers are over us?"

A voice called out to them from the appearance and said, "You must fight against them like this, for the rulers fight against the inner person. You must fight against them like this: come together and teach salvation in the world with a promise. And arm yourselves with my Father's power, and express your prayer,

---

13. Again, here Codex Tchacos reads "body part." 14. Or "lifeless realms," "lifeless aeons." 15. Lit., "this one." 16. Cf. *Gospel of Thomas* 22:6. 17. Or "lifeless bodies." 18. Here Codex Tchacos reads, "and something unlawful (Coptic *oua[no]mia*; it is also possible to read *oua[kos]mia*, "disorder," or the Coptic *anomia* could conceivably reflect the Greek *anomoia*, "different, dissimilar") occurred from the likeness that had come into being" (*Letter of Peter to Philip* 4). 19. Pleroma, here and below. Codex Tchacos uses the Coptic *jōk*. 20. On Jesus as the divine fullness sent down in the body to those who are his own, cf. *John* 1:1–18. 21. Or "offspring." 22. Or "lifeless model." Here Codex Tchacos seems to suggest that the seed came to a mortal model. 23. Here Codex Tchacos adds "That is who you are." 24. One possible restoration is the following: "And I took [him up to my Father. They were] filled [with rest] through his salvation" (cf. Bethge, in *Nag Hammadi Deutsch*, 2.672). Here Codex Tchacos reads, "And I took the one who is mine, and the aeons [were brought] to completion through his [salvation], for . . ." (*Letter of Peter to Philip* 5). 25. Archons, here and below.

and surely the Father will help you, as he helped you by sending me.[26] [138] Don't [be afraid. I am with you forever],[27] as I already said to you when I was in the body."

Then came lightning and thunder from heaven, and what appeared to them there was taken up to heaven.

The Apostles Return to Jerusalem (138,7–139,9)

The apostles thanked the Lord with every praise and returned to Jerusalem.

As they were going up, they spoke with each other on the way about the light that had appeared. And a discussion arose about the Lord. They said, "If even our Lord suffered, how much more are we to suffer?"

Peter answered and said, "He suffered for us,[28] and we must also suffer for our smallness."[29]

Then a voice called to them and said, "I often told you that you must suffer. You must be brought to synagogues and governors so that you will suffer. But the one who will not suffer also [will] not [139] ... [my] Father ... that he may ...."[30]

The apostles rejoiced greatly and went up to Jerusalem. They went up to the temple and taught salvation in the name of the Lord Jesus Christ, and they healed a crowd.

Peter Preaches (139,9–140,1)

Peter opened his mouth and said to his disciples,[31] "When our Lord Jesus was in the body, he indicated everything to us, for he came down. My brothers, listen to my voice."[32]

He was filled with holy spirit and spoke as follows:

"Our luminary Jesus [came] down
and was crucified.
He wore a crown of thorns,
put on a purple robe,
was hanged on wood,
was buried in a tomb,
and he rose from the dead.

---

26. The battle against the rulers is spiritual; cf. *Ephesians* 6:10–20. 27. The restoration is tentative. 28. Here Codex Tchacos reads, "He died for us." 29. Smallness or pettiness is synonymous with deficiency, and smallness often refers to the insignificance of mortal existence. Jesus suffered because of human beings; human beings suffer because of their own deficiencies and their own mortality, traceable to the transgression of the Mother. Here Codex Tchacos reads, "we ourselves are to die for humanity" (*Letter of Peter to Philip* 7). 30. On the lacuna (and partial restoration), cf. Bethge, in *Nag Hammadi Deutsch*, 2.674; Mark 8:34–38; Acts 14:22. 31. Or "his fellow disciples." Either Peter has his own disciples, or he and the others together are disciples of Jesus. 32. Cf. Acts 2:14–40 and other Petrine speeches in Acts.

"My brothers, Jesus is a stranger to this suffering.[33] But we are the ones who have suffered through the Mother's transgression.[34] For this reason he did everything symbolically among us.[35] The Lord Jesus, Son of the Father's immeasurable glory, is the author of our life.

"My brothers, let's not listen to these lawless ones nor walk in [140] . . . ."[36]

The Apostles Disperse to Preach (140,1–27)

Peter assembled [the others] and said, "[Our Lord] Jesus Christ, author of our rest, give us a spirit of understanding, so we also may perform great deeds."

Then Peter and the other apostles saw and were filled with holy spirit.[37] Each one performed healings, and they left to preach the Lord Jesus.

They gathered with their companions, greeted them, and said, "Amen."

Then Jesus appeared and said to them, "Peace be with [all] of you and everyone who believes in my name. When you go, you will have joy, grace, and power. Don't be afraid. Look, I am with you forever."

The apostles parted from each other with four words,[38] to preach. And they went in the power of Jesus, in peace.

---

33. Here Codex Tchacos reads, "Jesus is a stranger to death" (*Letter of Peter to Philip* 8). 34. The transgression of Sophia or Eve. Here Codex Tchacos reads "our Mother's transgression." 35. Lit., "in a likeness among (or to) us." Here NHC has *kata oueine hrai ᵉnhētᵉn* and Codex Tchacos has *hᵉn ouein[e]* . . . *etbēᵉtᵉn*. 36. Among the possible restorations is the following: "in [fear before them all]" (cf. Bethge, in *Nag Hammadi Deutsch*, 2.675). 37. Cf. John 20:19–23; Acts 2:1–41 (the Pentecost story). 38. Lit., "into four words" (Coptic *ehrai epiftoou ᵉnšaje*), perhaps "with four messages" (the four gospels?).

MELCHIZEDEK

NHC IX,*1*

Introduced and Translated by Birger A. Pearson

The tractate *Melchizedek* is extant only in the Coptic version found in Nag Hammadi Codex IX, a translation from the original Greek. But it is only partially extant, for it is in a very fragmentary state. Only 19 lines out of some 750 are fully preserved. Partially preserved are 467 lines, of which 199 have been restored by scholarly conjecture. What remains of the text is, therefore, open to different interpretations.

Melchizedek is one of several texts making up a corpus of literature associated with a type of ancient Gnostic thought labeled by scholars as Gnostic Sethianism, for which a special system of beliefs has been delineated.[1] Formally, the tractate is an apocalypse attributed to Melchizedek, the ancient "priest of God Most High" named in *Genesis* 14:18. In it he tells of revelations given to him by angels from heaven. The name of one of these revealers is given in the text (as restored): "[Gamal]iel" (5,18), who appears in other Gnostic texts of a "Sethian" stamp. Melchizedek is clearly a product of Christian Gnostic reflection; indeed, the revelations given in the text have largely to do with the work of "Jesus Christ, the Son [of God]" (1,1) as prophesied by Melchizedek. Melchizedek also assumes a special role in the text as a "high priest" and mediator of ceremonies involving baptism, spiritual offerings, and prayers.

The tractate is made up of three main parts: (1) a revelation mediated by the angel Gamaliel (1,1–14,15); (2) a liturgy performed by the priest Melchizedek on behalf of his community (14,15–18,bottom); and (3) a revelatory vision mediated to Melchizedek by unnamed heavenly "brethren," probably including Gamaliel (18,bottom–27,10).

Gamaliel begins the first revelation to Melchizedek with a prophecy of the earthly work of Jesus Christ, beginning with his descent from heaven (1,1–4,10ff.). His teachings will elicit the enmity of the world ruler and his archons, who will

---

1. Hans-Martin Schenke, "The Phenomenon and Significance of Gnostic Sethianism"; John D. Turner, *Sethian Gnosticism and the Platonic Tradition.*

have him crucified. But the Savior will rise from the dead and provide his disciples with postresurrection instruction. Gamaliel then tells of the false doctrine that will be propagated by enemies of the truth (5,1–17). They will deny the reality of Jesus's birth and earthly life, death, and resurrection. But Melchizedek's teachings of hope and life will provide a guide for the elect.

Gamaliel then reveals his name and tells of his special role in bringing to heaven the elect, the "assembly of the [children] of Seth" (5,17–22). He proceeds to invoke in prayer the divine beings who inhabit the heavenly world, beginning with the primal divine triad in Sethian Gnostic thought (5,23–6,22). The beings invoked are the ineffable primal Father, the "self-begotten" Son, the mother Barbelo, Doxomedon Domedon, Jesus Christ (in his heavenly role), the four "commanders in chief" and "luminaries" Harmozel, Oroiael, Daveithe, and Eleleth, Pigeradamas, and Mirocheirothetou (or Meirocheirothetou), all invoked "through Jesus Christ, Son of God." Gamaliel tells Melchizedek that he (Jesus Christ) is from the "race" of the heavenly high priest who is above all the aeons. Gamaliel then refers to the self-offering of the high priest and commands Melchizedek to renounce animal sacrifices and to undergo a special baptism (7,25–8,10ff.).

In a highly mutilated section of the text, Gamaliel recounts the history of humanity from the creation of Adam until the final battle at the end of time, when the elect "seed" of the primal Father will achieve their final salvation, and the Savior will destroy Death (8,28?–14,9). The first revelation concludes with a warning to Melchizedek to keep these things secret, reserved only for the elect (14,9–15).

The second main part of the tractate begins with Melchizedek recounting his reaction to the revelation he has received: he glorifies God the Father and undertakes a series of ritual actions (14,15–18,7). These include an affirmation of his vocation as a high priest, a spiritual offering, baptism, and trisagia ("Holy are you," thrice) addressed to the same divine beings in the heavenly world that were previously invoked by Gamaliel. This part of the text concludes, in a highly damaged portion of the manuscript, with exhortations presumably addressed to Melchizedek's community (18,8–22ff.), a community that also confesses the "chief commander of the All, Jesus Christ," the last of the heavenly beings invoked with a trisagion.

The revelatory vision in the third main part of the tractate is introduced by the appearance to Melchizedek of unnamed heavenly messengers, who encourage Melchizedek in the exercise of his priestly office (19,1–20,26ff.). This part of the manuscript is badly damaged; pages 21–22 are represented by two small fragments, pages 23–24 by only one (blank on the recto side, p. 23). Pages 25–26 are represented by a larger fragment from the top of the leaf, preserving parts of lines 1–14 of page 25 and 1–15 of page 26. On page 25 Jesus Christ is addressing his executioners, the archons, recounting his sufferings, crucifixion, and resurrection (25,1–9). What follows in what is preserved of lines 10–14 is subject to two opposing interpretations, a problem to which we shall return.

On top of page 26 Melchizedek is greeted by heavenly beings and congratulated for his victory over the archons: "Be [strong, O Melchiz]edek, great [high priest of God [Most High, for the] archons who [are] your [enemies made] war against you. You have [gained the victory over them, and] they did not prevail over [you. You have] persevered and [destroyed] your enemies . . . " (26,2–9). The tractate concludes on page 27 with a warning to keep the revelations secret and the ascension back to heaven of Melchizedek's angelic informants.

The juxtaposition of the victory of Jesus Christ over his enemies on page 25 and Melchizedek's victory over his enemies on page 26 poses a fundamental question: what is the relationship between Jesus Christ and Melchizedek? The solution favored here is that Melchizedek and Jesus Christ are identified in some way.[2] In his vision the ancient priest is given to understand that he will play a crucial role in the future as the incarnation of the great heavenly high priest Jesus Christ. An analogy to this is found in the "Parables" of 1 (Ethiopic) *Enoch* 37–71. Enoch sees a vision of the Messiah–Son of Man (cf. *Daniel* 13) who will play a role in the future judgment. In chapter 71, he is given to understand that he himself is that Son of Man. The notion of successive incarnations of Melchizedek is found in another Jewish apocalypse, 2 (Slavonic) *Enoch*. Melchizedek's role as an end-time warrior is found in a text from the Dead Sea Scrolls (11QMelch). Moreover, we know of several Christians in Egypt who made the identification of Jesus Christ with Melchizedek, probably on the basis of their interpretation of the Melchizedek midrash in the New Testament, *Hebrews* 7.[3]

An opposing point of view has been put forward by Hans-Martin Schenke, Jean-Pierre Mahé, and Claudio Gianotto. They reject the identification presented here and separate the roles played in the text by Jesus Christ and Melchizedek. The two views are based on opposing interpretations of the fragmentary passage on page 25 that follows Jesus Christ's reference to his resurrection. Lines 9–14 are translated in this volume as follows: ". . . came out of . . . to me. . . . my eyes [saw . . . they did not] find anyone . . . me . . . ." Schenke sees two "I's" in this passage: Jesus's speech to the archons concludes with the reference to the resurrection, and Melchizedek then reports his recovery from his visionary trance. Schenke translates, "[My thought] came out of [the heights] to me, . . . my eyes began [to see again] . . . ."[4] Mahé and Gianotto accept Schenke's differentiation of the two "I's."[5]

The interpretation favored here seems to be supported by other passages in the tractate. The heavenly Jesus Christ is the "true high priest" resident in the divine world, of whom Melchizedek is his "image" (15,12; cf. 6,17), a doctrine that is based on an interpretation of *Hebrews* 7:3 ("resembling the Son of God"). Accordingly, Melchizedek too is not only the ancient "priest of God Most High" of *Genesis* 14 (12,10–11; 19,14), but is also a high priest (5,15; 26,3). As such he

2. Birger A. Pearson and Søren Giversen, in Birger A. Pearson, ed., *Nag Hammadi Codices IX and X*, 29–30; Birger A. Pearson, "The Figure of Melchizedek in Gnostic Literature," 111–12.
3. On these and other texts, see Birger A. Pearson, "Melchizedek in Early Judaism, Christianity, and Gnosticism."
4. Hans-Martin Schenke, in Hans-Martin Schenke, Hans-Gebhard Bethge, and Ursula Ulrike Kaiser, eds., *Nag Hammadi Deutsch*, 2.681.
5. In Wolf-Peter Funk, Jean-Pierre Mahé, and Claudio Gianotto, eds., *Melchisédek*, 109, 159.

assumes a paradigmatic role in the worship life of his community (second part of the tractate).

The tractate *Melchizedek* poses for us some interesting questions from the standpoint of the history of its traditions. It reflects the use of Jewish apocalyptic traditions, Egyptian Christian interpretations of *Hebrews*, and Sethian Gnostic traditions reflected in its mythological sections and its praises of the denizens of the Sethian heavenly world. It has been suggested that it is a gnosticized Jewish-Christian apocalypse.[6] On the basis of its antidocetic orientation (combating the view that Jesus only "seemed" to be fully human, p. 5), Hans-Martin Schenke has suggested, instead, that it is a Sethian text that is "no longer Gnostic."[7]

Melchizedek in the form that we know it was probably written in the late second or early third century, probably in Egypt, where it was translated from Greek into Coptic. Its author is completely unknown to us. His audience was evidently a group of Gnostic Christians who had a special fascination with Melchizedek, whose priesthood occupied a prominent place in their worship services.

BIBLIOGRAPHY

Wolf-Peter Funk, *Concordance des textes de Nag Hammadi: Les Codices VIII et IX*; Wolf-Peter Funk, Jean-Pierre Mahé, and Claudio Gianotto, eds., *Melchisédek*; Claudio Gianotto, *Melchisedek e la sua tipologia: Tradizioni giudaiche, cristiane e gnostiche*; Jan Helderman, "Melchisedek, Melchisedekianer und die koptische Frömmigkeit"; "Melchisedeks Wirkung: Eine traditionsgeschichtliche Untersuchung eines Motivkomplexes in NHC IX,1,1–27,10 (*Melchisedek*)"; Birger A. Pearson, "The Figure of Melchizedek in Gnostic Literature"; "Melchizedek in Early Judaism, Christianity, and Gnosticism"; Birger A. Pearson, ed., *Nag Hammadi Codices IX and X*, 19–85 (Birger A. Pearson and Søren Giversen); Hans-Martin Schenke, "Die jüdische Melchisedek-Gestalt als Thema der Gnosis"; "The Phenomenon and Significance of Gnostic Sethianism"; Hans-Martin Schenke, Hans-Gebhard Bethge, and Ursula Ulrike Kaiser, eds., *Nag Hammadi Deutsch*, 2.677–89 (Hans-Martin Schenke); John D. Turner, *Sethian Gnosticism and the Platonic Tradition*.

6. Pearson and Giversen, in *Nag Hammadi Codices IX and X*, 31–36.
7. Schenke, in *Nag Hammadi Deutsch*, 2.680.

Melchizedek[1]

Melchiz[edek][2]

The Future Career of Jesus Christ (1,1–4,11ff.)

Jesus Christ, the Son [of God][3] . . . from . . . . . .[4] the aeons, that he might [pass through] all of the aeons,[5] and [see] in each one of the aeons the nature of the aeon, as to what [kind] it is, and that he might put on as a garment sonship and goodness.[6] O brother, ...[7] their end . . . . And he will [reveal to them] the truth . . . . . .[8] proverbs[9] . . . . . .[10] [2] [at] first in parables [and riddles] . . . .[11]

. . . [when he] proclaims them, Death will be troubled and become angry, not only he himself but also his [fellow] world-ruling archons and the principalities and authorities,[12] the female gods and the male gods, together with the [arch] angels. And the . . . . . .[13] all . . . world rulers . . . about him and about . . . and . . . . . .[14] they will . . . hidden [mysteries] . . . .[15] [3]

. . . . . .[16] [scandal] from . . . the All. They will . . . [because of] this, while the [righteous will] bury him in haste. [They will] call him "the impious man" and "the [impure] transgressor of the law."

But[17] [on] the [third] day he [will rise from the] dead . . . .[18] [4]

. . . and . . . them . . . the holy disciples. And the Savior will [reveal] to them [the word] that gives life to the [All].[19] And those in [heaven], those on earth, and those under the earth[20] pronounced the word . . . . . .[21] [5]

---

1. Coptic text: NHC IX,1: 1,1–27,10. Editions: *The Facsimile Edition of the Nag Hammadi Codices: Codices IX–X*, 5–31; Birger A. Pearson, ed., *Nag Hammadi Codices IX and X*, 19–85 (Birger A. Pearson and Søren Giverson); Wolf-Peter Funk, *Concordance des textes de Nag Hammadi: Les Codices VIII et IX*, 567–72; Wolf-Peter Funk, Jean-Pierre Mahé, and Claudio Gianotto, eds., *Melchisédek*; Hans-Martin Schenke, Hans-Gebhard Bethge, and Ursula Ulrike Kaiser, eds., *Nag Hammadi Deutsch*, 2.677–89 (Hans-Martin Schenke). 2. The superscript title is partially preserved, with decoration, on a small fragment. 3. The revelation given to Melchizedek by the angel Gamaliel begins rather abruptly, without an introductory account of the angel's appearance. 4. One line missing. 5. This passage probably refers to the descent of the Savior. Cf. Isaiah's vision of the Savior's descent in *Ascension of* *Isaiah* 10.7–31. 6. Or "messiahship," "Christhood," (*m^entkhrēstos*). The Greek word *khrēstos* means "good," but is often confused with *khristos*, "anointed, Christ." Cf. *Secret Book of John* II, 6; 15. 7. Five lines untranslatable, two missing. 8. Two lines untranslatable, one missing. 9. Cf. *John* 16:25. 10. Two lines missing. 11. One line missing. 12. *Colossians* 2:15; *Ephesians* 6:12. 13. One line untranslatable, three missing. 14. Two lines missing. 15. One line untranslatable, two missing. 16. Two lines untranslatable. 17. Taking *auō* as equivalent to Greek adversative *kai*. 18. One line untranslatable, about sixteen missing. 19. This passage probably refers to the Savior's postresurrection instruction. "The All" probably refers to the totality of the elect, as often in Valentinian gnosis. 20. Cf. *Philippians* 2:10; *Revelation* 5:3. 21. Four lines untranslatable, about sixteen missing.

True Versus False Belief (5,1–17)

. . . [which] will happen in his name. <Furthermore>, they will say of him,

"He was not born," though he was born;
"he does not eat," though he does eat;
"he does not drink," though he does drink;
"he is not circumcised," though he was circumcised;
"he is without real flesh," though he came in the flesh;
"he did not suffer death," <though> he did endure suffering;
"he did not rise from the dead," <though> he did rise from the dead.[22]

[But] all the [tribes] and all [the peoples] will speak [the truth],[23] who are receiving from [you yourself], O [Melchize]d[ek], holy one and high priest,[24] the perfect hope and the [gifts of] life.

The Angel Gamaliel Identifies Himself (5,17–22)

I [am Gamal]iel. It is to [snatch away][25] the assembly[26] of the [children] of Seth that I have come. For they are above [thousands of] thousands [and ten thousands] of ten thousands[27] [of aeons for ever and ever. Amen].

Liturgical Invocations of Celestial Divine Beings (5,23–6,10)

O essence of [every aeon, A]BA[BA AI]AIAI[28] ABABA,
O divine A[utogen]es[29] of . . . ,
O movement [of every nature, Mother] of the aeons, [B]arb[elo],
O firstborn of [the aeons,] [6] Aithops[30] Doxomedon Dom[edon],
O possessor of lives, Jesus Christ,
O commanders in chief, luminaries, powers—Harmozel, Oroiael,
    Dav[eithe], Elel[eth],
And you, luminous immortal aeon, Pigeradamas,
And you, good God of the virtuous worlds, Mirocheirothetou,[31]
I call upon all of you through Jesus Christ, Son of God.

---

22. For a similar prediction of false teaching, see *Ascension of Isaiah* 3.21–31. Here the polemic is directed against those who advocate a docetic view of Jesus Christ. Such a polemic is surprising for a Gnostic text. **23.** Perhaps read, with Schenke (in *Nag Hammadi Deutsch,* 2.683), [*an 'ntihe*], "will [not] speak [this way]." **24.** Cf. *Melchezedek* 10, where Melchizedek is called "priest of God Most High," as in *Genesis* 14:18. His designation as "high priest" is probably based on *Hebrews* 5:10; 6:10. His role here is that of recipient and bearer of heavenly revelations. **25.** Gamaliel is one of the angels in the Sethian system whose role it is to "snatch away" or "receive" the elect Sethians from earth to heaven. Cf. *Three Forms of First Thought* 48. **26.** Or "church" (*ekklēsia*). **27.** Cf. *Revelation* 5:11. **28.** Perhaps read [IAI]AIAI, which then makes the whole ineffable name a palindrome. This name is probably meant to refer to the primal Father; cf. *Melchezedek* 16. **29.** Or "Self-Generated." He is the son in the Sethian divine triad of Father-Mother-Son. **30.** "Splendid." **31.** Mahé proposes as a possible Greek etymology for this name "ordained with unction of holy oil" (*Melchisédek,* 36).

The Heavenly High Priest (6,10–22)

He[32] is the one whom I proclaim, inasmuch as [the one] who truly exists [among those who truly] exist has made his [visitation][33] . . . [those who] do not exist, Abel Bar[uch,[34] that] to you[35] [might be given as a gift] the knowledge [of the] truth, that he[36] is [from the] race of the high priest which is [above] thousands [of thousands] and [ten thousands] of ten thousands of the aeons.[37] The adverse [spirits] are [ignorant] of him and of their own destruction

The High-Priestly Offering (6,22–7,6ff.)

Not only that, but I have come to [reveal] to you the truth . . . among [the brethren]: he included himself [in the] living [offering], together with your offspring. He [presented the offering for the] All. [For] it is not [cattle that] you will offer up [for sins] [7] of unbelief, [and for the] ignorant things and all the evil [deeds] that they [do], for they[38] do [not] reach [the Father of the All . . . . the faith] . . . .[39]

Melchizedek and Baptism (7,25–9,4)

. . . [world] . . . world . . . to be [baptized . . . in the] waters . . . . For the [8] waters that are [above] . . . who is baptized . . . but [baptize yourself] in the waters that are [below] . . . as he is coming to . . . great . . . [baptism] as they . . . upon . . . . . .[40] by . . . of the . . . . Pray for [the offspring of the] [9] archons and [all] the angels, together with [the] seed <that> emanated [from the Father] of the All.[41] . . . the entire seed from the . . . .

True Adam and True Eve (9,5–11,12ff.)

[There were] begotten the [gods and the angels] and the humans [and the demons] from the seed. All of [the natures], those in [heaven and] those on earth and [those] under [the earth] . . . . . .[42] the nature of the women . . . among those who are in the . . . they were bound with [many] . . . .[43]

[But this] is [not] the true Adam [10] or the true Eve.[44] [For when they[45] ate] from the tree [of knowledge], they trampled upon [the cherubim] and the seraphim [with the flaming sword].[46] The world ruler and [his archons went to

---

32. Jesus Christ. **33.** Lit., "has visited." **34.** An ineffable name referring to God the Father, made up of "Father" (Hebrew *ab*), "God" (*'ēl*), and "blessed" (*baruk*). **35.** Melchizedek, addressed by Gamaliel. **36.** Jesus Christ. **37.** Cf. *Melchizedek* 5 and the note. **38.** Animal sacrifices; cf. *Hebrews* 9:12–13. Schenke (in *Nag Hammadi Deutsch*, 2.684) reads *etou[naaau semoout a]uō*, "which they will do; they are dead

and . . . ." But there is not enough space in the lacuna for that restoration. **39.** Four lines untranslatable, about fourteen missing. **40.** About fourteen lines missing. **41.** A Gnostic myth is reflected in this passage. **42.** Seven lines missing, seven untranslatable. **43.** Perhaps read, with Funk, *ha[h ᶜnsnah]*, "many bonds." **44.** Cf. *On the Origin of the World* 117. **45.** True Adam and true Eve. **46.** *Genesis* 3:6, 24.

meet the bride] of Adam[47] [who was with him], and they were [polluted by her. But] after they had begotten offspring of the archons with [their cosmic influences, those] who belong to . . . .[48]

. . . [light][49] . . . and the females with the [males, those who] are with [him[50] . . . hidden] from every nature. [And those] who will receive from him the . . . [will renounce] the archons. [11] For [they] have become worthy . . . [immortal] and [great] . . . and [great . . . and] great . . . [human] children[51] . . . [disciples . . . image]. And . . . from the [light] . . . holy . . . . For [from the] beginning . . . a seed . . . .[52] [12]

Other Revelations (12,1–15ff.)

. . . . But I will be silent . . . , for we [are the brethren who have] come down from the living [generations.[53] Revelations][54] will be [revealed to] you [through] the [chosen children] of Adam—[that is, Abe]l, Enoch, N[oah], . . .chi[55] . . . you, Melchized[ek, priest] of God [Most High][56] . . . those who have [become worthy] . . . women . . . .[57] [13]

The End Time (13,1–14,9)

These two who have been chosen[58] will [at] no time nor [in] any place be begotten. Whenever they are begotten,[59] [by] their enemies, by their friends, by strangers and those of their own kin,[60] by the [impious] and the pious, there will [arise all of] the opposing natures, whether visible or invisible, with those in heaven, those [on] earth, and those under the earth. They will make [war][61] . . . each one. For [they exist], whether in the . . . [holy] and . . . are numerous . . . in a . . . them . . . . But these in the . . . every [one] will . . . these will . . . with every blow [and in] [14] sicknesses. These will be confined in other forms and punished. But these others the Savior will take away, and they will overcome everything, [not] with their mouths and words, but through the deeds they will do. [He[62] will] destroy Death.

Final Warning to Melchizedek (14,9–15)

[These things] which I was commanded to reveal to you, reveal also to others [as I have done].[63] But [that] which is secret do not reveal to anyone, unless [it is revealed] to you to do so.

---

47. I.e., the lower Eve. Cf. *On the Origin of the World* 116–17. 48. Nine lines missing, four untranslatable. 49. Perhaps read [ⲣ̄ⲙ̄ⲉⲛⲟⲩⲟ]*ein*, "man of light"—i.e., the true Adam. Cf. *On the Origin of the World* 117. 50. The true Adam. 51. Lit., "sons of man." 52. About sixteen lines missing. 53. Cf. *Melchizedek* 27. 54. Or "apocalypses" (*apokalupsis*). 55. Adam, Abel, Enoch, and Noah are marked as *nomina sacra* ("sacred names") with a continuous supralinear stroke. What is left of this name, ". . .chei. . ." or ". . .chen. . ." is similarly marked. 56. *Genesis* 14:18. 57. Two lines untranslatable, about fifteen missing. 58. The two witnesses of *Revelation* 11:3? 59. The text seems to be corrupt here. 60. Lit., "those who are theirs." 61. Cf. *Revelation* 11:7. 62. The Savior. 63. Lit., "in my way."

Melchizedek's Glorification of God (14,15–15,7)

And [I immediately] arose—I, Mel[chizedek]—and I began to [glorify] God [Most High] . . . that I should rejoice . . . while he is [acting] . . . living . . . [I said], I . . . and I . . . [as an offering. And I] will not cease from [now on and forever], O Father of the [All, because] you have had pity on me, and [**15**] [you have sent] the angel of light, [Gamaliel], from your [aeons, that he might] reveal to me . . . . When he came he [caused] me [to be raised up] from ignorance and the fructification of death to life.

Melchizedek's Vocation (15,7–16,11)

For I have a name: I am [Melch]izedek, the priest of [God] Most High. I [know] that I am [the image of] the true high priest[64] of God Most High, and . . . the world. For it is [no] small [thing that] God . . . as he . . . and . . . [the angels] that [are on the] earth . . . is the sacrifice of . . . whom Death deceived. When he[65] [died], he bound them [with] the natures that lead [them] astray. Still, he presented [**16**] offerings[66] . . . of the animals . . . . I have given them over to Death . . . and the angels and the . . . demons . . . living offerings . . . . I have presented myself to you as an offering, together with those who are mine, to you yourself, O God, Father of the All, with those whom you love, who came forth from you who are holy and [living].

Melchizedek's Baptism (16,11–17)

And <according> to the [perfect] laws I shall pronounce my name as I receive baptism, [now] and forever, among the living and holy [names] and in the [waters]. Amen.

Liturgical Doxologies to Celestial Divine Beings (16,17–18,7)

[Holy], holy, holy are you, O [Father of those] who truly exist, [with those who] do [not] exist, Ab[el Bar]u[ch],[67] for [ever] and ever. Amen.[68]

Holy, holy, holy [are you, who exist before] . . .az,[69] [for ever and] ever. Amen.

Holy, holy, [holy are you, Mother of the] aeons, Ba[r]belo, for ever and ever. Amen.

[Holy], holy, holy are you, [first]born of the aeons, [Doxo]medon . . . [**17**] . . . [for ever] and ever. Amen.

[Holy, holy], holy are you, . . . man,[70] [for ever and ever]. Amen.

---

64. Cf. *Hebrews* 7:3. **65.** Presumably Jesus Christ. **66.** Perhaps read *henprosphor[a euonᵉh]*, "[living] offerings." Cf. *Melchizedek* 6; 16. **67.** Cf. *Melchizedek* 6 and the note. **68.** Cf. the invocations of celestial divine beings in *Melchizedek* 5–6. **69.** A mystical name.

There are almost sixty names ending in -az in the *Books of Jeu.* **70.** A mystical name ending in -man (or -mas), perhaps Akraman (or Akramas); cf. *Holy Book of the Great Invisible Spirit* III, 65.

[Holy, holy], holy are you, O [chief commander, luminary in the first] aeon, [Harmozel, for ever] and ever. [Amen].

[Holy], holy, [holy are you], commander, luminary [of the aeons], Oriael,[71] for [ever and ever]. Amen.

Holy, [holy, holy are you], commander [of the aeons, man of light, Daveithe], for ever [and ever]. Amen.

Holy, [holy, holy are you], chief [commander, Eleleth] . . . aeons . . . . . .[72]

. . . [chief commander, Pigerada]mas,[73] [for ever and ever]. Amen.

[Holy], holy, [holy] are you, good [god of] [18] the [virtuous] worlds, [O great] Meirochei[rothetou, for] ever and ever. [Amen].

[Holy], holy, holy are you, chief [commander of the All], Jesus Christ, [for ever and ever]. Amen.

Final Exhortation (18,7–23ff.)

. . . [prophecy] and . . . . Blessed is [the one who will make his confession. But the one who will not confess] him . . . now . . . will happen to [him] . . . fear and . . . fear and . . . disturbance . . . surrounding [him] . . . in the place wherein [there is] great darkness . . . and many . . . appear . . . there . . . [appear] . . . . . .[74] [19]

Appearance of Heavenly Messengers and Their Message (19,1–24,2ff.)

. . . and . . . they were clothed in . . . all . . . there . . . and . . . like . . . them . . . . . .[75] troubles. They [permitted me to hear] their words . . . and they said to me, "[Greetings, Mel]chiz[ed]ek, [Priest] of God [Most High]." They spoke as if . . . [their] mouths . . . in the All . . . and . . . .[76]

. . . [he][77] led astray . . . he . . . [20] and his [offerings and his] worship services [and his] . . . faith and his prayers. They [offered up animals], they . . . those who are [his] . . . beginning . . . .

But [as for me, they spoke to me, saying, "Do not][78] be concerned, for [this priesthood] which you exercise [and which is] from . . . [in the deceitful] counsels [of] Satan . . . they . . . his teachings . . . for your [thoughts] . . . of this age[79] . . . ."[80]

. . . exist [in] . . . lead [astray] . . . . . .[81] [21] and some . . . and . . he gave them to . . . and . . . and you . . . . . .[82] [22] throw [him] . . . in order that you . . . now . . . by him . . . under . . . . . .[83] [24] for . . . [which] is above . . . .[84] [25]

---

71. Probably read "Oroiael." 72. One line missing, two untranslatable. 73. The text reads [Pigerada]man. 74. One line missing, four untranslatable. 75. Two lines untranslatable. 76. Two lines untranslatable, three missing. 77. Satan? Cf. *Melchizedek* 20. 78. The restoration of this lacuna is that of Funk (in *Melchisédek*), but there are other possibilities. 79. Or "aeon." 80. Three lines missing, one represented by a single letter. 81. Two lines missing. 82. About twenty-two lines missing. 83. About twenty-two lines missing. P. 23, a single small fragment, is blank. 84. About twenty-six lines missing.

The Passion and Resurrection of Christ (25,1–14ff.)

. . . me.[85] And . . . you struck me [with the reed];[86] you threw me . . . fall.[87] And [you crucified me] from the third hour[88] [of Sabbath] Eve[89] until [the ninth hour].[90] And after [these things I rose] from the dead . . . . came out of . . .[91] to me. . . . my eyes[92] [saw. . . they did not] find anyone[93] . . . me[94] . . . .[95] [26]

Melchizedek's Victory (26,1–27,3)

. . . [they][96] greeted [me] . . . . They said to me, "Be [strong,[97] O Melchiz]edek, great [high priest] of God [Most High, for the] archons who [are] your [enemies made] war against you. You have [gained the victory over them, and] they did not prevail over [you. You have] persevered and [destroyed] your enemies . . . [you] will find rest in no other [place except the one who is] living and holy . . . exalt himself . . . flesh . . . ."[98]

. . . [27] [with] the offerings, working on that which is good, fasting with fasts.

Final Warning to Melchizedek (27,3–6)

Do not reveal these revelations to anyone who is in the flesh—it <is> something noncarnal—unless it is revealed to you to do so.[99]

Ascension of the Heavenly Brethren (27,6–10)

When the brethren who belong to the generations of life had said these things, they were taken up to the regions above all the heavens.[100] Amen.

---

85. Here Christ is speaking to his archontic executioners, part of a vision experienced by Melchizedek. The vision began on the bottom of p. 18. 86. *Matthew* 27:30 87. Or "corpse" (*ptōma*). 88. *Mark* 15:25. 89. Greek *prosabbaton*, which is Friday. Cf. *Mark* 15:42. 90. *Mark* 15:34. 91. These lacunae are crucial for the interpretation of the vision of Melchizedek and the tractate as a whole: . . . *ma ei eb[ol h]ᵉm . . . . . . [eho]un eroi*. Pearson and Giversen suggest in a note: [*apasō]ma ei eb[ol h]ᵉm [pᵉmhaau eho]un eroi*, "[my] body came out of [the tomb] into me," referring to the reuniting of Jesus's body and soul. Funk originally suggested (in *Concordance des texts de Nag Hammadi: Les Codices VIII et IX*, 572): [*auhar]ma ei eb[ol h]ᵉm [pjise eho]un eroi*, "[a chariot] came out of [the height] to me," referring to Jesus's ascent to heaven, as in *Secret Book of James* 14. In his more recent transcription, he leaves the first lacuna blank and suggests [*a . . .]ma ei eb[ol h]ᵉm [pjise eho]un eroi*, ". . . came out of [the height] to me." Schenke suggests for the first lacuna: [*apanoē]ma*, "my thought" (in *Nag Hammadi Deutsch*, 2.698). In his view, two speakers are referred to in the first person, Jesus and Melchizedek. Jesus's speech concludes with the resurrection, and Melchizedek's begins on the same line with an account of his recovery from his ecstasy. However, there is not room in the lacuna for [*apanoē]ma* or [*panoē]ma*, "my thought." Funk and Mahé nevertheless now accept the change of speakers at line 9, as suggested by Schenke. See the discussion in the introduction. 92. Jesus's eyes; Melchizedek's eyes according to Funk, Mahé, and Schenke. Schenke translates, "my eyes began to see [again]," referring to Melchizedek's recovery from his ecstasy. 93. A reference to the women at the tomb? Mahé translates, ". . . [without] finding anyone," referring to Melchizedek's eyes. Schenke translates, "[but they] found no . . . ." 94. The bottom of the page is missing; so the conclusion to Jesus's address to his executioners is lost. 95. About fourteen lines missing. 96. The heavenly brethren mediating Melchizedek's revelatory vision; cf. *Melchizedek* 27. 97. An ancient "holy war" slogan; cf. *Deuteronomy* 31:6–7. 98. One line untranslatable, about thirteen missing. 99. A similar warning appears at the end of the first revelation at *Melchizedek* 14. 100. Melchizedek's vision concludes with the ascension of the brethren. His awakening and reaction to the vision is not recorded. Contrast *Melchizedek* 14.

THE THOUGHT OF NOREA

NHC IX,2

Introduced by John D. Turner
Translated by Marvin Meyer

The fifty-two-line *Thought of Norea* is more properly an "ode to Norea," wife-sister of Seth, conceived as a manifestation of Sophia, the "fallen" divine Wisdom, who will be restored along with her spiritual progeny into the divine world by the very aeons from which she once departed. Named by modern editors after the phrase "the thought (*noēsis*) of Norea" toward the end of the text (29,3), this short poetic text was originally untitled, nor can it be identified with other works under the name of Norea mentioned by Epiphanius ("Norea," *Panarion* 26.1.3) and in the Nag Hammadi treatise *On the Origin of the World* (*First Book of Noraia* and *First Discourse* [*logos*] *of Oraia*, 102,10–11.24–25).

The biblical Norea (variously spelled Orea, Oraia, Horaia, Nora, Noria, Noraia, Nuraita, and Nhuraita, perhaps derived from the Hebrew root *nūr*, "fire," or *nhr*, "shine," or *'ōr*, "light") is probably to be identified as Na'amah ("pleasant one"), who in *Genesis* 4:22 is the daughter of Cainite Lamech and sister of Tubal-Cain, later taken to be the wife-sister of Seth. According to Pseudo-Philo *Book of Biblical Antiquities* 1.1, "Adam produced three sons and one daughter, Cain, Noba, Abel, and Seth" (cf. *Chronicles of Jerahmeel* 26.1: "Adam fathered three sons and three daughters: Cain and his twin, Qalmana, his wife, and Abel and his twin, Deborah, his wife; and Seth and his twin, Noba, his wife"). According to *Zohar* I, 55a; III, 76b, the Cainite Na'amah seduced the "sons of God" (*Genesis* 6:2, interpreted to mean angels) by her beauty; according to R. Abba b. Kahana, in *Midrash Genesis Rabba* on *Genesis* 4:22, "Na'amah was Noah's wife." The "other Gnostics" of Irenaeus (*Against Heresies* 1.30.9) held that after the birth of Cain and Abel, Seth was generated after Norea, by the providence of Prunikos (Sophia). Probably drawing from Irenaeus's *Against Heresies* 1.30, Epiphanius (*Panarion* 39.5.2–3) claims that Seth had a wife named Horaia (i.e., Norea; cf. Na'amah), who was produced as a spiritual power in her own right. In *Panarion* 26.1.7–9 Epiphanius tells us that Noria, who revealed Barbelo and the higher powers, burned the ark that the evil creator had commanded Noah to build, an episode also narrated in the *Nature of the Rulers* (91,30–92,26) as a prelude to the dialogue between Eleleth and Norea. Finally, according to Filastrius (*Various Heresies* 33.3), the Nicolaitans venerated Barbelo and a certain woman Nora.

Norea's plea to the "God of the All" in the *Nature of the Rulers* constitutes her initial action in the *Thought of Norea*, where she invokes the divine triad of Father (Mind, Adamas), Mother (Ennoia, "Thought"), and Son (Mind, Logos, Autogenes). Just as in the *Nature of the Rulers*, where the angel Eleleth comes to her aid, so also the *Thought of Norea* accords her the Four Luminaries (Harmozel, Oroiael, Daveithai, and Eleleth) as helpers who intercede for her with the Father of the All. Having entered a condition of deficiency, she will be allowed to find rest in the place of Epinoia ("Insight") with the divine Autogenes ("Self-Generated"). Just as the Epinoia of Light in *Three Forms of First Thought* and the *Secret Book of John* represents Sophia, so also Norea in the *Thought of Norea* is a symbolic equivalent of Sophia, who seeks restoration to the divine realm by correcting the deficiency that originated through her attempt to extend the supreme deity's creative power beyond the divine realm.

As the upper Sophia she cries out to the Father of the All (Adamas conceived as Thought) to be restored to her place in the light, perhaps by the agency of the Four Luminaries (Harmozel, Oroiael, Daveithai, and Eleleth) or their ministers (Gamaliel, Gabriel, Abrasax, and Samblo), which results in her restoration to her former place in "ineffable Insight" (perhaps the light Eleleth, to whom she cries in the *Nature of the Rulers*) and thus in the realm of the divine Self-Generated (Autogenes). On the other hand, she is also the lower Sophia, manifested as the daughter of Eve and wife-sister of Seth who is yet to be delivered from her deficiency. It is interesting that here Adamas is himself the Father of the All, yet he is also called Mind (*nous*) and Thought (*ennoia*) as well as Father of Mind, a set of identifications that may refer to the nature of Adamas as bisexual, both father and mother, or else as "Man" and "Son of Man" (which are perhaps the two names that make the "single name" Man in *Norea* 28,27–29,5).

The *Thought of Norea*, *Three Forms of First Thought*, and the *Holy Book of the Great Invisible Spirit* seem to assume or stress the innocence of Epinoia/Sophia such that her restoration to the Light no longer requires repentance for her unintentional but arrogant generation of the world creator without the aid of her appointed consort, as described in the *Secret Book of John*. Indeed, the *Holy Book of the Great Invisible Spirit* goes a step further than *Three Forms of First Thought* by attributing the origin of the archons Sakla and Nebruel to Gamaliel and Gabriel, the ministers of the two highest of the Four Luminaries, while Sophia's function is merely limited to producing the matter over which they rule. So also in the treatise *Zostrianos* (9,1–11,1) Sophia serves as the model for worldly things but is not the source of the world creator who shapes it.

BIBLIOGRAPHY

Bernard Barc and Michel Roberge, *L'Hypostase des archontes: Traité gnostique sur l'origine de l'homme, du monde et des archontes (NH II,4); Noréa (NH IX,2)* (Michel Roberge); Birger A. Pearson, "The Figure of Norea in Gnostic Literature"; Birger A. Pearson, ed., *Nag Hammadi Codices IX and X*, 87–99 (Birger A. Pearson and Søren Giversen); Hans-Martin Schenke, Hans-Gebhard Bethge and Ursula Ulrike Kaiser, eds., *Nag Hammadi Deutsch*, 2.691–96 (Ursula Ulrike Kaiser and Uwe-Karsten Plisch).

The Thought of Norea[1]

"Father of the All,
[Thought] of light,
Mind dwelling on high,
above the regions below,
light dwelling [on] high,
voice of truth,
upright Mind,
unattainable Word,[2]
ineffable voice,
[incomprehensible] Father!"

To these Norea[3] [calls] out.
They heard and received her
into her eternal place.
They granted her the Father of Mind, Adamas,
and the [two] voices of the holy ones, [28]
so that she might rest in ineffable Insight[4]
and inherit the First Mind,[5]
which <she>[6] has received,
and rest in the divine Self-Generated,[7]
and generate herself,
as [she] also has inherited the living Word,
and be joined to all the imperishable ones,
and [dwell] in[8] the Mind of the Father,
so as to speak with words of [life],

---

1. Coptic text: NHC IX,2: 27,11–29,5. Editions: *The Facsimile Edition of the Nag Hammadi Codices: Codices IX and X*, 31–33; Birger A. Pearson, ed., *Nag Hammadi Codices IX and X*, 87–99 (Birger A. Pearson and Søren Giversen); Michel Roberge, *Noréa*; Hans-Martin Schenke, Hans-Gebhard Bethge, and Ursula Ulrike Kaiser, eds., *Nag Hammadi Deutsch*, 2.691–96 (Ursula Ulrike Kaiser and Uwe-Karsten Plisch). The title is construed from the contents of the text; the text is sometimes entitled the *Ode on Norea*. 2. Logos, here and below. 3. Norea (or Orea) is also discussed in the *Nature of the Rulers* and *On the Origin of the World*. In this regard the latter text mentions two works that may be related to Norea, the *First Book of Noraia* and the *First Discourse of Oraia*. 4. Epinoia. 5. In Middle Platonism, First Mind is a term for the divine. 6. The Coptic text has *etafjitᵉf*, "he has received," and is emended to read *eta<s>jitᵉf*. 7. Autogenes. 8. Or "[speak] with."

and remain in the presence of the exalted one
by taking [possession] of what she received
before the world came into being.

She has the great Mind of the invisible ones,[9]
and she glorifies their Father[10]
and lives among those
who . . . in the Fullness,[11]
and she beholds[12] the Fullness.

Days will come
when she will [attain][13] fullness
and no longer be in deficiency.
She has four holy helpers[14]
who intercede for her with the Father of the All,
Adamas,[15] [29] who is within all Adams.[16]
While he has the thought of Norea,
while she speaks of two names,
they mean a single name.[17]

---

9. Or "invisible one." 10. If the singular is restored for "invisible one," just above, perhaps emend to read "<her> Father." 11. Pleroma, here and below. 12. Or "[until] she beholds." 13. Or "[behold]." 14. The four helpers are the Four Luminaries Harmozel, Oroiael, Daveithai, and Eleleth. 15. If "Adama" is taken as a vocative, the sentence could read as follows: "Adamas, you who are within all Adams, you have the thought of Norea . . ." 16. I.e., within all people. 17. The two names are most likely Adamas, and Norea or Adam as humankind; the single name is Adamas, the name of God; cf. Pearson, in *Nag Hammadi Codices IX and X*, 99. See also *Gospel of Philip* 54, and the introduction to the present tractate.

THE TESTIMONY OF TRUTH

NHC IX,3

Introduced and Translated by Birger A. Pearson

T he *Testimony of Truth* is extant only in the Coptic version found in Nag Hammadi Codex IX, a translation from the original Greek. Unfortunately, almost half of the text is lost, owing to the damaged condition of the manuscript. Enough remains, nevertheless, for us to gain a good picture of the tractate's content.

The original title of this tractate, if there was one, is unknown. It is possible that a title was supplied at the end of the tractate, but the last two pages of the codex are lost. The title now in regular use has been editorially assigned on the basis of a major theme found in the tractate ("word of truth," 31,8; "true testimony," 45,1), part of its polemical thrust. The author is intent upon presenting his version of the truth—a radically encratic Gnostic Christianity—and contrasting this with the false opinions and practices of his "heretical" opponents. His polemics are presented in the form of rhetorical antitheses (light-darkness, knowledge-ignorance, incorruptibility-corruption, etc.). The author's opponents are easily identifiable on the basis of how they are described. They consist for the most part of members of the catholic ("orthodox") church, who clearly constitute a majority of Christians in the author's locale. Interestingly enough, the author's opponents also include fellow Gnostics, such as the Valentinians, Basilidians, Simonians, and others, with whose practices he vehemently disagrees.

The *Testimony of Truth* exhibits rhetorical features commonly found in early Christian homilies. Indeed, the first part of the tractate consists of a well-constructed homily (29,6–45,6), addressed to fellow members of a Gnostic Christian community "who understand how to listen with spiritual ears and not with their physical ones" (29,6–9). Its purpose is to encourage its hearers to remain steadfast in their faith, warning them of the errors of (catholic) Christian opponents. The second part (45,6–end), where the manuscript has suffered considerable damage, consists of miscellaneous additions, based on various sources, elaborating on themes already sounded in the first part. It is in this section that the polemics against other Gnostics occur. The two parts are presented from the same point of view, so it is clear that the same author is responsible for both. The tractate as a whole can suitably be characterized as a "homiletic tract."

The first part opens with an exordium in which the author appeals to those with spiritual hearing. An attack is launched against the law, which for the author is summed up in the command to procreate (29,26–30,18). The descent of the Son of Humanity from "imperishability" is a sign that the dominion of the law has come to an end (30,18–30). A contrast is then set up between those with knowledge and "the foolish," who are willing to suffer martyrdom for the faith under the illusion that the Father desires human sacrifice, but they are ignorant of the true nature of Christ (31,22–34,26). These people are also criticized for believing that there will be a physical resurrection, not understanding that the resurrection is really something spiritual, consisting of self-knowledge (34,26–38,27).

The author then continues his attack on marriage and procreation, sarcastically attacking people who think that God created male and female sex organs for the purpose of human pleasure. Jesus's virgin birth is taken as a sign that Christians should instead lead a virginal life and renounce the things of this world (39,1–40,19). In a rather bizarre allegory, the author interprets the martyrdom of Isaiah (his being sawed in two) to refer to the divisions between those governed by corruptibility and darkness and those who belong to incorruptibility and light (40,21–41,4).

The capstone of the homily constituting the first part of the tractate is a description of the career of the archetypal Gnostic: his renunciation of the world and his reintegration into the realm of imperishability (41,4–44,30). This first part of the tractate concludes with a peroration:

> This, therefore, is the true testimony: When a person comes to know himself and God, who is over the truth, that person will be saved and crowned with the unfading crown. (44,30–45,6)

The second part of the tractate opens with a contrast between John the Baptizer, born of an aged womb, and Christ, who "passed through a virgin's womb" (45,6–22). The author admonishes his hearers to seek after the interpretation of "mysteries" found in scripture, thus introducing a Gnostic midrash on the biblical snake (45,23–49,10), which was probably based on a preexisting source.[1] It starts with a paraphrase of *Genesis* 2:16–3:22 and continues with reference to Moses's contest with the Egyptian magicians (*Exodus* 4:2–4; 7:8–12) and the serpent in the wilderness (*Numbers* 21:9). The paradise narrative is interpreted in such a way as to expose the biblical creator as malicious and envious. The author identifies the snake allegorically as a manifestation of Christ and the salvation brought by him through gnosis. The author then excoriates his opponents for not understanding Christ "spiritually" (49,10–50,3).

---

1. Birger A. Pearson, "Jewish Haggadic Traditions in *The Testimony of Truth* from Nag Hammadi."

The material that follows is very fragmentary, but a central theme is the contrast between the "generation of Adam," under the law, and the "generation of the Son of Humanity," consisting of those who have renounced the desires of the flesh and have come to know the Father of Truth (50,3–69,7). In a section following four pages that lack any translatable material, the followers of Valentinus are attacked (55,1–18ff.) as well as Basilides and his son Isidore (56,1–57,8ff.), the Simonians (58,2–4), and others whose names are lost in lacunae. These "heretics" are attacked for their practices, which include the use of water baptism and the acceptance of marriage and procreation.[2]

The attack against baptism is taken up again (69,7–32), followed by an accusation of idolatry against certain opponents, which is illustrated with a midrash on David and Solomon's harnessing demons in their building of Jerusalem and the temple (69,32–70,30ff.). This midrash too is probably based on a preexisting source.[3] The tractate's polemical tone continues in the fragmentary material that remains (71,12–74,30, where the text breaks off).

The chief concern of the tractate's author from beginning to end is his total rejection of sex, marriage, and procreation. It is the biblical creator who is "the father of sexual intercourse" (68,8) and who holds the "generation of Adam" in thrall with his command in "the law" to marry and beget children (30,2–5; cf. *Genesis* 2:24). Members of the "generation of Adam" are given over to wicked desires (67,9–13) and utilize their sex organs for carnal pleasure (39,1–6). But with the coming of the Son of Humanity the "dominion of carnal procreation" has come to an end. The Gnostic, who is of the "generation of the Son of Humanity," has renounced the things of this world and has "made himself male" (68,8–11; 41,4–13).

The theology of the *Testimony of Truth* and its allegorical interpretation of scripture based on Alexandrian Jewish (Philonic) and Christian precedents clearly situates its author in an Alexandrian milieu. Also very striking is the massive use of specifically Valentinian Gnostic teachings in the areas of theology, Christology, anthropology, and the doctrine of resurrection.[4] Yet, the author does not shrink from including followers of Valentinus in his polemics against "heretical" opponents. The reason for that is not hard to find, for the basis of his polemics is his radical encratism, his total rejection and renunciation of sex and marriage. He also takes his stance against opponents who practice baptism. Since the Valentinians included baptism in their ritual life and accepted the institution of marriage and procreation in their daily lives, they are included in our author's vituperations.

Who was this man? He was surely well schooled in the Valentinian tradition, even though he included Valentinians among his opponents, so we might look upon him as an ex-member of the Valentinian school. As it happens, Clement of

---

2. Birger A. Pearson, "Anti-Heretical Warnings in Codex IX from Nag Hammadi," 188–93.
3. Birger A. Pearson, "Gnostic Interpretation of the Old Testament in *The Testimony of Truth* from Nag Hammadi," 314–18.
4. Birger A. Pearson, in Birger A. Pearson, ed., *Nag Hammadi Codices IX and X*, 110–18; Annie Mahé and Jean-Pierre Mahé, *Le Témoignage Véritable*, 26–69.

Alexandria provides us with information in his *Miscellanies* (3.86–95) on a teacher of radical encratism, Julius Cassianus, who is said to have "departed from the school of Valentinus," presumably because he had come to disagree with Valentinian practices. There is considerable overlap between what Clement tells us about this man and the views expressed by the author of the *Testimony of Truth*, so it is not unreasonable tentatively to identify Julius Cassianus as the author of our tractate.[5] To be sure, this identification has been criticized on various grounds: the absence of attacks on martyrdom and baptism in what Clement tells us of Julius's teachings,[6] supposed differences between Julius and our tractate's author on the interpretation of *Genesis* 2–3,[7] and a more favorable view of the Old Testament attributable to Julius than is reflected in the *Testimony of Truth*.[8] It must be remembered that Julius's writings are not extant, and Clement's information about him is not extensive, so the question of the authorship of our tractate must remain open. In any case, whoever the author was, he wrote around the same time and in the same place as Julius Cassianus, in late second- or early third-century Alexandria.[9]

BIBLIOGRAPHY

Wolf-Peter Funk, *Concordance des textes de Nag Hammadi: Les Codices VIII et IX*; Claudio Gianotto, *La testimonianza veritiera*; Jean-Daniel Kaestli, "Une relecture polémique de *Genèse* 3 dans le gnosticisme chrétien: Le *Témoignage de vérité*"; Klaus Koschorke, "Der gnostische Traktat 'Testimonium Veritatis' aus dem Nag-Hammadi-Codex IX"; *Die Polemik der Gnostiker gegen das kirchliche Christentum*; Annie Mahé and Jean-Pierre Mahé, *Le Témoignage Véritable*; Birger A. Pearson, "Anti-Heretical Warnings in Codex IX from Nag Hammadi"; "Gnostic Interpretation of the Old Testament in *The Testimony of Truth* from Nag Hammadi"; "Jewish Haggadic Traditions in *The Testimony of Truth* from Nag Hammadi"; Birger A. Pearson, ed., *Nag Hammadi Codices IX and X*, 101–227 (Birger A. Pearson and Søren Giversen); Hans-Martin Schenke, Hans-Gebhard Bethge, and Ursula Ulrike Kaiser, eds., *Nag Hammadi Deutsch*, 2.697–712 (Uwe-Karsten Plisch).

5. Pearson, in *Nag Hammadi Codices IX and X*, 118–20.
6. Klaus Koschorke, "Der gnostische Traktat 'Testimonium Veritatis' aus dem Nag-Hammadi-Codex IX," 108.
7. Claudio Gianotto, *La testimonianza veritiera*, 51, 86; Mahé and Mahé, *Le Témoignage Véritable*, 49.
8. Uwe-Karsten Plisch, in Hans-Martin Schenke, Hans-Gebhard Bethge, and Ursula Ulrike Kaiser, eds., *Nag Hammadi Deutsch*, 2.699.
9. So also Plisch, in *Nag Hammadi Deutsch*, 2.699.

The Testimony of Truth[1]

The Law Versus the Truth (29,6–30,18)

Now,[2] I shall speak to those who understand how to listen with spiritual ears and not with their physical ones. For many have sought for the truth but have not been able to find it, because the old leaven[3] of the Pharisees and scribes of the law[4] has overcome them. By "leaven" is meant desire for the error of the angels, demons, and stars.[5] As for the Pharisees and scribes, they belong to the archons who have authority [over them]. For no one living under the law is able to lift his gaze to the truth, for they cannot serve two masters.[6]

For the law's defilement is clear, [30] but undefilement belongs to the light. The law commands one to take a husband or take a wife, and to produce children, to multiply like the sand of the sea.[7] But passion, which is their delight, controls the souls of those who are begotten down here[8]—those who defile and are defiled in return—so that the law might be fulfilled by them. They show that they are helping the world[9] and [turning] away from the light. For them it will be impossible to [pass by] the archon of darkness until they have paid the last [cent].[10]

The Descent of the Son of Humanity (30,18–31,22)

The Son of Humanity[11] came forth from an imperishable realm[12] as one who was a stranger to defilement. He came [to the] world upon the Jordan [River], and the Jordan immediately [turned] back. John bore witness to Jesus's [descent], for it is he who saw the power that came down upon the Jordan River. He realized that the dominion of carnal procreation had come to an end. By the "Jordan River" is

---

1. Coptic text: NHC IX,3: 29,6–74,30ff. Editions: *The Facsimile Edition of the Nag Hammadi Codices: Codices IX and X*, 33–74; Claudio Gianotto, *La testimonianza veritiera*; Klaus Koschorke, "Der gnostische Traktat 'Testimonium Veritatis' aus dem Nag-Hammadi-Codex IX"; Annie Mahé and Jean-Pierre Mahé, *Le Témoignage Véritable*; Birger A. Pearson, ed., *Nag Hammadi Codices IX and X*, 101–203 (Birger A. Pearson and Søren Giversen); Hans-Martin Schenke, Hans-Gebhard Bethge, and Ursula Ulrike Kaiser, eds., *Nag Hammadi Deutsch*, 2.697–712 (Uwe-Karsten Plisch). 2. The text has "but." Use of the Greek connective particle *de* here may indicate the existence of previous material, now lost. 3. For "old leaven," cf. 1 Corinthians 5:7; "leaven of the Pharisees," cf. Luke 12:1. 4. The "law" is summed up in the command to multiply, as indicated below. 5. Sexual desire is inspired by demonic forces, whose ruler is the archon of darkness (the creator). 6. *Matthew* 6:24. 7. *Genesis* 1:38; cf. 22:17. 8. Lit., "in this place"—i.e., on earth. 9. The cosmos (*kosmos*). 10. *Matthew* 5:26. 11. I.e., "the Son of Man," a title that Jesus regularly applies to himself in the New Testament gospels. 12. Lit., "imperishability."

meant the function of the body, its sensual [31] pleasures. The water of the Jordan is the desire for sexual intercourse. By "John" is meant the ruler of the womb.[13]

This is what the Son of Humanity reveals to us: it is proper for you to receive the word of truth, assuming one will receive it completely.[14] As for one who is [in] ignorance, it is scarcely possible[15] for him to diminish the works of [darkness] that he has done. On the other hand, those who have come to know imperishability have become capable of combating [passions] . . . .[16]

I[17] said [to you], "Do not build [or] accumulate things for yourselves where robbers break in,[18] but bring forth fruit to the Father."

True Versus False Confession (31,22–34,26)

Foolish people have it in their minds that if they simply make the confession, "We are Christians," in words but not with power, and ignorantly give themselves up to a human death, they will live. But they are in error and do not know where they are going [32] or who Christ really is. Instead, they are hastening toward the principalities and the authorities.[19] They fall into their clutches because of the ignorance that is in them.

For if only words of testimony were effective for salvation, the whole world would hold out for this and be saved. But it is in this way that they have drawn error to themselves . . . .[20] [they do] not [know] that they [will destroy] themselves. If [God] really wanted a human sacrifice, he would be conceited.

The Son of [Humanity] clothed himself with their firstfruits and went down to Hades.[21] There he performed many mighty deeds and raised the dead. And the world rulers [33] of darkness[22] became envious of him, for they did not find any sin in him. He also destroyed their works affecting humanity by granting healing to the lame, the blind, the paralyzed, and the demon-possessed.[23] And he walked on the waters of the sea.[24] For this reason he [destroyed] his flesh by . . . which he . . . and he [became] . . . salvation . . . his death . . . . . .[25] [everyone] . . . .

How numerous [they are! They are] blind [guides, like the disciples]. They[26] boarded [the ship, and at about four] miles[27] away they [saw Jesus walking] on the [sea. These people][28] are [hollow] martyrs who bear witness only [to] themselves. In fact, they are sick and cannot get themselves up. [34] But when they are full of passion, this is their motivating idea: "If we give ourselves up to death for the sake of the name,[29] we will be saved." That is not the way things are. Rather, impelled by planetary forces,[30] they say that they have "completed" their futile "course."[31] And they . . . say . . . . But these . . . they have [given themselves up to death] . . . . . .[32] his . . . and his . . . . They are like . . . and are not in possession of the life-giving word.

---

13. Probably a reference to the creator; cf. Heracleon, frag. 8. 14. Lit., "in a perfection." 15. Lit., "it is difficult." 16. One line missing. 17. Probably the Son of Humanity. 18. *Matthew* 6:19. 19. *Ephesians* 6:12. 20. One line missing, two untranslatable. 21. Coptic *Amente*, the Egyptian underworld. Here it refers to this world. 22. *Ephesians* 6:12. 23. *Luke* 7:21–22. 24. *Matthew* 14:25. 25. Four lines missing. 26. The disciples. 27. Lit., "thirty stades"; cf. *John* 6:19. 28. The text reverts to discussion of the opponents. 29. The name of Christ; cf. 1 *Peter* 4:14. 30. Lit., "wandering stars." 31. 2 *Timothy* 4:7. 32. Four lines missing.

There Is No Physical Resurrection (34,26–37,9)

Some say, "On the last day we will certainly rise again [35] [in the] resurrection." But they do not [know what] they are saying, for the last day [is when] those who are Christ's . . . the earth, which is . . . . When the [time] was ripe, he destroyed their [archon] of [darkness]³³ . . . souls . . . . . . .³⁴ [He took] his stand . . . .

They asked [what they had been] bound with, and how they might get [themselves] loose. [They came to know] themselves, [who they are] or where they are now, and [where] it is [36] they might find respite from their ignorance and [attain] knowledge.³⁵ [It is these people] Christ will bring to heaven,³⁶ since they have [renounced] ignorance and advanced to knowledge. And those who have knowledge . . . . . . .³⁷

. . . the great . . . [the spiritual]³⁸ resurrection . . . . [He has come to] know [the Son of Humanity], that is, [he has come to] know [himself. This] is the perfect life, [that] people come to know [themselves]³⁹ through the All.⁴⁰

Therefore, [do not] look for the carnal resurrection,⁴¹ [37] which [is] destruction. [Those who] go astray by [expecting] a [resurrection] that is empty [are not stripped] of the flesh.⁴² [They do] not [know] the power [of God], nor do they [understand the interpretation] of the scriptures, [owing to their] duplicity of mind.⁴³

The Life-Giving Word of the Son of Humanity (37,9–38,27)

[The mystery] that [the Son of Humanity taught] . . . in order that . . . destroy . . . . . .⁴⁴ [the Son of] Humanity, who . . . written [book] . . . for they have . . . [blessed] . . . within [them]. And they live before [God under the light yoke.⁴⁵ Those who do not] have the life-giving [word] in their [hearts will die]. In their thoughts they are apparent to [the Son] of Humanity in terms of [their] actions and their [error. [38] . . . those] of this type. They . . . he divides⁴⁶ the . . . . And they [do not] understand that it is from him⁴⁷ that [the Son] of Humanity is coming. [If they] come to . . . sacrifice, they die a human death, and they [give themselves up] . . . . . .⁴⁸ a death . . . . . . .⁴⁹ Those who . . . they are many . . . each [one] . . . pervert . . . gain . . . [their] minds.

But [those who will receive] him to themselves [with uprightness] and [power] and every knowledge [are the ones whom] he will bring [to] heaven,⁵⁰ to eternal [life].

---

33. Cf. *Testimony of Truth* 30. 34. Nine lines missing, two untranslatable. 35. Gnosis, here and below. 36. Lit., "to the heights." 37. Nine lines missing, two untranslatable. 38. On the "spiritual resurrection," cf. *Treatise on Resurrection* 45–46. 39. Lit., "man . . . himself." 40. "The All" probably means here what it often does in Valentinian texts, the totality of the Gnostic elect. 41. "Carnal" or "fleshly" resurrection is the resurrection of the body; cf. *Treatise on Resurrection* 45–46. 42. To be "stripped" of the flesh is the goal of the Gnostic. Cf. *Gospel of Truth* 20. 43. Lit., "double-mindedness" (*dipsukhia*); cf. 2 *Clement* 19:2; *James* 4:8. Another possible interpretation of the text is that it is the "ambiguity" of the scriptures that is at issue. Only the Gnostic has the proper key to interpreting the scriptures. 44. Three lines untranslatable. 45. *Matthew* 11:30. 46. Cf. *Luke* 12:51–52. 47. The Father; cf. *John* 16:28. 48. Two lines untranslatable. 49. One line missing, two untranslatable. 50. Cf. *Testimony of Truth* 36 and the note.

Sensual Pleasures Must Be Renounced (38,27–39,19)

[But] as for those who receive him to themselves with [ignorance], the defiled pleasures [39] prevail over them. It is [these] people who say, "God created [genitalia][51] for our use, for us to [grow in] defilement in order to enjoy [ourselves]." So they cause God to become an accomplice [in] actions of this [kind]. They are [not] steady [upon] earth, [nor will they reach] heaven. But . . . place will . . . four . . .[52] . . .[53] unquenchable [fire] . . . which is . . . . . .[54]

Born Again by the Word (39,21–40,19)

. . . word . . . upon [the Jordan River][55] when he came to [John at] the time he [was baptized]. The [Holy] Spirit [came] down upon him [as a] dove . . . accept for ourselves that [he] was born of a virgin and assumed flesh. He [dwelt with [40] us][56] and received power.

Were we also born from a virginal union [or] conceived by the word? [Rather], we [have been born] again by [the word]. So let us strengthen [ourselves] as virgins among male . . . . They dwell . . . the virgin[57] . . . through . . . in the word . . . . But the word of . . . and spirit . . . . . .[58] is the Father . . . for the man . . . .[59]

The Martyrdom of Isaiah Signifies Divisions (40,21–41,4)

. . . [like Isaiah, who was sawed with a saw and] became two.[60] [So too the Son of] Humanity [divides] us by [the word of the] cross,[61] dividing [the day from] the night, the light from the darkness, and the corruptible [from] incorruptibility. He also [divides the] males from the females. "[Isaiah]" symbolizes [41] the body. The "saw" is the word of the Son of Humanity that separates us from the error of the angels.[62]

Renunciation of the World (41,4–21)

No one knows the God of truth except the person who forsakes all the things of this world and renounces the whole place, grasping the hem of his garment. Such a person[63] has established himself with power and subdued desire within him in every [way]. He has made himself [male], and, with self-examination,[64] has returned to himself . . . in becoming . . . the mind . . . [from] his soul . . . he has . . . .

---

51. Reading, with Mahé and Mahé, [morion], "bodily parts, genitalia." 52. Perhaps read *ftoe ⁿn[gōnia ⁿmpkah]*, "four corners of the earth"; cf. *Revelation* 7:1. 53. Three lines missing. 54. Two lines untranslatable. 55. Cf. *Testimony of Truth* 30. 56. *John* 1:14.

57. Probably Mary. 58. Three lines missing, one untranslatable. 59. One line missing. 60. *Ascension of Isaiah* 5.1–14; cf. *Hebrews* 11:37. 61. Cf. *Hebrews* 4:12. 62. Cf. *Testimony of Truth* 29 and the note. 63. Lit., "he." 64. Lit., "having examined himself."

Existential Questions (41,22–42,27)

In what way . . . the flesh, which . . . ? In what way . . . out of it? And how many [powers does he have]? Who is it who has bound him, or who is it who will loosen him? What is the light, and what is darkness? Who is it who created [the earth], and who is God? [Who] are [42] the angels? What is soul, and what is spirit? Where is the voice? Who is it who speaks, and who hears? Who is it who causes pain, and who suffers? Who is it who has begotten the corruptible flesh? What is the order of things?[65] Why are some people lame, and some [blind], some [mute] and some [deaf], some rich [and] some poor? And why is it that some people are [weak] and [some] robbers? . . . neither . . . all . . . things . . . as he again . . . fighting against [thoughts] of the archons, authorities, and demons without giving them a place in which to settle.

The Salvation of the Archetypal Gnostic (42,28–44,30)

[But] he struggled against their passions . . . he condemned [43] their error. He purified his soul from the transgressions that he had committed with an alien hand. He stood upright within himself, for it is possible for every one[66] to have death and life within himself and to exist in the midst of both. When he had received power, he turned to the right side[67] and entered into the truth. He left behind everything that pertains to the left and became filled with wisdom, counsel, understanding, insight, and eternal power. He broke open his <bonds> and condemned those who had formed everything.[68] They did not find . . . latent within him.

He [took] himself [by the hand], and began to understand [himself] and to speak with his [intellect], which is the father of the truth.[69] He spoke about the unbegotten aeons[70] and about the virgin who brought forth the light. He thinks about the power that flows over [everything] [44] and encompasses it. As a disciple of his male intellect, he began to maintain silence within himself until that day when he would become worthy to be received above. He rejects for himself verbosity and disputations. He endures all things and bears up under them. He puts up with all kinds of evil and is patient with everyone. He makes himself equal to everyone, yet separates himself from them. And if someone [wants something, he brings it] to him [so that] he might become perfect and holy, since he is a [virgin] . . . grasped [him], having bound him upon . . . and he became filled [with wisdom] and bore witness to the truth. [He will receive his] power and go

---

65. Lit., "arrangement" (*oikonomia*). 66. Following Mahé and Mahé in taking *fšoop h^n ouon nim* as a rendition of the Greek impersonal *enesti panti* and modifying the following two clauses accordingly. The text reads "he exists in everyone," but that hardly makes sense. 67. Lit., "the parts of the right." 68. Lit.,

"the whole place"—i.e., the physical world. 69. In Platonic and Gnostic thought, the human intellect (*nous*) can be referred to both as "god" and "father." See, e.g., *Corpus Hermeticum* 1.6 (*Poimandres*). 70. This passage contains allusions to a Gnostic myth.

up to an imperishable realm,[71] the place where he originated, leaving behind the world, which resembles the [night], and those in it who cause the stars to revolve.

The True Testimony (44,30–45,6)

This, therefore, is [45] the true testimony:[72] When a person comes to know himself and God, who is over the truth, that person will be saved and crowned with the unfading crown.[73]

John and Elizabeth, Christ and Mary (45,6–22)

John was begotten by the word through a woman, Elizabeth; and Christ was begotten by the word through a virgin, Mary. What is the meaning of this mystery? John was begotten through a womb worn with age, but Christ passed through a virgin's womb.[74] When she had conceived, she gave birth to the Savior, and they found that she was still a virgin. Why, then, do you go astray by not seeking after the interpretation of these mysteries, which were prefigured for our sake?[75]

Midrash on the Biblical Snake (45,23–49,10)

It is written in the law[76] about this: God[77] commanded Adam, "From every tree you may eat, [but] from the tree that is in the middle of paradise do not eat, for on the day that you eat from it, you will certainly die." But the snake was wiser [46] than all the other animals in paradise, and he persuaded Eve by saying, "On the day that you eat from the tree that is in the middle of paradise, the eyes of your mind will be opened." Eve obeyed; she stretched out her hand, took from the tree, and ate. She also gave some fruit to her husband who was with her. Immediately they realized that they were naked. They took some fig leaves and put them on as aprons.

But at [evening] time [God] came along, walking in the middle [of] paradise. When Adam saw him, he went into hiding. And God[78] said, "Adam, where are you?" He answered, "[I] have come under the fig tree." At that very moment God [realized] that he had eaten from the tree about which he had commanded him, "Don't eat from it."

And God[79] said, "Who is it [47] who instructed you?" Adam answered, "The woman you gave me." And the woman said, "It is the snake who instructed me." He cursed the snake and called him "devil."[80] And God[81] said, "Look, Adam has

---

71. Lit., "imperishability." Cf. *Testimony of Truth* 30 and the note. 72. Or "martyrdom" (*marturia*). For our author the "true testimony" is gnosis, rather than the martyrdom advocated by ecclesiastical Christians. This passage has the appearance of a peroration. This may mark the end of what was once a "first edition" of the homily. See the discussion in the introduction. 73. 1 *Peter* 5:4. 74. This is a Valentinian doctrine, attested by Irenaeus *Against Heresies* 1.7.2. 75. Cf. 1 *Corinthians* 10:6. 76. *Genesis* 2:16–3:22. 77. It is only in this midrash that "God" refers to the lower creator. The text has "when God," but then the sentence is left incomplete, so "when" is best deleted. 78. Text, "he." 79. Text, "he." 80. The author refers here to the common Jewish and Christian identification of the paradise snake as the devil (*diabolos*). 81. Text, "he."

become like one of us now that he knows evil and good." Then he said, "Let's throw him out of paradise so he doesn't take from the tree of life, eat, and live forever."

What kind of a god is this? First, he begrudged Adam's eating from the tree of knowledge. Second, he said, "Adam, where are you?" God does not have fore-knowledge; otherwise, wouldn't he have known from the beginning?[82] He has certainly shown himself to be a malicious grudger. And [48] what kind of a god is this?

Great is the blindness of those who read such things, and they don't know him.[83] He said, "I am the jealous God; I will bring the sins of the fathers upon the children up to three and four generations."[84] He also said, "I will make their heart thick, and I will cause their minds to become blind, that they might not under-stand or comprehend the things that are said."[85] But these are things he says to those who believe in him and worship him!

[In] another place Moses writes, "He made the devil into a snake <for> [those] whom he possesses as his offspring."[86] Also, in the book called *Exodus*, it is written thus:[87] "He contended against the [magicians]. When the place was full of [snakes] as a result of their wickedness, [the rod] in Moses's hand became a snake and swallowed the magicians' snakes."

Again it is written,[88] "He[89] made a snake of bronze and hung it on a pole [49] ... which ... and ... for the one [who will gaze] upon[90] [this] bronze [snake] will escape [destruction].[91] And the one who will [believe in] this bronze snake [will be saved]. For this is Christ; [those who have] believed in him have [received life].[92] Those who did not believe [will die].

Right and Wrong Faith (49,10–50,3)

What, then, is this [faith? They] do not [serve] . . . . . .[93] [50] and you [do not un-derstand Christ spiritually when you say], "We [believe] in Christ."

The Generation of Adam (50,3–12ff.)

For [this] is the [way] Moses [writes] in every book. The "[Book of the] Genera-tion of Adam"[94] [is written for those] who are in the [generation] of [Adam].[95] They follow the law and they obey it. And . . . .[96] [55]

---

82. The text should read at line 22: *je mē nefsooun an.* 83. Or "know it." 84. *Exodus* 20:5. 85. Cf. *Isaiah* 6:10, where the prophet says, "The heart of this people has become thick." 86. No such Mosaic text exists. Cf. *Testimony of Truth* 47 and the note. 87. Cf. *Exodus* 7:8–12, where Aaron's rod is featured. For Moses's rod, see *Exodus* 4:2–4. 88. *Numbers* 21:9. 89. Moses. 90. Perhaps restore, with Wolf-Peter Funk (*Concordance des texts de Nag Hammadi: Les Codices VIII et IX*), *pe*[*tnapō*]*t era*[*tᵉf*], "the one [who will run] to-ward," which goes better with *era*[*tᵉf*]. In favor of our reading is "look at" (*epiblepein*) in *Numbers* 21:9. 91. Lit., "none will destroy him." 92. Cf. *John* 3:14. 93. About thirteen lines missing, five untranslatable. 94. *Genesis* 5:1. 95. Perhaps read "of [the law]." 96. About thirteen lines missing, six untranslatable. Each page of pp. 51–54 consists of a single small frag-ment lacking translatable text.

"Heretical" Leaders and Their Schools (55,1–60,4)

"... the Ogdoad,[97] which is the Eighth, and that we might receive redemption in that place." They do not know what redemption is. Instead, they enter into [misfortune] and into a ... in death in the [waters]. This [is] the baptism [of death which they observe] ......[98] come to death ... and this is ... according to ......[99] [56]

He[100] completed the course of Valentinus. He himself speaks about the Ogdoad, and his disciples resemble the disciples of Valentinus.[101] They, for their part, [are in error] and abandon the good. They also advocate[102] [worship of] the idols[103] ....[104] He has spoken [many words and] written many [books] ... words ....[105] [57]

.... They are revealed for what they are by the confusion in which they exist, [through the] deception of the world. For that is where they wind up, together with their empty knowledge.

Isidore also, [his son], was like [Basilides]. He too [wrote much], and [he] .... But he did not ... this .... His disciples too ... blind ... but he gave them ... [pleasures] ....[106] [58]

They do [not] agree [with] each other. For the Si[mo]nians get married and produce children, but the ...ans[107] abstain from their ... nature ... [to passion] ... the drops[108] of ... smear themselves ... we ... [they agree] with each other ... him ... they say ....[109] [59]

... [there is] no judgment ... for these because of ... them ... the heretics ... schisms ... with the males ... are men ... they will belong [to the world rulers of] darkness ... of the world ... they have ... the [archons ... power] ......[110] judge [them] ....

But the ...ians[111] ... words[112] ......[113] [60] speak ... [they will] become ... in [unquenchable] fire ... they are punished.

The Generation of the Son of Humanity (60,4–67,9)

[But those] who are [from the generation] of the Son of [Humanity have ... in] all [the activities] ....[114] But it is [difficult] to [find] ... and to find [one out of

---

97. The Ogdoad is a technical term in Valentinian gnosis, e.g., as the place of repose for the "spiritual" prior to their entry into the Pleroma. See especially *Excerpts from Theodotus* 63.1. This entire passage is a critique of the Valentinian school. 98. Six lines missing. 99. About eleven lines missing. 100. Probably Basilides; cf. *Testimony of Truth* 57. Plisch restores ᵉnci before "Valentinus" at the end of the line and translates, "after Valentinus completed the course"—i.e., after he died. But there is not enough space for ᵉnci, and one would also expect *pefpōt*, "his course," instead of *ppōt*, "the course." What may be in view is that Basilides continued to teach in Alexandria after Valentinus's departure for Rome. 101. The Basilidian system includes an Ogdoad; see Clement of Alexan-

dria *Miscellanies* 4.126. 102. Lit., "have." 103. Probably what is meant is eating meat offered to pagan gods, something Basilides is reported to have taught; see Eusebius *Church History* 4.7.7. 104. Six lines missing, one untranslatable. 105. About eleven lines missing. 106. About fourteen lines missing, one untranslatable. 107. Perhaps read ᵉn[koddi]anos, "Coddians"; cf. Epiphanius *Panarion*, 26.3.6. This passage probably deals with the practices of a "libertine" Gnostic sect. 108. Probably seminal fluid. 109. About sixteen lines missing. 110. One line missing. 111. It is not possible to restore the name of this group. 112. Or "word." 113. About eleven lines missing. 114. Two lines untranslatable.

a thousand] and two [out of ten thousand][115] . . . .[116] For the Savior [said to his] disciples, ". . . one in . . . ."[117] [61]

. . . and he has [great] wisdom and [prudence and] intelligence and [understanding] and knowledge [and power] and truth. [And he has] some . . . from above . . . the place where the Son [of Humanity] . . . power . . . guard against . . . . . .[118] [62] . . . he knows . . . [he] comprehends . . . and the All . . . worthy of him . . . true

. . . alien . . . . But . . . . . .[119] [physician][120] . . . misfortune in . . . . . .[121] he received [baptism] . . . and those who . . . . . .[122] [65]

. . . [in] a dream . . .[123] silver . . . . But . . . are [rich] . . . among the [authorities] . . . . But the sixtieth . . . thus . . . world . . . . But they . . . gold . . . .[124]

They think, ". . . we have been released from [66] the flesh." . . . but . . . not turn to . . . Jesus . . . . But . . . the beginning[125] . . . a son . . . whom they . . . out of . . . [which is] the type . . . light . . . .[126]

Those who derive from an [un]polluted realm, who . . . that they might . . . not blaspheming . . . [67] them not, nor is there any [pleasure] or desire, or [anything that] controls them. It is fitting that they should be undefiled, that they might [show] to everyone that [they are from] the [generation of the] Son of Humanity, since it is about [them] that the Savior bore witness.

The Generation of Adam (67,9–68,8)

But [those who are] from the descendants[127] of Adam are revealed by their [actions and by] their [work]. They have not ceased [from evil desire] . . . . But some . . . dogs . . . the angels . . . . For . . . [dogs] which are begotten . . . will come . . . with their . . . . . .[128] move as they . . . [on] the day when they will bring forth [children]. Not only that, they have sexual intercourse while they are still nursing.[129] [68]

But others are caught up in the death of . . . . They are [pulled] every which way, and find delight in unrighteous mammon.[130] They lend money [at interest] and [spend their time] doing nothing. But he who is the father of [mammon] is also the father of sexual intercourse.

Gnostic Renunciation (68,8–69,7)

The person who is able to renounce these things shows [that] he belongs to the generation of the [Son of Humanity] and has power to accuse [him.[131] . . . He is

---

115. A saying of Jesus; cf. *Gospel of Thomas* 23. 116. One line missing. 117. About eleven lines missing. 118. About sixteen lines missing, one untranslatable. 119. Two lines untranslatable. 120. Reading [*ia*]*tros*. Plisch restores [*pe*]*tros*, "Peter." 121. Two lines untranslatable. 122. Twelve lines missing, one untranslatable. Pp. 63–64 are missing. 123. Perhaps read [*ounoub m*ᵉ*n*], "[gold and]"; cf. the reference to gold below. 124. About sixteen lines missing, two un-

translatable. 125. Perhaps read [ᵉ*n*]*arkhē m*[ᵉ*n nexou-sia*], "the principalities and the authorities"; cf. *Testimony of Truth* 32. 126. About fifteen lines missing, one untranslatable. 127. Lit., "seed." 128. Six lines missing, three untranslatable. 129. Lit., "giving suck." This refers to the resumption of intercourse before a child is weaned. 130. Cf. *Luke* 16:9. 131. The father of mammon and intercourse—i.e., Sabaoth; cf. *Testimony of Truth* 73.

not] controlled [in these] regions[132] by . . . [from] wickedness, [and he makes the] outside like the [inside.[133] He is like] an angel that . . . . . .[134] [power] . . . said them.

But one . . . .[135] And having withdrawn . . . he became silent, resisting verbosity and disputations.[136] [69] The person [who has] found the [life-giving word and] has come to know [the Father of truth has found repose]. He has ceased [seeking], having [found],[137] and when he found he became silent. He would speak few words to those who . . . in their intellectual . . . hearts.

True Versus False Baptism (69,7–32)

There are some who, upon entering the faith, [receive] baptism on the ground that they have [that] as a hope of salvation. They call it the "seal,"[138] not realizing that the [fathers of] the world are manifest there.[139] But he,[140] for his part, [knows that] he is sealed.[141] For [the Son] of [Humanity] did not baptize any of his disciples . . . . As for those who are baptized, if they were headed for life, the world would be emptied. But[142] the fathers of baptism were defiled.

But the baptism of truth is something else; it is by renunciation of the world that it is found. [But those] who say [only] with their mouths[143] [that they] are renouncing it [are lying], and they will wind up in the terrible [place], where they will also be treated with contempt. Just as those to whom it[144] was given are condemned, they shall get something.[145] They are habitually wicked in their actions.

Consorting with Demons (69,32–70,24)

Some of them fall into [70] [idol] worship. [Others] have [demons] living with them, [as did] David the king. It is he who laid the foundation of Jerusalem.[146] And his son Solomon, whom he fathered in [adultery], is the one who built Jerusalem.[147] He did it with the help of the demons, because he got their power. When he [finished building, he imprisoned] the demons [in the temple], and [put them] into seven [water jugs. They stayed] there a long [time], left in the [water jugs].

When the Romans [went] up to [Jerusalem], they discovered the water jugs, [and right away] the [demons] ran out of the water jugs like people escaping from prison. The water jugs [remained] pure after that. And since those days [they[148] live] with people who are [in] ignorance, and [have remained on] earth.

---

132. I.e., on earth. 133. *Gospel of Thomas* 22. 134. One line missing. 135. Three lines missing, two untranslatable. 136. Cf. *Testimony of Truth* 44. 137. *Gospel of Thomas* 2. 138. Greek *sphragis*, a common early Christian designation for baptism. 139. I.e., in baptism. 140. The archetypal Gnostic. 141. I.e., without baptism in water. 142. Taking *auō* ("and") as equivalent to Greek adversative *kai*. 143. Lit., "with the tongue." 144. Baptism. 145. The meaning seems to be that they will get what they deserve. 146. 2 *Samuel* 5:9. 147. I.e., the temple; 1 *Kings* 6:1–7. Solomon's power over demons is celebrated in Jewish legend. 148. The demons.

The Mysteries of David and Solomon
(70,24–30)

Who, then, is "[David]"? And who is "Solomon"? And what is the "foundation"? And what is the "wall" that surrounds Jerusalem?[149] And who are the "demons"? And what are the "water jugs"? And who are the "Romans"? These [are mysteries] [71] . . . .[150]

The Victories of the Son of Humanity's Disciple
(71,12–73,10)

. . . victorious over . . . [the Son] of Humanity . . . [undefiled] . . . . . .[151] and he . . . whenever he . . . . For . . . is a great . . . to this nature . . . which . . . those who . . . all in a [blessed] . . . , and they . . . [like] a salamander. It goes into a very hot oven blazing with fire, and it slithers into the [furnace] [72] . . . . . .[152] the furnace . . . . . .[153] ovens, for . . . that they might see . . . and the power . . . sacrifice.

Great is the sacrifice . . . one . . . [but] in a . . . . And [the Son] of Humanity . . . , and [he has] been revealed through the immortal bubbling fountain.[154] [73] . . . he is pure . . . [he is] free. He is not envious; he is separated from everyone, from [every] kind of impudence and ill will, whose [power] is great. [He] is a disciple . . . form of law . . . these . . . only . . . .[155]

Those Who Are Under the Law (73,13–74,4)

. . . they placed him under a . . . a teaching . . . his teaching,[156] saying, "[Even if] an [angel] comes from heaven and preaches to you contrary to what we preached to you, may he be cursed."[157] They do not let the . . . of the soul . . . freedom . . . , for they are still immature.[158] . . . they are not able to [observe] the law that works through these heresies, though it is not they, but really the powers of Sabaoth. Through [74] . . . the doctrines . . . as they have been jealous of some . . . law in Christ.[159]

The Gnostic's Goal (74,4–30ff.)

[But] those who will have the power will pass by [all of the] bodies, and . . . the Twelve[160] [judge] . . . them . . . the immortal fountain . . . . . .[161] is good . . .

---

149. The wall, not mentioned above, may have been in a source used by our author, a "midrash" on David and Solomon. 150. Five lines missing, six untranslatable. 151. One line missing, one untranslatable. 152. Five lines missing, eight untranslatable. 153. One line missing. 154. *Gospel of Thomas* 13.

155. Two lines untranslatable. 156. The apostle Paul's? 157. *Galatians* 1:8. The opponents appropriate Paul's asseveration for their own purposes. 158. Cf. 1 *Corinthians* 3:1. 159. Cf. *Romans* 8:2. 160. Perhaps the constellations of the zodiac. 161. Two lines missing, five untranslatable.

the whole place . . . the enemies. He baptized himself, and the . . . . He became divine, and flew [up], and they did not grasp him . . . the [enemies] . . . since it was not possible [for them to] bring him down again.

If any . . . grasp him [in] ignorance, attending to those who teach in the corners with clever props[162] and artful tricks, they will not be able . . . .[163]

---

162. Lit., "carved things." 163. One whole folio is missing from the end of the codex. The tractate ended either on p. 75 or on p. 76.

MARSANES

NHC X

Introduced and Translated by John D. Turner

M *arsanes* is a fourth-century Coptic translation of an originally Greek revelation discourse produced in the late third or early fourth century. Based
on the labors of the original editor, Birger A. Pearson, it is generally accepted that
Codex X contained only one treatise, *Marsanes*. It is badly damaged, and only
a few blocks of continuous text survive on pages 1–10, whose numeration is certain, and on pages 13–22, 25–46, 55–58, and 61–68, with uncertain numeration;
the other pages are either lost or survive in small fragments. Even the title
"[M]arsanes" hardly survives. The text is written in what was formerly called Sub-
achmimic (presently named L6) Coptic as a somewhat unclear translation of an
original Greek treatise, whose traces remain in many Greek words and in the discourse on the phonetic properties of the Greek alphabet in the long section occupying pages 25–31.

Marsanes is a first-person revelation dialogue written to establish the authority
of its putative author and central character, the prophet-mystic Marsanes—whose
name seems to be of Syrian origin—as the inspired leader and teacher of a small
group of relatively well indoctrinated Sethian Gnostics. In his account of a group
of Sethian-like sectarians he calls the "Archontics," Epiphanius mentions among
their honored prophets "a certain Martiades and Marsianos, who had been
snatched up into the heavens and had come down after three days" (*Panarion*
40.7.6), and chapter 7 of the untitled text of the Bruce Codex[1] tells us that "the
powers of all the great aeons worshiped the power which is in Marsanes." Birger
Pearson[2] therefore concludes that "Marsanes" and "Marsianos" are almost certainly one and the same figure.

In addition to the figure of Marsanes, there are other interlocutors, mostly of a
divine sort, such as Gamaliel in 64,19; an otherwise unidentified revealer, "the
blessed Authority," in 20,16; and even the Aeon of Barbelo itself in 10,12–29.
There is also the putative audience of the treatise, referred to at various points in

---

1. Cf. n. 40 of the translation.
2. In Birger A. Pearson, ed., *Nag Hammadi Codices IX and X*, 230–33.

Marsanes' discourse by both the singular and plural second-person form of address, which presuppose a small community of Marsanes' disciples who have already received basic teaching about the structure and deployment of the transcendent realm typical of Sethian treatises like the *Three Steles of Seth, Zostrianos,* and *Allogenes the Stranger* as well as basic teaching concerning the powers and configurations of the zodiacal signs. This suggests a Sethian community that thrives on speculations about theurgic ritual, popular astrology and arithmology, the properties of language that symbolize the nature and relationships of the soul, and the nature and origin of the intelligible and sensible worlds.

Probably the latest of the four Platonizing Sethian treatises (along with *Zostrianos,* the *Three Steles of Seth,* and *Allogenes the Stranger*), *Marsanes* effected a rapprochement of traditions at home in Gnostic Sethianism with contemporary Greek grammatical theory and Middle Platonic/Neoplatonic metaphysics and epistemology as a means of expounding the true nature of the Sethian divine and cosmic hierarchy and assuring its recipients of their ultimate salvation. The author composed this treatise on the basis of both personal experience and mythologumena drawn from the theogonical, metaphysical, and ritual doctrine most evident in two Sethian treatises that in all probability were already at hand — *Zostrianos* and *Allogenes* — summarizing this in such a way as to claim that he or she has experienced the full measure and truth of this doctrine, and on this basis to advance beyond those treatises by propounding doctrine on subjects not treated in them. The initial enumeration of thirteen seals or levels of being extending from the earthly to the highest divine realms are given merely for the benefit of an audience already schooled in it; they are roughly the same as those mentioned in *Zostrianos* (and to a lesser extent in *Allogenes*). The highest of these levels are the object of a visionary ascent that the main speaker, presumably Marsanes, has just undergone (5,17–26). The following chart gives a visual impression of the relationships among these levels of reality and their inhabitants:

Seal 13	The Unknown Silent One
Seal 12	The Invisible Spirit
Seal 11	The Triple-Powered One
Seal 10	The Barbelo Aeon
Seal 9	(Kalyptos)
Seal 8	Protophanes (Mind)
Seal 7	Autogenes
Seal 6	The Self-Generated Aeons (incorporeal; the individuals?)
Seal 5	The Repentance (incorporeal; repentant souls "in Marsanes")
Seal 4	The Sojourn (incorporeal; disembodied souls)

Seal 3	The Third (noncorporeal but sensible; the planetary spheres?)
Seal 2	The Second (corporeal; the sublunar realm?)
Seal 1	The First (corporeal; the physical, material realm?)

All scholars who have had occasion to comment on *Marsanes* in relation to other Sethian literature have called attention to its unique postulation of a new supreme principle, the Unknown Silent One, which transcends the Invisible Spirit, who is otherwise the supreme principle of all the other Sethian treatises. This modification of Sethian theology is parallel to a similar phenomenon that occurs in Iamblichus (cf. Damascius *On First Principles* 1.21,11–14; 25,21–22) and his disciple Theodore of Asine (Proclus *Commentary on Plato's Timaeus* 2.274,10–20), who placed an ineffable One absolutely unrelated to anything else at the summit of all reality—including Plotinus's supreme One, which was at least "present to" subsequent reality. Of course, at least in the case of *Marsanes* and Theodore, this supreme One nevertheless has some relation to its inferiors, since for Theodore, the "second One" was the aspiration ("breathing"), self-contact, and intelligibility of the first One, and for *Marsanes*, the Invisible Spirit (which "has no breath," 15,1–4; 15,29–16,2) seems to share both the silence and the activity of the Unknown Silent One. On these grounds as well as the presence of the prophet's name in the Bruce Codex, one might date Marsanes to the late third or early fourth century, contemporary with Iamblichus and Theodore.

In the course of his visionary ascent, it seems that Marsanes, like Zostrianos, had posed various questions concerning the nature of the beings to which he contemplatively assimilates himself, such as Barbelo (4,24–10,29, especially 10,7–12), the Triple-Powered One (14,15–16,2), probably the Invisible Spirit, and the supreme Silent One (16,3–16). As in the *Three Steles of Seth*, the community's experience replicates that of the visionary (8,2–4): "Those that are within me were completed together with all the rest." As in *Allogenes the Stranger*, true insight is achieved in a cognitively vacant knowledge (8,16–25): "I would contemplate a power that I hold in honor. When the third power (the Barbelo Aeon) of the Triple-Powered One contemplated him, it said to me, 'Be silent, lest you should know and flee and come before me. But know that this One was [silent], and concentrate on understanding.'"

Even though *Marsanes* considers ultimate enlightenment to result from a visionary ascent to the highest realm, in 3,25–4,2 and 5,17–6,16 it mentions a saving descent of Autogenes through the instrumentality of Sophia into the lower world. Although this descent seems unrelated to the triple descents of Barbelo or her avatars in other Sethian treatises, it seems to function here as a prototypical anticipation of Marsanes' own function as a salvific prophet who ascends to the transcendental realm and descends to reveal what he has experienced there.

Marsanes contains traces of the Sethian baptismal rite. The terms "seal" (*sphragis*, 2,12–13; 34,28; 66,[4]; *sphragizein*, 66,[3]), "washing" (55,20), and "cleanse" (66,1) may suggest a connection between baptism and visionary ascent similar to that found in *Zostrianos*. Pages 64–66 seem to narrate Marsanes' vision of certain angels, which include the traditional Sethian "minister" or "receiver" Gamaliel, who is over the spirit(s); just as he raptures baptismal participants into heaven in *Three Forms of First Thought* (48,26–30) and *Melchizedek* (5,17–20), he "takes" Marsanes to see an ever-flowing fountain of "living" water, a "cleansing," and an adornment with a "celestial" seal.

Only the first twenty of *Marsanes'* sixty-eight extant pages delve into the transcendental metaphysics and epistemology expounded in *Zostrianos* and *Allogenes the Stranger* and presupposed in the *Three Steles of Seth*; the remainder seem for the most part dedicated to astral phenomena (the zodiac, stars, planets, and their powers), the configurations of the soul, the nomenclature for the gods and angels, and the judgment of souls. There are references to the use of waxen images and emerald stones (36,1–6) and extensive discussion of the theory of the letters of the Greek alphabet and their combinations (pp. 25–33), based on the speculative theories in the manuals on phonetics and grammar found in Dionysius Thrax and his commentators, as well as of arithmology (pp. 33–34), which seem to illustrate the construction of the cosmic soul and the incorporation of souls into human bodies in the psychogonia of Plato's *Timaeus* 35a–44d.

Among the Sethian treatises, discussion of the cosmic soul occurs elsewhere only in *Zostrianos* (31,2–11). The ability to classify the various configurations or states of the soul—both cosmic and individual, both disembodied and embodied—is related to the need for careful observation of the planets, stars, and zodiacal signs, characterized by qualities similar to those (shapes) of the soul and of the letters of the alphabet, and so on. The letters of the Greek alphabet symbolize not only the "configurations" of the soul, but also the celestial, angelic powers and the elementary constituents of the sensible world. Vowels and consonants are evaluated in terms of their stability (and thus superiority) both independently and in various combinations (prefixed and suffixed). In particular, the relations between the five spherical configurations of the soul and certain combinations of the seven vowels and the emphasis on similarity and difference suggest that these speculations are somehow based on the psychogony in Plato's *Timaeus* (35a–36d).

This theurgical material, which is reminiscent of the second-century teachings of Marcus the Magician (Irenaeus *Against Heresies* 1.21) and more distantly of Iamblichus's disciple Theodore of Asine in the early fourth century, focuses on the nature of the soul, both individual and cosmic, the nature of the astral powers that affect the soul, and the means by which the Sethian adept might manipulate these powers to his or her advantage by utilizing the appropriate nomenclature for these realities. Although previous treatises like the *Three Steles of Seth*, *Zostrianos*, and *Allogenes the Stranger* had concentrated on theology or the metaphysics of the highest principles and intelligible realities and the means of knowing these, *Marsanes*—even though it offers its own equally abstruse metaphysics—now offers a Sethian Gnostic physics and psychology based on astrology, theurgical technique, and a theory of language. In this sense, *Marsanes* offers a specific—theurgical—theory of natural language according to which the linguistic articulation of human thinking and contemplation facilitates or enables not merely human knowledge of both the perceptible and intelligible cosmos, but in fact the self-knowledge of the higher realities themselves. Humans and their ability to articulate reality by linguistic means occupy a pivotal place in the scheme of things: human contemplation of the souls of the very stars themselves enables one to know their individual and mutual identity and the limitations set for them even before they were brought into being. Of all the Sethian treatises, *Marsanes* is the only one to raise the possibility that the perceptible realm of becoming and sensation might indeed be worthy of preservation (5,17–6,1).

Of the four Sethian Platonizing treatises, *Marsanes* and the *Three Steles of Seth* stand out as representative of an emphasis on the practices of an entire community, while *Zostrianos* and *Allogenes the Stranger* are much more concerned with the enlightenment of the individual reader. Moreover, although the *Three Steles of Seth* is basically a structured collection of ecstatic doxologies to be used in the course of a communal practice of visionary ascent, *Marsanes* not only encourages its recipients to engage in a similar practice of ascent as well as to master certain theurgical techniques, but is also clearly concerned with the behavior of members of a community and their interaction with those outside its immediate boundaries who earnestly seek the truth. The chief interest of the author seems to be the process of community formation and building.

BIBLIOGRAPHY

Charlotte A. Baynes, *A Coptic Gnostic Treatise Contained in the Codex Brucianus*; Auguste Bouché-Leclercq, *L'Astrologie Grecque*; Christoph Elsas, *Neuplatonische und gnostische Weltablehnung in der Schule Plotins*; John Finamore, "Iamblichus, the Sethians, and Marsanes"; Wolf-Peter Funk, Paul-Hubert Poirier, and John D. Turner, eds., *Marsanès*; Birger A. Pearson, "The Tractate Marsanes (NHC X) and the Platonic Tradition"; "Gnosticism as Platonism, with Special Reference to Marsanes"; Birger A. Pearson, ed., *Nag Hammadi Codices IX and X*, 229–347 (Birger A. Pearson); Henri-Charles Puech, "Plotin et les gnostiques"; Hans-Martin Schenke, Hans-Gebhard Bethge, and Ursula Ulrike Kaiser, eds., *Nag Hammadi Deutsch*, 2.713–33 (Wolf-Peter Funk); Carl Schmidt, *Gnostische Schriften in koptischer Sprache aus dem Codex Brucianus*; *Plotins Stellung zum Gnosticismus und kirchlichen Christentum*; John D. Turner, *Sethian Gnosticism and the Platonic Tradition*; Gustavus Uhlig, ed., "Dionysii Thacis Ars Grammatica"; Robin Waterfield, ed., *The Theology of Arithmetic: On the Mystical, Mathematical and Cosmological Symbolism of the First Ten Numbers, Attributed to Iamblichus*.

Marsanes[1]

Exordium: The Steadfastness and Confidence of the Recipients of the Revelation (1,1–2,11)

. . . . . .[2] [material] . . . and a [power]. They found him[3] with a pure heart without their being afflicted by evils. Those who have received you will be given a choice reward for their endurance, and [they will] endure the evils.

[But] let none of us be distressed and think [in] his heart that the supreme Father [is aloof], for he looks upon the All and takes care of them all. And [he] has shown them his [command] since it is [they] who speak . . . .[4] [2]

Marsanes' Vision of the Nature, Structure, and Deployment of the All (2,12–18,14)

. . . . . .[5] [the things I said] at first.

The Thirteen Seals (2,12–4,24)

Word of Confirmation (2,12–16)

But as for the thirteenth seal, I have confirmed it together with the limit of knowledge[6] and the certainty[7] of rest.

Seals 1–3: The Worldly Corporeal and Material Levels (2,16–26)

The first [and the] second and the [third] are for the worldly and the material realms. I have [informed] you about these, that you should [guard] your bodies. And a perceptible [power[8]] will [conceal] those who will be at rest, and they will be kept [from the] passions and division [of the] union.[9]

---

1. Coptic text: NHC X: 1,1–68,18. Editions: *The Facsimile Edition of the Nag Hammadi Codices: Codices IX and X*, 87–140; Wolf-Peter Funk, Paul-Hubert Poirier, and John D. Turner, eds., *Marsanès*; Birger A. Pearson, ed., *Nag Hammadi Codices IX and X*, 229–347 (Birger A. Pearson); Hans-Martin Schenke, Hans-Gebhard Bethge, and Ursula Ulrike Kaiser, eds., *Nag Hammadi Deutsch*, 2.713–733 (Wolf-Peter Funk). 2. First nine lines missing. 3. Probably the supreme deity, the Father. 4. Last line missing. 5. First ten lines missing. 6. Gnosis, here and below. 7. Or "foundation," Coptic *tajro*. 8. These perceptible powers would probably be the "glories" (described in *Zostrianos* 46–47), spiritual powers that manifest themselves in the sensible world. In *Allogenes the Stranger* 45 and 50, Youel identifies the power granted to Allogenes as Mind. 9. Either the incarnational union of body and soul or the sexual union of male and female.

Seals 4–5: The Incorporeal Sojourn and Repentance (2,26–3,14)

The fourth [and the] fifth[10] above it [are the ones] you have come to know [as divine. The fourth, concerns what] [3] exists above[11] the [corporeal type] and nature that [is divided in] three. You [were informed] about [these and the] three-[dimensional realm] by these [two].[12] You [were told that it] is incorporeal . . . . . . and after . . . within . . . every . . . which . . . and the things within them.

Seal 5: Repentance (3,14–18)

The [fifth concerns the] repentance [of] those within [it] and those who sojourn in that place.[13]

Seal 6: The Self-Generated Ones (3,18–25)

The sixth concerns the self-generated ones, the incorporeal being that exists individually,[14] together with those who abide in the truth of the All [with] understanding and stability.

Seal 7: Autogenes, the Self-Generated One (3,25–4,2)

The [seventh] concerns the self-generated power, the third [perfect Mind, the second one[15] who extended to [4] the] fourth[16] for salvation [through] Sophia.[17]

Seal 8: Protophanes, the First-Appearing One (4,2–7)

The eighth concerns the [masculine] mind [that] appeared [in the beginning],[18] as well as [incorporeal] substance and the [intelligible] world.

Seal 9: Kalyptos, the Hidden One (4,7–10)

The ninth [concerns the name] of the power [that] appeared [in the beginning].[19]

Seal 10: The Aeon of Barbelo (4,10–12)

The tenth [concerns Barbelo, the] virgin [who is male]—that is, the Aeon.[20]

---

10. In *Zostrianos*, the fourth and fifth "seals" would be Sojourn and Repentance, temporary locations for disincarnate souls awaiting either reincarnation or final enlightenment. 11. Or "according to." 12. These two are probably the fourth (Sojourn) and the fifth (Repentance) "seals." 13. Probably the fourth "seal," Sojourn. 14. Such individually existing incorporeal beings are the "perfect individuals," probably located in the Self-Generated Aeons. According to *Zostrianos* 29, these souls alone have "self-generated power and eternal life." 15. The Self-Generated One (Autogenes) would be the "second Mind" after and immediately below the "first Mind," Protophanes, and is also the second one (after the Barbelo Aeon) to extend itself downward in order to save souls in the lower world of the first three "seals." In Neoplatonic thought, the Self-Generated One would play the role of Plato's demiurge. For Neoplatonists, the transcendent deities do not themselves descend into the lower world, so the Self-Generated One here acts through the instrumentality of Sophia, the divine wisdom located at the lower boundary of the divine world. 16. The fourth "seal," the Sojourn. 17. Wisdom. 18. "That which appeared in the beginning" translates Greek *prōtophanēs*, Protophanes or "First-Appearing One," a divine masculine intellect containing distinct intelligences and souls unified with their objects of contemplation. 19. This level corresponds to the Kalyptos ("Hidden One") Aeon of *Zostrianos* and *Allogenes*, the highest realm within the Barbelo Aeon, and contains the universal ideas or paradigms of Platonic metaphysics. 20. The Barbelo Aeon as the universal Intellect comprises the highest realm of pure, determinate being.

Seals 11–12: The Triple-Powered One and the Invisible Spirit (4,13–19)

[The eleventh] and [the twelfth] speak of the Invisible One who possesses three powers[21] and the insubstantial Spirit[22] who belongs to the first Ungenerated One.[23]

Seal 13: The Unknown Silent One (4,19–24)

The thirteenth speaks concerning [the Unknown] Silent One, even the foundation of the indistinguishable One.[24]

Marsanes' Insight into the Nature of Incorporeal and Corporeal Reality (4,25–6,1)

For it is I who have [contemplated] that which truly exists. [Whether] individually or [as a whole], by discrimination [I knew] that they [pre]exist [in the] entire place[25] that is [5] eternal, namely: all those that have come into existence whether with or without substance; those who are unbegotten; and the divine aeons together with the angels and the souls without guile, and the soul-[garments], the images of the simple ones.[26] And [afterward they] were mixed with [those[27] that were distinct from] them. But [even the] entire [perceptible] substance still resembles the [substance that is intelligible] and insubstantial. [I have known] the entire corruption [of the former] as well as the immortality of the latter.[28]

I have discriminated and have attained the boundary between[29] the partial, sense-perceptible world and the entire realm of the incorporeal essence. And the intelligible world knew by discrimination that in every respect the sense-perceptible world is [worthy] of being preserved entire,[30] [for] I have not ceased speaking [of] Autogenes, [lest anyone] be [ignorant] [6] in turn of the entire place.[31]

---

21. This "Invisible One" corresponds to the "Triple-Powered One" of *Zostrianos, Allogenes the Stranger,* and the *Three Steles of Seth.* In *Marsanes,* it seems that the first of its three powers coincides with the Invisible Spirit, the second power with the Triple-Powered One itself (as the Invisible Spirit's own indeterminate emanative power), which ultimately issues in its third power, the Barbelo Aeon. **22.** The Invisible Spirit, who in Marsanes is the first unbegotten power of the Triple-Powered One. **23.** Probably a designation for the supreme principle identified as the Unknown Silent One in seal 13. **24.** Probably the Invisible Spirit. **25.** The divine world of "aeons." **26.** Probably pure souls destined for enlightenment. **27.** Their "bodies."

28. The "former" would be the "perceptible substance," while the latter would be the "intelligible substance." **29.** Lit. "end of," probably in the sense of "boundary." **30.** Or, on the hypothesis of the possible omission of a main verb in line 20 and third-person (rather than first-person) subject pronouns in lines 22–23 (so Pearson and Funk), 5,19–26 could be restored: "Part by part <I have (or "he has") come to know> the entire realm of the incorporeal essence, and <I have (or "he has")> come to know the intelligible realm, while <I (or "he")> was deliberating whether in any respect the sense-perceptible world is [worthy] of being preserved entire." **31.** The divine world of "aeons."

The Saving Descent of Autogenes, the
Self-Generated One (6,2–16)

He[32] descended; again he descended from the Unbegotten One who is insubstantial, who is the Spirit. The one who exists before them all[33] extends [to the divine] self-generated ones. The one who is [substantial] examines [the All][34] and is [the All and] resembles [the All]. And from [the single one] they [are] divided, [so that] I experienced many things, it being clear that he saved a multitude.

Marsanes Inquires About the Aeonic Realm of the
Triple-Powered One (6,17–29)

But beyond all of these, I am seeking the kingdom of the Triple-Powered One, which has no beginning. Whence did he appear and act to fill the entire place[35] with his power? In what way did the ungenerated ones come into existence without being generated? What are the differences among the [aeons? And] how many ungenerated ones [are there]? In what respect [do they differ] from each other?[36] [7]

The Triple-Powered One Actualizes the Silence of the
Unknown Silent One (7,1–29)

When[37] I had inquired about these things, I perceived that he acted from silence. He exists prior to those that truly exist, that belong to the realm of Being. He is a preexistent otherness belonging to the one that actualizes the Silent One. And the silence of [the one who follows] him acts. For [so long as] the latter [acts], the former [acts also]. The [silence that belongs to the Un]begotten One is among [the aeons, and from] the beginning he is in[substantial]. But the activity of that one <is> the Triple-Powered One. The Unbegotten One[38] is prior to the Aeon, since he is in[substantial].

---

32. The subject ("he," "the one," "the one who is substantial") throughout this paragraph is probably the Self-Generated One. **33.** "Them all" probably refers to those "below" the realms of the Barbelo Aeon. **34.** The Barbelo Aeon. **35.** The aeonic realm. **36.** Cf. such questions with those of *Zostrianos* (e.g., 2–3; 7–8). **37.** The probable antecedents of the pronominal subjects and objects of this complex passage may be as follows: "When I had inquired about these things, I perceived that the Triple-Powered One acted from silence. He exists prior to those that truly exist, that belong to the realm of Being. The Triple-Powered One is a preexistent otherness belonging to the Invisible Spirit that actualizes the Silent One. And the silence of [the Triple-Powered One who follows] the Invisible Spirit acts. For [so long as] the Invisible Spirit

[acts], the Triple-Powered One [acts also]. The [silence that belongs to the un]begotten Invisible Spirit is among [the aeons, and from] the beginning he is in[substantial]. But the activity of the Invisible Spirit <is> the Triple-Powered One. The unbegotten Invisible Spirit is prior to the Aeon of Barbelo, since he is in[substantial]. Now as for the summit of the Silent One's silence: it is possible <for> the Invisible Spirit, the summit of the Triple-Powered One's activity, <to> behold it. And the Unknown Silent One who exists, who is silent, [who is] beyond [insubstantiality], manifested [the Triple-Powered, first] perfect one." **38.** Possibly "the Unbegotten One" is an appositive attribute of the Triple-Powered One rather than an epithet for the Invisible Spirit; in *Zostrianos* and sometimes in *Allogenes*, the two are sometimes indistinguishable.

Now as for the summit of the Silent One's silence: it is possible <for> the summit of the Triple-Powered One's activity <to> behold it.[39] And the One who exists, who is silent, [who is] beyond [insubstantiality], manifested [the Triple-Powered, first] perfect One.

The Self-Manifestation of the Triple-Powered One (7,29–8,18)

[When he appeared] [8] to the powers, they rejoiced. Those that are within me were completed together with all the rest. And one by one they all blessed the Triple-Powered One, who is the First-Perfect One, [blessing] him in purity, [every]where praising the Lord [who exists] before the All, [who is the] Triple-Powered One.[40]

[It did not happen that] their laudations [were audible], but [it was my part] to keep on[41] inquiring] how they had become silent. I would contemplate a power that I hold in honor.

The Barbelo Aeon Reveals Itself as the
Triple-Powered One's Third Power (8,18–29)

When the third power[42] of the Triple-Powered One contemplated him,[43] it said to me,[44] "Be silent, lest you should know and flee and come before me. But know that this One was [silent], and concentrate on understanding. For [the power still] keeps [guiding] me into [the Aeon that] is Barbelo, the male [virgin]." [9]

Marsanes Explains the Barbelo Aeon's Deployment
from the Invisible Spirit (9,1–21)

For this reason the virgin became male,[45] because she had separated from the male.[46] The knowledge stood outside of him, as if belonging to him. And she who

---

39. Or perhaps "The exalted silence of the Silent One can be beheld by the exalted energy of the Triple-Powered One" (so Wolf-Peter Funk). 40. Cf. the untitled text of the Bruce Codex 7: "The powers of all the great aeons worshiped the power which is in Marsanes. They said, 'Who is this who has seen these things in his very presence, that on his account he (Monogenes) appeared in this way?' Nicotheos also spoke of him (Monogenes) and saw that he is that One. He said, 'The Father who surpasses every perfect being, and has revealed the invisible perfect Triple Power.' Each of the perfect men saw him and spoke of him, giving him glory, each according to his own manner." See also chap. 8: "And the triple-powered one came down to the places of the Autogenes. And they saw the grace of the aeons of the light which was granted to them. They rejoiced because he who exists came forth among them." 41. Funk takes 8,13–18

as the beginning of the following section: "But I (Marsanes) [continued to inquire] how they (the silent ones) had become silent. I was in the process of contemplating a power that I held in honor: the third power of the Triple-Powered. When <I (text: "it," feminine)> contemplated it, it said to me . . . ." Here the first-person pronoun is taken as referring to the Barbelo Aeon. 42. The third power of the Triple-Powered One would be the Barbelo Aeon. 43. Probably the Triple-Powered One as the entire assemblage of his three powers. 44. Marsanes. 45. The Aeon of Barbelo emanates from the apparently masculine Invisible Spirit as an indeterminate and therefore feminine power (Greek *dunamis*), which finally becomes instantiated as a determinate (and therefore masculine) divine intellect (Greek *nous*), the masculine Aeon of Barbelo. 46. The Invisible Spirit.

exists <is>[47] she who sought. She is situated just as the Triple-Powered One is situated. She withdrew from [these] two [powers],[48] since she exists [outside of] the
great one,[49] [seeing what] is above [her, the perfect one[50]] who is silent, [who has]
this [commandment] to be silent. His knowledge and his existence and his activity[51] are those things that the power[52] of the Triple-Powered One expressed:

The Barbelo Aeon Describes the Praise of the
Triple-Powered One (9,21–29)

"We all have withdrawn to ourselves. We have [become] silent, and when we
[too] came to know [that he is] the Triple-Powered One, [we] bowed down; we
[glorified and] blessed him. [He conferred] upon us [a great revelation]."

[Again][53] the Invisible [Spirit] [10] hastened to his place. The entire place[54]
was revealed, the entire place unfolded <until> he reached the upper region.
Again[55] he went forth and caused the entire place to be illuminated, and the entire place was illuminated.

Marsanes Receives the Power of the Barbelo Aeon (9,29–10,12)

And [I] was given the third part of [the spirit] of the power[56] of the Triple-
[Powered One]! Blessed is [the Aeon]![57] It[58] said:

Through Marsanes the Barbelo Aeon Urges the
Ascent Toward the Invisible Spirit (10,12–14,15)

"O [inhabitants of these] places![59] It is necessary [for you to contemplate] those
that are higher than these[60] and tell them to the powers. For you will become
[better] than the elect [in the last] times. Upward mounts the Invisible Spirit!
And you [yourselves], ascend [upward] with him, since you have the great

---

47. The manuscript reads *de*, "but," for probable *pe*. Funk translates: "But the existing one, the one who sought, possesses also the Triple-Powered," with the implication that Barbelo is also triple-powered. 48. The first two powers of the Triple-Powered One, perhaps existence and activity. 49. The Invisible Spirit. 50. The Triple-Powered One. 51. Perhaps the "existence" (*hupostasis*), the "activity" (*energeia*), and the "knowledge" (*gnōsis*) as the Triple-Powered One's three powers are the equivalent of the "Existence," "Vitality," and "Mentality/Blessedness" triad in *Zostrianos*, *Allogenes*, and the *Three Steles of Seth*. 52. Barbelo. 53. Although *palin* here might have the contrastive sense of "on the other hand" rather than repetition, it is more likely a mistranslation of *palindromein*, "run back again" — i.e., "the Invisible Spirit

returned to his place." 54. The aeonic realm. 55. Perhaps merely "the Invisible Spirit returned to his place." 56. Knowledge, Marsanes' name for the third power of the Triple-Powered One, probably identical with the Barbelo Aeon. 57. The Aeon of Barbelo, whose "blessedness," as in *Zostrianos* and *Allogenes*, is equivalent to "self-knowledge," which is the third of the Triple-Powered One's powers that Marsanes has also received. 58. The Barbelo Aeon, now speaking to the lower realm through Marsanes. 59. "These places" would be the physical, sensible world. Funk supposes the text to have omitted Barbelo's direct addressee: "O <Marsanes, tarry not among> those who inhabit these places." 60. "These" would be the contents of the Barbelo Aeon.

[radiant] crown![61] But on that day you will see [as you hasten to] ascend above [with him]. And [even] the sense-perceptible [things that are] visible [to you] . . . and they . . . ." [13] . . . . . .[62] the intellection. He[63] exists eternally without substance in the One Who Is, who is silent, the One who is from the beginning, who] is with[out] substance . . . part of . . . indivisible. . . . consider a . . . . . . [ninth] . . . for [14] . . . .[64]

Marsanes' Ascent to the Triple-Powered One (14,15–16,3)

I [was dwelling] among the aeons that were generated. As I was permitted, [I] came to be among those that were un[begotten]. But I was dwelling in the [great] Aeon,[65] although I [was separate from it]. And [I saw the] three powers [of] the Triple-[Powered] One. The [first[66] power] . . . and . . . . . .[67] [15] the Silent One and the Triple-Powered One, [and the One] that does not have breath.[68]

We took our stand . . . we [contemplated] . . . . . .[69] we entered . . . breath[70] . . . . . . [the Spirit [16] that] does not have breath, [and he] exists in [unknowability].

Marsanes Sees the Supreme Deity (16,3–18,14)

And [through] him[71] I saw the great [unknowable power[72]. . . . . . the one without] limit . . . and [I saw the one who exists] alone . . . . . .[73] [17] is active? And why is there no knowledge [among the] ignorant? And . . . he runs the risk . . . that he become . . . . . .[74] and . . . on account of . . . in . . . . . .[75] those that are dis[similar].

But it is necessary that [that everyone who] is without image [be like] those of the [single] one [that] exists before [them all]. The thought that pre[exists] . . . the

---

61. For the crown, see *Three Steles of Seth* 120; *Holy Book of the Great Invisible Spirit* III, 42; and the figure of the glorious Esephech, child and crown of the Triple-Male Child/great Christ's glory (IV, 59; III, 49–50; 53–54; 55–56; 61–62); *Zostrianos* 56–58; and frequently in the untitled text of the Bruce Codex. **62.** Pp. 11–12 are missing; top fourteen lines missing from p. 13. **63.** I.e., as the third of the Triple-Powered One's powers, the Invisible Spirit prefiguratively exists also in the Unknown Silent One, which may coincide with its first power. **64.** The last three lines of p. 13 and the first fourteen lines of p. 14 are missing. **65.** The Aeon of Barbelo. **66.** Restoring Coptic *šarp*, "first" power, the Unknown Silent One, or possibly *šamte*, "third" power, the Barbelo Aeon. **67.** Last three lines missing. **68.** The Invisible Spirit. Concerning the breathlessness (see also *Marsanes* 15–16) of the Invisible Spirit subjacent to the Unknown Silent One, Proclus (*Commentary on the Timaeus* 2.274,18–23) claims that Theodore of Asine (early fourth century) posited two highest ones, a first One, who—like *Marsanes'* Un-

known Silent One—is ineffable and uncoordinated with anything below it, and a second, intelligible (*noēton*) One (Greek *hen*), who is the aspirated breath of the inaspirate ineffability of the first One and defines an intelligible triad represented by the Greek word *hen*, probably conceived as a primal monad, dyad, and triad, consisting of its "elements" or letters: (1) an unpronounceable aspiration (*h*) represented in characters by a dimensionless point (in later Greek writing, a rough breathing mark); (2) a pronounceable vowel (*e*), whose one-dimensional outer arc symbolizes its own reversion upon itself (cf. Plato *Parmenides* 148e–149d); and (3) a final consonant (*n*) symbolizing its intelligibility (*noēton*) by means of the intersecting lines of the N that define a two-dimensional triadic surface. **69.** Lines 6–12 missing. **70.** Restoring "breath" (*pnoē*) or perhaps "intelligible" (*pnoē[tos]*). Lines 15–28 are missing. **71.** Probably the Invisible Spirit. **72.** Probably the supreme Unknown Silent One. Lines 6–11 missing. **73.** Lines 15–29 missing. **74.** Lines 12–14 missing. **75.** Four lines missing.

one that . . . .[76] [18] [Now] these [are the images that I] saw in nine [cosmic] Hebdomads [that are] in a [single eternal] day.[77] . . . . . . thirty . . . . . . [herself] . . . .

The Need to Know the Nomenclature of the Cosmic Powers and of the Soul (18,14–20,16)

And [again after] many [years, as for me], when I saw the [Father,[78] I came to] know him, and . . . many . . . partial . . . forever . . . the material ones . . . worldly . . . above . . . in addition [19] . . . . . .[79] a deity . . . from . . . the things that . . . them into . . . .[80] Name [them according] to their nomenclature, [and let no] one [think that you are] inferior to [their knowledge] and their [reality].[81] And [in addition, so that] [20] . . . . . .[82] hidden . . . the third [power].

The Blessed Authority's Instructions on Preparing the Soul (20,16–29?)

And the blessed Authority said [to me], "Among these [may] she who [does not have it receive no glory]. For there is no glory . . . nor even the one who. . . . For indeed the one [without glory is] a . . . . For . . . .[83] [21]

The Configurations and Powers of the Zodiacal Signs (21,1?–25,21)

. . . . . .[84] and the [zodiacal signs] . . . and the . . . and . . . which do not have . . . acquire for . . . revolution . . . . And . . . soul . . . this . . . , namely, the celestial soul . . . [sur]rounds . . . . . .[85] configuration . . . which is [22] . . . . . .[86] [spiritual]. . . . And those that [have likeness] . . . those who . . . [the form] . . . all the images [of which I spoke. It is necessary that] all the forms [become] configurations, so that [a form may] be assigned to [the elements][87] themselves, [including the smooth] and the rough,[88] [like the voices] of animals . . . and the . . . .[89] [25] there. But their

---

76. Lines 23–26 are unrestorable; 27–29 are missing. 77. This suggests that Marsanes' vision culminated on his sixty-third year (nine times seven), the most critical climacteric stage (*klimaktēr*) in a man's life, here experienced as a single eternal day; see Auguste Bouché-Leclercq, *L'Astrologie Grecque*, 526–31, esp. 528, n. 2. Ages forty-nine through eighty-one that were divisible by nine (symbolizing the soul) and/or seven (symbolizing the body) were considered either most vulnerable or most auspicious. Lines 5–10 unrestorable and 11–12 are missing. 78. Pearson restores "Father"; also possible are "Spirit" or "Aeon" (Funk). 79. On p. 18, lines 25–26 are unrestorable; 27–29 are missing. On p. 19, the first twelve lines are missing. 80. *Marsanes* 19,14–18 might be restored: "[It is necessary that] a deity [transfer them] from [those who observe] the things that [act in] them into [actuality]." 81. Greek

hupostasis, in the sense of actual "status" or "reality." 82. On p. 19, lines 24–25 are unrestorable; 26–29 are missing. On p. 20, the first twelve lines are missing. 83. Last five lines missing. 84. Lines 1–12 missing. 85. *Marsanes* 21,20–24 may have read: "And [it is the] soul [that has] this [sort of] [corporeality], namely, the celestial soul [that sur]rounds [the world]." 86. On p. 21, the last three lines are missing. On p. 22, the first fourteen lines are missing or unreconstructable. 87. Greek *stoikheia*, the basic "elements," either of the physical world or of the individual letters or sounds of written language. 88. Smooth (unaspirated) and rough (aspirated) vowels/syllables of the Greek language are compared to animals that produce smooth (articulate) and rough (inarticulate) sounds. 89. Last two lines of p. 22 and all of pp. 23–24 missing.

powers, which are the angels, are in the form of beasts and animals.[90] Some among them are [polymorphous] and contrary to [nature]; they have [sounds] adapted to their names, that [is], they are [distinct] and [different] in [appearance] and [they are bi-formed].[91] But these that are [homo]phonic by a third originate from substance.[92] And concerning these, all of these remarks are sufficient, since we have already spoken about them. For [this] distribution takes place also in these regions[93] in [the manner] we have mentioned from the [beginning].

The Alphabet and the Configurations of the Soul
(25,21–39,17)

The Soul and Its Configuration (25,21–22)

However, the soul too [has] its configuration, although it is diverse. It is [in its] form that the configuration of the only-begotten soul resides.

Vowels and Diphthongs: The First and Second Configurations of the Soul (25,22–26,17)

Its configuration is [the second] [26] spherical part—EĒIOU—while the first goes around [it],[94] the self-begotten soul—AEĒIOUŌ.
[The] second configuration—EĒIOU—derives from those [having] two sounds.[95] The first that suffixes them is [the upsilon], and [the iota is its companion. And these are the ones you know] in [the radiance] of the light. [Control] yourselves, receive the imperishable seed, bear fruit, and do not be attached to your possessions.

Tones and Accents (26,18–27)

But know that the long vowels[96] exist among the vowels and the diphthongs beside them. But the [short][97] are deficient,[98] as well as the [other sounds that] originate through them. And those that [are drawn][99] are intermediate.

---

90. The powers of the twelve signs (often animals) of the zodiac. 91. Perhaps the doubling of zodiacal signs by position or appearance (conjoined like Gemini, disjoint like Pisces, or composite of distinct parts like Sagittarius and Capricorn; Bouché-Leclercq, *L'Astrologie Grecque*, 151–52) or mere numerical doubling, e.g., of the twelve zodiacal signs into the twenty-four letters of the Greek alphabet (Funk). 92. Homophony and the interval of the third suggest some theory of the harmony of the spheres (Poirier, referring to the dream of Scipio in Cicero *Republic* 6.18). 93. I.e., here on earth. 94. Lit., "follows it" (in a circle outside it). 95. The diphthongs. 96. The text reads *netjasi*, "those that are elevated," possibly meaning the *oxytonoi*, words with stress on the final syllable, but more likely designating the long vowels *ē* and *ō* as opposed to the short ones *e* and *o*. 97. The text reads *brakhu*, "short," which may mean either "short vowels" or *barytonoi*, words with stress on the next-to-last syllable. 98. Or "weak," "worse." 99. Reading [*tak*ᵉ*m*], "drawn out," possibly rendering Greek *perispōmenon*, vowels bearing a circumflex accent, occupying an intermediate value between long and short.

Consonants and Their Combinations
(26,27–27,26)

Among the [consonants], the [semi]vowels[100] are superior [27] to the voiceless.[101] And those that are double[102] are superior to the changeless semivowels.[103] And the aspirates[104] are better than the inaspirates[105] <of> the mute consonants. As for those that are intermediate,[106] their combinations are many. They are ignorant [of] the good combinations and are combined with the worse[107] ones in the [middle. As] in the case of the nomenclature for the [gods] and the angels, it is [not that] the consonants are combined with each other indiscriminately, but only that they are combined so as to have a beneficial effect. It just didn't happen that their intent[108] was apparent.

Don't [sin anymore], and don't dare to have anything to do with sin. Now [I] speak to you [concerning the three configurations of the form] of the soul.

Vowels and the Second and Third Configurations of the Soul
(27,26–29,2)

[The] third [configuration of the soul][109] is [a sphere and] [28] a spherical one goes around it.[110] From the simple vowels <AAA>, EEE, <ĒĒĒ>, III, OO, UUU, ŌŌŌ, the diphthongs were as follows: AI, AU, [E]I, EU, ĒU, OU, OI, ĒI, [U]I, ŌI, AU EI, EU ĒU, OI OU, [GG]G, GGG, GGG,[111] AI AU, [EI EU], ĒU, OI, OU, ŌU, GGG, [GGG], AUEIEU, OIOU, ĒU—three times for a male soul. The third configuration is spherical; the second configuration, since it goes around it, has two sounds.[112] The male soul's third configuration consists of the simple vowels: AAA, EEE, ĒĒĒ, III, OOO, UUU, ŌŌŌ, ŌŌŌ, ŌŌŌ. And this configuration is distinct [from] the first, but [they resemble] each other [and they] make some [easy sounds] of [this sort: AEĒ]OŌ. And [29] from these are made the diphthongs.[113]

---

100. Voiced consonants (Z, X, PS, L, M, N, R, S). 101. Mute consonants (B, G, D, K, P, T, TH, PH, KH), thought to be deprived of soul. 102. The affricatives Z, X, PS. 103. The liquids L, M, N, R. 104. PH, TH, KH. 105. K, P, T. 106. B, G, D. 107. Perhaps in the sense of weaker consonants. 108. The text reads *p-ouōše*, "the (or, with syncopation, "their") will, intent," or perhaps *pou-ōše*, "their utterance, pronunciation." 109. On these configurations of the soul, see the introduction, and for more detail, the introduction in Funk, Poirier, and Turner, eds., *Marsanès*, 57–76. 110. The configurations of the cosmic and individual soul are represented as five concentric spheres, moving from the stability of the outermost to the instability of the innermost. 111. Perhaps the gammas are

the numeral three; thus 28,9 ([3-3-]3 3-3-3 3-3-3), followed by 28,10-11 (3-3-3 [3-3-3]). The significance of the gammas is unclear; they may have some numerical significance, e.g., (3 x 3) + (3 x 3) + (3 x 3) = 27 and (3 x 3) + (3 x 3) = 18, having to do with certain phonetic repetitions. Perhaps the numerical patterns underlying this series of diphthongs is an adaptation of Plato's famous lambda (*Timaeus* 35ab), which symbolized the demiurge's sectioning of the stuff of the world soul into seven portions (1 2 3 4 9 8 27), which was schematized into two classes of intervals, the "double" (1 2 4 8) and the "triple" (1 3 9 27). 112. A diphthong. 113. By appending I or U to a single vowel. Funk translates: "And through the diphthongs (are) likewise also given/ produced the fourth and fifth."

Vowel Combinations and the Fourth and Fifth
Configurations of the Soul (29,2–30,2)

So also the fourth and the fifth: with regard to them, not everything was allowed to be revealed, but only those things that are obvious. You were taught about them, that you should contemplate them in order that they too[114] might seek and find [what] they all are—either through themselves alone or through one another—or seek to reveal [limits] set from the beginning—either with reference to themselves alone [or] with reference to one another. Just as [the letters] coexist with each other [in] speech, whether individually or by similarity,[115] [they are] prefixed or [they] are suffixed. Either their [part] is derivative and similar, whether through [the long] vowels,[116] or [through] those of [dual time value,[117] or] through [the short vowels],[118] which are short . . . . . . [30] or the oxytones or the intermediate tones or the barytones.[119]

Consonant-Vowel Combinations: Syllables (30,3–32,5)

And sometimes consonants exist with the vowels, and by turns they are prepended and appended. They constitute a nomenclature [for] the angels. And sometimes the consonants are independent,[120] and diverse—<they>[121] are prefixed and are suffixed to the hidden gods.[122] By means of beat and pitch and silence and attack [they] summon the semivowels, all of which are subjected[123] to a single [sound]. Just as it is only the [unchanging consonants[124]] <and> the double consonants[125] that exist among the semivowels,[126] the aspirates,[127] [the inaspirates],[128] and the [intermediates][129] constitute [the voiceless consonants. Contrary to nature, the consonants and vowels] are combined [with one another, and] they are separate [31] from one another. They are prepended and appended, and they constitute an ignorant[130] nomenclature. And the resulting syllables become one or two or three or [four] or five or six up to seven having a [simple] sound. These that [have] two [sounds][131] are grouped with [the seventeen consonants. Among] the previously named, [some] are deficient and they are as if [they] had no substance, or as if [they] were an image [of] substance, [or] as if they separate the good nature [from the evil one] in the [middle].

And you [will assemble] the patterns that resemble each other, the vowels [together with] the consonants. Some examples are: BAGAD[A]ZATHA, BEGED[E]ZETHE, [BĒGĒDĒ]ZĒTHĒ, [BIGIDIZITHI, BOGO]ZOTHO,

---

114. "They" seems to refer to these soul configurations, but might refer to either people in general (Poirier) or even the letters (Funk). 115. Perhaps "whether individually or formally" (Funk), reflecting the Platonic distinction between universal forms and particular copies. 116. Eta and omega. 117. Alpha, iota, and upsilon. 118. Epsilon and omicron. 119. "Oxytones" (*netjasi*) should perhaps be "long vowels," and "barytones" (*netcaj'b*) should perhaps be "short vowels." It is unclear whether the reference is to

vowel quantity (so Poirier) or accentuation (acute, circumflex, grave). 120. Or perhaps "self-existent." 121. The text reads "it." 122. "Hidden gods" may here designate the graphically unrepresented elements of speech. 123. "Subjected" in the sense of "prefixed." 124. L, M, N, R, S. 125. Z, X, PS. 126. Z, X, PS, L, M, N, R, S. 127. TH, PH, KH. 128. K, P, T. 129. B, G, D. 130. Perhaps "meaningless nomenclature" (Funk). 131. Diphthongs.

[BUGUDUZUTHU], BŌGŌDŌ[THŌ, and] the rest. [And some are]: BA[BEBĒBIBOBUBŌ]. **[32]** But the rest are different: ABEBĒBI[B]OB, in order that you might [assemble] them and become separate from the angels. And certain effects will follow!

Arithmology (32,5–33,9?)

A good point of departure[132] is from the Triad, and it [extends to that[133] which] has need of [the One that] confined [it in] a shape. <The> Dyad and the Monad do not resemble anything; rather they are principles. The Dyad [constitutes] a division [from the] Monad, [and it] belongs to the hypostasis. But the Tetrad received the [elements] and the Pentad received concord, and the [Hexad] was perfected by itself. The [Hebdomad] received beauty, [and the] Ogdoad [attuned its constituents to harmony, and the Ennead is honored much more]. **[33]** And the [Decad revealed] the entire place.[134] But the Hendecad and the [Dodecad] have passed over [into the boundless, and] it [is higher than] the Hebdomad [which is bounded].

Syllables and Nouns (33,10?–35,20)

. . . . . .[135] [nouns] . . . promise that [the articulation marks] begin [to separate] them by means of a sign and a point, the [uninflected[136] one] and the [inflected][137] one. So also [are the images] of being: they derive [from a joining] of the letters[138] in [a holy union] **[34]** according to a [juxtaposition] where they exist independently. And <they> exist with each [other] by generation or [by kinship. And] according to [their own generation] they do not have . . . these . . . . . .[139] [they have] . . . one . . . speaking the riddle. Just as in the sense-perceptible world there exists the temple [which measures] seven hundred [cubits], and a river which . . . within an eternity, they . . . three . . . to the four . . . seals . . . clouds **[35]** [and the] waters, and the [forms of the] wax images, and some emerald images.[140]

For the rest, I will [teach you] about them. This is the generation of the names. That which[141] [was not] generated . . . [from the] beginning . . . . . .[142] with regard to . . . stand . . . however, . . . [three] times, when [closed], when lengthened, when [short].[143]

---

132. On this section, see Pseudo-Iamblichus *Theology of Arithmetic*. The Greek terms Monad, Dyad, Triad, Tetrad, Pentad, Hexad, Hebdomad, Ogdoad, Ennead, Decad, Hendecad, and Dodecad signify the respective groups of 1, 2, 3, 4, 5, 6, 7, 8, 9, 10, 11, and 12. 133. The Dyad, or Two, the first even and feminine number (which lacks determinate shape), needs completion by the androgynous Monad, or One, to contain it in the first odd or masculine number (which alone supplies determinate form or "shape"), the Triad, or Three. 134. The aeonic realm. 135. Lines 9–16 unrestorable. 136. Lit., the "upright" one. 137. The comma. 138. The text has *stoikheia*, "letters" or "elements." 139. Lines 8–15 unrestorable. 140. Such images often had cultic, sometimes apotropaic applications; cf. wax images of Hecate in Chaldaean theurgy (Porphyry *On the Philosophy Extracted from Oracles*, ed. G. Wolff, 134–35) or of Hermes in the magical papyri (*PGM* IV, 2359–2361; Karl Preisendanz, ed., *Papyri Graecae Magicae*, 1.146). 141. A feminine entity. 142. Lines 9–14 missing. 143. Probably closed, long, and short syllables.

Words (35,21–39,17)

But there exists a quiet [discourse] and there exists another discourse [related to free] <association>[144] [by speaking] of [that which is invisible], and it [manifests] the difference [between the Same] and the [Different[145] and] [36] between the whole and a [part] of an [indivisible] substance. And [that] power has a share in [the joy]—in both discord and [unity—of the honor], whether . . . body . . . . . .[146] [it is] possible [to know that the things that] exist everywhere [are honored] always, [since they] dwell both with the corporeal and the incorporeal ones. This is the discourse on the hypostases that one should [know] in this way. If [they do] not [speak] with one another, [how then] does the discourse help [those who] are troubled [with the discourse about that which is] visible? [Therefore] if one [37] knows it, one will [speak] it.

But there are words, some of which are [dual, and others] that exist [separately, the ones that pertain] to [substance][147] . . . . . . and they . . . or those which . . . [according to those that endure] or according to [those that] have time.[148] And [these] are either separated or joined with one another or with themselves, whether the diphthongs, or the simple [vowels], or every . . . or . . . or . . . [exist] just as . . . [exist] . . . the [consonants] . . . [38] they exist individually until they are divided and joined. Now some are able [to generate the consonants letter] by [letter] . . . difference . . . . . .[149] become . . . [substance] . . . . [They[150] will count] once [or twice] and thrice [for the] vowels, and twice [for] the consonants, and once for the entire ensemble, and unpredictably for [those] subject to change[151] [as well as those that] originated [from them] and [everything] thereafter. And they are all [the names at once. They] were [39] hidden, but they were pronounced openly. They did not stop being revealed, nor did they stop naming the angels. The vowels [are joined with] the [consonants, whether] externally [or] internally, by means of . . . they said . . . [teach you] . . . again [in this way they were counted] four times, and they were [engendered] three times, and they became [twelvefold].

Being Worthy of and Safeguarding the Revelation (39,18–45,20?)

For these reasons we have acquired sufficiency; for it is fitting that each one acquire power for himself that he may bear fruit, and that we never heap scorn [on] the mysteries . . . the . . . . For . . . which [is] . . . soul . . . the signs of the zodiac . . . . . .[152] [40] a new hypostasis. And the reward that will be provided for such a one is salvation. But the opposite will happen there to the one who commits sin. Only [the one who commits] sin . . . will be [in a] . . . in a . . . of the [remainder . . . these. Ponder them], so that even before you examine what one might [convey] to another, [you may re-

---

144. Emending *ousia*, "substance," to <*sun*>*ousia*, "association," "intercourse." 145. Cf. the mixture (and circles) of the Same and the Different in the cosmic soul according to Plato *Timaeus* 35a–37c. 146. Lines 9–14 unrestorable. 147. Substantives, perhaps common nouns. Lines 8–12 unrestorable. 148. Refer-

ring either to temporary versus eternal entities or perhaps to vowels that have "dual time" (A, I, U). 149. Lines 9–11 unrestorable. 150. The letters. 151. I.e., those that undergo change in the process of conjugation and declension. 152. Last two lines missing.

ceive] exalted power and divine knowledge and an ability that cannot be resisted. But you shall examine who is worthy that he should reveal them, knowing that they [will . . . down] to the . . . who sin. Therefore . . . . . .¹⁵³ [**41**] that which is fitting. Do not desire to empower the sense-perceptible world by not attending to me, the one who has received the salvation that comes from the intelligible world.

But as for these <discourses>,¹⁵⁴ beware your [divulging] them to [any]one . . . . . . .¹⁵⁵ lest [he succeed in understanding them] and take [them away.¹⁵⁶ And as for the remainder], I [will speak to] them of the [completion of my discourse] lest the sinful person [divulge them to others]. They did not understand them, namely, the embodied souls upon the earth, as well as those outside of the body, who are in heaven, more numerous than the angels. The topic that we [discussed] in [every] discourse, these . . . stars . . . say . . . whether already . . . into the . . . those who . . . [**42**] whether he observes the two¹⁵⁷ or observes the seven planets or the twelve signs of the zodiac or the thirty-[six] decans¹⁵⁸ . . . . . . [which] are [the twelve zones¹⁵⁹ that total three hundred sixty] lots,¹⁶⁰ [to] the [loci]¹⁶¹ in [association] with [these] numbers,¹⁶² whether [those in heaven] or those upon the earth, and those that are under the [earth], according to the sympathies and the divisions¹⁶³ deriving from these and from the remaining [three hundred sixty] degrees [according to kind and] according to [species] . . . .

Further Discussion in Severely Damaged Text (42,26–46,20; 46,25–55,16; 55,20–60,28; 61,6–28; 62,11–29; 63,23–29; 64,6–15.22–29)¹⁶⁴

Marsanes' Concluding Vision Concerning the Destiny of Souls (45,21?–68,18)

The Vision of Marsanes (45,21?–58,1)

[**46**] . . . . . .¹⁶⁵ the voice of . . . names and . . . [for] ever . . . [names] . . . .

---

153. Last four lines unrestorable. 154. Or "<words>." 155. Lines 9–10 unrestorable. 156. The antecedent of "them" is unclear; if it is the "discourses," perhaps the sense is to realize their significance and to divulge them to other (unauthorized) persons. 157. Most likely "the two" would be the sun and the moon. 158. The division of the zodiac into thirty-six decans, or "houses," of 10 degrees each. Lines 8–10 unrestorable. 159. The twelve zodiacal zones, signs, or "portions" of 30 degrees each, the *dōdekatēmoria*. 160. "Lots," the *monomoiriai*, or distribution of planets among the 360 degrees, or "portions" (*moirai*), of the zodiac. 161. The twelve (sometimes eight) portions of the ecliptic successively occupied by the signs of the zodiac. 162. Numbers of the degrees traversed. 163. The text has *merismoi*, "di-visions," which may also signify "allotments"; perhaps this is an attempt to refer to a doctrine of cosmic sympathies and antipathies. 164. The remainder of p. 42 and pp. 43–45 apparently contained discussion of intelligible or ideal entities, possibly also the cosmic soul; the remainder of p. 46 may have mentioned the significance of baptismal naming; pp. 47–54 are entirely missing; p. 55 contains the end of a discourse apparently addressed to Marsanes, who becomes silent and requests further teaching ("Now when I became silent, [I said], 'Tell [me] . . . what is the . . .'"), possibly about baptism ("washing"), which may have occupied pp. 56–58; pp. 59–60 are entirely missing; and the top of p. 61 contains the phrase "[the] kingdom of [the Triple-Powered One]"). 165. First nineteen and last five lines unrestorable.

[55] . . . . . .[166] Now when I became silent, [I said], "Tell [me] . . . what is the [power] . . . will wash . . . entire generation . . . .

Marsanes' Response (58,1–62,4?)

[61] . . . for your daughters . . . . . . for just as . . . the kingdom of [the Triple-Powered One]. But this one . . . .[167] Don't . . . [62] [speak] on the basis of what [you] don't [know. And] . . . , for it is . . . that you . . . the one whose . . . [you did not] know . . . .

Marsanes' Apocalyptic Vision of the Fearsome Angels (62,4?–64,17?)

And I [said] . . . . . .[168] for the . . . . . .[169] [63] . . . in . . . the remainder down [against the] earth. And they spoke like the angels. [And one] was like the wild [beasts]. And he said, ... [for] ever . . . beast . . . . . .[170] beast . . . . . .[171] from . . . of my [soul] . . . I saw a . . . [standing] . . . and his [image] was [fearsome]. And [his face] was . . . . . .[172] [64] I . . . because I [saw] all of [the lights] around [me blazing with] fire. [And I looked at myself] in their midst . . . . . .[173] angels [attending] me.

Gamaliel Comes to Marsanes' Aid (64,17?–65,5?)

And . . . the [one] . . . Gamaliel, [the one] who presides over [those spirits . . . . . .[174] [65] the great] angels [who are those] that receive [all of them] . . . with their . . . .

Gamaliel's Revelation (65,5?–66,16?)

And he [guided me down], and he [bore] me . . . . . .[175] [her] members . . . the [invisible . . . . . .[176] judgment] . . . thrown . . . every . . . [who is placed . . . . . .[177] ever-flowing fountain] of the living [water] . . . the two . . . silent . . . [gods] . . . . . .[178] [66] cleanse it[179] from . . . . . . the one whom they [sealed] has been adorned [with the] celestial [seal] . . . . . .[180] to his . . . great . . . .[181]

Marsanes' Vision of the Judgment of Souls, and the Title (66,17?–68,18)

And I [saw . . . . . . unmixed] . . . those who . . . . . .[182] [67] they will become . . . of God . . . a woman . . . while she is in [travail] . . . after she begot . . . . . .[183] all of

---

166. First sixteen and last seven lines missing. 167. Last twenty-four lines unrestorable. 168. Last twenty-four lines unrestorable. 169. Lines 6–29 missing or unreconstructable. 170. Six lines missing. 171. Lines 11–16 unrestorable 172. Last seven lines missing. 173. Lines 6–15 unrestorable. 174. Last eight lines missing. 175. Lines 8–11 unrestorable. 176. Two lines missing. 177. Line 20 unrestorable. 178. Last four lines missing. 179. "It" (feminine) may here refer to the soul. 180. Lines 6–10 missing. 181. Lines 13–16 missing. 182. Last eight lines missing. 183. Lines 6–11 unrestorable.

them . . . thing . . . humans . . . and . . . women [and men of this sort] . . . it is others [that are upon the] earth. [Know] that they . . . every . . . them, . . . on these, [together with the] home-[born], for these will [be able to know] God[184] . . . . . . aeons [68] with those who will . . . who have . . . God . . . from the [beginning] . . . in the . . . awful . . . fear . . . . . . names . . . . . .[185] mysteries . . . in . . . God . . . . . .[186] manifest . . . those who will know.

[M]arsanes

---

184. 67,21–22 as restored by Funk; lines 23–25 unrestorable; last four are missing. **185.** Lines 10–11 unrestorable. **186.** Line 15 unrestorable.

THE INTERPRETATION
OF KNOWLEDGE

NHC XI,1

Introduced and Translated by Einar Thomassen

The title of the first tractate of Codex XI, "The Interpretation (*hermēneia*) of Knowledge (*gnōsis*)," is written both on the flyleaf of the codex and at the end of the text. The precise meaning of this title is not clear; it may well have been invented in the course of transmission. The genre of the work is that of a homily or, less likely, a letter. The text is poorly preserved, as is the case with Codex XI in general; more than half the text has been lost, and many lines can only be tentatively restored.

The main theme of the homily is humility, and ideas related to this theme, such as endurance in adversity and the importance of faith, are stressed in the text. Exhorting his audience to be humble and to remain steadfast in faith is the author's overriding concern. This concern probably reflects a situation of social tension, both between the community addressed by the homilist and its surroundings and within the community itself. A situation of internal disaffection is particularly tangible in the last part of the homily (from p. 15 on), where the community members are urged not to be jealous of one another if some display greater spiritual gifts than others. In this way, the *Interpretation of Knowledge* offers a rare glimpse into the social dynamics of a Gnostic Christian community.

That the outlook of the text is Gnostic is clear from the first page: "The world [is the place of] unbelief [and death]" (1,36–38). The Gnostic tenor is also evident in a statement such as: "While we were in the darkness, we used to call many people 'father,' because we were ignorant of the true Father. And this is the greatest of all sins" (9,35–37). More precisely, the tractate can be assigned to a Valentinian homiletic tradition on account of numerous parallels with other Valentinian texts: the distinction between faith and persuasion (p. 1) is also found in the *Treatise on Resurrection*; the statement that the Father knew his limbs from the beginning and will reveal them at the end (p. 2) is paralleled in the *Gospel of Truth*; the metaphor of the "trace" (2,31) is found in the *Gospel of Truth* and the *Tripartite Tractate*; the image of the human being as an inn (*pandokeion*) inhabited by demons (p. 6) is used in a letter by Valentinus (Valentinus, frag. 2); the picturing of the Savior as schoolmaster teaching the true letters (9) is also found in the *Gospel of Truth*; the association of the Sabbath with the cosmos, and the interpretation of the Savior's "work on the Sabbath" to retrieve the lost sheep as a metaphor for his incarnation and descent into the world (11) also occur in the *Gospel of Truth*; the Name (12) is a central Valentinian notion; the concern with avoiding jealousy (*phthonos*; 15ff.) is also found in the *Gospel of Truth*, the *Treatise on Resurrection*, and other Valentinian sources; finally, on page 19 there even seem to be references to Church and Life, Valentinian names of aeons.[1]

The soteriology and Christology of the tractate are shown by statements that affirm that the Savior suffered and died a vicarious death for mortal humans; that he made himself "small" (10,27–28)—a reference to his incarnation; that he humbled himself and endured scorn; and that he himself was redeemed by the Greatness that came down—obviously at his baptism. Moreover, he cried out and was separated—an allusion to the crucifixion—and showed the way to the Father. All these themes situate the *Interpretation of Knowledge* firmly in the context of Eastern Valentinian doctrine.

Soteriology and Christology are not, however, in themselves the main concerns of the homily. The descriptions of the suffering Savior are intended above all as a moral paradigm for the audience. The specific emphasis on the Savior's humility and his willingness to endure scorn and persecution is most probably to be understood from the point of view of its paraenetic function. This suggests that the situation of the community that the text addresses may be characterized by similar afflictions. It seems as if the community may be under pressure from outside opponents and critics—either other Christians, who ridicule the Valentinians in the manner of the heresiologists, or non-Christians, who oppose Christianity in general. The homily, then, encourages the members to remain steadfast in their faith against such outside pressure.

However, the trouble is internal as well. The final part of the homily (from p. 15 on) reveals that some members feel disgruntled because they are accorded a lower status in the community than others. There are members who excel in spiritual gifts: prophetic speech and rhetorical ability. Others do not possess such gifts. The homilist seeks to persuade the disaffected, first, by arguing that jealousy is a sentiment unworthy of spiritual people and, second, by using the image of the one body (from 1 *Corinthians* 12): all limbs of the body, large and small, are equally important, and what one limb accomplishes benefits the rest of the body as well. By this rhetoric the homilist apparently seeks to avert a crisis of disintegration and disaffiliation threatening the community.

Due to the fragmentary state of the text, many parts of the tractate remain obscure. This is the case above all with the parts that mention one or more female figures. We hear about a virgin (pp. 3–4, 7), a young girl (3–4, 8), a woman in distress (7–8), a mother (7–8, 13), a woman associated with the first human (11), a female who is the spouse of the Word (3), and a woman who is useful and gives

---

1. See the notes to the translation.

birth (3, 14). In a Valentinian context, the most natural referent for a female figure would be Sophia, the fallen and redeemed aeon who also plays the part of the world soul in Valentinian cosmology. Although this interpretation seems plausible in some of the passages, it may not fit all of them, and it is quite possible that some other type of narrative whose theme completely eludes us was told (e.g., on pp. 7–8).

The *Interpretation of Knowledge* is notable for its daring use of imagery—the association of the crucifixion with the "fixity" of faith (p. 1), the nailing to the cross used as a metaphor for the Savior being "held on to" in the church (5), and the image of the "head" that looks down on its limbs on the cross, pulling them out of Tartaros (13). The creative rhetorical use of images and the exploration of the metaphoric potential of the life and passion of the Savior in particular are characteristically Valentinian. The same may be said about the use of sayings and parables of Jesus (5–6, 9) and the extensive allusions to the letters of Paul. The words of Jesus (9,27–10, top) are quoted from a collection of his sayings also attested by Clement of Alexandria and Egyptian sources, rather than from the written gospels.[2] The text thus reflects a stage in the history of the canon where the sayings of Jesus and the Pauline letters are the chief sources of authority.

We do not know who wrote the *Interpretation of Knowledge,* nor do we have any certain indications as to when it was written. The text shows a congregation in crisis, but it does not for that reason have to be late. An informed guess would be toward the end of the second century, in Alexandria or elsewhere in Egypt.

BIBLIOGRAPHY

Stephen Emmel, "Exploring the Pathway That Leads from Paul to Gnosticism. What Is the Genre of *The Interpretation of Knowledge* (NHC XI,1)?"; Wolf-Peter Funk, Louis Painchaud, and Einar Thomassen, eds., *L'Interprétation de la gnose*; Charles W. Hedrick, ed., *Nag Hammadi Codices XI, XII, XIII,* 21–88 (John D. Turner and Elaine H. Pagels); Klaus Koschorke, "Eine neugefundene gnostische Gemeindeordnung: Zum Thema Geist und Amt im frühen Christentum"; "Gnostic Instructions on the Organization of the Congregation: The Tractate *Interpretation of Knowledge* from CG XI"; Uwe-Karsten Plisch, *Die Auslegung der Erkenntnis* (*Nag-Hammadi-Codex XI,1*); Hans-Martin Schenke, Hans-Gebhard Bethge, and Ursula Ulrike Kaiser, eds., *Nag Hammadi Deutsch,* 2.735–46 (Uwe-Karsten Plisch).

---

2. See Wolf-Peter Funk, Louis Painchaud, and Einar Thomassen, eds., *L'Interprétation de la gnose.*

The Interpretation of Knowledge[1]

The [Interpretation] of [Knowledge]

The Nature of Faith (1,1–2,24)

......[2] believe, [not] through [all kinds of] deceptive [signs and] wonders ... that have come into being from ... followed after him, but through ... and humiliations. Before ... or a vision, [they ... in the way] they had heard ... they crucified [him] ... generation, he is hastening, before .... [For Christ] ..., so that our faith [should] be holy and pure ... not ... in its working, but ... it, and it is fixed in [us, so that we may] say that [our] endurance is hanging upon the [cross] fixed with a nail.[3]

For every person is [persuaded by means of what] he already believes. If [he does not believe, nothing] may [persuade] him.[4] It is great for a person to possess faith [while still dwelling] in unbelief—[that] is, in the world. [For] the world [is the place of] unbelief [and death]. Now death exists [2] ....[5]

.... For ... [semblance] ... they will ... faith is a holy [thing] ... is the opposite ... the ones to whom he will give ... them. It was not possible [for] ... incorruptibility ... will become ...... reveal[6] ... [those who] have been planted in ....

Faith in the Savior as Precursor (2,25–3, top)

For ... [who] are in distress ... he is able to bring a [large] assembled [congregation] out from ... [small] .... He became a [reliable precursor].

For [some] say that [he] is grasped [by means of his] trace. The structure[7] is [ignorant of his] form, but God, [who knows] his limbs—[he knew them] even

---

1. Coptic text: NHC XI, 1: 1,1–21,35. Editions: *The Facsimile Edition of the Nag Hammadi Codices: Codices XI, XII and XIII*, 7–27; Charles W. Hedrick, ed., *Nag Hammadi Codices XI, XII, XIII*, 21–88 (Elaine H. Pagels and John D. Turner); Uwe-Karsten Plisch, *Die Auslegung der Erkenntnis*; Hans-Martin Schenke, Hans-Gebhard Bethge, and Ursula Ulrike Kaiser, eds., *Nag Hammadi Deutsch*, 2.735–46 (Uwe-Karsten Plisch). 2. Thirteen lines missing or untranslatable. Some letters on p. 1 are preserved by having been blotted onto the facing page (front flyleaf B). 3. Cf.

Ignatius *Smyrnaeans* 1:1. 4. Cf. *Treatise on Resurrection* 46. 5. Thirteen lines missing or untranslatable. 6. These readings are uncertain. 7. The "structure" or "system" (Greek *sustasis*) is a term used especially by the Valentinians to designate either the world or the configuration of aeons that spreads out from the Father. The latter is the case here; cf. *Tripartite Tractate* 59. The aeons are the Father's children, and his limbs, and ultimately they also include the spiritual elements living in the world as the offspring of the aeon Sophia.

before they were born, [while they were still ignorant] of him—and who [knew each] one from the [beginning, being within] them,[8] will [reveal them at the end]. For it is necessary that [3] . . . .[9]

Veneration of a Virgin (3, top–5, top)

. . .[10] [having concerned himself with her, the] Savior withdrew from there, leaving her [healed. She] knows [him], though not [carnally, since] it was the Word[11] [she had received] as husband. [She] exists, however, [in such a] way as [to be of use] as well. He [receives], while she, [on her part, hands] us over as intelligent [children]. This [is] a marvel on her part, [since] she makes us overcome [every] endurance [and every deficiency].

And he loves [whoever] defers [to a] virgin. [Indeed], it is right to [give heed] to her [beauty] . . . until the death . . . it is right to exert oneself [4] . . . .[12]

Because of that, . . . it . . . . It dimmed our vision [of her who is a] virgin, just as that of [every unbeliever] here below, and we see [her as if] she were dead . . . that [in] which there is light. She who is dead [possesses] the . . . these great [powers] will give it[13] to [her from] above . . . the . . . young girl . . . because of him. She [gave birth] to [Christ]; he became . . . in the . . . Word, because he . . . the . . . his fall [5] . . . .[14]

The Parable of the Seeds, and the Suffering Savior as a Model (5, top–6, top)

. . . go forth from here. [Some fell] on the road, others [on the rock]. Some he [sowed among thorns], others [produced] grain . . . .[15]

. . . and the shadow. Look, ...[16] to deliver us [to a power] of . . . before the souls have gone forth from . . . [that] are killing them.

But he was pursued there, on the trail produced by the Savior. He was crucified and he died—not [his] own [death, for] he did not deserve to die, [but for the sake of] the Church of mortals. He [was] nailed, so that [they] might hold on to him in the Church, [because he teaches] it by means of humiliations, having endured in his suffering. Jesus in fact is a model for us because of [6] . . . .[17]

The Parable of the Good Samaritan, and the Descent into the World (6, top–7, top)

. . . this . . . the whole . . . , and . . . the bitter . . . of the [world] . . . us and . . . by the brigands . . . [from] Jerusalem . . . down to Jericho . . . they received . . . .[18]

---

8. The text should perhaps be corrected to read "[when they were within] him." 9. Twenty-four or twenty-five lines missing. 10. This section is very fragmentary, and the restored text on which the translation is based is highly conjectural. 11. Logos, here and below. 12. Twenty-four lines missing. 13. Or "him." 14. Fifteen lines missing or untranslatable. 15. *Matthew* 13:1–9 and parallels. 16. Three and a half lines missing. 17. Fourteen lines missing. 18. Cf. *Luke* 10:30–36. Two lines are missing after the fragmentary references to the story of the good Samaritan.

... down [here] below. Look [at us], how [we] are in the grip of utter deprivation, to the last of our possessions taken from us, because the deprivation [brought] us down and bound [us] with chains of flesh. < ... > since the body is an inn that the principalities and [the powers] have as a dwelling place, the inner person, [having been] locked up in the modeled form, [had to endure every kind of] suffering, [because he] was forced to serve [them] and was coerced to obey [their] workings.[19] They split the Church, that they might obtain a part in [7] . . . .[20]

Fate of a Female (7, top–9, top)

...[21] this ... able to . . . . . .[22] is ... beauty that will ... all, they wanted[23] to ... and you[24] were with ... they were fighting with ... like ... virgin ... to destroy ... wound ... this ... destroy her, but she ... her, to ... her, after they had ... imperishable; this ... but that he should remain ... virgin ... her beauty ... faithfulness ... and because of this ... her. He hastened ... he did not accept ... beauty while they humiliated [her] . . . .

For after the mother had [8] . . . . . .[25] the mother ... her enemy ... instruct ... violence ... nature ... the young girl ... impossible for him ... first, however ... the opposite . . . . [In what] way, however, . . . the young girl ... he was unable to ... he became ... kill her ... living ... he regarded her ... [above] life ... he knows that even if ... the world, she lives ... him to raise ... [pass] upward out of ... upon the regions of the ... [those] who hold power over [them] . . . . But he emptied himself ... in [which] he was ... the Father of the All ... even more, to her ... him. He is [9] . . . .[26]

The Teacher of Immortality (9, top–27)

... just as ... into . . . . He possesses them, while they ... [all] and receives [every] one [who is] worthy [of] receiving him. And . . . . [But] although he conceals himself, he is divine and lets himself be entangled with the things of creation, and he destroys them.

For [by] speaking to the Church he [became] for it a teacher of immortality.[27] [He] destroyed the arrogant [teacher] who [taught] it to [die. This teacher brought] a school of [life]. For [this teacher has] a different kind of school. [He] taught us the [living] letters. He took [us] away from the letters of the world, the ones from which we were taught about our death.

---

19. Cf. Valentinus, frag. 2. 20. Eight lines missing. 21. The references to a female in this section could indicate the soul or Sophia. 22. Two and a half lines are untranslatable. 23. Or "you (feminine singular) wanted." 24. Feminine singular. 25. Six lines missing. 26. Eight lines missing. 27. For the Savior as a teacher, cf. Gospel of Truth 19.

His Teaching: The True Father (9,27–10, top)

And his teaching was the following: do not call anyone your father upon earth. One is your Father, who is in the heavens.[28] You are the light of the world,[29] my brothers and fellow companions who do the will of the Father.[30] For what does it profit you if you gain the world and forfeit your soul?[31] For while we were in the darkness, we used to call many people "father," because we were ignorant of the true Father. And this is the greatest of all sins [10] . . . .[32]

The True Good (10, top–27)

. . . pleasure, as we . . . soul . . . thought . . . you[33] . . . . The . . . , however, is . . . . [For] this [reason], the living teacher [came]. He [brought] ignorance [to an end] as well as dimness [of vision]. He made [our] mind remember the good things [of the] Father and its own parentage.

For he said, [Shun] the world, for it doesn't belong to you. Do [not regard] as profitable the delights that are in it. Rather, they are [harmful] and a punishment. But take [instruction from the one who was] scorned. [That], O soul, [is] what is profitable and . . . . And receive your[34] [form and that] shape, which exist in the [presence of the] Father. It is the status and the rank that you knew before you wandered astray and were sentenced to become flesh.

The Incarnation of the Savior and the Redemption of the Soul (10,27–11, top)

In the same way I made myself quite small, in order that by humbling myself I might bring you back to that high rank, the place from which you had fallen when you were brought down into this pit. So if you believe in me, I am the one who will bring you up above, by means of this shape that you see. I am the one who will carry you on my shoulders. Enter through the side from which you fell, and hide yourself from the beasts. The burden you carry now [is] not your own. If you enter [11] . . . .[35]

Oblivion, Cosmic Existence, Bestiality, and the Tunic of the Body (11, top–31)

. . . from his glory . . . as in the [beginning]. From [his union] with the woman, sleep [came into being], and the [Sabbath]. And this [is the] world. For as a result of the [oblivion about] the Father [through] sleep, [the Sabbath was observed.

---

28. Cf. *Matthew* 23:9. 29. *Matthew* 5:14. 30. Cf. *Matthew* 12:48–50 and parallels. 31. Cf. *Matthew* 16:26 and parallels. 32. Eight lines missing. 33. Feminine singular. 34. The second-person pronoun here and in the following lines, until the end of the page, is feminine singular and refers to the human soul. 35. Fourteen lines missing.

After that, the] beasts [issued] from the . . . . For the [world] is [oblivion] and [sleep].[36] Therefore, [he] who has gone astray [is not an] enemy.

And from the beasts that had come forth, a tunic was put on [him] as his sentence. For the woman [had] no other garment [to put] on her seed except [that] which she had brought forth on the Sabbath.

The Work and the Clothing of the Son (11,31–12, top)

In fact, nothing beastly exists in the aeon. For the Father does not observe the Sabbath. Rather, he works in the Son, and through the Son. Moreover, he gave him the aeons: the Father possesses living rational elements by which he clothes him with the [aeons] as garments. The human [12] . . . .[37]

The Self-Humiliation of the Savior (12, top–29)

. . . is the name . . . . [He] emptied [himself, and he] relinquished [his majesty], taking scorn [in] exchange for the name. [For] our [sakes he] endured the scorn. He appeared in flesh, and [came] as a [provider]. He has [no] need of a glory [that] is [not his own]. He possesses his [own glory] with the [Father], which is that of being the Son.

[He] came, moreover, so that we might be made glorious [through] his humiliation, [as he] dwelled in these humble [places]. Indeed, through him who was scorned we receive the [remission] of sins. From him [who] was scorned and redeemed we receive grace.

The Saved Savior (12,29–13,14)

Who [is it], then, who saved the one who was scorned? It is the emanation of the name. For just as flesh needs to have a name, so [this] flesh is an aeon that Sophia brought forth. [He] received the Greatness that came down, that the aeon might enter the one who was scorned, so that we might shed the disgraceful skin we were wearing and be born once more in the flesh and blood of [13] . . . .[38]

. . . Fate. He . . . and the aeons . . . they received the Son [and he was] all mystery, [throughout] each one of his limbs . . . grace.

He Showed the Way and Pulled the Church out of the Pit (13,14–14, top)

When [he] cried out, [that one] was separated from the Church, just as in the [beginning] darkness was separated from the Mother. His feet, however, made tracks, and [they paved] the way that leads [up] toward the Father.

---

36. The restoration of the last four sentences is conjectural. 37. Twelve lines missing. 38. Eight lines missing.

[What] sort of [way], then, is this? It became [for] them . . . . It made . . . the light [for those] who dwell in it, so that the Church [might] be seen when it proceeds upward. For the Head pulled it up and out of the pit, as [it] bent over from up on the cross and looked down to Tartaros, in order that those who were below should look up. For in the same way as when someone looks into a well, and the face of the one who had been looking down then looks up, thus, when the Head looked down from on high to its limbs, the limbs [hastened] up to where the Head was.

The function of the cross, on its part, was to nail fast the limbs, and only so that they should be able [14] . . . .[39]

Waiting for the Consummation (14, top–27)

. . . has . . . for they had been brought [into] slavery. The "consummation [of the All]" did indeed signify "[completion]" in [what it] signified. The seeds [that] remain, however, [will] be held [back] until the All is separated and [given] form—and in this way the expression will be confirmed.

For just as the woman . . . is honored until her death [makes] good use of the time she has, so [will she] too give birth. She, however, gives birth [that she may] acquire all the [modeled form][40] allotted to her. [The offspring that turns out] to be perfect possesses [a nature] free of envy, because the Son of God dwells in him. But if [he] wants to acquire everything, [that] which he has will be wiped out by the fire, because he has acted very disdainfully and has been arrogant < . . . > of the Father.

The Decree of Freedom (14,27–15, top)

When the older son, then, had been sent after his little brothers, he unfolded the decree of the Father and read it out, taking his stand against the whole world. And he annulled the old document of debt, that of condemnation. This is what the decree said: those who were made slaves and were condemned through Adam have been [brought] out of death, have obtained the [remission] of their sins, and have been saved by[41] [15] . . . .[42]

Generosity and Sharing (15, top–17, top)

. . . us when we are worthy [of receiving what is good], the [powers and the grace].

I say, however, [that] . . . and [jealousy] . . . and [these] . . . . For [whoever is] worthy of . . . God and the Father . . . Christ, has removed himself [from] all such things and loves [his brothers] with all his heart . . . his limbs [against one another. If] he is free of jealousy, [he will not be] separate from the other [limbs. Accept

---

39. Seven lines missing. **40.** The text reads *plasma*. The word probably refers to human beings, all of whom must be born and pass through earthly exis- tence before the final consummation. **41.** Cf. *Colossians* 2:14–15; *Gospel of Truth* 20. **42.** Nine lines missing.

the] good [we] see that [our] brother has. [He] considers us [as if we] were himself, praising the [one who accords him] the grace. Thus, each one of us should partake of the gift that he has received from [God], and should not be jealous, in the knowledge that whoever is jealous insults his [brother] and also excludes himself from the gift and is negligent of God. He should be happy and rejoice, and receive his share of the grace and the gift.

Someone has a prophetic gift. Share in it without hesitation. Do not approach your brother with jealousy, and do [16] [not] ....[43]

... empty, being ... separated from their ... ignorant that ... in this way they ... them in ... so that they should ... [small].

Concerning the things you wish [to know] about, if a ... you: [if] your brother [possesses] grace ... , [do not] lessen yourself, but [rejoice in this] special spiritual gift. Pray for that person, that you may share in the grace that is in him. Do not consider [it as something] alien to you but rather as something [that] is your own. What each [of] your fellow limbs has received, you [will receive as well]. For the head they have you have also—the head from <which> all those gifts flow that are in your brothers.

Does someone make progress as a speaker? Do not take that as a personal affront. Don't say, "Why does that one speak but I do not speak?" For whatever he says belongs to you as well. Moreover, one who thinks what is said and one who speaks it—this is the one and the same power. The words [17] ....[44]

We Are the Limbs of a Single Body (17, top–19,14)

For[45] ... [an eye] or a [foot or a hand because they] exist as a [single] body, [which consists of us] all, serving [the one single head]. Each of [the limbs depends on] it. The limbs [cannot] all become [a foot] or an eye [or a hand].[46] These limbs will not [live by themselves], but would die. We [know that they would] kill themselves.

Why, then, [do you] still [prefer] the dead limbs [instead of the ones that are] alive? How can you have knowledge [if you] are ignorant of the brothers? [For being] ignorant, hating [them], and being jealous of them, [you will not receive] the grace that is in [them], because you do not wish to be joined with them for the gift of the head. Rather, you should [give] thanks on behalf of the limbs and pray that you too may be given the grace that has been given to them.

For the Word is rich and generous, and it is good.[47] It grants gifts in this world to its own people[48] without jealousy, in accordance with [18] ....[49]

... [they] appear in such a way that [each] of the limbs [possesses his] own [gift],[50] and [they appear] without fighting [one another] over the differences of

---

43. Nine lines missing or untranslatable. 44. Twelve lines missing or untranslatable. 45. The imagery in this section is based on 1 Corinthians 12:12–30; also cf. Romans 12:4–8 (body and members); Ephesians 1:22–23; 4:15–16; Colossians 1:18; 2:19 (Christ as the head).

46. Cf. 1 Corinthians 12:17. 47. "Good": khrēstos. 48. Cf. Ephesians 4:8 (Psalm 67:19, Septuagint). 49. Eleven lines missing or untranslatable. 50. The restoration is tentative.

[their gifts, but] as suffering and working [together. If] one of them is [sick, they are] sick with him, and [if] one is healthy, they are healthy [with him].[51]

Now, if such people [as] those who break the harmony in the performance of music, so that it becomes [dissonant], must be trained to take [part in] music, how much more incumbent is it on [those who] belong to [absolute] unity to be joined with one another! Do not accuse your head for not having made you into an eye but rather a finger. Do not be jealous of the one who has been given the part of an eye or a hand or a foot.[52] Be thankful instead that you are not outside the body, but have the same head as that for which the eye exists, as well as the hand and the foot and the other parts.

Why do you hate [19] the one who has been made a . . . . [just as the head] wanted? [Why] do you slander [your brother instead of] embracing [him]? . . . undefiled body . . . superior . . . .[53]

. . . dissolve . . . of the aeon . . . the descent . . . .

The Roots (19,15–20,13)

< . . . >, however, . . . [uproot] us from the aeons [that are in] that place and [that we possess], existing in the [visible] Church, those who exist [as the hidden roots of][54] humans. Openly, however, they proclaim [through them] the Fullness of the . . . .[55] Some are . . . [of] Church; because of [that they are] hastening,[56] and exist for it [in particular]. Others, of Life; because of that they are such as love abundant life. And each of the others [receives] from his own root and brings forth the fruit that is like himself. Since the roots are joined to one another, and their fruits are indivisible, what belongs to anyone superior is owned in common with the others.

So let us resemble the roots, being equal [20] . . . us . . . that aeon . . . that [do] not belong to us . . . above the . . . grasp him . . . .[57]

Beware of the Powers (20,13–21, top)

Since, then, [you have entrusted him with] your soul, he will [save it if you] give yourself to him, if you purify [yourself in your] heart, if you bar [your soul against the] devil, and if you [stay away from] his powers, which [pursue you in order to] be together with you. [For if the soul] is dead, the principalities and the powers have still . . . it.

What are you thinking now? [That they] are spirit? No! [Why] do they pursue the humans in this way until they die? Isn't [because] they [revel] in being

51. Cf. 1 Corinthians 12:26. 52. Cf. 1 Corinthians 12:15–18. 53. Five and a half lines missing or untranslatable. 54. The restoration is tentative. 55. This may mean that the aeons are invisibly present in the Church, inspiring its members by giving them charismatic gifts. In the following sentences, the Valentinian aeons Church and Life seem to be mentioned in particular. 56. Perhaps understand "hastening to it." This text may be based on a pun on the word ekklēsia, the assembly of those who are "summoned"; the "hastening" may be a description of the response of those who are summoned. 57. Eight lines missing.

together with the soul and so go searching for it? All places are in fact [closed] to
them by [such] humans as belong to God for as long as these are in the flesh; and,
being unable to see them, since they are living their lives in the spirit, they tear
apart that which is visible,[58] hoping to find them in this way. But what do they
gain from this? They rave senselessly. They ravage their surroundings, they dig
the earth[59] [21] ... him as he ... [who] hid ... exist ... purify . . . .[60]

Conclusion: The Struggle Against Sin (21, top–35)

..., however, is the ... after God ... grasp us ... but we walk . . . . For [if] the sins
[have been forgiven], the [jealousy] now even more ... the Church of the Savior.
For ... did not have the strength ... transgression, [to the extent that a] fighter
and an untrained person would have one and the same strength. Thus, if we sin,
who are the fighters [of] the Word, we sin worse than the gentiles, but if we overcome all sin, we shall receive the crown [of] victory, just as our head was given
glory by the Father.

The Interpretation of Knowledge

---

58. I.e., the body. 59. Cf. *Interpretation of Knowledge*
6, where the human body is compared to an inn rav-
aged by intruders; presumably the inn as well as the
body was built from earth. 60. About nine lines
missing.

NHC XI,2

Introduced by Einar Thomassen
Translated by Einar Thomassen and Marvin Meyer

The second tractate of Codex XI is an untitled treatise that in scope and vocabulary resembles the Valentinian treatises presented by the church fathers. Unfortunately, more than half of the text has been lost, due to the extensive damage suffered by this codex. No title is given at the end, and the beginning of the first page is lost, where a title might also possibly have stood, though most likely the tractate was untitled.

The author of *Valentinian Exposition* (22,1–39,39)[1] presents his own version of the Valentinian mythical narrative, beginning with the Father and concluding with the eschatological restoration of the spiritual seed to the Pleroma, or Fullness. Occasionally he self-consciously situates his exposition in the context of internal Valentinian debates about certain issues, as when he discusses the various powers of the Boundary (pp. 26–27) or when he defines the Son in relation to the Father's Will and Thought (24). Thus, the tractate also gives us some idea about the relatively independent style of an individual Valentinian teacher.

Because of its poor state of preservation, it is often no longer possible to follow the argument of the treatise in detail. After a few lines of introduction, of which only some isolated words remain, the exposition begins with a section about the Father, "the root of the All," on page 22. The text then goes on to speak about his "manifestation," which is the Son. The following pages discuss details of the projection of the Pleroma, until the story of the passion of Sophia starts somewhere on page 31.

In its presentation of the protology, *Valentinian Exposition* seems to be combining different Valentinian traditions. According to one line of argument (22),

---

1. Translated by Einar Thomassen.

the All preexisted within the Father, and the Son, who is the Father's Thought and Will, revealed it. This version resembles the protologies of the *Tripartite Tractate* and the *Gospel of Truth*. Another model used in the tractate is the system of aeons familiar from Irenaeus and the other heresiologists. This consists of the primal pair Depth (Bythos) and Silence, which duplicates into a Tetrad (Four); this Tetrad (Four) produces another Tetrad (Four), from which a Decad (Ten) and a Duodecad (Twelve) are subsequently brought forth. (The further idea that the Decad in turn produces 100 and the Duodecad 360 aeons is a less commonly attested variant.) On pages 29–30 such a thirty-aeon model of the Pleroma is laid out in full, though for this particular presentation the author seems to be using yet another source, since the first Father is here called Ineffable rather than Depth. According to the thirty-aeon systems, at any rate, the Son (the Only Begotten) appears as Mind, forming a second pair with Truth, after the initial pair Depth-Silence. He is not conceptualized as the Thought existing first within and then outside the Father. Some of the difficulties of the text are probably caused by the author's attempt to combine the various protological versions.

On pages 25–28, a special item of Valentinian theology is extensively discussed—the doctrine about the Boundary. Normally this concept refers to the power that separates the All from the inferior regions, although a Boundary is also sometimes said to be placed between the ineffable Father himself and the aeons (Irenaeus *Against Heresies* 1.11.1). The Boundary discussed on these pages seems primarily to be the latter variant, although a Boundary separating the All from the fallen aeon Sophia is clearly presupposed later in the text (31; 33). In this section as well the use of different sources is evident. The author first endorses the view of "some people," who attribute to the Boundary a set of four powers (26–27), and later (27–28) he goes on to discuss the opinion of "others," that there are only two powers. The latter view in fact agrees with what we read in the great Valentinian treatises of Irenaeus and Hippolytus.

The account of Sophia's error, split, and separation from the Pleroma (31–32; cf. 34) is fairly standard Valentinianism. *Valentinian Exposition* does not profess the theory about the two Sophias, found in Irenaeus and Hippolytus. Instead, the split is described as the abandonment of Sophia by her son (33)—probably named Christ (32; 33)—a variant that is also attested in several other sources (Irenaeus *Against Heresies* 1.11.1; *Tripartite Tractate*; *Excerpts from Theodotus* 23.2; 32–33). It is no doubt the more primitive version of the separation theme.

As in the other versions of the Valentinian myth, Sophia then repents and prays (34), and in response (cf. 32) the Pleroma sends the Son (33), who is Jesus (35; cf. 33). In a lost part of the text (35), Jesus sets Sophia right and then, together with her, creates the world as a likeness of the Pleroma from her passions and her "seeds" (35–36). We are also told that he brings down with him angels from the Pleroma (36)—they probably reside in a region above the created cosmos. There is also an anthropogony (37–38); from what is left of the text we can infer that Sophia places her seed in the first human. A demiurge is also involved in the work of creation, though he most likely only plays the role of an unwitting tool for Jesus and Sophia—his normal role in Valentinianism.

An original feature of *Valentinian Exposition* is a section on the origin of the devil and biblical events after the fall of the first man (38–39), before the eschatological restoration. A short section describing the saving mission of Jesus to earth must have been lost at the top of page 39; when the text resumes, the theme is already the final unification into the Pleroma.

Although the general scheme of the system in *Valentinian Exposition* is unmistakably Valentinian, it offers some unusual and puzzling variations. One odd feature is that the usual tripartition into material, psychical, and spiritual is missing, apparently replaced by a dualistic division into spirit and matter, or flesh. No satisfactory explanation has so far been found for this major divergence from the normal doctrine. Also unusual is the important role played by Sophia's original partner in the Pleroma (36; 39): it is to her partner that she is restored at the end, instead of being united with the Savior, or Jesus, as the systems normally have it. Jesus on his part is said to be united at the end with Christ, another odd idea.

The date and provenance of *Valentinian Exposition* is an open question. The text contains some materials that are undoubtedly very old in the history of Valentinianism, since it uses a system that has a series of features similar to that attributed (though wrongly) by Irenaeus to Valentinus in *Against Heresies* 1.11.1: Sophia being abandoned by her son, the use of "Ineffable" as the primary name for the Father, and the idea that the Boundary separates the Father from the aeons. On the other hand, the author also has access to other Valentinian sources, and the tractate itself may be have been composed at a considerably later time than the materials incorporated into it. Thus, any time between 160 and 350 (the approximate date of the codex itself) is conceivable.

The *Valentinian Liturgical Readings* (40,1–44,37)[2] are five short texts that deal with ritual practices: anointing, baptism (two readings), and the eucharist (two readings). They are written immediately after *Valentinian Exposition* in Codex XI, and it is a plausible (though unprovable) assumption that they were used in worship by the same Valentinian group as was using that particular tractate for instruction.

The first reading is a prayer addressed to the Father that he send the Son to be present as the active divine power in the anointing rite. The prayer uses an exorcistic-sounding formula taken from *Luke* 10:19, which is also attested elsewhere in baptismal contexts (for Valentinianism, *Excerpts from Theodotus* 76.2; for orthodox Christianity, Cyril of Jerusalem and John Chrysostom). Because this reading comes first and because of its exorcistic elements, it is likely that the prayer and the anointing rite accompanying it were performed during the first phase of the initiation ritual, before the immersion of the candidate in water.

The two readings on baptism are not prayers, like the one on anointing, but rather homiletic exposés. Three aspects of baptism are highlighted: baptism provides the remission of sins, it transports from one region (the world) to another (the aeon), and it effects a birth or formation from seeds to fully formed beings.

---

2. Translated by Marvin Meyer.

The expression "the first baptism" (40,39; 41,10–11.21–22) is not quite clear. Irenaeus (*Against Heresies* 1.21.2) says that some Valentinians used that expression to characterize the "psychical" baptism performed by ordinary Christians while they themselves claimed to offer a higher, "spiritual" baptism. That can hardly be the meaning here, since this "first baptism" seems already to bring the initiate into the aeon and incorruptibility. The "second baptism" may therefore refer to something that happens after death, when the ascending spirit is integrated into the Pleroma—an initiation in the transcendent world of which the first baptism is an earthly image.

The last two readings are heavily mutilated, but the references to *eukharistein* (which may also mean "thanksgiving") and to food and drink make it likely that these are prayers spoken in connection with the eucharistic celebration.

Taken together, the five readings seem to reflect a Valentinian version of the Christian initiation ritual with three phases: anointing, water baptism, and a eucharistic meal. The order of the three rites is puzzling, since other sources indicate that the normal order among the Valentinians was water baptism, anointing, and eucharist. The Valentinianism of the liturgical fragments seems somewhat idiosyncratic, just like that of the treatise to which they are appended.

BIBLIOGRAPHY

Charles W. Hedrick, ed., *Nag Hammadi Codices XI, XII, XIII*, 89–172 (John D. Turner and Elaine H. Pagels); Hans-Martin Schenke, Hans-Gebhard Bethge, and Ursula Ulrike Kaiser, eds., *Nag Hammadi Deutsch*, 2.747–62 (Wolf-Peter Funk); Einar Thomassen, "The Valentinianism of the *Valentinian Exposition* (NHC XI,2)."

Valentinian Exposition
with Valentinian Liturgical Readings[1]

Introduction (22,1–19)

. . . . . .[2] my [mystery . . . those who] belong to me and [those who will be] mine. These, then, are the ones who have . . . are.

The Root of the All (22,19–31)

The Father, who [is the root] of the All and the [Ineffable One], exists as One-ness, [being alone] in silence—"silence" means tranquility—since [he was] in fact One, and nothing existed before him. He also exists [as] Twoness and as a pair—his partner is Silence. Further, he possessed the All dwelling [inside] him, together with Will, Being, Love, and Permanence. These are unborn.

The Generation of the Son (22,31–23, top)

God [came] forth, the Son, Mind of the All. This means that even his Thought takes its existence from the root of the All, since he had him in Mind. Indeed, for the sake of the All, he entertained a Thought of something other than himself. For nothing else was in existence before him. He was the one who moved out of that place [23] . . . .[3]

Spreading Out (23, top–32)

. . . gushing [spring]. This, then, [is the] root [of] the All, Oneness before whom there is no one; [he is also] Twoness, dwelling in Silence and speaking only with himself; and [Four], insofar as he kept himself [in] Four while also dwelling in

---

1. Coptic text: NHC XI,2: 22,1–39,39 (*Valentinian Exposition*); 40,1–44,37 (*Valentinian Liturgical Readings*). Editions: *The Facsimile Edition of the Nag Hammadi Codices: Codices XI, XII and XIII*, 28–50; Wolf-Peter Funk, *Concordance des textes de Nag Hammadi: Les Codices X et XIa*; Charles W. Hedrick, ed., *Nag Hammadi Codices XI, XII, XIII*, 89–172 (Elaine H. Pagels and John D. Turner); Jacques-É. Ménard, *L'Exposé valentinien; Les Fragments sur le baptême et sur l'eucharistie*; Hans-Martin Schenke, Hans-Gebhard Bethge, and Ursula Ulrike Kaiser, eds., *Nag Hammadi Deutsch*, 2.747–62 (Wolf-Peter Funk). The title is construed from the contents of the text. 2. The first fifteen and a half lines are missing or untranslatable. 3. About eighteen lines missing.

Three Hundred Sixty.[4] He brought himself forth. In Two he revealed his Will, and in Four he spread himself out.

So much for the root of the All.

The Son as the Revealer, the Father's Thought, and Will (23,32–25, top)

Now let's [move] on to his revelation, his goodness, his coming here below, and all the rest. This is the Son, the Father of the All, the Mind of the Spirit. Him he possessed before [24] . . . .[5]

. . . that . . . . [He is] a spring, being the revelation [from the] Silence, and a Mind of the All, being Two with [Depth].[6] For he is the producer of the All and the actualization[7] [of the thought] of the Father—which is [Desire][8]—and the descent down below. When the First Father willed it, he revealed himself in him.

Since, therefore, [it is] through [him that] the revelation of the All takes place, I call him, with reference to the All, the Will of the All, and since he[9] conceived this kind of Thought[10] concerning the All, I call him, with reference to the Thought, the Only One.[11]

For to see the God of Truth is to give glory to the root of the All. Therefore, it was himself that he revealed in the Only One, and through him he revealed the ineffable [25] . . . .[12]

Only the Son Can Go Inside the Boundary (25, top–26,22)

. . . truth. [They] saw him residing in Oneness, in Twoness, and in Four, bringing forth the Only One and the [Boundary].

And the Boundary . . . [separated] the All . . . .[13]

. . . is totally ineffable to the All, and the confirmation and actualization of the All, the veil of [silence]. He is the [true] High Priest, the [one who has] the authority to enter the Holies of Holies, revealing the glory to the aeons and bringing forth the abundant wealth to <fragrance>.[14] The east [26] . . . .[15]

. . . in [him. He is the one] who revealed [him],[16] being the original . . . , the treasure of [the All], and [the one] who contains the All, the one who is elevated [above the] All.

---

4. This passage is taken to mean that the root of the All—the Father—first spreads himself out into Two and then Four. From Four he also extends himself as far as Three Hundred Sixty, representing the ultimate edge of the Pleroma, although in a distinct dimension of his transcendent essence he keeps himself restricted to the primal Four. **5.** About seventeen lines missing. **6.** Reading [pši]kʰh, the Greek bathos or buthos. **7.** Hypostasis. **8.** Reading en[thumēsis] (conjectural). Another option: en[noia], "Thought." **9.** The subject seems to be the Father. **10.** At the end of

Valentinian Exposition 22 it is said that the Thought was the first other entity to come into being. This probably explains why the Son as the Thought is called "Only One," "Only Begotten," "Monogenes." **11.** Or "Only Begotten," "Monogenes," here and below. **12.** About seventeen lines missing. **13.** About six lines missing or untranslatable. **14.** Emending to read au<sti>noube. **15.** The revelation given by the Son is compared to the sacrifice offered by the high priest. About seventeen lines missing. **16.** Or "[himself]."

Concerning the Boundary (26,22–28,29)

These now . . . Christ . . . in the way [it] was given . . . the fathers . . . .[17]

. . . is [invisible] to [them], being . . . the Boundary. And it has four powers: a separating one, a strengthening one, a form-giving one, and a [substance-producing one. These, then], are the true [powers]. If we are going to understand their aspects, time span, and locations, which some [people][18] have established—for they have [27] . . . .[19]

. . . from these [places] . . . love . . . pour out . . . the entire Fullness . . . the Permanence [endures at] all times, and . . . . For even from . . . the time . . . this abundance . . . . . .[20] the demonstration of its . . . .

But why a [separating] power, a strengthening one, a substance-producing one, and a form-giving one, as others have [objected]? For [they] maintain that the Boundary has only two powers, a separating one and a strengthening one, in so far as it separates [the Depth] from the aeons in order that [28] . . . .[21]

. . . . These, then, . . . of the [Depth] . . . . For [this] is the form . . . , then, of the Father of [Truth] . . . say that Christ . . . the Spirit . . . of the Only One . . . which . . . has . . . .[22]

Exposition About the Fullness (28,29–31, top)

. . . it is necessary that we . . . [with] greater assurance . . . in the scriptures, and formulate the ideas. For that reason, in fact, the ancients say that [they] were proclaimed by God. Let [us] try to understand, therefore, his inscrutable richness. He wished [29] . . . .[23]

. . . servitude . . . he [did not] become . . . lead their lives . . . look carefully [in the] . . . of knowledge[24] . . . , however, toward their respective [aspects].[25]

The [first] Four, [in fact], produced [another Four, which is that] of [Word[26] and] Life, [and Man and Church] . . . . he produced Word and Life: Word [for] the glory of the Ineffable, Life for the glory of Silence, Man for his own glory, and Life [for] the glory of Truth. This, then, is the Four that was brought forth after the likeness of the unborn one. And [this] Four that is brought forth [30] . . . .[27]

. . . [the Ten] from [Word and Life] and the [Twelve from Man] and [Church became] Thirty.

Now, it is . . . [Thirty] of the [aeons] . . . from . . . enter into . . . go forth . . . the aeons [and the uncontainable] ones. [And once] the [uncontainable ones had] seen . . . [they] . . . because . . . [uncontainable and] exists in the Fullness. However, the Ten from Word and Life brought forth Tens, so that the Fullness became a Hundred, and the Twelve from Man and Church [brought] forth and

---

17. About four and a half lines missing. 18. Reading *haeine*. 19. About seventeen lines missing. 20. About three lines missing. 21. About seventeen lines missing. 22. About three lines missing. 23. About seventeen lines missing. 24. Gnosis. 25. The text has *pro[sōpon]*. This word is also used at the end of *Valentinian Exposition* 26. Here it probably refers to the characteristics of the individual aeons, to be expounded in the following section. 26. Logos, here and below. 27. About fifteen lines missing.

produced Thirty, so that Three Hundred Sixty came into being, as the fullness of the year. And the year of the Lord [31] . . . .[28]

The Fall of Sophia (31, top–32, top)

. . . [perfect] . . . perfect . . . and according to the . . . [Boundary] and . . . Boundary . . . . . .[29] Greatness, which . . . such goodness . . . life . . . suffer . . . through the . . . in the presence of the [Fullness] . . . that he wanted . . . and he wanted to go [out of] the Thirty, although he was [a member] of Man and Church—and this is Sophia—so as to surpass [the Boundary] of the Fullness. [32] . . . .[30]

The Reaction of the Fullness (32, top–33, top)

. . . , however, . . . and she . . . , who . . . and . . . . For . . . the All . . . . . .[31] they [remembered] . . . however, . . . themselves . . . the All . . . him. And he . . . he made . . . remembrance together with the . . . the Fullness, by means of the Word . . . his flesh. [These], then, [are the . . . which] . . . after [Christ] had entered into it,[32] just as [I] said before, and the . . . toward the Uncontainable One . . . [brought] forth [33] . . . .[33]

How the Error Must Be Corrected (33, top–34)

. . . before they . . . forth . . . hid himself from . . . the partner,[34] and . . . the movement and . . . put forth Christ . . . and the seeds. Jesus . . . the word . . . [correction] of the <error> . . . perfection . . . a perfect form.

[He who had] gone[35] up into the Fullness did not want [to] consent to the suffering, [but] he [was] prevented from [passing through] because he was [held back][36] by the Boundary—that is, by the partner. For the correction could not come about except by means of his[37] own Son, to whom belongs the entire divine Fullness. It pleased him to place within him the powers as his body, and he descended.[38]

The Repentance of Sophia (33,35–35, top)

Now, these things Sophia endured after her son had hastened up from her. [For] she knew that she was in [34] . . . .[39]

---

28. About seventeen lines missing. 29. Three lines missing. 30. About sixteen lines are missing. The lost portion of the text must have contained an account of the division of Sophia into two parts, one if which was perfect, the other deficient. In the *Valentinian Exposition*, as in some other variants of the Valentinian system, Sophia's perfect half is described as her son and is probably identified with Christ. In the remainder of the text her deficient part is described as Sophia herself. 31. About five lines missing. 32. "It" probably refers to a noun in the preceding lost text designating the unity of the Fullness. 33. About ten lines missing. 34. The text has the Greek *suzugos*. This is no doubt Sophia's "better half," to whom she was previously joined in the Pleroma. All aeons form syzygic pairs. 35. Restoring [pentah]bōk. 36. Restoring aue[i]n[e euama]hte. 37. I.e., the Father's, or perhaps "its," the Fullness's. 38. Cf. *Colossians* 2:9. 39. About nine lines missing.

. . . union and . . . are gone. Their . . . the seeds . . . these did not . . . , "I have become . . . they too . . . . [My] reasoning ability is gone, but [insight][40] has remained."

Then [she wept, saying] to [herself], ". . . look [at] me. Those [insights] that I pondered . . . are all gone, but the [memory][41] of them has remained."

She repented and prayed to the Father of Truth, [saying], "Granted that I have [abandoned] my partner. Because of [that, I] am outside the region of stability as well. I deserve the things I have to endure. I used to be in the Fullness, bringing forth aeons and producing fruit with my partner."

She realized what she used to be and what had become of her, and so she suffered on both accounts. It has been said that she laughs because she continued to be solitary and thus imitated the Incomprehensible One; it is said that she [weeps] because she had cut herself off from her partner. [35] . . . .[42]

The Creation of the World (35, top–36,19)

. . . [Jesus and] Sophia prepared[43] the creation. Now, since the seeds [of] Sophia were unfinished and without form, Jesus conceived a creation of [this] kind: he created it from the seeds, with Sophia working together with him. Since they were seeds, and without [form], he came down [and revealed to them] the Fullness. [He instructed] them about the place [of the] uncreated. All things [he made after] the type of the Fullness and the Father, the Uncontainable One. The uncreated [is the] type of the uncreated act of [bringing into being], for it is from the uncreated that the Father brings forth into form. The creation, however, is the shadow of the preexistent.

Jesus, then, fashioned the creation and performed his work[44] from the passions surrounding the seeds. He separated them from one another, and the better passions he put into spirit, but the bad ones into carnal things. First, from all these passions [36] . . . .[45]

[Since] Providence had provided the correction in order to put forth shadows and images of the preexistent, the present, and the future things, that was the economy that [was] entrusted to Jesus. For [that] reason, he inscribed the All with [imitations], images, and [shadows].

On the Angels (36,19–38)

[For] when Jesus came [down],[46] he [also] brought [the seeds of the words][47] of the All—those belonging to the Fullness and the partner—that [is], the angels. For at the same time her partner had, with the assent of the Fullness, put [forth] the angels, in agreement with the will of the Father.

---

40. Possibly e[*pinoia*]. **41.** The restorations are tentative. **42.** About nine lines are missing. This lost portion of the text probably told how Jesus, the Savior, was sent down to Sophia, and how he healed her sufferings. This is a precondition for the creation of the world by Jesus and Sophia, which will take place next. **43.** Restoring *aucō*[*rc*]. **44.** Greek *demiourgei*. **45.** About nine lines missing or untranslatable. **46.** Restoring ⸢*ntarefei* g[*a*]r a[*hrēi*]. **47.** The restoration ([*logoi*]) is tentative.

For this is the will of the Father: that no one in the Fullness shall be without a partner. Thus, the will of the Father is always to put forth and give fruit. That she should endure suffering, then, was not the will of the Father; for she was all by herself, without her partner.

More on the Creation of the World (36,38–37,31)

Let us [37] . . . .[48]

. . . another . . . the second . . . and the son . . . another . . . is the Four of the world. And next this Four put forth [Three], so that the fullness of the world came to be Seven.

[There] came [into it] images, [likenesses], angels, [archangels], gods, and . . . . When all [these things] had taken place through Providence, . . . Jesus, as he . . . the seeds . . . the Only One . . . . They consist of [spiritual] beings as well as of carnal ones—such as are in heaven and such as are upon the earth.[49] He[50] fashioned for them this kind of location, and this kind of school, that would provide them with instruction and with form.

The Creation of the Human Being (37,32–38, top)

This demiurge now began to fashion a human being, after his own image on the one hand, and on the other after the likeness of the preexistent ones. It was this kind of dwelling place that [Sophia] made use of for the seeds [38] . . . .[51]

The Fall and Its Consequences (38, top–39, top)

. . . God,[52] after they . . . because of the human. The devil in fact is one of God's beings, but he defected and took with him the entire army of angels, and he [plucked out] his own root from that place, by means of . . . and . . . .

For he [made the human] of God fall,[53] and the . . . him. For that reason, sons [were] born [to him] who [were angry with] one another: Cain [killed] Abel his brother. For [the devil] breathed into [him] his spirit.

There [was] fighting and desertion both among the angels and among humankind: between those on the right and those on the left, between those in

---

48. About eight lines missing. 49. Here the spiritual and the carnal beings are probably to be understood as subcategories of psychical powers. 50. I.e., the demiurge (cf. the following section), whose origins must have been explained in the preceding lost text. The Valentinian demiurge is basically no more than a tool used by the Savior Jesus and Sophia for putting the psychical and material components of the cosmos in order. The creation of the world is not evil, but serves a providential purpose in the economy of salvation. The Savior and Sophia cannot, however, enter into direct contact with the inferior substances from which the world is made, but instead they work through the intermediary of the demiurge, who himself possesses psychical substance. 51. About ten lines are missing. This lost part of the text must have contained an account of how Sophia inserted the spiritual seed into the first human without the demiurge's knowledge. 52. "God" here and in the following clearly refers to the demiurge. 53. Restoring af[ᵉrspha]lle (Greek *sphallein*).

heaven and those upon the earth, between the spiritual powers and the carnal ones,[54] and the devil against God. Because of that, the angels lusted after the daughters of the humans, and they descended into flesh—so that God made a flood, and almost regretted having created the world. [39] . . . .[55]

The Restoration (39, top–39)

. . . the partner, Sophia, the son, the angels and [the seeds], whereas [Sophia's] partner, Sophia, Jesus, [the angels], and the seeds are [images of] the Fullness. The demiurge, moreover, [is a] shadow [of] the partner, the Fullness, Jesus, Sophia, the angels, and the seeds. Sophia's partner is an image [of the Father] of Truth, and Sophia and Jesus [are images of Truth and] the Only One, [while the] male [angels] and the female . . . seeds [are] all [images of the] Fullness, [and these are ourselves].[56]

So when Sophia receives her partner, and Jesus receives Christ, and the seeds are united with the angels, then the Fullness will receive Sophia in joy, and the All will be joined together and restored. Then the aeons will have received their abundance, for they will have understood that even if they change, they remain unchanging.

Valentinian Liturgical Readings

On Anointing (40,1–29)

. . . . . .[57]
according to . . . ,
. . . symbol . . . see him.
It is fitting [for you] now
to send your Son Jesus Christ
to anoint us,
that we may be able
to trample on [snakes]
and [ward off] scorpions
and [all] the power of the devil,[58]
[through] the [supreme] shepherd
Jesus Christ.
Through him have we known you,
and we [glorify] you.

---

54. Here again the spiritual and the carnal beings are probably to be understood as subcategories of psychical powers. 55. About nine lines are missing. This lost part of the text probably contained an account of the mission of Jesus to earth in order to save the spiritual seed. 56. The restoration of this sentence is tentative. Previous attempts to restore it have proved unsatisfactory. 57. Eight lines missing or untranslatable. 58. *Luke* 10:19; see also *Mark* 16:18 (longer ending of *Mark*); *Acts* 28:3–6.

Glory be to you,
Father in the [aeon],
[Father] in the Son,
Father [in] the holy Church
and among the holy [angels].
From [the beginning]
he abides [forever],
[in the] harmony of the aeons,
[from] eternity,
to the boundless eternity
of the eternal realms.
Amen.

On First Baptism (40,30–41,38)

[This] is the Fullness
of the summary of knowledge,[59]
this, which was revealed to us
by our Lord Jesus Christ,
the Only[60] Son.
These things are sure and necessary,
so we may walk in them.
They are of the first baptism. [41]
. . . .[61]
[The first] baptism [is the forgiveness] of sins,
. . . one who said,
"[I baptize] you
for the [forgiveness] of your sins."[62]
This . . . is a symbol
of the . . . [work][63] of Christ
[that is] equal . . .
in him . . .
For the [work] of Jesus is . . . .

The first [baptism] is the forgiveness [of sins].
[Through it we] are brought
from [people of the left]
to people of the right,[64]
from [corruption]
to [incorruptibility],
[which] is the Jordan.

---

59. Gnosis, here and below. 60. Or "Only Begotten," "Monogenes." 61. Nine lines missing. 62. The restoration is tentative. 63. The restoration is tenta- tive. 64. In Valentinian thought, those of the left are material people and those of the right are psychical people.

But that place is of the world,
so we have been [brought] from the world
into the aeon.
The meaning of John[65] is the aeon,
the meaning of the Jordan
is the descent that is the ascent,[66]
[our] exodus[67] from the world
[into] the aeon. [42]

On Baptism (42,1–43,19)

. . . . . . ,[68]
[from the] world [to the Jordan],
from [the things] of world [to the sight][69] of God,
from [the carnal] to the spiritual,
from the physical [to the] angelic,
from [creation] to Fullness,
from the world [to the] aeon,
from [enslavements][70] to sonship,
[from] entanglements to virtue,
from [wayfaring] to our home,
from [cold] to warmth,
[from] . . . to . . . ,
and we . . . to . . . .

[This] is how we were brought
[from] seminal [bodies] into a perfect form.

The cleansing[71] is the symbol
through which Christ has saved us
through the [gift] of his Spirit.
[He] delivered us who are [in him].[72]
From this time forth
souls [will become] perfect spirits.
[What is] granted to us [by the first] baptism [43]
. . . . . .[73]
. . . invisible . . . ,
. . . [which] is his,
since [we have become eternal] . . . ,
we have received [the salvation of Christ].[74]

---

65. John the Baptizer. 66. The descent to the Jordan indicates the ascent to the realm of Fullness. 67. Or "[the] exodus." 68. Nine lines missing. 69. Or "[truth]" (so Funk, tentatively). 70. Tentative. 71. Or "bath," a term for baptism with water. 72. Tentative. 73. Fourteen lines missing or untranslatable. 74. Tentative.

On the Eucharist (43,20–38)

[We] thank [you]
[and celebrate] the eucharist,[75] Father,
[remembering] your Son [Jesus Christ],
come . . .
invisible . . .
your [Son] . . .
his love . . .
. . . . . .[76]
to knowledge . . . .
They do your will
[through the] name of Jesus Christ,
and will do your will
[now and] always.
They are complete
[in] every gift
and [every] purity.

Glory be to you
through your firstborn Son
Jesus Christ,
now and forever.
Amen. [44]

On the Eucharist (44,1–37)

. . . . . .[77]
we receive[78]. . .
the word . . .
holy . . .
. . . . . .[79]
food and [drink] . . .
[your] Son,
since you . . .
food . . .
to us . . .
in life . . .
. . . . . .[80]
he is . . .

---

75. Or "[and give you] thanks." 76. Two lines missing or untranslatable. 77. Thirteen lines missing. 78. Tentative. 79. Two lines missing or untranslatable. 80. Two lines missing or untranslatable.

that is . . .
the church . . .
. . . . . .[81]
you are pure . . . .

You, Lord,
when you die in purity,
you will be pure,
so everyone who receives
food and [drink] from this
will [live].

Glory be to you
forever.
Amen.

---

81. Two lines missing or untranslatable.

ALLOGENES THE STRANGER

NHC XI,3

Introduced and Translated by John D. Turner

*A*llogenes the Stranger is a pseudonymous apocalypse or revelation discourse narrating the otherworldly ascent of Allogenes (*allogenēs*, "of another [*allos*] kind [*genos*]," the "Stranger" or "Foreigner") and the revelations he received from various divine beings. It is extant in only a single copy, as the third treatise in Nag Hammadi Codex XI (45,1–69,20), the first of two Sahidic texts contained therein, which are written in the same hand as Codex VII. Of its twenty-five extant pages averaging thirty-six to thirty-nine lines apiece, only pages 59–64 are complete; the first four or five lines are missing from the rest, except for pages 65–69, which lack the first fourteen lines, and pages 55–56, of which only the outer half of the text column survives. As in most Nag Hammadi tractates, the title *Allogenes* appears as a subscript (69,20) after the closing lines of the tractate (69,16–19), which are also inset and decorated.

The major dramatis personae within the text include the following:

1. Allogenes: the central character and interlocutor of the treatise *Allogenes the Stranger,* whom the initial revealer figure Youel calls a great "power" and "name" that "has come to be in the world" (59,8–9). The term "Allogenes"—that is, "of another kind/race"—is evidently a play on the tradition in *Genesis* 4:25 of Seth's birth as "another seed" (*sperma heteron*) in contrast to Abel, born in the likeness and image of Adam (*Genesis* 5:3), who was the first to bear of the image of God (*Genesis* 1:26–27). It serves as a title or epithet not only for Seth and for his seven sons, but even for the Great Invisible Spirit, the Sethian supreme deity (in *Holy Book of the Great Invisible Spirit* IV 50,21; III 41,6–7 as *allogenios*) or as a title for the anonymous central revealer figure in the (non-Sethian) *Second Discourse of Great Seth* 52,8–10 ("I am a stranger to the regions below"). Both the generic character of the name and its association with Seth are brought out in the *Three Steles of Seth* (119,31–120,15), where Seth praises his father Pigeradamas, the heavenly Adam, as self-generated from "another kind" and deriving from the divine

Self-Generated One, a distinctiveness in turn inherited by Seth and his seed. More recently, the name Allogenes has shown up in a fragment from the *Book of Allogenes* from Codex Tchacos, where "Allogenes" seems to play the role of Jesus in resisting the temptations of Satan.

2. Messos: Allogenes' disciple, whose name is invoked five times, always by Allogenes as "my son Messos." He plays no role other than the sole and direct but silent recipient of Allogenes' account of his ascent and accompanying revelations. His name may be a play on that of "Moses" or, more likely, stem from a generic designation "Middle One," a middleman who mediates the account of Allogenes' enlightenment to others.

3. Youel, the "all-glorious" "[Mother] of the Glories" (55,17): the revealer figure who throughout the first half of the treatise delivers to Allogenes five revelation discourses on the subjects of the nature and deployment of the Barbelo Aeon, the Triple-Powered One, and the means by which they are to be known and praised.

4. Salamex, Semen, and Arme: the powers of the luminaries of the Barbelo Aeon. As in Zostrianos, these are the chief revealer figures throughout the second half of the treatise. They instruct Allogenes concerning the ascent through the three powers (from Mentality to Vitality to Existence) of the Triple-Powered One toward a vision of the supreme Unknowable One, at which point they deliver a negative theological "primary revelation" of the Unknowable One, who can only be known by not knowing him.

The divine hierarchy is populated with figures typical of Platonizing Sethian texts:

5. The Unknowable One: the supreme, preexistent divine principle, utterly beyond being and comprehension, who seems sometimes to be distinguished from and sometimes equated with the Invisible Spirit.

6. The Triple-Powered One: mediator between the Unknowable One and the threefold Aeon of Barbelo. Its three powers—Existence, Vitality, and Mentality (or Blessedness)—give rise to Barbelo and her Aeon in three phases: in its initial phase as a purely infinitival Existence (*huparxis* or *ontotēs*), it is latent within and identical with the supreme One; in its emanative phase it is an indefinite Vitality (*zōotēs*) that proceeds forth from One; and in its final phase it is a Mentality (*noētēs*) that—through the contemplation of its source in the One—takes on the character of determinate being as the intellectual Aeon of Barbelo.

7. The Aeon of Barbelo: the self-knowledge of the Invisible Spirit and his only direct product, appearing in many Sethian treatises as the androgynous (though dominantly feminine) first thought of the supreme

Invisible Spirit. It is conceived of by *Allogenes the Stranger* (and *Zostri-anos*, the *Three Steles of Seth*, and *Marsanes*) as a masculine aeon, a universal Intellect that forms the highest realm of pure, determinate being, wherein reside the archetypes of all true things. This Aeon is a One-in-Many, completely unified, yet also containing three distinguishable ontological levels presided over by Kalyptos, Protophanes, and the Self-Generated One (Autogenes). As their names reveal, they represent three phases in the unfolding of determinate being within the Barbelo Aeon: initial latency (unrealized, "hidden" potential existence), initial manifestation, and final, self-generated actualization (as determinate being). Once actualized, these three represent, respectively, the dwelling place of: "those that truly exist," the universal ideas or paradigms of Platonic metaphysics; the "all-perfect ones who exist together," that is, undifferentiated but potentially distinct intelligences and souls that contemplate the ideal forms in Kalyptos; and the "perfect individuals" who are differentiated, individual forms and souls. Autogenes' activity is demiurgical, directed to the ordering of the psychical and physical realms below the Barbelo Aeon.

8. The Triple-Male Child: a savior or mediator who brings undifferentiated beings in the Aeon of Protophanes into differentiated existence in the Aeon of Autogenes and, conversely, helps the differentiated beings in the Aeon of Autogenes to ascend to the Aeon of Protophanes.

Although no other treatise by the name "Allogenes" is extant, Epiphanius, writing around 375 CE, referred to a plurality of the "books called *Allogeneis*" (*Panarion* 40.2.2; 39.5.1) as well as to seven books written in the name of Seth's seven sons, themselves called "Strangers" (*Panarion* 40.7.4–5), as is their father Seth (*Panarion* 40.7.2). Epiphanius says that they were composed by the Archontics and Sethians (*Panarion* 39.5.1; 40.7.4). He has difficulty recalling where he encountered these Sethians, saying that they are not to be found everywhere, but now only in Egypt and Palestine, although, fifty years earlier, they had spread as far as Greater Armenia (*Panarion* 39.1.1–2; 40.1). He further indicates that the Archontics had inherited these books from tradition: "They are already using texts called *Allogeneis* too, for there are books identified in this way" (*Panarion* 40.2.2). Although *Allogenes the Stranger* neither mentions Seth nor gives any clear sign of having been written by or about Seth or his sons, the colophon of the text (69,16–19: "The seal (*sphragis*) of all the books [of] Allogenes") suggests that its author conceived it as the final work concluding, or "sealing off," a series of such books.

Around 300 CE, Porphyry's biography of Plotinus states that Plotinus attacked certain Gnostics who "produced revelations by Zoroaster and Zostrianos and Nicotheos and Allogenes and Messos and other such people" (*Life of Plotinus* 16.6–7). Most scholars agree that *Allogenes the Stranger* and *Zostrianos* can be identified with these revelations mentioned by Porphyry. Since *Allogenes* is addressed to Messos and *Zostrianos* bears the cryptogram subtitle "Words of Zoroaster," it is possible that Porphyry here refers to these two tractates by the names of their respective central characters or names found in their titles. But Porphyry goes on to speak of separate refutations: Amelius's of the "Book of Zostrianos"and his own of the "Book of Zoroaster," as if referring to separate revelations by each figure named.

Since Epiphanius speaks of multiple instances of works under this title, it cannot be determined from the name alone whether *Allogenes the Stranger* is Porphyry's "revelation by Allogenes." But the striking agreement in terminology and conceptuality between Plotinus's refutation of the Gnostics in *Ennead* II, 9 [33] and that found in *Zostrianos* virtually guarantees its identity with the revelation of that name mentioned by Porphyry, so it is highly likely that a Greek version of the Coptic *Allogenes the Stranger* was indeed known to Plotinus and Porphyry in Rome between 244 and 269 CE. Since Irenaeus and Hippolytus, writing from 180 to 220 CE, do not mention Seth's sons or any books called *Allogeneis*, these Allogenes traditions may have developed after 220 CE in the West, or if earlier, perhaps in non-Western regions such as Syria or Egypt. *Allogenes the Stranger* was probably composed in Greek in an eastern Mediterranean locale, perhaps Alexandria, somewhere around 240 CE, subsequently finding its way to Rome by mid-third century, where it was translated into Coptic near the beginning of the fourth century and circulated southward in various Coptic versions and dialects, one of which was included in Codex XI.

The basic function of *Allogenes the Stranger* is to provide its readers a model of spiritual progress in the person of Allogenes by emulating his ascent from earth through the levels of the Barbelo Aeon, through the three levels of the Triple-Powered One, to a final vision of the supreme Unknowable One. Its detailed description of transcendent reality enables readers not only to replicate the insights achieved by him, but also like Messos, to teach them to others.

As an ascent apocalypse, *Allogenes the Stranger* is modeled not so much on Jewish and biblical themes as it is on Platonic ones, generally inspired by the "revelations" contained in particular dialogues of Plato—for example, that of Diotima concerning the ascent to the vision of absolute Beauty in the *Symposium* 201d–212a, the parable of the cave in *Republic* VII 514–517a, and the revelation of Er in *Republic* X 614b–621b. Given that Allogenes addresses its entire content—including not only the revelations he has received but also an account of both the command to write the book and his compliance with it—directly to his son Messos, *Allogenes the Stranger* can also be considered as a literary testament.

Rather than its membership in the class of "Allogenes" books, the distinctiveness of *Allogenes the Stranger* has much more to do with its membership in a typologically defined group of Nag Hammadi Sethian treatises that may be called the "Platonizing Sethian treatises," a group that contains, besides the treatises *Zostrianos* and *Allogenes* mentioned by Porphyry, also the *Three Steles of Seth* and *Marsanes*. All four clearly share a metaphysics and ontological doctrine characteristic of Plotinus and later Neoplatonists as well as of certain Middle Platonic sources, such as the fragments of Numenius, the *Chaldaean Oracles*, and especially an anonymous *Parmenides Commentary* (which may be pre-Plotinian, even though Pierre Hadot originally ascribed it to Plotinus's disciple Porphyry).[1]

The negative theology of *Allogenes the Stranger*, a portion of which (62,27–63,25) contains a word-for-word parallel with the *Secret Book of John* (BG 8502 24,9–25,7; NHC II 3,20–33) and is similar to that found in the anonymous Turin *Commentary on Plato's Parmenides*, is ultimately inspired by the *Parmenides* (especially its first "hypothesis," 137c–142a), the modes of nonbeing in both the *Parmenides* and the *Sophist* (240b, 254d); and its hierarchical metaphysics looks back to the three kings of *Letter* II (312e) as well as the doctrines of the paradigm, demiurge, and receptacle of the *Timaeus*.

Although it is probably *Zostrianos* that was the primary target of the various anti-Gnostic critiques of Plotinus and his colleagues, by contrast, *Allogenes the Stranger* seems relatively free of the specific objectionable features explicitly criticized in Plotinus's anti-Gnostic work (*Enneads* III 8; V 8; V 5; and especially II 9), suggesting that *Allogenes* was composed partly as a revision of *Zostrianos*. *Allogenes the Stranger* eliminates all discussion of celestial aeonic levels below the Barbelo Aeon. The account of the Aeon of Barbelo's generation from the unfolding of the threefold potency of the Invisible Spirit, scattered about through *Zostrianos*, is gathered together into the initial revelations of Youel on pages 45–49 of the present text. Instead of limiting the visionary ascent to the Barbelo Aeon, *Allogenes the Stranger* portrays an additional ascent through the various levels of the Triple-Powered One. Although *Zostrianos* conceives the Triple-Powered One's three powers as inherent in the Invisible Spirit, *Allogenes the Stranger* conceives the Triple-Powered One as a separately existing entity interposed between the Invisible Spirit and the Barbelo Aeon. Rather than interpreting the stages of the ascent as a sequence of transcendent baptisms administered by a plurality of revealers, *Allogenes the Stranger* interprets the ascent as a graded series of mental insights culminating in a mystical union with the supreme Unknown One, characterized as non knowing knowledge, thus offering one of the earliest known examples of the doctrine of "learned ignorance."

In short, it seems that *Allogenes the Stranger* restructures the metaphysics of *Zostrianos* into a tighter, more systematic framework, limits the metaphysical exposition to the transcendent spheres extending from the intellectual levels of the Barbelo Aeon to the supreme Invisible Spirit, more clearly articulates the process by which the Barbelo Aeon emanates from the Invisible Spirit, frees the whole from a baptismal context, and omits most instances of ecstatic praise and lists of divine beings.[2] Omission of the role of Sophia and the creator archon as well as

---

1. See W. Kroll, "Ein neuplatonischer Parmenides-kommentar in einem Turiner Palimpsest"; Pierre Hadot, "Être, Vie, Pensée chez Plotin et avant Plotin"; "Fragments d'un commentaire de Porphyre sur le Parménide"; *Porphyre et Victorinus*, 2.64–113; A. Linguiti, "Commentarium in Platonis 'Parmenidem'"; and, most recently, G. Bechtle, *The Anonymous Commentary on Plato's "Parmenides."*

2. A notable exception is an ecstatic doxological hymn, portions of which *Allogenes the Stranger* 54,11–37 shares with two other Sethian Platonizing treatises, the *Three Steles of Seth* (125,24–126,17) and *Zostrianos* (51,24–52,8; 86,13–24; 88,9–25) as well as with the final lines of the fragmentary "prayer of Seth" in Papyrus Berolinensis 17207.

the extensive discussion on the various types of souls also entails a shift of attention away from the psychological doctrine of the *Phaedo* and the physical doctrine of the *Timaeus* toward the more specifically theological issues of the *Parmenides* and the negative theological interpretation of its first hypothesis (137d–142a). This shift of interest to the transcendent realm may have resulted in a work of enhanced acceptability to the critical concerns of Plotinus's circle without abandoning the essential divine beings of Sethianism and its commitment to the authority of revelation. Most significantly, *Allogenes the Stranger* is perhaps the earliest attempt in the history of Western mysticism to combine these resources into a contemplative technique in which, although beginning with acts of discursive discernment of both oneself and the supreme Unknowable One, complete intuition of the One is achieved only at the point where one abandons any positive attempt to know him.

BIBLIOGRAPHY

Catherine Barry, Wolf-Peter Funk, Paul-Hubert Poirier, and John D. Turner, eds., *Zostrien*; William Brashear, "Seth-Gebet"; Pierre Hadot, *Porphyre et Victorinus*; Charles W. Hedrick, ed., *Nag Hammadi Codices XI, XII, XIII*, 173–267 (John D. Turner and Orval S. Wintermute); Karen L. King, *Revelation of the Unknowable God*; Bentley Layton, *The Gnostic Scriptures*, 141–48; Hans-Martin Schenke, "Bemerkungen zur Apokalypse des Allogenes (NHC XI,3)"; "Gnosis: Zum Forschungsstand unter besonderer Berücksichtigung der religionsgeschichtlichen Problematik"; "The Phenomenon and Significance of Gnostic Sethianism"; Hans-Martin Schenke, Hans-Gebhard Bethge, and Ulsula Ulrike Kaiser, eds., *Nag Hammadi Deutsch*, 2.763–87 (Wolf-Peter Funk); Madeleine Scopello, "Youel et Barbélo dans le traité de l'Allogène"; John D. Turner, *Sethian Gnosticism and the Platonic Tradition*; Richard Valantasis, "Allogenes (Nag Hammadi Codex XI,3)"; Michael A. Williams, *The Immovable Race*; "Stability as a Soteriological Theme in Gnosticism."

Allogenes the Stranger[1]

Authorial Ascription in Missing Incipit (45,1–2?)

. . . .[2]

Youel's Five Revelations to Allogenes the Stranger
(45,3?–57,24)

Introduction to the Revelations (45,3?–6)

. . .[3] since they are [perfect individuals.[4] And they are] all [united, conjoined].

Youel's First Revelation Discourse and Response (45,6–50,17)

The First Revelation Opens (45,6–15)

The [Mind], the guardian [I provided for you], taught you. And it is the power[5] that [exists] in you that [extended itself], since [it][6] often [rejoiced] in the Triple-Powered One who [belongs to] all [those] who [truly] exist with the [immeasurable] one.

Barbelo Becomes an Aeon (45,15–47,9)

O eternal [light of] the knowledge[7] that has [appeared]![8]
O male virginal [glory]!

---

1. Coptic text: NHC XI,3: 45,1–69,20. Editions: *The Facsimile Edition of the Nag Hammadi Codices: Codices XI, XII and XIII*, 51–75; Wolf-Peter Funk, Madeleine Scopello, Paul-Hubert Poirier, and John D. Turner, *L'Allogène*; Charles W. Hedrick, ed., *Nag Hammadi Codices XI, XII, XIII*, 173–267 (John D. Turner, Orval S. Wintermute, and Antoinette Clark Wire); Karen L. King, *Revelation of the Unknowable God*; Hans-Martin Schenke, Hans-Gebhard Bethge, and Ursula Ulrike Kaiser, eds., *Nag Hammadi Deutsch*, 2.763–87 (Wolf-Peter Funk). 2. The absence of the opening six and a half lines makes it impossible to identify positively the initial speaker or determine the text's self-designation, purpose, or genre. 3. *Allogenes the Stranger* probably began with a lengthy revelation discourse spoken by Youel (see "again" in *Allogenes the Stranger* 50) that continues through p. 49, where its conclusion is marked by Allogenes' remarks to Messos on 49–50. 4. The "perfect individuals" are differentiated, individual forms and souls in the realm of the Self-Generated. 5. Cf. the "great power" mentioned in *Allogenes the Stranger* 50. 6. One may restore either "it" or "you" (singular). 7. Gnosis, here and throughout. 8. In this section Youel describes the step-by-step emanation of the Barbelo Aeon from the Triple-Powered One, who first contracts and then expands into its successive subaeons Kalyptos, Protophanes, and Autogenes (and the Triple-Male Child), who actualize themselves by contemplating their respective predecessors in the aeonic hierarchy. During its emanation, the Barbelo Aeon is considered as an indeterminate—and thus feminine—processing power who becomes successively determined—and thus male—as the Aeon (masculine) of Barbelo (dominantly feminine in Sethian tradition). See *Marsanes* 9.

[O first] aeon from a unique threefold [aeon]!
[O] Triple-Powered One who [truly exists]!

For after it [contracted, it expanded],
and [it spread out] and became complete,
and it was empowered [with] all of them
by knowing [itself in addition to the perfect Invisible Spirit],
and it [became an] aeon.

By knowing [herself] she knew that one, and she became Kalyptos.
[Because] she acts in those whom she knows, she is Protophanes,
a perfect, invisible Intellect, Harmedon.
Empowering the individuals, she is Triple-Male.
Since she is individually [46] . . . . . .[9] they are united.
[Since she] is [their Existence] and she [sees] them all [truly] existing,
[she] contains the divine Self-Generated One.

When she [knew] her Existence and
when she stood at rest [upon] this one,[10]
<she> saw them [all] existing individually just as [they] are.

And when [they] become as he is,
[they shall] see the divine Triple-Male,
the power that is [higher than] God.

[He[11] is the thought] of all those who [are] united;
when he [contemplates them],[12]
he contemplates the great male [perfect] Intellect [Protophanes].

He is their [procession]:
when [he] sees [it, he also sees the truly existing ones],
[since he is the] procession [for those who] are united.

And when [he has seen] these, he has seen Kalyptos.
And when he sees the unity of the hidden ones,
[he] sees the Barbelo Aeon, the unbegotten offspring of [that One].[13]

When one should [see] how it [lives [47] . . . . . .[14] you have heard about the]
abundance of each one of them certainly.
[Now], concerning the Triple-Powered Invisible Spirit One, hear!

The Triple-Powered Invisible Spirit (47,9–49,38)

He [exists] as an invisible One, incomprehensible for them all,
although he contains them all within [himself],

---

9. Five lines missing. 10. Probably the Self-Generated One. 11. The Triple-Male. 12. I.e., those who "exist together" in Protophanes. 13. The Triple-Powered One. 14. Five lines missing; the top line of p. 47 would have continued with the conclusion "one sees the Triple-Powered One."

for [they] all exist because [of him].
He is perfect and [greater] than perfect.
And he is blessed, since he is always one.

And [he] exists [in] them all,
ineffable, unnamable, [a One] who exists throughout them all,
whom—[should] one intelligize him—one [would not desire]
anything that [exists] before him among those [that possess]
    existence,
for [he] is the [source from which they were all emitted].

[He is prior to perfection];
[he was prior to every] divinity, and
prior [to] every blessedness,[15]
since he provides for every power.

And he is an insubstantial substance,
a god over whom there is no divinity,
one who surpasses his own greatness and <beauty>. [48]

. . . . . .[16] [power. It is not impossible for them] to receive a revelation of these things if they unite.[17] Since it is impossible that the individuals comprehend the totality [situated in the] realm that is higher than perfect,[18] they at least share in it through a preconception, not as Being per se; [on the contrary], it is with the hiddenness[19] of Existence that he provides Being, [providing] for [it in] every way, since it is this that [shall] come into being when he contemplates himself.

For he is a [Unity] that subsists as
a [true cause] and source of [Being],
even an immaterial [matter]
and an innumerable [number]
and a formless [form]
and a [shapeless shape]
and [a powerlessness with power]
[and an insubstantial substance]
[and a motionless motion]
[and an inactive activity],
[except that he is a] provider of [provision]
[and] a divinity [of] divinity.[20]

---

15. Perfection, divinity, and blessedness often occur, with slight variations, as a triad of the supreme deity's attributes; *Allogenes the Stranger* 47; 55; 58; 62; 63; cf. *Secret Book of John* II, 3 and *Zostrianos* 15. **16.** Five lines missing. **17.** I.e., unite in Protophanes, the place for intelligences and souls "who exist together" with their objects of thought. **18.** I.e., the "perfect individuals" residing in Autogenes cannot know entities higher than the Barbelo Aeon since they are be-

yond determinate being. **19.** "Hiddenness" suggests Kalyptos, the "Hidden One" in the sense of the initial, not-yet-manifest phase of the Barbelo Aeon's emanation, probably identical with Mentality, the third power of the Triple-Powered One. **20.** These oxymoronic attributes, restored through remaining traces, suggest that the Invisible Spirit and his Triple Power transcend knowable reality.

But if they share,[21] they share in the primary Vitality, even an indivisible activity, a reality[22] of the primary activity of the one that truly exists.[23]

Now a secondary [49] activity . . . . . . , however, is that . . . Male . . . . . . he is endowed with [blessedness] and goodness, because when the Triple-Powered One is contemplated as the traverser[24] of the indeterminateness of the Invisible Spirit [that subsists] in him,

> the indeterminateness causes [him] to revert to [the Invisible Spirit]
> in order that it might know what it is that is within the Spirit and how it
>   exists,
> so that the Triple-Powered One might guarantee the endurance of
>   everything
> by being a determining cause of truly existing things.

For through the Triple-Powered One, knowledge of the Invisible Spirit became available, since he is the one who knows what the Spirit is. But they brought forth nothing [beyond] themselves, neither power nor rank nor glory nor aeon, for they are all eternal.

> He is Vitality and Mentality and Substantiality.[25] So then:[26]
> Substantiality constantly includes its Vitality and Mentality, and
> {Life has} Vitality includes Nonsubstantiality[27] and Mentality;
> Mentality includes Life and Substantiality.

And the three are one, although individually they are three.

Allogenes' Response to Youel: Fear yet Persistence (49,38–50,17)

Now after I heard these things, O my son [50] [Messos, I was] afraid and [I turned toward] the crowd . . . thought . . . , ". . . [empowers those who are able] to

---

21. I.e., share in this kind of indeterminate being. 22. Hypostasis. 23. As in the thought of Plotinus, all productive entities have a secondary activity that proceeds forth from them, which in the case of the Triple-Powered Invisible Spirit is its second "power," an indeterminate "vitality" that becomes defined by turning toward itself in an act of self-contemplation, as in the following paragraph. 24. The Coptic translator possibly rendered an original Greek *diaperainōn* (from *diaperainein*, "delimit," "bring to an end") with *diaperōn* (from *diaperaō*, "traverse," Coptic *refjioor*). Ordinarily determinate being only arises when a processing indeterminateness is delimited and takes on determinateness and knowability by reverting upon its source (here, the Invisible Spirit). 25. Here *pē ete pai pe* (rendering an expected *to on*, "determinate being") is perhaps an attempt to translate *ontotēs* or *ousiotēs* ("substantiality" or potential being), normally rendered in this treatise by *huparxis*. 26. Cf. Proclus *Ele-*

ments of Theology 103: "For in Being (*to on*) there is Life and Intellect, and in Life there is Being (*einai*) and Intellection (*noein*), and in Intellect there is Being (*einai*) and Living (*zēn*)." Although it consists of three distinct powers or phases, the Triple-Powered One is a fundamental unity: any two of its three powers taken in cyclic permutations mutually imply and are included in the third; its three powers are in fact three aspects of a single, quasi-hypostatic entity, "that which is Triple-Powered" or the "Triple-Powered One," distinguishable from both its source, the Invisible Spirit, and its product, the Aeon of Barbelo. 27. One would expect here the term "substantiality" (*ousiotēs*; Proclus uses the infinitive *einai*). If "nonsubstantiality" (*anousiotēs*, Coptic *tm^entatousia*) actually stood in the translator's source, it may have functioned as an attribute or even synonym for "pure existence," as in the phrases "nonsubstantial existence" (53) and "nonsubstantiality and nonbeing [existence]" (55).

know these things [by a] greater revelation, but I was able—even though flesh was upon me—to hear from <you>[28] about these things. And because of the teaching that is in them, the thought within me distinguished things beyond measure from unknowable things. Therefore I fear that my wisdom has become excessive."[29]

Youel's Second Revelation Discourse and Response (50,17–52,12)

Allogenes Has the Power of Intellect (50,17–51,7)

And then again, O my son Messos, the all-glorious one, Youel spoke to me. She appeared [to] me and said:

No one is able to hear these things except the great powers alone. O Allogenes, you have been vested with a great power, that with which the Father of the All vested you before you came to this place,[30] so that

> those things that are difficult to distinguish you might distinguish,
> and those things that are unknown to the multitude you might know,
> and that you might be restored to that which is yours,
> which was already intact and so needs no restoration. [**51**]
> ......[31] [to] you a form [and a revelation].

The Barbelo Aeon: Kalyptos, Protophanes, the Self-Generated, the Triple-Male Child (51,8–52,6)

As for the triple-[powered] Invisible Spirit, outside of him [there is situated] a nondiscriminating, incorporeal, [timeless] knowledge:

> Like all the aeons, so <too>[32] is the Barbelo Aeon:
> it is {also} endowed with the types and forms of the things that truly exist,[33]
> the image of Kalyptos;
>
> and endowed with their intelligent rational principle,[34]
> it bears the male intellect Protophanes as an image,
> and acts within the individuals
> either with craft or with skill or with partial instinct;
>
> endowed with the divine Self-Generated One as an image
> that knows each one of these,[35]

---

28. The text has "from you (masculine)," which would mistakenly imply Messos rather than Youel as Allogenes' interlocutor. 29. Allogenes has acquired at least enough wisdom to see the difference between things unknowable in principle and things beyond the measure of ordinary thought. 30. This great power (of intellectual discrimination) was identified in *Allogenes the Stranger* 45 as intellect. 31. Five lines missing. 32. The Coptic adverb *on* ("too," "also") should

more likely modify [*e*]*fšoop* in line 13 rather than *euntaf* in line 14. 33. The ideal universal forms, the archetypes of everything that has determinate being. 34. I.e., the *logoi* that mold individual souls and forms of individual things that come to reside in the Barbelo Aeon's lowest, self-generated "image," according to the archetypes in Kalyptos. 35. I.e., each of the perfect individuals.

it acts separately and individually,
continually rectifying defects arising from nature;[36]

endowed with the divine Triple-Male
as a preservation of them all with[37] the Invisible Spirit;
he is a rational expression of deliberation,
the perfect child.[38]

And this substantial reality is a [52] . . . .[39]

Allogenes' Response (52,7–12)

. . . . [My soul went slack] and I took flight; I was very disturbed. And [I] turned
to myself and saw the light that [surrounded] me and the good that was in me,
and I became divine.

Youel's Third Revelation Discourse and Response (52,13–55,17)

Difficulties in Comprehending the Triple-Powered One (52,13–53,23)

And the all-glorious one, Youel, contacted[40] me again and empowered me.
She said:

Since your wisdom has become complete and you have known the Good that
is within you, hear concerning the Triple-Powered One, things you shall guard in
great silence and great mystery, because they are not to be spoken to anyone except those who are worthy and able to hear. Nor is it fitting to speak to an uninstructed generation concerning anything higher than perfect.

But you have <this capability to hear> concerning the Triple-Powered One,
who exists in blessedness and goodness, the cause of everything by virtue of encompassing a vast magnitude even though he is <singularly>[41] One. [53] . . . . . .[42]
of [preconception], not as if [through things that exist] within comprehension
[and knowledge] and [understanding].

And that one moved motionlessly in his governance, lest he sink into indeterminateness by means of another act of Mentality. And he entered into himself
and appeared all-encompassing.[43]

---

36. Autogenes imposes these individual souls and
forms upon the contents of the physical, sensible
realms below him, thus playing the role of the Platonic demiurge. 37. Coptic *m^en* ("and," "with") must
here have the force of "in the presence of" (*nahr^en-*);
surely the Triple-Male Child would not save or preserve the Invisible Spirit. 38. Rather than constituting
a separate ontological level or "image" of the Barbelo
Aeon, the Triple-Male Child seems to act as a sort of
bond between its three levels and the Invisible Spirit,
much as a child expresses the unity of its parents. 39.
Six lines missing. 40. Or "approached"; the Coptic
could also be translated "anointed me." 41. The

phrase at the end of the page was probably *h^enou[oua]*,
"unitarily," "singularly." 42. Five lines missing. 43.
Cf. *Allogenes the Stranger* 47. Proclus (*Commentary
on the Timaeus* 2.251,4–5) defines this motionless motion as intellect in distinction to the self-motion of
soul. According to Victorinus *Against Arius* 4.8.26–30:
"Infinitival being is a primary motion that is called immobile motion, the same as interior motion, for when
it actuates itself that it might exist, it is rightly named
interior motion and immobile motion; it is this motion that we call 'it lives' and 'to live.'"

Everything that is higher than perfect is anterior to knowledge. Just as there is no possibility for complete comprehension, so also he is not known by me. And that's the way it is.

Barbelo Becomes an Aeon: An Auditory Metaphor (53,23–35)

On account of the third silence of Mentality and
the undivided secondary activity[44] that appeared in
the first thought—that is, the Barbelo Aeon—and
the undivided semblance of division, even
the Triple-Powered One and the nonsubstantial Existence,
it[45] appeared by means of an activity that is stable and silent.

Youel Praises the Triple-Powered One According to Existence, Vitality, and Mentality (53,35–55,12)

The power uttered a sound in this fashion:[46] "ZZA ZZA ZZA." But when she[47] heard the power and she was filled [**54**] . . . . . .[48]

. . . . You are [great, Deiphan]eus! Solmis, [you are great]!

In accord with the Vitality [that is yours],
[even] the primary activity from which derives Divinity:
You are great, Armedon! You are perfect, Epiphaneus!

And in accord with that activity of yours,
the secondary power, even the Mentality from which derives blessedness:
Autoer, Beritheus, Erigenaor, Orimenios, Aramen,
Alphleges, Elelioupheus, Lalameus, Yetheus, Noetheus!
You are great! He who knows you knows the All!
You are one, you are one, O good one, Aphredon!
You are the aeon of aeons, O perpetually existing one!

Then she praised the entire One, saying,

Lalameus, Noetheus, Senaon,
Asineus, Oriphanios, Mellephaneus,
Elemaoni, Smoun,[49] Optaon!

---

44. I.e., Vitality. 45. "The power" is probably the as-yet-indeterminate feminine phase of Barbelo still identical with the processing vitality of the Triple-Powered One prior to its self-determination as the masculine Aeon of Barbelo. 46. See the similar doxologies in the *Three Steles of Seth* (126) and *Zostrianos* (51–52; 86; 88). 47. "She" is probably Barbelo, who in the process of her emanation is completed not only by her self-vision, but also by her own sound. 48. Five lines missing, which probably contained a phrase such as "In accord with the Existence that is thine from which derives Perfection," which prefaced Youel's first doxology. 49. The Coptic text reads "Elemaoni, Smoun," which should be corrected on the basis of "the Seth prayer" of Papyrus Berolinensis 17207 (ed. Brashear): *el[l]emm[aōn e]issmoun*.

He who is! You are he who is, the aeon of aeons!
O unbegotten one higher than the unbegotten ones, Yatomenos!
It is you alone for whom all the unborn ones were begotten,
O unnamable one! [55]

. . . . . .[50] knowledge.

Allogenes' Response (55,12–17)

[Now after I] heard these things, I [too glorified]
the [perfect] individuals
and the all-perfect ones [who are united],
and the [super-perfect ones[51] who] transcend the [perfect ones].

Youel's Fourth Revelation Discourse and Response
(55,17–32)

The Triple-Powered One's Transcendence of All Being (55,17–30)

[Then the mother of] the glories Youel spoke to me again:

[O Allogenes], you [shall surely] know that
the [Triple-Powered] One exists before
[those that] do not exist,[52]
[those that exist] without [truly] existing,[53]
and those that exist,[54]
[and those that] truly exist.[55]
[And all these] exist [in]
divinity and blessedness and existence,
even as nonsubstantiality and nonbeing [existence].

Allogenes' Response (55,31–32)

[And then I] prayed that [the revelation] might happen to me.

---

50. Ten lines missing. 51. Restoring *houepjōk* (Greek *hupertelioi*), the "super-perfect ones" (in Kalyptos) as a superlative to both the "perfect (*teleioi*) ones" (in Autogenes) and the "all-perfect (*pantelioi*) ones" (in Protophanes); alternatively one might restore "all-perfect" and translate: "the all-perfect ones [who are united], even the [all-perfect ones who] transcend the [perfect ones]." 52. Probably mere "bodies." 53. Probably the individual souls in the Self-Generated. 54. Probably those who are "unified" in Protophanes. 55. Probably the "authentic existents" in Kalyptos. Cf.

Zostrianos 117 for a similar use of the categories of being and nonbeing developed by Plato (*Sophist* 240b7.12; 254d1; *Parmenides* 162a3) and Aristotle (*On the Heavens* 282a4–b7). Cf. *Allogenes the Stranger* 55 and the untitled text of the Bruce Codex 237. According to Proclus *Commentary on the Timaeus* 1.233,1–4: "Certain of the ancients call the noetic realm 'truly existent,' the psychical 'not truly existent,' the perceptible 'not truly nonexistent,' and the material 'truly nonexistent.'"

Youel's Fifth Revelation Discourse and Response
(55,33–58,6)

The Revelation Opens (55,33–56,21)

[And then the] all-[glorious] One, Youel, said to me, While the [Triple]-Male is a self-begotten entity insofar as he is] substantial, the [Triple-Powered One] ... is [an insubstantiality] [**56**] ......[56] those who dwell [in association] with the [generation of those] who [truly] exist. The self-begotten ones dwell with the [Triple-Male].

If you [seek with perfect] seeking, [then] you shall know the [good that is] in you; then [you shall know yourself] as well, as one who [derives from] the God who truly [preexists].

The Advent of the Luminaries: The Problem of Positive Knowledge (56,21–57,24)

[And after a hundred] years there shall [come to you] a revelation [of that One] by means of [Salamex] and Semen [and Arme,[57] the] luminaries of the Barbelo Aeon.

And [she said to me], It is appropriate [that you know it[58]] at first, so as [not to forfeit your] kind. [And when you succeed], then < . . . >. When [you receive] a conception [of that One, then] you [are filled with] the Logos[59] [to completion]. And then [you become divine] and [you become perfect. You receive] them [**57**] ......[60] the seeking ...... the Existence ....

If it [apprehends] anything, it is [apprehended by] that One and by that which is comprehended, which amounts to the same thing.

And then that which comprehends and knows becomes greater
than that which is comprehended and known.
But if it descends to its nature, it is less,
for the incorporeal natures have not associated with any magnitude,
having the property of being both everywhere and nowhere,
since they are greater than every maximum and less than every minimum.

Allogenes' Response and Youel's Departure (57,24–58,7)

Now after the all-glorious one, Youel, said these things, she separated from me and left me. But I did not despair of the words I had heard. I prepared myself with them and deliberated with myself for a hundred years. And I rejoiced greatly that I was in such a great light and such a blessed path, since all those whom I was wor-

---

56. Nine lines missing. **57.** The name of the third luminary, *Armē*, is restored from *Zostrianos* 62 and 63. **58.** Perhaps the Barbelo Aeon. The restoration of lines 27–31 is extremely conjectural. **59.** Logos in the sense of discursive reason. **60.** Four lines missing.

thy to see as well as those whom I was worthy to hear were things fitting for the great powers alone. [58] . . . . . .[61] [of God].

One Hundred Years Later, Allogenes' Ascent and the Final Revelation: The Barbelo Aeon (58,7–26)

[When the completion of] the one hundred years [approached], there [came upon] me a blessedness of the eternal hope full of auspiciousness. I saw:[62]

> the good divine Self-Generated One;
> and the savior who is the perfect Triple-Male Child;
> and his goodness, the perfect intellect Protophanes-Harmedon;
> and the blessedness of the Kalyptos;
> and the pre-principle of the blessedness, the Barbelo Aeon full of Divinity;
> and the pre-principle of the unoriginate one, the Triple-Powered Invisible Spirit,
> the totality that is more than perfect.

Allogenes Is Caught Up to a Pure Place (58,26–59,1)

When I was seized by the eternal light, by the garment that was upon me, and was taken up to a pure place whose likeness cannot be revealed in the world, then by means of a great blessedness[63] I saw all those about whom I had heard. I praised them all and [59] [stood at rest] upon my knowledge.

The Revelation of the Powers of the Luminaries (59,2–7)

[I] turned to the knowledge [of] the totalities, the Barbelo Aeon, and by means of the luminaries of the male virginal Barbelo I saw [multiple] powers telling [me]:

Instructions on Ascending Through the Triple-Powered One (59,7–60,12)

O great power![64] O name that has come to be in the world! O Allogenes, behold your blessedness,[65] how silently it abides, by which you know your proper self, and, seeking yourself, ascend[66] to the Vitality that you will see moving.

---

61. Five lines missing. 62. Allogenes now receives a vision of each of the beings described by Youel in the reverse of the sequence of their original emanation. The ambiguity of coordinating conjunctions makes it unclear whether this list contain five or six entities (as is the case also in *Allogenes the Stranger* 45–46). 63. Blessedness refers both to Allogenes' self-knowledge of his innate divinity and to his receipt of Mentality, the third of the Triple-Powered One's three powers (which

Zostrianos generally calls Blessedness). 64. Coptic *tinac^emcom* should be read as "O great power" rather than "I will get power." Having ascended to the Barbelo Aeon, Allogenes now "stands" at the stable level of Mentality, the third of the Triple-Powered One's three powers. Ascent to the level of Vitality, its second (processing) power, entails a loss of stability that can be regained only by either descending back to Mentality or ascending on to its highest power, Existence,

And even if you cannot stand, fear not. But if you wish to stand, ascend to the Existence, and you will find it standing and still after the likeness of the one who is truly still and embraces all these silently and inactively.

And should you experience a revelation of that one by means of a primary revelation of the Unknowable One—should you know him, you must be incognizant! And if you become afraid in that place, retreat because of those activities.[67] And should you become complete in that place, stay still! And—as has been impressed[68] upon you—be further aware [60] [that] it's like this with [everyone], just as in your case!

And [do not] further dissipate, [so that] you may be able to stand, and do not desire to be active, [lest] in any way you fall away [from] the inactivity [in you] of the Unknowable One. Do not know him, for it is impossible; but if by means of an enlightened thought you should know him, stay incognizant of him!

Allogenes' Response: The Ascent Through the Three Powers (60,13–61,22)

While I was listening to these things as those there spoke them, there was within me a stillness of silence, and I heard the blessedness whereby I knew <my>[69] proper self.

Then I ascended to the Vitality as I sought it. And I mutually entered it and stood, not firmly but quietly. And I saw an eternal, intellectual, undivided motion, all-powerful, formless, unlimited by limitation.

And when I wanted to stand firmly, I ascended to the Existence, which I found standing and at rest, resembling and similar to that which[70] was covering me. By means of a revelation of the indivisible and the stable I was filled with revelation.

By means of a primary revelation[71] [61] of the Unknowable One, [as though] incognizant of him, I [knew] him and was empowered by him. Having been permanently strengthened, I knew that [which] exists in me, even the Triple-Powered One and the revelation of his own incomprehensibility.

And by means of a primary revelation of the universally prime Unknowable One—the God who is beyond perfection—I saw him and the Triple-Powered One that exists in them all. I was seeking the ineffable and unknowable God of whom—should one know him—one would be completely incognizant, the one

---

which is identical with the supreme Unknowable One. At this point Allogenes will transcend discursive revelation and enter the domain of "primary revelation," wherein all active discursive thought must be abandoned in favor of a quiescent, passive, and incognizant "learned ignorance." **65.** See note 63. **66.** Here *anakhōrein* means "ascend" rather than "withdraw backward" as on p. 59. Cf. Plotinus *Ennead* III, 8 [30] 9,29–32: "Intellect must first withdraw, so to speak, backward, and somehow give itself up to what lies behind it (for it faces in both directions); and there, if it

wishes to see that First Principle, it must not be altogether intellect." **67.** Any intentional activity would disrupt Allogenes' stability. **68.** Lit., "according to the stamp (*tupos*) that is in you." **69.** The text's erroneous "according to itself (feminine)," should be emended to "according to my own self." **70.** I.e., the standing and resting achieved by Allogenes. **71.** The Coptic probably translates Greek *prophaneia* in the sense of a precognitive, nondiscursive anticipation or prefiguration, which can only be expressed in negative terms: one "knows" the supreme One by knowing what it is not.

who mediates the Triple-Powered One, the one who subsists in stillness and silence and is unknowable.

The Powers of the Luminaries: Negative Theology
(61,22–64,36)

And when I was confirmed in these matters, the powers of the luminaries said to me, Cease dissipating the inactivity that exists in you by further inquiry after incomprehensible matters; instead, hear about him insofar as it is possible by means of a primary revelation and a revelation:

> Now he is an entity insofar as he exists, in that
> he either exists and becomes, or {acts} <lives> or knows,
> although he {lives} <acts> without Mind or Life or Existence
> —or Nonexistence—incomprehensibly.[72] [62]
>
> And although he is an entity along with its own attributes,
> he is not left over in any way,
> as if he yields something that can be assayed or purified [or]
> as if he receives or gives.
>
> Nor is he diminished[73] in any way,
> [whether] by his own desire
> or whether by giving or receiving through another.
>
> Neither does he have any desire, whether his own
> or that which would have been added by something else.
>
> But neither does he produce anything by himself
> lest he become diminished in some other way.
>
> Therefore, he requires neither Mind nor Life
> nor indeed anything at all.

---

72. In view of the clauses preceded by *ē* ("or," but often used in introducing questions), lines on *Allogenes the Stranger* 61 may also be translated interrogatively: "Now does he exist as something that exists, or is he something that is or will become, or does he act or know or live, even though he incomprehensibly has no mind or existence or nonexistence?" Cf. Victorinus *Against Arius* 4.23,18–31: "We are thus obliged to say that his being, living and thinking are incomprehensi-

ble, and what is more, that his being, living and thinking even seem not to exist, since he is beyond all things. That is why one says that he is *anuparktos, anousios, anous, azōn*, without existence, without substance, without thought, without life, not somehow by privation, but by transcendence." 73. Here and in seven other occurrences on pp. 62, 63, and 67, the unattested Coptic *šojᵉh* is conjectured to mean "diminish."

He is superior to the totality in his privation[74] and unknowability—which is nonbeing Existence—although he is endowed with silence and stillness lest he be diminished by the undiminishable.

He is neither Divinity nor Blessedness nor Perfection.[75]
Rather he is an unknowable entity, not an attribute.
Rather he is something else superior to Blessedness and Divinity and
    Perfection,
for he is not perfect, but he is another thing [63] that is superior.

He is neither boundless
nor is he bounded by another.
Rather he is something superior.

He is neither corporeal nor incorporeal,
neither great [nor] small,
neither a quantity nor a [<quality>].[76]

Nor is he something that exists that one can know;
rather he is something else that is superior that one cannot know.

Even if primary revelation and self-knowledge characterize him,
it is he alone who knows himself.

Since he is not among existing things,
he is something else superior to superlative,
even in comparison to what is
and is not proper to him.

He neither participates in eternity
nor does he participate in time,
nor does he receive anything from anything else.

---

74. Privation in the sense of lacking all determinate attributes. 75. On the following section, see the parallel passage in *Secret Book of John* II, 3 (translated here in such a way as to show the close similarities): "[He] is [the immeasurable light], pure, holy, [spotless]. He is ineffable, [perfect in in]corruptibility. He is not in [perfection or in] blessedness [or in] divinity, [but rather he is far superior. He is] neither corporeal [nor incorporeal], neither great, [nor] small. [There is no] way to say '[What is his quantity'? or 'What is his quality]?' for it is not possible [for anyone to contemplate him]. He is not anything among [existing things, but rather he is] far superior—not 'superior' in the comparative sense, but rather in the absolute sense. He [participates neither] in eternity nor in time. For one

who [participates in eternity] was previously anticipated. He [was not limited] by time, [since] he receives nothing, [for it would be something received] on loan. For what is prior does not [lack] so as to receive." See also Michael Waldstein and Frederik Wisse, *Apocryphon of John*, 184–87. These notions are probably drawn from the first hypothesis of Plato's *Parmenides* (137C–142A6). In terms peculiar to *Allogenes the Stranger*, the One is neither diminishable, nor diminishing, nor undiminishable. 76. The Coptic reads "neither a number (ēpe, here rendered as "quantity") nor a creation (tamio)"; the translator probably read an original Greek *poion* ("quality") as if it were Greek *poiēton*, "creature."

He is neither diminishable,
nor diminishing,
nor undiminishable.

But he is self-comprehension,
like something so unknowable
that he exceeds those that excel in unknowability.

Even if he is endowed with blessedness and perfection and silence,
he is not the Blessed One, nor is he Perfection or Stillness.
But he is something existing[77] that one cannot [64] [know]
and that is at rest.

Rather they are completely unknowable aspects of him,
while he is much superior in beauty than all good things.
And in this way he is universally unknowable in every respect,
and it is through them all that he is in them all.

Not only is he the unknowable knowledge that is proper to him,
he is also united with the ignorance that sees him.[78]

<Whether one sees>[79] in what way he is unknowable, or sees him as he is in every respect, or would say that he is something like knowledge, he has acted impiously against him, being liable to judgment because he did not know God. He will not be judged by that One, who is neither concerned for anything nor has any desire, but he is judged by himself because he has not found the truly existing origin. He was blind apart from the quiescent source of revelation, the actualization deriving from the Triple-Power of the first thought of the Invisible Spirit.

The Powers of the Luminaries: Positive Theology (64,37–67,20)

This one[80] thus exists from [65] . . . . . .[81] something . . . [established on . . . . It was with] beauty and [a dawning] of stillness and silence and tranquility and unfathomable magnitude that he appeared.

He needed neither time nor <did he participate> in eternity.
Rather he is self-derived, unfathomably unfathomable.
He does not act—not even upon himself—so as to become still.

---

77. Funk suggests emending *efšoop*, "existing," to *efsotᵉp*, "superior." 78. Since the attributes of the Unknowable One are themselves unknowable, the Unknowable One basically is its own unknowable (self-)knowledge and thus knows itself by not knowing itself, which means that anyone who would know it must do so by not knowing it. 79. This or something similar has been omitted from the beginning of this remonstration. 80. In this section the discourse uses a mixture of negative and affirmative predications. 81. Fourteen lines missing.

He is not an Existence lest he be in want.
Spatially he is corporeal, while properly[82] he is incorporeal.
He has nonbeing Existence.
He exists for all of them unto himself without any desire.

Rather he is a maximum of magnitude. And he transcends his stillness in order that [66] . . . . . .[83] [the In]visible [Spirit].

[Although] he [empowered them all],
[they do not] concern themselves with that One at all,
nor is he empowered if one should participate in him.

In accordance with his immobile unity, nothing acts on him.
For he is unknowable; he is a breathless place of the boundlessness.

Since he is boundless and powerless and nonexistent,
he was not providing Being.
Rather he contains all of these in himself,
being at rest and standing.

From the One who constantly stands, there appeared an eternal Life,[84] the Invisible and Triple-Powered Spirit, the one that is in all existing things and surrounds them all while transcending them all. A shadow [67] . . . . . .[85] he [was filled with power. And] he stood before [them], empowering them all, and he filled them all.

Concerning all these matters, you have heard certainly. Do not seek anything more, but go. We do not know whether the Unknowable One has angels or gods, or whether the One who is at rest contains anything within himself except that very stillness. For he < . . . >, lest he be diminished. It is not appropriate to dissipate further through repeated seeking. It was appropriate that <you alone>[86] know and that they[87] speak with another. Instead, you will lead them . . . . [68]

Conclusion: Instructions for Writing the Book (68,15–25)

. . . . . .[88] and he[89] said to me, "Write down [the things] that I shall [tell] you and of which I shall remind you for those who will be worthy after you. And you shall

---

82. The Coptic "in a house" must be an attempt to translate Greek *oikeiōs*, "properly." 83. Fifteen lines missing. 84. The discourse concludes with the kind of affirmative language found in the revelations of Youel and seems to distinguish the supreme One from the Invisible Spirit, here identified not only as Triple-Powered, but also as an eternal Life. 85. Sixteen lines missing. 86. Emending the Coptic "I alone" to "you alone." 87. "They" are presumably the worthy whom Allogenes is to lead, who must speak with someone, perhaps his disciple Messos, other than Allogenes, who nevertheless will somehow guide them. 88. Fifteen lines missing. 89. "He" is an unidentified masculine speaker, perhaps one of the three powers of the luminaries.

leave this book upon a mountain and you shall adjure the guardian, 'Come, Dreadful One!' "[90] And when he said these things, he separated from me.

Allogenes Writes the Book and Commissions Messos (68,25–69,16)

But I was full of joy, and I wrote this book. I was commissioned, my son Messos, to disclose to you the matters that were proclaimed before me. And I initially[91] received them in great silence and I settled into preparing myself.[92]

These are the things that were disclosed to me, O my [son [69] Messos], ...[93] [proclaim them, O my] son Messos.

Subtitle and Title (69,16–20)

The Seal[94] of All the Books [of] Allogenes.

Allogenes the Stranger

---

90. For the deposition and guarding of revelations, see *Secret Book of John* II, 31 (with a curse); *Holy Book of the Great Invisible Spirit* III, 68 (also on a mountain), and *Discourse on the Eighth and Ninth* 61–63. By contrast Zostrianos leaves the heavenly tablets he has inscribed in the atmospheric realm (*Zostrianos* 129–30). The association of written heavenly revelations (1 *Enoch* 81, 93, 106) and mountains seems to go back to Moses on Sinai; cf. *Jubilees* 1:4–5:26 and Josephus *Jewish Antiquities* 1.70. 91. Or perhaps "of first importance." 92. Perhaps also "I came to stand according to my proper self as I readied myself." 93. Fifteen lines missing. 94. In view of Epiphanius's testimony concerning multiple "books of Allogenes," the term "seal" here must have the sense of the final and concluding item in a series of such works.

HYPSIPHRONE

NHC XI,4

Introduced by John D. Turner
Translated by Marvin Meyer

*H*ypsiphrone, which means "high-minded one" or perhaps "arrogant one," is the fourth and last treatise of Nag Hammadi Codex XI (69,23–72,35). It presently consists of four large and two or three small fragments containing the lower portions of the inner and outer margins of two or three papyrus leaves, which must have originally contained the entirety of this short treatise. It is written in the same script as the much longer and better preserved treatise preceding it in the codex, *Allogenes the Stranger,* although there is no discernible further relationship between these two treatises. Unlike the other treatises of Codex XI, it is written in a standard Sahidic Coptic dialect. Its date can be fixed only at some point prior to a *terminus ad quem* of around 350 CE, the time of the burial of Codex XI along with the other Nag Hammadi codices, and its authorship is indeterminate. Although the conclusion of the treatise is not extant, it is possible that it bore the superscript title "Hypsiph[rone]," the remainder of the title being restored from other occurrences of this name within the treatise. Fragment 2 and probably fragment 1 of plates 81 and 82 of *The Facsimile Edition of the Nag Hammadi Codices: Codices XI, XII, and XIII* also belong to the text of Hypsiphrone (and—assuming a final inserted leaf without conjugate at the beginning of the codex—perhaps even fragment 4), but cannot be placed accurately, given the present state of the text.

Apart from the poor condition of the treatise, even its cryptic title affords little insight into its content. The incipit states, "The book [concerning the things] seen [by Hypsi]phrone when they were [revealed] in the place of [her] virginity." Although the work portrays a plurality of interlocutors speaking with one another in the first and second person (beside the figure of Phainops there are "brothers" who appear in 69,28–31 and perhaps another male figure in 72,21–29), it ought not to be classified as a dialogue. It is rather the record of a speech of Hypsiphrone narrating "what Hypsiphrone saw" during her experiences in the world beyond the "place of her virginity." One may conjecture that Hypsiphrone represents a somewhat haughty or even arrogant female who abandons her dwelling in the "place of her virginity," perhaps a realm where there are no distinctions of gender, to explore the earthly realms beyond it. There she encounters Phainops, who "breathes into her [wellspring of] blood," a term that may signify a vagina, but which in the medical literature of the day most often refers to the heart as source of blood. Although she is filled with fear from this apparently aggressive behavior, she does not accuse him of taking advantage of her, but responds to his invitation to follow him and hear his account about this fiery fount of blood.

The personal name Hypsiphrone ("haughty, high-minded"), which is not otherwise attested, may have to do with a figure associated with the attributes of Eleleth (called Phronesis, "sagacity," in *Nature of the Rulers* 93,8), one of the traditional Sethian Four Luminaries, whose name might be derived from an Aramaic pun on the Semitic roots ʿalh ("go up, elevate") and ʿall ("go, bring about") to yield a form like ʿaliuta ("perversity") or ʾel-ʿalītā ("god of the height"), which might be rendered by Greek *hupsiphronē*. In Gnostic literature, both the figure of Sophia and Eleleth (only in *Three Forms of First Thought* and the *Holy Book of the Great Invisible Spirit*) inappropriately busy themselves with the earthly realm beyond their assigned place in the divine world.

The only other named figure in *Hypsiphrone* is Phainops (*phainōps*, "he of the bright eye, or visage, or appearance)," whose more common form *phainops* is found as an astral epithet in astrological texts from the fourth century onward, perhaps suggesting a similar affiliation for terms like staying in or moving out of one's "house" of virginity. He is named by Hypsiphrone as one who apparently presides over a "wellspring" or "fount" (*pēgē*) of blood into which he breathes and that seems to produce a fiery effect, perhaps a metaphor for sexual passion. Since in *Leviticus* 20:18 the phrase "fount of blood" refers to the genitalia of a menstruating woman and in *Mark* 5:29 to those of a hemorrhaging woman, the reference to breathing into her fount or wellspring of blood seems a bit unusual, perhaps referring to an act of cunnilingus. Nevertheless, in the end, Phainops is characterized as a benign figure who "has not gone astray" or acted aggressively with Hypsiphrone.

BIBLIOGRAPHY

Wolf-Peter Funk and Paul-Hubert Poirier, *Concordance des textes de Nag Hammadi: Les Codices XIb, XII, XIII*; Charles W. Hedrick, ed., *Nag Hammadi Codices XI, XII, XIII*, 269–80 (John D. Turner); Hans-Martin Schenke, Hans-Gebhard Bethge, and Ursula Ulrike Kaiser, eds., *Nag Hammadi Deutsch*, 2.789–93 (Wolf-Peter Funk); John D. Turner, "Hypsiphrone."

Hypsiphrone[1]

Hypsiph[rone]

The book [concerning the things] seen [by Hypsi]phrone[2] when they were [revealed] in the place of [her] virginity.

[She is listening] to her brothers . . . Phainops[3] and S. . . ,[4] and they are speaking [together] in a [mystery].

I[5] was [first in] rank [**70**] . . . . . .[6] I left [the place] of my [virginity] and went out to the [world]. Those who abide in the [place] of my virginity told me [about] these things. I went out[7] to [the world], and they said to [me,[8] "Once again] Hypsiphrone has [departed] from the place [of her] virginity."

Then Phain[ops, who] breathes into her [wellspring of] blood, heard this and stretched [out] for her.[9] He said, [I am Phai]n[o]ps . . . . [**71**]

. . . . . .[10] go astray . . . desire . . . of [people] remaining . . . or that I may see a person, one in the likeness of blood, or . . . fire, and a . . . in his hands. Then I [said] to him, "Ph[ainops] has not come upon me; he has not gone astray."

[I] saw a person [**72**] . . . . . .[11] For what he said . . . Phainops . . . . I saw him, and [he said] to me, "Hypsiphrone, [why do you stay] away from me? Follow [me] and I shall tell [you about these things]."

I followed [him], for [I] was [very] fearful. He told [me] about a wellspring of blood that is revealed by burning . . . he spoke[12] . . . .[13]

---

1. Coptic text: NHC XI,4: 69,21–72,33. Editions: *The Facsimile Edition of the Nag Hammadi Codices: Codices XI, XII, XIII*, 75–78; Charles W. Hedrick, ed., *Nag Hammadi Codices XI, XII, XIII*, 269–79 (John D. Turner); Hans-Martin Schenke, Hans-Gebhard Bethge, and Ursula Ulrike Kaiser, eds., *Nag Hammadi Deutsch*, 2.789–93 (Wolf-Peter Funk). 2. The name Hypsiphrone is derived from Greek and means "woman of high mind" or perhaps "woman of arrogance" or "haughty woman." 3. The name Phainops is derived from Greek and means "bright-eyed one" or the like. 4. This lacuna may include another name, but the reading is uncertain. 5. Hypsiphrone is speaking. 6. About fifteen lines missing or untranslatable. 7. Perhaps "I went down." 8. The restoration of "[me]" is tentative. 9. Here and below the references seem to be sexual. 10. About twenty-two lines missing or untranslatable. 11. About twenty-four lines missing or untranslatable. 12. Perhaps restore to read "he spoke [to me]." 13. About eight lines missing or untranslatable.

THE SENTENCES OF SEXTUS

NHC XII,1

Introduced by Paul-Hubert Poirier
Translated by Marvin Meyer

The *Sentences of Sextus* in Codex XII is a partially preserved Coptic version of a work previously known in its entirety and entitled in Greek *Sextou gnōmai*, the *Sentences of Sextus*. The Greek text is attested by two complete manuscripts and an incomplete Greek papyrus. The *Sentences* enjoyed wide circulation in ancient and medieval Christianity, in the East as well as the West. Formally, they present themselves as a gnomology (a collection of sentences, or aphorisms, put into the mouth of an unnamed spiritual master addressing an undesignated audience) about proper religious and moral behavior. As demonstrated by the Greek manuscripts and some of the ancient translations, the collection contains a total of 610 sentences. The first 451 of these were rendered into Latin at the end of the fourth century by Rufinus of Aquileia; it may therefore be assumed that, in an earlier form, the *Sentences* consisted of only 451 pieces, and that the collection was augmented later.

The collection is ascribed to a certain Sextus. The earliest mention of this ascription is made by the Alexandrian Christian writer Origen (d. 254), who refers to the *Sentences* on five occasions. In his *Commentary on the Gospel According to Matthew* (15.3), he introduces sentences 13 and 273 as written by Sextus. On another occasion (*Commentary on Ezekiel* 1.11), he attributes sentence 352, without naming Sextus, to a "wise and faithful man." Hence, it would appear that Origen not only knew of the attribution of the *Sentences* to Sextus, but that he was convinced that this Sextus was a "faithful" man—that is, a Christian. Nevertheless, it seems that the real identity of the author of the aphorisms was no clearer for ancient readers than it is for us today. Indeed, at least since the fourth century, the given author of the *Sentences of Sextus* was believed to be the Roman Pope Sixtus II (d. 258). Rufinus and the Syriac versions of the *Sentences* echo this identification. Although not impossible, authorship by the Roman bishop remains highly improbable. It was ironically criticized by Jerome and is generally rejected by modern scholarship.

Many of the sentences show a close relationship with other gnomic collections, particularly the collection attributed to Clitarchus and the so-called *Pythagorean Sentences*. From a comparison of the maxims common to Sextus, Clitarchus, and the "Pythagoreans," it appears that many of them having a definite Christian flavor in Sextus lack this character in the other compilations. Therefore, either these sentences were originally Christian and were secondarily de-Christianized, or, on the contrary, they were pagan from the beginning and later underwent a Christian rewriting. A careful examination of the common stock of the three collections tends to confirm the second hypothesis. As Henry Chadwick puts it, "A Christian compiler has edited, carefully revised and modified a previous pagan collection (or collections)."[1] This view gains plausibility when one considers that about 60 aphorisms from the *Sentences of Sextus* are quoted or alluded to by the Neoplatonic philosopher Porphyry in his *Letter to Marcella* (written about 300 CE), along with many others taken from Clitarchus and the Pythagorean collection. In *Sentences of Sextus* 49, where the text reads, "God needs nothing; the faithful man (*pistos*) needs only God," Porphyry has "wise" (*sophos*) instead of "faithful." This example shows that Porphyry used either a non-Christian version of the *Sentences* or the collection that served as the basis for the Christianized version of the *Sentences*. The latter is described by Chadwick as a work of great skill and clear design, the product of a "single mind," who lived around 180–210 CE.[2]

Although it is established that Origen read a Christianized version of the *Sentences of Sextus*, nothing precise can be inferred from the five aphorisms he quotes (13, 22, 109, 273, and 352) about the extent of the collection he had at hand. But the situation is quite different for the 127 sentences preserved in the surviving pages of Codex XII: there is such agreement in sequence, content, and wording between the Coptic, the Greek, and the Latin of Rufinus that we may conclude that the (Greek) source of the Coptic translation is identical with the text known from the end of the fourth century until now. The same cannot be said of the translations of the *Sentences of Sextus* into Syriac, Armenian, Georgian, and Ethiopic: they are rearrangements, or excerpts, of the original collection, often with significant differences in phraseology and a stronger Christian emphasis.

The *Sentences of Sextus* is a product of the philosophical milieu of the Platonic tradition of the second and third centuries, labeled by scholars as Middle Platonism and Neoplatonism. The *Sentences* develops a doctrine of God and humanity based on several passages of Plato. These texts were widely read and commented upon in the first centuries CE in both pagan and Christian circles. They express the ideas that humans partake in divinity through their mind or intelligence; that it is possible to know God, but difficult if not impossible to express God's being by means of human language; and that the soul is the most important component of humanity. The relevant Platonic passages are *Theaetetus* 176ab, *Timaeus* 28c, *First Alcibiades* 133c, and *First Alcibiades* 130c. These

---

1. Henry Chadwick, *The Sentences of Sextus*, 138.
2. Chadwick, *Sentences of Sextus*, 159–60.

Platonic formulations were very positively received by the early Christian thinkers, mainly because of their accord with the biblical doctrine of the creation of humankind "according to the image and likeness" of God (*Genesis* 1:26–27). Furthermore, their invitation to neglect the material and bodily world in favor of the soul coincided with the ascetic tendency that the first Christians shared with many of their pagan contemporaries.

Since the aphorisms of the *Sentences of Sextus* were largely a development of, and a commentary upon, the Platonic propositions cited above, and also because of the concise and attractive expression they gave to them, they rapidly became the favorite reading material of many educated Christians. For the same reason, they were appropriated by the Gnostics who were the owners and readers of the Nag Hammadi texts.

The Coptic translation of the *Sentences of Sextus* is estimated to have covered thirty-nine pages of Nag Hammadi Codex XII, but of this total only ten have survived, in a very fragmentary condition. Pages 15–16 contain sentences 157–80, while pages 27–34 have sentences 307–97. The translation was made in the Sahidic dialect of the Coptic language; it is a faithful, sometimes slavish, but on the whole intelligent rendering of the Greek original, without any discernable doctrinal bias. This means that the Coptic translator did not slant the Greek *Sentences* in a Gnostic direction. When the Coptic translation differs from the Greek manuscripts, a comparison with other ancient translations, namely, the Latin and the Syriac, shows that the difference is not due to the initiative of the Coptic translator, but rather to his Greek model being different from the two Byzantine manuscripts known to us.

The *Sentences of Sextus* must have been composed or compiled at the beginning of the third century CE by an unknown author familiar with Greek philosophy; it was soon ascribed to a certain Sextus, later identified with Pope Sixtus II. Its exact provenance cannot be determined with certainty, but the philosophical milieu it presupposes and the fact that it was known to Origen suggest Alexandria as a likely place of composition. Of course, the Coptic translation is of (Upper) Egyptian provenance, and it is to be dated no later than the second quarter of the fourth century.

Portions of six pages from another edition of the *Gospel of Truth* survive among the fragments of Codex XII, along with two additional fragments (only one of which includes any significant amount of Coptic text) that may derive from another tractate. The Coptic that can be deciphered in the additional fragments seems to communicate ethical and religious teaching, and the lines include references to what "I" and "we" do in contrast to those ("a crowd"?) who speak and live in a wicked manner. "They" may be associated with error and ignorance, as opposed to righteousness, and mention is made of God, called "my Father" (by Jesus?). There is further comment about a philosopher or philosophers, and the world, in the few lines that can be read.[3]

---

3. See Frederik Wisse, in Charles W. Hedrick, ed., *Nag Hammadi Codices XI, XII, XIII*, 329–55.

BIBLIOGRAPHY

Henry Chadwick, *The Sentences of Sextus*; Richard A. Edwards and Robert A. Wild, *The Sentences of Sextus*; Charles W. Hedrick, ed., *Nag Hammadi Codices XI, XII, XIII*, 295–355 (Frederik Wisse); Paul-Hubert Poirier, *Les Sentences de Sextus*; Hans-Martin Schenke, Hans-Gebhard Bethge, and Ursula Ulrike Kaiser, eds., *Nag Hammadi Deutsch*, 2.795–806 (Uwe-Karsten Plisch and Hans-Martin Schenke).

The Sentences of Sextus[1]

(157)   . . .[2] is [a sign] of ignorance.

(158, 159) [Love] truth, and [treat] falsehood like poison.

(160)   [Let] the right moment come before your words.

(161, 162) [Speak] when you should not [remain silent], and then, [when] it is appropriate, [speak of] what you know.

(163a)   An inopportune [word exposes] an evil heart.

(163b)   [When you] should act, don't [say a] word.

(164a)   Do not be inclined [to speak] first when in the company of [a group of people].

(164b)   [It is] a skill [to speak] and also a skill [to remain silent].

(165a)   It is [better] for you to be overcome [speaking the truth] than to overcome [through deceit].

(165b)   [One] who overcomes through [deceit is overcome] by truth.

(165c)   [False words expose] evil people.

(165d)   [Only in] a great [crisis is] a lie [necessary].

(165e)   [There are times] when you [sin] by telling [the truth] and [you do not sin] when [you tell a lie].

(165f)   Do not deceive [anyone, especially] someone who needs [advice].

(165g)   [If you wait to speak] after [many other people speak, you will see more clearly] what is profitable.

(166)   That person is [faithful] who takes the lead in all [that is good]. [16]

(167)   Wisdom guides [the soul] to the place of [God].

(168)   [There is no one] of the household of [truth except] wisdom.

(169)   A [believing] nature cannot [be enamored of] lying.

(170)   A fearful [and enslaved] nature cannot share in faith.

(171a)   When you are [faithful], saying what is right [is no greater than] listening.

(171b)   When you [are] with believers, be more inclined [to listen than] to speak.

---

1. Coptic text: NHC XII,1: 15,1–34,28 (pp. 17–26 are missing). Editions: *The Facsimile Edition of the Nag Hammadi Codices: Codices XI, XII, and XIII*, 85–94; Charles W. Hedrick, ed., *Nag Hammadi Codices XI, XII, XIII*, 295–327 (Frederik Wisse); Paul-Hubert Poirier, *Les Sentences de Sextus*; Hans-Martin Schenke, Hans-Gebhard Bethge, and Ursula Ulrike Kaiser, eds., *Nag Hammadi Deutsch*, 2.795–806 (Uwe-Karsten Plisch and Hans-Martin Schenke). Some of the restorations and emendations of the Coptic text come from Paul-Hubert Poirier. The *Sentences of Sextus* is also known in Greek, Latin, Syriac, Armenian, and Georgian versions. 2. Here the Greek version has *makrologia*, "Using too many words."

(172) A [hedonist] is good [for nothing].

(173) Only if you have no [sin may you speak] of whatever is from [God].

(174) The sins of the [ignorant are] the shame of [their teachers].

(175) Those because of whom [God's name] is blasphemed [are dead] in the sight of God.

(176) [A wise person] is one who does what is good, after God.

(177) [Let your life] confirm [your words before those who] hear.

(178) Do not even think of [doing] what [you should not do].

(179) [Do not do what you do not] want to [happen to you].

(180) [What is] shameful [to do is also shameful] . . . .³ [27]

(307, 308) [A wise person stands up for God] before others, and [God] thinks more of a wise person than God's⁴ own [works].

(309) [After] God, no one is as free as a wise person.

(310) [Everything] God has a wise person has.

(311, 312) A wise person shares in God's [kingdom]; an evil person does not want God's providence to come to pass.

(313) An evil soul flees from God.

(314) Everything bad is God's foe.

(315) Say in your heart that what is within you that thinks is what is human.

(316) Where your thought is your goodness is.

(317) Do not seek goodness in flesh.

(318) What does [not] harm the soul does not harm humankind.

(319) After God, honor a [wise] person, [since this one] is a servant [of God].

(320) [To consider] the body of your [soul] to be a burden is [prideful], but to be able to [dismiss] it [28] [gently] when [necessary is] blessed.

(321) [Do not] cause your own death; do not get [mad at] someone who will snatch you [from] the body and kill you.

(322) If someone takes [a wise person] from the body in a violent way, that one actually [does something] good for the person, [for] this person has been liberated from bonds.

(323) Fear of [death] causes a person grief because of the ignorance of the soul.

(324) <It would have been better> for you if the sword that kills people had never come into existence; but when it is there, say in your heart that it does not exist.

(325, 326a) Someone who says, "I believe," and spends a great deal of time faking it, will not endure but will fall. As your heart is, so your life will be.

---

3. Here pp. 17–26 are missing from the Coptic text. The Greek version of this sentence reads: "What is shameful to do is also shameful to make someone else do." 4. Lit., "his."

(326b) A godly heart gives rise to a blessed life.

(327) A person who plots evil against another [is also] the first one to taste [evil].

(328) [Don't let] an <ungrateful> person make you stop doing [good]. [29]

(329) [Do not say in] your heart that what someone asked for and [you] immediately gave is worth more than [the person who] received it.

(330) You will manage [great] wealth if you give willingly to those [in need].

(331) Persuade a foolish brother [not to] be foolish. If he is demented, take care of him.

(332, 334) Try hard to overcome everyone in mindfulness. Be self-sufficient.

(333) You cannot acquire understanding unless you first know you do not have <it>.

(335) On every matter there is also this word.[5] The limbs of the body are burdensome to those who do not use them.

(336) It is better to serve others than to make others serve you.

(337) Let someone whom God will not take from the body not take on personal burdens.

(338) Do not hold any opinion that does not help the needy, [and do not] listen either.

(339) A person who gives [with] partiality[6] acts arrogantly [and sins].

(340) If you [care for] orphans, you will be parent[7] of many children and [30] God's loved one.

(341) One [whom you serve] for [honor you have] served for a reward.

(342) [If] you [give with the idea] of honoring yourself, [you have] given not for humankind but for your own gratification.

(343, 344) Do not [make] a crowd of people angry. [Know] what a rich person should [do].

(345) It is better to die [than] to bring darkness upon the soul because of gluttony.

(346) Say in [your] heart that the body [is] the garment of your soul. Keep it pure, since it is innocent.

(347) Whatever the soul does in the body she[8] has as evidence when she goes to judgment.

(348, 349) Unclean demons lay claim to a corrupt soul; evil demons cannot stop a faithful and good soul from walking in the way of God.

(350) Do not offer the word of God to everyone.

(351) It is not reassuring for [those] corrupted by [glory] to [hear] about God.

---

5. This comment is also found in the Syriac version.
6. Coptic ([h^en ou]ji ho (so Poirier). Also possible is [aj^en] ji ho, "[without] respect." 7. Lit., "father."

8. The soul is often personified as a female in ancient literature.

(352, 353) It is not a small [risk] for us to [speak the] truth about God. [Do not say [31] anything about] God until [you have] learned from [God].

(354, 356) [Do not] speak with the godless [about] God; if you are defiled [because of] dirty deeds, [do not] speak about God.

(357) A true [word] about God is the word of God.

(355) Say a word about God as if you are saying it in God's presence.

(358) If your heart first is convinced that you love God, then speak to anyone you wish about God.

(359) Let your deeds of love for God come before all your words about God.

(360) Do not be inclined to speak with a crowd of people about God.

(361) Be more reserved with a word about God than with a word about the soul.

(362) It is better to give up a soul than to throw out a word about God flippantly.

(363a) You conceive the body but cannot dominate the speech of a godly person.

(363b) As the lion rules over the body of [a wise person], so also the tyrant rules only [over the body[9]].

(364) If a tyrant [32] threatens you, [especially at that time] remember God.

(365) A person [who speaks] the word of God [to those] who should not hear it [betrays] God.

(366) It is better [for] you to remain silent about the word of [God] than to speak thoughtlessly.

(367, 368) Someone who tells lies about God lies to God; a person who has nothing truthful to say about [God] is abandoned by God.

(369) You cannot know God if you do not worship him.

(370) A person who harms someone cannot worship God.

(371) The love of humankind is the beginning of godliness.

(372) A person who cares for people and prays for them all is the truth of God.

(373, 374) It is for God to save whom he wishes, but it is for the godly to pray that God may save everyone.

(375) When you pray for something and it comes to pass for you through God, then say in your heart that [you can [33] accomplish things with God].

(376a, 376b) [A person] worthy of God is God among [people]. <There is God> and the child of God: the one is great, the other is next to the great.

(377, 378) It is better for a person to have nothing than to have much but give nothing to the needy; and you too, if you beg God, will get nothing from him.

---

9. Lit., "over it."

(379)   If with all your heart you give your bread to the hungry, the gift is small but the goodwill is great with God.

(380)   Someone who thinks that nothing is in God's presence is no less than <a godless> person.

(381)   Someone who conforms his heart to God as much as is possible honors God greatly.

(382)   God is not in need of anything, but he rejoices over those who give to the needy.

(383)   The words of the faithful are few, but their deeds are many.

(384)   A faithful person who loves learning is a doer of truth. [34]

(385)   [Adjust yourself to the] circumstances of life in order that [you may] not [be distressed].

(386)   [If you] harm no one, you will fear no one.

(387)   A tyrant cannot take away true wealth.

(388)   Do what is right to do, willingly.

(389a) Do not do what is not right to do or anything of the kind.

(389b) Promise anything rather than saying, "I am wise."

(390)   Say in your heart that whatever you do well God does.

(391)   No person who <looks> to the earth and to earthly tables is wise.

(392)   You should not honor a philosopher who is only a body on the outside, but rather honor a philosopher in accordance with the person within.

(393)   Keep yourself from lying; there is one who deceives and one who is deceived.

(394/395)   Understand who God is, and understand who thinks within you; a good person is God's good work.

(396)   How miserable are those because of whom the [word] is blasphemed.

(397)   Death cannot destroy . . . .[10]

---

10. The Coptic text breaks off at this point. The Greek version of this sentence reads, "It is not death that destroys the soul, but rather an evil life."

THREE FORMS OF
FIRST THOUGHT

NHC XIII,1

Introduced and Translated by John D. Turner

The sixteen papyrus pages containing *Three Forms of First Thought* (or *Trimorphic Protennoia*) and the first ten lines of another copy of *On the Origin of the World*, discovered inside the front cover of Nag Hammadi Codex VI, constitute the remains of what would have been an entire Nag Hammadi Codex (XIII). Since the center of the papyrus quire is found between the sixth and seventh pages of *Three Forms of First Thought*, and since the text of *On the Origin of the World* would have occupied another thirty pages, the original eighty pages of Codex XIII would have begun with at least one presently missing treatise of thirty-four pages, quite possibly another copy of the *Secret Book of John*, which occupies first place in Codices II, III, and IV. The pages of the extant text, of which there is only one known copy, have all suffered severe damage on the bottom five or six lines; damaged as well are the tops of pages 35–36 and 45–50. In a manner reminiscent of the *Three Steles of Seth*, which concludes Codex VII, *Three Forms of First Thought* is divided into three subtractates, each with a subtitle; the ensemble bears the subscript title "Three Forms of First Thought" followed by a brief Greek colophon.

Three Forms of First Thought is an early ("Barbeloite") Sethian treatise in the form of a tripartite aretalogy (recitation of the powers, deeds, and attributes) of Protennoia-Barbelo, the First Thought of the Sethian supreme deity (the Invisible Spirit), in a first-person self-predicatory style much like those of the Isis aretalogies and certain biblical wisdom poems. As in the monologue of Pronoia, or Forethought, that concludes the longer version of the *Secret Book of John* (II 30,11–31,27), Protennoia recites her three salvific descents into the lower world. These recitations are structured into an introductory aretalogy (35,1–32) identifying Protennoia as the divine First Thought followed by three similar aretalogies in the same style, the second and third of which form separately titled subtractates in *Three Forms of First Thought*.

First, Protennoia is the divine but as yet inarticulate Voice of the Invisible Spirit's First Thought who presides over the establishing of the heavenly dwellings for her members and descends into the realm of chaos to give shape to her "members," fragments of her spirit that have fallen into the world (35,32–36,27; 40,29–41,1). Second, Protennoia is the articulate Speech of the Thought who descends to overthrow the old aeon ruled by the evil powers and empower her fallen members to prepare for the coming new age by giving them spirit or breath (42,4–27; 45,2–12; 45,21–46,3). Third, Protennoia is the fully articulate Word, or Logos, of the Thought who descends in the likeness of successively lower powers and, entering the "tents" of her members, confers upon them the saving baptismal rite of the Five Seals by which they are immersed in divine "living water"—whose divine luminescence washes away their corporeal nature—whereupon they along with the crucified Jesus are raptured into the light (46,5–6; 47,5–22; 49,15–22; 50,9–12.18–20).

The underlying tripartite aretalogy has been expanded by means of six narrative doctrinal insertions (36,27–40,29, virtually identical with the theogony and cosmogony expounded by the shorter version of the *Secret Book of John* and by Irenaeus around 175–180 CE; 41,1–42,2; 42,27–45,2; 46,7–47,5; 47,22–49,15; 49,22–50,9). Of these six narrative insertions, whose third-person expository prose breaks the otherwise smooth flow of Protennoia's self-referential speech, the second, third, and fifth are designated as "mysteries" that Protennoia is said to have communicated to the sons of the light.

Throughout the revelatory discourses Protennoia is manifested successively as silent thought, audible sound or voice, uttered speech, and finally as the fully articulate Logos; she is the "Logos existing in the Silence," a "hidden Sound," and the "ineffable Logos," much as in *Thunder* (14,9–15; 20,26–35). This conceptuality was likely derived from the Stoic distinction between internal reason or thought (*logos endiathetos*) and external and uttered or expressed reason (*logos prophorikos*).[1]

The imagery of water, light, ascent, and descent found throughout *Three Forms of First Thought* is heavily indebted to the hellenized Jewish wisdom schools responsible for the personification of the figure of the divine Wisdom and the development of the myth concerning her role in the creation of the world and in the subsequent enlightenment of humankind as it is found especially in 1 *Enoch* 42, *Sirach* 24, *Wisdom of Solomon* 7–8, and Philo of Alexandria. It seems that Sophia's attempts to seek a dwelling in the created order, one unsuccessful (as in 1 *Enoch* 42) and one successful (as in *Sirach* 24), were combined into a total of three descents into the lower world, two resulting in partial liberation, and the third resulting in the final awakening and salvation of those who received her. This is the same pattern that underlies the Johannine prologue, an independent composition that also was likely to have been a product of a similar form of wisdom speculation. The unique contribution of the author of *Three Forms of First*

---

1. See the sequence *phonē, lexis, logos* in Diogenes Laertius *Lives of Eminent Philosophers* 7.57.

Thought lies in the interpretation of the three revelatory descents: first, in terms of a primal divine triad of Father, Mother, and Son (probably an adaptation of the Father, Mother, Child triad developed by Plato in *Timaeus* 50d); second, in terms of a theory of progressive revelation in which each successive appearance of the revealer is characterized by an increasing degree of articulateness and finality (Voice, Speech, and Word); and third, the association of the final descent with a Logos figure who confers final enlightenment in the form of the transcendental-ized baptismal rite called the Five Seals.

It appears that *Three Forms of First Thought* has been secondarily Chris-tianized. Three glosses identifying the Son Autogenes as the Christ in the first subtractate (37,[31]; 38,22; 39,6–7) probably derive from the traditional Barbeloite theogonical material common to the *Secret Book of John* and Irenaeus *Against Heresies* 1.29, upon which the author drew for the first narrative insertion. These Christian glosses would have been suggested by an equation between the Chris-tian designation of Christ as *monogenēs* and what seems to be a pre-Christian des-ignation for the third member of the Barbeloite Father-Mother-Son triad, namely, the Self-Begotten or Self-Generated (*autogenēs*) Son.

At various points throughout *Three Forms of First Thought*, the triple descent of Protennoia and the various forms in which she appears are interpreted by means of concepts drawn from the Sethian baptismal-ascensional rite of the Five Seals.[2] The fact that the author refers to the recipients of this baptismal ascent rit-ual in the first-person plural and as "brethren" suggests a Sethian community with a well-established tradition of water baptism that brings total enlightenment and salvation. *Three Forms of First Thought* shows traces of first-person plural liturgical responses that immediately precede and follow this short theogony (36,33–39,13) and suggest some kind of liturgical exchange between speaker and audience; these may be the remaining traces of a community litany consisting of communal responses to a spoken recitation of Protennoia's first-person singular revelations. Rather than designating a fivefold immersion in the Living Water, the Five Seals are interpreted as a five-stage ritual of psychical ascent: the investi-ture of the stripped Spirit with light, its enthronement, its baptism by Micheus, Michar, and Mnesinous in the spring of Living Water, its glorification with the Fatherhood, and its rapture into the light (perhaps the Four Luminaries) by the servants of the Four Luminaries, Kamaliel, . . .anen, and Samblo (48, 15–35). The stages of this visionary rite do not seem to follow in an intuitively obvious se-quence; in 45,13–20 one has the sequence glorification, enthronement, investi-ture, baptism, and becoming light. In the *Holy Book of the Great Invisible Spirit*, where baptism is clearly central, the emphasis seems to lie on the descent of the holy powers upon the baptizand (cf. also the seed who "receive his name upon

2. In the *Secret Book of John* II 31,22–25, Barbelo-Pronoia-Forethought confers the Five Seals on her earthly mem-bers as the culminating salvific act of her third and final descent. In the *Holy Book of the Great Invisible Spirit* IV 58,6–8 they are called "[the mystery] of [mysteries]"; in III 66,3–4 they are associated with certain renunciations in spring baptism, and in III 55,12 and 63,3 they are identified respectively with the Invisible Spirit, Barbelo, the triple-male Child (i.e., the great Christ or great Seth), Youel, and the Child of the Child Esephech.

(or in) the water" of the *Revelation of Adam*), while in *Three Forms of First Thought*, *Zostrianos*, and the Pronoia monologue concluding the *Secret Book of John*, where glorification and rapture are central, the emphasis lies upon the ascent of the baptizand to the light.

Three Forms of First Thought sustains obvious relationships to other Sethian literature. The structure, content, terminology, and dramatis personae of its doctrine of baptism sustain a close relationship especially to the *Holy Book of the Great Invisible Spirit*, *Zostrianos*, the *Secret Book of John*, and, more distantly, *Melchizedek*, the *Revelation of Adam*, and the untitled text of the Bruce Codex. In its development of the Father-Mother-Child triad as applied to Protennoia-Barbelo, *Three Forms of First Thought* makes use of a cosmology and a triple descent motif very similar to those found in the *Secret Book of John*, especially its concluding first-person self-predicatory monologue by Pronoia (II 30,11–31,25), which, even before its incorporation into the *Secret Book*, likely served as a model or direct source for the original composition of *Three Forms of First Thought*.

The third subtractate narrates the incognito descent of Protennoia as the Word disguised in the form of the sovereignties, powers, and angels, culminating in the final revelation of herself in the human form of her members below, but it seems to have been supplemented by an alien and tendentious Christological interpretation. In the third subtractate, traditional Christological titles such as Christ, Beloved, Son of God (i.e., "Son of the Archigenetor"), and Son of Man are polemically interpreted in a consciously docetic fashion so as to suggest that these titles were inappropriately applied to the human Jesus by the apostolic church. By implication, the apostolic Jesus is shown actually to be the Christ of the evil archons; the apostolic beloved is actually the Beloved of the archons; the apostolic Son of God is the Son of the ignorant world creator; and the apostolic Son of Man is only a human being among the sons of men.

It is interesting that most of these reinterpretations of the Christology of the apostolic church in *Three Forms of First Thought* seem to depend on key passages from the *Gospel of John* to score their point in any acute fashion. It seems that the key to the relationship between these two texts lies in the recognition that *Three Forms of First Thought* has undergone at least three stages of composition. First, there was the original triad of the aretalogical self-predications of Protennoia as Voice, Speech, and Word that were probably built up out of the Jewish wisdom tradition and maybe out of the *Secret Book of John*'s similar Pronoia aretalogy itself sometime during the first century CE; there is little here that seems specifically Gnostic or Christian or Sethian or Barbeloite. Second, this was supplemented, whether by the same or by a different author, by various narrative doctrinal passages based upon traditional Barbeloite theogonical materials similar to those of the *Secret Book of John* and Irenaeus *Against Heresies* 1.29. After circulation as a mildly Christian "Barbeloite" text in this form, the third and last stage of composition seems to have involved a deliberately polemical incorporation of Christian, specifically Johannine Christian, materials into the aretalogical portion of the third subtractate. One might assign the third compositional stage

of *Three Forms of First Thought* to the period of the struggle over the interpretation of the Fourth Gospel witnessed by the New Testament letters of John during
the first quarter of the second century.

BIBLIOGRAPHY

Carsten Colpe, "Heidnische, jüdische und christliche Überlieferung in den Schriften aus Nag Hammadi,
III"; Craig A. Evans, "On the Prologue of John and the *Trimorphic Protennoia*"; Charles W. Hedrick, ed.,
Nag Hammadi Codices XI, XII, XIII, 371–454 (John D. Turner); Yvonne Janssens, *La Prōtennoia trimorphe*;
"Une source gnostique du Prologue?"; "The Trimorphic Protennoia and the Fourth Gospel"; "Trimorphic
Protennoia"; Paul-Hubert Poirier, ed., *La Pensée Première à la triple forme*; Gesine Schenke Robinson,
"The Trimorphic Protennoia and the Prologue of the Fourth Gospel"; James M. Robinson, "Sethians
and Johannine Thought: The Trimorphic Protennoia and the Prologue of the Gospel of John"; Gesine
Schenke, *Die dreigestaltige Protennoia herausgegeben, übersetzt und kommentiert*; Hans-Martin Schenke,
Hans-Gebhard Bethge, and Ursula Ulrike Kaiser, eds., *Nag Hammadi Deutsch*, 2.807–31 (Gesine Schenke
Robinson); John D. Turner, "The Sethian Baptismal Rite"; "Sethian Gnosticism and Johannine
Christianity."

Three Forms of First Thought[1]

Protennoia's Identity as the Omnipresent Divine First Thought (35,1–32)

[I] am First [Thought,[2] the] thought that is in [light].
[I] am movement[3] that is in the [All],[4]
[she in whom the] All takes its stand,
the firstborn among those who [came to be],
[she who] exists before the All.
[She] is called by three names,[5] though she dwells alone,
[since she is complete].

I am invisible within the thought of the invisible one,[6]
although I am revealed in the immeasurable and the ineffable.
I am incomprehensible, dwelling in the incomprehensible,
although I move in every creature.

I am the life of my Epinoia[7]
that is within every power and every eternal movement,
and in invisible lights,
and within the rulers and angels and demons
and every soul in Tartaros,[8]

---

1. Coptic text: NHC XIII,1: 35,1–50,24. Editions: *The Facsimile Edition of the Nag Hammadi Codices: Codices XI, XII and XIII*, 105–20; Charles W. Hedrick, ed., *Nag Hammadi Codices XI, XII, XIII*, 371–454 (John D. Turner); Yvonne Janssens, *La Prōtennoia tri-morphe*; Paul-Hubert Poirier, ed., *La Pensée Première à la triple forme*; Hans-Martin Schenke, Hans-Gebhard Bethge, and Ursula Ulrike Kaiser, eds., *Nag Hammadi Deutsch*, 2.807–31 (Gesine Schenke Robinson). The text is also referred to as *Trimorphic Protennoia*. 2. Protennoia, here and throughout this and other Sethian texts, is often identified as Barbelo, the merciful Mother(-Father), Pronoia ("Forethought"), and so on. 3. Probably in the sense of the self-motion of the soul, for Plato the source of all movement (*Phaedrus* 245c; *Laws* 895e–896b; cf. the motion of the divine wisdom in *Wisdom of Solomon* 7:22–24). 4. I.e., the universe. 5. I.e., Father, Mother, and Child (or Voice, Speech, and Word). 6. The invisible one may allude to the Invisible Spirit; as his thought, Protennoia is the originator of the Pleroma, or divine Fullness. 7. Epinoia (or "Insight," here and below) is a projection or lower double of Protennoia, her "reflection" by which she acts upon the realms below her. The figure of Epinoia occurs four times in *Three Forms of First Thought* (as the Epinoia of Light identified with Sophia in 39; 40; 47), once in the *Thought of Norea*, and sixteen times in the *Secret Book of John*. 8. Tartaros is the realm of the dead, the underworld, and often the lower realm of the underworld, hell, the place of punishment.

and in every material soul.
I dwell in those who came to be.
I move in everyone and probe them all.
I walk upright, and those who sleep I awaken.[9]
And I am the sight of those who are asleep.
I am the invisible one within the All.
I counsel those who are hidden,
since I know everything that exists in the All.
I am numberless beyond everyone.
I am immeasurable, ineffable, yet whenever I [wish],
[I] shall reveal myself through myself.
I [am the movement of] the All.
I am before [all, and] I am all, since I [am in] everyone.

Protennoia's Self-Manifestation as the Masculine Voice of the First Thought (35,32–36,27)

I am a [softly resounding] voice.[10]
I exist from [the first].
[I am] in the silence [that surrounds] every [one] of them. [36]
[It is] the hidden [voice] that [is in] me,
[in] the incomprehensible, immeasurable [thought],
[in] the immeasurable silence.[11]
I [descended to the] midst of the underworld
and I shone [down on the] darkness.[12]
I made the [water] surge.[13]
I am hidden in [radiant] waters.
I gradually made the All radiant by my thought.
I am laden with the voice.
Through me comes knowledge.[14]
I inhabit the ineffable and the unknowable.
I am perception and knowledge,
uttering voice by means of thought.

---

9. See *Ephesians* 5:14 and *Secret Book of John* II, 30–31. 10. Restoring *hroo[u efsᵉnsᵉn ebol hēs]ukhē*. Protennoia's thought is manifested in three forms of increasing articulateness, first as Voice (masculine; Coptic *hroou*, Greek *phthongos*, *psophos*, or *ēchos* in the sense of inarticulate sound), second as articulate Speech (feminine; Coptic *smē*, Greek *phonē*), and finally as the fully articulate Word, Discourse, or Reason (masculine; Coptic, from Greek, *logos*). 11. Cf. *Three Forms of First Thought* 37; 46; *John* 1:5; *Secret Book of John* II, 30. 12. Cf. the concluding hymn of the Savior found in the longer version of the *Secret Book of John* II, 30–31. 13. Water refers not only to the divine light (cf. *Secret Book of John* II, 4) and to enlightenment in general, but also to the "living water" (identified as the spirit in *John* 7:37–39) received in the Sethian baptismal rite of the Five Seals. 14. Note the Protennoia's progressive self-manifestation from thought to voice to knowledge (gnosis).

I am the real voice.
I resonate in everyone,
and they know it, since a seed is in [them].
I am the thought of the Father,
and through me came the voice,
the knowledge of everlasting things.
I exist as thought for all,
being joined to the unknowable and incomprehensible thought.
I, I revealed myself among all who recognize me,
for I am joined with everyone
through hidden thought and exalted <voice>,[15]
a voice from invisible thought.

Response of the Auditors (36,27–37,3)

The voice[16] is immeasurable, since it is in the immeasurable one.
It is a mystery, it is an [unknowable] deriving from [the incomprehensible one].
It is invisible [to all who are] visible in the All.
[It is light] in light.

We too [have ourselves left the] visible [world], since we [are saved by] hidden [wisdom through the] [37] ineffable, immeasurable [voice]. And what is hidden within us confers the product of its fruit upon the water of life.[17]

Revelation Narrative on the Perfect Son, the Logos-Christ (37,3–38,16)

The Perfect Son, the Word (37,3–20)

The Son is perfect in every respect. He is the word[18] originating through that voice, who came from on high, who has within him the name,[19] who is light. He revealed everlasting things, and all that was unknown became known. Those things difficult to interpret and secret he revealed, and to those who are in silence with the first thought he preached. He revealed himself to those in darkness, and he showed himself to those in the abyss.[20] To those in the hidden treasuries he told ineffable mysteries, and he taught unrepeatable doctrines to all who became children of light.[21]

---

15. The Coptic text is emended to read *ou<h>roou*. **16.** In this section, note the shift to third-person description and the auditors' first-person plural liturgical response; cf. also *Three Forms of First Thought* 42 and n. 58. **17.** Informed by Protennoia's voice, her spirit is now hidden within her members as a wisdom that makes the baptismal waters "living," effectively enlightening and therefore salvific. **18.** Logos. **19.** Probably that of Protennoia. **20.** Cf. *John* 1:5. **21.** These are the Sethian Gnostics, Protennoia's "members" resident in the world.

Excursus on the Equivalence of the Triads Father-Mother-Child and Voice-Speech-Word (37,20–30)

Now the voice that came from my thought—it exists as three abiding entities:[22] the Father, the Mother, and the Child—exists as perceptible speech, and it has within it a word endowed with every <glory>.[23] It has three masculine aspects, three powers,[24] and three names. Thus they exist as the three □ □ □, three quadrangles,[25] secretly in ineffable silence.

[The anointed one, the Christ], alone came to be. I anointed him with [goodness][26] as the glory [of the] invisible [spirit.[27] The three][28] I established [alone in] eternal [glory] over [the eternal realms in] living [water]. This [is the glory surrounding the one] [38] who made the light of those exalted aeons radiate gloriously and in everlasting stability. And [he] stood in his own light surrounding him, the eye of light[29] shining gloriously on me. He provided aeons for the father of all the aeons.

Protennoia's Identity as the Divine Mother Barbelo (38,7–16)

This is I myself, the thought of the Father,
First Thought,
Barbelo,[30] the [perfect] glory,
the [immeasurable] invisible one who is hidden.
I am the image of the Invisible Spirit.
Through me all took shape.
I am the Mother,
and the light that she appointed as virgin,
she who is called Meirothea,
the incomprehensible womb,
the unrestrainable and immeasurable voice.[31]

---

22. "Abiding entities" translates Greek *monai*, which in *John* 14:2, 23 signifies permanent heavenly dwellings. This triad usually refers to the Sethian supreme divine trinity (*Secret Book of John* II, 2; 9; Irenaeus *Against Heresies* 1.29.4), but here seems to refer to the three successive self-manifestations of Protennoia's thought as voice, speech, and word (*logos*). 23. The Coptic text is emended to read <e>oou. 24. Cf. the Triple-Powered One of the Platonizing Sethian treatises, which brings into being the aeon of Barbelo. 25. Perhaps a symbol of the three-formed Barbelo, for whom W. W. Harvey has suggested the etymology *b'arb'a 'elō*, "in four (i.e., the tetragrammaton, YHWH) is God." 26. The Coptic *m^ent[khs]* can mean either "goodness" (*khrēstotēs*) or "Christhood" (*khristotēs*); cf. the pun on "anointing" (*khrisma*). 27. Cf. the Invisible Spirit's anointing of the Self-Generated Child in *Secret Book of John* II, 6; *Holy Book of the Great Invisible Spirit* III, 44. 28. Perhaps the three masculinities, powers, and names previously mentioned. 29. "Eye" in the sense of "focus" or "source" is here applied to Christ as a source of light

and in *Three Forms of First Thought* 46 to Protennoia as the "eye of the three abiding entities." In *Holy Book of the Great Invisible Spirit* IV, 61 and *Wisdom of Jesus Christ* III, 105, "eye of light" is applied to Adamas, probably playing on the Greek words *phōs* (with acute accent, "man") and *phōs* (with circumflex accent, "light"). 30. Barbelo is the name of the supreme deity's first thought, intellect, or forethought (*pronoia*, "providence") in Sethian texts. 31. Similar names or epithets for the divine are used in the *Secret Book of John* II, 4–5. Mirothea (or Meirothea) may be a feminization of "divine anointed one" (*muro-theos*) or "divine destiny" (*meiro-theos*) or "divine part" (*meros*, derived from *meiromai*). Here and in *Three Forms of First Thought* 45 Mirothea is a feminine cognomen for Barbelo; in *Holy Book of the Great Invisible Spirit* III, 49, *Three Steles of Seth* 119, and *Zostrianos* 6 and 30, Mirothea is the mother of the heavenly Adam Pigeradamas. In *Melchizedek* 6 and 18 one also finds Meirocheirothetos (perhaps "one anointed with myrrh") mentioned together with Pigeradamas.

The Perfect Son Establishes the Aeons (38,16–23)

Then the perfect Son revealed himself to his aeons that originated through him. He revealed and glorified them and gave them thrones,[32] and he stood in the glory with which he glorified himself. They blessed the perfect Son, the Christ, the only god.[33]

The Response of the Aeons (38,23–30)

And they gave glory and said,

> He is. He is.
> Son of God!
> Son of God!
> It is he who is!
> The aeon of aeons beholding the eternal realms that he generated!
> For you generated by your own desire.
> Therefore [we] glorify you:
> MA MŌ
> ŌŌŌ EI
> A EI
> ON EI![34]
> The [aeon] of [aeons]!
> The aeon that he <honored>![35]

The Ranking of the Four Luminaries as Four Aeons (38,30–39,13)

Then[36] the [god who was generated] gave the aeons the power of [life on which they might rely], and [he] established [them].

> The first aeon he established [over the first],
> Armedon, Nousanios, [Armozel];

---

32. Cf. the baptismal enthroning and glorification in *Three Forms of First Thought* 45 and 48. 33. Cf. *John* 1:18. 34. Here the Coptic may be taken as glossolalia, or the text may be understood to reproduce Greek: *ma, mō, ō ō ō ei, a ei, on ei*, "MA! MŌ! You are thrice Ō (omega, "last"). You are A (alpha, "first"). You are he who is." The superlineation on MA and MŌ suggests they may be abbreviations for M(irothe)a and M(irothe)ō (so Paul-Hubert Poirier). A less likely possibility is that the string may begin with three Coptic imperatives: *ma, mō, ōō, ō ei, a ei, on ei*, "Give! Receive! Conceive! You are last (Ō, omega). You are first (A, alpha). You are he who is." See *Holy Book of the Great Invisible Spirit* III, 66; Bentley Layton, *The Gnostic Scriptures*, 92; John D. Turner, in *Nag Hammadi Codices XI, XII, XIII*, 440. 35. Emending *taeif* ("gave") to *taei<o>f* ("honored"). 36. In Sethian tradition, Harmozel, Oroiael, Daveithai, and Eleleth are the Four Luminaries. Here in this section they are reconceived as aeonic dwellings; in the *Secret Book of John* they become the respective dwellings for the archetypal Adam, Seth, his primordial seed, and (together with Sophia) Seth's future descendants.

the second he established [over the second aeon], [39]
Phaionios, Ainios, Oroiael;
the third over the third aeon,
Mellephaneus, Loios, Daveithai;
the fourth over the fourth,
Mousanios, Amethes, Eleleth.

Now these aeons were conceived by the god who was generated, the Christ, and they received and gave glory. They came forth, exalted in their thought,[37] and each aeon gave myriads of glories[38] in great untraceable lights, and all together they blessed the perfect Son, the god who was generated.

The World Creator Originates from Eleleth's Epinoia-Sophia (39,13–32)

Then came a word from the great luminary Eleleth, and said, "I am king. Who is king of chaos and who is king of the underworld?"[39]

At that moment his light appeared radiant, endowed with Epinoia.[40] The powers of the powers did not entreat him. And immediately there appeared the great demon who rules over the lowest part of the underworld and chaos. He has neither form nor perfection, but rather he has the form of the splendor of those conceived in darkness.[41] He is called Sakla, Samael, Yaldabaoth,[42] who took power, who snatched it from the innocent one, who overpowered her beforehand. She is the Epinoia of light who came down, from whom Yaldabaoth originally came into being.[43]

Epinoia-Sophia's Restoration (39,32–40,4)

The Epinoia of the [luminary Eleleth] realized that [Yaldabaoth] had begged him for another [order, even though he was lower] than she, and she said to Eleleth, "Give [me another order], so that you may become for me [a dwelling place and I may not] dwell in disorder [forever."[44] The order of the] whole house of [40] glory agreed with her request. A blessing was brought for her, and the higher order yielded to her.

---

37. "Exalted" in thought suggests a willful predisposition to independent (creative) activity; cf. *Secret Book of John* II, 9–10. 38. In *Zostrianos*, glories are "patterns of salvation," spiritual helpers to those seeking enlightenment. 39. See *Holy Book of the Great Invisible Spirit* III, 56, where Eleleth (rather than Sophia herself as in the *Secret Book of John*) initiates the emergence of the world creator and ruler Yaldabaoth. 40. Epinoia, Protennoia's lower self-manifestation, now appears as Sophia (Wisdom), Eleleth's power of light. 41. Probably a reference to Yaldabaoth's de- monic assistants. 42. Cf. *Secret Book of John* II, 11; *Nature of the Rulers* 94–95. Here Yaldabaoth is spelled "Yaltabaoth," perhaps meaning "begetter of powers," "son of shame," or the like, and Sakla is spelled "Saklas." 43. As in *Three Forms of First Thought* 40 and *Secret Book of John* II, 23 (cf. "kindness" in Irenaeus *Against Heresies* 1.29.4), the innocent one is Sophia, here identified with Epinoia; see n. 7 and *Secret Book of John* II, 9. 44. Lest Yaldabaoth gain complete control, Epinoia-Sophia requests that she rather than he be restored into the divine world.

Yaldabaoth Makes a Human Being in Protennoia's Likeness (40,4–7)

And the great demon began to produce aeons in the likeness of the real aeons, except that he produced them out of his own power.[45]

Protennoia Intervenes (40,8–29)

Then I too revealed my voice secretly and said, "Stop, stop, you who tread on matter. Look, I am coming down to the world of mortals for my portion that was there from the time when innocent Sophia was conquered. She descended so that I might thwart their plot, which was devised by the one who came from her."

All were disturbed, and everyone in the house of the unknowable light and the abyss trembled. And the chief creator[46] of ignorance reigned over chaos and the underworld and produced a human being in my likeness. But he did not know that this creature would be a death sentence for him, nor did he recognize the power in the creature.[47]

Protennoia's Self-Manifestation to Her Members (40,29–41,1)

But now I have descended and reached chaos.[48]
I was [with] my own who were there.
I am hidden in them, empowering [them], giving them shape.
From [the first day] until the day [I shall grant] mighty [power]
to those who are mine,
[I shall reveal myself to] those who have heard [my mysteries], [41]
the children of light.[49]

The First Mystery: Nullification of the Lower Powers (41,1–42,3)

I am their father, and I shall tell you a mystery,[50]
ineffable and unspeakable by [any] mouth.
Every bond I loosed from you,
and the chains of the demons of the underworld I broke,
the very chains that bound and restrained my members.
The high walls of darkness I overthrew,
and the secure gates of those pitiless ones I broke,
and I smashed their bars.[51]

---

45. Yaldabaoth uses the power he had stolen from Epinoia to create a deficient copy of the archetypal realms above him, a parody on Plato's *Timaeus* 39e; cf. *Secret Book of John* II, 12–13. 46. Greek *arkhigenetōr*, here and below; cf. *Secret Book of John* II, 12. 47. The end of the first narrative and resumption of Protennoia's self-revelation. The diabolical ploys of the demi-urge are more fully documented in the *Secret Book of John* and other texts. 48. Cf. *Secret Book of John* II, 30. 49. Protennoia's spiritual members trapped in the physical world; cf. *Three Forms of First Thought* 37; 45; 49. 50. Cf. 1 *Corinthians* 15:51. 51. Cf. *Psalm* 107:16; *Isaiah* 45:2.

And the evil force and the one who beats and hinders you,
and the tyrant, the adversary, the king, and the present enemy,
all these I explained to those who are mine,
who are the children of light,
so that they might nullify them all,
be liberated from all bonds,
and return to the place where they were in the beginning.

I am the first one who descended
for my portion that remains,
the spirit in the soul,
which came from the water of life.[52]

And out of the immersion of the mysteries I spoke,
I with the rulers and authorities,
for I went below their language.[53]
I spoke my mysteries to my own,
a hidden mystery,[54]
and the bonds and eternal oblivion were nullified.
I bore fruit in them,
the thought of the unchanging aeon,
and my house, and their father.
And I went down [to those who were] mine from the first,
and I reached [them and broke] the first strands that [enslaved them].
[Then] everyone in me shone, [42]
and I prepared [a pattern] for those ineffable lights in me.[55]
Amen.

The [Discourse] of First Thought: [Part One][56]

Protennoia's Self-Manifestation as Feminine Speech of the First Thought (42,4–46,5)

Protennoia as the Mother of the Voice (42,4–17)

I am the voice that appeared through my thought.
I am he who is in union[57]

---

52. The spirit within human souls originates from Protennoia's spirit, which is the archetypal living water of the Sethian baptismal rite (mystery) of the Five Seals in which her devotees are immersed. 53. Protennoia evidently speaks in ordinary language, but in such a way as to disguise it from the evil celestial rulers; see *Three Forms of First Thought* 42; 47. 54. Cf. *Colossians* 1:26; *Ephesians* 3:9. 55. Cf. *John* 14:2–3. 56. The section title concludes the first descent of First Thought,

Protennoia. There follows a second (42; 47) and third (47) descent; cf. the three descents of Forethought, Pronoia, in the concluding hymn of the Savior in the longer version of the *Secret Book of John* II, 30–31. 57. Protennoia is an androgynous union of her masculine aspects, Father (the Invisible Spirit) and Voice, with her feminine aspects of First Thought, Mother, and Speech; in the following section, her feminine aspects are now dominant (cf. *Three Forms of First Thought* 42; 47).

since I am called the thought of the invisible one.
Since I am called the unchanging speech,
I am called she who is in union.

I am alone and undefiled.
I am the mother [of] the voice, speaking in many ways, completing
     the All.
In me is knowledge, knowledge of things everlasting.
I speak in every creature, and I was known by everyone.
I lift up the speech of the voice to the ears of those who have known me,
the children of light.

The Shift of the Ages (42,17–27)

Now I have come the second time in the likeness of a female, and have spoken
with them. I shall tell them of the coming end of this age, and teach them about
the beginning of the age to come, the one without change, wherein our[58] appearance will be changed.[59]

   We shall be purified in those aeons from which I revealed myself in the
thought of the likeness of my masculinity.[60]

   I settled among those who are worthy[61] in the thought of my changeless aeon.

The Second Mystery: The Impending Overthrow
of the Cosmic Powers (42,27–45,2)

For I shall tell you a mystery of this age and tell you about the forces in it. Birth
beckons [birth], hour gives birth to hour, day [gives birth to] day. Months inform
the month, [time goes around] following [time]. This age [43] was completed in
[this] fashion, and it turned out to be short, as a finger releases a finger and a joint
separates from a joint.[62]

   When the great authorities knew that the time of fulfillment had appeared—
just as the time of birth pains came,[63] so also the time of destruction approached—all the elements trembled, and the foundations of the underworld
and the ceilings of chaos shook,[64] and a great fire shone in their midst, and the

---

58. Protennoia speaks here with the voice of the community; for similar alteration between the first-person
singular and plural, see *Three Forms of First Thought*
36–37 and *John* 3:11–12; 4:22; 9:4–5. 59. Cf. 1 *Corinthians* 15:52 and the Judeo-Christian notion of two opposed ages, this present (evil) age and the coming new
age of salvation. The first-person plural represents
the confession of the audience's community. 60. I.e.,
Protennoia's first descent as Voice. 61. In addition
to the "seed" (i.e., of Seth; cf. *Three Forms of First
Thought* 50), "those who are worthy" is a frequent

Sethian self-designation; see *Three Forms of First
Thought* 45; *Secret Book of John* II, 7; 25; 26; *Holy Book
of the Great Invisible Spirit* III, 56; *Allogenes the
Stranger* 52; 68; *Zostrianos* 4; 24. 62. The inexorable
repetition of celestial time and the earthly reproduc-
tive cycles of the present age will be ended in a short
time (a finger's breadth away). 63. In apocalyptic literature the troubles accompanying the emergence of
the new age are frequently compared to birth pains;
cf. 1 *Thessalonians* 5:3. 64. Cf. *Secret Book of John* II,
14; 30.

rocks and the earth were shaken like a reed shaken by the wind. And the allotments of fate and those who apportion the celestial houses[65] were greatly disturbed by loud thunder. The thrones of the powers were disturbed because they were overturned, and their king was afraid.

And those who follow fate paid their allotment of visits to the path,[66] and they said to the powers, "What is this disturbance and shaking that has come over us through the voice of exalted speech? Our entire world has been shaken, and the entire circuit of our path of ascent has been destroyed, and the path upon which we go, which takes us up to the chief creator of our birth, is no longer steady for us."[67]

Then the powers answered and said, "We too are at a loss about it, because we did not know what caused it. But arise, let's go to the chief creator and ask him."

The powers all gathered and went up to the chief creator. They [said to] him, "Where is your boasting by which you boast? Didn't we [hear you say], 'I am God, [and I am] your father, [44] and it is I who engendered you, and there is no other but me'?[68] Now look, we have heard a voice of the invisible speech of [the aeon] that we do not know.[69] And we ourselves have not recognized to whom we belong, for the voice we heard is foreign to us, and we do not recognize it, we do not know where it came from. It came and terrified us and left us weak in our knees. So let us weep and mourn most bitterly. So let us take flight[70] before we are forcibly imprisoned and taken down to the bowels of the underworld. For already the slackening of our bondage is at hand, and the time is short,[71] and the days are brief, and our age is fulfilled, and the weeping of our destruction is near, so that we may be taken we know <not> where.[72] For the tree from which we grew has fruit of ignorance. Death is in its leaves, and darkness is under the shadow of its boughs. In deceit and lust we harvested the tree, and through it ignorant chaos became our dwelling place.[73] For look, even the chief creator of our birth, about whom we boast, did not know this speech."[74]

So now, children of thought, listen to me, listen to the speech of your merciful mother. You have become worthy of the mystery hidden from the beginning of the ages,[75] so that you [might receive] it. And the end of this age and of the evil life [is near, and there dawns [45] the] beginning of the [age to come], which [will never change].[76]

---

65. Astral determinism is overthrown. The "houses" are the celestial houses or domiciles in which the planets are enthroned relative to the twelve signs of the zodiac in Greco-Roman astrology. One's lot of fate or fortune is determined by the positions of the sun and moon relative to the horoscope or ascendant zodiacal sign at one's birth (Ptolemy *Tetrabiblios* 3.11.5; 4.7.1). The twelve houses or domiciles of the zodiac are allotted to each planet and its celestial deity (*Tetrabiblios* 1.17.37; 3.10.129). 66. The periodic revolution of the planetary deities on their fixed ("fated") orbits. 67. The diurnal circuit of the planetary powers below (the underworld) and above (in the sky) the horizon

has been upset. 68. Cf. *Secret Book of John* II, 11; 13; *Nature of the Rulers* 86, based on *Isaiah* 45:5–6, 21; 46:9. 69. Protennoia's Voice; see *Secret Book of John* II, 14; *Nature of the Rulers* 88–89; *Holy Book of the Great Invisible Spirit* III, 59. 70. Or "let us complete our (orbital) course" (Gesine Schenke Robinson, Paul-Hubert Poirier). 71. Cf. *Mark* 13:20. 72. The Coptic text is emended to read <*an*>, "not." Without the emendation the text reads "the place we recognize." 73. On the tree of ignorance, cf. *Secret Book of John* II, 21–22. 74. See n. 69. 75. Cf. *Colossians* 1:26; *Ephesians* 3:9. 76. This marks the end of the second narrative mystery.

Protennoia as Androgynous Mother-Father (45,2–12)

I am androgynous.
[I am mother and I am] father, since I [mate] with myself.
I [mate] with myself [since it is] myself that [I] love.[77]
Through me alone the All [stands firm].
I am the womb [that puts forth] the All[78]
by giving birth to light [shining] in splendor.
I am the age to [come].
[I] am the fulfillment of all, Meirothea,[79] the glory of the Mother.
I cast voiced speech into the ears of those who know me.[80]

Protennoia Promises the Five Seals (45,12–20)

And[81] I invite you into the exalted, perfect light.
When you enter the light,
you will be glorified by those who give glory,
and those who enthrone will enthrone you.
You will receive robes from those who give robes,
and the baptizers will baptize you,
and you will become exceedingly glorious,
as you were in the beginning, when you were light.

Protennoia Transforms Her Members and Reascends (45,21–46,5)

And I hid myself in everyone
and revealed [myself] in them,
and every mind seeking me longed for me,
for I gave shape to everything when it had no form.
I transformed their forms into other forms
until the time when form will be given to everything.
Through me came the voice,
and I put breath in my own.
And I cast the eternally holy spirit[82] into them,
and I ascended and entered my light.
I [went] up on my branch
and sat [there among the] children of [holy] light.[83]
And [I withdrew] to their dwelling place [46] . . . become [glorious] . . . .
[Amen].

[On] Fate: [Part Two][84]

---

77. Cf. *Secret Book of John* II, 5–7. 78. Restoring *etiouō ᵉmptērf*. On Protennoia as womb, cf. *Secret Book of John* II, 5; also cf. *Chaldaean Oracles* 30, where Hecate is "womb containing the All." 79. On Meirothea, see n. 31. 80. Or "loud speech"; cf. *Three Forms of First Thought* 42; 47. 81. For a more plausible order of the ritual components of the baptismal-ascensional rite of the Five Seals than in this section, see *Three Forms of First Thought* 48 and the introduction to the tractate. 82. Or "breath" (of life); cf. *Genesis* 2:7; *Wisdom of Solomon* 15:11; *John* 20:23. 83. Cf. *Secret Book of John* II, 30; Poirier suggests that

Protennoia's Self-Manifestation as the Logos of the First Thought (46,5–6)

I am the [Word in the] ineffable [voice].[85]
I am in undefiled [light].

Narrative on the Logos: Voice, Speech, Word, Light, and Living Water (46,7–32)

A thought [was expressed] perceptibly through [the great] speech of the Mother, although a male offspring[86] [supports me] as my foundation. The speech exists from the beginning in the foundations[87] of the All.

But light is hidden in silence, and it was first to appear. While the Mother alone exists as silence, I alone am the word, ineffable, incorruptible, immeasurable, inconceivable.

The word is hidden light, bearing fruit of life, pouring living water from the invisible, incorruptible, immeasurable spring. This is the inimitable voice of the glory of the Mother, the glory of the offspring of god, a male virgin[88] from hidden intellect, silence hidden from the All, inimitable, immeasurable light, the source of everything, the root of the entire aeon.[89]

It is the foundation that supports every movement
of the aeons of the mighty glory.
It is the foundation of every foundation.
It is the breath of the powers.
It is the eye of the three abiding entities,[90]
which exists as voice from thought.
And it is word from speech.
It was sent to illumine those in darkness.

The Third Mystery: Protennoia's Three Incognito Descents (46,33–47,34)

Protennoia's Mysteries (46,33–47,7)

Now look, I [shall] reveal to you [my mysteries], since you are my [brethren,[91] and you will] know them all [47] . . . .

---

aj[e]*npaklados* here means "without my branch," in the sense of the elect community, whom Protennoia temporarily leaves in the world. **84.** The section title concludes the second descent of Protennoia. **85.** Alternatively, "I am the [Word (*logos*)] in the ineffable [light]." **86.** I.e., Protennoia as the masculine Logos. **87.** *Kaas*, normally "bones," is here more likely a feminine derivative of *kō* ("put," "set," as in the previous line), meaning "basis," "foundation." **88.** The androgynous "male virgin" is Barbelo in *Holy Book of the Great Invisible Spirit* III, 62 (elsewhere Youel);

Zostrianos 83; 125; *Allogenes the Stranger* 59; *Three Steles of Seth* 121; and *Marsanes* 4; 8. **89.** As Voice, Protennoia is the spring or source of the "living water" of enlightenment, which she, as Logos, pours forth upon her earthly members during their baptism; cf. *John* 4:13–14. **90.** "Eye," perhaps in the sense of the present "focus" (the word) of Protennoia's three manifestations as voice, speech, and word. Cf. *Three Forms of First Thought* 37 and n. 22. **91.** Or "fellow brothers," here and below.

I told [all of them about my mysteries]
that exist in [the incomprehensible], inexpressible [aeons].

Protennoia's First Descent as Masculine Voice (47,7–11)

I taught [them the mysteries] through the [voice]
[that exists] in perfect intellect,[92]
[and I] became a foundation for all,
and [I] empowered them.[93]

Protennoia's Second Descent as Feminine Speech (47,11–13)

The second time I came as the [speech] of my voice.
I gave shape to those who [took] shape, until their consummation.[94]

Protennoia's Third Descent as Masculine Word (47,13–34)

The third time I revealed myself to them in their tents as the word,[95]
and I revealed myself in the likeness of their shape.
I wore everyone's garment.[96]
I hid in them,
and [they] did not know who empowers me.
For I am in all sovereignties and powers
and in angels and every movement in all matter.
I hid in them
until I revealed myself to my brethren.

None of the powers knew me, [though] I work in them.
[They] thought they created everything, because they are ignorant.
They did not know the root and place of their growth.[97]

[I] am the light illumining all.
I am the light rejoicing [in my] brothers and sisters.
I came down to the world [of] mortals
on account of the spirit left behind in what [descended]
and came from innocent Sophia.

---

92. Cf. "hidden intellect" in *Three Forms of First Thought* 46, here perhaps used adverbially, "intellectually complete." 93. Protennoia's first descent. 94. Cf. *Secret Book of John* II, 31: "I brightened my face with light from the consummation of their realm." 95. Cf. *John* 1:14: "The Logos became flesh and made its tent (*eskēnōsen*) among us"; cf. also *Sirach* 24:8–10, where God commands Sophia to "make her tent" in the temple on Mount Zion. Protennoia-Logos does not actually become flesh, but merely appears in human form; cf. *Philippians* 2:7. 96. In her descent, incognito, Protennoia disguises herself in the "garments," or external appearance, of the celestial and physical powers, only revealing herself to her brethren (fallen members). 97. Blind to the divine realm beyond them, they cannot know that Protennoia is the true source of the universe.

Protennoia Grants the Living Water of Enlightenment (47,34–48,15)

I [came] and delivered . . . and [went] [48] . . . that which he
   [originally] had.
[I gave him] some of the water [of life],
[that strips] him of the chaos
[in the] uttermost darkness [in] the whole [abyss],
which is [corporeal][98] and psychical thought.
All these I put on.
I stripped him of that thought,
and I clothed him in shining light,
the knowledge of the thought of the fatherhood.[99]

The Rite of the Five Seals (48,15–25)

I[100] delivered him to those who give robes,
Yammon, Elasso, Amenai,
and they clothed him with a robe from the robes of light.
I delivered him to the baptizers, and they baptized him,
Micheus, Michar, Mnesinous,[101]
and they immersed him in the spring of the [water] of life.[102]
I delivered him to those who enthrone,
Bariel, Nouthan, Sabenai,
and they enthroned him from the throne of glory.
I delivered him to those who glorify,
Ariom, Elien, Phariel,
and they glorified him with the glory of the fatherhood.
Those who rapture raptured,
Kamaliel, . . .anen, Samblo,[103]
the servants of \<the\> great holy luminaries,
and they took him into the place of the light of his fatherhood.
And he received the Five Seals from the light of the Mother Protennoia,
   First Thought,
and it was [granted] him to partake of the mystery of knowledge,
and [he became light] in light.

---

98. "Corporeal" (ᶜn[tsōma]tikē) may also be restored as "spiritual" (ᶜn[pnama]tikē) or (with Schenke Robinson and Poirier) as [tcom ᶜmpna]tikē, "the spiritual power" (along with the psychical). 99. Protennoia exchanges the garments of the brethren's corporeal and psychical ignorance (cf. *Colossians* 2:11–15) with the knowledge of the fatherhood as the garment of her own radiance. 100. This section presents the rite of the Five Seals, the Sethian rite of baptismal ascension. 101. The trio of baptizers Micheus, Michar, and Mnesinous appears in *Holy Book of the Great Invisible Spirit* III, 64; the *Revelation of Adam* 84; and *Zostrianos* 6 (and without Mnesinous in 6). 102. The spring of living water is mentioned in *Secret Book of John* II, 4; *Marsanes* 65; and the untitled text of the Bruce Codex 263. 103. The trio Gamaliel, Samblo, and Abrasax occurs in baptismal contexts in the *Revelation of Adam* 22–23 and, together with Gabriel, in *Holy Book of the Great Invisible Spirit* III, 64–65; in *Melchizedek* 5, Gamaliel is the one sent to rapture the congregation of Seth's children.

Protennoia's Incognito Descent Deceives the Hostile Rulers (48,25–49,22)

So, now, [49] . . .[104]
[I] was in them, [inhabiting each one's form].
[The rulers] thought [I] was their Christ.
In fact, I [dwell in] everyone.
Indeed, within those in whom [I revealed myself] as light,
[I eluded] the rulers.
I am their beloved, for in that place
I clothed myself [as] the son of the chief creator,
and I was like him until the end of his regime,
which is the ignorance of chaos.
And among the angels I revealed myself in their likeness,
and among the powers as if I were one of them,
but among the children of humanity as if I were a son of humanity,
even though I am father of everyone.[105]
I hid in them all
until I revealed myself among my members, who are mine.

The Five Seals Reserved for Protennoia's Members Alone (49,22–50,4)

I taught them about the ineffable ordinances and the brethren, but the ordinances of the Father are inexpressible to every sovereignty and every ruling
power, and expressible only to the children of light.

These are the glories that are higher than every glory, the Five Seals, complete
by virtue of intellect. One who possesses the Five Seals with these names[106] has
stripped off garments of ignorance and put on shining light. And nothing will appear to one who belongs to the powers of the rulers. In them darkness will dissolve
and [ignorance] will die. And the thought of the creature[107] that [is scattered] will
have a single appearance, and [dark chaos] will dissolve [50] and . . . .

The Future Salvation of Protennoia's Members, Including Jesus (50,4–16)

. . . incomprehensible . . . within the . . . until I reveal myself [to all my brothers
and sisters] and gather all [my] brothers and sisters in my [eternal kingdom].

---

104. For this section, see the incognito descent of the
Savior in *Second Discourse of Great Seth* 56–57; of
Jesus in *Ascension of Isaiah* 10,7–13; and of Simon
Magus in Irenaeus *Against Heresies* 1.23.5; and the
Naassene Psalm in Hippolytus *Refutation of All Here-
sies* 5.10.2. **105.** Traditional Christological titles such
as Christ, Beloved, Son of God ("son of the chief
creator"), and Son of Humanity are polemically inter-

preted in a consciously docetic fashion; see the introduction to the tractate. **106.** Probably the names of
those mentioned in *Three Forms of First Thought* 48.
In *Holy Book of the Great Invisible Spirit* (III, 66) and
Zostrianos (five times in 6–7; 53), one is baptized in
the name of the divine Self-Generated, Autogenes.
107. Or "the (entire) creation" (Schenke Robinson,
Poirier).

I proclaimed the ineffable [Five] Seals to them
so that [I might] abide in them
and they also might abide in me.[108]

And I put on Jesus.[109]
I bore him from the cursed wood
and established him in the dwelling places of his father.[110]
And those who guard their places did not recognize me.

The Final Restoration of Protennoia's Seed (50,16–21)

For my seed and I cannot be restrained.[111]
My seed is mine,
and I shall [place] it in holy light
within incomprehensible silence.
Amen.

The Discourse on the Appearance: Part Three[112]

Subtitle of the Entire Treatise (50,22)

Three Forms of First Thought, in Three Parts[113]

Colophon (50,23–24)

Sacred Scripture Written by the Father
with Perfect Knowledge[114]

---

108. See *John* 15:4–7. 109. In *Holy Book of the Great Invisible Spirit* III, 64, it is the Logos-begotten Seth who introduces the holy baptism and puts on Jesus, thus crucifying not Jesus, but the hostile powers themselves. 110. Cf. the "abiding entities" (*monai*) mentioned in *Three Forms of First Thought* 37 and 46 and the obvious reference to the rooms (*monai*) of the Father's house in *John* 14:2–3. Contrary to the Gospel of John, it was Protennoia in the form of the Logos rather than the risen Jesus who prepared heavenly dwellings for believers and in the process raised Jesus from the cursed—thus non-redemptive—cross into the aeonic dwelling places of his Father, the Invisible Spirit. 111. In Sethian treatises that feature the figure of the heavenly Seth, the "seed" of Protennoia become the seed or offspring of Seth. 112. The subtitle of the third section of the work. 113. The subtitle of the entire work. It and the concluding colophon are written in Greek. The colophon reads: *agiagraphē patrographos en gnōsei teleia*. 114. Cf. the colophons of the *Holy Book of the Great Invisible Spirit* (III, 69) and the *Three Steles of Seth* (127).

THE GOSPEL OF MARY
WITH THE GREEK GOSPEL
OF MARY

BG 8502,1; P. Oxy. 3525; P. Ryl. 463

Introduced and Translated by Karen L. King

The *Gospel of Mary* represents the only extant early Christian gospel ascribed to a woman. It gives an account of a postresurrection appearance of the Savior to his disciples, in which he answers their questions and offers a farewell discourse before commissioning them to go out to preach the gospel of the kingdom. After he departs, however, instead of going out joyfully, the disciples are weeping, frightened that what happened to him might happen to them — all, that is, except Mary. She steps in to comfort the other apostles and leads them into a discussion of the Savior's teachings.

At this point, Peter asks Mary to recount any teaching the Savior may have given her that the others do not know. She agrees and tells them about the rise of the soul past the powers of Darkness (the probable understanding of the text), Ignorance, Desire, and Wrath, who seek to keep the soul from ascending. When she is finished, she stands in silence, imitating the soul at rest. But the peace is soon disturbed when Andrew questions the "strangeness" of her teaching; then Peter challenges whether the Savior would give private instruction to a woman and thereby show that he actually preferred her to the other disciples. Mary cries, dismayed that Peter is accusing her of lying about the Savior. But Levi defends her, pointing out that Peter has always been hot-headed, and now his divisive actions are putting him on the side of their adversaries. Levi admonishes them instead to do as the Savior commissioned them and go out to preach the gospel. Levi (or all the disciples)[1] depart, and the gospel comes to an end.

Although scholars have suggested that the quarrel among the disciples might represent controversies among different groups of Christians, the core issue at

---

1. Contrast the conclusion of the Coptic text with that of the Rylands fragment.

stake concerns who has understood the teachings of the Savior. Who is able to go forth and preach the gospel? Mary's stability of character and advanced teaching present her as the model disciple. Peter, on the other hand, has not understood. He cannot get past the distinctions of the material body to see Mary's spiritual character. What ultimately matters is the state of one's soul, and hence leadership should be based upon the capacity to understand the Savior's teachings, to meet the needs of others, and to preach the gospel.

The controversy illustrates some of the key points of the Savior's teaching. When asked about the destruction of matter, the Savior had taught that in the end all material natures, including the body and the world, will dissolve back into their original state (whether formlessness or nothingness is unclear). People, he said, get sick and die because they love deceptive material nature. They should instead root themselves in the Good by pursuing the true spiritual image within (perhaps a reference to being created in the image of God, in *Genesis* 1:26–27, and/or to the Platonic idea of the Human). This image is also subsequently referred to variously as the human, the child of humanity, and the perfect human.

Although the generic terms here are masculine ("man," "son of man"), the work is struggling to represent a view of both the human and the divine as essentially genderless. The only term used in the *Gospel of Mary* for God is "the Good." Similarly, when Mary comforts the other disciples, she tells them the Savior "made us human beings." This point is important because it underscores Peter's mistake: he cannot see Mary's nongendered spiritual character beyond the superficial gender/sex differences of the body, which are destined to pass away. It is because of her spiritual character that the Savior loved her more than the others and considered her worthy to receive special teaching.

One of the more seemingly astonishing teachings in the *Gospel of Mary* lies in the Savior's statement, "There is no such thing as sin." His point is theological: God is the author of everything that exists, and God is completely good; hence sin cannot really exist. Rather, he talks about the alienation from God as "adultery," implying the improper attachment to the body. Human beings "make sin," the Savior says, when they turn away from God and are overcome by ignorance and erroneous passions.

Indeed, because the diseases of the soul are caused by ignorance and false belief, only sound teaching and accurate knowledge of the truth about reality can heal people of death and the diseases that wrack the whole self, body and soul. The Savior supplies this teaching by instructing the disciples about their true spiritual nature and orienting them away from the world to the Good (the true image of nature).

The Savior admonishes them to seek the child of true humanity within; "seek and you will find," the Savior promises. The path of seeking is illustrated by the rise of the soul, which figures not only the journey of the soul after death but also the spiritual path in this life. In order to become fully human, the soul must understand its true nature is spiritual. It must reject all law and false condemnation that seek to enslave it ("Judge not lest you be judged," said Jesus in *Matthew* 7:1).

Finally, it must renounce all violence. Only then can it attain freedom and rest beyond time and eternity.

Where are we to place this gospel in the history of Christianity? Although Jesus and his earliest followers were Jews, Christianity very early came to include gentiles, as the letters of Paul demonstrate. The *Gospel of Mary* represents a kind of Christianity that seems to have been formed in a largely gentile milieu that was permeated by popular forms of Greek philosophy, especially Platonizing cosmology and Stoic ethics concerning the passions. Although Judaism and other forms of Christianity in this period also had absorbed many such ideas, the *Gospel of Mary* differs from the New Testament gospels in that it shows no development of Jewish theological speculation such as apocalyptic or wisdom Christologies. Indeed, Jesus is referred to only as Savior, Lord, and the Blessed One—all terms that have no specifically Jewish content but that would resonate deeply in Greek piety. The one exception may be when the Savior cautions his disciples against making "law like the lawgiver"—a possible reference to Moses—but the point of the Savior's warning is rather to caution the disciples against the law they themselves set; the point is directed toward controversy over regulating Christian communities.

Although the *Gospel of Mary* is ascribed to Mary (most likely Mary of Magdala), it is impossible to imagine a Jewish author for this gospel. The ascription may point instead to an early Christian group that appealed to her for apostolic authority, much as other communities in the second century were appealing to Paul, Peter, Thomas, or other apostles to authorize their teaching. The gospel shows no knowledge of the later fiction that Mary of Magdala was a repentant prostitute, but instead agrees with the gospel portrait of her as a prominent disciple of Jesus and witness to the resurrection.

Three fragmentary copies of the *Gospel of Mary* have been found in Egypt. The first is a version in Coptic, discovered in 1896 near the area of Achmim.[2] Two additional fragments in Greek were later found on the garbage heap at the regional capital of Oxyrhynchus.[3] No copy is contained in the Nag Hammadi codices. Although the first six pages and four additional pages in the middle of the work are missing, the Coptic copy is the best preserved of the three. Translations of all three copies appear below.

Since the Greek fragments date to the early third century, scholars are unanimous in dating the *Gospel of Mary* to the second century. Egypt is a likely location for composition, since all copies of the text were found there, but Syria has also been proposed.

BIBLIOGRAPHY

Ann Graham Brock, *Mary Magdalene, The First Apostle*; Esther A. de Boer, *The Gospel of Mary: Beyond a Gnostic and a Biblical Mary Magdalene*; F. Stanley Jones, ed., *Which Mary? The Marys in the Early*

---

2. See Walter C. Till and Hans-Martin Schenke, *Die gnostischen Schriften des koptischen Papyrus Berolinensis 8502.*

3. See Dieter Lührmann, "Die griechischen Fragmente des Mariaevangeliums POxy 3525 und PRyl 463."

Christian Tradition; Karen L. King, *The Gospel of Mary*; *The Gospel of Mary of Magdala: Jesus and the First Woman Apostle*; Dieter Lührmann, "Die griechischen Fragmente des Mariaevangeliums POxy 3525 und PRyl 463"; Antti Marjanen, *The Woman Jesus Loved: Mary Magdalene in the Nag Hammadi Library and Related Documents*; Erika Mohri, *Maria Magdalena: Frauenbilder in Evangelientexten des 1. bis 3. Jahrhunderts*; Douglas M. Parrott, ed., *Nag Hammadi Codices V, 2–5 and VI with Papyrus Berolinensis 8502, 1 and 4*, 453–71 (Robert McL. Wilson and George W. MacRae); Anne Pasquier, *L'Évangile selon Marie*; Silke Petersen, *"Zerstört die Werke der Weiblichkeit!" Maria Magdalena, Salome und andere Jüngerinnen Jesu in christlich-gnostischen Schriften*; Walter C. Till and Hans-Martin Schenke, *Die gnostischen Schriften des koptischen Papyrus Berolinensis 8502*.

The Gospel of Mary[1]

BG 8502,1

The Savior Discusses the Nature of Matter with the Disciples (7,1–9)

"....[2] Will matter then be utterly [destroyed] or not?"[3]

The Savior replied, "Every nature, every modeled form, every creature exists in and with each other. They will dissolve again into their own proper root. For the nature of matter is dissolved into what belongs to its nature.[4] Whoever has ears to hear should hear."[5]

The Nature of Sin and the Good (7,10–8,11)

Then Peter[6] said to him, "You have been explaining every topic to us; tell us one other thing. What is the sin of the world?"[7]

The Savior replied, "There is no such thing as sin;[8] rather, you yourselves are what produces sin when you act in accordance with the nature of adultery, which is called 'sin.' For this reason, the Good came among you, pursuing the good[9] that belongs to every nature. It will set it within its root."

Then he continued. He said, "This is why you get sick and die: because [you love] [8] what deceives [you. Anyone who] thinks should consider these matters.[10]

---

1. Coptic text: BG 8502,1: 7,1–19,5 (pp. 1–6, 11–14 are missing). Greek fragments: P. Oxy. 3525; P. Ryl. 463. Editions: Michel Tardieu, *Écrits gnostiques*; Walter C. Till and Hans-Martin Schenke, *Die gnostischen Schriften des koptischen Papyrus Berolinensis 8502*; Esther de Boer, *The Gospel of Mary*; Karen L. King, *The Gospel of Mary of Magdala*; Douglas M. Parrott, ed., *Nag Hammadi Codices II,2–5 and VI*, 453–71 (Robert McL. Wilson and George W. MacRae); Anne Pasquier, *L'Évangile selon Marie*; Hans-Martin Schenke, Hans-Gebhard Bethge, and Ursula Ulrike Kaiser, eds., *Nag Hammadi Deutsch*, 2.833–44 (Judith Hartenstein). 2. Pp. 1–6 are missing from the manuscript. 3. Whether matter is preexistent (and therefore eternal) or created (and therefore subject to destruc-tion) was a topic of philosophical debate. 4. Cf. 1 Co-rinthians 7:31; *Mark* 13:31; 2 *Peter* 3:10–13; *Gospel of Philip* 53; *On the Origin of the World* 127. 5. Cf. *Mark* 4:9 and parallels. 6. On Peter, cf. *Matthew* 10:2; 14:29–31;16:17–19; *Mark* 1:16–18, 29–31; 3:16; 8:31–33; 9:5–6; 14:29–31, 37–38, 66–72; *Luke* 24:34; *John* 13:6–11; 18:10; 21:15–21; *Acts* 1–5; 8–11; 1 *Corinthians* 15:5; *Gala-tians* 2:7–14. Cf. also the *Secret Book of James*, the *Acts of Peter and the Twelve Apostles*, the *Revelation of Peter*, the *Gospel of Thomas*, the *Letter of Peter to Philip*, the *Gospel of Peter*, and the *Act of Peter*. 7. Cf. *John* 1:29. 8. Cf. *Romans* 4:15. 9. The words "the good" are added here for clarification. 10. The words "these matters" are added here for clarification.

"Matter gave birth to a passion that has no Image because it derives from what is contrary to nature. A disturbing confusion then occurred in the whole body. That is why I told you, 'Become content at heart,[11] while also remaining discontent; indeed, become contented only in the presence of every true Image of nature.'[12] Whoever has ears to hear should hear."[13]

The Savior's Farewell (8,11–9,5)

When the Blessed One had said these things, he greeted them all. "Peace be with you," he said. "Acquire my peace within yourselves.[14]

"Be on your guard so that no one deceives you by saying, 'Look over here' or 'Look over there.' For the Child of Humanity exists within you.[15] Follow it.[16] Those who search for it will find it.[17]

"Go then, preach the good news about the kingdom.[18] Do not [9] lay down any rule beyond what I determined for you, nor promulgate law like the lawgiver, or else you might be dominated by it."[19]

After he said these things, he departed from them.

Mary Comforts the Other Disciples (9,5–24)

But they were distressed and wept greatly.[20] "How are we going to go out to the rest of the world to announce the good news about the kingdom of the Child of Humanity?" they said. "If they didn't spare him, how will they spare us?"[21]

Then Mary[22] stood up. She greeted them all, addressing her brothers and sisters, "Do not weep and be distressed nor let your hearts be irresolute.[23] For his

---

11. Cf. *Luke* 24:38; *John* 14:1, 27. 12. Cf. *2 Peter* 1:1, 4; *Gospel of Philip* 67. The words "only" and "true" are added in this sentence for clarification. 13. Cf. *Romans* 7:3, 5–7, 9–11, 14, 22–25. Sickness and death indicate an attachment to what is perishable; such attachment disturbs the whole body. This attachment arises because matter brings forth wrong thinking and ignorance, which give rise to the passions of fear, grief, desire, and bodily pleasures that lead the soul to orient itself toward fleeting material concerns. Because passions are rooted in ignorance, they are contrary to the true nature of things instituted by God. The Savior teaches the disciples instead to orient themselves ("become rooted") toward the true nature (image) of the Good, which is divine and eternal. True contentment of heart comes from conforming to the true Images of nature that come from God. 14. Cf. *John* 14:27; 20:19, 21, 26; *Luke* 24:36; *Wisdom of Jesus Christ* III, 91; *Letter of Peter to Philip* 140. 15. Cf. *Matthew* 24:4–5, 23–27, 29–30; *Mark* 13:5–6, 21–26; *Luke* 21:8, 25–27; *Gospel of Thomas* 3 (cf. P. Oxy. 654.9–21); 113; *Luke* 17:20–24. Others translate "Child of Humanity" as "Son of Man." Rather than expect a "Son of Man" to arrive on the clouds of heaven, as in *Mark* 13, the disciples are to seek within. 16. Or "him," here and below. 17. Cf. *Mark* 8:34b and parallels; *Matthew* 10:38; *Luke* 14:27; *Matthew* 7:8; *Luke* 11:9–10; *Gospel of Thomas* 2; 38; 92; 94; *John* 7:34, 36; 13:33; *Dialogue of the Savior* 126; 129. 18. Cf. *Matthew* 4:23; 9:35; 24:14; 28:18–20; *Mark* 13:10; 16:15; *Luke* 21:13; 24:44–49; *John* 20:21; *Acts* 1:8. 19. Cf. *Matthew* 28:20. The Savior cautions them against making rules and laws beyond his commandments. 20. Cf. *Matthew* 28:17; *John* 20:19. 21. Cf. *John* 15:18–21; 16:1–3. "If they didn't spare him" is a reference to Jesus's death and indicates that the *Gospel of Mary* is set after the resurrection. 22. On Mary, cf. *Matthew* 27:55–56, 61; 28:1–7, 9–10; *Mark* 15:40–41, 47; 16:1–8, 9; *Luke* 8:1–3; 24:1–10; *John* 19:25; 20:1, 11–18; *Gospel of Philip* 59; 63; *Gospel of Peter* 12:50–13:57; *Gospel of Thomas* 21; 114; *First Revelation of James* 40; *Wisdom of Jesus Christ* III, 98; 114; BG 8502, 90; 117; *Dialogue of the Savior* 126; 131; 134; 137; 139; 140; 141; 142; 143; 144; 146; *Pistis Sophia* 26; see also 199–200; 218–19; 232–33; 328; 339; *Apostolic Constitutions* 5.3.14; *Manichaean Psalm Book* 192; 194. 23. Cf. *John* 14:27.

grace will be with you all and will shelter you. Rather, we should praise his greatness, for he has prepared us and made us human beings."[24]

When Mary said these things, she turned their heart toward the Good, and they began to debate about the words of [the Savior]. [10]

Peter Asks Mary to Teach (10,1–10)

Peter said to Mary, "Sister, we know that the Savior loved you more than all other women.[25] Tell us the words of the Savior that you remember, the things you know that we don't because we haven't heard them."

Mary responded, "I will teach you about what is hidden from you." And she began to speak these words to them.

Mary Discusses Vision and Mind (10,10–23ff.)

She said, "I saw the Lord[26] in a vision and I said to him, 'Lord, I saw you today in a vision.'[27]

"He answered me, 'Blessed are you for not wavering at seeing me.[28] For where the mind is, there is the treasure.'[29]

"I said to him, 'So now, Lord, does a person who sees a vision see it <with> the soul <or> with the spirit?'

"The Savior answered, 'A person does not see with the soul or with the spirit. Rather, the mind, which exists between these two, sees the vision,[30] and that is [what] . . . ."[31]

Mary Describes the Ascent of the Soul (15,1–17,9)

" ' . . . . . it.'[32]

"And Desire said, 'I did not see you go down, yet now I see you go up. So why do you lie, since you belong to me?'

"The soul answered, 'I saw you. You did not see me, nor did you know me. You mistook the garment I wore for my true self.[33] And you did not recognize me.'

---

24. Cf. *John* 17:11. Although this passage is often compared with *Gospel of Thomas* 114 (also a controversy between Peter and Mary), in which the Savior says he will make Mary "male," there is actually a crucial difference. Like English, both Coptic and Greek have a term "man," which can indicate either a male individual or humanity as a whole, and a term "male," which can only refer to a masculine-gendered person. In the *Gospel of Thomas*, the term is "male"; in the *Gospel of Mary*, it is "man." Since in the *Gospel of Mary* both men and women disciples are made "men," the intent is generic ("human beings"). 25. Cf. *Gospel of Philip* 63–64; *Dialogue of the Savior* 139; 141. Note too that Mary of Magdala appears first in lists of women followers of Jesus in the New Testament gospels. 26. Or "master," here and below. 27. Cf. *John* 20:18. 28. That Mary does not "waver" indicates her spiritual stability, which conforms to God's unchanging nature. 29. Cf. *Matthew* 6:21; *Luke* 12:34; Clement of Alexandria *Miscellanies* 7.12.77. 30. The mind is that part of the human soul which allows people to see visions of higher spiritual reality. 31. Pp. 11–14 are missing from the manuscript. 32. Mary's teaching from the Savior resumes in the midst of a description of the soul's rise past the powers (cf. *First Revelation of James* 33; 34). Although the name of the first power is lost in the lacuna, it is probably "Darkness" (see below). 33. The words "I wore" and "true" are added in this sentence for clarification.

"After it had said these things, it left, rejoicing greatly.[34]

"Again, it came to the third power, which is called 'Ignorance.' [It] examined the soul closely, saying, 'Where are you going? You are bound by wickedness. Indeed, you are bound! Do not judge.'

"And the soul said, 'Why do you judge me, since I have not passed judgment? I have been bound, but I have not bound anything. They did not recognize me, but I have recognized that the universe is to be dissolved, both the things of earth [16] and those of heaven.'[35]

"When the soul had brought the third power to naught, it went upward and saw the fourth power. It had seven forms. The first form is darkness; the second is desire; the third is ignorance; the fourth is zeal for death; the fifth is the kingdom of the flesh; the sixth is the foolish wisdom of the flesh; the seventh is the wisdom of the wrathful person. These are the seven powers of Wrath.[36]

"They interrogated the soul, 'Where are you coming from, human-killer, and where are you going, destroyer of realms?'

"The soul replied, saying, 'What binds me has been slain, and what surrounds me has been destroyed, and my desire has been brought to an end, and ignorance has died. In a [world], I was set loose [17] from a world and in a type, from a type that is above, and from the chain of forgetfulness, which exists in time. From this hour on, for the time of the due season of the age, I will receive rest in silence.'"[37]

After Mary said these things, she was silent, since it was up to this point that the Savior had spoken to her.[38]

The Disciples' Dispute over Mary's Teaching (17,10–19,5)

Andrew[39] responded, addressing the brothers and sisters, "Say what you will about the things she has said, but I do not believe that the Savior said these things, for indeed these teachings are strange ideas."[40]

Peter responded, bringing up similar concerns. He questioned them about the Savior, "Did he, then, speak with a woman in private without our knowing about it?[41] Are we to turn around and listen to her? Did he choose her over us?" [18]

---

34. Desire cannot perceive the spiritual nature of the soul, but only the bodily garment that clothes it; hence the power did not see the soul descend and does not understand its true nature. It tries to turn the soul back to the material world, but the soul's superior perception ("You didn't see me, but I saw you") overcomes Desire. **35.** The third power condemns the soul because of its "adulterous" relation with the body that binds it, but the soul, who understands the fleeting nature of the body and the world, rejects the judgment of Ignorance. Judgment here is not understood as the capacity for spiritual discernment, but as condemnation (cf. *Matthew* 7:1; *Luke* 6:37–38). **36.** The power of Wrath has seven forms, perhaps indicating the nature of the seven planetary spheres through which the soul must ascend. The names of these forms also indicate the nature of wrath (cf. Seneca *To Novatus on Anger*

1.1.1–2). On "the foolish wisdom of the flesh," cf. *1 Corinthians* 3:18–19; *2 Corinthians* 1:12. **37.** Wrath charges the soul with acts of violence: killing its own body by deserting the material world and destroying the realms of the powers through its ascent. The soul acknowledges that all that binds it has been destroyed— but it interprets these acts as being freed from desire and ignorance. It has achieved true rest in silence. **38.** Even as the soul who has overcome ignorance and desire rests in silence, so too Mary models that silence after recounting the teaching of the Savior. **39.** On Andrew, cf. *Matthew* 10:2; *Mark* 1:16–18; 3:18; *Luke* 6:14; *John* 1:35–42, 44; *Acts* 1:13; *Gospel of the Savior* 97:31–32. **40.** Cf. *Luke* 24:10–11. **41.** Cf. Irenaeus (*Against Heresies* 3.3.1), who denies the apostles had teaching given to them in private.

Then Mary wept and said to Peter, "My brother Peter, what are you imagining? Do you think that I have thought up these things by myself in my heart or that I am telling lies about the Savior?"[42]

Levi answered, speaking to Peter, "Peter, you have always been a wrathful person.[43] Now I see you contending against the woman like the adversaries. For if the Savior made her worthy, who are you then for your part to reject her? Assuredly the Savior's knowledge of her is completely reliable. That is why he loved her more than us.

"Rather, we should be ashamed. We should clothe ourselves with the perfect human, acquire it for ourselves as he commanded us,[44] and announce the good news, not laying down any other rule or law that differs from what the Savior said."

After [19] [he said these] things, they started going out [to] teach and to preach.

The Gospel According to Mary

---

42. Cf. Irenaeus (*Against Heresies* 3.2.1), who says heretics were inventing and preaching their own fictions. **43.** On Levi, cf. *Mark* 2:14; *Luke* 3:27–29; *Gospel of Philip* 63; *First Revelation of James* 37. Levi calls Peter a "wrathful person"—the same term as the name of the fourth power, Wrath. **44.** Cf. *Ephesians* 4:13; *Colossians* 1:28; *Galatians* 3:27.

The Greek Gospel of Mary

P. Oxy. 3525

The Savior's Farewell

. . . having said these things, he [departed].

Mary Comforts the Other Disciples

[But they were distressed, weeping greatly]. "How [are we to] go [to the rest of the world preaching the good] news of the kingdom [of the Child of Humanity?" they said. "For if] they [did not spare him], how will they keep [away from] us?"

[Then Mary stood up and greeted] them; she tenderly kissed [them all and said, "Brothers and sisters, do not weep, do not be] distressed nor be in doubt. [For his grace will be] with you, sheltering you. Rather, [we should] praise his [greatness], for he has united us and [made us] human beings."

[When] Mary [said these things], she turned their mind [toward the Good, and they began to debate] about the sayings of the Savior.

Peter Asks Mary to Teach

[Peter said to] Mary, "Sister, we know that you were greatly [loved by the] Savior, as no other woman. Therefore tell us [those words] of the Savior that [you know] but that we haven't heard."

[Mary replied, "I will] report [to you as much as] I remember that is unknown to you." [And she began to speak these] words [to them].

Mary Discusses Vision and Mind

"When [the Lord appeared] to me in a vision, [I said], 'Lord, today [I saw] you.'
   "He replied, '[Blessed are you . . .].'"

P. Ryl. 463

Mary Describes the Ascent of the Soul

"'. . . for the rest of the course of the [due] measure of the time of the age, I will rest in silence.'"

After she had said these [words], Mary was silent, for the Savior had spoken up to this point.

The Disciples' Dispute over Mary's Teaching

Andrew said, "Brothers and sisters, what is your opinion of what was just said? Indeed, I do not believe that the Savior said these things, for what she said appears to give views that are different from [his] thought."

After examining these matters, <Peter said>, "Has the [Savior] spoken secretly to a woman and <not> openly so that [we] would all hear? [Surely] he didn't [want to show] that [she] is more worthy than we are? . . . ."

". . . . . . about the Savior."

Levi said to Peter, "Peter, you are [always] ready to give way to your perpetual inclination to wrath. And even now you are doing exactly that by questioning the woman as though you're her adversary. If the Savior considered her to be worthy, who are you to disregard her? For he knew her completely and loved her steadfastly.

"Rather, [we] should be ashamed and, once we have clothed ourselves with the [perfect] human, we should do what we were commanded. [We] should announce the good news as the Savior said, and not be laying down any rules or making laws."

After he said [these] things, Levi [left] and began to [announce the good news].

[The Gospel According to Mary]

THE ACT OF PETER

BG 8502,4

Introduced and Translated by Marvin Meyer

T he *Act of Peter* is the fourth and concluding tractate in Berlin Gnostic Codex 8502, following the *Gospel of Mary*, the *Secret Book of John*, and the *Wisdom of Jesus Christ*. The text occupies pages 128–41 of the codex, although pages 133–34 are missing. There is a brief colophon on page 142, at the end of the codex. The title of the *Act of Peter* has been discussed rather extensively on account of the peculiarity of its use of the singular "The Act" (*tepraxis*) and the possibility of its relationship to the other (Vercelli) *Acts of Peter* (Actus Vercellenses). Such a use of the singular is also demonstrated in an instance of "The Act of Andrew," as Gilles Quispel has noted,[1] and hence it may be concluded that the story told in the *Act of Peter* represents one "act" in what is potentially a series of apostolic acts. Further, it is now assumed by a number of scholars, such as Wilhelm Schneemelcher,[2] that the *Act of Peter* may very well be a portion of the lost opening section of the *Acts of Peter*; Schneemelcher also guesses that that the Petrine story in the apocryphal *Epistle of Titus* may provide another episode from the opening of the *Acts of Peter*.[3] If the *Act of Peter* may belong to the opening of the *Acts of Peter*, then the events that are described in the present text were most likely thought to have taken place in Jerusalem. The *Acts of Peter and the Twelve Apostles* from Codex VI of the Nag Hammadi library is probably unrelated to either the *Act of Peter* or the *Acts of Peter*.[4]

The *Act of Peter* narrates a story about the apostle Peter and his daughter. A person in a crowd faults Peter for healing so many people but ignoring his virgin

---

1. Cf. Hans-Martin Schenke, in Hans-Martin Schenke, Hans-Gebhard Bethge, and Ursula Ulrike Kaiser, eds., *Nag Hammadi Deutsch*, 2.848.

2. Cf. Wilhelm Schneemelcher, ed., *New Testament Apocrypha*, 2.279. Conversely, see also Andrea Lorenzo Molinari, *"I Never Knew the Man": The Coptic Act of Peter*.

3. Cf. Schneemelcher, ed., *New Testament Apocrypha*, 2.57.

4. Here it may also be indicated that a Coptic translation of at least a portion of the *Acts of Peter* has been discovered by a team from the Polish Centre for Mediterranean Archaeology working at al-Gurna, near the Valley of the Kings in Upper Egypt. The only photograph initially available has been published in conjunction with an article in *Al-Ahram Weekly*, and that Coptic page can be identified as coming from a Coptic version of *Acts of Peter* 36–37. See *Al-Ahram Weekly* (http://weekly.ahram.org.eg/2005/730/he1.htm), February 17–23, 2005.

daughter, who is paralyzed. Peter proceeds to heal her in order to demonstrate the power of God, and then he allows her to return to her former disability. Peter explains that when she was young, his daughter proved to be a temptation to a man named Ptolemy, and at this point, at the lost pages 133–34, the text breaks off. From Augustine (*Against Adimantus* 17.5), however, we know that in these pages Peter seems to have reported that Ptolemy took Peter's daughter, by persuasion or force, and was about to have sexual relations with her when God stepped in and stopped the sex by bringing paralysis upon the young virgin. Ptolemy was overcome with grief, Peter continues on page 135 of the *Act of Peter*, and he wept so much that be became blind and even contemplated suicide, until he saw a vision of light and heard a revelatory voice. Ptolemy had his servants lead him to Peter; then he saw with both the eyes of the flesh and the eyes of the soul and changed his ways. Finally, in his will, Ptolemy leaves a piece of land in the name of Peter's daughter, and Peter in turn sells the land and donates the money to the poor. At the end of the *Act of Peter*, virginity and generosity are triumphant.

This story told in the *Act of Peter* is also alluded to, as we have noted, in Augustine, but there are further indications of this story or a similar story in the *Acts of Philip* 42 and the *Acts of Nereus and Achilleus* 15. The reference in the *Acts of Philip* is brief,[5] but the *Acts of Nereus and Achilleus* tells a longer tale, complete with names of the characters in the story and variations on the means employed for promoting virginity. In the latter text it is said that Peter's virgin daughter is named Petronilla, and a certain Roman official named Flaccus falls in love with her and comes with a band of soldiers to take her away to be his wife. (Within the tradition of the story from the *Acts of Nereus and Achilleus*, the person who complains to Peter about his daughter is sometimes named Titus.) Petronilla responds by recommending that Flaccus not send soldiers but women and virgins. Flaccus complies, and Petronilla spends several days in prayer and fasting, celebrates the eucharist—and she dies.[6]

There is nothing specifically Gnostic about the *Act of Peter*. Rather, this is an encratite text with a message proclaiming sexual self-control and extolling the value of virginity. Nonetheless, Douglas M. Parrott has suggested that the *Act of Peter* may have been included with Gnostic texts in the Berlin Codex because it could be interpreted in a Gnostic manner:

> Perhaps the sufficient reason is the rich possibilities for allegorization this story would have presented to the Gnostics. Ptolemy could have represented the soul, whose attraction to the things of the world (represented by the beauty of Peter's daughter) leads to ignorance (represented by grief and blindness), and would have led to death except for the coming of the light of true knowledge (in *Act Pet.*, the vision of light and the voice of Christ [136,17–137,17]), which removes blindness (138,7–10). The paralysis

5. Cf. Schenke, in *Nag Hammadi Deutsch*, 2.846.
6. Cf. Schenke, in *Nag Hammadi Deutsch*, 2.846–47.

of the daughter could have represented the power of divine knowledge over the powers of this world; and, of course, the daughter could also have been seen as a type of the fallen Sophia. (For related gnostic views in BG, cf. *Soph. Jes. Chr.* [BG,3] 103,10–106,9; 117,13–126,16). It may thus have been the deeper meanings seen in this text that attracted the gnostic compiler to it and led him too use it in the codex.[7]

Whatever we may think of Parrott's suggestion, the *Act of Peter* would have been very attractive to Christian folks, like monks or any who might have ascetic interests, at a time, for instance, around the end of the second century.

BIBLIOGRAPHY

Andrea Lorenzo Molinari, *"I Never Knew the Man": The Coptic Act of Peter*; Douglas M. Parrott, ed., *Nag Hammadi Codices V,2–5 and VI with Papyrus Berolinensis 8502, 1 and 4*, 473–93 (James Brashler and Douglas M. Parrott); Louise Roy, *L'Acte de Pierre*; Hans-Martin Schenke, Hans-Gebhard Bethge, and Ursula Ulrike Kaiser, eds., *Nag Hammadi Deutsch*, 2.845–53 (Hans-Martin Schenke); Wilhelm Schneemelcher, ed., *New Testament Apocrypha*, 2.271–321 (Wilhelm Schneemelcher).

---

7. Douglas M. Parrott, in Douglas M. Parrott, ed., *Nag Hammadi Codices V,2–5 and VI with Papyrus Berolinensis 8502, 1 and 4*, 476.

The Act of Peter[1]

Peter Heals His Paralyzed Daughter (128,1–130,18)

On the first day of the week, the Lord's Day,[2] a crowd gathered and brought many sick people to Peter so that he might heal them.[3] One person from the crowd boldly said to Peter, "Look, Peter, before our eyes you have made many of the blind to see and the deaf to hear and the lame to walk, and you have helped the weak and strengthened them. But why haven't you helped your virgin daughter, who has grown up to be beautiful and has [129] believed in the name of God? For look, she is completely paralyzed on one side and lies there in the corner, helpless. We see people you have healed,[4] but your own daughter you have neglected."

Peter smiled and said to him, "My son, it is clear to God alone why her body is not sound. Be assured that God is not weak or unable to extend his grace to my daughter. But so that your soul may be convinced and those here may increase their faith—"[5] [130]

He looked at his daughter and said to her, "Get up from your place without any help except from Jesus, and walk, before all these people, healed. Come to me."

She got up and went over to him, and the crowd rejoiced at what happened. Peter said to them, "Look, your hearts are convinced that God is not powerless regarding anything we ask of him." Then they rejoiced even more and praised God.

Peter Makes His Daughter Return to Her Paralyzed State (130,18–132,7)

Peter said [131] to his daughter, "Now go back to your place, lie down, and become an invalid again, for this is better for both of us."[6] The girl returned, lay down in her place, and became as she was before. The whole crowd wept and begged Peter to make her well.

---

1. Coptic text: BG 8502,4: 128,1–141,7 (pp. 133–34 are missing); 142,1–2 (colophon). Editions: Michel Tardieu, *Écrits gnostiques*; Walter C. Till and Hans-Martin Schenke, *Die gnostischen Schriften des koptischen Papyrus Berolinensis 8502*; Douglas M. Parrott, ed., *Nag Hammadi Codices II,2–5 and VI*, 473–93 (James Brashler and Douglas M. Parrott); Louise Roy, *L'Acte de Pierre*; Hans-Martin Schenke, Hans-Gebhard Bethge, and Ursula Ulrike Kaiser, eds., *Nag Hammadi Deutsch*, 2.845–53 (Hans-Martin Schenke). 2. Sunday. 3. Cf. Acts 5:16; *Acts of Peter* 31. 4. Lit., "People you have healed are to be seen." 5. The conclusion of the sentence is assumed. 6. Lit., "for you and me."

Peter said to them, "As the Lord lives, this is better for both of us.[7] For on the day she was born I had a vision, and the Lord said to me, 'Peter, today a great trial has been born to you. [132] For this girl will harm many souls if her body stays healthy.' But I thought the vision was mocking me.

Peter Tells the Story of His Daughter and Ptolemy (132,7–135,17)

"When the girl was ten years old, she became a temptation to many. A wealthy man named Ptolemy saw the girl bathing with her mother and sent for her to take her as his wife, but her mother would not agree. He sent for her again and again. He could not stop . . . .

"[The servants of][8] [135] Ptolemy [brought] the girl back and laid her down at the door of the house, and then they left. When her mother and I became aware of it, we went down and found the girl completely paralyzed and disabled on one side of her body, from head to toe. We carried her off, and praised the Lord for having saved his servant from defilement, shame, and [destruction]. This is the reason why the girl [remains] in this condition to this day.

What Happened to Ptolemy Thereafter (135,17–139,17)

"Now, you should know what happened to Ptolemy. [136] He was sick of heart and grieved night and day over what happened to him, and because of the many tears he shed, he became blind. He decided to go and hang himself. And look, in the ninth hour of that day,[9] when he was alone in his bedroom, he saw a bright light that lit up the whole house, and he heard a voice that said [137] to him, 'Ptolemy, God has not given vessels[10] for corruption and shame. And it was not right for you, a believer in me, to defile my virgin, whom you should recognize as your sister,[11] since I have become one spirit for both of you.[12] But get up and hurry to the house of the apostle Peter, and you will behold my glory. He will explain this to you.'[13]

"Ptolemy did not delay. He ordered his servants [138] to show him the way and bring him to me. And when he arrived, he told me everything that had happened to him, in the power of our Lord Jesus Christ. Then he saw with the eyes of his flesh and the eyes of his soul. Many people set their hopes in Christ, and Ptolemy did good things for them and gave them the gift of God.

"After this Ptolemy died. He departed this life and went to be with his Lord. [139] And [when he made] his will, he left a piece of land in the name of my

---

7. Lit., "for her and me." 8. Pp. 133–34 are missing from the manuscript. In these pages Peter seems to have claimed that Ptolemy, either by persuasion or by force, took Peter's daughter away and was about to have sex with her when God intervened by bringing paralysis upon her. Cf. Augustine *Against Adimantus,* where Augustine claims to know of such a story in an apocryphal text. 9. 3:00 P.M. 10. Human bodies. 11. Cf. 1 *Timothy* 5:2. 12. Cf. 1 *Corinthians* 12:13. 13. Cf. the story of the conversion of Paul in *Acts* 9:1–22.

daughter, since it was through her that he believed in God and was saved. I myself was entrusted with the administration of the will, and I attended to it most carefully.[14] I sold the land, and, God alone knows, neither I nor my daughter[15] kept anything from the price of the land, but I gave all the money to the poor.[16]

The End of the Story (139,18–141,7)

"So, O servant of Christ Jesus, understand that God [140] takes care of his own and prepares what is good for each one of them, even though we think God has forgotten us. Now then, brothers and sisters,[17] let's be penitent and watch and pray. The goodness of God will look down upon us, and we are awaiting it."

Peter continued speaking before them all and, praising the name [141] of the Lord Christ, he gave bread to them all.[18] When he had distributed it, he got up and went home.

The Act of Peter [142]

Colophon (142,1–3)

God of [Gods]
God of Gods
Lord of Lords
King of Kings[19]

---

14. Lit., "I myself watched over the administration entrusted to me most carefully." 15. Here the text mistakenly repeats "I sold the land" (a case of dittography). 16. Cf. *Acts* 5:1–11. 17. Lit., "brothers." 18. This is probably a reference to the celebration of the eucharist. 19. The colophon on p. 142 is badly faded but may be read as in the translation.

THE GOSPEL OF JUDAS

Codex Tchacos 3

Introduced and Translated by Marvin Meyer

The *Gospel of Judas*, the third tractate in Codex Tchacos, occupies pages 33–58 of the codex, where it follows the *Letter of Peter to Philip* and *James*, a version of the *First Revelation of James*, also found in Nag Hammadi Codex V. The *Gospel of Judas* was discovered in the 1970s and was first published in 2006,[1] but the title was known from Irenaeus of Lyon (*Against Heresies* 1.31.1), who denounced the *Gospel of Judas* in around 180 as a text read by people he called Gnostics and included in his denunciation a brief description of its contents. His précis fits quite well the Coptic translation of the *Gospel of Judas* from Codex Tchacos.[2]

The *Gospel of Judas* is given its title at the conclusion of the tractate. The Coptic title (based on the Greek) is *peuaggelion* ^e*nioudas*, the "Gospel of Judas" (58,28–29) — but not the "Gospel According to (*kata* or *pkata*) Judas," as we might expect on the basis of titles of other early Christian gospels. Thus Judas is not designated, pseudonymously, as the author of the gospel. Rather, this is the "Gospel About Judas" or even the "Gospel for Judas," and his relationship to Jesus and his role in the story of the last days of Jesus are focal points of the gospel.

The *Gospel of Judas* opens with an incipit that identifies the text as a "secret revelatory discourse" (*plogo[s] ethēp* ^e*ntapophasis*, 33,1–2)[3] that Jesus shares with Judas Iscariot shortly before the time of his crucifixion. After the summary of the career of Jesus (33,6–21), a scene is presented in which Jesus comes upon his disciples as they are celebrating a holy meal together, and he laughs (33,22–34,2). Jesus laughs a great deal in the *Gospel of Judas*, as he also laughs in the *Secret Book of John*, the *Wisdom of Jesus Christ*, the *Second Discourse of Great Seth*, and the *Revelation of Peter*. Here he maintains that he is not laughing at the disciples,

---

1. Rodolphe Kasser, Marvin Meyer, and Gregor Wurst, eds., *The Gospel of Judas*.

2. See the essay by Gregor Wurst, "Irenaeus of Lyon and the Gospel of Judas," in Kasser, Meyer, and Wurst, eds., *Gospel of Judas*, 121–35.

3. On the term *apophasis*, cf. Hippolytus of Rome *Refutation of All Heresies* 6.9.4–18.7, citing a work attributed to Simon Magus and entitled *Great Revelation* (or *Great Declaration, Great Exposition — Apophasis megalē*).

but at their overly scrupulous desire to do the will of their god. When they profess that Jesus is in fact the son of their god (34,11–13), Jesus himself begs to differ; it turns out that their god is the demiurge, the creator of this world, and not the transcendent deity who is exalted over all. The disciples are not pleased by any of this, but they cannot accept Jesus's invitation to stand before him — with the exception of Judas, who stands in front of Jesus but turns his eyes away out of respect.[4] Judas then utters the correct profession of who Jesus is. He says to Jesus, "You have come from the immortal realm (or aeon) of Barbelo, and I am not worthy to pronounce the name of the one who has sent you" (35,17–21). In Sethian texts, Barbelo is commonly understood to be the divine Mother, and the Barbelo Aeon is featured in a number of Sethian Gnostic texts, especially Platonizing Sethian texts. In the extant portions of the *Gospel of Judas*, Barbelo is mentioned only here, and the profession by Judas may be taken to affirm that Jesus is the son or manifestation of the transcendent deity.[5]

In the scenes that follow in the *Gospel of Judas*, Jesus appears several times to speak with the disciples and at times privately with Judas. Earlier in the text it is suggested that often Jesus appeared to his disciples not as himself, but perhaps as a child (33,20).[6] Much of the conversation between Jesus and his disciples addresses, in one way or another, the various groups of human beings and religious folks that may be distinguished, and Jesus stresses that a particular group of people is especially blessed. As in other Sethian texts, this group is claimed to derive from the realms above, and the group is described in the *Gospel of Judas* as the generation of Seth and "that generation" (*tgenea et^emmau*), in a manner that recalls the references to "those people" (*nirōme et^emmau*) in the Sethian *Revelation of Adam*. The disciples report a vision of the Jerusalem temple — or possibly a visit to the temple — and Jesus uses the occasion to interpret the account of the disciples allegorically (39,5–43,11). What the disciples have seen in Jerusalem is interpreted as a foreshadowing of the emerging orthodox church, with its proclamation of the sacrificial death of Christ and its commitment to the celebration of the eucharist and the practice of martyrdom, and the orthodox leaders are depicted in terms that are neither flattering nor politically correct. If Irenaeus lashes out at the people behind the *Gospel of Judas*, they come back with equal hostility against him and his friends.

Judas also has his own vision in the *Gospel of Judas* (44,15–46,4). He tells Jesus that he has seen himself being persecuted by the other disciples — an allusion to the increasingly negative place of Judas in much of early Christian tradition — and he asks for the opportunity to be at home in an exalted mansion above. Jesus responds:

---

4. Cf. *Gospel of Thomas* 46.

5. On Barbelo, see the *Secret Book of John* and other Sethian tractates published in this volume as well as the essay by John D. Turner, "The Sethian School of Gnostic Thought," in the Epilogue.

6. See the note to the translation. The Coptic reads *^nhrot*, which may be translated "as a child," but conceivably it could be taken to mean "as an apparition," or it may have some other meaning. Cf. Kasser, Meyer, and Wurst, eds., *The Gospel of Judas*, 20.

No person of mortal birth is worthy
to go into the house you have seen:
that place is kept for the saints,
where sun and moon will not rule,
nor the day,
but they will stand there always
in the eternal realm with the holy angels. (45,14–24)

Yet Judas is the thirteenth—the "thirteenth daimon" (44,21)[7]—and although he will be opposed and even cursed, in the end (and in the *Gospel of Judas*) he will be vindicated.

A central part of the discussion between Jesus and Judas involves Jesus revealing to Judas, at length, the nature of the divine and the way in which the divine extends itself through emanations and manifestations down to our world below (47,1–55,20). The divine light from above shines down into this world, and the transcendent deity—"the great invisible [Spirit]" (47,8–9), a well-known phrase used among Sethians to depict the highest deity[8]—comes to expression through the Self-Generated (Autogenes) and a host of angels, luminaries, aeons, heavens, firmaments, and even heavenly Adamas and, perhaps, Seth. The four unnamed angels who come forth to serve as attendants for the Self-Generated (47,18–26) may bring to mind the four luminaries of Sethian lore: Harmozel, Oroiael, Daveithai, and Eleleth. The massive assemblage of entities, termed the cosmos or universe, is called "corruption" (50,13–14), and demiurgic powers named Nebro, Yaldabaoth, and Saklas (or Sakla), familiar from other Sethian texts, set up a bureaucratic structure and create this world and human beings in this world (50,11–53,7).[9]

Much of this cosmological material in the *Gospel of Judas* recalls accounts, especially Sethian accounts, of the evolution, or devolution, of the divine. Close parallels may be noted between the *Gospel of Judas*, the *Secret Book of John*, and the *Holy Book of the Great Invisible Spirit* as well as *Eugnostos the Blessed* and the *Wisdom of Jesus Christ*.[10] Sophia, personified Wisdom, is not presented in this cosmological revelation of Jesus, although she is referred to once earlier in the tractate, in a rather fragmentary passage, as "corruptible Wisdom" (44,4). It is theoretically possible that she may be lurking in a lacuna in the revelation, but it may be difficult to find room for her in the available gaps within the text, and there may be no explicit fall of Sophia recounted in the *Gospel of Judas*. Further, except for a single mention of Christ in the cosmological revelation (52,5–6),[11] the

---

7. Or the "thirteenth spirit," the "thirteenth demon." Judas is the thirteenth in that he was excluded from the circle of the twelve disciples, and he is also connected with the thirteenth realm or aeon.

8. Here the phrase may also be read "a great invisible [Spirit]."

9. On these demiurgic powers and the interpretation of the story of creation in the book of *Genesis*, see the *Secret Book of John*, the *Holy Book of the Great Invisible Spirit*, and other Sethian texts.

10. See the notes to the translation.

11. The text reads "[Se]th, who is called Christ" ([s]ēth peteŝaumou[te e]rof je pekhs); although this reading of the Coptic seems plausible, other readings may prove to be possible.

entire revelation (though placed on the lips of Jesus) is reflective of Hellenistic Jewish thought, and this section may come from a Sethian Jewish account of the transcendent nature of the divine and the origin of the universe. If this is the case, a Jewish mystical or Gnostic source may lie behind this section of the *Gospel of Judas*, and Jewish speculation may have been taken over and lightly Christianized as the teaching of Jesus in the *Gospel of Judas* in a way that is reminiscent of the *Secret Book of John*, which also seems to have been composed as a Jewish text and Christianized as the revelation of Jesus to John the son of Zebedee.[12]

Near the end of the *Gospel of Judas*, Jesus turns to Judas and says, "But you will exceed all of them. For you will sacrifice the man who bears me" (56,17–21).[13] Here Jesus is indicating that Judas will do exactly what Jesus says he will do: the inner person of Jesus—the spiritual person, the true person—will be liberated from the fleshy body, and Judas will turn in the fleshy body of Jesus to the authorities to be crucified. Judas Iscariot, often demonized and marginalized in Christian tradition, is restored to a position at the side of Jesus as a loyal and insightful disciple in the *Gospel of Judas*, and here Judas is completely devoted to Jesus. Jesus goes on to remind Judas that he has now been fully informed about spiritual things, and he encourages Judas to look up to the heavenly cloud and the divine light and the stars. Throughout the text the role played by the stars seems to presuppose the influence of Platonic thinking upon the traditions within the text. We may think, for example, of the discussion in Plato's *Timaeus* 41d–42b on the way in which the creator assigned each soul to a star. Near the conclusion of the *Gospel of Judas*, Jesus tells Judas, "The star that leads the way is your star" (57,19–20). Judas lifts up his eyes, gazes at the light, and enters the light, and from within the light a voice speaks out and Judas is enlightened. What the voice actually says, alas, is largely lost to the deterioration of the papyrus, but the scene presents what may be described as the transfiguration of Judas or Jesus.

The *Gospel of Judas* concludes with the act of Judas handing Jesus over to the high priests and scholars. The text does not include a passion narrative or any account of the crucifixion of Jesus. The last words of the gospel read, "And Judas received some money and handed him over to them" (58,23–26). That, after all, is a primary message of the gospel. Judas, the disciple closest to Jesus does what Jesus declares he will do to the end.

The text of the *Gospel of Judas* has also been interpreted in a dramatically different fashion. At an international colloquium on the *Gospel of Judas* held in Paris in October 2006, April DeConick and John Turner presented papers in which they suggested that Judas in this gospel may be taken as essentially a tragic figure. The key passage that is open to different understandings is the statement in which Jesus declares that Judas "will exceed all of them" (56,17–21). DeConick

---

12. Something of the same relationship may be seen between *Eugnostos the Blessed* and the *Wisdom of Jesus Christ*. Cf. the essay by Marvin Meyer, "Judas and the Gnostic Connection," in Rodolphe Kasser, Marvin Meyer, and Gregor Wurst, eds., *The Gospel of Judas*, 137–69.

13. Or "For you will sacrifice the man who clothes me" (*etrphorei* ᵉ*mmoei*).

and Turner have proposed that this might mean that Judas will exceed all of those who sacrifice to the god of this world, Sakla, and who participate in the evil within this world, by actually being more evil than all of them. He, after all, will perform the act of betraying and sacrificing his master. According to this interpretation, the cloud of light that Judas may eventually enter is not the luminous cloud of the divine realm above but rather a lower cloud that is associated with the demiurge. Unlucky Judas, in this analysis of the *Gospel of Judas*, hears everything from Jesus but still ends up poorly. Whether such a reading of the *Gospel of Judas* leaves room for any sort of positive message in the gospel remains uncertain. In that understanding of the text, what is the gospel, or good news, of the *Gospel of Judas*?

In November 2006, at the Society of Biblical Literature Annual Meeting in Washington, D.C., Ismo Dunderberg suggested a somewhat more nuanced understanding of the conclusion of the *Gospel of Judas*. In the gospel, after Jesus says to Judas, "You will sacrifice the man who bears me" (56,19–21), four statements, reminiscent of lines from the *Psalms*, are added, and these statements appear to reflect the strength of spirit that is necessary if Judas is to hand Jesus over to the authorities. In addition to these observations, it may also be possible to compare the varied ways that Judas is described in the *Gospel of Judas* with features of the portrayal of the Wisdom of the divine within this world according to the *Pistis Sophia*, the *Books of Jev*, and Iranaeus of Lyon. In the *Pistus Sophia*, Wisdom, like Judas in the *Gospel of Judas* derives from the thriteenth aeon, is likened to a daimon, is oppressed in this world, and is destined to return to the thirteenth aeon.

The *Gospel of Judas* is a Sethian gospel preserved in a Coptic translation that may be dated with confidence to the late third or the early fourth century. Most of the Coptic text has been recovered, thanks to dedicated restoration and conservation efforts. Fragments of papyrus and one-half of a folio of the *Gospel of Judas* (pp. 41–42) may still be in the hands of collectors or institutions, although some of the text has clearly been lost forever. The work of the additional restoration of lacunae may well continue for some time to come. The *Gospel of Judas* was originally composed in Greek, and we may date the composition of the earlier Greek version of the *Gospel of Judas* to around the middle of the second century, before Irenaeus commented on the *Gospel of Judas* in about 180. This makes the *Gospel of Judas* an early text in the Sethian tradition and a key text for our interpretation of the Sethian school of thought. The place of composition is unknown.

The translation given here is somewhat provisional, and we should anticipate that additional restorations, reconstructions, and interpretations will be proposed as time passes.

BIBLIOGRAPHY

Bart D. Ehrman, *The Lost Gospel of Judas Iscariot*; Rodolphe Kasser, François Gaudard, Marvin Meyer, and Gregor Wurst, eds., *Codex Tchacos*; Rodolphe Kasser, Marvin Meyer, and Gregor Wurst, eds., *The Gospel of Judas*; Herbert Krosney, *The Lost Gospel*; Elaine H. Pagels and Karen L. King, *Reading Judas*; James M. Robinson, *The Secrets of Judas*.

The Gospel of Judas[1]

Opening (33,1–6)

The secret revelatory discourse that Jesus spoke with Judas Iscariot in the course of a week,[2] three days before his passion.[3]

The Life of Jesus (33,6–21)

When he appeared on the earth, he performed signs and great wonders for the salvation of humankind. Some [walked] on the path of justice, but others stumbled in their mistakes, and so the twelve disciples were called.[4]

He began to discuss with them the mysteries that transcend the world and what will happen at the end. Many a time he does not appear as himself to his disciples, but you find him as a child among them.[5]

Jesus Discusses the Prayer of Thanksgiving (33,22–34,18)

Now, one day he was with his disciples in Judea, and he happened upon them as they were assembled together, seated and practicing their piety. When he [drew] near to his disciples [34] as they were assembled together, seated and giving thanks[6] over the bread, [he] laughed.[7]

The disciples said to [him], "Master, why are you laughing at [our] prayer of thanksgiving?[8] What is it we have done? This is what is proper."

He answered and said to them, "I'm not laughing at you. You aren't doing this out of your own will, but because in this way your god [will be] praised."

They said, "Master, you . . . are the son of our god."[9]

---

1. Coptic text: Codex Tchacos 3: 33,1–58,29. Edition: Rodolphe Kasser, François Gaudard, Marvin Meyer, and Gregor Wurst, eds., *Codex Tchacos*. An English translation of the *Gospel of Judas* is published, with commentary, in Rodolphe Kasser, Marvin Meyer, and Gregor Wurst, eds., *The Gospel of Judas*. 2. Lit., "eight days." 3. Or "before he observed Passover." 4. On Jesus calling his disciples, cf. *Matthew* 10:1–4; *Mark* 3:13–19; *Luke* 6:12–16. 5. On Jesus seen as a child, cf. *Secret Book of John* II, 2; *Revelation of Paul* 18; *Gospel of Thomas* 4; *Acts of John* 88; Hippolytus *Refutation of*

All Heresies 6.42.2. Here the word translated "child" could also be understood as "apparition" or even "veil." 6. Or "offering a prayer of thanksgiving," perhaps even "celebrating the eucharist" (Coptic *eu^ereukharisti*). 7. On the laughter of Jesus, see also the *Secret Book of John*; *Wisdom of Jesus Christ* III, 91–92; *Second Discourse of Great Seth* 56; *Revelation of Peter* 81; Irenaeus *Against Heresies* 1.24.4 (on Basilides). 8. Or "eucharist." 9. The disciples profess that Jesus is the son of their own god, who is the creator of this world, but they are mistaken.

Jesus said to them, "How is it that you know me? [I] tell you the truth,[10] no generation will know me among the people who are with you."

The Disciples Are Angry (34,18–35,21)

When his disciples heard this, [they] began getting angry and hostile and blaspheming against him in their minds.

Jesus recognized that they did not [understand, and he said] to them, "Why has your concern produced this hostility? Your god who is within you and [his powers][11] [35] have become angry within your souls.[12] [Let] any of you who is a [strong enough] person bring forward the perfect human being and stand before my face."

They all said, "We are strong."

But none of their spirits dared to stand before [him], except Judas Iscariot. He was able to stand before him, yet he could not look him in the eye, but he turned his face away.[13]

Judas [said] to him, "I know who you are and from what place you have come. You have come from the immortal realm[14] of Barbelo,[15] and I am not worthy to pronounce the name of the one who has sent you."[16]

Jesus Speaks Privately with Judas (35,21–36,10)

Jesus understood that Judas[17] was contemplating the rest of what is lofty, and he said to him, "Move away from the others, and I shall explain to you the mysteries of the kingdom, not so that you can attain it, but you will go through a great deal of grief. [36] For somebody else will take your place, so that the twelve [disciples] may be complete once again with their god."[18]

Judas said to him, "When will you explain these things to me? And [how][19] will the great day of light dawn for the . . . generation?"

But when he said these things, Jesus departed from him.

Jesus Appears to the Disciples Again (36,11–37,20)

The next day, in the morning, he [appeared] to his disciples.

They said to him, "Master, where did [you] go and what did you do when you departed from us?"

Jesus said to them, "I went to a different generation, one that is great and holy."

His disciples said to him, "Lord,[20] what is the great generation that is exalted over us and is holy, but is not present in these realms?"[21]

---

10. Or "Amen (*hamēn*) I say to you," here and below. 11. The restoration is tentative; also possible is "[his servants]." 12. Lit., "along with your souls." 13. Cf. *Gospel of Thomas* 46. 14. Aeon, here and below. 15. Barbelo is the divine mother and the first emanation of the divine in a number of Sethian texts, e.g. the *Secret Book of John*. The name Barbelo may derive from Hebrew, and it may mean "God in four"—that is, God as known through the tetragrammaton, the ineffable name of God, Yahweh. 16. Cf. *Gospel of Thomas* 13:4. 17. Lit., "he." 18. This seems to be a reference to the appointment of Matthias to replace Judas in the circle of the disciples according to *Acts* 1:15–26. The reading "You can" remains tentative. 19. The restoration is tentative. Perhaps read "when." 20. Or "Master" (Coptic *pjois*). 21. Or "aeons."

When Jesus heard these things, he laughed and said to them, "Why are you reflecting in your minds about the generation that is powerful and holy? [37]

[I] tell you the truth,[22]
no one born [of] this realm[23] will behold that [generation],
no angelic host of the stars[24] will rule over that generation,
no human of mortal birth will be able to accompany it,
because that generation is not from . . .
that has come to be . . . .
The generation of people among [you]
is from the generation of humanity . . .
power, which . . .
powers . . .
[through] which you rule."

When [his] disciples heard these things, each one was troubled in spirit. They were speechless.

Jesus Appears Yet Again (37,20–26)

On another day Jesus approached [them]. They said to [him], "Master, we have had a [vision] of you, for we have seen [dreams] of great power[25] last night."
[He said], "Why have [you] . . . and hidden yourselves away?"[26] [38]

The Disciples Behold the Temple (38,1–39,5)

They [said, "We have] seen a huge [house[27] in which there was a] great altar, and twelve men—they were priests, we would say—and a name.[28] A crowd was in attendance at that altar,[29] [until] the priests [were done presenting] the offerings. We [also] were in attendance."
[Jesus said], "What kind of people are [the priests]?"
They [said, "Some abstain[30] for] two weeks. [Some] sacrifice their own children, others their wives, in praise and humility with one another. Some have sex with men. Some perform acts of [murder]. Some commit all sorts of sins and lawless deeds. And the men who stand [before] the altar call upon your [name], [39] and through all the actions of their deficiency,[31] that [altar] becomes full."[32]
After they said these things, they became silent, since they were upset.

---

22. Amen. 23. Aeon. 24. The stars are discussed at length later in the Gospel of Judas. 25. Lit., "great [dreams]." 26. This fragmentary section may conceivably be restored to refer to premonitions the disciples experience of the arrest of Jesus in the garden of Gethsemane and what happens thereafter, when the disciples run for their lives. 27. Or "building." The reference is to the Jewish temple in Jerusalem. 28. Probably thought to be the name of either God or Jesus. 29. The text inadvertently repeats the phrase "at the altar" (dittography). 30. Or "fast." The restoration is tentative; but see Gospel of Judas 40. 31. Or "their deficient actions," "their faulty actions," "their wrong actions"—the Coptic reads šōōt, which functions as a technical term for the deficiency of light in many Gnostic texts. The word šōōt may also be translated "sacrifice." 32. If "deficiency" is the preferred translation of šōōt, there may be a contrast here between fullness and deficiency.

Jesus Offers an Allegorical Interpretation of the Temple
(39,5–43,11)

Jesus said to them, "Why are you upset? I tell you the truth,[33] all the priests who stand at that altar call upon my name. I tell you again, my name has been written on the . . . of the generations of the stars through the generations of people. They have planted trees in my name, without fruit, in a shameful way."[34]

Jesus said to them, "You are the ones presenting the offerings at the altar you have seen. That is the god you serve, and you are the twelve men you have seen. And the cattle brought in are the offerings you have seen—they are the multitude you lead astray [40] before that altar. [The ruler of this world][35] will stand and use my name in this manner, and generations of pious people will cling to him. After him another man will come forward from [those who are immoral],[36] and another [will] come from the child-killers, and another from those who have sex with men, and those who abstain,[37] and the rest of those who are impure and lawless and prone to error, as well as those who say, 'We are like angels'; they are the stars that bring everything to its end. For to the generations of people it has been said, 'Look, God has received your offering from the hands of the priests,'[38] that is, a minister of error. But it is the Lord who commands who is the Lord of the All.[39] On the last day they will be put to shame." [41]

Jesus said [to them], "Stop [sacrificing] . . . that you have . . . on the altar, since they are over your stars and your angels and they have already come to their end there. So let them be . . .[40] before you, and let them go . . . . . .[41] generations . . . . A baker cannot feed all of creation [42] that is under [heaven]."

And [when the disciples heard these things], they said to [him], "Lord, help us, save us."

Jesus said to them, "Stop disputing with me. Each of you has your own star,[42] and everyone . . . . . .[43] [43] in . . . that has not come . . . [spring of water] for the tree . . . of this realm[44] . . . after a while . . . but that one[45] has come to provide water for[46] the paradise of God, and the [race][47] that will endure, because [that one] will not defile the [way of life of] that generation, but . . . from eternity to eternity."

Jesus and Judas Discuss the Generations of People
(43,11–44,14)

Judas said to [him, "Rabbi],[48] what fruit is it that this generation produces?"

---

33. Amen. 34. On trees and fruit, cf. also *Gospel of Judas* 43; *Revelation of Adam* 76; 85. 35. The restoration is tentative; also possible is "[The . . . overseer (or bishop)]" or "[The . . . minister (or deacon)]." 36. Or "[those who fornicate]." 37. Or "fast." Cf. *Gospel of Judas* 38. 38. Or "a priest." 39. Or "the universe." 40. Possibly restore to read "[ensnared]," "[quarreling]," "[in a struggle]," "[deficient]," "[diminished]," or the like. 41. About fifteen lines missing. 42. This teaching about people and the stars assigned to them seems to derive from Plato; cf. *Timaeus* 41d–42b. On Judas's star, cf. *Gospel of Judas* 57. 43. About seventeen lines missing. 44. Aeon. 45. Lit., "he" or "it." The antecedent of the pronoun is unclear. 46. Or, perhaps, "to drink of." 47. Or "[generation]." 48. Coptic [*hrabb*]*ei*, which is restored with some confidence because of the other instances of the word "rabbi" in Codex Tchacos. In the *Gospel of Judas*, the usual word translated "master" as a title for Jesus is Coptic *sah*.

Jesus said, "The souls of all generations of people will die. When these people, however, bring the time of the kingdom to completion and the spirit parts from them, their bodies will die, but their souls will be alive and will be taken up."

Judas said, "And what will the rest of the generations of people do?"

Jesus said, "Nobody can [44] sow seed[49] on [rock] and harvest its produce.[50] This is also how . . . the [defiled] race[51] and corruptible Wisdom[52] . . . the hand that created mortal people, and their souls ascend to the eternal realms[53] on high. I tell you the [truth,[54] there is no authority] or angel [or] power that will be able to behold those [realms] that [this great], holy generation [will behold]."

After Jesus said these things, he went off.

Jesus and Judas Discuss a Vision
(44,15–46,4)

Judas said, "Master, just as you have listened to all of them, now also listen to me. For I have seen a powerful vision."

Jesus heard this and laughed, and he said to him, "O thirteenth daimon,[55] why are you so excited? Speak your mind, then, and I'll hear you out."

Judas said to him, "I have seen myself in the vision as the twelve disciples were stoning me and [45] treating [me harshly]. And I also came to the place that . . . after you. I saw [a house] . . . , and my eyes could not [grasp] its dimensions. Important people moved around it. That house <had> a thatched roof, and within the house there was [a crowd] . . . . . . ,[56] 'Master, let me also come in with these people.'"

[Jesus] answered and said, "Your star has deceived you, Judas." Further:

No person of mortal birth is worthy
to go into the house you have seen:
that place is kept for the saints,[57]
where sun and moon will not rule,
nor the day,
but they will stand there always
in the eternal realm[58] with the holy angels.

"Look, I have told you the mysteries of the kingdom [46] and I have taught you the error of the stars, and . . . send . . . on the twelve realms."[59]

---

49. The word "seed" is added in the translation for the sake of clarification. 50. Here the pronoun translated "its" is plural. On this saying, cf. the parable of the sower in *Matthew* 13:1–23; *Mark* 4:1–20; *Luke* 8:4–15; *Gospel of Thomas* 9. 51. Or "generation." 52. Sophia. 53. Aeons. 54. Amen. 55. Or "spirit," "demon." Cf. the role of the spirit or daimon of Socrates in Plato's *Symposium*. 56. Two lines missing. Judas is speaking the following sentence in his account of the vision. 57. Or "the holy." 58. Aeon. 59. Aeons.

Judas Asks About His Own Fate (46,5–47,1)

Judas said, "Master, is it possible that my seed is subject to the rulers?"[60]

Jesus answered and said to him, "Come, that I may . . . [you, that] . . . . . . ,[61] but you will go through a great deal of grief when you see the kingdom and its entire generation."

When Judas heard these things, he said to him, "What advantage is there for me,[62] since you have set me apart from[63] that generation?"

Jesus answered and said, "You will be the thirteenth, and you will be cursed by the other generations, but eventually you will rule[64] over them. In the last days they will . . .[65] up [47] to the holy [generation]."

Jesus Teaches Judas About the Divine and the Universe (47,1–48,21)

Jesus said, "[Come], that I may teach you about the things . . . [that] no person will see.[66] For there is a great and infinite realm,[67] whose dimensions no angelic generation could see, [in] which is the[68] great invisible [Spirit],[69]

> which no eye of angel has seen,
> no thought of the mind has grasped,
> nor was it called by a name.[70]

"And a cloud of light appeared in that place. And he[71] said, 'Let an angel come into existence as my attendant.'[72]

"And a great angel, the Self-Generated, God of light, came from the cloud. Four more angels came into existence because of him, from another cloud, and they served as attendants for the angelic Self-Generated. And the Self-Generated said, [48] 'Let [Adamas] come into existence,' and [the emanation] came to be. And he [created] the first luminary to rule over him. And he said, 'Let angels come into existence, for adoration [of him],' and ten thousands without number came to be. And he said, '[Let] an eternal being[73] of light come into existence,' and he came to be. He established the second luminary [to] rule over him, with ten thousands of angels without number, for adoration. This is how he created the rest of the eternal beings[74] of light, and he made them rule over them. And he created for them ten thousands of angels without number, for assistance.

---

60. Archons. 61. A line and a half missing. 62. Lit., "What is the advantage that I have received?" 63. Or "for." 64. Lit., "you will come to rule." 65. This remains a difficult passage, and it may be possible to understand that Jesus is telling Judas that the others will try to do something to him so that—as the text seems to say—"you may not ascend up to the holy [generation]." 66. The reading is uncertain. Perhaps read "has seen"? 67. Aeon, here and below. 68. Or "a." 69. The highest expression of the divine is frequently called the Great Invisible Spirit in Sethian texts. 70. Cf. 1 *Corinthians* 2:9; *Gospel of Thomas* 17; *Prayer of the Apostle Paul* A. 71. Or "it"—i.e., the Spirit. 72. Or "assistant," "helper," here and below. 73. Aeon. 74. Aeons.

Adamas, Luminaries, Heavens, Firmaments (48,21–50,11)

"Adamas was in the first cloud of light, which no angel could see among all those who are called 'God.' And he [49] . . . that . . . [after] the image . . . and after the likeness of [this] angel, he revealed the incorruptible [generation] of Seth to the twelve [luminaries], twenty-four . . . . He revealed seventy-two luminaries in the incorruptible generation, by the will of the Spirit. The seventy-two luminaries in turn revealed three hundred sixty luminaries in the incorruptible generation, by the will of the Spirit, so that their number would be five for each.

"Their father consists of the twelve eternal beings[75] of the twelve luminaries, and for each eternal being there are six heavens, so that there are seventy-two heavens for the seventy-two luminaries, and for each [50] [of them five] firmaments, [in order that there might be] three hundred sixty [firmaments]. They were given authority and a [great] angelic host [without number], for honor and adoration, [and in addition] virgin spirits [as well],[76] for honor and [adoration] of all the eternal beings[77] and the heavens and their firmaments.[78]

Cosmos, Chaos, Underworld (50,11–51,23)

"Now, the multitude of those immortal beings is called 'cosmos,' that is, corruption, through the Father and the seventy-two luminaries with the Self-Generated and his seventy-two eternal beings.[79] There[80] the first human appeared, with his incorruptible powers. The eternal being[81] that appeared with his generation, the one in whom are the cloud of knowledge[82] and the angel, is called [51] El[83] . . . realm . . .

"After these things . . . said, 'Let twelve angels come into existence [to] rule over chaos and the [underworld].' And look, from the cloud an [angel] appeared, whose face blazed with fire[84] and whose countenance was fouled with blood.[85] His name was Nebro,[86] which is interpreted as 'rebel,' but others name him Yaldabaoth. And another angel, Sakla,[87] also came from the cloud. So Nebro created six angels, with Sakla, to be attendants, and these produced twelve angels in the heavens, and each one received a share in the heavens.[88]

Rulers and Angels (51,23–52,14)

"And the twelve rulers[89] talked to the twelve angels: 'Let each of you [52] . . . and let them . . . generation . . . . . .[90] [five] angels.'

---

75. Aeons. 76. Cf. *Eugnostos the Blessed* III, 88–89; *Wisdom of Jesus Christ* III, 113; *On the Origin of the World* 105–6. 77. Aeons. 78. Cf. *Eugnostos the Blessed* III, 83–84. 79. Aeons. 80. I.e., in the cosmos. 81. Aeon. 82. Gnosis. 83. Cf. Eleleth in other Sethian texts. 84. On the creator god with eyes flashing, cf. *Secret Book of John* II, 10. 85. On Sophia of matter defiled with blood, cf. *Holy Book of the Great Invisible Spirit* III, 56–57. 86. On Nebruel, cf. *Holy Book of the Great Invisible Spirit* III, 57. 87. Here and elsewhere in the text the name Sakla is spelled "Saklas." 88. The names Yaldabaoth and Sakla (or Saklas) are well-known names of the demiurge in Sethian and other texts. 89. Archons. 90. One line missing.

The first is [Se]th, who is called Christ.
The [second] is Harmathoth, who is . . . .
The [third] is Galila.
The fourth is Yobel.
The fifth is Adonaios.

These are the five who ruled over the underworld, and first over chaos.[91]

The Creation of Humanity (52,14–53,7)

"Then Sakla said to his angels, 'Let's create a human being after the likeness and after the image.'[92] They formed Adam and his partner Eve, who in the cloud is called Zoe. For all the generations seek him under this name, but each of them calls her with their own names. Now, Sakla[93] did not [53] [command] . . . except . . . the generations . . . this . . . . And the [ruler][94] said to him, 'Your life is extended for a time, along with your children.'"

Jesus and Judas Discuss the Destiny of Adam and Humanity (53,8–54, top)

Judas said to Jesus, "[What] advantage is there for a human being to live?"

Jesus said, "Why are you concerned about this, that Adam, along with his generation, has received the length of his life with a designated period of time,[95] in the place where he has received his kingdom, with a designated period of time with his ruler?"[96]

Judas said to Jesus, "Does the human spirit die?"

Jesus said, "This is the reason why God commanded Michael to give the spirits of people to them on loan, for adoration, but the Great One commanded Gabriel to give spirits to the great generation without a king[97]—the spirit and the soul. Therefore, the [rest] of the souls [54] . . . . . .[98]

Jesus Discusses the Destruction of the Wicked with Judas and Others (54, top–55,20)

". . . light . . . . . .[99] around . . . spirit within you,[100] [which] you have made to dwell in this [flesh] among the generations of angels. But God caused knowledge[101] to

---

91. Cf. *Secret Book of John* II, 10–11; *Holy Book of the Great Invisible Spirit* III,57–58. In the list in the *Gospel of Judas*, the second angelic power is Harmathoth; in the *Secret Book of John* and the *Holy Book of the Great Invisible Spirit*, the first two are Athoth and Harmas. Further, the apparent correlation of Seth and Christ as the first angelic power is unusual in the context of other Sethian texts. 92. Cf. *Genesis* 1:26. 93. Here the name is spelled "Sakla." 94. Archon, though the restoration is tentative. 95. Here and below this phrase reads, lit., "in a number." Could the first instance of this phrase be a case of dittography? 96. The meaning of this sentence is uncertain. 97. Or, "the kingless generation," "the generation with no ruler over it"—that is, the seed or offspring of Seth. 98. One line missing. 99. About two lines missing. 100. Plural. 101. Gnosis.

be [granted] to Adam and those who are with him, so that the kings of chaos and the underworld might not dominate them."

Judas said to Jesus, "Then what will those generations do?"

Jesus said, "I tell you[102] the truth,[103] the stars above all bring matters to their end. When Sakla completes his time designated for him, their first star will shine with the generations, and they will bring to completion what has been mentioned. Then they will do immoral things[104] in my name and slay their children, [55] and they will . . . and . . . . . .[105] [in] my name, and[106] your star will rule over the [thir]teenth eternal realm."[107]

And afterward Jesus [laughed].

[Judas said], "Master, [why are you laughing at us]?"

[Jesus] answered [and said], "I'm not laughing [at you] but rather at the error of the stars, because these six stars wander around with these five warriors, and all of them will be destroyed, with their creatures."[108]

Jesus Speaks of the Baptized, and of Judas's Act of Turning Him In (55,21–57,20)

Judas said to Jesus, "Those who have been baptized in your name, then, what will they do?"

Jesus said, "I tell [you] the truth,[109] this baptism [56] . . . [in] my name . . . . . .[110] to me. [I] tell you the truth,[111] Judas, those [who] bring sacrifices to Sakla . . . God . . . . . .[112] everything evil.

"But you will exceed all of them.[113] For you will sacrifice the man who bears me.[114]

> Already your horn has been lifted up,
> and your anger has flared up,
> and your star has burned brightly,[115]
> and your heart[116] has [grown strong].[117] [57]

"[I tell you] the truth,[118] your last [days] . . . become . . . . . .[119] grieve . . . . . .[120] the ruler,[121] since he will be overthrown. And then the image of the great generation of Adam will be magnified, for before the heaven, the earth, and the angels, that generation from the eternal realms[122] exists.

---

102. Plural. 103. Here the text reads *alēthōs* rather than *hamēn*. 104. Or "fornicate." 105. About six and a half lines missing. Cf. *Gospel of Judas* 38; 40. 106. Here the word "and" may be repeated (a case of dittography). 107. Aeon. 108. The wandering stars are usually understood to be the planets. Here the six wandering stars are probably the five known planets (Mercury, Venus, Mars, Jupiter, Saturn) and the moon. 109. *Alēthōs*. 110. About nine lines missing. 111. *Alēthōs*. 112. Three lines missing. 113. Probably the

other disciples. 114. Or "that clothes me" (Coptic *etrphorei ᵉmmoei*). Judas will help Jesus to rid himself of the fleshly body so that the true spiritual person within may be liberated. 115. Or "passed by," "grown dim." The meaning is uncertain. 116. Or "mind." 117. These lines recall passages from the *Psalms*. 118. *Alēthōs*. 119. About two and a half lines missing. 120. About two lines missing. 121. Archon. 122. Aeons.

"Look, you have been informed of everything. Lift up your eyes and behold the cloud and the light that is within it and the stars that are circling it. And the star that leads the way is your star."

Transfiguration (57,21–58,9?)

Judas lifted up his eyes and beheld the cloud of light, and he[123] entered it. Those who were standing on the ground heard a voice coming from the cloud and saying, [58] . . . great generation . . . image . . . and . . . .[124]

Conclusion: Judas Turns Jesus In (58,9?–29)

. . . [Now], their high priests murmured because [he][125] had stepped into the guest room[126] for his prayer. But some scholars were there watching closely in order to lay hold of him during the prayer, for they were afraid of the people, since he was regarded by them all as a prophet.

And they came over to Judas and said to him, "What are you doing in this place? You are Jesus's disciple."

He answered them in accordance with their wish.

And Judas received some money and handed him over[127] to them.

The Gospel of Judas[128]

---

123. Here Professors Sasagu Arai and Gesine Schenke Robinson suggest that "he" may refer not to Judas, but to Jesus (private communication). If that is the case, the transfiguration that takes place in the *Gospel of Judas* is that of Jesus, and it may be understood in the text that the spiritual person of Jesus returns through the transfiguration to the realm above and his fleshly body that is left behind in this world below is turned over to the authorities to be crucified. 124. About five lines missing. On the apparent transfiguration of Judas, cf. the transfiguration of Jesus in *Book of Allogenes* 61–62ff. The final fate of Judas according to the *Gospel of Judas* may remain somewhat uncertain, in part because of missing text here at the conclusion of the gospel. 125. Or "they." 126. *Mark* 14:14 and *Luke* 22:11 use the same word for "guest room" (*kataluma*). 127. Here the verb for "hand over" is *paradidou* (from the Greek *paradidōmi*), as in the New Testament gospels. 128. Coptic *peuaggelion ᵉnioudas*, "The Gospel of Judas," "The Gospel About Judas," "The Gospel for Judas"—not "The Gospel According to Judas."

THE BOOK OF ALLOGENES

Codex Tchacos 4

Introduced and Translated by Marvin Meyer

The *Book of Allogenes*, or the *Book of the Stranger*, is the fourth tractate in Codex Tchacos and the last tractate that can currently be identified within the codex. The *Book of Allogenes* comes immediately after the *Gospel of Judas*, occupying pages 59–62 and following of the codex; however, the portions of the text on pages 63–66 are so fragmentary that they cannot be restored to any appreciable extent. Whether the *Book of Allogenes* extended beyond page 66 of the codex and what the total length of the text might have been remain unknown. Gregor Wurst has discovered a papyrus fragment that seems to contain the page number 108 (*rē*), and if this is in fact a page number from Codex Tchacos, the issue of the contents of the codex could be broadened to include a number of interesting possibilities, including the length of the *Book of Allogenes*. Pages 59–62 of the tractate are fairly well preserved, though there are sizable lacunae at the tops of these four pages as well.

The missing lines of text on the first page of the *Book of Allogenes* make it difficult to interpret the opening of the text, but a few observations can be made. It appears that a title was written at the opening of the text, but only a letter or two can be deciphered from the ink traces that remain. What survives suggests *pj[ōōme]*, "The [Book]," and since the protagonist in the tractate is Allogenes the Stranger, it is not unreasonable to posit some such title as "The [Book of Allogenes]." In his *Panarion* 39.5.1 and elsewhere, Epiphanius of Salamis suggests that there were multiple books entitled *Allogeneis* ("Strangers"), and the Nag Hammadi tractate *Allogenes the Stranger* (or *Allogenes*) from Codex XI concludes with the line "The Seal of All the Books [of] Allogenes" (69,17–19). It is clear that ancient authors knew of more than one treatise published under the name of Allogenes or the Stranger.[1]

The name Allogenes (Greek *allogenēs*) means "of another kind," "of another race," or "stranger." The term is most well known as an epithet of Seth the son of

---

1. On the books with Allogenes or Allogeneis in the title, see the introduction to *Allogenes the Stranger*.

Adam and Eve, who according to the book of *Genesis* was born as the good son after the sad affairs with Cain and Abel in the context of the first dysfunctional family. According to *Genesis* 4:25 in the Septuagint, Adam announced when Seth was born that that he obtained "another seed" (Greek *sperma heteron*) from God to replace Abel. Although a considerable literature has developed around the figure of Seth, Seth is particularly prominent among Sethian Gnostics, who claim to be the people of Seth. Among Christian Sethians, Seth is frequently associated with Jesus, so that in the *Holy Book of the Great Invisible Spirit* it is stated that Seth is clothed with "the living Jesus" (III 64,1–3), and in the *Gospel of Judas* one of the cosmic powers is named "[Se]th, who is called Christ" (52,5–6). Such is also the case in the *Book of Allogenes*, where the Stranger, Allogenes, assumes the character of Jesus.[2]

On the pages within the *Book of Allogenes* that may now be read with comprehension, three scenes are evident. The text may open with a vocative, "My son" (59,4), and if so, this use of the first-person singular possessive pronoun may relate to the resumption of the first person in 62,10. This evidence, limited as it is, could imply that the first three and a half pages of the *Book of Allogenes* are words addressed to a recipient of the tractate, and that the use of the third-person masculine singular finds its place within the address of the speaker, who is Allogenes the Stranger. Conversely, it is also feasible that a transition to a first-person account occurred somewhere on the top of page 62 in the lines currently missing from the tractate. In the first scene (59,4–26), certain people, most likely the disciples of the Stranger, go up on Mount Tabor and pray for a spirit of knowledge.

In a manner typical of Gnostic texts, both in the opening statement and in the prayer itself, a series of questions is given as a catalogue of what needs to be known by people of knowledge. Similar prayers and a similar series of questions are to be noted in the *Letter of Peter to Philip* 133,8–135,8, where the prayers are also uttered by the disciples on a mountain (Olivet).[3] In the second scene (59,26–61,16), the Stranger is tempted by Satan, who is described as "the one who is in control of the [world]" (60,24–25). The Stranger in turn explains that he is, as his name suggests, "from another race" (60,21–22).[4] In general, the second scene seems to function as a Gnostic version of the temptation story also known from the New Testament synoptic gospels (*Matthew* 4:1–11; *Mark* 1:12–13; *Luke* 4:1–13). The Stranger successfully withstands the tempting onslaughts of Satan, and Satan retreats in defeat. In the third scene (61,16–62,25ff.), the Stranger is transfigured. After offering a prayer, the Stranger (now speaking in the first-person singular) is surrounded by a bright light, and a voice calls out of the light to let the Stranger know that his prayer has been heard and good news is on the way. Before it can arrive, however, the text breaks off. From what can be read of the third

---

2. On Allogenes the Stranger and Jesus in Sethian texts, see the essay "The Sethian School of Gnostic Thought" in the Epilogue.

3. Here it may be recalled that a version of the *Letter of Peter to Philip* is to be found as the opening tractate in Codex Tchacos.

4. Coptic *kaigenos*.

scene, it is presented as a theophany, and it resembles the accounts of the transfiguration of Jesus in the New Testament synoptic gospels (*Matthew* 17:1–17; *Mark* 9:2–13; *Luke* 9:28–36) and the transfiguration of Judas (or Jesus) in the *Gospel of Judas* (57,21–58,9?). If the allusion to what is to be given "before you depart" (62,24–25) means that the theophany is taking place prior to the death of Jesus, then the revelation is thought to be presented, like the New Testament transfiguration accounts, within the lifetime of Jesus the Stranger.

On the next several pages of the tractate (63–66), only words and brief expressions can be recognized. We may be able to pick out references to the Father, a female character, aeons, power, a human, a brother, and a cloud of light. There are second-person masculine singular pronominal forms, which may suggest that someone—perhaps the voice from the light—is speaking to Allogenes the Stranger. Other fragments have been located with first-person singular pronominal forms and more isolated words and phrases—"light," "power," "sin," "unrighteousness," "desire," "wish," "praise," "silence," "child (or son) of God," and so on—and the name Allogenes also occurs, as does a vocative reference to "my father Trismegistus," of Hermetic fame. A number of these fragments may belong to the *Book of Allogenes*, and the reference to Trismegistus may derive from a Hermetic text (so Jean-Pierre Mahé). It may be the case, though this remains in the realm of speculation, that what is given on pages 63–66 (and beyond?) is a divine revelatory response from the light in answer to the questions raised earlier in the text and with interests that have to do with the nature of the cosmos and the knowledge and insight needed for salvation and life.

The *Book of Allogenes* is a Sethian Gnostic text that thus seems to portray Jesus as the Stranger during his lifetime, before his passion and crucifixion. It was most likely composed in Greek, perhaps in the second century, but the circumstances of composition, like the text itself, remain obscure.

BIBLIOGRAPHY

Rodolphe Kasser, François Gaudard, Marvin Meyer, and Gregor Wurst, eds., *Codex Tchacos*; Rodolphe Kasser, Marvin Meyer, and Gregor Wurst, eds., *The Gospel of Judas*; Herbert Krosney, *The Lost Gospel*.

The Book of Allogenes[1]

The [Book of Allogenes][2]

The Stranger Speaks, and the Disciples Seek Knowledge (59,1–26)

"My son,[3] . . . .[4]

". . . , saying, '. . . revelation . . . [that] we[5] may know ourselves: where we [have] come from, where we are going, and what we should do in order to live.'[6]

"And they departed and climbed up a mountain called Tabor.[7] They got on their knees and prayed, saying:

O Lord God,
you who are above all the great eternal realms,[8]
you who have neither beginning nor end,
bestow upon us a spirit of knowledge
for the revelation of your mysteries,
to come to a knowledge of ourselves:
where we have come from,
where we are going,
and what we should do in order to live."[9]

The Stranger Is Tempted (59,26–61,16)

After the Stranger[10] uttered these words, [Satan][11] appeared [60] [on] earth . . . [he] said,[12] ". . . . . . ,[13] and [help] yourself to what is in my world,[14] and eat of my good things, and take for yourself silver, gold, and clothes."[15]

---

1. Coptic text: Codex Tchacos 4: 59,1–62,25ff. Edition: Rodolphe Kasser, François Gaudard, Marvin Meyer, and Gregor Wurst, eds., *Codex Tchacos*. The text may also be referred to as the *Book of the Stranger*. 2. The title is restored, provisionally, as *pj[ōōme ⁿnallogenēs]*. 3. Partially restored (*pašē[re]*); the restoration is tentative. 4. About four lines missing. 5. The disciples are speaking. 6. Such a list of questions or topics of what needs to be known (cf. here and below) is attested in a number of Gnostic sources, e.g., *Letter of Peter to Philip* 134–35. 7. Coptic *thambōr*. Mount Tabor is also mentioned in *Gospel of the Hebrews* frag. 3 and elsewhere, and the mountain is often linked to the Mount of Transfiguration in Christian tradition. 8. Aeons. 9. On this prayer, cf. *Letter of Peter to Philip* 133–34. 10. Allogenes, here and throughout. 11. The restoration is tentative. 12. Satan is speaking. 13. Nearly six lines missing. 14. Cosmos. 15. On the temptation of Jesus in the New Testament gospels, cf. *Matthew* 4:1–11; *Mark* 1:12–13; *Luke* 4:1–13.

The Stranger answered and said, "Get away from me, Satan, for I do not seek you but my Father, who is superior to all the great realms.[16] For I have been called the Stranger because I am from another race. I am not from your race."[17]

Then the one who is in control of the [world][18] said to him, "We [61] ourselves . . . .[19] Come . . . . . .[20] in my world."

The Stranger [answered] and said to him, "Get away from [me], Satan, go, for I don't [belong to] you."

Then Satan [left] him,[21] after he had angered him many times but had been unable to fool [him].[22] When he had been overcome, he retreated to his own place in great shame.

The Stranger Is Transfigured (61,16–62,25ff.)

Then the Stranger called out with a loud voice and said:

O God,
you who abide in the great eternal realms,[23]
hear my voice,
have compassion on me,
and save me from all evil.
Look down upon me
and hear me
while I am in this desolate place.
Now [let your[24]] ineffable [light] shine upon me [62]
. . . . . .[25]
. . . your light . . . .
Yea, Lord, come to my aid,
for [I] do not know . . . ,
forever and ever.

Now, while I[26] was saying these things, look, a cloud of light surrounded [me].[27] I was not able to gaze at the light around it, so brightly was it shining.[28] I heard a word from the cloud and the light, and it shed its light over me and said, "O Stranger, the utterance of your prayer has been heard, and I have been sent to you in this place to announce the good news to you. Before you depart from [this place],[29] in order to . . . ."[30]

---

16. Aeons. 17. Or "generation" (twice). 18. Cosmos. "The one who is in control of the [world]" is Satan. 19. About two lines missing. 20. About two lines missing. 21. Another possible reading: "[cursed] him." 22. Or "[them]." 23. Aeons. 24. Or "the." 25. About five lines missing. 26. Allogenes the Stranger, now speaking in the first-person singular. Cf. "My son" at the opening of the text. 27. On the transfiguration of Jesus in the New Testament gospels, cf. *Matthew* 17:1–13; *Mark* 9:2–13; *Luke* 9:28–36. In *Gospel of Judas* 57–58, Judas (or Jesus) most likely is said to have been transfigured. 28. Lit., "the way it was shining." 29. A reference to the death of Jesus? 30. Here at the end of p. 62 the text breaks off; pp. 63–66 are very fragmentary, and how far the text may extend beyond this point remains uncertain. On the fragmentary pages that follow there seem to be references to Allogenes, a father, a brother, perhaps a female figure, eternal realms or aeons, the underworld, and power. It may be assumed that the topics discussed on these pages could be the issues that are presented in the questions near the beginning of the *Book of Allogenes* (59). See the introduction to the text.

EPILOGUE:
SCHOOLS OF THOUGHT
IN THE NAG HAMMADI
SCRIPTURES

Among the texts in the Nag Hammadi library, Berlin Gnostic Codex 8502, and Codex Tchacos there are substantial differences of perspective and theological and philosophical point of view. Some texts in these codices may be considered Gnostic, while others certainly are not. Further, in scholarly discussions, the term "Gnostic" itself is an embattled term. Karen L. King and Michael A. Williams[1] have proposed that the term may need to be abandoned as inappropriate, while other scholars, including Bentley Layton, Marvin Meyer, and Birger A. Pearson,[2] have suggested that the term, said by Ireneaus of Lyon to have been used in a self-referential manner by some religious groups, particularly Sethians (or Barbelognostics) and the followers of Marcellina, may still have viability.

In this volume we shall not resolve this debate about terminology and taxonomy, but we do make use of the words "Gnostic" ("Knower") and "Gnostics" ("Knowers"), and we refer to "gnosis" ("knowledge"). We avoid the term "Gnosticism," however, in order to be scrupulous in the use of terms, since the words *gnōsis* (gnosis), *gnōstikos*, and *gnōstikoi* (from which the English words "Gnostic" and "Gnostics," respectively, are derived) are ancient Greek words, but the term "Gnosticism" (with the ending "-ism") is a modern word that was coined in the seventeenth century. Here we might also add that the term *manda*, which is Mandaic for "knowledge," is the virtual equivalent of the Greek term *gnōsis*, and the use of this term among those people who refer to themselves as *Mandaye*, Mandaeans or "Knowers" — Gnostics — parallels the occurrence of *gnōsis* among those who call themselves *gnōstikoi* in the Greco-Roman world.[3]

---

1. Karen L. King, *What Is Gnosticism?*; Michael A. Williams, *Rethinking "Gnosticism."*

2. Bentley Layton, *The Gnostic Scriptures*; "Prolegomena to the Study of Ancient Gnosticism"; Marvin Meyer, *The Gnostic Discoveries*, 38–43; "Gnosticism, Gnostics, and *The Gnostic Bible*," 1–19, in Willis Barnstone and Marvin Meyer, eds., *The Gnostic Bible*; Birger A. Pearson, *Gnosticism and Christianity in Roman and Coptic Egypt*, 201–23. For the ongoing debate, see Antti Marjanen, ed., *Was There a Gnostic Religion?*

3. On the Mandaeans, see Jorunn Jacobsen Buckley, *The Mandaeans*; Kurt Rudolph, *Gnosis*, 343–66; *Die Mandäer*; and Barnstone and Meyer, eds., *The Gnostic Bible*, 527–65.

Of the Nag Hammadi and Berlin texts that may be considered to be related to Gnostic thought, four groups of tractates are commonly thought to form identifiable collections that reflect particular approaches to Gnostic spirituality or even particular Gnostic schools of thought. These four groups of texts from the Nag Hammadi scriptures are those of (1) Thomas Christianity, (2) the Sethian school of Gnostic thought, (3) the Valentinian school of Gnostic thought, and (4) Hermetic religion. At least some of the texts of Thomas Christianity, such as the *Gospel of Thomas* and the *Book of Thomas*, are not classified as Gnostic texts in an unqualified way in this volume, but they are considered to be texts with an incipient Gnostic point of view. Although this literature of Thomas Christianity may not represent Gnostic religion as we understand it from Sethian and Valentinian texts, it nonetheless played a significant role in Syria and Egypt and may have influenced the thought of Valentinus and others. The texts of the Sethian and Valentinian schools of thought illumine the Gnostic forms of religion addressed by the heresiologists Irenaeus of Lyon, Hippolytus of Rome, Epiphanius of Salamis, and others, and they serve to clarify the teachings understood—or misunderstood—by the heresiological authors in their highly polemical writings. The literature of Hermetic religion (e.g., *Poimandres*, Corpus Hermeticum 1)[4] has been known for many years, and the three Hermetic texts from Nag Hammadi Codex VI (*Discourse on the Eighth and Ninth, Prayer of Thanksgiving*, and *Excerpt from the Perfect Discourse*) add to our knowledge of the Hermetic tradition.[5] Other texts from the Nag Hammadi library, including Gnostic texts, defy classification, and such texts cannot be easily assigned to one of these identifiable groups of texts and schools of thought.[6]

The following essays introduce these four expressions of gnosis found in the Nag Hammadi scriptures, and they provide an evaluation of the contributions of these remarkable texts to our knowledge of Gnostic religion.

---

4. On the text *Poimandres* and the hero of the text with the same name, see Poimael in the *Holy Book of the Great Invisible Spirit* (NHC III,2; IV,2).

5. On the Hermetic tradition, see André-Jean Festugière, *La Révélation d'Hermès Trismégiste*; Arthur Darby Nock and André-Jean Festugière, eds., *Corpus Hermeticum*.

6. On the texts whose affiliation remains uncertain, see Meyer, *Gnostic Discoveries*; Pearson, *Gnosticism and Christianity in Roman and Coptic Egypt*, 40–81.

Thomas Christianity

Marvin Meyer

O ne of the forms of Christianity represented among the tractates from the Nag Hammadi library initially came to expression in Syria, and since the figure of Thomas is the protagonist in the literature that emerged within this form of Christianity, it is sometimes called Thomas Christianity. The central figure in the texts of Thomas Christianity is named Thomas, though that is not really his name but his nickname, "Twin," in Aramaic and Syriac. Much of Syrian culture was bilingual during the first centuries of the common era, and texts representing Thomas literature could be composed or copied either in Syriac or Greek and the nickname Thomas could also be given as Didymos, "Twin" in Greek. In Syria, particularly in the region of the Osrhoëne in eastern Syria, with its dynamic community of Edessa, the tradition of the Twin was revered, and he was referred to as Judas Thomas or Didymos Judas Thomas.[7]

According to the New Testament gospels (*Matthew* 13:55; *Mark* 6:3), Jesus had several siblings, and one of his brothers is said to have been named Judas. The New Testament *Letter of Jude* is attributed to Judas the brother of James, also a brother of Jesus. In Syria, Judas the brother of Jesus is called Judas Thomas, so that he is not only the brother of Jesus; he is his twin brother. Judas Thomas and James, himself nicknamed "the Just," are considered in consecutive sayings in the *Gospel of Thomas* 12–13, and although both are praised, Thomas seems to get the better of it, as might be anticipated, in his own gospel. According to the *Acts of Thomas*, Jesus and Judas sometimes even look like each other. Eusebius of Caesarea (*Church History* 1.13.1–5) discusses the correspondence between King Abgar of Edessa and Jesus, and he suggests that after the ascension of Jesus, it was Judas Thomas who sent the apostle Thaddaeus (Addai) to Edessa to heal the infirm king. In a variety of ways Judas Thomas is linked to Edessa, and he becomes a patron saint of Syrian Christianity and an apostolic missionary to Parthia and, eventually, India, where, legend would have it, he was martyred. Both the *Acts of Thomas* and Ephraem Syrus report that after the martyrdom of Judas Thomas, his bones were returned to Edessa, and in her travel journal the Christian pilgrim

---

7. On Edessa, see A. F. J. Klijn, *Edessa, die Stadt des Apostels Thomas*.

Egeria recounts how she visited Edessa in 384 and viewed the bones of St. Thomas.[8]

Not everyone with connections to Syrian Christianity, however, was enamored of Judas Thomas. In the *Gospel of John* there is a very different assessment of Thomas, and Judas Thomas is most known for his lack of faith and lack of insight into the person of Jesus. Far from being one in the know, Judas Thomas throughout much of the *Gospel of John* does not know—until he is invited to see and touch the wounds of the crucified and risen Jesus in *John* 20—and he has become infamous as "doubting Thomas."[9]

Central to the scriptures of Thomas Christianity is the role of Judas Thomas as twin, and in the literature the concept of the twin not only is descriptive of the family connections between Jesus and Judas, but also functions as a metaphor for the relationship between a person and the spiritual counterpart of the person— Jesus or one's heavenly alter ego. Such an emphasis upon the twin is prominent in Gnostic literature, especially among Valentinians, and also in Manichaean texts, but Judas as Twin is already present in the earliest of the documents of Thomas Christianity, the *Gospel of Thomas*, the second tractate of Nag Hammadi Codex II.

The *Gospel of Thomas* was probably composed in Greek, perhaps as early as the first century, most likely in the vicinity of Edessa in Syria.[10] In its incipit the *Gospel of Thomas* presents itself as "the hidden sayings that the living Jesus spoke and Judas Thomas the Twin (Didymos Judas Thomas) recorded," and it goes on to describe the way of salvation for those who read the gospel: "Whoever discovers the interpretation of these sayings (*logoi* in Greek) will not taste death." Thomas is mentioned by name once more in the gospel, in saying 13, where he, and not Simon Peter or Matthew, has the most profound insight into who Jesus actually is. Unlike the New Testament gospels, the *Gospel of Thomas* is not a narrative gospel that tells the story of Jesus. Rather, the *Gospel of Thomas* is a sayings gospel with 114 sayings of Jesus (according to the conventional means of numbering) that need to be interpreted, and as such the gospel resembles other collections of wise sayings—*logoi sophōn*, "sayings of the sages," as James M. Robinson has termed this genre of literature.[11] The sayings of Jesus in the *Gospel of Thomas* have a spiritual tone and mystical overtones, and readers are encouraged to encounter Jesus and become one with Jesus by coming to an understanding of his sayings and living a life of the spirit.

As in other gospels, Jesus proclaims God's reign or God's kingdom in the *Gospel of Thomas*, but in the *Gospel of Thomas* Jesus insists that the kingdom is not simply up in the sky or down in the underworld. The kingdom is also within a

---

8. See Han J. W. Drijvers, "The Acts of Thomas," 325.

9. See Elaine H. Pagels, *Beyond Belief*, 30–73.

10. A few scholars suggest that the *Gospel of Thomas* was composed in Syriac and identify what they believe are Syriac characteristics in the text. On the plausibility of an early date for the *Gospel of Thomas*, cf. Meyer, *Gnostic Discoveries*, 63–64; Stephen J. Patterson, *The Gospel of Thomas and Jesus*, 113–20.

11. See James M. Robinson, "*LOGOI SOPHON: On the Gattung of Q.*"

person, and by knowing oneself one can attain the kingdom. Thus, Jesus says in saying 3: "The kingdom is inside you and it is outside you. When you know yourselves, then you will be known, and you will understand that you are children of the living Father. But if you do not know yourselves, then you dwell in poverty, and you are poverty."

Brief portions of the text of the *Gospel of Thomas* are also preserved in three fragments from Greek editions (P. Oxy. 1, 654, 655) uncovered in an ancient rubbish heap at Oxyrhynchus (modern-day Bahnasa), between Cairo and Akhmim in Egypt. This, along with the discovery of the Coptic translation of the *Gospel of Thomas* in the Nag Hammadi library, underscores the fact that Thomas Christianity made its way from Syria to the land of Egypt in the text of the *Gospel of Thomas*. In his discussion of what he calls the school of St. Thomas, Bentley Layton speculates that Thomas's mystical message of salvation through self-knowledge may have come to the attention of the great preacher of Alexandria, Valentinus, the probable author of the *Gospel of Truth* (NHC I,3) and the founder of the Valentinian school of Gnostic thought.[12]

A similar interest in sayings of Jesus, Judas the Twin, and the self-knowledge of a person committed to the spiritual life may be seen in another Nag Hammadi text of Thomas Christianity, the *Book of Thomas*, the seventh and concluding tractate of Codex II. The *Book of Thomas* (supplied with the subtitle "The Contender Writing to the Perfect") was probably written in the second century, and it opens with an incipit reminiscent of the opening of the *Gospel of Thomas*: "The hidden sayings that the Savior spoke to Judas Thomas, which I, Mathaias, in turn recorded. I was walking, listening to them speak with each other" (138,1–4). In the lines that follow, Jesus acknowledges that Judas Thomas is his "twin and true friend" and his brother and that Thomas has acquired knowledge of himself. In the dialogue between Jesus and Thomas, Jesus employs words and motifs that echo sayings of the *Gospel of Thomas*, but in several respects the *Book of Thomas* differs from the *Gospel of Thomas*. The *Book of Thomas* in large part is presented in the form of a dialogue between Jesus and his brother; the tractate makes a point of applying Platonic themes (especially from Plato's *Phaedo, Phaedrus, Republic*, and *Timaeus*) to the discussion of the fate of a person in this world; and the tractate emphasizes the fire of passion and the fire of hell for sinners who are in the hands of an angry God, as Jonathan Edwards puts it. And if Jesus in the *Gospel of Thomas* concludes with what seems to be a symbolic statement on the female becoming male (saying 114), Jesus in the *Book of Thomas* bluntly utters a woe against succumbing to the ways of the female and the flesh: "Woe to you who love intercourse and filthy association with the female" (144,8–10).

Whether a third text from the Nag Hammadi library, the *Dialogue of the Savior* (NHC III,5), should be classified as a part of the scriptures of Thomas Christianity remains uncertain, but what is clear is that the *Dialogue of the Savior*

---

12. See Layton, *Gnostic Scriptures*, 220.

makes use of ideas and phrases also found in the *Gospel of Thomas*.[13] In the *Dialogue of the Savior*, three disciples are named as partners in conversation with Jesus, Matthew, Mary (Mary of Magdala), and Judas, and Judas is usually thought to be Judas Thomas (however, he could also be Judas Iscariot). Although the *Book of Thomas* and especially the *Gospel of Thomas* cannot be designated Gnostic texts without qualification and may more appropriately be called works with incipient Gnostic perspectives, the *Dialogue of the Savior* is more explicitly interested in delving into issues of central importance to Gnostics—knowledge and self-knowledge, fullness and deficiency, light and darkness, life and death. Near the end of the *Dialogue of the Savior*, this text, like the *Gospel of Thomas* and the *Book of Thomas*, takes up the topic of femaleness, and Judas finally says, "The works of the [female] will perish" (145,4–5). Yet earlier in the text the *Dialogue of the Savior* also depicts Mary of Magdala pronouncing words of wisdom, and she is praised "as a woman who understood everything" (139,12–13).

A fourth text of Thomas Christianity, but one that is not in the Nag Hammadi library, is the *Acts of Thomas*. Apparently composed in Syriac in the early part of the third century and subsequently translated into Greek, the *Acts of Thomas* is in the form of a Christian romance that rehearses the legendary adventures of Judas Thomas as apostle to India. The hero of the story is once again Didymos Judas Thomas, and embedded within the narrative are statements that recall sayings of the *Gospel of Thomas*—for example, *Gospel of Thomas* 13, on Thomas's inability to find the words to articulate the grandeur of Jesus, is reflected and expanded in the formulation of *Acts of Thomas* 47. At the opening of the story, as the apostles are casting lots to determine the destinations for their missionary work, Judas Thomas is selected to go to India, but he refuses to go, even with the urging of Jesus. So Jesus forces the issue by striking up a conversation with an Indian merchant, Abban, sent by King Gundaphoros to obtain a carpenter. Jesus offers to sell his slave Judas to him, and a deal is struck. When asked if Jesus is indeed his master, Judas can only confess, "Yes, he is my lord" (2). Judas makes his way to India, initially to Andrapolis, the "City of Man," and as a "divine man" he performs mighty deeds and teaches the Indian people to forsake the ways of sexuality, marriage, and the flesh and embrace the spiritual life of the Mother (the Holy Spirit and Wisdom), the "fellowship of the male," and the heavenly bridal chamber. Many repent and follow a life of purity and holiness, but some object, and in the end Judas Thomas is subjected to martyrdom. The *Acts* closes as the king takes dust from where the bones of St. Thomas had been (by that time the bones had been taken back to Syria), and the apostolic dust brings healing to his sick son.[14]

Within the *Acts of Thomas* is the *Hymn of the Pearl*, a poem said to have been performed by Judas Thomas while he was in prison in India. The hymn has a prince from the East tell the story of how he is sent to Egypt to obtain a pearl

---

13. In their analysis of the text, Helmut Koester and Elaine H. Pagels catalog many of the sayings that are paralleled in the *Gospel of Thomas*. See their introduction to the text in Stephen Emmel, ed., *Nag Hammadi Codex III,5*, 1–17.

14. On the *Acts of Thomas*, see Drijvers, "The Acts of Thomas," 322–411; Klijn, *The Acts of Thomas*.

guarded by a serpent. He removes his robe and heads for Egypt, only to be lulled into forgetfulness and sleep when he eats the food there. His royal parents back in the East write a letter to rouse him and remind him of his glorious lineage, and when the letter is sent, it flies in the form of an eagle and becomes speech. The prince awakens, casts a spell on the serpent, grabs the pearl, and returns home, led by the letter. His robe is sent on ahead, and recognizing himself in his robe, he puts it on. Dressed in the robe once again, he arrives at the palace and joins his father and the members of court.

The precise meaning of the *Hymn of the Pearl* has proved to be somewhat elusive. Han J. W. Drijvers reads the hymn as the account of the departure of Adam from paradise and his loss and recovery of the image of God, told in the light of the parables of the prodigal son (*Luke* 15:11–32) and the pearl (*Matthew* 13:45–46).[15] Other scholars have understood the hymn as a Gnostic account of the fall of a human being into the forgetfulness of this world and the return to the fullness of the divine in response to the Gnostic call. Bentley Layton offers a variation on this interpretation by suggesting that the hymn provides a version of the myth of the soul, which comes from the spiritual realm to this world of ignorance and must be educated and awakened to its true self in order to attain rest. Layton judges that although such a myth may not be specifically Gnostic, it is compatible with aspects of the Gnostic story of the origin and destiny of the human being.[16] We might also note that the image of the prince and the robe that resembles him reiterates the theme of the twin.

With the emergence of Mani and Manichaeism, the *Gospel of Thomas* and the *Acts of Thomas* were accepted as sacred literature by the followers of that world religion. Sayings from the *Gospel of Thomas* are cited and alluded to in the *Manichaean Psalm Book* and *Kephalaia*, and the *Acts of Thomas*, along with other of the apocryphal acts of the apostles, were incorporated into the holy writings of the Manichaeans. Mani himself developed, doubtless under the influence of Thomas traditions, a heightened awareness of the divine twin that accompanied him, and in the text *On the Origin of His Body* (the Cologne Mani Codex) he declares that the Father sent him his "unfailing twin, the entire fruit of immortality," to provide redemption and true instruction from the Father.[17]

Further, although the sojourn of Judas Thomas in India seems to be a matter of legend, the Christian legacy of Thomas as the apostle to India remains strong, and Thomas Christians continue to be a significant part of the Indian religious landscape to the present day.

BIBLIOGRAPHY

Han J. W. Drijvers, "The Acts of Thomas"; A. F. J. Klijn, *The Acts of Thomas*; Helmut Koester and Elaine H. Pagels, "Introduction," in Stephen Emmel, ed., *Nag Hammadi Codex III,5*, 1–17; Bentley Layton, *The Gnostic Scriptures*; Marvin Meyer, *The Gnostic Discoveries*; Stephen J. Patterson, *The Gospel of Thomas and Jesus*; James M. Robinson, "*LOGOI SOPHON*: On the Gattung of Q."

---

15. See Drijvers, "The Acts of Thomas," 331–32.
16. See Layton, *Gnostic Scriptures*, 366–70.
17. See Ron Cameron and Arthur J. Dewey, *The Cologne Mani Codex*.

The Sethian School of
Gnostic Thought

John D. Turner

The name "Sethian" is a typological category applied by modern scholars to the authors and users of a distinctive group of as many as sixteen treatises, mostly from the Nag Hammadi library, and does not appear to have been an original self-designation. There is no historical record of any group, Gnostic or otherwise, who actually called themselves "Sethians," even though this convenient term was used by certain of the fathers of the early Christian church who opposed this form of Gnostic thought. During the period 175–475 CE, several of these fathers produced antiheretical writings in which they refer to Gnostic groups they call "Sethian": Pseudo-Tertullian *Against All Heresies* 2, Filastrius of Brescia *Various Heresies* 3, Theodoret of Cyrrhus *Summary of Heretical Fables* 1.14 (citing Irenaeus of Lyon *Against Heresies* 1.30), and Epiphanius of Salamis *Panarion* 26; 39–40.[18]

On the other hand, many of these treatises refer to a special segment of humanity called "the great generation," "strangers," "another kind," "the immovable, incorruptible race," "the seed of Seth," "the living and immoveable race," "the children of Seth," "the holy seed of Seth," and "those who are worthy." The terms "generation," "race," "seed," and "strangers" are all plays on the tradition of Seth's birth as "another seed" (*sperma heteron*) in *Genesis* 4:25 (J source) and as bearer of the same image and likeness to God as was his father Adam in *Genesis* 5:3 (P source):

> And Adam knew his wife again, and she bore a son and called his name Seth, for she said, "God has appointed for me another seed (Hebrew *kī šāt-li elohīm zera' 'ahēr*; Greek *exanestēsen gar moi ho theos sperma heteron*) instead of Abel, for Cain slew him." (*Genesis* 4:25, RSV)

---

18. The earliest main patristic testimonies are Irenaeus's *Against Heresies* (ca. 175) and the lost *Syntagma* of Hippolytus (ca. 210), on both of which are based the testimonies of Pseudo-Tertullian (225–250), Filastrius (380/90), Theodoret (around 453), and Epiphanius (ca. 475). The Sethians described in Hippolytus's *Refutation of All Heresies* seem quite different from those described in the former sources and may perhaps be connected with the non-Sethian treatise *Paraphrase of Shem* (NHC VII,1).

When Adam had lived a hundred and thirty years, he became the father of a son in his own likeness, after his image (Hebrew *wayyōled bidmūtō kᵉtsalmō*; Greek *egennēsen kata tēn idean autou kai kata tēn eikona autou*), and named him Seth. (*Genesis* 5:3, RSV)

Seth's status as bearer and transmitter (unlike Cain and Abel) and ultimately restorer of the authentic image of Adam, the original bearer of the divine image, was of great significance to the original composers and users of this literature, whether or not they called themselves Sethians or "the seed of Seth."

Based on the work of Hans-Martin Schenke,[19] the following texts are representative of Sethian thought: from the Nag Hammadi codices and the Berlin Gnostic Codex, the *Secret Book of John* (NHC II,1; III,1; IV,1; BG,2), *Nature of the Rulers* (NHC II,4), *Holy Book of the Great Invisible Spirit* (III,2; IV,2, also known as the *Egyptian Gospel*), *Revelation of Adam* (V,5), *Three Steles of Seth* (VII,5), *Zostrianos* (VIII,1), *Melchizedek* (IX,1), *Thought of Norea* (IX,2), *Marsanes* (X), *Allogenes the Stranger* (XI,3), *Three Forms of First Thought* (or *Trimorphic Protennoia*; XIII,1); from the Bruce Codex, the untitled text; from Codex Tchacos, the *Gospel of Judas* and a poorly attested *Book of Allogenes* (or *Book of the Stranger*); and from patristic authors, the accounts of Irenaeus's *Against Heresies* 1.29 (Gnostics later identified by Theodoret as Barbeloites), and Epiphanius's *Panarion* 26, 39, and 40 (Gnostics, Sethians, and Archontics, respectively).[20] In varying ways, these treatises display a number of recurrent mythological features that Schenke considers to form a core doctrine or myth on the basis of which one may characterize a document as "Sethian": the self-understanding of their readers as the spiritual "seed" (descendants) of Seth, who is also their heavenly-earthly savior, and a supreme trinity consisting of the Father (Invisible Spirit), the Mother (Barbelo), and the Child (Autogenes), who in turn establish Four Luminaries (Harmozel, Oroiael, Daveithai, and Eleleth, often conceived as the dwelling places of the heavenly Adam, Seth, and the seed of Seth), the last of whom is responsible for the appearance of Sophia and, through her, for the material world and its evil fashioner and ruler Yaldabaoth/Sakla (or Saklas)/Samael and his demonic powers, who try to destroy the seed of Seth by flood and fire but are thwarted by the Mother's saving interventions: as a divine voice revealing the existence of the archetypal

---

19. Hans-Martin Schenke, "Das sethianische System nach Nag-Hammadi-Handschriften"; "The Phenomenon Gnostic Sethianism."

20. To this list one might add *Thunder* (NHC VI,2; so Layton, in *The Gnostic Scriptures*), and the *Gospel of Judas* (Codex Tchacos). Among the Sethian treatises listed here, there is no mention of Seth in the *Thought of Norea*, *Three Forms of First Thought*, *Allogenes the Stranger*, *Marsanes*, or the untitled text of the Bruce Codex (which, like *Zostrianos*, contains the name "Setheus"), and but a single mention of the "children of Seth" in *Melchizedek*. Although the name Seth occurs in the titles of the *Second Discourse of Great Seth* and the *Three Steles of Seth*, Seth is mentioned in the body of the latter only. Although *Genesis* 4:25 is quoted by the *Nature of the Rulers* in connection with the birth of Seth to Eve, Seth plays no further role therein, and it is instead Norea who is the heavenly helper for future generations. And, like Irenaeus *Against Heresies*. 1.29, *Three Forms of First Thought* and the *Thought of Norea* do not mention Seth at all. This leaves the *Revelation of Adam*, the *Holy Book of the Great Invisible Spirit*, the *Secret Book of John*, and the *Three Steles of Seth* as the only Sethian works wherein the figure of Seth is truly significant.

human, as the spiritual Eve, and ultimately as the heavenly Seth or Christ, who bestows a saving baptism often called the Five Seals.

Sethian Gnostic thought had its roots in a form of Jewish speculation on the figure and function of Sophia, divine Wisdom, whom the Jewish scriptures some- times personified as the instrument through whom God creates, nourishes, and enlightens the world (*Proverbs* 1–8; *Sirach* 24; *Wisdom of Solomon* 7). In the hands of Sethian Gnostics, these biblical functions of Sophia were distributed among a hierarchy of feminine principles: (1) an exalted divine Mother named Barbelo, who, as the First Thought ("Protennoia," "Pronoia") of the supreme deity (the Invisible Spirit), is the ultimate savior and enlightener; (2) a lower fig- ure named Sophia, who gave rise to the actual creator ("Yaldabaoth," "Sakla," "Samael," the first archon) of the physical world, who in turn incarnated portions of the supreme Mother's divine essence into human bodies; and (3) the emissary figure of the spiritual Eve ("Epinoia"), who appears on the earthly plane to alert humankind (Adam) to its true affinity with the divine First Thought. Final salva- tion would be achieved by the supreme Mother's complete reintegration of her own dissipated essence into its original unity.

The functions of these various feminine wisdom figures were interconnected by means of a myth that narrated the vicissitudes of knowledge (gnosis) itself. The potential thinking and self-knowledge of the supreme deity (the Invisible Spirit) initially achieves full actuality in the person of his First Thought (Barbelo), whose intelligence obediently extends itself into a plethora of intelligent spiritual entities called aeons, culminating in the figure of Sophia. But at that point, the orderly unfolding of the divine thinking tragically enters a phase of decline and fallenness in Sophia's rash attempt to imitate the supreme deity by conceiving a thought of her own. The independent willfulness of her creative thought results in the birth of the archon creator, who then steals it and infuses it into Adam's mortal human body, where it is further weakened by fleshly and material con- cerns and undergoes oblivion.

The remainder of the myth narrates the steps by which the divine Mother re- stores this dissipated divine thinking to its original actuality. Appearing first as the spiritual Eve/Epinoia, she awakens Adam's dim knowledge of his divine origin and image and bequeaths this enlightenment to subsequent humanity through Adam's son Seth and his progeny, the seed of Seth. This ensures that humanity's knowledge of its essential divinity will be preserved among future humanity in spite of the archon's attempts to suppress it (by the expulsion from paradise, the bringing of the flood, the inauguration of sexual lust through the fallen angels, and the conflagration of Sodom and Gomorrah). The Mother's further salvific appearances throughout subsequent history in various guises (e.g., as a luminous cloud, as ethereal angels, as Seth himself, or as Jesus) and ritual contexts (mainly baptism) continue to awaken humanity's potential self-awareness of its essential divinity to full actuality. Salvation is thus the awakening of the fallen divine self- knowledge and a reintegration into its original condition, which is actualized through the individual Gnostic in the act of coming to know oneself by reenact- ing the myth of the vicissitudes of knowledge itself.

The Sethian treatises divide themselves into two basic groups depending on the way one attains salvific enlightenment. One group of tractates (*Secret Book of John, Revelation of Adam, Holy Book, Three Forms of First Thought, Gospel of Judas,* and perhaps *Nature of the Rulers*) conceptualizes the means of salvation as a horizontal, temporally successive sequence of revelatory descents into this world by a heavenly savior, while another group (*Zostrianos, Allogenes the Stranger, Three Steles of Seth,* and *Marsanes*) conceptualizes the means of salvation as a vertically oriented ascent by which a visionary practitioner enters a succession of mental states in which one is cognitively assimilated to ever higher levels of being (and those beyond being itself). In the first, "descent pattern" group of treatises, the salvational process is instigated by the Mother of the Sethian trinity, usually called Barbelo, who—unrecognized by the hostile cosmic powers—appears at crucial points in primordial history, although her final appearance in contemporary times often occurs in a masculine guise, such as the Logos (Word) or Seth or Jesus, and the instrument of salvation is frequently the baptismal rite called the Five Seals. In the second, "ascent pattern" group, the possibility of enlightenment is revealed by the visionary experience of various illustrious figures—Zostrianos, Allogenes, and Marsanes—who exemplify a contemplative technique to be implemented by the individual Gnostic either alone or in concert with other similarly instructed adepts.

The Sethian treatises also exhibit a number of textual interdependencies. Pronoia's first-person singular recitation of her three salvific descents narrated at the end of the longer version of the *Secret Book of John* seems to underlie the structure and much of the content of the closely related *Three Forms of First Thought*. *Three Forms of First Thought's* tendency to shift the blame for the origin and activity of the world creator Yaldabaoth from Sophia onto the Fourth Luminary Eleleth is shared by the *Holy Book of the Great Invisible Spirit* and possibly by the *Gospel of Judas*. The baptismal doctrine of the *Three Forms of First Thought* also seems to sustain a close relationship especially to the *Secret Book of John*, the *Holy Book*, *Zostrianos*, and—more distantly—to *Melchizedek*, perhaps *Marsanes*, and even the *Revelation of Adam*. The *Three Steles of Seth* (126,5–13), *Zostrianos* (86,13–23; 88,9–22; 51,24–52,8), and *Allogenes the Stranger* (54,6–37) share an ecstatic doxology directed to a specific group of divine powers. *Allogenes the Stranger* shares word-for-word a section of its initial negative theology of the supreme Invisible Spirit with the initial negative theology of the *Secret Book of John*, while *Zostrianos* (64,13–66,11 + 66,14b–68,13 + 74,17–75,21) shares almost word-for-word its negative theology of the supreme One with Book I, chapters 49,9–50,21 of Marius Victorinus's treatise *Against Arius*; indeed, all these negative theologies seem to be extracted from a Middle Platonic treatise or commentary on the first hypothesis of Plato's *Parmenides* (137a–142 a).

Many of the Sethian texts (*Secret Book of John, Three Forms of First Thought, Holy Book, Revelation of Adam, Melchizedek, Zostrianos, Marsanes,* and the untitled text of the Bruce Codex) contain allusions to rituals, especially a baptismal rite often called the Five Seals. Although some of these allusions could be understood as referring to an otherworldly mystical experience rather than to a literal water ritual, others are most naturally understood as references to a physical ritual practiced by sectarian group with its own social organization and communal identity.

Detailed analysis of the literary composition and interdependency of all the Sethian treatises suggests a relative compositional sequence of mutual priority and posteriority. There seem to be four important literary synchronisms between the Sethian treatises and non-Sethian literature, two well attested and two conjectural. First, sometime between 175 and 180 CE, Irenaeus, bishop of Lyon, knew of the *Gospel of Judas*, which he ascribed to certain "Gnostics," as well as some version of the *Secret Book of John*, whose theogony and cosmogony he summarized in his *Against Heresies* (1.29). Second, in his *Life of Plotinus* 16, Porphyry attests that versions of *Zostrianos* and *Allogenes* circulated among members of Plotinus's seminar in Rome in the period 240–265 CE, and the conclusion to Plotinus's anti-Gnostic text (*Ennead* III, 8 [30]; V, 8 [31]; V, 5 [32]; II, 9 [33]) has certain doctrines of *Zostrianos* clearly in view, and indeed appears to cite *Zostrianos* 9,17–10,20 in *Ennead* II, 9 [33] 10,19–33. Third, both *Zostrianos* (64,13–75,21) and Marius Victorinus's *Against Arius* I 49,9–50,21 utilize a common negative theological source that seems to be from a Middle Platonic commentary on Plato's *Parmenides* of uncertain date, but likely pre-Plotinian, and a similar origin may be posited for the negative theological source common to *Allogenes the Stranger* (62,28–63,25) and the *Secret Book of John* (BG 24,6–25,7; II 3,18–33). Fourth, the final section of *Three Forms of First Thought* (49,7–50,16) seems to reflect the debate over the interpretation of the Fourth Gospel that occurred around the time of the writing of the *First Letter of John*, perhaps around 125–150 CE.

The time line between Irenaeus around 175 CE and Porphyry around 260 CE may be extended both backward and forward. On the one hand, the compositional history of *Three Forms of First Thought* and the *Secret Book of John* suggests that they contain material—such as the Pronoia monologue concluding the longer version of the *Secret Book*—that antedates Irenaeus and seems to reflect debates over the interpretation of the Fourth Gospel as early as the first quarter of the second century. Accordingly, one may assign such precursory material to the first half of the second century. On the other hand, certain features of the treatise *Marsanes* link it with the Neoplatonic teaching of Iamblichus and Theodore of Asine in the late third century. Thus the *Three Steles of Seth*, *Zostrianos*, and *Allogenes the Stranger* would be assigned to the first half—and *Marsanes* perhaps to the later second half—of the third century.

Between these extremes, one may assign the earliest compositional stages of *Three Forms of First Thought*, the *Secret Book of John*, and perhaps even the *Gospel of Judas* to the first half of the second century, while their final (present) form as well as that of the *Nature of the Rulers*, *Thought of Norea*, *Revelation of Adam*, *Melchizedek*, and *Holy Book of the Great Invisible Spirit*—roughly in that order—would have appeared somewhere in the late second or early third century. Of course, since nearly every treatise has its own peculiar history of redactions, one cannot assume a simple unilinear dependence of one upon another, but rather a more complex process of cross-fertilization. Nevertheless, as one traces this compositional sequence, moving from what seem to be relatively early treatises to relatively later ones, there is a noticeable shift away from the descent pattern of the Pronoia monologue toward the ascent pattern characteristic of the Platonizing treatises. Although there are elements of ascent throughout the entire corpus, the ascent pattern clearly predominates in the Platonizing group, whose Platonic metaphysics resists the notion of salvific descents. Of course, it is possible that the ascent and descent patterns were merely alternative—rather than successive—conceptions of enlightenment from the beginning of the Sethian movement, but such an assumption cannot account for the elaborate multiplication of psychical realms and postmortem conditions of souls in *Zostrianos* (e.g., 42,10–44,22; 27,19–28,30; attested also by Plotinus and *Marsanes*) compared with the rather simpler four-level hierarchy of psychical realms and conditions within the Four Luminaries of the *Secret Book of John* (BG 64,14–71,2; NHC II 25,16–27,30).

BIBLIOGRAPHY

Hans-Martin Schenke, "The Phenomenon and Significance of Gnostic Sethianism"; "Das sethianische System nach Nag-Hammadi-Handschriften"; John D. Turner, "The Gnostic Threefold Path to Enlightenment"; "Sethian Gnosticism: A Literary History"; *Sethian Gnosticism and the Platonic Tradition*.

The Valentinian School of
Gnostic Thought

Einar Thomassen

One of the most successful Gnostic Christian movements was founded by Valentinus around 140. Toward the end of the second century Irenaeus of Lyon regarded the followers of Valentinus in the Valentinian school of Gnostic thought as the most dangerous of all the Gnostic heretics, and his *Against Heresies* was especially written to refute them. In the fourth century Valentinian communities still existed in the eastern part of the Roman Empire—victims, by that time, of increasing orthodox persecution.

About Valentinus himself very little is known.[21] Irenaeus says he was active in Rome from the late 130s until about 160. The tradition (cf. Epiphanius, ca. 390) that he originally came from Alexandria is uncertain. Valentinus wrote homilies, letters, and psalms, fragments of which have been preserved. It is doubtful that he himself composed a "system" in the manner of many of his disciples. (The report in Irenaeus *Against Heresies* 1.11.1 is untrustworthy.) His psalms, however, continued to be used in worship by later Valentinian communities. That he is the author of the *Gospel of Truth* remains a distinct possibility. Well-known Valentinian leaders and writers of the second century include Heracleon, Ptolemy, Marcus "the Magician," Axionicus, and Theodotus. Most of the Valentinian documents that have been preserved are, however, anonymous.

The most important sources for our knowledge of Valentinian theology are the grand systematic treatises reported by Irenaeus and Hippolytus, and the *Tripartite Tractate* from Nag Hammadi (NHC I,5). Other significant sources are *Excerpts from Theodotus*, by Clement of Alexandria, the fragments of Heracleon's commentary on the *Gospel of John*, mainly transmitted by Origen, and Ptolemy's *Letter to Flora*. Valuable information is also given by Tertullian, Clement of Alexandria, and other mainstream Christian writers such as Epiphanius.[22] Of the

21. On Valentinus, see Layton, *Gnostic Scriptures*, 215–64; Christoph Markschies, *Valentinus Gnosticus?*; Einar Thomassen, *The Spiritual Seed: The Church of the "Valentinians."*

22. For translations of texts on the Valentinians, especially in the church fathers, see Barnstone and Meyer, eds., *Gnostic Bible*, 239–355; Werner Foerster, ed., *Gnosis*, vol. 1; Layton, *Gnostic Scriptures*, 265–353.

Nag Hammadi tractates, the *Gospel of Truth* (I,3), the *Treatise on Resurrection* (I,4), the *Tripartite Tractate* (I,5), the *Gospel of Philip* (II,3), the *Interpretation of Knowledge* (XI,1), and *Valentinian Exposition* (XI,2, together with the *Liturgical Readings*) are most probably of Valentinian provenance.

Valentinian theology can be described as the earliest attempt to formulate a comprehensively theoretical interpretation of Christianity. Characteristic of the Valentinian vision is that the Christian message of salvation is explained by means of the opposition between spirit and matter, an opposition that in turn is derived from the even more basic polarity of oneness and plurality. The essential features of the system are as follows. A single first principle is the ultimate source of all. That principle is called the Father and is also named the "Depth" (Bythos or Bathos). He is inconceivable and indescribable, but he knows himself and wishes to be known. The Father's self-knowledge produces the Son, who is a Mind. The Father and the Son are ambiguously one and two at the same time, and that situation makes it possible for a plurality of beings to be generated, who represent an unfolding of the self-reflective, divine essence but are individual personalities in their own right as well. These spiritual entities are called "members of the All," "entireties," aeons, and the like—and collectively the Pleroma, "Fullness."

The tension between oneness and plurality inherent in the generative process ultimately leads to a crisis with the last and youngest of the aeons, usually called Sophia. She attempts to grasp the totality of the Father, but she fails because she is only an individual aeon. As a result, she suffers and is split in two. Her perfect, spiritual part returns to the Pleroma, whereas her imperfect part is cut off. A Boundary (*horos*) is set up to keep the inferior part of Sophia away from the Pleroma.

Sophia outside the Pleroma has been reduced to a state of deficiency, depriva-tion, and unfulfilled, irrational passion. From this negativity and passion, matter takes its origin. Perceiving these consequences, Sophia repents and prays for help from her fellow aeons in the Pleroma. This sentiment of repentance and conver-sion produces the substance characteristic of the soul—"psychical" substance. Moreover, in response to her prayer for help, the Pleroma unites to bring forth a Savior. He is a joint product of all the aeons and, being accompanied by a host of angels, manifests both the unity and the diversity of the Pleroma. By the vision of the Savior and his angels, Sophia is healed of her passions and experiences a third type of emotion: joy. In this state of mind she brings forth a third kind of off-spring: spiritual beings, who are images of what she has seen. Thus, the sub-stances of matter, soul, and spirit are all derived from the various emotions successively experienced by Sophia.

From these substances the cosmos is made. This work is carried out by the now rational Sophia and/or the Savior. The earth and the seven planetary spheres above it are made out of matter and psychical substance, with psychical archons ruling the spheres. The manual work of creation, however, is carried out by the chief archon, called the demiurge, who does not realize that he is only a tool used by the real creators, Sophia and the Savior. Sophia herself dwells, together with her spiritual children, in a region called the Ogdoad (Eight), or the Middle, located between the cosmos and the Pleroma.

The first human being is created in the same way as the cosmos. Moved by Sophia, the demiurge forms him out of matter and soul. In addition, however, Sophia secretly inserts into Adam a spiritual component, which derives from the children she bore during her joyful vision of the Savior and his angels. Humans thus possess a spiritual element—or at least some humans do—hidden in their body and soul. However, this element, "the inner man," is bullied and tormented by the demons residing in corporeality and passion and needs to be awakened and liberated by a saving agent from above.

For that reason the Savior descended to earth as Jesus. He taught the spiritual humans about their true Father and their origins in the Pleroma and vanquished for them the powers of materiality and death. After his return to the Pleroma, the Church continues his work, by giving instruction and administering the rite of Redemption—that is, baptism (water immersion and anointing). In baptism the initiate is redeemed from corporeality by partaking in the Savior's victory over the demons. Yet baptism also means that one is reunited with the Pleroma. This reunification is pictured as a "wedding" with one of the angels that have accompanied the Savior and appear as outward manifestations of the Pleroma; for this reason baptism is also called "the bridal chamber."

Ultimately, the unification with one's angel is conceived as healing the split that first arose when Sophia was separated from the Pleroma. In the redemptive process, Sophia herself is united with the Savior, as bride and bridegroom, and the individual spiritual people, who are Sophia's children, are united in the same way with the Savior's accompanying angels. The Savior represents the Pleroma as a totality and the angels its constituent plurality of aeons. Thus, the initial problem of reconciling oneness, duality, and plurality—which led to the passion of Sophia and her separation from the Pleroma—is resolved through the mechanism of reunification through baptismal initiation, resulting in the stabilization of the Pleroma as a harmonious unity-in-multiplicity. The end of this process is called "the restoration" (*apokatastasis*).

It is clear that the Valentinian school of Gnostic thought presupposes the ontology of Greek philosophy, and in particular the Neopythagorean monistic theories that attempted to derive everything, even materiality, from a single first principle. Like Neoplatonism, moreover, Valentinian thought aimed to reconcile oneness and plurality through a theory of emanation and restoration. However, Valentinian theology goes beyond these purely philosophical presuppositions in two ways: first, by positing a divine agent, whose descent, through an act of grace, into the world of matter and multiplicity makes possible the restoration of unity; and second, by insisting on the necessity of performing ritual acts for the restorative process to be realized. These two features of the system show that Valentinianism is a religion and not simply a philosophical theory.[23]

---

23. On the possibility that Valentinus may have been familiar with the *Gospel of Thomas* and on the similarities between Sethian and Valentinian thought, see Layton, *Gnostic Scriptures*; Meyer, *Gnostic Discoveries*.

Valentinianism split into two branches, an "Italian," or "Western," branch and an "Eastern" branch. According to Hippolytus (*Refutation of All Heresies* 6.35.5–7), the former taught that the body of Jesus was psychical, whereas the latter held it to be spiritual. Careful comparison of the various sources shows that an essential difference in fact exists between them in their views about the body of the Savior. Some texts claim that the Savior came with a spiritual body and allowed himself to be incarnated in a material body. His spiritual body consisted of the Church, the heavenly seed of Sophia, or a congregation of angels. Through his incarnation a mechanism of mutual participation was effected, so that the spiritual people living on earth could become members of his spiritual body—that is, of the spiritual Church—while he took upon himself the corruptible nature of their bodily existence. According to this theory, the Savior had to submit himself to human, corporeal existence, including suffering and death, in order to redeem the spiritual people from it. As a result, he himself had to be redeemed, and his redemption took place at his baptism in the Jordan: during that event, a power from above descended upon him that later enabled him to abandon his body on the cross.

In contrast, another group of texts affirms that the Savior neither suffered nor assumed a material body. Instead, he put on a "psychical Christ" when he was incarnated, and he was the one who suffered and was crucified, not the Savior himself. Associated with this theory is a strong focus on the psychical people as the class of humans who need salvation; the spiritual people, on the other hand, tend to be regarded as saved automatically, by virtue of their inborn nature, and not by any redemptive act of the Savior.

The first of these theories is attested in *Excerpts from Theodotus* 1–42, the *Tripartite Tractate*, the *Gospel of Truth*, the *Treatise on Resurrection*, the *Gospel of Philip*, and the *Interpretation of Knowledge*. The second theory is especially typical of the Valentinian treatises reported by Irenaeus and Hippolytus and *Excerpts from Theodotus* 43–65. It is in the latter group of texts that we find the idea that the Savior had a psychical body; according to them, the Savior had a spiritual and a psychical component but no material body. In the first group of texts, on the other hand, the Savior was spiritual but assumed a body of human flesh, but there is no mention of a psychical body. This crucial difference between the two groups of texts is sufficiently consistent with Hippolytus's report on the two branches to allow the conclusion that in all likelihood the first group of texts represents the Eastern and the second the Italian, or Western, form of Valentinian thought.

Two other important differences between the various texts should also be mentioned. In the Western texts, the Pleroma is most often described as a system of thirty aeons, who are accorded individual names, coupled in pairs ("syzygies"), and hierarchically organized (with Sophia as the last and youngest). The Eastern texts (most instructively the *Tripartite Tractate*) usually do not adopt this model, but describe instead how an unlimited number of aeons first exist in a hidden and seminal state within the Father, as in a womb, and then are born and made manifest as independent beings. This version of the pleromatogony—the unfolding of the Pleroma—appears to be more primitive than the other, since it may explain why "Depth" was chosen as a name for the Father, and because Valentinus himself seems to have entertained similar ideas (Tertullian *Against the Valentinians* 4.3).

Another point where the texts vary is in the description of the division of the fallen aeon. According to the best-known Western texts, Sophia is split in two, so that a higher Sophia is restored to the Pleroma while a lower Sophia (in Irenaeus's system called Achamoth) is left outside. In other systems, however, Sophia gives birth to a son, usually called Christ, and he hastens back into the Pleroma while Sophia herself remains outside the Pleroma, deprived of her spiritual element. The latter version is found in the system erroneously attributed to Valentinus in Irenaeus *Against Heresies* 1.11.1, and in *Excerpts from Theodotus* 32, *Valentinian Exposition*, and the *Tripartite Tractate* (in a slightly modified form). It is likely that this version is more primitive than the one that involves two Sophias. It is in any case important to realize that the separation of spirit from matter is the main motif of the myth of the fall of Sophia, and that this idea could be expressed by various forms of narrative.

The goal of salvation is the reintegration of the spiritual essence in humanity with the Pleroma, conceived of as the "bridal chamber."[24] Some texts are also concerned with the fate of the "psychics," and it is sometimes said that the good among these will obtain salvation on a lower level, being raised to the Ogdoad, where Sophia dwelled before her restoration (cf. Irenaeus *Against Heresies* 1.7.1). Whether this was thought to be their final destiny is an issue debated among scholars.

BIBLIOGRAPHY

Werner Foerster, ed., *Gnosis: A Selection of Gnostic Texts*, vol. 1; Christoph Markschies, *Valentinus Gnosticus?*; Antonio Orbe, *Estudios Valentinianos* (5 vols.); François Sagnard, *La gnose valentinienne et le témoignage de saint Irénée*; Einar Thomassen, *The Spiritual Seed: The Church of the "Valentinians."*

---

24. The concept of the bridal chamber is presented with particular insight in the *Gospel of Philip.*

Hermetic Religion

Jean-Pierre Mahé

N ag Hammadi Codex VI is the least Gnostic codex of the entire Nag Hammadi library. Only one of the eight writings it contains, the *Concept of Our Great Power*, is distinctly Gnostic, and the other tractates have various orientations. Yet we do find Hermetic materials at the end of this heterogeneous collection of tractates in Codex VI, and Hermetic religion has much in common with Gnostic spirituality. Both traditions emphasize a passionate quest for the ultimate origin of beings and an unlimited confidence in the redeeming virtue of knowledge.

As soon as the Greeks became acquainted with Egypt, they identified the Egyptian god Thoth, the inventor of the hieroglyphs, with Hermes, the most learned of their own deities. In Egyptian traditions, Thoth could be called "great, great, very great," as a superlative expression. Initially this phrase was literally translated into Greek as *megas, megas, megistos,* and eventually this expression was abridged as *Trismegas,* "Thrice Great," or *Trismegistos,* "Thrice Greatest." Since Greek speakers did not understand the meaning of this Egyptian superlative, they reinterpreted it in different ways.

Some Greek thinkers fancied Trismegistus as the third offspring of a lineage of ancient sages. As the son of Hermes-Agathodemon, he was thought to have translated into Greek and handed over to his son Hermes-Tat the hieroglyphic writings carved on steles before the flood by their ancestor Hermes-Thoth. Other Greeks said that this figure was called Trismegistus because he had discovered that the supreme God consists in a threefold great power (most likely the Unbegotten, the Self-Begotten, and the Begotten One). Still other Greeks explained that Hermes had come to this world three different times, before and after the flood. During his third advent he "recognized himself" and thus merited the epithet Trismegistus.

Ancient Egyptians ascribed to Thoth theological, liturgical, and technical writings copied in the "House of Life"—that is, the scriptorium of a temple. Consequently, as early as the third or second century BCE until the third century CE, there appeared Greek writings of astrology and alchemy as well as magical recipes and philosophical treatises said to have been translated from the Egyptian language and authored by Hermes Trismegistus.

Other collections of teachings of Isis to Horus and Hermes to Tat or to various other disciples, such as Asclepius or Ammon, are no longer extant. Gnomologies, such as the *Sayings of the Good Demon*, or textbooks for different levels of education, entitled *General Lectures* and *Detailed Lectures*, also have disappeared. We know of their existence only through later writings, excerpts, and fragments.

In addition to the classical editions of the philosophical Hermetica by Walter C. Scott and Alexander Stewart Ferguson,[25] or Arthur Darby Nock and A.-J. Festugière,[26] several other editions should also be mentioned: various fragments preserved in papyri of the second–third centuries CE; the *Definitions of Hermes Trismegistus to Asclepius*, a gnomology preserved in a sixth-century Armenian translation (with fragments of the Greek original in an Oxonian eleventh-century manuscript); Hermetic quotations in a Syriac collection of *Prophecies of Pagan Philosophers*; and Greek fragments on the soul in the Oxonian manuscript.[27] Three Hermetic texts are to be found in Nag Hammadi Codex VI, and all three have been translated into Coptic from Greek. The first Nag Hammadi text, the *Discourse on the Eighth and Ninth* (VI,6), was previously unknown; the others, the *Prayer of Thanksgiving* (VI,7) and the *Excerpt from the Perfect Discourse* (VI,8), are more or less parallel to chapters 41 and 21–29 of the Latin *Asclepius*.

Recent research on Hermetic religion has resolved several problems, and the Coptic Hermetic texts from Nag Hammadi have shed new light on these issues. First, with regard to the matter of Egyptian origins, we should note that Roman Egypt, where the philosophical Hermetica were written, is very different from Pharaonic Egypt. Roman Egypt displays an intellectual and religious syncretism that combines with the Egyptian cultural core several successive strata, from the Iranian conquest of Cambyses up to the Hellenistic and Roman periods. However, according to Hermetic dogma, Egypt, as the mother of human civilization, cannot possibly have received any foreign influence. On the contrary, she has always been the teacher of other nations. As the priest of Saïs explains to Solon (*Timaeus* 22b), the culture of the world has been periodically swallowed up by various cataclysms, except in Egypt, which has always been protected by the Nile. Therefore, the wise of other nations necessarily depend on Egypt. The truths found in Moses's *Genesis* and Plato's *Timaeus* can be traced back to the antediluvian writings of Hermes-Thoth. As a result, when Hermetic writers seemingly borrow ideas from Jewish or Greek sources, they are simply returning to Egypt her own heritage, stolen by foreigners. The recent discovery of the *Ancient Egyptian Book of Thoth*, a Demotic teaching to a disciple "who loves knowledge" and "wishes to learn," suggests that the Hermetic dialogues, which are so different from the Socratic genre, might well derive from Egyptian models. In any case, they are formally closer to Egyptian wisdom than to Plato.

Second, most scholars currently agree that Hermetism is not a philosophical system but a spiritual way. Consequently, despite apparent contradictions that we

---

25. Walter C. Scott, *Hermetica* (vol. 4 edited by Alexander Stewart Ferguson).

26. Nock and Festugière, *Corpus Hermeticum*.

27. See the additional items in the bibliography.

may note in the texts, we should not contrast Gnostic with non-Gnostic Hermetic writings. In fact, non-Gnostic Hermetic writings constitute the beginning of the quest for God: those searching for the divine first have to become aware of his invisible presence through his visible creatures. Other Hermetic treatises mirror a subsequent stage in which devotees understand that God is so far beyond what is perceptible that the world seems to be interposed as a screen between the human mind and the source of all beings. If we were to attempt to locate the three Hermetic writings of the Nag Hammadi scriptures on the "way of immortality" (*Discourse on the Eighth and Ninth* 63,11), we would say that the *Excerpt from the Perfect Discourse* belongs to the first stage of conversion and knowledge, whereas the *Discourse on the Eighth and Ninth* concerns the "the perfect one who is" (63,32) in the final stage of mystic enlightenment and spiritual rebirth. The *Prayer of Thanksgiving* recapitulates the three main stages in its reference to mind, word, and knowledge (64,9–10).

Third, the discovery of the Coptic Hermetica confirms that Hermetic religion, far from being a mere literary phenomenon, was an actual religious movement with a deep social impact, based on congregations quite similar to Gnostic communities. The Hermetic worshipers accepted popular religion and admired the traditional cults of Egypt, which they called the holy land of their ancestors (*Stobaei Hermetica* XXIV, 23), a country "more godly than any other country" (*Excerpt from the Perfect Discourse* 70,30–32), the "dwelling place of the gods" and the "school of religion" (71,32–22). Hermetic authors quote the aretalogies of Isis and Osiris (*Stobaei Hermetica* XXIII, 65–68) and sometimes paraphrase the hymns to Khnoum (*Corpus Hermeticum* V, 6–7). They adopt the Egyptian theory of statues that are empowered by souls (*Excerpt from the Perfect Discourse* 69,32–70,2).

Such religious practices, which allegedly are necessary for the balance of the universe (*Excerpt from the Perfect Discourse* 70,6–7; 73,12–22), should be assiduously observed. However, Trismegistus teaches his disciples how to make these religious practices more complete, profound, and spiritual. True piety consists in offering appropriate worship to all the levels of divinity.

Followers of Hermetic religion formed religious circles that convened around or inside the temples (*Asclepius* 1.41; *Corpus Hermeticum* VII, 2), and they devoted themselves to cultic and teaching activities. Based on the books ascribed to Trismegistus, Hermetic thinkers did not make a clear-cut distinction between philosophy and occultism. Thus, astrology could be practiced as a spiritual exercise leading to the admiration of the divine works and training the soul for mental ascent just as efficiently as aircraft pilots in the modern world avail themselves of flight simulators. Likewise, alchemy could help Hermes' disciples experiment on metals in order to achieve the same kind of radical transmutation they hoped to realize within themselves through the mystery of rebirth.

To age-old Egyptian ceremonies the Hermetic worshipers added more rituals: prayers, spiritual offerings, bloodless fraternal meals, and various initiations. Some scholars have regarded allusions to these liturgies as mere metaphors. Nevertheless, the reality of these activities is confirmed by the new Coptic Hermetic texts. For example, the liturgical rubrics at the beginning and end of the *Prayer of Thanksgiving* are quite similar to those that precede and follow the rite of ecstatic ascent in the *Three Steles of Seth* (NHC VII,5). The *Discourse on the Eighth and Ninth* presents a sacred ceremony taking place in a congregation of people, with prayers to be recited by the candidate being initiated or the officiant or both together. Such prayers are accompanied by appropriate gestures and a regenerating kiss. They display obvious analogies with the baptismal liturgies contained in the *Holy Book of the Great Invisible Spirit* (III,2; IV,2) and *Melchizedek* (IX,1).

Occultism provides a common background for Hermetic and Gnostic writings in the Nag Hammadi library. Hermes uses magical words and vowels to command the heavenly spheres (*Discourse on the Eighth and Ninth* 56,17–22). He teaches how to make gods by providing statues with souls (*Excerpt from the Perfect Discourse* 68,29–31). Like an alchemist, Hermes succeeds in transcending his own body, so that he may see himself (*Discourse on the Eighth and Ninth* 58,8). All of these magical, theurgical, and alchemical devices are also evidenced in Gnostic prayers and liturgies.

There are additional similarities with many writings of the Nag Hammadi scriptures, especially with the *Paraphrase of Shem* (NHC VII,1), which uses the same *Genesis* commentary as *Poimandres* (*Corpus Hermeticum* I), and with the so-called Sethian treatises, which also offer a threefold path of Gnostic enlightenment, as been demonstrated in the pioneering works of John Turner.[28] It would certainly be worthwhile in future scholarship to compare the Hermetic and the Sethian paths of spirituality.

BIBLIOGRAPHY

Sebastian Brock, "A Syriac Collection of Prophecies of the Pagan Philosophers"; "Some Syriac Excerpts from Greek Collections of Pagan Prophecies"; Régine Charron, "The *Apocryphon of John* (NHC II,1) and the Graeco-Egyptian Alchemical Literature"; Brian P. Copenhaver, *Hermetica*; Simonetta Feraboli, *Hermes Trismegistus, de triginta sex decanis*; A.-J. Festugière, *La Révelation d'Hermès Trismégiste*; Garth Fowden, *The Egyptian Hermes*; Richard Jasnow and Karl-Theodor Zauzich, *The Ancient Egyptian Book of Thoth*; Jean Letrouit, "Chronologie des alchimistes grecs"; Paolo Lucentini, Ilaria Parri, and Vittoria Perrone Compagni, *Hermetism from Late Antiquity to Humanism*; Jean-Pierre Mahé, *Hermès en Haute Égypte*; "La voie d'immortalité à la lumière des *Hermetica* de Nag Hammadi et de découvertes plus récentes"; "Preliminary Remarks on the Demotic *Book of Thoth* and the Greek *Hermetica*"; "The Definitions of Hermes Trismegistus to Asclepius"; Arthur Darby Nock and A.-J. Festugière, *Corpus Hermeticum*; Joseph Paramelle and Jean-Pierre Mahé, "Extraits hermétiques inédits dans un manuscrit d'Oxford"; Walter C. Scott, *Hermetica* (vol. 4 edited by Alexander Stewart Ferguson); Kevin van Bladel, "Sources of the Legend of Hermes in Arabic"; Anna van den Kerchove, "Pratiques rituelles et traités hermétiques" (new Hermetic fragments, pp. 291–94).

---

28. E.g., John D. Turner, *Sethian Gnosticism and the Platonic Tradition.*

TABLE OF TRACTATES IN THE NAG HAMMADI LIBRARY, THE BERLIN GNOSTIC CODEX, AND CODEX TCHACOS

This table of tractates lists the following for the thirteen Nag Hammadi Codices (NHC), the Berlin Gnostic Codex 8502 (BG 8502), and Codex Tchacos (Tchacos): the codex and tractate numbers, the standardized tractate titles (revised in this edition), the page and line numbers from the Coptic manuscripts, and abbreviations (where new abbreviations are given here, the older abbreviations from *The SBL Handbook of Style* are given in parentheses).

NHC I,1	The Prayer of the Apostle Paul	A,1–B,10	Pr. Paul
	(colophon)	(B,11–12)	
NHC I,2	The Secret Book of James	1,1–16,30	Scrt. Bk. Jas. (Ap. Jas.)
NHC I,3	The Gospel of Truth	16,31–43,24	Gos. Truth
NHC I,4	The Treatise on Resurrection	43,25–50,18	Treat. Res.
NHC I,5	The Tripartite Tractate	51,1–138,25	Tri. Trac.
NHC II,1	The Secret Book of John	1,1–32,9	Scrt. Bk. John (Ap. John)
NHC II,2	The Gospel of Thomas	32,10–51,28	Gos. Thom.
NHC II,3	The Gospel of Philip	51,29–86,19	Gos. Phil.
NHC II,4	The Nature of the Rulers	86,20–97,23	Nat. Rulers (Hyp. Arch.)
NHC II,5	On the Origin of the World	97,24–127,17	Orig. World
NHC II,6	Exegesis on the Soul	127,18–137,27	Exeg. Soul
NHC II,7	The Book of Thomas	138,1–145,19	Bk. Thom. (Thom. Cont.)
	(scribal note)	(145,20–23)	

NHC III,1	The Secret Book of John	1,1–40,11	Scrt. Bk. John (Ap. John)
NHC III,2	The Holy Book of the Great Invisible Spirit	40,12–69,20	Holy Book (Gos. Eg.)
NHC III,3	Eugnostos the Blessed	70,1–90,13	Eugnostos
NHC III,4	The Wisdom of Jesus Christ	90,14–119,18	Wisd. Jes. Chr. (Soph. Jes. Chr.)
NHC III,5	The Dialogue of the Savior	120,1–149,23	Dial. Sav.
NHC IV,1	The Secret Book of John	1,1–49,28	Scrt. Bk. John (Ap. John)
NHC IV,2	The Holy Book of the Great Invisible Spirit	50,1–81,2+	Holy Book (Gos. Eg.)
NHC V,1	Eugnostos the Blessed	1,1–17,18	Eugnostos
NHC V,2	The Revelation of Paul	17,19–24,9	Rev. Paul (Apoc. Paul)
NHC V,3	The First Revelation of James	24,10–44,10	1 Rev. Jas. (1 Apoc. Jas.)
NHC V,4	The Second Revelation of James	44,11–63,33	2 Rev. Jas. (2 Apoc. Jas.)
NHC V,5	The Revelation of Adam	64,1–85,32	Rev. Adam (Apoc. Adam)
NHC VI,1	The Acts of Peter and the Twelve Apostles	1,1–12,22	Acts Pet. 12 Apos.
NHC VI,2	Thunder	13,1–21,32	Thund.
NHC VI,3	Authoritative Discourse	22,1–35,24	Auth. Disc. (Auth. Teach.)
NHC VI,4	The Concept of Our Great Power	36,1–48,15	Great Pow.
NHC VI,5	Excerpt from Plato's Republic	48,16–51,23	Plato Rep.
NHC VI,6	The Discourse on the Eighth and Ninth	52,1–63,32	Disc. 8–9
NHC VI,7	The Prayer of Thanksgiving	63,33–65,7	Pr. Thanks.
	(scribal note)	(65, 8–14)	
NHC VI,8	Excerpt from the Perfect Discourse	65,15–78,43	Perf. Disc. (Asclepius)
NHC VII,1	The Paraphrase of Shem	1,1–49,9	Paraph. Shem
NHC VII,2	The Second Discourse of Great Seth	49,10–70,12	Disc. Seth (Treat. Seth)
NHC VII,3	The Revelation of Peter	70,13–84,14	Rev. Peter (Apoc. Peter)

NHC VII,4	The Teachings of Silvanus	84,15–118,7	Teach. Silv.
	(colophon)	(118,8–9)	
NHC VII,5	The Three Steles of Seth	118,10–127,27	Steles Seth
	(colophon)	(127,28–32)	
NHC VIII,1	Zostrianos	1,1–132,9	Zost.
NHC VIII,2	The Letter of Peter to Philip	132,10–140,27	Ep. Pet. Phil.
NHC IX,1	Melchizedek	1,1–27,10	Melch.
NHC IX,2	The Thought of Norea	27,11–29,5	Norea
NHC IX,3	The Testimony of Truth	29,6–74,30+	Testim. Truth
NHC X	Marsanes	1,1–68,18	Marsanes
NHC XI,1	The Interpretation of Knowledge	1,1–21,35	Interp. Know.
NHC XI,2	Valentinian Exposition	22,1–39,39	Val. Exp.
NHC XI,2a	On Anointing	40,1–29	On Anointing.
NHC XI,2b	On First Baptism	40,30–41,38	On Bap. A
NHC XI,2c	On Baptism	42,1–43,19	On Bap. B
NHC XI,2d	On the Eucharist	43,20–38	On Euch. A
NHC XI,2e	On the Eucharist	44,1–37	On Euch. B
NHC XI,3	Allogenes the Stranger	45,1–69,20	Allogenes
NHC XI,4	Hypsiphrone	69,21–72,33+	Hypsiph.
NHC XII,1	The Sentences of Sextus	15,1–34,28+	Sent. Sextus
	(beginning lost)		
NHC XII,2	The Gospel of Truth	53,19–60,30+	Gos. Truth
	(beginning lost)		
NHC XII,3	Fragments		Frm.
NHC XIII,1	Three Forms of First Thought	35,1–50,24	Three Forms (Trim. Prot.)
NHC XIII,2	On the Origin of the World	50,25–34+	Orig. World
BG 8502,1	The Gospel of Mary	7,1–19,5	Gos. Mary
	(beginning lost)		

BG 8502,2	The Secret Book of John	19,6–77,7	Scrt. Bk. John (Ap. John)
BG 8502,3	The Wisdom of Jesus Christ	77,8–127,12	Wisd. Jes. Chr. (Soph. Jes. Chr.)
BG 8502,4	The Act of Peter	128,1–141,7	Act Pet.
Tchacos 1	The Letter of Peter to Philip	1,1–9,15	Ep. Pet. Phil.
Tchacos 2	James	10,1–30,27	James
	(= The First Revelation of James)		1 Rev. Jas. (1 Apoc. Jas.)
Tchacos 3	The Gospel of Judas	33,1–58,28	Gos. Judas
Tchacos 4	The Book of Allogenes	59,1–66,25+	Bk. Allog.

BIBLIOGRAPHY

Brent A. Smith

Al-Ahram Weekly. February 17–23, 2005. http://weekly.ahram.org.eg/2005/730/he1.htm.
Aland, Kurt, ed. *Synopsis Quattuor Evangeliorum: Locis parallelis evangeliorum apocryphorum et partum adhibitis*. 15th rev. ed. Stuttgart: Deutsche Bibelgesellschaft, 1996. Corrected printing. With an Appendix by the Berliner Arbeitskreis für koptisch-gnostische Schriften, "Das Thomas-Evangelium / The Gospel According to Thomas," 517–46.
Alberry, C. R. C., ed. *Manichaean Manuscripts in the Chester Beatty Collection*. Vol. 2, *A Manichaean Psalm-Book, Part II*. Stuttgart: Kohlhammer, 1938.
Arai, Sasagu. *Die Christologie des Evangelium Veritatis: Eine religionsgeschichtliche Untersuchung*. Leiden: Brill, 1964.
Asgeirsson, Jon Ma., Kristin De Troyer, and Marvin W. Meyer, eds. *From Quest to Q: Festschrift James M. Robinson*. Bibliotheca Ephemeridum Theologicarum Lovaniensium 146. Louvain: Presses Universitaires de Louvain; Peeters, 2000.
Atiya, Aziz S., ed. *The Coptic Encyclopedia*. 8 vols. New York and Oxford: Macmillan, 1991.
Attridge, Harold W. "P.Oxy. 1081 and the Sophia Jesu Christi." *Enchoria* 5 (1975): 1–8.
——, ed. *Nag Hammadi Codex I (The Jung Codex)*. 2 vols. Nag Hammadi Studies 22–23. Leiden: Brill, 1985.
Badilita, Cristian. *Métamorphoses de l'Antichrist chez les Pères de l'Église*. Théologie historique 116. Paris: Beauchesne, 2005.
Barc, Bernard L., and Michel Roberge, eds. *L'Hypostase des archontes: Traité gnostique sur l'origine de l'homme, du monde et des archontes (NH II,4); Noréa (NH IX,2)*. Bibliothèque copte de Nag Hammadi, Section "Textes" 5. Québec: Les Presses de l'Université Laval; Louvain: Peeters, 1980.
Barns, John W. B., Gerald M. Browne, and John C. Shelton, eds. *Nag Hammadi Codices: Greek and Coptic Papyri from the Cartonnage of the Covers*. Nag Hammadi Studies 16. Leiden: Brill, 1981.
Barnstone, Willis, ed. *The Other Bible*. Rev. ed. San Francisco: HarperSanFrancisco, 2005.
Barnstone, Willis, and Marvin Meyer, eds. *The Gnostic Bible*. Boston: Shambhala, 2003.
Barry, Catherine, ed. *La Sagesse de Jésus-Christ (BG 3; NH III,4)*. Bibliothèque copte de Nag Hammadi, Section "Textes" 20. Québec: Les Presses de l'Université Laval; Louvain: Peeters, 1993.
Barry, Catherine, Wolf-Peter Funk, Paul-Hubert Poirier, and John D. Turner, eds. *Zostrien (NH VIII,1)*. Bibliothèque copte de Nag Hammadi, Section "Textes" 24. Québec: Les Presses de l'Université Laval; Louvain: Peeters, 1999.
Bauer, Walter. *Orthodoxy and Heresy in Earliest Christianity*. 2d ed. Philadelphia: Fortress, 1971.

Baynes, Charlotte A. *A Coptic Gnostic Treatise Contained in the Codex Brucianus (Bruce MS 96, Bod. Lib. Oxford)*: A Translation from the Coptic; Transcription and Commentary. Cambridge: Cambridge University Press, 1933.

Bechtle, Gerald. *The Anonymous Commentary on Plato's "Parmenides."* Berner Reihe philosophischer Studien 22. Bern: Haupt, 1999.

Bellet, Paulinus. "The Colophon of the Gospel of the Egyptians: Concessus and Macarius of Nag Hammadi." In *Nag Hammadi and Gnosis: Papers Read at the First International Congress of Coptology (Cairo, December 1976)*, edited by Robert McLachlan Wilson, 44–65. Nag Hammadi Studies 14. Leiden: Brill, 1978.

Bethge, Hans-Gebhard. "'Der Brief des Petrus an Philippus': Ein neutestamentliches Apokryphon aus dem Funde von Nag Hammadi (NHC VIII,2), herausgegeben, übersetzt und kommentiert, Diss. (B), Berlin, 1985." *Theologische Literaturzeitung* 114 (1989): 396–98.

———. "The Letter of Peter to Philip." In *New Testament Apocrypha*, edited by Wilhelm Schneemelcher, 1.342–47.

———. "'Nebront': Die zweite Schrift aus Nag-Hammadi-Codex VI, eingeleitet und übersetzt vom Berliner Arbeitskreis für koptisch-gnostische Schriften." *Theologische Zeitschrift* 98 (1973): 97–104.

———. "'Zweiter Logos des grossen Seth': Die zweite Schrift aus Nag-Hammadi-Codex VII, eingeleitet und übersetzt vom Berliner Arbeitskreis für koptisch-gnostische Schriften." *Theologische Literaturzeitung* 100 (1975): 97–110.

Bethge, Hans-Gebhard, Stephen Emmel, Karen L. King, and Imke Schletterer, eds. *For the Children, Perfect Instruction: Studies in Honor of Hans-Martin Schenke on the Occasion of the Berliner Arbeitskreis für koptisch-gnostische Schriften's Thirtieth Year*. Nag Hammadi and Manichaean Studies 54. Leiden: Brill, 2002.

Bethge, Hedda. "'Die Exegese über die Seele': Die sechste Schrift aus Nag-Hammadi-Codex II, eingeleitet und übersetzt vom Berliner Arbeitskreis für koptisch-gnostische Schriften." *Theologische Lituraturzeitung* 101 (1976): 93–104.

Betz, Hans Dieter, ed. *The Greek Magical Papyri in Translation*. 2d ed. Chicago and London: University of Chicago Press, 1992.

Bianchi, Ugo, ed. *Le Origini Dello Gnosticismo: Colloquia di Messina, 13–18 Aprile 1966*. Studies in the History of Religions (Supplements to *Numen*) 12. Leiden: Brill, 1970.

Biblical Archaeologist 42 (1979). Issue devoted to the Nag Hammadi discovery.

Blatz, Beate. "The Coptic Gospel of Thomas." In *New Testament Apocrypha*, edited by Wilhelm Schneemelcher, 1.110–33.

Blatz, Beate, and Einar Thomassen. "The Dialogue of the Savior." In *New Testament Apocrypha*, edited by Wilhelm Schneemelcher, 1.300–12.

Böhlig, Alexander, and Pahor Labib, eds. *Koptisch-gnostische Apokalypsen aus Codex V von Nag Hammadi im Koptischen Museum zu Alt-Kairo*. Wissenschaftliche Zeitschrift der Martin-Luther-Universität, Halle-Wittenberg, Sonderband. Halle-Wittenberg: Martin-Luther-Universität, 1963.

Böhlig, Alexander, and Frederik Wisse, eds. *Nag Hammadi Codices III,2 and IV,2: The Gospel of the Egyptians*. Nag Hammadi Studies 4. Leiden: Brill, 1975.

Bouché-Leclercq, Auguste. *L'Astrologie Grecque*. Paris: Presses universitaires de France, 1899.

Bovon, François, Bertrand Bouvier, and Frédéric Amsler. *Acta Philippi (Textus)*. Corpus Christianorum, Series Apocryphorum 11–12. Turnhout: Brepols, 1999.

Bowe, Barbara E. "Dancing into the Divine: The Hymn of the Dance in the *Acts of John*." *Journal of Early Christian Studies* 7 (1999): 83–104.

Brashear, William. "Seth-Gebet." *Archiv für Papyrusforschung* 42 (1996): 26–34.

Brashler, James. "The Coptic *Apocalypse of Peter*: A Genre Analysis and Interpretation." Ph.D. dissertation, Claremont Graduate University, 1977.

Brock, Ann Graham. *Mary Magdalene, the First Apostle: The Struggle for Authority*. Harvard Theological Studies 51. Cambridge, MA: Harvard University Press, 2002.

Brock, Sebastian. "Some Syriac Excerpts from Greek Collections of Pagan Prophecies." *Vigiliae Christianae* 38 (1984): 77–90.

——. "A Syriac Collection of Prophecies of the Pagan Philosophers." *Orientalia Lovaniensia Periodica* 14 (1983): 203–46.

Brown, S. Kent. "James: A Religio-Historical Study of the Relations Between Jewish, Gnostic, and Catholic Christianity in the Early Period Through an Investigation of the Traditions About James the Lord's Brother." Ph.D. dissertation, Brown University, 1972.

Bruns, P. "Noëma." In *Lexikon der antiken christlichen Literatur*, edited by Siegmar Döpp and Wilhelm Geerlings, 453. Freiburg-Basel-Wien: Herder, 1998.

Buckley, Jorunn Jacobsen. "Conceptual Models and Polemical Issues in the Gospel of Philip." In *Aufstieg und Niedergang der römischen Welt*, edited by Hildegard Temporini and Wolfgang Haase, II.25.2, 4167–94. Berlin: De Gruyter, 1988.

——. *Female Fault and Fulfillment in Gnosticism*. Studies in Religion. Chapel Hill and London: University of North Carolina Press, 1986.

——. *The Mandaeans: Ancient Texts and Modern People*. Oxford: Oxford University Press, 2002.

Bullard, Roger A. *The Hypostasis of the Archons: The Coptic Text with Translation and Commentary*. Patristische Texte und Studien 10. Berlin: De Gruyter, 1970.

Cameron, Ron. *Sayings Traditions in the Apocryphon of James*. Harvard Theological Studies 34. Philadelphia: Fortress, 1984.

——. "Thomas, Gospel of." In *The Anchor Bible Dictionary*, edited by David Noel Freedman et al., 6.535–40. New York: Doubleday, 1992.

Cameron, Ron, and Arthur J. Dewey, eds. *The Cologne Mani Codex*. Missoula, MT: Scholars Press, 1979.

Chadwick, Henry. *The Sentences of Sextus: A Contribution to the History of Early Christian Ethics*. Texts and Studies, New Series, 5. Cambridge: Cambridge University Press, 1959.

Charlesworth, James H., ed. *The Old Testament Pseudepigrapha*. 2 vols. New York: Doubleday, 1983, 1985.

Charron, Régine. "The *Apocryphon of John* (NHC II,1) and the Graeco-Egyptian Alchemical Literature." *Vigiliae Christianae* 59 (2005): 438–56.

——. *Concordance des textes de Nag Hammadi: Le Codex III*. Bibliothèque copte de Nag Hammadi, Section "Concordances" 3. Québec: Les Presses de l'Université Laval; Louvain: Peeters, 1995.

——. *Concordance des textes de Nag Hammadi: Le Codex VII*. Bibliothèque copte de Nag Hammadi, Section "Concordances" 1. Québec: Les Presses de l'Université Laval; Louvain: Peeters, 1992.

Chérix, Pierre. *Le Concept de notre grande puissance (CG VI,4): Texte, remarques philologiques, traducion et notes*. Orbis Biblicus et Orientalis 47. Fribourg and Göttingen: Vandenhoeck & Ruprecht, 1982.

Claude, Paul. "Approche de la structure des Trois Stèles de Seth." In *Colloque international sur les textes de Nag Hammadi (Québec, 22–25 août 1978)*, edited by Bernard Barc, 362–73. Bibliothèque copte de Nag Hammadi, Section "Études" 1. Québec: Les Presses de l'Université Laval; Louvain: Peeters, 1981.

——, ed. *Les Trois Stéles de Seth: Hymne gnostique à la triade (NHC VII,5)*. Bibliothèque copte de Nag Hammadi, Section "Textes" 8. Québec: Les Presses de l'Université Laval; Louvain: Peeters, 1983.

Colpe, Carsten. "Heidnische, jüdische und christliche Überlieferung in den Schriften aus Nag Hammadi, III." *Jahrbuch für Antike und Christentum* 17 (1974): 109–25.

Copenhaver, Brian P. *Hermetica: The Greek Corpus Hermeticum and the Latin Asclepius in a New English Translation*. Cambridge and New York: Cambridge University Press, 1992.

Crossan, John Dominic. *The Birth of Christianity*. San Francisco: HarperSanFrancisco, 1998.

——. *The Cross That Spoke: The Origins of the Passion Narrative*. San Francisco: Harper & Row, 1988.

——. *Four Other Gospels: Shadows on the Contours on Canon.* Minneapolis: Winston (Seabury), 1985.

Culianu, Ioan. "The Gnostic Revenge: Gnosticism and Romantic Literature." In *Religionstheorie und Politische Theologie, Band 2: Gnosis und Politik*, edited by Jacob Taubes, 290–306. Munich, Paderborn, Vienna, and Zurich: Wilhelm Fink/Ferdinand Schöningh, 1984.

——. *The Tree of Gnosis: Gnostic Mythology from Early Christianity to Modern Nihilism.* Translated by H. S. Wiesner. San Francisco: HarperSanFrancisco, 1992.

Davies, Stevan. *The Gospel of Thomas and Christian Wisdom.* New York: Seabury, 1983.

de Boer, Esther A. *The Gospel of Mary: Beyond a Gnostic and a Biblical Mary Magdalene.* New York and London: Clark International, 2004.

——. *Mary Magdalene: Beyond the Myth.* Translated by John Bowden. Harrisburg, PA: Trinity Press International, 1997.

——. "Mary Magdalene and the Disciple Jesus Loved." *Lectio Difficilior* 1 (2000): electronic journal (http://www.lectio.unibe.ch).

de Catanzaro, Carmino J. "The Gospel According to Philip." *Journal of Theological Studies* 13 (1962): 35–71.

DeConick, April D. "Corrections to the Critical Reading of the *Gospel of Thomas*." *Vigiliae Christianae* 60 (2006): 201–8.

——. "The *Dialogue of the Savior* and the Mystical Sayings of Jesus." *Vigiliae Christianae* 50 (1996): 178–99.

——. "The Great Mystery of Marriage: Sex and Conception in Ancient Valentinian Traditions." *Vigiliae Christianae* 57 (2003): 307–42.

——. *The Original Gospel of Thomas in Translation, with Commentary and New English Translation of the Complete Gospel.* Journal for the Study of the New Testament, Supplement Series. London: Clark, 2006.

——. *Recovering the Original Gospel of Thomas: A History of the Gospel and Its Growth.* Early Christianity in Context. New York and London: Clark International, 2005.

Denzey, Nicola F. "Genesis Exegetical Traditions in the *Trimorphic Protennoia*." *Vigiliae Christianae* 55 (2001): 20–44.

Dewey, Arthur J. "The Hymn in the Acts of John." *Semeia* 38 (1986): 67–80.

Doresse, Jean. "Les apocalypses de Zoroastre, de Zostrien, de Nicothée . . . (Porphyre, *Vie de Plotin*, §16)." In *Coptic Studies in Honor of Walter Ewing Crum*, edited by Michel Malinine, 255–63. Bulletin of the Byzantine Institute 2. Boston: Byzantine Institute, 1950.

——. "'Le Livre sacré du grand Esprit invisible' ou 'L'Évangile des Égyptiens.' Texte copte édité, traduit, et commenté d'après la Codex I de Nag'a-Hammadi / Khénoboskion." *Journal Asiatique* 254 (1966): 317–435; 256 (1968): 289–386.

——. *The Secret Books of the Egyptian Gnostics: An Introduction to the Gnostic Coptic Manuscripts Discovered at Chenoboskion.* Translated by Philip Mairet. London: Hollis & Carter, 1960.

Drijvers, Han J. W. "The Acts of Thomas." In *New Testament Apocrypha*, edited by Wilhelm Schneemelcher, 2.322–39.

Dubois, Jean-Daniel. "Contribution à l'interprétation de la *Paraphrase de Sem*." In *Deuxième Journée d'Études coptes, Strasbourg 25 mai 1984*, edited by Jean-Marc Rosenstiehl, 150–60. Cahiers de la Bibliothèque copte 3. Louvain and Paris: Peeters, 1986.

——. "Le *Traité Tripartite* (Nag Hammadi I,5) est-il antérieure à Origène?" In *Origeniana octava: Origen and the Alexandrian Tradition; Papers of the 8th International Origen Congress, Pisa, 27–31 August 2001*, edited by Lorenzo Perrone, 1.303–16. Bibliotheca Ephemeridum Theologicarum Lovaniensium 164. Louvain: Peeters, 2003.

Dunderberg, Ismo. "The School of Valentinus." In *A Companion to Second-Century Christian "Heretics,"* edited by Antti Marjanen and Petri Luomanen, 64–99.

Edwards, Richard A., and Robert A. Wild. *The Sentences of Sextus.* Society of Biblical Literature Texts and Translations 22, Early Christian Literature Series 5. Chico, CA: Scholars Press, 1981.

Ehrman, Bart. *Lost Christianities: The Battle for Scripture and the Faiths We Never Knew.* New York and Oxford: Oxford University Press, 2003.

———. *The Lost Gospel of Judas Iscariot.* New York and Oxford: Oxford University Press, 2006.

———. *Lost Scriptures: Books That Did Not Make It into the New Testament.* New York and Oxford: Oxford University Press, 2005.

Elsas, Christoph. *Neuplatonische und gnostische Weltablehnung in der Schule Plotins.* Berlin and New York: De Gruyter, 1975.

Emmel, Stephen. "Exploring the Pathway That Leads from Paul to Gnosticism: What Is the Genre of *The Interpretation of Knowledge* (NHC XI,1)?" In *Die Weisheit: Ursprünge und Rezeption: Festschrift für Karl Löning,* edited by Martin Fassnacht, 1–19. Münster: Aschendorff, 2003.

———. "A Fragment of Nag Hammadi Codex III in the Beinecke Library: Yale Inv. 1784." *Bulletin of the American Society of Papyrologists* 17 (1980): 53–60.

———. "The Recently Published *Gospel of the Savior* ('Unbekanntes Berliner Evangelium'): Righting the Order of Pages and Events." *Harvard Theological Review* 95 (2002): 45–72.

———. "Unbekanntes Berliner Evangelium = the Strasbourg Coptic Gospel: Prolegomena to a New Edition of the Strasbourg Fragments." In *For the Children, Perfect Instruction,* edited by Hans-Gebhard Bethge, Stephen Emmel, Karen L. King, and Imke Schletterer, 353–74.

———. "Unique Photographic Evidence for Nag Hammadi Texts CG V–VIII." *Bulletin of the American Society of Papyrologists* 16 (1979): 179–91.

———, ed. *Nag Hammadi Codex III,5: The Dialogue of the Savior.* Nag Hammadi Studies 26. Leiden: Brill, 1984.

Evans, Craig A. "On the Prologue of John and the Trimorphic Protennoia." *New Testament Studies* 27 (1980/1981): 395–401.

Evans, Craig A., Robert L. Webb, and Richard A. Wiebe, eds. *Nag Hammadi and the Bible: A Synopsis and Index.* New Testament Tools and Studies 18. Leiden: Brill, 1993.

The Facsimile Edition of the Nag Hammadi Codices. Published under the auspices of the Department of Antiquities of the Arab Republic of Egypt in conjunction with the United Nations Educational, Scientific and Cultural Organization. 12 vols. Leiden: Brill, 1972–84.

Fallon, Francis T. *The Enthronement of Sabaoth: Jewish Elements in Gnostic Creation Myths.* Nag Hammadi Studies 10. Leiden: Brill, 1978.

Feraboli, Simonetta, ed. *Hermes Trismegistus, de triginta sex decanis.* Corpus Christianorum, Continuatio Mediaevalis 144; Hermes Latinus IV.1. Turnhout: Brepols, 1994.

Festugière, André-Jean. *La Révelation d'Hermès Trismégiste.* 4 vols. Paris: Gabalda, 1949–54.

———, ed. *Les Actes apocryphes de Jean et de Thomas.* Cahiers d'orientalisme 6. Geneva: Cramer, 1983.

Filoramo, Giovanni. *A History of Gnosticism.* Oxford and Cambridge: Blackwell, 1990.

Finamore, John. "Iamblichus, the Sethians, and Marsanes." In *Gnosticism and Later Platonism: Themes, Figures, and Texts,* edited by John D. Turner and Ruth Majercik, 225–57. Atlanta: Society of Biblical Literature, 2000.

Fischer, Karl-Martin. "'Der Gedanke unserer großen Kraft (Noema)': Die vierte Schrift aus Nag-Hammadi-Codex VI, eingeleitet und übersetzt vom Berliner Arbeitskreis für koptisch-gnostische Schriften." *Theologische Literaturzeitung* 98 (1973): 169–76.

Foerster, Werner, ed. *Gnosis: A Selection of Gnostic Texts.* Translated by Robert McLachlan Wilson. 2 vols. Oxford: Clarendon, 1974.

Fowden, Garth. *The Egyptian Hermes: A Historical Approach to the Late Pagan Mind.* Cambridge and New York: Cambridge University Press, 1986.

Frankfurter, David. *Religion in Roman Egypt: Assimilation and Resistance.* Princeton, NJ: Princeton University Press, 1998.

Funk, Robert W., ed. *New Gospel Parallels.* 2 vols. Foundations and Facets 6. Philadelphia: Fortress, 1985.

Funk, Wolf-Peter. "'Authentikos Logos': Die dritte Schrift aus Nag-Hammadi-Codex VI, eingeleitet und übersetzt vom Berliner Arbeitskreis für koptisch-gnostische Schriften." *Theologische Literaturzeitung* 98 (1973): 251–59.

——. *Concordance des textes de Nag Hammadi: Les Codices VIII et IX.* Bibliothèque copte de Nag Hammadi, Section "Concordances" 5. Québec: Les Presses de l'Université Laval; Louvain: Peeters, 1997.

——. *Concordance des textes de Nag Hammadi: Les Codices X et XIa.* Bibliothèque copte de Nag Hammadi, Section "Concordances" 6. Québec: Les Presses de l'Université Laval; Louvain: Peeters, 2000.

——. "Ein doppelt überliefertes Stück spätägyptischer Weisheit." *Zeitschrift für Ägyptische Sprache und Altertumskunde* 103 (1976): 8–21.

——. "The First Apocalypse of James." In *New Testament Apocrypha,* edited by Wilhelm Schneemelcher, 1.313–26.

——. "Koptisch-gnostische Apokalypse des Paulus." In *Neutestamentliche Apokryphen in deutscher Übersetzung,* edited by Wilhelm Schneemelcher, 2.628–33. Tübingen: Mohr (Paul Siebeck), 1989.

——. "'Die Lehren des Silvanus': Die vierte Schrift aus Nag-Hammadi-Codex VII, eingeleitet und übersetzt vom Berliner Arbeitskreis für koptisch-gnostische Schriften." *Theologische Literaturzeitung* 100 (1975): 7–23.

——. "Notizen zur weiteren Textkonstitution der Zweiten Apokalypse des Jakobus." In *Nubia et Oriens Christianus: Festschrift für C. Detlef G. Müller zum 60. Geburtstag,* edited by Piotr O. Scholz and Reinhard Stempel, 107–14. Cologne: Dinter, 1987.

——. "The Second Apocalypse of James." In *New Testament Apocrypha,* edited by Wilhelm Schneemelcher, 1.327–41.

——. "Der verlorene Anfang des Authentikos Logos." *Archiv für Papyrusforschung* 28 (1982): 59–65.

——. *Die zweite Apokalypse des Jakobus aus Nag-Hammadi-Codex V.* Text und Untersuchungen zur Geschichte der altchristlichen Literatur 119. Berlin: Akademie, 1976.

Funk, Wolf-Peter, Jean-Pierre Mahé, and Claudio Gianotto, eds. *Melchisédek (NH IX,1): Oblation, baptême et vision dans la gnose séthienne.* Bibliothèque copte de Nag Hammadi, Section "Textes" 28. Québec: Les Presses de l'Université Laval; Louvain: Peeters, 2001.

Funk, Wolf-Peter, Louis Painchaud, and Einar Thomassen, eds. *L'Interprétation de la gnose.* Bibliothèque copte de Nag Hammadi, Section "Textes." Québec: Les Presses de l'Université Laval; Louvain: Peeters, forthcoming.

Funk, Wolf-Peter, and Paul Hubert-Poirier. *Concordance des textes de Nag Hammadi: Les Codices XIb, XII, XIII.* Bibliothèque copte de Nag Hammadi, Section "Concordances" 7. Québec: Les Presses de l'Université Laval; Louvain: Peeters, 2002.

Funk, Wolf-Peter, Paul-Hubert Poirier, and John D. Turner, eds. *Marsanès (NH X,1).* Bibliothèque copte de Nag Hammadi, Section "Textes" 27. Québec: Les Presses de l'Université Laval; Louvain: Peeters, 2000.

Funk, Wolf-Peter, Madeleine Scopello, Paul-Hubert Poirier, and John D. Turner, eds. *L'Allogène (NH XI,3).* Bibliothèque copte de Nag Hammadi, Section "Textes." Québec: Les Presses de l'Université Laval; Louvain: Peeters, forthcoming.

Gager, John G., ed. *Curse Tablets and Binding Spells.* New York: Oxford University Press, 1992.

Ghica, Victor Corneliu. "Les actes de Pierre et des douze apôtres (NH VI,1). La vie d'un écrit apocryphe: rédaction, remaniement, traduction." Ph.D. dissertation, École Practique des Hautes Études, 2006.

Gianotto, Claudio. *Melchisedek e la sua tipologia: Tradizioni giudaiche, cristiane e gnostiche (sec. II a.C.–sec. III d.C.).* Supplementi alla Rivista Biblica 12. Brescia: Paideia Editrice, 1984.

——. *La testimonianza veritiera.* Testi del Vicino Oriente antico 8.1. Brescia: Paideia Editrice, 1990.

Giversen, Søren. "The Palaeography of Oxyrhynchus Papyri 1 and 654–655." Paper presented at the Society of Biblical Literature Annual Meeting, Boston, November 1999.

Goehring, James E. "The Concept of Our Great Power." In *The Anchor Bible Dictionary,* edited by David Noel Freedman et al., 3.1125. New York: Doubleday, 1992.

Good, Deirdre. "Divine Noetic Faculties in Eugnostos the Blessed and Related Documents." *Le Muséon* 99 (1986): 5–14.

———. "Sophia in Eugnostos the Blessed and the Sophia of Jesus Christ (NHC III,3 and V,1; NHC III,4 and BG 8502,3)." In *Coptic Studies: Acts of the Third International Congress of Coptic Studies, Warsaw, 20–25 August 1984*, edited by Wlodzimierz Godlewski, 139–44. Warszawa: PWN-Éditions Scientifiques de Pologne, 1990.

Grant, Robert M. *Gnosticism and Early Christianity*. 2d ed. New York: Columbia University Press, 1966

———, ed. *Gnosticism: An Anthology*. New York: Harper, 1961.

Grenfell, Bernard P., Arthur S. Hunt, et al., eds. *The Oxyrhynchus Papyri*. London: Egypt Exploration Fund, 1898–.

Grobel, Kendrick. *The Gospel of Truth: A Valentinian Meditation on the Gospel, Translation from the Coptic and Commentary*. Nashville and New York: Abingdon, 1960.

Guillaumont, Antoine. "De nouveaux actes apocryphes: Les actes de Pierre et des douze apôtres." *Revue de l'histoire des religions* 196 (1979): 141–52.

Guillaumont, Antoine, Henri-Charles Puech, Gilles Quispel, Walter Till, and Yassah 'Abd al-Masih. *The Gospel According to Thomas*. Leiden: Brill, 1959.

Haardt, Robert, ed. *Gnosis: Character and Testimony*. Leiden: Brill, 1971.

Haas, Y. "L'exigence du renoncement au monde dans les Actes de Pierre et douze apôtres, les Apophtegmes des pères du désert et la Pistis Sophia." In *Colloque international sur les textes de Nag Hammadi (Québec, 22–25 août 1978)*, edited by Bernard Barc, 295–303. Bibliothèque copte de Nag Hammadi, Section "Études" 1. Québec: Les Presses de l'Université Laval; Louvain: Peeters, 1981.

Hadot, Pierre. "Être, Vie, Pensée chez Plotin et avant Plotin." In *Les sources de Plotin: dix exposés et discussions par E. R. Dodds [et al.] Vandoeuvres-Genève, 21–29 aôut 1957*, 107–57. Entretiens sur l'antiquité classique 5. Genève: Fondation Hardt, 1960.

———. "Fragments d'un commentaire de Porphyre sur le Parménide." *Revue des Études Grecques* 74 (1961): 410–38.

———. *Marius Victorinus, Traités théologiques sur la Trinité, II: Commentaire*. Paris: Cerf, 1960.

———. *Porphyre et Victorinus*. 2 vols. Paris: Études Augustiniennes, 1968.

———. "'Porphyre et Victorinus': Questions et hypotheses." In *Res Orientales IX*. Bures-sur-Yvette: Groupe pour l'Étude de la Civilisation du Moyen-Orient, 1996.

Haenchen, Ernst. "The Book Baruch." In *Gnosis*, edited by Werner Foerster, 1.48–58.

———. "Das Buch Baruch: Ein Beitrag zum Problem der christlichen Gnosis." *Zeitschrift für Theologie und Kirche* 50 (1953): 123–58.

Halm, Heinz. *Die islamische Gnosis: Die extreme Schia und die 'Alawiten*. Die Bibliothek des Morgenlandes. Zurich: Artemis, 1982.

Harvey, W. W., ed. *Irenaeus, Libros quinque adversus haereses*. Cambridge: Academy, 1857. Reprint, Ridgewood, NJ: Gregg, 1965.

Havelaar, Henriette. *The Coptic Apocalypse of Peter (Nag Hammadi Codex VII,3)*. Texte und Untersuchungen zur Geschichte der altchristlichen Literatur 144. Berlin: Akademie, 1999.

———. "Wie spricht Gott in der Schöpfungsgeschichte von Codex VII,1?" In *Der Gottesspruch in der koptischen Literatur*, edited by Walter Beltz, 117–24. Beiträge zur Orientwissenschaft 15. Halle-Saale: Institute für Orientalistik, 1994.

Hedrick, Charles W. *The Apocalypse of Adam: A Literary and Source Analysis*. Society of Biblical Literature Dissertation Series 46. Chico, CA: Scholars Press, 1980.

———. "The *Apocalypse of Adam*: A Literary and Source Analysis." In *The Society of Biblical Literature One Hundred Eighth Annual Meeting Book of Seminar Papers Friday–Tuesday, 1–5 September 1972, Century Plaza Hotel, Los Angeles, CA*, vol. 2, edited by Lane C. McGaughy, 581–90. Missoula, MT: Scholars Press, 1972.

———. "The *Apocalypse of Adam* Reconsidered." In *The Society of Biblical Literature One Hundred Eighth Annual Meeting Book of Seminar Papers Friday–Tuesday, 1–5 September*

1972, *Century Plaza Hotel, Los Angeles, CA*, vol. 2, edited by Lane C. McGaughy, 573–77. Missoula, MT: Scholars Press, 1972.

———. "Caveats to a 'Righted Order' of the *Gospel of the Savior*." *Harvard Theological Review* 96 (2003): 229–38.

———. "Kingdom Sayings and Parables of Jesus in the Apocryphon of James: Tradition and Redaction." *New Testament Studies* 29 (1983): 1–24.

———, ed. *Nag Hammadi Codices XI, XII, XIII*. Nag Hammadi Studies 28. Leiden: Brill, 1990.

Hedrick, Charles W., and Robert Hodgson, Jr., eds. *Nag Hammadi, Gnosticism, and Early Christianity*. Peabody, MA: Hendrickson, 1986.

Hedrick, Charles W., and Paul A. Mirecki. *Gospel of the Savior: A New Ancient Gospel*. California Classical Library. Santa Rosa, CA: Polebridge, 1999.

Helderman, Jan. "Das Evangelium Veritatis in der neueren Forschung." In *Aufstieg und Niedergang der römischen Welt*, edited by Hildegard Temporini and Wolfgang Haase, II.25.5, 4054–106. Berlin: De Gruyter, 1988.

———. "Melchisedek, Melchisedekianer und die koptische Frömmigkeit." In *Actes du IVe Congrès Copte, Louvain-la-Neuve, 5–10 Septembre 1988*, vol. 2, *De la linguistique au gnosticisme*, edited by Marguerite Rassart-Debergh and Julien Ries, 401–15. Publications de l'Institut Orientaliste de Louvain 41. Louvain: Université Catholique de Louvain, 1992.

———. "Melchisedeks Wirkung: Eine traditionsgeschichtliche Untersuchung eines Motivkomplexes in NHC IX,1,1–27,10 (*Melchisedek*)." In *The New Testament in Early Christianity: La réception des écrits néotestamentaires dans le christianisme primitif*, edited by Jean-Marie Sevrin, 335–62. Bibliotheca Ephemeridum Theologicarum Lovaniensium 86. Louvain: Louvain University Press/Peeters, 1989.

Helmbold, Andrew K. "The Apocryphon of James." In *The Nag Hammadi Gnostic Texts and the Bible*, edited by Andrew K. Helmbold. Baker Studies in Biblical Archaeology 5. Grand Rapids, MI: Baker, 1967.

Hills, Julian V. "The Dialogue of the Savior." In *The Complete Gospels: Annotated Scholars Version*, edited by Robert J. Miller, 343–56. San Francisco: HarperSanFrancisco, 1994.

———. "The Three 'Matthean' Aphorisms in *Dialogue of the Savior* 53." *Harvard Theological Review* 84 (1981): 43–58.

Hock, Ronald F., and Edward N. O'Neil, eds. *The Chreia in Ancient Rhetoric*. Vol. 1. Atlanta: Scholars Press, 1986.

Irmscher, Johannes. "Die gnostische Apokalypse." In *Apocalittica e gnosticismo: Atti del Colloquio Internazionale Roma, 18–19 giugno 1993*, edited by Maria Vittoria Cerutti, 29–42. Rome: Gruppo Editoriale Internazionale, 1995.

Janssens, Yvonne, ed. *Les Leçons de Silvanos (NH VII,4)*. Bibliothèque copte de Nag Hammadi, Section "Textes" 13. Québec: Les Presses de l'Université Laval; Louvain: Peeters, 1983.

———. "Les Leçons de Silvanos et le monachisme." In *Colloque international sur les textes de Nag Hammadi (Québec, 22–25 août 1978)*, edited by Bernard Barc, 352–61. Bibliothèque copte de Nag Hammadi, Section "Études" 1. Québec: Les Presses de l'Université Laval; Louvain: Peeters, 1981.

———, ed. *La Prôtennoia trimorphe (NH XIII,1)*. Bibliothèque copte de Nag Hammadi, Section "Textes" 4. Québec: Les Presses de l'Université Laval; Louvain: Peeters, 1978.

———. "Une source gnostique du Prologue?" In *L'Évangile de Jean: Sources, rédaction, théologie: Réimpression anastatique*, edited by Marinus de Jonge, 355–58. Bibliotheca Ephemeridum Theologicarum Lovaniensium 44. Gembloux: Duculot; Louvain: Louvain University Press, 1987.

———. "Trimorphic Protennoia." In *The Coptic Encyclopedia*, edited by Aziz S. Atiya, 7.2276–77. New York and Oxford: Macmillan, 1991.

———. "The Trimorphic Protennoia and the Fourth Gospel." In *The New Testament and Gnosis: Essays in Honour of Robert McLachlan Wilson*, edited by A. H. B. Logan and A. J. M. Wedderburn, 229–44. Edinburgh: Clark, 1983.

Jasnow, Richard, and Karl-Theodor Zauzich. *The Ancient Egyptian Book of Thoth: A Demotic Discourse on Knowledge and Pendant to the Classical Hermetica*. Vol. 1, text; vol. 2, plates. Wiesbaden: Harrasowitz, 2005.

Jeremias, Joachim. *Unknown Sayings of Jesus*. 2d ed. Translated by Reginald H. Fuller. London: S.P.C.K., 1964.

Jonas, Hans. *The Gnostic Religion: The Message of the Alien God and the Beginnings of Christianity*. 2d ed. Boston: Beacon, 1963.

———. *Gnosis und spätantiker Geist: Die mythologische Gnosis*. 3d ed. Forschungen zur Religion und Literatur des Alten und Neuen Testaments 51. Göttingen: Vandenhoeck & Ruprecht, 1964.

Jones, F. Stanley, ed. *Which Mary? The Marys of Early Christian Tradition*. Symposium 19. Atlanta: Society of Biblical Literature, 2002.

Jowett, Benjamin. *The Republic and Other Works*. New York: Anchor Books, 1973.

Junod, Eric, and Jean-Daniel Kaestli. *Acta Johannis*. Corpus Christianorum, Series Apocryphorum 1, 2. Turnhout: Brepols, 1983.

Kaestli, Jean-Daniel. "Une relecture polémique de Genèse 3 dans le gnosticisme chrétien: *Le Temoignage de vérité.*" *Foi et Vie* 80, no. 6 (1981): 48–62.

Kähler, Martin. *Der sogenannte historische Jesus und der geschichtliche, biblische Christus*. Leipzig: Deichert, 1956.

Kasser, Rodolphe. "Bibliothèque gnostique V: Apocalypse d'Adam." *Revue de Theologie et de Philosophie* 100 (1967): 313–33.

———. *L'Évangile selon Thomas: Présentation et commentaire théologique*. Neuchâtel: Delachaux & Niestlé, 1961.

———. "Un nouvel apocryphe copte." Paper presented at the 8ème Congrès International d'Études Coptes, Paris, July 2004.

———. *Oratio Pauli Apostoli*. In *Tractatus Tripartitus, Partes II et III; Oratio Pauli Apostoli; Evangelium Veritatis*, edited by Rodolphe Kasser, Michel Malinine, Henri-Charles Puech, Gilles Quispel, and Jan Zandee, 243–60. Supplementum photographicum. Bern: Francke, 1973, 1975.

Kasser, Rodolphe, François Gaudard, Marvin Meyer, and Gregor Wurst, eds. *The Gospel of Judas, Together with the Letter of Peter to Philip, the Book of James, and an Unknown Book of Allogenes, from Codex Tchacos: Critical Edition*. Washington, DC: National Geographic Society, forthcoming.

Kasser, Rodolphe, Michel Malinine, Henri-Charles Puech, Gilles Quispel, and Jan Zandee, eds. *Tractatus Tripartitus: Pars I, Pars II, Pars III*. 2 vols. Bern: Francke, 1973, 1975.

Kasser, Rodolphe, Marvin Meyer, and Gregor Wurst, eds. *The Gospel of Judas*. Washington, DC: National Geographic Society, 2006.

Khalidi, Tarif. *The Muslim Jesus: Sayings and Stories in Islamic Literature*. Cambridge, MA, and London: Harvard University Press, 2001.

King, Karen L. "The Apocryphon of John: Part II of the Gospel of John?" Paper presented at the annual meeting of the Society of Biblical Literature, Denver, CO, November 2001.

———. "Approaching the Variants of the *Apocryphon of John*." In *The Nag Hammadi Library After Fifty Years: Proceedings of the 1995 Society of Biblical Literature Commemoration*, edited by John D. Turner and Anne McGuire, 105–37. Nag Hammadi and Manichaean Studies 44. Leiden, New York, and Köln: Brill, 1997.

———. "The Gospel of Mary." In *The Complete Gospels*, edited by Robert J. Miller, 351–60.

———. *The Gospel of Mary*. Hermeneia. Minneapolis: Fortress, forthcoming.

———. *The Gospel of Mary of Magdala: Jesus and the First Woman Apostle*. Santa Rosa, CA: Polebridge, 2003.

———. *Revelation of the Unknowable God: With Text, Translation, and Notes to NHC XI, 3 Allogenes*. Santa Rosa, CA: Polebridge, 1995.

———. *The Secret Revelation of John*. Cambridge, MA, and London: Harvard University Press, 2006.

———. "Sophia and Christ in the Apocryphon of John." In *Images of the Feminine in Gnosticism*, edited by Karen L. King, 158–76.

———. *What Is Gnosticism?* Cambridge, MA: Harvard University Press/Belknap Press, 2003.

———. "Which Early Christianity?" In *The Oxford Handbook of Early Christian Studies*, edited by Susan Ashbrook Harvey and David Hunter. Oxford: Oxford University Press, forthcoming.

———. "Why All the Controversy? Mary in the *Gospel of Mary*." In *Which Mary?* edited by F. Stanley Jones, 53–74.

———, ed. *Images of the Feminine in Gnosticism*. Studies in Antiquity and Christianity. Philadelphia: Fortress, 1988.

Kirchner, Dankwart. "Das Buch des Thomas: Die siebente Schrift aus Nag-Hammadi-Codex II, eingeleitet und übersetzt vom Berliner Arbeitskreis für koptisch-gnostische Schriften." *Theologische Literaturzeitung* 102 (1977): 793–804.

———. *Epistula Jacobi Apocrypha: Die zweite Schrift aus Nag-Hammadi-Codex I*. Texte und Untersuchungen 136. Berlin: Akademie, 1989.

Kirchner, Dankwart, and Einar Thomassen. "The Apocryphon of James." In *New Testament Apocrypha*, edited by Wilhelm Schneemelcher, 1.285–99.

Klijn, Albertus Frederik Johannes. *The Acts of Thomas: Introduction — Text — Commentary*. Supplements to *Novum Testamentum* 5. Leiden: Brill, 1962.

———. *Edessa, die Stadt des Apostels Thomas: Das älteste Christentum in Syrien*. Neukirchener Studienbücher 4. Neukirchen-Vluyn: Erziehungsverein, 1965.

———. *Seth in Jewish, Christian, and Gnostic Literature*. Leiden: Brill, 1977.

Kloppenborg, John S. *Excavating Q: The History and Setting of the Sayings Gospel*. Minneapolis: Fortress, 2000.

———. *The Formation of Q: Trajectories in Ancient Wisdom Collections*. Philadelphia: Fortress, 1987.

———. *Q Parallels: Synopsis, Critical Notes and Concordance*. Sonoma, CA: Polebridge, 1988.

Kloppenborg, John S., Marvin W. Meyer, Stephen J. Patterson, and Michael G. Steinhauser. *Q–Thomas Reader*. Sonoma, CA: Polebridge, 1990.

Koester, Helmut. *Ancient Christian Gospels: Their History and Development*. Philadelphia: Trinity; London: SCM, 1990.

———. "Gnostic Writings as Witnesses for the Development of the Sayings Tradition." In *The Rediscovery of Gnosticism*, edited by Bentley Layton, 1.238–61.

Koester, Helmut, and Elaine H. Pagels. "Report on the *Dialogue of the Savior* (CG III,5)." In *Nag Hammadi and Gnosis: Papers Read at the First International Congress of Coptology (Cairo, December 1976)*, edited by Robert McLachlan Wilson, 66–74. Nag Hammadi Studies 14. Leiden: Brill, 1978.

Koschorke, Klaus. "Gnostic Instructions on the Organization of the Congregation: The Tractate *Interpretation of Knowledge* from CG IX." In *The Rediscovery of Gnosticism*, edited by Bentley Layton, 2.757–69.

———. "Eine gnostische Paraphrase des johanneischen Prologs: Zur Interpretation von 'Epistula Petri ad Philippum' (NHC VIII,2) 126,16–137,4." *Vigiliae Christianae* 33 (1979): 383–92.

———. "Eine gnostische Pfingstpredigt: Zur Auseinandersetzung zwischen gnostischem und kirchlichem Christentum am Beispiel der 'Epistula Petri ad Philippum' (NHC VIII,2)." *Zeitschrift für Theologie und Kirche* 74 (1977): 323–43.

———. "Der gnostische Traktat 'Testimonium Veritatis' aus dem Nag-Hammadi-Codex IX: Eine Übersetzung." *Zeitschrift für die neutestamentliche Wissenschaft und die Kunde der älteren Kirche* 69 (1978): 91–117.

———. "Eine neugefundene gnostische Gemeindeordnung: Zum Thema Geist und Amt im frühen Christentum." *Zeitschrift für Theologie und Kirche* 76 (1979): 30–60.

———. *Die Polemik der Gnostiker gegen das kirchliche Christentum: Unter besonderer Berücksichtigung der Nag-Hammadi-Traktate "Apokalypse des Petrus" (NHC VII,3) und "Testimonium Veritatis" (NHC IX,3)*. Nag Hammadi Studies 12. Leiden: Brill, 1978.

Krause, Martin. "The Letter of Eugnostos." In *Gnosis*, edited by Werner Foerster, 2.24–39.

———. "Die Petrusakten in Codex VI von Nag Hammadi." In *Essays on the Nag Hammadi Texts in Honour of Alexander Böhlig*, edited by Martin Krause, 36–58. Nag Hammadi Studies 3. Leiden: Brill, 1972.

Krause, Martin, and Pahor Labib. *Die drei Versionen des Apokryphon des Johannes im koptischen Museum zu Alt-Kairo*. Wiesbaden: Harrassowitz, 1962.

———. *Gnostische und hermetische Schriften aus Codex II und Codex VI*. Abhandlungen des Deutschen Archäologischen Instituts Kairo, Koptische Reihe 2. Glückstadt: Augustin, 1971.

Kroll, W. "Ein neuplatonischer Parmenides-kommentar in einem Turiner Palimpsest." *Rheinisches Museum für Philologie* 47 (1892): 599–627.

Krosney, Herbert. *The Lost Gospel: The Quest for the Gospel of Judas Iscariot*. Washington, DC: National Geographic Society, 2006.

Kubińska, Jadwiga. "L'ange Litakskuel en Nubie." *Le Muséon* 89 (1976): 451–55.

Kuntzmann, Raymond, ed. *Le Livre de Thomas (NH II,7): Texte établi et présenté*. Bibliothèque copte de Nag Hammadi, Section "Textes" 16. Québec: Les Presses de l'Université Laval; Louvain: Peeters, 1986.

Layton, Bentley. *The Gnostic Scriptures: A New Translation with Annotations and Introductions*. Garden City, NY: Doubleday, 1987.

———. *The Gnostic Treatise on Resurrection from Nag Hammadi: Edited with Translation and Commentary*. Harvard Dissertations in Religion 12. Missoula, MT: Scholars Press, 1979.

———. "The Hypostasis of the Archons, or *The Reality of the Rulers*: A Gnostic Story of the Creation, Fall, and Ultimate Salvation of Man, and the Origin and Reality of His Enemies; Newly Edited from the Cairo Manuscript with a Preface, English Translation, Notes, and Indexes." *Harvard Theological Review* 67 (1974): 351–425.

———. "Prolegomena to the Study of Ancient Gnosticism." In *The Social World of the First Christians: Essays in Honor of Wayne A. Meeks*, edited by L. Michael White and O. Larry Yarbrough, 334–50. Minneapolis: Fortress, 1995.

———, ed. *Nag Hammadi Codex II,2–7, Together with XIII,2*, Brit. Lib. Or. 4926(1), and P. Oxy. 1, 654, 655*. 2 vols. Nag Hammadi Studies 20–21. Leiden: Brill, 1989.

———, ed. *The Rediscovery of Gnosticism: Proceedings of the International Conference on Gnosticism at Yale, New Haven, Connecticut, March 28–31, 1978*. Studies in the History of Religions (Supplements to *Numen*) 41. Leiden: Brill, 1980–81.

Létourneau, Pierre, ed. *Le Dialogue du Sauveur*. Bibliothèque copte de Nag Hammadi, Section "Textes" 29. Québec: Les Presses de l'Université Laval; Louvain: Peeters, 2003.

Letrouit, Jean. "Chronologie des alchimistes grecs." In *Alchimie, art, histoire et mythes: Actes du 1er colloque international de la Société d'Étude de l'Histoire de l'Alchimie (Paris, Collège de France, 14–15–16 mars 1991)*, edited by Didier Kahn and Sylvain Matton, 11–93. Textes et travaux de Chrysopoeia 1. Paris-Milan: Séha-Archè, 1995.

Linguiti, Alessandro. "Commentarium in Platonis 'Parmenidem.'" In *Testi e lessico nei papiri di cultura greca e latina*. Studi e Testi per il Corpus dei Papiri Filosofici. Firenze: Olschki, 1995.

Logan, Alastair H. B. "The Epistle of Eugnostos and Valentinianism." In *Gnosis and Gnosticism: Papers Read at the Eighth International Conference on Patristic Studies (Oxford, September 3–8, 1979)*, edited by Martin Krause, 66–75. Nag Hammadi Studies 17. Leiden: Brill, 1981.

Lucentini, Paolo, Ilaria Parri, and Vittoria Perrone Compagni, eds. *Hermetism from Late Antiquity to Humanism*. Instrumenta patristica et mediaevalia 40. Turnhout: Brepols, 2003.

Lüdemann, Gerd, and Martina Janssen. *Bibel der Haretiker: Die gnostischen Schriften aus Nag Hammadi*. Stuttgart: Radius, 1997.

Lührmann, Dieter. "Die griechischen Fragmente des Mariaevangeliums POxy 3525 und PRyl 463." *Novum Testamentum* 30 (1988): 321–38.

Luttikhuizen Gerard P., ed. *Eve's Children: The Biblical Stories Retold and Interpreted in Jewish and Christian Traditions*. Themes in Biblical Narrative 5. Leiden: Brill, 2003.

———. *Paradise Interpreted: Representations of Biblical Paradise in Judaism and Christianity*. Themes in Biblical Narrative 2. Leiden: Brill, 1999.

Mack, Burton L. *Logos und Sophia: Untersuchungen zur Weisheitstheologie im hellenistischen Judentum*. Göttingen: Vandenhoeck & Ruprecht, 1973.

———. *The Lost Gospel: The Book of Q and Christian Origins*. San Francisco: HarperSanFrancisco, 1993.

MacRae, George W. "The Apocalypse of Adam (First to Fourth Century A.D.): A New Translation and Introduction." In *The Old Testament Pseudepigrapha*, vol. 1, *Apocalyptic Literature and Testaments*, edited by James H. Charlesworth, 707–19. Garden City, NY: Doubleday, 1983.

———. "The Apocalypse of Adam Reconsidered." In *Society of Biblical Literature Seminar Papers*, 2.573–77. Missoula, MT: Scholars Press, 1972.

———. "A Nag Hammadi Tractate on the Soul." In *Ex Orbe Religionum: Studia Geo Widengren*, edited by Claas Jouco Bleeker, Samuel Georg Frederik Brandon, and Marcel Simon, 471–79. Studies in the History of Religions (Supplements to *Numen*) 21. Leiden: Brill, 1972.

Mahé, Annie, and Jean-Pierre Mahé, eds. *Le Témoignage Véritable (NH IX,3): Gnose et Martyre*. Bibliothèque copte de Nag Hammadi, Section "Textes" 23. Québec: Les Presses de l'Université Laval; Louvain: Peeters, 1996.

Mahé, Jean-Pierre. "The Definitions of Hermes Trismegistus to Asclepius." In *The Way of Hermes*, edited by Clement Salaman, Dorine van Oyen, and William D. Wharton, 99–124. London: Duckworth, 1999.

———, ed. *Hermès en Haute Égypte (Tome I): Les textes hermétiques de Nag Hammadi et leurs parallèles grecs et latins*. Bibliothèque copte de Nag Hammadi, Section "Textes" 3. Québec: Les Presses de l'Université Laval; Louvain: Peeters, 1978.

———, ed. *Hermès en Haute Égypte (Tome II): Le Fragment du Discours Parfait et les Définitions hermétiques arméniennes*. Bibliothèque copte de Nag Hammadi, Section "Textes" 7. Québec: Les Presses de l'Université Laval; Louvain: Peeters, 1982.

———. "Preliminary Remarks on the Demotic *Book of Thoth* and the Greek *Hermetica*." *Vigiliae Christianae* 50 (1996): 353–63.

———. "La prière d'actions de grâces du Codex VI de Nag-Hammadi et le discours parfait." *Zeitschrift für Papyrologie und Epigraphik* 13 (1974): 40–60.

———. "La voie d'immortalité à la lumière des *Hermetica* de Nag Hammadi et de découvertes plus récentes." *Vigiliae Christianae* 45 (1991): 347–75.

Mahé, Jean-Pierre, and Paul-Hubert Poirier, eds. *Écrits gnostiques*. Bibliothèque de la Pléiade. Paris: Gallimard, 2007.

Malinine, Michel, Henri-Charles Puech, Gilles Quispel, Walter C. Till, Rodolphe Kasser, R. McLachlan Wilson, and Jan Zandee, eds. *Epistula Iacobi Apocrypha: Codex Jung F. I^r–F. VIII^v (pp. 1–16)*. Zurich and Stuttgart: Rascher, 1968.

Marcovich, Miroslav, ed. *Hippolyti refutationis omnium haeresium librorum decem quae supersunt*. New York and Berlin: De Gruyter, 1986.

Marjanen, Antti. "The Suffering of One Who Is a Stranger to Suffering: The Crucifixion of Jesus in the Letter of Peter to Philip." In *Fair Play: Diversity and Conflicts in Early Christianity: Essays in Honour of Heikki Räisänen*, edited by Ismo Dunderberg, Christopher Tuckett, and Kari Syreeni, 487–98. Supplements to *Novum Testamentum* 103. Leiden: Brill, 2002.

———. *The Woman Jesus Loved: Mary Magdalene in the Nag Hammadi Library and Related Documents*. Nag Hammadi and Manichaean Studies 40. Leiden, New York, and Köln: Brill, 1996.

———, ed. *Was There a Gnostic Religion?* Publications of the Finnish Exegetical Society 87. Helsinki: Finnish Exegetical Society; Göttingen: Vandenhoeck & Ruprecht, 2005.

Marjanen, Antti, and Petri Luomanen, eds. *A Companion to Second-Century Christian "Heretics."* Supplements to *Vigiliae Christianae* 76. Leiden and Boston: Brill, 2005.

Markschies, Christoph. *Valentinus Gnosticus? Untersuchungen zur valentinianischen Gnosis mit einem Kommentar zu den Fragmenten Valentins*. Tübingen: Mohr (Paul Siebeck), 1992.

Bibliography

815

Martin, Luther H. "The Anti-Philosophical Polemic and Gnostic Soteriology in 'The Trea-
tise on the Resurrection.'" *Numen* 20 (1971): 20–37.
McGuire, Anne. "Conversion and Gnosis in the *Gospel of Truth.*" *Novum Testamentum* 28
(1986): 338–55.
———. "Women, Gender, and Gnosis in Gnostic texts and Traditions." In *Women and Chris-
tian Origins*, edited by Ross Shepard Kramer and Mary Rose D'Angelo, 257–99. New
York and Oxford: Oxford University Press, 1999.
Ménard, Jacques-É., ed. *L'Authentikos Logos*. Bibliothèque copte de Nag Hammadi, Section
"Textes" 2. Québec: Les Presses de l'Université Laval; Louvain: Peeters, 1977.
———. *L'Évangile de Vérité*. Nag Hammadi Studies 2. Leiden: Brill, 1972.
———. *L'Évangile de Vérité: Rétroversion grecque et commentaire.* Paris: Letouzey & Ané,
1962.
———. *L'Évangile selon Philippe: Introduction, texte, traduction, commentaire.* Strasbourg
and Paris: Letouzey & Ané, 1967.
———. *L'Évangile selon Thomas.* Nag Hammadi Studies 5. Leiden: Brill, 1975.
———, ed. *L'Exposé valentinien: Les Fragments sur le baptême et sur l'eucharistie (NH XI,2).*
Bibliothèque copte de Nag Hammadi, Section "Textes" 14. Québec: Les Presses de l'Université Laval; Louvain: Peeters, 1985.
———, ed. *La Lettre de Pierre à Philippe: Texte établi et présenté.* Bibliothèque copte de Nag
Hammadi, Section "Textes" 1. Québec: Les Presses de l'Université Laval; Louvain:
Peeters, 1977.
———, ed. *Le Traité sur la resurrection (NH I,4).* Bibliothèque copte de Nag Hammadi, Sec-
tion "Textes" 12. Québec: Les Presses de l'Université Laval; Louvain: Peeters, 1983.
Meyer, Marvin. *The Gnostic Discoveries: The Impact of the Nag Hammadi Library.* San Fran-
cisco: HarperSanFrancisco, 2005.
———. *The Gnostic Gospels of Jesus: The Definitive Collection of Mystical Gospels and Secret
Books About Jesus of Nazareth.* San Francisco: HarperSanFrancisco, 2005.
———. "Gnosticism, Gnostics, and *The Gnostic Bible.*" In *The Gnostic Bible*, edited by Willis
Barnstone and Marvin Meyer, 1–19.
———. *The Gospels of Mary: The Secret Tradition of Mary Magdalene, the Companion of
Jesus.* San Francisco: HarperSanFrancisco, 2004.
———. *The Gospel of Thomas: The Hidden Sayings of Jesus.* San Francisco: HarperSanFran-
cisco, 1992.
———. "*Gospel of Thomas* Logion 114 Revisited." In *For the Children, Perfect Instruction*, ed-
ited by Hans-Gebhard Bethge, Stephen Emmel, Karen L. King, and Imke Schletterer,
101–11. Also in Marvin Meyer, *Secret Gospels*, 96–106.
———. "Judas and the Gnostic Connection." In *The Gospel of Judas*, edited by Rodolphe
Kasser, Marvin Meyer, and Gregor Wurst, 137–69.
———. *The Letter of Peter to Philip: Text, Translation, and Commentary.* Society of Biblical
Literature Dissertation Series 53. Chico, CA: Scholars Press, 1981.
———. "Making Mary Male: The Categories 'Male' and 'Female' in the *Gospel of Thomas.*"
New Testament Studies 31 (1985): 544–70. Also in Marvin Meyer, *Secret Gospels*, 76–95.
———. Review of Karen L. King, *What Is Gnosticism? Review of Biblical Literature* (2004)
electronic journal (http://www.bookreviews.org).
———. "The Round Dance of the Cross." In *The Gnostic Bible*, edited by Willis Barnstone
and Marvin Meyer, 351–55.
———. *Secret Gospels: Essays on Thomas and the Secret Gospel of Mark.* Harrisburg, New
York, and London: Trinity Press International/Continuum, 2003.
———. *The Unknown Sayings of Jesus.* Boston: Shambhala, 2005.
Meyer, Marvin, and Charles Hughes, eds. *Jesus Then and Now: Images of Jesus in History and
Christology.* Harrisburg, New York, and London: Trinity Press International/Continuum,
2001.
Meyer, Marvin, and Richard Smith, eds. *Ancient Christian Magic: Coptic Texts of Ritual
Power.* Mythos. Princeton, NJ: Princeton University Press, 1999.

Miller, Robert J., ed. *The Complete Gospels: Annotated Scholars Version*. Santa Rosa, CA: Polebridge, 1994.

Mohri, Erika. *Maria Magdalena: Frauenbilder in Evangelientexten des 1. bis 3. Jahrhunderts*. Marburger theologische Studien 63. Marburg: Elwert, 2000.

Molinari, Andrea L. *The Acts of Peter and the Twelve Apostles (NHC 6,1): Allegory, Ascent, and Ministry in the Wake of the Decian Persecution*. Society of Biblical Literature Dissertation Series 174. Atlanta: Society of Biblical Literature, 2000.

———. "The Acts of Peter and the Twelve Apostles: A Reconsideration of the Source Question." In *The Nag Hammadi Library After Fifty Years: Proceedings of the 1995 Society of Biblical Literature Commemoration*, edited by John D. Turner and Anne McGuire, 461–83. Nag Hammadi and Manichaean Studies 44. Leiden: Brill, 1997.

———. "*I Never Knew the Man*": *The Coptic Act of Peter (Papyrus Berolinensis 8502.4); Its Independence from the Apocryphal Acts of Peter, Genre and Legendary Origins*. Bibliothèque copte de Nag Hammadi, Section "Études" 5. Québec: Les Presses de l'Université Laval; Louvain: Peeters, 2000.

Montgomery, James A. *The Samaritans, the Earliest Jewish Sect: Their History, Theology, and Literature*, 255–63. Philadelphia: Winston, 1906.

Morard, Françoise-E., ed. *L'Apocalypse d'Adam (NH V,5)*. Bibliothèque copte de Nag Hammadi, Section "Textes" 15. Québec: Les Presses de l'Université Laval; Louvain: Peeters, 1985.

———. "*L'Apocalypse d'Adam* de Nag Hammadi: Un essai d'interpétation." In *Gnosis and Gnosticism: Papers Read at the Seventh International Conference on Patristic Studies (Oxford, September 8–13, 1975)*, edited by Martin Krause, 35–42. Nag Hammadi Studies 8. Leiden: Brill, 1977.

———. "Thématique de *l'Apocalypse d'Adam* du Codex V de Nag Hammadi." In *Colloque international sur les textes de Nag Hammadi (Québec, 22–25 août 1978)*, edited by Bernard Barc, 288–94. Bibliothèque copte de Nag Hammadi, Section "Études" 1. Québec: Les Presses de l'Université Laval; Louvain: Peeters, 1981.

Müller, Casper D. G. *Die Engellehre der koptischen Kirche: Untersuchungen zur Geschichte der christlichen Frömmigkeit in Ägypten*. Weisbaden: Harrassowitz, 1959.

Murdock, W. R. "The Apocalypse of Paul from Nag Hammadi." Th.D dissertation, Claremont School of Theology, 1968.

Nagel, Peter. *Das Wesen der Archonten aus Codex II der gnostischen Bibliothek von Nag Hammadi*. Wissenschaftliche Beiträge K3. Halle-Wittenberg: Martin-Luther-Universität, 1970.

Nock, Arthur Darby, and André-Jean Festugière, eds. *Corpus Hermeticum*. 4 vols. Paris: Sociéte d'édition "Les Belles lettres," 1945–54.

Oeyen, Christian. "Fragmente einer subachmimischen Version der gnostischen Schrift ohne Titel." In *Essays on the Nag Hammadi Texts in Honour of Pahor Labib*, edited by Martin Krause, 125–44. Nag Hammadi Studies 6. Leiden: Brill, 1975.

Orbe, Antonio. *Estudios Valentinianos*. 5 vols. Analecta Gregoriana 99. Rome: Pontificia Università Gregoriana, 1958.

Orlandi, Tito. *Evangelium Veritatis*. Testi del Vicino Oriente antico 8.2. Brescia: Paideia, 1992.

———. "La traduzione copta di Platone, Resp. IV, 588b–589b: Problemi critici ed esegetici." *Atti della Accademia Naziunale dei Lincei* (Rendiconti della Classe di Scienze morali, storiche e filologiche, Serie 8) 32 (1977): 45–62.

Pagels, Elaine H. *Beyond Belief: The Secret Gospel of Thomas*. New York: Random House, 2003.

———. *The Gnostic Gospels*. New York: Random House, 1979.

———. *The Gnostic Paul: Gnostic Exegesis of the Pauline Letters*. Philadelphia: Fortress, 1975.

———. *The Johannine Gospel in Gnostic Exegesis: Heracleon's Commentary on John*. Society of Biblical Literature Monograph Series 17. Nashville: Abingdon, 1973.

———. "The Mystery of the Resurrection: A Gnostic Reading of 1 Corinthians 15." *Journal of Biblical Literature* 93 (1974): 276–88.

Pagels, Elaine H., and Karen L. King. *Reading Judas: The Gospel of Judas and the Shaping of Christianity*. New York: Viking, 2007.

Painchaud, Louis. "La composition de l'Évangile selon Philippe (NH II,3): Une analyse rhétorique." In *Society of Biblical Literature Seminar Papers*, 35–66. Atlanta: Scholars Press, 1996.

———, ed. *Le Deuxième Traité du Grand Seth (NH VII,2)*. Bibliothèque copte de Nag Hammadi, Section "Textes" 6. Québec: Les Presses de l'Université Laval; Louvain: Peeters, 1982.

———, ed. *L'Écrit sans titre: Traité sur l'origine du monde (NH II,5 et XIII,2 et Brit. Lib. Or. 4926[1])*. Bibliothèque copte de Nag Hammadi, Section "Textes" 21. Québec: Les Presses de l'Université Laval; Louvain: Peeters, 1995.

———, ed. *Fragment de la République de Platon (NH VI,5)*. Bibliothèque copte de Nag Hammadi, Section "Textes" 11. Québec: Les Presses de l'Université Laval; Louvain: Peeters, 1983.

———. "The Literary Contacts Between the Writing Without Title 'On the Origin of the World' (CG II,5 and XIII,2) and 'Eugnostos the Blessed' (CG III,3 and V,1)." *Journal of Biblical Literature* 114 (1995): 81–101.

———. "Something Is Rotten in the Kingdom of Sabaoth: Allégorie et polémique en NH II 103,32–106,19." In *Acts of the Fifth International Congress of Coptic Studies, Washington, August 1992*, edited by Tito Orlandi, 339–53. Rome: C.I.M., 1993.

———. "The Writing Without Title of Nag Hammadi Codex II: A Redactional Hypothesis." *Second Century* 8 (1991): 217–34.

Painchaud, Louis, and Bernard Barc. "Les réécritures de l'Apocryphon de Jean à la lumière de l'hymne final de la version longue." *Le Muséon* 112 (1999): 317–33.

Painchaud, Louis, M.-P. Bussières, and M. Kaler. "The Coptic *Apocalypse of Paul*, Irenaeus' *Adv. Haer.* II.30.7, and the Second-Century Battle of Paul's Legacy." *Journal of Early Christian Studies* 12 (2004): 173–94.

Paramelle, Joseph, and Jean-Pierre Mahé. "Extraits hermétiques inédits dans un manuscrit d'Oxford." *Revue des Études Grecques* 104 (1991): 109–39.

Parrinder, Geoffrey. *Jesus in the Qur'an*. New York: Oxford University Press, 1965.

Parrott, Douglas M. "The Significance of the Letter of Eugnostos and the Sophia of Jesus Christ for the Understanding of the Relation Between Gnosticism and Christianity." In *Society of Biblical Literature Seminar Papers*, 387–416. Missoula, MT: Scholars Press, 1971.

———, ed. *Nag Hammadi Codices III,3–4 and V,1 with Papyrus Berolinensis 8502,3 and Oxyrhynchus Papyrus 1081: Eugnostos and the Sophia of Jesus Christ*. Nag Hammadi Studies 27. Leiden: Brill, 1991.

———, ed. *Nag Hammadi Codices V, 2–5 and VI with Papyrus Berolinensis 8502,1 and 4*. Nag Hammadi Studies 11. Leiden: Brill, 1979.

Pasquier, Anne. "Étude de théologie du nom dans le traité d'Eugnoste à partir d'un fragment de Valentin." *Le Muséon* 103 (1990): 205–14.

———, ed. *Eugnoste (NH III,3 et V,1): Lettre sur le Dieu transcendant*. Bibliothèque copte de Nag Hammadi, Section "Textes" 26. Québec: Les Presses de l'Université Laval; Louvain: Peeters, 2000.

———, ed. *L'Évangile selon Marie (BG 1)*. Bibliothèque copte de Nag Hammadi, Section "Textes" 10. Québec: Les Presses de l'Université Laval; Louvain: Peeters, 1983.

Patterson, Stephen J. *The Gospel of Thomas and Jesus*. Foundations and Facets. Santa Rosa, CA: Polebridge, 1993.

———. "Sources, Redaction and *Tendenz* in the Acts of Peter and the Twelve Apostles (NH VI,1)." *Vigiliae Christianae* 45 (1991): 1–17.

Patterson, Stephen J., James M. Robinson, and Hans-Gebhard Bethge. *The Fifth Gospel: The Gospel of Thomas Comes of Age*. Harrisburg, PA: Trinity Press International, 1998.

Pearson, Birger A. "Anti-Heretical Warnings in Codex IX from Nag Hammadi." In *Gnosticism, Judaism, and Egyptian Christianity*, by Birger A. Pearson, 183–93.

———. "The Apocalypse of Peter and Canonical 2 Peter." In *Gnosticism and the Early Christian World: In Honor of James M. Robinson*, edited by James E. Goehring, Charles W. Hedrick, Jack T. Sanders, and Hans Dieter Betz, 67–75. Forum Fascicles 2. Sonoma, CA: Polebridge, 1990.

———. "Christians and Jews in First-Century Alexandria." In *Gnosticism and Christianity in Roman and Coptic Egypt*, by Birger A. Pearson, 82–99.

———. "The Figure of Norea in Gnostic Literature." In *Proceedings of the International Colloquium on Gnosticism: Stockholm, August 20–25, 1973*, edited by Geo Widengren, 143–52. Stockholm and Leiden: Almqvist & Wiksell International, Brill, 1977.

———. "The Figure of Melchizedek in Gnostic Literature." In *Gnosticism, Judaism, and Egyptian Christianity*, by Birger A. Pearson, 108–23.

———. "Gnostic Interpretation of the Old Testament in *The Testimony of Truth* from Nag Hammadi (CG IX,3)." *Harvard Theological Review* 71 (1980): 311–19.

———. *Gnosticism and Christianity in Roman and Coptic Egypt*. Studies in Antiquity and Christianity. New York and London: Clark International, 2004.

———. "Gnosticism as Platonism, with Special Reference to Marsanes (NHC 10,1)." *Harvard Theological Review* 77 (1984): 55–72.

———. *Gnosticism, Judaism, and Egyptian Christianity*. Studies in Antiquity and Christianity. Minneapolis: Fortress, 1990.

———. "Jewish Haggadic Traditions in *The Testimony of Truth* from Nag Hammadi." In *Gnosticism, Judaism, and Egyptian Christianity*, by Birger A. Pearson, 39–51.

———. "Melchizedek in Early Judaism, Christianity, and Gnosticism." In *Biblical Figures Outside the Bible*, edited by Michael E. Stone and Theodore A. Bergren, 176–202. Harrisburg, PA: Trinity Press International, 1998.

———. "Philo, Gnosis, and the New Testament." In *Gnosticism, Judaism, and Egyptian Christianity*, by Birger A. Pearson, 165–82.

———. "The Tractate Marsanes (NHC X) and the Platonic Tradition." In *Gnosis: Festschrift für Hans Jonas*, edited by Barbara Aland, 373–84. Göttingen: Vandenhoeck & Ruprecht, 1978.

———, ed. *Nag Hammadi Codex VII*. Nag Hammadi and Manichaean Studies 30. Leiden: Brill, 1996.

———, ed. *Nag Hammadi Codices IX and X*. Nag Hammadi Studies 15. Leiden: Brill, 1981.

Peel, Malcolm. "The 'Descensus ad Inferos' in the 'Teachings of Silvanus' (CG VII,4)." *Numen* 16 (1979): 23–49.

Perkins, Pheme. "Apocalypse of Adam: The Genre and Function of a Gnostic Apocalypse." *Catholic Biblical Quarterly* 39 (1977): 382–95.

———. *The Gnostic Dialogue: The Early Church and the Crisis of Gnosticism*. New York: Paulist, 1980.

———. *Gnosticism and the New Testament*. Minneapolis: Fortress, 1993.

Peters, F. E. "Jesus in Islam." In *Jesus Then and Now*, edited by Marvin Meyer and Charles Hughes, 260–70.

Petersen, Silke. *"Zerstört die Werke der Wieblichkeit!" Maria Magdalena, Salome und andere Jüngerinnen Jesu in christlich-gnostischen Schriften*. Nag Hammadi and Manichaean Studies 48. Leiden: Brill, 1999.

Plese, Zlatko. *Poetics of the Gnostic Universe: Narrative and Cosmology in the Apocryphon of John*. Nag Hammadi and Manichaean Studies 52. Leiden: Brill, 2005.

Plisch, Uwe-Karsten. *Die Auslegung der Erkenntnis (Nag-Hammadi-Codex XI,1)*. Texte und Untersuchungen zur Geschichte der altchristlichen Literatur 142. Berlin: Akademie, 1996.

Poirier, Paul-Hubert, ed. *La Pensée Première à la triple forme (NH XIII,1)*. Bibliothèque copte de Nag Hammadi, Section "Textes" 32. Québec: Les Presses de l'Université Laval; Louvain: Peeters, 2006.

———, ed. *Le Tonnerre, intellect parfait (NH VI,2)*. Bibliothèque copte de Nag Hammadi, Section "Textes" 22. Québec: Les Presses de l'Université Laval; Louvain: Peeters, 1995.

Poirier, Paul-Hubert, and Louis Painchaud, eds. *Les Sentences de Sextus (NH XII,1), Fragments (NH XII, 3), suivi du Fragment de la République de Platon (NH VI, 5)*. Bibliothèque copte de Nag Hammadi, Section "Textes" 11. Québec: Les Presses de l'Université Laval; Louvain: Peeters, 1983.

Pouderon, Bernard. "Hélène et Ulysse comme deux âmes en peine: Une symbolique gnostique ou pythagoricienne?" *Revue des études grecques* 116 (2003): 132–51.

———. "'Paysages d'âmes' d'écrits gnostiques: L'Exégèse sur l'âme." In *Lieux, décors et paysages de l'ancien roman, des origines à Byzance: Actes du 2e colloque de Tours, 24–26 octobre 2002*, edited by Bernard Pouderon. Collection de la Maison de l'Orient et de la Méditerranée; Série littéraire et philosophique 8. Lyon: Maison de l'Orient et de la Méditerranée, 2005.

Pratscher, Wilhelm. *Der Herrenbruder Jakobus und die Jakobustradition*. Forschungen zur Religion und Literatur des Alten und Neuen Testaments 139. Göttingen: Vandenhoeck & Ruprecht, 1987.

Preisendanz, Karl, ed. *Papyri Graecae Magicae: Die griechischen Zauberpapyri*. Herausgegeben und übersetzt von K. Preisendanz; zweite, verbesserte Auflage von A. Henrichs. 2 vols. Stuttgart: Teubner, 1973, 1974.

Puech, Henri-Charles. "The Apocryphon of James (Apocryphon Jacobi)." In *New Testament Apocrypha*, edited by Edgar Hennecke and Wilhelm Schneemelcher, English translation edited by Robert McLachlan Wilson, 1.333–38. Philadelphia: Westminster, 1963.

———. "Les nouveaux écrits gnostiques découverts en Haute-Égypte. Premier inventaire et essai d'identification." In *Coptic Studies in Honor of Walter Ewing Crum*, 91–154. The Bulletin of the Byzantine Institute 2. Boston: Byzantine Institute of America, 1950.

———. "Plotin et les gnostiques." In *En quête de la Gnose*, vol. 1, *La gnose et le temps*, 244–48. Bibliothèque des science humaines. Paris: Gallimard, 1978.

Puech, Henri-Charles, and Gilles Quispel. "La Lettre de Jacques." *Vigiliae Christianae* 8 (1954): 7–22.

Riley, Gregory J. *Resurrection Reconsidered: Thomas and John in Controversy*. Minneapolis: Fortress, 1995.

Roberge, Michel. "Anthropogonie et anthropologie dans la *Paraphrase de Sem* (NH VII,1)." *Le Muséon* 99 (1986): 229–48.

———. "Chute et remontée du Pneuma dans la *Paraphrase de Sem* (NH VII,1)." In *Coptic Studies: Acts of the Third International Congress of Coptic Studies, Warsaw, August 20–25 1984*, edited by Wlodzimierz Godlewski, 353–63. Warszawa: PWN-Éditions Scientifiques de Pologne, 1990.

———. "La crucifixion du Sauveur dans la *Paraphrase de Sem* (NH VII,1)." In *Actes du IVe congrès copte, Louvain-la Neuve, 5–10 septembre 1988, II: De la linguistique au gnosticisme*, edited by Marguerite Rassart-Debergh and J. Ries, 381–87. Publications de l'Institut orientaliste de Louvain 41. Louvain-la-Neuve: Institut Orientaliste, 1992.

———, ed. "Noréa." In *L'Hypostase des archontes: Traité gnostique sur l'origine de l'homme, du monde et des archontes (NH 11,4) suivi de Noréa (NH IX,2)*, edited by Bernard Barc and Michel Roberge, 149–68. Bibliothèque copte de Nag Hammadi, Section "Textes" 5. Québec: Les Presses de l'Université Laval; Louvain: Peeters, 1980.

———, ed. *La Paraphrase de Sem (NH VII,1)*. Bibliothèque copte de Nag Hammadi, Section "Textes" 25. Québec: Les Presses de l'Université Laval; Louvain: Peeters, 1999.

———. "The *Paraphrase de Sem* (NH VII,1) as an Ascent Apocalypse." *Le Muséon* 113 (2000): 25–54.

———. "La *Paraphrase de Sem* (NH VII,1) et le problème des trois natures." In *Les textes de Nag Hammadi et le problème de leur classification: Actes du colloque tenu à Québec du 15 au 19 septembre 1993*, edited by Louis Painchaud and Anne Pasquier, 279–93. Bibliothèque copte de Nag Hammadi, Section "Études" 3. Québec: Les Presses de l'Université Laval; Louvain: Peeters, 1981.

———. "Le rôle du *Noûs* dans la *Paraphrase de Sem*." In *Colloque international sur les textes de Nag Hammadi (Québec, 22–25 août 1978)*, edited by Bernard Barc, 328–39. Bibliothèque copte de Nag Hammadi, Section "Études" 1. Québec: Les Presses de l'Université Laval; Louvain: Peeters, 1981.

Robinson, Gesine. "The Trimorphic Protennoia and the Prologue of the Fourth Gospel." In *Gnosticism and the Early Christian World: In Honor of James M. Robinson*, edited by James E. Goehring, Charles W. Hedrick, Jack T. Sanders, and Hans Dieter Betz, 37–50. Forum Fascicles 2. Sonoma, CA: Polebridge, 1990.

Robinson, James M. "Essays on the Original Reading Behind Q 12:27 in Codex Sinaiticus and P. Oxy. 655." In James M. Robinson, *The Sayings Gospel Q: Collected Essays*, edited by Christoph Heil and Joseph Verheyden, 711–883. Bibliotheca Ephemeridum Theologicarum Lovaniensium 189. Louvain: Presses Universitaires de Louvain; Peeters, 2005.

———. "From the Cliff to Cairo: The Story of the Discoverers and Middlemen of the Nag Hammadi Codices." In *Colloque international sur les textes de Nag Hammadi (Québec, 22–25 août 1978)*, edited by Bernard Barc, 21–58. Bibliothèque copte de Nag Hammadi, Section "Études" 1. Québec: Les Presses de l'Université Laval; Louvain: Peeters, 1981.

———. "The Jung Codex: The Rise and Fall of a Monopoly." *Religious Studies Review* 3 (1977): 17–30.

———. "*LOGOI SOPHON*: On the Gattung of Q." In *Trajectories Through Early Christianity*, by James M. Robinson and Helmut Koester, 71–113.

———. "Nag Hammadi: The First Fifty Years." In Stephen J. Patterson, James M. Robinson, and Hans-Gebhard Bethge, *The Fifth Gospel*, 77–110.

———. *The Secrets of Judas: The Story of the Misunderstood Disciple and His Lost Gospel*. San Francisco: HarperSanFrancisco, 2006.

———. "Sethians and Johannine Thought: The Trimorphic Protennoia and the Prologue of the Gospel of John." In *The Rediscovery of Gnosticism*, edited by Bentley Layton, 2:643–62.

———. "The Three Steles of Seth and the Gnostics of Plotinus." In *Proceedings of the International Colloquium on Gnosticism: Stockholm, August 20–25, 1973*, edited by Geo Widengren, 132–42. Stockholm and Leiden: Almqvist & Wiksell International, Brill, 1977.

———, ed. *The Nag Hammadi Library in English*. 3d ed. San Francisco: HarperSanFrancisco, 1988.

Robinson, James M., Paul Hoffman, and John S. Kloppenborg, eds. *The Critical Edition of Q: Synopsis Including the Gospels of Matthew and Luke, Mark, and Thomas with English, German, and French Translations of Q and Thomas*. Louvain: Peeters, 2000.

Robinson, James M., and Helmut Koester. *Trajectories Through Early Christianity*. Philadelphia: Fortress, 1971.

Rosenstiehl, Jean-Marc, and Michael Kaler. *L'Apocalypse de Paul (NH V,2)*. Bibliothèque copte de Nag Hammadi, Section "Textes" 31. Québec: Les Presses de l'Université Laval; Louvain: Peeters, 2005.

Rouleau, Donald. *L'Épître apocryphe de Jacques (NH I,2)*. Bibliothèque copte de Nag Hammadi, Section "Textes" 18. Québec: Les Presses de l'Université Laval; Louvain: Peeters, 1987.

Roy, Louise. *L'Acte de Pierre (BG 4)*. Bibliothèque copte de Nag Hammadi, Section "Textes" 18. Québec: Les Presses de l'Université Laval; Louvain: Peeters, 1987.

Rudolph, Kurt. *Gnosis: The Nature and History of Gnosticism*. English translation edited by Robert McLachlan Wilson. San Francisco: HarperSanFrancisco, 1987.

———. "Der gnostische 'Dialog' als literarisches Genus." In *Probleme der koptischen Literatur*, edited by Peter Nagel, 85–107. Wissenschaftliche Beiträge K2. Halle-Wittenberg: Martin-Luther-Universität, 1968.

———. *Die Mandäer*. Göttingen: Vandenhoeck & Ruprecht, 1960–61.

Sagnard, François. *La gnose valentinienne et le témoignage de saint Irénée*. Paris: Vrin, 1947.

Schäferdiek, Knut. "The Acts of John." In *New Testament Apocrypha*, edited by Wilhelm Schneemelcher, 2.152–212.

Schenke, Gesine. *Die dreigestaltige Protennoia herausgegeben, übersetzt und kommentiert*. Texte und Untersuchungen zur Geschichte der altchristlichen Literatur 132. Berlin: Akademie, 1984.

Schenke, Hans-Martin. "The Acts of Peter and the Twelve Apostles." In *New Testament Apocrypha*, edited by Wilhelm Schneemelcher, 2.412–25.
———. "Bemerkungen zur Apokalypse des Allogenes (NHC XI,3)." In *Coptic Studies: Acts of the Third International Congress of Coptic Studies, Warsaw, 20–25 August, 1984*, edited by Wlodzimierz Godlewski, 417–24. Warszawa: PWN-Éditions Scientifiques de Pologne, 1990.
———. "The Book of Thomas (NHC II,7): A Revision of a Pseudepigraphical Epistle of Jacob the Contender." In *The New Testament and Gnosis: Essays in Honour of Robert McLachlan Wilson*, edited by A. H. B. Logan and A. J. M. Wedderburn, 213–28. Edinburgh: Clark, 1983.
———. "Zur Faksimile-Ausgabe der Nag-Hammadi-Schriften." *Zeitschrift für Ägyptische Sprache und Altertumskunde* 102 (1975): 123–38.
———. "Gnosis: Zum Forschungsstand unter besonderer Berücksichtigung der religionsgeschichtlichen Problematik." *Verkündigung und Forschung* 32 (1987): 2–21.
———. "The Gospel of Philip." In *New Testament Apocrypha*, edited by Wilhelm Schneemelcher, 1.179–208.
———. *Die Herkunft des sogennanten Evangelium Veritatis.* Berlin: Evangelischer Verlag, 1958.
———. "Die jüdische Melchisedek-Gestalt als Thema der Gnosis." In *Altes Testament-Frühjudentum-Gnosis*, edited by Karl-Wolfgang Tröger, 111–36. Berlin: Evangelische Verlagsanstalt, 1980.
———. "The Phenomenon and Significance of Gnostic Sethianism." In *The Rediscovery of Gnosticism*, edited by Bentley Layton, 2:588–616.
———. *Das Philippus-Evangelium (Nag-Hammadi-Codex II,3).* Texte und Untersuchungen 143. Berlin: Akademie, 1997.
———. "The Problem of Gnosis." *Second Century* 3 (1983): 78–87.
———. "Das sethianische System nach Nag-Hammadi-Handschriften." In *Studia Coptica*, edited by Peter Nagel, 165–73. Berliner Byzantinische Arbeiten 45. Berlin: Akademie, 1974.
———. *Das Thomas-Buch (Nag-Hammadi-Codex II,7): Neu herausgegeben, übersetzt und erklärt.* Texte und Untersuchungen 138. Berlin: Akademie, 1989.
———. "Vom Ursprung der Welt: Eine Titellose gnostische Abhandlung aus dem Funde von Nag-Hammadi." *Theologische Literaturzeitung* 84 (1959): 243–56.
Schenke, Hans-Martin, Hans-Gebhard Bethge, and Ursula Ulrike Kaiser, eds. *Nag Hammadi Deutsch.* 2 vols. Die Griechischen Christlichen Schriftsteller der ersten Jahrhunderte, Neue Folge, 8, 12. Berlin and New York: De Gruyter, 2001, 2003.
Schenke, Hans-Martin, and Einar Thomassen. "The Book of Thomas." In *New Testament Apocrypha*, edited by Wilhelm Schneemelcher, 1.232–40.
Schmidt, Carl. *Gnostische Schriften in koptischer Sprache aus dem Codex Brucianus, herausgegeben, übersetzt und bearbeitet.* Leipzig: Hinrichs, 1892.
———. *Plotins Stellung zum Gnosticismus und kirchlichen Christentum.* Texte und Untersuchungen zur altchristlichen Literatur 20. Leipzig: Hinrichs, 1901.
Schmithals, Walter. *Gnosticism in Corinth: An Investigation of the Letters to the Corinthians.* Translated by John E. Steely. Nashville: Abingdon, 1971.
Schneemelcher, Wilhelm, ed. *New Testament Apocrypha.* English translation edited by Robert McLachlan Wilson. 2 vols. Cambridge: James Clarke; Louisville: Westminster/John Knox, 1991–92.
Schoedel, William R. "Jewish Wisdom and the Formation of the Christian Ascetic." In *Aspects of Wisdom in Judaism and Early Christianity*, edited by Robert L. Wilken, 169–99. Notre Dame, IN: University of Notre Dame Press, 1975.
———. "'Topological' Theology and Some Monistic Tendencies in Gnosticism." In *Essays on the Nag Hammadi Texts in Honour of Alexander Böhlig*, edited by Martin Krause, 88–108. Nag Hammadi Studies 3. Leiden: Brill, 1972.
Schoenborn, Ulrich. *Diverbium Salutis: Studien zur Interdependenz von literarische Struktur und theologische Intention des gnostishen Dialogs am Beispiel der koptischen 'Apokalypse*

des Petrus' aus Nag Hammadi (NHC VII,3). Studien zur Umwelt des Neuen Testaments
    19. Göttingen: Vandenhoeck & Ruprecht, 1995.
Scholem, Gershom. *Jewish Gnosticism, Merkabah Mysticism, and Talmudic Tradition*. New
    York: Jewish Theological Seminary of America, 1960.
Scholer, David M. *Nag Hammadi Bibliography 1948–1969*. Nag Hammadi Studies 1. Leiden:
    Brill, 1971.
——. *Nag Hammadi Bibliography 1970–1994*. Nag Hammadi Studies 32. Leiden: Brill, 1997.
Scopello, Madeleine. "Les citations d'Homère dans le traité de *L'Exégèse de l'âme*." In *Gnosis
    and Gnosticism: Papers Read at the Seventh International Conference on Patristic Studies
    (Oxford, September 8–13, 1975)*, edited by Martin Krause, 3–12. Nag Hammadi Studies 8.
    Leiden: Brill, 1977.
——. "The Concept of Our Great Power." In *The Coptic Encyclopedia*, edited by Aziz S.
    Atiya, 2.583–84. New York and Oxford: Macmillan, 1991.
——. "Contes apocalyptiques et apocalypses philosophiques dans la bibliothèque de Nag
    Hammadi." In *Apocalypses et voyages dans l'au-delà*, edited by Claude Kappler, 321–50.
    Paris: Cerf, 1987.
——. *L'Exégèse de l'âme, Nag Hammadi Codex II,6: Introduction, traduction et commen-
    taire*. Nag Hammadi Studies 25. Leiden: Brill, 1985.
——. *Femme, gnose et manichéisme: De l'espace mythique au territoire du réel*. Nag Ham-
    madi and Manichaean Studies 53. Leiden: Brill, 2005.
——. "Jewish and Greek Heroines in the Nag Hammadi Library." In *Images of the Feminine
    in Gnosticism*, edited by Karen King, 71–90.
——. "Les 'Testimonia' dans le traité de *L'Exégèse de l'âme* (Nag Hammadi, II, 6)." *Revue de
    l'histoire des religions* 191 (1977): 159–71.
——. "Youel et Barbélo dans le traité de l'Allogène." In *Colloque international sur les textes
    de Nag Hammadi (Québec, 22–25 août 1978)*, edited by Bernard Barc, 374–82. Biblio-
    thèque copte de Nag Hammadi, Section "Études" 1. Québec: Les Presses de l'Université
    Laval; Louvain: Peeters, 1981.
Scott, Walter C. *Hermetica*, 4 vols. Vol. 4 edited by Alexander S. Ferguson. Oxford: Claren-
    don, 1924–38.
Segal, Alan F. *Two Powers in Heaven: Early Rabbinic Reports About Christianity and Gnosti-
    cism*. Studies in Judaism and Late Antquity 25. Leiden: Brill, 1977.
Segal, Judah Benzion. *Edessa, "The Blessed City."* Oxford: Clarendon, 1970.
Segelberg, Eric. "The Coptic Gnostic Gospel According to Philip and Its Sacramental Sys-
    tem." *Numen* 7 (1987): 189–200.
——. "Evangelium Veritatis: A Confirmation Homily and Its Relation to the Odes of
    Solomon." *Orientalia Suecana* 8 (1959): 1–40.
Sell, Jesse W. "Jesus the 'Fellow-Stranger': A Study of CG VI 2,35–3,11." *Novum Testamentum*
    23 (1981): 173–92.
——. *The Knowledge of the Truth — Two Doctrines: The Book of Thomas the Contender* (CG
    II,7) *and the False Teachers of the Pastoral Epistles*. Bern: Laing, 1982.
Sevrin, Jean-Marie. *Le dossier baptismal séthien: Études sur la sacramentaire gnostique*. Bib-
    liothèque copte de Nag Hammadi, Section "Études" 2. Québec: Les Presses de l'Univer-
    sité Laval; Louvain: Peeters, 1986.
——, ed. *L'Exégèse de l'âme (NH II,6)*. Bibliothèque copte de Nag Hammadi, Section
    "Textes" 9. Québec: Les Presses de l'Université Laval; Louvain: Peeters, 1983.
——. *L'Exégèse de l'âme, Nag Hammadi Codex II,6: Introduction, traduction et commen-
    taire*. Nag Hammadi Studies 25. Leiden: Brill, 1985.
——. "Les noces spirituelles dans l'Évangile selon Philippe." *Le Muséon* 87 (1974): 143–93.
——. "Paroles et paraboles de Jésus dans les écrits gnostiques coptes." In *Logia: Les paroles
    de Jésus — The Sayings of Jesus*, edited by Joel Delobel. Bibliotheca Ephemeridum Theo-
    logicarum Lovaniensium 59. Louvain: Peeters, 1982.
——. "La rédaction de *l'Exégèse de l'âme* (Nag Hammadi II,6)." *Le Muséon* 92 (1979): 237–71.
Sieber, John H. "The Barbelo Aeon as Sophia in Zostrianos and Related Tractates." In *The
    Rediscovery of Gnosticism*, edited by Bentley Layton, 2.788–95.

——, ed. *The Nag Hammadi Codex VIII*. Nag Hammadi Studies 31. Leiden: Brill, 1991.

Silverstein, Theodore. *Visio Sancti Pauli: The History of the Apocalypse in Latin Together with Nine Texts*. Studies and Documents 4. London: Christophers, 1935.

Silverstein, Theodore, and Anthony Hilhorst. *Apocalypse of Paul: A New Critical Edition of Three Long Latin Versions with Fifty-four Plates*. Cahiers d'Orientalisme 21. Geneva: Patrick Cramer Editeur, 1997.

Smith, Jonathan Z. *Drudgery Divine: On the Comparison of Early Christianities and the Religions of Late Antiquity*. Chicago: University of Chicago Press, 1990.

Smith, Mitzi J. "Understand Ye a Parable! *The Acts of Peter and the Twelve Apostles* as Parable Narrative." *Apocrypha* 13 (2002): 29–52.

Smith, Terence V. "The Peter-Figure in Gnostic Sources." In *Petrine Controversies in Early Christianity*, by Terence V. Smith, 102–42. Wissenschaftliche Untersuchungen zum Neuen Testament 2, Reihe 15. Tübingen: Mohr (Paul Siebeck), 1985.

Stead, G. C. "The Valentinian Myth of Sophia." *Journal of Theological Studies* 20 (1969): 75–104.

Stroumsa, Gedaliahu A. G. *Another Seed: Studies in Gnostic Mythology*. Nag Hammadi Studies 24. Leiden: Brill, 1984.

Sumney, Jerry L. "The 'Teachings of Silvanus' as a Gnostic Work." *Studies in Religion* 21 (1992): 191–206.

Tardieu, Michel. *Écrits gnostiques: Codex de Berlin*. Sources gnostiques et manichéennes 1. Paris: Cerf, 1984.

——. "Recherches sur la formation de l'Apocalypse de Zostrien et les sources de Marius Victorinus." In *Res Orientales IX*, 7–114. Bures-sur-Yvette: Groupe pour l'Étude de la Civilisation du Moyen-Orient, 1996.

——. *Trois mythes gnostiques: Adam, Éros et les animaux d'Égypte dans un écrit de Nag Hammadi (II,5)*. Paris: Études augustinennes, 1974.

Tardieu, Michel, and Jean-Daniel Dubois. *Introduction à la Littérature Gnostique*. Paris: Cerf, 1986.

Thomassen, Einar. "How Valentinian Is *The Gospel of Philip?*" In *The Nag Hammadi Library After Fifty Years: Proceedings of the 1995 Society of Biblical Literature Commemoration*, edited by John D. Turner and Anne McGuire, 251–79. Nag Hammadi and Manichaean Studies 44. Leiden, New York, and Köln: Brill, 1997.

——. *The Spiritual Seed: The Church of the "Valentinians."* Nag Hammadi and Manichaean Studies 60. Leiden: Brill, 2006.

——. "The Valentinianism of the *Valentinian Exposition* (NHC XI,2)." *Le Muséon* 102 (1989): 225–36.

Thomassen, Einar, and Louis Painchaud, eds. *Le Traité tripartite (NH I,5)*. Bibliothèque copte de Nag Hammadi, Section "Textes" 19. Québec: Les Presses de l'Université Laval; Louvain: Peeters, 1989.

Till, Walter C. *Das Evangelium nach Philippos*. Patristische Texte und Studien 2. Berlin: De Gruyter, 1963.

Till, Walter C., and Hans-Martin Schenke. *Die gnostischen Schriften des koptischen Papyrus Berolinensis 8502*. 2d ed. Texte und Untersuchungen 60. Berlin: Akademie, 1972.

Torjesen, Karen Jo. *When Women Were Priests: Women's Leadership in the Early Church and the Scandal of Their Subordination in the Rise of Christianity*. San Francisco: HarperSanFrancisco, 1993.

Tröger, Karl-Wolfgang. "Die sechste und siebte Schrift aus Nag-Hammadi-Codex VI, eingeleitet und übersetzt vom Berliner Arbeitskreis für koptisch-gnostische Schriften." *Theologische Literaturzeitung* 98 (1973): 495–503.

Turner, John D. *The Book of Thomas the Contender from Codex II of the Cairo Gnostic Library from Nag Hammadi (CG II,7): The Coptic Text with Translation, Introduction and Commentary*. Society of Biblical Literature Dissertation Series 23. Missoula, MT: Scholars Press, 1975.

——. "The Book of Thomas and the Platonic Jesus." In *L'Évangile selon Thomas et la bibliothèque de Nag Hammadi, traditions et convergences: Actes du colloque tenu à Québec du*

29 *mai au* 1 *juin* 2003. Bibliothèque copte de Nag Hammadi, Section "Études" 9. Québec: Les Presses de l'Université Laval; Louvain: Peeters, forthcoming.

———. "The Gnostic Threefold Path to Enlightenment: The Ascent of Mind and the Descent of Wisdom." *Novum Testamentum* 22 (1980): 324–51.

———. "Hypsiphrone." In *The Anchor Bible Dictionary*, edited by David Noel Freedman et al., 3.352–53. New York: Doubleday, 1992.

———. "A New Link in the Syrian Judas Thomas Tradition." In *Essays on Nag Hammadi in Honour of Alexander Böhlig*, edited by Martin Krause, 109–19. Nag Hammadi Studies 3. Leiden: Brill, 1972.

———. "The Sethian Baptismal Rite." In *Coptica, Gnostica, Manichaica: Mélanges offerts à Wolf-Peter Funk à l'occasion de son soixantième anniversaire*, edited by Paul-Hubert Poirier. Bibliothèque copte de Nag Hammadi, Section "Études" 8. Québec: Les Presses de l'Université Laval; Louvain: Peeters, 2005.

———. "Sethian Gnosticism and Johannine Christianity." In *Theology and Christology of the Fourth Gospel: Essays by the Members of the SNTS Johannine Writings Seminar*, edited by Gilbert van Belle, Jan Gabriël van der Watt, and P. J. Maritz, 399–433. Bibliotheca Ephemeridum Theologicarum Lovaniensium 184. Louvain: Louvain University Press/ Peeters, 2005.

———. "Sethian Gnosticism: A Literary History." In *Nag Hammadi, Gnosticism, and Early Christianity*, edited by Charles W. Hedrick and Robert Hodgson Jr., 55–86.

———. *Sethian Gnosticism and the Platonic Tradition*. Bibliothèque copte de Nag Hammadi, Section "Études" 6. Québec: Les Presses de l'Université Laval; Louvain: Peeters, 2001.

Turner, Martha Lee. *The Gospel According to Philip: The Sources and Coherence of an Early Christian Collection*. Nag Hammadi and Manichaean Studies 38. Leiden: Brill, 1996.

Uhlig, Gustavus, ed. "Dionysii Thacis Ars Grammatica." In *Grammatici Graeci*, I, i, edited by Gustavus Uhlig. Leipzig: Teubner, 1883. Reprint, Hildesheim: Olms, 1965.

Uro, Risto, ed. *Thomas at the Crossroads: Essays on the Gospel of Thomas*. Edinburgh: Clark, 1998.

Valantasis, Richard. "Allogenes (Nag Hammadi Codex XI,3)." In *Ascetic Behavior in Greco-Roman Antiquity: A Source Book*, edited by Vincent L. Wimbush, 235–42. Studies in Antiquity and Christianity. Minneapolis: Fortress, 1990.

———. *The Gospel of Thomas*. New Testament Readings. London and New York: Routledge, 1997.

van Bladel, K. "Sources of the Legend of Hermes in Arabic." In *Hermetism from Late Antiquity to Humanism*, edited by P. Lucentini, I. Parri, and V. Perrone Compagni, 285–94. Instrumenta patristica et mediaevalia 40. Turnhout: Brepols, 2003.

van den Broek, Roelof. "The Authentikos Logos: A New Document of Christian Platonism." In *Studies in Gnosticism and Alexandrian Christianity*, 206–34. Nag Hammadi Studies 39. Leiden: Brill, 1996. Reprint, *Vigiliae Christianae* 33 (1979): 260–89.

———. "Juden und Christen in Alexandrien im 2. und 3. Jahrhundert." In *Juden und Christen in der Antike*, edited by Jacobus van Amersfoort and Johannes van Oort, 101–15. Kampen: Kok, 1990.

———. "The Teachings of Silvanus and the Greek Gnomic Tradition." In *Studies in Gnosticism and Alexandrian Christianity*, 259–83. Nag Hammadi Studies 39. Leiden: Brill, 1996.

———. "The Theology of the Teachings of Silvanus." In *Studies in Gnosticism and Alexandrian Christianity*, 235–58. Nag Hammadi Studies 39. Leiden: Brill, 1996. Reprint, *Vigiliae Christianae* 40 (1986): 1–23.

Van den Kerchove, Anna. "New Hermetic Fragments." In "Pratiques rituelles et traités hermétiques," 291–94. Ph.D. dissertation, École Practique des Hautes Études, 2005.

van Os, Bas. "Dispositio: Towards a Rhetorical Analysis of the Gospel of Philip." Paper presented at the Society of Biblical Literature Annual Meeting, Philadelphia, November 2005.

Van Unnik, W. C. "The Origin of the Recently Discovered 'Apocryphon Jacobi.'" *Vigiliae Christianae* 10 (1956): 149–56.

Veilleux, Armand, ed. *La premiére apocalypse de Jacques (NH V,3); La seconde apocalypse de Jacques (NH V,4)*. Bibliothèque copte de Nag Hammadi, Section "Textes" 7. Québec: Les Presses de l'Université Laval. Louvain: Peeters, 1986.

von Harnack, Adolf. *Marcion: The Gospel of the Alien God*. Translated by John E. Steely and Lyle D. Bierma. Durham, NC: Labyrinth Press, 1990.

Waldstein, Michael. "The Apocryphon of John: A Curious Eddy in the Stream of Hellenistic Judaism." Privately circulated preprint, August 1995.

———. "The Primal Triad in the *Apocryphon of John*." In *The Nag Hammadi Library After Fifty Years: Proceedings of the 1995 Society of Biblical Literature Commemoration*, edited by John D. Turner and Anne McGuire, 154–87. Nag Hammadi and Manichaean Studies 44. Leiden, New York, and Köln: Brill, 1997.

Waldstein, Michael, and Frederik Wisse, eds. *The Apocryphon of John: Synopsis of Nag Hammadi Codices II,1; III,1; and IV,1 with BG 8502,2*. Nag Hammadi and Manichaean Studies 33. Leiden: Brill, 1985.

Waterfield, Robin, ed. *The Theology of Arithmetic: On the Mystical, Mathematical and Cosmological Symbolism of the First Ten Numbers, Attributed to Iamblichus*. Grand Rapids, MI: Phanes Press, 1988.

Wekel, Konrad. "'Die drei Stelen des Seth': Die fünfte Schrift aus Nag-Hammadi-Codex VII, eingeleitet und übersetzt vom Berliner Arbeitskreis für koptisch-gnostische Schriften." *Theologische Literaturzeitung* 100 (1975): 571–80.

Wendland, Paul, ed. *Refutatio omnium haeresium*. Die Griechischen Christlichen Schriftsteller der ersten Jahrhunderte 26. Hildesheim and New York: Olms, 1977.

Whittaker, John. "The Historical Background of Proclus' Doctrine of the *authupostata*." In *De Jamblique à Proclus: 9 exposés suivis de discussions*, 193–210. Vandoeuvres-Geneva: Fondation Hardt, 1975.

———. "Self-Generating Principles in Second-Century Gnostic Systems." In *The Rediscovery of Gnosticism*, edited by Bentley Layton, 1.176–89.

Williams, Francis E. "The Concept of Our Great Power: Jumble, 'Coherent,' or Composite?" In *Abstracts: American Academy of Religion*. Society of Biblical Literature Abstracts 160. Atlanta: Scholars Press, 1997.

———. *Mental Perception: A Commentary on NHC VI,4, The Concept of Our Great Power*. Nag Hammadi and Manichaean Studies 51. Leiden, New York, and Köln: Brill, 2001.

———. "The Text of *The Concept of Our Great Power* (NHC VI,4)." In *Abstracts: American Academy of Religion*. Society of Biblical Literature Abstracts 267. Atlanta: Scholars Press, 1996.

Williams, Michael A. *The Immovable Race: A Gnostic Designation and the Theme of Stability in Late Antiquity*. Nag Hammadi Studies 29. Leiden: Brill, 1985.

———. "Interpreting the Nag Hammadi Library as 'Collection(s)' in the History of 'Gnosticism(s).'" In *Les textes de Nag Hammadi et le problème de leur classification: Actes du colloque tenu à Québec du 15 au 19 septembre 1993*, edited by Louis Painchaud and Anne Pasquier, 3–50. Bibliothèque copte de Nag Hammadi, Section "Études" 3. Québec: Les Presses de l'Université Laval; Louvain: Peeters, 1995.

———. *Rethinking "Gnosticism": An Argument for Dismantling a Dubious Category*. Princeton, NJ: Princeton University Press, 1996.

———. "Sethianism." In *A Companion to Second-Century Christian "Heretics,"* edited by Antti Marjanen and Petri Luomanen, 32–63.

———. "Stability as a Soteriological Theme in Gnosticism." In *The Rediscovery of Gnosticism*, edited by Bentley Layton, 2:819–29.

Williams, Michael A., and Lance Jennot. "Inside the Covers of Codex VI." In *Coptica, Gnostica, Manichaica: Mélanges en l'honneur de Wolf-Peter Funk*, edited by Louis Painchaud and Paul-Hubert Poirier, 1025–52. Bibliothèque copte de Nag Hammadi, Section "Études" 7. Québec: Les Presses de l'Université Laval; Louvain: Peeters, 1995.

Wilson, Robert McLachlan. *The Gospel of Philip: Translated from the Coptic Text with an Introduction and Commentary*. New York and Evanston: Harper & Row, 1962.

Wisse, Frederik. "After the *Synopsis*: Prospects and Problems in Establishing a Critical Text of the *Apocryphon of John* and Defining Its Historical Location." In *The Nag Hammadi Library After Fifty Years: Proceedings of the 1995 Society of Biblical Literature Commemoration*, edited by John D. Turner and Anne McGuire, 138–53. Nag Hammadi and Manichaean Studies 44. Leiden, New York, and Köln: Brill, 1997.

——. "The Apocryphon of John." In *The Anchor Bible Dictionary*, edited by David Noel Freedman et al., 3.899. New York: Doubleday, 1992.

——. "On Exegeting 'The Exegesis on the Soul.'" In *Les textes de Nag Hammadi: Colloque du Centre d'Histoire des Religions (Strasbourg, 23–25 octobre 1974)*, edited by Jacques-É. Ménard, 68–81. Leiden: Brill, 1975.

——. "The Nag Hammadi Library and the Heresiologists." *Vigiliae Christianae* 25 (1971): 205–23.

Wolff, Gustavus, ed. *Porphyrii De philosophia ex oraculis haurienda*. Hildesheim: Olms, 1962.

Wurst, Gregor. "Irenaeus of Lyon and the Gospel of Judas." In *The Gospel of Judas*, edited by Rodolphe Kasser, Marvin Meyer, and Gregor Wurst, 121–35. Washington, DC: National Geographic Society, 2006.

Zandee, Jan. "'Les Enseignements de Silvain' et le Platonisme." In *Les textes de Nag Hammadi, Colloque du Centre d'Histoire des Religions (Strasbourg, 23–25 octobre 1974)*, edited by Jacques-É. Ménard, 158–79. Nag Hammadi Studies 7. Leiden: Brill, 1975.

——. "'Les Enseignements de Silvanos' et Philon d'Alexandrie." In *Mélanges d'Histoire des Religions offerts à Henri-Charles Puech*, edited by P. Lévy and E. Wolff, 335–45. Paris: Presses Universitaires de France, 1974.

——. "Gnostische trekken in een apocryphe brief van Jacobus." *Norsk Teologisk Tidsskrift* 17 (1963): 401–22.

——. "Die Lehren des Silvanus: Stoischer Rationalismus und Christentum im Zeitalter der frühkatholischen Kirche." In *Essays on the Nag Hammadi Texts in Honour of Alexander Böhlig*, edited by Martin Krause, 144–55. Nag Hammadi Studies 3. Leiden: Brill, 1972.

——. "'Die Lehren des Silvanus' als Teil der Schriften von Nag Hammadi und der Gnostizismus." In *Essays on the Nag Hammadi Texts in Honour of Pahor Labib*, edited by Martin Krause, 239–52. Nag Hammadi Studies 6. Leiden: Brill, 1975.

——. "Origène et 'les enseignements de Silvain' (Nag Hammadi Codex VII,4)." *Laval théologique et philosophique* 46 (1990): 369–82.

——. "*The Teachings of Silvanus*" and Clement of Alexandria: A New Document of Alexandrian Theology. Mededelingen en Verhandelingen van het Vooraziatisch-Egyptisch Genootschap "Ex Oriente Lux" 19. Leiden: Ex Oriente Lux, 1977.

——. *The Teachings of Sylvanus (Nag Hammadi Codex VII,4): Text, Translation, Commentary*. Egyptologische Uitgaven 6. Leiden: Nederlands Instituut voor het Nabije Oosten, 1991.

ACKNOWLEDGMENTS

This volume, which offers a new English edition of the texts in the Nag Hammadi library, the Berlin Gnostic Codex, and Codex Tchacos, builds upon the scholarly efforts of many of our colleagues—colleagues like Hans-Martin Schenke, to whom the volume is dedicated—and those of us who have contributed to the volume acknowledge, with gratitude, that what we have done has been done in collaboration with such colleagues, past and present. On behalf of the contributors to this volume, I would like to express our particular gratitude to our friends at Laval University for their hospitality in welcoming us to their campus in order to discuss these texts. I also recognize the assistance of Brent Smith, who compiled the bibliography, and Leslie K. Hayes, who compiled the Index of Proper Names and served as an academic proofreader, as well as the help of the Institute for Antiquity and Christianity of Claremont Graduate University. I am pleased to acknowledge the support of Chapman University and the Griset Chair in Bible and Christian Studies for my research, support that has continued for well over two decades. HarperSanFrancisco has provided resources and encouragement to pursue this arduous task of translation and interpretation to its conclusion, and the publisher has supported us during our weeks in Québec. At HarperSanFrancisco, several people have proved especially helpful in the production of this volume, among them Michael Maudlin, Eric Brandt, Kris Ashley, Terri Leonard, and Lisa Zuniga. In an earlier incarnation John Loudon caught the vision of a new presentation of Nag Hammadi and related texts, and that vision comes to fruition here. Finally, I personally offer my deepest thanks to my wife and children, who for many years have walked with me through the cosmos of the demiurge and have glimpsed with me a bit of the light shining through from above and from within.

—*Marvin Meyer*
January 2007

INDEX OF PROPER NAMES

Leslie K. Hayes

This index of proper names includes the names of persons, places, powers, and personified concepts found in the texts from the Nag Hammadi library, the Berlin Gnostic Codex, and Codex Tchacos. The terms are usually listed in alphabetical order. The opening letters of a few terms cannot be restored, and they are listed at the end of the index. Additional historical terms have been incorporated, such as "assembly" and "baptism." While such terms are not necessarily to be taken as proper nouns, they appear in this index for the benefit of students of antiquity who seek to locate these texts in their historical milieu.

The complexity of thought and expression found in these texts continues to resist standardization. In an effort to leave complexity exposed, this index has taken an inclusive approach. In many cases it incorporates capitalized, ordinary, and adjectival forms of the listed term as it appears in the text. This strategy of inclusion is intended to allow the reader to explore the wider fields of meaning attached to the indexed terms. The index records terms only where they appear in the translations and footnotes to the translations. It excludes occurrences in the prefatory materials. For the convenience of the reader, terms are keyed to the pagination of this volume rather than the original codices. The index does not indicate how many times the term occurs on a given page nor whether the term occurs in the text or footnote of the given page.

One of the advantages of an index for this extraordinary collection of ancient texts is the opportunity it provides to see the ideas and terms that stimulated the religious, ritual, philosophical, and mythological imaginations of the authors and communities who produced and cherished these texts. For example, a glance at the index will show the ancient and enduring deployment of social terms of authority and hierarchy in the realm of myth and ritual by the frequent use of the terms "mother," "father," and "ruler." Special concerns for power, spirit, baptism, darkness, light, love, and truth are evident by the frequent occurrence of these terms. Moreover, the creative balance between tradition and innovation is evident in the many "invented" (technical) terms that stand alongside more familiar biblical and philosophical terms. Thus, the index is offered as a tool with which to explore these rich texts.